MW01487227

THE OXFORD ENCYCLOPEDIA OF
CHILDREN'S LITERATURE

EDITORIAL BOARD

THE OXFORD ENCYCLOPEDIA
OF

CHILDREN'S LITERATURE

Jack Zipes
Editor in Chief

VOLUME 3

LUCA–SLOT

OXFORD
UNIVERSITY PRESS
2006

OXFORD
UNIVERSITY PRESS

Oxford University Press, Inc., publishes works that further
Oxford University's objective of excellence
in research, scholarship, and education.

Oxford New York
Auckland Cape Town Dar es Salaam Hong Kong Karachi
Kuala Lumpur Madrid Melbourne Mexico City Nairobi
New Delhi Shanghai Taipei Toronto

With offices in
Argentina Austria Brazil Chile Czech Republic France Greece
Guatemala Hungary Italy Japan Poland Portugal Singapore
South Korea Switzerland Thailand Turkey Ukraine Vietnam

Published by Oxford University Press, Inc.
198 Madison Avenue, New York, New York, 10016
http://www.oup.com

Library of Congress Cataloging-in-Publication Data

The Oxford encyclopedia of children's literature / Jack Zipes, editor in chief.
p. cm.
Includes bibliographical references and index.
ISBN 978-0-19-514656-1

1. Children's literature—Encyclopedias. I. Zipes, Jack David.
PN1008.5.094 2006
809′.8928203—dc22

2005034390

9 8 7 6 5 4

Printed in the United States of America on acid-free paper

THE OXFORD ENCYCLOPEDIA OF CHILDREN'S LITERATURE

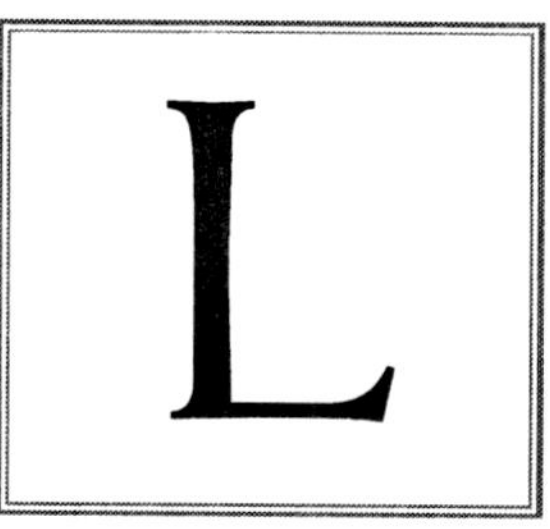

CONTINUED

Lucas, E. V. (1868–1938), prolific British writer, novelist, poet, essayist, critic, and editor of books for children. Edward Verrall Lucas is the editor of *Dumpy Books for Children* (40 vols., 1897–1908), which includes *The Flamp, the Ameliorator, and the Schoolboy's Apprentice* and *A Cat Book*, as well as *The Story of Little Black Sambo* by Helen Bannerman. As a good reader, Lucas was excellent in discovering new talent and seeking out old but valuable books. He revived and republished Mary and Charles Lamb's *Books for Children* (1903). Collections such as *Old-Fashioned Tales* (1905), *Forgotten Tales of Long Ago* (1906), *The Book of Shops* (1899), and *Four and Twenty Tailors* (1900) are big picture books illustrated by F. D. Bedford. *Playtime and Company* (1925) is an anthology of poems for children illustrated by Ernest H. Shepard. As one of the *Punch* table members and a friend of A. A. Milne, Lucas was aware that children love light humor, especially nonsense, repetition of words, and narrative twists. As chair of Methuen, he introduced Milne and Shepard to the British reading public. He also wrote, as early as 1896, a useful essay on poetry for children.

[*See also* Collections; Picture Books; Poetry; *and biographies of figures mentioned in this article.*]

Okiko Miyake

Ludwig, Volker (1937–), cabaret artist, playwright, and director of the Grips Theater for Children in Berlin, which he founded in 1972. Son of the well-known satirist Eckhart Hachfeld—which was also Ludwig's own real name—he began writing for cabaret and television in 1962. Among his early works were eight complete cabaret programs for the Reichkabarett Berlin, established in 1965. In 1966 this cabaret sponsored a children's theater called Theater für Kinder im Reichkabarett, which was later renamed the Grips Theater ("Grips" is slang meaning "noggin," or knowing how to use one's head in a smart way).

Ludwig has written eighteen plays for children, six plays for young adults, and six for all ages. Influenced by the cabaret and Bertolt Brecht, he is one of the chief representatives of an emancipatory theater for children and one of the most renowned playwrights for children in Germany and abroad. He has often collaborated with other authors, such as Reiner Lücker and Detlev Michel, and his plays have been produced in forty-seven countries and thirty-nine languages. Almost all his plays are available in books or have been recorded. They are all accompanied by rock music and deal with social and political issues in a provocative manner. For instance, *Mannomann* (Man Oh Man!, 1973), deals with sexism and the problems of a single mother with two children; *Ein Fest bei Papadakis* (A Party at Papadakis's Place, 1974), concerns racial discrimination; *Ab heute heisst du Sara* (From Now On Your Name Is Sara, 1989) involves anti-Semitism and the Holocaust; *Bella, Boss, und Bulli* (Bella, Boss, and Bully, 1995) treats the problem of bullying; and *Melodys Ring* (Melody's Ring, 2000) focuses on racism and the prejudical treatment of political émigrés. Thanks to Ludwig's leadership and creative talents, Grips remains one of the most important children's theaters in Europe and the world.

BIBLIOGRAPHY

Fischer, Gerhard. *Grips: Geschichte eines populären Theaters (1996–2000)*. Munich: Iudicium, 2002.

Zipes, Jack. "Political Children's Theater in the Age of Globalization." In his *Speaking Out: Storytelling and Creative Drama for Children*, 239–268. New York: Routledge, 2004.

Zipes, Jack, ed. *Political Plays for Children: The Grips Theater of Berlin*. St. Louis, Mo.: Telos, 1976.

Gina Weinkauff

Lugeba, Bonnie (1930–), Ugandan teacher and journalist. Lugeba taught for three years in Uganda, worked on various newspapers in Kampala for fourteen years, and then started and edited his own news magazine, *Ssanyu*. He later worked as news editor for the Ugandan Ministry of Information and became an information officer, a scriptwriter, and chief editor of an international features agency. Lugeba's interest in children's literature resulted in *Great Animal Land* (1971), about East Africa's national parks; it was audio-recorded for radio and television broadcasts. In his subsequent book, *Cry Jungle Children* (1974), which promotes wildlife preservation, Lugeba gives voice to rivers, animals, and birds in order to generate reading interest and environmental consciousness in children, and to inspire them to participate actively in environmental protection. He subtly appeals to young reader by informing them about wildlife societies' efforts to save the flora and fauna—"Africa's beautiful natural heritage"—from destruction.

MAHOUMBAH KLOBAH

Lullaby. Song to sooth babies and infants and make them go to sleep, lullabies are the beginning of all poetry and the beginning of all music, both in the life of each individual and in the history of mankind; the poets of the first epic poems and the first hymns were rocked and lulled to sleep by their mothers. Each of us is acquainted with the rhythm of rocking and lulling before we are born: it repeats the heartbeat heard in the womb, and thus our first literary and musical activities have a biological background. Typically, singing lullabies is accompanied with physical actions such as patting, walking, swaying, and cuddling.

The simplest form of a lullaby was a wordless humming, with a steady rhythm. Then the first words appeared: "Hush, hush, little baby, go to sleep!" And more words: reassuring the child, "mother is here"; comforting the child, "I will rock you"; caressing it, "my dearest one" or—in a Spanish cradle song—*lucerito de la mañana* ("my little morning star"). From this point the songs are no longer purely pragmatic—that is, meant to obtain a concrete result (sleep). They also reflect the mother's feelings: the persuasive text has become lyrical. Poetry is born.

New themes emerge, on the border of the two. Humoring the child with the promise of food—if you go to sleep, you'll get porridge—which is found all over the world, may appear to be pragmatic, a form of "negotiating." But an infant does not understand the words, so in fact they reflect the mother's intentions again. This is even more clear with other promises: famously that Papa's going to buy you mocking bird and a diamond ring.

Not all lullabies are so optimistic. In a song from South Uist, in the Scottish Hebrides, the mother complains that she has no breast milk for her baby, nor anything else to feed it. Other songs mention the many dangers that threaten the fragile life of a baby. And if the baby survives, the mother may die: who will take care of the little baby then? In such songs there is a strong opposition between the soothing melody and the distressing words. According to Marina Warner, spelling out these dangers might have a magical function: by naming the evil forces, we make them harmless (as in the fairy tale "Rumpelstiltskin").

In other lullabies the baby is threatened or cursed. Again, these might be related to magic or superstition. Some cultures believe that calling a baby ugly helps to divert evil beings, such as fairies or demons, who were supposed to steal babies; calling the baby precious could make the gods jealous, provoking an ill fate. In common language, relics of the same superstition are found in blessings in the form of a curse—for example, in English, the expression "break a leg."

These themes are found in lullabies from oral traditions all over the world. All forms still exist, and parents use simple and complex forms equally. In lullabies written by individual poets, there seems to be more diversity, related to cultural differences. But poets often use themes from the oral tradition, and some of the lullabies written by poets became very popular and returned to the oral tradition, often in a shorter form (sometimes only the refrain survived).

BIBLIOGRAPHY

Daiken, Leslie. *The Lullaby Book*. London: Edmund Ward, 1959.

Vries, Anne de. "The Beginning of All Poetry: Some Observations about Lullabies from Oral Traditions." In *Change and Renewal in Children's Literature*, edited by Thomas van der Walt, 159–169. Westport, Conn.: Praeger, 2004.

Warner, Marina. *No Go the Bogeyman: Scaring, Lulling, and Making Mock*. London: Chatto and Windus, 1998.

ANNE DE VRIES

Lunn, Janet (1928–), U.S.-born Canadian writer for children and young adults. Lunn has published novels, picture books, a collection of retold European fairy tales, a biography of Lucy M. Montgomery, and a history of Canada, the last coauthored with Christopher Moore. *Double Spell* (1968), her first novel, explores the theme that is fully developed in her most celebrated book, *The Root Cellar* (1981), which adheres to the British time-slip fantasy tradition of Alison Uttley, Lucy M. Boston, and Philippa Pearce, depicting a young protagonist's encounter with the past as a part of her identity quest. The novel operates with many familiar patterns from time fantasy, including a physical door that opens into another dimension, yet it also engages in creative dialogue with its predecessors, demonstrating the vitality of the

Mother GOOSE's *Melody.* 39

HUSH-a-by baby
On the tree top,
When the wind blows
The cradle will rock;
When the bough breaks
The cradle will fall,
Down tumbles baby,
Cradle and all.

This may ſerve as a warning to the proud and ambitious, who climb ſo high that they generally fall at laſt.

Maxim.

Content turns all it touches into gold.

C 4 LITTLE

Lullaby. Illustration from *Mother Goose's Melody* (London: T. Carnan, 1784), p. 38. Reproduced courtesy of the Cotsen Children's Library, Princeton University Library

genre. The protagonist, the archetypal orphan Rose, is displaced in time because of her profound discontent with her situation. She finds that she has a mission in the past, and her time travels are conscious and even controlled. Still, when Rose in the end realizes that the old woman who served as her magical helper during time displacement is Susan, whom she met as a young girl in the past, the story acquires a substantially more psychological tone. The narrative structure displays sophistication and some daring solutions of the inevitable time paradoxes that stimulate the readers' imagination. Rose's journey is not an escape into a world of dreams and ghosts but a journey home, toward full awareness of her own reality. As Rose's life receives meaning, the reader too sees a possibility for optimism in the open ending. Lunn's *Shadow at Hawthorn Bay* (1988) is another psychological story with a historical setting and supernatural elements, while *The Hollow Tree* (1997) is a more straightforward historical novel.

BIBLIOGRAPHY

Nikolajeva, Maria. "A Typological Approach to the Study of *The Root Cellar*." *Canadian Children's Literature* 63 (1991): 53–60.

MARIA NIKOLAJEVA

Lurie, Alison (1926–), American author and scholar. Lurie has contributed directly to children's literature with her books of retold folk tales: *The Heavenly Zoo* (1979), *Clever Gretchen and Other Forgotten Fairy Tales* (1980), *Fabulous Beasts* (1981), and *The Black Geese* (1999). She edited the *Oxford Book of Modern Fairy Tales* (1975) and coedited the *Garland Library of Children's Classics*. Her critical writings include *Don't Tell the Grownups: Subversive Children's Literature* (1990) and *Boys and Girls Forever* (2003), a collection of essays linked by the Peter Pan theme. Lurie's adult novels include the Pulitzer Prize–winning *Foreign Affairs* (1984), which gently satirizes an aging professor of children's literature.

FRANCES ARMSTRONG

Lurie, Morris (1938–), Australian writer. Lurie writes for both children and adults. His children's books are permeated with a wry sense of the absurd and a compassion for the young and powerless. In *The 27th Annual African Hippopotamus Race* (1969), illustrated by Elizabeth Honey, a favorite with young readers, Edward Day, a two-and-a-half-ton hippo, wins a race down the Zamboola River, defeating a devious opponent. *Arlo the Dandy Lion* (1971), illustrated by Richard Sawers, is a fable in which pride leads to downfall. Other books include *Toby's Millions* (1982), illustrated by Arthur Horner, *Alison Gets Told* (1990) illustrated by Ann James, *What's That Noise? What's That Sound?* (1991), illustrated by Terry Denton, *Racing the Moon* (1993), illustrated by Geoffrey Tate, *Boy in a Storm at Sea* (1997), and *Zeeks Alive!* (1997).

STELLA LEES and PAM MACINTYRE

Luther, Martin (1483–1546), German leader of the Protestant Reformation who wrote treatises, commentaries on Scripture, tracts on theology and ecclesiastical abuses, hymns, sermons, and the first translation of the Bible in a common German vernacular. The Weimar edition (1883) of his works contains 104 volumes. While combating abuses of the Roman Catholic Church and promoting religious reforms, Luther and other leaders of the Reformation also committed themselves to education in the church, school, and home. Numerous works of reformed catechism and other instruction were devoted to the schooling of the young, even if such intent is not obvious from the titles. For example, Luther wrote *Der kleine Catechismus / Fuer die gemeyne Pfarherr vnd Prediger* (The Little Catechism / For the Common Pastor and Preacher, 1529) for home instruction of adults and children (the "common" preachers), although the title may suggest that the book is for professional clergy. Luther's *Passionalbüchlein* (Little Book of the Passion, 1529) stands out among his writings for young people. The text of this brief collection of Bible excerpts, prayers, and illustrations appeared both in Latin and in German, demonstrating the Reformation's stated commitment to classical education as well as to popular knowledge of Scripture.

[*See also* Illustrations; *and* Religious Instruction and Education.]

LUKE SPRINGMAN

Luts, Oskar (1887–1953), Estonian writer. Luts studied pharmacology at the University of Tartu and served as a pharmacist in the Russian army during World War I. As a professional writer, he won recognition with his short stories and dramas. His juvenile story *Kevade* (1912; English trans., *Spring*, 1983) is one of the best-known children's books in Estonia. Based on the author's memories, it is a clear portrait of an Estonian country school at the end of the 19th century, with a detailed depiction of the children's psychology. The book was adapted for the stage and for a ballet; a screen version was released in 1969. The protagonists also appear in the subsequent books *Suvi* (Summer, 1918), *Tootsi pulm* (Toot's Wedding, 1921), *Ärpäev* (Weekday, 1924) and *Sügis* (Autumn, 1938). With the story *Nukitsamees* (1920; English trans., *Bumpy*, 1987), Luts exerted great influence on the development of fantasy for children in the Baltic states.

BETTINA KÜMMERLING-MEIBAUER

Luzzati, Emanuele (1921–), Italian writer and illustrator. One of the most important and prolific writer-illustrators of 20th-century Italy, Luzzati has produced his own illustrated texts, illustrations for other writers, an audio book, and countless animated cartoons (including his superlative *Magic Flute*). Typical of his work are nursery rhymes and stories in verse, as in *Tre fratelli, quaranta ladroni, cinque storie di maghi e burloni* (Three Brothers, Forty Thieves: Five Stories of Wizards and Jokers, 1983), with its verse versions of "Ali Baba," "The Firebird," "The Three Brothers," and others from various traditions. Often inspired by opera, Luzzati has also decorated *Pinocchio* and books by Gianni Rodari and Italo Calvino. Rodari claimed to envy Luzzati for the "naturalness with which he uses so many different languages: words, pictures, theater, cinema, pottery, puppets." Moving between fairy tale traditions and innovative surprises, his work resembles a witty and colorful theatrical game, the rhyming texts framed by illustrations suggesting busy stage action and brilliant décor. He founded a theatre in Genoa (with programs for children), where a multi-media museum also records his dynamic genius.

BIBLIOGRAPHY

Carandini, S., and M. Fazio. *Il sipario magico di Emanuele Luzzati*. Rome: Officina Edizioni, 1980.

ANN LAWSON LUCAS

Lyle Crocodile. *See* Waber, Bernard.

Lynch, Chris (1962–). Born in Boston, Massachusetts, the author Chris Lynch holds dual American and Irish citizenship and resides in Scotland. While pursuing an MA at Emerson College, a course he took with writer Jack Gantos served as the catalyst for Lynch's own career in children's literature. He is best known for his young adult novels, many of which contain an undercurrent of physical, sexual, or emotional violence. This undercurrent, along with sometimes rough language and an unflinching moral ambiguity, has often earned Lynch mixed receptions even as critics have acknowledged his fine sense of craft. *Shadow Boxer* (1993) was criticized for a scene in which two boys watch a video of their father's savage beating. The damaged, death-obsessed protagonist of *Iceman* (1994) turns his inner turmoil into bloodlust on the ice-hockey rink and befriends a reclusive mortician whose private life includes hints of necrophilia. *Gypsy Davey* (1994) presents squalid poverty and vicious abuse in excruciating detail, and in the trilogy of books that make up Blue-eyed Son (1996) Lynch explores drunkenness, drugs, and mindless violence in a working-class Irish neighborhood. But if a penchant for exploring the dark and bizarre aspects of human behavior characterizes his work, so does wild humor—from the wryly sarcastic to the outrageous and offbeat. These two elements may coexist in the same text: *Slot Machine* (1995) treats the subject of hazing through the eyes of an irrepressibly funny narrator. Anything but a formulaic writer, Lynch performed a bold stylistic experiment with the Printz Award Honor Book *Freewill* (2001); the novel travels through a moody, mysterious teenager's complex inner life via a startling second-person narrative. Lynch has also published several short stories in various anthologies and journals, as well as *The He-Man Woman Haters Club* (1997–1998), a series for middle-grade readers that uses broad humor to gently mock its angst-filled adolescent male characters.

MEERA LEE SETHI

Lynch, P. J. (1962–), Belfast-born illustrator, who studied art and design at Brighton School of Art. Patrick James Lynch won the Mother Goose Award while still a student for his collaboration with Alan Garner, *A Bunch of Moonshine* (1986). His approach is traditional, and influences include Arthur Rackham, Edmund Dulac, and Maxfield Parrish. His painterly style is founded on impressive drawing ability and mastery of tonal modeling and perspective; photographic reference is used both for composition and factual detail. By these means, in watercolor and gouache, Lynch achieves acutely heightened naturalism that functions as a sign for veracity; all depicted objects appear "true to life" whether such objects exist or not in reality.

Lynch's illustrations encompass two worlds: one of fantasy and fairy tale and the other of fictional realism; the compositions for the former display a Romantic visionary attitude, and settings for both are meticulously researched. Lynch visited Norway to study architecture, boats, and carvings for *East o' the Sun and West o' the Moon* (1991, translated by Sir George Webbe Dasent). In *Catkin* (1994), Antonia Barber's tale of a child taken by the Little People, the fairy-tale universe of the text is evoked through intense attention to effects of light. *The Steadfast Tin Soldier* (1991), translated by Naomi Lewis, inspired a bold interpretation that connects with the dark heart of Hans Christian Andersen's story, particularly through manipulation of scale and viewpoint. *Ignis* (2002), by Gina Watson, humorously records a young dragon's quest to find fire and gives Lynch the opportunity to create dramatic aerial scenes. His interpretation of Frank Stockton's classic tale of 1887, *The Bee-Man of Orn* (2003), includes paintings of brooding landscapes and ominous caverns intended to induce awe in the hero and viewer alike.

The sense of specific period and place is strongly conveyed in Lynch's work for realist texts. Susan Wojciechowski's *The Christmas Miracle of Jonathan Toomey* (1995), about an introverted widowed carpenter who unexpectedly finds the gift of love, won the Kate Greenaway Medal and the CBI/Bisto Book Award for its sequence of scenes that look mellowed by a varnish of time. Dramatic intensity comes through poses that lead viewers to believe they know how the characters think and feel, which is also a feature in the illustrations for *When Jessie Came across the Sea* (1997), written by Amy Hest, recording the adventures of a young Jewish girl on her transatlantic journey from Europe in the early years of the 20th century. This book brought Lynch his second Kate Greenaway Medal. For Douglas Wood's *Grandad's Prayers of the Earth* (1999), in which a boy recalls his deceased grandfather, Lynch's approach is more diffused and generalized, creating a sense of mood or atmosphere rather than catching an incident; natural settings and seasonal change are major symbols for regeneration and continuity.

JANE DOONAN

Lynch, Patricia (1894–1972), Irish novelist. Lynch, the author of about fifty books for children, was born in the city of Cork and spent most of her childhood moving with her family between Ireland, England, and Belgium. Her memoir, *A Story-Teller's Childhood* (1947), though not always to be relied on for specific details of her life, gives evidence of an upbringing in which the oral tradition of storytelling was particularly vibrant. Her most successful children's fiction recalls this early influence. Her first published writing, when she was in her twenties and living in London, was in the form of journalism. Her article "Scenes from the Rebellion" became famous as an eyewitness account of events in Dublin during Easter week, 1916. Following her marriage in 1922, she returned to Ireland and settled in Dublin. Her earliest children's stories appeared first in a newspaper, the *Irish Press*, in 1931. This newspaper also serialized her children's novel *The Turf-Cutter's Donkey* (book publication, 1934). This and its sequels became her best-known books and were translated into many languages. Another sequence of stories, featuring the leprechaun Brogeen and including such titles as *Brogeen Follows the Magic Tune* (1952) and *Brogeen and the Lost Castle* (1956), enjoyed equal popularity. Like the Turf-Cutter books, they are characterized by an emphasis on the kind of transformational magic that ensures a rapidly evolving narrative. Many of these novels may now seem whimsical and sentimental, but some of Lynch's other fantasies, such as *The Grey Goose of Kilnevin* (1939) and *Jinny the Changeling* (1959), retain their original, simple fairy-tale charm. Lynch's fantasy writing at its finest, however, resides less in her full-length fiction than in her numerous short stories, gathered in collections such as *The Seventh Pig, and Other Irish Fairy Tales* (1950), reissued as *The Black Goat, and Other Irish Fairy Tales* (1959), where her grasp of otherworldly atmosphere can be quite haunting.

In addition to her fantasy stories Lynch wrote in other genres, including historical fiction and realistic adventure. Of the former, the most interesting is *Fiddler's Quest* (1941), strongly imbued with the spirit of Romantic Irish nationalism. Her adventure stories, perhaps reflecting her own nomadic life as a child, often have young characters who confront rejection and loneliness. *Holiday at Rosquin* (1964), for example, sees its heroine becoming friends with a young boy confined to a wheelchair and, in the process, attaining a measure of self-worth and dignity. Lynch deals equally sympathetically in several of her novels with the theme of emigration; *The Bookshop on the Quay* (1956) depicts scenes of departure and farewell of the kind familiar in the Ireland of the 1940s, 1950s, and 1960s.

BIBLIOGRAPHY

Watson, Nancy. "A Revealing and Exciting Experience: Three of Patricia Lynch's Children's Novels." *The Lion and the Unicorn* 21, no. 3 (1997): 341–346.

ROBERT DUNBAR

Lyon, Elinor (1921–), British author. Born in Yorkshire, Lyon was educated at Oxford University, which she left early for the Women's Royal Naval Service during World War II. A prolific author in various genres, mostly holiday adventure stories, she began writing in the 1940s and produced almost a book a year in the 1950s and 1960s before tapering off in the 1970s, by which time her works (and holiday stories in general) were considered passé. Lyon's best-known stories are her eight books about Ian and Sovra, a doctor's children living on a remote Scottish estate. Beginning with *We Daren't Go A-Hunting* (1951), they include *Run Away Home* (1953), in which they are joined by Cathie, a runaway from an orphanage, and *Daughters of Aradale* (1957), which involves Ian, Sovra, and Cathie in reconstructing the journey of a Jacobite fugitive in order to prove the honor of Cathie's family. They continue into the next generation, with Sovra's children appearing in *The King of Grey Corrie* (1975) and *The Floodmakers* (1976). Outside this character-led series, Lyon wrote self-contained adventures such as *Dragon's Castle* (1956) and *Rider's Rock* (1958) using similar settings, mostly in Scotland and Wales. She also wrote *The Golden Shore* (1957), a time-travel adventure set in ancient Greece. Influences from the past shaped her plots, which are driven by good motives: typically the children set out on their adventures to correct an injustice, fight for freedom, or show compassion. Lyon's emphasis is on children acting resiliently on their own. She valued physical strength and courage; her characters are always resourceful, and she particularly favored girls, to whom she gave leading roles which they fulfilled with conviction. Unusually for this sort of fiction, Lyon painted adults too in a favorable light.

JULIA ECCLESHARE

Lyon, George Ella (1949–), American poet, picture-book author, and novelist. Although Lyon began as a poet for adults, the editor Richard Jackson encouraged her to try writing for children. Her compelling, poetic picture book texts often explore children's viewpoints on subjects from Lyon's Kentucky childhood, family history, regional culture and landscape, or travels to distant places such as the Bronx Zoo nursery and Anasazi pueblos. In *Who Came Down That Road?* (1992), a mother tells her son about people and animals traveling their road back into prehistoric times. *Come a Tide* (1990) and *Mama Is a Miner* (1994) depict hardship and togetherness in Appalachian life. *Borrowed Children* (1988) is a girl's coming-of-age novel, while *Gina. Jamie. Father. Bear.* (2002) shows Lyon's interest in blending family stories with magical themes. Her autobiography for children, *A Wordful Child* (1996), and other writings express Lyon's love for the physical and spiritual power of words.

[*See also* Catalanotto, Peter *and* Gammell, Stephen.]

BIBLIOGRAPHY

Herrin, Roberta T. "From Poetry to Picture Books: The Words of George Ella Lyon." In *Her Words: Diverse Voices in Contemporary Appalachian Women's Poetry*, edited by Felicia Mitchell, 166–177. Knoxville: University of Tennessee Press, 2002. Analysis of the relationship between Lyon's poetry and picture book texts, by a scholar of Appalachian literature.

TINA L. HANLON

Lyons, Mary E. (1947–), American historian and writer. A native of Macon, Georgia, Mary Evelyn Lyons attended Appalachian State University in North Carolina and the University of Virginia. Formerly a teacher and librarian, she is known especially for her biographies and profiles of African American artists, including the writer Zora Neale Hurston (*Sorrow's Kitchen*, 1990), the painter Horace Pippin (*Starting Home*, 1993), and the cabinetmaker Tom Day (*Master of Mahogany*, 1994). Her fascination with strong women and historical documentation is evident in her study *Keeping Secrets: The Girlhood Diaries of Seven Women Writers* (1995) and in fiction such as *Letters from a Slave Girl: The Story of Harriet Jacobs* (1996) and *Dear Ellen Bee: A Civil War Scrapbook of Two Union Spies* (coauthored with Muriel M. Branch, 2000). Of Irish descent, Lyons has also begun to explore the effects of the Great Famine in books such as her novel *Knockabeg* (2001).

PEGGY LIN DUTHIE

Lyra, Carmen (1888–1949), Costa Rican author, teacher and cofounder of Obrera University. Lyra, whose real name is María Isabel Carvajal, founded the children's journal *San Selérin*, edited several school primers, and established a reading room for children in the National Library of San José. After the dictator Federico Tinoco's downfall in 1919, Lyra was celebrated as a national author. In 1931 she joined the Communist Party and the women's liberation movement. During a civil war, she was expelled, and she spent her last years in Mexico. Costa Rica's national prize for children's literature was named after her in 1975 (the Premio Carmen Lyra). Her fairy tale collection *Cuentos de mi tía Panchita* (Stories of My Aunt Panchita, 1920) led to Lyra's being considered the founder of modern Costa Rican children's literature. In addition, she called attention to the cultural traditions of her country, which are influenced by Afro-Caribbean, Native American, and European sources.

BETTINA KÜMMERLING-MEIBAUER

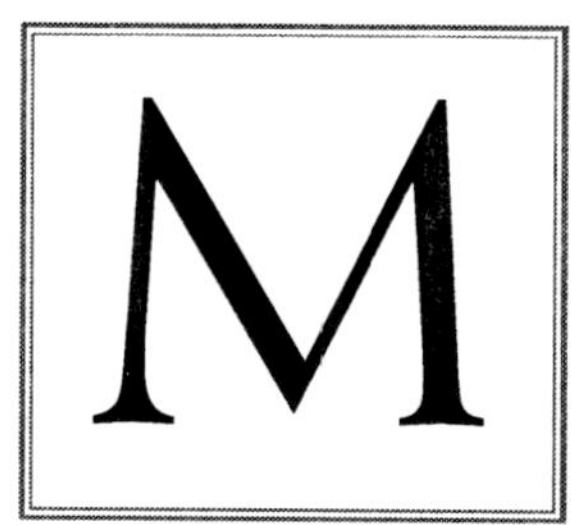

Maar, Paul (1937–), German author, illustrator, and playwright who enjoys both critical acclaim and widespread popularity. After studying art and working for six years as a teacher, he became a freelance author and illustrator. Since publication of his first volume of stories in 1968, he has written more than forty books or plays, providing the illustrations for most of his books himself. His work covers a broad spectrum of genres: stories and novels for beginner readers to young adults, picture books, fantasy and realistic stories, parodies, plays, and screenplays. He is currently the most frequently performed living playwright in German, Austrian, and Swiss theaters. Inventiveness, playfulness, and humor are the major features that characterize his work. His most famous creation is the fantastic figure Sams from his best-selling novel *Eine Woche voller Samstage* (A Week of Saturdays, 1973), its five sequels, and two film versions. Sams, who owes his existence to (virtually untranslatable) wordplay on the names of the weekdays, is an anarchic, carnivalistic creature who adopts the shy Herr Taschenbier as his father and undermines every form of order and authority that dictate the adult's everyday life. Sams likes to play with language, constantly inventing comic ditties and parodies, and causes endless trouble, confusion, and delight by taking words and sayings literally.

Such playful use of language dominates in Maar's work, together with a proximity to oral storytelling with uncomplicated sentence and plot structures for the younger age range. On the other hand, he is a self-conscious writer who uses intertextual references to authors and works of German Romanticism, for instance, in *Lippels Traum* (Lippel's Dream, 1984), who frequently makes narration itself thematic, as in the cycle *Der tätowierte Hund* (The Tatooed Dog, 1968), and likes to cast an unfamiliar perspective onto that which is familiar, as in his fairy tale parody "Geschichte vom bösen Hänsel, der bösen Gretel und der Hexe" (The Tale of Wicked Hansel, Wicked Gretel, and the Witch, 1968).

The visual image rather than an abstract idea is the impetus for much of his work. The orginal idea for his play *Kikirikiste* (Noodle Doodle Box, 1972), an absurdist piece that revolves around the relationship between two clownish characters, each living in his own brightly colored box and refusing to share it with the other, evolved from a vision of creating an optical illusion on stage using a box with different colored sides.

Maar has received several prizes, including the Deutscher Jugendliteraturpreis (the German State Prize for Children's Literature) for his life's work in 1996 and the Verdienstorden der Bundesrepublik Deutschland (Order of Merit of the Federal Republic of Germany) in 1998. His books and plays have been translated into more than twenty languages. Together with his wife, Nele Maar, he has translated a number of children's books from English.

Emer O'Sullivan

Macarthur-Onslow, Annette (1933–), Australian illustrator who creates detailed line drawings in carefully researched and expressionistic interpretations of nature. She has contributed illustrations to many overseas writers' books, including *Circus Boy* (1960) and *Animal Stories* (1961) by Ruth Manning-Saunders. *Birds: Poems* (1962) by Judith Wright gave her the opportunity to interpret her homeland, and she went on to illustrate *Half a World Away* (1962) and *The Roaring 40* (1963), by Nan Chauncy, and *Pastures of the Blue Crane* (1964), by Hesba Brinsmead. She captures the beauty of the Australian alps in *Winged Skis* (1964), *Silver Brumbies of the South* (1965), and *Silver Brumby Kingdom* (1967) by Elyne Mitchell. *Uhu* (1969), set in the Cotswolds, tells the story of an accident-prone owl and won the 1970 Children's Book Council of Australia Book of the Year Award. In *Minnie* (1971), an old white cat belonging to the same household wanders off and faces the terror of a fox and a dog before she is found. *Trim* (1975) is Matthew Flinders's account of his faithful and intelligent cat, written when Flinders was a prisoner on Mauritius. *Round House* (1975) illustrates a house in Gloucestershire and *The Giant Bamboo*

Happening (1982) interprets the twelve days of Christmas through magical events in a garden.

STELLA LEES and PAM MACINTYRE

Macaulay, David (1946–), American author and illustrator. Born in Burton-on-Trent, England, Macaulay moved to Bloomfield, New Jersey, at eleven years old, and obtained a BA in architecture from the Rhode Island School of Design. He briefly taught junior high school before returning to his alma mater to teach. Among his extensive contributions to informational books for children are those in which he uses detailed, assertive black pen-and-ink illustrations on oversized white pages to depict the process of building in *Cathedral: The Story of its Construction* (1973), *City: A Story of Roman Planning and Construction* (1974), *Pyramid* (1975), *Underground* (1976), *Castle* (1977), *Mill* (1983), *Ship* (1993), and *Mosque* (2003). These books go far beyond architectural content; they describe the historical, cultural, and social contexts that gave rise to the structures. The same artistic and narrative techniques mark *Unbuilding* (1980), a book that demonstrates central principles of assembly as it pictorially disassembles the Empire State Building. *Building Big* (2000), a companion to the public television series, looks at architectural wonders to highlight design problems and their innovative solutions that made way for future structures.

During a respite from writing about buildings, Macaulay spent four years drawing and explaining smaller engineering feats for the nearly four-hundred-page *The Way Things Work* (1988) and later produced the post-digital age expanded version, *The New Way Things Work* (1998); in both, color has been added to Macaulay's black-and-white drawings. These books, which are popular across ages and genders, amplify the quiet humor that infuses his other nonfiction works. A woolly mammoth leads readers through the mechanics, physics, and technologies that make possible such familiar machines as the lawnmower, the television, the refrigerator, and later the microchip, the personal computer, and the Internet. Visual puns and tongue-in-cheek jokes run throughout as they do in *Great Moments in Architecture* (1978), in which the Tower of Pisa is laid out on a tipsy drafting table, and *Rome Antics* (1997), in which the reader tours Rome by following the flight of a carrier pigeon.

Macaulay has received international recognition for his contribution to science and to informational books for young people; his honors include the Boston Museum of Science's Bradford Washburn Award, the Medal of the American Institute of Architects, the Deutscher Jugendliteraturpreis, and a Dutch Silver Slate Pencil Award. His two nominations for the Hans Christian Andersen Medal also note his distinctive achievement in fictional picture books. *Motel of the Mysteries* (1979) and *Baaa* (1985) offer ironic political commentaries on modern civilization, and *Why the Chicken Crossed the Road* (1991) turns Macaulay's understanding of cause and effect to wacky ends. *Shortcut* (1999), a seemingly simple journey story, proves anything but as its nine chapters refuse to follow the straight line of a clean narrative. He won the 1991 Caldecott Medal for *Black and White*, a bold, full-color picture book in which each page is divided into quadrants to tell four different stories until the visual elements of one story begin to appear in other stories. In *Black and White* Macaulay engages readers with his self-reflexive awareness that stories, like buildings, are mere constructions.

BIBLIOGRAPHY

Anstey, Michele. "'It's Not All Black and White': Postmodern Picture Books and New Literacies." *Journal of Adolescent and Adult Literacy* 45, no. 6 (2002): 444–457.

Hoare, Geoffrey. "The Work of David Macaulay." *Children's Literature in Education* 8, no. 1 (Spring 1977): 12–20.

McClay, Jill Kedersha. "'Wait a Second . . .': Negotiating Complex Narratives in Black and White." *Children's Literature in Education* 31, no. 2 (2000): 91–106.

CATHRYN M. MERCIER

MacDonald, Betty (1908–1958), American author of five children's books as well as autobiographical novels and screenplays for adults. Born Anne Elizabeth Campbell Bard, MacDonald tried her hand at a wide variety of jobs before publishing her first book, *The Egg and I*, in 1945. In 1947 she published *Mrs. Piggle-Wiggle*, a collection of linked short stories; it was followed by the sequels *Mrs. Piggle-Wiggle's Magic* (1949), *Mrs. Piggle-Wiggle's Farm* (1954), and *Hello, Mrs. Piggle-Wiggle* (1957). The charmingly eccentric protagonist, Mrs. Piggle-Wiggle, is all that a child could ask for. She is also the answer to the prayers of harried parents. In each tale the kindly, clever, and magical Mrs. Piggle-Wiggle provides a silly but satisfying solution to typical childhood problems—tattling, selfishness, poor table manners, pet neglect, interrupting, and many more. MacDonald's ability to reshape the tradition of didactic instructional tales for children into a witty and comic form accounts for her books' continuing popularity.

MEGAN LYNN ISAAC

Macdonald, Caroline (1948–1997), born in Taranaki, New Zealand. Macdonald was the youngest in her family by many years, and her siblings had all left home when she was still very young. Books became company for her and she read voraciously. Like so many writers, she worked at a variety of jobs after leaving school and before becoming a full-time writer. Macdonald wrote short stories as well as novels in a range of genres. Her work has a strong sense of place, and she used the landscape of New Zealand to provide the background for a number of her novels. She did not always write with a third-person narrator; for example, *Speaking to Miranda* (1991) is written in the first-person present tense, a form Macdonald felt was necessary, given the plot and the characters. This book also draws on Macdonald's interest in the unreliable narrator, where the reader is more aware of what is happening than is the character herself.

Macdonald's work is concerned with families and the alliances and strains that form within them. Beyond that, she explored the place of people in the world in general, especially in such works as *The Lake at the End of the World* (1988) and *The Eye Witness* (1991), which reveal Macdonald's interest in fantasy and science fiction. *Spider Mansion* (1994) has been described as a psychological thriller.

Although she had a short career, dying just fifteen years after her first book was published, Macdonald won many literary awards for her books, including the Esther Glen Memorial Award for her first book, *Elephant Rock* (1983), and the Victorian Premier's Award for *The Lake at the End of the World*. She was much in demand as a speaker at conferences, seminars, and schools, and her work remains popular today.

Margot Hillel

George MacDonald. The evil witch seeks revenge in "Little Daylight"; illustration by Arthur Hughes from *The Light Princess and Other Stories* (London, 1874). Collection of Jack Zipes

MacDonald, George (1824–1905), Scottish author of novels, fantasies, poetry, and sermons. MacDonald was raised in Huntly, Aberdeenshire, and the local landscape with its ruined castle informs much of his writing for both adults and children. He attended the University of Aberdeen, studying natural sciences and immersing himself in literature in several languages, notably German. From Aberdeen he went to London to study for the ministry at Highbury College. In 1850 he took a pastorate at Arundel in Sussex, but before long members of the parish engineered his resignation by lowering his salary and accusing him of heresy. The basis for that charge was MacDonald's belief in universal salvation and his interest in so-called German theology (in 1851 he had published translations of the German poet Novalis). Unable to support his young family in Arundel, MacDonald left the ministry and moved to Manchester. Later, influenced by F. D. Maurice, he joined the Church of England, but he made his living as a writer and never again used the title "Reverend."

In 1855 MacDonald published his first book, the play *Within and Without*. He followed this with *Phantastes: A Faerie Romance for Men and Women* (1858), and he then produced many novels, books of poetry, sermons, and essays over the next forty years. MacDonald's fiction for both adults and children occupies at least two genres, realism and fantasy, although his reputation largely rests on the latter. In 1864 his first children's tale appeared: "The Light Princess," later included in MacDonald's collection of short fantasy for children, *Dealings with the Fairies* (1867), and over later years appearing in single-volume editions illustrated by various artists, including Arthur Hughes, William Pene DuBois, and Maurice Sendak. "The Light Princess" shares a delight in linguistic play with *Alice's Adventures in Wonderland*

(1865), by MacDonald's friend Lewis Carroll. The difference between Carroll's work and MacDonald's lies in the latter's use of the traditional fairy tale and in his clear moral agenda. MacDonald parodies the traditional tale here and in works such as "Little Daylight" (first appearing in *At the Back of the North Wind*, 1872), "The Giant's Heart" (1863), and "The Carasoyn" (1871). These parodic fairy tales speak of self-sacrifice, obedience, and duty.

Of MacDonald's several short fantasies for children, none is more enigmatic than "The Golden Key" (1865), in which two young people, Tangle and Mossy, journey to the land whence the shadows come. MacDonald's intertextual references here range from Dante to Blake and Novalis. He offers his young readers a challenge and his older readers a gift. This, like much of MacDonald's work, is crossover writing, appealing to both adults and children.

MacDonald published four full-length fantasies for young readers: *At the Back of the North Wind* (1871), *The Princess and the Goblin* (1872), *The Princess and Curdie* (1882), and *The Wise Woman, a Parable*, also known as *The Lost Princess* (1875). Each initially appeared in serial form in *Good Words for the Young* or *Good Things*. They criticize the Victorian class system and challenge the comforts of orthodox politics and religion. *At the Back of the North Wind* is unusual in that it blends an element of fantasy with a Dickensian treatment of Victorian London. The main character, Diamond, is a preternaturally wise and good child who has experiences with Lady North Wind early in the novel and later takes his father's place driving a cab through the London streets. Once Diamond is immersed in city life, his experiences of North Wind are indirect rather than direct. Diamond is so good that he, like many fictional children in the Victorian period, goes to his reward while still in his childhood.

The most influential of MacDonald's children's books are the two *Princess* books. The first tells of Princess Irene, a plot by goblins to kidnap her and make her the bride of their Prince Harelip, and her adventures with the miner boy Curdie. The second tells of Curdie's adventures in the city of Gwyntystorm as he labors to liberate the king from the machinations of disloyal courtiers and politicians. Plot summary, however, cannot do justice to the symbolic richness of these two books. The most intriguing of the many elusive symbols is the figure of Irene's great-great-grandmother, who inhabits a room in the castle tower in the first book and shape-changes in the second. Together these two fantasies take the reader on a journey to the end of time, and on the way they touch on a great range of themes, from geology to spirituality.

Less well known are MacDonald's realistic children's books, such as *Ranald Bannerman's Boyhood* (1871), *Gutta Percha Willie, the Working Genius* (1873), and *A Rough Shaking* (1891). Like his fantasies, they were serialized before appearing in book form, and the first two (also like the fantasies) were illustrated by Arthur Hughes, a well-known painter and illustrator associated with the Pre-Raphaelites. The books combine the adventures of young people growing up with thoughts on education and parenting.

In 1893 MacDonald published an essay, "The Fantastic Imagination," in which he sets out his theory of the fairy tale. He equates the fairy tale with the sonata, a musical form of contrasts and formal balance. Like music, the fairy tale has form but no definite meaning. Its task is to wake meaning in the reader rather than tell the reader what to think. MacDonald's sense of the fairy tale derives from Romantic aesthetics, especially as set out by German (e.g., Novalis and Ludwig Tieck) and English writers (e.g., Samuel Taylor Coleridge and Percy Bysshe Shelley). MacDonald's influence is evident in the work of C. S. Lewis, J. R. R. Tolkien, Diana Wynne Jones, and Philip Pullman.

[*See also* Fantasy *and biographies of figures mentioned in this article.*]

BIBLIOGRAPHY

Avery, Gillian. "George MacDonald and the Victorian Fairy Tale." In *The Gold Thread: Essays on George MacDonald*, edited by William Raeper, 126–139. Edinburgh: Edinburgh University Press, 1990.

McGillis, Roderick, ed. *For the Childlike: George MacDonald's Fantasisies for Children*. Metuchen, N.J.: Scarecrow, 1992.

Reis, Richard H. *George MacDonald*. New York: Twayne, 1972.

Roderick McGillis

MacDonald, Margaret Read (1940–), American storyteller, folklorist, author, and children's librarian. MacDonald teaches storytelling at the University of Washington, has authored numerous picture books, and has written and edited collections of tales and books on storytelling. Perhaps her single most valuable contribution to storytellers and scholars is *The Storyteller's Sourcebook* (1982), a subject, title, and motif index to folklore collections for children that took eleven years to complete. A 2002 supplement updates this massive work. Her many books written for storytellers include *Twenty Tellable Tales* (1986, 2005), *Book Play* (1995), and *Three-Minute Tales* (2004). The collection *Earth Care: World Folktales to Talk About* (1999) followed *Peace Tales* (1992, 2005). *The Round Book: Rounds for Kids to Sing* (1999) contains eighty rounds, with information on their history and suggestions for singing. Working with a Thai librarian, Su Vathanaprida, she put together *Thai Tales: Folktales of Thailand* (1995) before visiting the country as a Fulbright scholar.

Linnea Hendrickson

MacDonald, Suse (1940–), American author and artist of innovative concept books for young children. Before turning to children's books, MacDonald worked as an illustrator of scientific textbooks in New York, and then as an architectural designer with her husband in a family construction business in Vermont. Her first book, *Alphabatics* (1986), which started out as a typography class project to turn a letter of the alphabet into an animal, won a Caldecott Honor Award. She next collaborated with writer Bill Oakes on a series of concept books beginning with *Numblers* (1988), in which numbers from 1 to 10 are transformed into shapes using brilliant paper collage. In *Sea Shapes* (1994) basic shapes are transformed into sea creatures. *Peck, Slither, and Slide* (1997) explores animal behavior with playful typography and includes factual notes about the animals. More recently, MacDonald has collaborated with Jean Marzollo on a series of rebus books.

Linnea Hendrickson

Machado, Ana Maria (1941–), Brazilian author for children and adults; scholar, linguist, and winner of the 2000 Andersen Medal. Regrettably, few of Machado's books, enormously popular in Brazil and throughout Latin America, have been translated into English, although several are available in the United States in Spanish translations. A title available in English is *Menina Bonita do laço de fita* (1986; Eng. trans., *Nina Bonita*, 1996), a picture book about a white rabbit who loves a little girl's black skin—when he finds out that she received her color from her grandmother, he marries a black rabbit and produces babies with spots and many shades of black and white. *Latin America* (2001), a comprehensive history for young people, is also available in English, as is *Bisa Bea, Bisa Bel* (1982; English trans., *Me in the Middle*, 2002), a work that the international scholar Maria Nikolajeva calls "a children's and female counterpart to Gabriel García Márquez's *One Hundred Years of Solitude*, a piercing, powerful, magical exploration of the invisible links between generations."

[*See also* Brazil; Nonfiction; *and* Picture Books.]

BIBLIOGRAPHY

Nikolajeva, Maria. "Ana Maria Machado: The Power of Language." *Bookbird* 38, no. 3 (2000): 6–10.

Linnea Hendrickson

Mack, Louise (1870–1935), Australian author, journalist, and war correspondent. Mack wrote several novels for adolescents, notably a trilogy tracing the lives of Lennie Leighton and her best friend, Mabel James: *Teens: A Story of Australian School Girls* (1897), *Girls Together* (1898), and *Teens Triumphant* (1933). She attended Sydney Girls' High School, where she was a classmate of the author Ethel Turner. On leaving school she published poems in the *Bulletin*, an influential Australian weekly periodical, as well as a column entitled "Sydney Women's Letter," under the pseudonym "Gouli-Gouli." In 1896 she published her first novel, *The World is Round*, but it was *Teens* that attracted the attention of adolescent readers. Regarded as the chief rival of Turner's *Seven Little Australians* (1894), this novel is notable for its depiction of intense female friendships and the liveliness of its style. It is set in an urban high school rather than the select private school favored by most writers of school novels of this period, and traces the interplay between the lives of its girl characters at home and at school. For many years an excerpt from *Teens* featured in the state school readers that were widely read by Australian children. *Girls Together* follows the progress of Mabel and Lennie two years later.

Mack traveled to London in 1901, where she published a number of adult novels before moving to Italy. She became editor of the *Italian Gazette* and was the first female war correspondent for two London newspapers, *The Daily Mail* and *The Evening News*. She returned to Australia in 1916 and divided her time between traveling and writing, mainly for newspapers and magazines in Australia and New Zealand. *Teens Triumphant*, her last novel, traces Lennie's life as an art student in London.

Clare Bradford

MacKay, Claire (1930–), Canadian author. Born in Toronto, MacKay studied politics and social work and was active as a social worker for many years before writing her first book, *Mini-Bike Hero* (1974), at the age of forty. Initially written for her youngest son, the book became a best seller and was followed by two sequels, *Mini-Bike Racer* (1976) and *Mini-Bike Rescue* (1982). Her interest in politics is depicted in the Ruth Schwartz Foundation Award–winning *One Proud Summer* (1981), a book cowritten with Marsha Hewitt about the hundred-day Dominion Textile strike of 1946 in Valleyfield, Quebec, and in *Pay Cheques and Picket Lines* (1987), a detailed history of unions in Canada. *The Toronto Story* (1990) brings to life the people and events that shaped the city of Toronto through history. Her nonfiction books *Bats about Baseball* (1995; cowritten with Jean Little) and *Touching All the Bases: Baseball for Kids of All Ages* (1994) deal with the history of baseball. In *The Minerva Program* (1984), a schoolgirl has to prove that she did not use her knowledge of computers to change her grade. In 1983 MacKay was honored with the Vicky Metcalf Award in recognition of her body of work.

Maria-Venetia Kyritsi

Macken, Walter (1915–1967), Irish novelist, actor, and playwright. Macken wrote two novels for children. In *Island of the Great Yellow Ox* (1966; filmed for U.K. television in 1971), children marooned on an island outwit villainous treasure hunters. In *The Flight of the Doves* (1968), Finn Dove and his sister run away from a wicked stepfather; their search for their grandmother involves adventures across rural Ireland. In both novels, the drama arises from children in conflict with malevolent adults. Clashing characters and lively action sequences give a theatrical flavor, though in *The Flight of the Doves*, the characters and plot are more fully integrated and developed.

Belinda Copson

MacLachlan, Patricia (1938–), American children's writer. She received the Newbery Medal for *Sarah, Plain and Tall* (1986), a frontier story about two children whose widowed father finds a wife through advertisement. This warm, idyllic book is different from MacLachlan's other novels, which show children in contemporary settings and in painful conflicts with parents. Each involves a serious issue: a stepmother or a new sibling, disability in *Through Grandpa's Eyes* (1979), or a foster parent in *Mama One, Mama Two* (1982). However, the didactic message is not imposed upon readers; coming to an insight demands strong empathy on the readers' part, as the characters continually refuse to see life for what it is. The adults are consistently portrayed as immature, unable to cope with their own problems, still less to provide security for their children. In *Arthur, for the Very First Time* (1980) the boy's parents have not told him about the imminent arrival of a new baby, because they are unprepared to take on the responsibility. The motif of parents who choose to suppress their emotions, thus evoking a strong sense of guilt in the child, is central, particularly in *Baby* (1993), where the mother gradually accepts the death of her newborn son. MacLachlan's protagonists often suffer from a trauma caused by being abandoned by the mother. The shock results in a mental block, conveyed through elaborate narrative techniques. It is especially prominent in *Journey* (1991), showing the protagonist with the highly symbolic name of Journey, who refuses to accept the truth about the disappearance of his mother. It is significant that the parents in MacLachlan's novels are intellectuals: artists, musicians, or writers. Their profession is to create illusions, and they hide themselves behind their own creations, instead of facing real problems, and thus betray their children.

In *Unclaimed Treasures* (1992), the eleven-year-old Willa is erotically attracted to a married man, a daring subject even for a young adult novel. Yet MacLachlan's subtle narrative makes the reader primarily see a confused adolescent's identity quest. The novel employs a complex structure with several narrative levels and sophisticated metafictional references. The protagonist learns to reevaluate her own life, to decide what is "important and extraordinary," two key words in the novel. It also shows a warm relationship between siblings, a motif that is echoed in *Seven Kisses in a Row* (1983). All MacLachlan's novels contain recurrent patterns and images such as babies and pregnant women, symbolizing the protagonists' insight about life and death. Many of her child protagonists are artistically talented: for example, a poet in *Cassie Binegar* (1982) or a musician in *The Facts and Fictions of Minna Pratt* (1988). More important, there are often various symbols for seeing such as binoculars or cameras, and the characters come to insights through using those instruments or through drawing or painting. The central metaphor from *Unclaimed Treasures*, "things beneath the surface" (unborn babies, unfinished paintings, unwritten books), is also the secret of MacLachlan's writing: telling things by not telling them, making the readers "see the unseen."

BIBLIOGRAPHY

Nikolajeva, Maria. "The Child as Self-Deceiver: Narrative Strategies in Katherine Paterson's and Patricia MacLachlan's Novels." *Papers* 7, no. 1 (1997): 5–15.

Russell, David L. *Patricia MacLachlan*. New York: Twayne, 1997.

Trites, Roberta Seelinger. "Claiming the Treasures: Patricia MacLachlan's Organic Postmodernism." *Children's Literature Association Quarterly* 18, no. 1 (1993): 23–28.

Trites, Roberta Seelinger. "Is Flying Extraordinary? Patricia MacLachlan's Use of Aporia." *Children's Literature* 23 (1995): 202–220.

MARIA NIKOLAJEVA

Macleod, Doug (1959–), Australian author, television writer and producer, librettist, poet, and playwright. His sense of the comic and his grasp of the absurd have contributed to some of Australia's funniest television series, such as *Kath and Kim*, and can be enjoyed in his collections of poems: *In the Garden of Bad Things* (1982), illustrated by Peter Thomson, and *The Fed Up Family Album* (1983), illustrated by Jill Brierley. *Sister Madge's Book of Nuns* (1986), illustrated by Craig Smith and "written by Sister Madge Mappin from the Convent of Our Lady of Immense Proportions," uses the incongruity of nuns being involved in biker gangs, cannibalism, and mixing magic potions. *On the Cards* (2002), illustrated by Craig Smith, parodies greeting-card rhymes. Macleod's witty novel for young adults is *Tumble Turn* (2003).

STELLA LEES and PAM MACINTYRE

Madeline. *See* Bemelmans, Ludwig.

***Mad* Magazine.** *Mad*, the longest-running humor magazine in America, was founded in 1952 by publisher William Gaines and editor Harvey Kurtzman. Famous for its trademarked image—the freckled, gap-toothed Alfred E. Neuman and his signature phrase, "What? Me worry?"—*Mad* featured such artists as Mort Drucker, Don Martin, Jack Davis, Al Jaffee, Dave Berg, and Sergio Aragones, who brilliantly satirized contemporary American life, entertainment, and politics. With the magazine reaching a high circulation of 2.8 million copies in 1973, its gleefully sardonic point of view paved the way for *Saturday Night Live*, *The Simpsons*, *National Lampoon*, *South Park*, *Late Night with David Letterman*, and other contemporary comedic institutions.

BIBLIOGRAPHY

Evanier, Mark. *"MAD" Art: A Visual Celebration of the Art of "MAD" Magazine and the Idiots Who Create It*. New York: Watson-Guptill, 2003.

DANIEL T. KLINE

Mado Michio (1909–), pen name of Ishida Michio, Japanese poet for children, born in Tokuyama, Yamaguchi Prefecture, and the recipient of the 1994 Hans Christian Andersen Author Award. In the mid-2000s he remained active in creating poems for children.

Mado started writing poetry at Taipei Technological School. In 1934 two of his poems were selected with the highest honors for *Kodomo-no-kuni*, a pictorial monthly magazine for young readers. This distinction led him to create many poems and rhymes for children. Mado was virtually unknown until he was over sixty years old, although his most famous poem, "Zo-san" (Little Elephant), with a composition by Dan Ikuma, was published in 1952.

Mado's first collection, *Tenpura Pri-pri* (Tempura Frying), was published in 1968 and won the Noma Children's Book Award. After this publication, he had no difficulty in having his poems published. In 1992, *Mado Michio Zen-Shishu* (The Complete Poetry of Mado Michio), containing more than 1,200 of his poems and songs, was published. This volume makes his complete work, including unpublished poems from his early career, accessible for the first time. The collection won the Education Minister's Art Encouragement Prize. In the same year, *The Animals: Selected Poems* (translated by the empress Michiko, illustrated by Anno Mitsumasa) was copublished in Japan and the United States as a bilingual edition. In the author's postscript, Mado describes his philosophy: "On this earth myriad living things of infinite number are given life. This is a wonderful blessing. Thanks to this life-sustaining force, humans enjoy the privilege of pursuing endless dreams and splendid lives." Here is a good example of his philosophy:

Kotori	A Little Bird
Sorano Sizuku?	A dewdrop from the sky ?
Utano Tubomi?	A bud of a song?
Me de nara Sawattemo ii?	May I touch you Just with my eye?

The Magic Pocket: Selected Poems (1998) was a sequel to *The Animals*. Mado's most poetic characteristic is his simplicity of expression, the relation of common creatures and everyday objects with the vast universe, and his sense of humor.

OKIKO MIYAKE

Maestro, Betsy (1944–), American nonfiction writer. Born in New York, Betsy Crippen Maestro earned a BS and

MS from Southern Connecticut State College and began her career as a kindergarten teacher. After her marriage to the illustrator Giulio Maestro, the two began to collaborate on picture books. Their first publication, a retelling of *A Wise Monkey Tale*, was published in 1975 and was a Junior Library Guild selection. They have collaborated on more than one hundred books. Their ongoing American Story series began with the acclaimed *The Discovery of the Americas* (1991) and continues to help young readers understand and appreciate American history and tradition. The books have been praised for the quality of their illustrations and for their clarity and accuracy.

NANCY J. KEANE

Maestro, Giulio (1942–), American illustrator and writer. Born in New York City, educated at Cooper Union, and initially an advertising designer, Maestro became a prolific and versatile children's illustrator. He uses a variety of media and has worked with writers including Franklyn M. Branley, Judy Delton, and Mirra Ginsburg. His closest collaborator is his wife, Betsy Maestro, with whom he produced *Lambs for Dinner* (1978), *The Story of Clocks and Calendars* (1999), and their series featuring Harriet the elephant (e.g., *Harriet Goes to the Circus*, 1977; *Harriet at Play*, 1984). Their ongoing American Story series began with the acclaimed *The Discovery of the Americas* (1991). Maestro is also the author-illustrator of works of humor, wordplay, and riddling, including *Halloween Howls: Riddles That Are a Scream* (1983). His illustrations for *The Tortoise's Tug of War* (1971) and Ginsburg's *Three Kittens* (1973) were chosen by the American Institute of Graphic Arts for its Children's Book Shows in 1971–1972 and 1973–1974.

ADRIENNE E. GAVIN

Magic. Magic is a considerably more frequent element in children's literature than in fiction for adults, presumably because children's writers expect their audience to have retained the belief in the supernatural. Magic, including magical beings or objects and magical events, is a natural part of mythical worlds (for instance, in J. R. R. Tolkien's, C. S. Lewis's, Ursula Le Guin's, or Philip Pullman's fantasy works), and it is also used as a means of passage from the ordinary world and an alternative world or, in time-shift fantasy, between times. Another kind of magic appears within the everyday world, for instance, in magical transformations or wish fulfillment, and often produces comic effect, showing that magic is out of place in the real world, as in many novels by E. Nesbit. Many stories distinguish between benevolent, or white, magic, and evil, dark, or black magic, but the boundary may be fluctuating. In contemporary works, such as *The Lives of Christopher Chant* by Diana Wynne Jones or the Harry Potter novels by J. K. Rowling, magic is comparable to knowledge and art that can be taught and trained and that can turn back on its performer. Magic can thus be viewed as a metaphor for power, creativity, imagination, life wisdom, and many other human features and experiences.

[*See also biographies of figures mentioned in this article*.]

BIBLIOGRAPHY

Nikolajeva, Maria. *The Magic Code: The Use of Magical Patterns in Fantasy for Children*. Stockholm: Almqvist and Wiksell International, 1988.

Wilson, Anne. *Magical Thought in Creative Writing*. Stroud, U.K.: Thimble Press, 1982.

MARIA NIKOLAJEVA

Magic Pudding, The. *See* Lindsay, Norman.

Magnet, The. Also published as The Magnet Library (1908–1940), *The Magnet* was a popular tabloid weekly paper for boys, published by Alfred Harmsworth's Amalgamated Press. This cheap illustrated small paper contained some adventure and detective stories, but its most prominent and best-known stories were by Charles Hamilton (writing as Frank Richards), featuring Greyfriars School, the schoolboy hero Harry Wharton, and the food-oriented, accident-prone antihero Billy Bunter. Bunter became the most famous of British schoolboys, appearing from the first issue; his increasingly outrageous behavior and importance within the stories reflected his immense popularity. In total, Hamilton wrote 1,380 Greyfriars instalments for *The Magnet*, in the 1930s writing almost the entire magazine. Like its companion paper, *The Gem*, *The Magnet*'s school stories perpetuated an unchanging world where fairness, loyalty, decency, and imperialist ideology informed the boys' responses to bullies, cheats, and criminals. Ultimately both papers fell victim not to a lack of readership but to wartime paper shortages.

[*See also* Gem, The; Hamilton, Charles; Harmsworth, Alfred; *and* School Stories.]

BRIDGET CARRINGTON

Magnier, Thierry (1956–), French publisher, chief editor for the Gallimard magazine *Lire et savoir* (Literacy and

Knowledge) from 1996 to 1998. He wrote the beautiful *Solange et l'ange* (1997; Eng. trans., *Isabel and the Angel*, 2000), illustrated by Georg Hallensleben, in which a little pig falls in love with the angel in the painting at the Louvre Museum. In 1998, he created the avant-garde Thierry Magnier publishing house for children's and young adult fiction and published his own picture books as Stéphane Labruyère. His publishing firm has received praise for Antonin Louchard and Katy Couprie's *Tout un monde* (A Whole World, 2000), for finely designed picture books and for boldly realistic social novels by Jeanne Benameur and Rachel Hausfater-Douïeb.

[*See also* Benameur, Jeanne.]

JEAN PERROT

Magnolia Buildings. *See* Stucley, Elizabeth.

Magorian, Michelle (1948–), British author, born in Southsea, Hampshire, and educated at the Bruford College of Speech and Drama, then at Marcel Marceau's École du Mime in Paris. She was working as an actress when her first novel, *Goodnight, Mister Tom* (1981), which won the Guardian Children's Fiction Award, appeared. The book tells the moving story of William Beech, an evacuee during World War II. Leaving behind his sin-obsessed, Bible-bashing mother, he blossoms under the care of the grumpy widower Tom, who helps him discover his many hidden talents, and his worth as a human being, and eventually adopts him after his mother's suicide.

None of her other four novels has matched the success of *Goodnight, Mister Tom*, now considered a modern classic, although *Back Home* (1985) deservedly won the American Library Association Award. It tells the story of Rusty, who returns home after five years in America as an evacuee, and of her mother Peggy's attempt to rebuild family life. Eventually, Peggy accepts that her wartime experience has made her unable to resume her role as a subservient wife, and she moves on to a new life with her children.

A Little Love Song (1991), *Cuckoo in the Nest* (1994), and *A Spoonful of Jam* (1998) also focus on the impact of war on family relationships and on the equally difficult return to peace. *A Little Love Song* additionally compares the First and Second World Wars, while the other two novels, set in the acting world, explore class and gender divisions and allow Magorian to reiterate her belief in the primacy of individual self-realization over conformity to established norms.

Magorian has also published some poetry, *Waiting for My Shorts to Dry* (1989) and *Orange Paw Marks* (1991); a picture book, *Jump* (1992); and two collections of short stories, *In Deep Water* (1992) and the emblematically titled *Be Yourself* (2003).

BIBLIOGRAPHY

Agnew, Kate, and Geoff Fox. *Children at War: From the Great War to the Gulf*. London and New York: Continuum, 2001.

ROSE-MAY PHAM DINH

Maguire, Gregory (1954–), American author, cofounder of Children's Literature New England. Spanning several styles and genres, Maguire's eclectic body of work includes fantasy, realism, humor, historical fiction, science fiction, and picture books, and he has written for audiences ranging from young prereaders through middle graders and young adults to adults.

The Dream Stealer (1983) is the first of his many works that reexamine classic literary or folkloric figures, in this case the Russian folk character Baba Yaga. Perhaps his most well-known title, *Wicked: The Life and Times of the Wicked Witch of the West* (1995), is a similar reexamination. Intended for adults but widely read by a young adult audience, the tale recounts the story of Oz prior to Dorothy's invasion from the perspective of Elphaba, the green-complexioned Wicked Witch of the West; in 2002 the story was adapted as a Broadway play. His subsequent adult crossover novels, *Confessions of an Ugly Stepsister* (1999) and *Mirror, Mirror* (2003), also use alternative perspectives to tell well-known stories; the former was adapted into a TV movie in 2002.

Yet he is also a talented writer of thoughtful realistic fiction, often—as in his fantasy novels—exploring the existence of the disenfranchised, as he does in *Missing Sisters* (1994) and *Oasis* (1996). The questions he raises of family, alienation, and trust are also paramount in *The Good Liar* (1999), his first true historical fiction novel, which treats the life of a young French boy during World War II. On quite a different note, his popular Hamlet Chronicles series for middle graders, which begins with *Seven Spiders Spinning* (1994), uses a realistic contemporary setting but spices it up with high-spirited humor and fantastical elements.

Maguire has also coedited collections of children's literature essays, including *Origins of Story: On Writing for Children* (1999) and *Innocence and Experience: Essays and Conversations on Children's Literature* (1987).

BIBLIOGRAPHY

Silvey, Anita, ed. *The Essential Guide to Children's Books and Their Creators*, 283. Boston: Houghton Mifflin, 2002.

ELISSA GERSHOWITZ

Mahy, Margaret (1936–), distinguished New Zealand writer born in Whakatane; honored with the Order of New Zealand in 1993. Mahy attended Auckland University College and graduated from Canterbury University College. After becoming a librarian in 1965, she moved permanently to Governor's Bay in Lyttleton Harbour. Her childhood was spent within a family adept in rhyme games, storytelling, verbal nonsense, and recitations; she read and listened to stories voraciously from an early age and wrote incessantly from the age of seven. This rich beginning may have helped her develop the multistranded humor in all her books and the deep characterization of her longer novels.

Mahy's place in New Zealand children's literature was hard-won; her early attempts to publish were thwarted by an inexperienced children's publishing world. Recognition came through her contributions to the *New Zealand School Journal*, whose editors included her work for a printing exhibition in New York. Consequently, after 1968, Franklin Watts in the United States and Dent in the United Kingdom began publishing her work. A prolific writer, she has published more than two hundred picture books, verse and story collections, plays, instructional readers, and, most notably, novels for all ages.

Margaret Mahy.

Mahy's first picture book, *A Lion in the Meadow* (1969), illustrates her ability to create dual worlds, an actively magical one alongside another of homely comfort. An imaginary lion becomes afraid of the dragon that has been invented by the unbelieving mother. The boy and the lion make an unexpected alliance, calmly retiring to a wardrobe. *The First Margaret Mahy Story Book* (1972) was a mix of ghost stories (in a tone that she used later in the short novel *Five Sisters*, 1996) and included incredible inventions (such as "The Strange Egg," which foreshadows the robust exaggeration in many of her picture books). In *The Three Legged Cat* (1993) Mahy's particular blend of wordplay, absurdity, and closure tells of Tom, a cat who swaps places with a swagman's hat and travels on the peripatetic swaggie's head. Many of her picture books are ebullient rhymes—*A Summery Saturday Morning* (1998) rollicks through a rhymed story of a dog chased by geese. In the comedic fantasy of her short novel *The Greatest Show off Earth* (1994), every detail, even the title, bespeak Mahy's propensity to call attention to words and rhyme, to story and the wider world of ideas, as she enlarges children's awareness. The longer novels, such as *The Other Side of Silence* (1995) for young teenagers and *Alchemy* (2002) for older teenagers, are underpinned by the idea that in making choices about life we need to use all our capacities. For Mahy this concerns not only family life, fiction, and thinking about truth, as in *The Other Side of Silence*, but also widening one's perspective to encompass science, the supernatural, philosophy, poetry, and love.

In Mahy's major novels for older readers, the light laughter and nonsense enlivening her narratives are transformed into complex psychological insight that reinforces her highly imaginative rendering of families and their restorative power. She is known particularly for her use of the supernatural as a site for agency. In *The Haunting* (1982) the family center is threatened by a challenge from the peripheral Great Uncle Cole, but the older sister, Troy, has stronger magic within the family. It is Troy's decision to use her powers that saves her brother Barney but, more necessary for her, it also enables her to assert her autonomy as she reenters family life.

In *The Changeover: A Supernatural Romance* (1984), Laura, the young heroine, who becomes a witch in order save her brother Jacko from the incubus Carmody Braque, is her brother's protector. Laura's transformation ensures Jacko's rescue and simultaneously secures family ties just as she begins her journey toward love and autonomy. Her next novel, *Dangerous Spaces* (1985), is closely connected to *The Changeover*. Indeed, all the novels tend to center on teenagers establishing autonomy through self-examination (and often transformation) in complex settings of family, fairy tale, and the supernatural. Dangerous spaces occur in the unreflected and unfeeling life.

The routines of family (kitchens, siblings, and food) in *The Haunting* and *The Changeover* enable sensitive girls to develop as tough human beings. It is different for Mahy's boy heroes; Ellis in *24 Hours* (2000) and Jonny in *Memory* (1987) do not live at home. In *Memory*, Jonny has left his family, and we meet him dragging his hangover around parking lots. He stumbles across and looks after confused old Sophie, another disoriented human being, acting as if he were her family, while he discovers his true self. In twenty-four hours Ellis breaks from his middle-class family to experiment with life, drama, and love. Maturation for each of these boys comes through their care of others; Jonny helps organize care for Sophie and sorts his own memories, and Ellis, after helping a suicidal bully, shakes off his grief over the death of a friend by suicide. Neither boy is bound to his family, and neither boy's powers are supernatural. We last see Ellis confidently pedaling his way into the dangerous world.

The lasting appeal of her work rests in such emotional and intellectual complexity. Mahy has won many awards, including Carnegie medals for *The Haunting* and *The Changeover*; several library association awards in the United States and Britain for *The Changeover*, *The Catalogue of the Universe*, and *Memory*; and several best-fiction prizes in New Zealand. Ten of her books are included among the Top One Hundred New Zealand Children's Books of the Twentieth Century, published as the *New Zealand Children's Literature Foundation Yearbook of 2001*.

BIBLIOGRAPHY

Gavin, Adrienne. "Apparition and Apprehension: Supernational Mystery and Emergent Womanhood in *Jane Eyre*, *Wuthering Heights*, and Novels by Margaret Mahy." In *Mystery in Children's Literature*, edited by Adrienne Gavin and Christopher Routledge, 131–148. Basingstoke, U.K.: Palgrave, 2001.

Lawrence-Pietroni, Anna. "The Trickster, the Changeover, and the Fluidity of Adolescent Literature." *Children's Literature Association Quarterly* 20, no. 1 (Spring 1995): 9–14.

Norton, Lucy. "Seeing is Believing: Magical Realism and Visual Narrative in Margaret Mahy's *The Changeover*." *Bookbird* 36, no. 2 (1998): 29–32.

Wilkie-Stibbs, Christine. "'Body Language': Speaking the Feminine in Young Adult Fiction." *Children's Literature Association Quarterly* 25, no. 2 (Summer 2000): 76–87.

Jill Holt

Maitland, Anthony (1932–), British illustrator who studied art in in the United Kingdom and abroad before becoming a freelance illustrator. For his first book commission, illustrations for Philippa Pearce's *Mrs. Cockle's Cat* (1961), he perfectly combines line and color wash to create the atmosphere of warm affection reflected by the text. The illustrations won him the Kate Greenaway Medal for 1961. His succeeding illustrations for the same author's *A Dog So Small* (1962) headed each chapter and once again established the appropriate mood with minimum detail. But Maitland is best known for his magnificent illustrations for Leon Garfield's stories, starting with *Jack Holborn* (1964) and finishing with some of the volumes in *The Apprentices* (1976–1978), the rest of which were illustrated by Faith Jaques. Maitland's swirling black ink drawings, with their looming shadows and unerring eye for dramatic detail, perfectly matched Garfield's gothic imagination, and his cover designs show him equally at home using a full palette of colors. Other commissions include illustrations for a new edition of Andrew Lang's classic *The Green Fairy Book* (1978), again in black and white and particularly effective in bringing out the humor in these tales. He has also worked with Eleanor Farjeon and Penelope Lively.

[*See also biographies of figures mentioned in this article.*]

Nicholas Tucker

Majerová, Marie (1882–1967), major Czech writer, critic and journalist and a representative of social realism, especially in her depictions of women's emancipation. She started her career as a children's writer by retelling folk tales, collected as *Magic World* (1913), while in *Fairy Tales from All Over the World* (1930), Majerová, a dedicated Communist whose real last name was Bartová, used the fairy-tale form for political and ideological purposes. In *Girl Robinson* (1940) she called for women's equality, yet was forced to show how her female protagonist must adapt to social pressure. Her last work for children, *The Tale of the Discontented Rabbit* (1946), addressed to younger readers, focused on children's everyday life and play. After World War II, in

Communist Czechoslovakia, Majerová turned her activity mainly toward criticism, fighting didacticism in children's literature and propagating for high artistic standards.

MARIA NIKOLAJEVA

Major, Kevin (1949–), Canadian writer honored with the Vicky Metcalf Award (1992) for a distinguished body of work. He was born in Stephenville, Newfoundland, and after graduating from Memorial University became a teacher in the outports. Realizing that his students had no books that they felt were relevant to their lives, he began writing about the problems of teens in Newfoundland's fishing villages. He achieved immediate success with his first three books, earning critical praise for combining local color and serious themes. He also became controversial: several schools banned his books because they spoke frankly about alcohol, drugs, and sex. Unwilling to repeat himself, Major continually changes narrative strategies and subject matter. His first three novels focus on destructive changes in outport life. In *Hold Fast* (1978), the experiences of the orphaned narrator, who must move from an outport village to the city, contrast traditional values with contemporary urban materialism and insensitivity. *Far from Shore* (1980) uses several narrators to paint the destruction, especially the disintegration of outport families, caused by chronic unemployment. *Thirty-six Exposures* (1984) is bleaker still, using its thirty-six vignettes, much like snapshots from the camera of the narrator, to convey the despair of young people who see no future for themselves in their island home. In *Dear Bruce Springsteen* (1987), in which a teen's letters to a rock singer explore his feelings about his separated parents, Major (perhaps in an attempt to gain American readers) moved away from explicitly mentioning a Newfoundland setting. In his next novel, *Blood Red Ochre* (1989), he made a dramatic departure in narrative method and genre. This novel alternates third- and first-person viewpoints, and its elaborate plot combines adolescent problem fiction with the historical novel and a time-shift fantasy. Although the fantasy and contemporary realism sections are logically and psychologically weak, the historical chapters are vivid and tense. Major again shifted gears with *Eating between the Lines* (1991), mixing adolescent problems with comic fantasy. The story of a boy who literally enters into books to find insight into ways that he can win the hand of a girl and simultaneously save his parents' marriage, this novel is notable for its humorous episodes, satiric jibes, and subtle sexual references. Major again showed his considerable talents as a comic writer in *Diana: My Autobiography* (1993), which simultaneously satirizes adulation of the British royal family and a teenage girl's superficiality and egocentrism. Although the death of Princess Diana has probably doomed it to obscurity, this farce about maturing identity is an engaging novel that has thematic depth because of its witty use of motifs of perception. In addition to novels, Major has also written a picture book, *The House of Wooden Santas* (1997), a tale about caring for others, and an alphabet, *Eh? to Zed* (2000), which celebrates the country by cataloguing heroes, objects, and places that make Canada unique. Major, who once noted the lack of respect accorded children's writers, has in recent years begun publishing both fiction and nonfiction for adults.

RAYMOND E. JONES

Makarenko, Anton Semenovic (1888–1939), Russian Soviet educator and writer. Makarenko received much international attention in the 1920s for his treatment of orphaned, abandoned, and criminal children in the wake of the Russian Revolution in 1917 and the ensuing civil war. The books in which he described his experience, *The Road to Life* (1933–1935; English trans., 1955) and *Learning to Live* (1939; English trans., 1953), became part of the official Soviet ideology, despite the books' lack of artistic quality. Makarenko's reform pedagogy implied building labor colonies for children, governed by hard military discipline and severe punishment. Since it produced various positive results, this inhuman method was enthusiastically greeted by many foreign visitors. It was criticized by some Russian educators, but had the strong support of the regime. Makarenko's endeavors gave rise to the child penitentiary system that still existed in Russia in the 2000s and also affected the sanctioned views on education. Amid Stalin's terror, Makarenko was lucky to die a natural death.

[*See also* Russia.]

BIBLIOGRAPHY

Bowen, James. *Soviet Education: Anton Makarenko and the Years of Experiment*. Madison: University of Wisconsin Press, 1962.

Lilge, Fredeick. *Anton Semyonovitch Makarenko: An Analysis of His Education Ideas in the Context of Soviet Society*. Berkeley: University of California Press, 1958.

MARIA NIKOLAJEVA

Mäkelä, Hannu (1943–), Finnish writer and poet. Mäkelä is best known for his nonsensical fantasy novels for children, *Herra Huu* (1973; English trans., *Mr. Boo*, 2002) and its sequels, which feature a small, weak, and powerless antihero who dreams of being strong and fearful. Mr. Boo has lost his magical powers and must therefore turn to ordinary children for help to survive, leading to all kinds of funny and surprising situations. The novels, illustrated by the author, are dynamic, action-oriented, and explicitly entertaining. Other fantasy novels by Mäkelä feature intelligent animals, for instance, the philosophical horse in *Hevonen joka hukkasi silmälasinsa* (The Horse Who Lost His Eyeglasses, 1977), or animated toys, as in *Kalle-Juhani ja kaverit* (Kalle-Juhani and Comrades, 1981). These works have a more serious tone than the extremely popular Mr. Boo stories, which have also been turned into stage and television versions.

MARIA NIKOLAJEVA

Makuszyński, Kornel (1884–1953), Polish poet, novelist, columnist, and theater critic. *Bezgrzeszne lata* (Sinless Years, 1925), Makuszyński's first, and autobiographical, novel for young readers met with an enthusiastic reception. The same is true of his other, mostly fantasy and adventure, novels: *O dwóch takich, co ukradli księżyc* (About the Two Who Stole the Moon, 1928), *Przyjaciel wesołego diabła* (The Merry Devil's Friend, 1930), *Wyprawa pod psem* (The Expedition in the Wretched Weather, 1935), *Awantura o Basię* (The Fuss over Barbara, 1936), *Szatan z siódmej klasy* (The Fiend from the Seventh Grade, 1937), and *Szaleństwa panny Ewy* (Miss Eve's Follies, 1940). Far from moralizing, Makuszyński's books are pervaded with warm humor and the belief in a person's good nature and inner strength. He also wrote neoromantic fairy tales for younger children, such as *Bardzo dziwne bajki* (Very Bizarre Fairy Tales, 1916), and coauthored comic books about the adventures of Matołek the Billy Goat and Fiki Miki the Little Monkey.

JUSTYNA DESZCZ-TRYHUBCZAK

Malerba, Luigi (1927–), Italian novelist and script writer. Malerba, whose real name is Luigi Bonardi, uses language that is realistic and nondidactic, designed to construct irrational, grotesque, or humorous worlds. He has published poetry, nursery rhymes, stories, and fairy tales such as *Mozziconi* (Butts, 1975), featuring the tramp Mozziconi, who is also a philosopher, and the unconventional and surreal *Storiette* (Little Stories, 1977), *Pinocchio con gli stivali* (Pinocchio in Boots, 1977), *Le galline pensierose* (Thoughtful Hens, 1980), and *Il cavaliere e la sua ombra* (The Knight and His Shadow, 1993), frequently leading to absurd and surreal plot lines and situations. The absurdist series featuring the knight Millemosche (A-Thousand-Flies, 1969–1973) provides a satire of Crusade epics. Malerba also wrote prefaces to Jules Verne's *Around World in Eighty Days* and Gianni Rodari's *Telephone Tales*.

KATIA PIZZI

Malot, Hector (1830–1907), French novelist, compared to Gustave Flaubert for his first book, *Les amants* (The Lovers, 1859). His realism, however, successively gave way to sentimentalism, which became prominent in his work for the young, starting with *Romain Kalbris* (1869). Because of the success of this novel, the publisher Hetzel encouraged him to write *Sans famille* (1878; Eng. trans., *No Relations*, 1880; also translated as *Nobody's Boy*, *The Adventures of Remi*, and *The Foundling*), in which a kidnapped boy travels across France and finally finds his mother. The success was immense and remains so, with the story having been translated into many languages and made into movies and cartoons. The publisher Flammarion brought out Malot's *En famille* (1893; Eng. trans., *Her Own Folk*, 1894), less known but interesting from the social viewpoint: a little girl shares the working-class life before her grandfather, a rich manufacturer, acknowledges her. During these temporary adventures, the characters live in utmost poverty, surviving on their own, like a Robinson Crusoe, although not on an island but in an unjust society.

BIBLIOGRAPHY

Diversité d'Hector Malot. Cahiers Robinson, no. 10. Arras: Université d'Artois, 2001.

Malot, Hector. *Le Roman de mes romans*. Paris: Flammarion, 1886. Autobiography republished in the *Cahiers Robinson*, no. 13 (2003).

FRANCIS MARCOIN

Mangut, Joseph (1955–), Nigerian writer for young adults. Born in Gwande, Plateau State, Nigeria, Mangut is an author of realist young adult novels that raise moral questions, are set in urban environments, and often feature characters who turn to crime. He is best known for his novels *Have Mercy* (1982) and *The Blackmailers* (1982), which focus on social conditions and the temptations toward committing crime. In *Women for Sale* (1984) the protagonist readjusts to the outside world after serving a prison sentence. Mangut's novels ask whether theft is ever justifiable and whether it is social inequality or individual immorality that instigates criminality.

ADRIENNE E. GAVIN

Man in the Moon. The face, and sometimes figure, supposedly seen in the full or crescent moon is often referred to as the Man in the Moon. Worldwide myths offer as many images in the moon as there are cultures to see them, including a rabbit, a woman weaving, a man carrying a basket on his back, a seated figure, and a four-eyed jaguar. In European tradition, the man is said to have arrived there because he scoffed at Sunday and was doomed to do without the day of rest forever in a world where it is always Monday. Inuit myth places him there as the keeper of souls. In Malaysia he is braiding a fishing line to catch everything on earth, while a rat gnaws the line and a cat chases the rat, ensuring equilibrium in the universe.

The Man in the Moon appears in Mother Goose rhymes ("The Man in the Moon came tumbling down, / And asked the way to Norwich") and other nursery rhymes; J. R. R. Tolkien ascribed to the hobbits a lengthy poem in which the Man in the Moon comes down to earth and gets drunk in an alehouse, and barely bundles back to where he ought to be before the Sun comes up.

Sometimes the personage is a woman, as is Chang O, the Chinese Moon goddess. With her also dwell Wu Kang, banished there endlessly to cut the branches of the cassia tree, and the jade hare, allowed to live there as a reward for his selflessness. In Nancy Willard's *The Nightgown of the Sullen Moon* (1983) the moon is a female who wants clothes. Numerous modern adaptations exist of this universal theme as well as original tales about the man (or woman), for example, Tomi Ungerer's *Moon Man*, 1967.

AMANDA COCKRELL

Manning, Rosemary (1911–1988), British novelist and teacher. Born in Weymouth, Dorset, Rosemary Joy Manning had unhappy experiences at boarding school which provoked recurrent mental illness and informed her adult novel, *The Chinese Garden* (1962). In her first, most enduring book for children, *Green Smoke* (1957), she speaks through an ancient and irascible dragon, R. Dragon, who flies the child Sue to a number of legendary sites relating their stories. This and its three sequels (1959, 1962, 1980) remain popular. Like her writing for adults, Manning's notable historical novel for young adults, *Arripay* (1969), celebrates the achievement of true and fearless self-knowledge.

BRIDGET CARRINGTON

Manning-Sanders, Ruth (1895–1988), Welsh writer. Manning-Sanders started her career as a poet, and from the 1950s on she brought retellings of folk and fairy tales to new audiences. Among her best work is the twenty-two-volume collection commencing with *A Book of Giants* (1962) and completed with *A Book of Magic Horses* (1984). Staple fare for eight- to twelve-year-olds in public libraries at the time, the series introduced a generation to a range of familiar and lesser-known tales from around the world. Manning-Sanders's distinctive style is characterized by a storyteller's ear for repetition and dramatic buildup, and a lively way with detail. She also wrote several children's novels, such as *Circus Boy* (1960), which draws on her own experience of two years with a traveling circus, and she produced four books of verse, receiving the Blindman International Poetry Prize in 1926.

BELINDA COPSON

Manushkin, Fran (1942–), American editor and author. A graduate of the Chicago Teachers College, Frances Manushkin worked as a teacher and tour guide before joining the staff of Harper and Row's children's department, where she worked from 1968 to 1978 and where her mentors included Ursula Nordstrom and Charlotte Zolotow. Her editing projects included Lillian Hoban's Arthur books, and she later worked for Random House (1978–1980) before becoming a full-time writer. Her first book, *Baby* (later editions titled *Baby, Come Out!*), appeared in 1972. It received mixed reviews but proved popular in nine languages and received a Dutch Silver Pencil Award. She has since written more than thirty books and is known for her simple yet lively delivery. In the 1990s, Manushkin's range expanded to Jewish stories such as *Latkes and Applesauce* (1992), *The Matzah That Papa Brought Home* (1995), *Miriam's Cup: A Passover Story* (1998), and *Daughters of Fire: Heroines of the Bible* (2001).

PEGGY LIN DUTHIE

Marcellino, Fred (1939–2001), American illustrator and author of children's picture books and novels. Marcellino attended New York's Cooper Union for the Advancement of Science and Art and Yale University and won a Fulbright fellowship. Early in his career he designed record album covers and book dust jackets. He insisted on reading completely the books he was assigned and often designed his jackets symbolically rather than relying on a tip sheet that highlighted details about a character's appearance and the novel's setting. His thoughtful work made him one of the preeminent book jacket artists of the late 20th century.

Marcellino's first children's book illustrations appeared in Tor Seidler's novel *A Rat's Tale* (1996). Its success inspired him to try his hand at illustrating fairy tales. His first picture book, *Puss in Boots*, retold by Tor Seidler (1990), won a Caldecott Honor. His pictures include tributes to earlier illustrators of the tale, for example, the French illustrator Gustave Doré, but are strikingly modern as well. His unconventional front cover for the book focuses so tightly on Puss's face that the title credits had to be moved to the back cover. Marcellino continued his work illustrating old tales with a version of *The Steadfast Tin Soldier* (1992), a collection of Edward Lear poems, a retelling of a Brothers Grimm story, a newly illustrated volume of E. B. White's *Trumpet of the Swan* (2000), and, most daringly, a reimagining of Helen Bannerman's *Little Black Sambo*, now titled *The Story of Little Babaji* (1996), which garnered praise for its smooth visual style and overtly Indian setting but also some criticism for its own cultural reductivism.

Marcellino provided original text for only one book, *I, Crocodile* (1999), which he also illustrated. In this wickedly funny tale, a proud crocodile archly narrates his adventures as he is kidnapped by Napoleon, relocated to France, and finally comfortably ensconced in the sewers of Paris. Its sequel, *Arrivederci, Crocodile*, was left unfinished at Marcellino's death.

MEGAN LYNN ISAAC

Marcet, Jane (1769–1858), British writer. Marcet wrote nearly thirty popular introductions to the physical, natural, and social sciences for female and young readers. One of twelve children of the Swiss merchant-banker Anthony Haldimand, she enjoyed an unrestricted education at home. In 1799 she married the physician Alexander Marcet, and their home in London's Russell Square became a meeting place of the Whig intellectual establishment. Regular visitors included Maria Edgeworth, the chemist Sir Humphry Davy, the botanist Augustin de Candolle, and the mathematician H. B. de Saussure, so Marcet kept abreast of new developments in science. Having the advantage of learning so much through conversations with scientists, she chose to present complex concepts through familiar dialogue, a format long considered suitable for teaching those who had had little exposure to abstract ideas. Her *Conversations*, all published anonymously, became an identifiable trademark. The best-known on both sides of the Atlantic were her volumes on chemistry (1806), political economy (1816), and natural philosophy (1819). Like works by her predecessors Mary Wollstonecraft, Dorothy Kilner, and Priscilla Wakefield, Marcet's dialogues feature a well-informed, articulate mother and children with different personalities and aptitudes—for example, Mrs. B and her adolescent daughters, the impetuous Caroline and the serious Emily, in *On Vegetable Physiology* (1829).

Marcet's scientific popularizations, notably *Chemistry*, were addressed to readers from well-educated, affluent families and introduced current theory and correct terminology as well as promoting experimentation through adroit use of laboratory equipment and chemicals. Michael Faraday claimed that reading *Conversations on Chemistry* had inspired him to pursue a life in science; it was widely adopted as a textbook in female academies, women's colleges, and mechanics' institutes. Although her popularizations were pitched quite high, Marcet's effective expositions expressed in a remarkably unpretentious style did much to close the gap between scholarly knowledge and ordinary life. By making the newest advances in science and social theory available to both young and adult readers, Marcet won the praise of David Ricardo, Thomas Babington Macaulay, and Thomas Malthus.

[*See also* Books of Instruction; Edgeworth, Maria; Kilner, Dorothy, and Mary Ann Kilner; Science Books; Wakefield, Priscilla; *and* Wollstonecraft, Mary.]

BIBLIOGRAPHY

Lindee, M. Susan. "The American Career of Jane Marcet's *Conversations on Chemistry*, 1806–1853." *Isis* 82 (1991): 9–23.

Polkinghorn, Bette. "Jane Marcet and Harriet Martineau: Motive, Market Experience, and Reception of Their Works Popularizing Classical Political Economy." In *Women of Value: Feminist Essays on the History of Women in Economics*, edited by M. A. Dimand, R. W. Dimand, and E. L. Forget, 71–81. Aldershot, U.K.: Edward Elgar, 1995.

Shteir, Ann B. *Cultivating Women Cultivating Science: Flora's Daughters and Botany in 1760–1860*. Baltimore: Johns Hopkins University Press, 1996.

PATRICIA DEMERS

Marchand, Pierre (1939–2002), French publisher. Marchand, who as an autodidact, founded the children's literature department of the prestigious publishing house Gallimard with his friend Jean-Olivier Héron in 1972. With a vision of books as a way to allow children to open up and discover the world, he created nonfiction series remarkable for their graphic and technical innovation. In 1978 he brought out texts by great writers illustrated by young artists in the series Enfantimages ("Childimages"). Wishing to have publications distributed to as wide an audience as possible, Marchand brought the paperback into general use in children's literature with the series Folio Junior and Folio Benjamin. In 1999 he left Gallimard and became the creative director at Hachette Livres.

SOPHIE VAN DER LINDEN

Marchant, Bessie (1862–1941), British writer of more than 150 girls' adventure stories, born in Petham, Kent. Marchant has been described as "the girls' Henty," usually setting her stories in the distant Empire, particularly Canada, or other "exotic" lands where restrictions of class, traditional female roles, and expectations could be subverted. In early books such as *The Half Moon Girl; or, The Rajah's Daughter* (1898), she permitted her adolescent heroines to rival male experience and display the freedom and intrepidity that typified the Edwardian "New Woman" in adult novels, although, at the books' conclusions, the girls return to an ultimately feminine role in England. Marchant's stories, like later girl detective series, combine accurate geographical detail with plots involving ransom, smuggling, and physical danger. In her story of espionage, *A Girl Munition Worker* (1916), Marchant was able to utilize the increasingly varied career roles that World War I made available to women.

[*See also* Adventure Books; Henty, G. A.; *and* Young Adult Literature.]

BRIDGET CARRINGTON

Marchant, John (fl. 1750), 18th-century English author of two volumes of children's poetry, *Puerilia* (1751) and *Lusus juvenilis* (1753). An admirer of Isaac Watts, Marchant composed poems in correct, colloquial language attempting to "enlarge ideas" about ethics and religion in an appealing way. Although he wrote poems about animals, Marchant rejected the fable as a model, arguing instead that subjects drawn from children's daily lives were more likely to make an impression because their relevance would be immediately apparent and the audience would quickly grasp it. He chose subjects he thought suitable to readers' ages and gender, such as a conversation with a doll for little girls or, for young ladies, the come-on of a madam. Written in a variety of meters and stanzaic forms, many of Marchant's poems could be sung to the well-known tunes listed in the table of contents, such as "For he's a jolly good fellow," reflecting his concern that children sang bawdy ballads and love lyrics because there was so little appropriate verse for them.

[*See also* Fables; Poetry; *and* Watts, Isaac.]

ANDREA IMMEL

Marchetta, Melina (1965–), Italian Australian author. Marchetta left school at fifteen, and subsequently trained to be a secondary school teacher. She is best known for her award-winning *Looking for Alibrandi* (1992), which explores the life of a seventeen-year-old Italian Australian girl in her last year of high school. As in Marchetta's more recent *Saving Francesca* (2003), the major theme is the protagonist's search for identity within the complexities of Australian multicultural society. *Alibrandi*, one of Australia's best-selling novels, was reissued in an adult edition, and was made into a successful feature film. Marchetta's script for the film won an Australian Film Institute award.

MARGOT HILLEL

Marchiori, Carlos (1937–), Italian Canadian illustrator. A native of Venice, Marchiori studied in Padua and emigrated to Canada in 1956. His early career included generating cartoons for CBC television and the National Film Board of Canada; his short animated film *The Drag* (1965) was nominated for an Academy Award. As a book illustrator, Marchiori is primarily known for the vibrant, colorful prints in Edith Fowke's *Sally Go Round the Sun: 300 Songs, Rhymes and Games of Canadian Children* (1969). His playful, seemingly artless designs incorporate thumbprints and other stamped patterns as well as skillfully painted detail. In 1970 the volume was named Book of the Year for Children by the Canadian Library Association; twenty years later, the Vancouver Public Library selected it as one of 133 "great Canadian books of the century." Now working as Carlo Marchiori, the artist later settled on a whimsically decorated estate in northern California and specializes in mural painting and furniture decoration.

PEGGY LIN DUTHIE

Mardrus, Joseph Charles (1868–1949), French physician and translator. Born in Cairo, Egypt, Mardrus traveled around the Middle East as a seafaring physician (1895–1899); he is best known as the author of a French translation of the *Arabian Nights*. After settling in Paris, he began to publish the *Mille et une nuits* (literally, Thousand and One Nights, 1899–1904), his most notable work. His translation is literal and voluptuous, retaining the inserted poems, unlike the first French translation by Antoine Galland (1704–1717), which was classical and elegant. Mardrus's translation was immediately very popular, but it continues to be controversial. Readily accessible, it shows the writer's undeniable skill as a storyteller. Furthermore, as with other oral tales, there is no fixed original. If Galland's chaste translation is the usual base text for youth literature, Mardrus's work is useful to storytellers, who can compare it with more recent translations and create their own versions.

NADINE DECOURT

Marino, Jan (1936–), American author of intermediate-grade and young adult novels. Marino looked into her own life when writing her first novel, *Eighty-Eight Steps to September* (1989), which concerns a girl who experiences the death of a sibling. This sensitive story established the author's ability to tackle complex emotional issues. She continued writing in that vein with *The Day Elvis Came to Town* (1991), in which a girl growing up in the early 1960s contends with her father's drinking and the racial prejudice met by her family's new boarder. Orphaned siblings dream of a better life in *The Mona Lisa of Salem Street* (1995), and a novel set in the Vietnam era, *Searching for Atticus* (1997), features a teenager who wishes her father were more like Atticus Finch in Harper Lee's *To Kill a Mockingbird*. In all her novels, Marino creates convincing characters who struggle with family ties, identity, and acceptance—of oneself and others—on their path to adulthood.

[*See also* Lee, Harper.]

PETER D. SIERUTA

Mark, Jan (1943–), British author. Mark's award-winning writing includes junior fiction, children's plays, picture books, fantasy fiction, realistic young adult novels, nonfiction, and short stories for children. She has also adapted her work for television and radio, edited poetry anthologies, and produced a novel and a short story collection for adult readers. She studied at the Canterbury College of Art and later worked as an art teacher. Mark has been awarded the Carnegie Medal twice.

Mark's literary style is characterized by its keenly observed detail, trademark wit, accurate rendition of dialogue, and an often somber view of the world as a brutal and unforgiving place. Her first novel, *Thunder and Lightnings* (1976), is about a developing friendship between two boys from different social classes. Written in realist style, it explores adolescent relationships and the impact of class divisions on them, as well as reflecting on the process of maturation. It was a popular and critical success, earning both a Carnegie Medal and Penguin/*Guardian* Award. *Handles* (1983), a novel which cleverly uses the story of a young female protagonist obsessed with motorbikes to interrogate gendered behavior, language, and language signification, won Mark a second Carnegie Medal.

Mark's short stories, rich in narrative detail and infused with wry humor, are outstanding examples of this genre. *Nothing To Be Afraid Of* (1980), a collection which focuses on the terrifying powers of the imagination, achieves a remarkable level of realism in its well-wrought characters and familiar settings. At the same time, Mark skillfully creates a genuinely frightening atmosphere and uses disturbing story twists to evoke a sense of the uncanny. A particularly innovative example of Mark's ability to combine realism with fantasy is her novel *They Do Things Differently There* (1994). Two girls, Charlotte and Elaine, who live in a stiflingly conventional English suburb, construct their own parallel fantasy world by redescribing the seemingly dreary suburban landscape of their daily lives. The novel seamlessly blends the realistic monotony of daily life with fantasy, and the result is intriguing, surreal, and frequently hilarious.

Mark's futuristic fantasy fiction for young adult readers, which includes the early trio *The Ennead* (1978), *Divide and Rule* (1979), and *Aquarius* (1984), stands apart from her more realist-oriented works of fiction. Here she uses a speculative fantasy world to examine the process of growing up in the shadow of the conflict between individuality and social institutions. Later fantasy develops a more political focus, through the frame of East-West relations in the apocalyptic *The Eclipse of the Century* (1999) or the regime of surveillance and oppression in *Riding Tycho* (2005). *Useful Idiots* (2004), a futuristic fantasy thriller set on an environmentally damaged and politically divided planet Earth in the year 2080, satirizes contemporary environmental, technological, and racial politics, providing a disturbing critique of the notion of a unified, homogenized Europe. Mark's diverse contribution to, and range across, most genres of English children's literature is significant because its intelligent and inventive thematic exploration of issues pertaining to identity, ethnicity, and cultural value always looks for an engaged intelligence in readers.

JOHN STEPHENS

Markham, Mrs. (c. 1779–1837), British writer of textbooks. After marriage in 1814 to a clergyman and the birth of three children, Elizabeth Cartwright Penrose published *A History of England from the First Invasion by the Romans to the End of the Reign of George III* in 1823, using the pseudonym she was to retain for the rest of her career, Mrs. Markham (Markham was a village where she had spent some of her childhood). This was a standard history textbook, a narrative of events followed by a catechism section designed to ensure that the user had learned the lessons of the previous chapter, couched as conversations between Mrs. Markham and her children. It stood out from other history textbooks because of Markham's friendly tone and her willingness to introduce children to the principles of Enlightenment historiography, particularly the idea that the purpose of studying history was to show how civilized society had gradually been formed. The illustrations that her new publisher, John Murray, introduced for the revised edition of 1826 helped to make the book distinctive and appealing, preparing the way for a sequel, *A History of France* (1828). *Historical Conversations for Young Persons* (1836) was written entirely in the form of conversations, and books of questions to supplement the two histories were published. The texts continued at the heart of school and home curricula in Britain and America until the late 19th century. They were still well enough known in the 20th century for the character Oswald to disparage them in the first chapter of E. Nesbit's *The Wouldbegoods* (1901), and Hilaire Belloc parodied them in his *Mrs. Markham's New History of England* (1926). *A Visit to the Zoological Gardens* (1829), *Sermons for Children* (1837), and *The New Children's Friend* (1832) were less successful.

MATTHEW GRENBY

Markoosie (1942–), Canadian Inuit writer, pilot, and translator. Markoosie Patsauq, who has published under his given name alone, was born in Inukjuak, Quebec, and schooled in Yellowknife, Northwest Territories. His book *Harpoon of the Hunter* first appeared in *Inuit Newsletter/Inuttituut*. He translated the book from his first language into English and published it in 1970. The narrative is importantly different from familiar Anglo-European narratives. The story follows one character, Kamik, as he hunts for a wounded polar bear across a bleak land. It is an uncompromising look at a dying culture, presenting the fate of a people with sadness and acceptance. Markoosie also wrote *Wings of Mercy* (1972).

RODERICK MCGILLIS

Marks, Alan (1957–), brought up in London's docklands, attended several art schools before working as a full-time illustrator. His first commission was for illustrations for Kevin Crossley-Holland's story *Storm* (1985), which won the Carnegie award for 1985. Since then Marks has collaborated with many distinguished authors, including Rosemary Sutcliff, Joan Aiken, and Jill Paton Walsh. Mostly working in black and white, his meticulously drawn figures are sometimes backed up by added watercolor washes. He is much in demand for illustrating traditional rhymes and stories, and his *Ring-a-Ring o' Roses and a Ding, Dong Bell* (1991) was a particular success, made up of rhymes chosen by the artist himself.

NICHOLAS TUCKER

Marrin, Albert (1936–), American award-winning author of historical nonfiction. Marrin worked as a social studies teacher before becoming a university lecturer and professor in the history department of Yeshiva College, New York. His work is aimed at young adults and takes a refreshing approach to chronicling American and world history. In books such as *The Yanks Are Coming: The United States in the First World War* (1986), *America and Vietnam: The Elephant and the Tiger* (1992), and *Virginia's General: Robert E. Lee and the Civil War* (1994), Marrin details the desperation and consequences of war. In *Hitler* (1987), *Stalin: Russia's Man of Steel* (1988), and *Napoleon and the Napoleonic Wars* (1991), he presents accurate portraits of national leaders who radically changed world history. His nonfiction books, which are historically precise, contain copious explanatory notes as well as references to primary sources where the young reader can find further information on the book's subject. *1812: The War Nobody Won* (1985), which describes the causes and key events of the early-19th-century conflict between Great Britain and the United States; *Unconditional Surrender: U. S. Grant and the Civil War* (1994), which studies Grant's life and his pivotal role in the Civil War; and *Tatan'ka Iyota'ke: Sitting Bull and His World* (2000), about the life of one of the best-known Native American leaders of the 1800s, were all named Boston Globe–

Horn Book Honor Books. Another one of his biographical books, *Commander in Chief: Abraham Lincoln and the Civil War* (1997), was a Booklist Children's Editors' Choice, an ALA Best Book for Young Adults, a VOYA Nonfiction Honor List selection, and a Capitol Choice. In 1995 Marrin was presented with the *Washington Post*–Children's Book Guild Nonfiction Award for his outstanding lifetime contribution to the quality of nonfiction for children.

Maria-Venetia Kyritsi

Marryat, Captain Frederick (1792–1848), a British Navy commander and fecund novelist. The son of a London magnate and member of Parliament, Marryat went to sea at age thirteen fired by Horatio Nelson's victory at Trafalgar (1805). He saw many conflicts and served in the Mediterranean, the Caribbean, and the Atlantic and Indian Oceans. After experiencing the harsh conditions belowdecks, he was given command of his own ship while in his twenties. His distinction in devising new signaling systems was recognized, as were his bravery and humanity; for rescuing men from drowning, he was awarded the Royal Humane Society's gold medal in 1818. His first novel was *The Naval Officer; or, Scenes and Adventures in the Life of Frank Mildmay* (1829). He resigned from the navy in 1830, devoting himself to writing full-time. Marryat's firsthand knowledge furnished his early maritime novels, *Jacob Faithful* (1834), *Peter Simple* (1834), and *Mr Midshipman Easy* (1836) with accurate detail, and in them he treated what became typical subjects: mystery at sea in *The Phantom Ship* (1839) and piracy in *The Pirate and the Three Cutters* (1836) and *The Privateer's-Man One Hundred Years Ago* (1846). His first non-maritime novel, *Japhet in Search of a Father* (1836), is the fictional autobiography of an orphan making his way in the world.

Though intended for adults, the picaresque adventures of *Peter Simple* and *Mr Midshipman Easy* were also enjoyed by the young, and, responding to his family's requests, Marryat turned to writing books for children: *Masterman Ready, or, The Wreck of the "Pacific"* (a retelling of the *Swiss Family Robinson* scenario) appeared in 1841–1842. Here his writing included elements of disguised didacticism and religious observance. Marryat then began to move away from contemporary sea stories: *The Settlers in Canada* (1844) introduced encounters with Indians, and—nowadays his best-known book—*The Children of the New Forest* (1847) is the first British historical novel for children to have a lasting place in children's literature. Set in England, with children (both girls and boys) as leading characters, it is a story of the Civil War (1642–1645) and espouses the Royalist cause. *The Mission; or, Scenes in Africa* (1845) was not a success, and *The Little Savage* (1848–1849), his last children's book, about a boy brought up on an island, was completed posthumously by his son, Frank.

Charles Dickens and Joseph Conrad admired Marryat's work: he had indeed a Dickensian skill and humor in developing idiosyncratic characters and in his narrative drive. Marryat's eventful stories were much translated and were soon followed by those of Mayne Reid and Ballantyne; they occupy an important place in the history of the adventure novel. A harbinger of future developments, *Masterman Ready* reached the pinnacle of its popularity during the 1870s fashion for adventure books. Taking up themes and locations first explored by Daniel Defoe, Marryat provided some of the earliest examples in children's literature proper of a genre and a subgenre always—and still—deeply rooted in English literary tradition: the adventure novel and the sea story.

BIBLIOGRAPHY

Butts, Dennis, ed. Introduction to *The Children of the New Forest*, by Frederick Marryat. Oxford, U.K.: Oxford University Press, 1991.

Conrad, Joseph. *Tales of the Sea*. London: Orlestone, 1919. On Marryat and James Fenimore Cooper.

Warner, Oliver. *Captain Marryat: A Rediscovery*. London: Constable, 1953.

Ann Lawson Lucas

Marsden, James (1908–1973), prolific and versatile English writer who wrote over five hundred books under seventeen separate names. Marsden, whose real name is John Creasey, wrote short stories, Westerns, romantic novels, and children's books, but is best known for his detective fiction, which often involved the use of popular series characters such as Gideon of Scotland Yard, John Mannering ("The Baron"), and Gordon Craigie from "Department Z." Most of his works are now out of print, but he is remembered for his exciting mysteries. His children's mystery novels include *Murder by Magic* (1937), *The Sacred Eye* (1939), and *Five Missing Men* (1940).

Patricia Kennon

Marsden, John (1950–), Australian author, born in Melbourne. Best known for his frank explorations of adolescence in realistic novels, he won immediate attention in 1987 with his first novel, *So Much to Tell You*, about a scarred and emotionally traumatized teenage girl who lives in self-imposed muteness at a boarding school. With this novel Marsden established his customary practice of representing youth characters through their own words, often by narration structured as diary entries or letters. Candid representations of teenage sexuality, and explorations of hard-hitting themes such as teenage violence in *Letters from the Inside* (1991) and *Dear Miffy* (1997), have earned him some controversy, but he is also known as a writer capable of humor, as evident in his popular book for younger audiences, *Staying Alive in Year 5* (1989). Although mostly identified as a writer for adolescents, Marsden has also published other works for younger readers, including several picture books, the most famous of these an allegory of race relations in Australia, *The Rabbits* (1998), illustrated by Shaun Tan. Marsden consolidated his career with his enormously popular speculative fiction series, the Tomorrow Series, beginning with *Tomorrow, When the War Began* (1993). The seven books of the series, narrated by a female teenager, Ellie, follow the lives of a group of youths after a fictional invasion of Australia. Ellie's struggles to come to terms with the collapse of Australian society and youth culture, and her ruminations on war, death, sex, and adolescence, establish her as an exemplary Marsden character: forthright, down-to-earth, and emotionally engaging. For many years a teacher, Marsden is well-known for his support of young people, in particular his encouragement of youth writing, evident in his nonfiction guide, *Everything I Know about Writing* (1993). His other major nonfiction work is *Secret Men's Business* (1998), a contentious exploration of teenage masculinity.

SHELLEY CHAPPELL

Marsh, James (1946–), English artist born in Yorkshire, studied graphic design at Batley College of Art and Design. Working for different agencies, he designed and illustrated numbers of record sleeves before establishing his own studio in 1969, known as "Head Office." Six years later he began freelancing, producing a stream of work ranging from covers for *Time* magazine to artwork for men's publications like *Penthouse* and *Men Only*. His work is always characterized by warm, rich colors achieved through his use of painting oils and acrylics. Illustrating book covers, too, he has worked extensively for Penguin Books, providing some excellent designs for the novels of William Trevor. For Trevor's *The Boarding House*, for example, Marsh provided an apparently blameless red door on the cover, hung with interior curtains. But in the slit where letters are posted, two yellow eyes are seen peeping out, promising no good at all.

Marsh's work for children is best represented by *Bizarre Birds and Beasts* (1991). Informed by a surreal vision where nothing is ever quite as it seems, its glowing pictures of real and mythical animals are clearly influenced by the work of Henri Rousseau, René Magritte, and Salvador Dali. *From the Heart* (1993), subtitled *Light-Hearted Verse*, continues in the same vein, with his colorful illustrations as always informed by a sense of mystery and wonder.

NICHOLAS TUCKER

Marshak, Samuil (1887–1964), Russian writer, playwright, critic, and translator; together with Kornei Chukovsky, one of the pioneers of Soviet children's literature. Besides being a brilliant translator of Shakespeare's sonnets into Russian, he translated English nursery rhymes and ballads, Robert Louis Stevenson, Rudyard Kipling, Edward Lear, and A. A. Milne. Marshak started writing his own poems for children in the 1920s. Most of them were produced in collaboration with prominent illustrators and published as picture books. Some of these are humorous, even nonsensical, animal tales and fables: *Babies in the Zoo* (1923), *The Tale of the Stupid Mouse* (1923), *The Poodle* (1927), or *Stripes and Whiskers* (1930). Some of these have clear morals, others are merely entertaining because the requirement for didacticism and social commitment was not yet established in Soviet children's literature. In *The Circus* (1925) and *The Ice-Cream Man* (1925; Eng. trans., 1943), the pictures by Vladimir Lebedev, reminiscent of the propaganda poster, carry the primary information, accompanied by a few lines with catchy rhymes. More typical for the new Soviet children's literature were verse stories focusing on the rapidly changing urban life: *The Fire* (1923), *Yesterday and Today* (1925), *Baggage* (1926; Eng. trans., *The Pup Grew Up*, 1989) or *Hail to Mail* (1927; Eng. trans., 1990). *The Absentminded Fellow* (1930; Eng. trans., 1999) is a magnificent nonsense poem in everyday, easily recognizable settings. Much of the irony present in these verses is too subtle for young readers and is addressed to adults. Marshak's later works for children fluctuate between the heroic—celebrating the achievements of socialism in *The War against the Dniepr* (1931) and the superior moral qualities of the new Soviet citizen in *The Tale of the Unknown Hero* (1938)—and the satirical, when he portrays an American millionaire's disastrous visit to Leningrad in *Mister Twister* (1933) or a young Nazi boy's successful en-

Samuil Marshak. Front cover illustration by Boris Kustodiev for *Pozhar* (Moscow: Raduga, c. 1926). REPRODUCED COURTESY OF THE COTSEN CHILDREN'S LIBRARY, PRINCETON UNIVERSITY LIBRARY

trance exam to join the Gestapo in *Young Fritz* (1942). While most of these verses have lost their relevance, they can still be appreciated for their marvelous rhythm, rhyme, and humor.

After the war, Marshak worked mostly as a translator and wrote lyrical poetry for adults, while he published poetry collections for children with a common theme announced by the titles: *The Multicolored Book* (1947) and *Around the Year* (1948). In addition, he wrote a counter-story to his earlier book, *The Tale of the Clever Mouse* (1956), and retold in rhyme some Russian, Ukranian, Lithuanian, and Oriental folktales as well as fairy tales by Hans Christian Andersen. Marshak is also known for his children's plays, many of which are still performed, notably *Pussy-Cat's House* (1922) and *The Month-Brothers* (1943; Eng. trans., 1983), based on a Slovak folktale, a version of "Mother Holle."

Marshak's status in Russian children's literature is comparable to that of Milne in England or Dr. Seuss in the United States; his verses are among the very first literary texts children read. As editor of several literary magazines for children in the 1920s and later chairman of the Soviet Children's Writers' Guild, Marshak made an outstanding contribution to the promotion of Soviet children's literature and the introduction of international children's literature in the Soviet Union.

BIBLIOGRAPHY

Bode, Andreas. "Humor in the Lyrical Stories for Children of Samuel Marshak and Kornei Chukovsky." *Lion and the Unicorn* 13, no. 2 (1989): 34–55.

Sokol, Elena. *Russian Poetry for Children*. Knoxville: University of Tennessee Press, 1984.

MARIA NIKOLAJEVA

Marshall, Allan (1902–1984), Australian author born in Noorat, Victoria. Marshall was crippled by infantile paralysis when he was six. He wrote short stories, accounts of his travels, and contributed a wealth of material to journals and newspapers. The first volume of his autobiography, *I Can Jump Puddles* (1955), recalls his rural childhood battling disability within a loving family. His determination to walk, ride, fight, and play is inspirational, and the book has been adapted for television and film. In *Whispering in the Wind* (1969), Peter sets off with a horse, a stock whip with supernatural properties, and a magical leaf to find a beautiful princess. Together with a wise kangaroo, Greyfur, he finds the princess, who has been locked up until she can pass her school examinations. *Fight for Life* (1972) has Bill surviving a bushfire and finding his fortune. Marshall draws on Australian folklore, bush culture, and colloquial idiom to write with optimism about the need for strength to survive life's hard times.

STELLA LEES

Marshall, Emma (1828–1899), British author known mainly for her children's literature, but also for poetry, religious works, and historical novels. After marrying a minister's son and starting a family, Marshall began to write many books for children, particularly young girls. Her first children's book, *The Happy Days at Fernbank: A Story for Little Girls*, was published in 1861. Most of her books are domestic stories imbued with religion, published by evangelical publishers, with the young heroes and heroines learning valuable lessons about society, faith, and love. *Lessons of Love; or, Aunt Bertha's Visit to the Elms* (1863) tells the story of Edith, a young girl whose parents depart for some months. Although her aunt arrives to care for the girls, Edith insists on taking control, and proceeds to learn many valuable lessons about respecting her elders and having love for and patience with her family. Marshall became a very popular writer and produced nearly two hundred books.

[*See also* Girls' Books and Fiction *and* Evangelical Writing.]

AMANDA THIBODEAU

Marshall, H. E. (1876–?), British writer who produced popular histories for children in the early 20th century. Few details about her life are known. Henrietta Elizabeth Marshall's most famous book is *Our Island Story* (1905), a history of England for children; the book was reprinted in 2005 with a view to instilling a love of history in British children as it did for earlier generations of Marshall's readers. She also wrote histories of France, Scotland, and the United States and of the British Empire in Australia and India. Marshall aims to amuse as well as instruct, and anecdotes are often mixed with facts. One of her most readable works is *English Literature for Boys and Girls* (1909), in which she surveys the development of English literature from oral narratives to the Victorian Age, enlivened by quotations and structured as a metastory about stories. Marshall has also produced children's versions of several legends, including those of Beowulf, Roland, and Robin Hood. Her last book was *Kings and Things* (1937).

SINDHU MENON

Marshall, James (1942–1992), American children's illustrator and author. Marshall is best remembered for his witty and gently satiric works, illustrated with his lively cartoons. He grew up on a Texas farm and loved drawing from an early age, but lacking any encouragement, he turned to music. He studied the violin and viola and won a scholarship to the New England Conservatory of Music. After only a year, he injured his hand and was forced to abandon his musical studies. Subsequently, he studied at Trinity College in Hartford, Connecticut, and Southern Connecticut State College. He briefly taught high school French and Spanish but soon returned to his first love, drawing. He presented a portfolio

James Marshall. Back cover of *George and Martha* (Boston: Houghton Mifflin, 1972). REPRODUCED COURTESY OF THE COTSEN CHILDREN'S LIBRARY, PRINCETON UNIVERSITY LIBRARY

to Houghton Mifflin, and the publisher showed an immediate interest in his work, commissioning him to illustrate Byrd Baylor's *Plink, Plink, Plink* (1971). The following year Marshall won acclaim with his own book, *George and Martha*, about two lovable hippopotamuses curiously named for Edward Albee's fiery characters in the play *Who's Afraid of Virginia Woolf?* In sharp contrast to Albee's creations, Marshall's comical figures are models of kindness and consideration. George and Martha appeared in six sequels and quickly became childhood favorites. Marshall himself claims inspiration from both Maurice Sendak and Edward Gorey, and critics have also seen the influence of Jean de Brunhoff and Roger Duvoisin. Like de Brunhoff's Babar the Elephant and Duvoisin's Petunia or the Happy Lion, Marshall's endearing cartoon characters are also the vehicles for a sharp and sophisticated wit.

In 1974 Marshall teamed with Harry Allard for *The Stupids Step Out*, the first of a wildly popular series of four books about a family of lovable simpletons, reminiscent of Lucretia Hale's Peterkin family (*The Peterkin Papers*, 1886). The family, whose surname is Stupid, is a parody of the nuclear family as portrayed on 1950s American television. Backward in every way but blithely ignorant of their own deficiencies, the Stupids (whose name and antics have needlessly distressed many adults) remain favorites of children, who are invited to enjoy a confident superiority. Marshall and Allard produced numerous popular sequels to *The Stupids* and teamed again for *Miss Nelson Is Missing* (1977). This is the hilarious tale of an unruly class of students who are at last tamed by a frightening substitute teacher, Miss Viola Swamp—who, the readers are allowed to discover, is in fact the students' regular teacher, Miss Nelson, in disguise. Miss Nelson, like the Stupids, returns in several sequels. Under the name Edward Marshall, Marshall wrote numerous easy-to-read books in the I Can Read Fox series, including *Fox and His Friends* (1982) and four sequels, all about how Fox is repeatedly outwitted, usually by his younger sister. Marshall brought his comic genius to folk tales and received a Caldecott Honor Award for his version of *Goldilocks and the Three Bears*. His strength was his genuine respect for his child audience—sharing with them his sophisticated humor, his social commentary, and his jovial illustrations.

DAVID L. RUSSELL

Marshall, John (c. 1755–c. 1825), British publisher instrumental in the expansion of the children's book market after John Newbery's death in 1767. Soon after inheriting his father Richard's chapbook printing business, Marshall introduced children's books to the line and identified several rising stars of the new generation of writers for the young. Sarah Trimmer produced her two steadiest sellers: the animal story *The History of the Robins* (1786) and the *Description of a Set of Scripture Prints* (1786), a pictorial introduction to the Bible. Lucy Peacock edited the *Juvenile Magazine* (1788–1789), the second English children's periodical. Dorothy and Mary Ann Kilner wrote moral tales about believable child characters, including *Jemima Placid* (1783), and charming animal "autobiographies" such as *The Life and Perambulation of Mouse* (1783). Lady Ellenor Fenn devised elementary readers like *Cobwebs To Catch Flies* (1783) and teaching aids, such as *A Set of Toys* (1792?), notable for their innovative child-centered pedagogy. These works, all nicely illustrated, drew favorable reviews. Marshall also issued Hannah More's *Cheap Repository Tracts*, but the author and publisher had a bitter falling out. (More may have been the victim, if Trimmer's characterization of Marshall as a sharp trader and slave driver was accurate.) Whether their quarrel may have also soured relations with Marshall's other women authors is unclear, but the literary quality of his backlist fell off as they took their new works to other firms. By 1800 Marshall was publishing chiefly picture books for young children, among the first with hand-colored engravings and color paper bindings with decorative labels, perhaps to compete more effectively with John Harris, the Darton family, and Benjamin Tabart. Among Marshall's most delightful productions were libraries of miniature books of instruction (some ostensibly for teaching dolls) sold in wooden boxes that looked like bookcases, a reissue of the nursery rhyme collection *Mother Goose's Melody*, and Richard Scrafton Sharpe's *Anecdotes and Adventures of Fifteen Gentlemen* (1821), which Edward Lear cited as an inspiration for his limericks.

[*See also* Bible in Children's Literature; Darton Family; Fenn, Ellenor; Harris, John; Juvenile Magazine; Kilner, Dorothy, and Mary Ann Kilner; Limericks; Miniature Books; More, Hannah; Nursery Rhymes; *and* Trimmer, Sarah.]

BIBLIOGRAPHY

Alderson, Brian. "Miniature Libraries for the Young." *Private Library*, 3rd series, 6, no. 1 (Spring 1983): 2–38.

ANDREA IMMEL

Martchenko, Michael (1947–), Canadian illustrator and author. Born in France, he emigrated to Canada at the age of seven. He studied visual art at the Ontario College of Art in Toronto and began a career in advertising. The children's author Robert Munsch and an editor from Annick Press saw his artwork at an exhibit and, admiring its playfulness, suggested he consider illustrating children's books. Martchenko is best known for his illustrations of Munsch's books, beginning with *The Paper Bag Princess* (1980). His childhood love of cartoons and comic books is reflected in his cartoon-style drawings and sly sense of humor. In Munsch's *Thomas's Snowsuit* (1986), Martchenko draws the school principal with whitening hair as he becomes more and more frustrated with Thomas. Some school districts complained that the book demonstrates lack of respect for authority. Martchenko also illustrates Allen Morgan's Matthew series, starting with *Matthew and the Midnight Tow Truck* (1984). These dream fantasies give Martchenko lots of opportunity for visual humor. His own stories are equally rich in comic exaggeration. In *Ma, I'm a Farmer* (2003), a computer programmer learns that too much technology on the farm can lead to serious mayhem. Martchenko works mostly in watercolor and pencil.

TERRI DOUGHTY

Martel, Suzanne (1924–), French Canadian author. Suzanne Chouinard Martel is the winner of numerous awards, including the Canada Council for the Arts Award (1984) and the Governor-General's Literary Award (Canada, 1992). Her science fiction novel *Surréal 3000* (1963; English trans., *The City Underground*, 1964) was a best seller. In the 1980s, she published other science fiction novels: *Nos amis robots* (1984; English trans., *Robot Alert*, 1985) and *Un orchestre dans l'espace* (A Space Orchestra, 1985). Martel also wrote historical fiction—*Jeanne, fille du roy* (1974; English trans., *The King's Daughter*, 1980)—which recalls the first French settlements in Canada. She began the Montcorbier series with her sister, Monique Corriveau (1927–1976); Martel continued this saga, a mixture of history and fantasy, after Corriveau's death.

[*See also* Corriveau, Monique.]

CLAIRE LE BRUN

Martí, José (1853–1895), Cuban poet, journalist, and patriot. At the age of sixteen, José Julian Martí y Pérez was arrested by the Spanish colonial authorities for subversive activities and sentenced to hard labor. At seventeen he was exiled to Spain (1871–1874), and from that point he dedicated his life to the pursuit of freedom and the overturning of tyranny. Often he settled in a country only to leave shortly thereafter when oppressive regimes took charge. He studied and taught in Europe and the Americas, but he never stopped dreaming of an end to Spanish colonialism. Invited back to Cuba in 1878 during a general amnesty (the Peace of Zanjon), he was expelled a second time in 1879. He did not return home again until the revolution began in 1895, and he died early in the fighting, becoming a martyr and cementing his status as national hero.

As a poet, Martí is praised for an honest style, free of the excesses of nationalism. He exerted an early influence on *modernismo* (Modernism) in Latin American poetry, a turning toward simplicity and the power of unique imagery. In his lifetime, he published only two volumes of poetry, although more work was collected and published posthumously. He was also a gifted journalist and social critic. Martí's *crónicas* (chronicles or reports) from New York included the oft-reprinted work "Coney Island," which provides a brutally honest description, rich in wonder and small details. Martí does not seek to disparage, but rather to provide an accurate picture of America from the perspective of an interested outsider.

Martí founded and contributed to many periodicals in his life, including *La edad de oro* (1889; English trans., *The*

Golden Age). This magazine represents Martí's commitment to children, but it produced only four issues; the financial backer discontinued funding because of the lack of religious content. Instead, Martí offered his own poetry, old stories translated from other languages, news articles, and history lessons. One of his most impressive poems is included—"Dos principes" (Two Princes)—which recounts the deaths of a prince and a peasant and the obliteration of their class distinctions. In an article titled "Pin the Tail on the Donkey: A New Game and Some Old Ones," Martí enlightens readers on cultural relativity through an examination of games in different countries and time periods. Volumes comprising all four issues of *La edad de oro* are still read today.

Despite his belief in the revolution and his desire to fight oppression, Martí's poetry can express a peaceful perspective. He is widely praised for *Ismaelillo* (1882), a tender book of verses to the son from whom Martí would be separated for most of his life. His most famous book of poetry, *Versos sencillos* (1891; English trans., *Simple Verses*), contains passionate descriptions of nature, a boundless love of the world, and the pain of betrayal, defeat, and death. "Cultivo une rosa blanca" (English trans., "I Cultivate a White Rose") is often taught to Spanish-speaking schoolchildren. In this poem, Martí offers a white rose not only to the true friend but also to the cruelest heartbreaker.

BIBLIOGRAPHY

Magill, Frank N., ed. "The Poetry of José Martí." In his *Masterpieces of Latino Literature*, 439–443. New York: HarperCollins, 1994.

Rotker, Susana. *The American Chronicles of José Martí*. Hanover, N.H.: University Press of New England, 2000.

MONICA FRIEDMAN

Martin, Ann M. (1955–), prolific American author primarily of realistic novels directed at preteenage girls. Martin graduated from Smith College with the intention of becoming an educator. She soon shifted to a career in publishing and then turned to writing. In 1985 at the request of the editor Jean Feiwel, Martin wrote a novel about four girls who form a babysitting cooperative. The book, *Kristy's Great Idea* (1986), and its sequels quickly blossomed into a publishing empire with hundreds of titles and several spin-off series such as the Baby-Sitters Club. Martin has also collaborated with Paula Danziger on two epistolary novels about a pair of best friends separated by a family move, in *P.S. Longer Letter Later* (1998) and *Snail Mail No More* (2000), and with Laura Godwin on *The Doll People* (1999), about a friendship between a Victorian doll and a modern doll inhabiting the same doll house, and its sequel, *The Meanest Doll in the World* (2003). Martin's most critically successful novel is her Newbery Honor–winning *A Corner of the Universe* (2002), a story of a girl's relationship with her mentally disabled uncle.

MEGAN LYNN ISAAC

Martin, Bill, Jr. (1916–2004), American editor, lecturer, and author. After attending Kansas State Teachers College (now Emporia State University), William Ivan Martin taught high school English, journalism, and drama. His first publication was *The Little Squeegy Bug* (1945), illustrated by his brother Bernard. The sales of the book rocketed after Eleanor Roosevelt mentioned it on the radio, and Martin's career as a writer took off. In 1960 Martin became an editor and children's textbook creator at Holt, Rinehart, and Winston. Having struggled with reading as a child, he gravitated toward an auditory approach to teaching reading. The Sounds of Language series (1966–1992) focuses on the relationship between the written word and its sound. He also produced the Owl Books (1971), four libraries of more than one hundred books that cover social studies, science, literature, and arithmetic. He wrote more than three hundred books, including the popular *Brown Bear, Brown Bear, What Do You See?* (1967), illustrated by Eric Carle, and *Chicka Chicka Boom Boom* (1989). All of Martin's books have limited text and are highly patterned and predictable so that beginning readers can feel the accomplishment of reading a whole book.

NICHOLE CORCORAN

Martin, John Percival (1880–1966), British Methodist missionary and author. The Reverend Mr. Martin wrote the Uncle series of six children's books in the mode of surreal fantasy. The first two books, *Uncle* (1964) and *Uncle Cleans Up* (1965), were published late in Martin's life, and the others posthumously. Uncle, an eccentric millionaire elephant in a purple dressing gown, lives at palatial Homeward with his main allies, Old Monkey and Cat Goodman. He engages in constant conflict with the inhabitants of squalid Badfort, including Beaver Hateman and Hitmouse. The last book in the series is *Uncle and the Battle for Badgertown* (1973). The books belong to some extent in the Lewis Carroll nonsense tradition.

SINDHU MENON

Martin, Patricia Miles (1899–1986), American writer. Born in Cherokee, Kansas, and educated at the University of Wyoming, Martin became a teacher before moving in 1942 to San Mateo, California, where she took a creative writing course at San Mateo College and went on to become a prolific writer for children. Characterized by careful research and a frequent focus on friendship, honesty, and various cultures and regions, especially Native Americans and the American Midwest, her many children's books include biographies, picture books, information books, and animal stories. The first of more than one hundred titles, *Sylvester Jones and the Voice in the Forest* (1958), was followed by titles including *The Pointed Brush* (1959), *The Little Brown Hen* (1960), and *The Rice Bowl Pet* (1962). Biographies for children include *Abraham Lincoln* (1964), *Daniel Boone* (1965), *Dolly Madison* (1967), and *Jacqueline Kennedy Onassis* (1969). Occasionally writing as Jerry Lane, Martin more frequently used the pen name Miska Miles, under which many of her best-known titles appeared. These include *Apricot ABC* (1969), which uses the letters of the alphabet to depict an apricot's life cycle. *Gertrude's Pocket* (1970) highlights the economic difficulties faced by characters in a coal town through the story of young Gertrude, whose prized hand-me-down dress is torn by a bully but then mended with a patch pocket sewn by her grandmother. Martin's best-known book is *Annie and the Old One* (1971). A Newbery Honor Book and winner of the Christopher Medal, among other awards, this gentle story represents death as part of the cycle of life by telling of a Navajo grandmother who, with calm acceptance, reveals that she will die when the weaving of a rug is completed, and of her young granddaughter who tries to prevent the finishing of the rug.

ADRIENNE E. GAVIN

Martin, Rafe (1946–), American award-winning author and storyteller born in New York and educated at the University of Toronto. Martin has written more than a dozen books for children and edited two books about Zen Buddhism for adult readers. His work is often inspired by folklore. For instance, he retells an Algonquin Indian version of Cinderella in *The Rough-Face Girl* (1992), and *Birdwing* (2005) is a sequel to the Grimm brothers' tale "The Six Swans." His picture book *Will's Mammoth* (1989), illustrated by Stephen Gammell, and its chapter book version, *The Boy Who Loved Mammoths* (1996), take us into the imaginative world of a boy who believes that mammoths exist. In *The Storytelling Princess* (2001) the heroine rebels against a fairy-tale-like prearranged marriage and goes on to become a storyteller and win the prince to whom she was initially promised. *The Hungry Tigress* (1999) brings to life stories from the Buddhist tradition, and *Mysterious Tales of Japan* (1996) introduces English-speaking children to traditional Japanese tales. Martin has received many awards, among them three American Library Association Notable Book Awards, and the Women's National Book Association has honored him with its Lucile Micheels Pannell Award.

MARIA-VENETIA KYRITSI

Martineau, Harriet (1802–1876), English writer. Born into a Unitarian family in Norwich, Martineau had a good education and later became a prolific writer. She wrote for adult readers on political economy, history, social reform, religion, family life, and philosophy; she also wrote guidebooks and an autobiography. Her works for children are similarly genre-spanning: historical and geographical fiction, moral tales, Sunday school stories, devotional exercises, and a school story. They include *Devotional Exercises for the Use of Young Persons* (1823), *Principle and Practice; or, The Orphan Family* (1827), and *Five Years of Youth; or Sense and Sentiment* (1831). She produced her best-known children's books during a long period of illness; these were published in 1841 as a series of four titled *The Playfellow: A Series of Tales*. The first, *Settlers at Home*, is a survival story set in the 17th century, involving the children of a Dutch Protestant family of settlers in Lincolnshire who are marooned by a flood caused by prejudiced neighbors. The second, *The Peasant and the Prince*, contains two French Revolution stories, the first involving the young Marie Antoinette and a peasant family and the second recounting the life and death of the Dauphin. The third is a popular Norwegian adventure, *Feats on the Fjord*, which features pirates, lovers, a hidden cave, and a dastardly villain. The fourth is Martineau's most significant children's book, *The Crofton Boys*, one of the earliest school novels. Set in a boys' boarding school, it reveals the horrors its protagonist faces, including the amputation of his foot after a playground accident, but it also emphasizes the importance of honor. Martineau's works for children deal with harsh situations and are important in the development of various genres of children's literature: school stories, adventure books, survival tales, and historical fiction.

[*See also* Adventure Books; Historical Fiction; *and* School Stories.]

BIBLIOGRAPHY

Pichanick, Valerie Kossew. *Harriet Martineau: The Woman and her Work*. Ann Arbor: University of Michigan Press, 1980.

Sanders, Valerie. *Reason Over Passion: Harriet Martineau and the Victorian Novel*. New York: St. Martin's, 1986.

ADRIENNE E. GAVIN

Martín Gaite, Carmen (1925–2000), Spanish novelist, poet, and essayist. She was the first woman to win Spain's Premio Nacional de Literatura in 1978 for her adult novel *El cuarto de atrás* (1978; English trans., *The Back Room*, 1983). She resisted attempts to draw clear boundaries between children's and adult fiction. Her three works published for children are all enchanting fairy tales that present endearing and often eccentric characters in a fantastic atmosphere, where dreams and imagination play a prominent role, as they do in all her fiction. *El castillo de las tres murallas* (The Three-walled Castle, 1981), illustrated by Juan Carlos Eguillor, received the 1981 Libros de Interés Infantil (Books of Interest to Children) prize. It is considered by some critics to be her best work and was published, along with her second children's tale, *El pastel del diablo* (The Devil's Cake, 1985), in a single volume for adults, *Dos cuentos maravillosos* (Two Marvellous Tales), in 1992. In 1990, a fairy-tale novel set in New York, *Caperucita en Manhattan* (Little Red Riding Hood in Manhattan), was published for readers "from eight to eighty-eight." The novel was inspired by a stay in New York as a visiting lecturer at Barnard College, and the cover illustration is Norman Rockwell's famous depiction of the Statue of Liberty. The author illustrated her novel with thirteen simple, childlike black-and-white drawings. The imaginative heroine, Sara, lives in an ugly apartment block in Brooklyn with her conventional parents; her free-spirited grandmother is a former music-hall singer who has had several husbands and lovers; and the wolf the little girl encounters in Central Park, and eventually hooks up with her lonely grandmother, is a millionaire cake king by the name of Edgar Woolf. Martín Gaite's children's books are a celebration of fantasy and the power of the imagination that address young and old alike.

BIBLIOGRAPHY

Brown, Joan Lipman. *Secrets from the Back Room: The Fiction of Carmen Martín Gaite*. University, Miss.: Romance Monographs, 1987.

Martín Gaite, Carmen. *El cuento de nunca acabar* (The Neverending Tale). Madrid: Trieste, 1983.

Servodidio, Mirella, and Marcia L. Welles, eds. *From Fiction to Metafiction: Essays in Honor of Carmen Martín Gaite*. Lincoln, Neb.: Society of Spanish and Spanish-American Studies, 1983.

SANDRA L. BECKETT

Maruki Toshi (1912–2000), Japanese artist, born in Hokkaido, Japan. She studied oil painting in Tokyo and married the Japanese artist Iri Maruki in 1941. Together they visited Hiroshima, her husband's hometown, just after the dropping of the atomic bomb there in August 1945. Deeply affected by the horror she saw, she started to draw images of the war in tableaus and picture books often in collaboration with her husband, as well as producing other books of nursery tales and illustrated works. Her most famous work is *Hiroshima no Pika* (1980; English trans., *The Hiroshima Story*, 1983), an acclaimed and controversial picture book in which she depicts painful images of people burned by the fire in the aftermath of the explosion. She has earned admiration for her honest and courageous attitude toward child readers in addressing this subject, but she has also been criticized on the basis that her images are too heavy and cruel for children. Some critics feel that the work is lacking in a relevant commentary on the issues of the atomic bomb. It has been translated into several languages.

TOMOKO MASAKI

Marvel Comics Group. *See* Comic Books.

Mary Had a Little Lamb. "Mary's Lamb" is the most famous of the *Poems for Children* (1830) by Sara Josepha Hale (1788–1879), written at the request of Lowell Mason, an American composer who introduced music into the public school curriculum. Two of three eight-line stanzas of the poem narrate an incident; the last draws the moral embodied in the story. Appropriated by 19th-century anthologies and McGuffey's *Eclectic Readers* without acknowledgment of the author, "Mary's Lamb" "slipped into the language uncredited, prey to the theft of ideas." Although Hale's authorship had been established by the publication of the poem under her name in the September-October 1830 issue of *Juvenile Miscellany*, her most serious challenge came in 1879 from John Roulstone, whose controversial authorship has been perpetuated by a 1926 plaque at the Little Red Schoolhouse in Sudbury, Massachusetts. Hale, a prolific author and longtime editor of *Godey's Lady's Book*, wrote literature for children that is integral with the objectives of her other literary works: to teach truth and build character while giving pleasure through story and verse. Ironically, while her most famous poem lives on in traditional nursery lore, her name is all but forgotten.

[*See also* Hale, Sara Josepha; *Juvenile Miscellany, The*; Nursery Rhymes; *and* Poetry.]

M. SARAH SMEDMAN

Mary Poppins. *See* Travers, P. L.

Marzollo, Jean (1942–), American writer of more than one hundred books for children and adults. Marzollo is probably most famous for the riddles that accompany Walter Wick's photographic puzzles in the "I Spy" series (including *I Spy: A Book of Picture Riddles*, 1992). Her experience in education (she worked for Harvard's Project Upward Bound) and her editorship of *Let's Find Out* (a magazine for kindergarten children), inspired her to write books relating to children's lives. Her first book, *Learning through Play* (1972), is a guide for parents and teachers and remained in print for twenty years. Marzollo's books are known for their use of rhythm and rhyme—something she attributes to the presence of poetry during childhood. She has collaborated on writing science fiction with her husband, Claudio Marzollo, and sports stories with her sons. Her work also includes science books for beginning readers, Bible stories, and easy readers starring Shanna, a vivacious African American heroine.

BIBLIOGRAPHY

Spodek, Bernard, Rosalinda B. Barrera, and Violet J. Harris. "In Touch with Kids: A Conversation with Jean Marzollo." *New Advocate* 15, no. 2 (Spring 2002): 91–99.

LINNEA HENDRICKSON

Masefield, John (1878–1967), British poet, playwright, and novelist, born in Ledbury, Herefordshire. He wrote six books for children, two of which are now recognized as classics. In 1930, when he was only thirty-two, he was appointed Britain's poet laureate.

John ("Jack") Masefield first attracted attention with his lyrical and inspiring verses about seafaring; his best-known poem begins, "I must go down to the sea again." In fact, though he spent two years in the British merchant marine as a teenage trainee, and was deeply moved by this experience, Masefield was unable to follow a career on shipboard since he became violently seasick. His unsympathetic guardians, who deplored his interest in writing, insisted that he join another ship, but at seventeen, he deserted from the service and spent two years wandering about the United States, taking odd jobs and living rough. Finally he returned to England, where he gradually became able to support himself as a writer. In 1903, he married Constance Crommelin, a teacher who was eleven years older than he. They had a son and a daughter.

Masefield's first works for children, *A Book of Discoveries* and *Martin Hyde*, appeared in 1910. The first, though presented as fiction, is really a series of informal lectures on local history and ecology. *Martin Hyde; or, the Duke's Messenger*, an adventure story set in the late 17th century, full of spies, disguises, midnight rides, battles, imprisonment, and escape, is more original.

Jim Davis, Masefield's next book for children, is simpler and more upbeat: it is the story of a boy who falls in with smugglers on the coast of Devon in 1821. It is equally full of incident: there are gypsies, mysterious night riders, a sea voyage, storms, fights, a sunken treasure—and a happy ending. Though less original than *Martin Hyde*, it was popular in its time and is still in print today.

The Midnight Folk (1927) and its sequel, *The Box of Delights* (1935), are wonderfully inventive adventure fantasies for younger children. The hero of the first book, Kay Harker, finds lost treasure with the help of several animals and his own forgotten toys. He is opposed by his governess, Sylvia, who turns out to be a witch, and by a wicked wizard called Abner Brown. *The Box of Delights* is even better. Sylvia and Abner are now married and searching for a magic box that makes it possible to travel in time and space. They are formidable opponents, who can turn into wolves and who own a fleet of sinister flying taxis. They kidnap Kay's guardian, two of his friends, and the clergy of the local cathedral. If the latter cannot be rescued, there will be no midnight service on Christmas Eve; thus the climax of the story becomes an exciting confrontation between good and evil.

BIBLIOGRAPHY

Dwyer, June. *John Masefield*. New York: Ungar, 1987.
Masefield, John. *Grace before Ploughing: Fragments of an Autobiography*. London: Heinemann, 1966.
Masefield, John. *In the Mill*. London: Heinemann, 1941.
Masefield, John. *So Long to Learn*. London: Heinemann, 1952.
Smith, Constance Babington. *John Masefield: A Life*. Oxford, U.K.: Oxford University Press, 1978.
Sternlicht, Sanford V. *John Masefield*. Boston: Twayne, 1977.

MARIA NIKOLAJEVA

Massee, May (1883–1966), American children's book editor, translator, and publisher. Born in Chicago to a family descended from the Puritans, Massee grew up a voracious reader and a fan of *St. Nicholas Magazine*. While she was very young, the family moved to Wisconsin, where she completed high school and attended the Wisconsin Library School. She spent five years at the Buffalo Public Library, working in the children's room. Her interest in spreading knowledge about the best children's books led to her editorship of the *A.L.A. Booklist*. In 1922, Doubleday, Page, and Company in New York invited her to create a department for children's books. She disliked the term "juvenile" and replaced it with "junior books." She supported and encouraged the publication of a wide range of pioneering children's books of outstanding quality, many of them reflecting cultures and traditions from around the world, such as Margery Clark's *Poppy Seed Cakes* (1924), illustrated by Maud and Miska Petersham. With the aid of her friend Ernst Reichl, a German émigré, she translated Erich Kästner's popular *Emil und die Detektive* into American English (1930) in a lively and widely read rendition. In 1933 she left Doubleday for Viking Press. An exceptionally gifted editor, she shepherded a substantial number of books to literary and artistic fame, including four that won the Caldecott Medal and nine that won the Newbery Award.

[*See also biographies of figures mentioned in this article.*]

J. D. STAHL

Mass Market Fiction. The availability of inexpensive, mass market paperback editions has transformed both children's literature and publishing in general, creating positive outcomes in making books readily available for children but also setting the stage for a largely negative commodification process that affects the kinds of books published. Educators, librarians, and parents have debated, since the onset of series fiction, a conceptual precursor to mass market fiction, whether the goal of increasing children's interest in reading outweighs the effect of making available masses of simplistic, formula fiction. This question has been debated since the mid-19th century, when the British penny dreadfuls and American dime novels were first sold to young readers on newsstands in Britain, America, and, in some reincarnation, in other countries such as France. Jules Verne's novels were partly sold in this fashion before they were collated into novels, usually for the holiday trade. Since the 1960s, most educators and librarians have embraced the positive good of catering to actual reading interests, and this, plus declining library budgets and competition from other forms of entertainment like radio, comic books, television, and video and computer games, has partially driven the acceptance of series fiction (like the *Nancy Drew* and *Hardy Boys* series of the Stratemeyer Syndicate, one of the first sources of the debate) into the school and public libraries, at least in the English-speaking world.

The Early Books

The mass market paperback, as package and as a marketing category, surfaced first in 1939 in the United States, when Pocket Books issued its first titles for twenty-five cents. This price held for most such books for ten years. Mass market paperbacks referred originally to small-format, paperbound titles that could fit into newsstand book racks. The success of these titles, most of which were for adults until the early 1960s, was largely driven by the fact that the majority of people could not afford hardcover books, nor would they go into bookstores, which were thought of as the purview of the scholarly and the upper classes. Sold at newsstands, in convenience and grocery stores, in train stations and airports, the books sold in the millions as opposed to under a hundred thousand for hardcover titles. The idea of this kind of marketing, pitching sensational stories to young readers through newsstands, began in the mid- to late 19th century. But it was not until the late 1950s that the phenomenon of creating mass market paperbacks for children really took hold.

In addition to the obvious advantages of increased marketing outlets for children's classics like those of Kenneth Grahame, A. A. Milne, and Laura Ingalls Wilder, this format has inherited content similarities from the penny dreadful and dime novel. For example, it favors series titles, as children and parents look for "another one just like the other one." Also, cover art is more a part of the marketing strategy than a representation of the contents. In the early mass market fiction of the 1940s and 1950s, cover art was unabashedly sensual. It was designed to appeal to young men's understanding of sensuality, both because that ideology dominated the period and because the people distributing and selling the books were usually males. This gave them the incentive to display the books prominently so that they, as well as their customers, could see the covers, and it also started the trend of divorcing cover art from contents. In fact, the convention of lurid covers with "fallen women" in suggestive stances was so dominant that J. D. Salinger's teen classic *The Catcher in the Rye* was first issued with such a cover by the New American Library mass market imprint, Signet, in 1953. And it was so objectionable to the author and the reading public that NAL lost the rights to his novel.

Publishers and Imprints

The growth period for mass market fiction directed at children was the 1960s, although the number of titles and imprints has steadily increased since an industry shakeout in the 1970s. By 1960, most major publishers in the United States had paperback children's lines, such as Dell Yearling Books, Penguin Puffin Books, Fawcett's Golden Library, and Ace, to name only a few. These lines were still being adjusted in the 1980s, as age-grouped fiction became standardized.

Children's mass market fiction tends to be slightly larger in size than adult paperback books, between the size of the trade paperbacks that increasingly dominate all other forms of publishing and the standard-sized mass market news-rack title. They are designed to appeal to a range of age groups, from the youngest readers to young adult readers. Illustrations and cover art are both important to the form, as are other devices of product recognition such as encomiums from established writers, comparisons to their work, and identification with literary subgenres such as mystery, fantasy, science fiction, and teen romance. Some fiction is even published in two formats; for instance, one can purchase the latest *Red Wall* series book by Brian Jacques in a standard mass market size or in a slightly larger, children's book oversize.

The Upside

Mass production of artistic work, as Walter Benjamin argues in "The Work of Art in the Age of Mechanical Reproduction," transforms the effect of the work, and not always for the better. Yet there are advantages to inexpensive, readily available books for children. First, the reduced price encourages children and their families to consider owning their own books. In 2005 the paperbacks published for children were still under five dollars, while hardcover picture and other kinds of books ranged from fourteen to nineteen dollars. Reprints of literary classics, both established and new, are readily available in mass market format, although sometimes in abridged forms. So mass market production allows children, and their libraries, to afford a greater range of fiction. Boxed holiday gift sets have become attractive purchases for parents of modest means. One might even argue that the giant U.S. bookstore chains like Borders which emerged at the end of the 20th century owe their existence to the paperback book, and such stores always have children's sections that are well stocked and are categorized by age and type. Thus when Ballantine issued J. R. R. Tolkien's *Lord of the Rings* in 1969 in mass market format, it was an instant best seller, and Tolkien's *The Hobbit*, likewise produced in a mass market edition, could become a children's classic. The wide range of fiction provided for by the paperback industry has allowed for a flowering of fantasy, science fiction, mystery, and romance for readers of all ages, but in the children's and teen categories, fantasy seems to dominate.

The Downside

There are many advantages to children's series fiction, as Nell Beram points out in her *Horn Book* article. Quoting the librarian Sarah Sugden, Beram affirms that having familiar characters and settings from book to book is helpful for less experienced readers. And, she adds, adults also read series fiction, using Agatha Christie as an example. In fact mystery fiction and science fiction and fantasy are two genres that have proliferated in the general mass market format, and since the advent of Tolkien's eminently popular trilogy (which was really five books), fantastic fiction and mystery have particularly dominated paperback publishing for children. Not all series are as formulaic as *Goosebumps*, *Baby-Sitter's Club* or the *A–Z* mystery series; nevertheless, one can observe the way in which Edward Stratemeyer's more than forty series on detectives and other kinds of adventurers has historically played a role in establishing the content of the children's mass market, by including stereotypes, simple writing, repeated characters, and repetitive plots. Stratemeyer seemed to have a series character for every taste, from the cozy mystery stories of Nancy Drew and the Hardy Boys to stories of aviators and other adventurers. And although the titles produced in his fiction factory were issued as hardbound books, they were of a smaller size than the standard hardcover and thus much less expensive.

It can be difficult to tell the good writers from the bad when sorting through mass market titles, as each is marketed with similar techniques of cover art, illustration, and back-cover encomiums. One often has to rely on preknowledge of the author or the series. But even this may fail. For example, Wilder's *Little House* series has made its way into many more children's libraries because it is available in a children's paperback edition. On the other hand, publishers' conservatism has lead to the creation of offshoot series by less dynamic and believable authors, and Wilder's original group of stories is now called *The Laura Years* and has been preserved with the artistry of the American illustrator Garth Williams. This series title is obviously a marketing ploy, to juxtapose it to *The Rose Years*, about Laura's daughter, and

The Caroline Years, about her mother—neither of which project the voice of authenticity that came from Wilder's lived experience. Because paperbacks are so cheap to produce, have a track record (especially in children's literature) for respectable sales, and are hooked into both traditional bookstores as well as the usual paperback distribution networks, editors can take some chances. But purchasing and marketing series—or, as in the case of Wilder, books that seem to be in the same universe with some of the same characters—appeal to editors and publishers, just as they do to the producers of the comics series, television series, and series movies that have increasingly dominated popular culture. Content, in effect, is irrelevant and is essentially regarded as commodity.

The tendency to repeat a good thing has brought about children's series and teen versions of the fantasy series, the current exemplar of which is the megaphenomenon of J. K. Rowling's *Harry Potter* series, and the extension of which are such pedagogically motivated books as the several American girls' series, where books, dolls, girls' dresses to match the dolls, cookbooks, cutouts, and so forth are all part of the package. Thus, although one can celebrate the increasing availability of children's literature brought about by paperbacks, the prevalent commodification presents us with a grim trade-off. How will young readers come to appreciate the richness of good children's stories when these are placed among so much repetitive, simplistic work? And how do we help children distinguish this richness in competition with the many other forms of entertainment? Catering to the desires of younger readers as they learn to appreciate both reading and the value for their mental development of good writing has never been as complicated as now.

[*See also* Canon, The; Cover Art; Dime Novel, The; Penny Books; Penny Dreadful; Publishers and Publishing; Series Books; *and titles of series and biographies of figures mentioned in this article.*]

BIBLIOGRAPHY

Davis, Kenneth C. *Two-Bit Culture: The Paperbacking of America*. Boston: Houghton Mifflin, 1984.

Pearson, Edward. *Dime Novels; or, Following an Old Trail in Popular Literature*. Port Washington, N.Y.: Kennikat, 1968.

Sullivan, Larry E., and Lydia Cushman Schurman, eds. *Pioneers, Passionate Ladies, and Private Eyes: Dime Novels, Series Books, and Paperbacks*. New York: Haworth, 1996.

Walters, Ray. *Paperback Talk*. Chicago: Academy Chicago, 1985.

Zipes, Jack. *Sticks and Stones: The Troublesome Success of Children's Literature from Slovenly Peter to Harry Potter*. New York. Routledge, 2001.

Janice M. Bogstad

Masson, Sophie (1959–), Australian writer for children and adults who draws on her French and Indonesian background in her novels. Original and complex family stories, other worlds, and other times are vividly imagined. *Fire in the Sky* (1990) links Dominique and Tad as they time travel into medieval France, a setting also evoked in *In Hollow Lands* (2004), where it is combined with Breton folklore. *A Blaze of Summer* (1992) moves to modern-day France. *The Opera Club* (1993), *The Cousin from France* (1993), *Winter in France* (1993), *The Secret* (1993), and *Family Business* (2000) comprise a series about the French Australian Seyrac children. *Sooner or Later* (1991) and *The Sun Is Rising* (1996) take up questions of white and Australian Aboriginal relations in a contemporary country town. Mythology, history, and folk tales are reworked in the fantasy trio *Carabas* (1996), *Cold Iron* (1998), and *Clementine* (1999). In *The Green Prince* (2000), Jack follows a merman and a water sprite to find his destiny in an underwater world. An alternative history is proposed in *The Hand of Glory* (2002), in which France is the colonizer of Australia rather than Britain.

Stella Lees and Pam Macintyre

Matas, Carol (1949–), Canadian writer. Matas, from Winnipeg, Manitoba, is best known for her young adult historical fiction about the Holocaust. Coming from a theater background, she has published children's and young adult prose as well as plays. Her successful novels *Lisa* (1987; American title, *Lisa's War*) and its sequel *Jesper* (1989; American titles, *Kris's War* and *Code Name Kris*), were both turned into plays. These stories concern the Danish resistance and the rescue of Danish Jews during the Nazi occupation of Denmark. They display, as do many of her other historical novels, the fate of persecuted Jews during or after World War II in various European contexts. Matas recounts less familiar incidents, such as the Jews' postwar journey to Palestine in *After the War* (1996) and its sequel *The Garden* (1997), or the persecution of Jews in General Grant's territory during the Civil War in *The War Within* (2001). Apart from drama and historical fiction, her work spans several genres, including fantasy, science fiction, and contemporary issues. Her fantasy series—*Of the Two Minds* (1995), *More Minds* (1996), *Out of their Minds* (1998), and *A Meeting of Minds* (1999), all coauthored with Perry Nodelman—displays the power of reading minds to create an imaginary world blending elements of fantasy, adventure, and fairy tale.

Jana Pohl

Mather, Cotton (1663–1728), New England minister, eldest son of Increase Mather, the most distinguished member of a dynasty of Puritan divines. He thought of himself as the leader of the Massachusetts church, and his ardent wish was to revive the waning spirit of his forefathers. He entered Harvard when he was twelve, received an MA in 1681, and became co-minister with his father at the Second Church in Boston, succeeding him on his death in 1723. He was a powerful preacher and an energetic writer, the author of more than 450 works on a wide variety of subjects, with a particular interest in the young; *Cares about the Nurseries* (1702) gives much thought to their upbringing, and his diary has many references to the anxious care he gave to his own children. Many of his sermons were preached at a child's funeral, when he would habitually urge the duty of early piety. He held up as an example his brother Nathanael who had died at the age of nineteen, "an Old Man without Gray Hairs upon him." He was much impressed by James Janeway's *A Token for Children* and added to the Boston edition of 1700 some Massachusetts examples. Though very brief and lacking in the emotional appeal of the Janeway narratives, they are noteworthy for being one of the earliest literary appearances of New England children.

[*See also* Janeway, James.]

GILLIAN AVERY

Mathers, Petra (1945–), American author and illustrator. Born in Germany and later settling in the United States, Mathers has created many imaginative and highly original picture books. Her books have appeared on the *New York Times* Best Illustrated List four times and have received numerous other awards, including the Boston Globe–Horn Book award for illustration for *Sophie and Lou* (1991), the story of a shy mouse who finds happiness when she bravely teaches herself to dance and opens herself to friendship. Mathers works in watercolors, with rich hues and flat perspectives that often include fascinating details. The first book she both wrote and illustrated is *Maria Teresa* (1985), the story of a chicken who accidentally escapes from her cage and ends up performing in a circus. *Theodor and Mr. Balbini* (1988) is about a quiet man who is not entirely pleased when his dog suddenly begins to talk. *Victor and Christabel* (1993), a mystery and a love story starring crocodiles, was inspired in part by the 15th-century painting *Saint Ursula's Dream* by Vittore Carpaccio. *Kisses from Rosa* (1995) is based on Mathers's own childhood in the Black Forest of Germany, when she was separated from her mother, who was ill with tuberculosis. In the 1990s, beginning with *Lottie's New Beach Towel* (1998), Mathers began a series of books about a white chicken named Lottie and her friend Herbie. Small in format and told in multiple panels, these stories explore themes of love, friendship, and courage. In addition to her own writings, Mathers has illustrated numerous works by other well-known writers, including Verna Aardema's retelling of a Mexican folktale, *Borreguita and the Coyote* (1991), Jacqueline Briggs Martin's *Grandmother Bryant's Pocket* (1996), Lynne Jonell's series of simple stories for young children, beginning with *Mommy Go Away!* (1997), the poet Jack Prelutsky's *The Frogs Wore Red Suspenders* (2002), and M. T. Anderson's picture book biography of the surrealist composer, *Strange Mr. Satie* (2003).

[*See also* Aardema, Verna.]

BIBLIOGRAPHY

Vandergrift, Kay E. "The Petra Project." http://eclipse.rutgers.edu/petra/index.jsp. An archive of the development of text and pictures in a picture book (*Kisses for Rosa*), with interview with the author.

LINNEA HENDRICKSON

Mathiesen, Egon (1907–1976), Danish painter and picture book artist. Together with several other Danish illustrators, he found inspiration in early Soviet experimental children's books, exhibited in Copenhagen in 1932, and thus started a radically new trend in children's book illustrations in Denmark. Mathiesen's picturebooks, beginning with *We Want to Fly* (1939), are characterized by simple plots in which the verbal story, often nonsensical, as in *Boogiewoogie and His Four Sons* (1946), is completely subordinate to the pictures. The illustrations, deliberately aimed at appealing strongly to the viewer's senses, use bright colors, clear-cut shapes, contrasts of shapes, colors, and sizes, and no backgrounds or unnecessary details, thus skillfully imitating children's drawings. Rhythm and repetition on the verbal as well as the visual level are important elements in the books that address a very young child. Mathiesen's most famous book, translated into many languages, *The Blue-Eyed Pussy* (1949; English trans., 1951), is elaborate in its simplicity, with the pictorial layout carrying the dynamic plot and the expressive black-and-white images cleverly complemented with the yellow and blue of the cats' eyes. It is a story about being an outsider and establishing one's own identity, told in a manner accessible for the youngest readers. All Mathiesen's books are explicitly didactic in the best sense of the word: they teach and preach, yet the message is never obtrusive, but presented through playfulness in words and images. *Fredrik with the Car* (1944) plays with the notions of right and wrong, but it also introduces the idea of internationalism, as the character takes an imaginary journey and meets and befriends children of all colors, allowing for gratifying visual solutions. *Oswald the Monkey* (1947; Eng. trans., 1959) depicts in an allegorical form a rebellion against dictatorship, a highly relevant subject at the time. This combination of high artistic quality and social commitment makes Mathiesen an outstanding picture book creator.

BIBLIOGRAPHY

Christensen, Nina. "Teaching Tolerance. A Comparative Reading of Two Danish Picture Books." *Bookbird* 37, no. 4 (1999): 11–16.

Maria Nikolajeva

Mathis, Sharon Bell (1937–), African American schoolteacher, writer, and librarian. Mathis was born in Atlantic City, New Jersey, and raised in the Bedford-Stuyvesant section of Brooklyn, New York. She began her literary career writing for her students—stories with high-interest topics and low-level vocabulary—and gained acclaim for her sensitive explorations of complex issues and warm portrayals of strong African American youth in *Listen for the Fig Tree* (1973) and other books. Like other writers for youth in the 1970s, Mathis challenged thematic boundaries and provoked some controversy by touching on serious issues such as senility, drug addiction, and death. She is particularly noted for her depiction of people in impoverished urban settings who, by working together in the face of hardship, discover individual and collective worth. Her awards include the Council on Interracial Books for Children Prize for *Sidewalk Story* (1971), a Coretta Scott King Author Award for *Ray Charles* (1973), and a Newbery Honor for *The Hundred Penny Box* (1975). Mathis continues to write stories for children and edits a column for *Ebony Jr.*

Sheri Anita Massey

Matsui Tadashi (1926–), president of Fukuinkan Shoten (one of Japan's leading publishers) from 1968 to 1985, played a pioneering role in shaping the contemporary Japanese picture book scene. He began his career as the editor of *Kodomonotomo* (Children's Companion; started in April 1956), which produces an original, high-quality picture book each month. Through Matsui's high editorial standards and vision, he launched the careers of now distinguished picture book makers, including Akaba Suekichi, Anno Mitumasa, and Tashima Seizou. As an author, Matsui wrote *Momotaro* (1965; illustrated by Akaba Suekichi) and *Pika: The Signal* (1966; illustrated by Choh Sinta). Since then he has worked as a lecturer, producer of exhibitions, critic of picture books, and advocate for children's books in Asia. His collected essays on picture books, including *What Is a Picture Book* (1973) and *Present Situation of Picture Books, Future of Children* (1992), provide powerful insights into the Japanese picture book world.

[*See also biographies of figures mentioned in this article.*]

Okiko Miyake

Matsutani Miyoko (1926–), Japanese children's writer, born in Tokyo, who began writing stories during World War II. Her first published book was *Kai ni natta kodomo* (A Child Who Becomes a Shell-Fish, 1951), a collection of short stories; the title story was a poetic fantasy about a child who is dead. Her early works were mostly fantasy, influenced by Hans Christian Andersen, but they gradually approached the Japanese legendary world. Her work includes first picture books for infants like *Inai Inai Ba* (Bopeep, 1967) and *Ii okao* (Your Good Face, 1967), books for young readers like *Chiisai Momo-chan* (Little Momo, 1964), and novels like *Futari no Ida* (Two Idas, 1969) and *Shinokuni kara no baton* (The Baton from the Land of the Dead, 1976). While her books for younger children focus on the relationship between mother and child, her novels for older readers show Matsutani's keen awareness about social problems, especially war, the environment, and the continuity of history. She also has been interested in Japanese local legends and folk tales, organizing a research group to collect and investigate oral tales. Besides publishing those collections and the picture book versions of folk tales, she wrote some literary folk tales herself. Among them, *Tatunokotaro* (Taro the Dragon Child) won the international Andersen Award in 1960. Matsutani based this work on a local legend of a poor mountainous area and invented a hero who overcomes poverty to create a new community. Her folklore stories address issues and problems of the interdependence between human beings and nature. In addition to the old traditional folk tales, she has been collecting modern legends among Japanese city dwellers.

[*See also* Fairy Tales and Folk Tales; Japan; *and* Legends.]

Ariko Kawabata

Matthiessen, Wilhelm (1891–1965), German author, best known today for his children's detective novel *Das rote U* (The Red U, 1932) and the collection of fairy tales *Das alte Haus* (The Old House, 1923). Matthiessen was one of the most popular and respected German children's authors during the 1920s and 1930s. His books of fairy tales show the child's world thoroughly populated by pixies, sprites, kobolds, and all manner of endearing spirits, which reassuringly depict nature as benevolent. Matthiessen's detective novels, including *Das rote U* and *Das Mondschiff* (The Ship to the Moon, 1949), center around children banding together to solve a mystery. He also capitalized on the immense fame of the German writer of American Wild West novels, Karl May, with adventure novels such as *Nemsi Bey* (1933), whose eponymous hero proves time and again the superiority of Germans over the wild mountain folk of Tibet.

LUKE SPRINGMAN

Mattingley, Christobel (1931–), Australian writer of over forty books for children. Her humanitarian concerns encompass insights into the very young and probe global questions of war, race, and disability. Her early work, *Windmill at Magpie Creek* (1971; illustrated by Gavin Rowe), *Tiger's Milk* (1974), *The Long Walk* (1976; illustrated by Helen Sallis), *The Big Swim* (1977; illustrated by Elizabeth Honey), *The Jetty* (1978; illustrated by Gavin Rowe), and *Brave with Ben* (1982; illustrated by Elizabeth Honey), explores the fears of childhood from learning to swim to walking home from school. *Rummage* (1981; illustrated by Patricia Mullins) won the inaugural Children's Book Council of Australia Junior Book of the Year Award in 1982; in it, Septimus Portwine runs a messy secondhand stall at the market. *Tucker's Mob* (1992; illustrated by Jeanie Adams) has been translated into a number of Australian Aboriginal languages. *The Angel with a Mouth-Organ* (1984; illustrated by Astra Lacis) and *The Miracle Tree* (1985; illustrated by Marianne Yamaguchi) contemplate the effect of World War II on children. Mattingley has taken the impact of war further in *No Gun for Asmir* (1993) and *Asmir in Vienna* (1995), both illustrated by Elizabeth Honey, and *Escape from Sarajevo* (1996), based on the experiences of an actual family caught up in the Bosnian conflict.

STELLA LEES and PAM MACINTYRE

Matute, Ana María (1925–), Spanish writer, considered one of the best postwar novelists, who was a finalist for the Andersen Medal. Her works reflect the trauma the civil war constituted for numerous Spanish writers. War appears as a fratricidal confrontation in many of her works. Her novels are intimate in scale and melancholic, but always leave a door open to hope. Her characters are lone children, often orphans, in search of their identity. Notable among her extensive output are the volumes *El polizón del Ulises* (Ulysses' Stowaway, 1965), *Sólo un pie descalzo* (Just One Bare Foot, 1983), and *El verdadero final de la Bella Durmiente* (The Real Ending of Sleeping Beauty, 1995), a tale in which she breaks with the structure of traditional European stories. Her best work is *Olvidado Rey Gudu* (King Gudu Forgotten, 1996), a long tale of fantasy giving characters and traditions from folklore a surprising treatment.

MARISA FERNÁNDEZ-LOPEZ

Maurois, André (1885–1967), French writer whose real name is Maurice Herzog. He started writing *Les silences du Colonel Bramble* (1918; English trans., *The Silence of Colonel Bramble*, 1930) in 1917, when he was a liaison officer for the British Army. Thanks to his novels, full of humanism, and his biographies about international writers, he was elected to the Académie Française. For young people, he wrote *Le pays des trente-six mille volontés* (1928; English trans., *The Country of the Thirty-Six Thousand Whistles*, 1930), a fairy tale about childhood, and *Le voyage au pays des articoles* (1928; English trans., *A Voyage to the Island of the Articoles*, 1929), a tale showing a utopian island where places and inhabitants are only addicted to the arts. His masterpiece, *Patapoufs et Filifers* (1930; English trans., *Fattypuffs and Thinifers*, 1969), illustrated in the original by Jean Bruller, portrays two young brothers in a fantasy world, where the big "Patapoufs" and the thin "Filifers" are enemies. Thanks to the children, the war is brought to an end, and readers are left with a message of peace and tolerance with humor.

JACQUES TRAMSON

Mavrina, Tatiana (1902–1996), Russian artist and book illustrator, winner of the Andersen Medal (1976). Most of her production for children concerns illustrations of fairy tales such as Aleksandr Pushkin's *The Tale of the Dead Princess and the Seven Heroes* (1949) and his epic fairy-tale poem *Ruslan and Ludmila* (1960), as well as collections of Russian fairy tales. Her original picture books include *Fairy-Tale Beasts* (1965), *Fairy-Tale ABC* (1969), and many others, in

André Maurois. Front cover Illustration by Fritz Wegner for *Fattypuffs and Thinifers* (New York: Alfred Knopf, 1968). REPRODUCED COURTESY OF THE COTSEN CHILDREN'S LIBRARY, PRINCETON UNIVERSITY LIBRARY

which texts are clearly secondary to pictures. Mavrina imitated the style of the Russian chapbook *lubok*, also drawing inspiration from traditional folk crafts. Her illustrations are not specifically addressed to children, and her books are often published as gift editions.

MARIA NIKOLAJEVA

Max and Ruby Books. *See* Wells, Rosemary.

Max und Moritz. *See* Busch, Wilhelm.

May, Karl (1842–1912), German writer. Karl Friedrich May was perhaps be the most popular and most controversial German author of all time. He is best known for his Wild West adventures and tales of exploits in exotic Middle Eastern lands, which to this day have a fanatic following and not a few detractors. May was born to a destitute family in Ernstthal, a village south of Leipzig, and suffered throughout his childhood from illnesses related to malnutrition, including blindness. By his own account, he also suffered from lifelong delusions and behavioral disorders. He passed his teacher's examination in 1861, but he had hardly entered a classroom before he was charged with theft and sentenced to his first term in prison. For almost two decades May survived as a thief and con artist, spending about as much time in jail as out. During one incarceration, May managed to work in the prison library and discovered writing as an outlet for his feverish imagination.

May's first novel, *Die Rose von Ernstthal* (The Rose of Ernstthal, 1874), attracted the attention of the publisher H. G. Münchmeyer, who employed May (now presenting himself as "Dr." Karl May) as an editor of popular magazines. Immediately May began contributing his own stories to periodicals, of which two in particular—*Deutscher Hausschatz in Wort und Bild* (German Household Treasure in Words and Pictures) and the children's magazine *Der gute Kamerad* (The Good Comrade)—became the vehicles for his mass popularity. May's tales of adventure overwhelmed his earlier "village tales" and pulp novels. Most of his Orient series, written between 1881 and 1888, appeared as novels in 1892 under such titles as *Durch die Wüste* (In the Desert), *Durchs wilde Kurdistan* (Through Wild Kurdistan), and *Von Bagdad nach Stambul* (From Baghdad to Istanbul; Eng. trans., *The Caravan of Death*). A year later May had reworked and published as novels his Wild West stories featuring the heroes Old Shatterhand and the noble savage Winnetou. Although these and his other travel adventures did not appear as children's literature, the devotion of young German readers to May's German heroes has begun to ebb only in the latest generation. Indeed, May's children's tales—such as *Der Sohn des Bärenjägers* (The Son of the Bear Hunter, 1890) and *Der Schatz im Silbersee* (The Treasure in Silver Lake, 1894)—contain no stylistic features that would distinguish them specifically as children's literature, other than having been serialized in a juvenile periodical.

May enhanced his popularity through masterful publicity events, which included photography sessions posing May in exotic costumes and tours of German cities. With his fame arrived campaigns to discredit May and his work. Critics publicized his criminal past, accused him of writing "trash" and "smut" harmful to young people, and exposed his fraudulent claims of having experienced the adventures he wrote about. By 1900 May had ceased writing adventures and dedicated himself to pacifism and world peace, becoming a friend and follower of the first Nobel Peace Prize laureate, Bertha von Suttner.

BIBLIOGRAPHY

Berman, Nina. "The Appeal of Karl May in the Wilhelmine Empire: Emigration, Modernization, and the Need for Heroes." In *A Companion to German Realism 1848–1900*, edited by Todd Kontje 283–305. Woodbridge, U.K.: Camden House, 2002.

Evenson, Brian. "Apaches, Aryan-Style: A Review of Karl May's Winnetou." *Denver Quarterly* 15, no. 2 (1958): 27–30.

Krinsky, Carol Herselle. "Karl May's Western Novels and Aspects of Their Continuing Influence." *American Indian Culture and Research Journal* 23, no. 2 (1999): 53–72.

LUKE SPRINGMAN

May, Sophie (1833–1906), American writer who, but for a brief stint of teaching in Indiana, spent her entire life writing in her hometown of Norridgewock, Maine. In her day, May, who was born Rebecca Sophia Clarke, was known as the "Dickens of the nursery." Publishing more than forty books, May distinguished herself by creating fun-loving, energetic, often naughty children in a time when most children were depicted as stiff examples of religious perfection. Her first stories, published in the *Little Pilgrim* in 1864, became the Little Prudy stories, starting with *Little Prudy* (1864). They were shortly followed by other series. The Dotty Dimple stories began with *Little Prudy's Dotty Dimple* (1865) and *Dotty Dimple at her Grandmother's* (1868). *Flaxie Frizzle* (1876) began another series, as did *Quinnebasset Girls* (1877), the latter for teenage girls. Although not many children read May's work today, she was praised and in high demand during her lifetime, particularly among children eager to discover the new adventures of their beloved characters.

[*See also* Girls' Books and Fiction *and* Series Books.]

AMANDA THIBODEAU

Mayer, Marianna (1945–), American author and illustrator known for her retellings of folk tales and fairy tales. Mayer studied at the Art Students League in New York and began creating children's books with her then husband, Mercer Mayer. The couple produced several wordless picture books and in 1978 collaborated on a version of *Beauty and the Beast*, with Mercer's illustrations and Marianna providing the text. Employing rich language, combining several variants of the tale, and adding depth to the main characters, Mayer created a retelling that emphasized the tale's romance. With *Beauty and the Beast*, Mayer found her niche and she has continued to write distinguished interpretations of fairy tales, folk tales, legends, and myths. Her work includes both old favorites such as *The Twelve Dancing Princesses* (1989) and *Baba Yaga and Vasilisa the Brave* (1994) and lesser-known tales such as *The Black Horse* (1984) and *Iduna and the Magic Apples* (1988). In *Iron John* (1999), Mayer explores the myth of the "noble wild man," finding inspiration in sources from Geoffrey of Monmouth to the Brothers Grimm and contriving plenty of adventure to accompany the underlying message: live in harmony with the natural world. She has also written original stories. *The Little Jewel Box* (1986) contains many fairy tale elements—a magic object, a blessing gone awry, and a spirited hero, who must perform impossible tasks for a reluctant father-in-law. But Mayer subverts traditional gender roles by giving the hero part to an adventurous young girl named Isabel. Mayer has expanded her focus, turning her attention to religious subjects and writing books that introduce children to the lives of figures such as Jesus of Nazareth; his mother, Mary; the twelve Apostles; and Saint Nicholas.

MELISSA SCHUTT

Mayer, Mercer (1943–), writer and illustrator known for his Little Critter books. After being discouraged from pursuing a career as a children's book illustrator by his instructors at the Honolulu Academy of Arts, Mayer persevered and published *A Boy, a Dog, and a Frog* in 1967. This wordless book is characteristic of much of his work. The warm illustrations feature the landscapes and animals of Mayer's childhood, the child protagonist is a little clumsy but accomplishes his goal in an unexpected fashion, and the work itself won a number of awards. He went on to create more than three hundred books for children, including more than a dozen with his wife, Gina Mayer, and several with his former wife, Marianna Mayer.

Mayer's most popular stories feature Little Critter, an anthropomorphic, buck-toothed hedgehog in overalls. Little Critter shares the dreams, fears, and daily life of a typical child and can be counted on to break, lose, or dirty any object in his possession, but he has a huge heart. A characteristic book in the series, *Just for You* (1975), catalogs his efforts to help his mother, which only create trouble until he realizes that a hug is the best gift. These simple tales appeal to very young children who dream of mastery of their world even as they recognize their own limitations.

Mercer Mayer. Front cover for *There's a Nightmare in My Closet* (New York: Dial Press, 1968). Collection of Jack Zipes

His visual style runs the gamut from the cartoon figure of Little Critter to a lush fantasy world, as in Jay Williams's *Everyone Knows What a Dragon Looks Like* (1976; a *New York Times* Best Illustrated Book). The pictures feature costumes and architecture specific to ancient China, as well as Mayer's ubiquitous little animals. Pen and ink drawings alternate with richly colored pages—for example, the beautiful illustration of the dragon revealing himself in all his splendor.

BIBLIOGRAPHY

Wheeler, Jill C. *Mercer Mayer*. Edina, Minn.: Abdo, 2005.

Monica Friedman

Mayhew, James (1964–), British author and illustrator. Born in Stamford, Lincolnshire, Mayhew graduated in 1987 from the Maidstone College of Art with a degree in illustration. Two years later he published his first picture book, *Katie's Picture Show* (1989). Further books featuring the character Katie include *Katie Meets the Impressionists* (1997) and *Katie and the Sunflowers* (2000). Mayhew uses his amiable fictional heroine to encourage children to enjoy art. In the first book we meet Katie at an art gallery. Once she is free from adult supervision, a fantasy sequence begins; she enters some of the paintings and interacts with the subjects to amusing effect. Mayhew has also published other picture books, has illustrated anthologies, and has worked with children's authors such as Joyce Dunbar and Elizabeth Beresford.

Phyllis Ramage

Maymat, Nicole (1939–), French publisher and writer. In 1978 she founded the Ipomée publishing house, named after the exotic flower, just as her own tales were inspired by the theme of the garden in *Le gang des chenilles rouges* (The Gang of the Red Caterpillars, 1973), *L'histoire d'Héliacynthe* (Heliacynth's Story, 1980), and *Histoire de Lilas* (Lilacs' Story, 1984). Her house was united in 1991 with Albin Michel Jeunesse and then with Le Seuil. She continued to publish major illustrators—Frédéric Clément, Alain Gauthier, Claude Lapointe, and the Russian Boris Diodorov (who illustrated Hans Christian Andersen's *The Little Mermaid* in 1998)—as well as writers like Martine Delerm. Maymat's narratives range from fantasy in *Maco des grands bois* (Maco of the Great Woods, 1985) to poetic realism in *La maison des dunes* (The House on the Dunes, 1995) to adventure in *Vanille, flibustière des Antilles* (Vanilla, a Buccaneer of the West Indies, 2001).

Jean Perrot

Mayne, William (1928–), British author, born in Hull and educated for a period at the Canterbury Cathedral Choir School. He is best known for his novels, though he has also been an anthologist and has written short stories and coauthored picture books. Mayne's work has consistently eschewed the usual reader-friendly features of much children's fiction. His writing avoids authorial explanations, direct informative description, and logically sequential dialogue. His oblique and evocative prose demands an attentive and diligent reader; better still, a second reading. This was unusual when he started writing in the 1950s, a period when children's fiction in Britain was still dominated by Enid Blyton and an unquestioned belief in the importance of an

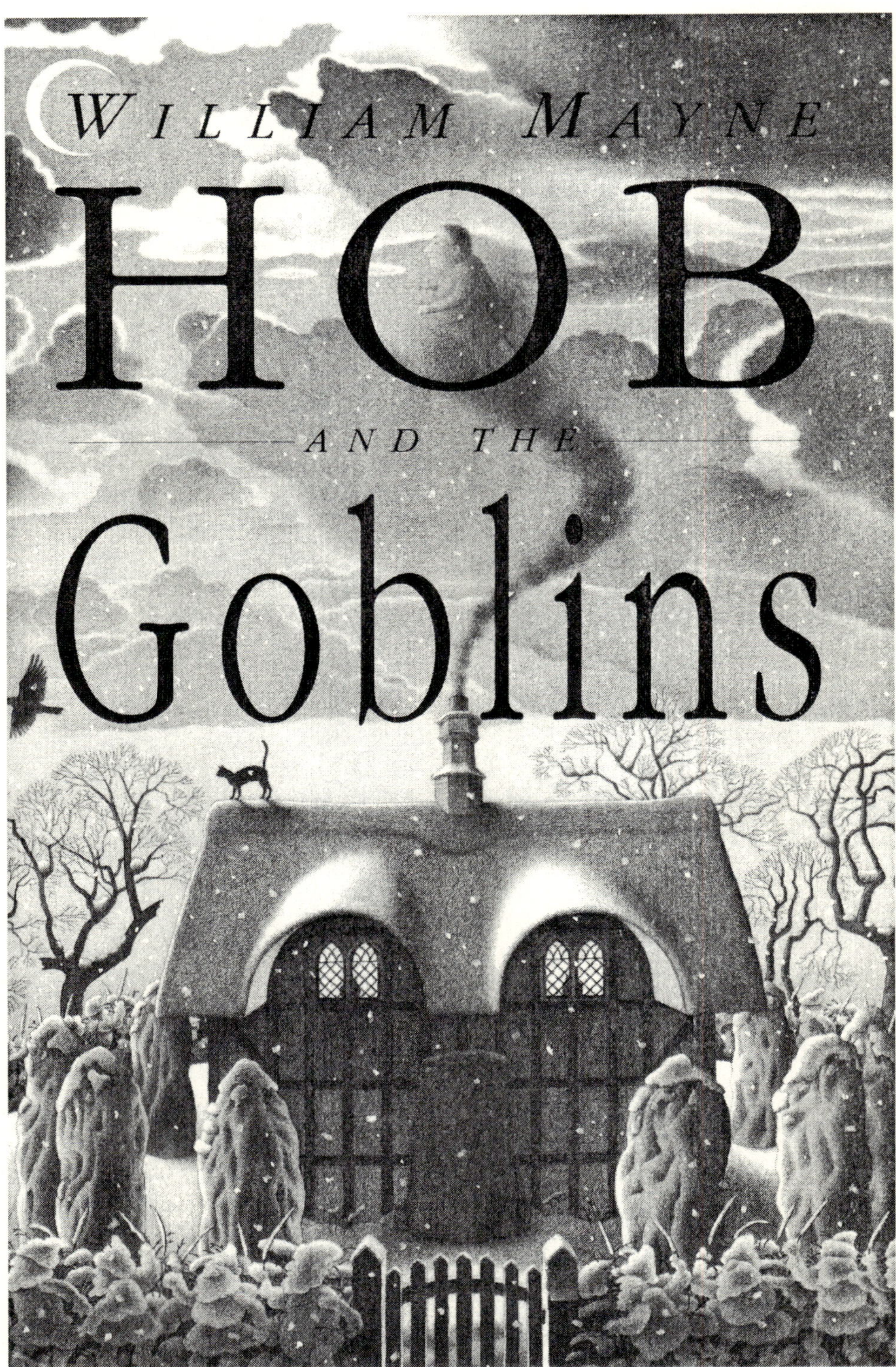

William Mayne. Front cover illustration by Norman Messenger for *Hob and the Goblins* by William Mayne (New York: D. Kindersley, 1994). COLLECTION OF ANDREA IMMEL

explanatory and reassuring authorial voice. In discussions about literary quality, Mayne and Blyton were frequently employed as exemplars of the two extremes, librarians in particular expressing a reluctance to spend public money on works that—however good—remained on the shelves.

In Mayne's early novels there is always a strong sense of place. This is not just a sociological interest in a specific locality and its people, but rather a fascination with soil, land, and rocks—and in particular the dynamic ways in which the land might change and reveal its historical or mythological past to its inhabitants. In an interview with Raymond Thompson in 1989, Mayne spoke of "reminiscences in the landscape" and, in many of the works, these reminiscences are manifested exclusively to children. This approach to landscape can be said to typify the way he represents history and character as well—his fiction seeks to reveal hidden treasures and subterranean meanings and structures. It is also fascinated by the way things work—how to make a raft or drain a marsh (*The Member for the Marsh*, 1956), how trucks might or might not run downhill on rusty tracks (*Sand*, 1964), how a group of children might run a school without a teacher (*No More School*, 1965), or why a wheel rolled from the top of a hill would always follow the same path (*The Rolling Season*, 1960). Similar qualities were apparent in the novels he wrote for younger readers (*The Last Bus*, 1962; *On the Stepping Stones*, 1963; *Plot Night*, 1963; *The Yellow Aeroplane*, 1968). An important feature of Mayne's fiction is that it shows young readers how to be curious about everything—archaeology, mythology (especially Arthurian), engineering, mining, landscape history, climate and weather, dialect, how families function in their homes, the relations between younger schoolchildren and prefects. His writing invites readers to be interested, and this invitation is equally present in his stories for very young readers—*The Patchwork Cat*, a picture book (1981), illustrated by Nicola Bayley, and the four books of Hob Stories (from 1984, reissued in one volume in 1991), illustrated by Patrick Benson.

Mayne has refused to explain his creative process in simple logical terms; it is, to him, mysterious, even perhaps magical. Speaking of *Earthfasts*, he said, "The links that are made are beyond mere reason. I didn't take some parts and put them together. They came together, and that's the only way to create anything. Construction isn't any good." He refers to this process as "fabulation." It is not surprising that Mayne's fiction is especially sympathetic to children with a capacity for faith. The most uncompromising expression of this is *The Grass Rope* (1957), which won the Carnegie Medal and tells the story of a little girl whose belief in fairyland and, specifically, unicorns is vindicated. Mayne's other award-winning novel is *Low Tide* (1992), which won the Guardian Children's Fiction Award; this too is a vindication of the power of magic and folklore, though with a bitter twist as the children here are bluntly condemned for lying. However, Mayne's admirers would probably give greatest honors to the Choir School quartet and the Earthfasts trilogy. The former (*A Swarm in May*, 1955; *Choristers' Cake*, 1956; *Cathedral Wednesday*, 1960; *Words and Music*, 1963) is based on his own experience as a chorister and established Mayne's unique ability to capture ephemeral experience seen from within a child's understanding and at the same time to suggest the engaging characteristics of this unusual cathedral community. *Earthfasts* was published in 1966 and did not become a trilogy until *Cradlefasts* (1995) and *Candlefasts* (2000) were issued. The trilogy combines many of the author's abiding interests—landscape, history, time, and the ways in which they fuse and overlap—and a narrative manner involving clues, puzzles, riddles, and anomalies.

In May 2004, Mayne was given a two-and-a-half-year sentence for sexually abusing six young girls more than thirty years previously. The fact that a major children's author was apparently guilty of using his position to groom children for sexual abuse was deeply shocking and left his publishers—along with booksellers, librarians, teachers, and parents—uncertain whether his works should be withdrawn and his entire contribution to children's literature obliterated. Catherine Bennett, in a carefully argued article in the *Guardian* in May 2004, wrote that "Mayne's particular gift for conveying, in prose of great assurance and spareness, the way in which children's minds work, also speaks of a fascination with juveniles that occasionally, criminally, knew no limits." It is perhaps true that an authorial preoccupation with children may, in certain circumstances, prompt an actual and illicit preoccupation with them, an idea explored by Nicholas Tucker, in an article in *The Independent*, with reference to a number of children's authors, including Charles Kingsley, J. M. Barrie, Lewis Carroll, and Ian Strachan. Many commentators, like Bennett, concluded that, whatever the author may have been guilty of, the books remain blameless.

When a children's writer is found to have been a child abuser, two irreconcilable views are articulated. One regards the abuser and the writing as entirely separate; the other sees the writing as inevitably tainted. However, it is possible to argue that good writing achieves an honesty and truth that transcends the troubled individual who creates it.

BIBLIOGRAPHY

Stephens, John. "Metafiction and Interpretation: William Mayne's *Salt River Times, Winter Quarters*, and *Drift*." *Children's Literature* 21 (1993): 101–117.

VICTOR WATSON

Mayne Reid, Captain T. (1818–1883), author of adventure stories and works of natural history. Of Northern Irish origin, he emigrated to America in 1840, where, after a variety of jobs, Thomas Mayne Reid became a journalist, traveling widely all over the continent. He was seriously wounded when fighting, as a volunteer, with the U.S. Army in the war against Mexico in 1847. He began to write in 1848 and *The Rifle Rangers*, published in 1850, became hugely popular. Like that first novel, *Scalp Hunters* (1851), was for adult readers. After Mayne Reid had settled in England, a publisher invited him to write for boys: *The Desert Home* came out in 1851 and *The Boy Hunters* in 1852, both before Christmas. Thereafter, one or more new books could be expected every year, reliably timed to provide Christmas presents; in all he wrote around ninety adventure novels. He also dramatized *The Quadroon* (1856), and Dion Boucicault used it as the basis for *The Octoroon* (1859). Between 1867 and 1870 he spent three more years in the United States.

Mayne Reid's highly successful stories were based on his own colorful experiences of the world, on his firsthand knowledge of American frontier life (the subject of most of his work), on his enthusiasm for and detailed knowledge of nature, and on literary inspiration: he greatly admired Lord Byron and something of the passionate Byronic hero is present in his work. Despite being the son of a Presbyterian minister, he did not offer the religious or moralizing messages of many contemporaries such as R. M. Ballantyne, Charles Kingsley, or W. H. G. Kingston. Nor is there an overt imperialist vein in the books. His stories were much translated, and the Italian adventure writer Emilio Salgari saw Mayne Reid as a boyhood inspiration.

ANN LAWSON LUCAS

Mazer, Harry (1925–), American writer. Mazer is the author of more than twenty popular young adult novels. He worked for many years as a teacher, brakeman, ironworker, welder, longshoreman, and pulp fiction writer before completing his first juvenile book, *Guy Lenny* (1971). Several of his coming-of-age titles follow a home-away-home pattern in which male protagonists caught in moral dilemmas run away from their problems, eventually to return with new resolutions. His edited collection *Twelve Shots: Outstanding Short Stories about Guns* (1997) explores the consequences of a social reality affecting adolescents everywhere. Mazer has also cowritten three novels with his wife, Norma Fox Mazer: *The Solid Gold Kid* (1977), *Heartbeat* (1989), and *Bright Days, Stupid Nights* (1992). In addition to numerous other awards and accolades, many of his books have been selected for the ALA Best Books for Young Adults list. In 2003 Mazer received the 2003 ALAN Award for Contributions to Young Adult Literature.

[*See also* Mazer, Norma Fox.]

BIBLIOGRAPHY

Reed, Arthea J. S. *Presenting Harry Mazer*. New York: Twayne, 1996.

BENJAMIN LEFEBVRE

Mazer, Norma Fox (1931–), American writer. Mazer is the author of more than thirty books of young adult realistic fiction, including three written with her husband, Harry Mazer. Her works focus primarily on female adolescents struggling to maintain a healthy sense of self, often in dysfunctional or difficult circumstances, but they resist neat resolutions; instead, her protagonists evolve as they gain a better understanding of the world around them. In *After the Rain* (1987), a Newbery Honor Book, Rachel struggles to redefine a relationship with her intimidating grandfather after he is diagnosed with a terminal illness; she matures as a result, and the experience affects in positive ways her relationships with other family members. In *Taking Terri Mueller* (1981), recipient of an Edgar Award for Best Juvenile Mystery, Terri discovers that her beloved father kidnapped her as a small child from her mother, whom she had been told was dead; she learns to forgive her father and to sustain new relationships with both her parents. In *When We First Met* (1982), which was adapted into a film for HBO, Jenny meets the boy of her dreams but struggles with her conflicting feelings and the pressure of her family when she discovers that his mother was responsible for a car accident that killed her sister. *Good Night, Maman* (1999) is a historical novel about a brother and sister who escape the Holocaust and emigrate to New York. *Dear Bill, Remember Me? and Other Stories* (1976) was voted a *New York Times* Outstanding Book of the Year and an ALA Notable Book, and *When She Was Good* (1997) was an ALA Best Book for Young Adults. Mazer (with her husband) was awarded the ALAN Award for Contributions to Young Adult Literature in 2003.

[*See also* Mazer, Harry.]

BIBLIOGRAPHY

Reed, Arthea J. S. *Norma Fox Mazer: A Writer's World*. Scarecrow Studies in Young Adult Literature 3. Lanham, Md.: Scarecrow, 2000. A good analysis of Mazer's major accomplishments in young adult literature, with extensive biography.

Benjamin Lefebvre

McBratney, Sam (1943–), Irish author who writes for a wide audience, from text for picture books to novels for young adults. His picture book *Guess How Much I Love You* (1994), illustrated by Anita Jeram, has achieved huge success internationally and toys and other products have been developed from the book. It is a tender book, in which Big Nutbrown Hare and Little Nutbrown Hare compete to say how much each loves the other. Reassurance is also the theme of other picture books; *The Dark at the Top of the Stairs* (1996), illustrated by Ivan Bates, is a well-constructed tale of a group of young mice full of bravado. *Just You and Me* (1998), also illustrated by Bates, attempts to repeat the success of *Guess How Much I Love You*. McBratney has written mostly for emergent readers, but the quality of his work varies. *Jimmy Zest* (1982) and subsequent Jimmy Zest titles display McBratney's empathy with children as does *Bert's Wonderful News* (1998). His young adult fiction is his best work, although he has written the least for this age group. These books also exude warmth and sympathy. With *You Just Don't Listen* (1994) he shows the affectionate struggle between a mother and daughter as each finds fulfillment in her own life. *The Chieftain's Daughter* (1993) hits a more somber note in its portrayal of a love story that symbolizes the tension arising from the clash between Christianity—the new religion—and the old pagan religion in Ireland. Stylistically complex, it marvelously delineates the ache of young love and family divisions in a changing society. In *Celtic Myths* (1997) he further explores the old stories of Ireland and other Celtic lands. Not many of McBratney's books have a discernibly Irish setting, but the intonation and atmosphere of his native Ulster underlie much of his writing, giving it freshness and a rich texture.

Valerie Coghlan

McCaffrey, Anne (1926–), American science fiction writer living in Ireland. McCaffrey is the author of several series that are popular with adults and young people alike. Her most famous books are science fiction fantasies set on a distant planet called Pern, where Earth has been all but forgotten and humans protect themselves from a harsh environment with the help of symbiotic dragons. The Harper Hall trilogy is most often classified as young adult literature, but other Pern books cross category boundaries as well. McCaffrey's Unicorn Girl books have explored more thoroughly fantasy settings, while works like *The Ship Who Sang* (1969), *To Ride Pegasus* (1973), and *Sassinak* (1990; in collaboration with Elizabeth Moon) are traditionally science fiction, complete with spaceships (occasionally as main characters). In all of McCaffrey's work, girls and women are depicted as both strong and lovable; they fight for their rights but remember to deal with boys and men as individuals rather than categories. Great talents can be used in the service of love rather than being subordinated to it.

The Harper Hall trilogy, in addition to being McCaffrey's best-known work for young adults, encapsulates several of McCaffrey's favorite themes. They feature a young woman named Menolly, who flees a harsh family situation where she is little more than a drudge and makes a new place for herself in the world. Menolly fights the establishment that tells her a young woman cannot pursue a musical career and eventually triumphs. Her heroines exist most comfortably outside the strictures of the traditional societies in which most of them are raised, eventually finding their place as gadflies or exiles.

McCaffrey's books have won major fiction awards, including the Hugo, the Nebula, the Ditmar (from Australia), the Golden Pen, and the Margaret A. Edwards Award. She has often worked with other writers on novel projects. In 2003, McCaffrey began collaborating on novels with her son, Todd.

BIBLIOGRAPHY

McCaffrey, Todd. *Dragonholder*. New York: Ballantine, 1999.

Marissa K. Lingen

McCarthy, Maureen (1953–), Australian writer, who was born in the state of Victoria and worked as an art teacher before becoming a scriptwriter for film and television and a writer for young adults. Large-scale and romantic in scope, McCarthy's books make a major contribution to the documentation of the lives of less affluent Australian adolescents and appeal to a wide readership. Her first books the In Between series—*Alex*, *Fatima*, *Angie*, *Saret* (all 1987)—were created from her television scripts. Continuing to write about young people from the various ethnic backgrounds that make up suburban Melbourne, McCarthy treated the cultural clash between Greek and Anglo-Australians in her next book, *Ganglands* (1991). Class divisions have also motivated the sweeping road-romance novel *Cross My Heart* (1993), whose central characters are a runaway pregnant teenager and a former criminal; and in *Queen Kat, Carmel, and St. Jude Get a Life* (1995) three young women from the same country town, but from very different social backgrounds, find themselves in a shared house during their first year at university. Politics also inspire McCarthy's stories. In *Chain of Hearts* (1999), Sophie, a rebellious seventeen-year-old, gains perspective from a similarly troubled Vietnam veteran, and from Minh and his family, Vietnamese refugees, while in *Queen Kat, Carmel, and St. Jude Get a Life*, Carmen pursues a man she believes was her father's torturer in Chile. Her most political novel is *When You Wake and Find Me Gone* (2002), in which twenty-year-old Kit visits Northern Ireland to find her father and attempt to understand her parents' active and violent role in the Irish conflict of the 1980s. *Flash Jack* (2001) is for a younger readership than McCarthy's crossover novels, but continues to pursue her hard-nosed examination of the difficulties of adolescence and family life, in the context of wider social and moral concerns.

Pam Macintyre

McCaughrean, Geraldine (1951–), prolific British writer for children and adults; author of retellings, novels, and plays; winner of the Whitbread, Carnegie, *Guardian*, and Blue Peter awards. After working for a television company, McCaughrean (pronounced "Ma-KOH-kran") was a subeditor for a London publishing house and began writing stories, becoming a full-time writer in 1988. Her numerous retellings from Greek mythology, English folklore, traditional tales from all over the world, and classics like John Bunyan's *Pilgrim's Progress* (1999) testify to her gift for storytelling and interest in literature and language. Her original stories, mainly aimed at teenagers, are carefully researched novels that combine adventure with a lively, evocative prose. They are often set in the past (from medieval England in *A Little Lower Than the Angels*, 1987, or medieval China in *The Kite Rider*, 2001, to 1890s Oklahoma in *Stop the Train!*, 2001) and draw on the conventions of traditional subgenres, like the pirate story *Plundering Paradise* (1996; U.S. title, *The Pirate's Son*). Halfway between a novel and a collection of stories, *A Pack of Lies* (1988) provides an oblique commentary on fiction through the elusive author figure of MCC Berkshire.

Virginie Douglas

McCaughren, Tom (1936–), Northern Irish journalist and writer of adventure novels for children. His popular fox series, such as *Run Swift, Run Free* (1986), chronicles the experiences of a community of foxes. His historical novels *In Search of the Liberty Tree* (1994) and *Ride a Pale Horse* (1998) are set during the 1798 Irish Rebellion, while *The Legend of the Golden Key* (1983) and *The Legend of the Corrib King* (1984) are fantasies based on Irish folklore. His acclaimed thriller for teenagers, *Rainbows of the Moon* (1989), set on the contested Irish border, emphasizes the need for peace and reconciliation.

Patricia Kennon

McCay, Winsor (1867–1934), American animation pioneer and visually innovative cartoonist. In his early career, McCay worked as a reporter, sign painter, dime museum artist, and live performer whose rapidly created sketches impressed the audience with his ability to get every detail right the first time. As a cartoonist, he created *Dream of the Rarebit Fiend* (1904–1911, 1913) for the *Evening Telegram*, and *Little Sammy Sneeze* (1904–1906) and *Little Nemo in Slumberland* (1905–1914, 1924–1926) for the *New York Herald*. Sammy's sneeze creates chaos in the penultimate panel of each *Sammy Sneeze*, but *Rarebit Fiend* is more adventurous in its conceit. McCay's first extended foray into dreams, *Rarebit* launches a dreamer into indigestion-inspired nightmares: paralysis, being buried alive, reverting

Winsor McCay. Gertie the Dinosaur by McCay (ink on tracing paper; 1914). J. Arthur Wood Jr. Collection of Cartoon Art, Prints and Photographs Division, Library of Congress

to infancy, a child's blocks toppling and causing a chain reaction that topples a city. In the final panel of each strip, the dreamer awakens, relieved.

At the end of each *Little Nemo* strip, the title character also awakens from his dream, usually glad to have escaped the fantasy but sometimes longing to return. Though based on McCay's son Robert, Nemo is an everyman (or everychild) whose name is Latin for "no one." Flip, a cigar-smoking, green-faced clown, serves as Nemo's companion and adversary, often (though not always) preventing him from reaching the Princess of Slumberland. More than either the characters or the mundane dialogue, McCay's stunning visual style makes this full-page, full-color Sunday strip appealing. Rendering buildings and landscapes in almost photographic detail, McCay's fine Art Nouveau line combines with both bold and subtle colors to depict vivid dreams. McCay departed from the comic strip's usual arrangement of panels, stretching and bending their shapes to suit his story's art. When Nemo and his companions grow distorted like people in funhouse mirrors, the panels grow taller and smaller along with the characters. In the most famous *Little Nemo* sequence, the panels get taller as Nemo's bed's legs grow longer and longer, carrying Nemo and Flip on a wild, precarious ride through the city. In 1908 *Little Nemo* became a Broadway musical, and, in 1911, one of the first animated comic strips. These adaptations, McCay's prolific output, and many vaudeville appearances made him a star, prompting William Randolph Hearst to hire him.

When McCay joined Hearst's newspapers in 1911, the *Herald* forced him to relinquish the title of *Nemo*: it appeared as *In the Land of Wonderful Dreams* in Hearst's *New York American*. McCay was then doing "chalk talks," drawing both editorial cartoons and *Little Nemo*, and creating short films like *Gertie the Dinosaur* (1914). Angry that McCay was spending time on other projects, Hearst demanded that he cease his vaudeville performances, stop drawing *Little Nemo*, and create editorial cartoons. Although McCay continued to work on animation in his free time, Hearst effectively ended his period of peak creativity. When his contract expired in 1924, McCay resigned from the *American* and created two more years of *Little Nemo* for the *Herald Tribune*, but the strip was neither as inventive nor as successful in its second incarnation. In 1927 he resumed working as an editorial cartoonist for Hearst's papers, a position he held until his death.

McCay's impact on children's literature and culture can be measured by the many artists who cite his influence. Chuck Jones has called McCay and Disney "the two most important people in animation," and Maurice Sendak pays homage to *Little Nemo* in his *In the Night Kitchen* (1970). Creator of the first masterpieces in two media (comics and animated films), Winsor McCay rendered dreams that inspire other artists to pursue theirs.

[*See also* Little Nemo.]

BIBLIOGRAPHY

Canemaker, John. *Winsor McCay: His Life and Art*. Introduction by Maurice Sendak. New York: Abbeville, 1987.

Marschall, Richard, ed. *The Best of Little Nemo in Slumberland*. New York: Stewart, Tabori and Chang, 1997. Includes appreciations by Maurice Sendak, Ron Goulart, Art Spiegelman, Charles M. Schulz, Chuck Jones, and Bill Watterson.

Philip Nel

McCloskey, Robert (1914–2003), American author and illustrator of children's books, who was born in Hamilton, Ohio. After studying art in Boston, he wrote and illustrated *Lentil* (1940), a humorous book for children in the

Robert McCloskey. Illustration from *Lentil* (New York: Viking Press, c. 1940 [reissued 1964]). Reproduced courtesy of the Cotsen Children's Library, Princeton University Library

middle grades. The detailed lithographs of *Make Way for Ducklings* (1941), a picture book describing the adventures of a pair of mallards raising their family in the middle of Boston, won him the Caldecott Medal. In *Homer Price* (1943), McCloskey returned to stories for older children, this time a series of six comical tales set in a midwestern town. The gentle satire targets modern technology, and the stories are nostalgic reminders of a simpler and safer time. The same themes are apparent in *Centerburg Tales* (1951), a collection of seven stories also featuring Homer Price. In 1948, McCloskey created *Blueberries for Sal*, a picture book portraying a humorous reversal featuring McCloskey's own daughter Sarah and her mother, McCloskey's wife, Margaret Durand. The lithographs, done in blue and white, are extraordinarily expressive and earned McCloskey a Caldecott Honor Award. *One Morning in Maine* (1952), in which he introduced Sarah's younger sister, Jane, brought McCloskey his second Caldecott Honor. And in the following year McCloskey won his third Caldecott Honor for his lively monochrome illustrations for *Journey Cake, Ho!* (1953), written by his mother-in-law, the Newbery Award–winning author Ruth Sawyer. *Time of Wonder* (1957), which won McCloskey his second Caldecott Medal, was his first work in watercolor, and the text consists of a prose poem text celebrating the wonders of nature along the Maine coast. In *Burt Dow, Deep-Water Man* (1963) McCloskey returned to the tall tale, recounting an old sailor's adventures, with brightly colored illustrations enhancing the nonsensical humor. McCloskey produced a relatively small number of children's books, but the quality is astonishing, and he remains a perennial favorite among children to this day.

BIBLIOGRAPHY

Fannin, Alice. "Robert McCloskey." In *The Dictionary of Literary Biography*, vol. 22, *American Writers for Children, 1900–1960*, edited by John Cech, 259–266. Detroit: Gale, 1983.

Schmidt, Gary D. "A Merger of Traditions: Sources of Comedy in Robert McCloskey's Homer Price Stories." *Studies in American Humor* 5, no. 4 (Winter 1986–1987): 287–298.

Schmidt, Gary D. *Robert McCloskey*. New York: Macmillan, 1990.

David L. Russell

McClung, Nellie Letitia (1873–1951), Canadian politician, feminist, and novelist. Helen Letitia Mooney McClung's reputation as an activist for the rights of women is well established, especially her role as one of the "Famous Five" who fought to have women recognized as "persons" under Canadian law. McClung was also a successful novelist. *Sowing Seeds in Danny* (1908), *The Second Chance* (1910) and *Purple Springs* (1928) follow the life of Pearl Watson, the oldest of nine children, who copes with the miseries of poverty, especially those caused by alcoholism, with courage and inventiveness. McClung's writing is lively and amusing, as befits one whose motto was "Never retreat, never explain, never apologize—get the thing done and let them howl."

Frances Armstrong

McClure, Gillian (1948–), British author and illustrator who was born in Bradford and educated at the University of Bristol. McClure wrote and illustrated her first book, *The Emperor's Singing Bird* (1974), while she was working as an infant and nursery school teacher in Scotland, and after that she went on to produce several acclaimed works, such as *What's The Time Rory Wolf?* (1982), in which the plot is narrated through freeze-frame-like illustrations, and *Selkie* (1999), which explores a traditional Shetland Island legend of seals who shed their skin to become human and is distinguished by McClure's use of a beautiful blue and green sea-color palette. She has collaborated with her father, the poet Paul Coltman, on three books: *Witch Watch* (1989), for which McClure has created Baba Yaga–reminiscent illustrations that heighten the mysteriousness of the plot with their fuzziness; *Tinker Jim* (1992); and *Tog the Ribber, or Granny's Tale* (1985), in which she uses illuminated borders and letters in order to enhance the sense of the heroine's fear while she is fleeing from Tog the Ribber's vengeful ghost. The last two books, based on Paul Coltman's dialect poems about children's self-imposed illogical fears, were both short-listed for the Smarties Book Prize. Other works containing illustrations by McClure include *The Little White Hen* (1996), by Philippa Pearce, in which the hen's and rooster's different personalities are highlighted through McClure's contrasting colors, and *Bruna* (2003), by Anne Cottringer, for which McClure provided very delicate and warm watercolor illustrations. In *Tom Finger* (2001), which she both wrote and illustrated, a cat mysteriously brings magical gifts every day to a little girl who has lost her own beloved tabby. The illustrations portray a wintery landscape of whites and light greens, and with her clever technique McClure manages to secretly disguise the imaginary witch of the story.

Maria-Venetia Kyritsi

McCord, David (1897–1997), American poet for children, noted for his deft use of language and his keen sensitivity to the child's world. Born in New York City, he spent part of his childhood in Oregon. He learned his love of words and sense of rhythm from the Bible and began writing poetry at fifteen. He was in his fifties, however, when his first book for children, *Far and Few* (1952), was published. He attended Harvard, studying physics and mathematics, and earning an MA in romance languages. In the mid-1920s he became executive director of the Harvard College Fund—a position he held for thirty-eight years (in 1956, the university awarded him its first honorary doctorate in humane letters). A man of enormous energy, he loved fly-fishing, painting (chiefly in watercolors), and writing essays and poems. Of his over 550 poems, some four-fifths were intended for children, and he especially loved giving poetry readings in elementary schools. His poetry is distinguished by its humor, linguistic agility, and sensitivity to the child's psyche. His childhood favorite was Robert Louis Stevenson and the influence is unmistakable. Like Stevenson, McCord had a knack for choosing subjects close to the child's heart, such as the secret place described in "This Is My Rock," one of his most widely anthologized poems. But McCord's range reaches far beyond Stevenson's, as revealed in his wordplay, his experimentation with rhyme schemes and rhythms and sounds (his popular "Pickety Fence" is an exquisite example of onomatopoeia), and his love of nonsense verse. Perhaps his most endearing quality is his ability to speak directly to his young readers on their own terms with his keen knowledge of their hopes, dreams, and observations. His poems are gentle, joyful, lyrical, and, not infrequently, insightful. The National Council for Teachers of English honored him with its first Award for Excellence in Poetry for Children in 1977. His poems have been collected in a single volume, *One at a Time: His Collected Poems for the Young* (1977).

David L. Russell

McCulloch, Derek (1897–1967), associated with the BBC *Children's Hour* from 1933 to 1950. Having been severely injured in World War I, McCulloch joined the BBC as an announcer in 1926. His aim when appointed London *Children's Hour* organizer in 1933 was to develop a somewhat homespun program along more professional lines, without ever losing the personal touch. In its early phase with "uncles" and "aunties" he was Uncle Mac; he later abolished these titles, and used his only in his children's publications. McCulloch rapidly became a national figure, and was particularly associated with the part of Larry the Lamb in S. G. Hulme Beaman's *Toytown* plays, possibly the program's best-loved series. In 1938, McCulloch was made *Children's Hour* director, an appointment coinciding with the loss of a leg in a traffic accident. After retirement he worked as children's editor for the *News Chronicle*. He edited several collections of stories and also wrote his own, the most popular being *Cornish Mystery* (1950).

[*See also* Children's Hour *and* Radio Shows for Children.]

Gillian Avery

McCully, Emily Arnold (1939–), American author and illustrator born in Galesburg, Illinois, and educated at Brown and Columbia Universities. McCully is best known for *Mirette on the High Wire* (1992), her Caldecott Award–winning picture book about a fiery young girl who inspires a retired high-wire walker in late-19th-century Paris. She has written and illustrated several dozen books and has illustrated over one-hundred books for other authors. McCully was working as a freelance magazine artist when she illustrated Meindert De Jong's novel *Journey from Peppermint Street* (1968), a book that won the 1969 National Book Award and changed the course of McCully's career. Her first solo effort was *Picnic* (1984), a wordless story about a family of mice. The watercolor drawings in *Picnic* were powerful enough to stand alone, and the book won the 1985 Christopher Award. McCully has since written four more books about the same mouse family: *First Snow* (1985), *School* (1987), *New Baby* (1988), and *Christmas Gift* (1988). McCully follows other characters through multiple books such as the Grandma series, three tales about a boy and his two grandmothers. Another series follows a family of theatrical bears through five unique stories. McCully's other subject matter remains grounded in historical fact. *The Ballot Box Battle* (1996), *The Bobbin Girl* (1996), *The Pirate Queen* (1995), and *Beautiful Warrior: The Legend of the Nun's Kung Fu* (1998) are lavishly illustrated picture books based on public figures or incidents; each one features a young female protagonist. McCully, who began drawing at age three, is a self-taught artist. Her writing and illustrations focus on characterization, typically highlighting her leading characters' emotions. She continues to write and illustrate and often travels to present teachers' workshops and participate in art exhibitions. Brown University awarded her an honorary degree in 2002.

Nichole Corcoran

McDermott, Gerald (1941–), American illustrator, author, filmmaker, and graphic designer. Born in Detroit, Michigan, and educated at the Pratt Institute in New York,

McDermott first encountered art at age four, when his parents enrolled him in classes at the Detroit Institute of Arts. He went on to become an internationally acclaimed author and illustrator, creating more than twenty-five books and animated films which have made him popular among both children and adults. When in college he worked as a graphic designer for the educational New York TV station Channel 13, and designed and directed his first animated film, *The Stonecutter* (1960), based on a Japanese folk tale; it was published in picture book form in 1975. *Anansi the Spider* (1972), McDermott's first book, received immediate acclaim and earned him a Caldecott Honor Award. He is widely known for his trickster tales, including *Zomo the Rabbit* (1992), *Coyote* (1994), *Jabutí the Tortoise: A Trickster Tale from the Amazon* (2001), and *Raven* (1993); the last received a Caldecott Honor Award and a Boston Globe–Horn Book Honor Award. McDermott received the Caldecott Medal for *Arrow to the Sun: A Pueblo Indian Tale* (1974), which recreates the Pueblo myth of how the spirit of the Lord of the Sun was brought into the human world. In his picture book *Creation* (2003), he visualizes how the world was created, inspired by Eastern and European religious traditions as well as the Bible. His friendship and cooperation with the mythologist Joseph Campbell, his consultant on several films, acquainted McDermott with the psychological aspects of mythology and influenced his later career. Increasingly he has made a point of integrating cultural and mythological symbolism in his art.

Maria-Venetia Kyritsi

McDonald, Megan (1959–), versatile American author of the Judy Moody series for newly independent readers and an unusually wide variety of other writing. *Judy Moody* (2000) and subsequent books have hit a chord with eight- and nine-year-old readers. According to McDonald, Judy, who *is* moody, is based on her own life and personality. Sprightly sketches by Peter Reynolds provide a sophisticated look, and large type makes the books relatively hefty. Her younger-looking Beezy series for beginning readers has not been as popular. McDonald's first book, *Is This a House for a Hermit Crab?* (1990), emerged from her work as a storytelling librarian. *The Potato Man* (1991) and the *Great Pumpkin Switch* (1992), both illustrated by Ted Lewin, were based on stories her father told. *Tundra Mouse* (1997) incorporates Eskimo Yup'ik storyknife tradition. McDonald has also written books on insects, penguins, and reptiles; several novels for older readers; and the haunting and poetic *The Bone Keeper* (1999).

BIBLIOGRAPHY

Broaddus, Karen, and Gay Ivey. "Surprising the Writer: Discovering Details through Research and Reading." *Language Arts* 80, no. 1 (September 2002): 23–30.

Linnea Hendrickson

McDonald, Meme (1954–), and **Boori Pryor** (1950–), Australian coauthors of children's fiction. Pryor is an Aboriginal author of Kunggandji and Birra-gubba ancestry, and McDonald is a non-Aboriginal author. The pair has worked collaboratively since 1988, when they published their first novel, *My Girragundji*. They have since produced several novels, including the much-lauded *The Binna Binna Man* (1999). Their books, which focus on the identity formation of urban Aboriginal characters and on race relations in Australia, are notable for their use of Aboriginal English, their judicious deployment of photographs, and their reliance on Aboriginal beliefs and practices, such as the coexistence of humans and spirits in everyday experience.

Clare Bradford

McElderry, Margaret K. (1912–), American editor of award-winning children's books and pioneer of international publishing collaborations. Born to Northern Irish immigrant parents in Pittsburgh and trained there as a librarian at the Carnegie Library School after graduating from Mount Holyoke College, McElderry began her career as an assistant to Anne Carroll Moore at the New York Public Library (1934 to 1943). After a stint as librarian for the Office of War Information in London and Brussels (1943–1945), McElderry became children's book editor at Harcourt Brace and, after 1971, started her own imprint at Atheneum, continued at Macmillan and Simon and Schuster. She edited a number of Newbery and Caldecott Award books (both in 1952) as well as Honor books, in addition to winners of the Mildred Batchelder, Boston Globe–Horn Book, Hans Christian Andersen, Canadian Library Association Book of the Year, Carnegie Medal, NCTE Award for Excellence in Poetry, and IRA Award for best novel. McElderry formed deep and lasting relationships with many authors, including Nancy Bond, Lucy Boston, Susan Cooper, Edward Eager, Elizabeth Enright, Eleanor Estes, James Houston, Margaret Mahy, Nicholas Mordvinoff, Andre Norton, Mary Norton, Joan Phipson, Virginia Sorenson, and Patricia Wrightson. The illustrators for her picture books also reflect a star-studded global cast: Mitsumasa Anno, Irene Haas, Felix Hoffman, Feodor Rojankovsky, Erik Blegvad, and Warwick Hutton, among others. Married to the publisher Storer Lunt, McElderry was active in IBBY, honored with the Women's National Books Association Award (1975), and selected to deliver the Arbuthnot Lecture (1994). Her impact was never more significant than when she published controversial books following World War II: a collection of Japanese stories (*The Dancing Kettle*, 1949) by Yoshiko Uchida, who also wrote novels about her family's experiences in U.S. detention camps, and a translation of Margot Benary-Isbert's stark novel *The Ark* (1953) about war-torn Germany. The indomitable courage, vision, energy, and humor of this creative editor helped shape children's literature for six decades.

[*See also biographies of figures mentioned in this article.*]

BIBLIOGRAPHY

Hearne, Betsy. "Margaret K. McElderry and the Professional Matriarchy of Children's Books." *Library Trends* 44, no. 4 (Spring 1996): 755–775. Explores the ties among 20th-century women in publishing and librarianship, with special emphasis on McElderry's contributions.

Marcus, Leonard. "An Interview with Margaret K. McElderry." *Horn Book Magazine* 69, no. 6 (1993): 692–704; 70, no. 1 (1994): 34–45. McElderry discusses the major aspects of her editorial direction in children's book publishing throughout the second half of the 20th century.

Betsy Hearne

McEwan, Ian (1948–), British novelist and screenplay writer, recipient of the prestigious Booker Prize for *Amsterdam* (1998). Although the theme of childhood underlies all his works, only one of them, *The Daydreamer* (1994), is actually aimed at adults and children alike. *The Daydreamer* evades categories: not only has it been published both in separate editions for adults (with a preface by the author) and children (illustrated by Anthony Browne), but it can equally be perceived as either a novel or a collection of stories. The seven episodes from ten-year-old Peter's life focus on the theme of metamorphosis, blurring the frontiers between reality and fiction and offering, through his daydreams, a metatextual commentary on writing. McEwan has also written the English text for the picture book *Rose Blanche* (1985), a war-time story illustrated by the Italian artist Roberto Innocenti and initially written in French by the Swiss author Christophe Gallaz.

[*See also* Browne, Anthony *and* Innocenti, Roberto.]

Virginie Douglas

McFarlane, Peter (1940–), Australian poet, writer, and educator who is involved in Australia's longest-running community poetry reading venue, Friendly Street Poets, located in Adelaide. His books include lighthearted comedies for young readers as well as hard-hitting critiques of contemporary society for young adults. McFarlane has coedited poetry texts for schools, such as *Orange Moon* (1975) with Garth Boomer. With Lisa Temple he has compiled two poetry anthologies for senior secondary students, *Blue Light, Clear Atoms* (1996) and *Among Ants, between Bees* (1998). *Exploring the Writer's Craft* (2000) is a text on the teaching of writing and *The Projected Muse* (1977) is a book of excerpts from Australian film scripts. He and Tessa Duder edited a collection of stories by Australian and New Zealand writers, *Personal Best* (1997). His own short stories are collected in *The Flea and Other Stories* (1992) and *Lovebird* (1993). A semiautobiographical novel, *The Tin House* (1989), evokes the fears of a twelve-year-old in a changing world. In *The Enemy You Killed* (1996) a group of young men's war games turn to violence and tragedy in a graphic story of troubled adolescents. *More Than a Game* (1999) is written in the voice of an intellectually disabled girl Tammy, whose enthusiasm for Australian-rules football leads her into moments of confrontation with her boyfriend and the team. McFarlane is also the author of several novels for younger readers: *Rebecca the Wrecker* (1995), *Betty the Balloon Buster* (1996), *Max the Man Mountain* (1997), *Soula the Ruler* (1997), *Barnaby the Barbarian* (1998), and *Michaela the Whaler* (1998), all illustrated by Stephen Axelsen. *Goat Boy* (2001), *Bomber Boy* (2002), and *Kart Girl* (2003) are humorous adventure stories for upper primary school-age children.

Stella Lees and Pam Macintyre

McFarlane, Sheryl (1954–), Canadian author of children's picture books. Since 1974 she has lived on the West Coast of Canada. Her love of this region, and particularly her connection with the coast, is reflected in her books. Her first book, *Waiting for the Whales* (1991), beautifully illustrated by Ron Lightburn's realistic paintings, uses the rhythm of the seasons, represented by the migration of orca whales, to teach a young girl about the natural cycles of birth and death. *Jessie's Island* (1992) and *Moonsnail Song* (1994), both illustrated by Sheena Lott, celebrate West Coast island life and show readers the pleasures of noticing the small details in nature. Even McFarlane's books that are not ostensibly about living on the coast, like *This Is the Dog*

(2003), still reflect coastal experiences, in this case when the runaway puppy makes his way onto the beach.

[*See also* Lightburn, Ron.]

Terri Doughty

McGinley, Phyllis (1905–1978), American poet and children's book author. Born in Ontario, Oregon, and educated at the universities of Southern California and Utah, McGinley began her career as a teacher but soon started writing professionally, mostly light verse but also children's books, essays, criticism, and song lyrics. Her first work for children, *The Horse Who Lived Upstairs* (1944), about a horse that learns to appreciate what he has, was written in verse and was followed by two Caldecott Honor Books: *All around the Town* (1948), an alphabet book narrated in verse about the many sites that can be found in a city, and *The Most Wonderful Doll in the World* (1950), in which a little girl idealizes her lost favorite doll. In *The Year without a Santa Claus* (1957), made into a popular television special in 1974, Santa resigns for a year from his duties, partly because he has a bad cold and partly because he is disappointed by the lack of belief in the Christmas spirit. McGinley wrote more than a dozen books for children, but she is best known for her technically skillful poetry, which won her a Pulitzer Prize for *Times Three: Selected Verse from Three Decades* (1960).

Bibliography

Wagner, Linda Welshimer. *Phyllis McGinley*. New York: Twayne, 1971.

Maria-Venetia Kyritsi

McGough, Roger (1937–), British poet, novelist, playwright, broadcaster, and anthologist. Born in Liverpool and educated at Hull University, Roger Joseph McGough taught in schools and art colleges. He was a member of the pop music/poetry group The Scaffold from 1963 to 1973. He began publishing poetry in 1965, achieving recognition as one of the "Liverpool Poets," with Adrian Henri and Brian Patten, included in *The Mersey Sound* (1967), one of the best-selling poetry books of recent times. His poetry has been consistently popular; his trademark wordplay, use of "run-together" words, impeccable timing, and skeptical irreverence encapsulate a distinctive late 20th century outlook. He has received various fellowships and honorary awards and was honored with the Order of the British Empire in 1997. McGough's first collection for children, *Mr. Noselighter* (1976), was made for his son; since then he has twice won the Signal Poetry Award, in 1984 for *Sky in the Pie* (1983) and in 1999 for *Bad, Bad Cats* (1997). Other notable collections of his own work include *Nailing the Shadow* (1987), *An Imaginary Menagerie* (1988), *Good Enough to Eat* (2002), a collection for younger children, *Pillow Talk* (1990), and *Another Custard Pie* (1993), a story in verse. Known for his anthologies of humorous poetry for children, he has also collaborated with other children's poets; in 1979 he and Michael Rosen produced *You Tell Me*, a collection for adolescents that includes poems in which McGough uses a child's viewpoint to observe adult experience, a device he continues in *The Way Things Are* (1999). His work also includes such comic novels as *The Great Smile Robbery* (1982) and *The Stowaways* (1983), and humorous factual books. In 1984 McGough wrote the lyrics for a U.S. stage adaptation of *The Wind in the Willows*. He has narrated his own work on audio book and CD, as well that of other authors, including Mick Inkpen's *Kipper* stories.

[*See also* Rosen, Michael.]

Bridget Carrington

McGraw, Eloise Jarvis (1915–2000), American author of children's fiction. McGraw earned her degree from Principia College and continued to study art intermittently at a variety of institutions. Over her long career, McGraw's work took a variety of shapes—eighteen books for young readers, short stories, and several pieces for adult readers. She achieved much success as a writer of historical fiction; both *Moccasin Trail* (1952) and *The Golden Goblet* (1961) were Newbery Honor books. Although McGraw was a careful researcher, not all of her fiction has aged well. *Moccasin Trail* features Jim Keath, a young white protagonist raised by Crow Indians. Jim struggles both to appreciate the Indian culture and eventually to reintegrate himself among his surviving family members. McGraw's portrayal of the Native Americans in her text lacks the depth, perspective, and sensitivity that would be expected in a modern novel.

McGraw was also successful with mysteries, including *Mara, Daughter of the Nile* (1953), the Edgar Award–winning *A Really Weird Summer* (1977), and *Tangled Webb* (1993). Additionally, she authored a variety of fantasy novels. She produced three novels for the Oz series originated by L. Frank Baum. Two of these were collaborations with her daughter Lauren McGraw Wagner: *Merry-Go-Round in Oz* (1963) and *Forbidden Fountain in Oz* (1980). She also received a third Newbery Honor for her novel *The Moorchild* (1996), which features Saaski, a changeling child who fits in with neither the wild magical Folk of the hillsides nor the human parents on whom she has been foisted.

Across this variety of genres, McGraw excelled at telling a compelling story and peopling it with young characters, often lacking family support, who struggle to find a place for themselves.

Megan Lynn Isaac

McKee, David (1935–), British picture book author. His most popular creations are the ongoing numerous books about Elmer the Patchwork Elephant (1968), also available as board, coloring, pop-up, flap, and hole-in-the-page books. Other successful ongoing series include *Mr. Benn* (1967) and *King Rollo* (1979). Among critics, McKee is especially appreciated for his postmodern, highly sophisticated picture books, in which words and pictures often contradict each other or tell different stories altogether. In *I Hate My Teddy Bear* (1982), the unimaginative conversation of two bored children stands in sharp contrast with the mysterious activities going on around them in the pictures. The flat verbal plot of *Charlotte's Piggy Bank* (1996) is counterbalanced by the many exciting visual subplots that often take a keen eye to discover. Both books employ exciting pictorial solutions, including the "impossible space" reminiscent of M. C. Escher. Yet in all their playfulness, McKee's books carry serious, if not directly disturbing, messages. *Not Now, Bernard* (1980), another book where text and images convey different stories, focuses on the total miscommunication between a child and his parents, resulting in the child being eaten up by a monster. While it is natural to assume that the monster is the product of the boy's self-therapeutic imagination, neither the text nor the pictures suggest that the events are merely the child's fancies, and the parents continue to ignore the monster just as they have ignored Bernard. The theme of the abandoned child who uses imagination to cope is developed in *The Monster and the Teddy Bear* (1989). These books use visual means to express a child's emotions and anxieties that are difficult, not to say impossible, to convey with words in a way comprehensible for a young child; images take over when words are no longer sufficient and appeal to the readers' empathy directly, without the mediation of language.

Maria Nikolajeva

McKillip, Patricia (1948–), well-respected author of fantasy and science fiction who initially wrote for children and young adults. McKillip's first works were illustrated children's books that explored both fantasy and real-world settings. *The Forgotten Beasts of Eld* (1974), her first full-length fantasy, received the World Fantasy Award for best novel. Her *Riddle of Stars* trilogy (1976–1979, also referred to as the Riddle-Master trilogy) has been compared to Ursula Le Guin's Earthsea trilogy. In the 1980s McKillip experimented with new genres, including a coming-of-age novel, *Stepping from the Shadows* (1982), and science fiction for a variety of ages. She returned to fantasy in the late 1980s. Often considered a feminist for her revisions of fantasy motifs, she has been praised by critics for her well-developed characters and her ability to address human questions in fantastic worlds. She is also noted for her writing style, often a combination of lyrical description and humor.

BIBLIOGRAPHY

Spivack, Charlotte. *Merlin's Daughters: Contemporary Women Writers of Fantasy*. New York: Greenwood Press, 1987.

Rachel B. Kapelle

McKinley, Robin (1952–), American author of fairy-tale retellings, short stories, picture books, and fantasy novels. McKinley's childhood was peripatetic owing to her father's military career. She studied English literature at Bowdoin College and then worked as an editor, researcher, and teacher. In 1992 she married Peter Dickinson, a renowned British fantasy author, and moved to England. McKinley is an accomplished reteller of classic stories, which she vividly reshapes for contemporary audiences. Her first novel, the highly regarded *Beauty: Retelling of the Story of Beauty and the Beast* (1978), subtly reworks the traditionally patriarchal significance of this fairy tale by making its heroine a self-conscious and seemingly plain young woman. The novel is as much about Beauty's self-awakening as it is about her discovery of the Beast's compassionate nature. A feminist discourse is always present in McKinley's writing, particularly in relation to her strong-willed female protagonists. *Deerskin* (1993), a version of the Perrault fairy tale "Donkeyskin," transforms the tale of a young woman raped by her father into a journey of feminine empowerment. In *Rose Daughter* (1997), McKinley revisits the story of Beauty and the Beast but importantly changes the ending: the story concludes by allowing Beauty to choose her own fate.

McKinley has also published a number of acclaimed fantasy novels. Like her fairy tales, these fantasies are set in carefully detailed worlds and feature assertive female heroines. *The Blue Sword* (1982), a Newbery Honor book, is a sword-and-sorcery fantasy about the spirited Harry, a girl who embodies many of the heroic qualities conventionally associated with masculinity. *The Hero and the Crown* (1984), which won the Newbery Medal, is a prequel to *The Blue Sword*. It is also a female coming-of-age story, exploring the future queen's progression from outcast to heroic dragon fighter. In 2003 McKinley published her first adult novel, *Sunshine*, an introspective, ruminative vampire thriller.

John Stephens

McKissack, Patricia (1944–), and **Fred McKissack** (1939–), African American authors who were born in Tennessee. The McKissacks, who met at Tennessee State University, began collaborating in 1984 and have published (either separately or together) more than one hundred books about African American experiences. In her early readers and picture books, Patricia McKissack draws on the folkloric patterns and southern vernaculars in tales told by her grandparents. Her picture books present strong African American children embedded in cultural traditions, as in, for example, *Flossie and the Fox* (1986); *Mirandy and Brother Wind*, a Caldecott Honor book and the recipient of the Coretta Scott King Illustrator Award for Jerry Pinkney's illustrations (1988); *A Million Fish . . . More or Less* (1992); and *Goin' Someplace Special*, a Bank Street Best Book and Coretta Scott King Award winner (2001). In these books Flossie outwits the cunning fox, as generations of slaves outsmarted masters; Mirandy dances with the invisible Brother Wind in the ritualistic cakewalk; Hugh Thomas reels off a very tall tale; and Tricia Ann takes a stand against Jim Crow laws. *The Dark-Thirty: Southern Tales of the Supernatural* (1992), an anthology that combines nail-biting suspense with significant events in African American history, won a Coretta Scott King Award and a Newbery Honor citation. Patricia McKissack has contributed to the Royal Diaries series, with *Nzingha: Warrior Queen of Matamba* (2000), and the Dear America series, with *Color Me Dark: Diary of Nellie Lee Love* (2000) and *Look to the Hills: The Diary of Lozette Moreau, a French Slave Girl* (2004). With her son, Fredrick McKissack Jr., she published *Black Diamond: A Story of the Negro Baseball League* (1994).

In their nonfiction, the McKissacks extend their celebration of African American heroes—sung and unsung—in histories and biographies. Extensive research, a solid use of primary sources, and reproduction of significant documents characterize their works about George Washington Carver, Frederick Douglass, Langston Hughes, Martin Luther King Jr., Satchel Paige, Sojourner Truth, Ida B. Wells, Michael Jackson, and others. The same careful research characterizes historical studies such as *The Civil Rights Movement in America from 1865 to the Present* (1987) and *Days of Jubilee: The End of Slavery in the United States* (2003). In the popular *Christmas in the Big House, Christmas in the Quarters* (1994), the authors combine genres as they describe events on a Virginia plantation in 1859. Details of pastimes, stories, and food preparation highlight differences between the Christmas celebrations in the master's house and those in the slaves' quarters. Educators hail the McKissacks for the relevance of their nonfiction to middle- and high-school curricula and for their emphasis on quieter chapters in history (as in *A Long Hard Journey: The Story of the Pullman Porter*, winner of a Coretta Scott King Award and the Jane Addams Peace Award, 1990; *Red Tail Angels: The Story of the Tuskegee Airmen of World War II*, 1995; and *Black Hands, White Sails: The Story of African-American Whalers*, 1999). The McKissacks received the Regina Medal in 1998 for their "distinguished contribution to children's literature."

BIBLIOGRAPHY

Wrobble, Lisa A. "Patricia C. and Fredrick L(emuel) McKissack." In *St. James Guide to Children's Writers*, 5th ed., edited by Sara Pendergast and Tom Pendergast, 734–737. Detroit, Mich., and London: St. James Press, 1999.

Cathryn M. Mercier

McLean, Andrew (1946–), and **Janet McLean** (1946–), Australian illustrator and writer respectively. Their thoughtful texts and detailed illustrations capture the minutiae of the child's world; the drama of professions that intrigue children, such as *The Riverboat Crew* (1978), *The Steam Train Crew* (1981), *Fire-Engine Lil* (1989), and the play of kindergarten children in *Make It I'm the Mother* (2000). Domestic pets are fondly evoked in *Oh, Kipper!* (1991), *Dog Tales* (1993), *Cat Goes to Sea* (1994), *Cat's Whiskers* (1995), and a series about a small dog: *Josh* (1997), *Josh and the Thumper* (1997), *Josh and the Ducks* (1998), and *Josh and the Monster* (1998).

Andrew McLean's black-and-white sketches capture the character and mood of novels such as *Antonio S and the Mystery of Theodore Guzman* (1997) and the Bartlett and the Hazel series by Odo Hirsch. Luminous watercolors bring to life landscapes, from rural Australia to war-ravaged Bosnia, in picture books such as *Highway* (1998), by Nadia Wheatley; *My Dog* (2001), by John Heffernan, which won the 2002 CBCA Award for Younger Readers; and *A Year on Our Farm* (2002), by Penny Matthews, winner of the 2003 Children's Book Council of Australia (CBCA) Award for Early Childhood. *You'll Wake the Baby!* (2000), by Catherine Jinks, which won the 2001 CBCA Award for Early Childhood, and *Reggie Queen of the Street* (2003), by Margaret Barbalet, reveal McLean's engagement with domestic drama.

Stella Lees and Pam Macintyre

McMillan, Bruce (1947–), American photo-illustrator and author of picture books. His ingenious presentation of math, science, and the natural world in concept books for young children and photo-documentary books for middle-graders attract wide readership and critical esteem and have won numerous awards. McMillan received a jump start at age five when his father presented him with his first camera. Soon after, McMillan and his family moved to Maine, which he continues to make his home and where he completed his formal education by earning a BS in biology. For McMillan, Maine plus photography plus biology do not equal destiny, but they inform the forty-plus books McMillan has authored to date. McMillan's own description of his work stresses that he is not a photographer shooting isolated images, but rather a photo-illustrator creating visual narratives dependent upon each photograph's advancing the story. A self-taught writer, McMillan shapes his narratives from his extensive research, passion for accuracy, desire to tell good stories, and irrepressible urge to promote creativity and delight in learning. Titles such as *Dry or Wet?* (1988), *One Sun: A Book of Terse Verse* (1990), *Eating Fractions* (1991), and *Jelly Beans for Sale* (1996), feature a multicultural cast of local children delighting in various activities: splashing and drying off, a day at the beach filled with discovery and rhymes, cooking and dividing food, and exchanging the correct coins for colorful candies. McMillan engages the young audience of his concept books through careful sequencing of technically sophisticated but clearly "readable" visual images, humorous wordplay, and his control of his books' entire design as a physical object. The latter control extends to his photo-documentaries, many of which implicitly suggest both the fragility and adaptability of life through McMillan's choice of subject (often birds, usually endangered) or setting (often cold places near water) or both, as in *Penguins at Home: Gentoos of Antarctica*, 1993, and *Nights of the Pufflings*, 1995. The latter is the first of five books set in Iceland, an ongoing connection marked by McMillan's 2004 arts residency in Akureyri, home of Iceland's cherished children's author, Nonni (1857–1944). Perhaps McMillan's characterizing *The Remarkable Riderless Runaway Tricycle* (one of his few photo-illustrated fantasies, 1978; film version, 1982) as autobiographical offers a clue to his divining inspiration from both austerity and bare concepts. When McMillan looks at the tricycle, he sees his own persistence, determination, and penchant for happy endings.

Janice M. Alberghene

McNaughton, Colin (1951–), British writer and artist, who, since the publication of his first title in 1976, has produced over eighty books, many of which he has both written and illustrated. The greatest influence on his work, which is steeped in popular culture, is comics art, with the result that dynamic layout and graphic continuity effortlessly move his cast of eccentric characters through space and time; ever-irreverent humour, fondness for spoofs, and intertextuality typify his texts. He has received many awards, including the Kurt Maschler Award for *Have You Seen Who's Just Moved in Next Door to Us?* (1990) and the British Book Design and Production Award for *Making Friends with Frankenstein: A Book of Monstrous Poems and Pictures* (1993). *Watch Out for Giant Killers!* (1992), an environmental fable, was adapted for the theater. In McNaughton's popular "Preston Pig" series, each book is an ingenious variation upon a single theme: will hungry, devious Mr. Wolf catch the boisterous little pig Preston? *Oops!* (1996), winner of the Smarties Prize, cunningly refers back to folk tales, and in *Hmm . . .* (1998), Preston tries and fails to get Mr. Wolf interested in a career. Originally McNaughton's effortless graphic style was influenced by line-based artists, but in later works it has become more painterly.

Bibliography

Alderson, Brian. "Pigs, Pirates, and Preposterous Pictures: Making Friends with Colin McNaughton." In *Daft as a Bucket: Inside the World of Colin McNaughton*, edited by Elizabeth Hammill. Newcastle upon Tyne, U.K.: HarperCollins, Centre for the Children's Book, 1998.

Lewis, David. "Colin McNaughton and 'Knowingness.'" *Children's Literature in Education* 29, no. 2 (1998): 59–68.

Jane Doonan

McNeill, Janet (1907–1994), Irish-born British writer and playwright, remembered in children's literature for her comic fantasy series *My Friend Specs McCaan* (1955) and sequels, echoing the works of E. Nesbit. The books describe a chain of episodes happening to an ordinary schoolboy who becomes invisible when a class photo is taken, witnesses a phoenix being reborn, hatches a baby dragon from an egg he has found, receives swimming lessons from a mermaid, and so on. *The Battle of St. George Without* (1966) and its sequel are realistic novels in a contemporary urban setting.

Maria Nikolajeva

McPhail, David (1940–), a prolific American illustrator and author. Although McPhail trained to be an artist at the Boston Museum of Fine Arts School, he discovered the world of children's book illustration while working as a shipping clerk for a book wholesaler. He began by illustrating textbooks but soon worked up the courage to write a book of his own. McPhail usually employs pen, ink, and watercolor, although he also works in acrylics. Over time his layouts have migrated from drawings contained in their own boxes to full-page illustrations that have the text imposed over them. He claims to know little about writing and to rely on his editors to polish his texts. He still occasionally illustrates the works of other authors.

Bears and pigs populate many of McPhail's titles. He attributes this in part to his love for his childhood teddy bear and for E. B. White's book about a pig, *Charlotte's Web* (1952). He fashioned a well-known series around the character "Pig Pig" (*Pig Pig Grows Up*, 1980) and another around anthropomorphized bears (*Emma's Pet*, 1985). Even his works that focus on a child character, such as his Edward series, contain animals in the background. McPhail creates animal characters in tense situations or engaging in inappropriate behaviors as a way to explore topics with children in a nonconfrontational way. In many of his books he uses very gentle humor to subtly communicate moral lessons. Very often it is the kindness of one character to another that becomes the focal point of a McPhail work. He details some of his creative processes in an autobiography he wrote for children, *In Flight with David McPhail* (1996).

Charlotte Cubbage

McRae, Rodney (1958–), New Zealand illustrator and animator who has lived in Australia since 1984. He blends reality and fantasy in books such as *My Mother's Kitchen* (1984), *Terrible Tracy: A Cautionary Tale* (1989), and *The Dragon in the Garden Shed* (1991). *The Gaping Wide-Mouthed Waddling Frog* (1989) is a counting book. Fine watercolors capture the degradation of a polluted river in *Cry Me a River* (1994), a moving plea for environmental awareness. His new illustrations for *Who Killed Cockatoo?* (1988), by W. A. Cawthorne, first published in 1860, use striking Australian Aboriginal motifs. *Dame Dearlove's Ditties for the Nursery* (1989) is one of a series aimed at reviving classic nursery rhymes from the 19th century. *Aesop's Fables* (1990) showcases McRae's artistry using computer graphics, collage, linocuts, torn paper, and scraper-board techniques to create alternate black-and-white and colored illustrations to pay tribute to the pictorial traditions of ancient Greece, South America, Australian Aborigines, Africa, Japan, ancient Egypt, and the caves of Lascaux. He has illustrated Robin Klein's *Brock and the Dragon* (1984), Jean Chapman's *Cockatoo Soup* (1987), and Edel Wignell's *Raining Cats and Dogs* (1987), among others, and animated for children's television programs including *Playschool*.

Stella Lees and Pam Macintyre

Meade, L. T. (1844–1914), Irish writer. Born in County Cork, Lillie Elizabeth Thomasina Meade moved to London in 1874, by which time she had already published her first adult novels. Although she wrote a total of some 250 books for a range of age groups, she is now chiefly remembered as a writer of girls' school stories. Her novel *A World of Girls: The Story of a School* (1886) is widely regarded as one of the pioneering works in this genre and was followed by, among many others, *Girls New and Old* (1895), *Betty: A School Girl* (1895), *Catalina: Art Student* (1896), *The Girls of St Wode's* (1898), and *The Manor School* (1903). In addition to her full-length fiction, Meade was responsible for a great deal of journalism and was one of the first editors of the girls' magazine *Atalanta*.

[*See also* School Stories.]

Robert Dunbar

Meader, Stephen (1892–1977), American author of adventure and historical fiction. Stephen Warren Meader's first novel, *The Black Buccaneer* (1920), which featured a fourteen-year-old boy captured by pirates, set the template for the author's stories of adolescent boys engaged in exciting adventures. Some were based on his own New England youth (*Red Horse Hill*, 1930; *Lumberjack*, 1934), while others, such as *Who Rides in the Dark?* (1935) and his Newbery Honor novel about young Bill Crawford's 1837 hike from New

Hampshire to Ohio (*Boy with a Pack*, 1937), are historical fiction of the first rank. Original copies are highly prized by book collectors, and new editions have been released for contemporary children.

PETER D. SIERUTA

Meaker, Marijane (1927–), prolific American writer better known by the pseudonym M. E. Kerr, under which she has published numerous pioneering books of realistic fiction for young adults. Ever a prankster and a provocateur, Meaker was once suspended from her boarding school in Staunton, Virginia—but that did not stop her from later finishing college at the University of Missouri with a concentration in English literature and journalism. Her first publication was a short story in *Ladies Home Journal* entitled "Devotedly, Patrick Henry Casebolt" (1951), a piece whose cheeky style, snappy dialogue, and boarding school setting prefigured the young adult books to come. Before she began her career in children's literature, Meaker published several adult mysteries under the name Vin Packer and nonfiction books for adults on lesbian life under the name Ann Aldrich.

Encouraged by her friend Louise Fitzhugh, author of *Harriet the Spy* (1964), and inspired by the potential for excellence in teenage writing that she saw in Paul Zindel's *The Pigman* (1968), Meaker wrote the first M. E. Kerr book, *Dinky Hocker Shoots Smack!* (1972). With it she joined the small group of writers who were at the vanguard of the newly emerging genre of young adult fiction. The novel, whose gutsy adolescent characters struggle with issues such as obesity, mental illness, and parental neglect, also won her a reputation as a writer who refuses to shy away from controversy and whose works deal with the vicissitudes of the underdog and those who exist on the fringes of society. *Gentlehands* (1978) explores evil and cruelty through a character whose grandfather was a Nazi war criminal; *Little Little* (1981) is narrated by a pair of teenage dwarfs; *Night Kites* (1986) dared to feature a young gay protagonist with AIDS before any other novel, for either teenagers or adults; and *Deliver Us from Evie* (1994) tells the story of a determined young lesbian dealing with community prejudice while growing up on a small southern family farm.

The vast majority of Meaker's narrators are male voices, a deliberate attempt to woo male readers without alienating female ones. She makes a habit of mining her own history for factual material to transform into fiction, and several of the experiences she had as a teenager and young adult have found their way into her writing. The autobiographical *Me, Me, Me, Me, Me: Not a Novel* (1983), written in answer to letters from readers curious about the origins of the events in her books, includes a codicil after each chapter connecting fictional characters to real-life counterparts. In *Blood on the Forehead: What I Know about Writing* (1998), Meaker shares the stories behind ten of her works in a chatty, no-nonsense book of advice for aspiring young authors. Her humor, her refusal to condescend to her readers, and her willingness to engage honestly with difficult issues have ensured her enduring popularity. In 1993 she won the Margaret A. Edwards Award, which recognizes a body of work that helps adolescents develop self-awareness and grapple with deep personal, social, and philosophical questions.

BIBLIOGRAPHY

Nilsen, Alleen Pace. *Presenting M. E. Kerr.* New York: Twayne, 1997. Accessible appraisal of Meaker's body of work; includes biographical profile and readable critical analysis of stylistic and thematic elements.

MEERA LEE SETHI

Means, Florence Crannell (1891–1980), American novelist and biographer. Means is best known for *The Moved-Outers* (1945), a novel about a Japanese American family forced to live in an internment camp during World War II. The book, told from the perspective of Sue (Sumiko) Ohara, a high school senior, portrayed diverse reactions to internment, ranging from resignation to rage. It went through more than a dozen printings during its first year and received a Newbery Honor citation. Means was the daughter of Philip Wendell Crannell, an influential Baptist minister, and her output included biographies of missionaries such as Clarence Salsbury (*Sagebrush Surgeon*, 1955) and Abigail E. Johnson (*Sunlight on the Hopi Mesas*, 1960). For her life of George Washington Carver (*Carvers' George*, 1952), Means's research included interviewing his college art instructor and other individuals who had known the scientist personally. During her lifetime, however, Means's reputation rested on her depictions of minority teens discovering their callings, in novels such as *Shuttered Windows* (1938) and *Great Day in the Morning* (1946). Means's gifts included depicting tension within minority subgroups as well as interracial conflicts. Although her own work has faded out of fashion, she helped pave the way for realistic fiction featuring non-Caucasian protagonists.

PEGGY LIN DUTHIE

Medals. *See* Awards.

Meddaugh, Susan (1944–), American illustrator and author of humorous picture books. After college, Meddaugh first worked as a "girl Friday" at an advertising agency in New York City before moving to Boston, where she served as a designer and art director in Houghton Mifflin's children's book department. One of her most popular characters, Martha the lovable pit bull, debuted in the picture book *The Witches' Supermarket* (1991). On Halloween, Helen and her dog Martha go into a supermarket where all the customers are dressed as witches. Realizing that the customers are *real* witches, Martha (dressed as a cat) creates a diversion to help them escape. In *Martha Speaks* (1992), Martha eats alphabet soup and gains the ability to talk but soon learns that some things are better left unsaid. Meddaugh is an inventive, witty storyteller, and as an illustrator she has also worked on books by such authors as Verna Aardema, John Ciardi, and Eve Bunting.

DEBRA MITTS-SMITH

Medearis, Angela Shelf (1956–), African American writer, known best as a children's book author, whose picture books realistically depict African American life and culture. In 1990 Medearis published her first book, *Picking Peas for a Penny*, a richly textured counting rhyme about life on the author's family farm during the Depression. She has since published more than seventy books in a variety of genres, ranging from picture books to biographies to adaptations of African folk tales to cookbooks. Some of her picture books are based on her own childhood experiences; others seek to recover and retell stories of the African American experience. Her body of work includes *Dancing with the Indians* (1991), *Come This Far to Freedom: A History of African-Americans* (1993), *Poppa's New Pants* (1994), *Kyle's First Kwanzaa* (1996), *The 100th Day of School* (1996), *Rum-a-Tum-Tum* (1997), and *The Biggest Snowball Fight* (2002).

BIBLIOGRAPHY

"Angela Shelf Medearis." In *Something About the Author*, edited by Alan Hedblad. Vol. 123. Detroit, Mich.: Gale Research, 2001.

CAROL JONES COLLINS

Medieval Children's Literature. The medieval period is generally recognized as that thousand-year period in Europe from the fall of Rome in 476 to the Reformation in 1517. When defining children's literature in the Middle Ages, it is important to recognize texts written specifically for children and also those produced for a mixed audience of adults and youths. At the same time, it is essential to include didactic works—that is, works intended to teach moral and religious lessons or the essentials of reading and writing—as well as literature whose purpose is to entertain. In fact, much of medieval literature arcs between purpose and pleasure or, as Chaucer writes in the *General Prologue* to the *Canterbury Tales*, between "sentence" (moral sense) and "solas" (pleasure). Additionally, it is instructive to consider texts that feature child protagonists, in order to ascertain the forms of subjectivity enabled by those texts.

While the legends and myths, ballads and sagas, songs and stories of oral tradition passed along by bards, courtiers, or family members probably constitute some of the earliest children's literature—versions of which survive today as fairy tales and folklore—many medieval written texts exhibit specific thematic, linguistic, grammatical, rhetorical, or codicological features that evidence their being written for younger audiences. Chaucer's *A Treatise on the Astrolabe*, written for his ten-year-old son, features simplified diction and sentence structure. Other examples of medieval literature directed primarily toward children and youth include didactic and moral literature (Caxton's *Book of Curtesye*, *The Lytylle Childrenes Lytil Boke*), courtesy and conduct literature (*The Babees Book*, "How the Good Wife Taught Her Daughter"), educational and instructional literature (*Eclogues of Theodolus*, *Distichs of Cato*) and school texts (Ælfric's *Colloquy*, "The ABC of Aristotle"), religious literature, entertainment and popular literature (recensions of *Sir Gowther* and Chaucer's *Melibee* or *Squire's Tale*), and drama (*Occupation and Idleness*, the N-Town *Mary Play*).

Even if they glance briefly backward to earlier literatures, the standard accounts of children's literature usually begin with the Puritan educational program and John Newbery's 1744 publication of *Little Pretty Pocket Book*, and for many years, the idea of medieval children's literature was a misnomer, if not an impossibility. This thesis was based on the argument that the medieval period neither recognized childhood as a distinct period of life nor understood children to be fundamentally different from adults; children were nothing more than "miniature adults," and since infant mortality was so high, medieval people did not invest emotionally in their children. Therefore, there could be no such thing as medieval children's literature. This thesis, argued by Philippe Ariés in his important 1961 book, *Centuries of Childhood*, has been superseded by contemporary historians like Shulamith Shahar, Barbara Hanawalt, Nicholas Orme, and

Ronald Finucane. Spurred by this new research, the realization that medieval children were indeed valued by their families and communities, and the wide variety of texts produced for younger audiences, literary critics in the 21st century are presented with the opportunity to move beyond a narrow definition of medieval children's literature to embrace and investigate the broad and varied textual culture of medieval youth.

BIBLIOGRAPHY

Adams, Gillian. "Medieval Children's Literature: Its Possibility and Actuality." *Children's Literature* 26 (1998): 1–24.

Ariès, Philippe. *Centuries of Childhood: A Social History of Family Life*. Translated by Robert Baldick. New York: Knopf, 1962.

Hanawalt, Barbara. *Growing Up in Medieval London: The Experience of Childhood in History*. London: Oxford University Press, 1993.

Harris, A. Leslie. "Instructional Poetry for Medieval Children." *English Studies* 74 (1993): 124–132.

Kline, Daniel T, ed. *Medieval Literature for Children*. New York: Routledge, 2003.

Shahar, Shulamith. *Childhood in the Middle Ages*. London: Routledge, 1990.

Shaner, Mary. "Instruction and Delight: Medieval Romances as Children's Literature." *Poetics Today* 13 (1992): 1–5.

DANIEL T. KLINE

Mee, Arthur (1875–1943), journalist, editor of *The Children's Encyclopedia* and *The Children's Newspaper*. Sir Arthur Henry Mee was described by Sir John Hammerton in his biography as "a child of wonder moving through a world of endless surprise to his questing mind." He succeeded in conveying this marveling excitement to young readers. The second son of a railway worker's ten children, he went to work with the *Nottingham Evening Post* when he was fourteen, getting his learning from books at the Nottingham Mechanics' Institute. Even in those early days he wrote with amazing speed and facility and had begun to form the massive collection of press cuttings to which he constantly added and which he was to use in his later educational works. He moved to work in London in 1896 and in 1905 was recruited by Lord Northcliffe, founder of the Amalgamated Press and one of the most powerful and frenetic of all press lords (he died insane in 1922), as literary editor of the *Daily Mail*. Always fertile in ideas, Mee, seeing the popular demand for easy educational works, suggested a children's encyclopedia to be published in periodical form. Northcliffe was dubious, but Mee, though much in awe of his chief, doggedly produced compelling samples of advertising copy, and the first fortnightly part appeared in March 1908. So great was its success that the Educational Book Company, a Northcliffe subsidiary, sold little else for twenty years. "Few men in England have such power as you," Northcliffe told Mee in 1910. His name was now enough to sell any book—and the ingredients of the *Children's Encyclopedia* and his cuttings collection were to be shuffled and presented anew in many of his other educational publications. Among these was the *Children's Newspaper*, which Mee initiated in 1919 and edited until his death in 1943.

[*See also* Children's Encyclopedia, The; Children's Magazines; Children's Newspaper, The; Journals and Periodicals; *and* Little Folks.]

GILLIAN AVERY

Meek, Margaret (1925–), influential British theorist in the areas of children, reading, and literature. One of her most important books is *How Texts Teach What Readers Learn* (1988), the title of which sums up her understanding that what children read plays an important part in their view of learning to do it, thus works of the imagination should be at the heart of the school curriculum. Dr. Margaret Meek Spencer has written extensively on these topics and on books for the young, in which area *The Cool Web*, which she coedited in 1977 (reprint, 1994), remains a classic of literary theory applied to children's literature. Other books include *On Being Literate* (1992), *Information and Book Learning* (1996), *Coming of Age in Children's Literature* (coauthor, 2003), and, as coeditor, *Language and Literacy in the Primary School* (1988) and *Achieving Literacy* (1983).

Among her wide-ranging interests are picture books, in which the text and the pictures enhance and extend each other. Meek also advocates the importance of listening to what children (including preschool children) say about the books they encounter. She has published many articles, especially in *Signal*, *Books for Keeps*, and the *School Librarian*, for which she was the reviews editor for twenty-one years. Meek has been associated with the London Institute of Education since 1968 and has frequently held guest appointments at universities internationally. Of the many awards and honors she has received, she values most the Eleanor Farjeon Award (1970) for services to children's literature.

VIRGINIA JOY LOWE

Meggendorfer, Lothar (1847–1925), Bavarian creator of movable and panoramic picture books. He was born in Munich and was the youngest of twenty-five children. When his father, a tax collector, died in 1860, Meggendorfer had to move from high school to trade school, where he was considered the worst pupil in the drawing class. Nevertheless, at age fifteen he enrolled in an art academy, supporting himself by playing the zither. In 1866 he began working for a comic paper, *Fliegende Blätter* (Flying Leaves), where Wilhelm Busch (1832–1908), creator of *Max und Moritz* (1865), was among his colleagues. Meggendorfer's first movable book, *Lebende Bilder* (Living Pictures, 1878), was made as a Christmas present for his son Adolf.

Considered the greatest innovator in this field, Meggendorfer included in his work dissolving views, animated figures moved by hidden levers, and panoramas, one of the most impressive of these being *Internationaler Zircus* (1887). His humor is slapstick: a riotous class of boys is instantly cowed when the master turns; a horn player is so bad that the cats on the roof outside join in. Some of his books were reproduced in Germany, the United States, and Britain in the late 20th century, and the originals are prized as collectors' items. Maurice Sendak, a great admirer, included an essay on Meggendorfer in *Caldecott & Co.* (1988).

GILLIAN AVERY

Meigs, Cornelia (1884–1973), American author and educator. The author of *Invincible Louisa* (1933), her Newbery Award–winning biography of Louisa May Alcott, Cornelia Lynde Meigs also received Newbery Honor citations for *Windy Hill* (1921), *Clearing Weather* (1928), and *Swift Rivers* (1932) and wrote more than twenty other books and numerous short stories for children, including four adventures as "Adair Aldon."

In addition, Meigs coauthored *A Critical History of Children's Literature: A Survey of Children's Books in English* (1953, revised 1969) with Anne Eaton, E. Nesbitt, and Ruth Viguers, serving also as project editor. The survey was lauded as a landmark study when it first appeared, but as with almost all of Meigs's other books, it has been superseded by more contemporary guides and is now out of print.

A graduate of Bryn Mawr, and later a professor there, Meigs was revered during her lifetime for her ability to combine her extensive research with vivid storytelling. A great-granddaughter of the war hero Commodore John Rodgers (1772–1838), Meigs infused many of her stories with patriotic themes, often contriving encounters between her fictional protagonists and real-life statesmen such as Benjamin Franklin and Ethan Allen. Meigs herself served in the War Department during World War II.

Meigs also enjoyed depicting plucky, resilient protagonists who defy conventional wisdom and uncomprehending, sometimes openly hostile adults in order to pursue missions such as reclaiming a farm (*Call of the Mountain*, 1940) or sailing across the Atlantic (*The Trade Wind*, 1927). Likewise, her biographies of Jane Addams (1970) and of Alcott celebrate women of stubborn personality, unstinting generosity, and determination to succeed in spite of ill health and limited resources. The blithe stereotypes and moral loftiness pervading Meigs's fiction have caused it to age badly on the whole, but *Invincible Louisa* has held up as an admiring yet candid introduction to the world of Alcott and her family.

BIBLIOGRAPHY

Miller, Bertha Mahony. "Cornelia Meigs—America Speaking." In *Newbery Medal Books, 1922–1955*, edited by Bertha Mahony Miller and Elinor Whitney Field, 117–121. Boston: Horn Book, 1955. See also Meigs's acceptance paper, pp. 122–124.

PEGGY LIN DUTHIE

Meireles, Cecília (1901–1964), Brazilian poet, writer, educator, and journalist. Meireles wrote a number of children's books, including many volumes of poetry, such as *Ou isto ou aquilo* (This or That, 1964). She also founded the Children's Library of Rio de Janeiro in 1934, the first children's library of Brazil. Meireles is one of only a handful of women integrated into the Portuguese-speaking literary canon. Although her fame rests principally on her work as a poet, during much of her early life she was known in Brazil for her work as a children's educator, an outgrowth of her experience as an elementary-school teacher (a position she took at the age of sixteen). From 1930 to 1934 she wrote a regular column on education for the prominent Rio newspaper *Diário de Notícias* in which she advocated the modernization of Brazilian public education. Her children's poetry is common reading in Brazilian elementary schools. It privileges aesthetics over didacticism and features appealing rhythm, cadence, and rhyme. The frequent themes in her adult poetry of death and life's transitory nature also find subtle expression in her poetry for children.

RICHARD VERNON

Melas, Leon (1812–1879), Greek jurist, politician, and author. Author of a number of educational volumes, Melas became famous for *Gerostathes* (Old Man Stathis, 1858), a classic children's novel in which an elderly man tells stories to the young boys of his village. Written simply yet evocatively in Katharevousa (the "purified" form of Modern Greek), the book taught its young readers, without being condescending, about proper ways of living and the virtues of the Greek spirit. Because of its educational and nationalistic qualities, it became one of the first children's books to be instituted as a reader in Greek schools and was so used for almost a century. Since then, the book has continued to be well loved, and its reissue in 1951 as an illustrated edition as well as its adaptation to demotic Greek (the colloquial form of Modern Greek) is proof of its enduring appeal.

DOMINIQUE SANDIS

Melcher, Frederic G. (1879–1963), American bookseller and editor. A native of Massachusetts, Frederic Gershom Melcher spent the first twenty-three years of his career as a retail bookseller, first for Estes and Lauriat in Boston and then for W. K. Stewart in Indianapolis. In 1918, he was appointed coeditor of *Publisher's Weekly*, eventually becoming president and later chairman of the R. R. Bowker Company.

Melcher was extraordinarily gifted at organizing and sustaining campaigns to promote children's literature, including National Children's Book Week (working with Franklin K. Mathiews, librarian of the Boy Scouts of America, who had first proposed such a program in 1915). As a delegate to the 1921 American Library Association conference, Melcher initiated the creation of the Newbery Medal and was instrumental in establishing the Caldecott Medal in 1937. Melcher also underwrote the Caroline M. Hewins lecture series on New England children's books (1947–1962). The ALA has issued Melcher scholarships to prospective children's librarians since 1955.

[*See also* Awards.]

PEGGY LIN DUTHIE

Melling, O. R. (c. 1952–), Irish-Canadian fantasy author. Born in Dublin, but raised in Canada, Melling, whose real name is Geraldine Whelan, received a BA in Celtic studies and an MA in medieval history from the University of Toronto. She is now a journalist in Ireland. Melling is best known for several time-shift fantasies in which troubled young people magically journey into mythic or fairy time and space, encounter figures from Celtic mythology, undertake quests that test their character, and, as a result, accept their identity in the mundane world. In Melling's first novel, *The Druid's Tune* (1983), the Irish epic *The Cattle Raid of Cooley* forms the basis for mythic events. By participating in the raid through a time shift, a Canadian brother and sister overcome their character flaws. The mythic material in *The Singing Stone* (1986) offers an explanation for the existence of fairies in Ireland, but the complex plot also conveys both the antiwar and identity themes evident in Melling's first novel. The independent adventures of the *Chronicles of Faerie* series—*The Hunter's Moon* (1993), *The Summer King* (1999), *The Light-Bearer's Daughter* (2001), and *The Book of Dreams* (2003)—have different protagonists, but each uses parallel characters and situations to focus on a girl's problematic identity. They also advance messages about respect for nature and racial tolerance. The lengthy conclusion to the series, Melling's only novel set predominantly in Canada, brings together the characters from the previous volumes for an epic contest between the forces of light and darkness. A heavily didactic journey through the geography and history of Canada, the book mixes myths and legends from Native tribes with those from Ireland, French Canada, India, and China. This unstable mixture overwhelms the drama of the fantasy quest and reduces the seriousness of the central character's dilemma about her identity.

[*See also* Fantasy *and* Irish Mythology.]

RAYMOND E. JONES

Meltzer, Milton (1915–), American author and illustrator, born in Worcester, Massachusetts. The son of Austrian Jewish immigrants, Meltzer attended Columbia University and lives in New York City. After leaving Columbia in 1936, he held a position as a staff writer for the Federal Theatre Project, sponsored by the Works Project Administration, for three years. From 1939 to 1969 he worked at a variety of jobs and published an occasional book, until 1968, when he left the Science and Medicine Publishing Company to take his chances as a full-time writer. From 1977 to 1980, Meltzer taught as an adjunct professor at the University of Massachusetts–Amherst. His manuscripts are kept in the Archives and Special Collections of the Gordon Library at Worcester Polytechnic Institute.

In his autobiography, *Starting from Home* (1988), Meltzer credits his beginnings as an historian, writer, and social activist to a teacher who introduced him to Thoreau's work and encouraged him to conduct independent, original research. He has published more than eighty informational books for children in a career that spans five decades. His first book, a collaboration with the poet Langston Hughes, was published for adults in 1956. Titled *A Pictorial History of the Negro in America* (retitled *A Pictorial History of Black Americans* when reprinted in 1983), it embodies the key qualities that mark Meltzer's work: a commitment to speaking out for and with the underrepresented in American society; an interest in human rights and social reform; a reliance on primary source material, including subject interviews, diaries, journals, speeches, newspaper articles, and pamphlets, to name a few; a skillful selection of details; and a multifaceted view of the biographical subject or historical period that includes political, social, cultural, and economic contexts. He writes about major historical figures such as the subjects of *The American Revolutionaries* (a 1987 ALA Best Book) and Lydia Maria Child, Benjamin Franklin, Thomas Jefferson, Mark Twain, and George Washington. Books such as *Ain't Gonna Study War No More* (1986; winner of the Jane Addams and Children's Book Award), *Bread and Roses* (1967), *Brother Can You Spare a Dime* (1970; winner of the Christopher Award), and *Poverty in America* (1986; winner of the Golden Kite Award) examine formative moments in American history: the peace movement, the labor movement, and the struggle against poverty.

Whether in a book about the potato, as in *The Amazing Potato* (a 1993 ALA Notable Children's Book), or about Jews, Hispanics, or Chinese or African Americans, in the A History in Their Own Words series (with more than one title named an ALA Notable Children's Book and one winning the Boston Globe–Horn Book Award for Nonfiction), Meltzer's writing serves as a form of social activism as he presents young readers with the people, events, and stories often left out of textbooks. He reaches beneath the celebrity of historical figures and around glamorous subjects to look at the ordinary words and works that effect social change. His ability to shape histories and biographies from the details of scrupulous research into compelling, original narratives has won child, adolescent, and adult readers alike. Meltzer's popularity is girded by literary acclaim. He has been short-listed for the National Book Award for *Langston Hughes* (1969), *Remember the Days* (1975), *World of Our Fathers* (1975), *Never Forget: The Jews of the Holocaust* (1977; winner of the National Jewish Book Award and the Jane Addams Children's Book Award), and *All Time, All Peoples: A World History of Slavery* (1981; a 1982 Notable Book). In 2000 Meltzer was awarded the Regina Medal from the Catholic Library Association for his continued distinguished contribution to children's literature, and in 2001 he received the Laura Ingalls Wilder Award from the American Library Association's division of services to children in recognition of lifetime achievement. As demonstrated by his influential 1976 *Horn Book* article, "Where Do All the Prizes Go?", Meltzer's activism also seeks to address the inequities that trouble the children's book world, calling attention to the literary establishment's favoring fiction over nonfiction and the major award committees' veritable silence about informational books for children.

[*See also* Information Books; Multicultural Books; Nonfiction; *and* United States.]

BIBLIOGRAPHY

Chatton, Barbara. "Milton Meltzer: A Voice for Justice." *Language Arts* 79, no. 5 (2002): 438–441.

Meltzer, Milton. "Where Do All the Prizes Go? The Case for Nonfiction." *Horn Book* 52, no. 2 (1976). http://www.hbook.com/exhibit/article_meltzer.html.

CATHRYN M. MERCIER

Melwood, Mary, British author and playwright influenced by the early-20th-century movement to adapt adult theatrical styles to children's theater. She is best known for her four unconventional children's plays *The Tingulary Bird* (1964), *Five Minutes to Morning* (1965), *Masquerade* (1974), and *The Small Blue Hoping Stone* (1976). The last is a Christmas drama about a struggling young couple who find meaning in a pebble on the beach. Melwood has also written two children's novels, *Nettlewood* (1975) and *The Watcher Bee* (1982), which are characterized by detailed settings and a leisurely pace.

KRISTA HUTLEY

Meniru, Teresa (1931–1994), Nigerian writer for children and young adults, was born in Ozubulu, Nigeria. Her children's books include *The Bad Fairy and the Caterpillar* (1970), *The Melting Girl and Other Stories* (1971), *Omalinze* (1971), *Unoma* (1976), *Unoma at College* (1981), *Drums of Joy* (1982), and *Ibe the Cannon Boy* (1987). In her stories Meniru highlights the problems of contemporary Nigeria: child abuse, kidnapping, and men of the underworld, as in *Drums of Joy*; or the second-class-citizen status of women, the burden of tradition, and the education of women, as is her focus in *Unoma at College*, whose protagonist rejects a "lucrative" marriage proposal in favor of a college education.

BIBLIOGRAPHY

Osa, Osayimwense. *African Children's and Youth Literature*. New York: Twayne, 1995.

MAWUENA KOSSI LOGAN

Meredith, Louisa Anne (1812–1895), born Louisa Anne Twamley, Birmingham, England, had achieved recognition as a poet and botanical illustrator before she married her cousin and traveled with him to Australia in 1839. She wrote nineteen books, fourteen of them in Australia, and poetry for adults and children about many subjects, including colonial life. *Loved and Lost! The True Story of a Short Life* (1860), a poem about her children's parrot, in 1869 became the first book of children's poetry published in Australia. *Grandmamma's Verse Book for Young Australians* (1878), later published as *Waratah Rhymes for Young Australians* (1891), poems extolling nature, was used extensively in Tasmanian schools. *Tasmanian Friends and Foes, Feathered, Furred, and Finned* (1880) has stories and poems loosely connected through the excursions of a family into the natural world and is enriched with Meredith's delicate colored illustrations. Her verse is lively and unaffected, urging children to appreciate the diversity of nature without interfering with it. Meredith was an early conservationist, a fiercely independent, gifted, and highly motivated woman.

BIBLIOGRAPHY

Rae Ellis, Vivienne. *Louisa Anne Meredith: A Tigress in Exile.* Sandy Bay, Tasmania: Blubber Head Press, 1979.

STELLA LEES

Merlin. Wizard, prophet, and adviser to King Arthur in retellings of the Arthurian legend, Merlin enters literature in Geoffrey of Monmouth's *History of the Kings of Britain* (1138), which introduces most key motifs associated with his early life. Merlin's mother was a Welsh princess, but his father was unknown and rumored to be a demon. The first story told of him relates his dream about the British king Vortigern's attempt to build a tower, his attempt to sacrifice Merlin, and his destruction by an invading army. The story has been retold as a picture book by Jane Yolen (*Merlin and the Dragons*, 1995). Merlin's next intervention in history was to arrange the conception of Arthur by shape-changing King Uther so that Queen Igrayne thought he was her husband. The third major story recounted by Geoffrey is of Merlin's construction of Stonehenge by moving the stone circle known as the Giants' Dance from Ireland to Salisbury. In about 1200, the French poet Robert de Boron attributed to Merlin the inspiration for the famous Round Table, although by Sir Thomas Malory's 15th-century retelling Merlin has become creator of the Table and mentor for all it stands for.

Merlin disappears at an early stage from the Arthurian story, removed by an enchantress (Vivien or Nimue) and sealed in a cavern beneath a rock (or within a tree in some versions). In Malory, she does this to escape Merlin's unwanted attentions, but two other motives shape later retellings: in an antifeminist version, popularized by Alfred, Lord Tennyson's poem sequence *Idylls of the King* (1859–1895), Vivien is a seductress who wickedly destroys Merlin after stealing his magic; in a second version, Merlin, frail and exhausted, willingly enters the cavern in search of final rest (as in Peter Dickinson's *Merlin Dreams*, 1988).

Among numerous Merlin stories for young readers, authors often dwell on his youth, as in Jane Yolen's The Young Merlin Trilogy (1996–1997) or T. A. Barron's *The Lost Years of Merlin* and its four subsequent volumes (1996–2000).

[*See also* King Arthur *and biographies of figures mentioned in this article.*]

JOHN STEPHENS

Merriam, Eve (1916–1992), American poet. A graduate of the University of Pennsylvania, Merriam worked as a clerk, copyeditor, and copywriter while establishing herself as a major writer of verse. She eventually composed more than fifty books for children, including biographies and picture books as well as poetry collections such as *There Is No Rhyme for Silver* (1962), *It Doesn't Always Have To Rhyme* (1964), and *Fresh Paint* (1986). She received the National Council of Teachers of English Award for Excellence in Poetry for Children in 1981.Her most controversial book was *The Inner City Mother Goose* (1969, revised 1982). Merriam updated traditional nursery rhymes with the plagues of contemporary ghettoes, including drug abuse, police corruption, and prostitution, and the book was banned from numerous classrooms and libraries. Her candor, however, was welcomed by fellow activists and artists, and the poems became the foundation for the musicals *Inner City: A Street Cantata* (1971) and *Sweet Dreams* (1984).

PEGGY LIN DUTHIE

Merrill, Jean (1923–), American author whose diverse publications include picture books, poetry, folk tale adaptations, and novels. Merrill began her literary career as an editor of youth-oriented magazines before publishing her first children's book, *Henry, the Handpainted Mouse*, in 1951. As an author, she always seemed to be ahead of her time, writing a sensitive story about death (*Blue's Broken*

Heart, 1960) at a time when that topic was generally considered taboo. She also frequently featured multicultural protagonists in her intermediate novels, such as *Maria's House* (1976) and *The Toothpaste Millionaire* (1972), the popular story of a boy who gets rich after inventing a new formula for toothpaste. Many regard *The Pushcart War* (1964) as a modern classic. Written in the form of a historical document, including footnotes and transcribed conversations, this wildly funny story about a battle between New York pushcart peddlers and truckers remains one of Merrill's most offbeat books in a career consistently marked by invention and innovation.

PETER D. SIERUTA

Merry's Museum (1841–1872). A long-running American children's periodical, *Merry's Museum* was founded by Samuel Griswold Goodrich, creator of *Parley's Magazine*. Originally called *Robert Merry's Museum*, the magazine featured Robert Merry, a kindly, one-legged old sailor who, like Goodrich's earlier persona Peter Parley, chatted with an audience of eagerly interested children. The format resembled that of *Parley's Magazine*, with which it competed until the two were merged in 1844. *Merry's Museum* was an illustrated literary miscellany, including fiction and articles on nature, history, science, everyday life. Among its popular features were the lively "Merry's Monthly Chat" in which contributors' letters figured, and its puzzles from "Aunt Sue's Puzzle Drawer." The magazine maintained a Christian perspective, and sought to exercise a wholesome influence, while educating. In 1850 Goodrich withdrew as chief editor, selling the magazine to Stephen T. Allen, who merged it with others in 1858. Other editors included John N. Stearns (1858–1866) and Louisa May Alcott (1868–1870), who tightened the editorial reins, changed the tone, and provided much of its content, including *Will's Wonder-Book* (1868) and her novel *An Old Fashioned Girl* (1869). Alcott left in 1870 to pursue other projects, and the magazine struggled on for a time but ceased independent publication in 1872.

[*See also* Journals and Periodicals; Parley's Magazine; *and biographies of firgures mentioned in this article*.]

BIBLIOGRAPHY

MacDonald, Ruth K. "Merry's Museum." In *Children's Periodicals of the United States*, edited by R. Gordon Kelly, 293–300. Westport, Conn.: Greenwood Press, 1984.

SUSAN R. GANNON

Messenger, Norman (1934–), English illustrator born and educated in Liverpool, and founding member of the Association of Illustrators in Britain. Like many children's book illustrators, Messenger has a background in illustration for the advertising industry, in which, before 1978, he worked as an art director with various London agencies. After becoming a freelance artist, his reputation soared with his illustrations for books, magazines, and design groups. Messenger's wordless picture books include *Annabel's House* (1988), *Making Faces* (1992), and *Famous Faces* (1995), all of which stimulate a young child's imagination and demand high-level audience participation. The exquisite *Annabel's House* is a pop-up book with doors, flaps, and lids that act as frames into which the reader is invited; it also has an envelope at the back of the book containing cutout characters that young children can use to create their own stories.

Messenger's delicate watercolor and line work is highly sophisticated, with meticulous attention to detail; *Annabel's House* received the *Redbook* Award in the United States. Although these particular books are relatively static, he is equally adept at conveying great energy and movement, evident in books such as Rosemary Wells's *Jack and the Beanstalk* (1997). Thumping fists, stamping feet, and quivering harps are evoked using soft watercolor illustrations on white space that beautifully complement this unusual retelling. Alan Garner's *Little Red Hen* (1997), Robert Southey's *Three Bears* (1998), and Barbara Baumgartner's *The Gingerbread Man* (1998) are also classic tales for early elementary students that feature Messenger's finely detailed, softly colored, and amusing illustrations. Later books are *The Creation Story* (2001) and *Imagine* (2005), a collection of picture puzzles and illusions.

SHARON REID

Metzenthen, David (1958–), a former advertising copywriter, is a prolific Australian writer for young people across readership and genres. Metzenthen's work for early and emerging readers in the Aussie Bites and Chomps series is quirky and hilarious. For slightly older readers *Brocky's Bananagram* (1994) is similarly humorous while pursuing themes of cultural ethnocentrism. *The Colour of Sunshine* (2000) and *Gilbert's Ghost Train* (1997) examine the effect of death on families and the young, male protagonists. Metzenthen's writing for young adults ranges across contemporary situations of the vicissitudes of work, rather than the more usual school setting, in *Falling Forward* (1998) and *Finn* *and the Big Guy* (1997), the effects of drought in *Johnny Heart's Heroes* (1996), and the "downsizing" of a key employing institution in a country town in *Stony Heart Country* (1999). Metzenthen is also motivated by the history of the settlement of coastal Victoria in *Wildlight* (2002), the picaresque story of a "wild child," and of the Western Front in World War I in *Boys of Blood and Bone* (2003). The young men who people Metzenthen's tough but optimistic stories are often outsiders who grapple valiantly with what life presents, with courage and the support of friendship.

PAM MACINTYRE

Mexico. Mexico is situated in the southern part of North America. It shares with most of the countries in Central and South America the Spanish language and an intercultural context that defines these countries' identities. Children's literature in Mexico can be divided into four great periods, with unique characteristics standing out in each.

Prehispanic and Colonial Periods

The agricultural development reached by the indigenous civilizations in Middle America allowed the sedentary life, the creation of an exact calendar, the institutionalization of education, and the oral transmission of their history and myths. The literary production to which children were exposed since an early age was transcribed by the Spanish missionaries who arrived during the colonial period. Many of the legends, songs, and tongue-twisters of that time are still part of the county's oral tradition. Also from this stage are preserved educational texts (*huehuetlatollis*) that parents recited to their sons and daughters: songs, poems, fables, and lullabies.

The conquest of Mexico by the Spanish began in 1521 and extended through three centuries. During this time three different literatures coexisted in the country: the prehispanic, the imported Spanish literature, and an oral literature of African origin. The Spanish brought with them books of chivalry that were very popular in Spain at that time. These rapidly became the most popular books among children and adolescents of the highest social classes in the New Spain. For the lower classes the Spanish had other intentions, especially the intent to evangelize the indigenous people into the Catholic faith. For the natives the Spanish turned to Bible stories, saints' lives, fables, catechisms, Christmas carols, and Christian modifications of the *huehuetlatollis*. The colonial period was marked by the cultural legacy of the Western civilizations and the prehispanic period. This was the beginning of the intercultural identity of Mexico.

The 19th and 20th Centuries

The War of Independence and liberation from Spain formed the Mexican political scenario of the 19th century. In the field of literature, Romanticism, and the passion for building a free country prevailed in the writers' production. Periodical publications appeared on the scene. José Rosas Moreno wrote fables that were later incorporated into educational literature. Other important works of the time include the poetry of Juan de Dios Peza and the edition of the *Biblioteca del Niño Mexicano* (Mexican Children's Library, 1899–1902), a novelized history of Mexico, published in eighty-five tiny volumes by Heriberto Frías.

Children's literature in Mexico in the 20th century was marked by the creation of the Public Education Office in 1921; this institution, spearheaded by the outstanding politician and thinker José Vasconcelos, became the most important promoter of children's literature in Mexico. Over the next eighty years it published almost three thousand titles for primary school children. It publishes books for children with different interests and ages, including books for disabled and indigenous children. The distribution of its books through school and public libraries reaches almost every place in the country. Among the most renowned authors of this period are Pascuala Corona, Armida de la Vara, Emilio Carballido, Mireya Cueto, Maria Luisa Valdivia, Gilberto Rendón, Felipe Garrido, Martha Romo, Francisco Hinojosa, Juan Villoro, Jaime Alfonso Sandoval, Antonio Granados, and Martha Sastrías.

The state-financed publishing house Fondo de Cultura Económica has also fostered children's literature in Mexico, making select editions in Spanish of national and international authors and working successfully to distribute these titles at book fairs, in bookstores, and in schools. Since the 1980s the production of high-quality children's books has increasingly become a focus of interest in Mexico, and publishing houses that formerly eschewed children's books began to publish them. One of the first publishers to expand into this field was Terra Nova publishing company. Later on, specialized publishers for children's literature began to appear. One of the most important of these is Petra, with internationally acknowledged titles, including *El guardagujas* (The Switchman, 1998) and *Cómo escalar un pastel* (How To Climb a Cake, 1997). Other publishing houses specializing in children books are Corunda, Cidcli, and Tecolote.

Mexican Riddles. Front cover of *Adivinanzas Mexicanas* by Jose Antonio Flores Farfan (Artes de México y del Mondo). COURTESY OF ISABEL SCHON

The main challenge children's book publishers all face is the distribution process. Mexico supports very few bookstores, and they are mainly concentrated in the large cities; bookstores specializing in books for children are even rarer. Many families cannot afford books, and public libraries are not common. The National Education Department has begun to address the problem by making large book purchases and distributing the titles in small classroom libraries in all the public schools in the country.

Illustration for children's books has also enjoyed considerable development in Mexico. Some of the country's most important illustrators are Felipe Dávalos, Fabricio Venden Broeck, Gerardo Suzán, Felipe Ugalde, Claudia de Teresa, Bruno González, Pablo Rulfo, Mauricio Gómez Morin, Guillermo de Gante, Claudia Legnazzi, Martha Avilés, Rafael Barajas, Antonio Helguera, Laura Fernández, and Maribel Suárez. The prestige of writing and illustrating for children has risen considerably: the awards have grown rapidly, and every year more children's books are published, the library networks are extended, and more books are exported to Hispanic countries. All of these changes are bringing about increases in the quality of Mexican children's books.

[*See also biographies of figures mentioned in this article.*]

BIBLIOGRAPHY

Arizpe Solana, Evelyn. *Cuentos mexicanos de grandes para chicos: Un análisis de su lenguaje y contenido.* Mexico City: Consejo Nacional para la Cultura y las Artes a través del Instituto Nacional de Bellas Artes, Universidad Nacional Autónoma de México, and Ediciones Mar y Tierra, 1994.

Corona Berkin, Sarah. "Los libros para niños en México: Las políticas editoriales de 1956 a 1993." In *Modernity and Tradition: The New Latin American and Caribbean Literature 1956–1994*, edited by Nelly S. González. Austin, Tex.: SALALM Secretariat, Benson Latin American Collection, the General Libraries, the University of Texas at Austin, 1996.

González Casanova, Pablo, ed. and trans. *Cuentos indígenas.* Mexico City: Universidad Nacional Autónoma de México, 1993.

Peredo, María Alicia. *Qué, cuánto, y dónde leen los niños de Jalisco.* Guadalajara: Red Estatal de Bibliotecas, 1994.

Rey, Mario. *Historia y muestra de la literatura infantil mexicana.* Mexico City: SM/Conaculta, 2000.

Schon, Isabel. *Books in Spanish for Children and Young Adults: An Annotated Guide*. Series 1–6. Metuchen, N.J.: Scarecrow, 1978–1993.

SARAH CORONA

Meyer, Carolyn (1935–), American author of more than fifty well-regarded fiction and nonfiction books for children and young adults. She began her writing career with *Miss Patch's Learn-to-Sew Book* (1969) and other crafts books. Her groundbreaking nonfiction series, beginning with *Voices from South Africa: Growing Up in a Troubled Land* (1986), was highly praised. The fictional *Rio Grande Stories* (1994) depicts a group of students engaged in family history and cultural research at a New Mexico high school. *White Lilacs* (1993) and *Jubilee Journey* (1997) are companion novels exploring issues of race in a small Texas town during the 1920s. *Where the Broken Heart Still Beats* (1993) is a fictionalized account of Cynthia Ann Parker, who, kidnapped by Comanches as a child, longed for her Indian life after she was reunited with her family twenty-five years later. More-recent books have included entries in the popular Scholastic Royal Diaries and Harcourt Young Royals series.

LINNEA HENDRICKSON

Meyer, Renate (1930–), painter and picture-book maker. She was born in Germany, and later became a naturalized British subject. She trained at the Regent Street Polytechnic School of Art, where she met her husband, the British illustrator Charles Keeping. Meyer brought a European perspective to the English picture book form. Her first work, *Vicki* (1969), the story of a lonely little girl who knits herself a friend whom she comes to prefer above real ones, is credited as being the first British wordless picture book. The narrative is conveyed through monoprint images that include textiles as a medium.

JANE DOONAN

Meynell, Laurence (1899–1989), versatile and prolific British author of novels for young people as well as biographies, thrillers, and romances for adults. Laurence Walter Meynell served in both world wars and taught for a while but spent most of his working life as a writer and editor, first at the Bodley Head and then on *Time and Tide*. He is best known for his school stories, written under the pseudonym A. Stephen Tring—the three Barry novels for boys (1947–1952) and the eight penny novels for girls (1949–1961)—and for career novels written under his own name and (for the four Bodley Head career stories for girls) the pseudonym Valerie Baxter. He completed the Nurse Carter trilogy after the death of its author (his first wife, Shirley Darbyshire), and he also wrote a series about Nurse Ross. Other pen names include Robert Eton and Geoffrey Ludlow. His work is well crafted, literate, and realistic, even in adventure mode and, though very much of its time, is still readable today.

ROSEMARY AUCHMUTY

Meyrink, Gustav (1868–1932), best known as the author whose novel *Der Golem* (Golem, 1915) inspired the famous film of the same name directed by Carl Boese and Paul Wegener (1920). As a house writer for the satirical magazine *Simplicissimus*, Meyrink, who was born Gustav Meyer in Vienna, established himself as a popular author for younger readers, noted for his mysterious, grotesque, and brilliantly witty stories. Meyrink's penchant for the occult matched his disdain for bourgeois propriety. His collection of stories *Des deutschen Spießers Wunderhorn* (The German Philistine's Magic Horn, 1913) parodied the classic children's collection of folk literature *Des Knaben Wunderhorn* (The Boy's Magic Horn, 1806–1808). Meyrink's own stories do not strictly belong to the genre of children's literature, nor do his translations of Rudyard Kipling's short stories and Charles Dickens's *The Pickwick Papers*. All his literary endeavors, however, bear the trenchant irony that has consistently attracted young readers.

[*See also* Children's Magazines; Dickens, Charles; Fairy Tales and Folk Tales; Kipling, Rudyard; *and* Parody.]

LUKE SPRINGMAN

Mhlophe, Gcina (1958–), South African storyteller. Born in Hammarsdale, near Durban, Mhlophe was educated in the Transkei and moved to Johannesburg in 1979. She has been central to the revival of South African traditional oral storytelling. A dynamic performer of African folk tales and her own stories, she is also a director, musician, writer, and storyteller on children's television. Her play *Have You Seen Zandile?* (1989) is based on her own childhood. Her books for children include *The Snake with Seven Heads* (1989) and *Queen of the Tortoises* (1990). In connection with her visits to rural schools to promote reading, she produced *Nozincwadi Mother of Books* (2001).

ADRIENNE E. GAVIN

Mikhalkov, Sergei (1913–), Soviet children's poet and playwright, the most typical representative of the official Communist literary doctrine and the epitome of a cultural conformist. His most famous character is an extremely tall police officer, intended as a role model of a new Communist hero. Mikhalkov's verses are primitive, tedious, and overtly didactic. Nonetheless, they received every literary award in the Soviet Union and the East European satellites, including the Lenin Prize, not normally given for children's literature. Mikhalkov also wrote satirical verses for adults and composed lyrics for the Soviet national anthem. In 2000, when the anthem was readopted in post-Communist Russia, Mikhalkov adapted it, inserting God instead of Stalin as the country's leading force. As a high executive within the Writers' Union and other power structures, Mikhalkov consistently persecuted and suppressed the genuinely talented writers and humanistic children's literature.

MARIA NIKOLAJEVA

Mickey Mouse. Walt Disney's most famous cartoon character. Mickey Mouse starred in the first sound cartoon, *Steamboat Willie*, in 1928, and formed the backbone of Disney's stable of cartoon figures, which later included Minnie Mouse, Donald Duck, Goofy, and Pluto. In the 1930s alone, Mickey appeared in nearly ninety shorts; his highest artistic moment came in the "Sorcerer's Apprentice" episode in the visionary *Fantasia* (1940). Voiced by Disney himself until 1946, the ubiquitous mouse has served as the Disney moniker for theme parks (Disneyland, 1955; Disneyworld, 1971; Disneyland Tokyo, 1983; Disneyland Paris, 1992), the original *Mickey Mouse Club* television series (1955–1959), and the *New Mickey Mouse Club* (1977–1979). The Disney Channel TV network revived a new *Mickey Mouse Club*, called simply MMC (1989–1994), which gave rise to a whole generation of pop stars, including Britney Spears, Christina Aguilera, Justin Timberlake, and Ryan Gosling.

[*See also* Disney, Walt *and* Donald Duck.]

BIBLIOGRAPHY

Finch, Christopher. *The Art of Walt Disney: From Mickey Mouse to the Magic Kingdoms*. New York: H. N. Abrams, 1973.

Santoli, Lorraine. *The Official Mickey Mouse Club Book*. New York: Hyperion, 1995.

Thomas, Bob. *Disney's Art of Animation: From Mickey Mouse to Beauty and the Beast*. New York: Hyperion, 1991.

DANIEL T. KLINE

Migdale, Lawrence (1951–), photographer. Born in Johannesburg, South Africa, Migdale studied photography at Central London Polytechnic, and has also lived in Israel. He became a U.S. citizen in 1982. He is best known for his photographs for Diane Hoyt-Goldsmith's multicultural series of books on celebrations (such as *Celebrating Kwanzaa*, 1993) and Native American culture (*Apache Rodeo*, 1995). In addition to photographing Hoyt-Goldsmith's books, he photographed Patricia Polacco's autobiographical *Firetalking* (1994), and he has also provided several covers for *Newsweek* magazine. His photographs for Hoyt-Goldsmith's books have been praised for crisply capturing their subjects in a relaxed and engaging manner. Migdale says he has been influenced by photographers Henri Cartier-Bresson, Irving Penn, and Robert Frank. He maintains a large archive of his photographs and images from his book covers on his Web site.

[*See also* Hoyt-Goldsmith, Diane; Multicultural Books; *and* Photography in Nonfiction for Children.]

LINNEA HENDRICKSON

Mighty Mouse. Created by Isidore Klein, Mighty Mouse was the most popular character in the Terrytoons comic universe. A caped, costumed mouse with superhuman powers, Mighty Mouse originally appeared in a theatrical short, *The Mouse of Tomorrow*, in 1942, and Mighty could be found thereafter rescuing Pearl Pureheart from the feline Oil Can Harry. In 1945, Mighty Mouse joined Terrytoon Comics, which later became Marvel, and appeared in different comics through the 1960s, singing his theme song, "Here I come to save the day!" The *Mighty Mouse Playhouse*, a half-hour Saturday morning cartoon show, was broadcast on CBS from 1955 to 1966, and the *Mighty Heroes* (featuring Mighty Mouse) lasted one season (1966–1967). Filmation studios produced new episodes in 1979, and Ralph Bakshi revived the character in the 1980s. A rumored live-action CGI film has not yet come to fruition.

[*See also* Comic Books *and* Television and Children.]

DANIEL T. KLINE

Mikolaycak, Charles (1937–1993), American illustrator and book designer, highly regarded in children's literature as well as the art world. Born in Scranton, Pennsylvania, Mikolaycak studied under Fritz Eichenberg and Richard Lindner at the Pratt Institute and credited them with his love of illustration and his ability to draw. His wife, the editor and writer Carol Kismaric, was a close associate as Mikolaycak served as the teller and illustrator for *The Boy Who Tried to Cheat Death* (1971), *Babushka* (1984), and *Orpheus* (1992). Before serving in the United States Army, Mikolaycak worked in advertising in Germany and later for Time-Life Books in New York. He then shifted to a career, as a full-time children's book illustrator. His method of working involved extensive research and thorough immersion in the work. *Orpheus*, for example, contains two full pages of notes and another page of bibliography and discography. He drew with a pencil, making numerous preliminary sketches that were discussed with his editor. A copy of the final sketch was mounted on illustration board, where he added color. Finally, he cut away the areas surrounding the illustration, revealing the clean white board underneath. His editor, Margery Cuyler, commented, "His work is classy with a capital C, and it's also deep. He goes right to the core of the unconscious" (Freedman, p. 96). Mikolaycak's work included Bible stories, European folk tales, contemporary stories, and poetry. *Babushka*, a story he had loved as a child, was named a *New York Times* Best Illustrated Book of the Year. He took as much care with book design as he did with illustrations, and each of his books is a work of art.

BIBLIOGRAPHY

Freedman, Russell. *Holiday House: The First Sixty-Five Years*. Rev. ed. New York: Holiday House, 2000.

Mikolaycak, Charles. "The Artist at Work: The Challenge of the Picture Book." *Horn Book* (March–April 1986): 167–173.

Yolen, Jane. "In the Artist's Studio: Charles Mikolaycak." *New Advocate* 3 (Spring 1990): 111–115.

LINNEA HENDRICKSON

Miles, Betty (1928–), American author of picture books and young adult fiction. A graduate of Antioch College, Miles has worked as an associate editor and as a consultant for *Sesame Street*. She has written more than two dozen books since her debut in 1958 with the picture book *A House for Everyone*, illustrated by Jo Lowrey. Among the prizes that she has received is the Child Association Book of the Year, for both *Save the Earth! An Ecology Handbook for Kids* (1974; revised as *Save the Earth: An Action Handbook for Kids*, 1991) and *The Real Me* (1974), a novel in which a mother and daughter seek to overcome gender inequities. Miles's fictional adolescents tackle not only the ordinary problems of daily life but also issues of social justice, including racial discrimination and censorship. She also wrote the innovative how-to-read book *Hey! I'm Reading!* (1995).

HELENE EHRIANDER

Milhous, Katherine (1894–1977), American artist and author whose books are set in her home state of Pennsylvania. As a teenager Milhous begged so fervently to attend art school that her mother pawned her wedding ring to pay the tuition. When a poster she designed drew the attention of a children's book editor, Milhous was asked to illustrate several volumes, including *A Book for Jennifer* (1940) and *The Silver Pencil* (1944), by Alice Dalgliesh. Soon she was writing and illustrating her own books. Holidays were the basis of several books, including *The First Christmas Crib* (1944) and *Snow Over Bethlehem* (1945), which is set not in the Middle East but in Bethlehem, Pennsylvania. She was awarded the Caldecott Medal for *The Egg Tree* (1950), which describes an unusual Easter tradition. The flat tempera paintings pay homage to Pennsylvania Dutch folk art and enhance the regional flavor of the text. This book remains Milhous's best known.

PETER D. SIERUTA

Millar, Harold Robert (1869–1942), Scottish illustrator. Born in Dumfriesshire, Millar studied at the Birmingham Municipal School of Art and began providing pen drawings for fiction, fairy tales, and children's stories for the *Strand Magazine* soon after it began publication in 1891. He was especially admired for the richness and authenticity of detail in pictures with exotic (both Western and Eastern) and historical settings, and in the 1890s provided hundreds of drawings for folk and fairy tales of Europe and Asia that first reached English audiences through the *Strand*. His work for F. Anstey's *Brass Bottle* (*Strand*, February-September 1900) was another early success, and in 1899 Millar began his long association with E. Nesbit, illustrating her magical tale for the *Strand*, "The Seven Dragons," and the many short tales and nine serialized fantasy novels for children that followed, from *Five Children and It* (1902) to *Wet Magic* (1913). He worked for other popular magazines of the day and illustrated numerous children's books, among them Rudyard Kipling's *Puck of Pook's Hill* (1906), but his work for Nesbit is his best.

ROSE LOVELL-SMITH

Miller, Bertha Mahony (1882–1969), American bookseller and reviewer and founding editor of *The Horn Book* magazine. In 1916 Miller established the Bookshop for Boys and Girls, as a philanthropic project of the Boston's Women's Educational and Industrial Union. With her colleague Elinor Whitney (later Elinor Whitney Field), she launched *The Horn Book* in 1924; its purpose, as described in the first issue, was to "blow the horn for fine books for boys and girls—their authors, their illustrators, and their publishers." Editor of the magazine through 1950, and subsequently the president of The Horn Book, Inc., until 1963, Miller is a key figure in the establishment in the United States of the importance of literary criticism and standards of evaluation to books for young people.

ROGER SUTTON

Milligan, Spike (1918–2002), radio comedian and writer of humorous books, including some specifically for children. Terrence Milligan was born in India and arrived in England in 1934. With his colleagues Peter Sellers, Harry Secombe, and Michael Bentine, he became famous in the 1950s for the weekly radio series *The Goon Show*. Milligan was principal writer as well as many-voiced performer, and the utterly new form of surreal, zany humor appealed strongly to young people in postwar Britain. The shows are still considered classics of radio, and Milligan published many of them in illustrated volumes. He wrote a humorous autobiography, including accounts of his war experiences, and his children's books of both poetry and stories are replete with the anarchic comedy that was his trademark. Among them are *Silly Verse for Kids* (1959), *The Bald Twit Lion* (1968), *Badjelly the Witch* (1973), and, with illustrations by W. Heath Robinson, *Goblins* (1978).

ANN LAWSON LUCAS

Mills, Claudia (1954–). This versatile and prolific American writer of fiction for children and young adults is also an associate professor of philosophy and a respected scholar in the field of children's literature. In the midst of her graduate studies, she impulsively took a secretarial job for the publisher Four Winds, wrote picture books and novels for children each day on her two-hour commute, and submitted them to the publisher under an assumed name. She had the sad task of writing rejection letters to herself, and at one point wrote a reader's report on her own work. Eventually, *At the Back of the Woods* (1982) was published under her own name. Mills's numerous books for young adults include several about the outgoing Dinah, beginning with *Dynamite Dinah* (1990). Her series West Creek Middle School for slightly younger readers includes *Losers, Inc.* (1997) and *You're a Brave Man, Julius Zimmerman* (1999). Mills has also written a popular easy-reader series, Gus and Grandpa.

LINNEA HENDRICKSON

Milly-Molly-Mandy. *See* Brisley, Joyce Lankester.

Milne, A. A. (1882–1956), British essayist, playwright, poet, editor, and writer of children's literature, Alan Alexander Milne is now principally known for his books about a young boy, Christopher Robin, his bear friend Winnie-the-Pooh, and their other animal friends. His fame as a children's

The Milnes and Pooh. A. A. Milne and his son Christopher; photograph by Howard Coster, 1926. NATIONAL PORTRAIT GALLERY, LONDON

author was the result of the casual request of a friend that he write something for her new children's magazine in 1923. The poem he produced, "The Dormouse and the Doctor," was an immediate success and launched a new stage in an already established literary career, but one that soon eclipsed all the others. Milne created a total of four books in the Pooh universe of the Hundred Acre Wood between 1923 and 1928, and the books have never been out of print since, having gradually made their way around the world and into the childhoods of several generations. The first book in the quartet, a book of verse titled *When We Were Very Young* (1924), is a book of poems written about Milne's then three-year-old son, Christopher Robin; the volume went through fifty-two printings in its first year. The most famous of the quartet is *Winnie-the-Pooh* (1926), which focuses more centrally on Christopher Robin's bear-toy friend. Another book of poetry, *Now We Are Six* (1927), followed. The much-beloved *The House at Pooh Corner* (1928) introduces Tigger and his bouncy personality into the Wood, gives Eeyore a house at Pooh Corner, and ends with an enchanted place that continues on its own as Christopher Robin goes off to school to learn the mysterious skills of reading and figuring.

After this fourth book, Milne abandoned Pooh Corner, although he wrote other books and plays for children, including *Toad of Toad Hall*, a play adapted from Kenneth Grahame's *Wind in the Willows* (1929) and produced in Liverpool in 1929. Despite an impressively long bibliography of drama and fiction for adults and children, and praise for his novels and his drawing-room, comic dramas by people of his own time, these four books are his best known and have traveled around the world and through eight decades of readers, young and old.

Milne's Literary History

Before writing these books, Milne lived the life of a scholar. His father was headmaster of Henley House School, and he and his brothers were able to attend the school with his father's pupils. Young Alan Milne apparently started to read simple words when he was three, significantly reflected in the fact that he started writing about his own son, Christopher Robin, when the boy was also three years old. Milne earned a BA degree in mathematics from Cambridge (1903) before he set out, with support from his father, to become a writer, and children's literature was the farthest thing from his mind. He first wrote essays—only two of which were published between 1902 and 1906—for the magazine *Punch* and was its assistant editor from 1906 to 1914, when he

A. A. Milne. Illustration by E. H. Shepard from one of the original Pooh books.

served in the Royal Warwickshire Regiment of the British Army. While editing *Punch*, he also contributed many essays focusing on a range of light topics such as golf and parties, which he represented with an entertaining wit. His career has in fact been divided into three parts by some critics: the first as an essayist and humorist for *Punch* from 1906 to 1914, the second as a playwright, and the third as a children's author. This is not a precise division, because he wrote and published plays and essays long after his Winnie-the-Pooh books became his signature work. In his "second stage" he added many well-received dramatic pieces to his bibliography, the first being *Wurzel-Flummery* (first produced in 1917), about two politicians who agree to change their last names to Wurzel Flummery to inherit money, and this is only the beginning of the nonsense wordplay. Another drama that became something of a signature piece, *Mr. Pim Passes By*, was so popular as a play that it was turned into a modestly successful novel, *Mr. Pim* (1922). Although he started writing during his military service, Milne wrote most of his best plays, many of which were produced in London and New York, in the ten years after leaving the service.

In reading his earlier essays, plays, and stories, one can readily establish the fascination for wordplay that allowed Milne to create such memorable characters in his children's books. Many critics have noted that the Winnie-the-Pooh books appeal to readers of all ages because their carefully crafted wordplay both typifies the characters and pokes lighthearted fun at them. But Milne was inspired to write the two books of stories and two books of verse by his son, Christopher Robin, who was born in 1920. When Christopher Robin was three, they were vacationing in the country and Milne, as usual, was working on his writing. The poet Rose Fyleman, a friend, had solicited a contribution for her new magazine, and as Milne interacted closely with his young son on their country vacation, a poem, "Dormouse," was inspired. Although this was the first Pooh poem published, the first one written was "Vespers" (1922), about Milne's son at his prayers, and both were later published in *When We Were Very Young*. "Dormouse" was so immediately successful that Milne was asked to produce more like it, and the Pooh books began. But Milne's son, Christopher Robin, asserts that many of the animal characters, developed from his own nursery toys, had already been given voices and personalities by his mother, Dorothy de Selincourt, who was herself a writer. Whether Milne was inventor or chronicler, the species of wit, based firmly on misunderstandings (usually of an innocent but self-satisfied type) between the various animals, is the center of each story.

Milne's Inspiration

The importance of the real Christopher Robin's nursery toys was so evident that they made their own visits to New York (1947) and to various parts of England before settling in New York City, where they are on display. The bear that is the center of these stories was originally named Edward and was given the name Winnie from a bear in the London Zoo. The toy animals served as inspiration for most of the characters and also for Ernest H. Shepard, who illustrated the four original books. Shepard's illustrations have become so intricately linked with the Pooh stories that they are inseparable, despite the fact that Milne did not originally like his work. Perhaps this is because, as one critic noted, his drawings of the animals both animate them and preserve their toylike nature so that, for example, when Owl uses Eeyore's tale for a bell pull there is no hint that it causes Eeyore any physical pain. Shepard's general outlines of the animal illustrations have been preserved through new print editions, but in other versions of the animals that have been created for animated Disney films and television productions, their subtle qualities are often eroded in the attempt to present them only as cute, brightly colored, lovable toys. Shepard's black-and-white line drawings rouse the imagination with their simplicity. The drawings of the boy character Christopher Robin are especially touching, as they preserve the sense of constant motion that characterizes self-confident, inquisitive children.

In discussing these children's classics, critics explore the relationship between Christopher Robin and the animals, as well as the character of each animal. Anita Wilson notes that the boy plays a dual role of listener and character, but other critics have noted that he also plays the adult to his children–animals. They look to him for direction and solutions to some of their problems, such as being caught in a tree or in the door of Piglet's house, as Pooh was after eating too much honey. And sometimes Christopher Robin dispenses distasteful advice, just as adults do. Wilson suggests that, while Christopher Robin could be any small child, Pooh as a character is unique, and a little more complex than the other animals. His gentle self-interest, assumption that he is the center of his universe, and touching reliance on Christopher Robin are juxtaposed with the fact that the other animals either look up to him, as do Piglet and Roo, or find themselves in need of his help, as do Tigger, Eeyore, and Rabbit.

Milne reveals in his autobiography that the character of Christopher Robin is as much himself as it is his son between the ages of three and six, and the adult Christopher Robin, increasingly uncomfortable with his timeless embodiment, asserted that his father was not as involved in his young childhood as critics may have believed. This is perhaps one of the appeals of the books. What some critics have called a sentimental portrayal of childhood is also a kind of nostalgia that many of us hold for a nonexistent childhood where our problems were straightforward and easily solved and a small patch of woods could be transformed into an enormous world of adventure. Other critics discuss the predictability of both characters and stories. We always know that Christopher Robin can help, even if we never know quite how. The other characters seldom surprise us with their actions, as they are both physically and behaviorally the embodiment of one narrow aspect of the whole emotional range. Tigger will almost always be bouncy, cheerful, and careless, and Eeyore, whose gloom was inherited by Puddleglum in Lloyd Alexander's Black Cauldron series and again by Marvin the Paranoid Android in Douglas Adams's *The Hitchhiker's Guide to the Galaxy*, will always see the underside of any situation. This predictability—comforting to young readers and amusing to older ones, who might see themselves or acquaintances in their antics—is often the source of the stories' delight.

Winnie-the-Pooh, a most un-bearlike bear, Piglet, Owl, Eeyore, Kanga, and Roo have become both cultural icons and cultural commodities. Their iconic status is typified by the facts that the critic Frederick C. Crews could be confident that his students would relate to Pooh as in the title of his critique of critical methodologies and that Benjamin Hoff could use Pooh and Piglet to introduce Taoism to Western readers. With the advent of a series of Disney Studios productions in the 1960s and, subsequently, use of the characters to sell products ranging from children's clothing to plastic chairs to wall stencils for children's rooms, children know of the boy and his bear without having read the books themselves. Although the books remain very popular, one must speculate that they can no longer be experienced for the first time. If children grow up with Winnie-the-Pooh hanging over their beds, or drawn large on their walls, will they ever be able to visit the idyllic nowhere-land of the Hundred Acre Wood and hold it in memory in their adulthood? Will they realize the power of Milne's simple writing, characterization, and creation of a truly fantastic place out of the stuff of childhood? If not, it is a sad loss.

[*See also* Animated Films; The Canon; Disney, Walt; *and biographies of figures mentioned in this article.*]

BIBLIOGRAPHY

Crews, Frederick C. *The Pooh Perplex: A Freshman Casebook.* New York: Dutton, 1963.

Hoff, Benjamin. *The Tao of Pooh.* New York: Dutton, 1982.

Hoff, Benjamin. *The Te of Piglet.* New York: Dutton, 1992.

Lurie, Alison. *Don't Tell the Grown-Ups: Subversive Children's Literature.* Boston: Little, Brown, 1990.

Milne, A. A. *Autobiography.* New York: Dutton, 1939.

Wilson, Anita. "Milne's Pooh Books: The Benevolent Forest." In *Touchstones: Reflections on the Best in Children's Literature*, vol. 1, 163–172. West Layfayette, Ind.: Children's Literature Association. 1985.

Wullschläger, Jackie. *Inventing Wonderland: The Lives and Fantasies of Lewis Carroll, Edward Lear, J. M. Barrie, Kenneth Grahame, and A. A. Milne.* New York: Free Press, 1995.

JANICE M. BOGSTAD

Minarik, Else Holmelund (1920–), Danish American author best known for creating the Little Bear books for beginning readers. Minarik taught first grade for many years and began writing stories because she found few books that met the needs of children who were just beginning to read. She eventually submitted some of her work to the editor Ursula Nordstrom, who published Minarik's *Little Bear* (1957) as the inaugural title in Harper and Row's I Can Read series. In *Little Bear*, Minarik combined a simple vocabulary and short sentences with graceful writing, well-drawn characters, and subtle humor, demonstrating that it was possible to create books of high literary quality for novice readers. The stories themselves exhibit keen insight into the concerns and needs of children: Little Bear explores his surroundings, using his imagination to test his own (and the world's) limitations, but he continually engages Mother Bear in conversations that reaffirm her love for him and the security her love provides. Minarik wrote four more books chronicling Little Bear's adventures: *Father Bear Comes Home* (1959), *Little Bear's Friend* (1960), *Little Bear's Visit* (1961; awarded a Caldecott Honor Award), and *A Kiss for Little Bear* (1968). Illustrations by Maurice Sendak supply each title with warm, witty representations of Little Bear's idyllic childhood world. Minarik's second contribution to the I Can Read series, *No Fighting, No Biting* (1958), features a pair of believably quarrelsome children who pester their long-suffering cousin into telling them tales about some equally quarrelsome alligators. Minarik is also the author of many picture books, including *What If?* (1987), which revisits a common theme in her work, imaginative play within a secure environment. Two kittens, Pit and Pat, contemplate a sequence of increasingly far-fetched possibilities but end up wondering what would happen if they scratched on their family's door.

[*See also* Nordstrom, Ursula *and* Sendak, Maurice.]

MELISSA SCHUTT

Miniature Books. Books designed in form and usually in content to be very much smaller than average, with a maximum dimension of three (or occasionally four) inches (76 or 100 millimeters). The smallness may serve practical purposes: Bibles and other devotional literature, dictionaries, almanacs, and travel timetables have all been produced in miniature. If the purpose is actually to conceal the book—of love poetry, espionage, pornography, or banned religious or philosophical texts—smallness is important.

More often, miniature books are too small to be really useful. They arouse admiration of the skill of their makers and often an amused sense of incongruity, especially when a title suggests grandeur. Tiny books usually have "cuteness," evoking tender protectiveness for something so small. Miniature books are precious and not intentionally thrown away—though easily lost.

Those miniature books for children that have survived are often sturdy, like the "thumb Bibles" produced (in about three hundred versions) from the 17th to the early 19th cen-

Miniature Books. The Doll's Library (London: J. Marshall, c. 1800). REPRODUCED COURTESY OF THE COTSEN CHILDREN'S LIBRARY, PRINCETON UNIVERSITY LIBRARY

tury. These copiously illustrated collections of Bible stories were valued for the education of children and the illiterate. The more delicate little books that John Marshall marketed in about 1800—The Child's Library, The Doll's Library, and others—fitted into little bookcases; Marshall hoped that these would be placed in toyhouses and used for doll education.

Although other publishers followed Marshall's example, and moderately small books for children have been published sporadically since, miniature books remain exceptional, not usually stocked in libraries or even bookstores. Yet, surprisingly large numbers of some miniature books were printed: David Bryce of Glasgow claimed to have published 100,000 copies of his English dictionary, about an inch high, and this was only one of his wide range, published around 1900. More recently, the stories of Beatrix Potter, who insisted on small volumes for small children, have been published in "miniature" size. Little Golden Books, not at all small, have shrunk themselves to Little Little Golden Books and Tiny Little Golden Books.

Miniature books made by children themselves have a special interest, the Brontës' juvenilia being the best known. Most famous and most inaccessible are the books of the library of Queen Mary's Dolls' House in Windsor, many handwritten for the occasion by the best authors of the day.

BIBLIOGRAPHY

Bondy, Louis W. *Miniature Books: Their History from the Beginning to the Present Day*. London: Sheppard Press, 1981.

FRANCES ARMSTRONG

Minority Literature in Anglophone Countries.

In English-speaking countries a European brand of children's literature arrived by way of Western colonizers. They consisted primarily of British citizens—people with a long-standing tradition of children's literature. This is not to imply that children in these countries had no literature prior to the arrival of the European model, although typically stories were not created exclusively for the young. Folklore and legend were richly represented in oral, and sometimes written, forms dating from ancient times, as in India (Khorana). The English tradition would, however, take on a unique shape in the colonies, since an imperialist perspective determined to some extent the themes in the settler-authored stories.

The numerical superiority of the indigenes, and their resistance to subjugation, created an aura of instability that colonial storytellers and officials found ways to address. For example, an innate inferiority was attributed to indigenes, and the notion of white superiority permeated literature and British-run schools. By whatever means possible, whites reassured themselves that their incursions were legitimate, and no matter how this propaganda may have affected colonized people, their prospects for retrieving their autonomy were nil. Their military disadvantage was simply insurmountable. As Victor Kiernan has explained, "Wherever settlements took place, the African would be exchanging the risk of kidnapping into slavery for the certainty of reduction to peonage."

In considering Anglophone India, South Africa, Australia, and the United States, we find similarities in the colonial-based literature and discover that the abuse of indigenous populations does not substantially change in cases where settler groups became the mainstream population. But in these four nations, various phases of imperialist thought and strategy are discernible, for example, the earliest, religiously bigoted, Anglo-Saxon incursions in India and the most explicitly antidemocratic system of domination in South African apartheid. In Australia we are in touch with the least studied region in the field of multicultural children's literature, and in the American "Westward movement" we find one of the most genocidal destructions of indigenous nationhood.

Other Anglo colonizers took control of Canada and New Zealand, as well as Tanganyika, Kenya, Rhodesia, and other areas in Africa. Many colonists left Africa, however, after national independence had been won—Tanganyika in 1961 (becoming Tanzania in 1964), Kenya in 1963, and southern Rhodesia in 1980 (becoming Zimbabwe). Nonetheless, in children's literature the departure of settlers did not mean the end of colonialist, anti-African sentiment. It continued to be blatantly represented in novels by former settlers, as in Eric Campbell's Tanzania-based *The Place of Lions* (1990), *The Year of the Leopard Song* (1992), and *Papa Tembo* (1997, published in the United Kingdom as *Elephant Gold*).

Put briefly, the basic failure in minority-settler literature was and is the inability of authors to conceptualize social equality or its achievement in society. Instead, a cultural and/or biological hierarchy has been among the myths passed to the next generation. From one century to the next, children's books have been tangible indicators of colonialist thought.

India

In India, British settlers, missionaries, and administrative personnel played a role in the earliest publications, for example, *Little Henry and His Bearer* (1812) and *The Last Days of Boosy* (1814). Author Mary Sherwood shows in these missionary stories the way the clergy could make model Christians out of wayward white children and also convert their servants. Sherwood's principal target is Hinduism, but the books illustrate an array of imperialist attitudes. India was where the initial pattern for British colonial administration was formed. In fact, according to Kiernan, "the whole complex of relationships among continents and races was deeply influenced" by the British presence in India. Well-known works such as Rudyard Kipling's *The Jungle Book* (1894) and *The Second Jungle Book* (1895) continued the 19th-century trend of promoting colonial rule and the myth of British superiority, while utilizing the traditions of the Indian fable (Khorana). In the 20th century Hinduism was still negatively compared with Christianity (as was Muslim culture). Theodora DuBois's *Tiger Burning Bright* (1964) uses such pejorative phrases as "ugly gods" and "repellent dancing gods and goddesses" (Khorana). In Margaret Dewrance's *Muthu* (1967) Christian schools and theology are benevolent forces, in stark contrast to the negative influence of Hindu gods. And, in a critique of Leslie Scrace's "Days in the Indian Sun: Stories of South India" (in Jean Head and Leslie Scrace's *Days in the Sun*, 1967), Khorana notes how "every psychological ploy is employed to win converts to Christianity." Her bibliographic study, *The Indian Subcontinent in Literature for Children and Young Adults*, includes more than nine hundred entries by nonnative writers (mostly Western), as well as writers native to the subcontinent.

Kathryn Castle's *Britannia's Children: Reading Colonialism through Children's Books and Magazines* is another helpful source, especially in its coverage of Indian characterization in children's magazines. Positive images of Indians reside in the characters' capacity to "absorb Britishness," but, as Castle notes, they must not be able to assimilate *too much* Britishness or do it on their own, as the question then arises: "Why keep the British there?" She cites stories from *Boys' Own Empire* as examples of how authors manage this dilemma. In stories published in *Girls' Empire*, added to the usual pulp fiction dangers is the threat of rape by the "depraved oriental" (Castle).

South Africa

Early settlers in South Africa (first the Dutch and then the British) created a children's literature that was essentially dominated by the English. In *King Solomon's Mines* (1885) H. Rider Haggard used African ceremonies to present his conception of the "primitive" and to associate Africans with animals. For example, when a dancer comes on the scene, "foam flew in flecks from her gnashing jaws, . . . her flesh quiver[ed] visibly . . . . Suddenly she . . . stiffened all over, like a pointer dog when he scents game."

In the 20th century, works such as Michael Williams's *Into the Valley* (1993) illustrate a continuation of the idea that Africans are inescapably backward. He is concerned about the impending "one person/one vote" election and implies repeatedly that South African blacks are unready for self-rule. A black storekeeper (used by Williams as his mouthpiece) explains factional conflicts: "The African National Congress wants power and the Inkatha Freedom Party wants power . . . But you ask one of the people—that woman, for example—what the ANC stands for, and she hasn't a clue, not a clue!" Williams also contrived characters reminiscent of blackface minstrel performers to underscore the absurdity of letting blacks vote in 1994.

This same antidemocratic scenario characterizes other novels published in the mid-1990s that feature black-majority political parties. The election is characterized as untenable, corrupt, or ludicrous in Dennis Bailey's *Thatha* (1994), Lawrence Bransby's *Outside the Walls* (1995), and *The Boy Who Counted to a Million* (1995).

Australia

Images of Australia's Aboriginal people often resemble the portrayals of Africans. Australian blacks are presented as naive, superstitious, bloodthirsty, and grotesque. In many books they are simply erased as participants in Australian history. Clare Bradford cites Ethel Turner's *Seven Little Australians* (1894) as an early example—all mention of Aboriginals was edited out in the 1900 edition. That omission, Bradford wrote, "works to silence any reference to the existence of an ancient indigenous culture, the illegitimacy of the colony's beginnings and its 'sorrowful history' of displacement and death." Schoolbooks managed the past in the same way, making the Aboriginal group already extinct and positioning "white child readers as natives of the country." In a contemporary novel, *Strange Objects* (1990), Gary Crew imagines early contacts between Europeans and Aboriginals resulting from shipwrecks off the Australian coast. As he interweaves two historical periods he creates a veritable catalog of stereotypes, perhaps intended as a way to expose both 17th- and 20th-century racism and Eurocentrism. Contemporary schoolboys view the Aboriginals as "winos" who are "horrible" in appearance and "ready to cut your throat." Crews places such content at center stage, making few credible references to Aboriginal people. The author's objection to racism becomes practically invisible as a result of his recurring slurs and insulting characterizations.

The United States

Arriving from many European locations, the first American immigrants contrived a notion of themselves as a "chosen people," a "civilization" divinely authorized to purge "uncivilized" populations (i.e., Native Americans). Richard Drinnon calls this the metaphysics of Indian-hating: those "deadly subtleties of white hostility that reduced native peoples to the level of the rest of the fauna and flora to be 'rooted out.'" American children's literature, in its depiction of Native Americans, has largely retained this perception from one era to the next. In 1893 William Osborn Stoddard (President Lincoln's wartime secretary) wrote numerous boys' books about "large, hideous, bronze-colored" savages. In 1986, Lynne Reid Banks introduced the Algonquins, whose faces were "wild, distorted, terrifying masks of hatred and rage" (*The Return of the Indian*). Patricia Willis, in *Danger Along the Ohio* (1997), described Indians in Pittsburgh as "shiftless, slouching men . . . beg[ging] money for whiskey"; others had "a fierceness that scared Amos to the ends of his toes."

In her article "A Sea of Good Intentions: Native Americans in Books for Children," Melissa Kay Thompson analyzes categories popular with novelists: pioneer stories, captivity narratives, and government-run boarding-school stories. At the same time, her study traces 19th- and 20th-century Supreme Court rulings that present the same stereotypes found in children's literature. She shows the extraordinary continuity in rulings that dehumanize native peoples and sees a similar continuity in books for the young.

Subordination

Taken as a whole, the irony of Western literature in Anglophone regions stems from its contradictory history. That is, settler populations opened the way for the sharing of a richly expressive art form, but in the end it was used to put the indigenous Anglophone in his or her "place"—an unjust, subservient place.

BIBLIOGRAPHY

Bradford, Clare. *Reading Race: Aboriginality in Australian Children's Literature*. Melbourne, Australia: Melbourne University Press, 2001.

Castle, Kathryn. *Britannia's Children: Reading Colonialism through Children's Books and Magazines*. Manchester, U.K.: Manchester University Press, 1996.

Drinnon, Richard. *Facing West: The Metaphysics of Indian-Hating and Empire-Building*. Minneapolis: University of Minnesota Press, 1980.

Khorana, Meena. *The Indian Subcontinent in Literature for Children and Young Adults: An Annotated Bibliography of English-Language Books*. New York: Greenwood Press, 1991.

Kiernan, Victor. *The Lords of Human Kind: European Attitudes to Other Cultures in the Imperial Age*. London: Serif, 1995. Reprint of 1969 edition.

MacCann, Donnarae, and Yulisa Amadu Maddy. *Apartheid and Racism in South African Children's Literature, 1985–1995*. New York and London: Routledge, 2001.

Thompson, Melissa Kay. "A Sea of Good Intentions: Native Americans in Books for Children." *The Lion and the Unicorn* 25 (September 2001): 353–374.

DONNARAE MACCANN

Mister Rogers. *See* Rogers, Fred.

Mistral, Gabriela (1889–1957), pseudonym of Lucila Godey Alcayaga, an educator, diplomat, and poet of Indian and Basque origin from Vicuña, Chile, who advocated Latin American children's literature and, in 1945, was the first South American winner of the Nobel Prize for Literature. In 1914, five years after her fiancé, accused of embezzlement, committed suicide, her entry "Los Sonetos de la Muerte" ("Sonnets of Death") under the name Gabriela Mistral won Chile's Laurel Crown and Gold Medal. In 1924, she published *Ternura* (English trans., *Tenderness*, 1970), a collection of children's poems including lullabies, rounds, stories, and tricks (*jugarretas*). The thematic elements of her emotional poetry—maternal love, her love of teaching, games, legends, nature's beauty—appear here. She hoped to encourage others to write specifically for children in Latin America, and in classrooms today, children still sing and dance to rounds from *Ternura*. In 1979, the Gabriela Mistral Inter-American Prize for Culture was created.

LYNDA G. ADAMSON

Mitchell, Elyne (1913–2002), Australian novelist who spent most of her life at a mountain cattle station, the backdrop for her well-loved novels. *The Silver Brumby* (1958), illustrated by Ralph Thompson, was the first of many Sibyl Elyne Mitchell's imaginative stories about the wild horses that breed in the mountainous country of southern Australia. Others include *Silver Brumby's Daughter* (1960), illustrated by Grace Huxtable, *Silver Brumby Kingdom* (1966), illustrated by Annette Macarthur-Onslow, and *Son of the Whirlwind* (1976), illustrated by Victor Ambus. All express Mitchell's passion for the Australian landscape. *Toowong Hill: Fifty Years on an Upper Murray Cattle Station* (1989) is her autobiography.

STELLA LEES and PAM MACINTYRE

Mitchell, Lucy Sprague (1878–1967), educator, author, and founder of the Bank Street College of Education in New York City. Established in 1916 as the Bureau of Educational Experiments, the school acquired its current name after moving to 69 Bank Street in 1930 (since 1970, its location has been 610 West 112th Street). Run by—and later named for—Harriet Johnson, Bank Street's nursery school was where Johnson, Mitchell, and other progressive educators tested and developed ideas about how children think and learn. Mitchell codified these ideas in the introduction to her *Here and Now Story Book* (illustrated by Hendrik Willem Van Loon, 1921), a collection for two- to seven-year-olds of stories adapted from their own "spontaneous expressions." Based on the premise that young children experience reality in the "here and now," these poems and tales reflect Mitchell's conclusions that children focus on sensory experiences, find the familiar world fascinating (and so have no need for fairy tales), think in terms of relationships, and understand language by playing with it—that is, the sound of words can be as important as their meaning. Although Mitchell wrote more than a dozen other children's books, her adult students had even greater success in promoting Bank Street's educational philosophy. The works of such former Bank Streeters as Margaret Wise Brown, Ruth Krauss, and Edith Thacher Hurd evince Mitchell's respect for the imaginative intelligence of children and answer her call for a literature that speaks the language of children and that, in her words, includes "children's first-hand experiences as a starting point."

[*See also* Brown, Margaret Wise; Hurd, Edith Thacher; *and* Krauss, Ruth.]

BIBLIOGRAPHY

Antler, Joyce. *Lucy Sprague Mitchell: The Making of a Modern Woman*. New Haven, Conn.: Yale University Press, 1987. The definitive biography.

PHILIP NEL

Mitchison, Naomi (1897–1999), British Left-wing intellectual and writer of historical novels, short stories, and children's books. She came from a notable scientific family: her father was the physiologist J. S. Haldane and her brother J. B. S. Haldane, the eminent geneticist. She studied science at Oxford but began to write historical novels in her twenties. Her first, *The Conquered* (1923), concerns the Roman conquest of Gaul. In 1928 she published a biography of Anna Comnena, the Byzantine princess and historian of the 12th century. Ancient Greece and Rome provided the settings for her finest fiction (for example, *The Corn King and The Spring Queen*, 1931); the life of the early Christians in Rome is treated movingly in *The Blood of the Martyrs* (1939). Throughout her life she was deeply engaged in sociopolitical thought and activity, writing wise and pioneering articles in the quality press and Socialist periodicals such as *The New Statesman*. Between the two World Wars she edited a volume of essays by prominent contributors assessing modern learning and opinion from the Left; *An Outline for Boys and Girls and Their Parents* was published by Gollancz in 1932.

After her marriage in 1916, she lived in the Highlands of Scotland and began to write for the young. Her many children's books include *The Big House* (1950), a socially critical time shift fantasy set in the western Highlands. In her later years she spent much time in Botswana, in southern Africa, where she was adopted as an honorary mother and chief. More books for children resulted from this experience, including *The Family at Ditlabeng* (1969) and *Sunrise Tomorrow* (1973). At home in Scotland or Africa, she was deeply concerned with the community, with fisheries and farming. She was named Baroness Mitchison and her seventy or more works record a distinguished and humane intelligence of the 20th century.

BIBLIOGRAPHY

Calder, Jenni. *The Nine Lives of Naomi Mitchison*. London: Virago, 1997.

Murray, Isobel, ed. *Scottish Writers Talking 2*. East Linton, U.K.: Tuckwell Press, 2002.

Murray, Isobel, ed. Introduction to *Beyond This Limit: Selected Shorter Fiction of Naomi Mitchison*. Edinburgh: Scottish Academy Press, 1986.

ANN LAWSON LUCAS

Miyake, Yoshi, world-famous American illustrator of children's books. Miyake's illustrations range in content, because he has worked on many diverse stories with many different authors. Numerous illustrations are included in children's books that focus on environmental issues, such as *Wonders of Rivers* (1982), by Rae Bains. He has also done work on children's mysteries, biographies, and religious stories. He illustrated *The Christmas Story* (1987), by Deborah Hautzig; *Writing* (1980), by Richard L. Allington and Kathleen Krull, which endeavors to show children how writing can be interesting; and Isaac Asimov's *The Disappearing Man and Other Mysteries* (1985). Yoshi Miyake has left a remarkable legacy of rich, colorful illustrations in all different genres of children's books, and his works continue to inspire children.

LAUREN HUGHES

Miyazaki Hayao (1941–), Japanese animator, writer, and director whose works are representative of Japanese *manga* (comics) and animation culture. Miyazaki's most persistent theme, reconciliation with nature, is evident in his early significant film *Kaze no tani no Naushika* (*Nausicaä of the Valley of Wind*, 1984), in which a young female hero, Nausicaä, struggles to bring peace to an ecologically devastated world threatened by giant insects and poisonous plants. The conflict between human and nature is further explored in *Mononoke hime* (*Princess Mononoke*, 1997), in which San, a young woman raised by wolf gods, and Ashitaki, a young man whose body has been poisoned by corrupted nature, battle to save the world. In his film *Sen to Chihiro no Kamikakushi* (*Spirited Away*, 2001), which won an Academy Award among other honors, ten-year-old Chihiro is robbed of her name and undergoes hardships in a mysterious world of pantheistic deities, where she gradually learns to live altruistically and so reclaims her identity.

BIBLIOGRAPHY

McCarthy, Helen. *Hayao Miyazaki: Master of Japanese Animation*. Berkeley, Calif.: Stone Bridge Press, 1999.

JUNKO YOSHIDA

Miyazawa Kenji (1896–1933), a conspicuously Buddhist Japanese poet, intellectual, and author of children's tales, also a natural scientist who taught agronomy and was interested in music and art. He grew up in an unfertile region of Japan, and he died at an early age of tuberculosis. He gave up teaching partially for altruistic reasons: to practice farming and follow artistic pursuits alongside the local community. Although his work was not well received during his lifetime, it gradually achieved recognition in Japan after his death, and he is now firmly established as one of Japan's foremost modern authors. All of his work is strongly imbued with his beliefs and is characterized by its intensely philosophical complexity, despite its syntactic simplicity and beauty. His original, idiosyncratic, and usually allegorical tales are taught across the curriculum in Japan, from primary school through university level; they include "Donguri to Yamaneko" (Wildcat and the Acorns), "Chûmon no Ôi Ryôriten" (The Restaurant of Many Orders), "Yamanashi" (Wild Pear), "Yukiwatari" (Snow Crossing), "Nametoko Yama no Kuma" (The Bears of Mount Nametoko), "Yodaka no Hoshi" (The Nighthawk Star), and "Serohiki no Gôshu" (Gôshu the Cellist), many of which began to be used in compulsory Japanese literature textbooks in the late 1970s. The first two tales come from *Chûmon no Ôi Ryôriten* (The Restaurant of Many Orders), a collection of children's tales published by the author at his own expense in 1924.

Many of his tales continue to be reissued, often as illustrated or picture book versions for both children and adults. Kenji, as he is known, has become the singularly most illustrated author in Japan, and several Japanese artists, educators, editors, and publishers have devoted a significant portion of their lives to promoting his work. In English, Junko Morimoto has illustrated four of Kenji's tales as picture books. The ever-increasing receptivity to Kenji's work is considered partially attributed to his spiritual and environmental themes, which offer solutions to the ubiquitous materialistic pursuits of the modern age.

[*See also* Morimoto, Junko.]

BIBLIOGRAPHY

Bester, John. *Once and Forever*. Tokyo: Kodansha, 1993.

Helen Kilpatrick

Moe, Jørgen. *See* Asbjørnsen, Peter Christen.

Moeyaert, Bart (1964–), Belgian author of children's books, poet, playwright, and translator. Moeyaert started his career with *Duet met valse noten* (Duet with False Notes, 1983), a love story. With his poetic style, he knows how to create atmosphere, and he usually offers deep insights into his characters' minds. Thus *Blote handen* (1995; English trans., *Bare Hands*, 1998) deals with transition, growing pains, and a boy's heartfelt inability to accept change. *Het is de liefde die we niet begrijpen* (1999; Eng. trans., *It's Love We Don't Understand*, 2001), a well-received story of child abuse and homosexuality, has a complex narrative structure and is expressed in sensitive language. Moeyaert has successfully collaborated with illustrators and musicians to create books that appeal to all the senses. For *Luna van de boom* (Luna from the Tree, 2001), based on a Slovakian fairy tale, Gerda Dendooven provided the pictures and Filip Bral the sound track. In 2002 Bart Moeyaert was one of the finalists for the Andersen Medal.

[*See also* Belgium *and* Young Adult Literature.]

Vanessa Joosen

Moffats, The. *See* Estes, Eleanor.

Mogridge, George (1787–1854), British children's writer and religious author. While apprenticing as a japanner, Mogridge contributed to Ackermann's *Poetical Magazine*. In 1811 he entered into partnership with his brother in the Japan trade in Birmingham, while contributing articles to the *Birmingham and Lichfield Chronicle* as Jeremy Jaunt. Two metrical tracts published under the signature X.Y.Z. by the Religious Tract Society (RTS), "Two Widows," and "Honest Jack," effectively launched Mogridge's writing career. His anonymous Houlston tract "The Juvenile Culprits" (1829), taught the consequences of cruelty to animals. Subsequently he wrote as Old Humphrey for the RTS's *Weekly Visitor*, as Ephraim Holding for Sunday school teachers and working men, and as Old Father Thames for the ragged schools. He also used the name Peter Parley, despite the objections of Samuel Griswold Goodrich, who had used the name in the United States. Never rich or even financially secure, Mogridge wrote 226 works under more than twenty pseudonyms and for a range of publishers. His widely marketed, moralizing work was well suited to the tastes of the laboring classes.

[*See also* Goodrich, Samuel Griswold *and* Religious Tract Society.]

BIBLIOGRAPHY

Memoir of Old Humphrey, with Gleanings from his Portfolio. London: RTS, 1860.

Williams, C. *George Mogridge: His Life, Character, and Writings*. London: RTS, 1856.

Patricia Demers

Mohr, Nicholasa (1938–), American author and artist best known for her realistic and richly evocative novels and short stories about life in New York's Puerto Rican barrio.

Herself the daughter of Puerto Rican immigrants, Mohr was born in Manhattan and grew up in Spanish Harlem and the Bronx. Trained as a fine artist and print maker, she became a full-time writer with the publication of her first novel, *Nilda* (1973). This story of a young girl's growing up in an impoverished barrio and striving to become an artist is the most autobiographical of her works. Although Mohr's primary focus is potential human resilience, she is able to capture the deep emotional component of childhood, and she is unsparing in her satirical approach to the barrio's schools and religious institutions. Her second and third books, *El Bronx Remembered* (1975) (a National Book Award finalist) and *In Nueva York* (1977), are collections of short stories linked by recurring themes and characters. In addition, Mohr has written six books for children and one short-story collection for adults. The State University of New York awarded her an honorary doctor of letters in 1989. Although clearly rooted in her own experiences, Mohr's work consistently addresses such universal considerations of childhood as prejudice, the plight of the outsider, and the struggle to endure.

BIBLIOGRAPHY

Forman, Jack. "Nicholasa Mohr." In *St. James Guide to Young Adult Writers*, 2d ed., edited by Tom Pendergast and Sara Pendergast, 597–598. Detroit, Mich., and London: St. James Press, 1999.

Mohr, Eugene V. *The Nuyorican Experience: Literature of the Puerto Rican Minority*. Westport, Conn., and London: Greenwood Press, 1982. Chapter 5, "A Woman's Perspective," 73–90, presents a thoughtful, in-depth analysis of the early fiction of Nicholasa Mohr (no relation to the author).

MICHAEL CART

Mole, John (1941–), English poet, teacher, and jazz enthusiast. Mole has written verse for both adults and children, although the sophisticated subjects, language, and references in his writing for children blur the distinction between the two. Among his numerous volumes of children's verse are *In and Out the Apple* (1984), *The Mad Parrot's Countdown* (1990), *The Conjurer's Rabbit* (1992), and *The Dummy's Dilemma* (1999). *Boo to a Goose* (1987) remains his most acclaimed collection, winning the Signal Award for outstanding contribution to children's poetry. Many of his poems have been illustrated by his wife, Mary Norman.

MATTHEW GRENBY

Molesworth, Mary Louisa (1839–1921), English novelist and children's writer; author of over one hundred works for a wide range of ages, from children still in the nursery to young ladies in the schoolroom, and a handful for adult readers. Her father—the illegitimate son of a Scottish army officer—became a prosperous businessman; but she married into the landed gentry and distanced herself from commerce.

Maria Louisa Stewart was born in Rotterdam, where her father was working; she then lived in Manchester, at first very close to the industrial center, until she was twenty-one. This background appears in a few of her books. In *The Carved Lions* (1895) she calls it Great Mexington; there, she depicts rich people who are showy, are "not always very refined," and speak with accents "both peculiar and ugly." In 1861 she married Captain Richard Molesworth, nephew

STORY SPINNING—p. 107.

Mrs. Molesworth. Illustration by Walter Crane from *The Tapestry Room: A Child's Romance* by Mary Louisa Molesworth (London, 1879). COLLECTION OF JACK ZIPES

of the seventh viscount Molesworth. Her husband was a man of uncertain, even violent, temper and was also recklessly extravagant. Their happiest years were the mid-1860s, when they were living at Tabley Grange in Cheshire, a dignified background often evoked in her books. In 1879 there was a legal separation, and thereafter it seems she had to support herself and her five surviving children, mainly by her writing.

Her first book, *Lover and Husband*, was a three-volume novel published in 1869 under the pseudonym Ennis Graham. Three more novels in similar style followed before she wrote her first children's book, *Tell Me a Story* (1875), which had illustrations by Walter Crane. It included "Goodnight, Winny," recalling the death of her six-year-old daughter Violet; and "The Reel Fairies," based on games she had played as a child. She habitually built stories around recollections such as these, and memories and observations of children she knew. *Carrots: Just a Little Boy*, one of her most successful books, was published in 1876; it too had drawings by Crane, who was to illustrate Molesworth's annual volume for Macmillan until 1891. This account of a six-year-old misunderstood by his irascible father and protected by his loving older sister was, Molesworth told her readers, based on a real little boy (her son Lionel). It is low on incident (as was typical in her books), but its three interpolated stories hold the reader because of Molesworth's empathy with her child characters. This was the great strength of her writing. She had many admirers, including the poet Swinburne, who considered her the equal of George Eliot.

Her next book, *The Cuckoo Clock* (1877), a fairy story, is the one that has survived longest. Griselda, sent to stay with two elderly aunts in an old town house, is lonely and frustrated by their restraints. She is befriended by a fairy cuckoo in her aunts' cuckoo clock, who tells her stories, takes her on adventures, and—being a stickler for good manners, like the author—gives her "improving" little lectures. Later, the pace of Molesworth's writing increased; her peak year was 1892, with eight publications. Her last book, *Fairies Afield*, was published in 1911.

BIBLIOGRAPHY

Cooper, Jane. *Mrs. Molesworth*. Crowborough, U.K.: Pratts Folly, 2002.

Green, Roger Lancelyn. *Mrs. Molesworth*. London: Bodley Head, 1961.

Keenan, Hugh T. "M. L. S. Molesworth." In *Writers for Children*, edited by Jane M. Bingham. New York: Scribner, 1988.

GILLIAN AVERY

Mollel, Tololwa M. (1952–), Tanzanian-born Canadian storyteller, picture book writer, and playwright. Mollel's works, which present familiar experiences through African folk tales retold with careful detail, or situate children in contemporary Tanzania, celebrate the courage, ingenuity, and self-reliance of children and small creatures. *Orphan Boy* (1990) won a Governor-General's Award for its illustrations by Paul Morin; more than fifteen other picture books have followed. Exploring new media, Mollel wrote *The Visit of the Sea Queen* (2000) for children's dance and *The Twins and the Monster* (2001), a narrated story accompanied by dance and a symphony. He adapted his picture book *A Promise to the Sun* (1992) into a play (2002).

ALAN RICHARDS

Molly Whuppie. An original Celtic folk tale collected in Joseph Jacobs's *English Fairy Tales* (1890), "Molly Whuppie" opens with the abandoned-children motif familiar from "Hop o' my Thumb," although these children are a burden because they are female. The story employs other familiar motifs, including the trickster, the youngest of three, the exchange of clothing, robbing a giant of three things, and "getting out of a sack." After the abandoned girls arrive at the ogre's house, Molly, the youngest, saves herself and her sisters by tricking the ogre into killing his own daughters in their place. After the girls have escaped to the king's palace, Molly wins royal husbands for her sisters and herself by returning three times to the ogre's castle to steal his sword, purse, and ring, escaping each time over a "bridge of one hair" too fragile to bear the ogre. The tale was popularized during the feminist movements of the 1970s, and is frequently retold and anthologized.

LISSA PAUL

Molnár, Ferenc (1878–1952), Hungarian writer who studied law in Budapest and Vienna. Molnár, whose real name was Ferenc Neumann, started working as a journalist in 1896, and became celebrated for his novels and dramas. In 1914 he was a war correspondent in Galicia. After numerous travels on the European continent, he emigrated to the United States in 1940 and lived in a hotel in New York until his death. His only children's book, *A Pál utcai fiúk* (1907, English trans., *The Paul Street Boys*, 1927), was inspired by Mark Twain's children's novels and has been required reading in Hungarian schools up to the present.

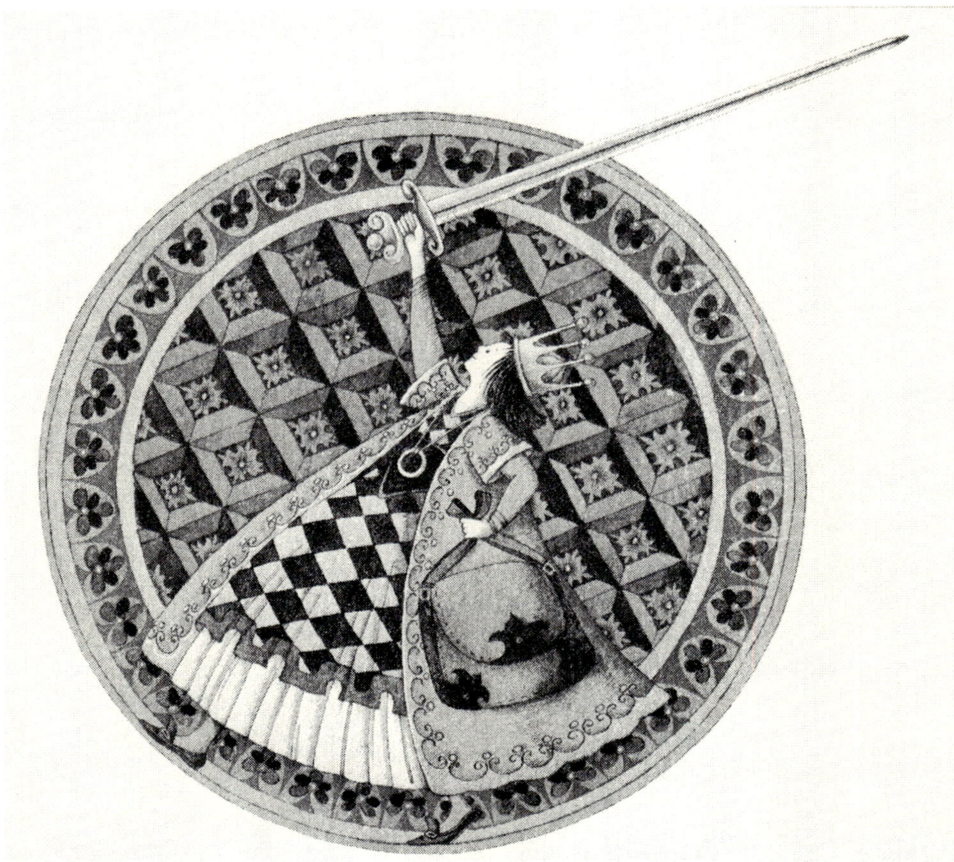

Molly Whuppie. Back cover illustration by Errol Le Cain for *Molly Whuppie,* retold by Walter de la Mare (London: Faber & Faber, 1983). Reproduced courtesy of the Cotsen Children's Library, Princeton University Library

Based on the author's memories about his youth in Budapest, this story deals with the quarrels of two school gangs over territorial rights to a deserted site. The extraordinary success of this book is due to Molnár's ability to combine styles from naturalism and romanticism, to provide his characters with compelling features, and to integrate satirical passages in the melancholy ending.

Bettina Kümmerling-Meibauer

Moloney, James (1954–), Australian author of children's books. He began his writing career with the publication of *Crossfire* (1992) and the intention of producing material that would encourage reluctant male readers. His work has a way of tapping into the cultural contexts of present-day Australia (politics, prejudice, reconciliation, sport, guns, rural and urban life), without losing sight of the bigger picture of the complexities of relationships and the dignity of the human spirit in a less than perfect world. This approach suits his intended audiences of adolescents, younger readers, and early readers and has resulted in his winning awards for a number of his books, including *Swashbuckler* (1996) and *A Bridge to Wiseman's Cove* (1997). His three related books, *Dougy* (1993), *Gracey* (1994), and *Angela* (1999), which dealt with the Aboriginal experience in urban Australia, caused extensive debate and were strongly challenged by some members of these communities because of his non-Indigenous origins. His other books include *The House on River Terrace* (1996), *Buzzard Breath and Brains* (1999), *Touch Me* (2001), *Intergalactic Heroes* (2002), and *Black Taxi* (2003). His continued commitment to the reading development of boys is demonstrated through his nonfiction text *Boys and Books* (2000).

Susan Clancy

Monjo, F. N. (1924–1978), American children's novelist and editor. Born in Stamford, Connecticut, and educated at Columbia University, Ferdinand N. Monjo was a children's book editor for several New York publishers, including Simon & Schuster's Golden Books (1953–1958) and American Heritage's Junior Library (1958–1961). Seeking to bring history alive and inspire young readers, he also wrote historical and biographical children's fiction and nonfiction; Monjo used historical incidents, a child's perspective, and humorous and interesting details in his books. For example, *Indian Summer* (1968), is about a pioneer family successfully defending against an Indian attack, told from a child's viewpoint. It has, however, been criticized for its portrayal of Native Americans. His best-known book, *The Drinking Gourd* (1970), tells of a young boy who helps escaped slaves on the Underground Railroad. *The One Bad Thing About Father* (1970) is told from the viewpoint of Theodore Roosevelt's sons, and *Letters to Horseface: Being the Story of Wolfgang Amadeus Mozart's Journey to Italy, 1769–1770, When He Was a Boy of Fourteen* (1975) consists of Mozart's (fictional) letters to his sister. Other titles include *Poor Richard in France* (1973), about Benjamin Franklin; *Gettysburg: Tad Lincoln's Story* (1976); and *The House on Stink Alley: A Story about the Pilgrims in Holland* (1977).

ADRIENNE E. GAVIN

Monteiro Lobato, José (1882–1948), Brazilian writer, editor, entrepreneur, artist, and translator; considered the father of Brazilian children's literature. In 1911 Lobato inherited the farm of his grandfather, the Viscount of Tremembé. His frustrations with politics that prevented the modernization of Brazil's agriculture were mirrored later by similar disappointments in his entrepreneurial efforts to revolutionize the Brazilian steel and oil industries. Lobato was influenced by U.S. capitalism, which he witnessed firsthand while serving as the Brazilian government's commercial attaché in New York City (1927–1931), as well as by the positivism of the French philosopher Auguste Comte (1798–1857) and the writings of Nietzsche. He was a materialist who believed Brazil could obtain economic and cultural independence through industrialization and mechanization—thus his interest in steel and oil. These varied influences can be seen in his books for young readers.

Lobato is also credited with commercializing Brazil's book industry. In 1918 he entered the editorial field and shortly thereafter started the first of a series of publishing companies dedicated to publishing not only his own works but those of new Brazilian authors. In 1920 he published his first children's book, *A menina do narizinho arrebitado* (The Snub-Nosed Girl). It was a great success and, like many of his later books, was used as a reader in Brazilian public schools. Although Lobato produced a nearly equal quantity of adult fiction, it is his seventeen volumes of children's books set in the Sítio do Pica-Pau Amarelo (Yellow Woodpecker Farm) that are his most famous and enduring works; they were even adapted for radio and television from the 1940s to the 1970s.

The Yellow Woodpecker Farm, first presented in *A menina do narizinho arrebitado*, is the setting for nearly all Lobato's children's books. It is a matriarchal utopia where the only activities are playing and learning and there are no parents, only a loving wise grandmother and her black serving woman, and where magic and fantasy mix with science and realism. Questions are encouraged, and answers are readily available. All learning takes place in a forum of discussion, through questions and debate. The series features Lúcia (the snub-nosed girl); her grandmother Dona Benta; another grandchild, Pedrinho; Lucia's stubborn and outspoken talking rag doll, Emília, who eventually comes alive; and a host of other characters, including the Viscount of Sabugosa, a noble talking corncob who is ready with a scientific explanation for every observed phenomenon. The series also contains adaptations of Brazilian and world myths, fables, children's classics such as *Peter Pan* and *Pinocchio*, and even encounters with such American popular-culture icons as the silent film cowboy Tom Mix and Felix the Cat—always in the setting of the Yellow Woodpecker Farm. Some books in the series, for example, *Emília no país da gramática* (Emília in the Grammarland), are dedicated to specific academic disciplines, in an effort to make these topics accessible and palatable to young readers.

Given his limited success with industrial reforms, Lobato came to believe that only by influencing the young would the reformist ideas he championed come to fruition. His children's books are unashamedly didactic and present theories and philosophies popular in Brazil in the first half of the 20th century. Nonetheless he is appreciated by Brazilians as much today as he ever was, largely because of his unique portrayal of children and the child–adult relationship. Despite having typical childhood imperfections, his characters evince a marked desire to learn and serve as examples of how understanding is gained and imagination cultivated in an environment of critical reason and judgment in which fear and tyranny are absent. Some of the superficial themes of his works may be dated, but the underlying lessons that children are reasoning individuals and that no authority is beyond question (for instance, religion in Lobato's books is seen as merely another cultural manifestation) have proved an important influence for Brazilian intellectuals, and even for many of Brazil's current ruling elite who grew up with Lobato's books and experienced the repressive Brazilian military dictatorship (1964–1985). Lobato himself was imprisoned for a time by the dictatorship of Getúlio Vargas (1937–1945), and at various points in the 1930s and 1940s his books were censored by both the government and the Catholic Church, which had many schools in Brazil. These events contribute to a tradition that regards Lobato as a progressive and reasoning enemy of blind totalitarianism, as well as to a view of children's literature as a locus for resistance against oppression.

[*See also* Brazil.]

BIBLIOGRAPHY

Azevedo, Carmen Lucia, de, Marcia Camargos, and Vladimir Sacchetta. *Monteiro Lobato: Furacão na Botocúndia* (Monteiro Lobato: Tempest in Botocúndia). São Paulo, Brazil: SENAC 1998.

Barbosa, Alaor. *O ficcionista Monteiro Lobato* (The Fiction Writer Monteiro Lobato). São Paulo, Brazil: Brasiliense, 1996.

Penteado, J. Roberto Whitaker. *Os filhos de Lobato: O imaginário infantil na Ideologia do adulto* (The Children of Lobato: The Imaginary World in Adult Ideology). Rio de Janeiro, Brazil: Dunya, 1997.

RICHARD VERNON

Montes, Graciela (1947–), author, publisher, and educator. Montes is a literature professor at the National University of Buenos Aires. For twenty years she was part of the Latin American publishing house Centro Editor, and she directed the children's literature series Los cuentos de Chiribital. In 1986 she cofounded the publishing house Libros del Quirquincho, where she was the publications director. The author of more than fifty children's books, her profound contribution to children's literature includes works of fiction, nonfiction, translation, and literary theory. Among her most popular children's stories are *Tengo un monstruo en el bolsillo* (1988, *I Have a Monster in My Pocket*), *La verdadera historia del Ratón Feroz* (*The True Story of a Ferocious Rat*), and *Otroso* (*Otherbear*). In her nonfiction work *El golpe y los chicos* (1996, *The Coup and the Kids*), she discusses state-sponsored terrorism and includes interviews with children of the *desparecidos*, people kidnapped and murdered during Argentina's Dirty War. Her essays on children's literature theory have been collected in two volumes: *El corral de la infancia* (1999, *The Playpen*) and *La frontera indómita* (1999, *The Indomitable Border*). She has been Argentina's candidate three times for the International Hans Christian Anderson Prize, in 1996, 1998, and 2000.

GENNY BALLARD

Montessori, Maria (1870–1952), eminent Italian education theorist whose progressive theories altered concepts of education, especially for the very young. Her child-centered system, based on science and informed by the new disciplines of psychology and psychiatry, was first described in 1909 and later in *The Montessori Method* (1912, revised 1919). The first woman to graduate with a medical degree from the University of Rome, as a young doctor she worked with mentally handicapped children, basing new techniques on French models to encourage learning. Skeptical about the existing norms of regimented, book-dominated education, she realized that her methods could be adapted for younger, normal children. Invited to establish nursery schools in housing projects, she opened her first Casa dei Bambini in Rome in 1907. She instructed schoolmistresses in her methods, and from this evolved the first training college for nursery-school teachers.

Montessori's methods relied on facilitation, spontaneity, and freedom from restraint. She redesigned school furniture and equipment in sizes appropriate to children. Sensory learning through play and a child's self-expression were emphasized; indeed, the fundamental concept was self-education. Her work contributed to the reassessment of the psychology and social role of children, who were no longer seen as imperfect adults but as having distinctive lives of their own. At first her reformed system was designed for children of three to six years old; by 1916 it had been adapted to suit older children in elementary (primary) school. Her ideas spread around the world, although they were opposed in Italy by the conventional education establishment. Montessori traveled the globe, advising on the founding of new schools, including those in India and China, and spent long periods in America. At the end of the 20th century she became the first woman to be depicted on Italian currency.

ANN LAWSON LUCAS

Montgomery, L. M. (1874–1942), writer of poetry and domestic fiction who gained an international reputation in the early 20th century as Canada's most prominent children's author. Most of Lucy Maud Montgomery's twenty novels and more than five hundred short stories are set in her home province of Prince Edward Island. That they focus disproportionately on protagonists who are unusually talented or who must cope with difficult family situations, or both, highlights the influence of her life on her work. Less personally, however, her characters and plots also implicitly comment on the tensions facing the intelligent woman who must reconcile society's expectations with her own desire for fulfillment.

Early Life and Career

After the death of her mother when Lucy was not quite two, her father sent her to be raised by her maternal grandparents, Lucy and Hector Macneill, in Cavendish, Prince Edward Island. Undemonstrative and strict, the Macneills provided for Montgomery a childhood that was physically safe but emotionally "starved," as she put it in a diary entry shortly before beginning the novel that was to make her famous, *Anne of Green Gables* (1908). The young Montgomery responded to the bleakness of her emotional surroundings by writing journals, fiction, and verse that provided an outlet for her feelings. Once she started to sell her work, she could take pleasure not only in imagining stories with happy endings for their underdog protagonists but also in developing a career that held out the possibility of financial as well as mental independence from her domineering grandparents; tellingly, criticisms of authoritarianism recur throughout her oeuvre.

Montgomery's earning capacities remained important in later life, when the mental illness of her husband, the Reverend Ewan Macdonald, became manifest eight years after their 1911 wedding. His bouts of depression were sometimes too debilitating for him to work, and Montgomery's income was intermittently crucial to the couple and their two sons. It is perhaps not surprising, then, that, as Catherine Sheldrick Ross contends in a contribution to Mary Rubio's *Harvesting Thistles*, Montgomery's literary stock-in-trade was "books that help readers to feel secure." Arguably, her fictions accomplish this by acknowledging and subsequently banishing an insecurity that Montgomery's circumstances made painfully familiar to her. Central figures in both Montgomery's magazine fiction and her best novels for children, such as *Anne of Green Gables*, *Emily of New Moon* (1923), and *Jane of Lantern Hill* (1937), endure orphanhood, poverty, unsympathetic and/or tyrannical relatives, and other constraints before finding happiness; Montgomery's fictional characters thus consistently move from instability to gratification, offering the reader the satisfactions of wish-fulfillment fantasies.

L. M. Montgomery. Illustration by Lauren Mills from *Anne of Green Gables* (Boston: David R. Godine, 1989), p. 226. COLLECTION OF ANDREA IMMEL

The Stories in Context

Montgomery's personal experiences and needs were not the only influences on her work; it is also helpful to consider the ways in which her fiction responds to the surrounding literary culture. *Anne of Green Gables*, for instance, may be seen in such contexts as the North American regionalist writing of the pre–World War I period (woman-centered and often subversive of dominant ideologies) and the sentimental adoption tale exemplified by, for instance, Hesba Stretton's *Jessica's First Prayer* (1867), Johanna Spyri's *Heidi* (1880; English trans., 1884), Frances Hodgson Burnett's *Little Lord Fauntleroy* (1886), and Kate Douglas Wiggin's *Rebecca of Sunnybrook Farm* (1903). These and many other fictions, the mass-market descendants of George Eliot's 1861 novella *Silas Marner*, purvey plots involving children—orphaned or otherwise separated from their parents—who after an uphill struggle bring out the unsuspected softer sides of crusty and forbidding elderly people.

Thus the eponymous heroine of *Anne of Green Gables* arrives at the home of dour Marilla Cuthbert and her reclusive brother, Matthew, through a mistake: the Cuthberts have requested a boy from the orphanage, meaning to give him a respectable home in exchange for his labor on their farm, but the message is garbled and a girl is sent instead. Matthew, the softer of the pair, feels Anne's charm from the start; Marilla takes longer to capitulate but eventually acknowledges that Anne has become the dearest object of her heart. Over six sequels, Anne acquires a devoted and successful husband and half a dozen attractive children, but her major emotional work is done at age eleven, when she turns the emotionally moribund Green Gables into a loving home. The thrust of such texts is not only to update the Cinderella tale by showing deserving protagonists win the regard of even the gloomy and inhibited but also to ratify the values of the private sphere, especially love, innocence, and a morality not based on money.

In Montgomery's hands, this affirmation of Victorian domestic and feminine ideals takes on feminist overtones as well. Her narratives applaud women and girls who exhibit executive ability, productivity, and assertiveness, whether these qualities are displayed in housekeeping (in *Jane of Lantern Hill* Jane learns to run her father's establishment at age eleven), romance (the heroine of Montgomery's 1926 novel *The Blue Castle*, deluded into thinking that she has a terminal illness, throws off the stultifying constraints imposed by her unappreciative family and proposes marriage to a disreputable-appearing man who later turns out to be a prime matrimonial catch), child care (Anne's teenage daughter Rilla takes on a "war baby," a task that bestows on her a new maturity and depth), or artistry (Anne and the protagonist of the Emily trilogy share writerly aspirations and talent). In a journal entry for 25 March 1922, Montgomery wrote of her husband's "medieval" assumption that "a woman is a thing of no importance intellectually—the plaything and servant of a man—and couldn't possibly do anything that would be worthy of real tribute"; her fictions consistently suggest both that women can compete with and occasionally surpass men intellectually and that "real tribute" is merited by women's achievements in the often undervalued domestic and emotional realms. While similar combinations of the traditional and the subversive may be found in many authors' works for children, Montgomery's novels also offer evocative settings and simple yet successful characterization, such that her debt to her predecessors in the field is fully balanced by her influence on her successors.

[*See also* Canada; Girls' Books and Fiction; Orphans; *and biographies of figures mentioned in this article.*]

BIBLIOGRAPHY

Epperly, Elizabeth Rollins. *The Fragrance of Sweet-Grass: L. M. Montgomery's Heroines and the Pursuit of Romance.* Toronto: University of Toronto Press, 1992.

Reimer, Mavis, ed. *Such a Simple Little Tale: Critical Responses to L. M. Montgomery's "Anne of Green Gables."* Metuchen, N.J.: Children's Literature Association and Scarecrow Press, 1992.

Rubio, Mary Henley, ed. *Harvesting Thistles: The Textual Garden of L. M. Montgomery; Essays on Her Novels and Journals.* Guelph, Ontario: Canadian Children's Press, 1994.

Wiggins, Genevieve. *L. M. Montgomery.* Twayne's World Authors Series. New York: Twayne, 1992.

CLAUDIA NELSON

Montresor, Beni (1926–2001), Italian author and illustrator of children's books and designer of productions for film and opera in the United States and Europe. Montresor was born in Bussolengo, Italy, and studied art at the Liceo Artistico in Verona, the Academia di Belle Arti in Venice, and the Centro Sperimentale di Cinematografia in Rome. He came to the United States in 1960, after working with the Italian film directors Federico Fellini, Roberto Rossellini, and Vittorio de Sica. In New York, Montresor designed sets and costumes for the Metropolitan Opera; he claimed that creating an entire world within the pages of a children's book was similar to creating a world onstage. He is best-known in children's literature for his illustrations for two classics: *May I Bring a Friend?* (1964) by Beatrice Schenk de Regniers, which won the Caldecott Medal, and *Little Red Riding Hood* (1991), which alarmed some readers because, true to Perrault's text (and harking back to Gustave Doré's illustrations), Montresor shows Red Riding Hood actually being devoured by the wolf and then floating peacefully, arms outstretched, in its red belly. One of Montresor's first books, *The Prin-*

Beni Montresor. Illustration from *Mommies at Work* by Eve Merriam (New York: Alfred A. Knopf, 1961), pp. 10–11. REPRODUCED COURTESY OF THE COTSEN CHILDREN'S LIBRARY, PRINCETON UNIVERSITY LIBRARY

cesses: Sixteen Stories about Princesses (1962), edited by Sally P. Johnson, was selected as a New York Times Best Illustrated Book. His own writings include *House of Flowers, House of Stars* (1962); *The Witches of Venice* (1963), based on an opera of the same name; *Cinderella* (1965), adapted from the opera *La Cenerentola* by Gioacchino Rossini; *I Saw a Ship a-Sailing* (1967), a fantasy based on the Mother Goose rhymes; *A for Angel* (1969); and *Bedtime* (1978). Montresor also illustrated many books for other writers, including *Belling the Tiger* (1961) and other books by Mary Stolz; Eve Merriam's *Mommies at Work* (1961); an adaptation by the poet Stephen Spender of Mozart's *The Magic Flute* (1966); and a second book by de Regniers, *Willy O'Dwyer Jumped in the Fire* (1968).

LINNEA HENDRICKSON

Moomin. *See* Jansson, Tove.

Moore, Anne Carroll (1871–1961), American librarian and critic. A graduate of the Pratt Institute, Moore became head of its children's library in 1897. When she joined the New York Public Library in 1906, she was charged with unifying and upgrading its services to children across the entire system, remaining its Superintendent of Work with Children until her retirement in 1941. She was the first chair of the American Library Association's Children's Section, and her insistence on professional training and standards was legendary. A regular reviewer for *The Bookman* (1918–1927), *The New York Herald Tribune Books* (1924–1930), and *Horn Book* (1939–1961), Moore was both revered and feared for her influence, clashing with editors such as Ursula Nordstrom but also mentoring Bertha Mahony Miller, Margaret K. McElderry, and many others. Her awards included a Newbery Honor citation for *Nicholas: A Manhattan Christmas Story* (1924) and honorary doctorates from the University of Maine and the Pratt Institute.

[*See also* McElderry, Margaret K.; Miller, Bertha Mahony; Nordstrom, Ursula; *and* Sayers, Frances Clarke.]

BIBLIOGRAPHY

Sayers, Frances Clarke. *Anne Carroll Moore: A Biography*. New York: Atheneum, 1972. One of Moore's protégés, Sayers succeeded her as Superintendent of Work with Children at the New York Public Library.

PEGGY LIN DUTHIE

Moore, Clement Clarke (1779–1863), American teacher and Hebrew scholar. The son of an academic minister, he became professor of Oriental and Greek literature at the General Theological Seminary in New York, but he remains famous solely as the reputed author of "A Visit from Saint Nicholas." Supposedly written for and first recited to his children on Christmas Eve 1822, the poem was, according to its legend, given by Moore's sister to the *Sentinel*, an upstate newspaper, and published anonymously on December 23, 1823. It incorporates characteristics of the Dutch New Yorkers described by Washington Irving (such as their sleighs, beards, leather boots, corpulence, and joviality) into the austere Father Christmas of English tradition presented in other contemporaneous verse to create the figure of Santa Claus and other popular aspects of modern Christmas tradition. The instant success and enduring appeal of the poem through many publications is attributable to its having been crafted to delight specific children, whose responses are said to have helped mold the final version.

CAROLE H. CARPENTER

Moore, Lilian (1909–2004), American editor, educator, storyteller, and poet. Moore is best-known for her spare, witty children's poetry and her simply but interestingly written fiction for young children, including *I'll Meet You at the Cucumbers* (1988) and the series The Little Raccoon. In 1985 Moore, who also wrote under the name Sara Asheron, received the National Council of Teachers of English Award for Excellence in Poetry for Children. Her books of poetry include *See My Lovely Poison Ivy and Other Verses about Witches, Ghosts, and Things* (1975); *Something New Begins* (1982); and *Poems Have Roots* (1997). Moore was also an influential editor and a founder of the Council on Interracial Books for Children.

LINNEA HENDRICKSON

Móra, Ferenc (1879–1934), Hungarian journalist, novelist, and writer of children's books. After completion of his studies, Móra lived in Budapest and worked in Szeged, Hungary as a librarian and later as director of the town museum. His novel *Ének a búzamezőkről* (1927; English trans., *Song of the Wheatfields*, 1930) and his children's books reflect the life and folklore of the peasants, workers, and miners of the Hungarian lowlands. Beginning in 1905, he published fairy tales, short stories, and poems for children. His best-known children's book in Hungary, *Kincskereső Kisködmön* (The Magic Coat, 1918), is a realistic, autobiographical story of rural childhood that contains additional fairy-tale elements and motifs. In it Móra describes the life of the village orphan Stepan and his struggles against illiteracy, poverty, starvation, disease, and death. The title of this melancholy, moving tale is based on a recurrent image: an embroidered coat made of sheepskin with magical qualities, which Stepan had received from his deceased father and which gets too tight whenever he lies.

BERND DOLLE-WEINKAUFF

Mora, Pat (1942–), an American poet, educator, and children's author who emphasizes her Chicana heritage and explores the challenges of bilingualism. Patricia Estella Mora taught in Texas public schools and colleges and served as a university administrator. In her essay collection *Nepantla* (1993), a Nahuatl word meaning "in the middle," Mora described for adult audiences her feelings about switching between two cultures. Her memoir, *House of Houses* (1997), presents her ancestors as they speak of their lives before and after leaving Mexico. Similarly, as a poet she addressed her Mexican American background (e.g., in *Chants*, 1984) and the political, social, and emotional attitudes that separate or unite people (e.g., in *Borders*, 1986). Mora's children's books draw on family stories for plot and character, use a poetic prose style, and emphasize concerns about assimilation and the maintenance of one's own cultural legacy. Her Aunt Ignacia stars as the protagonist in her first children's book, *A Birthday Basket for Tía* (1992). In 1997 she published *Tomás and the Library Lady* (dedicated to Tomás Rivera, a prominent leader in the Chicano literary movement). Other works include *Confetti: Poems for Children* (1995) and two Mayan folk tales, *The Race of Toad and Deer* (1995) and *The Night the Moon Fell* (2000).

Generally in Mora's writings the desert evokes a mother, fierce yet determinedly nurturing as wisdom is passed from the women in one generation to another. As an educator and activist, she advocates bilingual literacy and, with her siblings, established the Estella and Raúl Mora Award under the auspices of the National Association to Promote Library and Information Services to Latinos and the Spanish-Speaking (REFORMA). Her literary honors include a Creative Writing Award from the National Association for Chicano Studies (1983), a National Endowment for the Arts Fellowship (1994), the Tomás Rivera Mexican American Children's Book Award (1997), and the Premio Aztlán Literature Award (1997).

BIBLIOGRAPHY

Kanellos, Nicolás. "Pat Mora." In *Dictionary of Literary Biography: Chicano Writers*, 3d series, vol. 209, edited by Francisco A. Lomelí and Carl R. Shirley, 160–163. Detroit, Mich.: Gale Group, 1999.

LYNDA G. ADAMSON

Moral Tales. Moral tales for children, varying from short stories to full-length novels, particularly flourished in Britain from about 1780 to 1830, although their popularity survived well into the 19th century. Their main purpose was didactic—to instruct young readers how to behave—and their main technique was the narration of realistic stories about ordinary life, to show children what appropriate and inappropriate behavior might be.

The evolution of moral tales is complicated. F. J. Harvey Darton's *Children's Books in England* suggests that books about courtesy and conduct were known from the 16th century. The Puritan influence became important in the 17th century, when James Janeway's *A Token for Children* (1671), with its stories of young children who lived devoutly Christian lives, was immensely popular. This didactic tradition continued into the 18th century, although more secular influences became apparent. John Newbery's *Little Pretty Pocket-Book* (1744) provided children with entertainment, but its preface stressed the immeasurable value of prudence and reason. Margery, the heroine of *Goody Two-Shoes* (1765), is a model of patience and perseverance, finally rewarded with wealth and a title. A moral and didactic element is clearly present.

Rousseauism

During the late 18th century social and political developments associated with the French Revolution abroad and the Industrial Revolution at home, through which also swirled cross-currents of romanticism and evangelism, began to affect children's literature. The writings of John Locke and Jean-Jacques Rousseau stimulated a greater awareness of the child and illuminated the need for a serious and sustaining literature. Other French writers had considerable influence, particularly Mme. de Genlis (1746–1830), a friend of Maria Edgeworth's, whose *Tales of the Castle* was translated into English in 1785, and Arnaud Berquin (1747–1791), whose collection of stories *The Looking-Glass for the Mind* (1787) was enormously popular.

Thomas Day (1748–1789) was an ardent Rousseauist. His book *Sandford and Merton* (published in three volumes in 1783, 1786, and 1789) takes up Rousseau's ideas of education from *Émile* (1762) and articulates them through the story of a sympathetic clergyman, Dr. Barlow, and two contrasting pupils: Tommy Merton, the spoiled son of a rich sugar planter, and Harry Sandford, the good-natured son of a plain honest farmer. Through small domestic adventures, such as when Dr. Barlow denies Tommy a plate of cherries for refusing to do his share of gardening, and the use of contrasting moral attitudes embodied in the two boys, Day's story achieved great popularity and exerted a powerful influence on the subsequent development of the moral tale.

Not surprisingly, given that Day and her father were friends, Maria Edgeworth (1767–1849) owed a great deal to Day, and in such books as *The Parent's Assistant* (1796) and *Moral Tales* (1801) she also used such devices as the wise adult contrasting with child characters and real-life domestic incidents as instruments of moral education. "The Good French Governess," for example, shows how a French émigré governess educates Mrs. Harcourt's unruly children so that they not only enjoy formal learning after a visit to a "rational toyshop" but begin to develop morally, becoming more modest and affectionate. In the famous story "The Purple Jar" Rosamund discovers the folly of buying something that looks attractive but is really worthless, and so learns to be more rational. This emphasis on sense as opposed to sensibility appears in all of Edgeworth's books, and the depiction of a young heroine or hero gaining wisdom and maturity was taken up by many other writers.

Religious Themes

Edgeworth was a secular writer primarily interested in promoting rational and ethical values, but many of her contemporaries wrote from a Christian viewpoint. The works of Sarah Trimmer, Hannah More, and Mary Sherwood, the most prominent examples, were deeply influenced by the evangelical revival and fiercely opposed to Rousseau and the apparently godless support for the French Revolution.

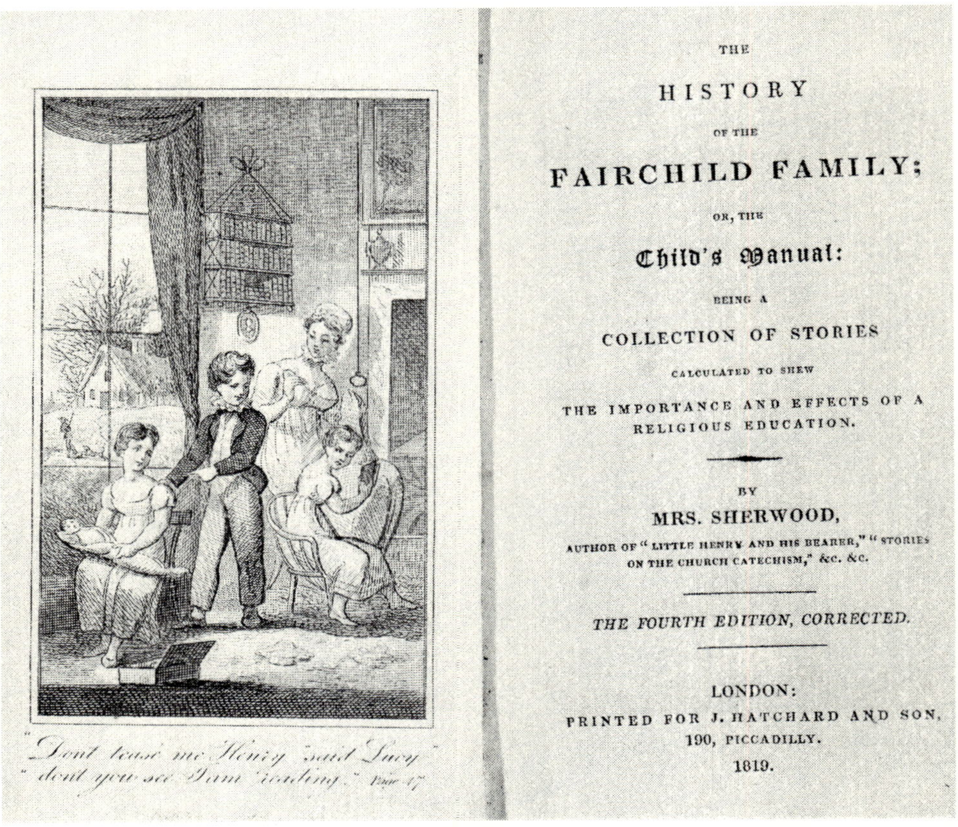

"Don't tease me Henry," said Lucy, "don't you see I am reading." Page 47

THE
HISTORY
OF THE
FAIRCHILD FAMILY;
OR, THE
Child's Manual:
BEING A
COLLECTION OF STORIES
CALCULATED TO SHEW
THE IMPORTANCE AND EFFECTS OF A
RELIGIOUS EDUCATION.

BY
MRS. SHERWOOD,
AUTHOR OF "LITTLE HENRY AND HIS BEARER," "STORIES ON THE CHURCH CATECHISM," &c. &c.

THE FOURTH EDITION, CORRECTED.

LONDON:
PRINTED FOR J. HATCHARD AND SON,
190, PICCADILLY.
1819.

Moral Tale. Frontispiece and title page from *The History of the Fairchild Family* by Mary Martha Sherwood (4th ed.; London: J. Hatchard, 1819). REPRODUCED COURTESY OF THE COTSEN CHILDREN'S LIBRARY, PRINCETON UNIVERSITY LIBRARY

Trimmer (1741–1810) was a firm supporter of the Church of England. Her most important book for children, *Fabulous Histories Designed for the Instruction of Children* (1786), achieved enormous popularity under its later title, *The History of the Robins*. This thoroughly didactic story contrasts the lives of a family of robins with those of the Benson family, in whose garden the birds nest. In one episode the young birds learn from their parents not to be wasteful, and in the next the Benson children learn not to be cruel to animals. Trimmer's *Instructive Tales*, first published in *The Family Magazine* in 1788–1789, represents her attempt to bring Christianity into the homes of the poor. "The Two Apprentices" tells the familiar tale of two lads, the industrious one making good and marrying his employer's daughter while his idle friend, who has neglected true religion, rapidly succumbs to consumption.

Hannah More's *Cheap Repository Tracts* (1795–1798) were not addressed directly to children, but their influence on the literary climate of the age was enormous. A prominent member of the Sunday School Movement, More (1745–1833) was asked to write against the Jacobin and atheistic literature circulating at the outbreak of the war with France. In a series of pamphlets she told simple stories, usually about village life, in which poor people, by practicing Christian virtues, found a peace and happiness that, the clear message was, no political or social change could hope to provide. "The Shepherd of Salisbury Plain," More's most famous story, is the tale of a poor but honest worker whose Christian patience is rewarded at last by a clergyman who appoints him as his new clerk. Other stories, such as "The History of Tom White the Postboy" and "The Two Shoemakers," make similar points about Christian virtues and temptations, and perhaps speak more directly to younger readers. The *Cheap Repository Tracts* were enormously popular, selling more than two million copies in their first year of publication, and they were widely circulated in North America by the American Tract Society.

By the late 18th century some sections of the evangelical movement wanted children's books to promote a fuller statement of evangelical principles, with more emphasis on sinfulness, self-examination, and the urgent need for Christ's forgiveness. Of the new books preaching this message for children, those by Mary Sherwood (1775–1851) were the most remarkable. Her power and variety in realistically depicting the joys and crises of ordinary life were evident as early as in *The History of Susan Grey* (1802), in which the clergyman-narrator draws the moral from the story of a young girl's Christian fortitude in the most difficult circumstances. Even more famous is Sherwood's full-length novel *The History of the Fairchild Family* (vol. I, 1818; vol. II, 1842; vol. III, 1847). In this story of middle-class family life she realistically depicts children playing with dolls, visiting neighbors, quarreling, even overeating. But her passionate desire to show how sinful children are, and how necessary it is for adults to bring them to Christian salvation, underpins the whole work. Although the third volume has a mellower tone, what remains in the memory is the episode in the first volume in which the caring father takes his children to view a hanging corpse.

Hard Work and Ethics

Between the extremes of Sherwood's intensely religious stories and Day's Rousseauistic ones flourished a vast number of writers showing varying degrees of didactic earnestness and religioethical meanings. The writings of Anna Laetitia Barbauld (1743–1825), especially her *Evenings at Home* (1792–1796), a collection of instructive dialogues and moralized tales that continued to be reprinted through the 19th century, and her *Hymns in Prose for Children* (1781) are traditionally Christian. In *Harry Beaufoy; or, The Pupil of Nature* (1821), by Maria Hack (1774–1844), a mother convinces her son of God's existence by showing him evidence of divine design in the universe.

Many writers were particularly intent on educating children to treat animals with kindness. In Priscilla Wakefield's *Instinct Displayed* (1817), for example, Caroline and Emily exchange very didactic letters about animal behavior. Within this subgenre of the moral tale are several appealing, imaginative stories, such as *Life and Perambulations of a Mouse* (1783), by Dorothy Kilner (1755–1836), and *Marvellous Adventures; or, The Vicissitudes of a Cat* (1802), by Mary Pilkington (1766–1839). Kilner also wrote *First Going to School; or, The Story of Tom Brown and his Sisters* (1804)—school stories were another variation of the moral tale. *Original Stories of Real Life* (1788), by Mary Wollstonecraft (1759–1797), is about two young girls taught not only about the importance of prayer but also about the need to behave properly to servants and animals.

Most moral tales, however, simply depict the struggles of ordinary people in everyday life, such as *The Orphan Boy* (1812), by Mary Belson Elliott (1794–1870), and *The Cottage in the Chalk-Pit* (1822), by Alice Catherine Mant (1788–1869). The anonymous *Life and Adventures of Lady Anne* (1823?), which portrays the pitiable state of orphaned children, is about a young heroine who endures various misfortunes before finally finding happiness. Barbara Hofland (1770–1844) wrote many moral tales about ordinary families struggling in adverse circumstances. *The Blind Farmer and His Children* (1816) is a typical expression of her belief that the practice of Christian virtues can lead to financial security. *Perseverance* (1826), by "Charlotte Elizabeth" (Charlotte Elizabeth Tonna, 1790–1846), is a family story about the education of African American children.

In general, moral tales describe and discuss human behavior realistically, relying on the moral and religious standards of the age. Sherwood's criteria tend to be intensely theological, but many writers, while praising Christian virtues, tend to concentrate on the importance of unselfishness and self-improvement, prudence, and reason. The Protestant work ethic is subscribed to, and the characters who practice its virtues often do well economically. In particular these tales stress the importance of kindly treatment of the poor and unfortunate, especially servants, African Americans, and animals.

These stories are often very formulaic. Wise and benevolent adults care for, educate, and control young children who sometimes behave badly or imprudently and must be corrected. Apart from Sherwood, most authors show children embarrassed by their errors rather than physically punished. The children themselves are often stereotyped, the wise and prudent contrasted with the lazy and thoughtless. These stories do not contain much physical detail or psychological subtlety; they often resemble fables.

The Waning of the Moral Tale

In the 19th century, however, the cultural climate began to change. Charles Lamb had denounced the works of Barbauld and Trimmer as early as 1802, and in 1839 Catherine Sinclair's *Holiday House* actually poked fun at the mischievous children's severe governess, Mrs. Crabtree. But the moral tale did not suddenly disappear; in the longer, more complex family stories that emerged, such as Harriet Mozley's *The Fairy Bower* (1841), Elizabeth Wetherell's *Wide, Wide World* (1851), and Louisa May Alcott's *Little Women* (1868), one can see traces of the moral tale. Even today, although authors may write about drug abuse, sex, and dysfunctional families, a strong amount of moral didacticism can be found in such books as Judy Blume's *Forever* (1975) and Anne Fine's *Goggle-Eyes* (1989).

Although the heyday of the moral tale may have been limited to the half century from 1780 to 1830, the phenomenon continues to provoke discussion and controversy. F. J. Harvey Darton's authoritative *Children's Books in England* (revised in 1982) criticized moral tales as propaganda and for overlooking the real child. Geoffrey Summerfield's *Fantasy and Reason* (1984) is even more hostile, arguing that the didactic realists showed a failure of feeling and the imagination.

More recently, however, there has been a vigorous attempt to rehabilitate the moral tale. Mitzi Myers, for example, argues that Maria Edgeworth's stories show a genuine knowledge of children and engage the reader's emotions quite as successfully as other genres. The tales of Dorothy Kilner and Barbara Hofland have similarly been reinvestigated. Almost all moral tales were written by women, and are increasingly repaying attention as examples of feminine storytelling.

[*See also* Cautionary Tales; Religious Instruction and Education; *and biographies of figures mentioned in this article.*]

BIBLIOGRAPHY

Avery, Gillian, with the assistance of Angela Bull. *Nineteenth Century Children: Heroes and Heroines in English Children's Stories, 1780–1900.* London: Hodder and Stoughton, 1965.

Butts, Dennis. *Mistress of Our Tears: A Literary and Bibliographical Study of Barbara Hofland.* Aldershot, U.K.: Scolar, 1992.

Clark, Beverly Lyon. "Reconstructing Dorothy Kilner: Anecdotes as Antidotes." *Children's Literature Association Quarterly* 14, no. 2 (1989): 58–63.

Cutt, M. Nancy. *Mrs. Sherwood and Her Books for Children.* London: Oxford University Press, 1974.

Darton, F. J. Harvey. *Children's Books in England: Five Centuries of Social Life.* 3d ed., revised by Brian Alderson. Cambridge, U.K.: Cambridge University Press, 1982.

Myers, Mitzi. "Romancing the Moral Tale: Maria Edgeworth and the Problematics of Pedagogy." In *Romanticism and Children's Literature in Nineteenth-Century England*, edited by James Holt McGavran Jr., 96–128. Athens, Ga.: University of Georgia Press, 1991.

Summerfield, Geoffrey. *Fantasy and Reason: Children's Literature in the Eighteenth Century.* London: Methuen, 1984.

DENNIS BUTTS

Mordvinoff, Nicholas (1911–1973), Russian painter, sculptor, and illustrator who was raised in Paris following the Russian Revolution. After graduating from the University of Paris, Mordvinoff spent thirteen years as an artist in the South Pacific and then emigrated to New York in 1946. His sixteen children's books were published under the pseudonym "Will and Nicolas," having been coauthored with William Lipkind. *The Two Reds* (1950), their first book, was a Caldecott Honor book and their second, *Finders Keepers* (1951), won the Caldecott Medal. *Circus Ruckus* (1954), *Chaga* (1955), and *The Magic Feather Duster* (1958) were chosen as among the best illustrated books of the year by the *New York Times*, and the American Institute of Graphic Arts awarded Mordvinoff a certificate of excellence for 1955–1957.

This immediate acclaim rests largely on Mordvinoff's superb linear technique and skill. In *The Two Reds* a thin line minimally outlines the form of red-headed Joey, and the other "Red" (an alley cat) is drawn with innumerable small lines suggesting form and furriness. As developed in the storyline, these two become friends, with matching red fur and hair reinforcing the point. *Finders Keepers* is notable for this linear style in combination with striking page designs. Here fragile lines coexist with bold, curving shapes as two dogs stroll along a hilly road. The total image is both comical and grandly panoramic. *The Tiny Little Rooster* (1960) shows off many Mordvinoff skills: infinite detail in the farm animals, five different roof textures, and an overall impression of movement through strong contrasts and rhythmic patterns. Taken as a whole, Mordvinoff's pictures brim with spontaneity and energy, a quality that probably stems from years of successful teamwork with the same collaborator, as well as from a highly sensitive and original treatment of composition and line.

DONNARAE MACCANN

More, Hannah (1745–1833), prolific English writer, now chiefly remembered for the Cheap Repository tracts, written to provide suitable reading for the newly literate pupils of the Sunday schools founded in the late 18th century. She was a delicate and precocious child, the fourth of five daughters of an Anglican schoolmaster who had charge of a school near Bristol. Her father began teaching her Latin and mathematics when she was eight, and "was frightened at his own success." In about 1757 her eldest sister, joined later by her other sisters, set up a school for young ladies in

Bristol. It became very successful; and there Hannah, who already knew French, acquired Spanish, Italian, and additional Latin from visiting masters. In 1762 she published a pastoral drama for schoolchildren.

In 1774 she went to London, where she met Samuel Johnson and many of his circle, including David Garrick, whose acting she much admired. Garrick, his wife, and More became great friends; Garrick produced More's play *Percy* in 1777 and supervised the writing of a second play. After his death in 1779, More lived from time to time—"twenty winters," as she later said—with his widow. More consorted with all the leading figures in society and was a member of the Blue Stocking circle of ladies. By 1780, however, she was beginning to lead a more serious life and was seeking friends from the Clapham Sect: evangelicals, philanthropists, and opponents of the slave trade, among whom William Wilberforce was prominent. In 1782 she published *Sacred Dramas*, verse plays with biblical subjects. In 1788 she published *Thoughts on the Importance of the Manners of the Great to General Society*, in which she castigated the morals of high society.

More had built a cottage in Blagdon, ten miles west of Bristol, where she spent the summer months with her sisters; and in 1789 she and her sister Martha, together with Wilberforce, visited Cheddar. Wilberforce was shocked by the ignorance and distress of the rural poor in Somerset, and urged the sisters to try to set up Sunday schools there. Out of this work the Cheap Repository Tracts eventually sprang. From March 1795 until November 1797 More was to write—under the initial L, M, or Z—some 50 of the 114 tracts, at the rate of three a month. Other writers included her sisters and friends from the Clapham Sect. She acquired a set of chapbooks and copied their format and their style, appealing to readers with titles that promised sensational reading: *Black Giles, the Poacher*; *Betty Brown, the St. Giles Orange Girl*; and *Robert and Richard, or the Ghost of Poor Molly*. She also gave practical advice on housewifery. Her best-known tale, *The Shepherd of Salisbury Plain*, which extols the meek acceptance of poverty and was extraordinarily popular in America, is the least typical. Though she supported the existing social order, she commended those with the initiative to better themselves, as in *The History of Tom White, the Postilion*. She had found the Somerset gentry and farmers hard and uncaring, and the clergy uncooperative and often inadequate; and she had great difficulties with them over the Blagdon Sunday school, some of which she described in *The Sunday School*.

With the help of influential friends, committees were set up all over England to distribute the tracts, which were enormously popular and were exported in large quantities to America. But success did not mean universal approval; the *Evangelical Magazine* wrote, "We think that danger of some kind usually lurks beneath the flowers of fiction"; and the Religious Tract Society was set up in 1799 because its founders deplored the lack of doctrine in More's works. They themselves soon found how difficult it was to write tracts for the young. But, interestingly, More herself was to echo their strictures on fiction. In *Coelebs in Search of a Wife* (1808), a father, commending his eight-year-old daughter's resolution to give up storybooks, says that "the early use of savoury dishes is not usually followed by an appetite for plain food."

[*See also* Chapbooks.]

BIBLIOGRAPHY

Primary Works

Cheap Repository Tracts, with a preface by James Silverman. New York and London: Garland, 1977. Contains "The Shepherd of Salisbury Plain," "The Two Wealthy Farmers," "The History of Tom White, the Postilion," "Black Giles the Poacher," and "Tawny Rachel."

Hole, Robert, ed. *Selected Writings of Hannah More*. London: William Pickering, 1996.

Secondary Work

Jones, M. G. *Hannah More*. Cambridge: Cambridge University Press, 1952.

GILLIAN AVERY

Morey, Walt (1907–1992), American writer. Born in Hoquiam, Washington, Morey later moved to Oregon. He worked variously as a mill worker, movie theater manager, boxer, filbert farmer, shipbuilder, and deep-sea diver. Beginning his writing career by producing short stories for pulp magazines, he turned to children's fiction in the 1960s, writing animal fiction and adventure books. Usually set in the wilderness of the Alaskan or Pacific Northwest, his fast-paced novels emphasize relationships between humans and nature. His best-known work, the award-winning best seller *Gentle Ben* (1965), tells of the bond between a boy and a Kodiak bear and inspired a movie adaptation and television series. Other titles include *Home Is the North* (1967), about a boy's adventures in remote Alaska; *Kavik the Wolf Dog* (1968), about a boy–dog friendship; *Scrub Dog of Alaska* (1971); *Run Far, Run Fast* (1974); and *The Year of the Black Pony* (1976).

ADRIENNE E. GAVIN

Morgan, Alison (1930–), British author whose stories are often set in the Welsh countryside of her childhood. The fictional village of Llanwern, modeled on a traditional Welsh farming community, is the background of Alison Mary Morgan's first four books: *Fish* (1971; published in the United States as *A Boy Called Fish*, 1973), *Pete* (1972), *Ruth Crane* (1973), and *At Willie Tucker's Place* (1975). *Leaving Home* (1979; published in the United States as *All Kinds of Prickles*, 1980) and *Paul's Kite* (1981) present a boy's search for acceptance and family after his grandfather's death compels him to leave his small farm and move to his aunt and uncle's suburban home and finally to the London apartment of his long-absent mother. Morgan also published books for younger readers, including *Christabel* (1984), about a goat, and *River Song* (1975), a chronicle of life in a bird community. *The Eyes of the Blind* (1986), aimed at teenaged readers, follows a young man's coming of age during the biblical King David's time. Themes of community, environmental awareness, family, and the trials of outsiders are prevalent in Morgan's writing.

KATHERINE M. ADAMS

Morgan, Sally (1951–), Australian Aboriginal author and artist who did not discover that she was descended from the Palku people of the Pilbara region until she was fifteen. Her autobiography *My Place* (1987) was enormously successful, and was adapted as *My Place for Younger Readers* (1990). Morgan has published several picture books, including *Little Piggies* (1991) and *Hurry Up Oscar* (1993). Her series of three books, *Just a Little Brown Dog* (1997), *Dan's Grampa* (1996), and *In Your Dreams* (1997), were illustrated by the noted Aboriginal artist Bronwyn Bancroft. Morgan's collection of short stories, *The Flying Emu*, contains several of her own illustrations.

[*See also* Australia; Bancroft, Bronwyn; *and* Picture Books.]

CLARE BRADFORD

Morgenstern, Christian (1871–1914), German poet, journalist, translator, publisher. Born into a family of painters, he studied law, economy, philosophy, and art history in Breslau and Berlin. He published from 1892 on (his first volume of poetry in 1895), cooperated with Bruno Cassirer's publishing house and with Max Reinhardt's Berlin Cabaret, and translated Henrik Ibsen and August Strindberg into German. Morgenstern suffered from tuberculosis, which caused his early death in 1914. He is best known for his nonsensical, satirical, and grotesque poems and cynical epigrams in *Galgenlieder* (1905) and *Palmström* (1910). While intended for an adult or "ageless" public, they were also published for children, in later editions—illustrated by Lisbeth Zwerger, Norman Junge, Jutta Bauer, and others—which enhanced the playfulness and absurd humor (related to dadaism) in his work. His works were also adapted to music by, for example, Hanns Eisler and Paul Hindemith. Morgenstern's absurdist, melancholy, and at the same time subtle and smooth poems, and his awareness of wordplay, have had great impact on the development of poetry in Germany and belong to the most beloved reading for both children and adults in the German-speaking countries.

BIBLIOGRAPHY

Morgenstern, Christian. *Lullabies, Lyrics, and Gallows Songs*, illustrated by Lisbeth Zwerger. Translated by Anthea Bell. New York: North-South Books, 1995.

ASTRID SURMATZ

Morgenstern, Susie Hoch (1945–), French writer. Morgenstern was born in Newark, New Jersey; she received her doctorate from Nice University (1972), where she became a professor. Her work derived from her observation of her growing daughters, who sometimes collaborated with her, as Aliyah did for *Terminale! Tout le monde descend* (Last Stop! Everyone Off, 1985). After starting with a book on the Hebrew alphabet in 1977, Morgenstern told the story of her Jewish grandmother in *Une vieille histoire* (An Old Story) in 1985. She is mainly concerned with family and with comical situations at school, as in *C'est pas juste* (It's Not Fair, 1983; published in the United Kingdom as *Stacey, the Unstoppable*, 1987); and with adolescents' difficulties, as in *Trois jours sans* (2001; *Three Days Off*, 2001). She emphasizes the pleasures of good cooking, as well as issues of obesity; but her real theme is love, as in *Lettres d'amour de 0 à 10* (1996; *Secret Letters from 0 to 10*, 1999), *Joker* (1999; *A Book of Coupons*, 2001), and *Un jour mon prince grattera* (1993; *Princesses Are People Too*, 2002). Her portrayal of a turbulent American girl in *L'Amerloque* (The Yank, 1993) made her a virtual ambassador of two countries.

JEAN PERROT

Mori, Kyoko (1957–), Japanese-American novelist and poet. Mori was born in Kobe, Japan. She emigrated to the

United States in 1977, earning a BA from Rockford College (1979) and a PhD from the University of Wisconsin–Milwaukee (1984), both degrees in English. Her mother's unhappy marriage and suicide when Mori was twelve are strongly reflected in her fiction: her first novel, *Shizuko's Daughter* (1993), tells the story of Yuki, who after her mother's suicide grows up in a restrictive, brutal home environment. The novel won a series of awards and was named an ALA Best Book for Young Adults. *One Bird* (1995), another story of a girl growing up alone in Japan in the 1970s, was awarded the Council of Wisconsin Writers Best Novel and named an ALA Best Book for Young Adults. Mori has also published an autobiography, *The Dream of Water: A Memoir* (1995); a book of essays, *Polite Lies* (1998), reflecting on differences between life for a young woman in the United States and Japan; and an adult novel, *Stone Field, True Arrow* (2000). She has also received awards for her poetry, published in magazines and in book form in *Fallout* (1994).

Janice M. Bogstad

Móricz, Zsigmond (1879–1942), Hungarian writer. The son of a farmer and building contractor, Móricz studied theology, law, and philosophy at the University of Budapest. He later contributed articles to the literary journals *Nyugat* and *Kelet Népe* and became known for his countryside novels and novellas.

Móricz's school story *Légy yó mindhalálig* (1937; English trans., *Be Faithful unto Death*, 1962) was initially written for an adult readership but is now regarded as a children's classic, as famous in Hungary as Ferenc Molnár's children's book *A Pál utcai fiúk* (1907; English trans., *The Paul Street Boys*, 1927). Móricz turned his own experiences of childhood and the Hungarian revolution into this novel of education, which describes the development of a student at the famous college in Debrecen. Bearing in mind his mother's admonition—the book's title—he decides to leave college to become a writer.

Bettina Kümmerling-Meibauer

Morimoto, Junko (1932–), internationally renowned Japanese Australian author-artist; born in Japan; emigrated to Australia in 1982. Many of her innovative picture books, which are characterized by Japanese themes and artistic style, have won awards from the Children's Book Council of Australia. *The White Crane* (1983), *The Inch Boy* (1984), and *A Piece of Straw* (1985) all won commendations, while *Kojuro and the Bears* (1986), an adaptation of a tale by Kenji Miyazawa, and *The Two Bullies* (1997), an adaptation of a traditional Japanese story, won the Picture Book of the Year in 1987 and 1998 respectively. Another well-known work, *My Hiroshima* (1987), is a graphic reflection on her experience of the atomic bomb. She has also illustrated a book of Zen stories, *One Hand Clapping* (1995), and more recently created an original fable with a Japanese motif, *Big Nuisance* (2003).

[*See also* Miyazawa Kenji.]

Helen Kilpatrick

Morpurgo, Michael (1943–), British writer who planned to become a professional soldier before turning to schoolteaching for ten years. Finding that his pupils enjoyed the stories he told them, he eventually decided to become a writer himself. His first book, *Long Way Home* (1975), describes how a boy living in care makes a new home for himself in a noisy, argumentative but fundamentally affectionate family. This was followed by a rush of other books, some aimed at junior readers and others catering to young teenagers, often with twin emphases on action and the emotional challenges characters have to come through in order to do what they know to be right. Animals also play an important part in his work, reflecting his efforts in the charity he runs with his wife, Farms for City Children. *War Horse* (1982), one of his own favorites, has been described as an equivalent of *Black Beauty* set during World War I. Seen through the eyes of Joey, a horse sent out to serve at the front, it describes the terrible carnage and acts of bravery taking place all around him. *Why the Whales Come* (1985) is set in the relative tranquillity of the Scilly Isles, where two children try to protect a stranded narwhal from the islanders, who want to kill it for its meat. *The Dancing Bear* (1994), set in the French countryside, continues with the theme of animals suffering at the hands of human beings. *Waiting for Anya* (1990), also set in a small village in France, describes how the people smuggle Jewish children over the border to Spain under the noses of their German occupiers. Morpurgo's next substantial novel, *The War of Jenkins' Ear* (1993), is one of his best. Drawing on his own unhappy experiences as a pupil, it describes the reaction of a harsh boarding school to a strange but magnetic new pupil. This boy sets out to do good whenever he can; he also believes he is Jesus Christ in his Second Coming. His time at the school finally ends in disaster when its brutal headmaster expels him on the spot.

An uncaring boarding school also features in *The Butterfly Lion* (1996), where a child turns back from running away from one such place after he meets an old lady who gives him the sympathy he wants. Hearing her sad story about her own young life inspires the pupil—whose name we never learn—to go back and face up to his own problems. But when he goes to revisit the old lady, he finds no evidence that she was ever there at all. This novel won the Smarties Book Prize and the Writers' Guild Children's Book Award for 1996. In 2003, Morpurgo was appointed children's laureate (a position he was instrumental in establishing) for two years, during which time he traveled to schools all over Britain. *Private Peaceful* (2003) came out during this time, one of his best novels and a powerful attack on the brutalities of war.

NICHOLAS TUCKER

Morris, Gerald (1963–), American novelist. Raised in Singapore, Morris studied English at Oklahoma Baptist University and earned his doctorate in Hebrew and Greek from Southern Baptist Theological Seminary. He began writing stories for young adults to leaven his academic studies and now balances his writing with his career as a pastor and teacher. His irreverent retellings of Arthurian legends draw from his familiarity with diverse sources, including Sir Thomas Malory, Wolfram von Eschenbach, and Chrétien de Troyes, and generally feature teenaged protagonists coming of age through their encounters with both Camelot and the world of fairies. Beginning with *The Squire's Tale* (1998), Morris has continued the series with *The Savage Damsel and the Dwarf* (2000) and several other volumes. Like its predecessors, *The Ballad of Sir Dinadan* (2003) combines humor and drama in its refusal to celebrate knightly posturing and courtly romance above intelligence and friendship.

[*See also* King Arthur.]

PEGGY LIN DUTHIE

Morris, Jill (1936–), Australian writer and publisher whose publishing company, Greater Glider Productions, produces books about the natural environment. Morris's books reveal the quirks of indigenous fauna, as in *Harry the Hairy-Nosed Wombat* (1970), *Kolo the Koala* (1971), and *Percy the Peaceful Platypus* (1972), all illustrated by Rich Richardson, and *Possums in the Roof* (1987), written and illustrated by Morris. *Australian Bats* (1992), illustrated by Lynne Tracy, and *The Wombat Who Talked to the Stars: The Journal of a Northern Hairy-Nosed Wombat* (1997), illustrated by Sharon Dye, are informational books. In the picture book *The Boy Who Painted the Sun* (1983), illustrated by Geoff Hocking, a boy who moves to the city re-creates the color and delights of country living.

STELLA LEES and PAM MACINTYRE

Morris, William (1834–1896), Pre-Raphaelite author and artist. Influenced by John Ruskin, Morris became an enthusiastic advocate of the idea of beauty in the midst of Victorian industrialism. Several of his prose romances became reading matter for children and young adults. Morris had a vision of England as a "splendid branch of the Germanic people, its life and thought nobly expressed in its songs and chronicles." His medieval romances include *A Tale of the House of the Wolfings* (1889) and *The Roots of the Mountains* (1890), which depicts the peoples of central Europe before the Roman conquest as a society "over which the shadow of Rome had never descended." Other romances read by children are *The Well at the World's End* (1896) and *The Sundering Flood* (1898). Morris's associates included Walter Crane, and his romances influenced 20th-century writers of fantasy, for example, J. R. R. Tolkien.

HELENE HØYRUP

Morrison, Lillian (1917–), American poet and anthologist. Morrison entered the field of children's books with a collection of autograph verses she had learned from the young patrons of the East Harlem library where she worked. *Yours till Niagara Falls* (1950) was followed by *Remember Me When This You See: A New Collection of Autograph Verses* (1961). She also compiled poetry books around the themes of school (*A Diller, A Dollar: Rhymes and Sayings for the Ten O'Clock Scholar*, 1955), sports (*Slam Dunk: Basketball Poems*, 1995), and food (*I Scream, You Scream: A Feast of Food Rhymes*, 1997). Her own spare, rhythmic verse was published in several accessible volumes. *The Sidewalk Racer, and Other Poems of Sports and Motion* (1977) focuses on basketball, boxing, and other athletic pursuits, while *Rhythm Road: An Anthology of Poems to Move To* (1988) will have readers tapping their feet to the cadences of music and dancing evoked in the verse.

PETER D. SIERUTA

Morse, Jedidiah (1761–1826), minister of the First Congregational Church in Charlestown, Massachusetts, active in missionary work among the Native Americans and also in opposing emergent Unitarianism. Morse's *Geography Made Easy* (1784), long the most popular book on the subject, was the first geography published in the United States and brought him the title of "father of American geography." At the time, geography was not taught scientifically, and in schools geography books were treated as readers. Morse, who compiled his book the year after graduating from Yale, provided not only information—often inaccurate but always interesting—about the settled areas of colonial America, but also travelers' tales and picturesque fables, such as the one (found in medieval bestiaries) about gray squirrels using their tails as sails when they cross rivers or lakes. The earliest edition of the book included a statement, subsequently removed, that inhabitants of Connecticut "though generally industrious sagacious husbandmen" were "intemperately fond of lawsuits and little petty arbitrations." Morse later wrote *A Compendious History of New England* (1804) with Elijah Parish, which brought accusations of plagiarism from Hannah Adams, author of *A Summary History of New England* (1799). Morse was the father of Samuel F. B. Morse (1791–1872), the artist and inventor who gave his name to the Morse code.

[*See also* Geography and Travel Books.]

BIBLIOGRAPHY

Johnson, Clifton. *Old-Time Schools and School-books* (1904). Edited by Carl Withers. New York: Dover, 1963.

Gillian Avery

Mortimer, Mrs. F. L. (1802–1878), evangelical English children's writer. Born in London, Mrs. Favell Lee Mortimer married London minister Thomas Mortimer in 1841. Following a religious conversion in 1827, she taught the poor, set up a school on her banker father's Wiltshire estate, and anonymously wrote readers, educational texts, and books of religious instruction for very young children. Her best-known work is the popular family devotional guide *The Peep of Day: or, A Series of the Earliest Religious Instruction the Infant Mind Is Capable of Receiving* (1833), which was followed by the similar *Line upon Line* (1837) and *More About Jesus* (1839). *Near Home: or, The Countries of Europe Described* (1849) and *Far Off: or, Asia and Australia Described* (1852) are geographical books with a religious flavor designed to steer children toward facts and away from fiction and fantasy. Mortimer also authored the successful *Reading Without Tears: or, A Pleasant Mode of Learning to Read* (1857).

Adrienne E. Gavin

Morton-Sale, John (1901–1990), and **Isobel Morton-Sale** (1904–1992), British illustrators. Fellow students at the Central School of Art, London, the couple married in 1924, set up separate studios near Dartmoor, and founded the Parnassus Gallery in London at the end of World War II. Individually engaged in book illustrating, in the 1930s the Morton-Sales began to produce collaborative work. Together they illustrated Mary Grigs's *The Yellow Cat* (1936) and Eleanor Farjeon's *Martin Pippin in the Daisy Field* (1937). Work for other Farjeon books followed, including *Cherrystones* (1942), *The Mulberry Bush* (1945), and *The Starry Floor* (1949). They also illustrated books such as Beverley Nichols's fantasy *The Tree That Sat Down* (1945). Influenced by the neo-Romantic movement, the Morton-Sales's illustrations depict child characters as natural beings who are part of the natural world. This is especially seen in their color and black-and-white illustrations of children for *Something Particular* (1955), by Ann Driver and Rosalind Ramirez, an account of an experimental venture by children in mime, music, and dance performed at St. James's Palace, London. The Morton-Sales's illustrations for this book have been said to evoke the whole spirit of childhood—a fairy-enchanted spirit.

Adrienne E. Gavin

Mosel, Arlene (1921–1996), American author, librarian, and professor of library science. Mosel is best known for two classic picture books: *Tikki Tikki Tembo* (1968) and *The Funny Little Woman* (1972), both retellings of traditional tales from Asia, and both illustrated by Blair Lent. The first was an ALA Notable Book and remains extremely popular, although there is controversy about the story's origin, which is probably Japanese rather than Chinese. Concerns have been raised that this tale, which purports to explain why Chinese children have short names, perpetuates stereotypes; however, it is liked by children and remembered fondly by many adults. It has been set to music for narrator and woodwind quintet by Harry Freedman (1974). *The Funny Little Woman*, which was awarded the Caldecott Medal, is based on "The Old Woman and Her Dumpling," Lafcadio Hearn's retelling of a traditional Japanese tale. The woman, who is funny because she laughs at everything, escapes from evil monsters by making them laugh too.

[*See also* Lent, Blair.]

Linnea Hendrickson

Moser, Barry (1940–), American book artist, illustrator, and writer from Chattanooga, Tennessee. Moser had a traditional southern upbringing in which he was taught to stand when a woman entered the room, to know about guns, and to know his place. He went to military school, which did little for his artistic development but did instill a love of order and symmetry. He credits his uncle with encouraging his artistic talent, insisting on quality work and severely criticizing anything less. Moser wanted to become an animator with Disney, but his family did not regard a career in animation a good choice, and he attended Auburn University to study industrial design, and then went to the University of Chattanooga. He was unhappy with the racism and occasionally the narrow views of his family (some members belonged to the Ku Klux Klan); some relatives were offended when he married a woman from Missouri whom they considered a Yankee. After teaching for several years in Tennessee he accepted a job in Massachusetts, and from that point his life as an artist flourished. More than one hundred public and private collections include his work, and besides writing and illustrating, he has taught at a number of universities and art institutes (Princeton, Vassar, and the Rhode Island School of Design, to name a few). He also cofounded a publishing company, the Pennyroyal Press.

Barry Moser. Illustration from *Earthquack* by Margie Palatini (New York: Simon and Schuster, 2002), p. 24. Reproduced courtesy of the Cotsen Children's Library, Princeton University Library

Moser works in a variety of media, often wood engraving and watercolor but also pencil; sometimes he uses pen or pencil with ink washes. For a time he gave up wood engraving because of the dearth of wood good enough to produce the results he desired, but he took it up again when he discovered a workable composite. He has illustrated books for both adults and young children, crossover books, and many classics, such as Dante's *Purgatorio* and the *Alice* books in 1982 and the *Adventures of Huckleberry Finn* in 1985. Moser's early training and sense of order are obvious in the wood engravings used for these stories. They are orderly, frequently symmetrical, and quite static, often showing portraits of the players in the story rather than depicting the action. They are stark and atmospheric and often view a figure from a low angle to make it appear more imposing. His 1983 illustrations for *Frankenstein* are a good example of this, as are those for *Dracula* (2000) and *Huckleberry Finn*.

Among Moser's earliest children's books were Van Dyke Parks's retellings of Brer Rabbit stories (*Jump! The Adventures of Brer Rabbit*, 1986; *Jump Again!*, 1987; and *Jump On Over!*, 1989). For these Moser switched to watercolors, which have the lighter touch appropriate for the very young. Here again, he chooses to show mostly characters rather than action, although action scenes are more numerous in *Jump On Over!* A highly meticulous illustrator and designer, Moser makes sure that each set of illustrations is suited to a story's overall tone. For Virginia Hamilton's *In the Beginning: Creation Stories from around the World* (1988) he used saturated colors for a more dignified and solemn feel. For the Brer Rabbit stories he used light watercolors, reflecting the carefree attitude of the text, and he illustrated *Earthquack* (2002), a delightful retelling of the Chicken Little story by Margie Palatini, with brighter, lighthearted watercolors. Rendered on white paper, the picture of the ermine in front of a white chicken in front of a white goose is a masterpiece of tonal expression. When asked by an editor to retell and illustrate Hans Christian Andersen's *The Tinderbox* (1990), he struggled until he heard the story in his head and told it in his aunt's voice. By setting it in the mountains in his home region of eastern Tennessee, he adapted a folk tale to his own time and place just as Andersen and the Grimm brothers had. Similar adaptations followed, for example, *Polly Vaughn* (1992), *Tucker Pfeffercorn* (1993), and *The Three Little Pigs* (2001). Moser is very prolific, having illustrated more than 120 children's and adult books, mostly by other authors. He has also continued to write and adapt children's stories, occasionally working with two of his daughters, Madeline and Cara.

[*See also* Illustrations *and biographies of figures mentioned in this article.*]

JACQUE ROETHLER

Moss, Elaine (1924–), British critic and librarian whose work as a commentator and reviewer brought serious critical attention to children's books. Moss trained as a librarian and worked as a teacher and in publishing before becoming a freelance journalist and broadcaster. As selector of the annual Children's Books of the Year exhibition and author of the accompanying catalog from 1970 to 1979, she played an important role in recognizing the trends and talents that developed in that period. Moss championed the promotion of picture books to older readers, overturning the traditional restriction of picture books to children who cannot yet read.

JULIA ECCLESHARE

Moss, Marissa (1959–), artist and author who has written and illustrated numerous books for children, most notably the popular *Amelia's Notebook* series. With a background in art history, Moss began as a picture book illustrator, eventually writing her own texts. Works include the self-illustrated *Regina's Big Mistake* (1990), *After-School Monster* (1991), *Hannah's Journal: The Story of an Immigrant Girl* (2000), and *Max's Logbook* (2003), as well as *Mighty Jackie: The Strikeout Queen* (2004), illustrated by C. F. Payne. The Amelia books, designed to look like school composition notebooks doodled in and written by a young girl, now number over fifteen. Moss currently lives and writes in Berkeley, California.

[*See also* Picture Books.]

MAGGIE HOMMEL

Mother Bunch. In chapbooks, Mother Bunch is an alewife and teller of tall tales and jokes. Inns then served as a distribution center for the chapbook trade. The 17th-century *Pasquil's Jest Book* presents the prototype mythical Bunch as a monstrous figure who died at the age of 175 and from whom "proceeded all our great greasie Tapsters and fat swelling Ale wives, whose faces are blown as bigge as the froth of their bottle Ale." The 18th-century Mother Bunch was often depicted as a purveyor of domestic advice. *The History of Mother Bunch of the West, Containing Many Rarities Out of Her Golden Closet of Curiosities* is a medley of recipes and charms to help girls find husbands. In the later 18th century the name was often given to collections of Madame d'Aulnoy's fairy stories. The poet John Clare (1793–1864) described how as a child he saved precious pennies to buy "penny histories," including "Mother Bunches Fairy Tales."

[*See also* Aulnoy, Marie Catherine, Comtesse d' *and* Chapbooks.]

GILLIAN AVERY

Mother Goose. A legendary crone in European popular traditions associated with fairy tales and nursery rhymes, this character is the modern-day descendant of an ancient type in western European folklore, which is related to the figures of the witch, the garrulous nurse, and the wise woman Mother Bunch—all regarded with suspicion because they possess either magic powers or secret knowledge (especially on sexual matters). Since 1650, Mother Goose has been connected in print with the old wives' tale, known in French as *un conte de ma mère l'oye* ("a story of Mother Goose"). The genre includes fairy tales, ghost stories, and "merry" (bawdy) tales, none of which were thought to have any literary merit or useful purpose beyond passing time during the short days of winter. The best-known representation of Mother Goose appears in the frontispiece of Charles Perrault's *Histoires ou contes du temps passé* (Stories and Tales of Times Past, 1697), where she is depicted as an old servant woman telling stories while spinning by the hearth.

Mother Goose was introduced to the English-speaking world when Robert Samber's translation of Perrault appeared in 1729, and since then her character has undergone a radical transformation in response to the gradual process of integrating popular vernacular literature into the literary canon. Mother Goose was described as the teller of Perrault's fairy tales on the title page of the Newbery edition for chil-

Mother Goose. Frontispiece by Feodor Rojankovsky for *The Tall Book of Mother Goose* (New York and London: Harper & Brothers, 1942). REPRODUCED COURTESY OF THE COTSEN CHILDREN'S LIBRARY, PRINCETON UNIVERSITY LIBRARY

dren, issued some time in the 1760s. She was connected to the nursery rhyme in another Newbery publication as the ostensible author of *Mother Goose's Melodies, or Sonnets for the Cradle* (1780). The association has persisted, even though it may have been nothing more than a clever marketing ploy. Isaiah Thomas introduced Mother Goose in her new capacity to Americans when he published an edition of *Mother Goose's Melodies* in 1785. By the 1820s, when Munroe and Francis were issuing their similarly titled collection of nursery rhymes, the term "Mother Goose rhymes" seems to have been established as a term for the genre in American English.

The character further metamorphosed into a comical fairy godmother, thanks to the runaway success of Thomas Dibdin's pantomime *Harlequin and Mother Goose; or the Golden Egg* (1806). The stage production also popularized a more fanciful version of the traditional conception of Mother Goose: an old woman with a hooked nose reaching her chin, a black brimmed hat with a steeple crown, and a stomacher and mantua. In this new guise, Mother Goose became a ubiquitous figure in the nursery, appearing in Victorian toy book anthologies of nursery rhymes, picture book versions of individual rhymes, and collections of nursery tales, which invariably included a selection of rhymes and fairy tales. Toward the end of the 19th century, illustrators such as W. W. Denslow began representing her as an actual goose dressed in the costume associated with the old lady. Mother Goose in the 20th century has continued to evolve into an unthreatening personage, the benign muse of harmless but liberating nonsense poetry—a far cry from her mysterious and dangerous antecedents. There have been various attempts to identify Mother Goose with a real person (some tongue-in-cheek, which have been swallowed whole by the unsuspecting), but they continue to circulate on the strength of the stories, not the evidence.

[*See also* Fairy Tales and Folk Tales; France; Mother Bunch; Nursery Rhymes; Pantomime; *and* Perrault, Charles.]

BIBLIOGRAPHY

Opie, Iona, and Peter Opie, eds. *The Oxford Dictionary of Nursery Rhymes*. New ed. New York: Oxford University Press, 1997.

Tsurumi, Ryoji. "The Development of Mother Goose in Britain in the Nineteenth Century." *Folklore* 10, no. 1 (1990): 28–35.

Warner, Marina. *From the Beast to the Blonde: On Fairy Tales and Their Tellers*. New York: Farrar, Straus and Giroux, 1994.

ANDREA IMMEL

Mother Hubbard. Mother Hubbard, a nursery rhyme character, became famous after *The Comic Adventures of Old Mother Hubbard and Her Dog* (1805) was published by John Harris; its author was Sarah Catherine Martin (1786–1826). Though Mother Hubbard was a character known in the 16th century, and Edmund Spenser published *Mother Hubbard's Tale* in 1590, these Mother Hubbard stories did not resemble nursery rhymes. Supposedly Martin invented the rhymes using traditional characters, and a familiar structure, such as that in *Old Dame Trot and Her Comical Cat*, issued by T. Evans in 1803. *The Comic Adventure of Old Mother Hubbard and Her Dog* became very popular, "with 16 Beautiful Designs, elegantly engraved on 16 Copper plates. Price 1s. plain, and 1s6d. coloured." Nonsense verses and simple illustrations are cleverly arranged together without any moral message in the first genuine nonsense picture book. The verses begins as follows:

Old Mother Hubbard
Went to the Cupboard,
To give the poor dog a bone,
When she came there
The Cupboard was bare,
And so the poor dog had none.

She went to the Bakers
To buy him some bread;
When she came back
The dog was dead!

She went to the Undertakers
To buy him a Coffin;
When she came back
The Dog was laughing.

Mother Hubbard goes on a series of errands and returns to find that the dog has done amusing things. The rhymes are easy to remember and enjoyable for young children as well as adults. In the last illustration, the dog appears in clothes that Mother bought for him. The Mother Hubbard rhyme has seen repeated publication as a picture book and has appeared in many nursery rhyme collections over the years. The same figure of Mother Hubbard with a large cloak has continued into the present. The Harris edition marked the advent of a new period in children's literature.

[*See also* Harris, John; Nonsense; *and* Nursery Rhymes.]

BIBLIOGRAPHY

The Comic Adventures of Old Mother Hubbard and Her Dog: A Facsimile. With a note by Carey S. Bliss. San Marino, Calif.: Henry E. Huntington Library and Art Gallery, 1962.

Okiko Miyake

Mother's Offering to Her Children, A. This was the first children's book published in Australia—for Christmas 1841. The complete title is *A Mother's Offering to Her Children by a Lady Long Resident in New South Wales*. It is full of lively dialogue between Mrs. S, an all-knowing mother, and her four children. Despite its didactic tone, it must have been entertaining and interesting. Charlotte Barton, the author, was herself the mother and governess of four children, and she clearly took notice of their interests. Stories of shipwrecks are frequent, as actual shipwrecks were on the Australian coast at that time. Barton also includes "Anecdotes of the Aborigines of New South Wales." Rather than recounting their capture and killing by "heroic" whites, these are tales of the suffering of children and their mothers. In Mrs S's view, "Some are very kind parents: but I do not think they are in general, to their infants" (p. 205). Some of her stories, and her attitude toward the indigenes, seem appalling today, though for her time she was tolerant and compassionate. Other topics covered are conchology, copper mining, Timor, and insects, all in a light tone, befitting a storytelling mamma.

Barton's name does not appear on the work; and although she was named in the announcement in 1841, for many years the author was thought to be Harriet, Lady Bremer. Bremer is so recorded in reference works, and even in the introduction to the facsimile published in 1979, though Rosemary Wighton, who wrote the introduction, expresses some doubt. In 1980 Marcie Muir established Barton as the true author; Muir also researched biographical details and published *Charlotte Barton, Australia's First Children's Author*.

BIBLIOGRAPHY

[Barton, Charlotte.] *A Mother's Offering to Her Children . . .* Facsimile edition. Milton, Queensland: Jacaranda, 1979.
Culican-Ward, Disny. "Charlotte Barton, Australia's First Writer for Children." *Margin: Life and Letters of Early Australia* 55 (2001): 10–22.
Muir, Marcie. *Charlotte Barton, Australia's First Children's Author*. Sydney: Wentworth, 1980.

Virginia Joy Lowe

Movable Books and Pop-Up Books. Throughout history readers have been enlightened, entertained, and engaged by books supplemented with innovative movable paper mechanisms. While it is not known who added the first such device to a book, one of the earliest examples was produced in the 13th century by the Catalan mystic and poet Ramon Llull of Majorca. His text was enhanced with revolving discs, or *volvelles*, that were used to illustrate his religious beliefs. The volvelles, consisting of two or more circular pieces on a single spindle, turned independently to reveal letters or terms of special significance to the reader. Other authors in the 14th and 15th centuries used volvelles as paper instruments to determine the duration of daylight, to predict the movement of the moon and planets, and to set the dates for religious holidays. In many of the early works the moving pieces were printed separately and the buyer had to assemble them and insert them into the book.

Books with movable parts were produced in the 16th and 17th centuries on a number of different topics. Medical texts included layered plates of anatomical illustrations that, when lifted, revealed the body's organs, muscles, and skeleton. Three-dimensional stand-up diagrams were used to teach perspective and to aid the understanding of optics. Landscape architecture books included movable plates with before and after scenes to show how professional garden designs could enhance the value of an estate.

Early Movables for Children

Movable books for children were first published in the 18th century. Until 1770, children's books were designed to instruct, not to entertain. The London book publisher Robert Sayer changed that with the production of turn-up or metamorphosis books, also called "harlequinades" because the popular stage character Harlequin often appeared as the main character. These small books, with limited text, were illustrated volumes produced from a single, printed sheet, folded perpendicularly into four. The sheets were hinged at the top and bottom of each fold and the picture was cut through horizontally across the center to make two flaps that could be opened up or down. When the flap was raised, a new picture was formed. Harlequinades became popular in the late 1700s and were widely copied by other publishers.

The peepshow, sometimes called a tunnel book, was another type of movable. Used by street entertainers in the 18th and 19th centuries, peepshows were often elaborate constructions depicting battle scenes, landscapes, distant cities, or topical events. Typically a peepshow book had accordion-pleated side panels attached to stiff front and back covers. The individual illustrated sheets that formed the peepshow had cut-out sections so that portions of each of the pictures, layered one behind another, could be viewed as one scene.

Pop-up Books. Front cover by S. Louis Giraud for *Animal Life in Fact, Fancy, and Fun* (London: Daily Sketch & Sunday Graphic, c. 1930). REPRODUCED COURTESY OF THE COTSEN CHILDREN'S LIBRARY, PRINCETON UNIVERSITY LIBRARY

When the observer looked at the peepshow through a hole in the cover, the book was extended lengthwise, and the layers of illustration formed a three-dimensional tableau.

Dean and Sons used the peepshow principle to add a three-dimensional effect to their books. The publisher, founded in London before 1800, was the first to produce movable books in large quantities, and by the 1860s the company claimed to be the originator of movable books for children. Dean established a special department of skilled craftsmen who prepared a variety of handmade mechanicals that formed their movable books. In the publisher's earliest books, a ribbon was used to raise layers of illustrations into a stand-up scene.

Dean also introduced movable books with transformational plates based on the jalousie, or Venetian blind, principle. The illustrations in these books had either a square or an oblong picture divided into four or five equal sections by horizontal or vertical slits. The pictures changed, or transformed, into a completely different picture by moving a tab on a side of the illustration. The London publishers Ward and Lock, Darton, and Read also sold movable books for children in the 19th century, but Raphael Tuck and Sons was the first publisher to seriously challenge Dean. In 1870, Tuck founded a company in London that produced a range of paper items including scrapbook pictures, postcards, greeting cards, puzzles, and paper dolls. Their product line also included a series of books with stand-up, three-dimensional displays.

Ernest Nister, another English publisher, began a printing business in 1877 and created a large number of movable books that used all of the major processes of the time: dissolving and revolving transformational slats, rotating intersecting wheels, and stand-up plates. One technique used die-cut figures to create movable scenes within a pictorial frame. When the page was turned, the figures, connected to the opposing page by paper hinges, stood up and formed a three-dimensional illustration.

Lothar Meggendorfer (1847–1925) created some of the most original movable picture books of the 19th century. The Munich artist had a rare comic vision that he transmitted through his art as well as through his ingenious mechanical devices. Meggendorfer's moving images were unique. He devised intricate levers, hidden between pages, that gave his characters enormous possibilities for movement. Tiny metal rivets, actually tightly curled thin copper wire, were used to attach the levers, so that a single pull tab could activate all of them, often with several delayed actions as the tab was extended. Some illustrations used more than a dozen rivets, and he often had five parts of the illustration moving simultaneously and in different directions. Meggendorfer's movable books were produced in German and many titles were translated into English and other languages. From the last decades of the 19th century until 1914 almost all of the notable movable books were printed in Germany, where the highest quality color printing was done. When World War I began, the German production of movable books stopped.

The 20th Century and the First Pop-Ups

Few movable books were produced during the war years or immediately thereafter, but a new series of books with stand-up scenes was introduced in 1929. The British book publisher S. Louis Giraud (1879–1950) conceived, designed, and produced books with movable illustrations that he described as "living models." While the term had yet to be coined, these books were the first authentic pop-up books. Each title contained at least five double-page spreads with pictures that came to life when the pages of the book were opened. Unlike their German-produced predecessors, Giraud's books were printed on coarse, absorbent paper with less sophisticated printing and color reproduction techniques, and they were moderately priced. Between 1929 and 1949, Giraud produced a series of sixteen annuals, first for the *Daily Express* newspaper and later as an independent publisher using the trade names Strand Publications and Bookano Stories. Each annual included stories, verses, and illustrations as well as five or more pop-ups.

As the Depression years deepened, Blue Ribbon Publishing Company of New York sought a way to rekindle sagging book sales. Their addition to the marketplace was "pop-up" books, a term Blue Ribbon registered to describe their movable books. Between 1933 and 1935 the publisher issued thirty pop-up titles featuring traditional tales, Mickey Mouse and Minnie Mouse, and such contemporary action characters as Buck Rogers, Tarzan, and Popeye.

An increasing number of books with moving parts was issued in the middle years of the 20th century. McLoughlin Brothers entered the movable book market in 1939 with the publication of their first Jolly Jump-up title. This series of ten titles, illustrated by Geraldine Clyne (1899–1979), had die-cut, stand-up pictures cut from a single sheet of paper. In 1942 the American artist Julian Wehr (1898–1970) began a series of books with tab-operated mechanicals, similar to those published in the 19th century. Wehr's full-page illustrations were slit at various points in the picture to permit arms, heads, legs, or other moving parts to protrude. A tab, encased between the printed pages, extended through the side or lower edge of the page. When the reader moved the tab, parts of the illustration were put in motion. The action was transmitted to many different parts of the picture at once: tails wagged, eyes moved, and legs danced.

Pop-up books began to change in the 1960s as artists and publishers were influenced by the remarkably innovative books created by the Czech artist Vojtech Kubašta (1914–1992). His work included bold, colorful drawings and equally bold pop-ups. Kubašta's three-dimensional illustrations often stood twelve inches off the printed page, and some also included tab-activated parts that added motion to the pop-ups. Many of the titles, reproduced in English and other languages, were reprinted in numerous editions. Kubašta's complex pop-ups inspired a renewed interest in movable books that had not been seen since the end of the 19th century.

Random House was one of the first major publishers to develop a line of pop-up books, and in 1965 it inaugurated what eventually became a numbered series of forty-five titles. Their children's pop-up books, which often included tab-operated mechanicals and rotating wheels, brought life to silly riddles, stories of everyday life, fairy tales, and the adventures of such characters as the Lone Ranger and Superman. Hallmark entered the pop-up market shortly thereafter and published nearly seventy titles during the late 1960s and the 1970s on a wide range of subjects from traditional tales, Bible stories, and riddles to nonfiction accounts of Benjamin Franklin and space travel. Mechanisms in other movable books of the period included lift-the-flaps, mix-and-match, and carousel books with covers that could be brought together to form a circular, three-dimensional display. The term "paper engineer" was created in the 1960s to identify the artist who envisions the paper structure, designs the interlocking pieces, and ensures that illustrations stand up when the book is opened and fold back within the pages when the book is closed.

In the 1980s and 1990s publishers produced an unprecedented number of pop-up books. Ranging from small-format books for young children with pop-up letters and numbers to sophisticated books with detailed illustrations and expanded text, pop-ups were used to depict a diverse range of topics from dinosaurs, transportation, and action heroes to human reproduction. Much of the growth and success of pop-ups in the last quarter of the 20th century was a result of the formation of packaging companies and the role they played in coordinating the creation of such books for publishers. Unique skills, equipment, and techniques are required in the production of pop-up books that are not needed to manufacture flat books. The stand-up illustrations that form pop-ups are printed and die-cut by machine. But, like the movable books produced centuries before, the individual pieces are all folded, glued, and assembled by hand. Because of the handwork required to assemble them, nearly all of the pop-up books published since the 1970s have been made in South America or Asia where labor costs have been traditionally lower. A packaging company could handle all of the production details from concept to delivered product. Many publishers were able to offer pop-ups for sale because they could acquire shelf-ready books from a packaging company and did not need in-house production specialists. Packagers were also able to reproduce the text in multiple languages without changing the pop-ups, thus contributing to the international distribution of popular titles.

During the 1980s and 1990s hundreds of pop-up books were produced each year, significantly surpassing all other previous publication rates. Yet, even though more than a thousand English-language pop-up titles were published in each of those decades, only a small number of people created the three-dimensional mechanicals. The most prolific and significant artists and paper engineers of the period included David Carter, Robert Crowther, James Roger Diaz, Dick Dudley, David Hawcock, Kees Moerbeek, Keith Moseley, Chuck Murphy, Ib Penick, Jan Pienkowski, John Strejan, Robert Sabuda, and Ron Van der Meer.

By the end of the 20th century, while pop-up book production was beginning to decline, many of the books that were being published included increasingly complex mechanicals. Paper engineers augmented pop-up pages with gate folds that extended the size of the printed page, encasing additional text and smaller displays underneath. Individual pop-ups often included complicated interlocking paper parts and were enhanced with glitter, foil, tactile inserts, and even sound chips and lights activated by the turning of a page.

Contemporary pop-up and movable books are not just ordinary books. Full of handmade paper sculptures, they are sophisticated creations with intricate mechanical devices, and their ingenious designs continue to surprise, entertain, and even educate readers as they have for centuries.

[*See also* Publishers and Publishing *and articles on counting and biographies of figures mentioned in this article.*]

BIBLIOGRAPHY

Balzer, Richard. *Peepshows: A Visual History*. New York: Abrams, 1998.

Dawson, Michael. "S. Louis Giraud and the Development of Pop-Up Books." *Antiquarian Book Monthly Review* 18 (1 May 1991): 218–222.
Haining, Peter. *Movable Books: An Illustrated History*. London: New English Library, 1979.
Meggendorfer, Lothar. *The Genius of Lothar Meggendorfer*. New York: Random House, 1985.
Montanaro, Ann R. *Pop-Up and Movable Books: A Bibliography*. Metuchen, N.J.: Scarecrow Press, 1993.
Muir, Percy. *English Children's Books, 1600–1900*. London: Batsford, 1954.

ANN R. MONTANARO

Mowat, Farley (1921–), one of the most famous and controversial Canadian writers, popular with adults and children. Mowat was born in Belleville, Ontario, but he lived in various places, gaining a knowledge of prairie wildlife and a love of the north. After military service in World War II, he studied biology at the University of Toronto. Summer fieldwork developed his concern for both the animals and the people of the Barrens and led to his first book, *People of the Deer* (1952), about the Ilhalmiut, a vanishing tribe of Inuit (Eskimos). Mowat's knowledge of the Arctic colors two children's books. *Lost in the Barrens* (1956) is a conventional but exciting wilderness survival tale in which two stranded boys learn that even the apparently hostile north can provide sustenance if one knows and respects nature. Mowat has called its sequel, *The Curse of the Viking Grave* (1966), a "potboiler": inadequacies in plotting and characterization undermine its discussion of serious issues, such as the plight of the Ilhalmiut. A third adventure novel for children, *The Black Joke* (1962), avoids didacticism in recounting the heroic efforts of three Depression-era boys who recover a boat that a sly businessman has taken from a Newfoundland fisherman. Mowat is most celebrated for his stories about animals. *Owls in the Family* (1961) is both an account of the humorous antics of two pet owls and a nostalgic look at a boyhood spent close to nature. The adult book on which it is based, *The Dog Who Wouldn't Be* (1957), a comic tale of an eccentric dog, is accessible to older children, as is *Never Cry Wolf* (1963), a fictionalized account of Mowat's university field study. This book sympathetically portrays a wolf family in order to destroy the myth that the wolf is a bloodthirsty killer.

BIBLIOGRAPHY

King, James. *Farley: The Life of Farley Mowat*. Toronto: Harper FlamingoCanada, 2002.
Lucas, Alex. *Farley Mowat*. Toronto: McClelland and Stewart, 1976.
Orange, John. *Farley Mowat: Writing the Squib*. Toronto: ECW, 1993.

RAYMOND JONES

Mphahlele, Es'kia (1919–), leading black South African writer, literary critic, and teacher. For some time during the period of apartheid, Mphahlele, whose first name was originally Ezekiel, lived in exile and his works were proscribed. His autobiography to 1957, *Down Second Avenue* (1959), contains memorable scenes of his childhood as a rural herd boy in a rundown Pretorian neighborhood, which make it suitable for young readers. The sequel is *Afrika My Music: An Autobiography 1957–1983* (1984). The narrator of the didactic youth novel *Father Come Home* (1984) tells his life story in episodic fashion with digressions, following the social history of the oppression of blacks through the 20th century. This is the only youth novel of the period by a black writer, and it gives an authentic picture of the customs and way of life of Mphahlele's people, with dialogue in English intended to convey the style of the mother tongue: "The ancestors are wise, wife of my brother, . . . hear me tell you." Mphahlele's short story for children, "The Dream of Our Time" (1991), teaches that knowledge will uplift them and change their country for the better.

ELWYN JENKINS

Mudrak, Edmund (1894–1965), Austrian ethnologist and editor of several collections of folk tales, legends, and myths for young people, some of which are still in print in German-speaking countries. At the University of Vienna Mudrak wrote his dissertation on the Wieland legend. Before 1945 he edited the series *Dürrs Sammlung deutscher Sagen* (Dürr's Collection of German Legends) and *Märchen der Ostvölker* (Folktales of the Eastern People). His nationalism led him to became a professor of ethnology at the University of Posen in occupied Poland. After World War II he published adaptations of traditional stories for young people: *Das grosse Buch der Volkssagen* (Big Book of Legends, written with Eduard Rothemund, 1959); *Die Sagen der Germanen* (Legends of the Germanic People, 1961); and *Nordische Götter- und Heldensagen* (Northern Legends of Gods and Heroes, 1961). Mudrak's sources were mostly northern and middle European tradition, medieval German chronicles, and 19th-century ethnological collections. Occasionally he drew on other cultures, as in *Das grosse Buch der Fabeln* (Big Book of Fables, 1962).

BERND DOLLE-WEINKAUFF

Mühlenweg, Fritz (1898–1961), German translator and author, mainly of travel stories. In 1927–1932 he accompanied the Swedish explorer Sven Hedin on three expeditions into the heart of Mongolia. Mühlenweg's first books for young readers are based on these experiences. His main work *In geheimer Mission durch die Wüste Gobi* (1950; *Big Tiger and Christian*, 1952) is considered one of the most beautiful adventure books in world literature. The story about a friendship between a Chinese and a German boy describes their adventurous trip and is an appeal to respect other people and cultures. *Nuni: Die Geschichte eines langen Heimwegs, bei dem die Sterne halfen* (Nuni: The Story of a Long Journey Home, Helped by the Stars, 1953) is also adventurous, but in this case the description is fablelike. This book, written as early as 1936, has been compared to Saint-Exupéry's *Little Prince*. Since the 1990s, Mühlenweg's works are being rediscovered.

[*See also* Germany.]

ANDREA WEINMANN

Muir, Percy (1894–1979), distinguished English antiquarian bookseller whose pioneering, elegant, erudite works about historical children's books helped define the subject as worthy of serious attention. Muir discovered the field in 1945 (and began collecting), when he purchased the F. R. Bussell collection. In 1946, inspired by Bussell's riches, he organized a landmark exhibition of over a thousand items at the National Book League and wrote the accompanying catalog, *Children's Books of Yesterday*. In 1954, Muir produced *English Children's Books* as an alternative to Darton's standard history of the genre, which was then out of print. Although indebted to Darton, Muir used a wider range of sources than had been available to his predecessor, as well as incorporating significant advances in scholarship since 1930, such as the the Opies' work. Muir's *Victorian Illustrated Books* (1971) was among the first sympathetic reappraisals of a traditionally undervalued era, including its children's books.

[*See also* Opie, Iona, and Peter Opie.]

BIBLIOGRAPHY

Book Collector 29, no. 1 (Spring 1980): 85–88. Unsigned obituary.

ANDREA IMMEL

Mukerji, Dhan Gopal (1890–1936), Indian American writer. Born near Calcutta into a Brahmin family, Mukerji became a Hindu priest before attending the University of Calcutta, Tokyo University, the University of California at Berkeley, and Stanford University. He emigrated to the United States in 1910. Although he wrote adult literature, including poetry, plays, nonfiction, and his 1923 autobiography *Caste and Outcast*, he is best known for his children's books, which render in English Hindu folklore and life and tell vivid stories of animals and humans in the Indian jungle. His first children's book, *Kari, the Elephant* (1922), was followed by the story collection *Jungle Beasts and Men* (1923) and *Hari, the Jungle Lad* (1924). His best-known book is the Newbery Medal winner *Gay-Neck: The Story of a Pigeon* (1927), about a carrier pigeon who serves in World War I. *Ghond, the Hunter* (1928) features a Hindu boy's training as a hunter. Other titles include *Hindu Fables for Little Children* (1929) and *Fierce-Face: The Story of a Tiger* (1936). The content of some of his work has been criticized as inappropriate for children, but he believed children understand mature themes. Mukerji committed suicide in New York City in 1936.

ADRIENNE E. GAVIN

Mullen, Michael (1937–), Irish novelist. Most of his work for children is in the form of historical fiction. It comprises *Sea Wolves from the North* (1983) and *The Viking Princess* (1988), set in Viking times; and a quintet of novels, including *The Little Drummer Boy* (1989) and *To Hell or Connaught* (1994), set in 17th-century Ireland. In later books, such as *Michelangelo* (1994) and *The Last Days of the Romanovs* (1995), he found his inspiration in European history. He has also written animal fiction; a nativity story; and a gently humorous fantasy, *Magus the Lollipop Man* (1981).

ROBERT DUNBAR

Müller, Jörg (1942–), Swiss illustrator and winner of the Andersen Medal in 1994. After attending the school of applied arts in Biel, Müller lived in Paris until 1967, working as a graphic designer. After returning to Switzerland, he produced a series of pictures showing the changes in a countryside over the course of twenty years, *Alle Jahre wieder saust der Presslufthammer nieder oder die Veränderung der Landschaft* (1973; English trans., *The Changing Countryside*, 1977). A similar work, *Hier fällt ein Haus, dort steht ein Kran und ewig droht der Baggerzahn oder die Veränderung der Stadt* (1976; English trans., *The Changing City*, 1977), is also impressive in its photographic accuracy. Working with the Swiss author Jörg Steiner, he produced many successful picture books, for example, *Der Bär, der ein Bär bleiben wollte* (1976; English trans., *The Bear Who Wanted to Stay a Bear*, 1986), *Die Kanincheninsel* (1977; English trans., *Rabbit Island*, 1978), and *Der Aufstand der Tiere oder Die neuen Stadtmusikanten* (The Animal's Rebellion; or, The New Town Musicians, 1989).

BETTINA KÜMMERLING-MEIBAUER

Mullins, Patricia (1952–), award-winning Australian creator of children's books whose interest in animals, toys, soft sculpture, and puppetry is reflected in many of her books. Her own works include *Fabulous Beasts* (1976), *Dinosaur Encore* (1992), *V Is for Vanishing: An Alphabet of Endangered Animals* (1993), and her reference book, *The Rocking Horse: A History of Moving Toy Horses* (1992). As an illustrator she has worked with authors such as Mem Fox (*Hattie and the Fox*, 1986, *Shoes from Grandpa*, 1989) and Christobel Mattingley (*Rummage*, 1981, *The Magic Saddle*, 1983). She is well known for her use of mixed media, an approach that enables her to extend her experimentation in technique and media and to individualize her artwork to suit the particular needs of a text. She is, however, best known for the softly textured effects she creates with tissue collages, as in *Dinosaur Encore* (1992) and *One Horse Waiting for Me* (1997).

[*See also biographies of authors mentioned in this article.*]

SUSAN CLANCY

Multiculturalism. Front cover of *Esperanza Rising* by Pam Muñoz Ryan (New York: Scholastic/Blue Sky Press, 2002). COURTESY OF ISABEL SCHON

Multiculturalism. Multiculturalism can be defined simply as the inclusion of, appreciation of, and respect for all cultures; but a more complex formulation includes a challenge to social inequality, and to the power structure that subordinates people on the basis of race, ethnicity, class, gender, sexual orientation, ability, age, and religion. Although multicultural literature is often perceived as literature by people of color or by others with a history of subjugation, the term as applied to children's books has been broadened. Children's book critics often connect multiculturalism with the educational and aesthetic impact of the literature, irrespective of long-standing oppression or discrimination. In any case, notions of culture, class, and political power are embedded in most definitions, and all involve some degree of controversy. Which populations, for example, are to be included, and which ones excluded? Who determines this? Is a specific group looked on as the "norm"? By emphasizing people of color, some scholars believe that centuries of exclusion can, to some degree, be redressed. Moreover, they argue, this historically underrepresented population will remain underrepresented if the focus shifts to criteria determined by socioeconomic class, gender, and so on. Some commentators contend that the group constituted of white, Protestant, European, middle-class males has a weaker claim for inclusion in a multicultural canon; but others argue that to exclude the "majority" establishes another norm, relegating nonmembers to a new version of "otherness." Besides, there are many distinct cultures represented by people with roots in European soil.

Another controversy revolves around authorship and its role in producing authentic, accurate literature. Several questions arise: Does membership in a group ensure authenticity, or are there as many differences within groups as between them? How can one discount the power of lived experience? When does social conscience become social consciousness? How can authors avoid condescension and stereotyping? How can educational "gatekeepers" prepare young readers to distinguish truth from invention?

Critics and Commentators

Historically, the National Council of Teachers of English (NCTE) was a leader in urging teachers and librarians to pay attention to an expanding world. In 1947, NCTE published *Reading Ladders for Human Relations*, although few books featured the diversity of cultures and classes that could advance a "human relations" project. Also under the aegis of NCTE, the African American librarian Charlemae Rollins had published her first book about materials appropriate for black children, *We Build Together*, in 1941. And even earlier, the African American librarian Augusta Baker started making such lists (the first in 1938) in connection with her work at the 135th Street Branch of the New York Public Library. It was difficult at that time to locate books in which African American characters held positions of power or stature. Nancy Larrick's article in the *Saturday Review of Literature*, "The All-White World of Children's Books" (1965), documented the number of books with "Negro" characters: only 6.7 percent of the publications from 1962 to 1964 contained one or more blacks, and among these, almost 60 percent were situated outside the continental United States. Most of the books, Larrick said, were "mediocre or worse." This article proved to be a trigger for changing publishers' attitudes toward books by and about African Americans. Beginning in 1966, the Council on Interracial Books for Children introduced *Interracial Books for Children Bulletin* (expanding the output from four to eight issues per year). Articles dealt with bias in books for children and also recommended constructive, multicultural titles. Largely as a result of this work, publishers actively began to seek artists and writers who could provide a more accurate and respectful picture of underrepresented people. The change, however, has not been essentially in the percentage of books published. For example, only about 8 percent of the nearly 5,000 children's books published in 2002 contained any characters of color. Nevertheless, a good percentage of these books were written by people of color and had a wide readership. In addition, a significant number of the picture books are of high aesthetic quality and offer realistic, well-conceived characterizations.

In 1972 Donnarae MacCann and Gloria Woodard edited *The Black American in Books for Children: Readings in Racism* (a second edition appeared in 1985). Many of its articles are reprints from *Interracial Books for Children Bulletin*. Essays such as these provided a scaffolding for analyzing books critically and contextually. In 1976 the first edition of Masha Kabakow Rudman's *Children's Literature: An Issues Approach* was published (there were subsequent editions in 1984 and 1995). This book broke ground by suggesting that societal issues and a sociopolitical context are legitimate concerns in evaluating the quality of a book. Rudman's first edition contained chapters about Native American and black characters as well as critical discussions of divorce, gender, war, ability, age, and sexuality. In *Shadow and Substance: Afro-American Experience in Contemporary Children's Fiction* (1982), Rudine Sims [Bishop] analyzes three categories: "social conscience" books (works intended to acquaint whites with blacks); "melting pot" books (stories positing black and white children as essentially the same); and "culturally conscious" books, which illuminate the African American experience from an African American perspective. In the field of Native American culture and experience, Oyate (founded in 1987 by Doris Seale and Beverly Slapin) provides advice and suggests materials for teachers and librarians. Scholars addressing educators and a variety of ethnic groups include Violet Harris (as in *Teaching Multicultural Literature*, 1993) and Mingshui Cai (as in *Multicultural Literature for Children and Young Adults: Reflections on Critical Issues*, 2002). Although the proportion of books by and about people of color has remained under 10 percent, an increasing number of critics are bringing a sensitive multicultural perspective to their scholarship.

Publishers have also played a key role in encouraging books with multicultural themes. Lee and Low is a multicultural children's literature publishing company that has issued over one hundred books representing different cultures. Children's Book Press focuses on bilingual books.

Awards

Critical acknowledgement of a literature supporting multiculturalism has grown over the years. This can be demonstrated partially by the number of awards granted for high-quality work. The Jane Addams Book Award, which began in 1953, recognizes books that "most effectively promote peace, social justice, world community, and the equality of the sexes and all races." The Council on Interracial Books for Children Award, established in 1968, was made annually for a number of years to encourage the publication of books written by people of color. Walter Dean Myers, Sharon Bell Mathis, Virginia Driving Hawk Sneve, and Juan Valenzuela were among the first recipients. The Coretta Scott King (CSK) Award, first presented in 1970, was established for African American authors who continued the dream of the late Martin Luther King Jr. Beginning in 1974, a similar CSK Award was presented to African American illustrators. The Carter G. Woodson Award, first presented in 1974, encourages treatment of topics concerning ethnic minorities and race relations. Awards such as the America's Award for Children's and Young Adult Literature, the Pura Belpré Award, and the Tomás Rivera Mexican American Children's Book Award honor Latino, Latina, and Caribbean authors and illustrators.

In the meantime, writers and illustrators of color were being recognized for their work through mainstream awards. Tom Feelings became the first African American artist to win the Caldecott Honor Award, in 1972. Nicholasa Mohr was the first Puerto Rican writer to win the Jane Addams Children's Book Award, in 1974. Virginia Hamilton was the first author of color to win the Newbery Medal, in 1975. Leo Dillon became the first artist of color—along with his wife, Diane—to earn the Caldecott Award; their work was honored in 1975. Ed Young became the first Chinese American to win the Caldecott Award, in 1990.

[*See also* Multiculturalism and Children's Books *and biographies of figures mentioned in this article* .]

BIBLIOGRAPHY

Bader, Barbara. "How the Little House Gave Ground: The Beginnings of Multiculturalism in a New, Black Children's Literature." *Horn Book* 78, no. 6 (November–December 2002): 657–673.

Bader, Barbara. "Multiculturalism Takes Root." *Horn Book* 79, no. 2 (March–April 2003): 143–163.

Bader, Barbara. "Multiculturalism in the Mainstream." *Horn Book* 79, no. 3 (May–June 2003): 265–280.

Cai, Mingshui. *Multicultural Literature for Children and Young Adults: Reflections on Critical Issues*. Westport, Conn.: Greenwood, 2002.

Gangi, Jane M. *Encountering Children's Literature: An Arts Approach*. Boston, Mass.: Pearson, 2004.

Harris, Violet. *Using Multiethnic Literature in the K-8 Classroom*. Norwood, Mass.: Christopher-Gordon, 1997.

Slapin, Beverly, and Doris Seale, eds. *Through Indian Eyes: The Native Experience in Books for Children*. Philadelphia, Pa.: New Society, 1992.

MASHA KABAKOW RUDMAN

Multiculturalism and Children's Books. It is often assumed in discussions of children's literature that self-evident and universal meanings attach to the term "multicultural books" and that this literature comprises texts that typically celebrate cultural plurality. However, both multiculturalism and its connections with children's literature involve complex and unstable concepts and ideologies. First, the concept "multiculturalism" is notoriously resistant to definition, largely because it is used in a variety of cultural settings to encode ideas about nationhood and citizenship, and because these ideas are formulated in response to diverse historical and political movements. Second, children's texts that incorporate characters from minority groups are not necessarily multicultural merely because they reflect cultural plurality; they may well treat minorities through superficial, stereotyped, or paternalistic representations.

Multiculturalisms: National Inflections

The global migrations and displacements that followed World War II and that have continued into the 21st century have radically reshaped the populations of nation-states. Discourses of multiculturalism have been mobilized to help regulate migrants in countries across the globe, including Australia, the United Kingdom, Germany, Italy, France, Canada, the Netherlands, India, New Zealand, and the United States. Governments and policy makers have called on multiculturalism as a framework for situating ethnic and cultural diversity within the unifying idea of the nation. At the same time, individuals and groups within nation-states have sought to use policies of multiculturalism in order to gain rights and opportunities.

But the term itself and its implementation in official and cultural practices is subject to vigorous debates wherever it is used. In Australia, the idea that the nation is built on a foundation of Britishness survives despite the fact that more than 20 percent of Australians were born in countries other than Australia, and among conservative groups, multiculturalism is blamed for the dilution of national identity. A defining factor in Canadian versions of multiculturalism is the proximity of the United States, which drives Canadian formulations of nationhood toward claims of unity and common purpose while members of minority groups resist homogenization. In the United States the term "multiculturalism" appears most often in debates about education; but this society's efforts to lump together ethnic, African American, and indigenous minorities have been predictably unsuccessful, given the different histories of these people as immigrants, slaves, and a rapidly exterminated population. As for Australian and Canadian Aboriginal people, as well as the Mao-

Multiculturalism and Children's Books. Front cover illustration by Eric Velasquez for his *Los discos de mi abuela* (New York: Scholastic/Lectorum Publications, 2002). COURTESY OF ISABEL SCHON

ris in New Zealand, they have strongly resisted incorporation into multicultural discourses, since their history involves invasion by a European power and not migration. In Germany, the Netherlands, and France, among other European nations, the concept of multiculturalism is bound up with rights to citizenship, especially in relation to guest workers and refugees.

During the 1960s and 1970s, activist groups in the United States and the United Kingdom drew attention to the fact that few children's books presented the lives of nonwhite characters or addressed issues of racism. In the United States the Council on Interracial Books for Children (CIBC) was founded in 1965, producing a publication, *Interracial Books for Children*, that advocated on behalf of minority groups and reviewed numerous new and best-selling children's books; for instance, this journal (published quarterly and then expanding to eight issues per year) carried reviews that sharply criticized William Armstrong's *Sounder* and Theodore Taylor's *The Cay* for privileging the dominant culture and for the reflex racism of their representations of African American characters and cultures. In Britain, the Writers and Readers Publishing Co-operative produced the influential publication *Racism and Sexism in Children's Books* (1975), which included critiques of Roald Dahl's *Charlie and the Chocolate Factory* and the *Doctor Dolittle* books, among other popular texts. In Australia and Canada, where national policies on multiculturalism were adopted in the early 1970s, educators and publishers recognized the importance of texts that afforded models of multiculturalism through representations of social practice.

Although civil rights activism, increasing migration levels, and national policy developments have since the 1960s focused attention on how children's books negotiate questions of race and plurality, the term "multicultural" books remains problematic. As Donnarae MacCann demonstrates in her introduction to *The Lion and the Unicorn*'s focus issue "Anti-Racism and Children's Literature" (2001), the political correctness debates of the 1990s provided ammunition for a conservative backlash against multiculturalism. Groups such as CIBC were charged with suppressing the rights of authors and promoting a Communist-inspired social realism. There are, however, more substantive questions to address in considering multiculturalism and children's literature: for instance, do children's books represent minority groups merely as a colorful backdrop to narratives of identity formation featuring white characters? Are such books "multicultural"? Are writers obliged to be from minority groups in order to write about them? What constitutes "authenticity" in representations of the cultures and practices of minorities?

The Production of Multicultural Books: A Question of Positioning

In *Language and Ideology in Children's Fiction*, John Stephens argues that the processes through which readers engage with texts are similar to interactions in which readers engage with other people; in other words, they involve negotiations of meaning. Additionally, texts replicate how language is used in the real world to conduct interpersonal relations. It follows that if children from minority groups are offered only texts that accept as natural the norms and values of the majority culture, they will be forced into a status as outsiders. They will have only remote ties to the imagined worlds offered in those books. On the other hand, a text whose narrative is enunciated from within a minority group has, potentially, two effects: it offers a meaningful subjective experience to children from this group, and it positions cultural outsiders to engage with difference.

Authors are themselves located in particular cultures, and construct themselves textually within narratives. When authors represent characters and practices outside their own experience and personal knowledge—especially when writers from dominant groups construct narratives located within minority cultures—they do not necessarily cast off the habits of thought and conditioned beliefs that have formed them as subjects. If authors' knowledge of minority groups is confined to what other members of the dominant culture have said or written about them, they may rely on received wisdom—that is, on stereotypes, cultural conventions, and impressions—rather than on firsthand knowledge or even on research. Thus, while most people would agree that authors are entitled to represent characters and perspectives outside their own cultures, such representations are by no means easy or unproblematic.

A crucial concern pertains to the effects of representation and the ethical considerations involved. Authors and illustrators who represent groups unfamiliar to them have an ethical responsibility to consider the effects of their representations. In children's literature, such considerations include scrutiny of the reading positions constructed by a text, and the ideologies promoted through language and narrative. However, because ideologies are to a large degree embedded in language and visual codes, they are not often apparent to authors and illustrators; nor are the good intentions of authors any guarantee that their texts will have positive discursive or material effects.

An example of the operation of implicit ideologies can be seen in an Australian picture book, *Mr. Plunkett's Pool* (1992), written by Gillian Rubinstein and illustrated by Terry Denton. Although this book won the Multi-Cultural Children's Literature Award in 1993, it presumes an Australia in which cultural diversity is subsumed into mass consumerism. The narrative involves a group of ethnically differentiated children (Asian, Greek, Anglo) who live on a street where an advertising executive, Mr. Plunkett, buys a mansion and installs a swimming pool. He refuses to allow the children to swim in his pool, until the children invent a "Vintoopling Machine," which enables them to propel themselves over Mr. Plunkett's fence and into the pool. This they do at the very moment that Mr. Plunkett's boss threatens him with the loss of his job unless he can devise the "Ultimate New Way" to sell lemonade. It occurs to Mr. Plunkett that the "Asian" children swimming in his pool among plastic dolphins look "just like a commercial." He uses the image of the children launching themselves from "a giant fizzy lemonade bottle into a giant fizzy lemonade pool," to generate a successful commercial, which makes the children (Kim and Lee) famous and rich. The children then install their own pool in which "everyone in the street" swims. Superficially, *Mr. Plunkett's Pool* may appear to be an endorsement of multiculturalism in its representation of ethnically diverse characters engaged in a common enterprise. However, there remains the implication that images of cultural diversity are positive insofar as they support global capitalism and consumerism—that is, insofar as they are "good for business." In this way the book promotes those weak versions of Australian multiculturalism that rely on images of happy, ethnically diverse citizens to construct a myth of a unified nation.

Authenticity and Universalism

The term "authentic" in discussions of multiculturalism and children's literature is frequently used as a synonym for "true" or "accurate." Applied to minority groups, "authentic" representations are generally held to be true to some "original" or, at least, "ancient" model. For instance, the assumption that African American culture is defined by an attachment to family or that Italians are always excitable—these are spurious and essentialized expressions of authenticity. Applied to individual characters, authenticity is most often associated with the idea that there exists a stable, permanent core of identity that, when discovered or uncovered, confers a sense of self.

These ideas of authentic selves and cultures derive from the Enlightenment and its privileging of individuality and rationality. They continue to exert a strong influence on children's literature, which often focuses on individual growth and identity formation. Questions must be asked about claims to authenticity: Who determines what is authentic? Who judges when authenticity is achieved? It is not the case that only members of minorities can deliver authentic versions of their cultures, even when such authors write out of their experience, because no one author can represent the diversity of experiences, views, and values across a culture. And since identity formation is forged out of multiple factors, such as gender, location, age, and education, there is no single mode of minority membership. Nor is it sufficient to invoke the real-life experience of minorities as a benchmark for authenticity, since fiction always operates to achieve narrative outcomes and does not simply mirror the real world. While it is clearly desirable that authors from minorities should be better represented in children's literature (which continues to be dominated by authors, illustrators, publishers, and editors from majority cultures), it does not follow that such authors will automatically address the diversity and complexity of minority experience.

The eponymous protagonist of the Canadian novel *Spud Sweetgrass* (1992), by Brian Doyle, describes himself as "part Irish and part Abo and part of a whole lot of other things" and his girlfriend, Connie Pan, as "half Vietnamese and half Chinese." Within the novel's formulation of Spud as a multicultural Canadian subject, the narrative privileges his Aboriginal heritage over other ethnicities. His progress toward self-actualization is plotted through his achievement of an "authentic" Aboriginal identity, figured through a narrow range of representations: that is, to be an Aboriginal subject involves environmental activism, disregard for authority, and respect for spirituality. The limitations of this mode of representation are apparent, as seen in the way they rest on a false premise—namely, the presence of a preexisting, fixed Aboriginal subjectivity. Moreover, whiteness is taken for granted as the standard against which Aboriginality is defined.

Notions of authenticity are especially troubling when they are applied to retellings of traditional stories. For indigenous peoples who have experienced the dislocations and traumas of colonization, orally transmitted stories often hold crucial cultural meaning, especially when they are associated with ritual practices. Moreover, in many indigenous groups, including Native American communities and Aboriginal clans in Canada and Australia, there exist cultural protocols as to who is entitled to tell and hear particular stories, and stories are often connected to places and kinship groups. The retelling of these stories by nonindigenous authors can be an act of textual colonization, especially as many retellings themselves rely on earlier retellings by nonindigenous "experts," as is the case with Paul Goble's picture books. Moreover, indigenous stories retold in English and other languages are often transformed into European tales that accommodate European narrative practices. Indigenous authors and illustrators are best equipped to produce retellings of their own narratives, and retellings should always include information about their traditional owners. The term "multicultural" is a misleading description when applied to retellings that have been so reconfigured that they bear scant relationship to the cultural traditions that they claim to represent. For example, stories drawn from Native American sources, but so unconnected with these sources that they distort a tale's content, include publications such as Penny Pollock's *The Turkey Girl: A Zuni Cinderella Story* (1996).

If notions of authenticity must be treated with care, the same is true for claims of universalism. When a text originating from a minority culture is said to have universal meanings, this frequently means that it has been interpreted in connection with values and ideologies prevalent in the dominant culture. However, insisting on diverse meanings does not imply that stories originating from minority cultures will be incomprehensible to mainstream readers. On the contrary, it suggests that different reading practices are required in order to understand and appreciate the stories. Such an approach goes far beyond notions of "tolerance," which merely reinstate the prevailing relations of power, or which merely offer the dominant group a chance to parade its superiority through forbearance of its "Others." Instead of "tolerance," there is this clear-cut maxim: the necessity of reading texts in relation to the narrative and linguistic traditions that inform them.

Reading Multiculturalisms in Children's Books

Multiculturalisms in children's books can be traced along a continuum of representational practices. At one end is the minimalist strategy of incorporating signs of cultural pluralism through unmarked references: in picture books, by way of visual representations of different ethnicities, and in novels, through details such as characters' proper names. Texts that merely signal the presence of ethnic minorities sometimes function in tokenistic ways, especially if characters from minority cultures are present predominantly as local color and are not attributed with individuality or agency, or if they are always figured as sidekicks to characters from the dominant culture. Another common narrative schema is one in which pluralism is represented as a resource or a benefit, so that characters from the dominant mainstream gain knowledge or advance in maturity through exposure to difference.

At the other end of the continuum are texts that engage explicitly with themes of interracial relations, or bring a meaningful emphasis to characters within minority cultures, or incorporate linguistic and narrative strategies characteristic of those cultures. In Laurence Yep's *The Star Fisher* (1991), for instance, the first-person narrator is the Chinese American Joan Lee, and the novel is set in a town in West Virginia where Joan's parents establish a laundry in 1927. The narrative traces the interplay between Joan's desire to be accepted into white culture and her sense of herself as a Chinese American subject. Her experience of navigating between cultures is symbolized by a Chinese story concerning a magical being (the star fisher of the title) who takes on human form and is trapped on earth when a farmer falls in love with her and hides the cloak that transforms her into a golden kingfisher. The star fisher story, with its themes of loss, change, and longing, operates as an analogue with the primary narrative, in which Joan Lee and her family struggle against racial prejudice. Although the novel's closure ostensibly celebrates the family's integration into the town's community, the significance of the star fisher story complicate, this happy ending, pointing to the effects of migration and their repercussions through generations of descendants.

The field of multicultural studies covers a broad spectrum of concepts and approaches. One common approach in children's texts and the critical discourses associated with them is that of "liberal multiculturalism." This critical method foregrounds inclusiveness and diversity, treating difference in terms of essentialized modes of being that are then realized "authentically" in certain children's books. Additionally, a way to approach the foregrounding of inclusiveness is to treat different literary works as connected with specific systems of aesthetics. This method takes its direction from the artistic philosophies and practices known to generations of literary artists and critics—people who have become immersed in the details of these aesthetic traditions. Native American aesthetics, black aesthetics, and so on are categories tied to historical group experience, but they have, arguably, a closer connection to art than to ultranationalism or a narrowly defined distinctiveness.

Another critical framework is one designated as "critical multiculturalism"—a conceptual approach outlined by Peter McLaren in his essay "White Terror and Oppositional Agency: Towards a Critical Multiculturalism." McLaren advocates a politicized and historicized approach that attends to the interplay between texts and the cultural conditions that shape them. Applied to children's literature, critical multiculturalism analyzes the political agendas of children's texts, whether implicit or explicit; it considers how subject positions are effected; it valorizes multiple narrative traditions; and it is attentive to the textual instabilities and contradictions that signal struggles over meaning.

The domain of postcolonial studies and the emerging fields of whiteness studies and diasporic studies offer further strategies and concepts relevant to multiculturalism and children's literature. Postcolonial studies deploy an array of concepts that emphasize the investigation of how texts represent colonialism and its effects in contemporary postcolonial nations. Whiteness studies draw attention to how the power and privilege of whiteness embedded in European colonialism is naturalized and invisible within multicultural societies. Diasporic studies attend to the consequences of dispersal and resettlement over successive generations, and to textual representations of memory, nationhood, and identities among diasporic groups. Of children's texts that pivot on the experiences of diasporic communities, Allen Say's *Grandfather's Journey* (1993) is a fine example, tracing the interior experiences of affection and attachment that characterize journeys to and from Japan and California by a Japanese family. As *Grandfather's Journey* demonstrates, interracial and cross-cultural relations involve complex negotiations between human subjects and between cultures; and increasingly, children's literature is a site where such negotiations are played out.

[*See also* Council on Interracial Books for Children; Critical Approaches to Children's Literature; Interracial Books for Children; Multiculturalism; *and articles on people, countries, and book types mentioned in this article.*]

BIBLIOGRAPHY

Bradford, Clare. " 'Oh How Different!': Regimes of Knowledge in Aboriginal Texts for Children." *The Lion and the Unicorn* 27, no. 2 (2003): 199–217.

Cai, Mingshui. *Multicultural Literature for Children and Young Adults: Reflections on Critical Issues*. Westport, Conn.: Greenwood, 2002.

Hage, Ghassan. *White Nation: Fantasies of White Supremacy in a Multicultural Society*. Annandale, Australia: Pluto, 1998.

MacCann, Donnarae. "Editor's Introduction: Racism and Antiracism, Forty Years of Theories and Debates." *The Lion and the Unicorn* 25 (2001): 337–352.

McLaren, Peter. "White Terror and Oppositional Agency: Towards a Critical Multiculturalism." In *Multiculturalism: A Critical Reader*, edited by D. T. Goldberg, 45–74. Oxford: Blackwell, 1994.

Stephens, John. *Language and Ideology in Children's Fiction*. London and New York: Longman, 1992.

CLARE BRADFORD

Bruno Munari. Illustration from *Gigi cerca il suo berretto* (Verona, Italy: Mondadori, c. 1945). REPRODUCED COURTESY OF THE COTSEN CHILDREN'S LIBRARY, PRINCETON UNIVERSITY LIBRARY

Munari, Bruno (1907–1998), prolific and prominent Italian illustrator and writer (as well as industrial designer, painter, sculptor, and photographer), whose innovative illustrations have adorned the publications of equally original writers, especially those of Gianni Rodari. Munari's work established itself as avant-garde even during the fascism of the 1930s, a culturally conservative period. He has used many techniques and styles, from the subdued elegance of trees in gray silhouette, to the surreal and linear, to potato and other vegetable prints, to faux-naif eruptions of penciled color in margins and between lines of text in imitation of children's daubs and doodles. Writing copiously for adults on art and design, Munari stressed the paradoxical importance of both the rules of art and a vision free from preconceptions. He paved the way for future generations of writers and artists through the fertility of his imagination and expertise. He reworked the traditional and the popular, in 1972 devising his impressive Green, Yellow, Blue, and White versions of Little Red Riding Hood and writing new nursery rhymes and verse stories in *Alfabetiere* (Alphabet Book, 1972). An earlier ABC had provided a primary school reader for use with new teaching methods (1960). Meanwhile he experimented not only with graphic style but also with book technology, employing different types of paper for *Nella nebbia di Milano* (In the Fog of Milan, 1968; U.S. title, *The*

Circus in the Mist, 1969) or nonpaper pages, such as the acetate used for the disintegrating blackbird of *Il merlo ha perso il becco* (The Blackbird Has Lost His Beak, 1987), besides various forms of mobile book construction, as in *Gigi cerca il suo berretto* (Louis Looks for His Cap, 1946).

BIBLIOGRAPHY

Munari, Bruno. *Bruno Books*. London: Harvill, 1953–. Trans. of *I libri Munari* (including *Georgie Has Lost His Cap*, trans. of *Gigi cerca il suo berretto*).

Munari, Bruno. *Design as Art*. Trans. by Patrick Creagh of *Arte come mestiere* (1966). Harmondsworth, U.K.: Penguin, 1971.

Munari, Bruno. *Facciamo assieme un libro da leggere: Alfabetiere secondo il metodo attivo* (Let's Make a Reading Book Together: The ABC by the Active Method). Torino, Italy: Einaudi, 1960.

Munari, Bruno. *Good Design*. Milan: All'insegna del pesce d'oro, 1963.

Munari, Bruno. *Jimmy Has Lost His Cap, Where Can It Be?* Cleveland, Ohio: World, 1959. Trans. of *Gigi cerca il suo berretto*.

Tanchis, Aldo. *Bruno Munari: From Futurism to Post-Industrial Design*. London: Lund Humphries, 1987.

Ann Lawson Lucas

Munoz, Claudio (1945–), illustrator and 1997 winner of the French Prix du livres de la mer for *The Little Captain* (1995), which he both wrote and illustrated. A native of Chile, Munoz attended college to study architecture but left to pursue a career in illustration. While he regularly publishes in magazines and newspapers, he also illustrated picture books such as *Little Pig Figwort Can't Get To Sleep* (2000), by Henrietta Branford, and *Just Another Morning* (2004), by Linda Ashman. Well respected in Britain, Munoz is admired for the versatility of his illustrations, which complement a wide range of vastly disparate texts.

Michelle H. Martin

Munro, Roxie (1945–), an American artist, dress designer, author, and illustrator of nonfiction picture books, especially the Inside-Outside series, which views famous landmarks from both their exterior and interior. Her first, *The Inside-Outside Book of New York City* (1985)—which made the *New York Times* list of Best Illustrated Children's Books—shows, for example, the Statue of Liberty from the outside as well as a view from the inside looking out over the harbor and the city. Munro has also illustrated books for other authors, including her husband, the Swedish photographer, artist, and writer Bo Zaunders, who has written three books, beginning with *Crocodiles, Camels, and Dugout Canoes: Eight Adventurous Episodes* (1998). Her illustrations for *The Inside-Outside Book of Libraries* (1996), written by Julie Cummins, depict libraries ranging from a one-room library in North Carolina to one on an aircraft carrier and another in a prison. Munro is also known for her many covers for the *New Yorker* magazine.

Linnea Hendrickson

Munsch, Robert (1945–), Canadian storyteller and picture-book writer. Born in Pittsburgh, Pennsylvania, one of nine children, Munsch was educated at Fordham, Boston University, and Tufts and spent seven years training as a Jesuit priest before turning to work in child care, where he developed his storytelling skills. After he and his wife emigrated to Canada in 1975, Munsch took a child care position at the University of Guelph, Ontario, where his storytelling talents were noticed and he began to publish picture books for children. He became a naturalized Canadian in 1983 and has since become the country's best-selling author. His stories usually begin as oral tales, which he performs over and over at festivals and (often unannounced) at child care centers, schools, and libraries. The stories that are requested most often are written down and adapted into picture books.

The books, many of them illustrated by Michael Martchenko, are characteristically humorous and nondidactic, deliberately retain a strong oral style, and often depict enterprising children triumphing over adults or over their own fears. *The Paper Bag Princess* (1980) is about an intelligent princess who rescues a prince but refuses to marry him. *Mortimer* (1983), developed from Munsch's first oral tale, concerns a boy who will not settle down after being put to bed and whose noisiness disturbs his family and the neighborhood until he eventually drifts off to sleep. Other books include *The Mud Puddle* (1979), *Murmel, Murmel, Murmel* (1982), *Good Families Don't* (1990), and *Alligator Baby* (1997), as well as films and audio recordings of his work. His best-selling book, *Love You Forever* (1986), illustrated by Sheila McGraw, differs from his usual style. It is a poignant story about the enduring love of a mother for her son that Munsch wrote in memory of his own two stillborn babies.

BIBLIOGRAPHY

Robert Munsch's Web site. http://www.robertmunsch.com.

Adrienne E. Gavin

Munsinger, Lynn (1951–), prolific American illustrator of picture and early-reader books. Munsinger loved drawing from an early age and graduated with an MFA from the Rhode Island School of Design in 1977. Her primary medium is ink washed with watercolor, and she excels at filling each drawing with action. Often without borders, her whimsical illustrations dominate pages by providing more detail than is given by the simple prose of her collaborating authors. A longtime partnership with the author Helen Lester began with *The Wizard, the Fairy, and the Magic Chicken* (1983). They have created numerous fables featuring animals, and continue to add to their popular penguin tales, the first of which was *Tacky the Penguin* (1988). In a departure from her usual picture books, Munsinger illustrated Janwillem van de Wetering's three-novel series about Hugh Pine the porcupine. She has collaborated with a number of other authors, including Joanna Cole, Judy Delton, James Howe, and Marjorie Weinman Sharmat.

CHARLOTTE CUBBAGE

Muppets. *See* Henson, Jim.

Murail, Marie-Aide (1954–), French writer; her doctoral dissertation at the Sorbonne was on the adaptation of the classics in children's literature. Murail is considered one of the great contemporary writers and is known for her humor, the liveliness of her dialogue, and her defense of new relationships between adults and children. She portrays males as responsible actors within the family, so that her hero Emilien becomes a new type of adolescent, capable of taking care of babies, in *Baby Sitters Blues* (1989). She has tackled nearly every genre—the playful initiation to languages in *Le hollandais sans peine* ("Dutch without Tears," 1989); the realistic novel in *Un séducteur-né* (A Born Seducer, 1991); the horror novel in *Amour, vampire, et loup-garou* (Love, Vampires, and Werewolves, 1998); and fantasy fiction based on games played on the Web in *Golem* (2001), written with her sister Elvire and her brother Lorris Murail.

JEAN PERROT

Murphy, Jill (1949–), British author and illustrator. Murphy's first book was *The Worst Witch* (1974). A witty version of a traditional school story, set in an academy for witches, it achieved instant popularity and was turned into a television series, a film, and a stage play. Three more Worst Witch titles followed. Murphy also produced picture books, creating affectionate and enduring series centered on the Large family (elephants) and the Bear family. These anthropomorphized characters experience situations familiar to all families in *Peace at Last* (1980) and *Five Minutes' Peace* (1986). More recently, *All for One* (2002) is a wry story of a young monster who always seems to be on the outside of the gang. Murphy works with colored pencils, building up layers of color to give depth and texture to her illustrations. The Worth Witch series is illustrated with detailed pen-and-ink drawings.

VALERIE COGHLAN

Murphy, Jim (1947–), American author especially noted for his nonfiction titles aimed at middle school students. Murphy graduated from Rutgers University and pursued graduate work at Radcliffe College. He began his career in publishing as an editorial secretary with Seabury Press (later Clarion Books) and worked his way up to become managing editor, leaving in 1977 to pursue his own writing.

Murphy's first book, *Weird and Wacky Inventions* (1978), foreshadows much of what is notable in his career. Using the resources of the U.S. Patent Office to research his book, Murphy profiles a variety of silly and generally unsuccessful gadgets, like the portable bathtub and jumping shoes. He reproduces the drawings that accompanied the original patent application and invites readers to interpret the inventions on their own. This willingness to introduce primary source material even to young readers, to present history from inviting perspectives and accessible angles, and to include a rich variety of original illustrative materials marks all of Murphy's nonfiction books; he also, with his in-text questioning of those primary sources, introduces to young readers the important concept of historiography.

Some of his most successful titles include the Newbery Honor book *The Great Fire* (1995), which explores the devastation caused by the blaze that destroyed much of Chicago in 1871; *Blizzard! The Storm That Changed America* (2000), which describes the terrible snowstorms of 1888, and *An American Plague: The True and Terrifying Story of the Yellow Fever Epidemic of 1793* (2003), which chronicles the course and effects of a devastating disease. Murphy intersperses his narration with personal accounts harvested from the historic record, drawing readers into the terror and excitement of these events. Careful research also forms the foundation of his other writing, such as the picture book *Dinosaur for a Day* (1992) and the young adult novel *The Story of James Edmond Pease: A Civil War Union Soldier, Virginia, 1863* (1998).

[*See also* Historical Fiction *and* Nonfiction.]

MEGAN LYNN ISAAC

Murphy, Shirley Rousseau (1928–), American writer and artist. Born in Oakland, California, Murphy was educated at the California School of Fine Arts and had an art career before moving to the Panama Canal Zone for a few years in the early 1960s, where she began writing for children and young adults. Her earliest books were realist fiction, including the horse books *The Sand Ponies* (1967) and *White Ghost Summer* (1967). *Poor Jenny, Bright as a Penny* (1974) tells the story of a girl who is happily adopted after facing such difficulties as an alcoholic and abusive birth mother. Murphy's young adult fantasies include the Ring of Fire quintet, which begins with *The Ring of Fire* (1977), and the Dragonbards trilogy culminating in *The Dragonbards* (1988). Humorous books for younger readers include *Mrs. Tortino's Return to the Sun* (1980). Murphy has recently achieved success with her adult Joe Grey cat detective series (1996–).

Adrienne E. Gavin

Musäus, Johann Karl August (1735–1787), German author and critic whose five volumes of fairy tales, *Volksmärchen der Deutschen* (German Folk Tales, 1782–1786), introduced the fairy tale as a modern form in Germany. In style, Musäus was a writer of the Enlightenment, and his fairy tale collections were based on chronicles, legends, and folk tales still in oral circulation in his time. In the tales old narrative traditions can be heard, but these have been revised by the author, who used them as his source of inspiration to develop the literary tale. Encouraged by Christoph Martin Wieland (1733–1813), another key writer of literary fairy tales in Germany. Musäus wrote and published with a bourgeois audience in mind. The tales are not children's literature in the sense that the works of the Grimm brothers and Hans Christian Andersen were—they contain no romantic retrospection on childhood, and they do not take place against the background of the adult world. Rather, Musäus's tales depict highly civilized realms, playing imagination, intellect, and irony against one another in order to delight and instruct. As early modern literary tales they had an important influence on Andersen's works.

Helene Høyrup

Musgrove, Margaret (1943–), African American author and educator. Musgrove has lived and traveled in West Africa; she spent 1997 in Ghana on a Fulbright grant to research children's stories. *The Spider Weaver: A Legend of Kente Cloth* (2001) is a story still told today about the master spider weaver's gift to the weavers of Ghana. In *Ashanti to Zulu: African Traditions*, with illustrations by Leo and Diane Dillon (1976), Musgrove provides a lesson in the diversity of African cultures. She spotlights African ethnicities from A to Z by briefly describing the legends, traditions, dwellings, garments, and ways of life of each ethnic group. This book, which won the Caldecott Medal in 1977, serves as a way to counter what she has called "the insidious forces that must be overcome for the good of all children," that is, "the overt and covert racism in children's literature."

[*See also* African American Literature *and* Dillon, Leo, and Diane Dillon.]

Mahoumbah Klobah

Mwangi, Meja (1948–), Kenyan filmmaker, satirist, and renowned author of some of the most highly regarded African thrillers for young readers. Born in Nyeri, Mwangi worked with the French Broadcasting Corporation and the British Council in Nairobi before turning to full-time writing. *The Bushtrackers* (1979), *Bread of Sorrow* (1987), and *Jimi the Dog* (1990) are some of his popular masterpieces of the thriller genre. His early novels, *Carcase for Hounds* (1974) and *Taste of Death* (1975), recapture the history and sociopolitical conditions in post-independence Kenya. His first successful novel, *Kill Me Quick* (1973), as well as *Going Down River Road* (1976) and *Striving for the Wind* (1990), explore his frequent theme of human degradation. More recently, *The Last Plague* (2002) tackles the threat posed by HIV-AIDS to the young generation. Mwangi has won the Kenyatta Prize for Literature, the Afro-Asian Writers Award, and the Adolf Lotus Grimme Award.

Aaron Mushengyezi

Myers, Christopher (1975–), African American illustrator. The son of Walter Dean Myers, Christopher Myers studied at Brown University and the Whitney Museum of American Art. *Harlem: A Poem* (1997), for which his father wrote the text, was named a Caldecott Honor Book and a Coretta Scott King Honor Book and received several other commendations. Known especially for evocative and deftly composed multimedia collages, Myers has also collaborated with his father on several young adult offerings, including *Shadow of the Red Moon* (1995), *Monster* (1999), and *A Time* *to Love: Stories from the Old Testament* (2003), as well as *Blues Journey* (2003), a picture book. Myers's solo efforts as author and illustrator include *Black Cat* (1999), *Wings* (2000), and *Fly!* (2001). A Coretta Scott King award runner-up, *Black Cat* was also an ALA Notable Book. Myers's dedication to celebrating African American culture is also visible in projects such as his adaptation and illustration of Zora Neale Hurston's *Lies and Other Tall Tales* (2005).

PEGGY LIN DUTHIE

Myers, Walter Dean (1937–), among the most important and prolific African American writers of contemporary young adult fiction. Myers is a nine-time winner of the Coretta Scott King Author Award for *Slam* (1998), *Now Is Your Time!: The African American Struggle for Freedom* (1991), *Fallen Angels* (1988), *Motown and Didi* (1984), and *The Young Landlords* (1979), the and Honor books *Monster* (1999), *Harlem: A Poem* (1997), *Malcolm X* (1993), and *Somewhere in the Darkness* (1992). Myers has also won the Newbery Honor Award twice (for *Somewhere in the Darkness* and *Scorpions*, 1988) and a Caldecott Honor Award (for *Harlem: A Poem*). In addition, Myers was the first to receive both the annual Virginia Hamilton Literary Award and the Michael L. Printz Award for Excellence in Young Adult Literature, for *Monster*. An impressively diverse writer, Myers has published picture books, fiction, nonfiction, adventure, science fiction, biographies, and mystery books, but he is best known for his young adult fiction. Named Walter Milton Myers in Martinsburg, West Virginia, Myers was born to a poor family in a segregated area still suffering from the effects of the Great Depression. When he was two years old, his mother died, leaving his father with eight children whom he could not support. When Myers was three, friends of the family, Herbert and Florence Dean, came to take two of Walter's sisters to live with them in Harlem, and decided to take Walter as well. Because the Deans raised him, Myers considers them his real family, and to acknowledge their role in nurturing him through a somewhat turbulent childhood and adolescence, he formally changed his name to Walter Dean Myers as an adult.

Walter Dean Myers.

Myers's works have been strongly influenced by a number of formative elements in his life. He had a severe speech problem as a child, one that plagued him for many years and that led to many conflicts with his peers. When he was four years old, his mother taught him to read, and he found that he could read words aloud that he otherwise had difficulty articulating. Though Myers learned only as an adult that his father was nearly illiterate, and though he dropped out of high school as a teenager, the value of literacy that Florence Dean instilled in him and the lively oral tradition that Herbert Dean passed on to him gave Walter a belief in books and literacy that, in effect, saved him from a life of delinquency. This high value on education and on the oral telling of family lore surfaces in many of Myers's texts. The strong bond between father and son also is a major theme in the many of his works.

Myers grew up in a Harlem, where church and the arts were integral parts of daily life and where most of the adults in the community felt it their duty and obligation to help raise children living there. Artists like Langston Hughes and James Baldwin were not only heroes whose work provided models for Myers's own, but they were also members of his community. As a young man, Myers took part in the Black Arts Movement, and because of his keen awareness of the historical stereotyping of African Americans in literature, when he began to write for young people, he wrote against this tradition, and throughout his career has sought to compose high-quality literature for young people in which they can see representations of themselves.

Myers's love of his Harlem home surfaces in titles as diverse as his first young adult novel, *Fast Sam, Cool Clyde, and Stuff* (1975) and his more recent picture book *Harlem: A Poem* (1997), illustrated by his son, Christopher. In *Fast Sam*, eighteen-year-old Francis, also known as "Stuff," who moved into his urban neighborhood when he was twelve, tells thirteen loosely related stories about his life. Like most of Myers's novels, this one has humor, but it also tackles some of the problems of black urban life such as black-on-black violence and the problematic relationship between the police and African Americans. Accessible to a younger audience, *Harlem* offers a songlike tribute to this diverse community that Myers calls home, and Christopher's visually rich collage illustrations bring it to life.

Myers also focuses in a number of his works on family and intergenerational relationships. *Won't Know Till I Get There* (1982) addresses the impact on the rest of the family when Earl Goins, a troubled teenage foster child with a criminal record, joins the household of fourteen-year-old protagonist Stephen Perry. When Earl, Stephen, and two of their friends get into trouble and are assigned community service at a home for senior citizens, the teens learn a great deal about themselves, as well as about how poorly the American social services system treats the elderly. Though Myers writes of many rich and positive father-son relationships, he creates a hauntingly complex one in *Somewhere in the Darkness* (1992). When fourteen-year-old Jimmy Little's father, Crab, who has been incarcerated for nine years, shows up one day, wanting somehow to gain his son's love and respect, Jimmy sees reflections of his own troubled teen self as he struggles to accept a man who has made so many bad choices.

Myers embraces diversity not only in terms of genres: he also experiments with different literary techniques. *Monster* (1999), for instance, is written in the form of a film script and a journal and integrates digitally manipulated photographs taken by Myers's son, Christopher. Sixteen-year-old Steve Harmon, an amateur filmmaker, faces the possibility of life in prison for being an accomplice to a drugstore robbery in which the storekeeper was murdered. While Steve uses his filmmaker's gaze to distance himself from this intensely emotional situation, his journal entries reveal the terror he feels. *Shooter* (2004), a narrative collage of sorts, combines interviews, newspaper articles, police, school, and a psychologist's reports, as well as the handwritten journal of Leonard Gray, the "shooter," to uncover what precipitated Len's murder of a star athlete and subsequent suicide. Though not directly involved in the plot, seventeen-year-old African American student Cameron Porter, who befriended Len, helps the authorities and readers piece together how this tragic event occurred. The picture book *Blues Journey* (2003), illustrated by Christopher Myers, celebrates blues music in picture book form. Given the diversity, number and, high quality of publications Myers has produced, he has undoubtedly played a significant role of defining contemporary young adult literature in general and African American children's literature in particular.

[*See also* African American Literature; Myers, Christopher; *and* Young Adult Literature.]

BIBLIOGRAPHY

Bishop, Rudine Sims. *Presenting Walter Dean Myers*. Boston: Twayne, 1991.

Burshtein, Karen. *Walter Dean Myers*. New York: Rosen, 2004.

Jordan, Denise M. *Walter Dean Myers—Writer for Real Teens*. Berkeley Heights, N.J.: Enslow, 1999.

Michelle H. Martin

My Friend Flicka. *See* O'Hara, Mary.

My Mother. *See* Taylor, Ann, and Jane Taylor.

Mystery and Detective Fiction. Critics generally agree that mystery fiction as a separate genre originated in the 19th century with Edgar Allan Poe. Tales he wrote in the 1840s, such as "The Murders on the Rue Morgue" and "The Purloined Letter" set a standard for both plot and character. The central figure of the narrative exemplifies the deductive powers of individuals in the use of encyclopedic knowledge and detailed observation to assemble clues to solve a mystery, usually involving a murder, and to uncover its perpetrator. From this point, mysteries evolved into types: "cozies," set in English country houses or university campuses, for which writers like Agatha Christie became famous; detective fiction, which emphasizes extensive reasoning from very little evidence, as exemplified by Sir Arthur Conan Doyle's detective Sherlock Holmes; and hard-boiled detective stories such as Dashiell Hammett's work in the early 20th century. Poe's and Doyle's popularity led to the found-

Nancy Drew Mystery. Front cover of *The Mystery of the Ivory Charm* by Carolyn Keene (New York: Grosset & Dunlap, 1936). REPRODUCED COURTESY OF THE COTSEN CHILDREN'S LIBRARY, PRINCETON UNIVERSITY LIBRARY

ing of the London Detective Club, fostered by the writer G. K. Chesterton in the 1920s. Readers also had heroes in series fiction published as dime novels; the best-known and perhaps longest-lasting was the Nick Carter series, beginning in the 1860s in America and passing through several transformations into novel and even radio series through the early to mid-20th century.

Mystery fiction lends itself to series writing as an author like Doyle develops a following for a central character who is not only intelligent and (usually) well educated, but also colorful and eccentric. Whether the emphasis is put on the powers of deduction and observation or on the investigator's personality, there is always some sort of crime at the story's core. The appropriateness of children being caught up in often grisly situations has disturbed educators, parents, and librarians, but, as Alison Lurie notes, such things excite child readers. Debate about what children should read and do read has consequently dominated discussions of children's mystery novels. Young readers may no longer start their interest in mystery by reading Doyle or Poe, but there are abundant references in subsequent mystery and detective fiction, from the Nancy Drew books to the recent award-winning mysteries by such authors as Joan Lowery Nixon and Kathryn Lasky. Additionally, mystery novels, with their emphasis on using one's mind both in the context of a puzzle plot and in the context of modern criminology, has given the mystery novel a better reputation than some other kinds of popular series fiction. A useful work for introducing the young reader to the historical mystery writers is *Detective Stories* (2001), edited by Philip Pullman. Among his selections from such writers as Doyle, Ellery Queen, Christie, and Dorothy L. Sayers, Pullman includes what is possibly the first young adult mystery novel, Erich Kästner's *Emil and the Detectives* (translated from the 1927 German work).

Children's Mystery Series and Their Critics

Children's mystery novels grew out of economic and cultural phenomena linked with increased literacy among the general population. As the children of the working class developed basic literacy in the 19th and 20th centuries, they became a potential audience. This inspired the development of penny dreadfuls (Britain) and dime novels (United States), followed by the inexpensive pulp magazines of the early 20th century, and the series fiction produced by such groups as the Stratmeyer Syndicate, which was responsible for more than sixty series titles of immense popularity from the 1880s through the 1960s. Within the mystery genre, two series with lasting appeal quickly emerged: the one hundred titles of the Hardy Boys series (sixty in the original series, begun in 1927), and the more than one hundred and twenty Nancy Drew novels (fifty-five in the original series, begun in 1930).

These series remained popular despite librarians' refusal or reluctance to stock them in public and school libraries, and despite many attacks by educators on their harmfulness as formulaic, sensationalized (according to pre-1960s standards), stereotypical, and simplistic writing. Each of these charges is true. The Hardy Boys series features two teenage brothers helping their father, a lawyer, solve grave legal cases, with sometimes dangerous and often unbelievable actions. Nancy Drew is both so accomplished and so successful that she cannot also be believable. The success of such works, however, has also led educators to revise their understanding of what and why children read. By the 1960s, librarians and educators began to agree that reading in itself was an important activity for young people, even if critiques of these and other series fictions still appear.

Mystery for Young Readers

Mystery fiction for young readers has undergone many transformations in the 20th century. Authors of mystery fiction are now recognized with major awards, and the genre also attracts authors who have become successful with other kinds of fiction. Additionally, mystery fiction is often combined with historical and supernatural genres, which can increase its pedagogical potential. The main shared characteristic of mystery fiction written for children from third to twelfth grade is that the detective is a young person, and one who is not always associated with an adult mentor. In some cases, especially in fiction written for the younger third-to-fifth-grade set, the detective might be an animal or have an animal companion, and the mystery may be historical in nature, removing the young detective from the immediate context of the crime.

Works for younger readers tend to emphasize the detection process and to involve their readers in problem solving. Donald Sobol's brilliant young sleuth in *Encyclopedia Brown, Boy Detective* (1963), and its sequels succeeds because of his keen observation and vast, always expanding knowledge. Young readers also enjoy James Howe's Bunnicula books, where the heroes are animals and the villain a vampire-bunny. Jane Yolen's character Piggins encounters many adventures, including those of Piggins the Detective.

Increasingly, however, problem fiction and mystery fiction are united, as in the work of one of the genre's most prominent writers, Joan Lowery Nixon. Author of more than a hundred books for children, Nixon has been the president of the Mystery Writers of America and has won the Edgar Allan Poe Best Juvenile Mystery Award for such works as *The Name of the Game is Murder* and *The Other Side of the Dark* (1986). Her mysteries are not series fiction, and they often set their heroes against formidable opponents. Stacy, of *In the Dark*, is in a coma from age thirteen to seventeen, having both seen her mother's murder and been herself gravely injured. She must overcome the lost years and the loss of her mother and catch the murderer by following clues locked in her own faulty memory. Nixon's mysteries are both popular and satisfying because of their complexity. In a lighter work, *The Weekend Was Murder* (1992), she spoofs both mystery plots and the contemporary culture of adult mystery fans by setting her murder mystery at a murder-mystery weekend in a Houston hotel. Her unlikely young detective, Mary Elizabeth Rafferty, has already solved one case, assisted by her boyfriend, Fran, and a hapless ghost. A tall, clumsy sixteen-year-old, she is both an actor for the entertainment of would-be-sleuth guests and herself a successful sleuth. Nixon's characters reference Christie, Doyle, and even Nancy Drew. *Nobody's There* (2000) pairs an angry young girl with an irascible old woman who fancies herself a private detective, and *The Specter* (1982) is simultaneously about child abuse and murder.

Cross-Genre Novelists

Other award-winning writers have written successful mystery novels that greatly influenced the development of the genre for younger readers. Virginia Hamilton, known for her historical and fantasy fiction, created *The House of Dies Drear* (1968) and its sequel around a modern boy's investigations of a safe house on the Underground Railroad of the Civil War era. Thomas Small is thirteen when his family moves from South Carolina to Ohio and plunges him into the exploration of Dies Drear's involvement with returning slaves to the South to rescue other slaves. Cynthia Voigt's mystery *The Callender Papers* (1983), another Edgar Award winner, is set in 1894 and deals with a family legacy hidden among thousands of family papers at an old estate. A young orphan girl, Jean, trained in Latin, is sent off to sort the papers, and she makes startling discoveries about the Callender family's history. Voigt delights in presenting female sleuths with unusual intellectual skills, as in *The Vandemark Mummy*, where teenaged Althea is studying Greek for her own entertainment and solves the mystery of why a minor Coptic mummy is desecrated. She in turn is saved from murder by starvation by her more outgoing brother, Phineas.

Zilpha Keatley Snyder is well known for her problem-fantasy novels, but she also wrote several problem-mystery novels, the most prominent of which are detective stories set in the context of role-playing gamers. *The Egypt Game* (1967) and its companion *The Gypsy Game* (1997) plunge a small gang into both cultural research and a deadly game of detecting. As with Voigt and Snyder, exotic settings and the historical adventure figure centrally in the archaeological mysteries of Lloyd Alexander's Vesper Holly series (*Drakenberg Adventure*, 1988, and others). Alexander creates an unlikely but likable orphan-sleuth with amazing intellectual and physical talents. Kathryn Lasky, Newbery Award-winning author of historical, mystery, supernatural, and science fiction as well as nonfiction, created the Starbuck Family mysteries, four stories in which two pairs of twins in one family solve historical murder mysteries in exotic locations. The older twins, July (male) and Liberty (female) are telepathic with each other and sometimes with their mirror-twin younger siblings. For example, they solve a Doyle-related, 19th-century mystery while visiting 20th-century London with their ecologist father, and another among Indian tribes of the American Southwest, mixing cultural history, detective skills, family dynamics, and adventure.

Supernatural Mysteries

Supernatural mystery for middle-grade readers has gained increasing popularity since one of its earliest practitioners, John Bellairs, created three series with young detectives, beginning with Lewis Barnavelt (*The House with the Clock In Its Walls*, 1973, and *The Figure in the Shadows*, 1975), and followed by Johnny Dixon and Anthony Monday. With elderly male and female friends, some of them librarians, others witches and warlocks, these intrepid sleuths persist through miasmas of evil and treachery, satisfying young readers' passion for frightful as well as thoughtful stories. Susan Cooper, well known for her fantasy fiction, portrays the delights of Scotland as young siblings Emily and Jess solve an old murder and the mystery of the Loch Ness monster with the help of a legendary mischievous spirit, the Bogart. Lasky's and Nixon's ghost players have already been mentioned, and Snyder's *The Trespassers* (1995) hints at ghostly intervention in a long-past disappearance of a young girl of a long-gone "cursed" family on California's coast. Philip Pullman's supernatural mystery stories, begun with the Victorian tale *Ruby in the Smoke* (1985) and its sequels, borrow the atmosphere of 19th-century London's docks and the wonder of emerging technologies such as photography in crime solving of the Holmes school of deductive reasoning.

Mysteries set in exotic and historical settings continue to be popular. In addition to Voigt, writers such as Laurence Yep weave long-dead people into their mysteries. Yep's *Mark Twain Murders* (1982) is set in San Francisco in 1864, when Mark Twain was briefly a newspaper reporter. The narrator, a fifteen-year-old boy, is involved in the crime investigation and simultaneously makes observations about the young Twain. Writers such as Beth Hilgartner and Lensey Namioka take the reader both back in history and away from everyday life. Hilgartner's engaging *Murder for Her Majesty* (1986) follows eleven-year-old Alice from the comfortable life of a nobleman's daughter in Queen Elizabeth I's 16th-century England to the streets and York Minster of historical York and into the middle of national intrigue. Even more exotic, Namioka, a Chinese American writer, evokes the samurai culture of 16th-century Japan and its first contact with the Portuguese Catholics of the time in her Zenta and Matsuzo mysteries *Valley of the Broken Cherry Trees* (1986), and *Samurai and the Long-Nosed Devils* (1976); the latter ends with references to the historically accurate expulsion of Westerners from Japan by the Meiji emperor.

Value of Mysteries

Mystery novels for young readers have become accepted and even celebrated by educators, librarians, and parents because they both stimulate the child's imagination and emphasize the importance of reasoning. That they also increasingly portray children in life-threatening situations, only makes them more realistic. As literary forms, mystery and detective fiction thus both encourage and educate, while providing the same gamelike entertainment that attracts adult readers.

[*See also* Dime Novel; Hardy Boys Series; Penny Dreadful; Stratemeyer Syndicate; *and biographies of figures mentioned in this article*.]

BIBLIOGRAPHY

Cox, J. Randolph. "Paperback Detective: The Evolution of the Nick Carter Series, from 1886–1990." In *Pioneers, Passionate Ladies and Private Eyes: Dime Novels, Series Books and Paperbacks*, edited by Larry E. Sullivan and Lydia Cushman Schurman, eds. New York: Haworth, 1996.

Gavin, Adrienne, and Christopher Routledge, eds. *Mystery in Children's Literature: From the Rational to the Supernatural*. Basingstoke, U.K.: Palgrave, 2001.

Magistrale, Tony, and Sidney Poger. *Poe's Children. Connections between Tales of Terror and Detection*. New York: Peter Lang, 1999.

JANICE M. BOGSTAD

Mythical Creatures. Mythical beasts have been a part of the literary tradition since Paleolithic times. The first records of such creatures in storytelling can be seen in the Lascaux cave paintings, dating around 17,490 B.C.E. Although these paintings depict the hunting of big game as practiced by *Homo erectus* for 2 million years, their central subjects are the animals, not the hunters—the animals are in the position of mythical superiority. Mythical creatures associated with children's literature are often amalgamations of common animals and sometimes combinations of beast and man. Some of the mythical figures known to children are dragons, griffons, satyrs, centaurs, unicorns, and Pegasus. Many of them have their origins in various world mythologies. Some, based on legends, are reported to have once been real animals. The Loch Ness monster and Bigfoot are two modern mythical creatures.

These creatures were cataloged in the bestiaries of medieval Europe, which drew heavily on the *Physiologus*, written in ancient Greece. A bestiary is a collection of brief, often narrative or poetic descriptions of animals—both real and invented—laced with annotations with a moral purpose. These descriptions were heavily illuminated and composed primarily in Latin. The bestiaries that began to develop in the 12th century linked teachings of Christianity with elements of myth, fable, folklore, allegory, and legend. The Aberdeen Bestiary, written in around 1200, is considered one of the best examples of its kind. David Day created a modern version, *A Tolkien Bestiary* (1979).

BIBLIOGRAPHY

Arnott, Michael, and Iain Beaven. *The Aberdeen Bestiary*. University of Aberdeen, U.K. http://www.abdn.ac.uk/bestiary/index.hti.

Evslin, Bernard. *Heroes, Gods, and Monsters of the Greek Myths*. New York: Four Winds Press, 1967.

VANESSA JOOSEN

Myths. At the beginning of the 21st century, as educational systems seem to offer diminishing space for the study of earlier cultures (literatures of the past, and early European history, religion, and sociology), and with the literature for young readers expanding into a vast and various selection, it would hardly be surprising if classical Greco-Roman

Norse Myths. Front cover illustration by Hannah Firmin for *The Norse Myths*, edited by Kevin Crossley-Holland (London: Penguin, 1982). COLLECTION OF JACK ZIPES

myths had disappeared from children's literature. Yet they survive, albeit as a minor genre, with new retellings consistently appearing. Three principal reasons may explain the improbable survival of classical mythology as a children's literature genre. First, literary retellings are produced under the assumption that myths are not only intrinsically interesting as stories but also perform important literary and social functions and have abiding implications for cultural life.

Second, mythologies of various origins are appropriated into popular culture, often in eclectic and anachronistic forms, in literature, film and television, commercial brand names, and even pop music. A high profile sword-and-sandal epic film such as *Troy* (2004) both keeps the ancient world within the gaze of the modern era and exemplifies elements of the reshaping process that guarantee accessibility (implausibly modern character motivation, for example). This presence in popular culture, especially in a cult series such as *Xena, Warrior Princess* (1995–2001), tends to encourage audiences to seek out other versions of the incorporated myths, especially as they become aware of the extent to which these borrowed myths deviate from their sources. *Xena* was in turn a spin-off from another TV series, *Hercules: The Legendary Journeys* (1995–1999), very loosely based on the labors of the classical hero. *Hercules* (1997), Disney's first foray into classical myth, also played fast and loose with the established story. It became just one more American male coming of age story in which the world is again saved from the forces of darkness; also, in its effective travesty of classical thought in constituting Hades (ruler of the underworld) as the villain and depicting him as killed in an uprising of his subjects, the film allegorically invokes contemporary notions of a new world order.

Xena, Warrior Princess draws primarily on classical mythology for source material but mingles it with elements from Hindu, Chinese, and other traditions, with an effect that is often paradoxical: its eclectic, postmodern pastiche of images, styles, and costumes resists any unified subject position, but its ethical stance in its representation of the struggle against evil and quest for redemption invokes archetypal connections beneath its narrative incidents. This tendency is symptomatic of the third way in which classical myth is figured in contemporary literature: as a component of a multicultural mythology that draws retellings of myths from around the world into a single volume or implies relationships among retold myths. Individual stories retold from classical or Scandinavian mythologies exist in relation to a larger system or pattern of narratives. When mythological systems are linked, the effect is to suggest an underlying commonality of human experiences as a basis for a multicultural approach to literary studies and human relationships.

Stories about the actions of deities or other supernatural beings explain why the world is as it is and why things happen as they do. Adults who retell these stories, however, generally assume that myths also perform important literary and social functions. A myth functions as a story with tangible links to a larger system or pattern of narratives, and this relational network guarantees that the specific story has a significance over and above mere story outcome: its meaning is determined by its relationship to that whole. In other words, any particular example is already interpretable as a moral fable or allegory whose significance is shaped by a powerful, sometimes indefinable emotional supplement and by its articulation within culture. This effect is often reinforced by parallels with biblical literature made or implied in the retelling. One of the stranger examples is the story "A Solstice Carol" from *Xena: Warrior Princess* (1996), a parody of Charles Dickens's *A Christmas Carol* relocated to an imaginary ancient Greek kingdom, with the classical Fates replacing the ghosts of Christmas Past, Present, and Future; the story overtly uses these connections to thematize compassion and altruism.

For adults who retell stories from classical mythology or write about these retellings, a myth may have five kinds of significance, in addition to the pragmatic classroom function of filling gaps in children's literary knowledge. First, a myth is invested with value as *story* itself. As a narrative that audiences may recognize as similar to other such narratives because it is patterned by archetypal situations and characterizations, a story transmits its latent value as a particular working out of perennial human desires and destinies. The structural pattern itself signifies without needing to be interpreted, because the meaning lies in the repeatability and the deep-laid similarity among otherwise apparently diverse stories. Underlying the structural pattern is a cultural assumption which could be explained according to a variety of theories—Jung's theory of the collective unconscious, or various structuralist theories as proposed by Vladimir Propp or Claude Lévi-Strauss, for example—but few retellers engaged in reproducing a story would articulate it in such terms. They might find more resonance with Ted Hughes's notion of Greek myth as "working anatomy of our psychic life."

Classical myth is deemed to embody putatively timeless and universal significances, and this in turn is combined with the second significance commonly attributed to classical myth: that it forms part of the cultural heritage of European and European-derived peoples, enabling them to understand Western art, literature, and ways of thinking. Within a cultural tradition that glorifies the value of classical antiquity, ancient wisdom is deemed to contain universal qualities and themes relevant to life today and to teach enduring moral and political lessons that can be used to improve our own society. Thus Roger Lancelyn Green's preface to his 1958 syncretic retelling argues that the stories "are a part of the world's heritage, they are part of the background of our literature, our speech, of our very thoughts." Green's carefully structured version implies a teleology according with this view. The position is implicitly challenged by Garfield and Blishen's Carnegie Medal–winning *The God beneath the Sea* (1970), probably the most interesting 20th-century retelling of a classical myth for young readers, and it is challenged anew by the more recent multicultural approaches. Although the underpinning assumptions about cultural capital have now become less prominent, quite modern retellings often still seem unaware that classical mythology was produced by and for a male-centered community, and the corollary production of subjective wholeness attributed to its influence is radically flawed by the individualism, imperialism, masculinism, and misogyny that pervade that mythology. As recently as 2001, Page Dubois has reiterated the argument that modern appropriations of the classics as timeless truth may be used to serve neoconservative ends, promoting patriarchy and associated family values, elitism, nationalism, and militarism. Many responses to the film *Troy* (2004) noted such connections.

The remaining significances attributed to myth are less obviously problematic. The third is that because myths are linked with religious urges and aspirations, they express spiritual insights in oblique narrative form. Fourth, as narrativized expressions of motions within the human unconscious, they distill psychic truth. And fifth, subsuming elements of the first three into a modern configuration, myths facilitate intercultural communication by bringing out the similarities between various world cultures, and hence they affirm the common humanity of the world's peoples. These last three significances offer intersections among mythologies drawn from diverse cultures and hence imply a frame so comprehensive that individual mythic systems appear to be only reflections of a common human impulse. Classical mythology might therefore seem to lose its preeminence and become one among many. A good example of this trend is Philip Wilkinson's *Illustrated Dictionary of Mythology* (1998), which is not organized around European mythologies (even though these are still allocated 40 percent of its available space). Introduced by a section dealing with "universal" themes—creation myths, gods and goddesses, heroes, monsters, supernatural animals, shape-shifting, and endings—the volume is arranged on principles of antiquity and region. A claim habitually made for classical myth—"A living part of all our heritage, myths are still some of the best stories of all time"—is here appropriated for a multicultural approach to myth.

Such a move seems particularly significant because any contemporary collection of myths is less likely to be yet another volume devoted to classical myths than a thematically organized international anthology. Often, however, the internationalism is largely an adjunct in a structure where classical myths function as nodes of significance within a larger web of Eurocentric relationships. This is perhaps inevitable because the target audience belongs mainly or wholly to European or European-derived societies, and because the function of transmitting cultural heritage always remains a residual if not a central concern, but it does constitute a problem in that the tendency of such collections is to privilege similarity over difference.

Myths are retold in contrasting ways. They can be self-referential, somewhat exotic stories, appearing to be of the same formulaic kind as modern fantasy action stories, or they can be retold within a frame that seeks to express or evoke their capacity to be seemingly simple narratives bodying forth abstract concepts. By displacing experience into the exotic—in practice, the archetypal—a retelling that evokes abstract concepts implies that everyday life does not consist merely of insignificant unique moments but is informed by some element of deeper mystery. *This* moment is like *that* moment in mythic time. What individuals experience in daily life is part of a cline of experience which culminates in transcendent human qualities. In effect, and no doubt at times in intention, the second kind of retelling opposes the first in a clash of cultural significances, although this may be more evident in acts of interpretation than in actual retellings. The extreme position sees the telling and teaching of myths, especially classical ones, as an aspect of cultural conservation central to the production of children as subjects who are unified and possess social integrity. This is to ascribe to classical myth a function earlier ages ascribed to the classics as a whole. Especially where young people are concerned, the purpose is to invoke an ethical vision capable of standing against the perceived self-absorption and fracturing of identity attributed to late 20th-century (post)modernism, materialism, and cultural relativism.

Modern retellings have addressed the possibility of an ethical vision by focusing particular attention on heroes, of which the Hercules stories and the Xena series are symptomatic. A more skeptical account is found in the carefully varied selection of four hero myths told cinematically in *Jim Henson's The Storyteller: Greek Myths* (1990): here the nature of heroism is interrogated through a tension between individualism and concern for others. Theseus is offered as a negative example; driven by male-centered attitudes, the cult of individualism, and his own ego, he is unable to think outside the frame of his own desires and ambitions, and at the end of the story he is haunted by the realization of his own monstrosity. Orpheus's failed attempt to bring Eurydice back from the underworld, and (in a new variant) his subsequent death at the hands of the women of his community when his grief causes him to fail to use his creative gift responsibly, offers a pointed contrast. His spirit assures the narrator that his lyre has never ceased to play but brings "tunes out of silence" and "love out of hate." This version thus emphasizes the creative rather than the destructive elements of the myth. Culture heroes from other traditions, whose stories have been widely represented—the African and African American Anansi or the Native American Coyote—likewise stress the creative role and its benefits and thereby suggest that comparative storytelling will affect how myth is understood more generally.

BIBLIOGRAPHY

Dubois, Page. *Trojan Horses: Saving Classics from the Conservatives*. New York: New York University Press, 2001.

Garfield, Leon, Edward Blishen, and Charles Keeping. *The God beneath the Sea*. Harmondsworth, U.K.: Kestrel, 1970.

Green, Roger Lancelyn. *Tales of the Greek Heroes*. Harmondsworth, U.K.: Penguin, 1958.

Philip, Neil. *The Illustrated Book of Myths: Tales and Legends of the World*. Illustrated by Nilesh Mistry. London: Dorling Kindersley, 1995.

Pilling, Ann. *Realms of Gold: Myths and Legends from Around the World*. Illustrated by Kady MacDonald Denton. London: Kingfisher, 1993.

Stephens, John, and Robyn McCallum. *Retelling Stories, Framing Culture: Metanarratives and Traditional Story in Children's Literature*. New York: Routledge, 1998.

Wilkinson, Philip. *Illustrated Dictionary of Mythology*. London: Dorling Kindersley, 1998.

JOHN STEPHENS

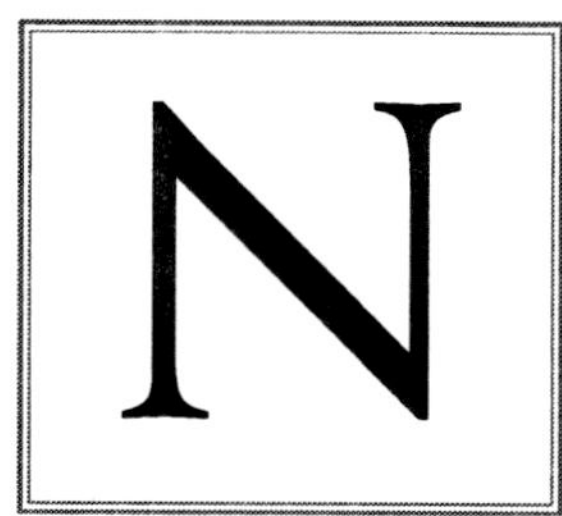

Na, An (1972–), Korean-born American recognized as an important voice reflecting the contemporary Korean immigrant experience. Na moved to San Diego, California, as a child, and received an MFA in writing for children from Vermont College. She is the author of *A Step from Heaven* (2001), in which a girl moves to the United States from Korea and faces the struggles of growing up as a new immigrant. The novel traces Young Ju's life, realistically portraying issues such as speaking English better than one's parents, and the culture gap between home and school. The book was well reviewed, was a National Book Award Finalist, and was winner of the Printz Award.

[*See also* Korea; Minority Literature in Anglophone Countries; *and* United States.]

LAURA E. ATKINS

Naidoo, Beverley (1943–), British novelist. Born and brought up in South Africa, Naidoo reacted strongly against the apartheid government of the time, joining the resistance and spending eight weeks in solitary confinement at the age of twenty-one. She moved to Britain in 1965 and became a teacher. Her first novel, *Journey to Jo'burg* (1984), tells of what happens after two black South African children realize that the baby they are in charge of is seriously ill. They make a journey of two hundred miles in order to find their mother, who is working for a white family in the big city. *Chain of Fire* (1989) describes how the same children later resist the government-backed forcible removal of everyone from their village to so-called homelands far away. *No Turning Back* (1995) focuses on the plight of Johannesberg street children trying to survive against all odds. Expertly plotted and peopled with fully rounded characters, these books all tell a good story while never succumbing to the temptation of preaching or polemics. *The Other Side of Truth* (2000) marks a departure: it describes the difficulties faced by two Nigerian children who are uprooted to Britain with their father after their mother has been shot by government-hired assassins. This novel won the Carnegie Medal in 2000. In its sequel, *Web of Lies* (2004), the younger of the two, Femi, is sucked into a criminal juvenile gang with a sinister young black leader who uses him as a convenient fall guy on dangerous adventures. In addition to her novels, Naidoo has published her doctoral thesis on teenage responses to literature and racism and has been an adviser for English and Cultural Diversity.

NICHOLAS TUCKER

Nakatani Chiyoko (1930–1981), Japanese artist who graduated from Tokyo National University of Fine Arts and Music, majoring in oil painting. She created 105 books, beginning with *The Lion and the Bird's Nest* (1960; U.K., Denmark, and Switzerland editions, 1972), with text by poet and friend Kishida Eriko. Nakatani's animal illustrations received high praise. In a happy collaboration with Kishida, Nakatani published *Hippopotamus* (1962; U.S. edition, 1963). It was translated into French as *Debut! Mon Brave Hippo* ("Album du Pere Castor No. 314," 1965). Nakatani produced both text and pictures for *Chiro the Stray Dog* (1965; Swiss edition, 1969), *Taro and Dolphins* (1969; U.K., U.S., and Switzerland editions, 1970), and twelve other books. She also illustrated *The Animal's Lullaby* (1966, with text by Trude Alberti), *The Brave Little Goat of Monsieur Seguin* (1966, with text by Alphonse Daudet), *The Little Old Woman in the Strawberry Patch* (1973, with text by Watari Mutuko), among others. Her drawing from close observation of objects and her illustrations' harmonious color tones appeal to young readers.

[*See also* Illustrations *and* Japan.]

OKIKO MIYAKE

Namioka, Lensey (1929–), award-winning Chinese American author of more than twenty books, especially noted for her series of adventure-mystery books set in 16th-century Japan and middle-grade domestic novels featuring a family of Chinese immigrants living in the United States. Namioka's own cosmopolitan family—her parents had been educated outside of China—moved frequently, and Namioka and her three sisters were often placed in the position of outsiders in regions of China markedly different from her native Beijing. The family's emigration to America shortly before World War II increased Namioka's need to adjust to a new culture. While studying mathematics at Berkeley, she met another outsider, Isaac Namioka, the grandson of a Christian Japanese man and a French woman, and married him in 1957. Namioka earned her MA degree in mathematics and worked as a college mathematics instructor. However, her love for stories led her away from mathematics and toward writing books for children that emphasize, in spare prose and with humor, the importance of celebrating cultural diversity and exploring one's cultural heritage—a theme she explores, for example, in *Half and Half* (2003), a novel about a biracial girl of Scottish and Chinese heritage. Namioka's works—such as her seven-book series about Zenta and Matsuzo, traveling unemployed samurai in feudal Japan, and begun in *The Samurai and the Long-Nosed Devils* and *White Serpent Castle* (both published in 1976 and recently reprinted); the series of four books about the Yang siblings (the first of which is *Yang the Youngest and His Terrible Ear*, 1992); and her picture books, such as *The Hungriest Boy in the World* (2001)—draw upon both her Chinese cultural heritage and also the Japanese cultural heritage of her husband.

[*See also* China; Japan; Multiculturalism and Children's Books; *and* United States.]

LYNNE VALLONE

Nancy Drew. Nancy Drew is the central character in a popular series attributed to Carolyn Keene and created by the Stratemeyer Syndicate. Beginning with *The Secret of the Old Clock* (1930), volumes in Nancy Drew Mystery Stories follow a similar pattern: Nancy uses her wit and common sense to solve mysteries usually set in her hometown of River Heights. Fifty-six volumes were published by Grosset & Dunlap until 1979 (the first thirty-four were revised between 1959 and 1977) and are considered the "original" texts. Simon & Schuster published new titles from 1979 to 2003 and launched a new series, Nancy Drew, Girl Detective, in 2004; it also published several concurrent series for older and beginning readers as well as spin-offs and tie-in titles with the Hardy Boys. Nancy Drew, who has been the subject of several academic studies, has also been featured on television, in graphic novels, and in several lines of spin-off products.

[*See also* Girls' Books and Fiction; Hardy Boys Series; Mystery and Detective Stories; Series Books; *and* Stratemeyer Syndicate.]

BIBLIOGRAPHY

Caprio, Betsy. *The Mystery of Nancy Drew: Girl Sleuth on the Couch*. Trabuco Canyon, Calif.: Source, 1992. Excellent analysis of the Nancy Drew series from a psychoanalytic perspective.

Dyer, Carolyn Stewart, and Nancy Tillman Romalov, eds. *Rediscovering Nancy Drew*. Iowa City: University of Iowa Press, 1995. Collection of essays dealing with various aspects of feminism, gender, race, and reading strategies.

Johnson, Deidre. *Edward Stratemeyer and the Stratemeyer Syndicate*. Twayne's United States Authors Series 627. New York: Twayne, 1993. An excellent overview of the Stratemeyer Syndicate and the majority of its series, including discussions of its methods of operation, key themes and patterns, and biographical information of key players. Also includes discussion of later series published by Simon & Schuster.

Mason, Bobbie Ann. *The Girl Sleuth: A Feminist Guide*. Old Westbury, N.Y.: The Feminist Press, 1975. A compelling account of Nancy Drew's early feminism.

Plunkett-Powell, Karen. *The Nancy Drew Scrapbook*. New York: St. Martin's, 1993. A detailed overview of the Nancy Drew books and spin-off products, with particular emphasis on her changing feminism and her changing world.

Romalov, Nancy Tillman, ed. "Nancy Drew." *The Lion and the Unicorn* 18, no. 1 (1994): 1–120. Special issue of the journal, presenting a collection of essays about Nancy Drew in the context of series fiction, girl culture, film adaptation, and international translation.

BENJAMIN LEFEBVRE

Nancy Drew Series. *See* Benson, Mildred Wirt.

Napoli, Donna Jo (1948–), American novelist for children and young adults and professor of linguistics at Swarthmore College. Napoli's middle-grade and young adult historical novels explore the life of Mary Magdalene during the Roman occupation of Israel, the Nazi occupation of Italy and eastern Europe, and Renaissance Venice. The protagonists of Napoli's contemporary realistic novels struggle with personal challenges and loss. Napoli's middle-grade trilogy that begins with *Soccer Shock* (1991) contains fantastical elements as the protagonist confronts his problems with the assistance of his talking freckles. In her sixteen-volume early-reader series Angelwings (1999–2001), a network of archangels guide little angels through tasks required to obtain their wings, tasks that involve assisting a child with a problem.

Donna Jo Napoli. Front cover illustration by Leo and Diane Dillon for *The Magic Circle* (New York: Dutton Children's Books, 1993). COLLECTION OF JACK ZIPES

More than any other writer for young adults, Napoli has mined the terrain of the folktale and fairy tale, re-creating stories with a depth of character and sophistication not achieved in their more familiar forms. Often writing from the viewpoint of the traditional villain, Napoli renders the character more human by revealing an emotional or psychological basis for his or her behavior. *The Magic Circle* (1993) tells "Hansel and Gretel" from the point of view of the witch, a tortured woman who fled to the forest precisely to prevent herself from eating children. *Zel* (1996) tells the story of "Rapunzel" and provides an explanation for the protagonist's imprisonment. *Spinners* (1999), cowritten with Richard Tchen, reveals the origin of Rumpelstiltskin's desire for the queen's child. *Beast* (2000) discloses the full extent of the Beast's punishment in "Beauty and the Beast." *Breath* (2003) revisits "The Pied Piper of Hamlin." *Sirena* (1998) mixes elements of Greek mythology with a retelling of "The Little Mermaid." Napoli has also written three intermediate novels which revisit the frog-prince motif with wry humor: *The Prince of the Pond* (1992); *Jimmy, the Pickpocket of the Palace* (1995); and *Gracie, the Pixie of the Puddle* (2004).

MARY ANN CAPPIELLO

Narnia. *See* Lewis, C. S.

Nash, Ogden (1902–1971), American humorist and poet. After meeting with failure as a teacher and a financier, Frederic Ogden Nash found work as an advertiser, honing his gift for short, catchy slogans. In his poetry, he was fond of pithy couplets that nearly rhymed, such as, "If called by a panther, / Don't anther." He referred to his own field as "the minor idiocies of humanity" and refused to take himself too seriously. Unlike the irreverent poet Hilaire Belloc, Nash deliberately used straggling lines and odd pronunciations rather than perfect poetic forms to convey his comic intent. Some of Nash's comic poetry is quite adult in content, but much of it is accessible to children as well as adults. As his career progressed, he spent more and more time on children's books, including *Girls Are Silly* (1962), *Parents Keep Out* (1951), and *Custard the Dragon* (1959).

BIBLIOGRAPHY

Axford, Lavonne B. *An Index to the Poems of Ogden Nash*. Metuchen, N.J.: Scarecrow, 1972.

MARISSA K. LINGEN

Nath, Pratibha (1931–), trilingual Indian author, who writes stories based on incidents inspired by everyday life, primarily for younger readers. Nath uses animals, their antics, and their idiosyncrasies to provide laughs—as in "Monkey at the Tap" (1987)—and to convey important messages. In *A Bowl of Water* (1985), three birds set out to quench their thirst. A bowl of water, provided by a kind boy, takes the place of all the natural resources. In *Barber at the Zoo* (1984), the Lion is annoyed when his tail is accidentally nicked. But the situation is diffused without unpleasantness, and Badlu escapes, a wiser and more careful man. *Indian Folk-Tales and Legends* (1995) presents the best in Indian tales, narrated with humor and sympathy, while *The Making* *of the Taj* (2003) re-creates a glorious period of Indian history.

[*See also* Animal Stories; Fairy Tales and Folk Tales; *and* India.]

NANDINI NAYAR

National Book Award. *See* Awards.

National Council of Teachers of English. The National Council of Teachers of English (NCTE) is a professional organization devoted to improving the teaching and learning of English and the language arts and providing support and resources to teachers in these disciplines at all levels of education. Founded in 1911, the NCTE has grown to include approximately 60,000 members in the United States and other countries. The NCTE works to fulfill its mission through a variety of methods. The organization publishes a newspaper, *The Council Chronicle*; about a dozen specialized journals (including *Language Arts*, *Voices from the Middle*, *English Journal*, *English Education*, and *College Composition and Communication*); and a new list of about twenty books each year. Annual conventions and conferences held across the country bring members together to share ideas and classroom techniques, learn about new books and materials, and provide an ongoing opportunity for teachers to continue their own education and polish their expertise. The NCTE also provides research funds for scholars and teachers, and it works to set professional standards on issues such as class size, workload, and instruction. Among its most deeply held commitments is fighting efforts to censor or restrict the curricular materials teachers use in their classrooms.

MEGAN LYNN ISAAC

National Velvet. *See* Bagnold, Enid.

Native American Children's Literature. "Native American" or "American Indian" refers to the indigenous peoples of the United States. Although children's books featuring these groups have been acclaimed for their alleged literary qualities, most of the books lack accurate portrayals of native peoples. To a large degree, they contain texts and illustrations that obscure the diversity within Native American cultures, stereotype Native American people as bloodthirsty savages or "noble savages," and tell stories that confine Native Americans to days long past. The majority of the books were written by authors who were not themselves Native American, and their books generally reflect images of native peoples in pulp fiction and the popular press. As far back as 1881, however, Native American authors wrote stories to counter these portrayals.

Susette LaFlesche (Inshata Theumba, Bright Eyes; Omaha) wrote "Nedawi" for *St. Nicholas Magazine* in January 1881. It depicts life in an Omaha hunting camp. Several stories by Charles Alexander Eastman (Ohiyesa; Dakota) appeared in *St. Nicholas* in 1893 and 1894 and were later published in *Indian Boyhood* (1902, 1933, 1971), a favorite in Boy Scout programs. Luther Standing Bear's (Ota K'te; Lakota) *My Indian Boyhood* (1931) is primarily autobiographical, while *My People the Sioux* (1928) and *Land of the Spotted Eagle* (1933) describe traditional Lakota culture. *I Am a Pueblo Indian Girl* (1939) was written by thirteen-year-old Louise Abeita (E-Yeh-Shure, Blue Corn; Isleta) and shares information about daily aspects of Pueblo Indian life and culture. The accompanying illustrations in this picture book were watercolors painted by Native American artists (for instance, Allan Houser, whose work would eventually become internationally renowned).

During the 1940s, the U.S. Bureau of Indian Affairs published the bilingual booklets known as the "Indian Life Readers" for use in the U.S. Government Boarding and Day Schools. Most of the books were written by nonnative author Ann Nolan Clark, but they were illustrated by native artists. Of particular interest is Navajo artist Hoke Denetsosie's attention to authenticity; according to Denetsosie, as quoted in Barbara Bader's *American Picturebooks from Noah's Arc to the Beast Within*:

> The nature of the series, being concerned with Navajo life, called for illustration genuine in every sense of the word. I had to observe and incorporate in pictures those characteristics which serve to distinguish the Navajo from other tribes. Further, the setting . . . had to change to express local changes as the family moved from place to place. The domestic animals . . . had to be shown in a proper setting just as one sees them on the reservation. The sheep could not be shown grazing in a pasture, nor the horses in a stable, because such things are not Navajo.

One reader, *In My Mother's House*, initially titled *Third Grade Home Geography*, was published by a mainstream

Native American Story. Illustration by Hoke Denetsosie from *Little Herder in Spring and Summer* by Ann Nolan Clark (Washington, D.C.: United States Indian Service, 1950). REPRODUCED COURTESY OF THE COTSEN CHILDREN'S LIBRARY, PRINCETON UNIVERSITY LIBRARY

press in 1941. D'Arcy McNickle's (Chippewa Cree) historical novel for middle school readers, *Runner in the Sun*, was published in 1954 and follows Salt, a teenager being trained to lead his people. Pablita Velarde (Santa Clara) retold and illustrated Pueblo stories told by her grandfather in *Old Father, the Storyteller* (1960). Velarde, also a world-renowned artist, provided information regarding the symbolism of elements she included in the illustrations.

During the 1970s, a magazine for children was published by the American Indian Historical Society. Titled *The Wee Wish Tree*, it contained short stories, poems, and essays written by Native American authors and children. Encouraged by the Council on Interracial Books for Children, Virginia Driving Hawk Sneve (Rosebud Sioux) wrote *High Elk's Treasure* (1972), *When Thunders Spoke* (1974), and *The Chichi Hoohoo Bogeyman* (1975). The prose poem by Simon Ortiz (Acoma), *The People Shall Continue* (1977, 1988), chronicles the history of Native Americans from creation to the present day and includes content omitted or glossed over in other narratives about the settlement of the United States. For example, Ortiz includes the forced removal of native peoples from their homelands, the involuntary separation of children from their families and their placement in government-controlled boarding schools, and the alliances formed in the 1960s among peoples of color. During the 1980s, Joseph Bruchac (Abenaki) wrote *The Wind Eagle and Other Abenaki Stories* (1985), which he would follow with similar collections as well as picture books, traditional retellings, historical and contemporary fiction, biography, and autobiographical works.

In the 1990s, publications by Native American authors represented a growing body of authentic literature for children. Among the best-known writers are Michael Dorris (Modoc), Louise Erdrich (Ojibwe), Joy Harjo (Creek), Michael Lacapa (Apache/Hopi/Tewa), Gayle Ross (Cherokee), Cynthia Leitich Smith (Creek), Joseph McLellan (Nez Perce), N. Scott Momaday (Kiowa), Cheryl Savageau (Abenaki/Metis), Craig Kee Strete (Cherokee), Jan Waboose (Anishinabe), and Bernelda Wheeler (Cree). The lived experiences Native American people bring to their writing infuses their work with a deep understanding of figures such as the trickster, a human who can shift his shape at will, becoming an animal such as a rabbit, raven, or coyote. The trickster engages in both chaotic and constructive endeavors, serving as a symbol of life in all its multiplicity, all its possibilities. Joseph McClellan's (Nez Perce) nine picture books about Nanabosho are particularly well done.

Four significant developments merit note here. First is the picture book retellings of traditional stories, in which the reteller documents sources and the changes he or she made to the story. Also important is the technique of framing these books by opening and closing with illustrations of a modern-day family who have gathered to hear the story. Gayle Ross's books are exemplary: *How Rabbit Tricked Otter and Other Cherokee Trickster Stories* (1994), *How Turtle's Back Was Cracked* (1995), and *Legend of the Windigo: A Tale from Native North America* (1996). Second are books that are centered on Native American peoples of today. Far too many books confine native people to the remote past. Working to correct that imbalance are authors such as Cynthia Leitich Smith (Creek) whose books *Jingle Dancer* (2000), *Rain Is Not My Indian Name* (2001), and *Indian Shoes* (2002) focus on contemporary children. Similarly, in nonfiction there is some emphasis on modern contexts: for instance, *We Are Still Here* (5 vols., 1992–1995) and *The First Americans* (5 vols., 1993–1995). Third are native-authored books that bring Native American issues to the body of children's literature. One example is *Battlefields and Burial Grounds* (1994). Written by two Pawnee men, Roger C. and Walter R. Echo-Hawk, the book describes efforts to recover from museums the remains of ancestors for reburial on tribal lands. Fourth is the work of contemporary Native Americans, who write critiques of popular books that inaccurately portray Native Americans. Among books severely criticized for stereotypical, biased, and erroneous depictions of Native Americans are *Brother Eagle, Sister Sky* (1991; illustrated by Susan Jeffers), *Little House on the Prairie* (1935, 1953) by Laura Ingalls Wilder, *Indian in the Cupboard* (1980) by Lynn Reid Banks, *My Heart Is on the Ground: The Story of Nannie Little Rose* (1999) by Ann Rinaldi, and *Arrow to the Sun* (1974) by Gerald McDermott. Also criticized are authors whose fraudulent claims to native identity have been exposed; most notable are Jamake Highwater and Forrest Carter. An additional problem is the retellings of traditional stories that are no longer recognizable as works from native sources, for instance, *The Turkey Girl: A Cinderella Story* (1996) by Penny Pollock and *Two Bad Boys* (1996) by Gail E. Haley.

[*See also* Fairy Tales and Folk Tales; Historical Fiction; Myths; Racism; United States; *and biographies of figures mentioned in this article.*]

BIBLIOGRAPHY

Seale, Doris, and Beverly Slapin, eds. *The Broken Flute*. Walnut Creek, Calif.: AltaMira, 2005. Includes hundreds of reviews of books about Native Americans.

Slapin, Beverly, and Doris Seale, eds. *Through Indian Eyes: The Native Perspective in Books for Children*. Philadelphia: New Society, 1998. The single most useful volume for understanding Native American literature.

Welcome to Oyate. http://www.oyate.org. Maintained by Slapin.

DEBBIE REESE

Naughton, Bill (1910–1992), writer of fiction, plays, and memoirs. Naughton, whose real name was William John Francis, was born in County Mayo, Ireland, but raised in Bolton, Lancashire. As an outsider, an Irish Catholic living among English Protestants, he wrote with an ethnographer's precision about life in the north of England. Naughton's autobiographical novel *One Small Boy* (1957) movingly charts a boy's dislocation from his motherland and his struggle to find a place in the world. It is also one of the most evocative depictions of a young Catholic struggling with his faith. Naughton was an intensely religious man, and a sense of the numinous in the everyday shines through his prose, whether he is describing the work of "night soilsmen" or the construction of a "trolley" racer, as in "Spit Nolan," his finest, much anthologized short story. In minimal words, this tale raises issues of religious difference, national identity, and Marxian notions of productive labor. However, these weighty themes are leavened with earthy humor, which also makes lesser works like *Pony Boy* (1946), *A Dog Called Nelson* (1976), and *My Pal Spadger* (1977) hilarious. Naughton writes about a lost world of "pals," where comradeship was essential for survival; and he often documents the emotionally fraught transition from boyhood to manhood.

BIBLIOGRAPHY

Rudd, David. "Betwixt and Between: The Canonization of Naughton and Nolan." *Signal* 91 (2000): 41–50.

DAVID RUDD

Naylor, Phyllis Reynolds (1933–), American author of several popular children's trade series. She has written fiction for readers of all ages, from children still at the picture-book stage to adults, with some nonfiction thrown in as well. Naylor had her first short story published when she was sixteen, and two years later she started selling regularly to magazines and Sunday school papers. She also taught school and worked as a secretary and an editorial assistant before becoming a full-time writer. Since the publication of her first novel, *What the Gulls Were Singing*, in 1967, she has published at least one new book each year.

Naylor has found a balance between series work and stand-alone books. In the Alice books, school and family tales about a girl in junior high whose mother has died, Naylor also finds a balance between underplaying her adolescent characters' development and obsessing about it. These books have been so popular that Naylor has added prequels for younger girls, chronicling Alice's grade-school days. From the first book, *The Agony of Alice* (1985), Alice's narrative voice is matter-of-fact about tampons and breasts and does not dwell on them. Schoolwork, music, friends, and family are at least as important in these books as boys and puberty; and Alice, although authentically adolescent, is not a caricature of a young person. Nor are Naylor's other young heroes and heroines caricatures; in the Bessledorf series, beginning with *The Mad Gasser of Bessledorf Street* (1983), strange and humorous things happen left and right, but Naylor keeps the characters in perspective even when they are losing their own. In her Witch series, she always remembers that young people will have difficulty being believed when they have strange stories to tell. These books, beginning with *Witch's Sister* (1975), feature two girls who try to fight the evil of a local witch. Naylor also wrote the York trilogy, about time travel to several different periods in British history.

Naylor has also addressed the theme of adolescents' choices and their separation from parents or other family members. *A String of Chances* (1982) depicts a minister's doubtful daughter, and *To Walk the Sky Path* (1973) deals with a traditional Native American family and the son's decision about whether to follow its ways or to assimilate with white people; in these two works, the protagonists face similar choices concerning their own values and their place in the world.

Naylor's work has received recognition and praise from several organizations, including the American Library Association. *Night Cry* (1984), her story of a girl who must overcome fear and prejudice to save a kidnapped child, won the Edgar Award from the Mystery Writers of America. Naylor won the Newbery Medal with *Shiloh*, the story of an eleven-year-old rural boy, Marty, whose empathy for animals leads him to take in an abused dog. Some educators consider Marty's behavior too good to be true, in the sense that it seems to be on an unrealistically mature developmental level; but readers of all ages have found the boy's protection of the little dog, Shiloh, true to life. Naylor wrote several sequels to *Shiloh*, and a successful film series was made of the books.

Naylor also drew on her background in psychology to write the How to Get Along books, teaching adolescents skills for coping with family and social situations.

BIBLIOGRAPHY

Naylor, Phyllis Reynolds. *How I Came to Be a Writer*. New York: Aladdin, 1987.

MARISSA K. LINGEN

Nazoa, Aquiles (1920–1976), self-taught Venezuelan writer, journalist, poet, and humorist. His vast literary production, based upon Venezuelan popular culture, is marked by an acute sense of humor and by an affectionate view of everyday life. Among the books he wrote for children are: *Poesía para colorear* (Poetry to Color, 1958), *Fábula de la ratoncita presumida* (Fable of the Conceited Little Mouse, 1982), *El espantapájaros* (The Scarecrow), *La niña, el pozo, el gato, el cojín bailador, y las siete piedritas* (The Little Girl, the Well, the Cat, the Dancing Cushion, and the Seven Little Stones, 1985), *Vida privada de las muñecas de trapo* (The Private Lives of the Rag Dolls, 1986), *Fábula de la avispa ahogada* (Fable of the Drowned Wasp, 1991), *El libro de los animales* (The Book of Animals, 1991), *Historia natural contada por Carlota* (Natural History as told by Carlota, 1994), *El perro, el chivo, y los tigres* (The Dog, the Goat, and the Tigers, 1994), *La historia de un caballo que era bien bonito* (The Story of a Horse That Was Very Beautiful, 1985), *Retablillo de Navidad* (Little Christmas Manger, 1991), *El libro de los cochinitos* (The Little Piggies Book, 1997), and *Retablo aragüeño* (Christmas Manger in Aragua, 1998).

MAITÉ DAUTANT

Nazor, Vladimir (1876–1949), prominent Croatian writer, who achieved fame in children's literature with his tales. After graduating in natural sciences in Graz, Austria, he returned to Croatia, working as a teacher. Joining the partisan movement, he was the first president of the Croatian Diet Presidium after World War II. A selection of his numerous works for children, previously printed separately, was collected in *Dječja knjiga* (1947; Children's Book). His dialogically structured children's poems are marked by a mixture of didacticism and aestheticism. In his children's plays and especially in his legends and tales of magic and animals, Nazor rewrote, often in allegorical mode, motifs and plots from popular international and regional fantastic literature, both written and oral traditions. His *Istarske priče* (1913; Istrian Tales), based on myth and folklore, as well as his autobiographical *Priče iz djetinjstva* (1924; Stories from Childhood) are considered sophisticated representatives of Art Nouveau style in literature. Although not intended for children, they are today recognized as children's literature.

MARIJANA HAMERŠAK

Needham, Violet (1876–1967), British children's writer. Amy Violet Needham's novels, many of them set in early 20th-century Ruritania, enjoyed enormous popularity. The trappings of royalty, integral to her plots, do not obscure her sure handling of character. Reluctant kingship and the conflict of duty with personal wishes are recurring themes in her writing, whether in her Ruritanian works such as *The Stormy Petrel* (1942), or in her historical novels, also set in imaginary countries, such as *The Changeling of Monte Lucio* (1946). Needham was in her sixties when her first book was published; long after her death, her works still have a devoted following of adult fans.

[*See also* Fantasy *and* Historical Fiction.]

BELINDA COPSON

Needle, Jan (1943–), a versatile writer who addresses diverse social issues in children's books that blend compassion and wit. *Albeson and the Germans* (1977), his first book, questions comic-book representations of Germans. In *My Mate Shofiq* (1978) and *Piggy in the Middle* (1982), Needle probes insidious institutional racism; other works explore bullying, oppression by the state, and ethical issues about killing in wartime. His themes, however, are always embedded in compelling and often very funny narratives. *A Fine Boy for Killing* (1979) begins a rich ongoing sequence of historical naval novels. Needle's most renowned work, *Wild Wood* (1981), wittily inverts the respectable tale of the River Bankers in Grahame's *The Wind in the Willows*, offering instead the view of the disgruntled workers (Stoats and Ferrets). Needle has prepared novels and novelizations of the popular television school series *Grange Hill*, and he himself is also a scriptwriter for children's programs.

BIBLIOGRAPHY

Inglis, Fred. "Social Class and Educational Adventures: Jan Needle and the Biography of a Value." In *Stories and Society: Children's Literature in Its Social Context*, edited by Dennis Butts. Basingstoke, U.K.: Macmillan, 1992, 84–96.

DAVID RUDD

Neill, John R. (1877–1943), illustrator considered by L. Frank Baum to be his chief collaborator on the Oz series. The fifth of eight children, John Rea Neill grew up in the Philadelphia suburb of Germantown. As a boy he often wandered away from home and got lost, absorbed in the creation of imaginary adventures. He attended the Pennsylvania Academy of Fine Arts for a year, then dropped out, feeling he could learn nothing more there. Neill was a busy and successful newspaper illustrator on staff at the *New York Evening Journal*, the *Philadelphia Inquirer*, and the *Philadelphia North American* when he agreed reluctantly in 1904 to succeed W. W. Denslow as the illustrator of the Oz books. Between 1904 and 1942, Neill provided pictures for thirteen of Baum's fourteen volumes in the series—an achievement for which the author conferred upon him the title "Imperial Illustrator of Oz"—then the nineteen titles by Ruth Plumly Thompson. After thirty-eight years realizing the land of Oz, Neill went on to author three stories of his own: *The Wonder City of Oz* (1940), *Scalawagons of Oz* (1941), and *Lucky Bucky in Oz* (1942). Upon his death, Neill left an unfinished manuscript, *Runaway in Oz*, which was first published with illustrations by Eric Shanover in 1995 by Books of Wonder. The finding aid for the Neill papers at the de Grummond Children's Literature Collection (at the University of Southern Mississippi) concludes, "The economy of style Neill brought to the Oz books gave Baum's characters and exotic locales form and substance, forever linking Neill to the Oz series.

Neill also brought his inimitable manner to Henry Wadsworth Longfellow's *Hiawatha* (1909), John Greenleaf Whittier's *Snowbound* (1909), and Edgar Allan Poe's *The Raven* (1910), as well as juvenile works published in magazines such as *Boy's Life*, *Ladies' Home Journal*, *McCall's*, and the *Saturday Evening Post*. Neill was also redrew illustrations for pirated editions of Beatrix Potter's *Peter Rabbit* and Helen Bannerman's *Little Black Sambo*, both of which circulated widely in America.

[*See also* Illustrations and *biographies of figures mentioned in this article*.]

MICHELLE H. MARTIN

Nekrasov, Andrei (1907–1987), Soviet Russian children's writer, best known for his book *The Adventures of Captain Wrungel* (1939), an ingenious and original contribution to the tradition of the tall tale in the spirit of Baron Münchhausen. The name of the main character alludes partly to Wrangel Island in the Arctic Ocean (named after a Russian explorer), and partly to *vrun*, the Russian word for "liar." The witty, dynamic first-person narrative tells about the incredible adventures of Captain Wrungel and his two bizarre companions during their voyage around the world. It abounds in puns, wordplay, and nonsense, but also presents geographical facts in an entertaining manner. The book is not completely devoid of the official Soviet ideology, as it portrays a Japanese admiral as the chief villain, but this figure is a generalized caricature rather than an example of ethnic prejudice. The book was extremely unusual for its time, when most Soviet children's literature was realistic and didactic.

Maria Nikolajeva

Nelson, Marilyn (1946–), American poet who writes for children and adults. In simple, colloquial, and powerful language, Nelson often melds the rhythms of African American speech with such traditional European forms as the sonnet and blank verse. After working on two collections of verse for children, including *The Cat Walked through the Casserole* (1984), she wrote half a dozen books for an adult audience, winning two Pushcart Prizes and becoming the poet laureate of Connecticut. Her *Carver: A Life in Poems* (2001) was marketed for young adults, in part, she says, because her usual publisher—a university press—was unwilling to reproduce photographs. This biography of George Washington Carver, celebrating (in the words of the poem "Goliath") "the slingshot of intelligence, and one / pebble of truth," earned honors in the Newbery and Coretta Scott King competitions. Urged by the editor Andrea Pinkney to take up lynching in a book for young adults, Nelson wrote a heroic crown of sonnets called *A Wreath for Emmett Till*; it was published in 2005, the fiftieth anniversary of Till's death.

BIBLIOGRAPHY

Flynn, Richard. "Consolation Prize." *Signal* 100 (2003): 1–19. After bemoaning the current state of poetry for children, Flynn turns to *Carver*, calling Nelson "a poet with intelligence, a poet with an ear."

Beverly Lyon Clark

Nesbit, E. (1858–1924), British children's writer. According to the critic Marcus Crouch, "no writer for children today is free from debt to this remarkable woman," and according to the critic Barbara Wall, Edith Nesbit is acknowledged as the creator of "the twentieth-century voice" in children's fiction. Forced into hack writing to support her family, Nesbit finally found her true calling in children's literature. In contrast to the dominant Victorian children's writers, Nesbit was one of the first British writers to take the part of the child and use a child first-person narrator endowed with a penetrating and genuine childlike view. Her immediate sources of inspiration in this respect were *The Golden Age* (1885) and *Dream Days* (1898) by Kenneth Grahame, adult novels about childhood written from the adult point of view, yet attempting to reconstruct a child's way of thinking and seeing the world. Nesbit applied and developed the attempt in her first full-length work *The Story of the Treasure Seekers* (1899) and its sequels, known as the Bastable trilogy and sometimes called the first contemporary realistic stories for children, employing a true and consistent child perspective. In addition, "The Reluctant Dragon" from *Dream Days*, an upside-down tale about a romantically minded dragon who refuses to fight St. George, inspired Nesbit to write a whole series of fractured fairy tales, first published in magazines and then collected in *The Book of Dragons* (1900) and *Nine Unlikely Tales* (1901). The essentially new feature in Nesbit's tales, as compared to those of earlier authors, was that she introduced tokens of her own time, such as elevators, telephones, diving bells, or cars, into traditional fairy tale settings, thus violating genre norms.

The principle of blending the everyday and the magic became the trademark of Nesbit's fantasy novels, all still read and appreciated today. In fact, she can be considered the founder of modern fantasy for children because she established certain patterns and trends. In her works, Nesbit explicitly postulated some rules for the use of magic that many of her successors within the fantasy genre have consciously or subconsciously followed. One of the primary rules is that, in order to function as an engine in a literary plot, magic cannot be omnipotent, but must have some laws and limitations. This principle is tangible already in Nesbit's first fantasy novel, *Five Children and It* (1902), obviously inspired partly by Mrs. Molesworth's *The Cuckoo Clock* (1877), where a wooden cuckoo plays the part of a good fairy for the child, and partly by two adult novels by F. Anstey, *Vice Versa* (1882) and *The Brass Bottle* (1900), both based on the idea of the absurdity of magic in modern world.

The type of fantasy Nesbit created is sometimes labeled "humorous fantasy" or even "nonsense," as opposed to heroic fantasy of the Tolkien fashion. The humorous effect often depends on the reader's failed expectations if the reader is familiar with the traditional folk tale patterns. In addition to its literary models Molesworth and Anstey, *Five Children and It* refers to the well-known folk tale about three wishes in which the third wish must be used to eliminate the devastating consequences of the first two. In the novel, ordinary British children find a strange creature in a sandpit, a hairy and bad-tempered Psammead, or Sandfairy, who can grant wishes. Yet whatever the children wish for, something is bound to go wrong. They wish to be "beautiful as the day," and have to go without lunch because the nurse does not recognize them. They wish for money, and get a sandpit full of ancient coins that cannot buy anything. Much like the folk

THE OPENING OF THE ARCH WAS SMALL, BUT CYRIL SAW THAT HE COULD GET THROUGH IT.

E. Nesbit. Illustration by H. R. Millar from *The Story of the Amulet* (London: T. Fisher Unwin, c. 1912). REPRODUCED COURTESY OF THE COTSEN CHILDREN'S LIBRARY, PRINCETON UNIVERSITY LIBRARY

tale hero, the children waste the magic wishes without gaining happiness. Among the restrictions appearing in the novel, the Psammead can only grant one wish a day, and magic is over by sundown, which constantly puts the children in precarious situations. Finally, they themselves refrain from taking the Psammead's magical help, thus demonstrating that magic is out of place in the modern world. In the sequel, *The Phoenix and the Carpet* (1904), the same children get hold of a flying carpet and a newborn Phoenix. Magical adventures start all over again, and once more Nesbit shows how tricky magic may be.

In *The Enchanted Castle* (1907), some further restrictions are proposed. Although the magic ring, featured in the novel, is a traditional fairy tale object, it works in an unusual and complicated manner: first twenty-one hours, then fourteen, then seven. Besides, the ring is whatever its bearer wants it to be: a wishing ring, an invisibility ring, a ring that makes you four yards tall or brings inanimate objects to life. Magic is irreversible, and, like the Niebelung ring, or the ring in Tolkien's novels, it corrupts the bearer. Magic thus appears a much more dangerous source of power in this novel, not pure entertainment as in the *Five Children* series. The idea of invisibility, although well known in folklore, was suggested to Nesbit by the science fiction novel *The Invisible Man* (1897) by H. G. Wells, who was a good friend of hers. *The Enchanted Castle* contains several direct parallels to *The Invisible Man.*

With *The Story of the Amulet* (1906), classified as the very first book of its kind ever written for children, Nesbit explored a radically new theme, definitely inspired by Wells's *The Time Machine* (1895). Although the idea of time displacement is similar in both texts, there is an essential difference in the nature of fantasy and science fiction with regard to both the purpose and the treatment of irrational events. Nesbit had no intention of foreseeing the future. Instead, she wanted to introduce young readers to history in a new and entertaining manner, therefore sending her time travelers—the five children from the previous novels—to exciting epochs of the past in places such as ancient Egypt and Babylon, Roman Britain, and legendary Atlantis. In *The Time Machine* the instrument of time travel is a gadget constructed by a scientist. Although the novel does not describe how the machine works, the point of departure is a rational explanation of a technically conceivable phenomenon. The amulet in Nesbit's story is a kind of time machine, but, unlike the science fiction gadget, it does not need any rational explanation. Nesbit's notion of time, however, is quite close to the modern scientific view of the world, expressed in *The Amulet* by the daring statement: "Time is only a mode of thought." Put into modern terms it means that time is not linear, that all times exist simultaneously. Nesbit was thus quite up to date on the theory of relativity, consciously or unconsciously.

The most important law introduced by Nesbit is that magic adventure does not take any real, primary time. The children come back from their journeys in time at exactly the same moment they went through the arch of the amulet. Primary time stands still in their absence. Their magical helper, the Psammead, explains that it would be wrong to mix up the present and the past or to cut bits out of one to fit into the other. This is a very convenient way to solve the time paradox and also build up the narrative without having to explain why the characters in the book are not missed by the adults while they are away.

When Nesbit's children arrive in ancient Egypt in 6000 BC, readers can expect them to have problems with communication. Nesbit dismisses these by saying that magic also allows the children to talk and understand other people even in the most distant epochs. Wells's adult novel does not admit of such explanations. His Traveler takes pains to learn the language of the secondary time he enters. While these references to Wells were conscious on Nesbit's part, she was obviously trying to articulate rules for magical time travels. More were to come in her later novels with the time shift motif, *The House of Arden* (1908) and *Harding's Luck* (1909). The mechanism of time traveling in *The House of Arden* is essentially different from that described in *The Amulet*. There is no visible time machine, but the children are taken on journeys in time by a magic helper, the Mouldiwarp, whom they summon by an incantation. The children themselves hit upon the idea that they want to travel into the past. They may be inspired by the sight of the Arden Castle and the memories of the Arden family glory; but they have also read *The Story of the Amulet*—an ingenious self-reference. Thus they are prepared for the marvelous things that happen. They are not surprised, and the adventure is much like a game. Besides, they always have the possibility to return instantly to the security of their own time as soon as the adventure becomes too scary.

In *The House of Arden*, Nesbit ponders still another dilemma of time displacement: whether the time traveler can affect history. Science fiction writers have depicted many frightening examples of how interfering with the past crucially changes the whole history of the world. The purpose of Nesbit's time fantasies was to present history in an entertaining way, not to depict an apocalyptic vision of distorted time. Neither did Nesbit wish to remove her characters definitely from the time and place to which they belong. The reason lies most probably in the poetics of children's literature in general, the significance of a happy ending. For a child, presumably, the permanent order of the world provides a sense of security. To allow the protagonist to shake this order by affecting history would be equal to undermining the child's faith in the stability of the world. Nesbit wanted to make sure that no calamity happens to her young heroes. Therefore she decided once and for all that time travelers could not affect history, a principle that most of her successors have followed, while some contemporary writers such as Diana Wynne Jones have rejected it.

In the sequel, *Harding's Luck*, cousin Richard, whom the Ardens met during their travels, becomes the protagonist. It is the same Mouldiwarp and his mighty brothers Mouldier Warp and The Mouldiest Warp who take Dickie, in the primary time a poor lame orphan, through different epochs. After a long while Dickie understands the mechanism of time displacement, which is more complicated than in the first book. In the past Dickie finds love and family, and in the end he decides to stay there forever. He thus definitely distorts linear time, escaping from the epoch to which he belongs. Nesbit leaves open the question of whether or not this implies meddling with history. *The Magic City* (1910) falls a step back in the exploration of fantasy genre, as it more closely follows the pattern of a heroic fairy tale, even though it is quite fascinating in its play with dimensions and the notions of fantasy and reality. *Wet Magic* (1913) features a mermaid as the magic helper. In *The Wonderful Garden, or The Three C's* (1911), the reader is compelled to question whether the events are indeed magical or have a rational explanation. Among Nesbit's many realistic novels, *The Railway Children* (1906) is perhaps the best loved.

Nesbit's most prominent talent lies in the storytelling and the innovative approach to genres, even though she undoubtedly created some colorful and memorable characters. Her overt socialist beliefs—she was a founding member of the Fabian Society—are prominent in her works for children, as she repeatedly lets her middle-class characters discover social injustice. She is also a very cautious feminist. While she obviously could not make her female characters fully emancipated, there are small details in many of her books pointing toward the idea of women being equal or even superior to men. Some of Nesbit's works were made into film and television series. Several major British and American children's writers have acknowledged Nesbit's impact on them, for instance, Edward Eager, Pamela Travers, and Mary Norton. Indirect traces of her influence can be also found in the fantasy works by Alison Uttley, C. S. Lewis, Philippa Pearce, and, most recently, J. K. Rowling.

[*See also* Fantasy; Magic; Science Fiction; *and biographies of figures mentioned in this article.*]

BIBLIOGRAPHY

Bell, Anthea. *E. Nesbit*. London: Bodley Head, 1960.
Briggs, Julia. *A Woman of Passion: The Life of E. Nesbit, 1858–1924*. New York: New Amsterdam, 1991.
Crouch, Marcus. *The Nesbit Tradition. The Children's Novel 1945–1970*. London: Benn, 1972.
Dorao, Marisol. *E. Nesbit, su vida y sus cuentos*. Cádiz, Spain: Universidad de Cádiz, 1987.
Lochhead, Marion. *The Renaissance of Wonder in Children's Literature*. Edinburgh, U.K.: Canongate, 1977.
Moore, Doris Langley. *E. Nesbit: A Biography*. London: Benn, 1967.
Prickett, Stephen. *Victorian Fantasy*. Hassocks, U.K.: Harvester, 1979.

Streatfeild, Noel. *Magic and the Magician: Edith Nesbit and Her Children's Books*. London: Benn, 1958.
Wall, Barbara. *The Narrator's Voice: The Dilemma of Children's Fiction*. London: Macmillan, 1991.

MARIA NIKOLAJEVA

Nesin, Aziz (1915–1995), Turkish novelist, playwright, short-story writer, and philanthropist. Nesin's voluminous writings cover a wide range of topics and have been translated into twenty-five languages. Nesin's preferred style is satirical, a reaction against the oppressive politics in Turkey during the middle 1900s, when the traditional government gave way to a multiparty system. Nesin's *Marko Paşa* (or *Marko Pasha*), an influential weekly publication that led to his arrest and a term in jail, exposed intolerance, conflicts, and cruelty in his politically changing society.

Nesin's struggle for human rights—including children's rights—is best expressed in his well-known autobiography *Böyle gelmişs böyle gitmez* (1966; *Istanbul Boy: That's How It Was but Not How It's Going to Be*, 1977). The subtitle of this book reverses a Turkish saying: "That's how it was and will always be." In 1972 Nesin established the Nesin Foundation, funded by royalties and donations, to contribute to the welfare of disadvantaged children.

RUSUDAN KILABERIA

Ness, Evaline (1911–1986), American artist and author. She was born in Ohio and raised in Michigan, where her father worked on an automobile assembly line. Ness worked as a commercial artist while studying at the Art Institute of Chicago, and then continued her studies at the Corcoran Gallery in Washington, D.C., and the Accademia di Belle Arti in Rome. She was married for twelve years to Elliott Ness, the famous crime fighter and pursuer of Al Capone. After a career as a commercial artist for *Seventeen Magazine* and a fashion artist for Saks Fifth Avenue, she illustrated her first children's book, *The Bridge* (1957), by Charlton Osborn. Subsequently she began to write her own books. She wrote and illustrated *Josefina February* (1963), *A Gift for Sufa Sufa* (1963), and *Exactly Alike* (1964). She adapted and illustrated the folk tales *Mr. Miacca* (1968) and *Long, Broad, and Quickeye* (1968). She received Caldecott Honor Awards for her illustrations in *All in the Morning Early* (1963), by Sorche Nic Leodhas; *Pocketful of Cricket* (1964), by Rebecca Caudill; and *Tom Tit Tot* (1965), adapted by Virginia Haviland. Ness won the Caldecott for *Sam, Bangs, and Moonshine* (1966), a book about a child's battle with truth-telling in which she captured a seaside setting with line drawings and blue-gray washes. Not surprisingly, Ness was in demand as an illustrator. She created pictures for Lloyd Alexander's *Coll and His White Pig* (1965), Elizabeth Coatsworth's *Lovely Maria* (1960), and Lucille Clifton's *Some of the Days of Everett Anderson* (1970), among other works. As an author-illustrator, Ness is known for strong story lines and for her care in adapting style and medium to the specific subject of each story she undertook. Most important, Ness was among the artistic standard-bearers of the late 20th century. Her work brims over with contemporary sensibility, originality, a flawless sense of design, and an unmistakable commitment to conception and technique.

BEVERLY VAUGHN HOCK

Netherlands. In the Netherlands, the first books written especially for children were published in the 16th century. They were schoolbooks, catechisms, and so on, made for didactic purposes. The first fiction for children appeared at the end of the 18th century, when Hieronymus van Alphen published his *Kleine gedigten voor kinderen* (3 vols., 1778–1782; English trans., *Poetry for Children*, 1856). His little poems were molded completely after the educational views of his time, concentrating on the moral content. He put model children on the stage. In poem after poem, virtues are shown to the reader. Written with a rare literary talent, his verses became classic and acquired a place in the literary history of the Netherlands.

Van Alpen's success stimulated other authors to make an effort. Within one year there was such a large supply of children's books that they were considered a separate literary category; besides poetry, other genres appeared. In the 19th century the moral perspective was gradually replaced by a more childlike point of view. And from the middle of the century, a great variety of picture books provided more entertainment. At the end of the century the girl's novel (in imitation of Louisa May Alcott's books) and the boy's novel came into vogue, genres that dominated the first half of the 20th century. A real classic, still in print, is C. Joh. Kieviet's *Uit het leven van Dik Trom* (From the Life of Dik Trom, 1891): the portrait of a "real Dutch boy," who plays all possible pranks but has a heart of gold.

From the turn of the 20th century there is even more attention paid to the emotions of children, their play and leisure. In poetry for children one finds a great influence from nursery rhymes, and themes such as dolls' tea parties and the arrival of a baby brother or sister. In prose, "domestic

The Netherlands. Illustration by Jan M. Verburg from *The Island of the Nose* by Annie Schmidt (London, New York, Toronto, Sydney: Methuen, 1977), p. 15. REPRODUCED COURTESY OF THE COTSEN CHILDREN'S LIBRARY, PRINCETON UNIVERSITY LIBRARY

realism" came into vogue, in which the world was reduced to the children's immediate surroundings. This genre produced a new classic: Nienke van Hichtum's *Afke's tiental* (1903; English trans., *Afke's Ten*, 1936), a story about a working-class family with ten children, kept together by a loving, self-effacing mother. In the 1950s the tone of children's literature gradually changed, especially in the work of the generation that made its debut after World War II. The most striking example is Annie M. G. Schmidt (1911–1995), generally recognized as the most versatile and talented children's book author in the Netherlands. She had a great influence on the next generations: the writers of the 1970s and

1980s are particularly indebted to her. In realistic stories for older children, the world grew larger, in more than one sense: more and more stories were set in other countries, often far away, while the border between the world of children and the world of adults was disappearing. Two authors stood out in this genre: An Rutgers van der Loeff-Basenau (1910–1990) and Miep Diekmann (1925–). Innovating picture books were also published by Dick Bruna (1927–). The 1960s were a period of further growth and consolidation, without really new developments. The most important new author of this period was Paul Biegel (1925–), who wrote a large number of fantasy stories. Max Velthuijs (1923–) became one of the most outstanding Dutch picture book artists, with an international fame.

The 1970s were dominated by a heated discussion about children's books, because of the rapid social changes. In these years Willem Wilmink (1936–2003) wrote his first poems for children. Like no other writer, he managed to immerse himself in the psyche of a child. Guus Kuijer (1942–) became famous as the author of five lively books about Madelief, beginning with *Met de poppen gooien* (1975; English trans., *Daisy's New Head*, 1980). They fitted into the tradition of everyday stories, but the tone was surprisingly new. Els Pelgrom (1934–) attracted much attention with one of the first novels about the German occupation of the Netherlands during World War II written by an author who was a child at the time: *De kinderen van het Achtste Woud* (1977; English trans., *The Winter When Time Was Frozen*, 1980). It was followed by numerous fantasy and realistic novels.

In the 1980s critics started paying more attention to literary aspects, and authors began to explore the borders of children's literature. As a result more and more children's books were interesting for adults; sometimes one could wonder who the intended reader was. An example is the work of Wim Hofman (1941–), also read by many adults because of its literary qualities. Hofman is a double talent, both author and artist. He writes fantasy and realistic novels, illustrated with childlike pictures. Another remarkable author is Joke van Leeuwen (1952–), a very individual, playful talent, who also illustrates her books herself, with smooth transitions from words to pictures. She writes from a strict child's point of view: many things that are self-evident for adults are unknown to her characters, which leads to all kinds of surprises. Imme Dros (1936–) works in heterogeneous genres, which makes it difficult to classify her. Her central work is a fantasy story, *Annetje Lie in het holst van de nacht* (1987; English trans., *Annelie in the Depths of the Night*, 1991). Typical for the postmodern children's literature of the 1990s is the appearance of many retellings. A remarkable example is a novel by Wim Hofman, *Zwart als inkt is het verhaal van Sneeuwwitje en de zeven dwergen* (Black as Ink Is the Story of Snow White and the Seven Dwarfs, 1997), in which the fairy tale of three thousand words has grown into a novel of thirty thousand words and eighty-eight pictures.

[*See also* Picture Books *and biographies of figures mentioned in this article.*]

BIBLIOGRAPHY

Linders-Nouwens, Joke, and Marita De Sterck. *Behind the Story: Children's Book Authors in Flanders and the Netherlands.* Translated from the Dutch by Jan Michael and Rina Vergano, with an introduction by Aidan Chambers. Antwerp, Belgium: Ministerie van de Vlaamse Gemeenschap; Amsterdam, Netherlands: Nederlands Literair Produktie- en Vertalingenfonds, 1996.

Vries, Anne de. "Literature for All Ages? Literary Emancipation and the Borders of Children's Literature." In *Reflections of Change: Children's Literature since 1945*, edited by Sandra L. Beckett, 43–47. Westport, Conn.: Greenwood, 1997.

Vrooland-Löb, Truusje, and Annelies Fontijne. *Dutch Oranges: Fifty Illustrators from Holland.* Translated from the Dutch by David Colmer. Zwolle, Netherlands: Waanders, 2001. Catalog of an exposition at the International Children's Book Fair at Bologna, April 2001.

ANNE DE VRIES

Nettell, Stephanie (1938–), children's book editor of the influential British newspaper the *Guardian* from 1978 to 1992. Nettell built on the already high standards established by her predecessor, the children's novelist John Rowe Townsend. Originally editor of the literary magazine *Books and Bookmen*, Nettell made the *Guardian* children's book pages superlative, often employing leading writers as reviewers. Closely involved with the annual Guardian Children's Fiction Award, she edited *Guardian Angels* (1988), an anthology comprising fifteen new stories by previous winners of the award. In 1992 she was awarded the prestigious Eleanor Farjeon Award in recognition of her outstanding work in children's literature journalism. Her *60 Creators of Favourite Children's Books* (1994) is an informal, very approachable introduction to some of the best writers and illustrators in contemporary British children's literature, with useful suggestions for further reading. She has also written a longer story, *The Gramercy Christmas Treasure* (2005), illustrated by Ian Penney.

[*See also* Journals and Periodicals; Publishers and Publishing; Townsend, John Rowe; *and* United Kingdom.]

NICHOLAS TUCKER

Neufeld, John (1938–), American author known for writing groundbreaking young adult books dealing with controversial social issues. Born in Chicago and educated at Yale, Neufeld hoped that his love of books and reading would lead to a career in editing original books. Instead he found himself working for various publishing houses in publicity and library promotions. When Neufeld heard of a real-life incident in which a white family faced community pressure after adopting an African American child, he decided it was perfect material for a book. *Edgar Allan* (1968) is the story of a minister's family that adopts a lovably guileless black child, only to give him up later. At less than a hundred pages, the tautly written novel stunned readers with its frank depiction of racial dissension and its uncompromising ending. Neufeld's next book, *Lisa, Bright and Dark* (1969), also broke new ground in young adult literature, exploring a previously taboo topic—a sixteen-year-old girl's descent into mental illness—with great candor. Broadcast as a "Hallmark Hall of Fame" television movie for which Neufeld wrote the script, the novel was hugely popular among teenage readers. *Freddy's Book* (1973) might have enjoyed similar success if it had been more widely available, but many libraries refrained from purchasing this blunt story of a boy's single-minded quest to discover the meaning of a sexual term he sees scrawled across a wall. The author has also written adult fiction, an historical novel for children (*Gaps in Stone Walls*, 1996), and several more young adult novels on hot button issues such as teenage pregnancy (*Sharelle*, 1983), homelessness (*Almost a Hero*, 1995), censorship (*A Small Civil War*, 1996), and sexual harassment (*Boys Lie*, 1999). However, by the time these books were published, the new realism in young adult fiction had already broken so many barriers that Neufeld's later titles, though generally well written, did not have the same impact as his earlier, most controversial novels.

PETER D. SIERUTA

Neverending Story, The. *See* Ende, Michael.

Neville, Emily (1919–), American author primarily of young adult novels. Emily Cheney Neville grew up in a large extended family clustered around the Cheney Silk Mills in Manchester, Connecticut, but her novels explore life in and around large cities. She attended Bryn Mawr College at age sixteen and completed an economics degree. She married Glen Neville, whom she met while they were working for the same newspaper, raised five children, and began writing fiction in 1961 when the youngest started school. Her first published novel, *It's Like This, Cat* (1963) won the coveted Newbery Medal. It introduces a first-person narrator, Dave Mitchell, a fourteen-year-old living with his lawyer father and homemaker mother in an apartment in New York City. Partly to spite his father, who prefers dogs, he acquires a cat and an elderly cat-lady friend, Kate. The stray cat's adventures plunge him into humorous and dangerous situations that ultimately result in his having a closer relationship with his father, as he starts to see both parents with new respect for their talents and their flaws. *Berries Goodman* (1965), in which a young boy confronts anti-Semitism while defending a friend, received the 1966 Jane Addams Children's Book Award. Neville published four more young adult novels between 1966 and 1975 and then took a break from writing to acquire a law degree in 1976 and practice law. In her 1988 novel *The Bridge*, written for younger readers, a boy watches the many large machines used to construct a new bridge to his driveway. *The China Year* (1991), about an eighth-grade girl's year with her family in Beijing just before the Tiananmen Square massacre, received mixed reviews. Yet this sensitive portrait of a young girl uses a child's natural curiosity to present the personal side of the daily life and growing unrest in that complicated country. Neville's understated setting is as much a character in this novel as the city is in the urban tales she wrote earlier in her career.

[*See also* Young Adult Literature.]

JANICE M. BOGSTAD

Newberry, Clare Turlay (1903–1970), American author and illustrator noted for her lifelike drawings of animals, particularly cats and kittens. Many of her books have been reissued since their original publication in the 1930s and 1940s, to delight a new generation of young readers. All her illustrations were done from life, and her apparently fanciful animal stories were actually derived from her experiences with her own pets. *Marshmallow* (1942), for example, is based on the true story of a friendship between a rabbit and Newberry's cat Oliver. Newberry wrote that she created the realistic-looking fur on some of her kittens by "painting rapidly with watercolor on wet paper." For other books she used different techniques, such as conté crayon on pastel paper for *Pandora* (1944). Although her first book, *Herbert the Lion* (1931), was illustrated "in a careful, exact manner," illustrations for some of her later books were life sketches "done at top speed," a style she preferred.

LINNEA HENDRICKSON

Newbery, John (1713–1767), London bookseller whose pioneering publication, the *Little Pretty Pocket-Book* (c. 1744), is considered the first modern children's book. Before Newbery, Thomas Boreman produced books in which text and illustrations were intended to amuse and instruct young readers exclusively and were distinctively packaged as products for that audience. But Newbery was the first bookseller to build a diversified list of works for children and to promote them through advertisements, reviews, and endorsements of the texts themselves, practices noted with amusement by essayists.

Children's books were a small part of Newbery's output: for adults, he published novels, periodicals, plays, poetry, satires, cookbooks, and medical works, as well as selling patent medicines, like Dr. James's Fever Powder, which were also puffed in books for the "rising generation." Steady-selling books of instruction were Newbery's real money-makers, and many stayed in print until 1800. They included: *The Circle of the Sciences* (1745–1748), a multivolume introduction to arithmetic, chronology, geography, grammar, logic, poetry, and rhetoric; readers such as *The Pretty Book for Children* (5th ed. 1751) and *The Museum for Young Gentlemen and Ladies* (1756); *The Holy Bible Abridged* (1757); a celebrated work of popular science, *Tom Telescope's the Newtonian System of Philosophy* (1761); *The New History of England from the Invasion* (1759); and Oliver Goldsmith's *History of England in a Series of Letters* (1764).

Newbery issued only a handful of entertaining books for children, but his fame rests upon such works as the *Lilliputian Magazine* (1751), the first children's periodical; *Nurse Truelove's New Year's Gift*, in which the nursery rhyme *The*

THE
NEWTONIAN SYSTEM
OF
PHILOSOPHY

Adapted to the Capacities of young GENTLEMEN and LADIES, and familiarized and made entertaining by Objects with which they are intimately acquainted:

BEING

The Subſtance of SIX LECTURES read to the LILLIPUTIAN SOCIETY,

By TOM TELESCOPE, A.M.

And collected and methodized for the Benefit of the Youth of theſe Kingdoms,

By their old Friend Mr. NEWBERY, in *St. Paul's Church Yard*;

Who has alſo added Variety of Copper-Plate Cuts, to illuſtrate and confirm the Doctrines advanced.

O Lord, how manifold are thy Works! In Wiſdom haſt thou made them all, the Earth is full of thy Riches.
Young Men and Maidens, Old Men and Children, praiſe the Lord. PSALMS.

LONDON,
Printed for J. NEWBERY, at the BIBLE and SUN, in *St. Paul's Church Yard*. 1761.

John Newbery. Frontispiece and title page from *The Newtonian System of Philosophy* by Tom Telescope with help from Mr. Newbery (London: J. Newbery, 1761). REPRODUCED COURTESY OF THE COTSEN CHILDREN'S LIBRARY, PRINCETON UNIVERSITY LIBRARY

House That Jack Built first appeared in print; and the *History of Little Goody-Two Shoes* (1765), the period's most popular novel for children (1757). Newbery aspired to be a publisher of polite literature, and his children's books were notable for their literary qualities, the encouragement to self-improvement through education, and the promotion of humane values such as kindness to animals. He continues to receive the credit for these pioneering publications because most have never been attributed definitively to particular authors, including ones he employed—most notably Giles Jones, who probably wrote *Goody-Two Shoes*, and Christopher Smart, who mostly likely edited the *Lilliputian Magazine*.

Newbery's successors continued to issue important children's books: his nephew Francis was the first to issue abridgments for children of important novels such as Samuel Richardson's *Pamela* (1740) or Henry Fielding's *Tom Jones* (1749); his stepson Thomas Carnan published one of the most important early collections of nursery rhymes, *Mother Goose's Melodies* (1780); Elizabeth Newbery issued many works by Richard Johnson illustrated by John Bewick and novels for young adults by Elizabeth Pinchard and Mary Pilkington. After three generations, the firm was sold to Elizabeth Newbery's business manager, John Harris, who was one of the early 19th century's great children's book publishers. Perhaps Newbery's greatest achievement was to create something analogous to a quality brand of children's books, which his successors maintained, that offered a benchmark for reviewers beginning with Sarah Trimmer in her magazine *Guardian of Education* (launched 1802) and continuing well into the 19th century. He is the namesake of the award presented by the American Library Association for the most distinguished American children's books of the previous year.

[*See also biographies of figures and titles of works mentioned in this article.*]

BIBLIOGRAPHY

Roscoe, Sydney. *John Newbery and His Successors, 1740–1814*. Wormley, U.K.: Five Owls Press, 1973.

Townsend, John. *John Newbery and His Books: Trade and Plumb-Cake Forever, Huzza!* Metuchen, N.J.: Scarecrow Press, 1994.

ANDREA IMMEL

Newbery Medal. *See* Awards.

Newell, Peter (1862–1924), American humorist and illustrator. Newell, a self-taught artist, captivated readers with his humorous pen-and-ink illustrations, quirky characters, and nonsensical captions. His drawings were reproduced in serial publications including *Harper's Weekly*, *Harper's Monthly*, and *St. Nicholas*; but he soon turned to books for children, creating clever, innovative works like *Topsys and Turvys* (1893), with pictures that could be read right side up and upside down. In *The Hole Book* (1908), a gun, accidentally discharged in the opening scene, sent forth a bullet that cut an actual hole in each subsequent page, resulting in funny situations. *The Rocket Book* (1912) again used a hole cut through the pages to show the amusing results of a rocket soaring from a basement through a twenty-one-story building. In *The Slant Book* (1910) Newell used another innovative device, a book in the shape of a parallelogram with story and illustrations printed on the diagonal. Newell also produced illustrations for editions of Lewis Carroll's Alice books, the Grimms' fairy tales, and books by Stephen Crane.

[*See also* Carroll, Lewis; Grimm, Jacob, and Wilhelm Grimm; St. Nicholas Magazine.]

ANN R. MONTANARO

New England Primer. This schoolbook was part of most American children's upbringing from the late 17th century until the mid-19th. No introduction to reading achieved anything like the same universality in England, or the same longevity; it has been estimated that the *New England Primer* sold an average of 25,000 copies annually for 150 years. George Emery Littlefield (in *Early Boston Booksellers*, 1900) described the primer as "the most remarkable book that was ever published in this country, and which has had such a mighty influence in moulding the mind, forming the habit, and coloring the creed of our ancestors." Its early history, a highly complex bibliographic problem, is debated in many specialist works. It was first printed in Boston sometime between 1686 and 1690. Its probable compiler was Benjamin Harris, a printer and political exile from London; he advertised a second edition in 1691. What the first version contained is not known, since the earliest extant copies (there are only two) are dated 1727. These differ slightly, but both include alphabets; a syllabarium; biblical texts; prayers and graces; and an account with an accompanying woodcut of the death, in 1554, of John Rogers, the first Protestant martyr during Mary Tudor's reign. Both end with John Cotton's catechism, "Milk for Babes."

The contents of the *New England Primer* were to vary according to the taste of printers and their customers, but John Rogers was almost always included. Another constant feature was the rhymed picture alphabet, which begins "In Adams Fall / We sinned all," although many of the subjects here varied, being sometimes predominantly religious and sometimes more secular. The alphabet as it originally appeared was taken from *A Guide for the Childe and Youth*, a primer signed "T.H." and printed in London in 1667. The catechism also varied; sometimes it was John Cotton's "Milk for Babes," but sometimes the Westminster "Shorter Catechism" (which was actually far longer) was used. Many editions contained a dialogue—probably by Benjamin Keach—between Christ, Youth, and the Devil, in which Youth, failing to heed injunctions to repent, is carried off to hell. Later editions usually included Isaac Watts's "Cradle Hymn," which introduced a gentler element into a book otherwise conspicuously austere.

BIBLIOGRAPHY

Carpenter, Charles. *History of American Schoolbooks*. Philadelphia: University of Pennsylvania Press, 1963.

Ford, Paul Leicester, ed. *The New-England Primer: A History of Its Origin and Development*. New York, Dodd, Mead, 1897. Reprinted 1962. Contains a facsimile reproduction of one of the two surviving copies dated 1727.

GILLIAN AVERY

Newfeld, Frank (1928–), book designer and illustrator born in Brno, Czechoslovakia. Raised and educated in England, he emigrated in 1954 to Canada, where he developed into one of the country's foremost book designers. His greatest contributions to children's literature are the illustrations for Dennis Lee's *Alligator Pie* (1974), *Nicholas Knock and Other People* (1975), and *Garbage Delight* (1977), works in which he fully realizes his philosophy of illustrating. He envisions a work holistically, seeking its overall rhythm and conceiving of each illustration in terms of what precedes and follows it, giving precedence to text when written by others. In his own works, *Simon and the Golden Sword* (1976) and *Creatures: An Alphabet for Adults and Worldly Children* (1998), he exerts more control over the balance between text and image, removing words to a glossary in the latter. The particular appeal of his illustrations rests in their capacity to stimulate children to take ownership of them through reacting playfully to the familiar, everyday things portrayed and imaginatively adding to them.

CAROLE H. CARPENTER

Newman, Leslea (1955–), American fiction writer, born in Brooklyn, New York. She earned a BS in education from the University of Vermont and a certificate in poetics from the Naropa Institute. The author of more than forty books, Newman has received many literary awards, mostly for her adult works. For young people, she has authored a variety of picture books and novels, some general interest (such as *Hachiko Waits*, 2004), some dealing with gay and lesbian or feminist themes (such as *A Fire Engine for Ruthie*, 2004). Newman is best known as the author of the groundbreaking and controversial *Heather Has Two Mommies* (1989), the first children's book to portray lesbian families in a positive way.

[*See also* Gay and Lesbian Literature for Children *and* Picture Books.]

NANCY J. KEANE

Newsome, Effie Lee (1885–1979), African American poet and writer of short fiction. Newsome was hired by W. E. B. Du Bois to carry on the work he had undertaken in *The Brownies' Book* (1920–1922). From 1925 to 1929 her job was to contribute a column, "The Little Page," for the magazine *The Crisis*. Her poems captured the child's love of fantasy, as in "We'll Break Our Camp and March Like Men" (*Crisis*, September 1928); her tales satirized white arrogance, as in "On the Pelican's Back" (*Crisis*, August 1928). Newsome was educated at Wilberforce, Oberlin, and the University of Pennsylvania. After marrying the Reverend Henry Nesby Newsome, she organized a boys' club in Birmingham and collected her nature poems in *Gladiola Garden* (1940). Her most distinctive works include lyrical poems about the value of an African heritage, and nonsense verses in the manner of Edward Lear. Her poems for adults (acerbic criticisms of white exploitation) were included in *The Poetry of the Negro, 1746–1949*, edited by Langston Hughes and Arna Bontemps (1949).

[*See also* Bontemps, Arna Wendell; Brownies Book, The; *and* Hughes, Langston.]

BIBLIOGRAPHY

MacCann, Donnarae. "Effie Lee Newsome: African American Poet of the 1920s." *Children's Literature Association Quarterly* (Summer 1988): 60–65.

DONNARAE MACCANN

Newth, Mette (1942–), Norwegian author, translator, and illustrator who started publishing picture books, children's and young adult novels and comics in 1969, some coauthored with her husband, Philip Newth. She has exhibited internationally and worked as a principal for Norwegian art schools. Her main focus is on (post)colonial power relations and the treatment of minorities like the Saami (Lapland), the Inuit (Greenland), and the Aboriginals. *Bortførelsen* (1987; English trans., *The Abduction*, 1989) portrays an Inuit girl and her friend, (abducted to Norway in the 17th century), who try to flee in a kayak into the open sea probably to face death, based on hundreds of similar stories of abductions of native people to Europe in that time. *Forandringen* (1997; English trans., *The Transformation*, 2000) shows the conflict of an Inuit girl who saves a missionary from starvation in late medieval times. *Det mørke lyset* (1995; English trans., *The Dark Light*, 1998) treats the story of a girl in 19th-century Norway suffering from leprosy. Newth is deeply engaged in defending the marginalized and combines this defense with detailed research, a lucid and vibrant style, and a surprising perspective.

BIBLIOGRAPHY

Crew, Hilary S. "Mette Newth's *The Abduction*, The Transformation, and Arctic Colonialism: A Postcolonial Perspective." *The Lion and the Unicorn* 28, no. 4 (2004): 429–445.

Astrid Surmatz

New Zealand. In the 19th century New Zealand children's books were published in England, and they commonly linked geographical instruction about the newly settled land and about the indigenous Maori with entertainment. Lady Barker, in *A Christmas Cake in Four Quarters* (1871), was a crisp pragmatic voice, and inflated accounts of Maori war practices helped sell G. A. Henty's adventure story *Maori and Settler: A Story of the New Zealand War* (1891); the ultimate triumph for the family being a return to England.

20th-Century Genres

In the early 20th century, fantasy creatures collated from Irish and English tales and Maori legends led young readers to learn about the land (considered empty) and the Maori through the spirit and fairy world. Edith Howes—the botanist known particularly for her widely published, fairy-guided sex education title *The Cradle Ship* (1916)—established a tradition. In the 1950s, Avis Acres (observing the commercial success of May Gibbs's comic tales of Australian bush fairies, *Gumnut Babies*, 1916), created her long-lasting cartoon characters Hutu and Kawa. Their fey quality echoed the children's pages of the 1930s and discomforted adults of the day.

The colonial family adventure genre, like its Australian counterpart, exemplified the child as knowledgeable about the bush and personally and physically effective. Isabel Maude Peacocke, who wrote *The Cruise of the Crazy Jane* (1932) among many others, and Esther Glen, author of *Six Little New Zealanders* (1917), drew suntanned girls as well as boys fording flooded rivers, just as the Australians fought bush fires. Mona Tracy's historical war novel *Rifle and Tomahawk* (1927) was emblematic of the period; the family remains central, the girl is stalwart, and the protagonist hopes to further Maori-Pakeha relations in the future. A dearth of well-written children's books in the 1930s to 1960s brought specific attention to Maurice Duggan's *Falter Tom and the Water Boy* (1958; reprinted 1984), an original fantasy evoking memories of Charles Kingsley's *The Water Babies* (1863).

In the 1970s the ubiquitous nation-building ethos surfaced in the work of Ruth Dallas (*Big Flood in the Bush*, 1972), Joan de Hamel (*Take the Long Path*, 1978), and Anne de Roo (*Jacky Nobody*, 1983). The New Zealander remained young, egalitarian, and competent in rural matters. Anne de Roo advanced the interracial discourse in that Jacky Nobody, a mixed-race orphan, came to the realization that he, like his nation, had to value both cultures. Representations of Maori as well as Pakeha (a term for non-Maori) New Zealand children became more sophisticated through the 1980s to post-2000. Writers such as Gaelyn Gordon, who explored interethnic spiritual cooperation, as well as Jack Lasenby, Margaret Mahy, Paula Book, and William Taylor, were now portraying a society as mixed as it was for children themselves.

Exploding in the 1980s was a burst of fantasy and science fiction writers whose protagonists make heavy decisions affecting the world. In Maurice Gee's O trilogy beginning with the *Halfmen of O* (1982), the hero has to balance democracy and free speech against authoritarian government in another world. Barry Faville, beginning with *The Keeper* (1986), investigates issues of genetic engineering in a postcataclysmic world. Sherryl Jordan's often violent and ceremonial fantasies closely engage the reader in issues of personal and social responsibilities; her popular *Rocco* (1990), where possible pasts and futures intersect, juxtaposes a simple peaceful society with a complex militaristic one. *Because We Were the Travellers* (1997) introduces a quartet by Jack Lasenby grappling with ideas of exclusion, survival, myth, and the nature of story. In its postdisaster setting, it is bleak writing in strong contrast not only to other writers for teenagers but also to Lasenby's great store of closely observed rural humorous stories and other novels for wide-ranging

New Zealand. Front cover of *The Adventures of Hutu and Kawa* by Avis Acres; told by Colleen Rea (Wellington, N.Z.: A. H. and A. W. Reed, 1958). REPRODUCED COURTESY OF THE COTSEN CHILDREN'S LIBRARY, PRINCETON UNIVERSITY LIBRARY

audiences. Lasenby's humor, including the tall tales in the Uncle Trev stories (about a saddle-eating horse) and a series of summer adventures like *The Battle of Pook Island* (1996) are embedded in rural New Zealand adventures certainly available to fewer children in the 21st century. In his skilled use of child slang and crudities, Lasenby laid the base for other humorists such as Vince Ford, who wrote *2Much4U* (1999).

Much discussed was William Taylor's exploration of gay relationships in *Blue Lawn* (1994) and *Jerome* (1999). Paula Boock, in *Dare Truth or Promise* (1997), depicts the complex lives of two girls in love who have to sort money and class issues as well as sexual orientation. Obsessive love in some of the stories in *Falling in Love* (1995), collected by Tessa Duder, and *Hostel Girl* (1999), by Gee, continued this theme.

Margaret Mahy, New Zealand's major writer for children, continues adding to her abundant body of work—picture books, verse, and novels. Mahy's concern with the idea of a life of integrity, her humor, a fast pace, and a mix of fantasy with family dialogue underpin all her work. Her work for older readers engages teenagers in a searching commitment to life, enhanced rather than negated by her employment of the supernatural. She won Carnegie Medals for *The Haunting* (1982) and *The Changeover: A Supernatural Romance* (1984) and has won other major international awards for *Catalogue of the Universe* (1985), *The Tricksters* (1986), and *Memory* (1987). She was initially not published in her homeland, but, generous with her time visiting schools and conferences, she is feted throughout the country and is a holder of the Order of New Zealand.

Illustrated Titles

Picture books were a major genre in New Zealand publishing from the 1980s. Lynley Dodd, whose *Hairy Maclary from Donaldson's Dairy* (1983) rollicked its way through a number of rhythmic rhymed stories, was extremely popular, and Miriam Smith's Maori-oriented stories reveal sociological depth in simple tales. Gavin Bishop illustrated and subtly retold English folk tales, such as *Three Billy Goats Gruff* (2003), and Maori legends, such as *Maui and the Sun* (1996). Although his talented painting and shrewd storytelling is locally underestimated, his books continue to delight New Zealanders, recognizing themselves in illustrations. Joy Cowley locates her stories in a realistic New Zealand setting—her idiomatic *Video Shop Sparrow* (1999) integrates a sardonic adult humor with a gentle account of two boys freeing a trapped sparrow.

A large body of illustrated work since the 1980s on Maori myths and legends has come from artists including Robert Jahnke, Para Matchitt, Peter Gossage, Robin Kahukiwa, Chris Slane, and Gavin Bishop. Some of these writers, Maori themselves, drew on the graphic novel or on ethnographic records. Gavin Bishop in *The House That Jack Built* (1999) represents culture clash in an English rhyme, and he and Robert Sullivan in *Weaving Earth and Sky* (2002) step in a new direction constructing the reader as Maori. Showing real Maori children, Patricia Grace in *The Trolley* (1993), writes a gritty account of a solo mother making her children a Christmas present. With the increasing profile of Maori writers, as Witi Ihimaera, author of *Whale Rider* (1987) might say, we look to the past as we move to the future.

[*See also* Colonial Fiction *and biographies of figures mentioned in this article.*]

Bibliography

Gilderdale, Betty. "Children's Literature." In *Oxford History of New Zealand Literature*, edited by Terry Sturm, 525–574. Auckland: Oxford University Press, 1998.

Khorana, Meena, ed. "Children's Literature of Australia and New Zealand." *Bookbird* 37, no. 1 (1999). Special issue.

Mahy, Margaret. "Finding Your Reflection in a Small Mirror: A Developing Children's Literature in New Zealand." *Bookbird* 37, no. 1 (1999): 50–56.

Melbourne, Sidney. "The Portrayal of the Maori in New Zealand's Children's Fiction." In *A Track to Unknown Water*, 90–103. Metuchen, N.J.: Scarecrow, 1987.

Jill Holt

Nichols, Grace (1950–), author of poetry and prose for all ages. Nichols was born in Guyana but has lived in Britain since 1977. She often takes a wry view of modern British life in her poetry for adults, but as a children's writer she is best known for poetry that takes the reader to the inspiring sights and language of her Caribbean childhood. The collection *Come on into My Tropical Garden* (1988) fuses Standard English and Caribbean Creole in conveying "back home" sounds, sights, and happenings, such as the telling of "jumbie" (ghost) stories and a rhythmic praise of a mother's practical skills and courage in "Wha Me Mudder Do." Nichols is also committed to introducing Caribbean poetry and poets to children through a number of excellent anthologies, many of them coedited with her partner John Agard. From *Poetry Jump Up* (1990) to *No Hickory, No Dickory, No Dock: A Collection of Caribbean Nursery Rhymes* (with Agard, 1991) to *A Caribbean Dozen: Poems from Caribbean Poets* (with Agard, 1994) and *From Mouth to Mouth* (with Agard, 2004), Nichols has found in both original and traditional verse a combination of sound and sense that appeals directly to young listeners.

[*See also* Agard, John; Caribbean Countries; *and* Poetry.]

Gillian Lathey

Nichols, Ruth (1948–), Canadian writer of fantasy and historical fiction. Nichols's first novel, *Ceremony of Innocence* (1969), invokes the theme that appears throughout her novels: the female hero's search for maturation and identity.

Song of the Pearl (1976) and *The Left-Handed Spirit* (1978) develop this issue while extending their scope to include the afterlife and the early Roman and Chinese empires. Nichols is best known for her two works of high fantasy, *A Walk Out of the World* (1969) and *The Marrow of the World* (1972); the latter was named the Canadian Library Association Book of the Year for Children. While *A Walk Out of the World* contains obvious Tolkienian overtones both in landscape and in Nichols's portrayal of dwarves, *The Marrow of the World* presents a unique marine atmosphere along with a powerful vision of female identity. Both novels provide satisfying syntheses of fantasy and realism.

[*See also* Fantasy; Girls' Books and Fiction; *and* Historical Fiction.]

BIBLIOGRAPHY

Jones, Raymond E., and Jon C. Stott. "Ruth Nichols." In *Canadian Children's Books: A Critical Guide to Authors and Illustrators*, 363–366. Toronto: Oxford University Press, 2000.

ANNE HIEBERT ALTON

Nicholson, William (1872–1949), British artist and author who is regarded as a pioneer in the field of children's picture books and was knighted in 1936. Born in Newark-on-Trent, Nicholson was an acclaimed painter of portraits, landscapes, and still lifes. His first book, *An Alphabet* (1897), features wood engravings of individuals identified by profession ("A was for Artist" is a self-portrait) or personality trait. *The Square Book of Animals* (1899) contains twelve block prints of ducks, swans, and other forms of wildlife. The two picture books that Nicholson both wrote and illustrated, *Clever Bill* (1926), the tale of a toy soldier separated from its child, and the adventure story *The Pirate Twins* (1929), are regarded as seminal works of the genre. Their tight, spare texts, dramatic plots, and symbiotic unity of prose and color art influenced generations of future picture books. Though these volumes are rarely read today, Nicholson remains known to contemporary readers for the watercolor illustrations he contributed to Margery Bianco's 1922 classic, *The Velveteen Rabbit*.

PETER D. SIERUTA

Nick Carter Dime Novels. Nick Carter, the most famous American dime novel detective, helped popularize standard literary conventions such as the child sidekick, the hero's reliance on assumed identities and disguises, and the use of specialized crime-busting gadgets. Carter, the first

Nick Carter. Front cover of *Nick Carter Weekly* no. 196 (29 September 1900). REPRODUCED COURTESY OF THE COTSEN CHILDREN'S LIBRARY, PRINCETON UNIVERSITY LIBRARY

series character to have his own eponymous publications, debuted on September 28, 1886, in Street and Smith's popular fiction periodical, *New York Weekly*, predating the introduction of Sherlock Holmes by over a year. According to most authorities, Carter was created by John Russell Coryell (1851–1924), a former journalist and unsuccessful author of children's books. Along with a number of other authors, most notably Frederick van Rensselaer Dey (1861–1922) and Eugene T. Sawyer (1846–1924), Coryell chronicled more than 1,200 gripping stories starring Carter, in *Nick Carter Library*, *New Nick Carter Library*, *Nick Carter Weekly*, *New Nick Carter Weekly*, and *Nick Carter Stories*. In October 1915, fearing that the public was growing tired of adventures dealing exclusively with Carter, Street and Smith relaunched *Nick Carter Stories* as one of the first pulp fiction magazines,

Detective Story, which included an occasional Carter mystery alongside serials starring new characters and backup features describing the minutiae of detective work. As early as 1908 Carter had become a movie hero; and as the dime novel era wound down, his admirers became older viewers and readers and radio audiences.

BIBLIOGRAPHY

Sampson, Robert. *Yesterday's Faces: A Study of Series Characters in the Early Pulp Magazines*, Vol. 1, *Glory Figures*. Bowling Green, Ohio: Bowling Green University Popular Press, 1983.

ERIC J. JOHNSON

Nic Leodhas, Sorche (1898–1969), American author and folklorist known for collections of Scottish tales. Born Leclaire Alger in Youngstown, Ohio, the author worked as a librarian for much of her life. Early in her career, she published a trio of children's novels (*Jan and the Wonderful Mouth Organ*, 1939; *Dougal's Wish*, 1942; and *The Golden Summer*, 1942). Nearly twenty years passed before she adopted the name "Sorche Nic Leodhas"—Gaelic for "Claire, daughter of Louis"—and began publishing Scottish folk tales in collections and individual volumes. *Heather and Broom: Tales of the Scottish Highlands* (1961) contains "seanachie" stories—tales originally told by wandering storytellers—such as "The Woman Who Flummoxed the Fairies" and "The Lass Who Couldn't Be Frightened." Written in beautifully cadenced prose that begs to be read aloud, the stories are sometimes humorous, sometimes thought-provoking, and at other times eerie. Her next book, *Thistle and Thyme: Tales and Legends from Scotland* (1962), was named a Newbery Honor book. Several of Nic Leodhas's later folk-tale collections were based on themes. *Gaelic Ghosts* (1963), *Ghosts Go Haunting* (1965), and *Twelve Great Black Cats, and Other Eerie Scottish Tales* (1971) all dealt with the supernatural. *Sea-Spell and Moor Magic: Tales of the Western Isles* (1968) contains stories that come from each of the Hebrides Islands. Gaelic songs inspired *By Loch and Lin: Tales from Scottish Ballads* (1969). She also published two individual picture books based on traditional poems, *All in the Morning Early* (1963), which earned a Caldecott Honor for Evaline Ness's illustrations, and *Always Room for One More* (1965), for which illustrator Nonny Hogrogian won the Caldecott Medal. Throughout her lifetime, Sorche Nic Leodhas gathered stories from anyone she met with a Scottish background and made a point of never including a previously published story in one of her books, thereby making a significant contribution not just to children's literature, but to the study of folklore in general.

PETER D. SIERUTA

Nicolai, Friedrich (1733–1811), German author. Son of a bookseller and publisher, Friedrich Christoph Nicolai took over his father's bookshop in Berlin in 1758 and became one of the leading publishers and authors of the German Enlightenment. He was friends with Gotthold Ephraim Lessing and Moses Mendelssohn, and in 1798 he was elected member of the Academy of Sciences in Berlin and in 1799 given an honorary doctorate by the university of Helmstedt. He published *Literaturbriefe* (Literary Letters, 1759–1765) and was very successful with the publication of *Allgemeine Deutsche Bibliothek* (General German Library, 1765–1805). His moral fables were often included in school primers. Nicolai's satirical Bildungsroman *Das Leben und die Meinungen des Herrn Magister Sebaldus Nothanker* (The Life and Meanings of Master Sebaldus Nothanker, 1773–1776) was quickly regarded as suitable reading matter for young adults and was published in abridged editions intended for children.

BETTINA KÜMMERLING-MEIBAUER

Nielsen, Kay (1886–1957), Danish illustrator. Born into a theatrical family in Copenhagen, Nielsen grew up among artistic people. He had aspirations of becoming a doctor, but his artistic talent was too obvious to be ignored. At seventeen he went to Paris where he came under the influence of Jean Paul Laurence and the Colorossi school. There he was exposed to the Japanese artworks that were popular at the time. After leaving school, he moved to London, where he began illustrating books. Along with Arthur Rackham and Edmund Dulac, he was prominent in the gift book phenomenon of the years before World War I. He came to the work later than Dulac and Rackham, but the war interrupted his promising career in book illustration, since people no longer had money to spend on these beautiful and expensive books.

Nielsen's fame rests on only four books: *Powder and Crinoline* (1913; U.S. title, *The Twelve Dancing Princesses*), *East of the Sun and West of the Moon* (1915), *Fairy Tales by Hans Andersen* (1922), and *Hansel and Gretel* (1925). These latter two were published after the war in an attempt to reinvigorate the gift book market, but they were not as successful as the first two. A fifth book, *Red Magic*, published in 1932, contained only eight plates of inferior quality, and it soon was out of print.

Kay Nielsen. Illustration of Rapunzel from *Hansel and Gretel and Other Stories by the Brothers Grimm* (New York: George H. Doran, 1925). REPRODUCED COURTESY OF THE COTSEN CHILDREN'S LIBRARY, PRINCETON UNIVERSITY LIBRARY

Nielsen returned to Copenhagen at the end World War I and was drawn once again into the theater world, designing sets and costumes. In 1936 he was invited to America to mount a production of *Everyman*. Nielsen stayed on in California to work at the Disney studios, but he was a slow worker and did not fare well in the fast-paced world of cartoon animation. Therefore, he allowed a leave of absence to become permanent, but he left an enduring stamp at Disney, as he designed the "Bald Mountain" and "Ave Maria" sequences for the 1942 movie *Fantasia*. He also did some design work in the late 1930s for *The Little Mermaid*, for which he received screen credit when the film was released fifty years later.

After returning to Denmark, Nielsen lived in near poverty until his death. During this time, he made some twenty illustrations for *A Thousand and One Nights*, but printing costs were prohibitive and they were not published until 1977 when Nielsen's work experienced a renascence.

His illustrations were meant primarily for an adult audience, and he has come to be viewed as a children's illustrator probably only because of the choice of books he illustrated. His drawings are very sophisticated, influenced by Art Noveau and the works of Aubrey Beardsley. They are distinguished by sinuous lines and a palette that mixes pastel colors with muted backgrounds—reflecting, some say, the half-light of Nordic winters. Objects are stylized, with flowing trees and impossibly long legs and dresses. Large open areas contrast with highly decorated areas. These qualities combine to give Nielsen's pictures an elegance rarely seen in children's book illustrations.

BIBLIOGRAPHY

Meyer, Susan E. "Kay Nielsen." In her *A Treasury of Great Children's Book Illustrators*, 195–209. New York: Abrams, 1983.

JACQUE ROETHLER

Nieritz, Gustav (1795–1876), one of the most successful German writers of popular tales during the 19th century. Son of a Dresden teacher, Nieritz became a teacher himself and assumed the same position his father had. When he started his career as a writer in the 1830s, he was influenced by the Catholic author Christoph von Schmied (1768–1854) and can be regarded as the Protestant counterpart of this author. Nieritz's stories are about common people leading virtuous and pious lives that save them from any adversity. The titles often contain the moral motto of the story: *Der kleine Bergmann oder Ehrlich währt am längsten* (The Little Miner, or Honesty Is the Best Policy, 1834), *Der junge Trommelschläger oder Der gute Sohn* (1838; English trans., *The Little Drummer*, 1858), *Das vierte Gebot oder Die ungleichen Brüder* (The Fourth Commandment, or The Unequal Brothers, 1840), and others. Nieritz claims in his autobiography (1872) that he had published 117 books for children and young people, some of which were translated in other European countries and in the United States. At the turn of the 20th century the work of Nieritz was criticized by members of the youth literature reform movement (Jugendschriftenbewegung) for being meaningless from a literary point of view and tendentious in its moral message.

[*See also* Germany *and* Moral Tales.]

BERND DOLLE-WEINKAUFF

Nightingale, The. *See* Andersen, Hans Christian.

Niimi Nankichi (1913–1943), Japanese poet and novelist for children. Nankichi, whose real name was Watanabe Shohachi, was born in the suburb of Handa, near Nagoya, and was interested in literature from a young age, submitting stories and poems for school journals. After graduating from high school, he worked briefly as a substitute teacher. During this period his literary talent was recognized by other poets, and his stories and poems began to appear in *Akaitori* (The Red Bird), a literary journal for children that was among the best of its time. He then entered the Tokyo School of Foreign Studies to major in English. He obtained a job in Tokyo, but after contracting tuberculosis he returned to his hometown. While working as a teacher, he continued to write stories and poems for children. In 1943, his illness worsened; he died as he was in the midst of preparing his second and third collections of short stories.

His fiction for children is characterized by clear story lines and vivid descriptions of scenes from his home country. Some works explore the feelings of young people; some depict village scenes. *Ojiisan no lamp* (Grandfather's Lamp, 1942) was his first published anthology. Other short stories were collected after his death in *Ushi wo tsunaida tsubaki no ki* (A Camellia Tree and a Cow, 1943) and *Hananokimura to nusubitotachi* (Thieves and Flower Tree Village, 1943). Some of his stories have been made into picture books and are loved by modern readers; among these works, "Gon gitsune" (Gon the Fox) has been adapted as an authorized textbook in elementary schools and has become one of the most popular children's stories.

In 1994, following a local movement to preserve his manuscripts, the Niimi Nankichi Memorial Center was opened in Handa city, encouraging research into his works as they relate to the local community and children.

ARIKO KAWABATA

Niland, Deborah (1952–), illustrator and twin daughter of the Australian writers D'Arcy Niland and Ruth Park, was born in New Zealand. Her witty and playful illustrations to Park's *The Gigantic Balloon* (1975), *Roger Bandy* (1977), and *When the Wind Changed* (1980), in which Josh becomes a hero despite the warnings he is given about making grotesque faces, express her distinctive design and larger-than-life exuberance. She has illustrated books by Jean Chapman such as *The Sugar Plum Christmas Book* and *The Sugar Plum Song Book* (both 1977); poetry books by Michael Dugan, including *Stuff and Nonsense* (1974); Hazel Edwards's series including *There's a Hippopotamus on Our Roof Eating Cake* (1980) and *Guess What? There's a Hippopotamus on the Hospital Roof Eating Cake* (1997); and *Fairy Strike* (1980) by Trevor Todd. *ABC of Monsters* (1976) and *Old MacDonald Had an Emu* (1986), which have Australian animals in whimsical attitudes and display her humor. With her sister Kilmeny she illustrated *Mulga Bill's Bicycle* (1973) and *The Drover's Dream* (1973), reviving for children two popular poems by the author of "Waltzing Matilda," A. B. Paterson.

STELLA LEES and PAM MACINTYRE

Niland, Kilmeny (1952–), illustrator and twin daughter of the Australian writers D'Arcy Niland and Ruth Park, was born in New Zealand. Her style as an illustrator is similar to that of her sister Deborah, capturing the quirky, self-deprecating, and "larrikin" (rowdy) quality of Australian humor. *Old Witch Boneyleg* (1978), by Ruth Manning-Saunders, and *Fairy Tale Picture Dictionary* (1979), by Jane Wilton-Smith, are collections of fairy stories. Niland illustrated Mem Fox's *Just Like That* (1986); *Grandad Barnett's Beard* (1988), by Christine Church; and *Fey Mouse* (1988), by Hazel Edwards. *How Many Dogs in the House?* (2003), by Beverley Boorer, is a counting book featuring comical dogs and cats. She wrote and illustrated *Feathers, Fur, and Frills* (1980), a book of Australian animals, and *A Bellbird in a Flame Tree: The Twelve Days of Christmas* (1989), which has native fauna sent as Christmas presents.

[*See also* Niland, Deborah *and biographies of other figures mentioned in this article.*]

STELLA LEES and PAM MACINTYRE

Nilsson, Eleanor (1939–), writer who was born in Scotland and emigrated to Australia in 1952. Her books for early readers include *The 89th Kitten* (1989), illustrated by Linda Arnold, *The Black Duck* (1991), illustrated by Rae Dale, and *Pearl's Pantry* (1996), illustrated by Betina Ogden. *The House Guest* (1991), winner of the 1992 Children's Book Council of Australia Book of the Year Award, Older Readers, is about Gunno and his friends who break into houses. A mystical connection beyond time and place develops between Gunno and the missing Hugh. In *Outside Permission* (1996), Simon and David infiltrate the House of Records, where they find the dates of their own deaths.

STELLA LEES and PAM MACINTYRE

Nimmo, Jenny (1944–), British author. Solitary children, family mysteries, and Welsh landscapes and legends figure frequently in Nimmo's fantasies, such as *The Snow Spider Trilogy* (1986–1989) and the Children of the Red King series, which started with *Midnight for Charlie Bone* (2002). Nimmo was producing and writing for the children's television series *Jackanory* when she wrote her first novel, *The Bronze Trumpeter* (1974), in which a Sicilian boy, Paolo, meets some commedia dell'arte players while his father is fighting in World War I. That war is also at the heart of a ghost story set in the present, *The Rinaldi Ring* (1999), which is rich in mystery and literary allusion. Conservation is a theme of *Ultramarine* (1990), its sequel *Rainbow and Mr Zed* (1992), and, for younger readers, *The Owl-Tree* (1997), which, like *The Snow Spider*, won a Smarties Award. The picture books *Gwion and the Witch* (1996) and *Branwen* (1997), illustrated by Jac Jones, retell Welsh myths.

PETER BRAMWELL

Niño, Jairo Anibal (1941–), Colombian fiction writer, poet, and dramatist for children and adults. Born in Boyacá, Colombia, Niño first explored the fine arts and was a member of La Mancha, a group of painters. Later he was an actor, puppeteer, theater director, and playwright. Among his books for children are *Zoro* (1977), *La alegría de querer* (The Joy of Liking, 1986), *Preguntario* (Questionairy, 1989), *El quinto viaje/The Fifth Trip* (1991), *La estrella de papel* (The Paper Star, 1992), *El músico del aire* (The Air Musician, 1994), and *Orfeo y el cosmonauta* (Orpheus and the Cosmonaut, 1995). His many awards include the ENKA Award for Children's Literature (1977), the Chamán Award (1990), and the IBBY Honor List (1992).

[*See also* South America, Spanish-Speaking.]

OLGA GARCÍA-LARRALDE

Nister, Ernest (1842–1909), publisher born in Oberklingen, Germany, best known for high-quality color printing and movable books. Nister began his printing business in 1877 when he acquired a small lithographic workshop in Nuremberg, Germany. By 1888 he had opened offices and design studios in London, but all of the printing was done in Germany, taking advantage of their high-quality chromolithographic printing processes. The Nister catalog included a full range of publications: annuals, storybooks, toy books, poetry, and religious stories, as well as calendars, greeting cards, embossed pictures, and even games. George Manville Fenn, Charles Kingsley, and E. Nesbit were but some of the well-known authors whose work was published by Nister.

Nister produced more than five hundred mostly undated illustrated books for children, but from the 1890s the firm's production was almost exclusively toy or movable books and Nister introduced many new mechanical techniques. *Land of Long Ago* (c. 1890) included three-dimensional scenes that lifted into view with the pull of a linen tab. The revolving pictures, as seen in *Magic Moments* (c. 1890), had two different pictures printed on intersecting, die-cut disks; with the pull of a tab one picture covered the second to show a completely new image. The cutting and construction of all of the movable books was done by hand and required considerable skill to align all of the separate pieces. The illustrations in Nister's books—typically featuring affluent, well-dressed, cheerful children at play—were produced by many different artists. The artist's name, however, was often either dropped or missing, while the signature of Nister, as lithographer, was usually found somewhere on the work—thus leading to confusion about attribution. Nister frequently reused illustrations, occasionally adding picture elements that were not in the original work.

Nister held both English and German patents for the revolving picture mechanism that first appeared in *Twinkling Pictures* (1899). The mechanism consisted of two disks that covered each other and were divided into six segments. Those segments in turn fit together in a star formation. When a tab in the frame was pulled, one disk slid over the other to reveal a kaleidoscopic picture. Nister publications ceased in 1916 but many of the publisher's books had a second life in 20th-century reproductions. Some of the books published in the 1980s and 1990s were exact reproductions, some were issued with different titles, and some were compilations of Nister illustrations and were not true replicas of 19th-century movable books.

[*See also* Germany; Movable Books and Pop-Up Books; Publishers and Publishing; Toy Books; *and biographies of figures mentioned in this article*.]

BIBLIOGRAPHY

Krahé, Hildegard. "The Importance of Being Ernest Nister." *Phaedrus* 13 (1988): 73–90.

ANN R. MONTANARO

Nix, Garth (1963–), Australian author of fantasy and science fiction novels, born in Melbourne and educated at the University of Canberra in the 1980s. Before becoming a full-time writer, Nix worked in most aspects of the publishing business, including stints as a bookseller, editor, publisher, and literary agent. He is best known for his trilogy of young adult fantasy novels: *Sabriel* (1995), *Lirael* (2001), and *Abhorsen* (2003), which follow the adventures of several protagonists whose inherited abilities enable them to traverse the boundary between the living and the dead in a magical world that borders and intertwines with a mundane world much like our own. Nix's inspiration for the series includes both a picture of Hadrian's Wall, in England, that shows green pastures on one side of the ancient stone border and snow-covered hills beyond it, and authors of strong female protagonists, like the fantasy writer Robin McKinley. Nix's earlier works include *Ragwitch* (1991) and *Shade's Children* (1997). Two series written in the early 2000s, The Seventh Tower (a six-book series) and The Keys to the Kingdom (a seven-book series), are aimed at a slightly younger audience. All of Nix's novels are noteworthy for striking a memorable balance between compelling heroes and unusually dark and vicious villains.

MEGAN LYNN ISAAC

Nixon, Joan Lowery (1927–2003), American author of more than 150 children's and young adult's mystery and historical fiction, as well as historical and science books and science fiction books. Principally known for her many mystery novels, including individual titles and mystery series such as *Case Busters*, *First Read-Alone Mysteries*, *Super Sleuth*, *Mary Elizabeth*, and *Thumbprint* (with her daughter Kathleen Nixon Bush), Nixon wrote almost one hundred books in this popular genre and is the only person to have won four Edgar Allan Poe Awards from the Mystery Writers of America. Her mystery novels are generally set in the present and depict teenagers who are really pursuing other goals or working at part-time jobs. The mysteries sometimes explore the supernatural, with ghosts, séances, haunted houses, and even the "mystery weekend" that has become a popular leisure activity of readers. She also wrote several history series for different age levels, focusing principally on the late 19th and early 20th centuries. Her Orphan Train series of eleven books was written for two age groups and engaged topics such as woman suffrage, the Civil War, and slavery at a very personal level. Her Ellis Island series featured girls in their early teens and told stories of the immigrant path to the United States, and her Young Americans was often praised for the resiliency of the pioneer-protagonists. Nixon's books are noted for both their effective plots and their characterizations, and thus are compelling reading despite their often simple language. Many of her novels make use of vivid settings in both the modern and the historical West, including Texas, where she spent most of her adult life. She also published a science series on volcanoes, glaciers, earthquakes, oil and gas, and underwater lands with her husband, H. H. Nixon, three of which received National Science Teachers Association and Children's Book Council awards. Despite this success, she preferred writing fiction. Shortly before her death she published *The Making of a Writer* (2002), a book about her own development as a writer, which described her reasons for turning from a planned career as a journalist to one as a children's writer.

[*See also* Easy Readers; Historical Fiction; Mystery and Detective Stories; *and* Science Books.]

JANICE M. BOGSTAD

Noddy. *See* Blyton, Enid.

Nolan, Dennis (1945–), American writer and illustrator. Born in San Francisco, California, and educated at San Jose State College (now University), Nolan currently lives in Williamsburg, Massachusetts. The illustrator and author-illustrator of numerous children's books, Nolan produces illustrations, often acrylics, characterized by close attention to detail. His author-illustrated works include *Monster Bubbles: A Counting Book* (1976), *The Castle Builder* (1987), the best-selling *Dinosaur Dream* (1990), and *Shadow of the Dinosaurs* (2001). Illustrations for texts by his wife, Lauren Mills, include *Fairy Wings* (1995), which won a Golden Kite Award for illustration, and *Fia and the Imp* (2002). Other collaborations include illustrations for Jane Yolen's *Dove Isabeau* (1989) and *Wings* (1991); for a 1993 edition of T. H. White's classic *The Sword in the Stone*; for some of Bruce Coville's Shakespeare retellings, including *William Shakespeare's A Midsummer's Night's Dream* (1996); and for Robert F. Kennedy Jr.'s *Saint Francis of Assisi: A Life of Joy* (2005).

[*See also* Counting Books; Illustrations; *and biographies of figures mentioned in this article.*]

ADRIENNE E. GAVIN

Nolen, Jerdine (1953–), African American educator and creator of imaginative picture books. Her first book, *Harvey Potter's Balloon Farm* (1994), was followed by *Raising Drag-*

ons (1998) and *Lauren McGill's Pickle Museum* (2003), among others. Nolen also writes about the values of home and family, in *In My Momma's Kitchen* (1999); and she tackles the subject of slavery in her original folktale *Big Jabe* (2000). Many of her books feature strong African American protagonists. She has been praised for the wit and vernacular flow of her stories, a strength she attributes to her family. Nolen was born in Mississippi but grew up in Chicago; throughout her childhood she was immersed in a rich blend of northern and southern dialects, and early on she acquired a good ear for language—as well as a sense of humor. Her appreciation for words and writing set her on the path to teaching, and *Harvey Potter* had its genesis in a classroom activity.

KATHERINE M. ADAMS

Nonfiction. In terms of quantity, the various categories of nonfiction make up the greatest part of all literature published for children. The term is often applied to all materials, including mythology, folk and fairy tales, poetry, drama, and biography, that are shelved in school and public libraries worldwide according to the numbers of the Dewey Decimal System. However, a narrower definition, and the focus of this article, limits the term to works variously described as "the literature of fact," or information, informational books. Biography, a large enough subtopic to warrant its own coverage, is excluded. Informational nonfiction books are written to impart information and to treat ideas relating to various topics in the social sciences, sciences, technology, fine arts, recreation, humanities, and history. Nonfiction trade books, as distinguished from textbooks, are often used by teachers to supplement textbooks, but they are also read by both children and adults for enjoyment, out of curiosity, and from a desire or need to know. In fact, the best way for an adult to learn about an unfamiliar subject may be by reading a good children's nonfiction book.

Despite the existence large numbers of children's nonfiction books (they typically make up from 60 to 75 percent of a library collection), they did not, until the late 20th century, receive much attention from critics and scholars, and they have tended to fall outside the scope of what is considered literature. There are several possible reasons for this neglect. First, many of the books have been and continue to be published in series. Although some of these are of high quality, many are formulaic, shallow, and hastily written. They are often purchased by libraries solely because they meet the needs of the curriculum, and there is nothing else suitable that is available. Second, much nonfiction is relatively ephemeral in nature. Timeliness is important, even in books for children, which are not necessarily immediately impacted by the latest research. There are relatively few informational books that can stand the test of time. (However, a study of these older books can provide important insights into the values and educational theories of the past.) How many books for adults on social issues, politics, science, geography, and history survive long enough to be considered classics? Literary analysis tends to focus on works with lasting value. Third, the power of narrative or story that often draws readers to fiction is often lacking in nonfiction, although the best often has both narrative power and imagination, and employs many of the literary techniques found in fiction. During the latter part of the 20th century, however, various political, economic, technological, and educational trends converged to revolutionize the nature of children's nonfiction and propel it into a role of greater importance. Increasing critical attention has followed.

History of Nonfiction

For practical purposes, the first well-known and widely available nonfiction book for children was the *Orbis Sensualium Pictus*, a nonfiction picture book published in Latin and High Dutch in 1657 by Johann Amos Comenius. Other early books include *The Knowledge of the Heavens and the Earth Made Easy* (1726) by Isaac Watts, John Newbery's *A Pretty Little Book of Pictures for Little Masters and Misses* (1759), and Sarah Trimmer's *Fabulous Histories* (1786). In the United States, early nonfiction included travel books such as Samuel Griswold Goodrich's *The Tales of Peter Parley about America* (1827) and, in the 1850s, Jacob Abbott's Rollo series. Arabella B. Buckley's *The Fairy-land of Science* (1879) was one of the late 19th-century science books that inspired Walter Wick's photographic essay *A Drop of Water* (1997). In Australia, the very first book published locally, *A Mother's Offering to Her Children by a Lady Long Resident in New South Wales* (1841), whose author was later identified as Charlotte Barton, was an informational book in a catechism format with questions and answers about Australia's plants, animals, and Aboriginal inhabitants. Selma Lagerlof's *The Wonderful Adventures of Nils* (1901), written to teach Swedish children their country's geography and inspire in them a love of their country, was widely translated into other languages.

Advances in technology in the early part of the 20th century led to the publication of books with colored pictures integrated with the text, such as E. Boyd Smith's *The Farm Book* (1910). Hendrik Van Loon's history of the world, *The Story of Mankind* (1921), was awarded the very first Newbery Medal in 1922. Other nonfiction books won Newbery Medals and Honor awards over the years, but they were primarily biographies. Katherine Shippen's *Men, Microscopes, and Living Things* (1955) was named a Newbery Honor book. Virginia Lee Burton's masterful 1962 nonfiction picture book, *Life Story*, showing the broad sweep of time from its possible beginning to the present, is one of a few nonfiction books from before the 1970s that remain in print. Others include Holling Clancy Holling's books such as *Paddle to the Sea* (1941), *The Tree in the Trail* (1942), *Minn of the Mississippi* (1951), and *Pagoo* (1957); Marguerite Henry's *Album of Horses* (1951), with illustrations by Wesley Dennis; *Stars: A New Way to See Them* (1952) by H. A. Rey; and the large-format *Colonial Living* (1951), with its detailed drawings by Edwin Tunis.

The launching of the satellite *Sputnik* by the Soviet Union in 1957 jump-started the space race, causing the U.S. Congress to pass the National Defense Education Act of 1958 to boost science education. Funding included the purchase of science books for libraries. One long-lasting result was the *Let's-Read-and-Find-Out* science series, originated in 1960 by Franklyn M. Branley and others and involving some of the best children's science writers of the day, including Millicent Selsam, Paul Showers, and Branley himself, and attracting top illustrators including Aliki, Ed Emberley, Nonny Hogrogian, and Paul Galdone. The series continues to publish new titles and update older ones with updated information and new illustrations. On the heels of the push for science education came Lyndon Johnson's Great Society program of 1964, which coincided with the civil rights movement and poured still more money into school libraries, leading to a demand for more nonfiction books on history, civil rights, and social issues. In 1969 Julius Lester's *To Be a Slave* was named a Newbery Honor book. In the 1970s, library funds dwindled, but changes in technology had enabled publishers to create more eye-catching nonfiction books, increasingly illustrated with photographs and full-color illustrations, and marketed to bookstores as well as to libraries. Rapid changes in the genre were also prompted by the influence of television and later computer technology. The Dorling Kindersley format of sharp photographic images placed on stark white backgrounds, introduced in the 1980s, has influenced the look of informational books. The amount of text in nonfiction books has decreased, while the amount of white space and space given to computer-generated graphics, colorful photographs, sidebars, and text boxes has increased. Printed books have taken on more and more of the characteristics of computer screens, allowing reader-viewers to jump from text box to image, and back again. Many of the changes in children's nonfiction reflect Eliza T. Dresang's theories as expressed in *Radical Change: Literature for Youth in an Electronic Age* (1998): changing formats, changing boundaries, and changing perspectives. Subjects that were formerly taboo in children's books are now being explored. Voices that have not previously been heard are finding expression.

Overview of Scholarship

Margery Fisher's *Matters of Fact* (1972) was the first full-length survey and critical examination of nonfiction for children. A major turning point was Melton Meltzer's article in the February 1976 issue of *Horn Book*, "Where Do All the Prizes Go? The Case for Nonfiction." In this much-reprinted and frequently quoted essay, Meltzer argued that the best of nonfiction involves "imagination, invention, selection, language and form" just as any other form of literature does, and that it should be judged accordingly. *Beyond Fact* (1982), edited by Jo Carr, is an important collection of essays on various aspects of nonfiction, including science, history, biography, and areas of controversy. It includes contributions by many well-known writers and scholars. *Lion and the Unicorn* 6 (1982) was an issue devoted to informational books for children, while the *Children's Literature Association Quarterly* 10, no. 4 (1987) included a section devoted to analyses of literary aspects of nonfiction. Rosemary Bamford and Janice Kristo's *Making Facts Come Alive: Choosing and Using Quality Nonfiction Literature K–8* (1998) contains sections on evaluation and selection, nonfiction relating to various disciplines, and nonfiction and children, as well as a series of response guides and information about Orbis Pictus winners. Linnea Hendrickson's "Lessons from Linnea: *Linnea in Monet's Garden* as a Prototype of Radical Change in Informational Books for Children," in *Children's Literature in Education* 30, no. 1 (March 1999), examines Christina Björk and Lena Anderson's 1985 book through the lens of Eliza Dresang's theory of "radical change," and focuses on historical precedents for utilizing fictional journeys and fictional guides to convey information. *The Best in Children's Nonfiction: Reading, Writing, and Teaching Orbis Pictus Award Books* (2001), edited by Myra Zarnowski, Richard M. Kerper, and Julie M. Jensen, contains essays discussing the characteristics of good nonfiction, perspectives by Orbis Pictus award-winning authors, and an annotated listing of all the Orbis Pictus–winning and honor books, 1990–2000. Sandip LeeAnne Wilson's doctoral dissertation, *Coherence and Historical Understanding in Children's Biography and Historical Nonfiction Literature: A Content Analysis of Selected Orbis Pictus Books* (2001), contains interesting observations on the way that good historical nonfiction provides both younger and older students with "the opportunity to learn the conventions of historical thinking" and how "authors select, interpret and question information." Kathleen Isaacs, chair of the 2005 Robert F. Sibert Award Committee, considers difficult questions about truth and documentation in "Truth in Informational Books," in *School Library Journal* 51, no. 7 (July 2005).

Awards and Prizes

In 1976, perhaps in response to Meltzer's plea, a separate Boston Globe–Horn Book Award for Nonfiction was established. In 1977, the annual Washington Post–Children's Book Guild Nonfiction Information Award was established to honor an author or an author-illustrator "whose total work has contributed significantly to the quality of nonfiction for children." In 1987, the Canadian Information Book Award sponsored by the Children's Literature Roundtables of Canada was awarded for the first time, and the New Zealand Library and Information Association Award for Nonfiction was established, with the first award given to *Gaijin: Foreign Children in Japan* (1986), by Olive and Ngaio Hill. In the United States, the National Council of Teachers of English established the Orbis Pictus Award for nonfiction in 1989, with the first award given in 1990. The Children's Book Council of Australia Book of the Year Award established the Eve Pownall Award for Information Books in 1993. The Giverny Award, for the author and illustrator of a children's science picture book that illustrates a scientific principle, was established by two scientists at the 15 Degree Laboratory at Louisiana State University in 1998. A second Canadian award for nonfiction, the Norma Fleck Award for Canadian Children's Nonfiction, was established in 1999. The American Library Association awarded the first Robert F. Sibert Medal for Nonfiction in 2001. The awards have encouraged higher standards for accuracy, creativity, and documentation, and have provided greater visibility for children's nonfiction, which has also increasingly received other awards, including recent Caldecott Medals and Honor awards.

Criteria for Evaluating

When asked to tell the difference between "fiction" and "nonfiction," elementary school children commonly describe nonfiction as "real, "true," or "facts" and fiction as "made up" or "not true." However, the lines between fact and fiction in children's literature are often blurred. Scholars, critics, and authors of nonfiction themselves continue to debate how much fiction, if any, is admissible in a work of nonfiction. Fictional devices, such as the imaginary journey and the fictional narrator, have been used to impart ideas and information, dating at least as far back as Samuel Griswold Goodrich's Peter Parley (1827) and Jacob Abbott's *Rollo in Paris* (1854). The presentation of factual information by a fictional guide was revitalized in the 1980s with the popular Magic School Bus series begun in the 1980s by Joanna Cole and Bruce Degen, in which the imaginary and imaginative teacher, Ms. Frizzle, drives her students on bus tours through the water works, the human body, and the solar system. In a later series, beginning with *Ms. Frizzle's Adventures: Ancient Egypt* (2001), Ms. Frizzle explores history.

There are generally agreed-upon criteria for evaluating informational books, most of them similar to the guidelines set forth by Beverly Kobrin in *Eyeopeners!* (1988), titled "How to Judge a Book by Its Cover—and Nine Other Clues." Kobrin's criteria include attractiveness, accuracy, authority, appropriateness, rhetorical style, stereotypes, tone, format, and book design. Even before reading a book, it is possible to quickly check for the qualifications of the author, the acknowledgments of authorities and sources consulted, the currency and thoroughness of bibliographies, and the existence of a glossary, index, and table of contents. The best information books, writes Jo Carr (1982), "go beyond fact" to make us "think deeply" and "feel deeply." "Gifted writers work with facts as sculptors work with clay—or artists with paint, composers with melody, poets with words—to give meaningful form to their perception of things."

Subjects, Scope, and Formats

Information books for children range from simple concept books aimed at very young children, such as Tana Hoban's classic photographic books (*Shapes, Shapes, Shapes*, 1986) and Lois Ehlert's *Color Zoo* (1989), with its colorful die-cut shapes, to lengthy and complex prose works written for adolescents. The topics and forms these books take are wide ranging. There are general and specialized reference books, including children's encyclopedias and almanacs, and books of records, such as *The Guinness Book of Word Records*, a work children find fascinating, whether or not it is actually intended for them. "Fact" books about dragons and ghosts, the Bermuda Triangle, and the aliens that purportedly crashed in Roswell, New Mexico, are always in demand.

Books on government include innovative picture books with child appeal, such as David Catrow's *We the Kids* (Dial, 2002), a wild and wacky gloss on the preamble to the United States Constitution, and more serious, full-length treatments such as Wilborn Hampton's Orbis Pictus honor book *Kennedy Assassinated!* (1997), which recounts the author's experiences as a young reporter covering the assassination. Books on civil rights include such titles as Walter Dean Myer's Coretta Scott King Award–winning *Now Is Your Time! The African-American Struggle for Freedom* (1991). Another children's book category, paralleling the self-help books of the adult world, includes books on subjects ranging from handling bullies to dealing with death, divorce, and handicaps and ranging in format from Aliki's picture book *Feelings* (1984) to *Girl Stuff* (2000) by Margaret Blackstone, a book with that combines illustrations and a substantial text that addresses issues facing girls approaching puberty.

Books on language include those on the development of the alphabet and the history of writing, alphabet books, foreign languages, and wordplay (including riddles and puns), grammar, and usage. Loreen Leedy's *There's a Frog in My Throat* (2003) illustrates animal figures of speech, and Marvin Terban writes entertainingly on idioms, homographs, and wordplay (for instance, *The Dove Dove*, 1988). A lavishly illustrated series by Ruth Heller discuss adjectives, adverbs, and other parts of speech (for instance, *Behind the Mask: A Book about Prepositions* (1995). Laura Rankin's *The Handmade Alphabet* (1991) contains exquisitely drawn hands depicting the alphabet in sign language. Greg Tang has created a series of innovative and entertaining math books, beginning with *The Grapes of Math: Mind-Stretching Math Riddles* (2001), and Stuart J. Murphy's *MathStart* series features stories designed to teach mathematics (for instance, *Betcha!*, 1997, teaches estimation).

Science writing is a huge category in terms of both subject matter and variety of texts, including books as simple as Lola M. Schaefer's *Sea Anemones* (1999), with one sentence per page facing a full-color photograph, and a glossary, index, and sources for further information, including Internet sites. More complex books for slightly older readers include how-to books such as Vicki Cobb's popular *Science Projects You Can Eat* (1994) and her Sibert Award honor book *I Face the Wind* (2003), a superb mix of text and graphics that explains principles of physical science to very young scientists. Seymour Simon's clearly written and breathtaking photo-essays on space, animals, the earth, machines, and human anatomy include titles for both younger and older readers. Science writing includes always popular dinosaur books ranging from pop-ups such as the ingenious *Encyclopedia Prehistorica: Dinosaurs* (2005) by Robert Sabuda and Matthew Reinhart, to engaging photo-essays such as Nic Bishop's *Digging for Bird-Dinosaurs* (2000), one of the well-regarded Scientists in the Field series. Comprehensive dinosaur encyclopedias such as *The Dinosaur Encyclopedia* (2001) by David Lambert, available with an accompanying interactive CD, update the groundbreaking volumes created by Helen Roney Sattler in the 1980s.

The versatile Laurence Pringle, who has written more than ninety thoughtful science books on topics ranging from global warming to the life cycle of the dragonfly, received the Orbis Pictus Award for *An Extraordinary Life: The Story of a Monarch Butterfly* (1997), with paintings by Bob Marstall, a book whose design was influenced by the work of Holling Clancy Holling. Books on evolution continue to be controversial, and sometimes invite censorship. Outstanding books in the early 21st century include Lisa Westberg Peters and Lauren Stringer's *Our Family Tree: An Evolution Story* (2003), which connects human life to that of the earth's earliest single-celled organisms. Two very different books, both called *The Tree of Life*, appeared in 2003 and 2004: the first, by Peter Sís, is an exploration of the life and ideas of Charles Darwin; the second, *The Incredible Biodiversity of Life on Earth*, is by Rochelle Strauss and Margo Thompson and presents the complex tree of classification in a stunning visual manner. Another relatively new and notable book among many on this topic is Steve Jenkins's *Life on Earth* (2002).

Books on human anatomy and physiology include the censored and celebrated *It's Perfectly Normal* (1994, 2004) by Robie Harris, illustrated by Michael Emberley, a book about puberty and sexuality for older children, and *It's So Amazing* (1999), a companion book for younger children. The classic *How We Are Born, How We Grow, How Our Bodies Work, and How We Learn* (1975) by Joe Kaufman, aimed at even younger children, contains a life-size picture of a newborn baby, and detailed drawings of the human skeleton and anatomy.

Innovative books on pets include *How to Talk to Your Dog* and *How to Talk to Your Cat*, both published in 2000, by Jean Craighead George, illustrated with a combination of drawings, photographs, speech balloons, and varied typefaces. One of the most prolific authors of informational books for young children is Gail Gibbons, who has written and illustrated more than 135 books, many on natural history topics, including several on domestic animals such as pigs, honeybees, ducks, and cows (*The Milk Makers*, 1983). Children's cookbooks include those with an international and multicultural scope and children's versions of popular cookbooks for adults (including a facsimile of the 1957 *Betty Crocker's Cook Book for Boys and Girls*). Other cookbooks involve literary tie-ins, such as *The Little House Cookbook* (1979), based on the popular series by Laura Ingalls Wilder; *The Grandma Poss Cookbook* (1985), with Australian specialties based on Mem Fox's popular picture book *Possum Magic* (1982); and the *The Narnia Cookbook* (1998), by Douglas Gresham with illustrations by Pauline Baynes, that includes a recipe for Turkish delight.

The best-known author and illustrator of books on architecture and technology is David Macaulay, who broke new ground with the publication of *Cathedral* (1973)—with its detailed black-and-white drawings depicting the building of a fictional medieval cathedral—followed by *City* (1974), *Pyramid* (1975), *Castle* (1977), *Mill* (1983), and *Mosque* (2003). Macaulay's most outstanding nonfiction achievement may be the encyclopedic *The Way Things Work*, originally published in 1988 and since updated with both print and electronic versions. Books on art, music, dance, opera, and sports, as well as the incredibly popular and numerous how-to-draw books by Lee J. Ames (for example, *Draw 50 Animals*, 1974) are part of children's nonfiction. *The Art Fraud Detective* (2000) by Anna Nilsen is an unusual, interactive book encouraging readers to look closely at a series of paintings, spotting differences and similarities. Neil Ardley's *A Young Person's Guide to Music* (2004) includes an accompanying music disc, while Aliki's *Ah, Music!* (2003) ambitiously tackles the entire field of music with lively, illustrated entries.

Outstanding writers of geography and history include the award-winning authors Mark Aronson, Susan Campbell Bartoletti, Rhoda Blumberg, Jean Fritz, Russell Freedman, James Cross Giblin, Kathryn Lasky, Patricia and Fredrick McKissack, Milton Meltzer, Jim Murphy, Judith St. George, and Shelley Tanaka. History books range from sweeping, multivolume sets such as Joy Hakim's engaging *History of US* (1993–2003) to books that focus on specific incidents, such as Janes Yolen and Heidi Stemple's *The Salem Witch Trials: An Unsolved Mystery from History* (2004). Steve Jenkins, best known for the outstanding cut-paper collages that illustrate his award-winning books on natural history, wrote and illustrated a book on climbing Mount Everest (*The Top of the World*, 2002). Jennifer Armstrong, in her Orbis Pictus award–winning *Shipwreck at the Bottom of the World: The Extraordinary True Story of Shackleton and the Endurance* (1998), made use of archival photographs and painstaking original research to tell an exciting story. The photographer George Ancona has produced dazzling photo-essays on multicultural subjects, including *Barrio* (1998), the story of young boy growing up in the Mission District of San Francisco, and *Pablo Remembers: The Fiesta of the Day of the Dead* (1993). A series titled What's It Like, Grandma?, published in 2002–2003 by Ann Morris, focused on visits with American grandmothers representing various ethnic groups: Jewish, Arab, Vietnamese, New Mexican Spanish, and Shoshone. The role and perspectives of women, African Americans, Native Americans, Hispanic Americans, and other minorities have received greater attention since the late 20th century, and more members of cultural minorities are writing and speaking for themselves, although there are still few books written by Native American authors and finding accurate representations of their history and current lives is difficult.

The years 2000–2005 saw an unprecedented flurry of books on the Lewis and Clark expedition to mark its two hundredth anniversary. Tiles included Rhoda Blumberg's *York's Adventures with Lewis and Clark* (2004), winner of the 2005 Orbis Pictus Award; Dorothy Hinshaw Patent and William Muñoz's pair of books on the animals and plants on the trail; and Laurence Pringle's *Dog of Discovery* (2002), an account of Meriwether Lewis's Newfoundland dog, Seaman, who accompanied the expedition.

[*See also* Awards; Biography; Books of Instruction; Geography and Travel Books; How-To Books; Information Books; Multiculturalism and Children's Books; Photography in Nonfiction for Children; Science Books; *and biographies of figures mentioned in this article*.]

BIBLIOGRAPHY

Bamford, Rosemary, and Janice V. Kristo, eds. *Making Facts Come Alive: Choosing and Using Quality Nonfiction Literature K–8*. Norwood, Mass.: Christopher-Gordon, 1998.

Carr, Jo, ed. *Beyond Fact: Nonfiction for Children and Young People*. Chicago: American Library Association, 1982.

Fisher, Margery. *Matters of Fact: Aspects of Non-Fiction for Children*. New York: Crowell, 1972.

Freeman, Evelyn. "Nonfiction: A Genre Comes of Age." In *Children's Literature Remembered: Issues, Trends, and Favorite Books*, edited by Linda M. Pavonetti, 101–115. Westport, Conn.: Libraries Unlimited, 2004.

Giblin, James Cross. "From *The Story of Mankind* to Studies of AIDS: A Hundred Years of Informational Books for Children." In *Children's Literature Remembered: Issues, Trends, and Favorite Books*, edited by Linda M. Pavonetti, 91–100. Westport, Conn.: Libraries Unlimited, 2004.

Hendrickson, Linnea. "Lessons from Linnea: *Linnea in Monet's Garden* as a Prototype of Radical Change in Informational Books for Children." *Children's Literature in Education* 30, no. 1 (March 1999): 35–45.

Isaacs, Kathleen. "Truth in Information Books." *School Library Journal* 51 (July 2005): 28–29.

Meltzer, Milton. "Where Do All the Prizes Go? The Case for Nonfiction." *Horn Book* (February 1976): 17–23.

LINNEA HENDRICKSON

Nonsense. Nonsense writing comes in two forms: the kind of silly explorations of sound and sense often generated by young children, and the much more complex body of work that can be called literary nonsense, best known through Victorian writers such as Edward Lear and Lewis Carroll. The two kinds of nonsense share some characteristics: both are ludic and delight in wordplay and rhythm, but whereas nonsense by children is largely spontaneous, fugitive, and essentially meaningless, literary nonsense has a distinguished intellectual tradition and some examples have survived through the generations.

When applied to the literary tradition, the term "nonsense" is misleading, and perhaps deliberately so. In one of the earliest studies of the genre, Elizabeth Sewell observes that nonsense is equated with "inconsequence, pointlessness, senselessness, incongruity—all negatives which lead us to equate Nonsense with disorder." With the exception of "incongruity," these are not terms of disorder but of dismissal. The label "nonsense" invites us to skim the surface of its products and implies that they are beneath consideration. Such insistence invites scrutiny, beginning with Edward Lear, who revived the term after a century or more when it had fallen from use, and applied it to the humorous verses and drawings he did alongside his more serious paintings. Far from being the inconsequential products of a fatigued brain in the way Lear suggests, the best literary nonsense requires a high degree of technical knowledge and intellec-

Nonsense. Front cover of *The Great Panjandrum Himself* by Randolph Caldecott (London: George Routledge & Sons, n.d.). REPRODUCED COURTESY OF THE COTSEN CHILDREN'S LIBRARY, PRINCETON UNIVERSITY LIBRARY

tual sophistication for its effects, which is why it is important to distinguish nonsense from comic and silly verse such as "I am silly / You are silly / All of us are silly, / Willy. / All of us but cousin Millie. / She's upside down." Although it may have a certain kind of anarchic appeal, writing of this kind is not good nonsense since it employs a limited number of nonsense devices and operates at only one level. John Goldthwaite identifies such writing with what he calls the fanciful mood in nonsense, which tends to be populist and derived from the oral tradition, as distinct from its logical mood, which is always literary and often, he claims, moral.

Early Nonsense Writing

The conventions of nonsense have a long and elevated pedigree. In his study of 17th-century nonsense, Noel Malcolm demonstrates that the popular belief that nonsense grew from folk traditions is erroneous; in fact, literary nonsense derives from highly specialized discourses in high culture. For instance, many of the early examples of nonsense were created to be performed at the Inns of Court and consist of parodies of the kinds of rhetorical and courtly skills on which the legal profession depended and in which its practitioners needed to excel. Nonsense works through logic, and one of its underlying intellectual puzzles is whether it is possible—and if so, how—to use grammatically correct language or other signifying systems recognizable to the reader in order to write something that is entirely without meaning. One of the earliest and most extreme examples of such an attempt is found in the work of John Taylor, the so-called "water poet," writing in the late 16th and early 17th centuries. Taylor devised special languages to try to subvert meaning, as in "Epitaph in the Bermuda Tongue, which must be pronounced with the accent of the grunting hog," and begins "Hough gruntough wough Thornough / Coratough, Odcough robunquogh."

Probably the best-known effort to create a sustained piece of meaningless text in English is Samuel Foote's *The Great Panjandrum Himself*, devised to test the ability of an actor-friend to learn lines. It consists of a series of separate sentences linked by false cohesive ties: "So she went into the garden to cut a cabbage leaf to make an apple pie, and at the same time a great she-bear, coming down the street, pops its head into the shop. What! No soap? So she died." Despite the deliberately random nature of the sentences, the ties suggest a linear progression to the events, which do seem to make a story despite Foote's best efforts—particularly when illustrated as the text famously was by Randolph Caldecott. In this way, readers subvert the effort to deny meaning, showing that far from being easy, thoughtless writing, literary nonsense is extremely demanding. A writer who has tried to move beyond language to create pure nonsense is Christian Morgenstern, whose *The Fish's Night Song* (1903) is a particularly witty example of nonverbal nonsense:

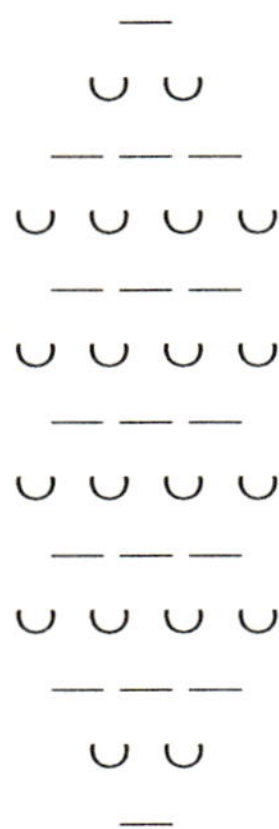

Morgenstern's poem makes use of a nonsense tradition that privileges form over content and delights in codes, anagrams, acrostics, transpositions of letters and words, highly evolved numerical patterns, and other systems for concealing meanings. This tradition appealed strongly to Lewis Carroll, one of the most influential writers of nonsense. It combined his fascination with both words and mathematics. Central to the rules of logic is that there *are* rules that can be identified and applied: literary nonsense cannot work on purely personal information, and craftsmanship involves abiding by the rules. Carroll makes a similar point in his preface to *Through the Looking-Glass*, which explains that despite a few liberties with sequence, every move in the chess game on which the story is based is "strictly in accordance with the laws of the game." The conventions of literary nonsense are numerous. In addition to following the laws of grammar, it employs wordplay, mixes together unrelated or contradictory items (usually suggesting an affinity between them through the use of rhyme or parallelism), and tends to present actions and behaviors in terms of extremes. Another strong nonsense tradition is parody, often a form of inversion, such as Carroll's parodies of Isaac Watts's *Divine Songs* in *Alice's Adventures in Wonderland*.

The device of concealing information in nonsense writing has been used in various ways: Carroll often hid invitations or information about surprises in coded messages to his young friends, while Edward Lear concealed psychologically revealing self-portraits in many of his verses. It is easy to find correspondences between the stout, bespectacled, lonely man with the unfortunate nose and many of the characters who feature in Lear's nonsense verse and drawings, perhaps most obviously the Yonghy-Bonghy-Bo. Although nonsense *may* conceal meanings, it does not always do so. The tendency for critics to unveil hidden meanings was itself parodied by a critic in the *New Yorker* in a piece on the great American nonsense writer Theodore Geisel, better known as Dr. Seuss. Geisel was given the task of writing a book using only the 225 words his editor had selected for their ability to teach phonics, and eventually came up with *The Cat in the Hat*—a book undoubtedly in the nonsense tradition. The *New Yorker* article offered readers a tongue-in-cheek analysis of the text as a story about an "alarmingly polymorphous cat" intruding on a scene of repression against the wishes of the household superego (the fish) to introduce two uptight little persons to their libidos—Thing One and Thing Two!

Some think that because of its stress on rationality and logic, nonsense has always been a peculiarly male-dominated genre; interestingly, a common strand in nonsense writing is the nostalgic desire to return to childhood and a premasculine way of being. This is typified by the first poem in Hilaire Belloc's *Cautionary Verses* (1940):

> And when your prayers complete the day,
> Darling, your little tiny hands
> Were also made, I think, to pray
> For men that lose their fairylands.

Another area that may lurk beneath the surface of nonsense is an exploration of the relationship between ways of knowing and ways of being. Nonsense in the 19th century, for instance, can be seen as a response to the overconfident and highly rigid systems of education and morality of the day, and the Victorian obsession with collecting, classifying, and so spuriously assuming possession over information about the world, past and present—particularly once many of the "certainties" on which they depended were thrown into doubt by developments in the natural sciences. For those, like Carroll, professionally involved with the church, it was not always prudent to enter too vigorously into teleological debates, but the *Alice* books show ample evidence of his interest in and knowledge of Darwin's theories and natural science generally. In this instance nonsense offered a good-natured and discreetly concealed response to a topical and potentially troubling issue. Carroll, like many other nonsense makers, was also alert to its potential to give expression to political and social observations that in other forms might have been contentious.

Nonsense Writing in the 20th Century

More recently, nonsense has had resurgence in literary modernism, with its questioning of the relationship among language, self, and reality. Arguably, in its rejection of grand narratives and the conventions and subjects of "serious" realist fiction, nonsense anticipated and was called into the service of the modernist movements in literature and art such as those arising from futurism and Dadaism. But modernism is not the mode best suited to nonsense: in its playful testing of boundaries, evocations of false histories, experimentation with identities and subjectivities, and its iconoclastic mixing of styles and forms, nonsense finds its natural place in literary postmodernism. Resistance and transformation are at the heart of Salman Rushdie's *Haroun and the Sea of Stories* (1990), a children's book that owes a strong debt to nonsense writers of the past, from the Beatles to Norton Juster's excellent *The Phantom Tollbooth* (1961). In *Haroun*, Rushdie employs a vast array of nonsense conventions: literal-mindedness, lexical exhibitionism, inversion, parody, juxtapositioning of literary styles, incongruity, blending the ordinary and the extraordinary, and an intertextual patchwork that stitches together ancient oral tales and examples from the postwar culture industries. The text begins with an acrostic puzzle spelling out the name of Rushdie's son, Zafar, from whom Rushdie was separated as a consequence of the fatwa against him. The text rejects the conventions of realism as a false way of making sense of the world; nonsense is presented as the more meaningful and truthful idiom. Like Carroll, Rushdie, who found himself constrained and marginalized by the imposition of the fatwa in 1989, also used the strategies of nonsense to give expression to his frustrations. Through the nonsense devices in *Haroun*, he weaves together thoughts on individual liberty, censorship, linguistic diversification, and the need for fantasy in everyday life, and he does so without complaining about his circumstances or capitulating to a nihilistic world view.

As a text that is characterized by its use of nonsense, *Haroun and the Sea of Stories* offers a paradigm of the dichotomous nature of children's literature itself. On the one hand, it is dependent on and respectful of the education system and the didactic tradition; on the other, it is subversive and liberating, mocking and critiquing the values and practices of these same systems and the institutions and individuals responsible for upholding and disseminating them. Nonsense is associated with popular culture and held in low esteem by some, but many of its practitioners have been major literary figures. It is simple and directed at an inexperienced audience, yet it can deal in philosophy, psychology, and linguistic theories beyond the levels of most young readers. Nonsense can be slight, but it can equally be a courageous mode, offering opportunities for giving expression to opinions and experiences that might otherwise be silenced.

[*See also* Alice Imitations; Humor; *and biographies of figures mentioned in this article.*]

BIBLIOGRAPHY

Goldthwaite, John. "Do You Admire the View? The Critics Go Looking for Nonsense." *Signal* 76 (January 1992).

Malcolm, Noel. *The Origins of English Nonsense*. London: Harper Collins, 1997.

Sewell, Elizabeth. *The Field of Nonsense*. London: Chatto and Windus, 1952.

Tigges, Wim. *An Anatomy of Literary Nonsense*. Amsterdam: Rodopi, 1988.

KIMBERLEY REYNOLDS

Noonan, Diana (1960–), author of over eighty works of fiction and nonfiction for children and young adults. Born in Dunedin, New Zealand, and educated at the University of Otago, Noonan initially worked as a teacher before embarking on a full-time writing career with *The Silent People* (1990), a novel about preservation of the environment focusing on a girl's friendship with an ancient tribe of moa hunters in an isolated part of New Zealand. This novel was short-listed for the Esther Glen Award. Other books include *Leaving the Snow Country* (1991) and its sequel *A Sonnet for the City* (1992), about a girl who leaves her country home in order to attend university in the city and the problems and difficulties she encounters there. Books for younger readers include *The Best-Loved Bear* (1994) and its sequel *The Best-Dressed Bear* (2002), *A Dolphin in the Bay* (1993), which won the Aim Children's Book Award for Junior Fiction, and the educational *The Know, Sow, and Grow Kids' Book of Plants* (1997), illustrated by her husband Keith Olsen, which was awarded the New Zealand Post Children's Books Award for Non-Fiction. Noonan is also editor of the New Zealand *School Journal*.

[*See also* Ecology and Environment *and* New Zealand.]

MARIA-VENETIA KYRITSI

Noonuccal, Oodgeroo (1920–1993), activist, artist, and author of poetry, short stories, plays, and essays. Oodgeroo, otherwise known as Kath Walker, was a member of the Noonuccal people of the Yuggera group in Queensland, Australia. She left school at thirteen to become a domestic servant, and during World War II spent four years in the Australian Women's Army Service (1941–1944). She later trained as a secretary and bookkeeper. In 1964 she published her first collection of poetry, *We Are Going*, which was succeeded by two further collections. Her poetry was highly influential among Aboriginal and non-Aboriginal readers and presented a politicized and forthright perspective on colonization in Australia and the continuing marginalization of Aboriginal cultures and people. *Stradbroke Dreamtime* (1972) combined retellings of stories she learned as a child with accounts of her life as a child, under the colonial regime that operated on Stradbroke Island. This collection was immediately popular with children, ushering in a period of increasing production for children by Aboriginal authors and artists. Oodgeroo's collection of traditional stories *Father Sky and Mother Water* (1981) was illustrated with her own paintings. She combined writing and painting with a distinguished career as an activist, fostering the maintenance of Aboriginal culture and the education of Aboriginal children.

[*See also* Australia *and* Multiculturalism and Children's Books.]

CLARE BRADFORD

Nordic Countries. The five Nordic countries—Sweden, Denmark, Norway, Finland, and Iceland—have much in common geographically, historically, and culturally. Yet, in order to assess the development of children's literature in the region, it is necessary to understand the region's profound diversity. The most elementary difference is linguistic: although Danish, Norwegian, Swedish, and Icelandic are related, Finnish is not a Scandinavian, and not even an Indo-European, language. Sweden, Denmark, and Norway are monarchies, while Iceland and Finland are republics. Sweden and Denmark have a glorious past as nation states, while Norway gained independence only in 1905, Finland in 1917, and Iceland in 1944. Sweden has maintained its famous neutral policy, which has kept it out of wars since 1814, but Norway, for instance, was invaded by Nazi Germany. All this is naturally reflected in the fictitious universe of children's books. For instance, the war theme is conspicuously absent from Swedish children's literature other than in historical novels. National identity is seldom discussed in Swedish children's literature, whereas it is often central in Norwegian or Icelandic, and so on.

Nordic Children's Literature. Illustration from *Tant Grön, Tant Brun och Tant Gredelin* by Elsa Beskow (Stockholm: Åhlén & Åkerlun, c. 1930), p. 16. REPRODUCED COURTESY OF THE COTSEN CHILDREN'S LIBRARY, PRINCETON UNIVERSITY LIBRARY

The Norwegian literary language has only existed as such, and not as a Danish dialect, for less than two hundred years, which naturally delayed the emergence of a national literature. Finnish, spoken by 94 percent of Finland's population, hardly had any written literature until the publication of the national epic *Kalevala* in 1835–1836. Instead, children's literature written in Swedish emerged in 19th-century Finland, being at the same time a natural part of metropolitan Swedish literature. Although Finland was politically included in the Russian Empire from 1809 to 1917, it stayed culturally close to Sweden, and the intellectual elite in Finland was almost exclusively Swedish-speaking.

Since Denmark is geographically adjacent to Germany, Danish literature has always had close connections to German literature, even though the German cultural influence was also strong in Sweden and Norway at least until World War II. Such a universal classic as Daniel Defoe's *Robinson Crusoe* reached Scandinavia through a German adaptation. Iceland was for obvious reasons still more culturally isolated. Today the minority cultures in Greenland and on the Faeroe Islands, and the Sami (Lappish) culture in the far north of Finland, Sweden, and Norway also struggle for a children's literature of their own. Internationally, children's literature of the Nordic region enjoys a strong reputation—its authors have repeatedly received the Hans Christian Andersen Award, including Astrid Lindgren, Tove Jansson, Maria Gripe, Cecil Bødker, and Tormod Haugen, and the illustrators Ib Spang Olsen and Svend Otto S. Nordic children's books are translated into many languages, and Hans Christian Andersen, Astrid Lindgren, and Tove Jansson enjoy world fame.

Before the 20th Century

Although fables, ABC books, and books of courtesy aimed at young readers can be found in the Nordic countries already in the 16th century, children's literature proper did not emerge until Romanticism, through the double impact of the period's interest in the child and in folklore. Romantic poets such as the Danish B. S. Ingemann (1789–1862) and the Norwegian Henrik Wergeland (1808–1845) published collections of poetry addressed to children. In Denmark and Sweden, folk tales were not incorporated into children's reading until the turn of the 20th century. In contrast, in Norway, which was part of Denmark until 1814 and afterward in union with Sweden until 1905, the study of folklore was closely connected to the emergence of national identity, which contributed to the early inclusion of fairy tales in young people's education. The world-famous collection of Norwegian folk tales by Peter Christen Asbjørnsen and Jørgen Moe, adapted for children in 1883, laid the foundation for a national children's literature. Moe also wrote an original fairy tale story, *I brønden og i kjærnet* (In the Well and in the Pond, 1851), one of the first Norwegian children's books. The other Nordic countries lack a folk tale treasury as part of the national consciousness. However, Denmark produced one of the most famous children's authors of all times and nations, Hans Christian Andersen (1805–1875), "the father of the literary fairy tale," whose impact on the development of a national children's literature cannot be overestimated. With his fairy tales, Andersen created a completely new and original literary genre that influenced many generations of writers not only in Scandinavia but throughout the world.

Zacharias Topelius (1818–1898) is considerably less known internationally than Andersen; however, he is regarded as the creator of Swedish-language children's literature. Topelius belonged to the Swedish-speaking minority in Finland and thus contributed to both countries. His multivolume *Läsning för barn* (Reading Matter for Children, 1865–1896) contains edifying fairy tales, stories, poems, and plays for the young. Another significant Swedish writer was Victor Rydberg (1828–1895), whose fairy tale *Lille Viggs äfventyr på julafton* (Little Vigg's Adventure on Christmas Eve, 1875) shows a mixture of didacticism and entertainment.

Otherwise, foreign books in translation and adaptation—German, and later English—dominated children's reading

Nordic Children's Literature. Illustration by Arne Ungermann from *Jørgens hjul* by Edvard Heiberg (Copenhagen: Mondes Forlag, 1932). REPRODUCED COURTESY OF THE COTSEN CHILDREN'S LIBRARY, PRINCETON UNIVERSITY LIBRARY

until the end of the 19th century. Since compulsory elementary education was legislated already in the first half of the 19th century, the level of literacy was high and the need for reading matter great. In Denmark and Sweden, by 1900, the regular publication of cheap children's books, distributed through schools, was established, including both translated classics and original works. The numerous children's magazines contributed to a wide dissemination of children's literature.

The Turn of the Century

The turn of the 20th century brought about debates on child education, when the famous book *Century of the Child* (1900), by Sweden's Ellen Key, drew the attention of educators and writers to the reading needs of children. This period was the heyday of the literary fairy tale, much in the wake of Andersen and reflecting the strong neo-Romantic movement beginning in the 1890s. The abundance of children's and Christmas magazines provided new channels for publication of fairy tales, verses, nursery songs, and short stories with religious and moral content. The Swedish Helena Nyblom (1843–1926) was the leading author of fairy tales. In Finland, the literary fairy tale tradition continued well into the 1930s, for instance, by Nanny Hammarström (1870–1953) and Anni Swan (1875–1958).

Picture books for children became a prominent genre, thanks to the development of printing technology that enabled mass production of four-color illustrations, but they were also influenced by the British models. The most famous Swedish picture book maker, whose work is still enjoyed today, was Elsa Beskow (1874–1953). Idyllic images of a small Swedish town in *Aunt Green, Aunt Brown, and Aunt Lavender* (1918) alternate in her works with breathtaking adventures in enchanted forests in imaginative stories about gnomes.

The major early-20th-century Swedish classic was written by Selma Lagerlöf (1858–1940), winner of the Nobel Prize for literature and, together with Andersen, the best internationally known Scandinavian writer. *The Wonderful Adventures of Nils* (1906–1907), originally commissioned as a schoolbook in geography, made use of a typical fairy tale plot in which a lazy boy is punished by being transformed into a midget and forced to improve in order to become human again. Less known internationally, but equally important for the development of national Swedish children's literature, was *The Children of the Moor* (1907), by Laura Fitinghoff (1848–1908), which depicts a group of poor orphans walking through Sweden in search of a better life. In Norway this period is referred to as the golden age, with several mainstream authors such as Dikken Zwilgmeyer (1853–1913) and Barbara Ring (1870–1955) publishing significant works for children and thus raising the prestige of a national children's literature.

Between the Wars

The years between the wars is generally referred to as the least glorious in children's literature, with little worth remembering today. In all the Nordic countries, this period can be characterized by the expansion of a strongly gendered literature: books for boys and books for girls. The former were often flying adventures, airplanes being the foremost symbol of the rapid advancement of modernity, for instance, in the books by the Norwegian Leif Hamre (1914–) and the Swedish Harald Viktorin (1889–1960). Books for girls were typical Cinderella stories in which poor, but nice and hardworking girls win their princes. Among the most prominent authors were the Swedish Marika Stiernstedt (1875–1954) and Jeanna Oterdahl (1879–1965), the Finno-Swedish Rut Forsblom-Sandman (1912–1964) and Harriet Clayhills

(1920–), and especially the Danish Karin Michaëlis (1872–1950), whose Bibi books became exceptionally popular on the international scene. The series by the Swedish Martha Sandwall-Bergström (1913–2000) about Kulla-Gulla (Anna in English), although starting in 1945, continued the same tradition.

The 1930s saw the evolution of Danish picture books, strongly influenced by the Soviet avant-garde posters and picture books exhibited in Copenhagen in 1932, and free from Beskowian idyll and fairy tale settings. In the same year a truly modernistic picture book was published, *Jørgens hjul* (Jørgen's Wheel), illustrated by Arne Ungermann (1902–1981), and the most famous Danish picture book, *Paul Alone in the World* (1942), by Jens Sigsgaard (1910–1991) and Ungermann, was part of the same trend, the full impact of which, however, emerged in the late 1940s and the 1950s.

Nordic Children's Literature. Illustration by Ib Sprang from *Hokus Pokus* by Halfdan Rasmussen (Copenhagen: Carlsen Illustrations forlaget, 1967). REPRODUCED COURTESY OF THE COTSEN CHILDREN'S LIBRARY, PRINCETON UNIVERSITY LIBRARY

In general, the between-the-wars period was important for the evolution of children's literature because many foreign classics were translated, and they stood as models for Nordic authors and helped to establish children's literature as a literary system. The publication of children's books occurred on a regular basis, specialized publishing houses were started, children's literature began to be reviewed in the press, and a number of critical works on children's literature appeared.

The Postwar Generation

The postwar period can be characterized by the emergence of a radically new kind of children's literature both in form and in content. In 1945 several pathfinders made their appearance in Sweden: first and foremost Astrid Lindgren (1907–2002), but also the brilliant nonsense poet Lennart Hellsing (1919–) and the master of domestic stories Hans Peterson (1922–). That same year Tove Jansson (1914–2001) published the first Moomin novel. These writers were soon followed by Åke Holmberg (1907–1991) in Sweden, the author of witty detective stories for children; the nonsense poets Inger Hagerup (1905–1985) in Norway, Halfdan Rasmussen (1915–2002) in Denmark, and Kirsi Kunnas (1924–) in Finland; and the magnificent humorists Zinken Hopp (1905–1987), Torbjørn Egner (1912–1990), and Alf Prøysen (1914–1970) in Norway—Prøysen being internationally famous for his comic figure Old Mrs. Pepperpot.

The common denominator for all these writers was a more generous attitude toward the child and hence children's literature. The postwar generation appealed to the child's senses and imagination and took the child's side against oppressive adults. The new writers explored the child inside themselves, writing from their own childhood experiences, genuine or fictitious. In Finland, Denmark, and Norway, the war rendered earlier children's literature irrelevant, and the postwar optimism called for positive models. Sweden, which did not participate in the war, could nevertheless learn from its neighbors, which presented both earlier idyll and traditional adventure in a new light, and therefore brought new subjects, forms, styles, and values into children's literature. In Denmark the postwar period was the primary place for exciting experiments with picture books, seeking new expressive means in the narrative interaction of words and images. Noteworthy names include Egon Mathiesen (1907–1976), Arne Ungermann, Svend Otto S. (1916–), and Ib Spand Olsen (1921–).

However, no other Nordic writer of the postwar generation can compete in importance and popularity with Astrid Lindgren. Writing in almost every possible genre and style, she consistently broke conventional rules and norms, in regard to pedagogical concepts as well as artistic principles. Her work is characterized by the superb mastery of plot, poignant and poetic language, powerful characterization, and deep understanding of human relationships. Her internationally best-known book is *Pippi Longstocking* (1945), a plea for the child's imagination, integrity, and power in confrontation with the world of adults. However, she also wrote domestic stories, detective stories, naughty-boy and tomboy-girl stories, and comic and high fantasy, and in each case she contributed something new and unusual to the genre as well as blending the genres to create a unique form, as in *Ronia, the Robber's Daughter* (1981). Lindgren did not stop at depicting difficult topics such as death. Yet she never left the child without hope, as can be seen in the controversial fantasy novel *The Brothers Lionheart* (1973). She never followed trends; rather, she set them.

Tove Jansson (1914–2001) was a genius of equal caliber but of a different kind. Like Topelius, Jansson represented the Swedish-speaking minority in Finland, and her Moomin novels reflect this minority's marginal and isolated position, combining traumatic memories of the past with optimistic hopes of the future. The Moomintrolls resemble ordinary people with their faults and virtues rather than fairy tale trolls. Jansson's compatriot Irmelin Sandman Lilius (1936–) created a mythical world of her own that had clear ties to reality.

The Rise of Psychological Literature: The 1960s and 1970s

The 1960s and 1970s in Scandinavia are marked by growing social awareness and commitment in children's literature. Imaginative writing was by many critics and educators pronounced harmful and undesirable. Responding to this, writers focused on the everyday experiences of the child by highlighting domestic realism. While the Norwegian Anne Catharina Vestly (1920–) and the Icelandic Magnea frá Kleifum (1930–) emphasized family values and positive relationships between children and adults, and the Danish Cecil Bødker (1927–) portrayed a utopian society in her poetic pseudo-historical series about Silas, the Swedish Hans Peterson, Kerstin Thorvall (1925–), and Rose Lagercranz (1947–) and the Finno-Swedish Marita Lindqvist (1918–) chose to concentrate on the issues that readers could recognize from their own lives in the rapidly urbanizing Scandinavia: single and divorced parents, moving into a big city, sibling rivalry, and school problems. The increasing rate of immigration was also reflected in children's novels. Previously taboo subjects such as death became prominent. Although much of this literature feels outdated today, some works by Gunnel Linde (1924–), Barbro Lindgren (1937–), the Finno-Swedish Bo Carpelan (1926–), and particularly Maria Gripe (1923–), with her Hugo and Josephine series (1961–1966) and *Elvis and His Secret* (1972), are existential novels of exceptional quality, because of their sophisticated narrative strategies.

The period saw the blossoming of the young adult novel, influenced by J. D. Salinger's *Catcher in the Rye*. The focus was on sexuality, gender roles, violence, alienation, suicide, drug abuse, and parental revolt. Gunnel Beckman (1910–) attained international acclaim with her young adult novels depicting teenagers' dilemmas, such as abortion; yet she was far from alone in this genre in Sweden. The Finnish Uolevi Nojoen (1939–) and Merja Otava (1935–) and the Norwegian Tor Fretheim (1946–) wrote novels about teenage protagonists lost in a complicated modern world, and the most prominent contemporary Icelandic children's writer Gudrún Helgadóttir (1935–) made her appearance.

Picture books of this period were also concerned with the everyday experience of very young children and sought simple but effective artistic means to convey the most common events in a child's life. The leading Swedish picture book creators in this tradition are Inger and Lasse Sandberg (1930– and 1924–); Gunilla Bergström (1942–), the author of several dozen Alfie Atkins books; and Gunilla Wolde (1939–), with her internationally popular Thomas and Betsy books. These authors definitely break with the elaborate Beskow tradition. Instead they imitate children's own drawings with plain forms and scarce details. This trend continued in part into the early 1980s with the tremendously successful Wild Baby books by Barbro Lindgren and Eva Eriksson (1949–).

Nordic Children's Literature Comes of Age: The 1980s and 1990s

The last decades of the 20th century were characterized by a return to imaginative writing after years of social commitment and issue-oriented fiction. Children's and young adult literature became more focused on the individual, and a larger variety of genres emerged, along with a palpable convergence of genres. Maria Gripe wrote a series of psychological gothic novels, and younger Swedish writers such as Mats Wahl (1945–) and Per Nilsson (1954–) wove elements of adventure and thriller into their everyday stories. Ulf Stark

(1944–) used comedy of errors, gender transgression, and makeover in his extremely popular novels for younger teens. The most remarkable Swedish novel of this period is *Johnny My Friend* (1985), by Peter Pohl (1940–), a piercing and multidimensional first-person narrative. Complex narrative techniques with unreliable and multiple narrators, multiple temporal levels, open and alternative endings, elaborate intertextuality, and indeterminacy concerning the credibility of the described events are especially evident in the novels by Danish writers such as Bjarne Reuter (1950–), Louis Jensen (1943–), Bent Haller (1946–), and Kim Fupz Aakeson (1958–). The Finnish Jukka Parkkinen (1948–), Hannele Huovi (1949–), and Tuula Kallioniemi (1951–) were hailed as innovative young adult authors. In Norway Tormod Haugen (1945–) became the leading writer of psychological novels, working extensively with symbols and metaphors. His compatriot Jostein Gaarder (1952–), the author of the international best seller *Sophie's World* (1991), wrote novels combining realism, mystery, and magic.

Historical novels, reflecting the everyday experience of children in various historical epochs rather than focusing on battles and other grand events, became a prominent genre in the 1980s, represented by Maj Bylock (1931–) and Mats Wahl in Sweden and Torill Thorstad Hauger (1943–) in Norway. Fantasy novels, obviously influenced by the Tolkien revival and the success of Philip Pullman and J. K. Rowling, started appearing in the late 1990s in Sweden, Norway, and particularly Iceland, which is the only Nordic country where myth and folklore have always been a living tradition. Although Nordic children's writers have started exploring multiculturalism, few works have so far gone beyond mere issue novels. For the most part, children's novels depicting immigrants and minorities confirm stereotypes rather than interrogate them, even when written by immigrant authors.

The picture book continued to flourish in Sweden, adding to its world reputation Sven Nordqvist (1946–) with his hilarious series about Festus and Mercury. New playgrounds for sophisticated postmodern picture books emerged with such names as the Norwegian Fam Ekman (1946–), the Danish Dorte Karrebæk (1940–) and Lilian Brøgger (1950–), and the Icelandic Sigrún Eldjárn (1954–). Many contemporary Nordic picture books are characterized by elaborate styles, existential themes, and sophisticated narrative techniques.

New Perspectives in the New Millennium

The present state of Nordic children's literature is characterized by its diversity and eclecticism. No genres are given preference; fantasy and realism, high and low genres exist side by side and often mix within the same work. Although all taboos concerning subjects and themes have been eliminated, the authors experiment with forms and expressive means, resulting in blurred borders between children's and adult literature. Even picture books, ostensibly addressed to very young readers, have become more complex and sophisticated, abounding in intertextuality and metafiction beyond a child's comprehension. The idea of an easily accessible literature for children has apparently been completely abandoned by the new generation of authors, and children's publishers have accepted this trend. Nordic children's and young adult literature has come a long way from the didactic and straightforward messages of the 1970s. Today the best writers attend more to creating aesthetic values in their books than to making them politically correct. Finally, it is essential to remember that in all the Nordic countries translations make up at least half of the production for children, and the need for many kinds of children's literature, especially mass-market products, is satisfied by translated works.

[*See also* Fairy Tales and Folk Tales *and articles on figures and topics mentioned in this article.*]

BIBLIOGRAPHY

Aðalsteinsdottír, Silja, ed. *Raddir barnabókanna*. Reykjavik, Iceland: Mál og mennning, 1998.

Bache-Wiig, Harald. *Norsk barnelitteratur—lek på allvor*. Oslo: Cappelen, 1996.

Birkeland, Tone, and Frøydis Storaas. *Den norske biletboka*. Oslo: Cappelen, 1993.

Birkeland, Tone, Gunvor Risa, and Karin Beate Vold. *Norsk barnelitteraturhistorie*. Oslo: Det Norske Samlaget, 1997.

Bookbird 37, no. 4 (1999). Special issue: "Children's Literature in the Nordic Countries."

Christensen, Nina. *Den danske billedbog 1950–1999*. Roskilde, Denmark: Roskilde University Press, 2003.

Edström, Vivi, ed. *Vår moderna bilderbok*. Stockholm: Rabén and Sjögren, 1991. With a summary in English: The Modern Swedish Picture-Book.

Klingberg, Göte. *Till gagn och nöje—svensk barnbok 400 år*. Stockholm: Rabén and Sjögren, 1991. With a summary in English: For Instruction and Delight, the Swedish Children's Book—400 Years.

Lehtonen, Maija, and Marita Rajalin. *Barnboken i Finland förr och nu*. Stockholm: Rabén and Sjögren, 1984. With a summary in English: Children's Books in Finland.

Lundqvist, Ulla. "Some Portraits of Teenagers in Modern Junior Novels in Sweden." In *The Portrayal of the Child in Children's Literature*, edited by Denise Escarpit, 117–124. Munich: Saur, 1985.

Lundqvist, Ulla. *Tradition och förnyelse: Svensk ungdomsbok från sextiotal till nittiotal*. Stockholm: Rabén and Sjögren, 1994. With a summary in English: Traditional Patterns and New Ones,

Swedish Books for Young Adults from the Sixties to the Nineties.
Nikolajeva, Maria. "Similar but Separate: National Features in Scandinavian Children's Literature." *Bookbird* 37, no. 4 (1999): 6–10.
Rättyä, Kaisu. "The Image of Finland in Finnish Children's Literature." In *Europe: A Dream in Pictures*, edited by Jean Perrot, 79–86. Paris: L'Harmattan, 2000.
Sønsthagen, Kari, and Lena Eilstrup, eds. *Dansk børnelitteraturehistorie*. Copenhagen: Høst and Søn, 1992.
Stybe, Vibeke. *Fra billedark til billedbog: Den illustrerede børnebog i Danmark indtil 1950*. Copenhagen: Nyt nordisk forlag, 1983.
Zweigbergk, Eva von. *Barnboken i Sverige 1750–1950*. Stockholm: Rabén and Sjögren, 1965.

MARIA NIKOLAJEVA

Nordqvist, Sven (1946–), Swedish writer and illustrator. Nordqvist is best known for picture books about the old man Festus and his cat Mercury. These started with *Pancake Pie* (original and English version, 1985) and have been translated into many languages. Nordqvist breaks with the picture book tradition dominant in Sweden during the 1960s and 1970s, characterized by scarce details and backgrounds and a focus on the young child's everyday experience. Instead, his picture books, such as *Willie in the Big World* (1985; English version, 1986) and *The Hat Hunt* (1987; English version, 1988), abound in details, substantially expanding the verbal narrative, and they feature hilarious events and funny, imaginative nonexistent characters. Nordqvist's work is notable for unusual perspectives, daring compositions, the use of graphic means to convey movement, and other innovative visual devices. He has also produced picture books in collaboration with other authors, as in the extremely popular series about Mamma Moo, the naughty cow; however, Nordqvist is considerably more restrained in illustrating other writers' texts than in his own works.

BIBLIOGRAPHY

Nikolajeva, Maria, and Carole Scott. *How Picturebooks Work*. New York: Garland, 2001.

MARIA NIKOLAJEVA

Nordstrom, Ursula (1910–1988), American editor, publisher, and writer. Nordstrom was probably the most significant figure in American children's literature of whom most people have never heard. She joined the children's books division at Harper and Brothers, later Harper and Row and now HarperCollins, in 1936 and became its director in 1940; she remained with Harper until her retirement nearly forty years later. Nordstrom's reach was considerable, and her editorial oeuvre groundbreaking and classic. In picture books, she edited Margaret Wise Brown's beloved *Goodnight, Moon* (1947), Russell Hoban's enduring *Bedtime for Frances* (1960), and the definitive modern picture book, Maurice Sendak's *Where the Wild Things Are* (1963). In the vanguard of the beginning-reader movement, she developed the I Can Read series, beginning with Else Holmelund Minarik's *Little Bear* (1957), illustrated by Maurice Sendak. Novels that took shape under her direction include E. B. White's *Charlotte's Web* (1952) and Louise Fitzhugh's *Harriet the Spy* (1964). She shrewdly negotiated controversies over full-frontal toddler nudity in Sendak's *In the Night Kitchen* (1970) and youthful homosexual encounters (the first in American literature for youth) in John Donovan's *I'll Get There. It Better Be Worth the Trip* (1969). She spotted Shel Silverstein's work in *Playboy* and convinced him to write his modern fable *The Giving Tree* (1964), and she nurtured a wary teenaged John Steptoe into creating *Stevie* (1969). As an author, Nordstrom produced only one book, *The Secret Language* (1960), a boarding-school story based on her own childhood experiences; it proved popular with young readers and was named an American Library Association Notable Book. The first woman at Harper to be named a vice president, she remained steadfast in her devotion to children's literature, rejecting a proffered "promotion" to the adult division in order to continue to produce creative, compelling, and appealing literature for real, not idealized youth—as she irreverently phrased it, "good books for bad children."

BIBLIOGRAPHY

Marcus, Leonard. *Dear Genius: The Letters of Ursula Nordstrom*. New York: HarperCollins, 1998.

DEBORAH STEVENSON

Norman, Lilith (1927–), Australian writer who, with her contemporaries Patricia Wrightson, Joan Phipson, and others, developed a new realism in Australian writing, in her case incorporating magical elements. She frequently examines families in crisis, as in *Climb a Lonely Hill* (1970), in which Jack and Sue survive a car accident to find a closer relationship, and *The Shape of Three* (1971), which deals with a hospital muddle over a set of twins. *The Flame Takers* (1973) and *A Dream of Seas* (1978; a provocative novel dealing with death and grief), have elements of magic realism. For younger readers, *My Simple Little Brother* (1979), illustrated by David Rae, is a collection of humorous episodes about a five-year-old. *The Paddock* (1992), illustrated by

Robert Roennfeldt; *Grandpa* (1998), illustrated by Noela Young; and *Aphanasy* (1994; based on a story by Svetlana Svetlanova) and *The Beetle* (1995; retold from a Hans Christian Andersen story), both illustrated by Maxim Svetlanov, are picture books.

STELLA LEES and PAM MACINTYRE

Norriss, Andrew (1947–), British writer; a former history teacher and conjuror. Norriss's children's books (and their television adaptations) display the light touch with dialogue and comic timing that also characterize his popular sitcoms for adults. His stories emphasize friendship and cooperation and take up children's problems, dilemmas, and decisions, but are never moralistic. Applying straight-faced rationality to fantastic situations—a fortune (*Matt's Million*, 1995); a flying machine (*Aquila*, a Whitbread winner, 1997); the power to stop time (*Bernard's Watch*, 1999)—Norriss entertains readers with flights of wish fulfillment, but he always suggests even greater flights: of confidence, self-esteem, and imagination.

PAMELA KNIGHTS

North, Sterling (1906–1974), American author and editor, best known for his animal stories. North grew up on a Wisconsin farm, worked for newspapers in Chicago and New York, and served as the editor for Houghton Mifflin's North Star imprint. He published some of his own titles under this imprint, including *Abe Lincoln: Log Cabin to the White House* (1956). The story of a farm boy raising a ram, *So Dear to My Heart* (1947), was one of North's many adult books and was made into a motion picture. His best-known work is *Rascal: A Memoir of a Better Era* (1963), an autobiographical account of the baby raccoon who shared North's life when he was twelve years old. This classic story was named a Newbery Honor book and has been translated into nearly twenty languages. The Edgerton, Wisconsin, home that Sterling North and Rascal shared is now a museum honoring the author.

[*See also* Animal Stories.]

PETER D. SIERUTA

Norton, Andre (1912–2005), American author best known for her series novels in the genres of fantasy and science fiction or space opera. Born Alice Mary Norton in Cleveland, Ohio, Norton legally changed her name in 1934. She attended Western Reserve University (1930–1932), now Case Western Reserve University, and worked as a children's librarian for the Cleveland Public Library from 1930 to 1950. Although she also wrote historical, gothic, and mystery fiction, Norton is known best for her science fiction and fantasy. Her first novel to gain notoriety was *Star Man's Son, 2250 A.D.* (1952). Seen as "space opera"—adventure novels that appeal to both adult and young adult readers—most of her books are in series, including the Time Traders series, beginning with Time Traders (1958), as well as the Forerunner, Astra, Planet Warlock, and Janus science fiction series, and the Witch World fantasy series. She wrote or collaborated on more than 140 novels. She received several lifetime achievement awards, including the Nebula Grand Master Award (1984), the Jules Verne Award (1984), and induction into the Science Fiction and Fantasy Hall of Fame (1996). She wrote fiction for younger readers, such as in the Star Ka'at series (four novels, 1976–1981), and collaborated with other well-known authors such as Rosemary Edgehill and Mercedes Lackey.

Norton drew her material from research in anthropology, myth, and classical Greek and Latin literature. She demonstrated an interest in animals and concern about the misuse of science. Set in the far future, like *Star Man's Son* and *Sargasso of Space* (1955), in the far past, like the Time Traders novels, or on alternate worlds, like the Witch World series, her works question our assumptions about past and present. Moreover, it is difficult at times to distinguish between her science fiction and fantasy, as the aliens sometimes possess powers like telepathy that human characters consider fantastical. Her heroes (male and female) are loners, outsiders whose abilities make them uncomfortable in the modern, conventional world but perfect for the challenges that face them. This common theme attracts the adolescent reader, who can identify with their distress.

[*See also* Fantasy; Science Fiction; *and* Young Adult Literature.]

BIBLIOGRAPHY

Elwood, Roger, ed. *The Book of Andre Norton*. New York: DAW, 1975.

Schlobin, Roger C. *Andre Norton*. Boston: Gregg, 1979.

JANICE M. BOGSTAD

Norton, Mary (1903–1992), British children's author, one of the foremost representatives of postwar British fantasy. Her first novel, *The Magic Bed-Knob* (1945), is written in the true spirit of E. Nesbit, bringing magic into the everyday

Mary Norton.

and elaborating in humorous details. Three ordinary children befriend a nice neighbor, Miss Price, who takes a correspondence course in black magic. This magical helper, the equivalent of Nesbit's Psammead or Pamela Travers's Mary Poppins, enchants a bed, turning it into a modernized variant of the fairy tale flying carpet. The children fly to London, where they are arrested for disorderly conduct in public—that is, an unmade bed in the middle of the street. Then they go to a Pacific island where they are very nearly eaten up by cannibals, a clear echo from Nesbit's *The Phoenix and the Carpet*. *The Magic Bed-Knob*'s sequel, *Bonfires and Broomsticks* (1947), develops Nesbit's idea of magical time travel. The bed turns out to have the property of transporting the children in time as well as in space. They visit the epoch of Charles II and also bring a young man, Emelius, from the past to their own time, where he is amazed by water pipes, cars, and other wonders. The episode, reminiscent of the visit of the Babylonian queen to modern London in Nesbit's *The Story of the Amulet*, is humorous and even nonsensical, based on the total puzzlement of the visitor from the past when confronted with an unfamiliar society. Norton is both ironic and didactic over her characters' poor knowledge of history, as Carey tells Emelius that the king will be executed, whereupon her brother points out that it was Charles I who was executed. Carey suggests that they go back to their own time and look it up. Then they can also warn Emelius about the Great Fire of London that will take place a week later in his time. In fact, Miss Price agrees to let the magic bed take the children to the past, providing that they went "somewhere really educational." Norton thus adheres to the tradition of time-shift fantasy that combines entertaining and didactic purposes without adding any ethical or psychological dimensions. Time travel is rather mechanical and does not involve any identity problems that otherwise often constitute the central dilemma of time displacement. Yet the novel acquires a more serious tone toward the end, especially as Miss Price and Emelius choose to stay together in the past. The two books were brought out together in a revised version as *Bed-Knob and Broomstick* (1957) and made into a Disney movie. Norton's tribute to Nesbit is also tangible in *Are All the Giants Dead?* (1975), a charming story featuring fairy tale creatures who retire after the hero and the princess start living happily ever after.

Considerably better known is Norton's Borrowers series, starting with the Carnegie Medal–winning *The Borrowers* (1952), which portrays a family of miniature people, Pod, Homily, and their daughter Arrietty, who live secretly in the world of humans, "borrowing" everything they need, basic necessities as well as objects of luxury. The origin of the Borrowers is obscure, but it is hinted that their ancestors once were normal people, but grew tinier with each generation because of being scared—an interesting way of describing the powerless and the oppressed. A short prequel, *Poor Stainless* (1966), depicts the happy times when the house was full of Borrowers. Now the remaining three despise "human beans" (incidentally, a pun picked up or repeated by Roald Dahl in *BFG*) and believe that they exist exclusively to supply the Borrowers with all they need. It is the unwritten rule that Borrowers must never reveal themselves to people, yet the curious and enterprising Arrietty, the epitome of a rebellious teenager, befriends a boy who helps them survive, but also causes their reluctant move away from the old house.

The narrative frame of the story presents a metafictional question. Kate, a young girl featured in the frame (in a later edition, she is also changed into a first-person narrator), hears the story of the Borrowers from her distant relative Mrs. May, who in her turn heard it from her little brother when they were children. The little brother is the boy of the main story, but as the story is thus twice detached even from its recipient within the novel, Kate, there is a strong reason to question its credibility. In other words, the Borrowers can be either the boy's or Mrs. May's invention—most likely the latter's, as she explains to Kate where all the small lost objects in the house go. However, the boy might have made up the story for himself, when he was bedridden, and later told it to his sister during hot nights in India. This marvelously enticing hesitation concerning the source and reliability of the Borrowers' story continues in the sequels *The Borrowers Afield* (1955), *The Borrowers Afloat* (1959), and *The Borrowers Aloft* (1961) that follow the three Borrowers' search for a home, during which they experience the thrill of freedom and the dangers of the wide world. Not least, they face the threat of being exploited by greedy humans. In *The Borrowers Avenged* (1982), Norton completes the series by letting the characters find a final refuge, reunited with their lost relatives.

The humor and excitement of the Borrowers series, as well as many other stories of miniature people, lies in the description of details and all the ways the Borrowers use ordinary objects—a defamiliarization effect that Norton employs with great ingenuity. A more serious dimension is found in the metaphorical picture of the Borrowers representing children—small, weak, and powerless—in their relationship to adults. The Borrowers live in conflict with the world of humans and in constant threat from them. At the same time, they are dependent on humans for their survival. The balance between dependence and autonomy, the longing for independence and the insight of its impossibility, is the essence of the stories. Yet the series conceals other levels of meaning, including the clash between tradition and modernization, or an allegory of the Holocaust.

[*See also* Fantasy *and* Nesbit, E.]

BIBLIOGRAPHY

Hopkins, Chris. "Arrietty, Homily, Pod: Homes, Size, Gender, and Relativity in *The Borrowers*." *Children's Literature Association Quarterly* 25, no. 1 (2000): 21–29.

Hunt, Caroline C. "Dwarf, Small World, Shrinking Child: Three Versions of Miniature." *Children's Literature* 23 (1995): 115–136.

Kuznets, Lois R. "Mary Norton's *The Borrowers*: Diaspora in Miniature." In *Touchstones: Reflections of the Best in Children's Literature*, edited by Perry Nodelman, vol. 1, 198–203. West Lafayette, Ind.: Children's Literature Association, 1985.

O'Malley, Andrew. "Mary Norton's 'Borrowers' Series and the Myth of the Paternalist Past." *Children's Literature* 31 (2003): 71–89.

Stott, Jon C. *Mary Norton*. New York: Twayne, 1994.

Thacker, Deborah. "Real or Story? *The Borrowers*." In *Introducing Children's Literature from Romanticism to Postmodernism*, edited by Deborah Thacker, Deborah Cogan, and Jean Webb, 130–135. London: Routledge, 2002.

Watson, Victor. *Reading Series Fiction: From Arthur Ransome to Gene Kemp*. New York: Routledge, 2000.

MARIA NIKOLAJEVA

Nosov, Nikolai (1908–1976), Russian children's writer. His work encompasses several genres: humorous short stories about boys' everyday pranks in *Tall Tales* (1945); a rather conventional school story, *Vitya Maleyev at School and at Home* (1951); and one of the most popular fantasy novels of all time in Russia, *The Adventures of Dunno and His Friends* (1954). In this last book we meet a community of miniature people, living in an autonomous, perfectly harmonious world. After some innocent pranks involving the protagonist—the "naughty boy," Dunno—several male Mites take an expedition in a balloon, arriving in another town populated exclusively by girls, who promptly set about socializing the ill-behaved boys. The (rather mild) conflict involved is that Dunno claims to be the inventor of the balloon. The novel thus shows a picture of an ideal society where there is nevertheless room for improvement and where collective labor, friendship, and honesty are presented as the highest virtues. In a sequel, *Dunno in Sun City* (1958), the protagonist and two companions travel to another community that has reached a higher technological level. There is also a parallel didactic plot, once again showing how society can improve the individual. Finally, in *Dunno on the Moon* (1964–1965), the characters discover a ruthless capitalist world of miniature people inside the moon, where the masses are impoverished, exploited, and oppressed. The visitors from Earth initiate a revolution, and a communist paradise is established. The trilogy thus develops from a bucolic utopia through a technological utopia to a political utopia. Apart from their overt ideology, their didacticism, and their egregious gender and class stereotyping, the three "Dunno" novels are witty, skillfully plotted, and marvelous in characterization. These positive features made the novels enjoyable for several generations of young readers, although the irony and social satire were most likely lost on them.

BIBLIOGRAPHY

Nikolajeva, Maria. "A Utopia of Mites." In *From Mythic to Linear: Time in Children's Literature*, 70–76. Lanham, Md.: Scarecrow, 2000.

MARIA NIKOLAJEVA

Nöstlinger, Christine (1936–), Austrian novelist, dialect poet, newspaper columnist, writer for radio and TV, and winner of the first Astrid Lindgren Memorial Award (2003, with Maurice Sendak) and the Andersen Medal (1984). From her earliest published work in the early 1970s, Nöstlinger has been "a reliably bad child-rearing influence of the same caliber as Astrid Lindgren" (Lindgren Award Jury). Her works have been best sellers in numerous languages, including Russian, Japanese, French, and Spanish—but never in English. Indeed, few of her translated works are still in print in English, and most of her recent work has not been translated.

Christine Nöstlinger. PHOTOGRAPH BY JULIA MAETZ/ASTRID LINDGREN MEMORIAL AWARD

Nöstlinger was raised in Hernals, a working-class district of Vienna. Her father was a watchmaker, her mother a kindergarten teacher. When her much-loved father was called off to war in 1940, he became her fantasy protector as she rebelled against the home-front authority of women and the elderly. Upon his return in 1945, it took her years to emancipate herself from the idealized model of the father that she had created and then "chased after like a panting puppy." Her experiences with the final days of the war and the occupation and with her coming of age in postwar Austria are captured in two tautly written, densely atmospheric autobiographical works, *Maikäfer flieg!* (1973; English trans., *Fly Away Home*, 1975), and *Zwei Wochen im Mai* (Two Weeks in May, 1981), which show her life as a young girl and then as an increasingly independent teenager.

Like many other German-language children's writers of her generation, among them Renate Walsh and Peter Härtling, Nöstlinger's writing of the 1970s represents a settling of accounts with the authoritarianism and the patriarchy of 20th-century German-Austrian society—forces that lingered in schools and in the family long after their ostensible removal from the political sphere. Her novel *Wir pfeifen auf den Gurkenkönig* (1972; English trans., *The Cucumber King*, 1975), perhaps her greatest work and certainly her most popular, examines patriarchal authority at three levels. There is the political and historical level, as represented by the fantastically grotesque Kumi-Ori II, an eighteen-inch crowned cucumber with white gloves and red-lacquered toenails, ousted from his cellar kingdom by the oppressed Gurkingers. The discovery of this unlikely monarch in the Hogelmann family's kitchen sets up the second level of struggle against patriarchal authority, namely within the family, for Kumi-Ori, though ridiculous in appearance, quickly wins the allegiance and complicity of Mr. Hogelmann, an old-school Austrian pater familias, much to the consternation of twelve-year-old Wolfgang Hogelmann and his sister Martina, who see through to the evil core of the ludicrous intruder. (Indeed, in a plot the children discover, Kumi-Ori plans to drown his former subjects in the cellar—with their father's help.) Wolfgang and Martina seek to rescue their father from Kumi-Ori's influence, but Nöstlinger leaves open until the end whether they are successful. On the other hand, Nöstlinger leaves no doubt when it comes to the despotic and sadistic math teacher Mr. Haslinger, a virulent holdover of

Nazi rule. The school represents the third level of patriarchal authority in *The Cucumber King*.

Nöstlinger's accomplishment in *The Cucumber King* and in her other great works of the 1970s, among them her very first work, *Die feuerrote Friederike* (1970; English trans., *Fiery Frederica*, 1975), and *Konrad oder Das Kind aus der Konservenbüchse* (1975; English trans., *Conrad: The Factory-Made Boy*, 1976), is not solely the translation of a socially critical message into convincing and entertaining children's fiction. These are also works that rehabilitate fantasy as an auctorial strategy in an era otherwise often dominated by sober and tediously humorless social realism. In the wake of the 1968 student revolts, the prevailing Marxist-inspired school of antiauthoritarianism accepted only unflinching, taboo-blind "problem literature," rejecting fairy tale and fantasy alike as escapist and (as it was said then) *systemerhaltend*, that is, pro-establishment. Nöstlinger, by contrast, innovatively crafts an uncompromising critical message, completely and undogmatically aware of the subtle metaphorical paths of literary reception taken by young readers. In *Fiery Frederica*, for example, the heroine's flaming red hair provokes rejection by classmates unwilling to tolerate diversity. Yet the same hair ultimately becomes the source of Frederica's inner strength and even magical powers. In *Conrad*, an eccentric middle-aged woman acquires an impeccably behaved seven-year-old boy from a mail-order catalog. Delivered in a large can, she must pour a nutrient solution over his head to unshrivel him—and within moments, he is the perfect, mass-produced son. Ultimately, however, Conrad must learn bad manners to avoid being reclaimed by his manufacturer, who wants to deliver him to a different family. For this novel, Nöstlinger introduces a compelling fantastic vehicle to convey a socially critical message, further enriched by her gift for situational humor and dialectal wordplay, much of which succeeds remarkably well in English translation—thanks to the art of the translator Anthea Bell, who, it should be noted, translated all of Nöstlinger's great works of the 1970s.

Beginning in 1984, with *Geschichten vom Franz* (Stories about Franz), Nöstlinger turned her attention mainly to creating works for younger children. In 1992, Nöstlinger introduced eight-year-old Mini, an alert and convincing heroine with the whole palette of concerns and interests of children her age. In her books for younger readers as in her earlier works for teenagers, Nöstlinger never compromises in her respect for a child's perspective on the world, at the same time not shrinking from the complexities that characterize a child's life. In *Mini ist verliebt* (Mini in Love, 1999), for example, young readers soon understand what Mini herself does not: that the object of her affection is just a big show-off.

In light of her consistent antiauthoritarian and emancipatory message, her engagement for the rights of children, her irreverent humor, and her documented international, transcultural appeal, it is no surprise that Christine Nöstlinger was the first world writer to win the Astrid Lindgren Memorial Award, sharing the prize with that other great mold breaker, the American Maurice Sendak.

[*See also* Austria; Fantasy; Translation; Young Adult Literature; *and biographies of figures mentioned in this article.*]

BIBLIOGRAPHY

Cubbage, Charlotte, and Jeffrey Garrett. "*Väterdämmerung*: Fact, Fiction, and Fathers in Nöstlinger's *The Cucumber King*." *Bookbird: A Journal of International Children's Literature* 39, no. 2 (2001): 21–27.

Fetz, Nancy Tillman. "Christine Nostlinger's Emancipatory Fantasies." *The Lion and the Unicorn* 10 (1986): 40–53.

Lathey, Gillian. *The Impossible Legacy: Identity and Purpose in Autobiographical Children's Literature Set in the Third Reich and the Second World War*. Bern, Switzerland, and New York: Peter Lang, 1999.

Rogers, Mike. "Christine Nöstlinger and the Force of Tradition." In *"Other" Austrians: Post-1945 Austrian Women's Writing*, proceedings of the conference at the University of Nottingham, 18–20 April 1996, edited by Allyson Fiddler, 47–56. Bern, Switzerland: Peter Lang, 1998.

JEFFREY GARRETT

Nursery Rhymes. Verses of early childhood from birth through kindergarten—many derived from and still active in oral tradition, together with literary versions purposefully composed for children—abound in literature for youngsters worldwide. Many commentaries attempt to define the genre by listing types of verses, most commonly in terms of their uses or forms—for example counting rhymes, bouncing rhymes, lullabies, riddles, short nonsense narratives, and such. This approach neither captures the essence of the category nor offers insight into its defining characteristics: a common audience of children and, frequently, their caregivers; strong and insistent rhythm; strict rhyme; and repetition, often incremental in nature. The rhymes are commonly described as being short, yet many have existed in numerous stanzas. Years of passage through childhood culture have effectively preserved in these verses just the amount of content that is capable of engaging youngsters through its familiarity—typically several stanzas at most. This effect of familiarity exists for the published verse as well, indicated

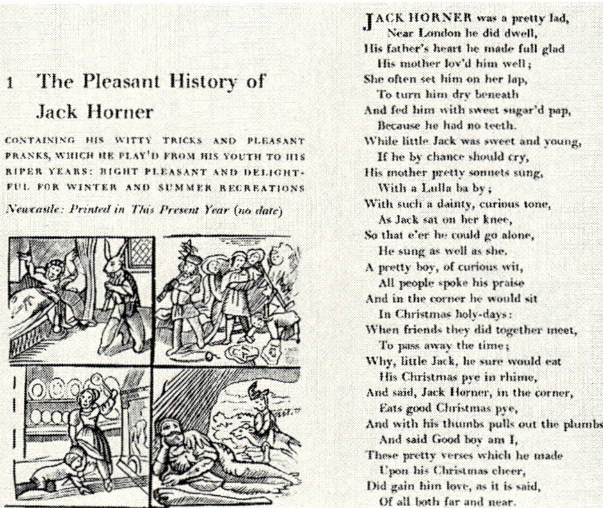

1 The Pleasant History of Jack Horner

CONTAINING HIS WITTY TRICKS AND PLEASANT PRANKS, WHICH HE PLAY'D FROM HIS YOUTH TO HIS RIPER YEARS: RIGHT PLEASANT AND DELIGHTFUL FOR WINTER AND SUMMER RECREATIONS

Newcastle: Printed in This Present Year (no date)

JACK HORNER was a pretty lad,
Near London he did dwell,
His father's heart he made full glad
His mother lov'd him well;
She often set him on her lap,
To turn him dry beneath
And fed him with sweet sugar'd pap,
Because he had no teeth.
While little Jack was sweet and young,
If he by chance should cry,
His mother pretty sonnets sung,
With a Lulla ba by;
With such a dainty, curious tone,
As Jack sat on her knee,
So that e'er he could go alone,
He sung as well as she.
A pretty boy, of curious wit,
All people spoke his praise
And in the corner he would sit
In Christmas holy-days:
When friends they did together meet,
To pass away the time;
Why, little Jack, he sure would eat
His Christmas pye in rhime,
And said, Jack Horner, in the corner,
Eats good Christmas pye,
And with his thumbs pulls out the plumbs,
And said Good boy am I,
These pretty verses which he made
Upon his Christmas cheer,
Did gain him love, as it is said,
Of all both far and near.

Nursery Rhymes. From *The Pleasant History of Jack Horner* (Newcastle, England, c. 1850). COLLECTION OF JACK ZIPES

by the not-uncommon disenchantment of child listeners with too much of the same thing or the fatigue of adult readers through repetition beyond the portion of the rhymes preserved as icons of their childhood.

Early Traditions

The oldest verses of this nature were indubitably orally derived, for they represent one of the primary ways adult humans seek to interact and communicate with their young. "Peek-a-boo, I see you" is a simple and widespread example of this adult-child interactive play that can logically be assumed to have ancient roots, owing to the pervasive existence of variations on this form in child-rearing traditions worldwide. Another universal form is that of rhymes associated with making gestures, actions, and mime while touching parts of the child's body. Examples include the well-known toe game "This little piggy" and the tickling rhyme "Round and round in the garden, goes the teddy bear." Lullabies are a third universal form; these typically gentle tunes are not always matched in gentleness by the accompanying verse, as, for instance, in "Rock-a-bye baby." Other verse set to music is commonly used to create various amusements, such as the dandling game "There was a nimble pony, whose name was Dapple Gray," and here again comparable examples exist in languages and cultures throughout the world.

The significance of these very early traditional communications has been demonstrated in a Toronto program called Parent-Child Mother Goose, developed for new parents who are recent immigrants separated from their families. Encouraged to use nursery rhymes from their specific cultures, these parents feel more comfortable and competent in interacting with their infants and less isolated from parents of other backgrounds because they, too, are seen to have similar verses.

Some of these very early verses enter children's active repertoires as they begin to socialize with other children, but mostly these verses are etched in memory to be used with subsequent generations, as they are when the need to communicate with an infant arises. The remembrances go beyond normal memory, for persons who as preliterate children heard rhymes or songs in a different language or dialect that they themselves never actively spoke will reproduce in comparable circumstances those items as they received them in their infancy.

The specific origins of nursery rhymes—as of most folklore—continue to intrigue people, but such details are lost to the ages because (like so much concerning childhood culture in the past) they were never adequately recorded. The basic characteristics of nursery rhymes are common traits of oral traditions in general, and the enduring popularity of the verses owes much to the ownership engendered in the littlest of people through resonance with that most familiar and personal of all human communication. Another stream in the nursery rhyme tradition, however, comprises those verses written by adults specifically to educate or amuse children, and the history of this category, while complex and open to debate, is much easier to document. Iona and Peter Opie have demonstrated that the actual term "nursery rhyme" first appears in 1824 but is preceded by several centuries of related texts—ballads, bawdy or historical or satirical—that some 19th-century folklore scholars argued, in keeping with evolutionary theories of the time, were the detritus of high culture preserved mimetically among children (or the common folk). Such ideas prompted research into the sociocultural sources for the rhymes, offering allegorical referents for persons and events depicted in them: for instance, "Mary, Mary quite contrary" reputedly being Mary, Queen of Scots. A number of studies of this nature exist, among which *The Annotated Mother Goose* (1962), compiled by the Baring-Goulds, is a good example.

From the mid-18th century onward, nursery rhymes became increasingly prominent in the developing literature for children. John Newbery's heirs published a collection, *Mother Goose's Melody; or, Sonnets for the Cradle* (c. 1766), that helped cement the enduring link between Mother Goose and rhymes—rather than a link between Mother Goose and

Nursery Rhymes. The Cat and the Fiddle: frontispiece to *Mother Goose's Melodies, or Songs for the Nursery*, edited by William A. Wheeler (Boston and New York: Houghton, Mifflin, 1869). REPRODUCED COURTESY OF THE COTSEN CHILDREN'S LIBRARY, PRINCETON UNIVERSITY LIBRARY

tales, as first presented in Charles Perrault's 1697 collection for children, *Histoires ou contes du temps passé* (English trans., *Histories or Tales of Past Times, Told by Mother Goose* (1729). The chapbooks that became popular in the early 19th century were ideal outlets for a single nursery rhyme or a small collection and helped standardize and cultivate a reading audience for the rhymes. Robert Chambers's *Popular Rhymes of Scotland* (1826) is one of the larger anthologies of the period, which also gave rise to significant publications in the United States and Canada, such as *Mother Goose's Melodies* (1833), but similar collections appeared only later in Britain's remaining colonies such as Australia, where W. A. Cawthorne's influential *Who Killed Cockatoo?* did not appear until 1870.

The practice of creating relatively inexpensive but elaborately illustrated books of nursery rhymes commenced in 1881 with the publication of *Mother Goose; or, The Old Nursery Rhymes* by Kate Greenaway. Subsequently, Randolph Caldecott's highly successful and extended series of relatively short picture or toy books appeared, each presenting one or several rhymes in large print with few words on a page accompanied by elaborate, colored illustrations. A pattern was thus established for accomplished illustrators to use nursery rhymes as the stimulus for their creativity, resulting in such works as *The Baby Opera* (1877) by Walter Crane, *Mother Goose: The Old Nursery Rhymes* (1913) by Arthur Rackham, *The Real Mother Goose* (1916) by Blanche Fisher Wright, and works by many others such as Raymond Briggs, Maurice Sendak, and Richard Scarry throughout the 20th century.

There is no standard canon of Mother Goose verses, although modern works presented as "Mother Goose" tend to focus on the most popular or well-known verses in the attenuated forms in which they have survived—"Jack and Jill" and "Mary had a little lamb," for example. These rhymes and songs are so familiar that it was possible for Janet Ahlberg to create *Each Peach Pear Plum* (1973), a picture book for wee ones based on the traditional game "I spy," using just names of characters from the verses as well as traditional children's tales.

While some nursery rhymes still have oral currency among children despite the onslaught of media on their culture, the abundant anachronisms and archaic words incorporated in the rhymes have caused many of them to fall into disuse. For instance, few now know what a "tuffet" or "whey" might be, and wordplay seems insufficient to fascinate a child who does not. Further, societal concerns about bullying, violence, and abuse mitigate against preserving "Georgie Porgie," "Tom, Tom, the piper's son," "The Old Woman who lives in a shoe," and many more Mother Goose rhymes, no matter how humorous they might formerly have seemed. The strong element of nonsense and the ridiculous that courses through nursery rhymes is the source of the humor in them, but those very elements are targeted by many adults as stimulating more fear than pleasurable laughter in the contemporary child.

Yet, modern scholars, such as the Opies from their canonical *The Oxford Book of Nursery Rhymes* (1951) to their later works, have made the same argument for nursery rhymes that J. R. R. Tolkien made for "Faerie" (in his frequently reprinted 1975 essay "On Fairy Stories"), and Bruno Bettelheim (in *The Uses of Enchantment*, 1976) argued for not only the value but also the necessity of fairy tales. Nursery rhymes "help children deal with the conflicts and complexities of real life" by presenting a nonsensical "world of kindness and cruelty, history and fantasy, morality and amorality, peace and aggression, and the multitude of paradoxical forces that permeate human life" (Rollin). Simply, nursery rhymes offer children access to the truth in a form that they can accept and handle. The apparently simple or nonsensical verses, then, bear powerful meaning for the young, whose obvious attachment to them has indicated that they are matters of consequence.

Role in Children's Lives

Nursery rhymes serve various functions for the young far beyond any amusement value. They are a primary means of language acquisition; indeed, some researchers argue that they are central to language acquisition and should be a part of a child's life within the first eighteen months in order for the youngster to develop the necessary synapses to develop his or her full literacy potential. Nursery rhymes also fulfill the goal of enabling children to see themselves in literature, for the world seems to be nonsensical to children and they are thus gratified to identify with the many vulnerable characters to whom things happen in fairy tales.

As children age, they are the first to put behind them "childish things," and they frequently use variants on nursery rhymes to express their maturation. The result is an endless variety of parodies on familiar forms that have themselves, in recent years, become the basis for numerous books. Especially fine examples of this genre are the compilations by June Factor (with Gwenda Davey and others) of children's own submissions, starting with *Far Out, Brussel Sprout* (1983), in which one of the most popular of childhood verses appears as "Mary had a little lamb, Her father shot it dead. Now it goes to school, beneath two slices of bread." Children mark their passage through childhood by rejecting what went before and declaring supremacy over it, as in the following "elevated" version of "Three Blind Mice" by a ten-year-old:

> Three rodents with defective vision,
> Three rodents with defective vision.
> Observe how they perambulate.
> They all perambulated after the agriculturalist's mate,
> Who severed their extremities with a kitchen utensil.
> Have you ever observed such a phenomenon in all
> your existence
> As three rodents with defective vision?

The Opies' volume *I Saw Esau: The Schoolchild's Pocket Book*, illustrated by Maurice Sendak (1992), is a fine collection of older children's reactions of this nature to nursery rhyme.

A substantial number of books have explored the way that nursery rhymes may be a means of instilling identity—most obviously national identity, but sometimes cultural or religious identity as well. Around the beginning of the 20th century, when nationalist movements were common and immigrants to new lands were searching for their identity, numerous nursery rhyme collections with overtly nationalist themes appeared—for instance, David Boyle's *Uncle Jim's Nursery Rhymes for Canadian Children* (1908), which was the first four-color illustrated Canadian work for children. Boyle, an avocational scholar of folklore, integrated his Argylleshire background with the Canadian environment to produce a work intended to promote a sense of Canadianness. Robert Holden has documented that around the same time in Australia, there emerged verses obviously involved with what we might now call "identity politics"—such as "Twinkle, Twinkle, Southern Cross," which played on the distinctiveness of the antipodes. There were also publications promoting American verse, as documented in the retrospective *Yankee Doodle's Literary Sampler of Prose, Poetry, and Pictures: Being an Anthology of Diverse Works Published for the Edification and/or Entertainment of Young Readers in America before 1900*, edited by Virginia Havilland and Margaret Coughlan (1974). Modern versions of the same type include Colin Thiele and Wendy DePaauw's *The Australian Mother Goose* (2d. ed., 1992), which enjoys success as a children's, as well as a tourist, book. Works attempting to manipulate nursery rhymes to fulfill overt agendas have seldom captivated significant audiences. Children continue today, as they undoubtedly have throughout the history of nursery rhymes, to engage with the rhymes directly and to make of them what matters to their understanding of the world and operation in it.

[*See also* Chapbooks; Fairy Tales and Folk Tales; Lullaby; Picture Books; Toy Books; *and biographies of figures mentioned in this article.*]

BIBLIOGRAPHY

Baring-Gould, William S., and Ceil Baring-Gould. *The Annotated Mother Goose*. New York: Branhall House, 1962.

Holden, Robert. *Twinkle, Twinkle, Southern Cross: The Forgotten Folklore of Australian Nursery Rhymes*. Canberra: National Library of Australia, 1992.

Factor, June. *Far Out, Brussel Sprout*. Melbourne, Australia: Oxford University Press, 1983.

Opie, Iona, and Peter Opie. *I Saw Esau: The Schoolchild's Pocket Book*. Illustrated by Maurice Sendak. Cambridge, Mass.: Candlewick, 1992.

Opie, Iona, and Peter Opie, eds. *The Oxford Book of Nursery Rhymes*. Oxford: Clarendon Press, 1951.

Rollin, Lucy. *Cradle and All: A Cultural and Psychoanalytic Reading of Nursery Rhymes*. Jackson: University of Mississippi Press, 1992.

Carole H. Carpenter

Nurse Truelove's New-Year's Gift; Or, The Book of Books for Children. This easy reader, published (perhaps in 1753) by John Newbery, was frequently reprinted in colonial America. Its secularism distinguished it from other contemporary readers. Less space was devoted to religious instruction, and more was devoted to short fiction teaching middle-class values and the work ethic. For example, "Mrs. Williams and Her Plum-Cake" demonstrated why individual merit should take precedence over social rank. *Nurse Truelove* also contains the first appearance in print of the nursery rhyme "The House that Jack Built." *Nurse Truelove* was advertised as free to all children visiting Newbery's bookshop; they would pay just twopence for the binding of Dutch floral paper, "but not unless you are good." Actually, this was no bargain, as similar pamphlets normally sold for the same price. This strategy, satirized by Edward Moore in 1755, in an essay in the *World* on misleading promotional ploys, undoubtedly contributed to Newbery's reputation for skilled (and shameless) advertising.

Andrea Immel

Nusic, Branislav (1864–1938), one of the greatest Serbian comedy writers, as well as a novelist, storywriter, essayist, and journalist. In 1900, he was a secretary for the Ministry of Education. Afterwards he became a dramatist for the National Theater in Belgrade and in 1904 was selected to be head of the Serbian National Theater. Nusic initiated the production of social comedy in Serbia, presenting local merchants, regional chiefs, police clerks, homemakers, and villains as symbols for power and money in present-day society. A prolific author famous for his distinguished sense of humor, Nusic used satire, caricature, and irony as main vehicles with an intent to bring about social improvement, especially in children's literature. Although Nusic wrote primarily for adults, in the 1930s he published the very first Serbian children's novels. He is considered the follower of the late-19th-century poet Jovan Jovanovic Zmaj, thus marking the second period of Serbian children's literature. He left his trace as a classic on the entire 20th century and was also dominant in the repertoire of modern Serbian theater.

[*See also* Drama *and* Eastern European Countries.]

MILENA MILEVA BLAZIC

Nutcracker, The. This German story by E.T.A. Hoffmann was first published in 1816 as *Nussknacker und Mausekönig* (The Nutcracker and the Mouse King). Hoffmann's tale has at least three narrative layers: reality, dreams, and storytelling. It begins on Christmas Eve, when little Marie gets a nutcracker in the shape of a man. During the night, she witnesses a battle between the nutcracker's army of toy soldiers and a group of mice. It is she who gets hurt, and during her recovery she hears the story of the nutcracker, who is an enchanted prince. According to Isa Schikorsky, the multiple layers of this work resist any definite categorization. It has been described as a fairy tale, as a typical fantasy story, and as a realistic story about a sick girl who has bad dreams. Alexandre Dumas's adapted version, *Les aventures d'un casse-noisette* (1845), served as the basis for Tchaikovsky's ballet (1892), from which the famous "Nutcracker Suite" is extracted. In the 20th century, Hoffmann's tale was illustrated by Maurice Sendak (1984) and Lisbeth Zwerger (2003).

[*See also* Fairy Tales and Folk Tales; Fantasy; Germany; *and* Hoffmann, E. T. A.]

BIBLIOGRAPHY

Schikorsky, Isa. "Ernst Theodor Amadeus Hoffmanns Wirklichkeitsmärchen 'Nussknacker und Mausekönig.'" In *Klassiker der Kinder- und Jugendliteratur*, edited by Bettina Hurrelmann. Frankfurt am Main: Fischer, 1995, 520–539.

VANESSA JOOSEN

Nwankwo, Nkem (1936–2001), Nigerian novelist, schoolteacher, poet, journalist, newspaper editor, and writer for young adults, born in Nnofia, Nigeria. He earned a reputation as a member of "the first generation of African literary voices" with the publication of his first adult novel, *Danda* (1964), followed by *My Mercedes Is Bigger Than Yours* (1975) and *The Scapegoat* (1984). He also authored *Tales out of School* (1963) and *More Tales out of School* (1965), two young adult adventure stories that remain popular in Nigerian secondary schools. Although attracted to some features of modernity, Nwankwo was equally wary of wholesale rejection of traditional values, which he often promoted in his works.

BIBLIOGRAPHY

Osa, Osayimwense. "The Rise of African Children's Literature." *Reading Teacher* 38 (April 1985): 750–754.

MAWUENA KOSSI LOGAN

Nwapa, Flora (1931–1993), Nigerian writer, educator, and publisher. Born in Oguta, East Central State, Nigeria, and educated at University College, Ibadan, and the University of Edinburgh, Nwapa worked variously as an education officer for the Nigerian Ministry of Education, as assistant registrar at the University of Lagos, as a state minister responsible for reuniting children with their parents after the Biafran war, and as a teacher and lecturer. The publication of *Efuru* (1966) made her Nigeria's first published woman novelist, and she continued writing adult literature. In the 1970s she founded two publishing companies, Tana Press and Flora Nwapa Books, which published much of her later work. Her first children's book, *Emeka, Driver's Guard* (1972), was followed by titles including *Mammywater* (1979), about an Igbo water goddess, a similar story for younger children called *The Adventures of Deke* (1980), *Journey to Space* (1980), *The Miracle Kittens* (1980), and *My Animal Number Book* (1981).

[*See also* Africa: Sub-Saharan Africa; *and* Publishers and Publishing.]

ADRIENNE E. GAVIN

Nyblom, Helena (1843–1926), Danish-Swedish poet and writer of short stories. She was best known as the prolific and popular author of Swedish literary fairy tales for children, published between 1896 and 1920; a selection is available in English under the title *The Witch of the Woods* (1968). Nyblom's fairy tales include versions of "Beauty and the Beast" and a variant of Andersen's "The Little Mermaid." She can be counted among the most faithful followers of the Andersen tradition in Nordic literature, yet her writing is unmistakably original and fresh. Many of her tales, mixing Swedish folklore, ancient myths, and Romantic motifs, contain clear feminist messages typical of her time. They also reflect the general didacticism of Swedish literature for children at the turn of the 20th century. Nyblom's tales are little known and little appreciated today; at best, they are included in anthologies of fairy tales. Yet she made a significant contribution to the development of Swedish children's literature as a social and literary system.

BIBLIOGRAPHY

Nordlinder, Eva. *Sekelskiftets svenska konstsaga och sagodiktaren Helena Nyblom*. Stockholm: Bonnier, 1991. With a summary in English: "The Kunstmärchen in Turn-of-the-Century Sweden: Helena Nyblom and Her Tales."

MARIA NIKOLAJEVA

Nye, Naomi Shihab (1952–), American writer and anthologist who has celebrated her Arab American heritage in poems, picture books, novels, and essays. The daughter of an American mother and a Palestinian father, Nye was born and raised in St. Louis, Missouri, spent a year living in Jerusalem, then moved to San Antonio as a teenager. She has produced many volumes of poetry for young people as both an editor (*The Same Sky: A Collection of Poems from around the World*, 1992) and as an author, including *Nineteen Varieties of Gazelle: Poems of the Mideast* (2002), which sensitively describes life in the troubled Middle East, as well as the experiences of young Arab Americans growing up in the United States. Her compelling first novel, *Habibi* (1996), places an Arab American girl in contemporary Jerusalem, where she learns about her Palestinian heritage and falls in love with a Jewish boy. This book, like much of the author's work, celebrates cultural diversity while exploring the universal human experiences that link us all.

PETER D. SIERUTA

Nye, Robert (1939–), English writer and critic. At the age of sixteen Nye quit school and had his first poetry published. In 1961 he moved to Wales in order to write full-time. The experience proved to be productive in many ways. He earned critical recognition with a collection of poetry, *Juvenilia I* (1961), started writing reviews for different British literary journals and newspapers, and developed an interest in Welsh and Celtic legends—material he would make use of in his children's books *Taliesin* and *March Has Horse Ears* (both 1966). Besides novels and poetry, he has continued writing children's books. *Beehunter: Adventures of Beowulf* (1968) is a retelling of the Anglo-Saxon epic; Nye makes the story accessible to young readers and puts his own twist on some of the incidents. The Beowulf book was followed by *Wishing Gold* (1970), based on Irish folklore. Nye has also edited a collection of folk tales, *The Classic Folktales from around the World* (1994).

BJÖRN SUNDMARK

Nygren, Tord (1936–), Swedish artist. Nygren is a highly sought-after illustrator of children's books, for which he usually makes black-and-white drawings; but he has also created a number of remarkable picture books, such as *I'll Take Care of the Crocodiles* (1977; English version, 1978) and *Come into My Night, Come into My Dream* (1978; English version, 1981), with text by Stefan Mählqvist. These, as well as Nygren's wordless picture book *The Red Thread* (1987–1988), are characterized by richness of detail and postmodern play with visual allusions, which address the adults who are reading along with children.

BIBLIOGRAPHY

Nikolajeva, Maria, and Carole Scott. *How Picturebooks Work*. New York: Garland, 2001.

Scott, Carole. "Dual Audience in Picture Books." In *Transcending Boundaries: Writing for a Dual Audience of Children and Adults*, edited by Sandra Beckett, 99–110. New York: Garland, 1999.

MARIA NIKOLAJEVA

Oakley, Graham (1929–), English author and illustrator. Oakley is best known for his series of books about a church inhabited by a cat and a large number of mice. Experienced in set design, and with an interest in buildings, Oakley planned to tell the story of a village, beginning with its church. But he populated the church with mice and with a cat who had listened to too many sermons and had made a moral decision that killing mice was wrong. *The Church Mouse* (1972) was followed by many sequels, almost one a year from 1972 to 2000. The adventures of mice and cat and some of the humans in the village are related with a humor and innuendo that appeals to adults as well as children. While admiring the detailed illustrations of the cats entered in a cat show, for instance, the reader suddenly notices that three mice have climbed into the judge's coat pocket to taunt the cats. The text has only indicated that the mice had a plan to ensure that their friend Sampson, comfortable in the presence of mice, would win. Another series chronicles the escapades of the Foxbury Police Department, beginning with *The Foxbury Force* (1994).

[*See also* Animal Stories *and* Anthropomorphism.]

Frances Armstrong

Obaldía, María Olimpia de (1891–1985), Panamanian writer. Born in the province of Chirquí and known as "La alondra chiricana" (The chiricana skylark), de Obaldía is one of the most highly esteemed modernist poets of Panama. Her poems for children can be found in *Parnaso infantil* (1948; A Parnassus for Children) and *Breviario lírico* (1929; Lyrical Compedium). Her other writing for children is based on traditional Panamanian tales. The subject of a multitude of honors, she was the first female member of the Academia Panameña de la Lengua (Panamanian Academy of Language) and in 1949 was dubbed "Maria Olimpia of Panama." Written at the time of her country's independence, her poems reflect nationalistic as well as Christian sentiments. Her main themes reflect her love for home and children but the poems are also intimately linked to the native landscape and include a deeply felt solidarity with the destitute local Guaymí Indians.

Evelyn Arizp

Obaldia, René de (1918–), French poet and novelist; member of the French Academy. Obaldia is best known for his plays, such as *Génousie* (1960) and *Le vent dans les branches de sassafras* (1965; *Wind in the Branches of the Sassafras*, 1979). He was recognized as a writer for young people with his book of poems *Innocentines, poèmes pour enfants et quelques adultes* (Innocent Rhymes: Poems for Children and a Few Adults, 1969). Many illustrated editions of this book have been published, and a play was derived from it. Obaldia sees the world ironically and with a touch of madness, in keeping with postmodernism. Puns and wordplay involving sounds as well as meanings are the basis of his writing, which perpetually strays off the beaten track. For instance, he uses English words, which he transcribes phonetically (thus *weekend* becomes *ouiquenne*). One of his poems is an homage to Tom Sawyer.

Jean Foucault

Obele, Cheryl Ann, an American married to an Igbo Nigerian, and the author of two Nigerian juvenile novels in the Macmillan Winners series. Both feature children who deviate from the expectations of Igbo society, the majority group of southeastern Nigeria. *Nwogo the Witch* (1987) concerns the superstition and persecution occasioned by a shy girl's prominent birthmark. Fleeing pressures of school and home, Nwogo finds refuge with a kind family and gains the self-confidence to stand on her own. In *Stepping Out* (1988), twelve-year-old Sunday's determination to develop his artistic talent leads to conflict with his ambitious father over choice of career. Eventually, his father is won over as Sunday proves his worth through art.

Virginia W. Dike

O'Brien, Robert C. (1922?–1973), American journalist and fabulist whose real name was Robert Leslie Carroll Conly. His year of birth is disputed; according to some sources it is 1918, but according to others it is 1922. O'Brien was a professional journalist, working for prominent magazines such as *Newsweek* and *National Geographic*, and did not start publishing fiction until he was in his late forties. His first two books, *The Silver Crown* (1968) and *Mrs. Frisby and the Rats of NIMH* (1971), were for younger children; his last two, *A Report from Group 17* (1972) and *Z for Zachariah* (1975), are appropriate for older children or for adults. *The Silver Crown* tells of a girl taken away to a kingdom whose ruler is influenced by horrible machinery. O'Brien's best-known work is his second novel, *Mrs. Frisby and the Rats of NIMH*, which won the Newbery Medal when it was published. It also won the Lewis Carroll Shelf Award, the Mark Twain Award, the Pacific Northwest Library Association Young Readers' Choice Award, and the William Allan White Children's Book Award; and it came in second for the National Book Award. In this book, laboratory rats at the National Institute of Mental Health have developed phenomenal intelligence, which they apply to build a safe haven—complete with electricity and elevators—for themselves and all of their kind. The rats then decide that self-sufficiency is vital and move their haven away from the curious eyes and dangerous machinery of human beings. O'Brien's last two books were darker in their subject matter: *A Report from Group 17* portrays the cold war as heated up to biological warfare; *Z for Zachariah* is about a girl fleeing from a sadist in a world ravaged by a nuclear holocaust. *Z for Zachariah* was published posthumously, having been completed by members of O'Brien's family after his death. O'Brien's daughter, Jane Leslie Conly, also wrote two sequels to *Mrs. Frisby: Racso and the Rats of NIMH* (1986) and *R-T, Margaret, and the Rats of NIMH* (1990).

MARISSA K. LINGEN

O'Connor, Jane (1947–), American publisher and author of more than forty books for beginning readers and young adults. O'Connor uses a humorous approach to family and friendship conflicts in such young reader books as *Lulu and the Witch Baby* (1986), in which Lulu casts a disappearing spell on her annoying baby sister. Other works include the Here Come the Brownies series for Girl Scouts, *Super Cluck* (1991), written with her son Robert, and *The Ghost in Tent Nineteen* (1988), written with her husband Jim O'Connor. Her young adult novels include *Yours Till Niagara Falls, Abby* (1979), which explores friendship and camp life. O'Connor has published several nonfiction works for children, including *Magic in the Movies: The Story of Special Effects* (1980). Coauthored with Katy Hall, the New York Academy of Sciences Honor book explores camera tricks and makeup techniques. O'Connor combines humor with nonfiction in *If the Walls Could Talk: Family Life at the White House* (2004), which explores presidential experiences from George Washington to George W. Bush.

[*See also* Nonfiction *and* Young Adult Literature.]

ERICA HARTNETT

Odaga, Asenath (1938–), born in Rarieda, Kenya, a prominent and prolific writer and publisher of materials in English and Luo for children of all ages. Odaga Asenath Bole has been a teacher, founder, and first headmistress of a girls' school; secretary of the Kenya Library Services; assistant director of a curriculum development program; research fellow; editor; chair (the Kenya Women's Literature Group and the Children's Literature Association of Kenya); founding member of the Writers' Association of Kenya; and a member of the executive committee for the International Board on Books for Young People. She believes that children's literature is significantly important in the image-forming process of young readers, and that oral literature serves to project the image of one's society with a clear picture of the African world through events that are familiar to the members. *The Hare's Blanket, and Other Tales* (1967), *Thu Tinda: Stories from Kenya* (1980), and *Kenyan Folk Tales* (1981) draw on the oral tradition of Odaga's community to depict everyday activities in children's lives at home and at school. These activities are, according to her, "the bits and pieces that fit into the stream of [children's] existence and make their life whole." And it is from these bits that she tries "to create realistic and objective work." She adheres to the African concept of the functionality and the practical use of art beyond its entertainment value to the people: *Jande's Ambition* (1966) shows a young girl determined to complete her education and become a teacher. The Kip series—*Kip on the Farm* (1972), *Kip on the Coast* (1977), *Kip Goes to the City* (1977)—are educational stories about adventures in the farm, market, and travel to the city. *Ogilo and the Hippo* (1991), a story about the secret pact of boys who are determined to protect and save a pregnant hippo from being killed by poachers for meat, conveys morals to children and young adult readers.

MAHOUMBAH KLOBAH

O'Dell, Scott (1898–1989), American writer principally known for his historical fiction aimed at middle-grade readers and based in the 18th- and 19th-century American Southwest, West Coast, and Mexico. O'Dell was born in Los Angeles with the name of Odell Gabriel Scott, but changed his name to Scott O'Dell after a printer's mistake. While he made his living as a novelist, technical director for Paramount, and cameraman for Metro Goldwyn-Mayer, he was sixty-two when his first children's novel, *Island of the Blue Dolphins*, earned him an international reputation. He was to complete twenty-six novels for young readers in the next thirty years, most of them historical and twenty-two of them with non–European American heroes. He was still in the midst of writing two books, later completed by his wife, Elizabeth Hall, when he died of cancer at ninety.

In addition to the Newbery Medal for *Island of the Blue Dolphins* (1960), later made into a popular movie by Universal Studios in 1964, he received awards and citations from the American Library Association, Horn Book, and many other national and international organizations. After *Island of the Blue Dolphins*, his second most honored novel is probably *The King's Fifth* (1966), in which the story is told by the same narrator/hero but from alternating time perspectives: one in 1538, when the narrator first sets out on a voyage of discovery, and the other in 1541, when he is in jail in Vera Cruz, New Spain (on the coast of the Gulf of Mexico), awaiting his trial for not delivering "the king's fifth" of the reputed gold gleaned during his expeditions among the natives. While in jail, the narrator is encouraged to write down his story, ostensibly because his jailer, and many others around him, think it will help them to find the gold. What emerges instead is a tale of horror and death as his Spanish companions kill, torture, and destroy on their way across the Mexican peninsula in search of the Seven Golden Cities of Cibola. In the course of the journey, most lose their lives, but not before crossing paths with Captain Coronado.

O'Dell's novels can be characterized stylistically by his reliance on first-person narration and, in most cases, by their straightforward exploration of historical characters and situations; his four modern novels are regarded as his least successful. O'Dell is both praised for the many Native American narrators and characters in his novels and criticized for using stereotypes in their descriptions, although this is more characteristic of his Hispanic than of his Native American characters. While a few of his novels are set in medieval Europe (*The Road to Damietta*, about St. Francis of Assisi, 1985) or colonial America (*Sarah Bishop*, 1980, and *The Serpent Never Sleeps*, about Pocahontas, 1987), many, like *Island of the Blue Dolphins*, are set in his familiar ground of the Southwest and chronicle the cruelties with which native populations were treated by European invaders, from the conquistadors and priests of the 16th through 18th centuries, to the northern Europeans of the 19th and 20th. *Island of the Blue Dolphins* and its sequel, *Zia* (1976), explore the Spanish destruction coastal Indian cultures. His pre-Colombian trilogy of *The Captive* (1979), *The Feathered Serpent* (1981), and *The Amethyst Ring* (1983) focuses specifically on 17th-century Spanish expeditions to the Inca, Aztec, and Mayan cultures. His narrator is, atypically, an adult, Julian Escobar, whose amazing facility with languages and range of travels have elicited some skepticism. While presenting the reader with one man's often critical perspective on these destructive periods in the history of the Americas such as the fall of the Aztec empire, O'Dell often strains the reader's credulity that one person could survive so many harrowing adventures over such ranges of time and space.

From his very first success with *Island of the Blue Dolphins*, O'Dell clung to the use of the first-person narrator, which to some detracts from the realism of his works. At the same time, as many critics have noted, this technique also personalizes the reading experience, making it suitable for the younger imagination. O'Dell's stories usually involve high adventure, deep moral dilemmas, and glimpses of a maturing process that lead the works to be evaluated as Bildungsromans. In many of his novels, the heroes (male or female) are isolated from civilization and must learn to live in harmony with the animals and plants around them, as well as pursue their own self-determined paths to survival. O'Dell is also noted for his use of female narrators and heroes who survive on their own in hostile and complicated situations, such as Karana of *Island of the Blue Dolphins*; the eponymous narrators Zia, Alexandra (from *Alexandra*, 1984), Carlota (from *Carlota*, 1977), and Sarah Bishop; Bright Morning, the Navaho girl in *Sing Down the Moon*; and Bright Dawn, the Inuit girl who guides a dog team in the Alaskan Iditarod in *Dark Star, Bright Dawn* (1988). These young adults are compelling characters, often challenging the expectations of their cultures, yet O'Dell also conveys respect for the very traditions his characters challenge.

O'Dell demonstrated a great facility for speaking in the many voices of these very different characters, for which he has been both praised and criticized. Yet he maintained consistently that his stories were written with a didactic intent out of his own convictions, which included a strong moral code but an equally strong wariness of established religions and constricting social customs. Though some critics challenge his protagonists' tendency to accept tragedy with little emotional response, his books are admired for their ability to compel young readers of many races to appreciate both O'Dell's writing and his moral lessons about nature, native and historical traditions, self-reliance, and survival.

[*See also* Historical Fiction; United States; Westerns; *and* Young Adult Literature.]

BIBLIOGRAPHY

Maher, Susan. "Encountering Others: The Meeting of Cultures in Scott O'Dell's *Island of the Blue Dolphins* and *Sing Down the Moon*." *Children's Literature in Education* 23, no. 4 (1992): 215–227.

Russell, David L. *Scott O'Dell*. New York: Twayne, 1999.

Tarr, C. Anita. "Apologizing for Scott O'Dell: Too Little, Too Late." *Children's Literature* 30 (2002): 199–204.

Townsend, John Rowe. "Scott O'Dell." In *A Sense of Story: Essays on Contemporary Writing for Children*, 154–162. Boston: Lippincott, 1971.

JANICE M. BOGSTAD

Odgers, Sally (1957–), Australian author of books about country life and farm animals. The trials of dairy farming are featured in *Her Kingdom for a Pony* (1977), illustrated by Noela Young, and *The Days the Cows Slept In* (1979). Rosina loves horse riding in *Rosina and her Calf* (1983), *Rosina and the Show* (1985), and *Rosina and Kate* (1988). Short books for beginning readers include *Maria and the Pocket* (1987), illustrated by Jane Tanner, and *Emma Jane's Zoo* (1986), illustrated by Janet Ayliffe. The latter has split pages showing a girl who creates her own zoo of pets. Odgers, who is also known as Sally Farrell, has written a number of novels incorporating the supernatural, such as *The Ghost Collector* (1988), *Welcome to the Wierdie Club* (1989), and *The Magician's Box* (1991). Based on the films of Yoram Gross, she has adapted the series on Dorothy Wall's Blinky Bill, and has contributed to a number of reading schemes.

STELLA LEES and PAM MACINTYRE

O'Faoláin, Eileen (1900–1988), author of children's stories, notably illustrated by Nano Reid, Muriel Brandt, Nora McGuinness, and Brian Wildsmith. Her "fairy" stories, as she calls them, include *The Little Black Hen* (1940) and *Miss Pennyfeather and the Pooka* (1944) and draw on motifs from Irish folklore. Two collections of myths and legends, *Irish Sagas and Folktales* (1954) and *Children of the Salmon and Other Irish Folktales* (1965), are considered classics. *An circín dubh* (The Little Black Hen) and *Púca bán Chorcaighe* (The White Pooka from Cork, 1955) were translated into Irish by Brighid Ní Loinsigh. Eileen O'Faoláin is the wife of the writer Sean O'Faoláin.

[*See also* Wildsmith, Brian.]

MARY SHINE THOMPSON

Ofurum, Helen (1941–), Scottish-born Nigerian author of the children's books *Iheoma* (also written as "Theoma") *Comes to Stay* (1982), and *A Welcome for Chijoke* (1983). Born to a British mother and a Nigerian father, Ofurum attended primary school in Nigeria and secondary school in Scotland. Ofurum's first book, a short novel, tells of how Dr. Uche and his family deal with a newborn baby they find dropped off on the doorstep of Dr. Uche's new hospital. *A Welcome for Chijoke* tells the story of eleven-year-old Chijoke Igwe, who goes in search of his estranged father after the death of his beloved mother.

MICHELLE H. MARTIN

Ogawa Mimei (1882–1961), Japanese novelist. Influenced by European Romanticism, Ogawa Kensakus began writing for adult readers, then gradually turned to children's fiction. With the "Manifesto of the Children's Story" (1926), he declared that children's stories were his own special form of expression. He felt a deep sympathy with Suzuki Miekichi, the editor of the children's journal *Akaitori* (The Red Bird), sharing her Romantic ideal of children's innocence. His literary fairy tales are characterized by lyrical description with a strong underlying sense of humanism, as in such masterworks as "Nobara" (A Wild Rose, 1920) and "Akai rousoku to ningyo" (A Red Candle and a Mermaid, 1921). Indeed, he was called the father of the modern Japanese fairy tale, which he raised to an art. During World War II he was forced to write propagandistic stories; afterward, he endeavored to reconstruct children's literature. However, his Romantic idealization of the child was criticized by some reviewers and authors, who in 1959 took up the slogan "Good-bye, Mimei," and began a new, realistic trend in children's literature.

ARIKO KAWABATA

Ogiwara Noriko (1959–), Japanese writer of fantasy for an audience of primarily female young adult readers. Noriko J. Ogiwara has been an extensive reader of western fantasy since her childhood and first wrote fiction for children while she was a university student. When she first published *Sorairo Magatama* (1988), she was honored with an award for new writers of children's literature in Japan. It was then translated into English as *Dragon Sword and Wind Child* in 1993. The books in her best-known Magatama (a comma-shaped bead) trilogy—*Sorairo Magatama*, *Hakucho Iden* (1991), and *Usubeni Tennyo* (1996)—are all based on Japanese classics and set in ancient Japan. This is a unique concept for modern Japanese fantasy. She creates not only in Japanese historical contexts, but also creates fictions with western settings, such as the Nishi no Yoki Majo (Good Witch of the West) series, and has been awarded many prizes of Japanese children's literature.

[*See also* Japan.]

MACHIKO YANO

O'Hara, Elizabeth. *See* Sally Series.

O'Hara, Mary (1885–1980), American novelist, composer, and screenwriter. Mary O'Hara Alsop was born in New Jersey; was raised in Brooklyn Heights, New York; and was educated in America and in Europe, where she studied music and languages. In her early twenties she moved with her first husband to Los Angeles; they had two children before the marriage ended. After her daughter's death from cancer, O'Hara became a screenwriter during the silent era of film; this was when she took Mary O'Hara as her pen name. With her second husband she moved to Wyoming in 1931. Inspired by the wild horses of the open Wyoming plains, she wrote the trilogy of novels for which she is best-known: *My Friend Flicka* (1941) and its sequels, *Thunderhead* (1943) and *Green Grass of Wyoming* (1946). *My Friend Flicka*, about a boy who raises a wild filly, is important in the development of stories about horses and of novels that focus on the bond between humans and animals. It was a best seller; the two sequals were also successful, and all three works were filmed. In 1947 O'Hara, again divorced, moved to Connecticut, where she wrote and composed works including an autobiography, *Flicka's Friend* (1982); and a musical, *The Catch Colt*.

ADRIENNE E. GAVIN

O. Henry (1862–1910), American master of the art of short-story writing, whose real name was William Sidney Porter. During an unsettled childhood he became an avid reader, and as a young man he dabbled with art and writing to little effect. He then took up a post as a bank clerk and was subsequently imprisoned for embezzlement. During his incarceration he altered his middle name to Sydney, adopted his pen name, and began to write the short stories that made him famous. Thereafter he wrote hundreds of tales, selling them to prestigious magazines and newspapers. O. Henry's stories were about people in all walks of life, from down-and-outs to millionaires. Many of his plots were set in the New York City of his day; others had New Orleans, the Midwest, California, and Mexico for their backgrounds. In "The Caballero's Way" (1907), he created the Cisco Kid, a character now long famous on both the large and small screens.

Many of O. Henry's stories are little more than three thousand words long, the shortest no more than three pages. An example of this brevity can be found in "Witches' Loaves" (1911). His plots are convoluted and invariably lead to unexpected conclusions, as in "The Gift of the Magi" (1906), "The Cop and the Anthem" (1906), and "The Ransom of Red Chief" (1910). Although not traditionally categorized as children's literature, O. Henry's stories are not infrequently used in high schools and middle schools—despite their dated settings and his penchant for obscure vocabulary. Their appeal to juveniles might well be attributed to their brevity, their unexpected endings, and their human interest. "The Gift of the Magi" was published as a children's book in 1994.

[*See also* Short Story.]

GEOFFREY FENWICK

Okoro, Anezi (1929–), Nigerian author. Born in Arondizuogu, Nigeria, Anezionwu Nwankwo Okoro is a professor of medicine at the University of Nigeria, Nsukka. His fictional works are mainly for children between ages ten to fourteen, and are primarily adventure stories in African settings. They tell stories about childhood ingenuity and predilection for hair-raising escapades: *The Village School* (1966) offers an exciting description of a life in a village primary school in southeastern Nigeria in the 1930s; in *The Village Headmaster* (1967) a new headmaster's efforts to implement changes in the school are met with opposition and problems; in *One Week One Trouble* (1972), Wilson Tagbo goes off to secondary school and there gets into one trouble after another; in *Double Trouble* (1990), the sequel, Tagbo cuts school to be initiated into a secret cult, but instead finds himself in far more serious trouble. Other adventure chronicles are *Febechi in Cave Adventure* (1971) and *Febechi down the Niger* (1975).

MAHOUMBAH KLOBAH

Okoye, Ifeoma (1937–), Nigerian writer. Okoye has many years of experience teaching in primary school and college, and her books deal with childhood education. In *Eme Goes to School* (1979), a little girl is reluctant to go to school but finds it enjoyable in the end. *No School for Eze* (1980) deals with truancy; Eze thinks that staying at home will be more fun than going to school—until he tries it. In *The Adventures of Tulu the Little Monkey* (1980), Tulu escapes from the zoo only to find that life is hard outside. *No Supper for Eze* (1980) shows the consequence of Eze's refusing to take an afternoon nap.

MAHOUMBAH KLOBAH

Okpi, Kalu, Nigerian writer for young adults. Okpi focuses his writing specifically for African youth and seeks to entertain, edify, and instruct, and to forge a common cause with ordinary people. In *The Smugglers* (1977) Jonnie Malu, a journalist and Special Services agent, fights against a Nigerian and international crime syndicate. Its sequel, *On the Road* (1980), continues with Malu once again answering the "S" Squad's call for help to find out who is behind the rash of daring armed robberies perpetrated against Nigeria's most prestigious financial institutions. *Love Changes Everything* (1993) describes a failed amorous relationship between Gavinah, a stylish young girl in exile in Nigeria, and Onyeuku, a law student and rock musician.

MAHOUMBAH KLOBAH

Olaleye, Isaac (1941–), award-winning Nigerian writer. He draws upon his childhood in Nigeria to inform, challenge, entertain, and inspire young readers. *Bitter Bananas* (1994), featuring a boy's determination to see a problem through to the bitter end, is a story told by the author's father; it is about thwarting baboons that steal palm sap. The book was cited by the Parent Council Limited as among the outstanding books of the year. Olaleye's second book, *Distant Talking Drum: Poems from Nigeria* (1995), is a collection of poems, each describing a different aspect of life in a Nigerian rural village—aspects such as preparing food on a grinding stone, washing laundry by a stream, and weaving cloth by hand. The American Library Association honored this work as a Notable Book. *In the Rainfield: Who Is the Greatest?* (2000) is a Nigerian folk tale about the battle among the elements—and its surprising resolution.

[*See also* Africa: Sub-Saharan Africa; Fairy Tales and Folk Tales; *and* Poetry.]

MAHOUMBAH KLOBAH

Old King Cole. A familiar figure in a children's nursery rhyme. The rhyme's original reference is obscure, but it is usually linked to an early Welsh king named Coel. It is also conjectured that the king's "pipe and bowl" may have been musical instruments, because tobacco was not introduced until 1585. In Gaelic *ceol* means "music," and this may explain the source of the rhyme. The rhyme has been refashioned into many forms. It was a Disney short film (1933), in which the king throws a jazz party for the citizens of storyland; it was elaborated by Edwin Arlington Robinson (1869–1935) into a long ballad about experiencing worldly failure but gaining spiritual wisdom; and L. Frank Baum retold it in *Mother Goose in Prose* (1897) as a rags-to-riches story.

[*See also* Adaptation *and* Nursery Rhymes.]

JESSICA J. BURKE

Oliver, Narelle (1960–), Australian author and illustrator who grew up in Toowoomba, Queensland. *Leaf Tail* (1989), *High above the Sea* (1991), *The Best Beak in Boonaroo Bay* (1993), and *The Hunt* (1995) reflect Oliver's interest in natural history and in the preservation of the environment and threatened wildlife. *Sand Swimmers: The Secret Life of Australia's Dead Heart* (1999) is a dual narrative that contrasts the failed efforts of an early European explorer, Charles Sturt, to survive in the seemingly inhospitable Simpson Desert with Aboriginal knowledge of the land and its "secret" supply of natural desert vegetation and wildlife. Oliver's illustrations are linocuts hand-colored with pencil or wash. *Baby Bilby, Where Do You Sleep?* (2001) invites readers to play a hide-and-seek game to discover the secret hiding places of some Australian desert creatures. *Mermaids Most Amazing* (2001) explores the human fascination with mermaids through history, folk tale, and fantasy. The playful lift-the-flap book *The Very Blue Thingamajig* (2003) is a concept and counting book, offering young children a subtle lesson in difference, and is a departure from Oliver's previous work in style, format, and subject. Oliver's reputation rests on her ability to combine information and story in a visually arresting format.

[*See also* Australia; Ecology and Environment; *and* Information Books.]

KERRY MALLAN

Onadipe, Kola (1922–), Nigerian executive of a business corporation, teacher, and a prolific author of children's literature. Onadipe made his name with his first children's book, *The Adventures of Souza* (1963), an exciting story of the adventures and misdeeds of a naughty village boy who goes hunting, joins a secret cult, and meets a magician. *The Magic Land of the Shadows* (1970), a story about an orphan girl in the strange land of shadow people living under the earth, confirms Onadipe's proficiency in expanding folk tales with imagination and skill to produce new and refreshing stories. This success in transforming folklore into appealing narratives that aim to make children laugh is further evidenced in *The King Is Naked, and Other Stories* (1985). He also uses stories relating to traditional beliefs and practices as material in his children's books to either corroborate the values of those practices or refute their importance in light of modern civilization. *Koku Baboni* (1962) refutes the belief in the evil nature of twins and other multiple-birth children. *Sugar Girl* (1964) repudiates the belief in witches, wizards, and other men and women with supernatural powers. *The Boy Slave* (1966) and its sequel *The Return of Shettima* (1972) denounce the evil deeds of slavery.

MAHOUMBAH KLOBAH

Once and Future King, The. *See* White, T. H.

Oneal, Zibby (1934–), American author of picture books and nonfiction for children and novels for young adults. Elizabeth Oneal was born in Omaha, Nebraska, and was educated at Stanford University and the University of Michigan, where she has also taught writing. Although she has been interested in writing stories as long as she can remember, the progress of her career parallels the growth of her own children. Her first picture books—*War Work* (1971) and *The Improbable Adventures of Marvelous O'Hara Soapstone* (1972)—began as stories for them. Later, as her children grew up, Oneal turned to writing the young adult novels for which she is most highly acclaimed: *The Language of Goldfish* (1980), *A Formal Feeling* (1982), and *In Summer Light* (1985). All three feature teenage heroines struggling with the changes adulthood brings. Unlike many authors for young adults, Oneal eschews dramatic plots and heightened emotion in favor of the quiet interior conflicts and development of her characters. This restrained elegance has earned her accolades that include the Christopher Award and the Boston Globe–Horn Book Award. She has also explored women's history in a biography of Grandma Moses and has created a picture book about female suffrage.

MEGAN LYNN ISAAC

One Hundred and One Dalmations, The. *See* Smith, Dodie.

O'Neill, Judith (1930–), Australian writer. O'Neill's strongly situated historical novels, which focus on feisty girls experiencing the vicissitudes of early Australia, include *Jess and the River Kids* (1984), set during World War II; *Stringybark Summer* (1985), about early logging families in southeastern Victoria; and *Deepwater* (1988), which examines wartime prejudice against German settlements around the Murray River. *So Far from Skye* (1992) and its sequel, *Hearing Voices* (1996), are based on the experiences of Scottish crofters arriving in Victoria in the 19th century. *Transported to Van Diemen's Land: The Story of Two Convicts* (1977) recalls Tasmania's convict heritage through a success story of restored fortune. O'Neill's interest in exclusive communities led her to depict a pseudo-religious cult and the power struggles within it in *The Message* (1989). *Sharp Eyes* (1993) and *Whirlwind* (1999) are aimed at less confident readers.

STELLA LEES and PAM MACINTYRE

O'Neill, Mary (1908–1990), American author and poet. Mary LeDuc O'Neill is best known for a single book of poetry, *Hailstones and Halibut Bones: Adventures in Color* (1961). The original edition of these twelve poems of color metaphors was elegantly illustrated with understated colors by Leonard Weisgard. The book was reillustrated by John Wallner in 1989, with brighter colors and a sprightlier design. It has also been published in braille and continues to be popular with children and teachers. The unforgettable title comes from the poem "What Is White?": "White is a dove / And lily of the valley / And a puddle of milk / Spilled in an alley—." Two of O'Neill's other poems are the basis for *The Sound of Day, the Sound of Night* (2003), a picture book illustrated by Cynthia Jabar. The day sounds of "Bus honks and bells, / dishes and shoes" contrast with the hushed sounds of night ("Distant dog bark, / Kitten purr"). O'Neill published several volumes of poetry, among them *People I'd Like to Keep* (1964) with illustrations by Paul Galdone, *What Is That Sound!* (1966) with illustrations by Lois Ehlert, and *Take a Number* (1968), a poetic introduction to basic number concepts. She also wrote picture books, fiction, and nonfiction. *The White Palace* (1966), a nonfiction account of the journey of a Chinook salmon, was illustrated by Nonny Hogrogian. O'Neill began to write for children after a successful career as an advertising copywriter, ending up as vice president of a New York advertising agency. She resigned to work as a freelance writer, contributing articles, stories, and verse to *Woman's Day*, *Scholastic*, and other magazines. When she was in her sixties, O'Neill joined the Peace Corps, where she taught journalism and writing in Ghana and Costa Rica from 1970 to 1974. In the 1980s she wrote a series of nonfiction books for Troll Associates on dinosaurs, air and water pollution, and conservation.

[*See also* Poetry *and biographies of figures mentioned in this article.*]

LINNEA HENDRICKSON

O'Neill, Rose (1874–1944), American author and illustrator, and inventor of the kewpie doll. Kewpies had a rounded cuteness similar to that of Mabel Lucie Attwell's toddlers, but O'Neill characterized them in more detail. They were versions of cupids, but where cupids brought problems, kewpies fixed them. Their main weapon was laughter. Kewpies appear to be of neutral gender, but they are referred to with masculine pronouns, yet also support the rights of women. Scootles is the only outright female in Kewpieville, a real child drawn much larger than the kewpies, into whose company she is welcomed as the "Baby Tourist."

O'Neill's kewpies first appeared in the *Ladies' Home Journal* in December 1908, and her rhymed stories of their adventures, copiously illustrated, were soon to be found in other magazines and newspapers. In one example, when a small girl is criticized by her family for overeating at Christmastime, a number of kewpies invade her home and remind family members of the importance of occasional indulgence. O'Neill sculpted a sample from which bisque kewpies were made in Germany, and soon kewpie dolls were everywhere.

[*See also* Atwell, Mabel Lucie; Illustrations; Doll and Toy Stories; *and* Series Books.]

FRANCES ARMSTRONG

Onobrakpeya, Bruce (1938–), a versatile artist and printmaker. Onobrakpeya has been a major voice in African art for both children and adults for almost fifty years; his major contribution to children's literature is mainly in the area of illustrations. His captivating illustrations are well integrated, enhance visual literacy, and draw children as well as adults to books. The bold and vibrant black and white lines that characterize his charming illustrations in Cyprian Ekwensi's *An African Night's Entertainment* (1962; number 1 in the African Readers Library of African Universities Press), Rosemary Uwemedimo's *Akpan and the Smugglers* (1965; number 9 in the African Readers Library), and Wole Soyinka's translated version of D. O. Fagunwa's *Forest of a Thousand Daemons: A Hunter's Saga* (1982) typify most of his illustrations in other books for children and for adults as well. Today, this patriarch of African art and illustrations is encouraging young aspiring artists in his Ovuomaroro Studio in Lagos and Agbarha-Otor, Nigeria, and through the Bruce Onobrakpeya Foundation, the goal of which is to train and nurture first class artists.

OSAYIMWENSE OSA

Opie, Iona (1923–), and **Peter Opie** (1918–1982), husband-and-wife team of independent British scholars who documented the continuity of children's folklore and traditional games. Among the 20th century's most important folklorists, the Opies gave equal weight to direct observation and archival research: Iona undertook the fieldwork, and both sifted through printed sources for additional evidence. Peter did the writing, with considerable input from Iona. They were also distinguished scholar-collectors in the mold of the 18th-century antiquarian Joseph Ritson.

Practicality and insatiable curiosity, not Romanticism, were the wellsprings of the Opies' lifelong fascination with the apparently ephemeral but enduring aspects of children's culture. Shortly before the birth of their first child, they decided to compile a new work on the origins of nursery rhymes when they were unable to find a satisfactory account of the source and meaning of "Ladybird, Ladybird." It took the couple seven years of painstaking research to produce the

The Opies in the Playground. Frontispiece to *Children and Their Books: A Celebration of the Work of Iona and Peter Opie*, edited by Gillian Avery and Julia Briggs (New York: Oxford University Press, 1989). COLLECTION OF JACK ZIPES

Oxford Dictionary of Nursery Rhymes (1951), which immediately superseded the standard work, James Orchard Halliwell-Phillips's *Nursery Rhymes of England* (1842), thanks to its entries containing each rhyme's fullest version, unusual variants, and Continental analogues, a chronological list of appearances in print sources, and commentary. Because the *Dictionary* was a surprise academic bestseller, its royalties provided the Opies with the means to tackle the next work on their long list of projected studies. In addition to the *Dictionary* they compiled several nursery rhyme anthologies, including *The Oxford Nursery Rhyme Book* (1955), illustrated by Joan Hassall, and *A Family Book of Nursery Rhymes* (1964), illustrated by Pauline Baynes. Research on the *Dictionary* also inspired them to collect literary evidence of parents' less tender feelings toward their young, which was eventually published in *Babies: An Unsentimental Anthology* (1990).

Another of the *Dictionary*'s by-products was a collection of playground rhymes, *I Saw Esau* (1947), the forerunner of the Opies' 1959 study, *The Lore and Language of School Children*. *Lore* demonstrated that children's oral culture was flourishing, not dwindling away, as their predecessor Norman Douglas feared. Their next two studies on children's culture were taxonomies of games other than party, Scout, or team games: *Children's Games in Street and Playground* (1969) focused on the activities that children aged six to twelve engage in outdoors without supervision or equipment, and *The Singing Game* (1985) on the singing and clapping games most commonly played by girls between the ages of seven and nine. Although the Opies were indebted to the pioneering folklorists Joseph Strutt, Alice Bertha Gomme, and W. W. Newell, Iona's extensive fieldwork—visiting schools, conducting surveys, and organizing the raw data—was unprecedented. All three volumes are distinguished by the precision and sophistication of the Opies' classification system, which makes it possible to find the description of individual items without knowing the various names they may have gone by over time or in different regions.

To support their ongoing research, Peter had amassed by the late 1960s one of the most remarkable 20th-century collections of rare children's books and toys, including the common, cheap ones of celluloid and plastic. Their two sons inherited the collecting gene; James is an expert on British die-cast toys and toy soldiers, and Robert specializes in packaging design. The Opies drew on their collection's incredible riches in compiling several notable anthologies of historical children's literature: *The Oxford Book of Children's Verse* (1973), 332 British and American poems with notes showing how they reflect literary trends and changing social values; *The Classic Fairy Tales* (1974), the first known texts of the twenty-four best-loved fairy tales, lavishly illustrated; *Three Centuries of Nursery Rhymes and Poetry for Children* (1977), an enumerative bibliography based on the 1973 exhibition of the same title; and *A Nursery Companion* (1980), annotated full-color facsimiles of two dozen early-19th-century picture books.

When the Opies were interviewed in 1981 by Jonathan Cott for a *New Yorker* profile, they were considering ways to keep the Opie Collection of Child Life and Literature intact, including the conversion of Westerfield, their house in Surrey, into a study center for scholars. Shortly after Peter's sudden death in 1982, Oxford's Bodleian Library offered to purchase the collection for a million pounds. Iona contributed £500,000 toward the purchase, and a nationwide appeal raised the remaining £500,000. Some of the funds came from the sales of three publications: *Tail Feathers from Mother Goose* (1988), compiled by Iona and illustrated by leading British artists; *The Treasures of Childhood* (1988), a coffee-table book describing the Opie Collection's riches; and *Children and Their Books* (1989), a festschrift.

Since the collection's transfer to the Bodleian, University Microfilms has published a microfiche series of the collection's holdings, permitting greater access to its superb resources.

Having secured the collection's future, Iona resumed full-time work alone, producing *A Dictionary of Superstitions* (1989), a revised edition of *I Saw Esau* (1992) illustrated by Maurice Sendak; *The People in the Playground* (1993), a diary of her visits to a local school over a three-year period that shows how children transmit lore during free play; *Children's Games with Things* (1997), describing games such as marbles, hopscotch, and ball bouncing; and a revised edition of the *Oxford Dictionary of Nursery Rhymes* (1997). She also found time to write essays and introductions for such works as the *International Companion Encyclopedia of Children's Literature* (1996); *My Very First Mother Goose* (2000), illustrated by Rosemary Wells; and the *Cambridge Guide to Children's Books in English* (2001). Having completed the life's work that the couple had laid out at the beginning of their collaboration, Iona retired from scholarship.

The Opies' achievements are all the more remarkable in light of the fact that they conducted their research for decades without the benefit of university training or institutional support. That the Opies were able to live on the royalties from their learned publications while devoting all their energies to the next project was due partly to their willingness to make extraordinary sacrifices but also, more important, to the unusual character of their work. General readers as well as specialists found the Opies' brand of impeccable scholarship irresistible because formidable erudition was always presented with clarity, elegance, and enthusiasm, then deliciously leavened with wry, clear-headed insights into human behavior.

[*See also* Collecting and Collectors *and* Playground Rhymes.]

BIBLIOGRAPHY

Alderson, Brian. "Collecting Children's Books: Self-Indulgence and Scholarship." In *Children and Their Books: A Celebration of the Work of Iona and Peter Opie*, edited by Gillian Avery and Julia Briggs, 7–17. New York: Oxford University Press, 1989.

Cott, Jonathan. "'When the Voices of Children Are Heard on the Green': Iona and Peter Opie." In his *Pipers at the Gates of Dawn: The Wisdom of Children's Literature*, 2421–2302. New York: Random House, 1983.

Hurst, Clive. "Selections from the Accession Diaries of Peter Opie." In *Children and Their Books: A Celebration of the Work of Iona and Peter Opie*, edited by Gillian Avery and Julia Briggs, 19–44. Oxford: Oxford University Press, 1989.

Treasures of Childhood: Books, Toys, and Games from the Opie Collection, edited by Iona and Robert Opie and Brian Alderson. New York: Arcade, 1989.

ANDREA IMMEL

Optic, Oliver (1822–1897), pseudonym for William Taylor Adams, Horatio Alger's primary competitor. Born in Medway, Massachusetts, Optic was a popular and prolific author for boys during the latter half of the 19th century. A teacher and administrator in Boston schools for twenty years, he began publishing in 1841. His first two novels, published in 1853 and 1854, were directed at adults; but in 1855 he published *The Boat Club*, his first novel for children. An immediate success, it remained popular for a long time, going into over sixty editions. This book inaugurated the *Boat Club* series. Optic wrote many more series, among them the Great Western, Boat Builder, All-Over-the-World, Army and Navy, The Blue and the Gray, Riverdale, Yacht Club, and Blue and Gray on Land. He died before finishing the penultimate book in the Blue and Gray on Land series; it was completed by Edward Stratemeyer. At the time of his death Optic had published 107 books for boys.

Optic began editing *The Student and Schoolmate* in 1858, and in 1867 he started *Oliver Optic's Magazine: Our Boys and Girls*, for which he wrote many of the stories himself. This weekly serial, which contained puzzles, articles, and poetry, as well as stories, makes an attempt to appeal to girls. It remained successful until 1875, when the publishers, Lee and Shepard, experienced financial difficulties and discontinued it. Optic's fiction concentrates on character. Like Alger, Optic often worked the rags-to-riches story, making it clear that success was the result of sterling character. For example, in *Now or Never*, Bobby Bright is provided with a companion who engages in the same business as Bobby (door-to-door book sales), but since his character is impure and he is not penny-wise, he fails, while Bobby—pure of heart and motive—succeeds. Some of Optic's plots are quite improbable. While his didacticism sounds stilted today, he was very popular, selling 100,000 copies of his books per year in his heyday. Optic was attacked as a sensational writer by figures such as Louisa May Alcott and some attendants of the first American Library Association in 1876, but he also had his champions, and his popularity among the reading public was undeniable.

[*See also* Alger, Horatio; Boys' Books and Fiction; Children's Magazines; Series Books; *and* Stratemeyer, Edward.]

BIBLIOGRAPHY

Jones, Delores Blythe. *An "Oliver Optic" Checklist: An Annotated Catalog-Index to the Series, Non-series Stories, and Magazine Publications of William Taylor Adams.* Westport, Conn.: Greenwood, 1985. Contains a short biography.

Jacque Roethler

Oram, Hiawyn (1946–), author born in South Africa and educated at the University of Natal before moving to the United Kingdom. A writer of picture books, poems, and plays, Oram focuses primarily on books dealing with emotions in young children, as in *Angry Arthur* (1982). In this work, Arthur's tantrum is illustrated using a weather metaphor, and in *Billy and the Babysitter* (1994) and *The Second Princess* (1994) Oram tackles childhood jealousies and insecurity. She collaborated with illustrator Sonia Holleyman on the *Mona the Vampire* series for older readers (books such as *Mona the Vampire and the Big Brown Bap Monster*, 1995).

[*See also* Africa: Southern Africa *and* Picture Books.]

Phyllis Ramage

(276)

CXXXVI.

Ludi Pueriles.

Boyes-Sports.

Orbis Sensualium Pictus. Illustration from an English edition; *Orbis* was originally published in Nuremberg, Germany, in 1658. Reproduced courtesy of the Cotsen Children's Library, Princeton University Library

Orbis Sensualium Pictus. First published in Nuremburg in 1658, *Orbis Sensualium Pictus* (Illustrated World of the Senses), by the Czech John Comenius, was a pioneering educational work. It was designed not only to teach Latin and the vernacular language but to give "a Picture and Nomenclature of all the chief Things that are in the world, and of Men's Employments therein," as announced in 1659 on the title page of the English translation by Charles Hoole. Comenius wanted to reform both the method and the content of teaching. Children learn through their senses; therefore, pictures should be provided to illustrate every object and function named. "Come, boy! Learn to be wise," says the master. "What doth this mean, to be wise?" asks the boy; and he is told, "To understand rightly, to do rightly, and to speak out rightly, all that are necessary." The book opens with an ingenious alphabet of sounds, beginning "The crow cryeth a a A a" and finishing with a horsefly who says "ds ds Z z." Then come the world; the heavens above; the earth below; earth's creatures, its animals and plants, man and woman and their anatomy; trades; occupations; astronomy; and geography—followed by more abstract matters such as the religions of the world and moral philosophy. Universal God-centered knowledge, Comenius felt, was the key to a peaceful God-fearing world.

Comenius devised *Orbis Sensualium Pictus* when he was faced with a school in Hungary where the pupils needed something far more elementary than the earlier work, *Janus linguarum reserata* (The Gate to Languages Unlocked), that he had written for his abler classes in Poland. However, religious persecution in Hungary drove him away before it could be printed. Both books were greatly esteemed, but *Orbis pictus*, with over 300 pages and some 150 engravings, was expensive, and the information and the illustrations inevitably became out of date. *Orbis pictus* lasted longer in Germany than in England, and an American edition illustrated by Alexander Anderson was published in 1810.

BIBLIOGRAPHY

Comenius, John Amos, with an introduction by John Sadler. *Orbis pictus*. Oxford: Oxford University Press, 1968.

Gillian Avery

Orczy, Baroness (1865–1947), Hungarian author born in Tarnaörs into a landed family with a literary and musical background. Following agricultural and financial problems, the family moved to Budapest and then to Brussels, to allow her father to pursue his musical career; Emma Magdalena Rosalia Marie Josepha Orczy and her sister attended convent schools there. In 1880 the family settled in London, where her father achieved some success as a composer, while she added English to her fluent Hungarian, German, and French. Orczy then attended art school, where she was a contemporary of Angela Brazil and met her future husband, Henry Montague Barstow, whom she married in 1894 and with whom she produced several children's books, including *Old Hungarian Fairy Tales* (1905); she did the translation and Barstow illustrated. Throughout her career, Orczy's output included crime and historical novels, her earliest works in 1899 being short crime stories for magazines. Following a visit to Paris in 1900, she wrote her best-known historical romance, *The Scarlet Pimpernel*, in five weeks, but failed to get it published until after the successful reception of a dramatized version in 1905 that starred Ellen Terry's youngest brother, Fred, as Sir Percy Blakeney, the apparently effete English aristocrat who daringly rescues condemned French aristocrats from the guillotine in revolutionary France. Blakeney became an immensely popular character, epitomizing the ideal English hero—honorable, resourceful, courageous, and dashing—and appeared in eleven further Scarlet Pimpernel novels between 1908 and 1940, all read enthusiastically by adolescents, as well as inspiring numerous film and TV adaptations, the best known being the 1934 film starring Trevor Howard. Orczy also developed a series of crime stories around *Lady Molly of Scotland Yard* (1910), an aristocratic female detective. Orczy and Barstow moved abroad after World War I, but when Barstow died in 1943, Orczy returned to London.

[*See also* Adventure Books; Brazil, Angela; Fairy Tales and Folk Tales; Films: Film Adaptations of Children's and Young Adult Literature; *and* Historical Fiction.]

Bridget Carrington

Orgel, Doris (1929–), Jewish American children's book author and translator. Born in Vienna, Austria, Doris Adelberg Orgel was forced to flee with her family in 1938 when the Nazi Party took power. They fled first to Yugoslavia, then to New York, an experience she retold in fictionalized form in *The Devil in Vienna* (1978). She graduated from Barnard College in 1955, and wrote and translated fairy tales as well as realistic children's books such as *Sarah's Room* (1963, published under the name Doris Adelberg). She won the Lewis Carroll Shelf Award in 1960 for her translation of Wilhelm Hauff's literary fairy tale *Zwerg Nase* (*Dwarf Long-Nose*, illustrated by Maurice Sendak). She has written a series of realistic contemporary books about Becky Suslow, daughter of a divorced doctor-mom, beginning with *My War with Mrs. Galloway* (1985), and the young adult novel *Risking Love* (1985). She has also retold a number of Greek myths in accessible modern language, as in *The Princess and the God* (1996), a version of the story of Cupid and Psyche.

J. D. Stahl

Original Poems, for Infant Minds, by Several Young Persons. *See* Taylor, Ann and Jane.

Orlando the Marmalade Cat. *See* Hale, Kathleen.

Orlev, Uri (1931–), Israeli writer best known in Israel and abroad for his books about the Holocaust from a child's perspective. He has published more than thirty children's books in Hebrew and in translation. In 1996 he was the first Israeli author to be awarded the Hans Christian Andersen Award, the highest international recognition given to a living children's author. Orlev was born Jerzy Henryk Orlowski to an assimilated Jewish family in Warsaw, Poland. When World War II erupted, his father was captured on the Russian front and only reentered Orlev's life in 1954. His mother was murdered in her hospital bed by Nazi soldiers. Orlev spent the war years in the Warsaw Ghetto, hiding among Polish farmers, and in the Bergen-Belsen concentration camp. After liberation, he and his brother emigrated to Israel (then Palestine).

Orlev's wartime childhood is reflected in books such as *HaEe B'Rechov HaTziporim* (1981; English trans., *The Island on Bird Street*), *HaEish Min HaTzad HaAcher* (1988; English trans., *The Man from the Other Side*), *HaGiveret Em HaMigbaat* (1990; English trans., *The Lady with the Hat*), and *Rutz Yelid, Rutz* (2001; English trans., *Run, Boy, Run*), all of which won the Mildred L. Batchelder Award, given to an American publisher by the American Library Association to encourage the translation of outstanding works of international children's literature. Orlev's novels read like adventure stories, evidence of his childhood reading and his ability to protect himself imaginatively from the horrors of the war years through fantasy and play, a process he details in the memoir *Hayalei Oferet* (1956; English trans., *The Lead Sol-*

diers). Almost unknown outside Israel are his many picture books, which combine humor, fantasy, and satire, as in the popular *Savta Soreget* (Grandma Knits, 1980), a fable about a grandmother forced by intolerance and prejudice to unravel her knitted house, pets, and grandchildren. Orlev has also written fantasies for middle-grade readers, such as *Shirat HeLeviyatanim* (The Song of the Whales, 1997) about a boy who inherits his grandfather's power to repair dreams.

[*See also* Historical Fiction; Holocaust Literature for Children; Israel; *and* Picture Books.]

BIBLIOGRAPHY

Khorana, Meena. "Uri Orlev: Celebrating the Indomitable Spirit of Childhood." *BookBird* 34, no. 2 (1996): 6–8.

Kokkola, Lydia. *Representing the Holocaust in Children's Literature*. New York: Routledge, 2003.

Tal, Eve. "Beneath the Surface: The Untranslated Uri Orlev." *The Looking Glass* 8, no. 2 (2 April 2004). http://www.the-looking-glass.net.

Eve G. Tal

Ormai, Stella (1949–), American illustrator of over a dozen books. The daughter of artists, Ormai graduated from the Rhode Island School of Design with a degree in illustration. She began her career by illustrating such works as *Mystery at Mouse House* (1980) and the *Bizzy Bones* books by Jacqueline Briggs Martin, quickly earning herself a reputation for drawing animals, particularly mice. A versatile artist, Ormai has also illustrated nonfiction works for children, including *Heartbeats: Your Body, Your Heart* (1983) and *Shadow Magic* (1985). An admirer of the early-20th-century illustrator Arthur Rackham, she works in pen and ink and watercolors to achieve quick, clear images, and takes inspiration from a love of nature instilled by childhood summers at her grandfather's farm. Ormai has also done some writing for children, but her primary focus is her art. In 1980 she received the Don Freeman Memorial Grant from the Society of Children's Book Writers.

[*See also* Illustrations; Nonfiction; Picture Books; *and* Rackham, Arthur.]

Katherine M. Adams

Ormerod, Jan (1946–), author and illustrator. Born in Western Australia, Ormerod studied art and design at the Western Australian Institute of Technology. She moved to England in 1980, and has lived there since. Ormerod illustrates her own and others' work, having written and illustrated over sixty books. Her award-winning *Sunshine* (1981), which won both the Children's Book Council of Australia Picture Book of the Year and The Mother Goose Award, and its sequel *Moonlight* (1982) are wordless picture books with the whole of the narrative being conveyed by the illustrations. These two works mirror Ormerod's own life at the time, living in London with a small child. They are closely observed vignettes of family life in the morning and at night. *Sunshine* uses a number of different page designs to move the narrative along—on some pages there are whole-page spreads, on others a number of small, rapidly-changing illustrations that resemble a film. Both books contain a wealth of detail about life at home at the time of getting up, getting ready for work or school, and getting ready for bed. The books implicitly valorize the two-parent family as well as emphasizing the importance of the father helping with household chores and looking after children. As the story is carried by the illustration only, things such as body language, gesture, and facial expression are especially important in conveying both emotion and action. All of these things convey the security of this particular child and the closeness of her relationship with both parents. At a time when there is some disquiet about the lack of picture books for very young children and the Children's Book Council of Australia has set up a special award for such books in the hope of encouraging their publication, *Sunshine* and *Moonlight* remain popular for very young children. The books also encourage interactivity, as children can verbalize the story portrayed in the illustrations.

Ormerod continues to produce numerous books and, over the years, she has produced a range of work, including counting books, a sticker book that contains reusable stickers for children to use with their toys, and a series of books designed for parents to share with babies. She has also illustrated a number of fairy tales such as *The Story Of Chicken Licken* (1985), *Peter Pan* (1987), and *The Frog Prince* (1990). Her work is remarkable for its careful draftsmanship and design as well as the range of media she uses—water color, pen and ink, and gouache, among other things. Her work is also characterized by her close observation of her subjects. There are frequently touches of humor in the illustrations too, such as when the little girl points out the burning toast to her newspaper-reading father in *Sunshine*, and a baby crawls on the stage in *Chicken Licken*. Ormerod also captures the feelings of childhood in a number of books—feeling frightened in *Be Brave Billy* and the need to follow one's dreams in *Jump!* a book written by Michelle Magorian and illustrated by Ormerod.

Margot Hillel

Orphans. Orphans as archetypal figures in children's literature can be traced back to myths and folk tales, in which the symbolic removal of parental figures is the foremost requirement for a successful rite of passage. The most common hero of myth and folk tale is an underprivileged child or young person, a youngest son or youngest daughter, often a child of unknown origin. At the end, the hero finds his fortune, "the princess and half the kingdom," and triumphs over those who at first seemed cleverer and stronger. In children's fiction, the absence of parents is a condition for the protagonist's unhampered exploration of the world. The degree of abandonment can vary from a simple excursion by the parents to their emotional indifference to their actual death. Tom Sawyer's, Anne Shirley's, Mary Lennox's, Dorothy's, and Harry Potter's parents are dead. The March sisters' father is away at war. Peter Rabbit's mother goes shopping. The parents in *The Lion, the Witch, and the Wardrobe* remain in London while the children are sent to the country. Gilly Hopkins's mother has deserted her. Jess's parents in *Bridge to Terabithia* neglect his intellectual and emotional needs. Such children, whose parents are alive, but do not care about them, can be called "functional orphans."

BIBLIOGRAPHY

Nikolajeva, Maria. *The Rhetoric of Character in Children's Literature*. Lanham, Md.: Scarecrow, 2002.

MARIA NIKOLAJEVA

Orr, Wendy (1953–), Australian writer. Wendy Ann Orr, also known as Sally George, was born in Canada and lives in Australia. Her writing, full of humor and intensity, represents the multicultural make-up of the Australian community, its mix of classes, big cities, and small country towns. A thematic concern across her work is the development of self and finding one's place in the world. *Arabella* (1998), illustrated by Kim Gamble, is a picture book exemplifying Orr's subtlety. Matthew, the main character, learns to sail on his grandfather's small sailing boat. When his grandfather's precious model boat the "Arabella" is lost in a storm, Matthew bravely rescues it. Beyond the story, a careful reader of text and illustration will discover a hidden depth to Matthew and the rescue. Orr has written lively and appealing books for younger children, including *The Tin Can Puppy* (1990), illustrated by Brian Kogler, and *Bad Martha* (1991), illustrated by Carol McLean-Carr. Sophie, in *Ark in the Park* (1994), longs for a pet, which is forbidden in the inner-city apartment where she lives, and the pet shop in the park becomes her salvation. In *Leaving It to You* (1992) Linda finds out much about herself as she visits an elderly woman with arthritis. *The Bully Biscuit Gang* (1995), illustrated by Mike Spoor, describes a creative solution to bullying. For older readers, *Peeling the Onion* (1996) follows the anguish of athletic Anna, as she reinvents herself, physically and mentally, after a debilitating car accident. *Yasou Nikki* (1995), illustrated by Kim Gamble, is autobiographical, but Orr transfers her experience as an expatriate child in France to a Greek girl, Nikki, in an Australian kindergarten. Elements of the supernatural enliven *Spook's Shack* (2003), illustrated by Kerry Millard. As Sally George, Orr has contributed *Breakfast in Bed* (1994), *Bad Dog, George!* (1994), and *George at the Zoo* (1994) to the Voyages series.

STELLA LEES and PAM MACINTYRE

Ortiz, Simon (1941–), Native American poet, writer, and human rights activist. A member of the Acoma Pueblo Nation, Ortiz is best known for his children's book *The People Shall Continue* (1977, 1988), his historical epic poem about five centuries of Native American themes and struggles. The cultural themes center on the preservation and "balance of the Earth," as well as on the mutual respect to be practiced among all nations. In addition, Ortiz chronicles the imperialist invasions and the Native-led resistance. Designed as a picture book and illustrated by Sharol Graves, this is among the few children's books touching upon First Nation history by a Native American. Ortiz has also written *The Good Rainbow Road* (2004; illustrated by Michael Lacapa), an original, folk-inspired tale telling how two courageous boys save their village. The book is written in English and Keres (a language spoken in Acoma and six other Pueblo communities in New Mexico) and includes a translation in Spanish.

[*See also* Lacapa, Michael; Multiculturalism and Children's Books; *and* Native American Children's Literature.]

LINNEA HENRICKSON

Ortiz Cofer, Judith (1952–), Puerto Rican poet, essayist, and novelist, raised in both Puerto Rico and New Jersey. Ortiz Cofer's characters illustrate the confusion created by dual identity—by having American citizenship rights (minus voting rights) if you reside in Puerto Rico, but having only local voting rights in Puerto Rico, where one has no independent citizenship. *The Line in the Sun* (1989) and *Call Me Maria* (2004) depict the literal and symbolic consequences of residing in these two worlds, and pinpoint especially the consequences in a young girl's identity formation. *A Line in the Sun* indicates the author's familiarity with the social milieu of tenement buildings in New Jersey and rural towns in Puerto Rico. Readers see a stream of laborers searching for jobs in the United States; they witness the interdependence of family members; they realize how "family" includes numerous and sometimes eccentric townsfolk. *Silent Dancing: A Partial Remembrance of a Puerto Rican Childhood* (1990) offers a poetic treatment of this material, underscoring how autobiographical writing can be a deeply expressive art form. *An Island Like You: Stories of the Barrio* (1995) shows the challenges youngsters face when they negotiate close relationships in two dissimilar locales: Puerto Rico and the United States. This book received the Pura Belpré Medal.

[*See also* Interracial Books for Children; Multiculturalism and Children's Books; South America, Spanish-Speaking; *and* United States.]

BIBLIOGRAPHY

Acosta-Belen, Edna. "A Melus Interview: Judith Ortiz Cofer." *Melus* 18 (Fall 1993): 84–98.

LUCILLE HERNÁNDEZ GREGORY

Ørvig, Mary (1918–1993), Swedish librarian. She was the founder and first director of the Swedish Children's Books Institute (1965–1983). Ørvig received her professional training in the United States and brought to Sweden many valuable ideas about introducing books to children. Her position in Sweden is comparable to that of Jella Lepman in Germany or Francelia Butler in the United States. Indeed, with her vision and vigor, Ørvig personified the world of children's literature. She was the coauthor of a number of standard general surveys; she annotated anthologies of children's literature; and she wrote two original scholarly works on girls' fiction. She also initiated the publication series of the Swedish Children's Books Institute and edited yet another series of scholarly volumes. Ørvig served as secretary of the International Research Society for Children's Literature in 1974–1978 and contributed considerably to international cooperation in scholarship on children's literature. In 1986 she was awarded a doctor's degree *honoris causa* by Stockholm University.

[*See also* Butler, Francelia; International Research Society for Children's Literature; *and* Lepman, Jella.]

MARIA NIKOLAJEVA

Orwell, George (1903–1950), British author of political and literary essays, realistic novels, and fantasy fiction. The son of a British civil servant, Eric Arthur Blair was born in Bengal, India, and raised in Henley-on-Thames, England. After graduating from Eton, he worked for several years as a police officer in Burma, taught school, clerked in a bookstore, and produced educational radio programs for the British Broadcasting Corporation. His early literary works—published under the name George Orwell—contain autobiographical components. *Down and Out in Paris and London* (1933) recounts his own experiences living among the poor, while the novel *Burmese Days* (1934) draws on the years he spent in Colonial Burma. In 1936 the author traveled to Spain to write about the Spanish civil war, but quickly joined the militia and was wounded in combat. A self-described "democratic socialist," Orwell's contempt for totalitarianism and fascism led to the creation of his two best-known works. The novella-length *Animal Farm* (1945) utilizes the elements of a "talking animal" tale as a group of domesticated farm creatures stage a revolt against their human owner only to have their "animalist" society devolve into tyranny. A political allegory for the Russian Revolution, the story's characters represent historical figures, with the idealist pig Snowball typifying Trotsky, and the despotic pig Napoleon standing in for Stalin. Four years later, Orwell published *Nineteen Eighty-Four*, a futuristic fantasy about a totalitarian society in which "Big Brother" alters history, controls thought and language, and even bans human emotions such as love. Though the Russian Revolution has faded from public consciousness and the year 1984 has now come and gone, Orwell's dystopian novels remain enduring classics. Though not specifically written for young readers, these accessible books have become middle- and secondary-school staples, introducing students to allegory and political satire written in the guise of compelling and thought-provoking speculative fiction.

BIBLIOGRAPHY

Bowker, Gordon. *Inside George Orwell*. New York: Palgrave, 2003.
Kirschner, Paul. "The Dual Purpose of Animal Farm." *Review of English Studies* 55, no. 222 (2004): 759–786.

PETER D. SIERUTA

Orwin, Joanna (1944–), New Zealand writer, born in Nelson and, in the early 2000s, living in Christchurch, New Zealand. Orwin's background lies in the natural sciences, plant ecology, science editing, and freelance nonfiction and science writing. A writer of fiction for children and young adults, Orwin is known for well-researched novels that reveal New Zealand's environment and heritage, especially Maori mythology and history, and that link past and present. Her first children's novel, *Ihaka and the Summer Wandering* (1983), and its sequel, *Ihaka and the Prophecy* (1984), set around nine hundred years ago, tell of a young boy's maturation. *The Guardian of the Land* (1985) won the New Zealand Children's Book of the Year Award. Other titles include *Watcher in the Forest* (1987), the picture book *Tar Dragon* (1997), and the young adult novels *Owl* (2001), which was winner of the 2002 Senior Fiction category of the New Zealand Post Children's Book Awards, and *Out of Tune* (2004), in which a contemporary teenager finds echoes of her own feelings in the diary of her 19th-century ancestor. Orwin has also produced the adult nonfiction titles *Four Generations from Maoridom: The Memoirs of Syd Cormack as told to Joanna Orwin* (1997) and *Kauri: Witness to a Nation's History* (2004).

Adrienne E. Gavin

Osborne, Mary Pope (1949–), American author of series books, picture books, historical fiction, realistic fiction, young adult novels, retellings, and nonfiction, and editor of story, poetry, and song collections. While Pope's writing is noted for its clarity, readability, scholarship, and compassion, she is perhaps best known for her ability to write well in a variety of genres and over a broad range of subject matter, with an oeuvre totaling almost one hundred titles. In her most popular and enduring series, the Magic Tree House collection of short chapter books, readers learn about history and literature through the time-travel adventures of siblings Jack and Annie. The Magic Tree House Research Guide nonfiction series provides doorways of informational reading beyond the level explored in the original series, while the *Merlin Missions* books take the brother and sister on longer quests based in Arthurian myth. In addition to several short chapter books featuring animal characters—including *Mo to the Rescue* (1985) and *Spider Kane and the Mystery under the May-Apple* (1992)—Pope has written four young adult novels treating the effects of mental illness, racism, war, and divorce, including *Run, Run, as Fast as You Can* (1982); many retellings of Greek myths, presented with feminist twists; and six full-length, middle-grade novels, three of them within the historical fiction series My America. She has been a deft adapter of folk tales for picture books (as in *Brave Little Seamstress*, 2002), and a sensitive editor of folklore collections (*Mermaid Tales from Around the World*, 1993). Her stand-alone nonfiction covers religious themes and American historical figures.

[*See also* Easy Readers; Historical Fiction; *and* Nonfiction.]

Timnah Card

Osborne Collection. *See* Libraries *and* Collections.

O'Shea, Pat (1931–), Irish author of two children's books inspired by Celtic mythology: *The Hounds of the Mórrígan* (1985) and *Finn MacCool and the Small Men of Deeds* (1987). In *Hounds* Catherine Patricia Shiels O'Shea depicts both present-day Ireland and Tír-na-nóg, a fairyland inhabited by both legendary and original characters. This four-hundred-page novel tells the adventures of two children who embark on a quest to prevent the Mórrígan, Celtic goddess of war, from regaining her powers. In 1987 *Hounds* appeared on *Horn Book*'s honor list. Spanish, French, German, Danish, and Italian translations of the book have been published. *Finn MacCool* is shorter, aimed at a younger audience, and illustrated (by Stephen Lavis). It retells a legend in which the hero, Finn, aids the king of the giants. Both works are noted for their inventive language, their humor, and their lively treatment of traditional material.

BIBLIOGRAPHY

"(Catherine) Pat(ricia Shiels) O'Shea." In *Contemporary Authors*, New Revision Series, Vol. 84. Detroit: Gale Research, 1999.

Donlon, Pat. "O'Shea, Pat." In *Twentieth-Century Children's Writers*, 4th ed., edited by Laura Standley Berber, 725–726. Detroit: St. James, 1995.

Rachel B. Kapelle

Osorio, Ana de Castro (1872–1935), Portuguese writer. Born at Mangualde, in the middle of Portugal, she died in Setúbal, a historical city near Lisbon, the capital of Portugal. Osorio was one of the most important cultural figures of her country from feminist, educational, and literary points of view. As a feminist, she wrote a book dealing with Portuguese women and created "A Liga das Mulheres Portuguesas" (The League of Portuguese Women) in the year 1908, which marked the demise of the Portuguese monarchy. Osorio also worked as a primary school teacher in Brazil, where she lived, and some of her books were used as school textbooks in Brazil as well as in Portugal. Many scholars consider her as the founder of children's literature in Portugal. She translated the tales of the Grimm brothers and Hans Christian Andersen into Portuguese, and some of her works were translated into French, Spanish, and Italian. From 1897 to 1935 she published collections of various kinds of texts under the title *Para as crianças* (For the Children). She was also a journalist, and adapted many of the rich texts from the Portuguese traditional literature to a child's perspective.

[*See also* Andersen, Hans Christian; Fairy Tales and Folk Tales; Grimm, Jacob, and Wilhelm Grimm; Portugal; *and* Translation.]

MANUELA FONSECA

O'Sullivan, Mark (1954–), writer of novels for young adults. He lives in County Tipperary, and many of his novels are set in small-town Ireland. However, one of his works follows the heroine from Ireland, during its civil war, to New York: this is *Wash-Basin Street Blues: Nora in New York* (1995), the sequel to his first novel, *Melody for Nora* (1994, winner of the Bisto Eilís Dillon Memorial Award in 1995). The burning of Erich Kästner's books inspired the surreal plot of O'Sullivan's *Angels without Wings* (1997), set in Berlin in 1934. The burden of saving the real world from the Nazis' evil delusions falls to the fictional characters created by the novel's writer-protagonist, Axel. O'Sullivan's feisty central characters are given to self-recrimination and doubt; their moodiness—sometimes amounting to aggression—shapes his tight plots. Examples include Lida's self-hatred in *More Than a Match*, Nance's misplaced anger at her parents in *White Lies* (1997), and Robby's struggle to overcome his dead father's paramilitary legacy in *Silent Stones* (1999).

[*See also* Kästner, Erich.]

MARY SHINE THOMPSON

Otis, James (1848–1912), American journalist and author of boys' books. During the course of thirty years, Otis, whose real name is James Otis Kaler, wrote some 130 books for boys, but it was only his first, *Toby Tyler, or Ten Weeks with a Circus* (1881) that had great success. In an introduction to later editions of the book, Kirk Munroe, then editor of *Harper's Young People*, described his first meeting with the author, and how "a shabbily dressed stranger, unwashed and unkempt" appeared in his office, explaining that he was in desperate need of ready money. He had been editor, he said, of an American paper in London that had folded up, had traveled steerage back to New York, and on the way over had written "a bang-up yarn." Over lunch he read it to Munroe, and his career as a boys' writer began. Kaler's privations on his journey back are reflected in the description of runaway Toby's perpetual gargantuan appetite. The story owed its popularity to its vivid and authentic account of circus life (Kaler himself had been connected with a circus), and also to the character of the wayward monkey Mr. Stubbs, Toby's companion. A sequel, *Mr. Stubbs's Brother* (1883), was also successful. *The Boys' Revolt* (1894), a powerful story about New York newsboys, is equally compelling and is perhaps Kaler's best work, but, lacking the exotic setting of *Toby Tyler*, it made less of an impression.

[*See also* Boys' Books and Fiction *and* Harper's Young People.]

GILLIAN AVERY

Ottley, Reginald (1909–1985), Australian author who came from the United Kingdom in 1924. Somber novels such as *No More Tomorrow* (1971) and *Jim Grey of Moonbah* (1970) praise working people for their resilience and integrity, and depict the dry, isolated areas of Australia, particularly the landscape of the Centre. His trilogy about a lonely, hard-working boy on an outback cattle station—the award-winning *By the Sandhills of Yamboorah* (1965), illustrated by Clyde Pearson; *The Roan Colt of Yamboorah* (1966), illustrated by David Parry; and *Rain Comes to Yamboorah* (1967), illustrated by Robert Halles—captures life in a remote community as an unnamed boy forms a friendship with a dour cattleman. In *The Bates Family* (1969), eight siblings traverse rural Australia earning their living as itinerant drovers. *Black Sorrow* (1980), illustrated by John Van Loon, tells of a horse rehabilitated by grieving Jody. Sydney gangs are the focus in *The War on William Street* (1971), Ottley's only urban novel.

[*See also* Australia.]

STELLA LEES and PAM MACINTYRE

Ouida (1839–1908), prolific British writer of novels, essays, and short stories, born Marie Louise de la Ramée. Although children read *A Dog of Flanders* (1872), an animal story, only *Bimbi* (1882), a collection of tales, and *Meleagris Gallapavo: A Story for Children* were specifically written for children. Flamboyant and vividly written, her novels concern well-born men in high society, and her best-known work, *Under Two Flags* (1867), shaped the popular view of the French Foreign Legion. Ouida's sensational and fast-moving social romances were much read by adolescent girls in Britain and America, despite the vehement disapproval of parents, critics, and educators.

[*See also* Animal Stories; Crossover Books; *and* Girls' Books and Fiction.]

BRIDGET CARRINGTON

Our Exploits at West Poley. *See* Hardy, Thomas.

Our Young Folks. Subtitled *An Illustrated Magazine for Boys and Girls*, *Our Young Folks* was published in Boston from 1865 to 1873, initially by Ticknor and Fields (later Fields and Osgood, then James R. Osgood). The founding editors were John Townsend Trowbridge, Gail Hamilton (Mary Abigail Dodge), and Lucy Larcom, all of whom wrote for the magazine. New England in flavor and pro-Union, antislavery in its sympathies, it had a wide American following—as the correspondence columns show—catering to serious-minded, well-educated readers, ranging in age from about ten to eighteen. There were many distinguished contributors, including Louisa May Alcott, Thomas Bailey Aldrich (*The Story of a Bad Boy* appeared as a serial), Dinah Maria Craik (who contributed the poem "The Little Jew: A True Story"), Charles Dickens (*A Holiday Romance* appeared in four parts in 1868), Lucretia Hale (*Peterkin Papers*), Henry Wadsworth Longfellow, Thomas Mayne Reid, Harriet Beecher Stowe, and John Greenleaf Whittier. *Our Young Folks* merged with *St. Nicholas* in 1874.

[*See also* Children's Magazines; Journals and Periodicals; St. Nicholas Magazine; *and biographies of figures mentioned in this article.*]

BIBLIOGRAPHY

Friedberg, Joan Brest. "*Our Young Folks*." In *Children's Periodicals of the United States*, edited by R. Gordon Kelly. Westport, Conn.: Greenwood, 1984.

GILLIAN AVERY

Outcault, R. F. (1863–1928), American cartoonist. Outcault's best-known creation, the Yellow Kid, changed the role of comic strips in American newspapers. Ohio-born Richard Felton Outcault began his career as an illustrator for Thomas Edison's laboratories, but he found fame with his *New York World* comic strip "Hogan's Alley," which featured a group of disadvantaged characters mocking the conventions of upper-class society. Outcault's strip was among the first to utilize sequential panels, dialogue balloons, and color art, and it proved that individual comic strips could increase newspaper circulation. One bald, big-eared character, Mickey Dugan—known as the Yellow Kid because of his oversized, canary-colored nightshirt—became the first comic figure to be widely merchandised (products ranged from dolls to cigarettes). Outcault's move from the *New York World* to the *New York Journal* led to a lawsuit between rival publishers Joseph Pulitzer and Randolph Hearst, and the term "yellow journalism"—sensationalistic news reporting—may have been coined because of the flamboyant journalistic style typically employed by both papers that published the Yellow Kid. Outcault's strip lasted until 1898, at which time he devoted himself to "Buster Brown," a comic that is long forgotten yet continues to be merchandised to this day, most notably as a brand of children's shoes.

PETER D. SIERUTA

Outhwaite, Ida Rentoul (1888–1960), Australian illustrator, born Ida Sherbourne Rentoul in Melbourne, and educated at Presbyterian Ladies' College. She is a major figure in the development of children's book illustration in Australia. During her life she gained an international reputation, exhibiting in London and Paris as well as in Australia. Her first book (*Mollie's Bunyip*) was published in 1904, when she was sixteen, and contained written text by her sister Annie R. Rentoul. Both sisters took part in the First Australian Exhibition of Women's Work, held in Melbourne in 1907. *Elves and Fairies* (1916) was the first picture book to be published in Australia in high-quality color. Outhwaite also illustrated in black and white, with such drawings showing great light and shade, acknowledging her interest in the works of artists such as Aubrey Beardsley.

She was one of a number of Australian illustrators of the fairy books that became very popular in the interwar years. Some of her major works were written by her husband, Grenbry Outhwaite. Ida Outhwaite had a comic strip in the Melbourne *Weekly Times* for many years and also illustrated the works of other authors. Her work continues to be reprinted today, both in book form and in such ephemera as greeting cards.

MARGOT HILLEL

Overton, Jenny (1942–), British writer and editor, who has worked for Macmillan and Lutterworth Press and has written four children's books. In *Creed Country* (1969), investigating historical documents is an absorbing project, testing the bonds of family and friendship. In the sequel, *The Nightwatch Winter* (1973), enacting a mystery-play cycle is a way of both escaping and processing adolescent experience. Overton explores friction and relationships within and beyond a large family, using a cultural and social setting already unfashionable at the time of writing. Her well-read middle-class children share interests in music and history, and the vocabulary is demanding even to older readers. These books share similar themes and events, and a pleasure in language and literature, with the Marlow Family stories of Antonia Forest, though Forest's characterization is superior. Unusually for children's books of the period, both writers assume an interest in religion as an integral and serious part of family debate.

Overton's other books are simpler in style. *The Thirteen Days of Christmas* (1972) offers a comic twist on a traditional song. *The Ship from Simnel Street* (1986) is a family story set in an early-19th-century baker's shop. Her writing pinpoints family tensions and loyalties, and her small output is less well-known than it deserves.

[*See also* Forest, Antonia.]

Belinda Copson

Owen, Gareth (1936–), British poet, born in Southport, England. He became a teacher and then for many years was a lecturer in a college of education in the Midlands. His first collection of poems for children, *Salford Road* (1976), was initially published privately. It was followed by *Song of the City* (1985), which has often been acknowledged as one of the finest collections of the 1980s and for which he won The Signal Award for Poetry. Another collection, *My Granny Is a Sumo Wrestler*, appeared in 1994. Owen often appears to be writing about his own childhood. Frequently anthologized, he combines humor and warmth and avoids sentimentality.

Geoffrey Fenwick

Owl and the Pussy-Cat, The. *See* Lear, Edward.

***OWL* Magazine.** Originally published as a science magazine for children, *OWL* is now a general-interest magazine for children aged nine to thirteen. Founder Annabel Slaight launched the magazine in 1976, and it merged with Bayard Canada in 1997. Regular features in the magazine include dramatic photography, a calendar that highlights Canadian cultural events, cartoons, commentaries on animals, controversial subjects, poetry and stories written by readers, puzzles, and feature articles on themed topics. The companion magazines published by Bayard Canada, *ChickaDEE* and *Chirp*, are for children aged six to nine. *OWL* has an approximate circulation of 78,000 in Canada and the United States. See also *Owlkids Online* at http://www.owlkids.com.

[*See also* Canada; Children's Magazines; *and* Nonfiction.]

Roberta Seelinger Trites

Oxenbury, Helen (1938–), British picture book author and illustrator. She made an outstanding contribution to the development of the board book, having created, in the 1980s, three series for babies that are now regarded as internation classics. *Tickle, Tickle* (1987), in her Big Board Books, was the first winner of the Sainsbury's Baby Book Award. Other successful series are Heads, Bodies, and Legs (1980); First Picture Books (1983); and a set of eight Pippo Books, which originated as a comic strip in the French children's magazine *Popi* and feature episodes in the life of a little boy and his toy monkey. Although Oxenbury's early work included some detail, she later developed a more minimalist style in which communication is achieved through a contour line drawn with varying pressure, together with watercolor. Oxenbury has been awarded the Kate Greenaway Medal twice: for her collaboration with Edward Lear and Margaret Mahy, *The Quangle Wangle's Hat and The Dragon of an Ordinary Family* (1987); and for Lewis Carroll's *Alice's Adventures in Wonderland* (2000), which also won the Kurt Maschler Award. Her interpretation for the latter, including Alice in a skimpy blue dress and white sneakers, renders Carroll's classic accessible for today's child. In order to reflect the reality and the fantasy engaging a family in *We're Going on a Bear Hunt* (1989), Michael Rosen's rendition of a traditional rhyme, Oxenbury alternated black-and-white and color wash illustrations. This work won the Smarties Book Prize and has been adapted as a story play book. Her collaboration with Martin Waddell, *Farmer Duck* (1991), won the British Book Award for Children's Illustrated Book of the Year, and the Smarties Book Prize. *So Much* (1994), with text by Trish Cooke, also won the Smarties Book Prize, as well as the Kurt Maschler Award.

[*See also* Preschool Books.]

BIBLIOGRAPHY

Martin, Douglas. "Helen Oxenbury." In *The Telling Line*, 202–214, London: Julia MacRae Books, 1989.

JANE DOONAN

Oxenham, Elsie J. (1880–1960), British writer of books for young adults. Oxenham's best-known work is the Abbey series, novels spanning two generations of girls growing up near a ruined abbey. Her real name was Elsie Jeanette Dunkerley, but she adopted the pen name of her father, the writer John Oxenham. Her approximately ninety books are characterized by a strong sense of place, whether set in London (where she grew up), Sussex (where she lived from 1922), Scotland, Wales, or Switzerland. She loved a rags-to-riches tale but focused on the ways her heiress characters used their wealth rather than how they won it: noblesse oblige is the dominant ethic of her work. In her school stories, she gave prominence to activities like Camp Fire and folk dancing, with which she was personally involved. Oxenham linked her various series to one another through the friendships of the different characters, thereby creating a huge interconnected and almost wholly female cast which ensured her enduring popularity.

ROSEMARY AUCHMUTY

Oxley, James MacDonald (1855–1907), Canadian lawyer, civil servant, and novelist. Educated at Dalhousie and Harvard, Oxley worked as a lawyer in Halifax before taking up a governmental position. He also worked for the Sun Life Assurance Company before trying his hand at boys' adventure stories. His output was prodigious—twenty novels between 1889 and 1905, as well as articles and nonfiction. Historical Canadian settings, often invoking the invigorating hardships of the north, are his forte. His most famous novel today is *Fife and Drum at Louisbourg* (1899), which depicts the siege of Louisbourg and the British and French struggle over Canada in the 1740s from the point of view of two realistically portrayed twin boys. His nonfiction includes *My Strange Rescue and Other Stories of Sport and Adventure in Canada* (1895), one of the first accounts of Canadian sports, including tobogganing, lacrosse, and ice hockey.

[*See also* Adventure Books; Boys' Books and Fiction; *and* Nonfiction.]

BJÖRN SUNDMARK

Oz. *See* Baum, L. Frank.

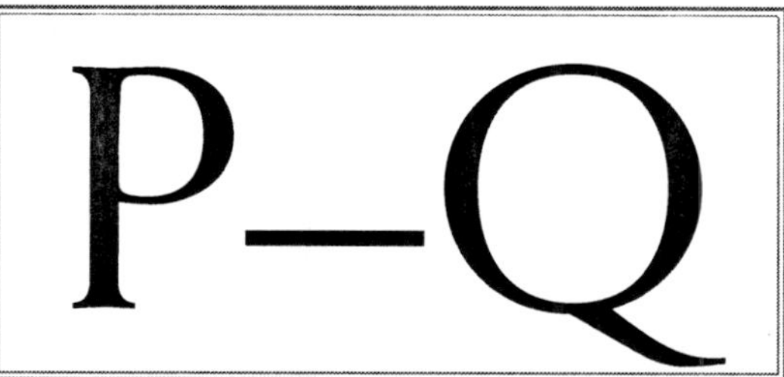

Paddington Bear. *See* Bond, Michael.

Padmanabhan, Manjula (1953–), Indian illustrator, writer, artist, and cartoonist. Born in Delhi, India, Padmanabhan was raised in Sweden, Pakistan, and Thailand, and lived in Delhi in the early 2000s. An exhibiting artist, novelist, short storyist, and prize-winning playwright, she produced the cartoon strip *Suki* for many years and is also a regular columnist and blogger. Her contribution to children's literature lies in her illustration and author-illustration of over twenty children's books. Highly detailed and with a clear sense of setting and pattern, her illustrations reveal matters of concern to her, for example, issues surrounding the positions of female characters and the situations of marginalized or alienated people. She is also interested in the hybridity of animals and humans, and she has produced work in both black and white and color. She began her children's literature career by illustrating many texts by other writers. One of the most popular early texts on which she collaborated was Tara Ali Baig's *Indrani and the Enchanted Jungle* (1979), which Padmanabhan illustrated in vibrant and atmospheric color. She also illustrated Indi Rana's *The Devil in the Dustbin* (1989), a book for middle readers about a boy who thinks he is a tamarind tree devil. Her author-illustrated works include the picture book *A Visit to the City Market* (1985), which has been admired for its vivid and colorful depiction of an Indian market. Recently she has author-illustrated two animal action-adventure novels for children, written under the shortened form of her name, Manjula Padma. *Mouse Attack* (2003) is about an intelligent albino "Action Mouse" named Arvee. Underlying the action are issues prevalent in Padmanabhan's adult work, such as alienation and marginalization and questions about how to battle a corrupt oppressor, in this instance a gangster rat. In the sequel, *Mouse Invaders* (2004), Arvee again has to save his mouse friends.

Adrienne E. Gavin

Page, Thomas Nelson (1853–1922), Virginia writer and upholder of the traditions of the Old South. Edmund Wilson in *Patriotic Gore* (1962) said of Page that "it was hard to make the Civil War seem cosy, but Thomas Nelson Page did his best." Born on a small plantation in Oakland, Virginia, a lawyer like his father, he saw the old regime during his most impressionable years, and was to idealize it in many romantic novels. He wrote three books for children, of which *Two Little Confederates*, which first appeared in *St. Nicholas* in 1888, is by far the best known. It views the Civil War and its aftermath through the eyes of two boys, and is set in Oakland, in a decaying plantation house staffed with devoted black slaves who have no wish for freedom. Page's books were so successful that he gave up law to write. His literary career came to an end when he was appointed ambassador to Italy in 1913. He held the post until 1919, and wrote *Italy and the World War* (1920).

[*See also* St. Nicholas Magazine *and* United States.]

BIBLIOGRAPHY

Primary Works

Among the Camps (1891)
Pastime Stories (1894)

Secondary Works

Elbert, Sarah. Preface to *"Two Little Confederates" and Annie Fellows Johnston's "The Little Colonel"*. New York: Garland, 1976.

Wilson, Edmund. *Patriotic Gore: Studies in the Literature of the American Civil War*. New York: Oxford University Press, 1962.

Gillian Avery

Paget, Francis (1862–1882), antiquarian and author, rector of Elford, near Lichfield, Staffordshire. Paget wrote papers on local history and tales of village life. Between 1844 and 1849 he edited *The Juvenile Englishman's Library*, to which he himself contributed stories, notably "The Hope of the Katzekopfs" (1844), generally regarded as the earliest literary fantasy for children. Written under the name William Churne, supposedly a 17th-century authority on "all matters connected with Fairyland," it was designed, according to the preface to the second edition, to see whether "children's hearts could be moved . . . to shake off the hard, cold, calculating, worldly, selfish temper of the times." It tells the story of Prince Eigenwillig, whose name means "self-willed." He so ill-treats the good child Witikind, whom the fairy Abracadabra has given him as a companion, that the exasperated fairy elongates him into "a coil of living catgut" and kicks him all the way to Fairyland. Prince Eigenwillig falls into the hands of the evil sprite Selbst (self), who becomes a monstrous burden from which the schoolmaster Discipline finally frees him, teaching him to deny himself and think of others first.

[*See also* Fairies *and* Fantasy.]

GILLIAN AVERY

Pai, Anant (1929–), Indian author and editor of comic books, audiotapes, and magazines. Pai joined the Times of India Books Division in 1961 and first worked on comics. His contribution to Indian children's literature is nothing short of phenomenal. The comic book series, Amar Chitra Katha (literally "Immortal Pictorial Tales") under his series editorship, filled a huge lacuna in the Indian child's reading list. Amar Chitra Katha was launched in 1967 with *Krishna*. Pai was motivated to introduce tales from Indian history and mythology when he realized that Indian children were unaware of their cultural inheritance. Amar Chitra Katha is now a venerated institution, synonymous with all that is acceptable. The series is organized into various sections: Mythology, Ancient Indian History, Tales from the Epics and the Vedas, Freedom Struggle, and Makers of Modern India, among others. There are also two subseries, Pancharatna (Indian mythology, epics, Jatakas, or freedom fighters, and brave Rajputs, great rulers of India) and Special Issues (on the Ramayana, Jesus Christ, Sanskrit plays, Indian emperors, and Buddhist tales). Men and women invariably possess physiognomic features and wear costumes that are identifiably northern Indian. Demons are dark-skinned (like southern Indian races), and there is a clear patriarchal bias in the portrayal of women (even "heroic" women such as the Rani of Jhansi). Pai's greatest innovation was his adaptation of the comic-book format, which until then had been used primarily to narrate Western stories, to tell Indian tales. In 1980 Pai started *Tinkle*, a fortnightly children's comic that featured stories, poems, and jokes. *Kapish* and *Kalia the Crow*, Pai's comic-book creations, reveal a great influence of the *Panchatantra*. Here smaller animals outwit animals like the tiger and even, on occasion, man. Pai's stories often end with the triumph of meek, good animals over larger, evil ones.

NANDINI NAYAR

Paine, Albert Bigelow (1861–1937), American editor and writer whose works include several children's books. Paine is remembered by later generations as Mark Twain's secretary and as the author of the three-volume biography of Twain (1912), of which a version for children appeared in 1916. His life of Joan of Arc, *Girl in White Armor* (1927), was condensed from his adult biography. For ten years from 1899 he conducted the St. Nicholas League, which published reader contributions to that journal—illustrative as well as literary—and awarded certificates and medals to the winners. His own *Hollow Tree* stories ("How Mr. Dog Got Even," "How Mr. Rabbit Lost His Tail"), written for *St. Nicholas*, are reminiscent of *Uncle Remus*, but his *The Arkansaw Bear* (1898) is entirely original, a touching and delightful story of the comradeship between Bosephus, a homeless boy, and Horatio, a highly articulate fiddle-playing bear; they wander through the South, singing and fiddling for their living. Paine gives the text of the songs and their music.

[*See also* Biography; Clemens, Samuel Langhorne; *and* St. Nicholas Magazine.]

BIBLIOGRAPHY

Paine, Albert Bigelow. *The Boys' Life of Mark Twain*. New York and London: Harper, 1916.

Paine, Albert Bigelow. *The Hollow Tree*. New York: R. H. Russell, 1898.

Paine, Albert Bigelow. *In the Deep Woods*. New York: R. H. Russell, 1899.

GILLIAN AVERY

Pak, Soyung (1968–), writer born in South Korea and raised in New Jersey. Pak completed a bachelor's degree in fine arts, a master's in education, and an MBA from the Chicago Graduate School of Business. She worked in publishing at Simon and Schuster and Prudential Securities, and subsequently as an assistant manager at PepsiCo. She won the Ezra Jack Keats Award in 2000 with her first picture book, *Dear Juno* (1999; illustrated by Susan Kathleen Hartung), a story about a small Korean American boy's creative communication with his grandmother in Korea by means of drawings and found objects. Pak explored further the theme of communication across cultures in *A Place to Grow* (2002), a book based on her family's migration to the United States but given universal application by the illustrator Marcelino Truong's Vietnamese settings. *Sumi's First Day of School Ever* (2003) presents a positive view of migrant experience through a child's discovery of acceptance in her first day at school.

[*See also* Multiculturalism and Children's Books.]

SUNG-AE LEE

Pakistan. Formed from two geographically separate areas of India in 1947 as an Islamic nation, Pakistan has a small but growing collection of literature for children available. In 1971 the eastern section of Pakistan seceded and became Bangladesh. Pakistan is bounded by India, Iran, Afghanistan, and China; its primary cultural influences are its origin nation India, and its bordering Islamic countries Iran and Afghanistan. Nearly half the population is under the age of fifteen, so there is a large market for children's literature, if it can be developed in a country in which 35 percent of the population lives below the poverty line. The national infrastructure to support children's literature is small but growing; the National Library of Pakistan was founded in 1993. The adult literacy rate is 45 percent and improving dramatically. In 1980 the youth literacy rate was 37 percent and in 2002 it had improved to 59 percent, although these numbers do not highlight the great disparity in literacy between girls and boys. The overwhelming majority of boys attend primary school, which is free by government mandate. Studying the literature of Pakistan is a complex endeavor because there is such a diversity of languages spoken across the country. Urdu is the first official language of Pakistan, although only 8 percent of the population speaks Urdu at home; other languages include Punjabi, Pashto, Sindhi, and English (Pakistan's second official language, primarily used by government offices and the academic elite). Most literate children can read Urdu, and the majority of Pakistani children's literature is published in Urdu, with a small amount available in English, usually in translation.

Before India gained independence from Britain, most children's books published on the Indian subcontinent were educational texts in English or Urdu published by missionaries. In reaction, Islamic nationalists pushed for the publication of Urdu children's literature focusing on Islamic themes. The substantial amount of the development of Urdu children's literature in Pakistan has been through children's magazines rather than books. The most prominent was *Phool* (Flowers), founded in 1909 and still published today, though not in its original form. Along with children's magazines, short stories for children flourished in textbooks in the preindependence period. Even today, textbooks are still a major medium for transmission of children's short stories in Pakistan. Maulvi Nazir Ahmed, the first novelist writing in Urdu, also contributed to the development of early Urdu children's literature with his didactic stories.

After the partition from India that created Pakistan as an independent nation, much of the production of books was taken over by the National Book Foundation in Karachi. During this immediate postpartition period, children's literature was a didactic tool for educating the new generation in nationalist ideals and Islam. Early children's books in the postindependence period (1947–1960) covered issues of nationalism and Islamic pride. A large number of idealized biographies of Islamic and national heroes were produced to provide literary support to ideas of national identity.

In the 1960s and 1970s Pakistan experienced a period of relative stability during which the main controversy was between pro-Islam Rightists and pro-Soviet Leftists. Many prominent authors in all genres produced works based on socialist ideals, which included a distaste for religion in general and Islam in particular. In reaction, more children's books were produced with an emphasis on Islamic ideology. This clash of ideologies was fruitful, as it led to the discovery of new talents and the founding of new publishing houses to support the markets for the different factions. A new wealth of material—albeit controversial material—emerged in the Pakistani children's literature market.

The conflict between Left and Right ended with a solid victory for the Rightists after the Soviet invasion of Afghanistan. Because of Pakistani sympathy with the Islamic freedom fighters in Afghanistan, Islamic ideology once again came to dominate Pakistan's culture and, therefore, its children's literature market. Pro-Islam magazines such as *Ankh Micauli* (Hide and Seek, 1986–1997) were created during this period. *Ankh Micauli*, whose design of short and diverse articles was strongly influenced by *Reader's Digest*, had a philosophy that included entertainment and production quality as well as ideology. Children's publishing in Pakistan in the 21st century is dominated far less by ideological pieces, with far more room for pieces focused on entertainment, although there is still a strong didactic tradition dominating the children's market. The state-sponsored textbook industry is still very heavily influenced by current political mores, and textbooks are still heavily influenced by nationalism and pro-Islamism. Children's magazines such as *Phool* and *Masoom* have more of an entertainment focus, and roughly parallel English children's magazines in the intent to entertain. The many Urdu children's magazines print original poems and short stories written for children as well as stories in translation from other languages. Nonetheless, support for Islam is the common thread that runs through nearly all the magazines.

The government of Pakistan does have some efforts under way to increase the amount of quality children's literature in Pakistan, but given the poverty of the country, the efforts are slow-moving. The National Book Council (a government agency that merged in 2001 with the National Book Foundation) in 1965 initiated an official effort to develop children's literature. In 1987 the Da'wah Academy at the International Islamic University in Islamabad founded a Children's Literature Department. There are very few professional authors for children in Pakistan; much of the published work is done by volunteers or by individuals and organizations with other motives. Entertaining and humorous writing for children, especially, is primarily done by amateurs. However, government initiatives, academic support, and decreasing costs of publication are all leading toward a growing field of possibility.

A small number of books for children are published in or translated to English every year, although these are primarily intended for internal and expatriate markets, and not for the general book markets of English-speaking countries. Import and export of materials in Urdu is complicated by Pakistan's trade ban with the primary potential market for Urdu-language literature, India.

Popular writers for children include Ishtiaq Ahmed, Jamil Jalibi, and Shazia Farheen. The most prominent publishers of children's books include the National Book Foundation, Ferozsons, Sheik Ghulam Ali and Sons, and Saeed Kitab.

[*See also* India.]

BIBLIOGRAPHY

Mughal, Raees Ahmed. "Five Decades of Children's Literature in Pakistan." *Bookbird* 38 (2000): 10–15.

Rahman, Mahmudar. "Humor in Urdu Children's Literature." *Bookbird* 38 (2000): 37–39.

DEBORAH KAPLAN

Pal, George (1908–1980), Hungarian American animator and film director. Pal's early filmmaking career took him from Hungary to Germany, and then to Czechoslovakia, France, and the Netherlands. When World War II erupted in 1939, Pal and his wife, Czoka, were in the United States on a lecture tour; they stayed and eventually moved to Hollywood. By then he was already famous for his "Puppetoons," a portmanteau word formed from "puppet" and "cartoon." Puppetoons depend on stop-animation technique, with each shot framing a separate carved wooden puppet (or puppet part). On average, Pal would use as many as nine thousand puppets for each film, but the models could be reused and filmed from different perspectives—an advantage over standard animation, and something Puppetoons have in common with modern animation techniques such as Claymation and computer animation. Originally, Pal's Puppetoons were conceived as advertisements for Horlick's Malted Milk ("South Sea Sweets," 1939), Philips Radio ("The Little Broadcast," 1935), and other products, but because of their popularity, theaters soon started showing them without charging the advertisers for screen time. When Paramount Pictures started sponsoring the Puppetoons, the link to advertising was dropped altogether. Puppetoons from the American period include the anti-Nazi film *Tulips Shall Grow* (1942), where a sieg-heiling "screwball army" invades Holland but ultimately rusts to a standstill. Other significant Puppetoons are *John Henry and the Inky-Poo* (1946), based on African-American folklore, and the last and probably best-known Puppetoon short, *Tubby the Tuba* (1947), featuring an unhappy tuba who wants to play melodies rather than just going "oompah-oompah." Pal's success as an animator paved the way for him as a director of fantasy films such as *Destination Moon* (1950), *When Worlds Collide* (1951), and *War of the Worlds* (1953), all of which received Academy Awards for special effects.

BJÖRN SUNDMARK

Palgrave, Francis (1824–1897), English educationalist and anthologist. Palgrave's *Golden Treasury* of poetry was first published in 1861, and in 1875 he selected poems for a *Children's Treasury*. "Poetry for poetry's sake" was what he offered, according to his preface: poetry "fit to give pleasure,—high, pure, manly, (and therefore lasting)—" to children. Palgrave excluded poems of "morbid melancholy" and those exalting "love as personal passion," as well as directly didactic poems; he was sure that "the powerful operation of really good poetry" would in itself convey all the "useful lessons" that might be necessary.

[*See also* Collections *and* Poetry.]

FRANCES ARMSTRONG

Palmer, C. Everard (1930–), Jamaican teacher and writer born in Kendal, Jamaica, and resident since the 1950s in Canada. Many of Cyril Everard Palmer's stories are inspired by memories of his village childhood and exhibit humor, strong characterization, and vibrant dialogue. It was only after independence in the 1960s that children's literature other than folk tales began to emerge in the Caribbean, and Palmer's earliest contributions were *The Cloud with the Silver Lining* (1966), *Big Doc Bitteroot* (1968), *The Sun Salutes You* (1970), and *A Cow Called Boy* (1972). He incorporates traditional character types in his texts; in *The Wooing of Beppo Tate* (1972), which depicts a typical postemancipation rural settlement, his major protagonist, Teppy, the affable trickster, shows the influence of oral and traditional folk tale: like Anancy, Teppy is a survivor and a human parasite. *Full Circle: The Rami Johnson Story* (2003) continues the story begun in his excellent novel for young adults, *My Father, Sun-Sun Johnson* (1974).

[*See also* Anancy or Ananse, The Spider Man *and* Caribbean Countries.]

BRIDGET CARRINGTON

Pansy (1841–1930), American author, editor, and coauthor of numerous books for the Sunday-school market. Pansy, whose real name was Isabella MacDonald Alden, wrote evangelical fiction for children and young adults that included domestic novels, emblem books, and twenty-five collections of short stories from *The Pansy* (1874–1896), a magazine "for Sunday reading." Many of her novels appeared first in that magazine, which she edited and whose name capitalized on her enormous popularity. During a period of evangelical revival in the United States, her works spurred involvement in Sunday-school teaching, the Young People's Society of Christian Endeavor, and the Chautauqua movement. Despite their didacticism, Pansy's novels feature lively dialogue and sharp social satire, and her protagonists transform their families and communities. Representative works include *Four Girls at Chautauqua* (1876), *Ester Ried, Asleep and Awake* (1870), and *Tip Lewis and His Lamp* (1867), translated into German, Japanese, Hungarian (2003), and Bulgarian. Since the 1990s twenty-five of her works have been republished, principally as Christian romances for the adult market.

LAUREEN TEDESCO

Pantheon, The, or Ancient History of the Gods of Greece and Rome. *See* Godwin, William, and Mary Jane Godwin.

Pantomime. Pantomime is a composite British theatrical entertainment for children that presently consists of song, music, dance, and slapstick comedy; has gender- and age-crossing leads, a loose fairy-tale plot, and topical humor; and is associated with the Christmas season. It is a participatory form of theater, for at certain key moments the audience may sing along with the music or shout out phrases to the performers.

Possessing a long theatrical history in Western culture dating back to classical theater, the pantomime has links with the 16th-century commedia dell'arte tradition of Italy and the mime tradition in France. In Denmark the pantomime was an influential Romantic form that affected the work of Hans Christian Andersen. Productions in the Romantic style can still be seen at the theater in the Tivoli Gardens in Copenhagen. On the British stage the pantomime has links with 17th-century masques.

Most histories of the English pantomime date from the Reformation. In terms of audience attendance it has always been a popular form just as it is has always been both an expensive and profitable endeavor for theaters to produce. In the 18th century the audience spanned all ages and classes, although, because of the substantial audience of apprentices that attended the theater in this period, pantomime could be considered as an instance of early youth culture. Pantomimes were based on many topics including topical satire but gradually throughout the Regency and especially in Victorian England the themes of pantomime became associated with childhood and an audience of children due to the reliance on fairy tale and folk tale topics for the plots. By the 1890s the pantomimes assumed the form that they have today.

Pantomime is often thought of as being devoid of speech, as is mime, and being a comic form. However, the presence or absence of speech and the dramatic mode have changed over time. In the late 1710s and 1720s the dancing master John Weaver, who is credited with bringing the term to popularity, staged serious mute dramas based on myth, such as *The Loves of Mars and Venus* (1717) and *Orpheus and Eurydice* (1718), "in imitation of the Antient Greeks and Romans," where the narrative is transmitted by music and dance only. The first practitioner to popularize the form, John Rich "Lun" (1692–1761), initially appeared in another Weaver pantomime, *The Cheats; or, The Tavern Bilkers*, which placed some of the commedia characters, Harlequin, Scaramouch, and Punch, in London. Rich took over the role and staged pantomimes at Covent Garden, where he added

Pantomime. Panels 2 and 3 from *Harlequin's Invasion* (London: Robert Sayer, 1777). REPRODUCED COURTESY OF THE COTSEN CHILDREN'S LIBRARY, PRINCETON UNIVERSITY LIBRARY

a serio-comic second section comprising the love affair of Harlequin and Columbine and their pursuit by Pantaloon. Central to these antics were the transformation scenes that Harlequin performed thanks to his magic bat, usually given to him by a benevolent agent. This basic structure was retained until late in the 19th century. The silent Harlequin remained the norm until after Rich's retirement, supported as well by theatrical bans on spoken drama outside the two Patent Houses. David Garrick's Harlequin spoke in *Harlequin Invasion* (1759), and Garrick also initiated the scheduling of pantomimes in the Christmas season at Drury Lane.

The next actor-manager who in turn transformed the pantomime was Joseph Grimaldi (1778–1837), who from 1806 until 1823 at Covent Garden developed the role of clown into the central character. It was because of Grimaldi that audiences were encouraged to participate in the entertainment by singing the popular songs along with the actors; and clowns to this day are called Joey. Now neither Harlequin nor clown-people pantomimes exist although the legacy of the Harlequinade still exists in the transformation scenes, slapstick physical comedy, and chase scenes in modern-day pantomimes. The main characters today are those of the Victorian period: Dames (usually older men) and Principal Boys (usually young women). Dames have a bawdy sense of humor, outrageous costumes, and extrovert characters. They interact with the audience, initiate slapstick, and play tricks on the other performers. The costumes they wear play a large part in the jokes and are often visual puns. Principal Boys played by young women have their origin in the breeches parts of the 18th century and in the rise of the ballerina. By the 1880s the male lead was always played by a woman. Animal roles played by humans (skin parts) have been popular since the 19th century, and traces of this can be seen in the film production of the *Wizard of Oz* (1939) where the character of the cowardly lion is played by Bert Lahr.

Over the centuries, different British writers were interested in the pantomime, such as Joseph Addison and Richard Steele, Henry Fielding, and Leigh Hunt. In terms of writers associated with children's literature, Charles Dodgson (Lewis Carroll), William Makepeace Thackeray, and Charles Dickens all enjoyed attending pantomimes, the last editing Grimaldi's memoirs.

Some specific types of children's texts have been associated with pantomime, particularly the English toy theater sheets of Regency and Victorian England. In the late-18th and early-19th centuries a type of flap book became associated with the pantomime to the extent that it came to be called the Harlequinade. The relation of pantomime to children's theater appears to be indirect. *Peter Pan* (1904), considered the first children's play, has aspects of pantomime, in that Peter is usually played by an actress in the tradition of the principal boy. On occasion a popular novel such as *The Pantomime Cat* (1949) by Enid Blyton may feature pantomime characters, and Pantomime *Annuals* were published in the 1940s and 1950s in Britain.

[*See also* Toy Theaters.]

BIBLIOGRAPHY

Frow, Gerald. *"Oh, Yes It Is!": A History of Pantomime*. London: British Broadcasting Corporation, 1985.

Mayer, David. *Harlequin in His Element: The English Pantomime, 1806–1836*. Cambridge, Mass.: Harvard University Press, 1969.

O'Brien, John. *Harlequin Britain: Pantomime and Entertainment, 1690–1760*. Baltimore: John Hopkins University Press, 2004.

JACQUELINE REID-WALSH

Parables from Nature. *See* Gatty, Margaret.

Parent's Assistant, The. *See* Edgeworth, Maria.

Parish, Peggy (1927–1988), born Margaret Cecile Parish, an American author and educator best known for her popular easy reader series beginning with *Amelia Bedelia* (1963), in which puns and misunderstandings result in domestic chaos. *Dinosaur Time* (1974), an easy reader profiling eleven popular dinosaurs, also received positive critical and popular attention. Other Parish offerings include the four-volume board book set, *I Can—Can You?* (1984), celebrating the new skills of toddlers; several nonfiction craft books describing very simple projects; and the Liza, Bill, & Jed mystery series (1968–1986) for middle graders. Some controversy exists over the Granny Guntry easy reader stories, in which a nearsighted elderly woman plows through a variety of fiascos on the frontier, and *Good Hunting, Blue Sky* (1989), a revised edition of *Good Hunting, Little Indian* (1962); these books received some censure for perceived stereotyping of Native Americans.

TIMNAH CARD

Park, Barbara (1947–), American author of humorous fiction and picture books, respected for her ability to craft hilarious yet poignant narratives. Park began her career by writing middle-grade fiction—works such as *Skinnybones* (1982) and *Almost Starring Skinnybones* (1988), detailing the adventures of a diminutive ten-year-old pitcher who finds fame as a television celebrity—then expanded her repertoire to include young adult fiction with *Mick Harte Was Here* (1995), in which Mick's sister describes how his death has impacted the family. A picture book, *Psssst! It's Me . . . the Bogeyman* (1998), plays with the conventional representation of that imaginary monster. The author is probably best known for her extended series of short chapter books, beginning with *Junie B. Jones and the Stupid Smelly Bus* (1992), which follow a hyperactive, vociferous, well-intentioned but badly behaved young protagonist through kindergarten and into first grade.

[*See also* Humor; Picture Books; *and* Young Adult Literature.]

TIMNAH CARD

Park, Linda Sue (1960–), American author. A native of Illinois, Park attended Stanford University, earned graduate degrees at Trinity College (Dublin) and Birkbeck College (London), and worked as a corporate copywriter, journalist, and teacher. The daughter of Korean immigrants, Park set her first four books in Korea, with characters ranging from twelfth-century potters to World War II–era schoolchildren. *A Single Shard* (2001) received the Newbery Medal, and

When My Name Was Keoko (2002) was cited as a Best Book for Young Adults by the American Library Association, in addition to several other honors. Park's other works include *Project Mulberry* (2005), a contemporary novel featuring an opinionated Korean American seventh-grader, and an assortment of picture books. Park is notable both for the gracefulness of her prose and for her realistically nuanced portraits of families in different eras. While Park's stories are inspired and informed by Korean history and culture, it is the energy and intelligence of her protagonists that render her narratives compelling.

PEGGY LIN DUTHIE

Park, Ruth (1923–), Australian writer. She began her career in children's literature as the author of humorous animal stories, *The Muddle-Headed Wombat* (1962) and sequels, originally written for radio. Her many novels for older children include the psychological fantasy *My Sister Sif* (1986), about a girl who discovers that she has mermaid ancestry. Park's prize-winning novel *Playing Beatie Bow* (1980) is her best and most famous. Its young protagonist, Abigail, is displaced in time, finding herself living in horrible conditions in 19th-century Sydney, but also enjoying the loving, caring family that she lacks in her own time. In this novel, Park breaks away from several conventions used in earlier fantasies of time travel. Whereas the common principle is that time travelers cannot change history, it turns out that the purpose of Abigail's displacement is to interfere with history, although she is unaware of her task. Abigail is ambivalent about her experience. Her transportation to the past is involuntary and causes her pain and discomfort rather than excitement; and she retains her 20th-century mentality and knowledge. Yet she contemplates staying permanently in the past, not least when she becomes emotionally involved. In the end, she makes an important ethical choice, giving up her romantic dreams, and is rewarded by finding love in her own time. The novel has been unanimously appraised by critics as one of the finest and most poignant stories of a young person's maturation through time displacement. It has a skillfully wrought plot with subtle foreshadowing and many false threads; fascinating yet unobtrusive historical details; and a delicate balance between events and reflection. It is also one of the few time-shift novels in which the specifically female experience is emphasized and explored, and a feminist agenda is explicitly proposed. In particular, the powerful characterization makes the novel stand out among many other fantasy works, in which characters are subordinate to the plot.

BIBLIOGRAPHY

Nikolajeva, Maria. *From Mythic to Linear: Time in Children's Literature*. Lanham, Md.: Scarecrow, 2000.

Nodelman, Perry. "Interpretation and the Apparent Sameness of Children's Literature." *Studies in the Literary Imagination* 18, no. 2 (1985): 5–20.

Scott, Carole. "A Century of Dislocated Time: Time Travel, Magic, and the Search for Self." *Papers* 6, no. 2 (1996): 14–20.

MARIA NIKOLAJEVA

Parker, Nancy Winslow (1930–), American illustrator and writer. Born in Maplewood, New Jersey, and educated at Mills College, California, and the Art Students League and the School of Visual Arts, New York, Parker was a sales and sports promoter, art director, and graphic designer in New York City before becoming a freelance illustrator and writer in 1972. In the children's book field, she produces work characterized by humor and simplicity and with a fondness for depicting animals. Her author-illustrated works include *The Man with the Take-Apart Head* (1974), *Poofy Loves Company* (1980), and *The Christmas Camel* (1983). Her nonfiction includes *The President's Car* (1981) and *Land Ho! Fifty Glorious Years in the Age of Exploration with Twelve Important Explorers* (2001). Parker has also illustrated the texts of many authors, and for her work on Mildred Kantrowitz's *Willy Bear* (1976) and Caroline Feller Bauer's *My Mom Travels a Lot* (1981) she won the Christopher Award, a prize created to promote Judeo-Christian traditions.

[*See also* Illustrations; Nonfiction; *and* Picture Books.]

ADRIENNE E. GAVIN

Parker, Richard (1915–1990), English author of realistic, historical, and fantasy novels for middle-grade readers. A father of five and a longtime schoolteacher, Parker often based his stories on the experiences of his children and his students. His family's move to Australia was fictionalized in *New Home South*, which was published in the United States as *Voyage to Tasmania* (1961), and their later home at Britain's Herne Bay was memorialized in *Private Beach* (1964). *He Is Your Brother* (1974) was inspired by an autistic student who joined Parker's class. He was equally adept at realistic stories (*Second-Hand Family*, 1965, recounts the experiences of a neglected foster child), fantasies (in *M for Mischief*, 1965, siblings use a magic cookbook to humorous effect), and historical adventures concerning 9th-century Anglo-Saxons and 19th-century English smugglers. Although he never won major literary awards, Parker was a dependably solid writer whose work capably crossed a wide spectrum of genres.

PETER D. SIERUTA

Parker, Robert Andrew (1927–), American illustrator and painter notable in the gallery world. Parker was born in Virginia, was educated at the Art Institute of Chicago, and has been employed as a teacher at the Parsons School and the Rhode Island School of Design. His work is in many permanent collections (including those of the Museum of Modern Art and the Whitney Museum). Parker's numerous book assignments include *Pop Corn and Ma Goodness* (1972), a Caldecott Honor book; *Oliver Hyde's Dishcloth Concert* (1977); *The Magic Wings: A Tale from China* (1983); and *The Woman Who Fell from the Sky: The Iroquois Story of Creation* (1993). His work combines a seemingly tentative, nervous line with colors that animate the surface, simulate light and shadow, and reinforce the forms defined by the line. It is a loose, poetic style, both sketchy and vibrant, and used for sensitive portraits as well as a full range of moods in landscapes and seascapes.

DONNARAE MACCANN

Parkinson, Siobhan (1954–), Irish author. She lives in Dublin and is coeditor of *Bookbird* and former editor of *Inís: The Magazine of Children's Books Ireland*. A prolific writer of fiction for young adults, she has also published *The Thirteenth Room* (2003), an adult novel. *All Shining in the Spring: The Story of a Baby Who Died* (nonfiction, 1994), *The Dublin Adventure*, and *The Country Adventure* (1992) are for younger readers. Parkinson's narrative experiments are daring and intelligent. *Sisters . . . No Way!* (1996) comprises diverging accounts of stepsisters' tribulations, arranged back-to-back: the reader may begin with either. *Four Kids, Three Cats, Two Cows, One Witch (Maybe)* (1997) successfully parodies the Blytonesque adventure form, and explores personal identity through tale telling. *The Moon King* (2000) shifts between the fragmented interior monologue of the fragile, isolated Ricky and an omniscient third-person narrative. *The Love Bean* (2002) juxtaposes a contemporary tale of Irish immigrant tensions with an ancient story of invasion, each commenting upon the other. *Call of the Whales* (2000) employs a lyrical adult voice reflecting on coming of age in an Arctic wilderness. *Kathleen the Celtic Knot* (2003) describes, in acute detail, Dublin in 1937. Parkinson combines formal experiment, well-defined character, and assured narration to create accessible, intellectually rewarding fiction that respects children's emotional resources.

[*See also* Ireland *and* Young Adult Literature.]

MARY SHINE THOMPSON

Parks, Van Dyke (1943–), American musician, composer, adapter, and producer. His music has been marked by an unconventional approach and diverse interest in everything from pop music to minstrelsy. While Parks is most widely recognized for his work with popular musicians such as Brian Wilson of the Beach Boys and in scoring movies and commercials, in 1984 he recorded *Jump!*, subsequently creating the "Jump!" trilogy with the illustrator Barry Moser: *Jump!* (1986), *Jump Again!* (1987), and *Jump On Over!* (1989). This series of children's books follows the adventures of Brer (Brother) Rabbit and his neighbors in Briar Patch. Responding to criticism of Joel Chandler Harris's 19th-century rendition of the folk tales, Parks's adaptation omits the heavy dialect and leaves out the controversial figure of Uncle Remus, an older African American man who looks back fondly on Southern plantation life before the Civil War.

LUISA FRONTINO

Parley's Magazine. *Parley's Magazine: For Children and Youth* (1833–1844), an influential American miscellany, was the creation of Samuel Griswold Goodrich, who would later run the more literary *Merry's Museum*. Though Goodrich soon withdrew from *Parley's Magazine*, owing to health problems, he had effectively charted its course. Dr. William Alcott, an experienced educator and editor, succeeded him (1834–1837). *Parley's Magazine* promoted nonsectarian Christian values and the virtues of hard work, self-improvement, honesty, and patriotism. Its fiction, often unsigned and undistinguished, was realistic and down-to-earth, since Goodrich found fantasy, fairy tales, and even nursery rhymes distasteful. There was little humor, and illustrations were often recycled from other periodicals. In 1844 *Parley's* was merged with *Merry's Museum*. One journalistic legacy of *Parley's* was Goodrich's invention of "Peter Parley," a kindly old gentleman whose role was to charm young readers and win their allegiance for the magazine. This effective technique was widely imitated, both in America and in England.

BIBLIOGRAPHY

Marcus, Leonard S. "*Parley's Magazine: For Children and Youth.*" In *Children's Periodicals of the United States*, edited by R. Gordon Kelly, 345–357. Westport, Conn., and London: Greenwood, 1984.

SUSAN R. GANNON

Parnall, Peter (1936–), American illustrator and author from Syracuse, New York. He was educated at Cornell University and the Pratt Institute of Art. Disenchanted with a career in advertising, Parnall shifted to design and illustration in the early 1960s and has since won numerous awards and commendations, including multiple Caldecott Honor awards and *New York Times* citations for best illustrated books for children. He is especially known for his sensitive line drawings of children and animals. In *Annie and the Old One* by Miska Miles (1971), Parnall conveys the relationships between the people and the desert through delicate drawings augmented with touches of brown and gold desert colors. The characters are Navajo, and Parnall sensitively represents their culture and their relationships with each other as Annie comes to terms with her grandmother's impending death. He again draws from his knowledge of nature and Native American cultures for Byrd Baylor's *Hawk, I'm Your Brother* (1976; a Caldecott Honor Book). The drawings of Rudy Soto climbing a mountain to capture a young hawk let readers see the boy's determination to experience "hawkness." When Rudy understands that caging the hawk does not forge the bond he hoped for, Parnall realistically conveys the insights that lead the boy to free the hawk. Parnall's lifelong interest in animals and ecology prompts most of the work he writes and illustrates for children. *Alfalfa Hill* (1975), with its evocative depiction of how the first snow of a New England winter changes the landscape, and *Water Pup* (1993), about a lost puppy adopted into a family of foxes, exemplify how beautifully Parnall combines his love of the natural world with his art and writing.

[*See also* Baylor, Byrd; Ecology and Environment; Illustrations; *and* Native American Children's Literature.]

LINDA BENSON

Parody. The *Oxford English Dictionary* (OED) defines parody as "a burlesque poem or song," literally "beside, in subsidiary relation, mock-, etc. + song, poem"; and it is in this literal sense that parody initially appears in what could be considered the first children's novels: *Alice's Adventures in Wonderland* and *Through the Looking-Glass*. Lewis Carroll's parodic nonsense songs are often thought to be addressed to the knowledgeable adult rather than the child; but, if we understand parody to constitute a "skewed imitation," then it is possible to consider children's novels, in their post-Carroll form, as skewed imitations of adult reality. Thus, following Carroll, E. Nesbit quite consciously parodies the conventions of the didactic domestic novel, most pointedly in *The Would-Be-Goods*. The connection between parody and the children's novel reflects the fact that children's play is itself profoundly parodic. In their study of playground culture, the Opies provide considerable evidence of the transgressive nature of children's play and give a number of examples of how children parody "Mary Had a Little Lamb" (p. 90). More generally, students of children's play have suggested that when young children play, they do not imitate adult behavior but parody it. As Brian Sutton-Smith points out, the phantasmagoric play of young children "is a deconstruction of the world in which they live" (p. 166). Thus we might consider parody not as peripheral to the children's novel but as constituting its very essence.

BIBLIOGRAPHY

Opie, Iona, and Peter Opie. *The Lore and Language of Schoolchildren*. Oxford: Oxford University Press, 1959.

Sutton-Smith, Brian. *The Ambiguity of Play*. Cambridge, Mass.: Harvard University Press, 1997.

JOHN MORGENSTERN

Parœmiologia Anglo-Latina. A collection of proverbs for schoolchildren, compiled by John Clarke (d. 1658) in both English and Latin, *Parœmiologia Anglo-Latina* (1639) was modeled somewhat on Erasmus's *Adages*. Clarke, the headmaster of Lincoln grammar school, states in his preface that he has gathered material "from Erasmus, scholars and friends and over and beyond my own observations of many golden proverbs dropping from vulgar mouths." "Spare the rod and Spoil the child" is Clarke's version of the same sentiment expressed by William Langland's *Piers Plowman* in 1377. We also have "Children are unquestionable concern and dubious comforts!" and "Jack Sprat teaches his grand dame!" There is plenty of practical advice mixed with humor, as in "Bare words are no good bargain," "To forget a wrong is the best revenge," and "The pot calls the pan black-arse!" Even the Benjamin Franklin almanac version of "Early to bed, and early to rise" is to be originally found in *Parœmiologia Anglo-Latina*.

SINDHU MENON

Parrish, Maxfield (1870–1966), American painter and illustrator. Much of Parrish's prolific output—which encompassed murals, illustrations for children's and adult books and magazines, advertisements, posters, and calendars—was permeated with childhood imagery, especially themes from nursery rhymes and fairy tales. An early mural study, *Old King Cole* (1894), gained Parrish a reputation for whimsy and inventiveness, which led to further mural work and to his first cover commission for a national magazine, *Harper's Bazaar*, in 1895. Numerous magazine illustrations followed over the next two decades, among them covers for *Century*, *Scribner's*, *Collier's*, and the *Ladies' Home Journal*. In 1897 Parrish was invited to illustrate L. Frank Baum's first book, *Mother Goose in Prose*. The commercial success of this project resulted in commissions for two of Kenneth Grahame's early works, *Dream Days* (1898) and *The Golden Age* (1899). Parrish went on to illustrate *Poems of Childhood* (1904), *Arabian Nights* (1909), and Nathaniel Hawthorne's *A Wonder Book and Tanglewood Tales* (1910). However, the best known of his illustrated books is the *Knave of Hearts* (1925), which uses humor, spectacular color, and a brilliant intertwining of fantasy and reality to create a precisely rendered, luminous dreamworld. Eager to be associated with his enormous popular appeal, advertisers inundated Parrish with requests for artwork. His advertisements for Ferry's Seed, Swift's Premium Ham, and Jell-O, which featured nursery rhyme characters, and his "girl-on-the-rock" paintings for Edison Mazda became ubiquitous in America. Indeed, Parrish remains the most reproduced artist in history, as works created originally for books, magazines, murals, and advertisements were by the 1920s being replicated in art posters, calendars, and greeting cards. Yet he never compromised the quality of his work. He was a meticulous draftsman and a technical innovator, using his own system of glazes and varnish to create rare effects of light and color. Best remembered for his trademark "Parrish blue," his fairy tale characters, and his romantic landscapes, he helped shape the golden age of American illustration when print was as much a mass medium as television is today.

Parrish's Humpty Dumpty. Illustration by Parrish from *Mother Goose in Prose* by L. Frank Baum (Chicago: Way & Williams,1897), plate facing p. 212. REPRODUCED COURTESY OF THE COTSEN CHILDREN'S LIBRARY, PRINCETON UNIVERSITY LIBRARY

Maxfield Parrish. PRINTS AND PHOTOGRAPHS DIVISION, LIBRARY OF CONGRESS

[*See also* Illustrations; Journals and Periodicals; *and biographies of figures mentioned in this article.*]

BIBLIOGRAPHY

Ludwig, Coy. *Maxfield Parrish.* New York: Watson-Guptill, 1973. Still the best account of Parrish's life and work; also has a good bibliography and a comprehensive listing of his work.

NADIA CRANDALL

Partridge, Francesca (1968–), and **Franck Dubuc** (1966–), an Australian French collaborative pair of author-illustrators. Each studied art in France. Using pastel crayon and collage on a ridged brown-paper background, they have created a quartet of deceptively simple philosophical stories for elementary school children called *In a Field, On a Path, On a Plain,* and *In a Tree* (1998). The recurring theme of these verbally and visually challenging texts is "thinking," with one "questioning" animal character featured in each book. The pair has also illustrated Gretel Killeen's *Cherry Pie* (1998), *What'll We Get For Grandma?* (1999), and Martine Murray's *A Dog Called Bear* (2000).

[*See also* Easy Readers *and* Illustrations.]

SHARON REID

Pascal, Francine (1938–), American series creator and author. After writing award-winning books for young adults such as *Hangin' out with Cici* (1977), *My First Love and Other Disasters* (1979), and *The Hand-Me-Down Kid* (1980), Pascal became famous for her series fiction, including *Sweet Valley High* (starting 1983), *Sweet Valley Twins* (starting 1986), *Sweet Valley University* (starting 1994), and *Fearless* (starting 1999). The Sweet Valley series centers on the beautiful blonde identical twins Elizabeth and Jessica Wakefield and their countless romantic trials and tribulations. Although critics often decry the books for their superficiality, they have been extermely popular with young female readers, as evidenced by more than four hundred titles that have sold more than 120 million copies. In 1985, the Sweet Valley High Super Edition *Perfect Summer* became the first young adult novel to feature on the *New York Times* best-seller list. However, except for a few of the first Sweet Valley High books, Pascal is not the actual author of "her" series; she outlines the plots, and others complete the narratives.

[*See also* Girls' Books and Fiction; Series Books; Sweet Valley High Series; *and* Young Adult Literature.]

JULIE BARTON

Pastoral. In the context of children's literature, "pastoral" is used to denote a genre: books depicting characters, either children or anthropomorphic animals, in autonomous rural settings, in complete harmony with nature, untouched by civilization in the form of government, law, labor, money, or generally adult concerns and anxieties. The pastoral world, also referred to as "felicitous space," is normally liberated from death and sexuality, thus conveying a sense of innocence and primeval happiness—paradise before the Fall. Children's novels frequently identified as pastoral are Spyri's *Heidi* (1881), Potter's *Peter Rabbit* (1902), Grahame's *The Wind in the Willows* (1908), Montgomery's *Anne of Green Gables* (1908), Burnett's *The Secret Garden* (1911), Milne's *Winnie-the-Pooh* (1926), and Ransome's *Swallows and Amazons* (1930). William Empson includes *Alice in Wonderland* in his study of the pastoral, and Jon Stott also discusses such books as Boston's Green Knowe series (1954–1976) and George's *Julie of the Wolves* (1972) as a kind of pastoral. The essence of pastoral literature stems from the creation of a sense of permanent harmony, which in children's literature indicates that childhood is not only a benevolent space but an everlasting one. Some critics view this feature as an inherent characteristic of children's literature. Contemporary children's fiction and especially young adult fiction strongly challenge this attitude.

BIBLIOGRAPHY

Carpenter, Humphrey. *Secret Gardens. The Golden Age of Children's Literature.* London: Unwin Hyman, 1985.

Empson, William. *Some Versions of Pastoral. A Study of the Pastoral Form in Literature.* London: Chatto and Windus, 1968.

Evans, Gwyneth. "The Girl in the Garden: Variations in a Feminine Pastoral." *Children's Literature Association Quarterly* 19, no. 1 (1984): 20–24.

Francis, Elizabeth. "Feminist Versions of Pastoral." *Children's Literature Association Quarterly* 7, no. 4 (1982): 7–9.

Hunt, Peter. "Arthur Ransome's Swallows and Amazons: Escape to a Lost Paradise." In *Touchstones: Reflections of the Best in Children's Literature,* edited by Perry Nodelman, Vol. 1. West Lafayette, Ind.: Children's Literature Association, 1985, 221–231

Hunt, Peter. *The Wind in the Willows: A Fragmented Arcadia.* New York: Twayne, 1994.

Inglis, Fred. *The Promise of Happiness. The Value and Meaning in Children's Fiction.* Cambridge: Cambridge University Press, 1981.

Kuznets, Lois. "The Fresh-Air Kids, or Some Contemporary Versions of Pastoral." *Children's Literature* 11 (1983): 156–168.

Nikolajeva, Maria. *From Mythic to Linear: Time in Children's Literature.* Lanham, Md.: Scarecrow, 2000.

Stott, Jon C. "From Here to Eternity: Aspects of Pastoral in the Green Knowe Series." *Children's Literature* 11 (1983): 145–155.

Stott, Jon C. "Jean George's Arctic Pastoral: A Reading of Julie of the Wolves." *Children's Literature* 3 (1974): 131–139.

MARIA NIKOLAJEVA

Patel, Mickey (1941–1994), Indian illustrator, writer, painter, and cartoonist. Patel's illustrations are interpretative and embody a personal vision of the world, vaulting the limits of the text. The humor is a shade too sophisticated for children's books. Patel isolates one central feature of the animal/person and exaggerates it. In Tara Tewari's *Sona's Adventures* (1973) the camel's long neck is exaggeratedly, even grotesquely, elongated. In *Rupa the Elephant* (1974) the elephant is a large gray bulk, but Patel's story infuses her with the gentleness and goodness that characterizes the mammal. Here Patel's pictures evidence a great influence of the bright minimalism of cartoons.

NANDINI NAYAR

Patent, Dorothy Hinshaw (1940–), American writer. Born in Rochester, Minnesota, and raised in Marin County, California, Patent studied biological sciences at Stanford University and received a PhD in zoology from the University of California, Berkeley. In 1964 she married fellow zoologist Greg Patent, with whom she engaged in graduate research in the United States and Italy before settling in Missoula, Montana. A prolific and award-winning author of more than one hundred works for children and young adults, Patent specializes in books about nature, especially animals. Characterized by careful and comprehensive research and enthusiasm for the subject, her books present scientific material about individual species through clear, easily understood explanations. Her first book, *Weasels, Otters, Skunks, and Their Family* (1973), was followed by titles including *Frogs, Toads, Salamanders, and How They Reproduce* (1975), *Plants and Insects Together* (1976), and *Evolution Goes On Everyday* (1977). Many of these early books were illustrated by Matthew Kalmenoff, but in the 1980s Patent began a collaboration with photographer William Muñoz, whose photographs have became integral to many of her books and with whom she often travels while researching her material. Titles with Muñoz's photographs include *A Picture Book of Cows* (1982), *Buffalo: The American Bison Today* (1986), *Flowers for Everyone* (1990), *Nutrition: What's in the Food We Eat* (1992), three Lewis and Clark books (*The Lewis and Clark Trail: Then and Now*, 2002, *Animals on the Trail with Lewis and Clark*, 2002, and *Plants on the Trail with Lewis and Clark*, 2003), and *The Right Dog for the Job: Ira's Path from Service Dog to Guide Dog* (2004). Patent was awarded the 1987 Eva L. Gordon Award by the American Nature Study Society and the 2004 Washington Post Children's Book Guild Award, both for her overall contributions to writing for children.

[*See also* Nonfiction; Photography in Nonfiction for Children; *and* Science Books.]

ADRIENNE E. GAVIN

Paterson, Andrew Barton (1864–1941), Australian balladist. Usually known as "Banjo" Paterson, the former journalist, lawyer, and poet is remembered today for his ballads of Australian bush life. Typically, these show the rural man overcoming natural adversity and difficulties created through the erroneous perceptions of others. Laconic, honest, and possibly naive, the man of the outback epitomizes the necessary qualities for survival and even success. He is contrasted with the people of the city, who are venal, untrustworthy, and deprived. This dichotomy is most clearly seen in "Clancy of the Overflow." Paterson's heroes have come to represent an ideal and a national identity. Women and Aborigines have no part in those poems. His ballads continue to be popular, and are anthologized and published as picture books where the illustrations reinforce a nostalgic and often sentimental view of the Australian outback and its associated mythologies. His popularity today is partly a function of the successful film *The Man from Snowy River* (1982). From the poem of the same name, this is the story of a young man showing courage and horsemanship to earn the respect of his elders. Paterson is also remembered for "Waltzing Matilda," a ballad of a shearer's suicide, which has become the unofficial national song of Australia.

ALISON HALLIDAY

Paterson, Katherine (1932–), American children's writer, winner of the Andersen Medal (1998) and numerous other awards, one of the foremost innovators of the contemporary psychological novel for children. Her most famous, Newbery-winning novel, *Bridge to Terabithia* (1977), was among the first American children's books portraying a child's response to a friend's death. However, it is not about "coping with death," but about the hard work of growing up, told not from the perspective of an omniscient adult, but from that of an inexperienced and vulnerable child. Jess is spiritually underprivileged, and his friendship with Leslie opens a new world for him, literally a magical world that Leslie creates with her imagination. In Terabithia, Jess becomes a glorious knight. Yet in reality he is not ready to leave his dull and confined, but secure, world. Leslie's death leaves him without support, and he goes successively through denial, rage, and reconciliation. On the realistic level, Leslie's death is an inconceivable tragedy. On the symbolic level, Leslie, as Jess's spiritual guide, has served her purpose. Moreover, Jess carries his insights further, as he builds a bridge across the river and invites his little sister to enter Terabithia as the new queen.

Katherine Paterson. At the Library of Congress National Book Festival, 2004.

The other Newbery-winner, *Jacob Have I Loved* (1980), abounds in clichés from classic girl fiction: rivalry between twins, a sense of imprisonment, a romantic infatuation with an older man, liberation through a profession, and the inevitable marriage. However, the novel is truly remarkable because of its exciting tension between the narrating and the experiencing self. The adult Louise is telling the story of her adolescence during World War II. As a character, she lacks the ability to evaluate herself and the people around her. As a narrator, she is highly unreliable; she may omit facts, she may pass wrong judgments, or her memory may fail. In this ambiguity lies the psychological charge of this novel.

The Great Gilly Hopkins (1978) and *Park's Quest* (1988) are two variations on a similar theme, a girl seeking her mother and a boy seeking his father. *The Great Gilly Hopkins* could be an ideal illustration of an "issue novel": a problem child placed in a foster home after a series of earlier failures. Yet all the events are refracted through Gilly's immature mind. Gilly is strong and impudent on the surface, but profoundly insecure deep inside. While Gilly believes she is witty and cunning, and in complete control of the situation, she is in fact gradually getting emotionally dependent on her ugly foster mother, the blind neighbor, and the helpless foster brother. When the ideal image of the absent mother fails, this peculiar trio becomes Gilly's first real family, and the superficially happy ending, in which Gilly finds her biological kin, is deeply ironic.

The protagonist of *Park's Quest* knows that his father was killed in Vietnam, but when Park goes to visit his grandfather, it appears that his mother has concealed from him that he has a half sister, one almost his own age and Vietnamese. Thus the emotional betrayal of the mother proves more important for Park than the physical absence of the father. Likewise James in *Come Sing, Jimmy Jo* (1985) feels betrayed by his mother. Not only has she been a poor mother, cold and emotionally absent, not only has she failed to tell him about his real father, but she is jealous of his success on stage. James is exposed to tangled loyalties, and the ending, with a reunion and reconciliation, is, like that in *The Great Gilly Hopkins*, profoundly ironic, not to say scornful. James has taken a decisive step in renouncing his biological father in favor of his stepfather, and the choice is essential so that James can go further. However, going further means that there is no going back to the illusions of childhood.

Vinnie's father in *Flip-flop Girl* (1994) is dead, and since her little brother has taken the worst damage from it, Vinnie feels neglected. She reacts by having a crush on her schoolteacher and by becoming increasingly destructive. Her self-pity makes her maltreat her brother, alienate herself from her well-wishing mother and grandmother, and have preconceived opinions about the only classmate who tries to be friendly. In all these novels, Paterson chooses to let her narrative voice remain in the background, so that the readers must themselves decide whether Jess has betrayed Leslie, or whether Gilly is as great as she imagines. The delicate balance between confidence in the reader's ability to disengage from characters and enough empathy to involve the reader is one of Paterson's foremost achievements.

Further, although praised as "the ultimate realism," the novels have myths as underlying textual structures, and each character is a reincarnation of the traditional mythical hero. In *Bridge to Terabithia*, Paterson offers Jess and the readers the *Narnia Chronicles* as a matrix for interpretation. Both Narnia and Terabithia are sacred places where the hero is taken to be initiated. Also, other novels can be translated into mythical dimensions, and many hints are given in the texts to assist the reader, for instance, the Parcival legend in *Park's Quest*. It has been noted that Paterson does not offer young readers any hope. Indeed, the novels present disharmonious endings, suggesting that the character has gained something, but lost something else. Here the mythical levels provide a clue. Despite failures, Paterson's characters can go on. They have been dubbed knights in their sacred places. They have drunk from their holy grails. Thus they can continue their life quests.

Paterson's early children's novels are based on her experience of the Orient. Born and raised in China, she also spent four years in Japan, which inspired the historical adventure novels *The Sign of the Chrysanthemum* (1973), *Of Nightingales That Weep* (1974), *The Master Puppeteer* (1975), and *Rebels of the Heavenly Kingdom* (1983). Skillfully plotted, these books do not reach the psychological depth of Paterson's novels in contemporary settings. Later, Paterson turns her attention to her own country's history in *Lyddie* (1991), a piercing story of a young woman's way toward emancipation and social awareness, and *Jip: His Story* (1996), a modern reply to *Uncle Tom's Cabin* that attempts to provide a more accurate picture of slavery. *Preacher's Boy* (1999), also set in the past, adheres to the naughty-boy tradition and lacks the psychological dimension of the two other books. Paterson's vast output also includes picture book texts, retellings of fairy tales, nonfiction, and several collections of critical essays.

[*See also* Historical Fiction; Myths; Realism; *and* Young Adult Literature.]

BIBLIOGRAPHY

Chaston, Joel D. "Flute Solos and Songs That Make You Shatter: Simple Melodies in Jacob Have I Loved and Come Sing, Jimmy Jo." *The Lion and the Unicorn* 16, no. 2 (1992): 215–222.

Chaston, Joel D. "The Other Deaths in Bridge to Terabithia." *Children's Literature Association Quarterly* 16, no. 4 (1991–1992): 238–241.

Chaston, Joel D., and Sarah Smedman, eds. *Bridges for the Young: The Fiction of Katherine Paterson*. Lanham, Md.: Scarecrow, 2001.

Huse, Nancy. "Katherine Paterson's Ultimate Realism." *Children's Literature Association Quarterly* 9, no. 3 (1984): 99–101.

McGavran, James Holt Jr. "Bathrobes and Bibles, Waves and Words in Katherine Paterson's Jacob Have I Loved." *Children's Literature in Education* 17, no. 1 (1986): 3–16

Nikolajeva, Maria. "The Child as Self-Deceiver: Narrative Strategies in Katherine Paterson's and Patricia MacLachlan's Novels." *Papers* 7, no. 1 (1997): 5–15.

Powers, Douglas. "Of Time, Place, and Person: The Great Gilly Hopkins and Problems of Story for Adopted Children." *Children's Literature in Education* 15, no. 4 (1984): 211–219.

Schmidt, Gary D. *Katherine Paterson*. New York: Twayne, 1994.

Smedman, Sarah. "'A Good Oyster': Story and Meaning in Jacob Have I Loved." *Children's Literature in Education* 14, no. 3 (1983): 180–187.

Smith, Karen Patricia. "Literary Pilgrimages to the Gates of Excellence." *Bookbird* 36, no. 3 (1998): 6–10.

Westwater, Martha. "Abjection in the Novels of Katherine Paterson." In *Giant Despair Meets Hopeful: Kristevan Readings in Adolescent Fiction*, 65–90. Edmonton, Canada: University of Alberta Press, 2000.

Maria Nikolajeva

Paths of Learning Strewed with Flowers, The, or English Grammar Illustrated. *The Paths of Learning Strewed with Flowers* was published by Harris and Son in 1820. The preface to this sixteen-page book explains that its purpose is "to obviate the reluctance children evince to the irksome and insipid task of learning the names and meaning of the component parts of grammar." Elegant hand-colored copper engravings illustrate the brief and simple explanations of vowels, articles, nouns, adjectives, pronouns, verbs, participles, adverbs, prepositions, and interjections. Examples of interjections are given as "ah! alas! O! la! fie! hush! behold!" The text is accompanied by a scene of a seashore with a sinking boat in the distance, whose passenger shouts "alas!" while a little girl on land calls "Ah! my Brother" as a young midshipman advances toward her bearing a parrot who exclaims "O dear!" John Marshall produced a rival publication in 1822 with the title *The Path of Learning Strewed with Roses*. Iona and Peter Opie reproduced the Harris *Path* in *A Nursery Companion* (1980).

[*See also* Books of Instruction *and biographies of figures mentioned in this article.*]

Gillian Avery

Patten, Brian (1946–), British poet and fiction writer. Patten was born and educated in Liverpool, England. At an early age, with Roger McGough and Adrian Henri, he made an impact with the Mersey Sound, a loosely organized group concentrating initially on performance poetry. Patten is a prolific and versatile writer. Although best known as a poet, he has written a number of fiction books for children, including *Mr. Moon's Last Case* (1975), which won acclaim both in Britain and the United States, and *Grizzelda Frizzle and Other Stories* (1992). He has edited two anthologies of poems for children: *The Puffin Book of 20th Century Children's Verse* (1991) and *The Puffin Book of Utterly Brilliant Poetry* (1998). His collections of his own poetry for children include *Gargling with Jelly* (1988) and *Juggling with Gerbils*

(2000). Patten's wordplay and droll humor are typically Liverpudlian. He has contributed consistently and with distinction to poetry for children for more than three decades.

GEOFFREY FENWICK

Paul, Korky (1951–), illustrator. Paul was born Hamish Vigne Christie in Harare, Rhodesia (now Zimbabwe), and in the early 2000s was based in Britain. He studied at the Durban School of Art and subsequently worked in advertising and later studied film animation. Perhaps this background is responsible for the humor, energy, and immediacy that characterize his work. He plans his books meticulously, likening the process to creating a film set, and detailed settings are an essential part of Paul's books. For instance, Winnie's mansion in his series *Winnie the Witch* (with text by Valerie Thomas) has a ramshackle look and is full of extraordinary contraptions.

Originality as well as humor is a hallmark of Paul's work, epitomized in *Captain Teachum's Buried Treasure* (1989; text by Peter Carter), in which a rascally pirate is revealed to be rather forgetful. Paul's collaboration with Robin Tzannes has resulted in a number of books, including *Mookie Goes Fishing* (1994). Paul has also collaborated with Jonathan Long, John Agard, and Michael Rosen.

Paul has produced pop-up books, and some of his titles have been adapted for CD-ROM. His scratchy black lines give boldness and expression to the bodies and faces of his characters, implying movement. Paul draws with dip pen and ink, coloring in with watercolors, and uses computers to do his own layout and typography.

VALERIE COGHLAN

Paul Bunyan. A fictitious character in American tall tales, Paul Bunyan was the greatest lumberjack that ever lived. Bunyan's legend reportedly began as local campfire anecdotes in the mid-1800s, which James MacGillivray drew upon when he first penned the legendary tales of Bunyan in "The Round River Drive" (1910); the oversized lumberjack subsequently garnered most of his fame through lumber company advertising pamphlets that expanded his legend. Bunyan quickly became a national legend, and with his size and strength cleared trees throughout the northern U.S. frontier. Helping Bunyan was Babe, the blue ox, his giant pet from the Blue Snow. Other minor members of Bunyan's camp are Johnny Inkslinger, the famous bookkeeper who invented the pen, Big Ole, Sourdough Sam, and the Seven Axemen. Some of their exploits include digging the Great Lakes, battling giant mosquitoes, building the Rockies, surviving the year of two winters, and gouging out the Grand Canyon.

[*See also* Legends *and* Tall Tales.]

BIBLIOGRAPHY

Hoffman, Daniel. *Paul Bunyan: Last of the Frontier Demigods*. East Lansing: Michigan State University Press, 1999.

CATHLENA MARTIN

Paulding, James Kirke (1778–1860), writer and collaborator with Washington Irving, and the earliest American author of fairy stories. *A Christmas Gift from Fairyland* (1838), which purported to be by "Sampson Fairlawn of Chicago," was one of the most beautifully illustrated books of its time (the anonymous artist was John G. Chapman). The book is prefaced by a frame story relating how Mr. Simeon Starkweather, a hunter, one morning finds fairies in his trap. They fly away, leaving a roll of birch bark on which the four ensuing tales are inscribed. All four tales reflect Paulding's passionately felt views on the importance of imagination and the unique freedom of the New World. The most interesting is "The Nameless Old Woman," with its setting of New Amsterdam and Connecticut, where the Old Woman travels to be turned into a witch so that she can plague her avaricious and surly neighbor. Saint Nicholas then arrives to sort out their dispute and restore harmony. The story includes adventures with Native Americans and an exuberant account of witches' revels.

[*See also* Fairy Tales and Folk Tales *and* Irving, Washington.]

GILLIAN AVERY

Paulsen, Gary (1939–), one of the most prolific and popular American authors of young adult fiction and nonfiction. Three-time Newbery Honor winner, for *Dogsong* (1985), *Hatchet* (1987), and *The Winter Room* (1989), as well as the 1997 recipient of the American Library Association's Margaret A. Edwards Award for lifetime achievement in writing books for teens, Paulsen was born in Minneapolis, Minnesota, to alcoholic parents and had a miserable childhood. The son of an army officer, Paulsen moved so much that he disliked and performed poorly in school. Between 1946 and 1949 he lived in the Philippines, roaming the streets unsupervised. In his teens, his parents sent him to live with his grandmother and several aunts, which provided the stability

Gary Paulsen.

he lacked. During this time a librarian offered him a library card, and he discovered a love of books, devouring everything offered him.

After barely graduating from high school, he supported himself as a trapper and attended college. When he flunked out after two years, he joined the army, serving from 1959 to 1962. He fell into writing when working as a field engineer. Composing a fictional résumé, Paulsen got a job as an associate editor for a men's magazine in Hollywood. Since the appearance of his first book, *The Special War*, in 1966, he has published more than 175 books and more than 200 articles and short stories for both children and adults. The theme of survival surfaces in many of his books—be it a protagonist's survival of slavery, survival of dysfunctional family situations, or literal survival in the wilderness. *Hatchet*, for instance, tells the story of thirteen-year-old Brian Robeson, whose plane crashes in the Canadian wilderness on his way to visit his father. With only the clothes he is wearing and a hatchet his mother gave him, Brian lives by trial and error. Contending with adverse weather conditions, aggressive animals, and his own ignorance about the outdoors, Brian achieves a self-sufficiency that changes his worldview. Paulsen's trademark is his sensitive and introspective portrayal of adolescent protagonists—usually male—who transform while learning to respect and appreciate the natural world.

As a result of having run the Iditarod, the 1,180-mile Alaskan dogsled race, twice, Paulsen wrote *Dogsong*, a fictional story of an Inuit boy's coming of age as he learns to run sled dogs; *Woodsong* (1990), an autobiographical account of the Iditarod for young adults; and *Winterdance: The Fine Madness of Running the Iditarod* (1994) for adults. Paulsen also writes historical fiction, such as his slavery novels *Nightjohn* (1993) and its sequel *Sarny, a Life Remembered* (1997). True to Paulsen's style, these works deal with conflict with uncompromising frankness. In *Nightjohn*, the title character loses two toes to the axe of the slave master for teaching the protagonist to read.

[*See also* Adventure Books; Historical Fiction; *and* Young Adult Literature.]

BIBLIOGRAPHY

Salvner, Gary M. *Presenting Gary Paulsen*. New York: Twayne, 1996.

MICHELLE H. MARTIN

Pausacker, Jenny (1948–), author born in Adelaide, South Australia. She graduated with a PhD in children's literature from Flinders University, Melbourne, in 1981. A versatile writer for children, young adults, and adults, she has published works covering a range of genres: picture book, fantasy, realist fiction, anthology, crime, horror, historical fiction, and romance. Fantasies for younger readers include the humorous *Fast Forward* (1989) and the medieval adventure *The Perfect Princess* (2003). *Can You Keep a Secret?* (1989), set in Melbourne in the 1930s, provides a vivid social history of the Depression years. *What Are Ya?* (1984), *Mr. Enigmatic* (1994), and *Hide and Seek* (1996), an anthology of gay literature, challenge conventional writing on gay and lesbian sexuality. Young adult series fiction includes *Home Grrrls* (1998) and *The Blake Mysteries* (1998–1999). The *Central Secondary College* quartet, comprising *What Are Ya?*, *Mr. Enigmatic*, *Getting Somewhere* (1995), and *Sundogs* (2001), follows the lives of the characters in their final year of schooling at a fictional Melbourne high school. *Dancing on Knives* (2004) deals with many relationship and personal issues relevant to teenagers. Some of Pausacker's teenage and adult romances are published under various pseudonyms: Jaye Francis, Jade Forrester, Mary Forrest, and Rosa Tomaselli.

[*See also* Australia; Gay and Lesbian Literature for Children; Historical Fiction; *and* Young Adult Literature.]

KERRY MALLAN

Pausewang, Gudrun (1928–), one of Germany's most prolific and socially committed writers, whose work for young people is driven by a didactic urge arising from her childhood in the Third Reich. Pausewang's parents were determined to lead an "alternative" existence and brought up their six children on a smallholding in a German-speaking area of Czechoslovakia known at the time as the Sudetenland. At the end of World War II, the family was forced to leave Czechoslovakia, a period during which Pausewang was rapidly disabused of the belief she had shared with her adored father in the values of the Third Reich. After spending sixteen years in South America, Pausewang began to write a series of autobiographical texts that tread a cautious line between descriptions of her family's loss and suffering and historical contextualization through narrative commentary. Pausewang's reckoning with the past and acknowledgment of German guilt reach a climax in *The Final Journey* (1992; Engl. 1996), a fictional account of the last train journey of a young Jewish girl to the extermination camp at Auschwitz. It was indeed a courageous act for a German to attempt to address the fate of German Jews in a book that details all aspects of the degradation of the victims and the casual cruelty of German guards.

Pausewang is also known in the English-speaking world as the author of the two dystopian novels *The Last Children* (1983; Engl. 1988, also as *The Last Children of Schevenborn*) and *Fall-out* (1987; Engl. 1994), which depict the aftermath of a nuclear war and the collapse of a nuclear power plant, respectively. Both include searing scenes of injury and suffering. Pausewang's uncompromising approach to her subject matter and her young readers stems from her belief that children's literature should confront political, social, and environmental issues, in the hope that the young will become actively engaged in protecting their own futures.

[*See also* Germany *and* Holocaust Literature for Children.]

BIBLIOGRAPHY

Tebbutt, Susan. *Gudrun Pausewang in Context*. Frankfurt, Germany: Peter Lang, 1994.

Gillian Lathey

Pavey, Peter (1948–), Australian illustrator. Pavey was born in Melbourne and studied graphic design at Swinburne Institute of Technology. He illustrated Olaf Ruhen's *The Day of the Diprotodon* (1976) but is best known for his three books: *One Dragon's Dream* (1979), an award-winning counting book with a narrative; *I'm Taggerty Toad* (1980), about a boastful toad who gets his "come-uppance"; and *Battles in the Bath* (1983) where a child's bath toys take on a life of their own. He has also published *Is Anyone Hungry?* (1987). His works include fantasy, anthropomorphic animals, elements of the absurd, and humor. He uses cross-hatching in the earlier books to enhance visual depth and texture.

Margot Hillel

Paz, Marcela (1902–1985), writer from Santiago, Chile. Paz, whose real name was Esther Huneeus, was made famous by her *Papelucho* stories. For twenty-five years Paz was the secretary of the Society of Saint Cecilia, and in 1964 she became a founding member of the International Board on Books for Young People (IBBY), serving as its director until 1967. Paz gained international recognition in 1947 with the introduction of her novels featuring Papelucho, a nine-year-old schoolboy. In these stories (which have been translated into several languages) the protagonist is transformed into a number of characters, such as a doctor, a hippy, a historian, and a detective (for instance, *Papelucho Historiador*, 1955, and *Papelucho Detective*, 1956). Paz was the founder and director of the magazine *Pandilla* from the publishing house Zig Zag, and she edited the children's page in *La Nación*, Chile's flagship newspaper. In 1982 she won the Chilean National Literature Prize.

[*See also* IBBY; Latino and Latina American Literature; *and* South America, Spanish-Speaking.]

Genny Ballard

Peacock "At Home," The. *The Peacock "At Home"* (1807) is a sequel by Catherine Ann Dorset (1750–1817) to William Roscoe's poem *Butterfly's Ball and Grasshopper's Feast* (1806), both runaway best sellers published by John Harris. Dorset mixed high and low diction with accurate ornithological detail in fast-moving anapests. The reviewer in the prestigious *Gentleman's Magazine* thought it superior to the original and praised *Peacock* for its elegance and sly satire on the great, in which animal characters mock the affectations and pretensions of the society types. Driven to distraction by the success of the insects' entertainment, the peacock decides to host an exclusive affair on Valentine's Day that will establish the birds as leaders of the fashionable world. Those birds unable to attend the event offer amusing excuses appropriate to each one's character—the turkey must nurse her ailing brood, the solitary woodcock hates social crushes, and so on. The peacock receives his distinguished guests (many in finery run up by the tailorbird) and the evening's entertainments begin with a splendid concert by the songbirds, followed by a dance. Distinguished elderly birds and those past their prime play cards, gossip, and intrigue until the luxurious supper is served, with the razorbill carving the barbecued mouse and the spoonbill ladling out the soup. The guests chirp until dawn, when the lark's call and cock's crow signal the party's end. Dorset revised the poem in 1809 and added footnotes about the various species of birds mentioned in the text. It was reissued with new color illustrations in Harris's *Cabinet* in the 1820s and remained in print until the 1840s. *Peacock* inspired more than twenty imitations within a few years of its publication, including Ann Taylor's *The Wedding among the Flowers*, Mary Cockle's *Fishes Grand Gala* and *The Elephant's Ball and Grand Fete Champetre*, as well as numerous Victorian toy books such as *Miss Mouser's Tea Party* and *Master Mousie's Supper Party*.

[*See also* Animal Stories; Harris, John; Poetry; Roscoe, William; Taylor, Ann, and Jane Taylor; *and* Toy Books.]

BIBLIOGRAPHY

Ruwe, Donelle. "Satirical Birds and Natural Bugs: J. Harris' Chapbooks and the Aesthetic of Children's Literature." In *The Satiric Eye: Forms of Satire in the Romantic Period*, edited by Steven E. Jones, 115–137. London: Palgrave/Macmillan, 2003.

ANDREA IMMEL

Mervyn Peake. Front cover illustration by Peake for *Ride a Cock-Horse* (London: Chatto & Windus, 1940). REPRODUCED COURTESY OF THE COTSEN CHILDREN'S LIBRARY, PRINCETON UNIVERSITY LIBRARY

Peake, Mervyn (1911–1968), British novelist, poet, playwright, theatrical designer, artist, and illustrator of books for adults and children. Born in revolutionary China to missionary parents, Mervyn Laurence Peake drew on memories of his colorful boyhood in his work. His family returned in 1923 to England, where Peake studied at the Royal Academy Schools from 1929 to 1932, winning the Arthur Hacker Prize and exhibiting at the Royal Academy in 1931. In 1933 he joined an artist's colony on Sark, the Channel Island that moved his imagination and featured in his comic novel *Mr. Pye* (1953). Returning to England in 1935, Peake taught at Westminster School of Art, where he met and married his student Maeve Gilmore. She tirelessly promoted Peake's creations after his death, as exemplified by her eclectic selection of his work, *Peake's Progress* (1978). Peake's contribution to children's literature is significant, and his achievements as an illustrator—*Ride a Cock-Horse and Other Nursery Rhymes* (1940), *The Hunting of the Snark* (1941), *Alice's Adventures in Wonderland and Through the Looking-Glass* (1946), the Grimms' *Household Tales* (1946), and *The Swiss Family Robinson* (1949)—are widely recognized. His deft line drawings for *Treasure Island* (1949) masterfully capture the narrator's ambivalent response to Long John Silver and suggest an affinity with travel adventures common to Peake's own writing for children. His first publication was a children's picture book, *Captain Slaughterboard Drops Anchor* (1939), an absurd piratical adventure clearly influenced by Ballantyne and Stevenson. *Letters from a Lost Uncle* (1948) is a conceptually sophisticated children's book, forming a collection of letters from an eccentric uncle to his unknown nephew. The letters, stained with ink and food, are "pasted" over Peake's powerful sketches and provide a comic, metafictive commentary to the uncle's outlandish search for the mysterious White Lion.

Peake is probably best known for the grotesque and darkly humorous Gormenghast trilogy—*Titus Groan* (1946), *Gormenghast* (1950), and *Titus Alone* (1959)—charting the attempts of Titus, Seventy-Seventh Earl of Groan, to escape the confines of his crumbling inheritance of futile ceremony and corruption. Though the series was published for adults, Titus's progress to maturation has clear relevance for adolescent readers. Indeed, *Boy in Darkness* (1956), a Gormenghast spinoff, was later published as a children's book (1996). In this macabre novella, Titus flees Gormenghast only to be captured by the gruesome Goat and Hyena on behalf of the White Lamb, a malign deity that feeds on human souls. Peake's theological stance is not explicit here, but, along with the spiritual climax of *Letters from a Lost Uncle*, it contributes to the theological discourse of children's literature advanced by writers such as C. S. Lewis and Philip Pullman.

Peake was also a master of nonsense poetry, a form suited to his exaggerated illustrative style. Published in full color, *Rhymes Without Reason* (1944) is by turns farcical and bathetic, earning Peake a rightful place in the tradition associated with Lewis Carroll and Edward Lear. His recognition of the playful relationship between words and pictures is also evident in *Figures of Speech* (1954), reissued for children in 2003.

BIBLIOGRAPHY

Gardiner-Scott, T. J. *Mervyn Peake: The Evolution of a Dark Romantic*. New York: Peter Lang, 1989.

Gilmore, M. *A World Away: A Memoir of Mervyn Peake*. London: Gollancz, 1970.

Yorke, M. *Mervyn Peake: My Eyes Mint Gold—A Life*. London: John Murray, 2000.

LISA SAINSBURY

Peanuts. *See* Schulz, Charles M.

Pearce, Philippa (1920–), British children's writer. Before starting on a literary career, Pearce worked for BBC educational programs, where she wrote radio adaptations of literary texts, and for book publishers. Her first children's book, *Minnow on the Say* (1955), based on her childhood memories, is a somewhat conventional treasure-seeking adventure in an everyday English environment. However, her next children's novel, *Tom's Midnight Garden* (1958), won her the Carnegie Medal and world fame.

Pearce's works for children are diverse in form and themes. *A Dog So Small* (1962) portrays a child who copes with loneliness by inventing for a companion "a dog so small" that you can only see it with your eyes shut. *Mrs. Cockle's Cat* (1960), first published as a picture book and developed into a longer story, is a nonsensical animal tale. *The Squirrel Wife* (1971) presents an original retelling of the well-known fairy tale about a wonderful spouse. *The Battle of Bubble and Squeak* (1985) is a nice domestic story involving two pets and the children's struggle to be allowed to keep them. The psychological novel *The Way to Sattin Shore* (1985) is focused on child/parent conflict and a young girl's investigation of her father's mysterious death. While plots may not be Pearce's forte in any of these books, she nevertheless creates engaging portraits of children and adults. Pearce has also published several collections of short stories for children, for instance *The Shadow-Cage and Other Tales of the Supernatural* (1977) and *Who's Afraid? and Other Strange Stories* (1986).

Pearce's unsurpassed masterpiece is, however, *Tom's Midnight Garden* (1958), a time-shift fantasy universally acknowledged as one of the best novels in this genre. It features a young boy, Tom, who is sent away to stay with boring relatives in a house without a garden in which to play. At night, Tom discovers that there is after all a garden, but he does not initially realize that the garden exists in a different dimension—in fact, in a different time. He befriends Hatty, an orphan girl from the past, and experiences a few weeks of complete bliss, visiting her every night. The novel is preoccupied with the idea of time. The grandfather clock in the house, with the adequate inscription "Time No Longer" (Revelation 10:1–6), has an ambivalent function: its measurable time takes Tom closer to his departure home, away from the garden and Hatty, while in the magical time, it is his passageway to the garden. The most marvelous example of the time paradox is Tom and Hatty skating on the same pair of skates: Hatty hid them in the house in her time, Tom finds them in his time and is able to take them with him into Hatty's time where they already exist. Yet Tom does not seem to notice that Hatty is growing up, and the realization comes as a shock. An even greater shock when Tom meets Hatty as an old woman in his own time.

Unlike most earlier time-travel novels for children with their educational and entertaining tone, *Tom's Midnight Garden* carries a strong psychological charge, as the protagonist's involvement with the past significantly affects his life. The novel explores the tension between Tom's desire to stay forever in the childhood paradise of the garden and his acknowledgment of the necessity to grow up and return to real life. However, from the aged Hatty's account of the events in the last chapter, it also turns out to be a tragic story of an old woman who knows from experience that time is irreversible. The garden, which Tom is able to enter during the magical thirteenth hour of the night, exists in Hatty's memory time, evoked by Hatty's nostalgic memories of her happy, albeit lonely, childhood. It is a paradise where there is always summer, since memory is selective. The garden symbolizes irretrievably lost childhood and offers the child merely a temporal retreat. In the garden, both protagonists step out of their normal time into timelessness: Hatty by returning to her childhood and becoming a little girl again, Tom by going into the past. Yet, after having met the old Hatty, Tom longs to go home. He has escaped from the temptation of the garden and is psychologically prepared to grow up.

[*See also* Fantasy.]

BIBLIOGRAPHY

Jones, Raymond E. "Philippa Pearce's *Tom's Midnight Garden:* Finding and Losing Eden." In *Touchstones: Reflections of the Best in Children's Literature*, edited by Perry Nodelman, vol. 1, 212–221. West Lafayette, Ind.: Children's Literature Association, 1985.

Nikolajeva, Maria. "Midnight Gardens, Magic Wells." In *From Mythic to Linear: Time in Children's Literature*, 103–113. Lanham, Md.: Scarecrow, 2000.

Philip, Neil. "'Tom's Midnight Garden' and the Vision of Eden." *Signal* 37 (1982): 21–25.

Scott, Carole. "A Century of Dislocated Time: Time Travel, Magic, and the Search for Self." *Papers* 6, no. 2 (1996): 14–20.

MARIA NIKOLAJEVA

Peare, Catherine Owens (1911–), American biographer. A graduate of New Jersey State Teachers College, Peare worked as a stockbroker until 1951. As a freelance writer, she first chose to focus on *Albert Einstein* (1949), *Mahatma Gandhi* (1950), and *Mary McLeod Bethune* (1951), selecting each individual as an outstanding representative of his or her race and nation. Peare then trained her gaze on *Stephen Foster* (1952), *Mark Twain* (1954), *Jules Verne* (1956), and other luminaries in the arts. She was also intrigued by the lives of Presidents *Franklin Delano Roosevelt* (1962), *Woodrow Wilson* (1963), and *Herbert Hoover* (1965), and statesmen such as *William Penn* (1958). Respected as a thorough researcher, Peare traveled extensively and prided herself on her firsthand knowledge of her subjects' connections with a particular region. She won two regional Children's Choice awards for *The Helen Keller Story* (1959) and a Boys Club of America Medal for *Mahatma Gandhi*. Her popularity declined, however, after the 1960s.

[*See also* Biography.]

PEGGY LIN DUTHIE

Pearson, Kit (1947–), Canadian author born in Edmonton, Alberta, and educated at the University of Alberta. She received an MLS from the University of British Columbia and an MA from the Simmons College, Boston, Center for the Study of Children's Literature. Pearson worked as a children's librarian and as a reviewer and teacher of juvenile literature. Her first novel, *The Daring Game* (1986), describes the friendship between Eliza and her dormmate Helen, who suggests a game daring Eliza to break school rules. Pearson's second novel, *A Handful of Time* (1987), depicts the relationship of mother and daughter, using time travel. Her first of the *Guests of War* trilogy, *The Sky Is Falling* (1989), concerns British children evacuated to Canada during World War II. Ten-year-old Norah and her five-year-old brother Gavin have to overcome homesickness and find their place in a different culture. Its sequels are *Looking at the Moon* (1991) and *The Lights Go On Again* (1993). In the latter, Gavin, now ten years old, has to decide which country he should belong to. *Awake and Dreaming* (1996) describes nine-year-old Theo, who dreams of the ideal family and secure life that her irresponsible mother cannot afford. Pearson frequently refers to classic children's books in her works; such references reflect her belief in the power of stories and imagination. Her characters, often displaced and isolated, not only receive solace from those books but also try to cope with their difficulties in the real world. Pearson has won many awards, including the Canadian Library Association's Book of the Year for Children for *A Handful of Time* and *The Sky is Falling*, the Geoffrey Bilson Award for Historical Fiction for Young People for *The Lights Go On Again*, and the Governor General's Award and the Ruth Schwartz Award for *Awake and Dreaming*.

[*See also* Historical Fiction *and* Young Adult Literature.]

HIROKO MATSUSHITA

Peck, George Wilbur (1840–1915), American journalist and politician. Born in New York, he was brought to Wisconsin at the age of three and stayed the rest of his life. His reputation as a popular comic writer swept him into politics, and he became mayor of Milwaukee in 1890 and governor of Wisconsin in 1891. His accounts of the crude jokes played on his father by a hostile adolescent first appeared in *The Sun*, a Wisconsin paper that Peck himself had founded, and were collected in *Peck's Bad Boy and His Pa* (1883) and in *Mirth for the Million* (1883), where they appeared "with other gems of wit, humor, sarcasm and pathos."

Compared to Thomas Bailey Aldrich's "bad boy," Peck's is malevolent, an ingenious deviser of tricks such as sending his parents to church with cheese so strong that the congregation thinks there is an infiltration of sewage gas. Every chapter describes a physical humiliation inflicted on Pa. "Of course all boys are not full of tricks, but the best of them are. That is, those who are the readiest to play innocent jokes . . . are the most apt to turn out to be first-class business men." There were several sequels, where the bad boy can be seen variously abroad, with a circus, with cowboys, and finally (c. 1908) in an airship.

[*See also* Aldrich, Thomas Bailey; Boys' Books and Fiction; *and* Humor.]

GILLIAN AVERY

Peck, Richard (1934–), American author of fiction, especially for young adults. Peck was born in Decatur, Illinois, attended the University of Exeter in England from 1954 to 1955, and received a BA from DePauw University in 1956 and an MA from Southern Illinois University in 1959. Peck came to writing children's books through his first career as a high school English teacher. He left teaching in 1971 and, at the age of forty-seven, began writing for young adults. He has since published more than thirty books addressed to this audience, and he is considered one of the founders of young adult literature. A novelist, poet, essayist, and short-story writer, Peck moves beyond the problem novel to center his stories on characters who must trust themselves and must learn to think and to act as independent individuals. In 1972, Peck published his first book, the realistic novel *Don't Look and It Won't Hurt*, about a teenage girl faced with the challenges of divorce, an embittered mother, and a pregnant sister. Other realistic novels include *Father Figure* (1978), about a fatherless boy who raises his brother, *Are You in the House Alone?* (1976; an ALA Best Book), about a girl being stalked, and *Remembering the Good Times* (1985; ALA Notable and Best Book), a tough look at suicide. Peck pushes the serious coming-of-age novel to include comedies, such as *Princess Ashley* (1987) and *Teacher's Funeral: A Comedy in Three Parts* (2004); horror stories, such as *Ghosts I Have Been* (1977; a New York Times Outstanding Book of the Year); mysteries, such as *Dreamland Lake* (1973); light fantasy, such as *Lost in Cyberspace* (1997) and *The Great Interactive Dream Machine* (1998); and regional stories, such as *A Long Way from Chicago: A Novel in Stories* (1999; a Newbery Honor book) and *Fair Weather* (2001). Peck uses dialogue in various forms. At times it is sharp, witty, and feisty, as in the 2001 Newbery Award–winning *A Year Down Yonder*; at other times it is eerily true, as in *Close Enough to Touch* (1981); and at yet other times it is historically accurate and resonant, as in *Voices after Midnight* (1989) and The *River between Us* (2003). Recurring characters (such as the telepathic Blossom Culp, who appears in four novels, and Grandma Dowdel and her grandchildren, Joey and Mary Alice) and edgy topics of relevance to young adults keep loyal Richard Peck readers coming back for more. Although major literary recognition eluded Peck until the 1990s, when he received (1990) the Margaret A. Edwards Lifetime Achievement Award and attention from the 1999 and 2001 Newbery committees, Peck has always enjoyed a dedicated base of young adult readers, and reviewers have praised his books. The de Grummond Collection at the University of Southern Mississippi holds Peck's papers.

Richard Peck. At the Library of Congress National Book Festival.

[*See also* Realism *and* Young Adult Literature.]

BIBLIOGRAPHY

Gallo, Donald. *Presenting Richard Peck.* New York: Twayne, 1989.

CATHRYN M. MERCIER

Peck, Robert Newton (1928–), prolific American writer of novels with a rural setting, born in Vermont to a farming family. Although his six siblings did not attend school, Peck did. In his one-room school he met a devoted teacher, Miss Kelly. Some of his works show her impact on him, notably *Soup and Me* (1975), which is dedicated to her. After graduating from college, Peck worked at a wide range of occupations, from lumberjack and paper-mill worker to New York City advertising executive. His first novel, the award-winning *A Day No Pigs Would Die* (1972), established him as a writer for the young. This semiautobiographical novel depicts the harsh life of a family in which the sixteen-year-old son must become the breadwinner after his father falls ill. The depiction of the butchering of a pig is graphic but the result is emotionally touching. The sequel, *A Part of the Sky*, was published in 1994. Another series features two mischievous boys, Rob and his pal Soup. It began with *Soup* (1974), the first of fourteen tales set in 1930s Vermont. This humorous series is considered ideal for reluctant readers. Given its echoes of Tom and Huck, it seems appropriate that the third book, *Soup for President* (1978), received a Mark Twain Award.

[*See also* Young Adult Literature.]

JUNKO NISHIMURA

Pedley, Ethel Charlotte (1859–1898), Australian musician and writer, buried in Waverley, New South Wales. Pedley, the daughter of a homestead family, is remembered for her single book, *Dot and the Kangaroo* (1899), an Australian fairy tale, published posthumously. This work tells the story of a small girl lost in the bush and saved by a kangaroo. Dot is able to understand the animals, and learns about their lives, but is subsequently tried by them for the harm the white settlers have done to the indigenous creatures. On her safe return home, her father vows never again to shoot bush animals. Pedley dedicated her book to "the children of Australia in the hope of enlisting their sympathies for the many beautiful, amiable, and frolicsome creatures of their fair land, whose extinction, through ruthless destruction, is being surely accomplished." An Australian classic, *Dot* was dramatized in 1924, and made into a live action and animated film in 1977.

[*See also* Australia.]

BRIDGET CARRINGTON

Peet, Bill (1915–2002), American author and illustrator whose first career was as an animator for Walt Disney studios. Peet, who was born William Bartlett Peed, loved drawing as a child, and upon leaving high school received a scholarship to the John Herron Art Institute, Indianapolis. He worked first as an artist and then as a story developer on many Disney classics between 1937 and 1964, including *One Hundred and One Dalmatians* (1961) and *The Sword in the Stone* (1963). He decided that he needed more artistic control than allowed at the Disney studios, and resigned in 1964. Publishing his first children's book in 1959, Peet produced more than thirty-five before his death, twelve of which are in verse, such as *Hubert's Hair-Raising Adventure* (1959). He was a Caldecott Medal Honor Book winner for *Bill Peet: An Autobiography* (1989). The stories in Peet's books are fables of everyday life, mostly portrayed by animal characters. Despite his years at Disney, he drew somewhat realistic, as well as humorous, cartoons for his books, excelling at expressive faces that children love. Some plots highlighted typical foibles of childhood, such as bullying in *Big Bad Bruce* (1977), or lack of bravery in *Cowardly Clyde* (1979), while others focused on social issues such as environmental destruction in *Wump World* (1970).

[*See also* Animal Stories; Animated Films; Disney, Walt; *and* Poetry.]

BIBLIOGRAPHY

Fordyce, Rachel. "Bill Peet." In *St. James Guide to Children's Writers*, edited by Tracy Chevalier, 771–772. 3d ed. Chicago and London: St. James, 1989.

CHARLOTTE CUBBAGE

Pef (1939–), French author and illustrator whose real name is Pierre Ferrier. After literary studies, he drew humorous sketches for the press, then worked for twenty years for children's magazines before finally turning to children's books. Whether as writer or illustrator, he never hides his opinions, be they antiracial, antiwar, social, or simply human. His characters, antiheroes for the most part, look at the world with wide-open eyes, satisfying children's endless quest for what is real in life. To this end, he deftly plays with words and uses humor, which is sometimes dark, but always tender. He wrote more than 120 books. The author-illustrator of *Moi, ma grand'mère* (1978; My Grandmother, She Did This and That), *La belle lisse poire du Prince de Motordu* (1980; The Prince of the Twisted Words), *Le monstre poilu* (1984; English trans., *The Hairy Monster*, 1984), *Noël père et fils* (1985; Christmas, Father and Son), *Graine-de-calcaire* (1987; Limestone-Seed), *Vent latéral* (1989; Blowing from the North), *Moi, je m'appelle Adolphe* (1996; My Name Is Adolph), and *Zappe la guerre* (1998; Zapping Wars), he illustrated picture books such as *On lit trop dans ce pays* (2000; Too Much Reading in This Country), *Il faut désobéir* (2002; Disobedience Is Necessary). For Pef, a writer should definitely be part of the social landscape, pushing words, lines, and colors into their rightful place.

Denise Escarpit

Pelgrom, Els (1934–), Dutch author of a many-sided oeuvre, consisting of realistic and fantasy novels. Pelgrom's breakthrough came with *De kinderen van het Achtste Woud* (1977; English trans., *The Winter When Time Was Frozen*, 1980), describing the experiences of an eleven-year-old girl during her evacuation in the last winter of World War II. It has an almost idyllic atmosphere: the child from the city experiences her stay at a farm as a long holiday. But the war is always present in the background, and sometimes it comes grimly close. This book was truly innovating: it was the first book dealing with the German occupation of the Netherlands during the war inspired by childhood memories (although Pelgrom refused to call it "autobiographical").

Pelgrom also attracted much attention with *Kleine Sofie en Lange Wapper* (1984; English trans., *Little Sophie and Lanky Flop*, 1987), which relates the dreams of a little girl who is terminally ill. In those dreams, symbolizing her situation in reality, she performs a play in a cardboard toy theater, together with her dolls, about "What life has to offer." This book, greatly appreciated by the critics, is considered one of the highlights of Dutch children's literature in the 1980s.

Another remarkable book is *De eikelvreters* (The Acorn-Eaters, 1989), consisting of the childhood memories of Pelgrom's Spanish husband, who grew up in very poor circumstances in the first years of the Franco regime, when there was an incredible gap between rich and poor. Not only did the poorest people, living in caves, sometimes feed themselves with acorns—collecting them in the woods of the rich, they even risked their lives. The impressive events are told in a plain style, probably close to way the stories were originally told to the author; this makes it seem as though the protagonist is telling his stories directly to the reader.

[*See also* Historical Fiction; Netherlands; *and* Toy Theaters.]

Anne de Vries

Pellicer López, Carlos (1948–), Mexican artist educated at the National School of Plastic Arts. Pellicer López started illustrating children's books in 1982 and has participated in many exhibitions. As an author and illustrator he has created *Julieta y su caja de colores* (Julieta and Her Colored Pencil Box, 1993), *Juan y sus zapatos* (Juan and His Shoes, 1997), *El cuento de la abuela* (Granny's Tale, 1999), and *El tigre de Naim* (The Tiger of Naim, 2002). His illustration style is childlike and is characterized by strong colors that burst like explosions.

[*See also* Illustrations *and* Mexico.]

Maité Dautant

Pellowski, Anne (1933–), American storyteller and author who traced her family's history in a five-volume series of novels. Born in Pine Creek, Wisconsin, Pellowski spent most of her career working with children and books. Beginning as a children's librarian in Winona, Minnesota, she was an assistant storytelling and group work specialist with the New York Public Library, and served as director of the Information Center on Children's Cultures for UNICEF. She has published several volumes about multicultural storytelling, such as *The Story Vine: A Source Book of Unusual and Easy-to-Tell Stories from Around the World* (1984) and *The Storytelling Handbook: A Young People's Collection of Unusual Tales and Helpful Hints on How to Tell Them* (1995). Pellowski has celebrated her own heritage in a number of books, including *The Nine Crying Dolls: A Traditional Polish Folktale* (1980) and a delightful series of family stories originally called the *Four Farms* series and now known as the *Polish American Girls* series. *Willow Wind Farm: Betsy's Story* (1981), *Stairstep Farm: Anna Rose's Story* (1981), *Winding Valley Farm: Annie's Story* (1982), *First Farm in the Valley: Anna's Story* (1982), and *Betsy's Up-and-Down Year* (1998) feature several generations of Polish American girls growing up on farms and having fun with family and friends from the late 1800s through the 20th century.

[*See also* Historical Fiction; Librarians; *and* Multiculturalism and Children's Books.]

Peter D. Sieruta

Pender, Lydia (1907–), poet who immigrated to Australia from the United Kingdom in 1920. Her first book of verse was *Marbles in My Pocket* (1957), illustrated by Pixie O'Harris, and she later collaborated with the eminent poet Mary Gilmore on *Poems to Read to Young Australians* (1968), illustrated by Jane Gulloch. Two picture books about a small boy, *Barnaby and the Horses* (1961), illustrated by Alie Evers, and reillustrated by Inga Moore in 1980, and *Barnaby and the Rocket* (1972), illustrated by Judith Cowell, have a small boy experiencing the delights of a bonfire night and the rural landscape. In *Sharpur the Carpet Snake* (1967), originally illustrated by Virginia Smith, later by both Allan Stomann (1976) and Tony Oliver (1982), Benjamin Colley's snake escapes in a Sydney market, causing pandemonium. *The Land and the Spirit* (1992), illustrated by Kilmeny Niland, is a verse alphabet.

STELLA LEES AND PAM MACINTYRE

Pène du Bois, William (1916–1993), prolific American author and illustrator who was born in New Jersey but received much of his schooling at the Lycée Hoche in Versailles and the Lycée de Nice. Pène du Bois credits as an early influence his exposure to Jules Verne's novels, and especially to the novels' drawings. Following service in the U.S. Army (1941–1946), he became a founding editor of the *Paris Review*. He is best known for blending fantastic and often humorous narratives with realistic and highly detailed illustrations. This blend creates a tension between the real world and the otherworldly nature of the plot, while at the same time further strengthening his audience's belief in fantasy. In *The Three Policemen* (1938), a boat in the guise of a sea monster allows the artist to design a playful cross section of the vessel after its mutation to a floating hotel (with gymnasium, concert hall, and other luxuries). In *The Squirrel Hotel* (1952, 1979), the artist's detailed renderings of the bee orchestra, the Squirrel Hotel, and the toy shop visually anchor the mysterious nature of the story in the real world. In his picture book *The Forbidden Forest* (1978), two kangaroos and a bulldog are awarded medals of honor for their courageous feats during World War I. The potentially whimsical nature of his plot is undercut by the realistic depictions of the violence of war. *The Alligator Case* (1965) is a more straightforward narrative accompanied by fantastical illustrations. In this more traditional mystery, involving the arrival of a circus and three strangers in a small, sleepy town, Pène du Bois used the repetition of certain phrases and geometrical concepts to establish the credibility of the young detective's story. The colored illustrations, which expand on the actions and settings of various plot points, contain less detail and tend to be more abstract. Further, unlike in *The Squirrel Hotel*, the author-artist keeps this mystery lighter through the amusing narrative and the self-deprecating remarks of the detective.

William Pène Du Bois. Illustration from *Forgotten Forest* (New York: Harper & Row, 1978), p. 15. REPRODUCED COURTESY OF THE COTSEN CHILDREN'S LIBRARY, PRINCETON UNIVERSITY LIBRARY

Pène du Bois also illustrated stories by other authors. His realistic illustrations for Mark Strand's *The Planet of Lost Things* (1982) recall Pène du Bois's own stories and his use of precisely drafted illustrations to render a narrative believable. For Claire Huchet Bishop's novel about children in occupied France, *Twenty and Ten* (1952), Pène du Bois's black-and-white drawings make visible the emotions of the children, hence making the story more immediate to its audience.

Pène du Bois received a Newbery Medal for his gentle satire about greed, *The Twenty-One Balloons* (1947). This novel underscores a common theme in his work, namely, problems surrounding excess, especially the impending threat of sheer chaos. But his tone is playful rather than admonitory. Caldecott Honor Awards were bestowed on *Bear Party* (1951) and *Lion* (1956), and his numerous additional awards included the Child Study Award (1952), several New York Times Best Illustrated Book citations, and the Lewis Carroll Shelf Award.

[*See also* Fantasy; Illustrations; *and* Picture Books.]

DEBRA MITTS-SMITH

Pennac, Daniel (1944–), French author of children's books, adult novels, and nonfiction. Born into a military fam-

Daniel Pennac. © J SASSIER/GALLIMARD

ily, Pennac, born Daniel Pennacchioni, spent his childhood traveling the globe, from his birthplace in Casablanca, Morocco, to stints in Europe, Asia, and Africa. Because his first publication, *Le service militaire au service de qui?* (Whom Does Military Service Serve?, 1973), satirized the army in which his father served, the author chose to disguise his name and has used the pseudonym "Daniel Pennac" since. Among his adult books is the best-selling Malaussene series—comic thrillers featuring a beleaguered book publisher with an offbeat family. Pennac's children's books include *Cabot-Cabouche* (1982; U.S. and U.K. title, *Dog*), in which a canine narrator faces rejection and finds a home. Some critics found the book's tone uneven and the conclusion unconvincing. *L'oeil de loup* (1982; U.S. title, *Eye of the Wolf*, 2002) is an affecting, if surreal story of the relationship between an Alaskan wolf and an orphaned boy. Pennac has also written a series of children's mystery adventures (*Kamo et moi*, 1992; *L'evasion Kamo*, 2004) and *Comme un roman* (English trans., both *Better Than Life* and *Reads Like a Novel*), a 1992 nonfiction volume examining the role of reading in modern life—with a particular emphasis on children and books.

PETER D. SIERUTA

Penny Books. Cheaply printed illustrated books for children published in the latter half of the 19th century and the early years of the 20th century, penny books evolved out of chapbooks and shared their physical format. The books had small trim sizes, no hard covers, and were typically printed on one sheet of paper folded into a single gathering with between 16 and 24 pages—though sometimes they had as many as 32 pages. Penny books, which ranged in quality from crude to charming, derived their name from their humble cost. The new technologies that became available to publishers during the Industrial Revolution—including lithographic printing and the ability to make paper and bind cloth mechanically rather than by hand—drove down production costs considerably. As a result, for the first time it became possible for publishers to offer, on a much larger scale than ever before, mass-produced books that came complete with illustrations. This, in combination with a sharp increase in the demand for juvenile literature and the passing of a compulsory education law in England in 1876 that helped to create a large audience of newly literate children, contributed to an explosion in the publication of inexpensive children's books intended for a mass market. At the beginning of the 19th century, most works of literature written specifically for young readers were by intention didactic and moralistic; their primary purpose was to impart useful information or moral advice. In addition, only the children of rich parents could afford to read at all. Penny books reflected the start of a new age in books for children—an age in which the enjoyment and entertainment of the child audience was as important a consideration as the educational value of what the children read. At the same time, the books' tiny sizes and equally tiny prices put them literally within the reach of their young readers—readers who now came from both poor, working-class households and well-to-do families. In many ways, penny books represented the 19th century's most significant form of popular literature, and they contained fairy tales, folk tales, riddles, stories, songs, jests, and nursery rhymes as often as cautionary tales or religious teachings. British publishers famous for their penny books included James Kendrew, who produced a copious number of these cheap publications. Among his titles were *The History of Whittington and His Cat* (c. 1820) and *The Entertaining Story of Little Red Riding Hood* (published sometime between 1815 and 1841). Other important publishers of penny books included John Marshall and John Golby Rusher, who was responsible for the charming volume *The Book of Beasts for Young Persons* (c. 1820) and *The Interesting Story of Cinderella and Her Glass Slipper* (c. 1814). Penny books should not be confused with "penny dreadfuls" (United Kingdom) or "dime novels" (United States), terms used to describe

Penny Books. Front cover of *The Boy's Miscellany*, London, 7 March 1863. COLLECTION OF JACK ZIPES

similarly economical works of pulp fiction that were aimed at young, working-class audiences and that usually contained lurid tales of horror and adventure.

[*See also* Book Design; Chapbooks; Dime Novel, The; Penny Dreadful; Publishers and Publishing; *and biographies of figures mentioned in this article.*]

MEERA LEE SETHI

Penny Dreadful. The English "penny dreadfuls" surfaced in the early 19th century as a cheap source of printed entertainment, principally to attract the emerging literate working class of major industrial cities such as London or Manchester. They were called "penny dreadfuls" or "penny bloods" because the papers were issued in penny-parts—eight-page folios on cheap paper—sold for a penny per weekly issue. Also, while the content varied from paper to paper, the stories were characterized by sensationalized, even lurid detail designed to arouse basic emotions of horror and disgust, and thus lure readers to purchase more papers. Some stories ran for more than two hundred issues, and their sources were as varied as lightly rewritten gothic stories of the 19th century, with their vampires, werewolves, pirates, and evil monks, or stories of criminals, brigands, and highwaymen taken from historical accounts, actual news stories, or even from the work of established contemporary novelists such as Charles Dickens (without his permission).

Contexts

It can be difficult to define the term "penny dreadful" because critics used it, usually pejoratively, to designate a disparate body of work. The scholar John Springhall interprets this confusion by identifying it as: 1) a generic abusive term for the fiction of the 19th century or 2) the penny-issue novels of the 1830s and 1840s, and 3) their successors, for a juvenile audience, in the boys' papers of 1850s and later Fleet Street publishers. He further asserts that the pre-1850s works should properly be called "penny bloods." Michael Anglo adds that the term also often denoted the contents of the publications. While it is clear that young men of both the middle and working classes read the "dreadfuls" of the earlier 19th century, the term itself was used more widely for the later works because they reached a large juvenile audience and simultaneously came under critical scrutiny for their alleged evil influence on developing youth. It is the later period, from the 1850s through the early 20th century, when the penny dreadful had the most influence on children's literature.

Penny dreadfuls as a publishing phenomenon were made possible by the conjunction of specific social and economic conditions. First, increased levels of literacy among the general population became an economic necessity. Clerks, link boys, messenger boys, and even factory boys and girls needed basic literacy skills and, in creating that literacy, the state also created an audience with little chance to develop discernment. Second, both printing and paper technology had improved in the 19th century to make cheap, disposable, multicopy issues feasible for entrepreneurs with little capital. Third, the papers, like mass-market fiction of the later 20th century, used distribution networks such as newsagents rather than bookstores or lending libraries. Thus they were readily accessible to an audience who had little time to select and enjoy their forms of entertainment while going to and from twelve-hour-per-day jobs. Finally, there was a large population of young people; by midcentury over 40 percent of the population of England and Wales were under the age of twenty-one and ripe for cheap escape from their dreary lives.

Contents

Some of the more famous serials would be recognizable today. The Gothic tales of Horace Walpole and Ann Radcliffe, in the hands of struggling authors, usually from the middle class, became serial fiction, such as James Malcolm Rymer's *Varney the Vampire*, which ran 220 chapters with an astounding body count of murdered young women. Writers also turned to crime history for Dick Turpin, both a central figure and a background character in many stories. The famous publisher Edward Lloyd was possibly responsible for resurrecting an interest in highwaymen when he published *Lives of the Most Notorious Highwaymen* (1836), so that by the 1850s readers had been treated to the exploits of Captain MacHeath, Sixteen String Jack Rann, Tom King, Claude Duval, and even such fantasy females as May Turpin, Starlight Nell, and Bonnie Parker. The urban thief Jack Sheppard also received attention, in *The History of Jack Sheppard* (1869).

Another characteristic of the papers was their profusion of lurid pictures of vampire attacks, murders, holdups, and pitiful female victims, all designed to draw readers to the newsagent's stand. Probably the most famous recurrent villain was not a thief but a notorious murderer, the "Demon barber of Fleet Street," also known as Sweeney Todd, whose dark deeds were lavishly illustrated. The plot originated in an 1825 tale, *Les rues de Paris*, and was replayed as early as *The String of Pearls*, serialized in Lloyd's *The People's Periodical* (1846), but it was reincarnated in many forms, including a stage play by George Dibdin Pitt that was first shown in England in 1847. As late as 1883, a version appeared in *The Boy's Standard*, and it was later produced as a musical in the 21st century. *Spring Heeled Jack* was a penny-dreadful serial in 1838, as well as a play in 1863 and a forty-penny-part serial of that name published in 1867 by Newsagents Publishing Company (NPC).

By midcentury, the juvenile market for easily accessible leisure reading was both understood and exploited by a new breed of publisher and writer. Many of the same publishers who flourished in the early days of the "penny blood" launched successful "boys' papers." Chief among these was Edwin J. Brett (1828–1895) of NPC, whose major, but far from only, penny paper was *Boys of England* (1866–1899), an upgraded version of his earlier, more sensationalized works. The papers themselves flourished from 1855 to 1940, but it is the earlier versions by Brett, Emmett, George Vickers, and Lloyd that earned the name "penny dreadful." *Wild Boys of London* and *Wild Boys of Paris* were two of Brett's most notorious series. Other well-known names in this trade were G. W. M. Reynolds, author of the serial *The Mysteries of London* (1845–1848) and sequels (1856). George Vickers, through authors such as Harry Hazelton, published tales of sex and violence in titles about women and girls of London. Eventually, Brett and his competition attempted to court both readers and their parents by featuring boy heroes and some of the same rags-to-riches stories that were popular in the American "dime novels" of a similar period. There is much evidence of crossover between the two literary forms. By the 1880s adventure tales became popularized from such sources as the Aldine Publishing Company, whose "Deadwood Dick" series, set in the Black Hills of South Dakota, fed into the American Wild West fever of British as well as American boys. Buffalo Bill was another featured character. The turn-of-the-century rage for science and invention led to Franke Reade, a fictional inventor who became most famous for his "steam man" in the old West.

Inheritors

The penny dreadful had set the stage for adventure and science stories that filled the pulp magazines of the early 20th century by creating a venue for the kind of simple, fast-paced, sensational stories that appealed to unsophisticated readers with little time for education and little hope of significantly improving their lives. It also created a publishing format that led to the wide distribution of works by such enduring authors as Jules Verne and Edgar Allan Poe. The boys' papers have become the focus of Victorian studies and a source for scholars who examine the social mores of the time, from the conservative class values of the majority of papers to changing expectations for manliness and gender roles. Clearly the rich soup out of which the modern concept of mass-market entertainment grew, from early-20th-century film serials to comic books and radio and television series of the 1940s and 1950s, this form of fiction reinforced the primacy of story and the durability of taste for horror and adventure in children's literature.

BIBLIOGRAPHY

Anglo, Michael. *Penny Dreadfuls, and Other Victorian Horrors.* London. Jupiter Books, 1977.

Boyd, Kelly. *Manliness and the Boys' Story Paper in Britain: A Cultural History, 1855–1940.* London: Palgrave/Macmillan, 2003.

Carpenter, Kevin. "Introduction." In *Penny Dreadfuls and Comics: English Periodicals for Children from Victorian Times to the*

Present Day. London: Victoria and Albert Museum, 1983. Exhibition catalog.

Dunae, Patrick. "Penny Dreadfuls: Late Nineteenth-Century Boys' Literature and Crime." *Victorian Studies* 22 (1979): 133–150.

Haining, Peter. "Introduction." In *The Penny Dreadful; or, Strange, Horrid, and Sensational Tales!*, edited by Peter Haining. London: Victor Gollancz, 1975.

Springhall, John. "A Life Story for the People?: Edwin J. Brett and the London "Low-Life" Penny Dreadfuls of the 1860s." *Victorian Studies* (Winter 1990): 223–246.

Turner, E. S. *Boys Will Be Boys: The Story of Sweeney Todd, Deadwood Dick, Sexton Blake, Billy Bunter, Dick Barton, et al.* London: Joseph, 1948, 1957.

Janice M. Bogstad

Penrod. *See* Tarkington, Booth.

Peppe, Rodney (1934–), English author-illustrator born in Eastbourne, Sussex. He was educated at the Eastbourne School of Art and the London County Council Central School of Art. Peppe worked in advertising and design consultancy before becoming a prolific author-illustrator of picture and pop-up books for young children, beginning with *The Alphabet Book* (1968). His most characteristic illustrations are based on model toys he has built, as in his Henry series about an elephant (1975–), his Mice series about mice who live in a shoe (1981–), and his Huxley Pig series that was also televised in Britain (1989–).

[*See also* Illustrations *and* Movable Books and Pop-Up Books.]

Adrienne E. Gavin

Percy, Graham (1938–), illustrator born and raised in New Zealand, where he drew and painted as a young child. Percy is now based in Wimbledon, England. He has authored and/or illustrated more than one hundred books for young children during his award-winning freelance illustration career, receiving the Prix d'Italia in 1983 for *The Emperor and the Nightingale* (television program). Percy graduated in 1967 from the Royal College of Art with their Silver Medal and Travelling Scholarship to the United States. His work has been exhibited and published by the Association of Illustrators and European Illustration, among others, as well as at a one-person show at Storyopolis gallery, Los Angeles. In most of his illustrations Percy chooses a watercolor wash overlaid with colored pencil, incorporating the texture of the original paper. His appealing anthropomorphisms extend well beyond the humanization of elephants, chickens, and mice to include mittens, clouds, and even a stick of butter (*A Cup of Starshine*, 1991). Although his works include many updated or reimagined folk tales (*Children's Favourite Animal Fables: Retold and Illustrated by Graham Percy*, 2000), Percy has also illustrated books with contemporary themes (*When Dad Cuts Down the Chestnut Tree*, 1988; *Elympics* [poems about elephants competing in the Olympics], 1999). His body of work is mainly in the genres of lullabies, classic nursery rhymes, and favorite children's animal stories and fables. Percy has contributed to many series, as well as authored his own Shape series (1986), Animal Tails series (1995; board books with "real" animal tails), and twenty-title Picture Tales series of children's classics accompanied by sound recordings (2001, Peralt Montagut Publishers, Barcelona; eleven languages available). Percy designed the full-length animated film *Hugo the Hippo* (1970–1972, Hungary). Occasionally Percy speaks on the subject of children's book illustration. He maintains a Web site at http://www.grahampercy.com.

[*See also* Animal Stories; Illustrations; *and* Picture Books.]

Gretchen Leigh McCormack

Père Castor (1898–1967), French publisher whose real name was Paul Faucher. His innovative educational picture books are distinguished by the high quality of their design, typography, and illustrations. Originally a bookseller, Faucher was well connected with European intellectual circles, including the progressive educators to whom he dedicated the collection *Éducation* (1927), an anthology of essays on educational theory. He also promoted progressive education at the Bureau Français d'Éducation Nouvelle (French Office for New Education), which he helped found.

Inspired by the Czech educator Frantisek Bakulé, Faucher abandoned theory for pedagogy and began to work on the concept for a vast publishing project that would put into practice his ideas about how books could serve as instruments to initiate and incite reading while satisfying the child's fundamental need for self-expression. Images were essential to Faucher's project because of their potential to document, narrate, and facilitate creative play as an integral part of learning. He was equally convinced of images' power to influence a child's subconscious, and he therefore believed that illustrations should be neither frightening nor troubling. Picture books should, in his view, convey a clear vision of reality without distortion or caricature, while also transmitting human values. In 1931 the Paris publisher

Flammarion began issuing Faucher's picture books as the Père Castor series with its distinctive logo of a beaver, an animal selected for its association with building and construction. Having engaged the talents of émigré Russian artists, Faucher was able to produce relatively inexpensive, thin, color-printed paperbacks whose contents and formats fulfilled his ambitious educational and aesthetic program in age-appropriate ways. The series was especially strong in activity books (*albums d'activités*) intended to help children acquire the sensory and motor skills and the psychological and intellectual aptitudes necessary for independent reading. More than eighty Père Castor titles of four distinct types appeared between 1932 and 1939: nursery books, such as *ABC jeux du Père Castor* (Père Castor's ABC), illustrated by Feodor Rojankowsky; picture books for beginning readers, such as Teffi's *Baba Yaga*, illustrated by Nathalie Parain; game books, such as *6 métiers* (6 Jobs) illustrated by Nathan Altman; and activity books, such as *Je fais mes jouets avec des plantes* (I Make My Toys with Plants). Faucher's books quickly won international acclaim and were particularly successful in the United States, where the Artists and Writers Guild issued at least seven in translation.

After World War II, Faucher formed a new team of illustrators including Pierre Belvès, Gerda, and Hélène Guertik, and added new types of books to the line, such as *L'imagier du Père Castor* for babies, the series *Le montreur d'images* comprising photographically illustrated documents for teenagers, and the series *Les enfants de la terre* (Children of the World), intended to promote the values of peace and internationalism in the aftermath of World War II. Faucher also opened a school, which included a class for the mentally retarded; it became a center for exchange and debate about education. When Faucher died in 1967, he had been involved in the production of more than 320 titles, many of which had been adopted for use in schools, as well as so widely appreciated by the general public that 20 million copies had been sold around the world.

BIBLIOGRAPHY

Le Père Castor: Paul Faucher, un nivernais inventeur de l'album moderne. Actes du colloque de Pougues-les Eaux. Varennes-Vauzelles: Conseil général de la Nièvre, 1998.

ANNIE LALLEMENT-RENONCIAT

Pergaud, Louis (1882–1915), French novelist, son of a teacher and a teacher himself, killed in the First World War. He wrote short stories about nature: *De Goupil a Margot* (From Goupil to Margot, 1910), *La revanche du corbeau* (1911; English trans., *The Vengeance of the Crows*, 1930), *Le roman de Miraut, chien de chasse* (The romance of Miraut, the Retriever, 1912). Neglected nowadays because they have often been read in schools, these superficially quiet, yet rather cruel stories depict a world, seen from an animal point of view, where human beings are shown as a powerful and often distant enemy. Morality is subordinate to the struggle for survival in these epic narratives reminiscent of Selma Lagerlöf's. This harshness seems far from Pergaud's most famous novel, *La guerre des boutons* (The War of the Buttons, 1912), which takes place in a rural school setting.

FRANCIS MARCOIN

Perkins, Lucy Fitch (1865–1937), American author and illustrator. She is best known for her series of twenty-six Twins books, published between 1911 (*The Dutch Twins*) and 1938 (*The Dutch Twins and Little Brother*). Perkins said that her aim was to help in making "a unified nation out of a heterogeneous mixture of races," by showing how children live or lived in particular times and places. The twins, almost always a boy and a girl, are in some ways typical of their time and place, but Perkins tried to avoid stereotypes by showing how individuals are affected by the expectations of their society, sometimes conforming and sometimes rebelling. She even satirized the notion of stereotypes, as when the Scottish twin Jock, having decided to laze in bed, sticks to his decision "like a true Scotchman." She liked to sketch from a kneeling position, to be on a child's level, and similarly avoided describing her characters from an omniscient point of view.

[*See also* Interracial Books for Children *and* Multiculturalism and Children's Books.]

FRANCES ARMSTRONG

Perl, Lila, the daughter of Polish-Russian Jews, born in Brooklyn in the 1920s. Although she graduated from high school at age fifteen, she did not begin writing until her children were old enough to read. She is probably best known for her nonfictional works, which deal mostly with aspects of America's cultural history (in books such as *Slumps, Grunts, and Snickerdoodles: What Colonial America Ate and Why* and *It Happened in America: True Stories from the Fifty States*) as well as with the historical events related to specific ethnic groups (such as European immigrants, Chinese railroad builders, and Cherokees). She has also written on non-American topics such as Mayans and Egyptians. Her main fictional works are the Fat Glenda quartet featuring a teenage girl who struggles with weight issues. Perl's fiftieth book, *Four Perfect Pebbles*, was coauthored with Marion Blumenthal Lazan. Marion and her family were caught up in the Holocaust and incarcerated in Westerbork and Bergen-Belsen. The book received numerous awards including ones from the American Library Association, the International Reading Association, and the Association of Jewish Libraries.

[*See also* Holocaust Literature for Children; Multiculturalism and Children's Books; *and* United States.]

Lydia Kokkola

Perodi, Emma (1850–1918), one of the early women writers for children who became prominent in late-19th-century Italy. Like many others, Perodi worked in the new field of journalism for the young. In 1883 she became editor of the high-quality children's newspaper *Il giornale per i bambini* published in Rome, in succession to its ambitious founder, Ferdinando Martini, and Carlo Collodi. Subsequently Perodi moved to Palermo in Sicily to work for the publisher Salvatore Biondo. Her life was thus devoted to the new processes of cultural production for children.

In her own prolific writing, she produced a volume of short biographies of a hundred Roman women, a tale of brigands, a tale about the circus, stories of children in their own lands, and an account of Jewish history. She employed predominantly two quite different modes of narration. On the one hand, she emulated Edmondo De Amicis in writing realist novels concerned with social justice and reform, such as *Cuore del popolo: Libro per l'adolescenza* (The Heart of the People: A Book for Adolescents, 1892); her modernity may be noted here since adolescence was a new concept, and she boldly addresses the problem of the opposition of the Church to the state in the creation of Italy. On the other hand—and more important—she developed a remarkable vein of fantasy in numerous books of fairy tales, especially successful in *Le novelle della nonna* (Grandmother's Tales, 1892), which had many editions and inspired other writers; eclipsed for a time, it is now recognized as a major contribution to the genre and her chief legacy. The forty-five original tales are set within a realist frame story illustrating the life of a peasant family in Tuscany, and are told at intervals throughout a year's work, hardships, and family events. Even though the tales are told for didactic or therapeutic reasons, their often weird and macabre character contrasts vividly with hard reality. Perodi's interest in the fairy tale was inspired by the substantial anthropological work then being conducted in various regions of Italy by the pioneers of folklore studies: important collections of oral stories had already been published in the 1870s for both Sicily and Tuscany. Sicilian fairy tales and legends informed Perodi's volume *Al tempo dei tempi* (Long Ago, 1909–1910); these narratives were grouped respectively as tales of the Sicilian Mountains, Sea, and Cities. Folk legend is the basis also of her *Fate e fiori* (Fairies and Flowers, 1909). The best of her own stories display marked originality, lively imagination, and sophisticated literary skills.

[*See also* Fairy Tales and Folk Tales; Fantasy; Italy; *and biographies of figures mentioned in this article.*]

Bibliography

Faeti, Antonio, ed. *Fiabe fantastiche: Le novelle della nonna*, by Emma Perodi. Turin, Italy: Einaudi, 1974. See Faeti's introduction.

Ann Lawson Lucas

Perrault, Charles (1628–1703), French writer, poet, administrator, and member of the Academie Française. Born in Paris into one of the more distinguished bourgeois families of the time, Perrault is regarded as one of the founders of the literary fairy tale in Europe. Almost all of his fairy tales—and he only wrote eleven, even if one includes his verse tales—have become part of the classical canon in the West, and they prepared the way for the Grimms' tales, which have also become canonized. In fact, Perrault's tales have been reprinted in thousands of different versions for children and adults up through the 21st century and have often been confused with the Grimms' tales if not blended with them. Indeed, modern editions of his tales in English have often been attributed to the Grimms. Yet Perrault's works are distinctly different from the tales collected and edited by the Grimms and are complex.

Education and Career

Perrault began studying at the Collège de Beauvais (near the Sorbonne) in 1637, and at the age of fifteen he stopped attending school and largely taught himself all he needed to know to pass his law examinations in 1651 at the University of Orléans. After working three years as a lawyer, he left the profession to become a secretary to his brother Pierre, who was the tax receiver of Paris. During this time he published some minor poems and began taking more and more of an interest in literature. In 1659 he produced two important poems, "Portrait d'Iris" and "Portrait de la voix d'Iris," and

Charles Perrault. Frontispiece to *Les contes de Perrault* (Paris: Émile Guérin, c. 1890). COLLECTION OF JACK ZIPES

by 1660 his public career as a poet was in full swing when he published several poems in honor of Louis XIV. In 1663 Perrault was appointed secretary to Jean Baptiste Colbert, controller general of finances, perhaps the most influential minister in Louis XIV's government. For the next twenty years, until Colbert's death, Perrault was able to accomplish a great deal in the arts and sciences because of Colbert's power and influence.

In 1671 he was elected to the French Academy and was also placed in charge of the royal buildings. He continued writing poetry and took an active interest in cultural affairs of the court. When Colbert died in 1683, Perrault was dismissed from government service, but he had a pension and was able to support his family while concentrating more on literary affairs. In 1687, he helped inaugurate the famous "Querelle des anciens et des modernes" (Quarrel of the Ancients and the Moderns) by reading a poem entitled "Le siècle de Louis le Grand" (The Century of Louis the Great). Perrault took the side of the moderns and believed that France and Christianity—here he sided with the Jansenists—could progress only if they adapted and cultivated pagan beliefs and folklore and developed a culture of enlightenment. On the other hand, Nicolas Boileau, the poet and literary critic, and Jean Racine, the dramatist, took the opposite viewpoint and argued that France had to imitate the great empires of Greece and Rome and maintain stringent classical rules in respect to the arts. This literary quarrel, which had great cultural ramifications, lasted until 1697, when Louis XIV decided arbitrarily to bring it to an end in favor of Boileau and Racine. However, this decision did not stop Perrault from trying to include his "modernist" ideas in his poetry, prose, and fairy tales.

Literary Works

Perrault had always frequented the literary salons of his niece Mlle Lhéritier, Mme d'Aulnoy, and other women, and he had been annoyed by Boileau's satires written against women. It was in these salons that the French women had created an unusual vogue of literary fairy tales. Thus, influenced by them, Perrault wrote three verse tales, "Griseldis" (1691), "Les souhaits ridicules" (The Foolish Wishes, 1693), and "Peau d'âne" (Donkey Skin, 1694), along with a long poem, "Apologie des femmes" (1694), in defense of women. Whether these works can be considered pro-women today is questionable. Despite extolling the intelligence and capabilities of women, Perrault maintained that their talents should be put to use in the domestic and social realm (a perspective seen in most of his fairy tales). However, Perrault was definitely more enlightened in regard to women than either Boileau or Racine, and his poems make use of a highly mannered style and folk motifs to stress the necessity of assuming an enlightened moral attitude toward women and exercising just authority.

In 1696 Perrault embarked on a more ambitious project of transforming several popular folk tales with all their superstitious beliefs and magic into moralistic tales that would appeal largely to adults, demonstrate a modern approach to literature, and convey his views on the development of French civility. Like most writers of that period, he wrote fairy tales for his peers in the literary salons and not (as many critics claim) directly for children. Indeed, children's literature per se did not exist in France at that time. While preparing a manuscript of several fairy tales in 1695, he finished a prose version of "La belle au bois dormant" (Sleeping Beauty), which was published in the journal *Mercure Galant* in 1696, and in 1697 he published an entire collection of tales entitled *Histoires ou contes du temps passé*, based on the 1695 manuscript, which consisted of a new version of "Sleeping Beauty," "Le petit chaperon rouge" (Little Red Riding Hood), "Barbe bleue" (Blue Beard), "Cendrillon" (Cinderella), "Le petit poucet" (Tom Thumb), "Riquet à la houppe" (Riquet with the Tuft), "Le chat botté" (Puss in Boots), and "Les fées" (The Fairies). Each tale was accompanied with two ironic morals (*moralités*) in verse at the end that challenge the reader to interpret the tale from different perspectives.

Although *Histoires ou contes du temps passé* was published under the name of Pierre Perrault Darmancour, Perrault's son, and although some critics have asserted that the book was indeed written or at least coauthored by his son, evidence has shown clearly that this could not have been the case, especially since his son had not published anything up to that point. Perrault was simply using his son's name to mask his own identity so that he would not be blamed for reigniting the Quarrel of the Ancients and the Moderns.

Perrault's tales made their way into children's literature through a curious route. In the 18th century they were published as chapbooks and other kinds of inexpensive editions and were translated into English, German, Spanish, and other European languages. The tales were often abridged and adapted to appeal to popular taste and were easy for children to read. During the 19th century they were often printed as separate picture books for children, and they became part of the classical heritage for children in France and elsewhere. In the 1890s, with the invention of film, the famous French filmmaker Georges Méliès began adapting such Perrault tales as "Bluebeard," "Cinderella," "Little Red Riding Hood," and others for the cinema, and eventually Perrault's fairy tales became part of the cinematic staple of the Disney studio and many other film studios.

There is no doubt but that, among the writers of fairy tales during the 1690s, Perrault was the greatest stylist, which accounts for his tales having withstood the test of time. Furthermore, Perrault claimed that literature must become modern, and his transformations of folk motifs and literary themes into refined and provocative fairy tales still speak to the modern age, ironically in a way that may compel us to ponder whether the age of reason has led to the progress and happiness promised so charmingly in Perrault's tales.

[*See also* Fairy Tales and Folk Tales; France; Grimm, Jacob, and Wilhelm Grimm; *and* Moral Tales.]

BIBLIOGRAPHY

Hannon, Patricia. *Fabulous Identities: Women's Fairy Tales in Seventeenth-Century France*. Amsterdam: Rodopi, 1998.

Lewis, Philip. *Seeing through the Mother Goose Tales: Visual Turns in the Writings of Charles Perrault*. Stanford, Calif.: Stanford University Press, 1996.

Malarte, Claire. *Perrault à travers la critique depuis 1960*. Paris and Seattle, Wash.: Biblio 17, 1989.

Seifert, Lewis. *Fairy Tales, Sexuality, and Gender in France, 1690–1715: Nostalgic Utopias*. Cambridge, U.K.: Cambridge University Press, 1996.

Soriano, Marc. *Les contes de Perrault: Culture savante et traditions populaires*. Paris: Gallimard, 1977.

JACK ZIPES

Perrot, Jean (1937–), French critic and emeritus professor of comparative literature at the University of Paris. Perrot received his doctorate from the department of comparative literature at the Sorbonne with a dissertation on Henry James. He is the director of the Institut International Charles Perrault, a center for research in children's literature that he founded in Eaubonne in 1994. His publications include *Art baroque, art d'enfance* (Baroque Art, Children's Art, 1991), *Carnets d'illustrateurs* (Illustrators' Notebooks, 2000), and *Jeux et enjeux du livre d'enfance et de jeunesse* (Play and Games: Books at Stake for Children and Young Adults, 1999), which was a 2001 IRSCL Honour Book. Perrot has organized a host of international conferences and edited many important collections of essays. His indefatigable promotion of international exchange and collaboration in the study of children's literature has had a major impact on the field. In 2001 he was awarded the International Brothers Grimm Award.

[*See also* Critical Approaches to Children's Literature; France; Perrault, Charles; *and* Teaching Children's Literature.]

SANDRA L. BECKETT

Pestalozzi, Johann Heinrich (1746–1827), Swiss educator and author, whose writings and practical work influenced the development of educational systems in 19th-century Europe. Pestalozzi is sometimes called the "father of general education," and his school in Yvedon was visited by contemporary teachers and educationalists from many countries. Appalled by the physical and emotional misery among homeless children, Pestalozzi ran a school for neglected children from 1774 to 1780. His teaching methods attracted considerable attention in influential circles, and he was asked to set up an asylum for homeless children in Stanz in 1798 and in Burgdorf in 1799, where his institute included poor and middle-class children as pupils and simultaneously functioned as a teacher training college. The longest period of his life, 1800 to 1825, was spent in Yverdun, where he further developed his educational methods. Greatly influenced by Rousseau, Pestalozzi believed in the idea of the child's organic growth. What he termed "the principle of the organic" was first developed in *Die Abendstundne eines Einsiedlers* (The Evening Hour of a Hermit) in 1780. As a fundamental element in his views of education, he argued that the child's intellectual development should be seen as an integral part of its general growth. Moreover, teaching methods should be adapted to the developmental stage of the child, with a focus on perception and the practical world. Pestalozzi's views of childhood—together with those of Friedrich Froebel, whom he inspired—helped to shape 19th- and 20th-century views of childhood. The construction of the child reader, such as the play between word and image, objects and meaning, in the picture book or the concept book, could be seen as in line with Pestalozzi's views of the child's aesthetic relation to the world. His major ideas on education were published in *Meine Nachforschungen über den Gang der Natur in der Entwicklung des Menschengeschlechts* (My Inquiries into the Course of Nature in the Development of Mankind, 1797).

[*See also* Froebel, Friedrich; Language Acquisition and Children's Literature; *and* Piaget, Jean.]

Helene Høyrup

Peter Pan. *See* Barrie, J. M.

Peter Parley. *See* Goodrich, Samuel Griswold.

Peter Parley's Magazine. *Peter Parley's Magazine* was an English children's magazine that ran from 1839 to 1863. Founded and edited by William Martin (1801–1867), *Peter Parley's Magazine* was similar to other writings by "Peter Parley," a pseudonym originated by the American children's writer Samuel Goodrich (1793–1860) and adopted by several English imitators, including Martin. Like all Peter Parley work, Martin's magazine sought to communicate interesting and useful knowledge to children while eschewing highly fanciful writing, such as fairy tales and ghost stories, in the belief that such fiction was not only foolish because untrue but also potentially injurious to impressionable young minds. The avuncular editor of *Peter Parley's Magazine* addressed his juvenile readers with matter-of-fact cheerfulness, offered them "improving" advice, and piqued their curiosity about the real world in which they lived. The magazine contained informative articles on a wide variety of topics including natural history, biography, history, and sports, as well as poems and stories designed, as the editor put it, to "convey to the young reader some useful and valuable lessons in a pleasant manner." Arguably the best of the English Peter Parleys, Martin wrote in a lively if derivative manner and marketed his magazine with intelligence; as a result *Peter Parley's* sold well and circulated widely. As was common practice in the 19th century, separate issues of the magazine were bound together at the end of each year and sold as an annual, which appeared from 1840 until 1892, nearly thirty years after the monthly magazine itself had ceased publication. The magazine had featured black-and-white illustrations (block prints and engravings) from the beginning, and in response to competition from other English children's periodicals, colored plates were added to the annual in 1845. An attractive volume that served well as a gift or reward book, *Peter Parley's Annual: A Christmas and New Year's Present for Young People* was also offered in a less expensive version, without color plates.

[*See also* Children's Magazines; Goodrich, Samuel Griswold; Journals and Periodicals; Nonfiction; *and* Parley's Magazine.]

Bibliography

Darton, F. J. *Children's Books in England: Five Centuries of Social Life*. 3d rev. ed. Cambridge, U.K.: Cambridge University Press, 1982. Contains an overview of six "*English Peter Parley's*," including the editor of *Peter Parley's Magazine*, William Martin.

Carol A. Bock

Petersham, Miska (1888–1960), and **Maud Petersham** (1890–1971), American husband-and-wife author-and-illustrator team, who created more than one hundred picture books. Miska, born Mikaly Petrezselyem, in Hungary, was educated at the Royal Academy of Art in Budapest, studied in Italy, emigrated to England, and moved to New York in 1912. There he met and married Maud Fuller, a minister's daughter who was educated at Vassar. Initially they illustrated textbooks and works by others, including Carl Sandburg's *Rootabaga Stories* (1922), Charles and Mary Lamb's *Tales from Shakespeare* (1923), Johanna Spyri's *Heidi* (1932), and Carlo Collodi's *Pinocchio* (1932). In *The Poppy Seed Cakes* (1924) by Margery Clark they introduced a bright palette of colorful, eastern European motifs. They wrote *Miki* (1929) to introduce their son to Hungary, the home of his ancestors. They also collaborated on a series of Bible stories—*The Ark of Father Noah and Mother Noah* (1930), *The Christ Child* (1931), *David* (1938), *Joseph and His Brothers* (1938), *Moses* (1938), *Ruth* (1938)—always conscious of total book design. Some titles feature American history and customs: *An American ABC* (1941), a Caldecott Honor book; the Caldecott Medal–winning *The Rooster Crows: A Book of American Rhymes and Jingles* (1945), often called "The American Mother Goose"; *America's Stamps: The Story of One Hundred Years of U.S. Postage Stamps* (1947); *A Bird in the Hand: Sayings from "Poor Richard's Almanac"* (1951); *The Story of the Presidents of the United States of America* (1953); and *The Silver Mace: A Story of Williamsburg* (1956). The Petershams greatly influenced the genre of the information book. They are remembered for their engaging illustrations and stories of other times and lands, and they are credited with creating some of the earliest examples of books with themes exploring multiethnic and racial consciousness.

[*See also* Clark, Margaret; Collodi, Carlo; Lamb, Charles, and Mary Lamb; Sandburg, Carl; *and* Spyri, Johanna.]

Beverly Vaughn Hock

Petkevicius, Výtautas (1930–), Lithuanian novelist. Working within the totalitarian regime, Petkevicius resorted to children's fairy tale and allegory not only to convey criticism of society, but also to defend common human values against the Soviet censorship. *Acorn's Adventures in the Land of Vices* (1964) portrays a young oak tree as a protagonist who eventually recognizes his own shortcomings. *Mìkas Pùpkus, the Great Hunter* (1969) has a strong ecological agenda in fairy tale disguise. *Clay Matthew—the King of Men* (1978) is considered the most important contemporary Lithuanian children's novel. Presented as a dynamic adventure story about the fictitious Bread Land, it is an allegorical depiction of Lithuanian history, including its loss of independence and struggle against oppressors. The novel shows how people become indifferent and conformist under a dictatorship, a pessimistic view that was understandable at the time when the novel appeared.

[*See also* Censorship *and* Eastern European Countries.]

Maria Nikolajeva

Petry, Ann (1908–1997), African American author who wrote adult novels, short stories, and children's books with African American protagonists. Trained as a pharmacist, Ann Lane Petry graduated from the University of Connecticut in 1931 and worked in her family's drugstores. However, she had a great desire to become a writer, and in 1938 she moved to New York City, where she found a job as a reporter and taught in a Harlem experimental school, which allowed her to observe ghetto life affecting African American children. Petry's first short story, "Marie of the Cabin Club," was published in 1939 in the *Afro-American*, a Baltimore newspaper. With a Houghton Mifflin Literary Fellowship Award (1945), she wrote her first novel, *The Street* (1946, 1985, 1992), a work acclaimed for its naturalistic contrast of city and country. Petry's first children's book, *The Drugstore Cat* (1949), featured a country cat living in an urban pharmacy. Unhappy that few children's books with African American characters existed, in her second work, *Harriet Tubman: Conductor on the Underground Railroad* (1995), she featured the African American slave who led over three hundred other slaves to freedom. In another historical novel, *Tituba of Salem Village* (1964), Petry presents a Barbadian slave accused in the Salem witch trials of 1692. Petry's awards include honorary doctorates from Suffolk University (1983), the University of Connecticut (1988), and Mount Holyoke College (1989).

[*See also* African American Literature; Historical Fiction; *and* Multiculturalism and Children's Books.]

BIBLIOGRAPHY

Mobley, Marilyn. "Ann Petry." In *African American Writers*, edited by Valerie Smith. 347–359. New York: Scribners, 1991.

Lynda G. Adamson

Pevsner, Stella (1921?–), American author of young adult novels that usually chronicle the everyday experiences of suburban girls. Though the stories sometimes contain serious elements, the tone of the writing is generally lighthearted, with welcome doses of humorous dialogue. Among Pevsner's most popular titles are a story about an eighth grader's quest for identity, *Cute Is a Four Letter Word* (1978), and *Sister of the Quints* (1987), a story about Natalie's consternation when her father and his new wife have quintuplets, which has a follow-up that reintroduces Natalie's siblings at age thirteen, *I'm Emma: I'm a Quint* (1993). Pevsner occasionally experimented with different types of narratives, such as a grim story of teenage suicide, *How Could You Do It Diane?* (1989), a few books with male protagonists, including *Jon, Flora, and the Odd-Eyed Cat* (1994), and a novel, based on fact, about a girl's childhood in war-torn Vietnam (*Sing for Your Father, Su Phan*, 1997). These far-ranging titles demonstrated Pevsner's continuing growth as a writer.

[*See also* Girls' Books and Fiction.]

PETER D. SIERUTA

Peyton, K. M., (1929–), British writer. Kathleen Wendy Peyton grew up in Surrey and wrote her first book at the age of nine. Six books later, *Sabre, the Horse of the Sea* (1948) was published under the pseudonym Kathleen Herald. This was followed by two more pony stories, written (as she later admitted) in order to work off her frustration about not owning a horse herself. After she studied painting at Manchester Art School, she taught for three years before marrying in 1950 and starting a family. Soon thereafter she moved to rural Essex and produced *North to Adventure* (1958), an orthodox children's story written with her husband, Michael Peyton—the 'M' in their joint pen name, K. M. Peyton—who helped with plot ideas. This collaboration continued until *Windfall* (1962), about a 19th-century Essex fisherman's son who is generously rewarded for saving a man's life, only to lose everything by the end. *The Maplin Bird* (1964) also has a Victorian setting, this time with two orphans who help a young smuggler escape from the law. *Thunder in the Sky* (1966) is set at the start of the World War I, with a boy suspecting that his older brother may be a spy.

Peyton's great success came with *Flambards* (1968), a dashing, emotional tale of a landed family set just before the start of World War I, written in an involving style reminiscent of Daphne du Maurier at her most engaging. It tells the story of twelve-year-old Christina Parsons, an orphan who comes to stay for five years with her tyrannical uncle and two male cousins at Flambards, their crumbling Essex estate. As she gets older, Christina senses that huge changes are about to happen, with machines and a money economy beginning to displace immemorial country loyalties and practices. In *The Edge of the Cloud* (1969), Christina runs away with her cousin Will, who is obsessed with flying and designing airplanes. This book won the Carnegie Medal for 1969. In *Flambards in Summer* (1969) Christina, now a war widow, comes back to the big house on the edge of ruin. Determined to put things straight, she is overjoyed at the return of Dick, the stable boy who was once dismissed for trying to help her. Romantic but realistic, nostalgic but also forward-looking, with a keen eye for telling detail and a sure sense of historical change and continuity, the Flambards trilogy was made into a popular television series in 1979. Peyton eventually produced a fourth novel, *Flambards Divided* (1981), in which Christina finally marries Will, bringing down the wrath of the local gentry. But some fans found this conclusion too politically correct, preferring the more ambiguous ending of the third novel.

Peyton followed the Flambards trilogy with *Pennington's 17th Summer* (1970), a story for older teenagers and the author's own favorite, with its cover illustrated by herself. Pennington is a contemporary working-class boy with a gift for playing the piano. Misunderstood and sometimes beaten by his father, he is often in trouble with the law as well as at school. But just when everything is going badly, a famous music teacher offers to take him on as a pupil after hearing him play. In *The Beethoven Medal* (1971), Pennington is still in trouble despite making his concert debut, But he gains strength from the somewhat submissive love of his middle-class girlfriend, Ruth Hollis. The story ends with his going to prison for assaulting a policeman. *Pennington's Heir* (1980) finds Ruth pregnant and living with Pennington in poverty. It concludes as he plays the piano to would-be sponsors, with the couple still together, facing a future that is beginning to look more promising.

Writing many good but no longer outstanding titles subsequently, as she puts it herself "out of habit more than anything else," Peyton gradually reverted to the pony stories she started out with, though now with real horses of her own to enjoy. At her best, she brought a passionate energy to teenage novels that was much appreciated by readers of all ages.

NICHOLAS TUCKER

Pfister, Marcus (1960–), Swiss author and illustrator of several dozen children's picture books. Pfister's tales generally star young animals exploring their environment, like *Penguin Pete* (1987), or confronting small social problems, like *The Sleepy Owl* (1986). Simple and often moralistic, they appeal most to young or sentimental readers.

Artistically, Pfister's work is more distinguished. His cartoon-style animals reside in warmly inviting, watercolored landscapes. Pfister rose to international prominence after his story *Rainbow Fish* (1992) won a number of awards. In this tale an iridescently colored fish learns to make friends by sharing his beautiful scales. Pfister's use of holographic foil to produce the glittering fish scales makes the book visually memorable. He made use of the technique again in several sequels and in a number of other books like *The Christmas Star* (1993), *Dazzle the Dinosaur* (1994), and *Milo and the Magical Stones* (1997).

MEGAN LYNN ISAAC

Phaedrus (1973–1988). Edited by James Fraser of Fairleigh Dickinson University, *Phaedrus* was one of the earliest journals to document international scholarly research in children's literature. The journal began with a bibliographical focus, with the first issue consisting of a note about the purpose of the International Research Society for Children's Literature and listings of children's literature journals, selected dissertations, recent bibliographies and studies, and antiquarian and new booksellers. The journal constantly evolved, changing its subtitle and its publishers along the way. It began to include occasional substantial critical articles, such as an essay on the textless picture book by Joseph H. Schwarcz (1982), but most of the articles continued to be surveys of current research or of the children's literature of particular countries, similar to the country surveys in *Bookbird*. Later issues (*Phaedrus* became an annual in 1981) were indexed in the *MLA International Bibliography* and *Library Literature*. The thirteenth and final issue was published in Madison, New Jersey, in 1988.

[*See also* Critical Approaches to Children's Literature; International Research Society for Children's Literature; *and* Journals and Periodicals.]

LINNEA HENDRICKSON

Phantom Tollbooth, The. *See* Juster, Norton.

Phillips, Mary (1915–), English-born writer of children's books mostly set in South Africa. Three novels feature the early Dutch settlers. *The Bushman Speaks* (1961) and *The Cave of Uncle Kwa* (1965) were pioneering but inaccurate attempts to incorporate authentic bushman (San) lore in fiction. Two novels feature an African American detective based in Washington, D.C. As Nandi D'lovu she also wrote two novels about a South African–born detective who lives in the United States; in *Murder by Magic* (1990), he returns to Zululand and investigates a case involving a "witch-doctor"—an anachronistic, sensational portrayal of traditional beliefs and practices.

[*See also* Africa: Southern Africa; Colonial Fiction; *and* Multiculturalism and Children's Books.]

ELWYN JENKINS

Phipson, Joan (1912–2003), Australian writer. Born in Sydney, Phipson celebrated the pleasure of a rural childhood in her early novels. Her sensitive and tentative characters, often facing a rite of passage, act out their adventures within a strongly realized Australian landscape. *Good Luck to the Rider* (1953) and *The Family Conspiracy* (1962) each won the CBCA Book of the Year Awards and *It Happened One Summer* (1957) was highly commended. During the 1970s Phipson's novels became more urban, complex, and tense and featured older teenage protagonists. She examined fear in books such as *The Haunted Night* (1970), *The Cats* (1976), and *Keep Calm* (1978), and explored mystic and emotional forces in *The Way Home* (1973), *The Watcher in the Garden* (1982), and *A Tide Flowing* (1981). Phipson's capacity to portray troubled teenagers against a generally supportive world grew as her oeuvre expanded.

STELLA LEES

Photography in Nonfiction for Children. Photography first made its impact on children's literature amid the general flowering of illustration in the early 20th century. No less a photographer than Edward Steichen provided illustrations for Mary Steichen Martin's *The First Picture Book* (1930) and *The Second Picture Book* (1931), but Martin's concerns about the effect of fictionalized representation on developing children opposed the more fanciful tastes then prevalent. Nonetheless, other books with photographic illustrations began to appear. Notable among these is *Men at Work* (1932), by the noted social documentarian Lewis W. Hine, a book that may have done more to promote the strongly illustrative book for adults than the use of photography in books for children, but which nonetheless presages the photodocumentaries of the present day. An early example of the creative employment of archival, rather than purpose-taken, photographs is *Skyscraper* (1933), by Elsa H. Naumburg, Clara Lambert, and Lucy Sprague Mitchell, which tells in verse and prose of the construction of the Empire State Building. The most notable photographer in children's literature, however, was undoubtedly Ylla, whose animal photography was internationally popular, with the same photographs sometimes set to completely different texts in different countries (the photos that were treated to text by Jacques Prévert as *Le petit lion* in France in 1947 were, in the same year, produced as *The Sleepy Little Lion*, with text by Margaret Wise Brown, in America). Her vivid portraiture drew on the traditional appeal of animals, especially baby

Photography. Photograph from *Two Little Bears* by Ylla (Kamilla Koffler) (New York: Harper & Brothers, 1954), p. 28. REPRODUCED COURTESY OF THE COTSEN CHILDREN'S LIBRARY, PRINCETON UNIVERSITY LIBRARY

animals (a subject whose automatic interest has often meant careless employment), but brought the subject a freshness and immediacy that lifted her images above the stock. Nature continued to be a popular subject for photography, with artists such as the United States' Lilo Hess and Denmark's Astrid Bergman featuring animals wild and domestic in the 1950s and 1960s, while documentary photo-essays by photographers such as the Swedish Anna Riwkin-Brick (whose photographs were often partnered with text by Astrid Lindgren) chronicled the daily doings of children from different countries and different walks of life.

Since then, photography's use has expanded considerably, and a multitude of talented photographers employ their talents for child audiences of a considerable range of ages. Concept books for very young children, a genre that requires clarity as well as imagination, have produced several stars, such as Tana Hoban, one of the pioneers of photographic concept books, who remains one of its most reliable and imaginative practitioners; Margaret Miller, who brings a playful sensibility to the genre; and Bruce McMillan, who can translate daunting mathematical concepts into bright, accessible visuals. Increasingly prevalent are counting or alphabet books, some more successful than others, that find or create the subject figures photographically, as in Zoran Milich's *The City ABC Book* (2001), which finds shapes of the letters of the alphabet in the urban landscape.

The natural world continues to be a popular subject in photography. As author and photographer, Bianca Lavies brings her *National Geographic* experience to providing eye-opening investigations of creatures not always considered photogenic, as in *Compost Critters* (1993); Lavies is unusual in providing in each book a detailed explanation of how she obtains her startling images. The noted photographer William Muñoz is a regular partner of the author Dorothy Hinshaw Patent in her books about nature domestic and wild, while Jerome Wexler brings the same spirit of discovery in his text and photographs for small domestic pets. The New Zealander Nic Bishop embraces intimate closeups and stunning stop-motion to bring animals and their world into the audience's lap in books such as Joy Cowley's *Red-Eyed Tree Frog* (1999). Nor does work in this category have to feature animals: the work of the photographer Lennart Nilsson in Sheila Kitzinger's arresting *Being Born* (1986) chronicles the prenatal growth of a human embryo, then fetus, and Walter Wick's *A Drop of Water* (1997) uses stunning visuals to re-awaken viewers' appreciation of this everyday substance.

It is perhaps in recording the human world that photography finds its most important task; such photography can introduce youngsters to unfamiliar aspects of the world or reflect their own experience and appearance as valid. The photo-essayist George Ancona brings a matter-of-fact sensibility to titles such as *Barrio* (1998). Lawrence Migdale provides photography for Diane Hoyt-Goldsmith's multicultural books on celebrations and pastimes, such as *Celebrating a Quinceañera: A Latina's 15th Birthday Celebration* (2002), documenting vivid chapters of American life. Ray Bial takes an intriguing tack in his approaches to historical topics and contemporary ways of life, making the settings and equipment, rather than people, the photographic subjects. With books such as *Nights of the Pufflings* (1995), Bruce McMillan combines a naturalist subject, the puffins of Iceland, with a human story, the work of the children who ensure that the confused chicks make it safely to sea. The multitalented Susan Kuklin creates works for a variety of age groups, with subjects both technological and human, interweaving prose on often challenging, emotional subjects with evocative images.

Many books rely not on original photographs but on archival material gathered for the purpose. While the result is sometimes randomly scattered stock photographs bent to fit through the use of purposive captions, archival photographs can also result in dramatic and creatively considered visuals. Whether in books on the planets or the human body, Seymour Simon makes use of the most technologically advanced images and works his factual narrative in response to them, rather than merely allowing them to fill up page space. Dramatic, magazine-influenced design allows historical photographs to serve as background, narrative partner, and visual appeal in books such as K. M. Kostyal's *Trial by Ice: A Photobiography of Sir Ernest Shackleton* (1999), published, appropriately enough, by National Geographic, which developed a line of photobiographies. Toni Morrison pulls together images from the an aspect of the civil rights movement in *Remember: The Journey to School Integration* (2004) and inserts smatterings of provocative text that query the events and contemplate the thoughts of the subjects, who are often children.

While photography is generally associated with nonfiction, it has never entirely accepted that relegation (even Ylla's works supported an essentially fictional rather than documentary narrative). Especially with the advent of digital manipulation, audiences young and old are increasingly aware that images may be photographic without being faithfully documentary, a development that has led to more creative employment of photographs as story illustrations. Perhaps the most notable practitioners of the creative photographic tradition are Nina Crews and Jane Wattenberg, who defy convention by employing manipulated photographs to illustrate highly fanciful stories and folklore adaptations. With photo manipulation becoming a factor even in more apparently documentary images, it seems clear that photography is on the brink of working out a new illustrative identity for itself.

DEBORAH STEVENSON

Phukan, Mitra (1953–), Indian author and translator whose works move between culture-specific references and larger themes. Dipu in *Terrorist Camp Adventure* (2003) and Munu in *The Biratpur Adventure* (1997) are contrasted with the educated upper-middle-class protagonists. Phukan presents an informed childhood, shaped by the realities of the world the protagonists inhabit. Her children characters recognize the order of things and respect it. In *Mamani's Adventure* (1987), Mamani chases away the elephant but leaves a share of the sugarcane for it. Phukan questions the simplistic demarcation of human nature into good and bad, exploring the possibility of an in-between gray area. Girls possess an innate strength that manifests itself during crises. Mamani, for instance, displays remarkable courage and resource in saving the precious crop of sugarcanes. Phukan is one of two major children's writers—the other is Arup Kumar Dutta—from northeast India.

[*See also* Dutta, Arup Kumar *and* India.]

NANDINI NAYAR

Piaget, Jean (1896–1980), pioneering Swiss child psychologist who developed and continually refined an empirically researched paradigm-defining model of children's intellectual and cognitive development. Classic 20th-century writers (C. S Lewis, Jane Yolen, and J. R. R. Tolkien, for example) were able to grasp Piaget's concepts, and engaged with their young readers rather than write down to them. Piaget's published and collaborative works, primarily in French and English, number in the hundreds, and his articles in the thousands. Piaget's two early works are perhaps the best access points: *La langue et la pensée chez l'enfant* (1923; English trans., *The Language and Thought of the Child*, 1926) and *La représentation du monde chez l'enfant* (1926; English trans., *The Child's Conception of the World*, 1929). He received a BA (1915) and PhD (1918) from the University of Neuchâtel and continued postgraduate study at the University of Zurich, the University of Paris, and the Sorbonne. Though Piaget resisted being pigeonholed as a child (or developmental) psychologist, it was for this work that he is most remembered. Because of his earlier training in the sciences, he made significant links between biological and cognitive development that had profound implications for the epistemological basis of the process of a child's knowledge acquisition. Moving from philosophical speculation to the scientifically describable and reportable results, Piaget was effectively able to contest and overthrow the paradigm that children learned as little adults, or that their knowledge acquisition process was akin to writing on a blank slate. His work also put greater weight on a child's immediate physical environment and reduced the significance of factors such as ethnic background or heredity. It was his belief that the human mind was an active agent in all aspects of the learning process.

[*See also* Language Acquisition and Children's Literature *and biographies of figures mentioned in this article.*]

PHILIP E. KAVENY

Piatti, Celestino (1922–), Swiss commercial artist and picture book author and illustrator. Piatti worked in the Zurich studio of Fritz Buehler from 1944 to 1948 and by the 1950s was exhibiting his posters worldwide. He designed book jackets for Deutsche Taschenbuch Verlag in Munich (1961–1963) before creating picture books. His bold graphic style features simple, chunky figures drawn in thick black strokes and deep color against a white background. His work has often been likened to poster art and to stained glass. Three books were especially acclaimed in the United States: *The Happy Owls* (1963; American edition, 1964), *Celestino Piatti's ABC* (1967), and Aurel von Juechen's *Die heilige Nacht* (1968; English trans., *The Holy Night: The Story of the First Christmas*). Three more were in collaboration with other authors and were published internationally: *Zirkus Nock* with Ursula Haber (English trans., *The Nock Family Circus*, 1968), *Der golde Apfel* with Hans Bolliger (English trans., *The Golden Apple*, 1970), and *Der kleine Krebs* with Ursula Piatti (English trans., *The Little Crayfish*, 1973).

[*See also* Illustrations *and* Picture Books.]

MARGARET BUSH

Picard, Barbara Leonie (1917–), British author of five historical novels for older children, several collections of original fairy tales in a traditional style, and various retellings including *The Odyssey of Homer* (1952) and *Stories of King Arthur and His Knights* (1955). Picard's absorbing interest, which shaped all her writing, was mythology, legend, and folklore. Of her novels, the best known are *Ransom for a Knight* (1956) and *One Is One* (1965), both of which received Carnegie commendations. As in a quest legend, Picard's characters typically grow in experience and self-knowledge through a journey or series of encounters with the wider world.

[*See also* Fairy Tales and Folk Tales; Historical Fiction; *and* Myths.]

BELINDA COPSON

Picture Books. In the context of children's literature, picture books are a special kind of book in which the meaning is created and conveyed through the interaction of the verbal and the visual media. In many reference sources, picture books are treated as identical with books for very young children, who cannot yet read themselves. Although many picture books do indeed address the youngest readers in their themes and issues, picture books should be defined not through their implied readership but rather through their aesthetic characteristics. Until recently, scholarship of picture books has been strictly divided into two separate categories: studies by art historians and studies by children's literature experts. Whereas those in the first category paid attention to aspects such as line, color, light and dark, shape, and space, ignoring not only the textual component but frequently also the sequential nature of the picture book narrative, those in the second category treated picture books as any other children's books, applying either literary or educational approaches without taking into consideration the importance of text–image interaction. Recent influential studies of picture books have demonstrated that picture books cannot be satisfactorily analyzed with tools either from art history or from literary criticism but need a theory and a scholarly metalanguage of their own.

Definition

Most researchers make a clear distinction between picture books and illustrated books. In the former, in which a preexisting text has been supplied with illustrations, pictures are subordinated to words. The same story, for instance, a fairy tale, can be illustrated by different artists, and although these may impart different interpretations to the text, the pictures have primarily a decorative function; the story can still be read and understood without pictures. In a picture

Picture Books. Illustration by Maurice Sendak from his *Where the Wild Things Are* (New York: Harper & Row, 1963), p. 32. REPRODUCED COURTESY OF THE COTSEN CHILDREN'S LIBRARY, PRINCETON UNIVERSITY LIBRARY

book proper, words and images constitute an indivisible whole, and the overall impact of the work is achieved by the interaction of the two expressive means. This process and the result of this interaction have been described in terms such as iconotext, imagetext, composite text, synergy, polysystemy, counterpoint, contradiction, and congruence, which all emphasize that the true meaning of a picture book is created only by the joint efforts of the verbal and visual communication. The variety in the terminology reveals clear difficulties: while "iconotext" or "composite text" refers to the static unity of text and pictures, "counterpoint" or "synergy" refers to the complex dynamics of interaction in the process of making meaning.

In terms of the relationship between words and images, picture books present a wide continuum, from wordless picture books, in which the title offers the only verbal guidance to the interpretation (for instance, Mitsumasa Anno's *Journey*, 1977; Jan Ormerod's *Sunshine*, 1981, and *Moonlight*, 1982), to nonsequential, nonnarrative picture dictionaries and concept books (Helen Oxenbury's *I See, I Hear, I Touch*, 1985), in which words and images repeat and support each other, to picture storybooks, in which the narrative is carried collaboratively by words and pictures. However, the quantitative and qualitative ratio of text and images may vary substantially in different types of picture books. Words and pictures may convey more or less the same information and thus be symmetrical and even mutually redundant. Conversely, words and images may be mutually complementary, filling each other's gaps and compensating for each other's inadequacies. For instance, images are by far superior to words when it comes to descriptions of characters and settings, but words are superior in conveying relationships and emotions, as well as direct speech. Images are unsurpassed in conveying space, while words are indispensable for temporal aspects. A clever picture book makes use of the best of both means. In other cases, pictures may substantially add to the story conveyed by words, expanding and enhancing it, or occasionally words can expand the meaning of images. If words and images tell two different stories—as in Pat Hutchins's *Rosie's Walk* (1968), John Burningham's *Come Away from the Water, Shirley* (1977), and David McKee's *I Hate My Teddy Bear* (1982)—the tension creates an ironic counterpoint, which can occasionally continue so long as to become contradictory and even confusing, as in McKee's *Not Now, Bernard* (1980). Scholars suggest a variety of typologies concerning the balance between text and image, but all the approaches clearly demonstrate that the corpus of picture books is far from homogeneous.

Picture Books throughout History

Picture books are a relatively late phenomenon in the history of children's literature. Although one of the earliest books unquestionably intended for young readers, *Orbis sensualium pictus* (1658), by Johann Amos Comenius, was exactly what we today call a picture book, with pictures supporting words, the full-scale emergence of picture books was impossible until the development of printing technology enabled mass production of color illustrations. One of the earliest examples of true picture books was *Struwwelpeter* (1845; English trans., *Slovenly Peter*, 1900), by the German Heinrich Hoffmann, a collection of versified cautionary tales in which the verbal narrative is supported by a sequence of pictures, a structure reminiscent of contemporary comics. Another German classic, *Max and Moritz* (1865; English, 1871), by Wilhelm Busch, has a similar word–image collaboration. The development of British picture books received impetus from such outstanding 19th-century illustrators as Kate Greenaway, Randolph Caldecott, and Walter Crane. In Beatrix Potter's *The Tale of Peter Rabbit* (1902) and her other picture books, images substantially enhance the narrative, adding new dimensions to the verbal story, including irony. Although her books have a conventional layout, with text on one page and picture on the opposite page, Potter alternated pictures between right-hand and left-hand pages, creating a dynamic tempo by this subtle means that emphasized the dynamic nature of the story.

The foundation for the development of the picture book in the United States was to a large extent established by immigrants from Europe or their immediate descendants, including such renowned picture book makers as Wanda Gág (*Millions of Cats*, 1928), Ludwig Bemelmans (*Madeline*, 1939), H. A. Rey (*Curious George*, 1941), and especially Maurice Sendak, whose *Where the Wild Things Are* (1963) has changed the very concept of what a picture book is and how it works thematically, aesthetically, and psychologically. This remarkable story, consisting of just a few sentences, uses the images not simply to support or enhance the verbal narrative but to reflect a complex and subjective inner world of a very young child, who lacks the capacity to express himself with words. Among many noteworthy visual devices are the expansion of the picture area, reflecting the emotional state of the character, and the use of three wordless double spreads to illustrate "the wild rumpus," impossible to describe with words. No subsequent Western picture book maker could be totally free from the influence of *Where the Wild Things Are*. With it, Sendak opened the way for picture books that depict psychological states rather than external events; this is clearly seen in Sendak's own books, such as *Outside Over There* (1981).

Dr. Seuss's picture books, such as *And to Think That I Saw It on Mulberry Street* (1937) and *The Cat in the Hat* (1957), similarly externalize a child's internal world in the pictures, while some of them also interrogate the simple relationship between words and images, introducing visual concepts that lack correlation in language, such as a Grinch, a Who, a duck-dog, and a Zizzer-Zazzar-Zuzz. Seuss's *Green Eggs and Ham* (1960) is based on the incongruity between a linguistically correct phrase and the absence of its correspondence in the perceptible world. While Seuss's books are often treated as representative of the genre of nonsense, they undoubtedly illustrate one of the many potentials of the picture book medium. Some other milestones in American picture book art include *The Story of Ferdinand* (1936), by Munro Leaf and Robert Lawson; *Make Way for the Ducklings* (1941), by Robert McCloskey; *The Little House* (1943), by Virginia Lee Burton; *Goodnight Moon* (1947), by Margaret Wise Brown and Clement Hurd; *The Very Hungry Caterpillar* (1969), by Eric Carle; and *Sylvester and the Magic Pebble* (1969), by William Steig. Although some of the famous picture books were produced in collaboration between an author and an illustrator, the best examples are the creations of one single picture book maker, which once again emphasizes the intrinsic unity of the verbal and the visual aspect of the work.

Among the European picture books of the first half of the 20th century, the French Jean de Brunhoff has been most influential with his many Babar stories, beginning in 1931 (English trans., *The Story of Babar, the Little Elephant*, 1933). Although they have been rightfully criticized for their colonial ideology, they have substantially contributed to the development of picture book aesthetics with their unconventional and varied layout and composition, the use of picture sequences to convey the flow of time, the contrast between verso and recto, and other distinctive characteristics. Scandinavian picture books of the 1930s through the 1950s, inspired by the Soviet avant-garde picture book and poster art, experimented with shapes and colors and also introduced the use of negative space, black background areas devoid of unnecessary details. Thus the picture book developed a great variety of styles and its own narrative language, distinct from illustration art.

Typical for picture books in the second half of the 20th century is the further development of the specific picture book aesthetics, including the use of whole double spreads rather than placement of text and pictures on alternate pages, the experiments with different formats and layouts, integrating text into pictures, frame breaking (for instance, allowing images to "bleed" into the white edges around the panel), the dynamic composition of the double spread that stimulates page turning, the balance between the left-hand page (verso) and the right-hand page (recto), and the full utilization of endpapers, title pages, and covers as part of the narrative. Further, distorted and "impossible" space, inspired by expressionism and surrealism in art, multiple narrative levels, complex and sometimes contradictory points of view, playing with objective and subjective perception, and sophisticated intertextuality and metafiction become trademarks of what has been labeled as postmodern picture books. Janet and Allan Ahlberg's books, such as *The Jolly Postman* (1986), are good examples of this trend.

A significant feature of contemporary picture books, following *Where the Wild Things Are*, is their attempt to use the images to convey the subverbal states, the landscape of the mind. Anthony Browne's *The Tunnel* (1989) is an example of a picture book narrative in which images, contrary to words, emphasize that the story is taking place in the character's mind, reflecting her fears and anxieties. Similarly, in Browne's *Gorilla* (1983), the character's real experiences are transformed in her imagination, conveyed by images alone. John Burningham is another extraordinary master of psychological picture books. In *Granpa* (1984) images are used to depict a warm but complicated relationship between a child and her grandfather, as well as their internal reality, including dreams, visions, and memories, while the verbal dialogue conceals more than it reveals. In *Aldo* (1991) pictures totally contradict the verbal story, and in *Oi! Get Off Our Train* (1989) the initial rational explanation of the adventure as a dream is at the end shattered by words.

The best of modern picture books show a clear tendency toward counterpoint and contradiction in their text–image interplay. In such books as *The Trouble with Mum* (1983) and *Princess Smartypants* (1986), by Babette Cole; *Lily Takes a Walk* (1987), by Satoshi Kitamura; and *John Patrick Norman McHennesy—The Boy Who Was Always Late* (1987), by John Burningham, pictures subvert the verbal narrative, making the reader aware of discrepancies between the information received through the two media. Often this device enables the picture book maker to interrogate adult authority and generally to emphasize the plurality of perception. Many contemporary picture book makers, notably the Australian Colin Thompson in *Looking for Atlantis* (1993) and other books, elaborate with visual details, adding new dimensions to the story and offering a wide range of intertextual connections. Among the outstanding contemporary British picture book makers are Edward Ardizzone, Michael Foreman, Quentin Blake, and Raymond Briggs.

During the last decades of the 20th century, picture books in Europe, North America, Africa, and Australia received new inspiration through multiculturalism, bringing elements of indigenous cultures and styles into the visual aspect, as in *Why Mosquitoes Buzz in People's Ears* (1975), by Leo and Diane Dillon, and *The Rainbow Serpent* (1975), by Dick Roughsey. It should, however, be pointed out that the picture book in the Western sense does not necessarily exist in all countries; for instance, although in many Eastern European countries there are excellent illustrators, the phenomenon of the picture book proper is practically unknown.

Kinds and Genres of Picture Books

In most standard textbooks, histories, and thematic essay collections on children's literature, picture books are treated as a genre, alongside fairy tales, fantasy, adventure, domestic stories, animal stories, and so on. However, even a very brief look at the examples discussed in such sources reveals that picture books encompass all of these genres. Hundreds of picture books are based on classical and contemporary fairy tales; books such as *Where the Wild Things Are* and *The Tunnel* have all the unmistakable features of fantasy; *I Hate My Teddy Bear* is formally a domestic story; and animal stories would include books as diverse as *The Tale of Peter Rabbit*, *Babar*, *The Cat in the Hat*, and *Sylvester and the Magic Pebble*. Obviously, genre is not a sufficient category to differentiate picture books from other kinds of children's literature, and within the scope of picture books we can distinguish a number of separate genres or kinds. While some of these are similar to genres in fiction for older children (fantasy, adventure, family story), picture books display a few unique generic categories, for instance, picture dictionaries, ABC books, counting books, concept books, and wordless picture books. In all these genres, the images can be simple as well as complex. ABC books and picture dictionaries are often treated merely as educational tools used for language acquisition. However, contemporary ABC books have moved from a simple, symmetrical relationship between word and image ("A is for Apple") toward a complex and playful interaction, engaging children's imaginations and developing their sense of language as well as visual perception, as in *The Z Was Zapped* (1987), by Chris Van Allsburg. Such picture books can enhance young readers' understanding of literature not merely as a simple reflection of the external reality (a direct connection between word and object) but also as a complex network of referential relationships.

Illustrated poetry—that is, books containing at least one poem or verse on each double spread, accompanied by at least one illustration—seems to be a marginal category; some classic examples are C. M. Barker's *Flower Fairies* and the Swiss Ernst Kreidolf's floral fairy tales; good modern examples are Michael Rosen's illustrated verses. A special category of picture books is nonfiction, or information books, which differ from nonfiction for older readers mainly in the density of illustrations. There seem to be few, if any, nonfiction picture books that seriously take the specific picture book aesthetics into consideration, allowing pictures to be more than either mere decorations or educational implements.

The vast majority of picture books fall under the loosely defined category of picture storybooks, that is, narratives in which words and pictures are used together to convey a meaning. The verbal text can be written in prose or in verse, and the word–image interaction is one of the types discussed above, for example, symmetrical, complementary, or enhancing. Themes vary from everyday stories to fantasy, and styles vary from refined to grotesque. The characters can be human beings, animals, toys, animated objects, and even abstract notions, like the blots of color in Leo Lionni's *Little Blue and Little Yellow* (1959). The dominance of anthropomorphic animals in picture books can be accounted for in several ways, from the prejudices about young readers' preferences to the visually gratifying variety of animals as compared with human children. In most cases, however, the use of animals is hardly motivated, and the characters of such books as *Sylvester and the Magic Pebble*, the Frances books (1964–), by Russell and Lillian Hoban, and the Frog and Toad books (1970–), by Arnold Lobel, should be seen as humans in disguise. In some cases the verbal text does not even mention that the characters are anything other than humans. In other cases, however, the fluctuating border between human and animal is cleverly explored, as in Beatrix Potter's books, while many books play with the specific nature of the animal depicted, such as Curious George's monkeylike agility or the snake's particular body shape in *Crictor* (1958), by Tomi Ungerer. Many picture books feature animated machines, for instance, *Little Toot* (1939), by Hardie Gramatky; *Mike Mulligan and His Steam Shovel* (1939), by Virginia Lee Burton; and *The Little Train* (1973), by Grahame Greene and Edward Ardizzone.

Many contemporary picture books deconstruct traditional fairy tales, adding new dimensions in the pictures that take the story toward unusual interpretations, especially feminist ones. Outstanding creators of modern fairy tale picture books include Bernadette, Paul O. Zelinsky, and Trina Schart Hyman. Picture books by Jon Scieszka, such as *The Stinky Cheese Man* (1992), illustrated by Lane Smith, are both intertextual and highly metafictional.

The Dual Audience of Picture Books

An essential aspect in discussing picture books is their dual audience, which falls within the recent critical concept of cross-writing. Picture books, more than any other kind of children's literature, are read and appreciated by children and adults together, most often with the adult reading the book to a child or a group of children. Contemporary picture book creators seem to be very much aware of this reading situation, addressing the adult coreader parallel to the child, for instance, through specific intertextual and intervisual references. It has become common for picture book makers to include extensive and ironic visual allusions to famous art objects as well as aspects of popular culture—for instance, in Browne's *Gorilla* (1983) and *Piggybook* (1986)—that most likely are not immediately perceived by young readers. Sendak brings in images of the Holocaust in *We Are All in the Dumps with Jack and Guy* (1993), based on two nursery rhymes; the visual allusions are most likely lost on young readers. This does not, however, imply that the adult is addressed at the expense of the child (the infamous "double address"); on the contrary, a clever picture book takes into consideration the dual audience, offering both parties something to appreciate and enjoy.

[*See also* Book Design; Illustrations; *and articles on figures and topics mentioned in this article.*]

BIBLIOGRAPHY

Bader, Barbara. *American Picturebooks: From Noah's Ark to the Beast Within.* New York: Macmillan, 1976.

Doonan, Jane. *Looking at Pictures in Picture Books.* Stroud, U.K.: Thimble Press, 1993.

Hürlimann, Bettina. *Picture-Book World.* Translated and edited by Brian W. Alderson. London: Oxford University Press, 1968.

Kiefer, Barbara. *The Potential of Picturebooks: From Visual Literacy to Aesthetic Understanding.* Englewood Cliffs, N.J.: Prentice Hall, 1995.

Lewis, David. *Reading Contemporary Picturebooks: Picturing Text.* London: Routledge, 2001.

Nikolajeva, Maria, and Carole Scott. *How Picturebooks Work.* New York: Garland, 2001.

Nodelman, Perry. *Words About Pictures: The Narrative Art of Children's Picture Books.* Athens, Ga.: University of Georgia Press, 1988.

Schwarcz, Joseph H. *Ways of the Illustrator: Visual Communication in Children's Literature.* Chicago: American Library Association, 1982.

Schwarcz, Joseph, and Chava Schwarz. *The Picture Book Comes of Age.* Chicago: American Library Association, 1991.

Stewig, John Warren. *Looking at Picture Books.* Fort Atkinson, Wis: Highsmith, 1995.

Thiele, Jens. *Das Bilderbuch: Ästhetic, Theorie, Analyse, Didaktik, Rezeption.* Oldenburh, Germany: Isensee, 2000.

MARIA NIKOLAJEVA

Pied Piper of Hamelin, The. "The Pied Piper of Hamelin" is the legend of a magical piper who frees a medieval town from a plague of rats during the 13th century and who, after due payment has been refused, lures away the town's children, never to be seen again. Numerous references to the legend, which began about 1430, survive from the mid-15th century, but the influential literary sources are the 1816/1818 compilation from several versions by the Grimm brothers in *Deutsche Sagen* (German Legends) and Robert Browning's poem, "The Pied Piper of Hamelin" (1849). Browning's poem, with its moral concerning the repayment of debt and surmise that the children became part of the medieval colonization of eastern Europe, is the favored pretext for most subsequent retellings. It was illustrated by Kate Greenaway in 1885, and many other picture books that closely retell the poem have since been published, such as the versions retold and illustrated by Michèle Lemieux (1993) and Peter Weevers (1991).

Novelized versions have preferred other explanations for the events of the legend. In *What Happened in Hamelin* (1979), Gloria Skurzynski explains the tale's sinister events through a mixture of historical and scientific facts: the piper poisons the children with ergot and then sells them to a slave trader recruiting for the Children's Crusades. Slavery is also the motif in Alan Wheatley's time-slip novel *Merchant of Death* (1994), while ergot poisoning is favored by Donna Jo Napoli in her young adult novel *Breath* (2003), which depicts a medieval society plagued by disease and superstition, eager to find something on which to blame their misfortunes. Her story explores social marginalization by detailing the ways in which the narrator, a sick boy unable to follow the piper, is persecuted. Terry Pratchett's first Discworld novel for children, *The Amazing Maurice and His Educated Rodents* (2001), narrated primarily from the perspective of a group of rats, comically refashions the legend as an elaborate scam.

[*See also* Adaptation; Legends; *and biographies of figures mentioned in this article.*]

The Pied Piper. Illustration by H. J. Ford from *The Red Fairy Book*, edited by Andrew Lang (London: Longman, Green, 1890). REPRODUCED COURTESY OF THE COTSEN CHILDREN'S LIBRARY, PRINCETON UNIVERSITY LIBRARY

BIBLIOGRAPHY

Frante, Wolfgang. "Browning's Pied Piper of Hamelin: Two Levels of Meaning." *Ariel* 2, no. 4 (1971): 90–97.

Mieder, Wolfgang. "The Pied Piper of Hamelin: Origin, History, and Survival of the Legend." In *Tradition and Innovation in Folk Literature*, 45–83. Hanover, N.H.: University Press of New England, 1987.

Wunderlich, Werner. "The Pied Piper of Hamelin in History and Literature." *Michigan Germanic Studies* 19, no. 1 (Spring 1993): 1–17.

JOHN STEPHENS

Pieńkowski, Jan (1936–), illustrator and designer of children's books and pop-ups. Pieńkowski was born in Warsaw and relocated to England with his parents in 1946, after World War II. He read classics and English at Kings College, Cambridge; cofounded a greeting card company, Gallery Five; and worked in publishing, advertising, graphic design, and children's television before focusing on children's book illustration. Pieńkowski's illustrations for Joan Aiken's *A Necklace of Raindrops* (1968) mark his first venture into children's books, and his second collaboration with Aiken, *The Kingdom by the Sea* (1971), won Pieńkowski the Kate Greenaway Medal. Often set against richly colored backgrounds, the pen-and-ink silhouettes lend drama to Aiken's magical tales, and the absence of specific detail echoes the distant, fairy tale timescape of "once upon a time" in the verbal narrative. Pieńkowski's silhouette technique was also used in other books, notably the *Fairy Tale Library* (1977) and *Christmas* (1984). Pieńkowski is perhaps best known for the *Meg and Mog* series that he created with Helen Nicoll, depicting the comic antics of witch and cat in acid-bright, bold designs. The first of this series, *Meg and Mog*, appeared in 1972; by 2005 there were sixteen books in the series alongside a wide range of spin-off texts, a theatrical production, and a television series (first screened in the United Kingdom in 2003). Pieńkowski is not simply an illustrator, however; he is also a pioneer of the contemporary pop-up book, creating numerous witty and technically complex movables such as *Haunted House* (1979), another Kate Greenaway Medal winner. *Botticelli's Bed and Breakfast* (1996) might be termed a crossover text, since its irreverent take on art history implies a sophisticated readership. Pieńkowski's most recent project is *The First Noel*, an intricate pop-up lantern of vignettes in snowy silhouette.

[*See also* Aiken, Joan; Book Design; Illustrations; *and* Movable Books and Pop-Up Books.]

LISA SAINSBURY

Pierce, Meredith Ann (1958–), American writer of young adult fantasy. Her trilogy comprising *The Darkangel* (1982), *A Gathering of Gargoyles* (1984), and *The Pearl of the Soul of the World* (1989) takes place on the moon, which has been abandoned by human civilization after an attempt to re-create a technological paradise. The plot, involving a struggle of good and evil, may seem conventional, yet the trilogy presents one of the rare examples of a genuinely female identity quest, in which the adolescent protagonist is forced to define herself not in relation to men, but in relation to other women, peers as well as elders. It also conveys strong ecological and ethical messages and contains exhilarating play with language. *The Woman Who Loved Reindeer* (1985) and another trilogy, *Birth of the Firebringer* (1985), *Dark Moon* (1992), and *The Son of Summer Stars* (1996), continue to develop Pierce's peculiar mythic universe.

[*See also* Fantasy; Girls' Books and Fiction; *and* Science Fiction.]

MARIA NIKOLAJEVA

Pierce, Tamora (1954–), American author born in South Connellsville, Pennsylvania. Pierce worked in a variety of jobs, including as an editor for a literary agency, before becoming a full-time writer. She is renowned for her sword-and-sorcery fantasy fiction for children. Her first published fantasy series was the Song of the Lioness quartet (1983–1988), which featured the feisty Alanna, a young girl who successfully disguises herself as a boy to undertake her training as a royal knight in the (Arthurian-influenced) kingdom of Tortall. Pierce has also published a number of other sword-and-sorcery fantasy series, such as The Immortals quartet (1992–1996), The Circle of Magic quartet (1997–1999), The Protector of the Small quartet (1999–2002), and The Circle Opens quartet (2000–2003). The heroines of these series are free-spirited and independent, and in challenging the limiting assumptions that their societies make about appropriate feminine behavior they overturn the masculine heroic model that has traditionally dominated this fantasy genre.

[*See also* Fantasy *and* Girls' Books and Fiction.]

VICTORIA FLANAGAN

Pierrot. The pathetic, naive clown in French pantomime, Pierrot descends from the hapless, moonstruck Pedrolino, Harlequin's foil, in the Italian commedia dell'arte. Over time

Pierrot has evolved from the personification of unrequited love and undeserved sorrow to an icon in his own right. The ballooning white costume with black trimmings, chalk-white makeup, and earnest, often melancholy demeanor—now inseparable from the character—were the creation of the great 19th-century Parisian mime Baptiste Deburau, who made the role his own. Pierrot has also inspired authors such as Alexandre Dumas, Tomie De Paola, and Anita Lobel to create new works for children that go beyond traditional plots and themes.

[*See also* Pantomime *and biographies of figures mentioned in this article.*]

PEGGY LIN DUTHIE

Pieterse, Pieter (1936–2002), much loved South African writer whose oeuvre embraced the essence of the region. His murder was an enormous loss. He wrote many children's stories in Afrikaans, usually translated into English by his wife, the writer Jenny Winter. He put into his writings his intimate knowledge of landscapes, wildlife, and the sea, while the exciting plots were often set in the regional liberation and civil wars of the 1970s and 1980s. Typically, *Geheim van die Reënwoud* (Secret of the Rain Forest, 1984; English trans., *The Misty Mountain*, 1985) has as its theme the struggle to survive.

ELWYN JENKINS

Pilgrim's Progress. *See* Bunyan, John.

Pilkey, Dav (1966–), American author and illustrator, who infuses most of his books with slapstick humor (often with a bent toward the bathroom) and a strong sense of irony. His illustrations extend from straightforward line drawings to campy collage to elegant paintings. In the Captain Underpants books (1997–)—comic-book-style easy readers with interactive flip-action pages—protagonists George and Harold save the world from villains such as the Wicked Wedgie Woman. Pilkey's picture book *The Paperboy* (1996) provides a quieter perspective, its deeply hued acrylic paintings following a newspaper delivery boy and his dog as they traverse the boy's morning route. Other books return to the daffy comedy Pilkey is best known for: *Kat Kong* (1993) and *Dogzilla* (1993) spoof monster movies with layouts featuring outsized photos of pets as the main characters, while the Dragon series (1991–1993) introduces an absentminded reptile whose misadventures turn on his inability to focus on any single activity.

[*See also* Book Design; Easy Readers; Humor; *and* Illustrations.]

TIMNAH CARD

Pilkington, Mary (1766–1839), prolific British writer of fiction for young people between the ages of fourteen and twenty. Published by Elizabeth Newbery, John Harris, and Vernor and Hood, Pilkington's works were also translated into Italian, French, and Portuguese. Her novels *Edward Barnard* (1797) and *Henry* (1799) follow the plights of apparently poor orphans who patiently endure the insults of youngsters in their foster families and who nevertheless behave charitably and benevolently; both orphans are eventually reunited with their noble parents. In *The Force of Example* (1797), orphans benefit from the good example and instructive conversations of their aunt and uncle and from interaction with their cousins. Interspersed are discussions of historical figures and geography. Pilkington's *New Tales of the Castle* (1800) describes the experiences in Wales of aristocratic refugees from the French Revolution. The industry of the family and their attention to the distressed prevail in spite of their own straitened circumstances.

[*See also* Harris, John; Moral Tales; *and* Orphans.]

SYLVIA KASEY MARKS

Pillai, Keshaw Shankar (1902–1989), political cartoonist, journalist, and pioneer on behalf of Indian children's literature; known as Shankar. In 1957 he founded the Children's Book Trust, a company designed to create books for recreational reading, and in 1976 he founded the Association of Writers and Illustrators for Children, a forum for the study of children's literature. He was instrumental in advancing the cause of the Indian picture book (for instance, his Indraprastha Press provided the special equipment needed for illustrations), and he created a reading room and library to showcase picture books from around the world. Shankar's works include the self-illustrated books *Life with Grandfather* (1965), which is autobiographical, and *Sujata and the Wild Elephant* (1965), featuring a unique relationship between a girl and a rogue elephant. Works illustrated by other artists include *Hari, and Other Elephants* (1967; illustrated by Pulak Biswas) and *The Scare* (1982; illustrated by Reboti Bhushan). Shankar's *The Lion and the Elephant*

(1991), as well as others, was selected for an exhibition of Indian children's literature organized in Japan by the Buddhist organization Soka Gakkai. The Children's Book Trust's competition for writers of children's books, a contest that encourages works with an Indian background, honors the most outstanding contestant with the Shankar Gold Medal.

[*See also* India; Picture Books; *and* Publishers and Publishing.]

Donnarae MacCann

Pilling, Anne (1944–), British writer who was an English teacher before turning to full-time writing in 1981. Pilling coedited the *Kingfisher Treasury of Bible Stories* (2000) and retold two collections of creation stories, but is best known as a novelist. Her books for younger children, like *Dustbin Charlie* (1988), deal reassuringly with young children's loneliness, anxieties, and yearnings. Pilling's novels for older children also offer happy endings (consonant with her Christian beliefs), but are much grimmer. In her first children's novel, *Black Harvest* (1983), 20th-century children are haunted by sounds, sights, and smells of the Irish famine. Pilling has written many adolescent problem novels; her books of the 1980s are unusually explicit for their era in their treatment of money problems, the stigma of poverty, and its seemingly endless humiliations. She evokes the terrors of being pursued by violent criminals in *Stan* (1988) and the everyday wretchedness of being bullied in *The Big Pink* (1987) and *The Year of the Worm* (1984). Mothers in her novels generally mean well but fail to protect their children. Some intact families put the practice of Christian charity above care for their own children, as in *Mother's Daily Scream* (1995). In other novels, the husband has abandoned his wife, who neglects their child in her struggle to earn enough money, as in *Henry's Leg* (1985). This novel, which won the Guardian Award, follows the Blyton tradition with its missing treasure, mystery, and secret passage, and like the Famous Five, Henry outwits criminal adults and less-than-competent police. The book's blend of humor and the uncanny is, however, unlike anything in Blyton's work. Pilling also writes ghost stories under the name of Ann Cheedham.

[*See also* Blyton, Enid; Realism; Religious Instruction and Education; *and* Young Adult Literature.]

Alice Mills

Pimentel, Alberto (1849–1925), Portuguese politician, journalist, and writer. As a creative writer, he produced about two hundred works in several genres: history, biography, the historical novel (for example, *O descobrimento do Brasil* [The Discovering of Brazil, 1895]), the chronicle, and the anecdote (for example, *As amantes de D. João V* [John the Fifth's Lovers, 1892]) were all cultivated by Pimentel, who also wrote a memoir and collected folk songs. The Porto and the northern regions of Portugal serve as the settings in *O Porto há trinta anos* (Oporto Thirty Years Ago, 1893) and *As alegres canções do norte* (The Happy Songs from the North, 1905). Pimentel admired the celebrated Portuguese writer Camilo Castelo Branco and became a known Branco scholar, writing many texts about him, such as *Os amores de Camilo* (Camilo's Loves, 1899). Though Branco is not primarily known for children's literature or juvenile reading, his production of historical novels is important in Portuguese literature.

[*See also* Historical Fiction; Nonfiction; *and* Portugal.]

Manuela Fonseca

Pinchard, Elizabeth Sibthorpe, late-18th- and early-19th-century British writer of fiction for young people between the ages of fourteen and twenty, whose works were also published in the United States. In *The Blind Child* (1791), Pinchard's best-known novel in dialogue form, Helen regains her sight, but in the course of the story the Wyndham family discusses topics typically found in the fiction of this period: reciprocal duties, treatment of animals, fairy tales, parental indulgence, true and false sensibility, and education. In *Family Affection* (1816), Montrose Beresford endures much as a schoolboy in England and as an adult in India. He finally concludes that "real virtue, and real felicity, may be found in every rank and in every situation in life." Other works include *Dramatic Dialogues* (1792) and the sophisticated novels *Mystery and Confidence* (1814), *The Ward of Delamere* (1815), and *The Young Countess* (1820).

[*See also* United Kingdom *and* Young Adult Literature.]

Sylvia Kasey Marks

Pinkney, Andrea Davis (1963–), African American author of picture books and novels that focus on African American history and culture; the wife of the illustrator Brian Pinkney. Pinkney was editorial director of Hyperion Books for Children from 2001 to 2002 and became vice president and publisher of Houghton Mifflin's children's books in 2002. Having grown up in a family that participated in the civil rights movement, Pinkney considers herself a product of the movement, and the ideology of "black empowerment" certainly surfaces in such books of hers as *Seven Candles for Kwanzaa* (1993) and *Duke Ellington: The Piano Prince and His Orchestra* (1998), both of which are collaborations with her husband, Brian.

[*See also* African American Literature; Pinkney, Brian; *and* Publishers and Publishing.]

MICHELLE H. MARTIN

Pinkney, Brian (1961–), African American illustrator. Educated at the University of the Arts in Philadelphia and at the School of Visual Arts in New York City, Pinkney is the son of the illustrator Jerry Pinkney and the author Gloria Jean Pinkney, who encouraged him to pursue the arts as a child. Pinkney's career began with illustrations created for the *New York Times*, *Woman's Day*, and *Ebony Man*, and much of his work focuses on African-American history, culture, folklore, and art. For instance, *Alvin Ailey* (1993), the first collaboration between Pinkney and his wife, Andrea Davis Pinkney, tells the story of a famous black dancer whose "dances told stories." This picture book explores how Ailey incorporated his early experiences of the black church into the choreography and music of the Alvin Ailey American Dance Theater. *Bill Pickett, Rodeo Ridin' Cowboy* (1996), another of their collaborations, tells of an African-American cowboy who gained fame for "bulldoggin'" (rodeo steer wrestling). Pinkney specializes in scratchboard illustrations created with luma dyes, and in *Bill Pickett* the light underpaint shows through the scratches on brown and black images. This technique brings life and motion to the scenes depicting the cowboy's unique skill. In *Max Found Two Sticks* (1994), the story of a boy who "talks" with two sticks serving as drumsticks, the illustrations are unlike most of Pinkney's other work because the page layouts resemble those of comic strips. Both this tale and *Duke Ellington: The Piano Prince and His Orchestra* (1998) include the skillful use of curved lines to suggest music visually. Pinkney received both a Caldecott Honor Award and a Coretta Scott King Honor Award for his illustrations in Robert D. San Souci's *The Faithful Friend* (1995), an adaptation of a tale from Martinique.

MICHELLE H. MARTIN

Pinkney, Gloria Jean (1941–), American writer and wife of the acclaimed illustrator Jerry Pinkney. After many years of assisting her husband Jerry in his illustration work, she collaborated with him to produce *Back Home* (1992) and *The Sunday Outing* (1994), a pair of semiautobiographical picture books that follow young Ernestine on her first solo train trip, and offer a warm, nostalgic look at African American family life in the 1940s in a northern city and on a southern farm. Pinkney also authored a spiritual memoir, *In the Forest of Your Remembrance* (2001), illustrated by her husband as well as by her two sons, Brian Pinkney and Myles C. Pinkney.

[*See also* African American Literature *and biographies of figures mentioned in this article.*]

KARA REUTER

Pinkney, Jerry (1939–), African American illustrator. This prolific watercolorist has won five Caldecott Honor awards for his illustrations in Patricia McKissack's *Mirandy and Brother Wind* (1988), Robert D. San Souci's *The Talking Eggs* (1989), Julius Lester's *John Henry* (1994), Hans Christian Andersen's *The Ugly Duckling* (1999), and Pinkney's own *Noah's Ark* (2002). Pinkney is the husband of the children's author Gloria Jean Pinkney and father of the illustrators Brian and Myles Pinkney. He was born in Philadelphia, Pennsylvania, and grew up with five siblings, all of whom were encouraged in their artistic pursuits. When he was twelve, he met John Liney, creator of the "Little Henry" comic strip, and this encounter made him consider making a living as an artist. Receiving art training at Dobbins Vocational Art School and the Philadelphia College of Art (PCA), Pinkney left PCA after the birth of his first child and began freelancing. He later obtained a job with Rustcraft, a greeting card company, and moved his family to Boston. At Rustcraft and also at the Barker-Black Studio (an illustration house), Pinkney gained invaluable experience both in illustration and design. He illustrated his first book in 1964: Joyce Cooper Arkhurst's *Adventures of Spider: West African Folktales*.

In 1970 Pinkney moved his family to New York, and because publishers had started seeking out African American authors and artists to create children's books, he found new opportunities. As he developed as an artist, he began to focus more on African and African American subjects, but he continued to illustrate books from a variety of cultures. Although Pinkney's first efforts were in black and white, his signature illustrations are luminescent watercolor paintings through which can often be seen the original, underlying pencil sketches. He does not remove these sketches because he

Jerry Pinkney. "Rosebud Yellow Robe"; illustration by Jerry Pinkney from his *Tonweya and the Eagles and Other Lakota Tales* (New York: Dial, 1979). COLLECTION OF JACK ZIPES

wants readers to see some of the processes he uses and because these lines add a sense of motion to the pictures. Regardless of whether Pinkney is illustrating traditional stories such as Arkhurst's *More Adventures of Spider* (1972), poetry such as Thylias Moss's *I Want to Be* (1993), biographies like Alan Schroeder's *Minty: A Story of Young Harriet Tubman* (1996), retellings like Julius Lester's *Sam and the Tigers: A New Telling of Little Black Sambo* (1996), or novels such as Mildred Taylor's *Roll of Thunder, Hear My Cry* (1976), his illustrations bring light and life to the story and often round out details not suggested in the text.

In Julius Lester's *Sam and the Tigers*, for instance, young Sam, who lives in Sam-sam-sa-mara, chooses his own outfit for his first day of school. In the town live many animals, and while Pinkney takes great pains to draw anatomically accurate animals, in making them anthropomorphic he adds minute details that comment on their character: Mr. Giraffe wears round spectacles, a dress coat, and a green and yellow scarf, and even the spider wears a jacket. But the tigers who threaten to eat Sam wear no clothes at all. Pinkney's attention to detail—from painting faces on the trees to hiding insects in the grass—demonstrates his respect for young readers and his efforts to challenge them with the finest artwork he can produce.

As Pinkney has continued to grow as an artist, he has undertaken more individual projects. *Aesop's Fables* (2000) and *Noah's Ark* are two such works, and although he retells familiar stories in these volumes, his watercolor illustrations make the old stories new. In the illustration of the Ark in its formative stages, the ship covers a double-page spread and spills off the page, emphasizing the colossal dimensions of a craft large enough to transport every type of animal. Pinkney depicts flooded cities, sharks swimming above the towns, and the hull of the Ark floating safely on the water's surface.

In a career spanning more than forty years, Pinkney has helped raise artistic standards in children's literature. He has also served as a role model and mentor for other African-American artists seeking entrance to the field—beginning with his own children, three of whom are involved in writing and illustrating children's books.

[*See also* African American Literature.]

BIBLIOGRAPHY

Bishop, Rudine Sims. "The Pinkney Family: In the Tradition." *Horn Book* 72 (1996): 42–49.

Darigan, Daniel L. "Sorting Out the Pinkneys." *Language Arts* 80 (2002): 75–80.

MICHELLE H. MARTIN

Pinkney, Myles (1963?–), American photographer and son of the acclaimed illustrator Jerry Pinkney. His photographs have illustrated books by notable authors, including *It's Raining Laughter* (1997), a collection of poems by Nikki Grimes; *Can You Imagine?* (1997), an autobiography by Patricia McKissack; and *Sitting Pretty: A Celebration of Black Dolls* (2000) by Dinah Johnson. He collaborated with his wife Sandra L. Pinkney on *Shades of Black: A Celebration of Our Black Children* (2000) and *A Rainbow All around Me* (2002), contributing crisp, lively portraits honoring children of diverse cultures. With his father and brother, Brian, he also coillustrated his mother Gloria Jean Pinkney's memoir *In the Forest of Your Remembrance* (2001) with stately and serene photographs.

[*See also* African American Literature; Multiculturalism and Children's Books; Photography in Nonfiction for

Children; *and biographies of figures mentioned in this article.*]

KARA REUTER

Pinkney, Sandra, African American author of books that highlight diversity. In collaboration with her husband, the photo-illustrator Myles Pinkney, Pinkney authored two picture books that portray the many variations in children. *Shades of Black: A Celebration of Our Children* (2000) showcases African American beauty by representing the range of skin tones, eye color, and hair texture within the black community. *A Rainbow All around Me* (2002) is a book of colors, illustrated with photographs of children from a variety of ethnic groups. In both books, Pinkney's rhythmic language complements her husband's lively photographs and evokes texture and taste as well as color.

[*See also* African American Literature; Multiculturalism and Children's Books; *and* Pinkney, Myles.]

KARA REUTER

Pinkwater, Daniel (1941–), American author of humorous children's books, some of which he illustrates. Pinkwater (who has also published as Manus Pinkwater) studied art, and especially sculpture, attaining a BA from Bard College in 1964. He went on to study at the Art Institute of Chicago and at Harvard University and in the early 2000s was an occasional and much beloved National Public Radio commentator. He is known principally for his humorous children's books with unlikely titles, some of which he illustrates himself and some of which are illustrated by his wife, Jill Pinkwater. The books often include autobiographical elements from his childhood in Chicago; he also wrote a fictionalized biography, *The Education of Robert Nifkin* (1998).

Daniel Pinkwater.

Pinkwater's early children's fiction, *Wizard Crystal* (1973), *Magic Camera* (1974), *Lizard Music* (1976), *The Hoboken Chicken Emergency* (1977; made into a PBS movie in 1984), and *Fat Men from Space* (1977), drew attention because of their strange titles, their highly intelligent but usually socially marginalized main characters, and their science fiction content. The language is entertaining and the situations quirky, like the moose waiter in the remote restaurant in *Blue Moose* (1975), who talks like a headwaiter at a fancy hotel. Pinkwater has been called a "dadaist" and a "surrealist" because of the way the extraordinary intrudes into ordinary life. In *Lizard Music*, a boy left alone by his parents finds that his television will play only shows with lizards singing and concludes that some kind of conspiracy is afoot. *Fat Men from Space* tells of a crisis caused when alien fat men come to either steal or eat up all the junk food on earth, especially potato pancakes and hamburgers.

Five of Pinkwater's most popular novels were republished as *5 Novels* in 1997. They include *Alan Mendelsohn, the Boy from Mars* (1979), *Slaves of Spiegel* (1982), *The Snarkout Boys and the Avocado of Death* (1982), *The Last Guru* (1978), and *Young Adult Novel* (1982). *Young Adult Novel*'s satirical approach to the "problem novel" delights young and older readers with its references to Kevin's vegetative father, alcoholic mother, social worker, and checkered student career at, of course, Himmler High. It chronicles the ease with which a few intelligent, irreverent boys can foment rebellion in a traditional school. Their group, the Wild Dada Ducks, picks an imaginary boy to be elected class president. When he turns out to be real and does not want the job, the fun starts.

Many of Pinkwater's characters have casual relationships with equally odd adult males. Harold Blatz of *The Last Guru* is friendly with his Uncle Roy, whose job allows him to spend a lot of time in Mike's Bar and Grill. In *Alan Mendelsohn* Leonard and the eponymous Alan meet two odd bookstore owners, William Lloyd Floyd and Samuel Klugarsh, whose side business is selling mind-control lessons. These relationships enable Pinkwater to present people and comic situations from the perspective of an eleven- or twelve-year-old boy, and the humor arises in part because the boy's delightful interpretation of strange events may or may not be reliable. The efforts of the boys to create meaningful experiences out of otherwise dull lives, social settings, and institutions seemingly ranged against them reveal a kind of heroism that is at once funny and poignant, entertaining readers of all ages.

[*See also* Fantasy; Humor; Parody; Pinkwater, Jill; *and* Young Adult Literature.]

JANICE M. BOGSTAD

Pinkwater, Jill (1941–), American author and illustrator. Born Jill Miriam Schutz, in 1969 she married the writer and illustrator Daniel Manus Pinkwater, with whom she collaborated on more than thirty picture books. Pinkwater's vivid, cheerful artwork, executed in pen and marker, perfectly complements their stories. *At the Hotel Larry* (1998) is one of several books featuring a large, muffin-loving polar bear and his adventures in the world of humans. In 1977 the Pinkwaters coauthored the well-received nonfiction book *Superpuppy: How to Choose, Raise, and Train the Best Possible Dog for You.* On her own, Pinkwater has published one cookbook and five novels, including *Buffalo Brenda* (1989) and *Tails of the Bronx* (1991) for middle schoolers.

[*See also* Illustrations; Nonfiction; Pinkwater, Daniel; *and* Picture Books.]

MONICA FRIEDMAN

Pinocchio. Pinocchio is the protagonist of the novel by the Italian writer Carlo Collodi (Carlo Lorenzini). Written serially from 1881 to 1883, *The Adventures of Pinocchio* first appeared as a full-length novel in 1883, was translated for British audiences in 1891, and arrived in the United States in 1892. It has since been rendered in all major languages and in at least twenty distinct English translations. Written with both adults and children in mind, *Pinocchio* is a tale of growing up, where the comically hyperactive, headstrong, troublemaking puppet symbolizes an egocentric, self-preoccupied child who, in a dialectical process, gradually recognizes his impact on and connection to others, and who, after many troubles, matures into a responsible, empathic young adult. The tale depicts parental vexation, acknowledges conflicts within the family to be normal, and shows how children can learn to prosper emotionally in a corrupt world from the good examples of others. Pinocchio's spiritual transformation begins when, ignoring himself, he risks his life to save his father Geppetto, who has been swallowed by a fantastical shark. His metamorphosis continues when he empathizes with a dying donkey and makes sacrifices to provide for his ailing parent and to help his fairy benefactress, whom he believes to be ill and destitute. At the end she certifies Pinocchio's internal evolution by transforming him outwardly into a real boy, or person. Fundamental changes in the telling of the story did not occur until Yasha Frank

Pinocchio. Illustration by Charles Folkard from *Pinocchio: The Tale of a Puppet* by Carlo Collodi (London: T. Fisher Unwin, 1911). COLLECTION OF JACK ZIPES

(in a 1937 play performance in Los Angeles) altered Pinocchio's personality radically by making him naive, innocent, and passive; changed Geppetto into a father who loves but does not get angry; and revised the novel's theme from transformation and coming of age into a celebration of family solidarity and childhood obedience to proper authority. Though its plot differed, Walt Disney's famous film (1940) uses the same character and thematic changes introduced by Frank. Other writers afterward, beginning with Roselle Ross (1939), followed Frank's model, but made Pinocchio active, mischievous, and lovable. Because of the abundance of adaptations of Collodi's novel today, readers may easily mistake the adaptations for his original. That Collodi's story captures the imagination is attested to not only by children's continuations such as *Pinocchio in Africa* (by Eugenio Cherubini, 1903), *The Heart of Pinocchio* (by Paolo Lorenzini,

1917), *Pinocchio in America* (by Angelo Patri, 1928), *Puppet Parade* (by Carol Della Chiesa, 1932), and *Hi! Ho! Pinocchio* (by Josef Marino, 1940), but also by contemporary adult fiction such as *Pinocchio's Nose* (by Jerome Charyn, 1983), *Pinocchio in Venice* (by Robert Coover, 1991), "Pinocchio's Wife" (by Michael Kenyon, 1992), and films like *A.I.: Artificial Intelligence* (by Steven Spielberg and Stanley Kubrick, 2001).

[*See also* Adaptation; Collodi, Carlo; Italy; *and* Young Adult Literature.]

BIBLIOGRAPHY

Wunderlich, Richard. *The Pinocchio Catalogue: Being a Descriptive Bibliography and Printing History of English Language Translations and Other Renditions Appearing in the United States, 1892–1987*. Westport, Conn.: Greenwood, 1988.

Wunderlich, Richard, and Thomas J. Morrissey. *Pinocchio Goes Postmodern: Perils of a Puppet in the United States*. New York and London: Routledge, 2002.

RICHARD WUNDERLICH and THOMAS J. MORRISSEY

Pippi Longstocking. *See* Lindgren, Astrid.

Pistelli, Padre Ermenegildo (1862–1927), priest, philologist, teacher, and scholar in Italian, Greek, and Latin literature, and—as "Omero Redi"—a noted writer for Italian children. From 1906 to 1911 he contributed a regular column to the leading children's weekly, *Il giornalino della domenica* (The Children's Sunday Paper), in which he discussed, with witty informality and a zest for polemic, the people and events of contemporary Florence. Adopting the persona of an enfant terrible who recounted the "funny things" that happened at school, Pistelli headed his letters "Le Pistole d'Omero." The boyish confusion between "epistles" and "pistols" illustrates his entertaining technique for avoiding sermonizing while advancing shrewd comment in the style of a misspelled, blotted copybook. The intention was serious, but the joking disguise was new, original, and influential. Pistelli's objectives included educational and literary change, but were above all political and patriotic. Critics are divided about his legacy, especially because in later years Pistelli supported Fascism.

[*See also* Humor; Italy; *and* Journals and Periodicals.]

ANN LAWSON LUCAS

Pittman, Helena Clare (1945–), American author, illustrator and teacher. Pittman was educated at New York's Pratt Institute (B.F.A., 1969). Inspired by the birth of her youngest child, she created her first book, *A Grain of Rice* (1966), illustrating it with well-drafted pencil drawings. The book is based on a Chinese tale about a peasant who outsmarts an emperor and marries his daughter. In *The Gift of the Willows* (1988), Pittman's spirited watercolor paintings are enhanced by split-screen composition, harmonious framing, and the integration of type within the total design. Her dynamic technique corresponds to her central theme: the resilience of two willow trees as they symbolize a Japanese potter's ability to celebrate beauty while challenging hardship. Among Pittman's other picture book narratives is *The Snowman's Path* (2000; illustrated by Raúl Colón). She has also been a teacher of drawing, painting, design, and illustration at the State University of New York and the Parsons School of Design.

SANDRA BOLTON

Pitz, Henry Clarence (1895–1976), American illustrator. Born in Philadelphia and educated at the Philadelphia Museum School of Art and the Spring Garden Institute, Philadelphia, Pitz became an art teacher and a prolific and award-winning illustrator of children's literature, producing more than 160 books. His works include illustrations for Clarence Stratton's *Robert the Roundhead* (1930), Mary MacLeod's *The Book of Arthur and His Noble Knights* (1949), Patricia Cecil's *Kata, Son of Red Fang: Wolf Dog of the North* (1954), and editions of classics—including a 1954 edition of Robert Louis Stevenson's *Treasure Island*. Pitz also wrote *Illustrating Children's Books: History, Technique, Production* (1963).

[*See also* Illustrations.]

ADRIENNE E. GAVIN

Pitzorno, Bianca (1942–), major contemporary Italian writer for children, whose numerous novels address a multitude of social and political problems while remaining imaginative, stylish, and amusing. A left-wing feminist who is critical of hypocrisy, convention, stereotype, and the commonplace, Pitzorno tackles controversial and complex issues from ecology and consumerism to political corruption, social class, and race (*Tornatrás*; Throwback, 2000). Imaginative plotting, narrative verve, inventive characterization, humor, and the involvement of the reader, whether very young or adolescent, are Pitzorno's hallmarks. (Her stories for young children are usually told orally several times before being written down.) Early on, she began challenging the limitation of human norms and wittily addressed the idea of "aliens" in the partly botanical heroine of *Clorofilla dal cielo blu* (Chlorophyllis from the Blue Sky, 1975) and Mo, of indeterminate gender, in *Extraterrestre alla pari* (The Extraterrestrial au pair, 1979). Even in her treatment of antiquity *La giustizia di Salomone* (The Judgement of Solomon, 1978) or *La bambina col falcone* (The Little Girl with a Falcon, 1992), she queries common assumptions. While Pitzorno typically combines acid criticism with sunny laughter, *Principessa Laurentina* (Princess Laurentina, 1990) expresses the powerful emotions connected with adolescence and family difficulties, and the moving *Ascolta il mio cuore* (Listen to My Heart, 1991) is a psychological landmark. In *A letto, bambini!* (Bedtime, Children!, 1990) she created a vivid verse interpretation of Sylvia Plath, while her substantial novel, *La bambinaia francese* (The French Governess, 2004) is an intertextual, historical tale weaving together elements of Charlotte Brontë's *Jane Eyre* with Parisian and Caribbean revolutionary society. A favorite character has returned in a collection of old and new stories *Magie de Lavinia & C.* (The Magic of Lavinia & Co., 2005), illustrated by Quentin Blake. Pitzrono has explicated her own writing in *Storia delle mie storie* (The Story of My Stories, 2002), while also encouraging the young to write in *Manuale del giovane scrittore creativo* (The Young Creative Writer's Manual, 1996), which provides lessons and exercises.

[*See also* Fantasy; Italy; *and* Realism.]

ANN LAWSON LUCAS

Piumini, Roberto (1947–), Italian writer whose hundred or more publications include novels, stories, plays, translations, songs, rhymes, and collections of poetry. Piumini's literary identity has been created by a dazzling mixture of tradition and invention: different kinds of intertextuality are often present, and many of his works can be seen as modern—or postmodern—variations composed on themes from fairy tale, mythology, folklore, or literature.

His inspiration is international and polyglot, prompting, variously, retellings of ancient Greek myths in a work charged with both epic and lyric qualities—*Il circo di Zeus* (Zeus's Circus, 1986)—and in an imaginative explanation of Easter Island's history and mythology—*Motu-Iti: L'isola dei gabbiani* (Motu-Iti: Seagull Island, 1993). *Lo stralisco* (Dartwort, 1987) is an inspiring addition to the *Arabian Nights* legacy: the moving tale of a Turkish painter creating beauty for the dying months of a child, this meditation on art, humanity, and death is a masterpiece by any standards. The acceptance of death by young and old recurs in *Mattia e il nonno* (1993; English trans., *Mattie and Grandpa*, 1993). Piumini's internationalism is itself new in Italian children's literature and a hallmark of the postwar generation that experienced the European student movement of 1968. Utopianism is also present in his work; freedom of speech being insufficient, he tries to find "the speech for freedom," too. *Il giovane che entrava nel palazzo* (The Boy Who Went into the Palace, 1978) examines the significance of power. The normal narrative process of addition is reversed by subtraction: at the end of this quest, the authority of the governor of Milan matches his diminished stature (50 centimeters); simultaneously, a fundamental premise of fairy tales—namely, heroic initiation—is itself undermined. Concerned with humanity and civilization, good and evil, time and space, Piumini is a major Italian voice, both learned and lyrical.

[*See also* Fairy Tales and Folk Tales; Italy; Myths; *and* Utopia and Dystopia.]

ANN LAWSON LUCAS

Place, François (1957–), French illustrator and author born in Ezanville, a northern suburb of Paris. As a child, Place had a special interest in adventure books, which he read in scholastic settings, since his mother was a schoolteacher. After studies in the Estienne Art School and some illustrating of novels, his artistic ambitions turned quickly toward specializing in travel and adventure picture books for young readers. In 1992 he wrote and illustrated *Les derniers géants* (English trans., *The Last Giants*, 1993), the story of an expedition at the beginning of the 18th century in an unknown country inhabited by fascinating giants. Since then, Place has been best known for his remarkably precise and poetic watercolor paintings and his stories enhanced by maps, engravings, and travel sketchbooks. The success of his first book allowed him time to realize an immense project that demanded four years of work: *L'atlas des géographes d'Orbae* (The Orbae Geographers' Atlas), a masterly description of imaginary countries presented in alphabetic order, mixing tales and scientific plates. This illustrated book has received several awards. With *Le vieux fou de dessin* (1997; English trans., *Old Man Mad about Drawing: A Tale of Hokusaï*, 2004), Place conveys to young readers his passion for the work of the eminent Japanese artist Hokusai.

[*See also* Adventure Books; France; Geography and Travel Books; *and* Illustrations.]

SOPHIE VAN DER LINDEN

Planché, James Robinson (1796–1880), English dramatist and historian who wrote nearly two hundred theatrical pieces, including several "extravaganzas" based on translations of French fairy tales, especially those of Madame d'Aulnoy and Charles Perrault. Planché's work was popular with English audiences because of the contemporary social, cultural, and political references that he added to the original stories. His extravaganzas, based on the French *folie féerie* (fairy comedy) and English pantomime, employed intricately mechanized sets, fairy motifs, sumptuous decoration, music, dance, and historically accurate costumes. Because the plays' effects depend largely upon elaborate spectacles and contemporary references, it is challenging for readers today to appreciate their artistry. Planché's innovative use of puns and burlesque may have influenced W. S. Gilbert. Planché's most popular productions include *Puss in Boots* (1837), *Blue Beard* (1839), and *The White Cat* (1842). He also published several collections of fairy tales translated from French, including *The Fairy Tales of the Countess D'Aulnoy* (1855) and *Four and Twenty Fairy Tales Translated from Perrault* (1858).

[*See also* Adaptation; Aulnoy, Marie Catherine, Comtesse d'; Fairy Tales and Folk Tales; Pantomime; *and* Perrault, Charles.]

SIGRID ANDERSON CORDELL

Playbox. One of a group of children's annuals published in Britain by the Amalgamated Press, *Playbox* is considered the first comic annual. Originating as a children's supplement to the magazines *Home Chat* (1898) and *The World and His Wife* (1904), *Playbox* was launched as an annual in 1909 and was published until 1956. It starred the famous comic character "Tiger Tim," who went on to feature in a number of AP annuals and weeklies. Tiger Tim and his friends, a group of anthropomorphized animals attending "Mrs. Hippo's Kindergarten," later to become "Mrs. Bruin's Boarding School," appeared in several strips per annual (usually three pages) and in full-page illustrations. Also included were fantasy and adventure stories, additional comics, humorous poetry, and activities. Intended for young children, *Playbox* was profusely illustrated with color plates, text illustrations, and photographs. In 1925 the AP relaunched *Playbox* as a weekly comic aimed at girls, starring Tim's sister Tiger Tilly and her pals the Hippo Girls. Later redesigned for a mixed-sex readership, *Playbox* (weekly) ran until 1955.

[*See also* Animal Stories; Annuals; Children's Magazines; *and* Comic Books.]

BIBLIOGRAPHY

Clark, Alan. *The Children's Annual: A History and Collector's Guide.* London: Boxtree, 1988.

MARTHA SCOTT

Playground Rhymes. The most common form of children's poetry is also the most commonly overlooked: playground rhymes. A kind of folk poetry, playground rhymes exist somewhere between original composition and received oral tradition, and as such, they question dominant notions of the individual authorial genius, while simultaneously complementing adult literary poetic traditions through parody and appropriation. Playground rhyme—or playground poetry—is a term that refers to many forms of childhood folk poetry, each form serving multiple aesthetic and social functions. Some playground rhymes, for instance, are used to choose players in games ("Eenie meanie minie moe, / Catch a tiger by its toe"), while others facilitate jump-roping ("Cinderella dressed in yellow / Went upstairs to kiss her fellow") or hand-clapping games ("Miss Mary Mac, Mac, Mac, / All dressed in black, black, black"). Still others censure poor behavior ("No cuts, no butts, no coconuts"), mock authority ("Joy to the world, the teacher's dead, / I barbecued her head / Don't worry 'bout the body, / I flushed it down the potty"), mock peers ("I'm a monkey / You're a donkey; / I smell sweet and you smell funky"), or defend against mockery ("Sticks and stones may break my bones / But words will never hurt me"). However, a common characteristic of all good playground rhymes is the flaunting of lyrical inventiveness and language play.

Like the nursery rhymes of Mother Goose, no one owns these poems; they belong to each child equally, and each child retains the right to alter and revise the poems as mood or situation dictates. One child, for instance, might chant, "Greasy grimy gopher guts, / Mutilated monkey meat, / Little dirty birdie feet," while another might say, "Greasy grimy gopher guts, / Marinated monkey meat, / Vulture vomit at my feet." Similarly, children feel free to insert the names of friends (or enemies) into the following common rhyme, personalizing it and thereby winning their peers' esteem: "X and Y sitting in a tree, / K-I-S-S-I-N-G. / First comes love, / Then comes marriage, / Then comes Z in a baby carriage."

In different communities one finds either different rhymes or competing versions of the same rhyme, which vary from street corner to street corner, playground to playground. With playground poetry, variety is the rule, each new generation reproducing and reimagining their rhymes, forming a canon of culturally specific poetry shared by all, internalized through memory and public recitation. Unlike children's poetry produced by adults, the production of playground rhymes is not monitored by authority figures. Thus they often contain vulgar, violent (and quite comical) imagery, resisting conventions of decorum and politeness while favoring the lewd and scatological. Their very nature makes it unlikely that playground rhymes would ever be anthologized *for* children, and thus most rhymes exist only in memory, in performance, or in collections made by folklorists. The most notable exception to this rule is Iona and Peter Opie's *I Saw Esau: The Schoolchild's Pocket Book*, which, in its most recent incarnation, is illustrated by Maurice Sendak in an obvious bid for a child audience.

Playground rhymes resist nostalgic notions of the innocent and obedient child, and thus tend to disturb adults, implying, as they do, sexualized, complicated children able to control their world through wordplay and sometimes violent imagery. The authors and performers of these rhymes rarely hesitate to employ so-called adult language, crafting a kind of children's poetry that would be impossible to find in children's literature produced by adults:

Abraham Lincoln
Was a good old soul.
He washed his face
In a toilet bowl.
He jumped out the window
With his dick in his hand,
And said, "'Scuse me, ladies!
I'm superman."

The following parody of "Twinkle Twinkle Little Star" suggests the scatological and antiauthoritarian impulses common in playground rhymes:

Twinkle, Twinkle, little star,
Who the hell do you think you are?
Up in the sky you think you're it;
Down on earth you're a piece of shit.

As these rhymes illustrate, playground poetry demonstrates the child's preoccupation with the body and bodily functions, even as they promote group play, physical exchange, and unrestrained noise. They are composed and performed with the aim of producing strong *bodily* reactions: laughter, guffaws, gasps, groans, or, in the case of jump-rope rhymes, vigorous play. As they center on taboo subjects, the rhymes can be racist or can resist racism, as does this rhyme, first recorded in east Texas at the height of the civil rights movement:

Two, four, six, eight,
We ain't gonna integrate.
Eight, six, four, two,
Bet you sons-of-bitches do.

Other playground rhymes parody adult poetry. The best-known set of playground parodies includes the many variations on Isaac Watts's hymn "Joy to the World." With these poems, playground poets ally themselves with Lewis Carroll, an adult poet who used Watts's verse as a source for poetry. Based on Psalm 96:11–13, the hymn's religious theme is in conflict with the violence and revolutionary impulses of its many schoolyard variations, all of which question the hierarchical values implied by the hymn. One version reads:

Joy to the world, the school burned down,
And all the teachers died.
We're going to take the principal
And hang her from the toilet bowl
With a rope around her neck,
A rope around her neck,
A rope, a rope around her neck.

Other playground rhymes parody adult-produced television shows like *Barney*, which construct children as sweet and loving little angels ready and willing to learn politically correct lessons from equally sweet and loving adults:

I hate you, you hate me.
Let's tie Barney to a tree,
Pull the trigger,
Hit him on the head.
Whoopsy daisy, Barney's dead.

I hate you, you hate me.
Let's get together and kill Barney.
With a knife in the stomach and a bullet in the head
Aren't you glad that Barney's dead?

Although not respected by most adults, the rhythms and rhymes of playground poetry have influenced the writing of many poets, from Allison Joseph to Theodore Roethke, who, for instance, in "I Need, I Need," includes these lines, which seem more at home on the playground than in a collection of adult poetry:

A one is a two is
I know what you is:
You're not very nice,—
So touch my toes twice.

Roethke sees the poetic value in these oft-neglected rhymes, a kind of poetry too commonly put away with childish things. Inexhaustible and culturally relevant, these rhymes are part of a dense poetic tradition consisting of equally dense and rewarding texts.

[*See also* Carroll, Lewis; Grotesque; Nonsense; Opie, Iona, and Peter Opie; *and* Poetry.]

BIBLIOGRAPHY

Abrahams, Roger D., ed. *Jump-Rope Rhymes: A Dictionary*. Austin: University of Texas Press, 1969.

Butler, Francelia. *Skipping Around the World: The Ritual Nature of Folk Rhymes*. Hamden, Conn.: Library Professional Publications, 1989.

Sherman, Josepha, and T. K. F. Weisskopf. *Greasy Grimy Gopher Guts: The Subversive Folklore of Childhood*. Little Rock, Ark.: August House, 1995.

Thomas, Joseph T., Jr. "Child Poets and the Poetry of the Playground." *Children's Literature* 32 (Spring 2004): 152–177.

Thomas, Joseph T., Jr. *Poetry's Playground: The Culture of Contemporary American Children's Poetry*. Detroit, Mich.: Wayne State University Press, 2006.

JOSEPH T. THOMAS JR.

Plays. Stage adaptations have long been made of literature—legends, folk tales, fables, and fairy tales—intended for children and young adults. However, it was with the publication of Lewis Carroll's two children's books, *Alice's Adventures in Wonderland* (1865) and *Through the Looking Glass and What Alice Found There* (1871), that stage adaptations of literature for children and young adults by identified authors emerged. Many adaptations of contemporary literary works followed, with the *Alice* plays (1880 and 1882), F. Anstey's *Vice Versa* (1883), William Makepeace Thackeray's *The Rose and the Ring* (1890), Charles Kingsley's *The Water Babies* (1902), and Heinrich Hoffmann's *Struwwelpeter* (1903). Several of these continue to be performed in modern readapted versions. Frances Hodgson Burnett's own adaptation of her novel *Little Lord Fauntleroy* (1886; dramatized 1888) became immensely popular in Britain and the United States, creating a new fashion for boys' clothes, while Burnett also adapted her short novel *Sara Crewe* (1887) for the stage as *A Little Princess* (1902), incorporating and extending the stage version into the 1905 novel we know by this title today. Among musical adaptations, a version of *Alice* appeared in 1886, and Frank Baum's own musical *The Wizard of Oz*, loosely based on his 1900 book, was performed in 1902. In 1929 A. A. Milne adapted Kenneth Grahame's *The Wind in the Willows* (1904) as *Toad of Toad Hall*, a play with songs. Retrospective adaptations include those of Laura Ingalls Wilder's *Little House* series, Roald Dahl's books, and C. S. Lewis's *The Lion, the Witch and the Wardrobe*. Recent notable plays include Jacqueline Wilson's own versions of *Double Act* (1995) and *The Lottie Project* (1997), and literary award winners such as Louis Sachar's *Holes* (1998), David Almond's *Skellig* (2003), and Philip Pullman's 1995–2001 trilogy *His Dark Materials*, which became a two-part six-hour National Theatre production in 2003.

[*See also* Adaptation; Drama; Films: Film Adaptations of Children's and Young Adult Literature; *and biographies of figures mentioned in this article*.]

BRIDGET CARRINGTON

Pletsch, Oskar (1830–1888), German illustrator, educated at the Dresdner Kunstakademie, where he came to know Ludwig Richter and was commissioned to execute wood carvings for him. Later Pletsch became Richter's pupil, something that becomes evident in his genre pictures of pretty, rosy-cheeked children. Pletsch often rendered animals and playing children in rural homes. The girls wear aprons and play being housewives caring for their dolls, while the boys play being soldiers. Often his illustrations were framed by flowers or other objects. Pletsch's illustrations of domestic comfort and idyll were beloved by the German bourgeoisie, and his drawings were frequently used both at home and abroad, particularly in children's periodicals and to illustrate children's verse and doggerel. Among his best-known works are *Die Kinderstube* (1860; English trans., *The Nursery*), in which he introduces his distinctive style; *Wie's im Hause geht nach dem Alphabet* (Things Happen in the House According to the Alphabet, 1862) in folio size; and illustrations to a splendid edition of Hans Christian Andersen's *Märchen* (Fairy Tales, 1874).

[*See also* Andersen, Hans Christian; Germany; Illustrations; *and* Richter, Ludwig.]

HELENE EHRIANDER

Plowman, Stephanie (1922–), British writer of historical fiction. Formerly a teacher, Plowman is a history graduate, and her out-of-print novels for teenagers are now eagerly sought after by devoted adult collectors. Her books portray societies in decline and highlight the effect of such decline on individuals, as in *The Road to Sardis* (1965). Here the focus is on classical Greece, recording the war between Athens and Sparta and the decline of democracy. *Three Lives for the Czar* (1970) and *My Kingdom for a Grave* (1971) chart both the progress of the Russian Revolution and the decline of the Romanov dynasty through the experiences of an engaging young hero. Like other writers of historical fiction (such as Hester Burton), Plowman uses personal stories of fictional characters to shed light on historical figures and national events. For the reader, the narrators' helplessness in the face of events brings the poignancy of hindsight to her novels.

[*See also* Burton, Hester *and* Historical Fiction.]

BELINDA COPSON

Pludra, Benno (1925–), one of the most celebrated and successful East German children's writers. Pludra is the author of more than forty books for children and young adults, frequently translated and made into feature films, such as *Lütt Matten und die weiße Muschel* (1963; English trans., *The White Sea-Shell*, 1967), *Insel der Schwäne* (Swans' Island, 1980), and *Herz des Piraten* (The Pirate's Heart, 1985). Pludra's first career, as a sailor, was interrupted by World War II. After working as a journalist and a teacher, in 1952 he became an author of children's stories, novels, fairy tales, picture books, radio plays, and film scripts. His work conveys his admiration of his young readers and also conveys—through stories that are often set in the rural environment of the Baltic Sea coast—his love for the sea. For Pludra, the sea symbolizes both mankind's search for adventure and freedom and its desire to explore, and also the great dangers awaiting man on his journey to unknown lands. This journey, undertaken by Pludra's young heroes either in real life or in their world of dreams, is employed as a metaphor for the heroes' growing up. Pludra recounts their quest for happiness and fulfills his readers' longing for the exotic and adventurous by poetically exploring distant places in, for instance, *Die Reise nach Sundevit* (The Journey to Sundevit, 1965). Pludra's books are captivating because of the close tie between children and adults, the verve and imagination of his storytelling, his individualized heroes, and the friction between reality and children's imagination. He also wrote for young adults on themes such as first love, the quest for love, and children's need for a sense of belonging. Among many awards, Pludra won the prestigious Alex-Wedding-Preis in 2000.

[*See also* Adventure Books; Germany; Sea Stories; *and* Young Adult Literature.]

SYLVIA WARNECKE

Poetry. Poems intended for children are not substantially different from poems written to appeal to adults. In fact, "children's poems," like most good children's literature, may greatly delight an older audience. Conversely, the works of many distinguished poets who write for adults are read and enjoyed by younger readers. The differences between "adult" and "children's" poems, when such exist, occur in subject matter—topics relative to children's interests and activities; in wording—more concrete words favored over more abstract and general ones; in the greater emphasis on sense impressions; in the use of more "formal" techniques, such as rhythm and rhyme; and in the insistent prevalence of humor. Poetry for the child, like all poetry, is an imaginative arrangement of words, phrases, and lines that will make something vital "happen"; it is the skillful interweaving of music and meaning that elicits a "felt discovery." Such a discovery often relies on familiar experiences, what the child has observed and come to know. Through sensuous description and artful form, the ordinary is recreated and enhanced, as in "Night Creature" by Lilian Moore.

For the child, "voice" is especially important, as in the soothing voice of the Hopi lullaby (in Neil Philip's collection *Weave Little Stars into My Sleep: Native American Lullabies*, 2004):

> Sleep, sleep sleep
> Baby, shut your eyes
> On the trail the little beetles
> Have all shut their eyes.

Certainly, the child is entranced by both voice and sound—the Caribbean beat of James Berry and the vigor of the Caribbean dialect excite the ear in these lines from "Mek Drum Talk, Man" (*When I Dance*, 1988):

> Lawks O, slap the drum, slap it Buddy
> Slap it like ye mad somebody—
> budoom—a budoom—abudoom—a ba dap,
> budoom—abudoom—a ba dap.

Imaginative wordplay attunes the young ear to new ways of saying and understanding, rhymes create a sense of structural unity and reinforce meaning, and rhythm assists the

Poetry. Frontisiece and title page by Stephen Reid for *The Magic Casement: An Anthology of Fairy Poetry* edited by Alfred Noyes (London: Chapman & Hall, 1908). COLLECTION OF JACK ZIPES

relationship between sound and sense. Poetry can radiate thoughts and emotions through its images, which may be intensified by figures of speech, as in Nikki Giovanni's "The Drum" (*Spin a Soft Black Song*, rev. ed., 1985):

> Daddy says the world
> Is a drum
> Tight and hard
> And I told him
> I'm gonna beat out my own rhythm.

Forms of Poetry and the Range of Effects in Poetic Expression

Poems for children are often more lyrical, narrative, or dramatic than discursive or reflective. The forms vary: limerick, haiku, ballad, concrete or shaped poem, even the more formal types such as sonnet or elegy, or less formal excursions into free verse. Some forms are successful in achieving particular effects; for example, the limerick often teases, the haiku frequently rouses to wonder or mystical awareness, the ballad tells a story.

Whether the poem reveals a tragic insight or provides the young person with a moment of good-natured amusement, whether the verse is in free form or a more traditional form, poetry encourages acute observation, emotional participation, and intellectual pleasure.

From the Oral Heritage to the Romantic Period

What we can accept as the "first" poems for children—as well as for adults—derived from oral traditions: riddles, spells, tongue-twisters, songs, counting-out rhymes, cumulative rhymes (for example, "This is the house that Jack built"),"infant amusements" ("Here we go 'round the mulberry bush"), lullabies, and all kinds of anonymous verse.

Many of these "nursery rhymes" were collected in various editions of what would later be termed "Mother Goose." As early as 1744, Mary Cooper published *Tommy Thumb's Pretty Song Book*, edited by "Nurse Lovechild," which included such verses as "Sing a Song of Sixpence" and "Mistress Mary." In 1765 John Newbery published *Mother Goose's Melody*; this English edition was reprinted by Isaiah Thomas in Worcester, Massachusetts, in 1786 and 1794.

Even before Mother Goose rhymes, children had access to published poems, such as rhymed versions of *Aesop's Fables*. John Bunyan's popular *A Book for Boys and Girls* (1686) was designed to bring children to God through its seventy-four poems. Chapbooks (small paper booklets circulated during the 17th through the 19th centuries) were another source of poetry that appealed to child and adult audiences alike. Both the "broadside ballads" and the secular and biblical rhymed narratives must have had a wide audience. Printed specifically for children in 1715 and influential for at least two centuries was *Divine Songs Attempted in Easie Language*, by Isaac Watts. While these poems, like Bunyan's, instruct in moral virtue, they also reveal a sensitive awareness.

Yet the 18th century also held many unadulterated amusements for children. In 1734 Jean de La Fontaine's sprightly verse *Fables* were translated into English, and even the poet Dorothy Kilner, generally a moralist, could have fun with her subjects. Although Christopher Smart's "My Cat Jeoffry," included in *Jubilate Agno* (1758/59–1763), is not directed specifically at children, the poem has "childlike" appeal in its imaginative sense of how the feline spirit participates in God's creation. *Hymns for the Amusement of Children* (1772) expresses that same wonder, even ecstasy. As Morag Styles (in her excellent book *From the Garden to the Street: Three Hundred Years of Poetry for Children*) rightly acknowledges, in both style and voice Smart anticipates William Blake.

From the Romantic to the Victorian Period

In *Songs of Innocence* (1789) William Blake, like Smart, perceives the divinity in nature and writes in a more relaxed verse form; like Watts, he writes in the hymn tradition. Blake also uses dramatic voices to heighten social criticism, as here in "The Chimney Sweeper":

> When my mother died I was very young,
> And my father sold me while yet my tongue
> Could scarcely cry " 'weep! 'weep! 'weep!"
> So your chimneys I sweep and in soot I sleep.

Morag Styles believes that *Songs of Innocence* (1789) and *Songs of Experience* (1794) were undoubtedly written for both children and adults in order to provide a critical discourse and raise social awareness.

The first anthology of poems for children, called simply *Poetry for Children* (1801), was edited by Lucy Aikin, herself a nature poet. Like most subsequent anthologists for children, she included poetry by prominent adult poets she regarded as appropriate voices for the young. Much more influential in the first half of the 19th century was the collection *Original Poems for Infant Minds* (1804) by two sisters—Jane Taylor, known for writing "The Star" ("Twinkle, twinkle, little star," 1806), and her sister, Ann.

Although early-19th-century poetry for children, like the poetry of the previous century, was usually moral in direction, amusement became distinctly more important. The appeal to fantasy, play, and nonsense released both voice and meter. Written in 1807, William Roscoe's "Butterfly's Ball and the Grasshopper's Feast" begins, "Come take up your Hats, and away let us haste / to the Butterfly's Ball, and the Grasshopper's feast . . ." Another poem about animal festivities, also written in 1807, is *The Peacock "At Home,"* by Catherine Dorset. The poetry of John Clare (1793–1864) was not intended for children, but some of his poems have been collected specifically for a child audience because of their careful depiction of the rural landscape in simple and exacting language. Clare, along with other Romantic poets, has frequently been anthologized for children in later Victorian collections such as *The Children's Garland* (1862), edited by Coventry Patmore, and *The Blue Fairy Book* (1892), edited by Andrew Lang.

In "Lost from the Nursery: Women Writing Poetry for Children, 1800 to 1850," Styles comments on how few female poets are represented in anthologies of children's poems. This is particularly the case for earlier periods; Styles reminds us of female English Romantic poets who have been largely omitted, including Anna Barbauld, Sara Coleridge, Felicia Homans, Mary Howitt, and Dorothy Wordsworth. Add to this list the American poet Elizabeth Follen (1787–1860), who wrote *New Nursery Songs for All Good Children* (1832) and penned the favorite "Three little kittens lost their mittens . . ." Other notable poems from America in the early 19th century include Clement Clarke Moore's "A Visit from St. Nicholas" (1823) and Sara Josepha Hale's "Mary Had a Little Lamb" (1830).

Two Victorians, Edward Lear and Lewis Carroll, changed the nature of children's poetry forever. Both were exceptionally receptive to children; each had a remarkable sense of

Poetry. Frontispiece by Erick Berry to *Little Brown Baby* by Paul Dunbar (New York: Dodd & Mead, 1940). REPRODUCED COURTESY OF THE COTSEN CHILDREN'S LIBRARY, PRINCETON UNIVERSITY LIBRARY play, a gift for absurdity, eccentricity, and pure frolic; and each created wonderful scenarios with "sound-arios" to match.

Lear's many books of nonsense began with *The Book of Nonsense* (1846) and concluded with *Laughable Lyrics* (1877). Lewis Carroll (Charles Lutwidge Dodgson) wrote his nonsense verse in the Alice books: *Alice in Wonderland* (1865) and *Alice through the Looking-Glass* (1872). From the first *Alice* comes the bathos of "The Mock Turtle's Song" and from the second comes the mock-chivalric "Jabberwocky," set in a dangerous yet delectable dream landscape of "tulgey wood" and "borogroves," where lurk the "Jubjub bird" and "Bandersnatch." Creating portmanteau words and a language that awakens sound-image into unconscious understanding, Carroll anticipates surrealism.

In contrast to Lear and Carroll are three women poets: Jean Ingelow, Christina Rossetti, and Kate Greenaway, an illustrator as well as a poet. Known primarily for her fantasy novel *Mopsa the Fairy*, Ingelow wrote many volumes of sentimental verse and songs, some for children, these were collected in one volume in 1898. A much more renowned poet is Christina Rossetti; *Sing-Song* (1872) is her one collection for children—lyrics with immaculate diction and controlled rhythms, images that often startle, and a playfulness that is often profound. Greenaway often writes about the more genteel aspects of childhood, set in idyllic landscapes; her illustrations show delicate girls dressed in frilly gowns and prim boys in white-collared suits. Nonetheless, she has a good sense of the whimsical, as in "The Cats Have Come to Tea" in *Marigold Garden: Pictures and Rhymes* (1885). Although Robert Browning wrote only a single poem for children, "The Pied Piper of Hamelin" (1842), it is significant for its magic and realism intertwined in a mythical and mesmerizing narrative. Two popular American poets should be noted here: James Whitcomb Riley and Eugene Field.

Robert Louis Stevenson (1850–1894) is another Victorian poet who changed the nature of children's poetry; he becomes the child that he creates in his poems and seems to speak in the child's own words and with the child's own rhythms. *A Child's Garden of Verses* (1895) is centered in that "garden" of long ago when the child stayed in the quiet of his own house and enjoyed creating his own "media" experiences.

The 20th Century: Transitions into the Modern

For the most part, 20th-century poetry for children relinquished didacticism for delight. Nonsense verse appeared even in periodicals for children that often relied on sentimental themes and pious appeals, such as the well-known *St. Nicholas* magazine (Nov. 1873–Mar. 1940; some issues in 1943).

In fact, the 20th century offered poems that play with didacticism, mock stories of incautious or unpleasant children who come to harm. The poems of Hilaire Belloc (1870–1953) titillate with these pretend hazards: dangerous animals in *The Bad Book of Beasts* (1895) and miseries or fatalities that occur to the young—all genteel children—in *Cautionary Tales for Children* (1931). Belloc is the master of the straight-faced and gothic extravaganza usually set to tetrameter couplets.

Quite different for the melody and sensibility in his poetry is Walter de la Mare. Many of his poems in *Bells and Grass* (1942), his last collection, are about dreams and illusions but also include closely observed descriptions of the natural world. His earlier collections, *The Listeners, and Other Poems* (1912) and *Peacock Pie* (1932), are well known; the latter includes several character studies, as well as "magical" poems. *Come Hither* (1932) is his anthology of poems for "the young of all ages."

Several other poets born toward the end of the 19th century are noteworthy for their contributions: Rose Fyleman for her well-known fairy poems; Carl Sandburg for his good-natured appeals to children, some gathered in *Wind Song* (1960); Vachel Lindsay for his rhythmic energy and soaring rhymes; and Eleanor Farjeon for the religious elements in her poems and the delicacy of her vision. Some mention should also be made of Elizabeth Madox Roberts, who in *Under the Tree* (1930) expresses a real sense of how children think and feel; her poems have a natural grace.

Brilliant for his recognition of how the child perceives, for his immaculate rhymes, and for his humorous observations is A. A. Milne. His poems appear in *When We Were Very Young* (1924) and *Now We Are Six* (1927), and are collected in *The World of Christopher Robin* (1958). In a poem such as "The King's Breakfast," in which his Royal Highness whines, complaining there is no butter—will not even accept marmalade—we hear the stubborn refusals of a child. In "Binker" the little boy cherishes his invisible companion. "Sneezles," a masterpiece of sounds, persuades the reader of all the respiratory infirmities suffered by a small child. It realizes how successfully the child can dramatize an illness in order to stay pampered in bed.

A number of other poets born at the close of the 19th century and known primarily for their "adult" poems also wrote poems for children, such as T. S. Eliot (*Old Possum's*

Book of Practical Cats, 1939) and Robert Graves (*The Penny Fiddle*, 1960). Many of the poems by e.e. cummings have delighted older children for their humorous inventions in space and sound and, of course, for their wordplay.

Born at the end of the 19th century and widely renowned, David McCord (1897–1997) wrote prolifically for more than a half century. *One at a Time* (1974) offers a good representation of his poems—poems that give a human meaning to objects, reveal the experiences of children, and suggest the nature of our world. The child in "Tooth Trouble" records an experience known to most of us.

When I see the dentist
I take him all my teeth:
Some of me's above them,
But most of me's beneath.

In "Take Sky," sound evokes image and emotion. "Remember, words are life," McCord says.

Words taken one by one
Are poems as they stand—
Shore, beacon, harbor, land . . .

The ideology regarding poetry for children has changed rapidly in the 20th century. In 1924 Walter Barnes in *The Children's Poets* considered that children's poetry should present an idealized world for readers where children are "good and amiable" and reason is set aside for "poetic faith." Furthermore, Barnes felt that poems of a psychological or philosophical nature were totally unsuitable for children, who need not concern themselves with all "the baffling tragedies of humanity." Although some of this ideology may still be acceptable, especially as it concerns small children, poetry in the 20th century and later, especially since the 1960s, registers all the angst and anxieties, all the confusions and conjectures increasingly faced by the young. The young audience is no longer a privileged one, nor can it be protected; "poetic faith" in contemporary times means a truth stated and crafted not only to affect young minds and emotions but to bring the young mind to a larger awareness.

In the last decades of the 20th century the sense of the "global village" became increasingly important. Multiethnic experience is advanced both through having access to cultures of other countries and through the cultural diversity we experience in most of our neighborhoods. Thus, there developed new terminologies, a new rhetoric, different rhythms, another sense of the relationship between poet and reader. Subject matter expanded to include a wider recognition available to children, in human relationships as well as in environment and technology.

Poems Published from the 1940s to the 1970s

It seems inevitable that poems for children will always be exceptional for their ability to divert and amuse. Evidence Carl Withers's collection *Rhymes from a Rocket in My Pocket* (1948) and William Cole's anthology *Oh, What Nonsense!* (1966); included in the latter are poems by William Jay Smith, James Reeves, John Ciardi, Shel Silverstein, and, of course, "Anonymous." Eve Merriam's *The Inner City Mother Goose* (1969) can often be funny even while it provokes; through irony and satire and in skilifully rhymed verses, Merriam demonstrates for her reader instances of social injustice, hypocrisy, and oppression. Myra Cohn Livingston, the editor of *What a Wonderful Bird the Frog Are: An Assortment of Humorous Poetry and Verse* (1973), chooses well-crafted and thoughtful comedic poems from many sources, including Alexander Pope, Theodore Roethke, Maxine Kumin, and Richard Wilbur.

Many imaginative and challenging anthologies appeared, especially during the 1960s. One early anthology, *An Inheritance of Poetry* (1948), edited by Gladys L. Adshead and Annis Duff, includes admirable selections but too many that are remote from a child's sensibility and understanding. *The Crystal Cabinet: An Invitation to Poetry* (1962) contains more contemporary poets than does the Adshead and Duff anthology, as well as several more unusual poets for a young audience (Anna Akhmatova, Matya Zaturenska, Gaius Valerius Catullus, and Constantine Cavafy). The child reader is also enticed to speculate beyond his own more limited experiences (poems by Robert Graves, Archibald MacLeish, and Hart Crane), although too many may be accessible only to adults. Much more successful is the anthology edited by Louise Bogan and William Jay Smith entitled *Golden Journeys: Poems for Young People* (1965); the poems are carefully chosen for "being where the child is at" and then taking that child to a "beyond" from which he or she may come back transformed. The choices are eclectic—Debendranath Tagore, Robert Herrick, Barbara Howes, Stephen Spender, and Eleanor Wylie, to name a few.

While the once-acclaimed anthology by Stephen Dunning, Edward Lueders, and Hugh Smith, *Reflections on a Gift of Watermelon Pickle, and Other Modern Verse* (1966), was intended for an adolescent audience when first published, in the 21st century it seems relevant to a preadolescent reader who has more mature leanings and can identify with the experiences and emotions that high-school students had in the 1960s. Livingston's *A Tune beyond Us: A Collection of Poems* (1968) includes many well-selected poems, among which are poems from Asia, such as those by Yamabe no Akahito and Li Po, as well as poems by such Europeans as Aleksandr Sergeyevich Pushkin, Bertolt Brecht, Giuseppe Ungaretti, and Yevgeny Yevtushenko. Following the English translations are poems in the original language. Also published in 1968, Nancy Larrick's anthology *On City Streets* includes black-and-white photographs to realize the confusion and loneliness of those caught in the tangle of alleyways and buildings. Such visual-verbal relationships also recognize the wonder and beauty existing in rare spaces and in relationships with others. Poems such as "Emma's Store," by Dorothy Aldis, and "Mother to Son," by Langston Hughes, open the reader to the sighs and sounds of a metropolis.

David Mackay's collection, *A Flock of Words: An Anthology of Poetry for Children and Others* (1969), is a surprise. There are no topical headings; rather, poems are placed in a sequence that suggests a category. The inclusions are delightful, such as John Heath-Stubbs's "The History of the Flood." The reader learns that there were not precisely two of each animal boarding the ark, because "cats / Do not obey regulations; / And, as you might expect / A quantity of rabbits." There are poems by Prem Chaya (Thailand), Miroslev Holub (Czech Republic), and Wole Soyinka (Nigeria). Daisy Aldan's *Poems from India* (1969) introduces a cultural heritage not often recognized, and the collection includes many affecting poems.

Many poets wrote predominantly or significantly for children during the first seventy years of the 20th century; these mentioned represent some well-known voices. Langston Hughes (1902–1967) and Gwendolyn Brooks (1917–2000) sensitively recorded the experience of being black in America, especially during troubled times. In *Bronzeville Boys and Girls* (1956) Brooks seems especially attuned to the feelings of the solitary child, as in "Keziah":

> I have a secret place to go.
> Not anyone may know.
>
> And sometimes when the wind is rough
> I cannot get there fast enough.

Ogden Nash and William Jay Smith are fine humorists, as are John Ciardi and Eve Merriam, both of whom realize some wry awareness of social conditions. May Sarton often takes children to imaginary worlds where they become more fully aware of their own realities. Theodore Roethke and James Reeves wrote poems about the natural world. Aileen Fischer published numerous books, most intended for small children and revealing how simple, direct language as well as skillful rhymes can trigger surprising recognitions. A unique collection of poems about animals is *Prayers from the Ark* (1962), by Carmen Bernos De Gasztold and translated from the French by Rumer Godden. The speakers in these poems are all animals who give praise to God but frequently question his justice and ask for favors. Another interesting collection is *Poems to Solve* (1966), by May Swenson (1919–1989), consisting entirely of riddle poems; although the language may be complex, the images are precise and an invitation for the reader to search for a solution. These poems can be "played" over and over again. Charles Causley (1917–2003) wrote well-crafted poems from many perspectives—haunting, surprising, delighting. While known primarily as an urban and witty "adult" poet, Richard Wilbur has written a number of books for children in which he somersaults words to turn ideas on their heads, as in *Opposites* (1973).

From the 1970s into the 21st Century

Certainly, during the latter part of the 20th century and expanding into the 21st, poetry for children has become more varied in style, expression, subject matter, and complexity of form—and there are simply more poetry books, many profusely illustrated. Of particular significance in children's poetry is the continued and increasing recognition of other cultures and other countries; the voices of ethnic and racial groups previously unfamiliar or unknown give us new sounds and another sensibility. A small sampling of these diverse collections includes *Songs of the Dream People* (1972), edited by James Houston, containing Indian songs and chants and poems of North American Eskimo peoples; *The Luminous Landscape: Chinese Art and Poetry* (1981), edited by Richard Lewis; and *If I Had a Paka: Poems in Eleven Languages* (1982). Thirteen African and African American poets are represented in *Soul Looks Back in Wonder* (1993), compiled and illustrated by Tom Feelings.

Other anthologies are valuable for their discriminating selection of poems, such as the compilations of modern poetry edited by Paul B. Janeczko, one of which is *Looking for Your Name: A Collection of Contemporary Poems* (1993). *The Random House Book of Poetry for Children* (1983), edited by Jack Prelutsky, is satisfying for its humorous poems; *Classic Poetry: An Illustrated Collection* (1998), selected by Michael Rosen, for its imaginative selection and visual displays; and *Knock at a Star: A Child's Introduction to Poetry* (rev. ed., 1999), edited by X. J. and Dorothy Kennedy, for its sprightly appeal to small children.

A good number of contemporary poets for children are from England, for example, Ted Hughes, whose many poems about animals are especially strong and vigorous, often mythic in texture and meaning. Hughes identifies with the creatures he describes and often finds, through that relationship, a unity in the cosmos. Allan Ahlberg may be considered one of a group writing in "the streetwise school" of poetry; that is, he uses colloquial speech and uneven rhythms, and the smart-aleck interplays that quite naturally occur in the schoolroom and on the playground. Roger McGough and Michael Rosen also register the high energy and good-natured rowdiness in children's activities and, in the child's own language, deliver their acute perceptions. McGough's boisterous invention is illustrated in "Mafia Cats"—felines who pretend to lead a life of crime when in fact they are the pampered and precious pets of their owners. Quite different in voice and approach is John Mole; one of the few poets for children who is often reflective, he is remarkable for his craftsmanship. Jackie Kay in *Two's Company* (1992) includes poems in the voice of Carla Johnson, a child of divorced parents who divides her time and identities when she moves from one parent's house to the other's. Among the other significant British poets for children who warrant acknowledgment are Wendy Cope, Roald Dahl, Mick Gowar, Philip Gross, Adrian Henri, Adrian Mitchell, Gareth Owen, Brian Patten, Jon Whyte, and Kit Wright. Many of the British poets cited herein have been Signal Award recipients, the prize granted by the English journal *Signal* during 1970–2000. (*Signal* ceased publication in 2000.)

There has been an exciting outpouring of American poetry for children. Humorous poems are generally irresistible to a young audience, and Jack Prelutsky's rhymes seem to dance off the tongue in *Frogs Wore Red Suspenders* (2002). Prelutsky is also the editor of *For Laughing Out Loud: Poems to Tickle Your Funnybone* (1991), and the promise is realized. Some of the poets whose works appear in this volume are William Cole, Dennis Lee (Canadian), Colin McNaughton, and the popular Shel Silverstein. Silverstein's works include *Where the Sidewalk Ends* (1974), *A Light in the Attic* (1981), and *Falling Up* (1996), collections of rhymed narrative verse, often zany and extravagant, with bizarre drawings to match.

Forms range from the ingenious images in Mary O'Neill's *Hailstones and Halibut Bones: Adventure in Color* (1961, 1989) to the lilting rhymes of Karla Kushkin, collected in *Moon, Have You Met My Mother?* (2003) to the expansive discoveries in minimalist form by Natalie Babbitt in *small poems again* (1975) and by Valerie Worth in *All the Small Poems and Fourteen More* (1994), with any number of significant poems between and beyond. There are the "patterned poems" of Joan Bransfield Graham in *Splish Splash* (1994) and Paul Janeczko in *A Poke in the I: A Collection of Concrete Poems* (2001) and poems that focus on particular locales. In *City Kids* (2001) Patricia Hubbell chose to write on such subjects as those named in "Skyscrapers," "Stickball," and "Baglady." Lee Bennett Hopkins, the editor of *Spectacular Science* (1999), included poems about outer space. Surreal spaces of the imagination appear in *Night Garden: Poems from the World of Dreams* (2000), written by Janet Wong.

Still, it is the natural world that appeals to most poets—plants, animals, and the geographic variations of our land. A fine book among Constance Levy's many books on nature is *Splash!: Poems of Our World* (2000). Among Deborah Chandra's books on nature is *Rich Lizard, and Other Poems* (1993). Animal poems are especially enjoyed by children, and there are many choices, such as *I Am the Cat* (1999), by Alice Schertle; *Insectopedia* (1998), by Douglas Florian; *Mouse of My Heart: A Treasury of Sense and Nonsense* (2001), by Margaret Wise Brown; and *Animal Sense* (2003), by Diane Ackerman. Patrick J. Lewis, an unusually versatile poet, explores topography in *A World of Wonders: Geographic Travels in Verse and Rhyme* (2002), as does Diane Siebert in three books about various regions: *Mojave* (1988), *Sierra* (1991), and *Mississippi* (2001). Jane Yolen has published several books of nature poems that transport through both her own verbal images and the photographic images of Jason Temple; two such titles are *Color Me a Rhyme: Nature Poems for Young People* (2000) and *Wild Wings: Poems for Young People* (2002).

Most significantly, poems incisively suggest and reveal the human condition. Although all poets who write for children need to feel the pulse of the child's world, this is especially important for those who write about human relationships. A few such poets are Barbara Juster Esbensen, Mary Ann Hoberman, Sara Holbrook, Shirley Hughes, Bobbi Katz, Lilian Moore, Pat Mora, Marilyn Singer, and Judith Viorst.

The sense of human connection has widened for all of us. African American poetry, in particular, has increased in both volume and significance. In the later 20th century, such poets as Mari Evans, Eloise Greenfield, Nikki Giovanni, and Nikki Grimes all wrote for children. Grimes's *A Pocketful of*

Poems (2001) is particularly inventive for its use of poetic forms. Another African American poet, Joyce Carol Thomas, explores a young girl's family and heritage in *Brown Honey in Broomwheat Tea* (1993). Two gifted black voices from England are Jackie Kay and Benjamin Zephaniah. The Caribbean experience is lavishly illustrated in *Under the Moon and over the Sea: A Collection of Caribbean Poems* (2003). Poets represented in this volume include John Agard, James Berry, Valerie Bloom, and Grace Nichols.

Native American poems are of continued interest, for example, those in Brian Swann's *Touching the Distance: Native American Riddle Poems*. More recently, the Hispanic experience has been expressed in poetry, as in Francisco X. Alarcón's bilingual poems about summer in Mexico, *From the Bellybutton of the Moon, and Other Summer Poems* (1998), and Lori Carlson's *Sol a Sol* (1998), poems—in both English and Spanish—that follow the daily life of a Latino family. Asian cultures are also represented in a variety of poetic formats. Through paintings and Tang Dynasty translations, the Chinese heritage is beautifully conveyed in *Maples in the Mist* (1996), by Minfong Ho. In *A Suitcase of Seaweed, and Other Poems* (1996) Janet Wong demonstrates her multiethnic background; she writes poems about her Korean and Chinese heritage in an American setting.

Poems written by children have become recognized for their artistry and appeal; frequently these reflect the influence of ethos, race, and culture. One such collection is *The Palm of My Heart: Poetry by African American Children*, edited by Davida Adedjouma (1996). Two earlier collections are important for registering diverse children's voices: *Miracles: Poems by Children of the English-Speaking World* (1966), edited by Richard Lewis, and *I Heard a Scream in the Streets* (1970), edited by Nancy Larrick. Remarkable for their expressions of hope and longing and sensitivity to others' suffering are the poems written by children in *I Never Saw Another Butterfly: Children's Drawings and Poems from Terezén Concentration Camp, 1942–1944* (1978).

Increasing Significance

In the 21st century, poetry meets increasing obstacles. Influenced by media, computers, and other technologies, children, like their parents, live in the "fast lane," and, while they are likely to be more sophisticated and knowledgeable, they are also likely to be more distracted and more remote from the poetic disposition. Nonetheless, the continued publication of poems for children—and books on the writing of poems for children—as well as the existence of so many opportunities for children to write their own poems testifies to the genre's continued well-being.

Many books acknowledge the interest children have in poetry and in writing their own poems; Kenneth Koch, in *Wishes, Lies, and Dreams: Teaching Children to Write Poetry* (1970), recognizes how children can use their imagination to craft poems. Other writers provide understanding and inspiration for young writers: these include Arthur Alexander, Avis Harley, and the poet Paul B. Janeczko. In *Seeing the Blue Between: Advice and Inspiration for Young Poets* (2002) Janeczko presents poets' guidance on writing, as well as a selection of their poems.

Critical discussions on poetry—these can be read with interest by both children and adults—are included in Livingston's *Climb into the Bell Tower: Essays on Poetry* (1990); other critical works are *Let's Do a Poem: Introducing Poetry to Children* (1991), by Nancy Larrick; and *Pass the Poetry, Please* (1998), by Lee Bennett Hopkins, the latter a valuable anthology as well as commentary on the more prominent 20th-century American poets.

New developments have occurred in the orchestration of voices in poems for children—that is, how a poem may be read and interpreted. In Paul Fleischman's *Big Talk: Poems for Four Voices* (2000), each voice is appointed a color that an individual reader selects; three stories range from simple to complex "harmonies." Poetry has also moved into other genres, such as the memoir, for example, Cynthia Rylant's *Waiting to Waltz: A Childhood* (1974) and Janeczko's *Brickyard Summer* (1989). Novels in poetic form include *Out of the Dust* (1997), winner of the Newbery Medal, by Karen Hesse; and *The Way a Door Closes* (2003), by Hope Anita Smith, winner of the Coretta Scott King and John Steptoe New Talent Award.

Some critics have questioned the very concept of a separate realm of "children's poetry"; the claim is that the appeal to a juvenile audience narrows the range and reduces the worth of poetry. Certainly many poems published for children may be doggerel and without subtlety or substance—that same claim can be made for many "adult poems." But other critics have recognized how the poet can imaginatively enter the child's world and identify with his or her feelings and perceptions. Such a poet neither condescends nor forces the child to absorb what he cannot yet understand. The poem is thoughtfully crafted and resists an overwrought jokiness or easy sentimentality; rather, it engages through its respect for language and human concerns. At some level the poet meets the child, may share a confidence or delight, may become a witness for children to encourage them to make their own discoveries. The poet trusts his audience and respects the power of his craft.

Poetry for children is now recognized as an important genre. Two poets have been honored with the Newbery Medal, the annual award granted to "the author of the most distinguished contribution in American literature for children": Nancy Willard, for *A Visit to William Blake's Inn: Poems for Innocent and Experienced Travelers* (1982), and Paul Fleischman, for *Joyful Noise: Poems for Two Voices* (1989). The National Council of Teachers of English grants an Award for Excellence in Poetry for Children; such an award was instituted in 1977 and is given every three years. Many of the poets mentioned in this article have been recipients of this award—and poets will continue to aspire toward excellence in poetry worthy of the child.

[*See also* Nursery Rhymes; Playground Rhymes; *and biographies of figures mentioned in this article.*]

BIBLIOGRAPHY

Barnes, Walter. *The Children's Poets: Analyses and Appraisals of the Greatest English and American poets for Children, for Use in Normal Schools, Library Schools, and Homes*. Yonkers-on-Hudson, N.Y.: World, 1924.

Booth, David, ed. *Till The Stars Have Fallen: Canadian Poems for Children*. London and New York: Viking, 1990.

Delamar, Gloria T. *Mother Goose from Nursery to Literature*. Jefferson, N.C.: McFarland, 1987.

Hall, Donald, ed. *The Oxford Book of Children's Verse in America*. Oxford: Oxford University Press, 1985.

Morse, Brian. *Poetry Books for Children*. Stroud, U.K.: Thimble Press, 1992.

Nye, Naomi Shihab, ed. *Salting the Ocean: 100 Poems by Young Poets*. New York: Greenwillow, 2000.

Opie, Iona, and Peter Opie. *The Lore and Language of School Children*. Oxford: Clarendon, 1959.

Philip, Neil, ed. *The New Oxford Book of Children's Verse*. London: Oxford University Press, 1996.

Styles, Morag. *From the Garden to the Street: Three Hundred Years of Poetry for Children*. London: Cassell, 1998.

Styles, Morag. "Lost from the Nursery: Women Writing Poetry for Children 1800 to 1850." *Signal* 63 (September 1993): 177–205.

Wooden, Warren W. *Children's Literature of the English Renaissance*. Lexington: University of Kentucky Press, 1986.

MARILYN JURICH

Pogany, Willy (1882–1955), Hungarian-born illustrator and writer. Vilmos Andreas (Willy) Pogany moved steadily westward during his life: from Hungary to England, to New York City, and subsequently to Hollywood, though he ended his days in New York. Pogany's English sojourn produced luxurious and ornate editions of *The Rime of the Ancient Mariner* (1910), three Wagner volumes (1911, 1912, and 1913), and his first version of *The Rubaiyat of Omar Khayyam* (1909). He returned to *The Rubaiyat* several times and later claimed to be "The *Omar Khayyam* Illustrator." His English period also saw the abundantly illustrated *Treasury of Verse for Little Children* (1908), which remained in print for over thirty years. Further children's titles were the *Welsh* and *Hungarian Fairy Books* (1907 and 1913), *Folk Tales from Many Lands* (1910), *The Witch's Kitchen, or The India-Rubber Doctor* (1910), *The Fairies and the Christmas Child* (1912), five volumes of the *Willy Pogany Children* series (1914), and four volumes in the *Pogany Nursery Book* series (1915).

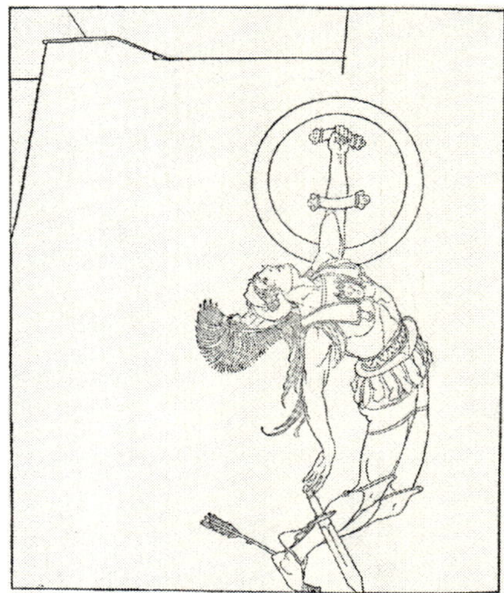

Willy Pogany. Illustration from *The Adventures of Odysseus and the Tale of Troy* by Padric Colum (London: George C. Harrap, 1930). REPRODUCED COURTESY OF THE COTSEN CHILDREN'S LIBRARY, PRINCETON UNIVERSITY LIBRARY

When Pogany went to the United States in 1914, he produced truly notable children's books. From 1916 to 1921 he teamed up with Padraic Colum to revitalize the Greek and Northern myths for children, some of which remain in print. His Art Deco illustrations for *Alice's Adventures in Wonderland* (1929) provided a refreshingly modern Alice, and his version of *Mother Goose* (1928) became an American standard. His long-running series of covers in the 1940s for Hearst's *American Weekly* newspapers, with bold pictures of classic myths and legends, made an immense impact on children throughout the United States. His many other children's books, *Fairy Flowers* (1926), *Looking out of Jimmie* (1927), *The Wimp and the Woodle* (1935), and others, showed continuing originality. He also provided murals for a series of Fairy Tale Cottages on William Randolph Hearst's Wyntoon

Estate in Northern California, produced an animated cartoon called *Scrambled Eggs*, and created *The Children's Window*, a large stained-glass window still to be seen at the Forest Lawn Funeral Home, Los Angeles.

[*See also* Adaptations; Collections; *and* Illustrations.]

Robin Greer

Pogodin, Radi (1925–1993), Russian children's writer, author of philosophical and existential novels and short stories in which fantasy and realism are skillfully blended. Unlike most Soviet children's books, Pogodin's are totally free from ideology and didacticism, and he takes the child's part without reservation, describing the world from the point of view of the weak and the inexperienced, be it a child, a mouse, or a completely imaginary being. Pogodin makes use of some traditional Russian fairy tale patterns and characters, combining them with contemporary settings and allowing ordinary children to experience adventures in magical countries where poetry, art, and imagination are the foremost virtues. His seemingly realistic novels and stories have mythical and allegorical dimensions. The central idea in Pogodin's works is the tension between the innocence and creative power of childhood and the burden and corruption of adulthood.

[*See also* Fairy Tales and Folk Tales; Fantasy; Realism; *and* Russia.]

BIBLIOGRAPHY

Nikolajeva, Maria. "On the Edge of Childhood." *Bookbird* 35 (1997) 2: 16–20.

Maria Nikolajeva

Pohl, Peter (1940–), Swedish writer of children's and young adult novels. His first novel, *Johnny My Friend* (1985; English trans., 1991), is considered his best and one of the most important landmarks in Swedish juvenile literature. It is remarkable not only because of its ruthless depiction of reality, but also because of its authentic narrative voice and intricate composition. Pohl is universally acknowledged in Sweden as a trendsetter, while he, in turn, shows great affinity with the British writer Aidan Chambers. Pohl's later novels, including *Alltid den där Anette!* (Always That Anette! 1988), *I Miss You, I Miss You* (1992; English trans., 1999), *När alla ljuger* (When Everybody Tells Lies, 1995), and *Man kan inte säga allt* (You Cannot Tell Everything, 1999), take up hot social issues, such as the school and health systems, bullying, crime, coping with a close relative's death, incest, and so on. Some are written in collaboration with adolescents. Pohl actively seeks new forms and expressive means, using narrative devices from film and other media. While all the novels are interesting in their themes and passionate social engagement, none has attained the artistic level of *Johnny, My Friend*.

[*See also* Chambers, Aidan; Nordic Countries; *and* Young Adult Literature.]

BIBLIOGRAPHY

Nikolajeva, Maria. "Deeper and Deeper into Dark Mysteries of Life." In *From Mythic to Linear: Time in Children's Literature*, 207–215. Lanham, Md.: Scarecrow, 2000.

Maria Nikolajeva

Pohl, Victor (1886–1979), writer born of an Afrikaans-speaking family in South Africa. Pohl wrote English fiction and nonfiction that was central to South African children's literature of the mid-20th century in embodying the love of white South Africans for their pioneers, for the unspoiled regions of the land, and for its wildlife. Most of his books, most notably *Bushveld Adventures* (1940), were autobiographical. The novel *Farewell the Little People* (1968) was a well-meaning but inaccurate tribute to the persecuted San. His books were immensely popular in South Africa, prescribed for school reading in that country and in New Zealand, and translated into various European languages.

[*See also* Africa: Southern Africa *and* Colonial Fiction.]

Elwyn Jenkins

Pokémon. A bestiary of nearly four hundred Japanese "Pocket Monsters," Pokémon was originally created for Nintendo by Satoshi Tajiri. Released in Japan in 1996, the Pokémon trading card game became a marketing phenomenon in the late 1990s in the United States, aided by the catch phrase "Gotta Catch 'Em All!" Pokémon soon expanded into an animated TV series, anime, and manga, videos and DVDs, feature films, collectibles, board games, and multiple video game platforms (primarily Nintendo and Gameboy systems). Pokémon characters combine familiar animal and insect characteristics with unusual powers, like the best-known Pokémon, named Pikachu, who is a playful yellow lightning mouse. Pokémon are caught and trained by Pokémon Trainers, like Ash Ketchum, protagonist of the anime cartoon. Pokémon Trainers then develop the animals' powers in battles against other Trainers and their Pokémon. As a Pokémon gains strength, it evolves into a more powerful creature. For example, a Pikachu evolves into the more powerful Raichu form. Pokémon Trainers like Ash then travel throughout the virtual environment, capturing new Pokémon and challenging other Pokémon Trainers in the hope of becoming a Pokémon Master. The cultural genius of the Pokémon phenomenon rests in the seamless overlap of commercial objectives and entertainment value in a creative, compelling, competitive game-playing environment of seemingly limitless combinations, a pattern followed by other Japanese cartoons like Dragon BallZ and Yu-Gi-Oh.

[*See also* Animal Stories; Computer Games; *and* Japan.]

DANIEL T. KLINE

Poláček, Karel (1892–1944), Czech author who first worked as an office employee. Beginning in 1923 he became a journalist and editor in Lidovy´ch, well known for his humorous novels for adults. After the German occupation of Czechoslovakia, he was arrested by the National Socialists because of his critical and satirical articles. Deported to the concentration camp Tabor in 1943, he was murdered in Auschwitz the next year. Poláček is author of the children's classic *Edudant a Francimor* (Edudant and Francimor, 1933), with illustrations by Josef Čapek. This fantastic story about the strange adventures of two witch brothers is clearly inspired by the British nonsense tradition. The combination of poetic language, colloquial language, and school slang especially contributes to the book's humorous impact. In addition, Poláček integrated stylistic devices of literary modernism like convoluted plots, cinematic narration, and irony, thus creating a major contribution to Czech fantasy for children.

[*See also* Fantasy *and* Nonsense.]

BETTINA KÜMMERLING-MEIBAUER

Poland, Marguerite (1950–), influential South African author for children and young adults, who has since moved on to writing adult fiction. The high quality of her writing lifted local children's books from the doldrums of the mid-20th century. Her volumes of short stories *The Mantis and the Moon* (1979) and *The Wood-ash Stars* (1983) were deservedly the only books to be awarded the Percy FitzPatrick Prize for South African English children's books in the first ten years after its establishment. Drawing on her childhood in the eastern Cape and her knowledge of African languages and culture (in which she is academically qualified), she wrote stories about the creatures of the bush in which they were characterized as indigenous people. Her prose—poetical, and with hints of the syntax of other languages—was criticized as too difficult for young children, though her books were very popular. Reacting to this criticism, she produced a revised, collected version entitled *Sambane's Dream* in 1989. Shorter, simpler stories, in the style of indigenous folk tales, appeared in *The Wood-ash Stars* (1983) and *The Small Clay Bull* (1986), strikingly illustrated by Shanne Altshuler. *Marcus and the Boxing Gloves* (1984) and *Marcus and the Go-kart* (1988) showed that she could write lively, contemporary stories for eight-year-olds in their own language. Turning to young adult fiction, Poland learned her craft with *The Bush Shrike* (1982), and then wrote *Shadow of the Wild Hare* (1986), considered by most critics as a landmark novel in that it adopted an indigenous worldview to understand the spiritual dimension of ecological survival. The story of a white girl who learns to appreciate these mysteries was a timely message for South African readers in the riches to be gained from interracial understanding.

[*See also* Africa: Southern Africa; Interracial Books for Children; *and* Young Adult Literature.]

ELWYN JENKINS

Politi, Leo (1908–1996), American author and illustrator of Italian descent, a pioneer of multicultural picture books. *Song of the Swallows* (1949), about the swallows' annual return to the Mission of San Juan Capistrano, won the Caldecott Medal. Born in Fresno, California, Politi returned with his family to his mother's home near Milan, where he lived for seventeen years and studied art before returning to California. There he settled in the Spanish barrio in Los Angeles, a setting that inspired *Pedro, the Angel of Olvera Street* (1946), a Christmas story, and *Juanita* (1948), about the pre-Easter ceremony, the Blessing of the Animals. Politi also wrote about a Chinese New Year celebration in *Moy Moy* (1961), and about life in the Los Angeles Japanese community in *Mieko* (1969). *The Mission Bell* (1953) features the 18th-century Franciscan Junipero Serra. Politi's illustrations are colorful, folklike watercolors filled with a gentleness, rhythm, and simplicity well suited to his stories. Many of the books also include music.

[*See also* Multiculturalism and Children's Books *and* Picture Books.]

LINNEA HENDRICKSON

Pombo, Rafael (1833–1912), Colombian poet, newspaper founder, translator, and author of fables and tales for children. After studying engineering, Pombo went to the United States to work for the Colombian Foreign Ministry. He stayed in the United States, mainly in New York, from 1855 to 1872. He then returned to Colombia, where he lived until his death. As a preadolescent Pombo was engaged in writing, and he assembled his own translations into a book. During his years in the United States he became a famous poet and a celebrated representative of Colombia's national romanticism. In 1905, Pombo was named the first Poeta Nacional (National Poet) in Colombia, and seven years later he was elected to la Academia Colombiana de la Lengua (the Colombian Academy of Language).

It was something of an accident that Pombo became one of Latin America's most famous authors of children's literature. When a political situation forced him to leave the Colombian Foreign Ministry in 1866, he began to select verses and prose by Colombian authors for school primers, working with Luis F. Mantilla. The following year Pombo published a collection of adaptations of fables in Spanish: *Cuentos pintados para niños* (Illustrated Tales for Children). The book consisted of twelve narratives in verse and prose. Four of these narratives, written in verse, are among the most famous of Pombo's work: "El renacuajo paseador" (The Strolling Frog), "La pobre viejecita" (The Poor Little Old Lady), "Simón el Bobito" (Simon the Little Fool) and "El gato bandido" (The Bandit Cat). Through these narratives the child reader is taught that he should listen to his parents and appreciate life, that even the foolish have dignity, and that crime is never a good option. The characters that Pombo created in his fables are vivid, and the rhythm and the use of such devices as alliteration make the verses easy to learn; for example, many Latin Americans can recite the fable of the strolling frog Rinrín Renacuajo.

In his writing, Pombo was driven by the idea that children are not born with an instinct for empathy; they must be taught it through religion and moral training. He saw verses as an efficient vehicle for providing such instruction.

Because much of Pombo's work refers directly to the writings of other authors, his originality has been challenged. But he did not make literal translations, nor did he versify translations; he adapted the original work developing an appropriate literary style involving lyrical beauty, humor, and free verse. He managed to entertain as well as convey ideas and values with agility, and his style was lucid and witty. Even though many of Pombo's poems were adaptations of classic children's literature, such as English nursery rhymes, his *cuentos* (stories) were so brilliant that they achieved importance all over the Spanish-speaking world.

KATARINA ERIKSSON

Pomerantz, Charlotte (1930–), American author of more than thirty picture books. Born in Brooklyn and educated at Sarah Lawrence College, Pomerantz began her long career in 1965 with *The Bear Who Couldn't Sleep*, illustrated by Meg Wohlberg. Her picture book texts, many appearing on annual lists of best books for children, include lullabies and poems as well as stories, and her poetry has appeared in anthologies. Her numerous illustrators include Jose Aruego, Byron Barton, Marilyn Hafner, Susan Jeffers, Anita Lobel, James Marshall, Catherine Stock, and Nancy Tafuri, among others. In 1974 Pomerantz won the Jane Addams Peace Association Children's Book Award for *The Princess and the Admiral*. In 1983 she won an honor award from the same association for *If I Had A Paka*. She also won the Christopher Award twice—in 1984 for *Posy* and in 2000 for *The Mousery*.

[*See also* Picture Books; Poetry; *and biographies of figures mentioned in this article*.]

MARGARET BUSH

Pommaux, Yvan (1946–), French author and illustrator. In 1970, Pommaux began working as a layout artist for the publisher L'École des loisirs, where he discovered the books of Maurice Sendak and Tomi Ungerer. He illustrated several texts by other authors, but soon began writing his own. *L'aventure* (The Adventure, 1976) was the first of his unique picture books influenced by cinema and comics. Later he also published comics, including a popular series about a crow couple, Corbelle and Corbillo. Inspired by the thriller, Pommaux revisits classic tales in a series about a black cat detective who solves the cases of Little Red Riding Hood in *John Chatterton détective* (John Chatterton, Detective, 1993), Snow White in *Lilas* (1995), and Sleeping Beauty in *Le grand sommeil* (The Big Sleep, 1998). Feline protagonists are also featured in *Une nuit, un chat . . .* (One Night, a Cat . . . , 1994), *La fugue* (The Escapade, 1994), and *Libérez Lili* (Free Lili, 1999). Pommaux won the Goncourt Jeunesse 2003 prize for his documentary picture book *Avant la télé* (Before TV).

[*See also* Comic Books; France; Illustrations; Sendak, Maurice; *and* Ungerer, Tomi.]

SANDRA L. BECKETT

Ponti, Claude (1948–), French author and illustrator born in Luneville, Lorraine. A graduate of the École des Beaux-Arts in Aix-en-Provence, Ponti has published three novels and more than sixty picture books, the most famous of which are *Pétronille et ses 120 petits* (Petronille and Her 120 Children, 1990), *L'arbre sans fin* (The Never-ending Tree, 1992), *Ma vallée* (My Valley, 1998), and the series *Tromboline et Foulbazar* (Tromboline and Foulbazar, 1993–). In 1986 Ponti entered the world of children's literature with *L'album d'Adèle* (Adele's Album), a wordless picture book that considerably transformed books for young children in France. Well-read and versatile, Ponti shows his abilities through dense intertextuality and remarkable respect for the traditional literary arts. Ponti develops lively imagination, and both his visual and his verbal languages are complex and equivocal. If his picture books offer varied, dynamic, and exhilarating reading experiences, they also arouse the reader's attachment to long and profound stories.

[*See also* France *and* Picture Books.]

Sophie Van der Linden

Pope, Elizabeth Marie (1917–1992), American author of historical fantasy and scholar of Renaissance literature. Long before Pope's children's fiction was published, she wrote a scholarly work called *Paradise Regained: The Tradition and the Poem* (1947). Her scholarship informed but did not overwhelm her two children's novels, *The Sherwood Ring* (1958) and *The Perilous Gard* (1974). Pope earned a doctorate from Johns Hopkins and was active in several historical societies. *The Sherwood Ring* deals with time travel and ghosts from the American Revolutionary War when a British girl moves to New York. It is more lighthearted but not as well known as its successor, *The Perilous Gard*, which was a Newbery Honor Book. Its take on the Tam Lin legend is colored by the author's background in the Tudor era of British history: the details of politics and contemporary society are note-perfect. The young heroine, exiled to Elvenwood Hall, finds romance but must save her love and unravel the truth about the Fair Folk beneath the aptly named castle. The plot is complicated by the religious and political conflicts of the British monarchies, which switched from Roman Catholic to Anglican to Roman Catholic and back to Anglican again over four reigns. Pope's scrupulous research allows even the most historically informed child or adult to lose him or herself in these books.

[*See also* Historical Fiction *and* Tam Lin.]

Marissa K. Lingen

Popeye, the sailor-man. With his spinach-eating antics, Popeye the sailor-man hit big with Depression-era children. Created by Elzie Crisler Segar (1894–1938), Popeye premiered as a minor character in the *Thimble Theatre* comic strip in 1929. He was so popular that the strip eventually was renamed after him. Most fans of Popeye remember him from his more than five hundred cartoon movies, the first of which debuted in 1933. Max Fleischer, of Fleischer Studios, brought Popeye from the comic strip to film; his attention to detail keeps the cartoons looking bright and energetic more than seventy years later. Jack Mercer gave Popeye his true voice in the 1940s, first for Fleischer and then for Paramount Studios. He would continue for forty years, eventually working for Hanna-Barbera in 1978 to recapture the earlier Fleischer magic. In December 1980 Popeye starred in a feature film with Robin Williams as Popeye and Shelley Duvall as Olive Oyl.

[*See also* Animated Films *and* Comic Books.]

Anthony S. Burdge

Popov, Nikolai (1938–), prominent Russian painter and illustrator. Popov grew up in Saratov on the Volga River and graduated from Moscow's Polygraphic Institute. He has since worked in various visual arts, including children's book illustration and animation. For years he contributed illustrations to the children's magazine *Murzilka*. He has won international recognition and many prizes, including the prestigious Grand Prix BIB (Bratislava International Biennale) in 1975 for his illustrations of Defoe's *Robinson Crusoe* (1974), and the Plaque BIB award in 1981 for illustrations in *Skazki i legendy Portugalii* (Tales and Legends of Portugal, 1980). He has two gold medals from the International Book Fair in Leipzig, and in 1998 was named Honored Artist of Russia. Recognition of Popov's talent spread throughout western Europe, Asia, and North America with the publication of his wordless picturebook *Why?*, published first in Switzerland in French (*Pourquoi?*) and German (*Warum?*, 1995), followed quickly by publication in English, Spanish, Chinese, Danish, and Italian. This title earned him a place in the 2000 Honour List of IBBY, the International Board on Books for Young People, an Honor Book award from the Society of School Librarians International, and a Notable Children's Trade Book in the Field of Social Studies award from the National Council for the Social Studies–Children's Book Council.

Popov's childhood experiences during the war years made a deep impression on him, evident in *Why?* This eloquent fable explores the nature of discontent and war. Frog's peaceful enjoyment of a wildflower is disrupted when Mouse erupts from underground, spearheaded by an umbrella. In a masterful double-spread, Mouse pounces from one side of the page to invade Frog's side and seize the flower. In greens and browns these opening scenes explore choices: coexistence and peace vs. greed and war; harmony with nature vs. destructive technology and domination over it. Facial expressions show the naïveté of the frog contingent as the mice escalate by rolling out more sophisticated weaponry—a cannon-like boot on wheels. Frogs in retaliation abandon hand-to-hand combat, learn cunning, and resort to dirty tricks and weapons of their own. Neither side perceives the next lurking threat, though readers get a glimpse from their privileged point of view. The usual forward flow of picturebook action (aided by right-facing characters) is repeatedly reversed as first one side, then the other returns to counterattack, but all victories are temporary and only serve to destroy the landscape. Epic significance is evoked by the large format and borderless design. In the final battle, sky is reduced to a thin discolored layer and greens turn brown/black. Up to that point the tone has been light, the animals cute, and the weapons amusing, but this sobering scene conveys the antiwar message unmistakably. The concluding double-spread reinstates the dividing line between Mouse and Frog, each looking thoughtful, but perhaps neither yet understanding "why." Readers, though, will perceive that, unlike the faceless soldiers in so many antiwar picturebooks, the protagonists here are real characters who bear responsibility for their actions. The title, the book's only text, subtly urges children to ponder the futility of war.

CHRISTINA M. DESAI

Porte, Barbara Ann (1943–), American author whose children's books cross a wide spectrum of genres. A librarian by profession, Porte entered the field of children's literature with *Harry's Visit* (1983), the first in a series of gently comic early readers about the trials and triumphs of Harry, a young boy living with his widowed father. Intended for middle grade readers, *Jesse's Ghost and Other Stories* (1983) is a collection of folkloric and original tales that range from fancifully humorous to spooky. Porte utilizes folklore in her young adult novels as well. Made up of interconnected family tales and vignettes, *I Only Made Up the Roses* (1987) concerns a teenager growing up in a biracial family, while *Something Terrible Happened* (1994) features a girl from another racially mixed family who receives emotional sustenance from the folk tales and family legends she learns as her mother suffers from AIDS. Porte's wide-ranging output makes her difficult to categorize, but demonstrates the breadth of her talent.

[*See also* Easy Readers; Fairy Tales and Folk Tales; Interracial Books for Children; Librarians in the United States; *and* Young Adult Literature.]

PETER D. SIERUTA

Porter, Eleanor (1868–1920), American author of the international best seller *Pollyanna* (1913) and its first sequel, *Pollyanna Grows Up* (1915), though the many Pollyanna stories that followed are works by other writers. Eleven-year-old Pollyanna Whittier is an eternally cheerful and optimistic orphan who goes to live with her stern Aunt Polly. Encouraged by her father to find the bright side in every situation, Pollyanna continually plays what she calls the "just being glad game," a game she relies on after a car accident threatens to make her lame for life, and a game that turns her cross Aunt Polly into a loving, maternal figure. Porter also wrote a series of novels about another orphan, Billy Neilson, who goes to live with an unknown relative, in this case an Aunt Hannah in Boston (*Miss Billy*, 1911; *Miss Billy's Decision*, 1912; and *Miss Billy Married*, 1914). Porter's first novel was *Cross Currents* (1907).

[*See also* Orphans.]

KELLY HAGER

Porter, William Sidney. *See* O. Henry.

Portugal. As in other European countries, if upper-class Portuguese children had books before and during the 18th century, these works had not been written particularly for them. Until Jean-Jacques Rousseau's *Émile: ou, De l'éducation* (1762), children were considered as miniature adults, and it was believed that they did not need special books. Primers and catechisms were exceptions. Oral literature played a prominent part in the transmission of traditional tales in Portugal. Children's literature proper appeared in Portugal during the Enlightenment, when important foreign texts were translated into Portuguese, and Portuguese authors began to produce their own works for children, often with a pedagogical aim.

Portuguese children's literature soared during the second half of the 19th century. While foreign books continued to

Portugal. Illustration by Carlos Botelho from *The Children's Book* by Antonio Botto, translated by Alice Lawrence Oram (Lisbon, c. 1935), p. 43. REPRODUCED COURTESY OF THE COTSEN CHILDREN'S LIBRARY, PRINCETON UNIVERSITY LIBRARY

be translated, the number of Portuguese texts kept increasing. Their main goal was to form character and influence the mind. Children's newspapers appeared at the same time. This propitious evolution, however, affected a minority of children, since three quarters of Portuguese children were still illiterate at the end of the 19th century. At the beginning of the 20th century, one of the key figures in the development of Portuguese children's literature was Henrique Marques Júnior. A children's author himself, he translated many foreign texts for children (Hans Christian Andersen, the Brothers Grimm, Charles Perrault, the Countess of Ségur, and so on). He also compiled one of the first important descriptive bibliographies of early children's books. This important reference book shows, among other things, that new collections for the young, often of good quality, appeared in Portugal at the end of the 19th and beginning of the 20th century. Further, it shows that publishing for children continued to grow during the same period. The titles were henceforth numerous. It also tells us that Portuguese children's theater developed in an interesting way.

At the beginning of Antonio de Oliveira Salazar's dictatorship (Estado Novo) and, above all, after World War II, two main kinds of subject matter coexisted in Portuguese children's literature. On the one hand, there were books whose goal was to magnify the virtues of traditionalism, patriotism, and nationalism. On the other hand, Portuguese children had texts that took the new social realities into account. In other words, Portuguese children's literature became more critical, and humor and irony appeared. During the following decades, Portuguese children's literature expanded quickly. New authors began producing some innovative works. Comic books appeared. New topics aimed at teenagers emerged: sexuality, friendship, parents, divorce, drugs, AIDS, and so on. Rural emigration and its consequences (the countryside in utter neglect; growing urbanization), social disparities, and racism were denounced, and environmental issues began to appear.

Illustration has been an important aspect of children's books in Portugal. During the Enlightenment, Portuguese children's books were rarely illustrated; the only engraving was the frontispiece. The artists often were anonymous. At the end of the 19th century, Portuguese artists started collaborating with children's books authors. Nowadays some Portuguese children's books illustrators have acquired an international reputation.

[*See also biographies of figures mentioned in this article*.]

BIBLIOGRAPHY

Gomes, José António. *Para uma história da literatura portuguesa para a infância e a juventude*. Lisbon: Instituto português do livro e das bibliotecas, 1997.

BERNARD HUBER

Postgate, Oliver (1925–), and **Peter Firmin** (1928–), British writing and illustrating team. Postgate was educated at Kingston College of Art and the London Academy of Music and Dramatic Art; Firmin, at Colchester School of Art and the Central School, London. They collaborated and operated as Smallfilms, producing children's animated programs from 1958. In addition to animating popular literature such as Violet Drummond's *Little Laura* books, they created and produced series that appealed to the imagination of the young: stories about small creatures that seemed to coinhabit the human world, as well as tales of distant, romantic cultures. Series titles include *Ivor the Engine*, *The Saga of Noggin the Nog*, *The Pingwings*, *Pogle's Wood*, *The Clangers*, and *Bagpuss*. A number of publications for children were produced as offshoots from the series, mainly in the form of annuals and large-format picture books containing stills from the animations. *Clangers: Major Clanger's Rocket* (1970), the story of an iron chicken shot down by rocket, which then causes havoc on the Clangers' planet, is told in a mixture of photographic stills and Firmin's line drawings. *The Pogles: The Magic Milk Cart* (1968) uses the same format to tell the story of how, when a young Pogle and his companion find what they believe to be a magic milk cart, only to realize that it belongs to some local children, they try to return it without being seen.

Firmin has had independent success with the character Basil Brush, a puppet he made for television and wrote subsequent stories about, such as *Basil Brush on the Trail* (1979). Postgate and Firmin's contributions to children's television and literature has had an enduring effect on the British public, with BBC viewers voting *Bagpuss* the Most Popular BBC Children's Film Ever in 1999.

[*See also* Animated Films; Series Books; *and* Television and Children.]

BIBLIOGRAPHY

Postgate, Oliver. *Seeing Things: An Autobiography*. London: Pan, 2000.

Linda Knight

Potok, Chaim (1929–2002), Jewish American novelist, historian, and author of children's books. Potok is best known for his novels *The Chosen* (1967), *The Promise* (1969), and *My Name Is Asher Lev* (1972). Raised in a traditional Jewish home, Potok received an orthodox Jewish education, was ordained as a rabbi, received his PhD in philosophy at the University of Pennsylvania, and taught Jewish studies and American literature at the university level. Because his novels mainly follow children's and adolescents' lives, they are often described as contemporary bildungsromans (novels of education), as the novels trace the maturing of children into young adults. The relationship between child and parent is regularly highlighted, and an important theme in his novels is the confrontation between traditional Orthodox Judaism and Western secular culture. *My Name Is Asher Lev*, which follows the maturation of a young Orthodox Jewish artist, is the most famous of these. Although he is best known for his novels, Potok also published three children's books late in his career, books that address the issues of change, fear, and the search for truth: *The Tree of Here* (1993), *The Sky of Now* (1995), and *Zebra and Other Stories* (1998).

[*See also* Bildungsroman or Novel of Education; Multiculturalism and Children's Books; *and* Young Adult Literature.]

BIBLIOGRAPHY

Kremer, S. Lillian. "Chaim Potok." *Contemporary Jewish-American Novelists: A Bio-Critical Sourcebook*. Westport, Conn.: Greenwood, 1997.

Sternlicht, Sanford V. *Chaim Potok: A Critical Companion*. Westport, Conn.: Greenwood, 2000.

Melinda Wilson

Potter, Beatrix (1866–1943), British author-illustrator whose work is central to the development of the modern picture book. She was clearly influenced by author-illustrators such as Randolph Caldecott and Kate Greenaway, but Potter's books are innovative in their integration of text and illustration. In *Peter Rabbit* (1901), narrative progresses through words and pictures as, for example, Potter visually anticipates Peter's violation of Mrs. Rabbit's instructions not to "go into Mr. McGregor's garden" by setting him apart from his siblings; Peter faces away from his sisters and does not seem to be listening to his mother. Another unique quality of Potter's books is the minute realism conveyed in her illustration of domestic scenes and landscapes, providing a concrete backdrop for her anthropomorphic fantasies.

Though the miniature format of the Peter Rabbit books implies a child readership, Potter is never patronizing, using sophisticated language and intricate narrative structures. Her books are of differing length and complexity, from her nursery books *Miss Moppet* (1906) and *The Story of a Fierce Bad Rabbit* (1906), to longer works such as *Little Pig Robinson* (1930). She also conveys the cruelty of nature through some of the most convincing villains in children's literature,

Beatrix Potter. At age nineteen, with her pet mouse Xarifa. REPRODUCED COURTESY OF THE COTSEN CHILDREN'S LIBRARY, PRINCETON UNIVERSITY LIBRARY

including Samuel Whiskers, Mr. Tod, and Tommy Brock, though the potential for terror is often tempered by comedy. In *Mr. Tod* (1912), Tommy Brock kidnaps the Flopsy Bunnies and they remain in peril for sixty-two pages; thus Potter seems almost to revel in the distress of the trembling rabbit babies, sustaining tension while her villains attempt to outwit each other.

Though British tourism invests in the pastoral idyll, and occasional sentimentality, evoked by Potter, this idyll is threatened by predators and undermined by the irony underpinning Potter's work. In the manner of Jane Austen, Potter satirizes Victorian and Edwardian convention, often producing social comedy through anthropomorphic play. Potter constantly dresses and undresses her characters, encouraging readers to reflect on the absurdity of human behavior. In *Tom Kitten* (1907), for example, Tom's mother tries to defy natural instinct in the dressing of her kittens for a tea party, and the consequent comical disrobing seems inevitable. In the process of ridiculing adult pretensions, Potter also provides a carnivalesque space in which her child characters can temporarily escape from adult authority. Indeed, her books are full of naughty children, such as Peter Rabbit, Squirrel Nutkin, and Tom Kitten, and though their behavior is usually punished, their naughtiness is celebrated as it takes center stage, thus questioning prevailing constructions of childhood in the style of Lewis Carroll and of Potter's contemporary Edith Nesbit. Potter's books are exquisitely balanced—between word and picture, fantasy and realism, child and adult, animal and human—and the equilibrium of her work may, in part, explain her lasting popularity.

Potter's talent was inadvertently nurtured by her upbringing. Helen Beatrix Potter was born in South Kensington, London, on 28 July 1866 to Helen and Rupert Potter. Inheritors of fortunes from the Lancashire cotton industry, her parents lived a life of middle-class gentility that made few concessions to the needs of a child. Until the birth of her brother, Bertram, in 1872, Beatrix spent her childhood in the company of her Scottish nurse, Miss McKenzie. Although she and Bertram became close, Beatrix mostly had to amuse herself in his infancy, reading widely and nurturing a talent for painting and drawing. The breadth of her reading is reflected in the rich intertextuality of her books: in *Squirrel Nutkin* (1903), traditional riddles contribute to characterization and narrative rhythm; *Pigling Bland* (1913) is structured around two nursery rhymes, "This Little Piggie Went to Market" and "Tom, Tom the Piper's Son," while *Little Pig Robinson* makes a hero of Edward Lear's piggy-wig in "The Owl and the Pussycat."

To suggest that the Potters lived a typical life of social rounds is inaccurate; Rupert Potter's love of art opened up a cultural oasis to Beatrix. As a respected amateur photographer, Rupert often photographed sitters for his friend, John Everett Millais, and he was a keen collector of Caldecott's work. As she matured, Beatrix attended art exhibitions with her parents and visited Millais's studio with her father. That she was becoming an incisive art critic is evident in her journal entries, written in secret code from 1881 through 1897. Until Leslie Linder's transcription of these journals in 1966, it was commonly accepted that Beatrix Potter's girlhood was isolated and unhappy. Though her parents discouraged friendships, her journals reveal an active interest in politics, art, photography, literature, and nature. Indeed, in the journals she developed her talent as writer and illustrator, recording the world around her through word and image with the wit and irony to be found in her later books.

Perhaps Beatrix's most important influences came from regular family excursions around the British Isles. Every

Beatrix Potter. Illustration from *Peter Rabbit* (London: F. Warne & Co., [1930s]), p. 26. REPRODUCED COURTESY OF THE COTSEN CHILDREN'S LIBRARY, PRINCETON UNIVERSITY LIBRARY

April, the Potters vacationed at the coast, and for three months every summer their London home, Bolton Gardens, was closed up and the entire household traveled to a rented home. Scotland became the regular backdrop to Beatrix's childhood holidays; from the age of five to fifteen, she spent summers at Dalguise House, a Perthshire mansion, along with her parents' guests, such as Millais and William Gaskell. Beatrix roamed the Dalguise estates, exploring and painting the natural landscape. In 1882, the family was dismayed to discover that Dalguise was no longer available, but when there was talk of a return in 1884, Beatrix reacted unfavorably in her journal, providing an insight into her views on her own childhood and her books:

> I am afraid there is a chance of going back to Dalguise. I feel an extraordinary dislike to this idea, a childish dislike, but the memory of that home is the only bit of childhood I have left. It was not perfectly happy, childhood's sorrows are sharp while they last, but they are like April showers serving to

> freshen the fields and make the sunshine brighter than before . . . The place is changed now, and many familiar faces are gone, but the greatest change is in myself. I was a child then . . . Everything was romantic in my imagination . . . Half believing the picturesque superstitions of the district, seeing my own fancies so clearly that they became true to me, I lived in a separate world. Then just as childhood was beginning to shake, we had to go, my first great sorrow. I do not wish to have to repeat it . . . let me keep the past.

The lyricism of these reflections anticipates the sensitivity of her best writing, and it is possible that Beatrix found a way of returning to this past world of romantic imagining through her children's books, which demonstrate the tension implicit in this passage; while there is a fanciful and picturesque quality to her much of her work, this is often sharpened by an expression of danger, cruelty, or sorrow. Clearly these sojourns to Dalguise had a lasting impact, but it was at the Potter's next family retreat, in the Lake District, that Beatrix formed a relationship with the natural world that was to transform her life.

During her childhood years and early womanhood, these trips provided only a short-term escape from Bolton Gardens, where Bertram and Beatrix created an idiosyncratic schoolroom through their collection of live creatures, such as lizards and bats, studying them closely in life and death. Bertram was sent away to school in 1883, and, now seventeen, Beatrix imagined her own education over, so it was with apprehension that she received the arrival of Annie Carter, employed to teach her German. The two soon became friends, however, and since Annie was only three years older than Beatrix, she had a friend of her own age for the first time. Though their time together was brief—for Annie announced her engagement in 1885—they remained lifelong friends, and it was for Noel Moore, Annie's first child, that Beatrix wrote the first version of *Peter Rabbit*.

In 1890, Bertram suggested that Beatrix send her sketches of a pet rabbit, Benjamin H. Bouncer, to a greeting card publisher. Hildesheimer & Faulkner requested further designs and subsequently produced her first publication, *A Happy Pair* (1890), a booklet of her pictures set to verse by Frederic Weatherly. Between 1892 and 1894 the Potters returned to Scotland for their summer holidays, and it was now that Beatrix began writing picture letters to the Moore children, including the famous Peter Rabbit letter in 1893. Beatrix also acted on her interest in fungi, writing a paper on spores with the support of her uncle, Sir Henry Roscoe, which was presented at the Linnean Society of London in 1897. Had she not encountered hostility from this patriarchal establishment, Beatrix Potter's career might have developed differently, for her theories were later proved correct.

Now began the second phase of Potter's life, marked by the cessation of journal entries, as she was about to embark on the most productive period of her literary career. Hoping to publish *Peter Rabbit*, Beatrix approached Hardwicke Rawnsley, the Vicar of Crosthwaite, honorary secretary of the National Trust and a poet, who had become a close friend in the Lake District. Frustrated by lack of interest, Beatrix decided to publish the book herself, and in December 1901, *The Tale of Peter Rabbit* appeared in a first edition of 250 copies. The firm of Frederick Warne eventually agreed to publication, and their edition appeared in 1902. The book was immediately successful and Beatrix finally had the means of supporting herself.

Beatrix gradually established a relationship with Norman Warne, who oversaw the publication of *The Tale of Squirrel Nutkin*, *The Tailor of Gloucester* (1903), *The Tale of Benjamin Bunny* (1904), *The Tale of Two Bad Mice* (1904), *The Tale of Mrs. Tiggy-Winkle* (1905), and *The Pie and the Patty-Pan* (1905). He proposed to Beatrix in 1905, to the dismay of her parents, who relied on Beatrix and abhorred the idea of her marrying "into trade." Beatrix persisted in the engagement only to be devastated by Norman's sudden death in the same year. Beatrix increasingly took refuge in Hill Top, a farm in Near Sawrey in the Lake District, which she had purchased earlier that year, and there began work on her next book, *The Tale of Jeremy Fisher* (1906), which was followed by two panorama books for younger readers: *The Story of a Fierce Bad Rabbit* and *The Story of Miss Moppet*. With the exception of *The Tale of the Flopsy Bunnies* (1909), all of her books in the subsequent period are set in and around Sawrey, including *The Tale of Tom Kitten*, *The Tale of Jemima Puddleduck* (1908), *The Roly-Poly Pudding* (1908; retitled *The Tale of Samuel Whiskers*, 1926), and *The Tale of Ginger and Pickles* (1909). In 1909, Beatrix purchased Castle Farm, close to Hill Top, meanwhile producing *The Tale of Mrs. Tittlemouse* (1910), *The Tale of Timmy Tiptoes* (1911; written with American readers in mind, it is her only book to feature creatures—chipmunks, gray squirrels, and a bear—that are not indigenous to the British Isles), and *The Tale of Mr. Tod*. As a significant landowner in the Lake District, Potter sought the advice of William Heelis, a solicitor, who proposed marriage in 1912. Once again her parents opposed the idea, but on 15 October 1913 they married, shortly after the publication of *The Tale of Pigling Bland*.

Beatrix now referred to herself as Mrs. Heelis, and this name change marks a shift in priorities. The farming and breeding of Herdwick sheep was now her consuming passion, and she became a respected expert on this breed. She also purchased land on behalf of the National Trust, bequeathing them much of her estate on her death. Her literary output slowed, though she produced *Appley Dapply's Nursery Rhymes* (1917) to help Warne's, who were close to bankruptcy, followed by *The Tale of Johnny Town Mouse* (1918). Her final books, *Cecily Parsely's Nursery Rhymes* (1922), *The Fairy Caravan* (1929), and *Little Pig Robinson* and *Sister Anne* (1932), were written at the behest of American fans and publishers. Two stories were published posthumously, "Wag-by-Wall" (1944) and *The Faithful Dove* (1956).

[*See also* Animal Stories; Anthropomorphism; Nursery Rhymes; Picture Books; Publishers and Publishing; *and biographies of figures mentioned in this article.*]

BIBLIOGRAPHY

Kutzer, M. D. *Beatrix Potter: Writing in Code*. New York and London: Routledge, 2003.

Linder, L. *A History of the Writings of Beatrix Potter*. London: Frederick Warne, 1971.

Mackey, Margaret. *The Case of Peter Rabbit: Changing Conditions of Literature for Children*. New York: Garland, 1998.

Potter, B. *The Journal of Beatrix Potter from 1881 to 1897*. Transcribed from her code writings by Leslie Linder. London: Frederick Warne, 1966.

Taylor, J. *"So I Shall Tell You a Story . . .": Encounters with Beatrix Potter*. London: Frederick Warne, 1993.

Lisa Sainsbury

Poulin, Stéphane (1961–), French-Canadian illustrator and author who studied graphic arts at Montreal's Ahuntsic College. Poulin claims various artistic influences, from the French Impressionists to Norman Rockwell. His first children's book, *Ah! Belle Cité / A Beautiful City ABC* (1985), is a bilingual alphabet book about Montreal; it received immediate critical acclaim. Among Poulin's most famous books are *As-tu vu Joséphine* (1986; English trans., *Have You Seen Josephine?* 1986), *Les amours de ma mère* (1990; English trans., *My Mother's Loves*, 1990), *Un voyage pour deux* (1991; English trans., *Travels for Two*, 1991). Poulin has illustrated more than a hundred books, including the anthology *The Outspoken Princess and the Gentle Knight* (1994), edited by Jack Zipes. Although his award-winning texts have been translated into several languages (English, Japanese, German, Korean, Swedish), he confesses to feeling more comfortable as an illustrator. He frequently collaborates with authors from Canada, the United States, and Europe—authors such as Denis Côté, Dominique Demers, Thierry Lenain, Raymond Plante, and Gilles Tibo. Poulin generally works in oil. The characteristics of Poulin's drawing are realistic settings and objects, in contrast to strange-eyed, somewhat cartoonish characters. He favors detailed pictures with primary colors. Poulin has won numerous national and international awards, including the Governor-General's Literary Award for *Benjamin et la saga des oreillers* (1989; English trans., *Benjamin and the Pillow Saga*, 1989) and *Poil de serpent, dent d'araignée* (Snake Bristle, Spider Tooth, 1997).

[*See also* ABC Books or Alphabet Books; Illustrations; Picture Books; *and biographies of figures mentioned in this article.*]

Claire Le Brun

Power, Rhoda (1890–1957), British author educated at Girton College, Cambridge, and known for historical fiction, retelling of folk tales, and pioneer work with the BBC on programming for schools. With Eileen Power, she wrote *Boys and Girls of History* (1926) and *More Boys and Girls of History* (1928), in which everyday life is narrated from the perspective of children. Power uses imaginary characters as eyewitnesses from different social milieus in *We Were There* (1955) and *From the Fury of the Northmen* (1957). Other texts include *The Age of Discovery from Marco Polo to Henry Hudson* (1927), *Great People of the Past* (1932), and the *Kingsway Histories for Juniors* (4 vols.; 1937, 1938). Her historical novel *Redcap Runs Away* (1953), in which a young boy joins minstrels, is set in 14th-century England. Power's collections of folk tales include *Stories from Everywhere* (1931), reissued as *The Big Book of Stories from Many Lands* (1970), *How It Happened: Myths and Folk Tales Retold* (1930), *Here and There Stories* (1945), and *Ten Minute Tales and Dialogue Stories* (1943).

[*See also* Fairy Tales and Folk Tales; Historical Fiction; *and* Nonfiction.]

Hilary S. Crew

Powling, Chris (1943–), British author, teacher, and lecturer. For many years Powling was the editor of the magazine *Books for Keeps*, during which time it was awarded the Hans Christian Andersen medal for its all-around excellence. A prolific author for younger readers, he has produced fifty-seven titles to date, ranging from picture books to adventure stories including *Where the Quaggy Bends* (1992), *Kit's Castle* (1996), and *Blade* (2005). He has also written widely about books and reading, including short, user-friendly biographies of Roald Dahl, Dick King-Smith, Quentin Blake, and Anne Fine, plus a popular guide for younger readers, *The Book About Books* (2001). A leading critic of the U.K. government's policies on teaching and encouraging reading in schools, he was one of five authors who contributed to *Meetings with the Minister* (2005), in which he makes clear his reservations about the U.K. National Curriculum, and specifically the Literacy Hour in primary schools.

[*See also* Biography; Literacy; United Kingdom; *and biographies of figures mentioned in this article.*]

Nicholas Tucker

Pratchett, Terry (1948–), British fantasy writer who published his first story at fifteen and has gone on to write over thirty books in a series called Discworld, in two trilogies for young readers, in three young adult books, and in several more books of one kind or another. The Discworld series appeals to a range of readers, young and not so young. It tells stories that take place on a planet flat as a disk, resting on the back of four enormous elephants who, in turn, stand upon the back of a huge turtle that swims through space. This description indicates the irreverent perspective Pratchett delights in taking. The tone in the Discworld books is firmly established in *Witches Abroad* (1991), when the three witches are traveling by boat on an underground river. They hear a sound and then they see a small gray creature following them on a log. This creature looks something like a frog, and it speaks in an Ovidian manner, drawing out the letter "s." The witches stare at the creature for a few moments, and then one of the witches, Granny Weatherwax, picks up an oar and bops the creature over the head. It curses as it splashes into the water. The witches go on their way. So much for Smeagol; so much for Tolkien. As Pratchett says on his Web site, he began Discworld (first book, *The Colour of Money*, 1983) intending to satirize fantasy, but he has gone on to satirize just about everything, from ancient Egyptian culture, to Hollywood movies, to the opera, to Shakespeare. The character in *Wyrd Sisters* (1988) who represents Shakespeare, the dwarf Hwel, finds himself writing dialogue from a Marx Brothers film. Pratchett's invoking of the Marx Brothers is instructive. His humor borders on the parodic, and sometimes satiric, nonsense we find in comedy by the likes of the Marx Brothers or the Monty Python group.

Terry Pratchett.

Pratchett's young adult books, *The Amazing Maurice and His Educated Rodents* (2001), *The Wee Free Men* (2003), and *A Hat Full of Sky* (2004), are set on the Discworld and contain familiar characters such as Granny Weatherwax and Death. *The Amazing Maurice* is something of a parody of the Pied Piper story, and the other two books follow the adventures of an eleven-year-old girl, Tiffany Aching, as she deals with various villains aided by the tiny Nac Mac Feegle, a race of bellicose warriors who shout like wee Scotsmen. The presence of Death in these books is indicative of Pratchett's many speculations on death. His children's book *Johnny and the Dead* (1993) tells the story of Johnny and his friends who work to save a local cemetery from being destroyed to make room for high-rise buildings. The message is that living people need to remember the past, whereas the dead can just let the past go. *Johnny and the Dead* is one of three books about Johnny Maxwell and his friends Wobbler, Bigmac, Yo-less, and sometimes Kirsty. The other two books are *Only You Can Save Mankind* (1993), about video games, and *Johnny and the Bomb* (1996), a time-slip fantasy in which Johnny returns to the time of World War II.

Pratchett's finest achievement in children's literature is the Bromeliad trilogy, *Truckers* (1989), *Diggers* (1990), and *Wings* (1990), about a group of Nomes long ago fallen from the sky. Finding themselves in a strange land, the Nomes created their own scripture and mythology, and now seek to return to their home in a faraway galaxy. Pratchett's interest in miniature worlds appeared from his first book, *The Carpet People* (1971), and takes flight in this series. As always, Pratchett's world is deeply Platonic in its logocentricity. Language has a way of creating the reality his characters experience, and the story of the Nomes is the story of a people emerging from an oral condition into literacy. Intertextual references range from the Bible to *Gulliver's Travels*, *Alice's Adventures in Wonderland*, and the British television program *Red Dwarf*. The books introduce young readers to the concept of interpretation and the construction of reality. And finally, they parody the narrative of exodus.

[*See also* Fantasy; Parody; Science Fiction; *and* Young Adult Literature.]

BIBLIOGRAPHY

Butler, Andrew. "Terry Pratchett and the Comedic Bildungsroman." *Foundation* 67 (1996): 56–62.

Kutzer, Daphne. "Thatchers and Thatcherites: Lost and Found in Three British Fantasies." *The Lion and the Unicorn* 22, no. 2 (1998): 196–210.

Sawyer, Andy. "Narrativum and Lies-to-Children: 'Palatable Instruction' in the Science of Discworld." *Journal of the Fantastic in the Arts* 13, no. 1 (2002): 62–81.

RODERICK MCGILLIS

Prater, John (1947–), British illustrator who worked in advertising before becoming a children's illustrator. Prater's first book, *On Friday Something Funny Happened* (1982), was runner-up for the Mother Goose Award. Since then he has written and illustrated various picture books for young readers. Prater's only wordless picture book, *The Gift* (1985), follows two children's journey in a flying cardboard box. The richly colored illustrations tell the story through the imaginative use of different-size frames. In *Once upon a Time* (1993) and *Once upon a Picnic* (1997), Prater joined with Vivian French to produce two fascinating intertextual picture books. The stories use traditional characters and patterned language to involve young readers. French's simple rhyming language is juxtaposed with Prater's narrative illustrations that paint a picture of fairy tale chaos within a rural setting. Recently, with the Baby Bears series, Prater has focused on books for very young children. *Oh Where, Oh Where?* (1998) and *Number One, Tickle Your Tum* (1999) are two titles in the series. The books contain simple, engaging story lines that encourage physical interaction between the young child and the adult reader. Prater's uncluttered line drawings of the young bear and parent make this collection of books very engaging.

[*See also* Illustrations; Picture Books; *and* Preschool Books.]

FIONA M. COLLINS

Prelutsky, Jack (1940–), American poet for children, born and raised in the Bronx in New York City. Prelutsky has been credited with revitalizing poetry for children in the latter half of the 20th century. As a child, Prelutsky was brilliant and multitalented; especially noted for his beautiful singing voice, for a time he wanted to be an opera singer. Curiously, poetry was not among his early loves. He briefly attended Hunter College, but dropped out to pursue the more exciting bohemian life in Greenwich Village. Among other things, he dabbled in photography, sculpting, folksinging, and taxi driving. Then, while working in a book and music store, he fancied he would become an artist and created a series of illustrations of fantastical animals. On a whim, he decided to write a poem to go with each illustration. He showed his work to an editor who immediately rejected the art—but accepted the poetry. The result was *A Gopher in the*

Jack Prelutsky. Illustration by Arnold Lobel from *Nightmares* (New York: Greenwillow, 1976), p. 29. REPRODUCED COURTESY OF THE COTSEN CHILDREN'S LIBRARY, PRINCETON UNIVERSITY LIBRARY

Garden and Other Animal Poems (1967), and so began his career as a one of America's most popular children's poets. In the tradition of Edward Lear, Lewis Carroll, and Hilaire Belloc, Prelutsky writes comical verse, dominated by rhyme and rhythm. His poems are generally inspired by everyday experiences and ordinary people, which are transformed by his wildly vivid imagination, concocting such unlikely creations as the boneless chicken who lays scrambled eggs. His work is a combination of the gross, the grotesque, and the purely silly, albeit without depth or challenge. Collections such as *Nightmares: Poems to Trouble Your Sleep* (1976), *The New Kid on the Block* (1984), and *My Parents Think I'm Sleeping* (1984) hold immense appeal for children, and their very titles suggest Prelutsky's ability to meet his young readers on their own terms.

[*See also* Nonsense; Poetry; *and biographies of figures mentioned in this article.*]

DAVID L. RUSSELL

Premchand (1880–1936), Indian writer in Hindi and Urdu well known for his novels and short stories. His works have been translated into English and several Indian languages. Though he is not exactly a children's writer, several of Premchand's short stories are meant for children and narrated from a child's perspective or have children as the central figures. Premchand. whose real name was Dhanpat Rai, was a political activist involved with the Indian freedom struggle, and an ardent believer in Gandhian philosophy. He wrote twelve novels, more than three hundred short stories, several essays, and journalistic pieces, as well as dramas and translations. His style is most remarkable for its realism at a time when Hindi fiction dealt mostly with legend and mystery. Despite the rather stark atmosphere of his major works like *Godan* (The Gift of a Cow, 1936), he also had a keen sense of humor, as is particularly evident in his stories for children like "Idgarh" and "The Story of Two Bullocks." In "Idgarh" Premchand tells the story of a poor boy who spends his scanty money at the fairground not on sweets or toys but on a pair of tongs for his grandmother. The story is appealing in the way the boy manages to convince his wealthier friends that his purchase is better than theirs as toy, weapon, or tool. "The Story of Two Bullocks" is an animal story, with the bullocks (who have quite philosophical talks between themselves) running away from a series of unkind masters and having several adventures until they finally wind up at their original happy home. Premchand's stories, which children enjoy, are mainly in the collection *Kishor Sahitya Mala* (2000). His complete short fiction appears collectively as *Manasarovar* (8 vols.; 1936–1941). Also notable is *Ram Charcha* (1998), a retelling for children of the epic *Ramayana*.

[*See also* India *and* Realism.]

SINDHU MENON

Prentiss, Elizabeth (1818–1878), American author of children's fiction and religious fiction for adults (such as *Stepping Heavenward*, 1869). Prentiss had a story published in the *Youth's Companion* when she was only sixteen, but in later years writing was made difficult by the frequent illnesses and deaths of her children. By 1856 Prentiss had recovered sufficiently to write *Little Susy's Six Birthdays*, a story that emphasizes the need to treat children differently as they grow older. *Little Susy's Six Teachers* (1856) and *Little Susy's Little Servants* (1856) followed, with the same thoughtful advice on how a child's life should be guided.

[*See also* Moral Tales *and* Religious Writing.]

FRANCES ARMSTRONG

Preschool Books. In general the term "preschool books" encompasses all books written and published for children from the age of about twelve months until six years. Preschool books apply to both fictional and nonfictional works, thus covering the range from the so-called baby books to picture books for small children, but also including books to read aloud, song books, movable books, and coloring books. As for literary genres, prose texts and poetry are predominant, but the number of dramatic works for preschool children is increasing. The majority of preschool books have illustrations in order to catch the eye of the small child who has not yet gained the ability to read the books by him or herself. For this reason preschool books imply an adult mediator who either reads the texts aloud or contemplates the pictures together with the small child.

Classification

The first type of book that infants normally encounter are baby books, often made of thick cardboard, but also of wipeable plastic, even wood or cloth ("rag books"). These handy books typically contain several pages that show pictures of common everyday objects a child will probably come in contact with. However, these books contain no text, with the possible exception of a single word denoting the object pic-

Preschool Books. Front cover illustration by Helen Oxenbury for *Dressing* (New York: Wanderer Books, a division of Simon & Schuster, c. 1981). REPRODUCED COURTESY OF THE COTSEN CHILDREN'S LIBRARY, PRINCETON UNIVERSITY LIBRARY

torially represented. The pictures are color drawings or photographs. The baby books drawn by Dick Bruna are well known. The famous *The First Picture Book* (1930) by Edward Steichen was highly influential in the development of photo books for small children. In order to appeal to toddlers these baby books are often disguised as playthings, for example, with the possibility of lifting up flaps in the pages or by the combination of baby book and stuffed animal or puzzle, encouraging the small child to use the baby book as a tool. In contrast to these baby books, "theme books" or "concept books" go a step further in that they depict objects, activities, and situations that are connected in some way—for example, board books about animals, vehicles, colors, shapes, or sizes. This type of book is intended for children who are already accustomed to baby books, and introduces them to bigger conceptual classes, either various dimensions of an object, a class of objects, or abstract ideas. A step ahead are those books for infants that are characterized by showing on each double spread an object on one side, and on the other side an activity that could be done with the object, as shown in Helen Oxenbury's popular board book series, which revolutionized the genre. In addition, these books most often show a main figure—either a child or an animal—that does appear on each double spread, thus introducing the small child to a preliminary concept of story. Another book type is the "I spy books." These picture books, which show a scene with many objects and figures, stimulate the child to play a recognition or seeking game, looking for hidden objects, as for example in Allan and Janet Ahlberg's *Peepo* (1981). Although a progressive narrative seldom appears in books for very young children, short and simple texts occur both in picture books and in illustrated books containing rhymes and poems for children. A transition from the theme books is the descriptive picture book, which describes everyday activities like doing the washing, going shopping, or working in the garden. Illustrated anthologies with traditional jingles, finger plays, lullabies, riddles, tongue twisters, or nursery rhymes entertaining children from birth to the age of about five are the young child's first poetry experience and evoke the child's aesthetic pleasure. Because of their brevity and their strongly marked rhymes, they ensure memorability. In addition, these verses could be regarded as concise narratives in four or six lines, thus preparing the listening child for longer and more complex texts.

At about three years of age children are normally accustomed to a simple concept of story. For this reason they will from then on encounter books with longer stories showing a more complex narrative structure. To this category belong fairy tales, fables, legends, picture books, and anthologies with short stories or poetry. Whereas picture books intended for children aged three show an episodic structure centered around one main figure, for example, *The Very Hungry Caterpillar* (1969) by Eric Carle or *Mr. Gumpy's Outing* (1970) by John Burningham, picture books for children already accustomed to stories with more than one protagonist are often distinguished by a more complex structure. These introduce the viewer to narrative and visual items essential for an understanding of fictional texts. To make access to these literary abilities easier, picture books in a series and centered around one popular figure were established with increasing success, for example, *Madeline* (from 1939 on) by Ludwig Bemelmans, *Babar* (from 1931 on) by Jean de Brunhoff, and *Curious George* (from 1941 on) by H. A. Rey. Wordless picture books like *Clown* (1995) by Quentin Blake and *Up and Up* (1979) by Shirley Hughes, with their high degree of complexity, require an audience already accustomed to sophisticated stories. To develop a sense of the specificities of literature, even metaliterary elements are often included in picture books, that is, metaphors, intertextual allusions, and even irony. Intertextuality in picture books mainly refers to well-known nursery rhymes or fairy tales in order to help the child to grasp the book's meaning. Effective examples of this procedure are the picture books *The Jolly Postman* (1986) by Janet and Allan Ahlberg and *Snow White in New York* (1986) by Fiona French. The ironic relationship between pictures and text—the pictures reveal something that is not mentioned in the text and vice versa—is shown in the ironic picture books *Rosie's Walk* (1968) by Pat Hutchins, *Nothing Ever Happened on My Block* (1966) by Ellen Raskin, and *Come Away From the Water, Shirley* (1977) by John Burningham. These delight even small children, thus presenting a first step toward an understanding of the concept of irony. Special types of picture books are the ABC book, which teaches children the letters of the alphabet—from the humorous *A Apple Pie* (1886) by Kate Greenaway to the sophisticated *Anno's Alphabet* (1974) by Mitsumaso Anno; counting books, which teach numbers and enable first encounters with arithmetic; and picture dictionaries, which can enlarge the child's vocabulary.

Poets such as Walter de la Mare, A. A. Milne, and Robert Louis Stevenson wrote children's poetry that both continue the tradition of the orally transmitted nursery rhymes, prayers, and folk songs, and also create new lyrical styles appropriate for even very young children. This tendency to produce simple but expressive poems for small children is evident in almost every European country, as shown by poets Halfdan Rasmussen (Denmark), Bertolt Brecht and James Krüss (Germany), Gianni Rodari (Italy), Julian Tuwim (Poland), Kornej Chukovsky and Samuil Marshak (Russia), and Lennart Hellsing (Sweden), and also applies to the poems written by Cecilia Meireles (Brazil), Gabriela Mistral (Chile), Kitahara Hakushi (Japan), and Manuel Felipe Rugeles (Venezuela).

The most complicated literary genre preschool children will encounter is children's novels written for children from the age of four onward. These novels are characterized by three features that should help the listening child grasp the story's sense: they contain illustrations; they keep to the oral tradition in terms of narrative structure; they are arranged in short chapters, each telling a captivating event that finds its closure at the end of the respective chapter. These features are obvious in many renowned children's books that now are regarded as children's classics, for instance, Michael Bond's *A Bear Called Paddington* (1958), Thorbjørn Egner's *Folk og røvere i Kardemomme by* (When the Robbers Came to Cardamom Town, 1955), Josef Lada's *Kokour Mikeš* (Purrkin, the Talking Cat, 1934), Astrid Lindgren's *Alla vi barn i Bullerbyn* (The Children of Noisy Village, 1947), and Otfried Preußler's *Die kleine Hexe* (The Little Witch, 1957). Other famous books for smaller children are distinguished by a perfectly matched combination of prose text and poems, like Rudyard Kipling's *Just-So Stories* (1902) or A. A. Milne's *Winnie-the-Pooh* (1926), thus connecting the child's delight in verses with an exciting story.

Past and Present Trends

During the Enlightenment, first attempts to amuse younger children were made by editions of nursery rhymes. Based on John Locke's claim for the child's entertainment by means of children's literature, the publisher John Newbery edited the *Mother Goose's Melody* (1760), probably compiled by Oliver Goldsmith. The discovery of small children as a serious audience goes back to Romanticism, especially to Johann Gottfried Herder's concept of early childhood as a lifespan that reflects earlier stages of human development. This idea caused an awareness for folk poetry that was established on pedagogical claims. Accordingly, the German poets Achim von Arnim and Clemens Brentano, who edited the three-volume *Des Knaben Wunderhorn* (The Youth's Magic Horn, 1805–1808) containing an appendix with children's songs, maintained that the orally transmitted songs and rhymes for children represent an adequate literary form, especially for small children. Jacob and Wilhelm Grimm's *Kinder- und Hausmärchen* (Children's and Household Tales, 1812–1815) also fitted into this tradition, stressing the young child's strong interest in orally transmitted folk tales. The success of these tales among children and adults encouraged the publication of such editions in other European countries, for example, Peter Christen Asbjørnsen and Jørgen Moe's *Norske Folkeeventyr* (Norwegian Folktales, 1835–1848) and Joseph Jacobs's *English Fairy Tales* (1890). Another important children's book especially intended for small children was Heinrich Hoffmann's *Der Struwwelpeter* (*Slovenly Peter*, 1845).

The interest in the earliest years of the child's development increased during the first half of the 19th century. The educationalists Friedrich Froebel and Johann Heinrich Pestalozzi claimed that books play a crucial role in early learning by providing accessible images of the world. In order to spread his newly developed educational theory, Froebel edited the volume *Mutter- und Koselieder* (Mother's Songs, Games, and Stories, 1844), which demonstrates the connection between play and language acquisition and the affection between mother and baby, which was also stressed by Christina Rossetti's *Sing-Song* (1872). At the end of the 19th century new types of picture books for small children were established. Because of improvements in woodblock printing that made colored illustrations on a large scale relatively cheap, "toy books," banking on the popularity of illustrators like Walter Crane, were produced in collectible series. At the same time, the first baby books and movable books appeared. At the turn of the century the program of reform pedagogy and the movement of art education that arose in England, Germany, and the Nordic countries caused an increasing interest in the young child's literary development, above all giving rise to heightened artistic endeavors in picture books. This tendency, noticeable in the picture books of Elsa Beskow, Kate Greenaway, Ernst Kreidolf, and many others, was continued until the 1930s by the Bauhaus movement in Germany, and also by artists in Denmark, Italy, and Russia, who created high-quality picture books for young children. Since 1945 the publication of preschool books has increased dramatically. An astonishing number of types and genres was developed for infants and kindergarten children, emphasizing the importance of the preschool years of learning by stimulating the child's knowledge of words, images, and concepts. These tendencies coincide with the growing interest in emergent literacy since the 1980s. Studies in linguistics, cognitive psychology, educational theory, and children's literature demonstrated that children's literature is fundamental to language acquisition, visual literacy, and literary literacy. The research into children's literary competence has emphasized the importance of listening to stories and rhymes. The analysis of joint picture book reading of mother and small child has shown that it produces verbal interaction and also builds a connection between early book usage and later skills in reading. The importance of emergent literacy has been stressed by the Bookstart Project, initiated in 1993 at the University of Birmingham and designed to investigate book sharing among families with infants. Many similar baby literacy projects have been set up throughout the United Kingdom, the United States, Germany, and Japan.

[*See also* ABC Books or Alphabet Books; Book Design; Counting Books; Movable Books and Pop-Up Books; Picture Books; Toy Books; *and biographies of figures mentioned in this article.*]

BIBLIOGRAPHY

Appleyard, Joseph Albert. *Becoming a Reader*. Cambridge, U.K.: Cambridge University Press, 1991.

Apseloff, Marilyn. "Books for Babies: Learning Toys or Pre-literature?" *Children's Literature Association Quarterly* 12 (1987): 63–66.

Butler, Dorothy. *Babies Need Books*. Sevenoaks, U.K.: Hodder and Stoughton, 1980.

Butler, Dorothy. *Cushla and Her Books*. Sevenoaks, U.K.: Hodder and Stoughton, 1979.

Ewers, Hans-Heino. "Children's Literature and the Traditional Art of Storytelling." *Poetics Today* 13 (1992): 169–178.

Kümmerling-Meibauer, Bettina. "Metalinguistic Awareness and the Child's Developing Sense of Irony: The Relationship between Text and Pictures in Ironic Picture Books." *The Lion and the Unicorn* 23 (1999): 157–183.

Kümmerling-Meibauer, Bettina, and Jörg Meibauer. "First Pictures, Early Concepts: Early Concept Books." *The Lion and the Unicorn* 29 (2005): 324–347.

Nodelman, Perry. *Words about Pictures: The Narrative Art of Children's Picture Books*. Athens: University of Georgia Press, 1988.

Tucker, Nicholas. *The Child and the Book: A Psychological and Literary Exploration*. Cambridge, U.K.: Cambridge University Press, 1981.

Vandergrift, Kay, ed. *Ways of Knowing: Literature and the Intellectual Life of Children*. Lanham, Md.: Scarecrow, 1996.

White, Dorothy Neal. *Books before Five*. Wellington: New Zealand Council for Educational Research, 1954.

Bettina Kümmerling-Meibauer

Pressler, Mirjam (1940–), German author and translator who studied arts at the academy of visual arts in Frankfurt am Main and languages in Munich. After working for one year in a kibbutz in Israel, she returned to Germany and began to write texts for children and teenagers. In her books she often deals with childhood and adolescence in difficult social circumstances, for example in *Nun red doch endlich* (Talk Now Finally, 1981), *Kratzer im Lack* (Scratch in Paint, 1981), and *Stolperschritte* (Stumble Steps, 1981). These books include autobiographical elements of Pressler's childhood, which she spent with foster parents, in a children's home, and in a residential school. Loneliness is a further topic in her books, for instance in *Bitterschokolade* (Bitter Chocolate, 1980), her first work, which was honored with the Oldenburger Children's and Juvenile Book Prize. In *Malka Mai* (2001; English trans., *Malka*, 2003), *Die Zeit der schlafenden Hunde* (The Time of the Sleeping Dogs, 2003), and other titles she treats the historical subject of anti-Semitism and persecution of the Jews under the Nazis. Many of her works have been translated into different languages. Pressler herself translated more than two hundred Dutch, Flemish, Hebrew, English, and Afrikaans books addressed to children, teenagers, and adults into German, including her major work *Anne Frank Tagebuch* (Anne Frank Diary, 1998). In *Ich sehne mich so: Die Lebensgeschichte der Anne Frank* (I Yearn So Much: The Story of Anne Frank's Life, 1992), Pressler presents a biography of Anne Frank. For her children's book *Wenn das Glück kommt, muss man ihm einen*

Stuhl hinstellen (If Fortune Comes You Have to Set a Chair for It, 1994) Pressler received the German Youth Literature Prize, and for her complete works as a translator she received the Special Prize of the German Youth Literature Prize.

[*See also* Germany; Holocaust Literature for Children; Translation; *and* Young Adult Literature.]

EVA GRESSNICH

Preussler, Otfried (1923–), is one of the best-known German authors of children's books of our times. Generations of German children have grown up with his books, and he is also famous beyond German borders: about 40 million copies have been printed of his total work worldwide, and his books have been translated into fifty-two languages. At least two of them, *Die kleine Hexe* (1957; English trans., *The Little Witch*, 1961) and *Krabat* (1971; English trans., *The Satanic Mill*, 1972), now belong to the classics of the international children's literature.

Preussler grew up in Reichenberg (now Liberec) in Czechia. He describes himself as a storyteller developing his skill through his father, who always collected fairy tales while hiking through the Ore Mountains. The son re-created the art of storytelling as a literary form suitable for children. In Preussler's view, adult problems, love stories, and politics are not subjects worth telling to children. In the 1970s, when there was demand that juvenile literature be emancipatory and critical, his books were called "heile Welt" ("ideal world") and rejected by critics.

Preussler's figures and literary topics come from the legends, myths, and fairy tales of his home area. His first two books resulted from a family context in the form of bedtime stories. His intention was to demythologize certain ominous figures: *Der kleine Wassermann* (1956; English trans., *The Little Water-sprite*, 1961), *The Little Witch*, and later *Das kleine Gespenst* (1966; English trans., *The Little Ghost*, 1967). The little witch, a witch disciple 127 years young, violates a ban issued by the Supreme Witch. As a punishment she has to act as a "real" witch for one year. Because she misunderstands the meaning of "real" witch, she helps many people in poverty, plays tricks on evil people, and saves animals. At the end of the year, she learns that a "real" witch is only permitted to do evil things and she is expelled. She avenges herself by burning the magic brooms and spell books of the other witches. She now is the only witch on earth who knows how to practice magic.

From the German folk tradition came the stories of the *Räuber Hotzenplotz* (3 vols., 1962, 1969, 1973; English trans., *The Robber Hotzenplotz*, 1965, and *The Further Adventures of Robber Hotzenplotz*, 1971) and stories about the Gothamites (*Bei uns in Schilda*, 1958; English trans., *The Wise Men of Schilda*, 1963), and from the Slavic culture came the stories *Die Abenteuer des starken Wanja* (1968; English trans., *The Adventures of Strong Vanya*, 1970). The fantastic novel *The Satanic Mill* is based on a Sorbic legend from the 17th century and deals with the poor orphan Krabat, who enters a bond with the Devil, a bond that finally is dissolved only by the love of a girl. More recently, Preussler has acted as a publisher of legends by following in his father's footsteps (*Zwölfe hat's geschlagen* [At Midnight on the Dot], 1988; *Mein Rübezahlbuch* [My Book of Rübezahl, Master of the Riesengebirge], 1995).

[*See also* Fairy Tales and Folk Tales; Germany; *and* Myths.]

ANDREA WEINMANN

Prévert, Jacques (1900–1977), French poet, dramatist, and scenarist. Prévert has been called the most popular French poet of the 20th century. He appealed effortlessly to a young audience because he never ceased to see the world through the intransigent, wonder-filled eyes of a child. Prévert satirizes the social conventions of which the child is so often a victim, condemns materialism and colonialism, and rebels against anything that obstructs happiness, love, and freedom. He wrote provocatively about controversial topics that were generally avoided in children's literature. His fantasy, poetic images, colloquial language, playfulness, and verbal games appeal spontaneously to children. Prévert's first collection of poems, *Paroles* (1945; English trans., *Selections from Paroles*, 1958), was immensely successful, with a vast popular audience that included young people. His famous poem "Pour peindre le portrait d'un oiseau" (1943; English trans., "To Paint the Portrait of a Bird," 1958), dedicated to the artist Elsa Henriquez, was published with Henriquez's illustrations in a bilingual children's edition in the United States in 1971. Henriquez illustrated Prévert's children's classic, *Contes pour enfants pas sages* (Tales for Naughty Children, 1947). The subversive title is explained in the first tale, "L'autruche" (The Ostrich), a provocative retelling of Perrault's "Le Petit Poucet" (Tom Thumb), in which the abandoned hero is encouraged by the ostrich who has devoured his stones to forget his insensitive parents and run away. Animals, often exotic, figure prominently in Prévert's work, and their goodness and wisdom contrast with the cruelty and stupidity of humans. In "L'opéra des girafes"

(The Opera of the Giraffes), mute giraffes sing a tragic song about their slaughter, and in "Scène de la vie des antilopes" (Scene from the Life of Antelopes) readers witness the sad meal of antelopes whose sister has provided the joyous feast of the white men. *Le petit lion* (The Little Lion, 1947), with photographs by Ylla, and *Bim, le petit âne* (1952; English trans., *Bim, The Little Donkey*, 1973), with photographs by Albert Lamorisse, are both stories about the escape of an imprisoned animal.

Prévert worked in very close collaboration with his illustrators, who were generally friends. Appearing in 1952 were *Lettre des îles Baladar* (Letter from the Baladar Islands) with drawings by André François, and also the play *Guignol* with illustrations by Henriquez. When Jacqueline Duhême wanted to do a children's book, Prévert offered to write the text and the result was *L'opéra de la lune* (The Opera of the Moon, 1953), with music by Christiane Verger. In a dream atmosphere, it relates the story of an orphan who is only happy on the moon. After Prévert's death, Duhême illustrated numerous of his poems for children's editions. *Page d'écriture* (1980; English trans., "Page from a Notebook," 1988), about the magical disruption of a teacher's math lesson by a lyrebird, was followed by *En sortant de l'école* (Getting out of School, 1981), *Le gardien du phare aime trop les oiseaux* (The Lighthouse Keeper Is Too Fond of Birds, 1984), *Chanson des escargots qui vont à l'enterrement* (1988; English trans., Two Snails They Would Aburying Go, 1989), *Le cancre* (The Dunce, 1989), *Chanson pour les enfants l'hiver* (Winter Song for Children, 1992), *Au hasard des oiseaux* (Birds, at Random, 1992), and *Le chat et l'oiseau* (The Cat and the Bird, 2000). In 1995, Duhême also illustrated an unpublished text, *Prosper aux enfers* (Prosper in Hell), which was probably intended for theater or cinema. Prévert was an extraordinary screenplay writer, and he collaborated with the brilliant animator Paul Grimault to produce two film versions of Hans Christian Andersen's "The Shepherders and the Chimney Sweeps" with the titles *La bergére et le ramoneur* (1950; English trans., *The Curious Adventures of Mr. Wonderbird*, 1952) and *Le roi et l'oiseau* (The King and the Bird, 1979), which won international prizes.

[*See also* Fantasy; France; Poetry; *and biographies of figures mentioned in this article.*]

BIBLIOGRAPHY

Baker, William E. *Jacques Prévert*. New York: Twayne, 1967.

Beckett, Sandra L. "'L'Eternel enfant du siècle' écrit pour les enfants: *Contes pour enfants pas sages* de Jacques Prévert." In *Trois fous du langage: Vian-Queneau-Prévert*, edited by Marc Lapprand, 161–170. Nancy, France: Presses Universitaires de Nancy, 1993.

SANDRA L. BECKETT

Price, Susan (1955–), multi-award-winning British author of fantasy, contemporary realism, historical fiction, folk tales, framed collections, and ghost stories. Born into a working-class family in the West Midlands, Price made an astonishing debut as an author with the publication of *The Devil's Piper* in 1973, a fantasy novel written when she was sixteen. Her natural storytelling ability, which cleverly uses tension, curiosity, or humor to compel readers to turn the page, is evident in her reshaping of existing stories, such as those of *The Carpenter and Other Stories* (1981), and also in her ingeniously framed stories like *The Ghost Drum*, winner of the Carnegie Medal. Narrated by a "learned cat" tethered by a chain to a tree, the chains of each story are wound and unwound by the cat's movements.

The industrialized areas in which Price was raised and continues to live often supply her narrative settings: *Twopence a Tub* (1975) is a historical novel set in the industrial center of England, as is *Sticks and Stones* (1976). *From Where I Stand* (1984), a realist novel for young adults that deals with the expression and experience of institutionalized racism in a British school, also draws upon Price's working-class background. Setting generally has an expressive function in her writing, where it is used to reinforce a sense of the past. This is not the past of British high culture, however, but the past of everyday life, with its own cultural traditions and history of oppression. The time travel fantasy *The Sterkarm Handshake* (1999), awarded the Guardian Children's Fiction Prize, provides a good example of Price's persistent interrogation of historical and contemporary cultural values. Despite differences in genre and style, Price's writing constantly discloses a strong desire to encourage young readers to question the social and educational structures and practices that may disempower them.

[*See also* Fantasy; Historical Fiction; United Kingdom; *and* Young Adult Literature.]

JOHN STEPHENS

Price, Willard (1887–1983), Canadian-born editor and writer who spent most of his life in the United States. Price accompanied a number of Geographical Society expeditions to various countries, and this experience prompted him to become a travel writer. Price published many adventure books for children that were popular on both sides of the Atlantic, such as *Amazon Adventure* (1951) and *Gorilla Adventure* (1969). Although some of the books' action was farfetched, the background material was authentic. The main theme—seasoned explorers, accompanied by youths, hunting for specimens for zoos and museums—now seems rather dated.

[*See also* Adventure Books *and* Geography and Travel Books.]

GEOFF FENWICK

Priceman, Marjorie (1958–), American author and illustrator known for her colorful, whimsical, free-flowing watercolor and gouache paintings. A graduate of the Rhode Island School of Design, where she studied with David Macaulay, Priceman worked at fashion sketching and fabric design before entering the field of children's books. Her first book, *Friend or Frog* (1989), contained the memorable lines, "Kate's best friend was green and spotted, which is unusual in a friend but attractive in a frog." Her imaginative illustrations for Lloyd Moss's *Zin! Zin! A Violin!* (1995) received many awards, including a coveted Caldecott Honor. She has illustrated and retold *Froggie Went a Courting* (2000) and created a pop-up version of *Little Red Riding Hood* (2001). She has also illustrated several collections of poetry compiled by Jack Prelutsky. *Hot Air: The Mostly True Story of the First Hot-Air Balloon Ride* (2005), which tells the story of the 1783 Montgolfier balloon launch, was praised for its comic details and dynamic design.

LINNEA HENDRICKSON

Primers. Primers were originally prayer books used by the laity. Because children learned to read from these devotional manuals, by the late Middle Ages the term came to mean any book used to teach reading. Though the *Oxford English Dictionary* gives 1799 as the date for the first use of "readers" (to indicate "books containing the passages for instruction or exercise in reading"), the link between teaching children to read and teaching them to become good Christians remained strong until well into the late 19th century. Only then did the religious term "primers" gradually give way to the more secular term "readers."

The creation of a program of study explicitly designed to teach children reading and the Protestant religion is credited to Benjamin Harris, an Anabaptist London printer who escaped religious persecution by fleeing to Boston in 1686. His American invention, *The New-England Primer* (c. 1690), was adapted from an earlier work, *The Protestant Tutor*, "instructing children to spel and read English, and grounding them in the true Protestant religion, and discovering the errors and deceits of the Papists" (1679). The rhyming alphabet ("In Adam's Fall / We sinned All") decorated with little woodcuts was a revolutionary pedagogical idea at the time, appearing just a few years after the Czech theologian and teacher Johann Amos Comenius (1592–1670) published his *Orbis Sensualium Pictus* in 1658, an illustrated encyclopedia designed to entice children into learning to read Latin. Harris's *New-England Primer* begins with a hymn by Isaac Watts, then moves sequentially from the letters of the alphabet (uppercase and lowercase), through lists of "easy syllables" (ba, be, bi, bo, bu), through syllabaries (words of one to six syllables), then to the rhyming picture alphabet and catechisms, and in early-18th-century editions, the famous bedtime prayer, "Now I lay me down to sleep." No copy of the *New-England Primer* survives earlier than 1727, but in a little more than another hundred years, 360 editions had appeared.

The late 18th and early 19th centuries ushered in an important period in the development of reading instruction, partly predicated on the influence of the new child-centered educational philosophies, especially John Locke's *Some Thoughts Concerning Education* (1693) and Jean-Jacques Rousseau's *Emile, or On Education* (1762). Locke's recommendation that children be given "some easy pleasant book," and Rousseau's belief that children should be raised in harmony with the natural (that is, the real as opposed to the spiritual) world produced a quantum leap in approaches to reading instruction. Suddenly children were believed to need encouragement and pretty stories about their everyday lives—rather than threats designed to frighten them into obedience for fear of losing their immortal souls. And for a time in the 18th and early 19th centuries, reading instruction lost its authoritarian, masculine tone and became distinctly maternal and affectionate.

Although it is likely that maternal pedagogies were beginning to take hold during the early part of the 18th century, the evidence is sketchy. By chance, a set of little handmade books, mobiles, and instructional books created by Jane Johnson (1707–1759), the wife of a British clergyman, survives—in the Lilly Library in Indiana. Their existence suggests that a more widespread culture of domestic teaching materials in the period may have existed. Only after the invention of a distinctive trade in children's book publishing in the middle of the 18th century did the first secular little

Primers. Illustration from the Guidebook by William Gray for the basic primer *Fun with Dick and Jane: Family Fun* (Chicago: Scott, Foresman and Company, 1940), p. 8. REPRODUCED COURTESY OF THE COTSEN CHILDREN'S LIBRARY, PRINCETON UNIVERSITY LIBRARY

books designed specifically to teach young children to read begin to appear.

Anna Laetitia Barbauld (1743–1825) usually receives credit for inventing the prototype for the modern reader. Her *Lessons for Children* (1778–1779) were original in content and design, providing for the first time "*good paper, a clear and large type*, and *large spaces*"—all elements that 21st-century reading teachers take as normal. Other inventive, intelligent 18th-century women were commissioned by children's publishers to write books that could be used by mothers or governesses to teach young children to read. Lady Ellenor Fenn (1743–1813), who published under the name of Mrs. Lovechild, wrote many instructional books, including *Juvenile Correspondence; or, Letters Suited to Children, from Four to Above Ten Years of Age* (1783). Dorothy Kilner (1755–1836) produced *Little Stories for Little Folks, in Easy Lessons of One, Two, and Three Syllables* (1785). And most famous was Maria Edgeworth (1767–1849), whose *Early Lessons* (1801) was a huge success and helped secure her reputation as an educationalist.

The feminine, domestic, affectionate model of reading instruction was, however, relatively short-lived—primarily because it was expensive, elite, and labor-intensive. By the late 19th century, once the Education Act of 1870 came into effect in England, there was an urgent need to figure out how to educate masses of children cheaply and effectively. The factory model systems devised earlier in the century first by the Scottish educator Andrew Bell, then implemented in London by Joseph Lancaster, depended primarily on rote learning but enabled a single teacher to instruct large numbers of children simultaneously. The rise of mass education resulted in the need for mass-produced educational books with which to teach reading.

In the United States, with the religious primer giving way to the secular reader, a search for something that would reflect the scientific and progressive feel of the age got under way. The series of readers produced by William Holmes McGuffey filled the bill and came to dominate the American market in the middle of the 19th century. McGuffey's *Eclectic First and Second Readers*, first published in 1836, boasted that they incorporated the "most approved ideas regarding the teaching of reading." That meant a shift from the methods used by early primers (moving sequentially from letters to syllables to words), to a "new" scientific method that advocated the idea that competent readers took in complete words grasped at a glance, not letter by letter. This development, in turn, gave rise to the fashion for the look-say method in which children were introduced to a small range of specially chosen (controlled) words that could be recognized and spoken at a glance. The specialist in reading development William S. Gray joined the educational publishing house Scott, Foresman, and created the Elson-Gray readers (in 1930), the precursor of the series that dominated American education for much of the middle of the 20th century, *Fun with Dick and Jane*—introduced in 1940.

The look-say method was marked by its severely limited word lists, which resulted in stilted sentences and in conversations not likely ever to have been spoken by real people. The assault on it, in 1955, by Rudolf Flesch in *Why Johnny Can't Read—and What You Can Do About It*, produced a return to direct phonics instruction. By the mid-1980s, phonics instruction was looking dated and a new philosophy called "whole language" (promoted by Professor Kenneth S. Goodman) advocated a literature-based approach, focused on the idea that children could be taught to read from the beginning using real books written by real authors, not by reading specialists. The backlash to this movement involved a return to phonics and a call for "leveled" reading, making sure that children proceed in a lockstep and controlled fashion.

[*See also* ABC Books or Alphabet Books; Easy Readers; Literacy; Reading Schemes; *and biographies of figures mentioned in this article.*]

BIBLIOGRAPHY

Avery, Gillian. *Behold the Child: Early Modern Children and their Books 1621–1922*. Baltimore: Johns Hopkins University Press, 1994.

Hilton, Mary, Moral Styles, and Victor Watson, ed. *Opening the Nursery Door: Reading, Writing, and Childhood, 1600–1900*. New York: Routledge, 1997.

Houston, R. A. *Literacy in Early Modern Europe*. 2d ed. Harlow, U.K.: Longman, 2002.

Whalley, Irene. *Cobwebs to Catch Flies: Illustrated Books for the Nursery and Schoolroom, 1700–1900*. Berkeley: University of California Press, 1974.

LISSA PAUL

Prince and the Pauper, The. *See* Clemens, Samuel Langhorne.

Princess Books, The. *See* MacDonald, George.

Pringle, Laurence (1935–), American writer and photographer. Pringle has drawn on his background in wildlife biology to create many compelling and distinguished information books on nature themes. He was born in Rochester, New York, but grew up in rural Mendon nearby. There he attended a one-room schoolhouse and explored the surrounding countryside. When he was twelve, he got his first camera and began to study and photograph birds, which led to his first publication at age seventeen, an article on crow behavior in *Open Road* magazine. He earned a degree in wildlife conservation at Cornell University in 1958 and an MA from the University of Massachusetts in 1960, and was pursuing a PhD in wildlife biology at Syracuse when he realized that the nonfiction articles and photographs he was continuing to publish were what he really wanted to do as a career. After a brief stint in journalism school, he took a position as an editor for the American Museum of Natural History's children's magazine, *Nature & Science*. While there, he was encouraged to try writing books for children, and his first, *Dinosaurs and Their World*, was published in 1968. Although he has written several well-received fiction picture books, he is best known for his nonfiction photo essays on nature and animals—many of which are considered the best children's books on their topics. He won the Orbis Pictus Award for Outstanding Nonfiction for Children in 1996 and 1998, for his titles *Dolphin Man: Exploring the World of Dolphins* (1995) and *An Extraordinary Life: The Story of a Monarch Butterfly* (1997), respectively. His body of work—more than books—has earned him many awards throughout his career: a Special Conservation Award for the National Wildlife Federation in 1978, the Eva L. Gordon Award from the American Nature Society in 1983, and the Nonfiction Award from the *Washington Post*/Children's Book Council in 1999.

REBECCA HOGUE WOJAHN

Propaganda. Much of children's literature has a political subtext. However, when a children's book is created with the primary intent of promoting a specific political agenda or governmental policy, the result is not so much a literary work with a political subtext but rather a propagandistic work that employs some of the conventions associated with children's literature. Governmental officials and leaders of various political parties and movements have long attempted to use children's reading material as a tool win the support of the younger generation and thus build their political base. However, since these books usually lack literary merit, they tend to fade into obscurity soon after their sponsoring organizations lose power.

In the history of state-sponsored propaganda, Nazi Germany stands out as the government that had the best-organized and most extensive propaganda machine. Even before Adolph Hitler came to power in 1933, his National Socialist German Workers' Party (more commonly known as the Nazi Party) began producing propagandistic books intended for children. Officials with the Nazi Party sponsored the publication of history textbooks in which Germany's role in European history was distorted in order to reflect the positions of the Nazi Party. Nazi officials also sponsored children's books, including *Quex, the Hitler Youth* (1932), which encouraged children to participate in Nazi youth organizations, and *The Poisonous Mushroom* (1938), which promoted anti-Semitism.

Germany was not the only country to sponsor propaganda directed at children during the World War II era. The United States, for instance, launched its own propaganda campaign that focused primarily on the production and distribution of films that supported the war effort. Some of these films were aimed at young people, including many animated films produced by the Disney Studio. The Office of War Information as well as the Office of Inter-American Affairs commissioned Disney to produce such animated films as *Der Fuehrer's Face* (1943), which made fun of Hitler, and *Saludos Amigos* (1942), which promoted the State Department's policy toward South America. Some of these films also spun off related children's books, such as H. Marion Palmer's *Donald Duck Sees South America* (1945).

It is no coincidence that there was a proliferation of propaganda directed at young people during World War II. Government agencies often initiate propaganda campaigns during times of war or when they are facing some other national crisis. These campaigns tend to subside when the war or crisis comes to an end.

BIBLIOGRAPHY

Shull, Michael S., and David E. Wilt. *Doing Their Bit: Wartime American Animated Short Films, 1939–1945*. Jefferson, N.C.: McFarland, 1987.

MARK I. WEST

Provensen, Alice (1918–), and **Martin Provensen** (1916–1987), American illustrators and writers. Both were born in Chicago and followed similar educational paths at the Art Institute of Chicago and the University of California, Los Angeles; they met in 1943 and married the following year. The Provensens then moved to New York City, began working as illustrators, and traveled in Europe gathering material that could inspire later illustrations. They settled on a farm in Staatsburg, New York. Collaborative illustrators and author-illustrators, their work is characterized by its variety, humor, thorough research, and detailed illustrations, plus a warmth of tone that avoids sentimentality. The first book on which they collaborated as illustrators was *The Fireside Book of Folksongs* (1947) edited by Margaret Bradford Boni. This was followed by illustrations for many classics, including a 1951 edition of Robert Louis Stevenson's *A Child's Garden of Verses*, Jan Werner Watson's 1956 adaptation of *The Iliad and The Odyssey*, a 1964 edition of Alfred Tennyson's *The*

Charge of the Light Brigade, and *The Provensen Book of Fairy Tales* (1971). Their illustrations for Nancy Willard's Newbery Medal–winning *A Visit to William Blake's Inn: Poems for Innocent and Experienced Travelers* (1981) earned the book a Caldecott Honor. The Provensens also produced author-illustrated work, beginning with *The Animal Fair* (1952) and followed by works such as *Karen's Curiosity* (1963), *My Little Hen* (1973), and a series of books based on their farm, including *The Year at Maple Hill Farm* (1978). Their Caldecott Medal–winning *The Glorious Flight: Across the Channel with Louis Blériot, July 25, 1909* (1983) has been praised for its accurate information, humor, and exceptionally strong sense of design. After Martin's death in 1987, Alice continued to author-illustrate books including *The Master Swordsman and the Magic Doorway: Two Legends from Ancient China* (2001).

[*See also* Illustrations *and biographies of figures mentioned in this article.*]

ADRIENNE E. GAVIN

Provoost, Anne (1964–), Belgian author of young adult fiction. Her debut, *Mijn Tante is een Grindewal* (1990; English trans., *My Aunt is a Pilot Whale*, 1994), combines a theme of sexual abuse with a story about saving whales. Provoost likes to explore the unpredictability of adolescents. Every good novel, she argues, has to contain a moment of alienation and should not merely satisfy a reader's longing for identification. That definitely applies to *Vallen* (1994; English trans., *Falling*, 1997), in which a teenager feels attracted to neo-Nazism when he explores his grandfather's past. This novel was adapted into an English film by Hans Herbots. More recently, Provoost has rewritten two famous tales: *De Roos en het Zwijn* (The Rose and the Swine, 1997) is based on Straparola's version of *Beauty and the Beast*, and *The Arkvaarders* (2001; English trans., *In the Shadow of the Ark*, 2004) retells the biblical story of Noah from the perspective of the people who built the ark, and were predestined to drown.

[*See also* Belgium *and* Young Adult Literature.]

VANESSA JOOSEN

Prøysen, Alf (1914–1970), Norwegian writer, internationally renowned for his collections of humorous magic tales about Little Old Mrs. Pepperpot (1957–1966). Mrs. Pepperpot ("Teskjekjerringa" in Norwegian; literally, "Teaspoon Lady"), an old farmer's wife, shrinks to the size of a teaspoon at whim and is then able to understand the language of animals. In this shape she experiences all sorts of funny adventures, acting as a magical helper to both people and animals. Unlike Lewis Carroll's Alice, she is empowered by her transformation. Prøysen also wrote fairy tales involving traditional folklore characters, like trolls and dwarfs, as well as animal tales. Continuing the tradition of Hans Christian Andersen, Prøysen uses everyday language and tones, and combines everyday settings with folk tale elements—as when he lets his comic figure Mrs. Pepperpot meet the famous Norwegian folk tale character, Valemon the White Bear (from the Norwegian version of "Beauty and the Beast").

[*See also* Fantasy; Magic; Nordic Countries; *and biographies of figures mentioned in this article.*]

BIBLIOGRAPHY

Hagen, Helge, and Dag Solberg. *Med en fiol bak øret: en bok om Alf Prøysen*. Oslo, Norway: Tiden, 1984.

Imerslund, Knud, ed. *Graset er grønt for aeille: ei bok om Alf Prøysen*. Bergen, Norway: Fagbokforlag, 2002.

MARIA NIKOLAJEVA

Publishers and Publishing. While following the historical arc of children's book publishing, it is important to keep the following in mind: The production of children's books is an enterprise conducted by adults for children in order to make a profit. This means that the books produced for children are ones that resonate with adults' imaginations of who and what children are as well as with the adults' sense of responsibility toward children. This also means a book must be of sufficient interest to a sustainable market; there must be enough buyers with enough money to allow the publisher to continue in business. Over time societies' imaginations of children and societies' senses of responsibility toward children shift and different books for children are produced. Changes in ownership have also created shifts in what an acceptable profit might be. Key moments and movements in children's book publishing occur at these shifts.

The Printing Press and the Protestant Reformation

There were few books until the means existed to mass-produce them. The first printing presses appeared in western Europe in the late 15th century. Curiously, the word "publisher" does not appear in the English language until the mid-18th century. Early publishers were "booksellers," and that meant that they printed the books, edited the books, bound the books, hand-colored them, and sold them in their own bookshop. In some cases they wrote the books as well. It was the 19th century before specialists emerged in each of these areas.

Religious groups were among the first to publish books explicitly for children. By the beginning of the 17th century the Protestant Reformation was in full swing in the British Isles and in its colonies in North America. Believing that a person risked spiritual damnation in the absence of living a proper spiritual life, Puritan clergy produced a number of religious tracts written for children for the purposes of teaching children proper morals and to enable them to read the Bible. These books introduced the alphabet, included a catechism, and told stories of the lives and deaths of exemplary Christian children. Notable titles are John Cotton's *Spiritual Milk for Boston Babes in Either England: Drawn Out of the Breasts of Both Testaments of Their Souls' Nourishment, but May Be of Like Use to Any Children*, which was later incorporated into *The New England Primer* and James Janeway's *A Token for Children, Being an Exact Account of the Conversion, Holy and Exemplary Lives, and Joyful Deaths of Several Young Children*. The Puritans saw children as sinners in need of salvation, and the books they provided were written to put the fear of God into their children.

Newbery and Locke

The 18th century ushered in the Enlightenment in Europe, and philosophers such as John Locke and Jean-Jacques Rousseau developed theories of childhood and advocated methods for the proper education of children. It was John Locke who argued that children ought to learn through their play and that children needed "easy, pleasant books." Locke could list only two books he thought appropriate for children, *Reynard the Fox* and *Aesop's Fables*. John Newbery, a mid-18th-century London bookseller and an admirer of Locke's educational philosophy, published books that were intended to delight children and invite them to play. He often sold his books with an accompanying toy such as a ball or a pincushion to aid in the connection between reading and play. The types of books published by Newbery show that he was publishing to a different market of children. His first book was entitled *A Pretty Little Pocket-Book, Intended for the Instruction and Amusement of Little Master Tommy and Pretty Miss Polly, with an Agreeable Letter to Read from Jack the Giant-Killer as also a Ball and a Pincushion, the Use of Which Will Infallibly Make Tommy a Good Boy and Polly a Good Girl. . . .* Child readers were being instructed, to be sure, but in a playful way, unlike the heavy-handed didacticism of the Puritan clergy. Including the ball and pincushion was Newbery's way of following Locke's advice to instruct in a playful manner. Newbery also was among the first publishers to use product placement in his books. Newbery was also a broker of patent medicines such as Dr. James' Fever Powder. This powder often made an appearance in Newbery's books, curing whatever ailments the books' characters were suffering. Newbery's books sold well enough, but it was the powder that made him a wealthy man.

Universal Literacy and the Emerging Middle Class

The growth of the business of children's books is directly related to the emergence and continued fiscal health of the middle class, for it took a middle-class income to be able to afford to purchase books and a middle-class lifestyle to provide children with the leisure time to read. By Newbery's time the reading market of middle-class children was large enough to support the business of children's book publishing. Poor, working-class children were not left out entirely of the business of children's books. Child laborers would pick rags to make the paper for books and would hand-color the woodblock illustrations with watercolor washes. Some working-class children were able to afford "chapbooks," a cheaply produced book sold by peddlers, or chapmen. Copyright laws were sparse and often ignored, so chapbook pirated editions of Newbery's and other publisher's books were widespread.

In the 19th century the business of children's books grew rapidly. The wealth generated by the British Empire and the rapidly expanding United States greatly increased the middle class. Universal literacy movements were active in both the United Kingdom and the United States. As a result more children could read and more children came from families who could afford to buy books. By the end of the century copyrights were protected by international treaty, halting, or at least slowing, the pirating of British works by American publishers and vice versa. Annually, the United Kingdom was producing around nine hundred new children's books a year, and the United States around four hundred.

Rise of a Profession

Children's book publishing became an entity of its own in the first half of the 20th century. Public libraries, many funded through gifts from Andrew Carnegie, became mainstays of any community of any size. Many of these libraries had space set aside for children's books and programming for children such as storytelling. There was now organized training of children's librarians, usually conducted at the largest city libraries. These (mostly) women were charged with purchasing children's books. To meet their need to make informed selections, reviewing journals such as *The Horn Book Magazine* began publication. Beginning with Macmillan, publishers created children's books departments in their houses, staffed with editors and marketing directors who specialized in producing and selling children's books. By the 1960s most major publishers had their own children's department with editors and marketing directors who specialized in children's books.

The launch of Sputnik by the Soviet Union in 1957 shocked much of the western world. The United States Congress, believing that American children were lagging behind Soviet children in their education, passed several important pieces of legislation, including the National Defense Education Act and the Elementary and Secondary Education Act. Children were seen as soldiers, reserves to be used later in the struggle against communism. These laws provided federal money for school libraries to purchase books. Suddenly, schools were awash with funds that could only be used for purchasing library books. Many publishing houses had difficulty meeting orders, especially orders for nonfiction.

In "The All-White World of Children's Books," a 1965 article in *The Saturday Review*, the educator and critic Nancy Larrick noted that very few children's book characters were black and argued that children of all colors needed books that showed characters who were like them. There were books being published for African American children, but these books were coming from within the African American community—W. E. B. Du Bois's *The Brownies Book*, a literary magazine for African American children begun in the 1920s, was one of many efforts by African American organizations and churches to provide quality reading material for African American children. The larger, mainstream publishers, however, virtually neglected children of color as characters and readers of children's books. Larrick's essay helped to change this. The civil rights movement was happening at this time and book-buying professionals, flush with federal money for purchasing books and with raised consciousness, demanded that publishers address this gap. What emerged from this were many pedestrian informational books and a handful of noteworthy authors and illustrators of color. "Children" now included children of all races, ethnic groups, religions, and capabilities, and the project of producing a body of quality children's books about the whole range of children moved into the consciousness of publishers, provided that the books would sell. By the mid-1980s, however, public funding for libraries had diminished. Institutions—schools and public libraries—no longer made up the majority of the children's book market, having been replaced by the bookstore.

Globalization and Reaction

Until the 1960s most children's book publishers were family owned, modest-sized businesses. Changes in governments' economic policies created an environment suited for large corporations. Many publishing houses became incorporated, and shares of their stocks were sold publicly. Publishing houses also merged into larger publishing houses. The mergers of the 1980s and 1990s left the bulk of children's book publishing in the select hands of a few large houses: HarperCollins, Penguin Putnam, Random House, Simon and Schuster, Scholastic, Houghton Mifflin. These large publishing houses are no longer family-owned businesses dedicated to books; instead, the children's book industry is owned by large, media conglomerates, such as Viacom, The News Corporation, Pearson Corporation, Bertelsmann, Reed Elsevier, von Holtzbrinck, Scholastic, and a consortium of the investment companies of Lee, Bain, and the Blackstone Group. All of these corporations, save the investment consortium, operate internationally in producing children's books.

These corporations' interests in children's books differ from the publishing companies' previous owners. Previous owners viewed their business as a tension between making a profit and publishing worthwhile books and believed that the company was doing well if it could earn a 3 to 5 percent margin of profit. These previous owners were aware, as were their ancestors in children's book publishing, the Puritans and John Newbery, that they had a responsibility to the intellectual, psychological, and social well-being of their readers. This was a fundamental difference between publishing books for children and publishing books for adults—editors of both children's books and books for adults had to ask the question "Is this a good book?" with "good" implying that the book would sell. Children's book editors had to ask a second question, "Will the book be good for children?" Corporate owners, however, are primarily responsible to their stockholders and have a fiduciary obligation to maximize profits. The interests of the corporate owners run to "branding," "licensing," and "cross-promoting" because these are the paths to greater corporate sales and profits. Well-known book characters such as Clifford the Big Red Dog, Madeline, Curious George, and Harry Potter became "brands," a kind of stand-alone meaning that could fit into a variety of commodities besides books, such as toys, television shows, clothing, and games. Every publishing company with a powerful brand is trying to establish a relationship with consumers (children) that resonates deeply with the consumer's (the child's) sense of identity. In other words, these corporations are hoping that children are attracted not to books so much as to any product that carries the brand's name. In the 21st century, the corporations that control children's book publishing understand that what they truly own are ideas and that they can make lots of money by selling licenses of their ideas to other companies. For example, Pearson (parent company of Penguin Putnam publishers) has sold the license for Ludwig Bemelman's Madeline to Eden Toys, which in turn has produced an extraordinary range of toys, dolls, doll houses, games, clothing, and other merchandise based on the Madeline stories.

Perhaps the most troubling effect of licensing is that the book and each spin-off piece of merchandise and each retelling across another medium becomes a promotion for every other product based on that story. This ubiquitous cross-promoting blurs, if not erases, the line between advertisement and entertainment. What used to be a cultural and intellectual pursuit—children reading books—has now become an act of consumption.

In previous decades, sales to schools and libraries would have provided a counterbalance. But government funding for library books was and continues to be scarce. In the 1980s the bulk of children's book sales shifted from schools and libraries to bookstores. Initially, these bookstores tended to be independently owned, and many of them specialized in selling children's books. These owners were experts in their own right in children's literature. By the 1990s large Internet bookstores such as Amazon.com and BN.com, and large "big-box" chain bookstores such as Barnes and Noble, Borders, and Blackwell's dominated the bookstore market. At independent bookstores, books were sold "hand to hand," that is, the owner would point out new titles to a customer the owner likely knew. The special book could find its way to the special reader. The owner knew something about children's books. In the big boxes clerical workers have a high turnover, thus they cannot develop their knowledge of the stock or the customers. So the big boxes depend on books that can sell themselves. These books are often celebrity-authored books, books with television or film tie-ins, or popular series books. The big boxes also sell display table space; for a publisher to have its books displayed prominently, the publisher must pay the bookstore chain. The quirky and unique children's book produced by a small, independent publisher is difficult to find among the thousands of other books stocked.

Some editors, disgusted by the changes in doing business, quit their jobs at the corporate-owned houses and started their own children's book publishing companies, oftentimes bringing with them well-established authors and illustrators. Walker Books, Templar Publishing, and Barefoot Books in the United Kingdom, and Candlewick, Front Street, and Roaring Brook are among the smaller, independently owned children's book publishers. Since 2000 these companies have won an impressive number of awards for literary quality, including the Newbery Medal, Caldecott Medal, and Kate Greenaway Medal.

[*See also* Chapbooks; Libraries; Mass Market Fiction; Specialist Publishing Houses; *and biographies of figures mentioned in this article.*]

BIBLIOGRAPHY

Darton, F. J. Harvey. *Children's Books in England: Five Centuries of Social life.* 3d ed. Revised by Brian Alderson. Cambridge, U.K.: Cambridge University Press, 1982.

Reynolds, Kimberley, and Nicholas Tucker, eds. *Children's Book Publishing in Britain since 1945.* Aldershot, U.K.; Brookfield, Vt.: Scolar, 1998.

Townsend, John Rowe. *Written for Children: An Outline of English-Language Children's Literature.* Lanham, Md.: Scarecrow, 1996.

DANIEL HADE

Pudney, John (1909–1977), British poet and author. Pudney worked as a journalist, a writer-producer for the BBC, and a publishing executive while also being actively engaged as a poet and writer for adults. His first children's book, *The Saturday Adventure: A Story for Boys* (1950), features "Fred and I" and their eccentric Uncle George. It was followed by further adventures assigned to the different days of the week. Then he created *Spring Adventure* (1961), part of a series linked to the seasons. These are all exciting if improbable adventure stories, frequently involving spies or strange inventions. They feature a direct style and a substantial amount of humor, qualities that are also characteristic of a series Pudney created for a younger audience. Included in that series is *The Hartwarp Light Railway* (1962), a novel about a derelict railroad.

FERELITH HORDON

Puffin Books. The children's imprint of Penguin Books, Puffin Books was founded, together with Puffin Picture Books, in 1941, by Penguin's publisher Allen Lane. Like Penguin books, Puffins were paperbacks designed to be both attractive and affordable; Lane's idea was to encourage young readers to turn into adult readers of Penguins, and initially the children's books were designed to look like Penguins, though they were fully illustrated.

The first editor of Puffin Books was Eleanor Graham, whose vision for the children's division was uncompromisingly focused on high literary and artistic merit; Noel Carrington, the first editor of Puffin Picture Books, was equally dedicated to high artistic and reproduction values. The conditions for launching the new imprint were difficult: it was a time of paper shortages, the idea of paperback children's books was alien and not welcomed by influential groups such as librarians, and other publishers were reluctant to negotiate paperback rights. Eventually Graham, who was Puffin's editor for twenty years, prevailed, and Puffin became the leading paperback children's book publisher with a diverse and extensive list. Under successive editors including Graham's influential successor Kaye Webb—founder of the Puffin Club, which provided a wide range of activities for members—Puffin books became more eclectic, less concerned with promoting middle-class values and tastes, and added young adult books to its activities. In 1978 the company acquired the hardback imprint Viking Kestrel and commenced operations in the United States. While the U.K. and U.S. companies are separate entities, they share authors and titles and cooperate on projects, including the copublished Puffin Classics series.

[*See also* Publishers and Publishing.]

KIMBERLEY REYNOLDS

Pullein-Thompson, Christine (1925–), **Diana Pullein-Thompson** (1925–), and **Josephine Pullein-Thompson** (1924–), British authors and sisters, postwar leaders in the pony book genre. Born in Wimbledon, Surrey, the sisters were educated briefly at Wychwood School, Oxford, until parental financial crises and dislike of school prompted their removal at ages fifteen and fourteen. Daughters of Joanna Cannan, novelist—who hoped they would marry Masters of Fox Hounds—nieces of May Cannan, poet, sisters of Denis Cannan, playwright, the sisters were part of a feisty family, described in their joint childhood autobiography *Fair Girls and Grey Horses* (1996): "The Pullein-Thompsons were *brave* . . . we taught ourselves to jump into nettles without flinching." Home had a pony book atmosphere; as teenagers they opened a riding school and together wrote *It Began with Picotee* (1946). Thereafter they wrote separately; as well as adult books, Josephine wrote thirty-nine, Diana thirty-one, and Christine seventy-four pony books. (Christine also wrote a series about Jessie, a black Labrador.) The pony books resound with Cinderella/Ugly Duckling/Rags to Riches themes. Poor but determined horse-mad heroes and heroines ride into adventure, win events, and rescue horses—who are equally strong characters in the books—from disasters. Protagonists are enterprising, hands-on, and eccentric.

The books open up a rural, horsey world in which laws and rituals are enmeshed in a tenderly pretty, severely practical, and merciless Beatrix Potter–like countryside; (foxes kill; hounds have bloody muzzles). Pullein-Thompson books instruct. Explanations of riding methods and horse psychology, punctuated with incantations of vocabulary—of hogged manes, white socks and stars, and the "leu in, leu in there, forrard away" of hunting cries—include the reader in an exclusive literary pony club.

[*See also* Horse and Pony Stories.]

MARY SEBAG-MONTEFIORE

Pullman, Philip (1946–), British writer and essayist whose outstanding work has been translated into at least eighteen languages and circulated worldwide. Pullman was

Philip Pullman. PHOTOGRAPH BY ROLF MARRIOT/ASTRID LINDGREN MEMORIAL AWARD

born in Norwich, England, and educated at primary schools in different parts of the world because his father was in the Royal Air Force. After secondary education in Harlech, North Wales, Pullman studied English at Exeter College, Oxford, and later completed a postgraduate teaching qualification. After teaching in a variety of schools, where several of the plays he wrote for the children were to form the basis for later published novels, he was appointed to the English department at Westminster College, Oxford, where he lectured on adults' and children's literature. He became a full-time writer after the publication of *Northern Lights* (1995; U.S. title, *The Golden Compass*, 1996).

The versatile and consistently high quality of Philip Pullman's writing is demonstrated by the large number of awards and prizes he has won. By 2005, he had won the Whitbread Children's and Book of the Year Awards, the Carnegie Medal, the Smarties Prize, the Guardian Children's Fiction Prize, the Astrid Lindgren Memorial Award, and the Hans Christian Andersen Medal. Pullman's writing covers a wide range of genres and styles, from the witty exuberance of what he calls his "semi-graphic" novels, for example *Spring-Heeled Jack* (1989) and *Count Karlstein* (1982), through "fairy tales" such as *The Firework-Maker's Daughter* (1996), *Clockwork, or All Wound Up* (1996), *I Was a Rat* (1999), and *The Scarecrow and His Servant* (2004), to historical thrillers set in the late 19th century: *The Ruby in the Smoke* (1985), *The Shadow in the Plate* (1986; U.S. title, *The Shadow in the North*, 1988), *The Tiger in the Well* (1991), and *The Tin Princess* (1994), all featuring a strong and unconventional female protagonist, Sally Lockhart. However, Pullman's outstanding contribution to children's literature is his controversial epic trilogy (or "one book in three volumes," as he prefers to call it), entitled *His Dark Materials: Northern Lights*, *The Subtle Knife* (1997), and *The Amber Spyglass* (2000). *Lyra's Oxford* (2003) appears to be, among other things, the start of a "new episode from the universe of 'His Dark Materials'" but, as the preface puts it, "It's not easy to tell."

Throughout his work, Pullman emphasizes the importance of stories: "Stories are the most important thing in the world. Without stories, we wouldn't be human beings at all." When asked *why* he believes stories are so important, he replied, "Because they entertain and they teach; they help both enjoy life and endure it. After nourishment, shelter and companionship, stories are the thing we need most in the world." Three such stories must serve to illustrate the different phases of Pullman's work. First, *The Ruby in the Smoke* ("That was the book in which I first found the voice that I now tell stories in"), a fast-paced, exciting thriller, set against a Victorian London "of docks and warehouses, of crumbling tenements and rat-haunted alleys, of narrow streets [and] blind brick walls" reminiscent of Leon Garfield or Dickens. The sixteen-year-old protagonist, Sally Lockhart, is an orphan with an unconventional education: her father taught her military tactics and bookkeeping and bought her a pistol for her fourteenth birthday. Sally is plunged into a labyrinth of evil and villainy, at the center of which is the Ruby of Agrapur, whose heart seems "to swirl and part like smoke, to reveal . . . a fantastic landscape of gorges, peaks and terrifying abysses."

The second text, *Clockwork, or All Wound Up*, Pullman considers "the best short book I've done," and it illustrates the delight in mechanical objects and narrative games, puns, and jokes that is evident in many of his works. The story, with its atmosphere of German Romanticism and gothic horror, is centered on a tall old clock in a German town square surrounded by a landscape of dark forests. The initial idea for the story was "something that worked like clockwork, something that fitted together in that very tight, mechanical way, where everything was connected, so that if you moved one bit something else would move," but among the many meanings of the title are "metaphors for the story-making process and the story itself." It begins like a traditional story, but, in a postmodern twist, Fritz, the storyteller, finds himself "at the mercy of characters and events (in his story) over whom he has lost control." The line drawings and captions that accompany the written text are "used by Pullman to reflect upon—in a playful, ironic or serious way—characters, events and situations in the primary narrative(s)" (Jones).

The text that marks the third phase of his work, *His Dark Materials*, Pullman describes as "'Paradise Lost' for teenagers," and it is epic in length (1,200 pages) and scope. The trilogy combines mystery and romance with metaphysics and philosophy, in stories that draw upon comics such as "Superman and Batman, gangster and cowboy serials, movies and stories of adventurers" (Lenz). Over the three books, the story moves through several parallel universes, some of which resemble ours but are subtly different. This enables Pullman to explore more clearly his ideas about good and evil, in particular the story of innocence and experience, and of innocence becoming experience. The daemons, which are an integral part of the characters' world, enable Pullman to symbolize the difference between "the infinite plasticity, potentiality and mutability of childhood and the fixed nature of adulthood." But behind the books lies another story, important for understanding a work written within the dissenting tradition of Milton and Blake. What Pullman calls the myth of the Republic of Heaven is a story of creation and rebellion, of development and strife, "a story that explained how there had once been a kingdom of heaven, and what had happened to that kingdom, and why there must now be a republic of heaven, and what part we have to play in keeping it alive . . . essential in an age in which God is dead." The myth gives a "sense of meaning and joy" because it involves a "passionate love" of this world, the physical world "of nature and food and drink and sex and music and laughter," and an understanding that "it will both grow out of and add to the achievements of the human mind such as science and art. . . . Established religion with its guilt-inducing distrust of the human spirit must be resisted in favour of the republic of heaven which is found in the whole world of stories. . . . Within them we can find the most memorable, life-enhancing glimpses of human beings at their very best."

[*See also* Fantasy; Historical Fiction; Horror Stories; *and* Young Adult Literature.]

BIBLIOGRAPHY

Carter, James. *Talking Books: Children's Authors Talk about the Craft, Creativity, and Process of Writing*. London: Routledge, 1999.

Gooderham, David. "Fantasizing It as It Is: Religious Language in Philip Pullman's Trilogy, His Dark Materials." *Children's Literature* 31 (2003): 155–175.

Jones, Dudley. "Only Make-Believe? Lies, Fictions, and Metafictions in Geraldine McCaughrean's *A Pack of Lies* and Philip Pullman's *Clockwork*." *The Lion and the Unicorn* 23 (January 1999): 86–96.

Lenz, Millicent. "Philip Pullman." In *Alternative Worlds in Fantasy Fiction*, edited by Peter Hunt and Millicent Lenz, 123–169. London: Continuum, 2001.

Wood, Naomi. "(Em)Bracing Icy Mothers: Ideology, Identity, and Environment in Children's Fantasy." In *Wild Things: Children's Culture and Ecocriticism*, edited by Sidney Dobrin and Kenneth Kidd, 198–214. Detroit: Wayne University Press, 2004.

TONY WATKINS

Punch and Judy. Front cover of *Punch and Judy* (Derby, England: Thomas Richardson, c. 1840). REPRODUCED COURTESY OF THE COTSEN CHILDREN'S LIBRARY, PRINCETON UNIVERSITY LIBRARY

Punch and Judy. Punch and Judy are the stars in a traditional hand-puppet show that was once ubiquitous on the streets of major cities and seaside resorts in Great Britain. The male puppet, Punch, is instantly recognizable for his oversized, hooked red nose, hunched back, bright red cheeks, and long club. Judy is his nagging but beleaguered wife. In the Punch and Judy shows, Punch murders his wife, their infant, the Policeman, the Beadle (civic official), the hangman Jack Ketch, the Devil, or anyone else who happens to come along. With his trademark club he bashes his victims over the head and then whirls them away. The first theatrical experience many British children have is watching a Punch and Judy show as toddlers, laughing at the comic violence.

The puppet of Mr. Punch himself and some, though not all, of his traditional form arrived in England in the middle of the 17th century, derived from the Italian commedia dell'arte shows and their Pulcinella character. Pulcinella was anglicized as Punchinello and then shortened to Punch. The show is also related to the Guignol tradition in France and has analogs in the puppet theaters of Greece, Turkey, North Africa, Germany, Austria, Spain, Holland, the Czech Republic, Romania, Russia, Burma, India, Thailand, and China. Once Punch acquired a wife, who was at first named Joan, then Judy, the story evolved into its modern version. Sometimes the Punch and Judy stage also features an "interpreter," a man who stands on the audience's side of the stage and tells it what is supposedly going on, often incorrectly and to the annoyance of Mr. Punch.

Punch and Judy stages have ranged from full-size, elaborate puppet theaters to tiny boxes carried through the streets on the backs of the puppeteers. Many played on the median islands between streams of traffic, their audiences risking life and limb to dart across and witness Punch's trademark violence. Today they commonly appear at funfairs and birthday parties, since the governments of urban centers are more reluctant to have pedestrians crowding street corners or running out into traffic to watch a puppet show. In recent years, some parents have been concerned about the effects of Punch's violence on their offspring, but defenders of the Punch and Judy show claim that its violence is a way for its viewers to release frustrations harmlessly. The sexual content of Punch and Judy shows has, however, decreased, making Punch less a leering rogue and more just a grinning trickster.

Punch and Judy make appearances in the plots of some British children's fiction, including as a wizard in John Masefield's *The Box of Delights* (1935). In Diana Wynne Jones's *The Magicians of Caprona* (1980), the main characters are shrunk to puppet size and compelled to enact the violence of a Punch and Judy show. More often, however, a Punch and Judy show is background, scenery that sets a familiar locale for the reader: the seaside, or a holiday, or a certain era of British urban history.

[*See also* Toy Theaters *and* United Kingdom.]

BIBLIOGRAPHY

Leach, Robert. *The Punch and Judy Show*. Athens: University of Georgia Press, 1985.

MARISSA K. LINGEN

Pushkin, Alexander (1799–1837), Russian national poet, also considered a major children's writer because of his fairy tales, which have been widely used in juvenile reading even though they were not specifically written for a young audience. Easily recognizable in plots, Pushkin's verse fairy tales are highly original in style and details. *The Tale of Tsar Saltan* (1831), based on a popular Slavic chapbook, is reminiscent of "The Girl Without Hands," and *The Tale of the Dead Princess and the Seven Heroes* (1833) is a rather unusual version of "Snow White," while *The Tale of the Fisherman and the Fish* (1833), unlike the Grimms' version, emphasizes social injustice in letting the conceited woman alone benefit from the wish granting. In *The Tale of the Golden Cockerel* (1834) Pushkin retold the story of the Arab astrologer from the *Alhambra* by Washington Irving, making it into a biting political satire on czarist Russia. *The Tale of the Priest and Balda, His Hired Hand* (1830; published 1840), with the plot also found in the Grimms' tales, is another example of satirical usage by Pushkin of the fairy tale; the tale was censored for its disrespectful portrayal of the clergy, and was published only posthumously with many alterations—for instance, the priest was changed into a merchant. Foreign sources notwithstanding, Pushkin's fairy tales have very tangible details of Russian settings, as well as the Russian historical and social context. They also have brilliant characterization, unusual for traditional fairy tales. The language, often imitating folk songs or ballads, is distinctly colloquial and abounds in poetical figures. Many punch lines from the fairy tales have become incorporated into the canon of Russian proverbs. Lauded by the authorities as a national and truly democratic poet in 1937, along the lines of the overall patriotic campaign, Pushkin became a figurehead in Soviet children's literature. His fairy tales were thus robbed of their satirical charge and banished to the nursery.

[*See also* Fairy Tales and Folk Tales; Poetry; *and* Russia.]

BIBLIOGRAPHY

Orlov, Janina. "Playful Magic in Pushkin's Tale of Tsar Saltan." In *Children's Literature as Communication*, edited by Roger D. Sell, 39–54. Amsterdam: John Benjamin, 2002.

MARIA NIKOLAJEVA

Puss in Boots. The central character and title of a classic literary fairy tale, Puss in Boots is possibly of oral origin. It was Charles Perrault, in his *Histoires, ou contes du temps passé* (1697; English trans., *Histories, or Tales of Past Times*, 1729), who guaranteed the place of Puss in Boots in children's literature and culture. Perrault's "Le Maistre Chat" (The Master Cat) contains several fairy tale archetypes: a clever talking animal, a third son who inherits nothing, a king, an ogre, and trickery. The cat rescues his master from penury by benign guile, duping "superior" beings. The lesson is socially subversive: intelligence, courage, and flair win against status and tyranny and enrich the humble; it is a fantastic version of the many scenarios, from the commedia dell'arte to Mozart, in which the servant is worth more than the master and is, indeed, in charge—a narrative ultimately congenial to French Revolutionary ideology (1789) and its successors.

The earliest known version of "Puss in Boots" is, however, Italian and gentler. Along with original stories and retellings of folk tales, it occurs in *Le piacevoli notti* (The Delightful Nights) by Straparola, a two-volume compendium arranged within a frame story and published in Venice in 1550 and 1553. Here the magical cat is female, never dons boots, and sympathetically helps her master (Night XI, i). In the following century, Basile incorporated Neapolitan dialectal versions of—some now classic—fairy tales in his Baroque masterpiece, *Lo cunto de li cunti* (The Tale of Tales, 1634–1636),

Italianized as *Il Pentamerone* (The Pentameron). In this fantastically and grotesquely framed collection, heavy with magic and Oriental influences, where elite and popular cultures meet, cat and ungrateful nouveau riche master end in bitter conflict. A French translation of Straparola was printed in 1560, but Perrault's precise relationship to the Italian antecedents is unknown. In the 18th century "Puss in Boots" appeared in chapbooks; in the 19th the story was criticized for its immorality but was also adapted for the stage. It still makes a popular pantomime.

[*See also* Fairy Tales and Folk Tales *and biographies of figures mentioned in this article.*]

BIBLIOGRAPHY

Bottigheimer, Ruth B. *Fairy Godfather: Straparola, Venice, and the Fairy Tale Tradition.* Philadelphia: University of Pennsylvania Press, 2002.

Bottigheimer, Ruth B. "Straparola's *Piacevoli notti*: Rags-to-Riches Fairy Tales as Urban Creations." *Merveilles et Contes* 7 (December 1994).

Canepa, Nancy L. *From Court to Forest: Giambattista Basile's "Lo cunto de li cunti" and the Birth of the Literary Fairy Tale.* Detroit: Wayne State University Press, 1999.

Canepa, Nancy L. *Out of the Woods: The Origins of the Literary Fairy Tale in Italy and France.* Detroit: Wayne State University Press, 1997.

Mazzacurati, Giancarlo. *Conteurs italiens de la Renaissance*, edited by Anne Motte Gillet. Paris: Gallimard, 1993.

Petrini, Mario. *La fiaba di magia nella letteratura italiana.* Udine, Italy: Del Bianco, 1983.

Petrini, Mario. *Il gran Basile.* Rome: Bulzoni, 1989.

Seifert, Lewis. *Fairy Tales, Sexuality, and Gender in France, 1690–1715.* Cambridge, U.K.: Cambridge University Press, 1996.

Soriano, Marc. *Les Contes de Perrault.* Paris: Gallimard, 1968.

Soriano, Marc. *Le dossier Perrault.* Paris: Hachette, 1972.

Zipes, Jack. "Of Cats and Men." In *Happily Ever After: Fairy Tales, Children, and the Culture Industry*, 15–38. New York: Routledge, 1997.

Ann Lawson Lucas

Pye, Trevor (1952–), New Zealand illustrator, author-illustrator, and artist. Born in Te Awamutu, and in the early 2000s living in Tauranga, New Zealand, Pye is an artist, sculptor, and the illustrator of numerous children's books. Characterized by vibrant color, cartoon-like style, and humor, his illustrations are used regularly in texts by authors such as Andrew Crowe, Joy Cowley, and Jenny Hessell. He illustrated Vivienne Joseph's *The A.O.K. Project* (1999), which was a finalist in the 2001 UNESCO Awards for Children's Literature. His author-illustrated books include *Ben and the Alien Invasion* (1995), *The Nest* (1995), and *The Big Race: A Very Tall Tale* (1999).

Adrienne E. Gavin

Pyle, Howard (1853–1911), the most important American writer and illustrator of children's books in the late 19th century. Best known for his versions of the medieval heroic tales of Robin Hood and King Arthur, Pyle also composed pirate narratives, modern fables, and fairy tales. His style of illustration featured strong-lined, stylized figures, producing what has been described as the "Pyle look."

Pyle was born in Wilmington, Delaware, to Quaker parents who recognized that his considerable abilities would be stifled by conventional schooling and therefore sent him to art school in Philadelphia, where he developed his technical resources, but his creativity was thwarted. After a period in New York City, working especially for Harper Brothers, *Scribner's Monthly*, and *St. Nicholas*, he returned to Wilmington in 1879 and began teaching at the Drexel Institute before setting up the Brandywine School in 1898. His teaching philosophy demanded technical control, but it also emphasized creative engagement with the subject, as he noted

Howard Pyle. With his daughter Phoebe. Photograph by Frances Benjamin Johnston, 1890s. Frances Benjamin Johnston Collection, Prints and Photographs Division, Library of Congress

in a letter: "I subordinate the technical training entirely to the training of the imagination." Pyle's pupils included such prominent illustrators and painters as Maxfield Parrish, Jessie Willcox Smith, and N. C. Wyeth. His teaching and performance radically changed American illustration; Jessie Willcox Smith said he "simply blew away all that depressed atmosphere and made of art an entirely different thing."

Pyle was immensely productive; he illustrated and wrote thirteen books for children, most published simultaneously on both sides of the Atlantic. The first book for which he composed both text and illustrations—and the only one he himself regarded as potentially a classic—was *The Merry Adventures of Robin Hood* (1883). With *Otto of the Silver Hand* (1888), set in 16th-century Germany and Dürer-like in style, and the four-book Arthuriad, *Robin Hood* witnesses to Pyle's lifelong fascination with the medieval period. If his approach as an illustrator in these historical books developed out of traditional practice, medieval and medievalist, his illustration for American magazines tended toward American subjects and was generally more delicate and realistic. For Pyle, the artist should address the whole text, not simply particular incidents; text and illustration should "round the circle instead of advancing in parallel lines." In the event, this principle is amply displayed in the notably different styles he developed for illustrating works on a range of subjects, in different kinds of publications. His illustrations for works of American history differ in character from those for his various literary fairy tales—*Pepper and Salt* (1885), *The Wonder Clock* (1888), and *Twilight Land* (1895)—and those in turn differ greatly from his opulent medievalizing illustrations to Tennyson's *Lady of Shalott*.

Pyle's *Robin Hood*, indebted to Thomas Percy's *Reliques* and Joseph Ritson's Robin Hood ballads, articulates tale to tale ("the one stepping upon the heels of another," to quote from the third part), constructing something like a heroic biography; Robin, indeed, is elevated eventually to the earldom of Huntingdon by Richard the Lionheart. In the typical early tale, a disaffected but remarkable youth falls into conflict with Robin or one of his band, and often betters his outlaw opponent, or at least certainly makes an impression such that he is invited to join Robin's household in Sherwood forest—for "three suits of Lincoln green each year and forty marks in pay." Many of the stories challenge established authority, especially the king's representatives or those of the Church—the sheriff of Nottingham or the bishop of Hereford. Besides traditional delight in undermining authority, Pyle's *Robin Hood* offers special pleasure in trickery, violence, and gang loyalty, reconstructing chivalric parody as a boy's game and a youth's story. In one of his pirate tale collections, Pyle half-jokingly asks what boy would not prefer to be a pirate than to be a member of Parliament.

In Pyle's overall design, serious things of this world are mixed with merry things. The stories are told with a zest that makes them irresistible, despite archaism. The images brilliantly enliven and inform the action: full-page illustrations, initials, headpieces, and tailpieces. The decorative element is considerable: full-page pictures are framed in deliberate, if not exact, imitation of medieval manuscript illumination. The same is true of the four Arthur novels composed between 1903 and 1910; their greater stylization reflects a greater idealization. The *Robin Hood* illustrations, however beautifully composed, constantly depict action; so, for instance, in the frontispiece Friar Tuck is portrayed carrying Robin across a stream, his gleeful expression utterly individual. In the Arthur stories, however, action is comparatively insignificant, the accumulating narrative force being carried by portraits. The frontispiece of the first book exemplifies general practice in its iconic figuring of Arthur himself. In his foreword, Pyle represents the Round Table heroes as perfect examples of courage and humility; Arthur himself is "the most honorable, gentle Knyght who ever lived in all the world."

Like its medieval predecessors, Pyle's Arthuriad is a monumental enterprise. Despite taking four novels to complete the story, it is still a digest of the available Arthurian material; he incorporated stories from the Mabinogian (especially Geraint and Enid), and his reworking of Thomas Malory's stories recalls Chrétien de Troyes, Lancelot becoming a dominating presence in consequence. There is much compression, including the conflation of Elaine of Astolat with Elaine the daughter of Pelles, in order to provide Lancelot with the opportunity to sire a more or less legitimate Galahad. The consequence is considerable confusion at times, not least in the handling of Guinevere. Nevertheless, Arthur's is a marvelous story and, despite marked archaism, this Arthuriad still impresses, not least because Pyle so patently trusted and valued the stories themselves.

For the most part Pyle employed pen-and-ink drawing, since he depended on wood-block engraving. N. C. Wyeth claimed Pyle's drawings stood with the greatest work of all time done in this medium. In his later career, however, in books like *Men of Iron* (1892) and his pirate adventure *The Story of Jack Ballister's Fortunes* (1895), Pyle was able to employ photoengraving and use halftones to create an image suggesting a more substantial, real world. In due course he appears to have tired of being associated with medievalist texts and, indeed, with illustration, eventually choosing to work with murals. It was on his first trip to Europe, undertaken to expand his knowledge of mural painting by studying Renaissance works, that he fell ill and died. In a letter written late in life Pyle admitted to a long-held ambition to write a "really notable" book for adults, but also claimed to be satisfied that he had "made literary friends of the children rather than older folk," since "the stories of childhood leave an indelible impression."

[*See also* Adventure Books; Illustrations; King Arthur; Robin Hood; United States; *and biographies of figures mentioned in this article.*]

BIBLIOGRAPHY

Abbott, Charles D. *Howard Pyle, a Chronicle*. New York: Harper and Brothers, 1925.

Nesbitt, Elizabeth. *Howard Pyle*. London: Bodley Head, 1966.

CLAUDIA MARQUIS

Pyle, Katharine (1863–1938), American illustrator and children's author. Pyle began her career by contributing verses and illustrations to her brother Howard Pyle's fairy tale collection, *The Wonder Clock* (1888). In addition to publishing what she termed "fugitive" poems, Pyle wrote three fantasy novels for children: *The Counterpane Fairy* (1898), *The Christmas Angel* (1900), and *As the Goose Flies* (1901), all featuring Pyle's own pearlescent half-tone illustrations. *Nancy Rutledge* (1906), a semiautobiographical novel, draws on Pyle's Quaker childhood in Delaware's Brandywine Valley. Pyle also wrote and illustrated many story collections, including *Fairy Tales from Many Lands* (1911) and *The Katharine Pyle Book of Fairy Tales* (1925).

[*See also* Fantasy *and* Pyle, Howard.]

CAROLYN SIGLER

Pym, T. (fl. 1880s–1890s), prolific late-Victorian English children's book illustrator whose style imitated that of Kate Greenaway. Her real name was Clara Creed. Although Pym's work was popular and received positive reviews, it has largely lost its appeal for contemporary audiences. Her line drawings are highly sentimental and not very well executed; the figures, often rendered in stiff, unnatural poses, are at times out of proportion, having too large, balloon-shaped heads. Although the children are meant to be attractive in a conventional way, the faces are often insipid or flattened and asymmetrical, giving them pained or nightmarish looks. Although little is known about her life, her work illustrated many well-known tales, such as Hans Christian Andersen's *Snow Queen* (1883) and L. T. Meade's *Autocrat of the Nursery* (1886). She also produced a series of coloring books for children, such as *Outlines for the Little Ones to Colour* (1881), *Drawn and Coloured* (c. 1890), and *Pretty Pictures for Little Paint Brushes* (1882).

[*See also* Andersen, Hans Christian; Greenaway, Kate; Illustrations; *and* Meade, L. T..]

SIGRID ANDERSON CORDELL

Quackenbush, Robert M. (1929–), prolific American illustrator and author, whose lifelong approach to learning includes degrees in art (BA, 1956) and social work (MA, 1994), and a certificate in psychoanalysis (1991). An early interest in drawing led Quackenbush to study at the Los Angeles Art Center College of Design and afterward to move to New York City to work as a commercial art director. His encounters with printmaking techniques prompted him to take more art classes and to freelance as a professional artist. A publisher asked him to use woodcuts to illustrate Hans Christian Andersen's *The Steadfast Tin Soldier* (1964), the first of sixty books he designed for other authors before he decided to write books himself. He segued into authorship with a series of books that interpreted folk songs, beginning with *Old MacDonald Had a Farm* (1972), in which his own story is combined with his illustrations to explain the lyrics. Quackenbush credits the birth of his son Piet, in 1974, with inspiring the bulk of his written work. Although he wrote biographies (focusing on 19th-century icons like Charles Darwin and Annie Oakley), humorous easy readers (such as *Too Many Lollipops*, 1975, featuring "Henry the Duck"), and books that deal with childhood problems, he is best known for his easy reader mystery stories. Most of these feature anthropomorphized animal detectives (with the exception of his Piet Potter series), including Detective Mole, Miss Mallard, and Sherlock Chick. His *Detective Mole and the Halloween Mystery* (1981) won an Edgar Allan Poe Special Award in 1981. As with his songbook series, his humorous illustrations add content to the story. Quackenbush illustrates all his work, favoring ink-and-watercolor drawings, sometimes returning to woodcuts, and continues occasionally to illustrate works of other writers.

[*See also* Easy Readers; Illustrations; Mystery and Detective Stories; *and biographies of figures mentioned in this article.*]

CHARLOTTE CUBBAGE

Quaye, Kofi (1947–), alternate spelling Cofi(e), writer of a number of stories for young children and young adults. He was born in Ghana and self-educated after leaving school in the ninth grade. His early stories came out in the monthly journal *When and Where*, and in 1970 his first book, *Sammy Slams the Gang*, was published. Quaye has written many books since. Two of the children's stories, *Foli Fights the Forgers* and *Jojo in New York* were published as part of the MacMillan Publishing Mactracks series for children and teenagers learning English as a second language.

RONADIN CAREY

Quayle, Eric (1921–2001), British writer, collector, and historian. While pursuing a successful career in business, Eric Quayle built up an important collection of over twelve thousand books, and his acquisition of materials by the 19th-century adventure-story writer R. M. Ballantyne led him to publish his well-researched biography *Ballantyne the Brave: A Victorian Writer and His Family* in 1967. A whole series of lavishly illustrated books followed, including *The Collector's Book of Books* (1971), *The Collector's Book of Children's Books* (1971), *The Collector's Book of Boy's Stories* (1973), and *Early Children's Books: A Collector's Guide* (1983). Although the emphasis of these books tends to be on collecting, their enthusiasm and illustrations contributed to their considerable popularity. Later in his career, Quayle also published attractive retellings of Cornish and Japanese legends under the titles *The Magic Ointment* (1986) and *The Shining Princess* (1989), both superbly illustrated by Michael Foreman.

DENNIS BUTTS

Queneau, Raymond (1903–1976), French writer of literary works in several genres, including novels, poems, criticism, and translations. Queneau is considered to be one of the most important children's poets, and his work influenced many contemporary authors and illustrators. In 1933 he published his first novel, *Le Chiendent* (English trans., *The Bark Tree*, 1968), though he became known as a poet with *Chêne et chien* (Oak and Dog) in 1937. The same year, his novel *Odile* distanced him from the surrealist movement, with which he had been associated. In 1960 Queneau cofounded Oulipo (Ouroir de Littérature Povential, or Workshop of Potential Literature), indicative of his experimental spirit. Queneau works language by elaborate manipulations or mathematical rules. In *Cent mille milliards de poèmes* (One Hundred Thousand Billion Poems, 1961), inspired by a children's book, the cut lines of each sonnet of the book can be interchanged with corresponding lines in another sonnet. *Un conte à votre façon* (A Fairy Tale in Your Own Way, 1967) and his famous *Exercises de style* (Exercise in Style, 1947) are based on a similar playfulness. Queneau's novel *Zazie dans le métro* (1959; English trans., *Zazie*, 1960) is well known by children, especially for its wordplay. But most of all, Queneau is an important poet for children, and his work lives on in the work of several contemporary authors and illustrators.

[*See also* France *and* Poetry.]

SOPHIE VAN DER LINDEN

Quiller-Couch, Arthur (1863–1944), British author, academic, and anthologist who adopted the pen name Q. Born in Bodmin, Cornwall, his love of that county and of the sea influenced much of his fictional output. His first novel, *Dead Man's Rock* (1887), an adventure story, so closely resembled the style of Robert Louis Stevenson that he was asked to complete Stevenson's unfinished novel, *St. Ives* (1898). Remembered particularly for his Oxford anthologies of English verse (1900 and 1939), Quiller-Couch also wrote a number of children's books, including *The Splendid Spur* (1889) and *Fort Amity* (1904), both historical novels, and *The World of Adventure* (1889–1891). His spirited retellings of fairy tales were graced by the work of exceptional artists such as H. R. Millar in *Fairy Tales, Far and Near* (1895), Edmund Dulac in *The Sleeping Princess and other Fairy Tales from the Old French* (1910), and Kay Nielsen in *In Powder and Crinoline* (1913).

[*See also* Adventure Books; Collections; Fairy Tales and Folk Tales; *and* Historical Fiction.]

BRIDGET CARRINGTON

Quinn, John (1941–), Irish writer born in County Meath. Quinn worked as a teacher before becoming an award-winning radio broadcaster, a career he maintained for twenty-five years. He concurrently became a writer and has produced novels, nonfiction, and a memoir for adults. His first children's novel, *The Summer of Lily and Esmé* (1991), won the 1992 Bisto Book of the Year Award; it is about a Dublin boy who spends the summer in the country, befriends two elderly women, and becomes involved in the mystery of a boy named Albert who died seventy years earlier. This novel was followed by the adventure story *The Gold Cross of Killadoo* (1992), which is set in Dublin during Viking times, and *Duck and Swan* (1993), about two children suffering difficulties, one a runaway from a children's home and the other having an ill mother; they find friendship and face adventure together. *One Fine Day* (1996) concerns a boy and his family who, during the height of the Irish troubles in the early 1970s, leave Belfast for a new life in County Clare, which reveals its own social issues.

[*See also* Ireland *and* Young Adult Literature.]

ADRIENNE E. GAVIN

Quiroga, Horacio (1878–1937), Uruguayan author who published his first book in 1900 after traveling in Europe. Quiroga lived several years in Argentina, working as a photographer and teacher, and for four years was lay magistrate in San Ignacio (Misiones). After the suicide of his wife in 1915, he received a position at the Uruguayan consulate in Buenos Aires. He became famous with *Cuentos de amor, de locura y de muerte* (Stories of Love, Madness, and Death, 1917), founded the literary group Anaconda in 1920, and worked as secretary at the Brazilian embassy. In 1927 he married a school friend of his daughter's, but after being left by her and falling sick with cancer, he committed suicide in 1937. First told to his children Eglé and Dario, eight of Quiroga's stories were published in different journals. Since the Uruguayan ministry of education refused to edit it because of supposed grammatical mistakes and the representation of cruel incidents, *Cuentos de la selva para los niños* (1918; English trans., *Jungle Tales*, 1923) was originally published in Argentina. The book's title alludes to Rudyard Kipling's classics *The Jungle Book* (1894) and *The Second Jungle Book* (1895), which Quiroga deeply admired. The relationship between animals and human beings and the contrast between nature and civilization pervade Quiroga's stories, all of which make use of the jungle area of Misiones as their setting. The author presents the jungle as a magical force that threatens people's lives on the one hand, but on the other hand evokes a feeling of mystical union. Because of the combination of realistic and fantastic elements and the representation of psychological processes, Quiroga paved the way for the renewal of Latin American children's literature. His stories, which continue to be essential parts of school readers, were translated into several languages (English, French, German, and Russian).

[*See also* Kipling, Rudyard; Latino and Latina American Literature; *and* Spanish-Speaking Countries.]

BETTINA KÜMMERLING-MEIBAUER

Qur'an in Children's Literature, The. It is clearly stipulated in the holy Qur'an that it tells the stories of previous nations: "We do relate unto thee the most beautiful of stories, In that we reveal to thee this (portion of the) Qur-ān: before this, thou too was among those who knew it not" (Surat Yusuf 12, verse 3). Similar verses stressing the importance of storytelling recur throughout this holy book. The stories present answers to the questions that face the prophet and his followers. They show the struggles that previous prophets and Muhammad himself undertook to win the hearts and minds of the nations to which they were sent.

The stories have been significant for children's writers in two main ways. First, most of the stories in the Qur'an have been rewritten for children in a language and style considered suitable for them. Various children's books deal with the lives of prophets preceding Muhammad, such as Jesus, Moses, Abraham, Solomon, and Noah. Such stories constitute a major part of children's literature in the Arab world. Second, a large number of the stories written for children in the Arab world are what might be labeled morality tales; most of the stories display a struggle between good and evil, as do all the stories in the Qur'an. Almost a quarter of modern children's literature in the Arab world explicitly addresses the lives and deeds of the prophet and his followers or other historical figures, such as Saladdin, who devoted their lives to the protection of Islam. Furthermore, even when writing books not directly about figures in the Qur'an, Arab authors generally agree that a basic function of children's literature is to spread Islamic moral values. In the West, the Qur'an figures in a few nonfiction titles that describe Muslim customs, but in the Arab world it permeates publications for children.

[*See also* Arab World; Moral Tales; Religious Instruction and Education; *and* Religious Writing.]

BIBLIOGRAPHY

The Looking Glass 8, no. 2 (April 2004). http://www.the-looking-glass.net/rabbit/v8i2/index.html. Special issue devoted to Arab children's literature.

Mdallel, Sabeur. "Translating Children's Literature in the Arab World: The State of the Art." *Meta* 48 (2003): 298–306.

SABEUR MDALLEL

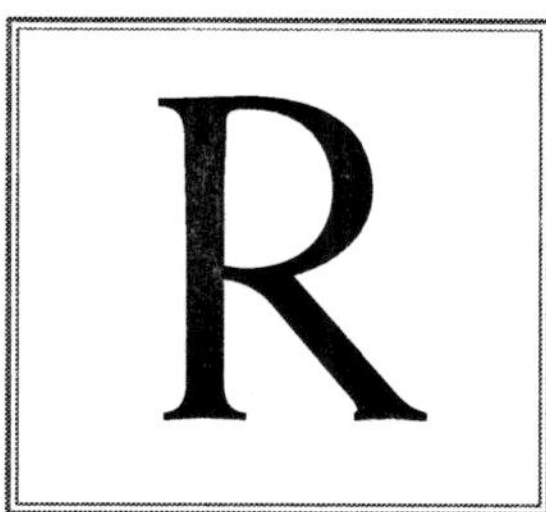

Racism. A combination of institutional power and prejudice against members of racial or ethnic groups other than one's own, racism has been a discernible feature in European and American children's literature from at least the early 1800s. In the United States, children's literature began to expand rapidly after the Civil War, at the very time when Ku Klux Klan violence and discriminatory Jim Crow laws were affecting the country at large. Children's books have always been firmly situated in the larger national context, and an egregious political environment overlapped with the rise of racism as a clearcut component of juvenile literature. In Europe, it was colonial domination that was on the increase at the end of the 19th century. Between 1878 and 1914, "European control extended over 84.4 percent of the earth's surface" (Pieterse, 1992, p. 76). In children's novels this fact was reflected in the way storytellers increasingly used colonial empires as settings for adventure novels. These developments contributed to the presence of more people of color in children's literature, but ex-slaves and colonized peoples were consistently characterized as the inferiors of whites and as threats to civilization.

It is difficult to explain the development of racism in America, including its presence in children's books, unless we examine the extensive consensus among the white population on the subject of white supremacy. Although at odds over slavery, the North and South were never far apart on the question of white superiority, and a perusal of abolitionist and postbellum children's books reveals such a unified perspective. For example, there are strong similarities in the characterization of blacks in John Townsend Trowbridge's *Cudjo's Cave* (1864) and the Southern novels *Diddie, Dumps, and Tot: A Plantation Child's Life* (1882) by Louise Pyrnelle and *Two Little Confederates* (1888) by Thomas Nelson Page. In the 20th century, the white supremacist tradition continued in Edward Stratemeyer's syndicated series books (e.g., the Rover Boys series in the early 1900s and the Nancy Drew books beginning in 1930). The dialect-speaking fools and the brutish black villains in these inexpensive series books did not start fading out until their creators faced civil rights reformers in the 1950s.

In addition to the racism based on a black/white color line, there is a persistent "savage" construct imposed on Native Americans. This image has remained steady throughout American history, from the captivity narratives of the colonial period to the present day. This longevity stems in part from assumptions connected with the Westward Movement. Every year a new crop of novels glorifies that movement and introduces tomahawk-wielding Native Americans who scalp hapless homesteaders. Examples dating from 1997 include Patricia Willis's *Danger along the Ohio*, William Durbin's *The Broken Blade*, and Ann Rinaldi's *The Second Bend in the River*. These and many similar titles have received glowing praise from children's-literature professionals. Accordingly, the lifespan of the "savage" is perpetually extended (Thompson, 2001, pp. 365–370).

Not all groups that are part of America's expansionist history have made a strong appearance in children's literature; for example, books featuring Chinese, Japanese, Mexican, and Puerto Rican protagonists have been relatively few. In 1975–1976, the Council on Interracial Books for Children (CIBC) brought together a team of Asian-American book reviewers to study sixty-six titles with Asian-American characters. This survey revealed an Asian cast of characters embracing obsolete, alien customs, ancient superstitions, and a lifestyle preoccupied with traditional folk festivals. This treatment of Asian culture had its antecedents in the fashions for chinoiserie in the 18th century and the Japanese taste in the 19th, art styles that filtered Chinese and Japanese aesthetics through a Western lens. With only a few exceptions, since the CIBC study Asian-Americans have remained associated in children's books with a largely mythical China and Japan (e.g., in Amy Tan's *The Chinese Siamese Cat*, 1994, with grotesque décor and offensive stereotypes by illustrator Gretchen Schields). Vietnam became a recurring subject in Cold War epics stressing the pro-American war effort. *Literature for Children about Asians and Asian Americans* (1987) by Esther C. Jenkins and Mary C.

Austin covers Vietnam as well as China, Japan, Korea, and other nations in Southeast Asia.

CIBC had already undertaken surveys similar to the Asian study: one in 1972 covering Puerto Rican books, and another in 1974 about Chicano/Chicana literature. Mexicans were regularly represented as indolent, superstitious, and unprepared for contemporary living. In Paula G. Paul's *You Can Hear a Magpie Smile* (1980), folk healers can have limited success with a mix of herbs and pseudo-psychology, but the novel is essentially a pitch about trading in the old Mexican world for the new one defined by Anglos. In a similar vein, Elizabeth Spurr's *Lupe . . . Me* (1995) foregrounds Mexican customs through the characterization of an "undocumented" housekeeper—a throwback to the stereotypical contented servant who giggles incessantly, gazes with wonder at modern appliances, and bonds effortlessly with her seven-year-old overseer. Such works reverberate with a colonialist mentality, implying an endless Anglo stewardship and an indefinite relegation of most Hispanics to menial occupations.

The colonial-promoting scenario developing outside the United States contains elements of the American Westward Movement motif: an assumption of empty space awaiting the colonizer, and (illogically) a belief in the legitimacy of waging war against dwellers in that "empty" space. Arguing on behalf of colonization, authors often depicted the indigenous group as hopelessly backward and less than fully human. In books for children, writers reinforced those notions through an array of stereotypes—the native as Stone Age primitive, perennial child, unwitting clown, exotic seducer, self-immolating servant, brutish assailant, cunning thief, sadistic warrior. Africans have been a primary target of this Western-contrived mythology, as seen in 19th-century British novels by Frederick Marryat, Robert Ballantyne, and George A. Henty. In the 1990s and beyond, similar stereotypes have flowed from the pen of the British adventure writers Eric Campbell (*The Year of the Leopard Song*, 1992) and Peter Dickinson (*AK*, 1992), and the American novelists Nancy Farmer (*Do You Know Me*, 1993) and Cristina Kessler (*No Condition is Permanent*, 2000).

In addition to the heavy concentration on Africa, the history of children's literature encompasses depictions of India and people in the Indian diaspora. Stories that were in essence missionary tracts set the pattern in the early 1800s (e.g., Martha Butt Sherwood's *The History of Little Henry and His Bearer*, 1814). The climax of such tales involves a conversion to Christianity, but the overall texture, as Meena Khorana notes about *Little Henry*, involves a denunciation of Hinduism as "ineffectual, superstitious, and caste-ridden" (p. xxvi). In other novels about India, two additional types emerged: colonial stories with British, polo-playing governors, and novels of "progress" with British technicians upstaging Indian technicians (Khorana, pp. xxvi–xxvii). By the mid-20th century, children's authors had become more adept at contriving "progressive" plotlines, yet even in 1998 we find updated reflections of *Little Henry* in Julia Holland's *Nothing To Remember*. A lack of respect for Indian culture pervades the novel as Indian immigrants express their devotion to Australia and their abhorrence of their homeland. Bombay is allegedly "crazy"—a teeming city of extreme filth and political corruption. Introducing a love interest between an Indian and a white Australian does little to offset the book's anglocentrism.

In a different English genre—the comic fanciful novel—stereotyping seemed largely unnoticed by the "gatekeepers" until challenged by those singled out for derision. Hugh Lofting's *The Story of Dr. Dolittle* and its sequels (1920–1948), Pamela Travers's *Mary Poppins* (1934), and Roald Dahl's *Charlie and the Chocolate Factory* (1964) were all revised at their publishers' insistence when school systems began pinpointing the white supremacist content and discarding the books. The new editions were either pruned or rewritten to eliminate the maligning of non-Western people.

In the United States, efforts to combat racism were given an organized base of operation in the Council on Interracial Books for Children, especially between 1967 and 1984 under the direction of Bradford Chambers, a social worker by training. In Britain, educators launched Teachers Against Racism (TAR) in 1972 and the National Committee on Racism in Children's Books was founded in 1976. This committee established an award to encourage writing that reflects a multiracial Britain and published articles in *Race Today* (Britain's leading race relations journal) and *CRC Journal* (the work of the Community Relations Commission of Great Britain). In 1985, racism in schoolbooks was carefully pinpointed in Beverley Naidoo's *Censoring Reality: An Examination of Books on South Africa* (published by the ILEA Centre for Anti-Racist Education and the British Defense/Aid Fund for Southern Africa). On the European continent, Germany was also active, especially through the work of Jorg Becker, a research fellow at the Hessen Foundation for Peace and Conflict Research in Frankfurt, and Klaus Doderer, the director of the Institute for Research and Youth Literature, an affiliate of J. W. Goethe University. Conferences were organized and papers published in *Beiträge zur Kinder- und Jugendliteratur*.

By the 1990s, the antiracist movement had become more dispersed, and a growing number of institutions took notice of racial and cultural bias, if only indirectly. For example, in the United States, specialized ethnic presses were established, such as Arte Público with its Piñata imprint for children's books. New prizes were created, such as the Pura Belpre Award for Latino/Latina authors and illustrators, and the Tomás Rivera Mexican-American Children's Book Award for encouraging authenticity in images of Mexican-Americans in the Southwest. Journals such as the *Children's Literature Association Quarterly* made room for ongoing coverage (as in *ChLAQ*'s "Cultural Pluralism Column"), while focus issues have appeared intermittently in *The Lion and the Unicorn*. *Multicultural Review* is a well-informed resource covering adult and children's literature. List-making is an activity of the Cooperative Children's Book Center at the University of Wisconsin (*Multicultural Children's and Young Adult Literature*) and the National Council of Teachers of English (*Kaleidoscope: A Multicultural Booklist for Grades K-8*). The result has been an increase in specific information about cultural and racial diversity; however a continuing challenge arises with fears of national "Balkanization" and the proverbial slippery slope of censorship. Since social justice is by definition a structural question, educational institutions that unduly aggravate such fears can become part of the problem. CIBC and its British and German counterparts realized as much when they opted explicitly to combat institutional racism.

The mythical "white man's burden" took shape as a way to meet "the needs of established colonialism," both internal and external (Pieterse, pp. 88, 166–171). It made its appearance in the cultural institutions and children's books of Germany, France, and the Netherlands as well as Britain and America. But the affinity of colonialism with racism did not come into clear focus until the decolonization of Asia and Africa after World War II, and the revival of the civil rights movement in the United States (Pieterse, p. 50). In the end, whether there is an internal colony (a term referring to slavery and the ongoing restricted prospects for blacks) or an external colony (when another's land base comes under foreign domination), the point is the maintenance of social inequality and the increase of benefits for the dominating group. As a player in this destructive endeavor, children's literature has much to answer for and much unfinished business.

BIBLIOGRAPHY

Gregory, Lucille H. "The Puerto Rican 'Rainbow': Distortions vs. Complexities." *Children's Literature Association Quarterly* 18 (1993): 29–35.

Harris, Violet J., ed. *Teaching Multicultural Literature in Grades K–8*. Norwood, Mass.: Christopher-Gordon, 1993.

Jenkins, Esther C., and Mary C. Austin. *Literature for Children about Asians and Asian Americans: Analysis and Annotated Bibliography*. New York: Greenwood, 1987.

Khorana, Meena. *The Indian Subcontinent in Literature for Children and Young Adults: An Annotated Bibliography of English-Language Books*. Westport, Conn.: Greenwood, 1991.

MacCann, Donnarae, and Gloria Woodard, eds. *The Black American in Books for Children: Readings in Racism*. 2nd ed. Metuchen, N.J.: Scarecrow, 1985.

Maddy, Yulisa Amadu, and Donnarae MacCann. *African Images in Juvenile Literature: Commentaries on Neocolonialist Fiction*. Jefferson, N.C.: McFarland, 1996.

Pieterse, Jan Nederveen. *White on Black: Images of Africa and Blacks in Western Popular Culture*. New Haven, Conn.: Yale University Press, 1992.

Thompson, Melissa Kay. "A Sea of Good Intentions: Native Americans in Books for Children." *The Lion and the Unicorn* 25 (2001): 353–374.

DONNARAE MACCANN

Rackham, Arthur (1867–1939), British illustrator whose lovely, otherworldly watercolor paintings set a style that has had lasting influence on fantasy illustration. Born in London, Rackham was sickly as an adolescent, and a sea voyage to Australia for his health inspired him to paint a series of watercolors of the scenery. On his return his father urged him to prepare himself for a more reliable career than art. So, in 1885 he took a job in a London insurance office, where he worked for the next seven years. During this time he also took night courses at the Lambeth School of Art, and in 1892 he went to work as a staff artist for illustrated magazines. Rackham began to do illustrations for books, and his first children's book commission, in 1896 for S. J. Adair Fitzgerald's *The Zankiwank and the Bletherwitch*, began to show the style that made him famous. His reputation grew with the commercial success of *Fairy Tales of the Brothers Grimm* (1900), and in 1902 he had his first exhibition of work at the Royal Watercolor Society.

His color illustrations for an edition of the Washington Irving classic *Rip Van Winkle* were shown at the Leicester Galleries in London in 1905, and it was those illustrations that truly made his reputation. The fifty-one color plates, in sinuous lines and transparent watercolors laid down wash over wash, give Rip Van Winkle's world its ethereal quality. In all Rackham's work, his lovely, often eldritch, maidens, his ogres and trolls, inhabit a land of looming trees with twisting roots and, occasionally, faces. Hidden images fill the backgrounds. They are often beautiful, yet there is something mildly sinister about them. His scantily clad sprites and knobby-limbed goblins offered a thrilling beauty and a

The Witch Curses Sleeping Beauty. Illustration by Arthur Rackham from *Fairy Tales of the Brothers Grimm* translated by Mrs. Edgar Lucas (London: Archibald, 1909). COLLECTION OF JACK ZIPES

glimpse of the dark and forbidden to the sheltered Edwardian children whose parents could afford the books. In the early 20th century, photo separation and reproduction techniques made Rackham's richly detailed illustrations possible, but the color sheets had to be inserted by hand, rather than printed on the page, a time-consuming process that made these lavishly illustrated editions an indulgence for those with the means to buy them. Rackham, a lanky figure with balding head and spectacles, often drew his own caricature, complete with carpet slippers, in his gnomes and elves, allowing himself a residency in his own fantastic netherworld.

Rip Van Winkle was followed in 1906 by one of Rackham's acknowledged masterpieces, *Peter Pan in Kensington Gardens*, although the *Times* of London criticized the book for giving more attention to sales to parents and grandparents enthralled by its beauty than to whether actual children would like it. Rackham was the center of further criticism in 1907 when he was commissioned to reillustrate *Alice in Wonderland*. Rackham's style gave Wonderland a dark overlay, with a realistically drawn Alice, a beaky-nosed, long-fingered hatter, and a truly frightening Red Queen. When Alice encounters the White Rabbit looking for his gloves, it is under a gnarled and limbless tree in a blighted landscape. The paintings outraged fans of the original illustrator, John Tenniel, whose work was so closely identified with the text. However, the book was a commercial success.

During his long career, Rackham illustrated more than fifty books, nearly all of them for children, and was acknowledged as the premier illustrator of his time. Among his forays into adult editions were his pictures for English translations of *The Rhinegold and the Valkyrie* (1910) and *Siegfried and the Twilight of the Gods* (1911), products of an 1897 trip to Bayreuth, Germany, where Rackham saw the classic Wagner opus *Der Ring des Nibelungen*, whose imagery and themes, drawn from German mythology, he borrowed for his illustrations. Among the children's books published at the height of his success were *Mother Goose: The Old Nursery Rhymes* and *Arthur Rackham's Book of Pictures* (both 1913). During World War I he illustrated *The Allies' Fairy Book* (1916), a collection of fables about the American, French, and British war effort. The publishing industry changed after the war, however, and postwar printing allowed cheaper methods of production less well suited to his work. Younger artists were coming to the fore, and sales of Rackham's books slowed in Britain, although he became increasingly popular in the United States.

In 1933, when he was invited to select twenty-three tales for *The Arthur Rackham Fairy Book*, he wrote in his preface to the collection about his belief in the importance of fairy tales. Rackham's work shows his innate understanding of the power of myth and fable, and of the dark longings that lie beneath their surface. His splay-fingered, bat-eared gnomes, as well as his delicate, sprightly fairies, belong to the older world of fairy, where it is often beautiful but where it is not a good idea to trespass without the pages of a book to guide you back. His illustrations in the 1930s for Christina Rossetti's *Goblin Market* (1933) and Robert Browning's *The Pied Piper of Hamelin* (1934), despite their bright colors, admirably show Rackham's continued awareness of the darker side of fantasy. Among his other wartime and postwar works were illustrations for Sir Thomas Malory's *The Romance of King Arthur* (1917), Shakespeare's *The Tempest* (1926), and John Ruskin's *King of the Golden River* (1932).

In the late 1930s, Rackham's health declined as he developed cancer. He had illustrated *A Midsummer Night's Dream* (1939) for the Limited Editions Club in New York, and from them received his last commission: new illustrations for Kenneth Grahame's *The Wind in the Willows*. Rackham took the assignment eagerly, as he loved the book (he had been offered the job of illustrating the original 1908 edition, but had had to turn it down because of other commitments). Despite his ill health, he set about creating a new set of pictures, many of them done from his bed, and finished the last one just before his death in 1939. The edition was published posthumously in 1940. Since his death, early editions of Rackham's books have become collectors' items, and many remain in print.

[*See also* Book Design; Fantasy; Illustrations; *and biographies of figures mentioned in this article*.]

BIBLIOGRAPHY

Adams, Gillian. "Arthur Rackham's Fairy Book: A Confrontation with the Marvelous." In *Touchstones: Reflections on the Best in Children's Literature*, edited by Perry Nodelman, vol. 3, pp. 107–121. West Lafayette, Ind.: Children's Literature Association, 1989.

Hamilton, James. *Arthur Rackham*. New York: Arcade, 1990.

Hudson, Derek. *Arthur Rackham: His Life and Work*. New York: Scribners, 1973.

Amanda Cockrell

Radford, Dollie (1858–1920), British poet, novelist, playwright, and children's author married to poet and political activist Ernest Radford. Dollie Radford, who was born Caroline Maitland, was a socialist and feminist activist, whose friendships included both eminent authors and political radicals such as Eleanor Marx, William Morris, W. B. Yeats, Olive Schreiner, George Bernard Shaw, and D. H. Lawrence. Like her writings for adults, Radford's collection of seasonal poems for children, *The Young Gardener's Kalendar* (1904), and her children's fantasy novel, *Sea Thrift: A Fairy Tale* (1904), use vivid natural detail to explore more complex themes of loss and renewal.

[*See also* Fantasy *and* Poetry.]

Carolyn Sigler

Radio Shows for Children. Listening to a story broadcast on radio has been described as the modern equivalent of the tribal campfire. Proponents of children's radio suggest that while television encourages passive viewing, radio requires active listening. Radio, in other words, is a participatory medium that engages the imagination of the listener. Nowhere has this active listening happened more enthusiastically than with *Children's Hour*, which aired on the BBC from 1922 to 1964. As Longfellow's verse recommended, "The Children's Hour" occupied the space "between the dark and the daylight / When the night is beginning to lower," that is, between 5 P.M. and 6 P.M., seven days a week. Four days (Wednesday, Thursday, Friday, and Sunday) were devoted to children's literature in one form or another, either poetry, readings of short stories, or the dramatization of original plays. Whether it was T. S. Eliot reading from *Old Possum's Book of Practical Cats* or a dramatization of the latest work from Rosemary Sutcliffe, *Children's Hour* provided unprecedented exposure to the best contemporary children's literature. Among other authors featured were Malcolm Saville, Arthur Ransome, and Dorothy Sayers. Dramatic presentations of Sherlock Holmes and readings of the *Just So Stories* and *Winnie the Pooh* were popular. One of the best-known series featured on *Children's Hour* was *Toytown*, created by the illustrator Hulme Beaman. First broadcast in the 1930s, and continuing for thirty-six episodes, *Toytown* featured beloved characters such as Larry the Lamb. The popularity of *Children's Hour* spawned the publication of numerous books including *The Children's Hour Annual* and Anthony Buckeridge's Jennings at School series.

Although *Children's Hour* was occasionally described as paternalistic or as an advocate of middle-class values, it garnered a loyal following, being perhaps the most popular program in the history of BBC Radio. Particularly during World War II, it has been argued, *Children's Hour* provided a unifying familial element to children who had been separated from loved ones. When the show was canceled in 1964, the event was met with a public outcry and debate that reached as high as the House of Commons.

The BBC's commitment to children's literature has always reached beyond *Children's Hour*, however. H. E Todd's *Bobby Brewster* series was launched after its appearance on the BBC in 1946. *Radio Fun* (1939–1960), was an annual comic book that featured well-known BBC personalities. The radio program *Listen with Mother* was created in 1950, ran for thirty-two years, and was conceived as a program for children too young for *Children's Hour*. Its opening line, "Are you sitting comfortably? Then I'll begin . . ." led into a format that used repetition to teach and emphasized the importance of the mother's role in child development. *Listen with Mother* regularly featured nursery rhymes and readings from popular anthologies. In the 1960s, dramatizations such as Alan Garner's *Elidor* (1965) were featured alongside popular series like Michael Bond's *The Herbs* or Ted Hughes's *Poetry in the Making*, a series devoted to creative writing that emphasized the genius of the ordinary child. In the 1970s Elaine Moss, a driving force behind the children's literature journal *Signal*, provided the BBC with book reviews. Dramatizations continued as well, such as Willis Hall's *The Summer of the Dinosaur*. In 1982 *Listen with Mother* was replaced by the five-minute program *Listening Corner*. Ruth Corrin, David Hill, and Anthony Horowitz all provided material to the BBC in the 1980s. A highlight in this era was *Treasure Islands*, a series of essays and recollections about children's literature and reading habits. The Bulmershe Library at the University of Reading has collected and maintains a *Treasure Islands* archive consisting of sound recordings of 170 programs.

While the BBC continues to maintain an interest in children's literature, specific mention should be made of the "schools radio" service, an educational channel delivered directly to schools in the United Kingdom since its inception in the 1920s. Schools radio went digital in 2003, allowing for greater flexibility for the downloading and playback of material. In the early 2000s programming for schools radio features a Meet the Authors series and a program of Reading Tree Stories that uses texts from stages eight and nine of the Oxford Reading Tree. Books featured on schools radio include abridgments of Robert Westall's *The Machine Gunners* and Berlie Doherty's *Street Child*, as well as retellings of European folk tales.

The Australian Broadcast Corporation (ABC) has also maintained a commitment to programming for children. *Kindergarten of the Air*, broadcast first in 1942, provided the inspiration for the BBC's *Listen with Mother*. Authors such as Colin Thiele (in the 1940s and 1950s) and Ruth Park (in the 1960s) wrote material for ABC. Park's *The Muggle Headed Wombat* was featured on the program *The ABC Argonauts*. And children's nature writer Jill Morris wrote sixty-five episodes of the ABC radio program *Bangotcher Junction*, beginning in 1985.

In the United States early children's radio consisted of science fiction, adventure, thrillers, and educational programs. Creative, musically engaging productions based on children's books included Danny Kaye's *Tubby the Tuba* and various interpretations of Prokofiev's *Peter and the Wolf*.

Cabbage Soup, produced by the Children's Radio Theater in the 1980s, included ALA notable productions of *Rapunzel* and *Beauty and the Beast*.

In the early 1990s Minneapolis-based WWTC-AM founded the first children's radio network in the United States, Radio Aahs (or "Radio Oz"). By 1996, Radio Aahs was available on thirty-two stations nationwide. The company was forced out of business by the founding in 1997 of Radio Disney, a network that now includes sixty-one stations. While Radio Disney is primarily music oriented, the network ostensibly maintains a commitment to children's books via promotional events at shopping malls, public libraries, and schools. Events such as "Reading Together with Laura Bush" (2002), for example, included readings of *The Chicken Sisters* by Laura Numeroff and *Martin's Big Words* by Doreen Rappaport.

Nationally syndicated programming is available today in the United States on XM Radio's XMKiDS and National Public Radio's *Pickleberry Pie*. Among the more successful locally produced programs are KTOO-FM's *We Like Kids* (Juneau, Alaska), WAMC-FM's *Knock On Wood* (Albany, New York), WERS's *The Playground* (Boston), and the Miami Children's Hospital's *Radio Lollipop*.

Radio commentary on children's literature was begun in America by Louise Seaman Bechtel, the founding editor of the first children's book department in the United States (Macmillan), who hosted a weekly review program. *Horn Book Magazine* has occasionally presented author profiles on NPR, such as features on Robert McCloskey and Chris Van Allsburg. In 2000 the University of Florida's WUFT-FM began producing *Recess*, a daily three-minute program frequently devoted to commentary on children's books.

[*See also* Children's Hour *and biographies of figures mentioned in this article*.]

BIBLIOGRAPHY

Hartley, Ian. *Goodnight Children . . . Everywhere: An Informal History of Children's Broadcasting*. London: Midas, 1983.

McKenna, Linda M. "The Relationship Between Attributes of a Children's Radio Program and Its Appeal to Listeners." *Educational Technology Research and Development* 41 (1993): 17–28.

Oswell, David. "Early Children's Broadcasting in Britain, 1922–1964: Programming for a Liberal Democracy." *Historical Journal of Film, Radio, and Television* 18.3 (August 1998): 375–393.

Kevin Shortsleeve

Rae, Gwynedd (1892–1977), British children's writer of the Mary Plain stories (1930–1965), about a bear cub from the bear pits at Bern. As in other talking animal stories, Mary is alternately constructed as an animal and as a child. The series started with *Mostly Mary* (1930), which focuses on her interactions with the other bears in Bern. Thereafter the books detail Mary's adventures in the wider world, accompanied by her friend the Owl Man (so-called because of his spectacles), first to England in *All Mary* (1930) and, later, to the United States in *Mary Plain Goes to America* (1957). Episodic in structure and comic in tone, the books revolve around the way that Mary's curiosity, combined with her misunderstanding of words and social routines, inevitably leads to trouble. One of the contributing factors to the popularity of the series in Britain in the 1930s and 1940s was Rae's relationship with the radio program *Children's Hour*.

[*See also* Animal Stories; Anthropomorphism; *and* Children's Hour.]

Simon R. D. Flynn

Raffi (1948–), America's leading folksinger for children. Born in Wolverhampton, England, Raffi Cavoukian, or Raffi, as he is better known to his fans, emigrated to Canada as a teenager. Raffi's enormous respect for children and his concern for the environment have combined to make his music unique. Not only does he delight children with his mixture of various musical styles, positive values, and his own brand of silly fun, he also delights their parents. This singer-songwriter financed his first children's album *Singable Songs for the Very Young* (1976), which launched his career as an entertainer for children.

Raffi felt that music made a tremendous impact on the education of a child. He knew how to allow children to learn best: through natural play. The details and concerns of children became important components of his music. The pattern to Raffi's songs has evoked feelings, images, and moods, allowing children to remember them easily. Many of Raffi's songs have been so well received that they were made into illustrated children's books, for example, *Down by the Bay* (1987) and *Baby Beluga* (1990).

After achieving international popularity, as well as selling millions of albums, Raffi decided to produce songs and albums for adults. His environmental concerns became the focus for his first album for grown-ups, *Evergreen Everblue* (1990). He sought to educate his listeners about global problems, such as toxic waste, the dwindling rain forest, and rapid destruction of the ozone layer, and help them develop an appreciation of the earth's beauty. He advocates the protection of the earth and world peace through Canada's Environmental Youth Alliance.

This child entertainer and environmental activist has been nominated for Grammy Awards (1987–1988), has won several platinum awards (1987), and has garnered numerous other awards including Canada's highest distinction, The Order of Canada, in 1983 for contributing to the educational lives of children.

BIBLIOGRAPHY

Cavoukian, Raffi. *The Life of a Children's Troubadour: An Autobiography*. Vancouver: Homeland Press, 1999.

Spies, Karen Bornemann. *Raffi: The Children's Voice*. Minneapolis, Minn.: Dillon Press, 1989.

JESSICA J. BURKE

Raggedy Ann and Raggedy Andy. *See* Gruelle, Johnny.

Rai, Bali (1971–), English author who specializes in fiction featuring multicultural (mostly British Asian) teenagers in English settings. His *(Un)arranged Marriage* (2001) is about a Punjabi teenage boy pushed by his family toward an arranged marriage, and explores the conflict between the immigrant parents and their English-born son. Rai followed with *Dream On* (2002), a British Asian football story; *The Crew* (2003), a thriller featuring a multicultural gang; *What's Your Problem* (2003), about racism in an English village, and *Rani . . . Sukh* (2004), a love story that moves between 1960s Punjab and modern-day Britain. Rai's books are often written with reluctant readers in mind.

LAURA E. ATKINS

Raible, Alton (1918–), American artist known primarily for illustrating the work of Zilpha Keatley Snyder. Born in Modesto, California, Raible was teaching art at the College of Marin in Kentfield, California, when his fellow teacher Snyder had her first novel, *Season of Ponies* (1964), accepted for publication. She submitted samples of Raible's artwork to her editor, who in turn offered him the opportunity to illustrate the book. His illustrations for this mystical story are appropriately surreal, as abstract images of fanciful horses trot across misty landscapes. Raible's dark-toned illustrations tend to have a pebbly, speckled, textured quality that is well suited for Snyder's magic-laced novels, which include three Newbery Honor books, *The Egypt Game* (1967), *The Headless Cupid* (1971), and *The Witches of Worm* (1972). Although he has illustrated a handful of children's books by other authors, Raible's atmospheric artwork is most closely associated with Snyder's novels.

[*See also* Illustrations *and* Snyder, Zilpha Keatley.]

PETER D. SIERUTA

Raikes, Robert (1736–1811), English editor and founder of Sunday schools. Born in Gloucester, Raikes was educated at schools there and in 1757 succeeded his father as editor and proprietor of the *Gloucester Journal*. Concerned about conditions in Gloucester jail, he published appeals for prison reform in his journal. Regarded as the founder of Sunday schools, he began together with the curate Thomas Stock by employing four women to teach children on a Sunday, and in 1780 he set up his own school for the children of chimney sweeps. In the following years, aided by publicity he gave the fledgling Sunday school movement in the *Gloucester Journal*, Sunday schools opened swiftly across the United Kingdom and the United States. Highly significant in the education of working-class children through their teaching of reading, writing, and other skills, as well as religion, Sunday schools also encouraged the rise of literature for children.

[*See also* Journals and Periodicals *and* Religious Instruction and Education.]

ADRIENNE E. GAVIN

Ramona Series. *See* Cleary, Beverly.

Ramos, Vicky (1960–), Costa Rican artist educated at the Escuela de Artes Plásticas de la Universidad de Costa Rica. Ramos has participated in individual and collective exhibitions, and her work for "Zurquí," a children's supplement in the newspaper *La Nación*, has allowed her to experiment in the art of illustration. She has been included twice in Costa Rica's IBBY Honor List, and her illustrated books include *Mo* (1991) by Lara Ríos, *Pedro y su teatrino maravilloso* (Pedro and His Wonderful Puppet Theater, 1992) by Carlos Rubio, *Niñas y niños del maíz* (Girls and Boys of the Corn, 1995), and *Poemas con sol y son* (Poems with Sun and Sound, 2000) by Rodolfo Dada.

[*See also* Illustrations; Latino and Latina American Literature; *and* Spanish-Speaking Countries.]

MAITÉ DAUTANT

Rand, Gloria (1925–), American author whose varied picture books are often based on true events. All are illustrated by her husband, Ted Rand. *Salty Dog* (1989), the first story about Salty, a clever dog who would grow up to accompany his owner on many adventures, was based on a newspaper story about a ferry-riding dog. In *Salty Takes Off* (1991), Salty falls out of an airplane over a snowy Alaskan wilderness and survives. *Prince William* (1992) centers on a seal pup affected by the 1989 oil spill in Prince William Sound. Another incredible adventure, based on a real-life incident that took place in Alaska in 1917, is the subject of *Baby in a Basket* (1997), in which a sled is overturned and a baby washed downriver, to be rescued miraculously by a group of trappers. Rand's stories, many about the relationship between humans and animals, have been praised for their pacing and emotional resonance.

[*See also* Animal Stories; Picture Books; *and* Rand, Ted.]

LINNEA HENDRICKSON

Rand, Ted (1915–2005), American artist and illustrator who began his children's book career at age sixty-five and illustrated seventy-nine books before his death. Rand was self-taught, making drawings throughout his elementary and high school years. Upon graduation he went to work as an artist for a Seattle department store, and by 1938 he had saved enough money to take a year off to see the world. He reported to a Seattle newspaper reporter, Cecilia Goodnow: "I saw Hitler speak in Munich, and I saw Mussolini speak in Rome. . . . I was too dumb to be scared." After serving for four years in the Naval Air Corps in the Pacific, he married Gloria Kistler, with whom he would later collaborate on a dozen books. He taught illustration part-time at the University of Washington and painted portraits of governors, university presidents, corporation heads, and Saudi Arabia's King Khalid. He also illustrated numerous books and reference works. At the urging of the author Bill Martin Jr., Rand illustrated his first children's book, Bill Martin and John Archambault's atmospheric *The Ghost-Eye Tree* (1985), followed in quick succession by other Martin and Archambault titles. Rand said he never enjoyed anything as much as illustrating children's books. "The technical freedom, the opportunity to work in a great variety of styles, the people I work with, the common goal of getting children to read, all these combine to put this at the top of my list." *Salty Dog* (1989) was his first collaboration with his wife, Gloria Rand. One of Ted Rand's last projects was Jack Prelutsky's *If Not for the Cat* (2004), a book of playful animal haiku, quite different from anything either Prelutsky or Rand had ever done before. The book received enthusiastic reviews and was named an ALA Notable book.

[*See also* Illustrations *and biographies of figures mentioned in this article.*]

LINNEA HENDRICKSON

Randolph, Vance (1892–1980), folklorist and foremost scholar of Ozark life. Randolph earned an education degree in his native Kansas and a master's degree in psychology at Clark University before embarking on his career as a teacher and writer. In 1919 he moved to Missouri with his bride and began learning about the Ozarks. At the outset he worked as a ghostwriter, but later as an author in the Haldeman-Julius Little Blue Books. These widely distributed works undoubtedly touched many children's lives, but Randolph's real influence derives from more than twenty books about Ozark tall tales, dialects, superstitions, songs, and jokes—all written in the storytelling voice that lends appeal to even the most scholarly endeavors. None were specifically targeted at children, but many have enjoyed a wide youth readership, especially the subversively bawdy *Pissing in the Snow and Other Ozark Folktales* (1976), which has sold over a hundred thousand copies. Numerous scholars of folk tales for children, such as Richard Chase, acknowledge a profound debt to Randolph.

[*See also* Chase, Richard; Fairy Tales and Folk Tales; Tall Tales; *and* United States.]

CAROLE CARPENTER

Rands, William Brighty (1823–1882), British journalist and man of letters. While earning his living primarily as a parliamentary reporter, Rands, sometimes under pseudonyms, also wrote adult poetry, fiction, literary criticism, and essays, but he is best known as a children's writer. *Lilliput Levee* (1864) contains some attractive verse, with near-classics like "Topsy-Turvey-world" and "Gypsy Jane." *Lilliput Lectures* (1871) is a series of talks intended for children on topics such as cities and the family, but also contains such poems as "Great, Wide, Beautiful, Wonderful World." *Lilliput Legends* (1872) is a collection of short stories, for example, "Prince Hydrangea," which mix fantasy and realism in ways sometimes reminiscent of George MacDonald. James Payn called Rands "the laureate of the nursery," and his works sometimes memorably capture the mind, the voice, and the imagination of a child.

DENNIS BUTTS

Rangachari, Devika (1969–), Indian writer of family fiction in which the worlds of school and home blend seamlessly. Rangachari explores the world of girls in greater detail than any other Indian author. Girls from affluent, educated backgrounds seek success measured by good academic performance and general good behavior. Home represents and defines the protagonist's very character. Radhika in *Growing Up* (2000) is appreciated because she overcomes the challenge of a poor background, while Mala is excused of her sins because of her parents. Rangachari's three books chart the growth of the characters (and in that sense may qualify as Bildungsroman). A new person—Anu in *Company for Manisha* (1999), Patti in *When Amma Went Away* (2002)—is often the catalyst of the growth, forcing the girls to revise attitudes and opinions.

[*See also* Girls' Books and Fiction *and* India.]

NANDINI NAYAR

Rankin, Joan (1940–), South African author and artist. Trained in fiber and ceramic arts as well as illustration, Rankin has created or contributed to over two dozen picture books since entering the field in 1986, winning the 1991 Katrine Harries Award (a biennial South African illustration prize). Characterized by soft colors and expressive typography, Rankin's humorous stories often feature anthropomorphized animals coping with traumas such as the first day of school. Her titles include *The Little Cat and the Greedy Old Woman* (1995) and *Wow! It's Great Being a Duck* (1998), as well as Karma Wilson's *A Frog in the Bog* (2003).

[*See also* Africa: Southern Africa; Anthropomorphism; Illustrations; *and* Picture Books.]

PEGGY LIN DUTHIE

Rankin, Laura (1953–), American illustrator and author of children's picture books. Rankin grew up in western New York and earned a BA in speech and drama at the University of New Hampshire. Subsequently she worked as a courtroom illustrator for a television station in Buffalo, and from 1977 to 1992 she was an editorial artist for the *Buffalo News*. Rankin has written and illustrated such titles as *The Handmade Alphabet* (1991) and *The Handmade Counting Book* (1998), which use American Sign Language, and she has also illustrated texts for other writers, such as *The Fabulous Fish From Lake Wiggawalla* (1991) by Teddy Slater and *The Wriggly, Wriggly Baby* (2002) by Jessica Clark. Critics have described Rankin's illustrations as expressive and magnificently detailed; in fact, the detail makes many of her picture books just as appropriate for preschoolers as for middle-grade readers and young adults.

[*See also* ABC Books or Alphabet Books; Counting Books; Illustrations; *and* Picture Books.]

MICHELLE H. MARTIN

Ransome, Arthur (1884–1967), English novelist. Arthur Mitchell Ransome is a major figure in the history of British children's literature; more than any other writer, he established a successful mode of direct address to his child readers, and he did much to invent the "holiday story." His twelve Swallows and Amazons novels are suffused with codes of behavior and intertextual awareness that hark back to the 19th century, but his plotting, his character drawing, and his attitudes to children and society are thoroughly modern and were highly influential.

Arthur Ransome.

Ransome was the son of a professor of history at what is now the University of Leeds, and he spent his childhood holidays in the English Lake District. His schooldays were unhappy, partly because of undiagnosed nearsightedness, and when he was seventeen he moved to London to work for the publisher Grant Richards. His early books, some of which he later disowned, were on any subject that would sell; some, like *The Souls of the Streets* (1904), copy the fashionable neo-paganism of the *Yellow Book* writers and Kenneth Grahame; *The Elixir of Life* (1915) is a novel in the manner of Poe; *The History of Storytelling* (1909) ventures into literary theory and criticism. These early years are described in Ransome's romanticized *Bohemia in London* (1907).

In 1913, after a traumatic libel action against him by Lord Alfred Douglas had failed, and to escape an unhappy marriage, Ransome went to St. Petersburg, where he learned Russian and studied folk tales. The resulting book, *Old Peter's Russian Tales* (1916), remains a classic. From 1915 to 1924 Ransome worked as a reporter, covering the Russian Revolution for the *Daily News* and then the *Manchester Guardian*. He was sympathetic to the Bolsheviks to the extent that the British Foreign Office considered trying him for treason; it is unclear whether he was manipulated by the Russians or worked for the British secret service. His *Six Weeks in Russia in 1919* (1919) is a vivid and compassionate account of the condition of the country. In the early 1920s Ransome lived with his new partner, Evgenia Shelepin (who had been Trotsky's secretary), in Estonia and published an account of building and sailing his "perfect" yacht, *Racundra's First Cruise*, in 1923. He worked for the *Manchester Guardian* as a foreign correspondent and fishing columnist until 1929, when he resigned and moved to the Lake District to become a full-time writer. His years as a journalist had honed his style to one of verb-centered economy.

Swallows and Amazons (1930) and its sequel, *Swallowdale* (1931), had a minor initial success, but the series became popular both in Britain and America with the pastiche of *Treasure Island*, *Peter Duck* (1932). The success of the series, which ended with *Great Northern?* in 1947, enabled Ransome to devote much of the rest of his life to fishing and sailing. The series is distinctive primarily because Ransome solved the problem of the tone of address for children's books. Perhaps because he felt that an interest in certain activities—sailing, fishing, camping—and valuing certain codes of conduct and certain places erased surface differences of gender, class or age, he was able to speak to his readers as peers. As he observed in 1937: "You write not *for* children but for yourself, and if, by good fortune, children enjoy what you enjoy, why then you are a writer of children's books." He also illustrated his books in a simple style, insisting on technical accuracy in practical details.

The books provide a secure background for their child characters' serious play, which is often based on their reading of fiction. Five of the books—the first two plus *Winter Holiday* (1933), *Pigeon Post* (1936), and *The Picts and the Martyrs* (1943)—are set in a fictionalized version of the Lake District and concern two or three family groups of children sailing, camping, fishing, prospecting, signaling, and at their most adventurous, rescuing a cragfast sheep or being involved peripherally in a fell fire. They do nothing that well-disciplined children could not be expected to achieve, and they live by carefully defined codes of conduct. Their apparent freedom is engineered by the adults: as in many 19th-century books, the mothers stand in for absent fathers but are ultimately responsible to them. There is much practical advice and little emotional life, but the characters do grow and mature across the series, so that even the slow-paced *Secret Water* (1939), ostensibly about children exploring Suffolk backwaters, has undercurrents of the tensions of developing adolescence.

Ransome's masterpiece is often considered to be *We Didn't Mean to Go to Sea* (1937), in which four children drift out into the North Sea in a yacht in a fog, and by dint of skills, teamwork, and mutual support, sail safely to Holland. The book is based on folk tale patterns: the first half is about the children learning survival skills, and the second about applying them. Ransome's knowledge of narrative structures and their appropriateness to developing readers can be seen across the whole series: *Swallows and Amazons* has a very strong structural closure, *Great Northern?* none at all. The series also includes a respected detective novel, *The Big Six* (1940), and a fanciful adventure story that uses Ransome's experience as a correspondent in China, *Missee Lee* (1941).

Ransome's last book is *Mainly About Fishing* (1959), but two collections of short pieces and fragments have been published since his death: *The War of the Birds and the Beasts* (1984) and *Coots in the North and Other Stories* (1988). The extensive archive of his papers at the University of Leeds is still yielding new materials: *Racundra's Third Cruise*, edited by Brian Hammett, appeared in 2002. The Arthur Ransome Society (formed in 1990) produces journals, newsletters, and an annual subscription volume.

BIBLIOGRAPHY

Brogan, Hugh. *The Life of Arthur Ransome*. London: Cape, 1984.

Hammond, Wayne G. *Arthur Ransome. A Bibliography*. Winchester, U.K.: St. Paul's Biographies; New Castle, Del.: Oak Knoll, 2000.

Hunt, Peter. *Arthur Ransome*. Boston: Twayne, 1991; rev. ed., *Approaching Arthur Ransome*, London: Cape, 1992.
Wardale, Roger. *Arthur Ransome and the World of Swallows and Amazons*. Skipton, U.K.: Great Northern, 2000.

PETER HUNT

Ransome, James (1961–), African American illustrator who was born in North Carolina and educated at the Pratt Institute in New York. Influenced by artists such as Mary Cassatt and Winslow Homer and usually working in oils, Ransome illustrates with rich, vibrant colors, a realistic style, and characters often modeled on people he knows. His variations in style are carefully designed to make each book unique. Ransome has illustrated works by many authors and is especially well known for assignments connected with African American culture, such as Angela Johnson's *Do Like Kyla* (1990), Deborah Hopkinson's *Sweet Clara and the Freedom Quilt* (1993), J. J. Reneaux's *How Animals Saved the People: Animal Tales From the South* (2001), and Jacqueline Woodson's *Visiting Day* (2002). In addition, Ransome has collaborated with his wife, Lesa Cline-Ransome, illustrating such titles as *Satchel Paige* (2000), *Quilt Counting* (2002), and *Major Taylor, Champion Cyclist* (2004). Winner of the Coretta Scott King Award for his illustrations in James Weldon Johnson's *The Creation* (1994), and recipient of a Coretta Scott King Honor Award for illustrating Margaree King Mitchell's *Uncle Jed's Barbershop* (1993), Ransome has also designed young adult book covers and produced murals for buildings, including the mural for the Children's Museum in Indianapolis.

[*See also* African American Literature; Illustrations; *and biographies of figures mentioned in this article.*]

ADRIENNE E. GAVIN

Rameshwar Rao, Shanta (1924–), Indian writer of myths, legends, folk tales, short stories, and picture books for children. Rameshwar Rao has retold tales from Indian scriptures and reworked folk tales and myths from little-known tribal communities and far-flung areas of India. In *Tales of Ancient India* (1960) she retells original stories like "How the Stork Got Its Long Neck" and "Why Snakes Have Forked Tongues." *Children's Mahabharata* (1968) and *In Worship of Shiva* (1998), drawn from Hindu myth and scripture, have demons, gods, and humans as characters. Rameshwar Rao treats religious icons in a secular fashion: gods are shown as capable of failings and weaknesses, demons achieve near-divinity via meditation and prayer, and humans share the characteristics of both. Rameshwar Rao draws on India's rich mythological heritage in her work. She stresses the importance of wise action and compassion in opposition to good intentions and social status. In *Seethu* (1980) she uses a doll that comes to life to comment on the problems that wealth and class pose in a society that sets great store by these things. In *Matsya* (1985) and *Bekanna and the Musical Mice* (2000) Rameshwar Rao continues to present protagonists who succeed owing to well thought out, decisive action.

[*See also* Fairy Tales and Folk Tales; India; *and* Myths.]

ANNA KURIAN

Rapunzel. The tale known as "Rapunzel" was first published in German in the Grimm brothers' *Kinder- und Hausmärchen* (1812–1815, 1822; English trans., *Children's and Household Tales*, 1909). This fairy tale depicts the struggles of a pregnant woman who craves a type of lettuce (rapunzel) growing in her neighbor's enclosed garden. She persuades her husband to steal some of the plant, but the couple pays dearly for this transgression when the husband promises to give their child to the garden's owner, an old witch. When the child, named Rapunzel, turns twelve, the witch locks her up in a tower in the woods and visits her by climbing her long hair. When the witch discovers that a prince has been visiting Rapunzel, harsh punishment befalls the girl (banishment to a desert) and the prince (blindness). After many years of wandering, the lovers eventually find each other, Rapunzel's tears restore the prince's sight, and the couple live happily ever after.

The roots of the Rapunzel tale can be traced back to oral and literary sources. The earliest known literary tale, "Petrosinella," was included in Giambattista Basile's collection *Il Pentamerone*, published in a Neapolitan dialect in 1634. This collection was known and admired by the Brothers Grimm. The name Petrosinella is related to the Neapolitan word for parsley, the plant the woman craves in this version. The French tale "Persinette" (1697), by Charlotte-Rose de Caumont La Force, was inspired by "Petrosinella" but also shares some characteristics with the Grimms' version. In recent years Diane Stanley illustrated a translation of the Neapolitan tale (*Petrosinella*, 1981) and later used these same illustrations in her own simpler retelling of the tale published in 1995.

The Grimms' version of the tale has frequently been illustrated and adapted in the United States. The Caldecott

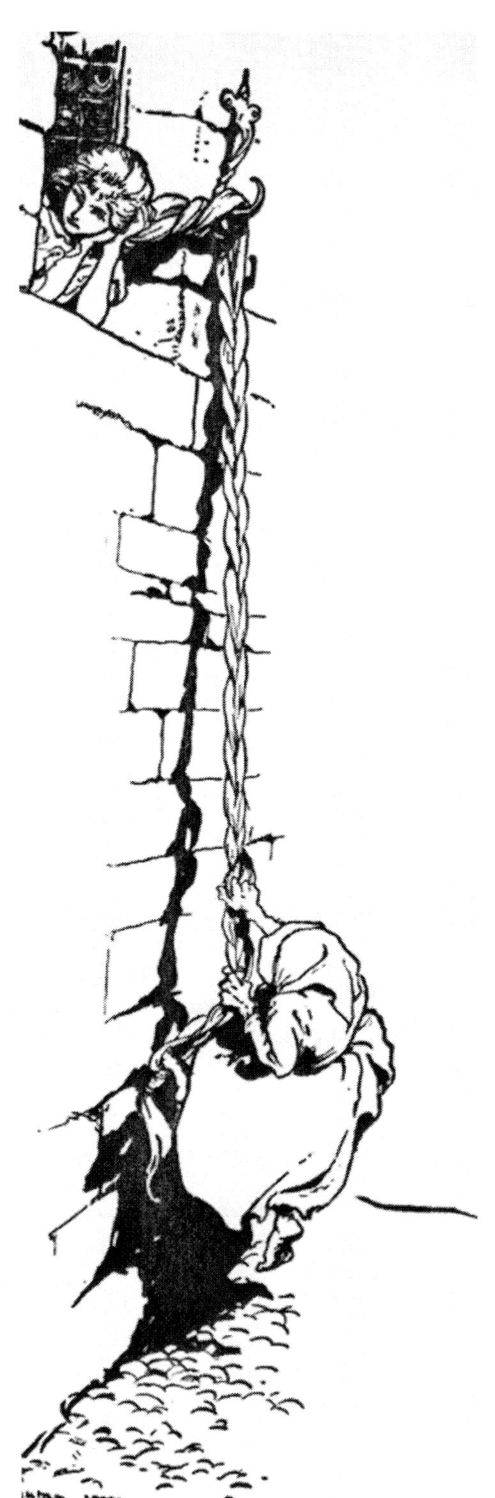

Rapunzel. The witch climbs the tower; illustration by Arthur Rackham from *Fairy Tales of the Brothers Grimm*, translated by Mrs. Edgar Lucas (London: Archibald & Co., 1909). COLLECTION OF JACK ZIPES

Award-winning picture book by Paul O. Zelinsky (1997) is especially notable, with its allusions to the Italian landscape and Renaissance art hinting at the tale's earlier Italian origins. *Zel* (1996), a novel-length expansion of the tale by Donna Jo Napoli, explores psychological issues such as adolescent isolation, the mother-daughter relationship, and forbidden love.

BIBLIOGRAPHY

Getty, Laura. "Maidens and Their Guardians: Reinterpreting the 'Rapunzel' Tale." *Mosaic* 30, no. 2 (June 1997): 37–52.

Hendrickson, Linnea. "The View from Rapunzel's Tower." *Children's Literature in Education* 31, no. 4 (December 2000): 209–223.

NATALIE ZIARNIK

Raschka, Chris (1959–), American author and illustrator. Raschka's bold, distinctive style and attention to design are constants throughout his body of texts and illustrations. The first picture book that he wrote and illustrated burst out of the biography genre, as *Charlie Parker Played Be Bop* (1992) presented the music of the jazz saxophone great through textual and visual rhythm, rather than standard biographical information. 1993's *Yo! Yes*—a monosyllabic yet vibrant conversation between two little boys, one black, one white—was a Caldecott Honor Book. 2000's *Ring! Yo?* continues the boys' dialogue, and 1999's *Like Likes Like* anthropomorphizes the books' similar themes of alienation, loneliness, and friendship. *Arlene Sardine* (1998), a book controversial in its straightforward portrayal of death, also presents the wills and desires of animals combined with an environmental message, as the title character's dream of becoming a sardine is fulfilled. Raschka is not afraid of color, either in his explosively vibrant picture book art or as an exploration of racial dynamics, and his works—including Margaret Wise Brown's posthumously published *Another Important Book* (1999)—consistently feature a multicultural cast of children. He has twice teamed with African American feminist writer and pioneer bell hooks to illustrate celebratory tales of African heritage and childhood (1999's *Happy to Be Nappy* and 2002's *Be Boy Buzz*). In 2001 Raschka collaborated with fellow author/illustrator Vladimir Radunsky for the mixed-media extravaganza *Table Manners*. Also in 2001 Raschka paired with compiler Paul Janeczko on *A Poke in the I: A Collection of Concrete Poems*. This groundbreaking title introduced a new generation of readers to concrete poetry while incorporating every element of illustration associated with Raschka: color, music, rhythm, energy,

Chris Raschka. Cover of *Arlene Sardine* (New York: Orchard Books, c. 1998). COLLECTION OF ANDREA IMMEL

mixed media, and seamless design to create an end product of seemingly carefree exuberance.

[*See also* Brown, Margaret Wise *and* Janeczko, Paul.]

ELISSA GERSHOWITZ

Raskin, Ellen (1928–1984), American author and illustrator. Raskin began her career in children's literature as a graphic artist, having previously designed and illustrated over a thousand book covers. Before writing her own stories, she illustrated a wide array of picture books. The first picture book she both wrote and illustrated was 1966's *Nothing Ever Happens on My Block*. In 1971 she published her first novel, *The Mysterious Disappearance of Leon (I Mean Noel)*, a story that set the precedent for her trademark blend of unique characters, imagination, humor, wordplay, puzzles, and mystery. Her 1974 title *Figgs and Phantoms*, the story of an extremely quirky family, won a Newbery honor, and the next year *The Tattooed Potato and Other Clues* won the Mystery Writers of America's Edgar Allan Poe Special Award.

In 1978 Raskin's *The Westing Game* was published. This book, set against the backdrop of Lake Michigan in Raskin's hometown of Milwaukee, Wisconsin, defies genre, as an atmospheric mystery full of humor and pathos. Its cast of characters is strongly drawn, their relationships reflecting social hierarchies, stereotypes, and prejudices. *The Westing Game* won the Boston Globe–Horn Book Award and the Newbery Medal. It was Raskin's last book.

ELISSA GERSHOWITZ

Rasmussen, Halfdan (1915–2002), Danish writer and poet, famous for his socially committed poetry. Beginning in the 1960s, Rasmussen wrote primarily for children, following the tradition of Nordic modernistic children's verse, represented in Sweden by Lennart Hellsing and in Norway by Inger Hagerup. He collected Danish folk and nursery rhymes, but mainly wrote his own nonsense verse, published in numerous collections, most of which were illustrated by Ib Spang Olsen. In Denmark his verses are appreciated by children as well as adults, and he was known as "the master of the rhyme." A selection is available in English as *Halfdan's Nonsense and Nursery Rhymes* (1973), illustrated by three leading Danish artists. Some of his rhymes, such as *Halfdan's ABC* (1967) or *Tante Andante* (1985), have been made into picture books. Many verses were set to music and became popular children's songs.

MARIA NIKOLAJEVA

Rathmann, Peggy (1953–), American illustrator and author of picture books that underscore the importance of visual images in the unfolding of a plot. A typical Rathmann work is the sparsely texted *Good Night, Gorilla* (1994), which relies on the illustrations to convey the action of the story as the zoo's expressive-faced animals secretly follow the zookeeper home after his nightly rounds and then settle down for the night in his bedroom. In 1996 Rathmann, born Margaret Crosby, won the Caldecott Medal for *Officer Buckle and Gloria* (1995), in which Officer Buckle's poker-faced safety lectures are hilariously interpreted in the illustrations by his canine partner, Gloria. *10 Minutes till Bedtime* (1998) again entices young viewers to share the illustrative joke, with a cavalcade of hamster tourists streaming through a boy's house at bedtime. The notion of the child audience's inclusion in a humorous secret recurs throughout Rathmann's work, making her lively images all the more appealing.

[*See also* Animal Stories *and* Picture Books.]

DEBRA MITTS-SMITH

Raverat, Gwendolen Mary (1885–1957), English wood engraver and pen-and-ink illustrator, born in Cambridge, educated at home and boarding school. She wrote

Period Piece (1952), an autobiography of her Victorian Cambridge childhood; illustrated the work of Hans Christian Andersen, Walter de la Mare, and others and the reprinted editions of Elizabeth Anna Hart's *The Runaway* (1936) and Charlotte Yonge's *Countess Kate* (1947). Her work shows a nostalgic zest for place, as in her description of her grandfather Charles Darwin's veranda: "I adored those pebbles. I mean literally, adored, worshipped. This kind of feeling is probably the most important thing in life." Her passion for accurate observation is defined in the black-and-white small scale of her art. After suffering a stroke, she smothered her terminally ill husband and committed suicide.

BIBLIOGRAPHY

Raverat, Gwen. *Period Piece*. London: Faber & Faber, 1952.
Spalding, Frances. *Gwen Raverat: Friends, Family and Affections*. London: Harvill Press, 2001.

MARY SEBAG-MONTEFIORE

Rawlings, Marjorie Kinnan (1896–1953), American author primarily of works for adults, including novels, autobiographical essays, short stories, a cookbook, and poetry. *The Yearling* (1938) is her only major contribution to the field of children's literature, but it is one of the American classics in the field and was the 1939 Pulitzer Prize winner. Rawlings was interested in writing from childhood and published a prizewinning story in the *Washington Post* at age eleven. She graduated from the University of Wisconsin in 1918 and worked for nine years as a journalist in Rochester, New York. She also wrote short stories but failed to find a publisher for them. After a trip to Florida in 1928, Rawlings purchased a seventy-two-acre farm and orange grove called Cross Creek in the scrub country of the northern part of the state. The transition to Florida reinvigorated her writing. She sold her first short story, a series of sketches called "Cracker Chidlings: Real Tales from the Florida Interior," to *Scribner's Magazine* in 1930. To her great fortune, her work caught the eye of the Scribner's editor Maxwell Perkins.

Marjorie Kinnan Rawlings.

The success of Rawlings's work is due in large part to her portrayal of the crackers and the landscape of northern Florida. The term "cracker" derives from the sound of the whips the frontier folk of the region used to drive cattle to the ports. Although frequently discussed as a regional writer, she loathed being labeled as such. In her adult works, her portrayal of the relationships between the black and white members of the community is ahead of her time, but in many ways is no longer appealing to modern readers for whom her affectionate, but nonetheless still somewhat condescending, tone is at best awkward.

The Yearling is the novel that both made and sustains Rawlings's reputation. The book grew out of a suggestion made by Perkins, but as it developed Rawlings decided that it was not going to be a book for boys after all; instead it would be a book about a boy, and it was marketed as adult fiction. The story follows a year in the life of Jody, a lonely eleven-year-old living on a north Florida subsistence farm with his parents Penny and Ora Baxter. After a fawn called Flag becomes his pet, Jody finds a new level of joy to temper the many dangers and deaths that haunt his life. After Flag destroys the family's crop, however, the fawn must be shot. Jody's initial despair and then painful acceptance of the harsh realities of life marks his shift toward unsentimental maturity. In 1946 the book was made into a film.

Rawlings's only other book for children is the posthumously published picture book *The Secret River* (1955). In this slight tale Calpurnia discovers a river rich with fish that enables her to provide food for her family during a difficult period, but she is never again able to find it. Most critics have found illustrator Leonard Wiesgard's pictures more notable than the story. Rawlings's most popular adult works include *South under Moon* (1933) and *Cross Creek* (1942).

[*See also* Animal Stories.]

BIBLIOGRAPHY

Bellman, Samuel I. *Marjorie Kinnan Rawlings*. New York: Twayne, 1974.

Silverthorne, Elizabeth. *Marjorie Kinnan Rawlings: Sojourner at Cross Creek.* Woodstock, N.Y.: Overlook, 1988.

MEGAN LYNN ISAAC

Rawlins, Donna (1956–), Australian artist, designer, illustrator, and printmaker. Her vigorous illustrations express the multicultural nature of modern Australia. *My Place* (1987), by Nadia Wheatley, traces the changing landscape and population of Australia back to Aboriginal times through its exploration of a Sydney Harbour setting. It won the 1988 CBCA Book of the Year Award: Younger Readers. In *Digging to China* (1988) Alexis tries to unearth a birthday present, and the hole he makes becomes a pathway for two Chinese children. *The Kinder Hat* (1985) and *Tucking Mummy In* (1987), both by Morag Loh, are witty picture books for preschool children about small incidents in happy families. *My Dearest Dinosaur* (1992), by Margaret Wild, a series of letters from a mother dinosaur to her missing mate, is enriched with lush illustrations, adding poignancy to the story. Rawlins's spirited and spare illustrations to Simon French's *Guess the Baby* (2002) present a cheerful and supportive classroom.

[*See also* Australia; Illustrations; Multiculturalism and Children's Books; Picture Books; *and biographies of figures mentioned in this article.*]

STELLA LEES AND PAM MACINTYRE

Rawls, Wilson (1913–1984), American writer of two coming-of-age novels, *Where the Red Fern Grows* (1961) and *Summer of the Monkeys* (1976). Part Cherokee, Rawls was raised on a farm in northeastern Oklahoma where he and his siblings were instructed in reading and writing by their mother. Later, he divided his time between working to support himself and his family and writing on every available scrap of paper. Eventually he completed five novels, which he later burned because he was ashamed of the poor mechanics of his writing. With his wife's help as editor, he rewrote one of his novels as the mainly autobiographical *Red Fern.* The story of Billy Colman and the lives and deaths of his two hounds is a classic tale of love, friendship, and devotion, much in the tradition of *Old Yeller* (1956). Both this novel and the completely fictional *Monkeys* have received numerous awards and critical acclaim, and have been adapted as motion pictures.

[*See also* Animal Stories *and* Young Adult Literature.]

KATHERINE M. ADAMS

Ray, Deborah Kogan (1940–), American author and illustrator of more than sixty children's books; also well-known as a painter, with some books published under the name Deborah Ray. Some of Ray's illustrations have been done in soft black-and-white pencil, others in luminous watercolors. Books by other writers that she has illustrated include Jeanne Whitehouse Peterson's *I Have a Sister, My Sister Is Deaf* (1977), also adapted for Reading Rainbow, Patricia MacLachlan's *Through Grandpa's Eyes* (1980), and two poems by E. E. Cummings, *Little Tree* (1987) and *Hist Whist* (1989), which was praised for its haunting illustrations. Ray's own books include *My Dog, Trip* (1987) and *My Daddy Was a Soldier* (1990). She has also written and illustrated two picture book biographies, *Hokusai* (2001), about the famed Japanese printmaker, and *The Flower Hunter* (2004), about the American naturalist William Bartram. Nature has always been one of Ray's strong interests and figures prominently in many of her books.

[*See also* Illustrations; Picture Books; *and biographies of figures mentioned in this article.*]

LINNEA HENDRICKSON

Ray, Jane (1960–), British illustrator and artist, with an instantly recognizable style. Her illustrations, with their variety of painting techniques including the use of collage and printed fragments, display jewel-like color and glisten with decorative accents in gold; characters are portrayed with stylized features and poses. She is well known for her interpretations of literary fairy tales, biblical stories, and operas: these include a spirited version of *The Twelve Dancing Princesses* (1996), *Noah's Ark* (1991), and *The Story of Creation* (1992), which won the Smarties Book Prize. She wrote the text for her own *Can You Catch a Mermaid?* (2002).

JANE DOONAN

Ray, Sukumar (1887–1923), Indian writer, playwright, poet, and illustrator, father of the filmmaker Satyajit Ray. Ray made a special place for himself when he introduced nonsense verses for the first time in Bengali literature. Until then there had been no unmitigated fun free from malice in Bengali. His poems first appeared in *Sandesh*, a children's magazine started by his father Upendrakishore, from 1914 onward. Ray himself edited *Sandesh* (Sweetmeat) from 1915 to 1923 and wrote for it many of the stories, poems, plays, and essays that make up the bulk of his writing. Many of these poems, compiled later, resulted in his famous collection *Abol-Tabol* (Rhyme without Reason) published in 1923, nine days after his death. It contains lasting creations such as the "Lug-headed Loon," "Pumpkin Puff," and "Grifonling." His other works include *Heshoramer Diary* (Heshoram's Diary), a spoof on Arthur Conan Doyle's Professor Challenger; *Pagla Dashu* (Crazy Dashu), a collection of hilarious stories; *Jhalapala* (Cacophony), a collection of plays; and *Haja-ba-ra-la* (A Topsy-turvy Tale), considered one of the finest pieces of nonsense in Bengali prose. Ray was influenced by Edward Lear and Lewis Carroll. But unlike the figures in "Jabberwocky," Ray's creations belong to our everyday world, funny but recognizable. Ray illustrated his work himself; his illustrations are considered brilliant even though he had no formal training in art.

[*See also* India; Nonsense; *and biographies of figures mentioned in this article.*]

SWAPNA DUTTA

Rayner, Mary (1933–), British author and illustrator known for her picture books about Mr. and Mrs. Pig and their ten piglets. *Mr. and Mrs. Pig's Evening Out* (1976) displays the parents' carelessness in employing Mrs. Wolf—clearly an unsuitable babysitter—and the young pigs' resourcefulness in foiling her greedy plans. Rayner's many successful sequels about the young piglets show increasingly well-defined characterizations, especially in the personality of Garth. Throughout the series Rayner takes an entertaining look at some of the familiar issues of the preschool years, for example, fussy eating habits in *Mrs. Pig's Bulk Buy* (1981). She also developed a recognizable painterly style that was sought after for covers in the 1990s, as when she produced new dust jackets for Dick King-Smith's titles, such as *The Sheep-Pig* (1983). Her versatility as a writer is seen in her novel for adolescents, *The Witch-Finder* (1975), and one about a highly observant cat, *Reilly* (1987).

[*See also* King-Smith, Dick *and* Picture Books.]

JULIA ECCLESHARE

Reading Schemes. Sets of books mass produced at reasonable cost per text so multiple copies can be acquired for classroom use are called reading schemes. Their stories of Dick and Jane or Janet and John (to cite examples from the 1950s and 1960s) are designed to support readers in school settings to develop their reading skills. Terms used for individual texts include readers, primers, and basal readers. They are characterized by controlled vocabulary that often leads to stilted or unnatural use of language, whereby meaning suffers because of the need to conform to predetermined reading levels, a limited range of interesting and varied syntactical structures, and simplistic illustrations. The page layout is conventional so that written text moves systematically from top to bottom, left to right, and for early readers such books often use only one sentence per line. Historically, as education became available to a larger percentage of the population, these texts were deemed necessary because books were expensive and not common in most households. There was little variety, with a set text being allocated per term per grade. The quality of paper was poor, covers were often soft cloth, and illustration was minimal.

Production of such materials has now become a profitable area of commercial publishing. Readers are only one part of a package that may include a large range of different readers, organized by levels, content, themes and genre. These are, in turn, supported by extensive teacher handbooks that include notes on the overall organization of the scheme, background information on the reading theories which underpin the scheme, teaching ideas and plans as well as books of reproducible black line masters with activities and exercises, wall charts, audio tapes, and computer-related materials.

The reading theory and methodology around which schemes are constructed are dependent on what is currently in favor within both educational and political circles. Early theories corresponded to a "bottom-up" approach to reading that focused on isolating letters and words and a systematic approach to phonics. During the 1970s "top-down" theories placed a strong focus on the "meaning-making" process, cueing systems and predicting and confirming meaning. Interactive or transactive theories recognize the role of social purpose in reading and require the explicit teaching of skills in a contextualized manner. It could be argued that in terms of cycles, because of political imperatives, many educational systems are reverting to a bottom-up approach, as reflected in the newer schemes now available. Although the ways in which readers are used within classrooms vary considerably, their use often means that children are restricted to working with these texts and are expected to work through them sequentially, regardless of how well they correlate to their reading ability.

The value of reading schemes in teaching reading is highly contested by many educators who argue that "real" literature—works by well-known children's authors and illustrators such as Cynthia Voigt, Katherine Paterson, Margaret Mahy, Gary Paulsen, Maurice Sendak, John Burningham, Anthony Browne, Bob Graham, and Raymond Briggs—is of far more benefit to children because it gives them access to more interesting materials, better-quality models of language with which to work, and greater access to extensive vocabularies and contexts for understanding them.

SUSAN CLANCY

Realism. Realistic literature seeks to offer an adequate, truthful representation of reality. The term "realism" is used to describe both content and style. The suggestion of an authentic mimetic representation can be supported, as John Stephens argues, by "conventions which affirm the text's veracity," such as a first-person narrator, the present tense, and the use of slang, or "by avoiding discoursal elements which foreground its literariness," such as ambiguity and figurative language (*Language and Ideology*, p. 251).

In adult literature, realism was the popular mode in the mid-19th century. Novels such as Louisa May Alcott's *Little Women* (1868) and Hector Malot's *Sans famille* (1878; English trans., *The Adventures of Remi*) have become classics of children's literature that address the harsher aspects of everyday life, such as poverty and death. Noel Streatfeild's *Ballet Shoes* (1936) and Eve Garnett's *The Family from One End Street* (1937) are two early-20th-century realistic novels that deal with social problems. Especially since the 1970s, a remarkable increase in the number of realistic fictions for the young can be noticed in most Western countries (also called new realism or neorealism). Opinions of what constitutes a truthful representation of reality inevitably differ: realistic fiction, as all fiction, cannot avoid being subjective, selective, and ideological.

Different degrees of realism have been discerned, and the realistic novel has several subtypes. For preschool children, the everyday-life story is its most common form, mixing both happy and unhappy events that are familiar to many children (such as a visit to the dentist, a birthday party, or the death of a pet). For older readers, the genre of realistic fiction is often considered synonymous with social critical literature and the problem book. The issues addressed concern both the life of the individual child/adolescent (including child abuse, divorce, and bullying in the works of, for instance, Anne Fine or Jacqueline Wilson) or they may affect the whole of society or even the world (such as ecological problems, war, and racism, in the works of, for instance, Beverly Naidoo). Some realistic fiction for older readers has documentary value, describing historical events or social problems with numerous accurate details. Dagmar Grenz notices an evolution in German children's literature after the 1970s from the "outward depiction of the world" to books that "discover the reality of the human inner self" ("Realist Stories for Children," p. 142): this shift toward the realistic psychological novel is by no means limited to the German context. The evolution frequently entails an increasing complexity in narrative techniques, as illustrated in the works of the British writer Aidan Chambers, the Swedish writer Peter Pohl, and the Belgian writer Bart Moeyaert.

The terms "hyperrealism," "ultrarealism," and "hard" or "harsh" realism denote novels that depict the darkest sides of (social) reality, often refraining from happy endings. Examples include the works of Melvin Burgess (U.K.), Peter Pohl, and Gudrun Pausewang (Germany). The desirable degree of realism in a children's book is debatable, and some topics still remain sensitive; for instance, detailed and realistic representations of the horrors of the Holocaust. Some critics argue that childhood should be carefree, and that children will soon enough learn about the harsher sides of reality—there is no need to confront them with it in literature. Defendants of hard realism argue that children encounter these problems in real life, and literature can make them aware of certain issues and offer them possible models to deal with the problems.

[*See also* Historical Fiction; Young Adult Literature; *and biographies of figures mentioned in this article.*]

BIBLIOGRAPHY

Grenz, Dagmar. "Realistic Stories for Children in the Federal Republic of Germany, 1970–1994: Features and Tendencies." In *Reflections of Change: Children's Literature Since 1945*, edited by Sandra Beckett, 141–151. Westport, Conn.: Greenwood, 1997.

Stephens, John. *Language and Ideology in Children's Fiction*. London: Longman, 1992.

VANESSA JOOSEN

Rebecca of Sunnybrook Farm. *See* Wiggin, Kate Douglas.

Recheis, Käthe (1928–), Austrian author who writes in the tradition of educational storytelling and social involvement. Her novel *Das Schattennetz* (The Shadow Net, 1964) tells the story of a survivor of a Nazi concentration camp. Recheis depicts the psychological suffering caused by the

Holocaust and touches on areas that had long been taboo. Reicheis was one of the first Austrian writers following World War II to treat the crimes committed by the Nazi regime. Later works by Recheis were also about dealing with the past, such as *Lena, unser Dorf, und der Krieg* (Lena, Our Village, and the War, 1987). In addition to examining her own history, Recheis became known for her depiction of Native American culture for a German public. Numerous short stories and novels, including *Kleiner Adler und Silberstern* (Little Eagle and Silver Star, 1961) and *Kleiner Bruder Watomi* (Little Brother Watomi, 1974), tell realistic stories about the history of Native Americans and often focus on loners and outsiders. Through social action the protagonists mature and find their place in society. Characteristic of Recheis's stories is a great emphasis on the representation of nature and on one's connection to nature, as in *Kleiner Waschbär weiß alles besser* (1999; English trans., *Little Raccoon Always Knows Best*, 2002). Recheis has also collected and edited fairy tales, myths, and sagas such as *Sagen aus Österreich* (Legends from Austria, 2001) and *König Arthur und die Ritter der Tafelrunde* (King Arthur and the Knights of the Round Table, 1974). She also wrote her own stories in this genre: *Die Wolfssaga* (The Wolf Saga, 1994) and *Der weisse Wolf* (The White Wolf, 1982).

[*See also* Austria; Collections; Holocaust Literature for Children; *and* Native American Children's Literature.]

Caroline Roeder

Red Fox. *See* Roberts, Charles.

Red Shoes, The. *See* Andersen, Hans Christian.

Redwall Series. *See* Jacques, Brian.

Reed, Talbot Baines (1852–1893), British writer of boys' fiction who, through influential works such as *The Fifth Form at St. Dominics* (serialized in the *Boy's Own Paper*, 1881–1882) and his stories about Parkhurst School, helped popularize and establish the conventions of the school story as a genre, largely by turning away from piety and providing strong plots. Reed himself was not educated at the kind of boarding school in which he sets his stories, but he sympathized with their purported ethos (many failed to live up to this rhetoric) of combining sports, religion, duty, and national pride. His characters are often excellent athletes, like Jim Halliday, one of the young men whose story is told in *The Adventures of a Three-Guinea Watch* (1880). Jim is "a strapping youth," "a good bat, a famous boxer, a desperate man in a football scrimmage, and a splendid oar."

Although most of his stories are set in schools, Reed's characters share many of the qualities familiar from the more established genre of boys' adventure stories; this means that they are ready to stand up for the underdog and sort things out with their fists, and as well as being trained athletes, are notable for their pluck. Reed's stories depart from the conventions of adventure fiction in the range of characters they include: he often pairs a strong character with one who is deficient in some way, and not all of his characters thrive. Each is presented with a trial of character that usually both corrects minor faults and shows him (Reed's characters are invariably male) to be free from the taint of sneak, duffer, bully, or other of the ungentlemanly traits Reed detested and lampooned in a popular series for the *Boy's Own Paper*. Usually the weak-strong partnership plays an important role in the development of each boy's personality and integrity. An example of this is found in his final book, *Tom, Dick, and Harry* (1892), in which the well-intentioned but foolish and impressionable Tom is befriended by a variety of steady fellows whose efforts help him rise to the top of his class. In the process, Tom inadvertently galvanizes his schoolhouse, raising it from the worst in the school to the best. Although many of Reed's characters go through crises—often related to their struggle to conform to the ideal of masculinity in the Victorian setting—Reed's stories work through action rather than emotion: they contain little in the way of self-examination or inner reflection.

Many of Reed's stories first appeared in the *Boy's Own Paper*; his story "My First Football Match, by an Old Boy" appeared on the front page of its first number. He gave his copyrights to the Religious Tract Society, publishers of the *BOP*, for negligible sums to support their work. In addition to writing boys' fiction, Reed worked full-time in the family type-foundry and his *The History of Old English Letter Foundaries* (1887) became a standard work.

[*See also* Adventure Books; Boy's Own Paper, The; Boys' Books and Fiction; *and* School Stories.]

Kimberley Reynolds

Rees, David (1936–1993), British novelist and critic. His children's novels include work for a range of age groups, and many of them have their origins in autobiographical details. Rees's Irish roots serve as the basis for his historical novel *The Green Bough of Liberty* (1979), set in County Wicklow in 1798, while events in Ireland that followed the Easter rising and the civil war provide an important background for *Miss Duffy Is Still with Us* (1980). For most of his academic life he taught at the University of Exeter, a city that features in several works, including *The Exeter Blitz* (1978), a story of World War II, for which he was awarded the Carnegie Medal. Memories of the same war provided the inspiration for *The Missing German* (1976), set on the north Devon coast. His novels of gay adolescence, including *Quintin's Man* (1976), *In the Tent* (1979), and *The Milkman's On His Way* (1982), were among the first in Britain to deal with this particular theme. Rees also published three volumes of critical essays on children's literature, *The Marble in the Water* (1980), *Painted Desert: Green Shade* (1984), and *What Do Draculas Do?* (1990).

[*See also* Critical Approaches to Children's Literature; Gay and Lesbian Literature for Children; Historical Fiction; *and* Ireland.]

ROBERT DUNBAR

Rees, Leslie (1905–2000), Australian journalist, editor, and drama critic. Rees has written histories of Australian drama, and edited and written plays, travel books, and novels for children. His first books for children were a series about a tiny character, Digit Dick, in the tradition of Tom Thumb and the Gingerbread Boy, originally appearing in *Digit Dick on the Barrier Reef* (1942), illustrated by Walter Cunningham. Rees wrote twelve books about Australian animals, eight illustrated by Cunningham, beginning with *The Story of Shy the Platypus* (1944). *The Story of Karrawingi the Emu* (1946) won the inaugural CBCA Book of the Year Award in 1946. These books were a successful combination of accurate and detailed life cycles of personalized indigenous animals in stories of dramatic survivals. Rees's realistic adventure stories for older readers—*Quokka Island* (1951), illustrated by Arthur Horowicz and set on Rottnest Island; *Danger Patrol* (1954), set in New Guinea; and *Boy Lost on Tropic Coast* (1968), illustrated by Frank Beck and set in the Torres Strait—feature Dexter Hardy, a bush pilot who also appears in *Panic in the Cattle Country* (1974). Rees's autobiography is *Hold Fast to Dreams: Fifty Years in the Theatre, Radio, and Books* (1982).

[*See also* Animal Stories; Australia; *and* Cunningham, Walter.]

STELLA LEES AND PAM MACINTYRE

Reeves, James (1909–1978), British poet, playwright, novelist, educationist, critic, editor, anthologist, and broadcaster. A tireless ambassador for literature and imaginative language—poetry above all—Reeves insisted that young readers deserved the highest standards. Essential qualifications were "imagination, technique, and taste" (*How to Write Poems for Children*, 1971). After studying English at Cambridge, he served a twenty-year apprenticeship, writing for adults and teaching (1933–1952), publishing his first children's collection, *The Wandering Moon*, in 1950. From the enigmatic couplets of "Spells" to the swirl of "Miss Petal," Reeves practiced his precept that children needed surprise and variety—of mood, subject, emotional tone, and form. A self-declared romantic, he believed that poems open up magic, mystery, and wonder. Taking the imagination into strange regions ("Under Ground") or transfiguring a familiar scene ("The sea is a hungry dog"), such effects were best achieved, he argued, through precise, "matter-of-fact" approaches. Whereas, in Reeves's view, adult poetry explored the interior mind, Reeves's children's reported the outer world of the senses. Charged with ignoring town-bred children, Reeves explained that for him "poetry was in the country"; cities were "prose."

Perhaps because of his failing eyesight, Reeves often spoke of the appeal of aural subjects, creating his most vivid scenes through the ear: in *The Blackbird in the Lilac* (1952; the first book to be illustrated by his lifelong collaborator Edward Ardizzone), in his laconic "Cows," written for choral speaking, in the onomatopoeic to-and-fro of "The Grasshopper and the Bird," or in the chilling ballad "Pluto and Prosperine." Stimulating interest in words for their own sake, rhythmic and verbal effects remained a delight: whether in the alphabetic *Ragged Robin* sequence (1961), or in the collections of *Prefabulous Animiles* (1957, 1975). Embracing the sheer exuberance of nonsense, Reeves displays his master touch with neologism. He animates lurking creatures, neither scientific nor mythic—precursors of those who stalk the grounds in J. K. Rowling's Hogwarts: the "supercilious Nimp," "the fearful Hippocrump," afflicted with toothache, or the "aimless Doze," snuffling like a head cold and looking, in Ardizzone's illustrations, like an amiable groundhog.

Reeves's notable, scholarly retellings introduced a richly diverse literary heritage—from fables, Greek myth, and Bible stories to the Brothers Grimm (*The Cold Flame*, 1967; illustrated by Charles Keeping), Cervantes (1959), and Bunyan (1976). He edited *The Idiom of the People* (1958) from the manuscripts of the English folksong collector Cecil

Sharp, and folkloric traditions permeate his work, from *Pigeons and Princesses* (1956), to the unfortunate *Rhyming Will*, who speaks only in verse (1967). Viewing such stories as strongest when factual, not atmospheric, he emphasized action in longer fictions, too: the adventures in *Mulbridge Manor* (1958), and the literary fantasy *The Strange Light* (1964). In the lively picture book *Mr Horrox and the Gratch* (1969; illustrated by Quentin Blake), Reeves caricatured an artist's (his own?) old-fashioned pastoral preferences: "So far as London is concerned, cows are definitely out." Suspicious of inflated, "inspirational" platitudes, he articulated his passions and principles in clear, unpretentious guides. Books such as *Teaching Poetry* (1958), *Understanding Poetry* (1965), and his wide-ranging selections and anthologies influenced generations of readers in schools and beyond.

[*See also* Ardizzone, Edward; Blake, Quentin; Collections; Fairy Tales and Folk Tales; Nonsense; *and* Poetry.]

Pamela Knights

Rego, Paula (1935–), British painter and printmaker. Rego, of Portuguese birth, trained at London's Slade School in the 1950s. A leading figurative artist, she is best known for a series of pastels executed in the mid-1990s, many of them a subversive response to the films of Walt Disney, and for powerful and troubling illustrations in children's books. Rego spent her childhood in Portugal, where the twin repressions of Salazar's dictatorship and the Catholic Church, as well as an ambivalent relationship with her mother, instilled an awareness of the complex dynamics of control and domination. She often explores these themes in a domestic setting, using anthropomorphic images of animals to express emotional turmoil. While many of her works incorporate multiple characters and their narratives, she is most interested in the experiences of her robust and earthy women.

Rego is essentially a storyteller, drawing inspiration from diverse sources. In the 1970s she began to research fairy tales with the aid of a grant from the Gulbenkian Foundation. This work found expression in *Contos Populares Portugueses* (*Portuguese Folk Tales*, 1974–1975) and later in *Nursery Rhymes* (1989), a series of thirty-three aquatint etchings. Many of these images explore Rego's favorite themes of control and domination, as well as adolescent sexuality: "Baa Baa Black Sheep" becomes a huge ram embracing a young girl; an anthropomorphic spider makes a predatory approach to Little Miss Muffet. Similar preoccupations emerge in her illustrations for *Peter Pan* (1992), where Captain Hook's attentions to Wendy are distinctly unsettling. Disney cartoons provided the inspiration for Rego's Dancing Ostriches (1995), Pinocchio (1995–1996), and Snow White series (1995). However, these huge pastels on canvas are hardly fare for young children. Snow White's gaze is knowing, not timid. She expresses a Freudian attachment to her father and rivalry with her stepmother, and her pose as she lies poisoned hovers somewhere between agony and sexual ecstasy. For Rego, there are no happy endings.

Bibliography

McEwen, John. *Paula Rego*. London: Phaidon, 1992, 1997.

Nadia Crandall

Reid, Barbara (1957–), Canadian illustrator and author trained at the Ontario College of Art in Toronto, where she starting working with the children's modeling clay plasticine for a class project. Although she uses other media, such as inks and paints—as in her early books like Betty Waterton's *Mustard* (1983)—Reid is best known for her plasticine sculpture illustrations, which she began using for Edith Newlin Chase's *The New Baby Calf* (1984). Plasticine works well for children's picture book illustration as it creates a playful tone. Reid mixes her own colors and juxtaposes them to brighten or darken them. She builds her illustrations layer by layer, so they have depth, and uses a variety of tools to create the level of intricate detail for which she is famous. Sometimes she adds materials, such as glitter or silver paint, for effect; in *The Subway Mouse* (2003), she adds pieces of candy wrappers and graphite shavings as dirt to create a realistically grungy subway station. When she finishes a sculpture, her photographer husband photographs it under bright lights to highlight its three-dimensionality. *The Party* (1997)—a book that Reid also wrote and for which she earned the Canadian Governor-General's Award for children's book illustration—about two sisters reluctantly attending a backyard family birthday party, demonstrates the kind of detail that can be achieved in the medium. The picnic table is laden with food: chip dip covered in plastic wrap, deviled eggs with paprika, a glistening jelly salad, and more. There is much for readers to pore over in Reid's lively illustrations. Her other books include *Have You Seen Birds?* (1986), *Sing a Song of Mother Goose* (1991), the Zoe books (1991), and *The Golden Goose* (2000).

[*See also* Illustrations *and* Picture Books.]

Terri Doughty

Reid, Meta Mayne (1905–1991), novelist. Born in Yorkshire, England, of Irish descent, she spent most of her life in Northern Ireland, which provided the setting for the majority of her children's books. These include historical novels, time-slip fantasies, and a few contemporary stories. In historical fiction such as *The Silver Fighting Cocks* (1966), *The Two Rebels* (1969), *Beyond the Wide World's End* (1972), and *The Plotters of Pollnashee* (1973), she focuses on the Ulster of the late 18th and early 19th centuries, convincingly recreating its conflicting ideologies and loyalties. Their Ulster settings give these novels considerable modern relevance.

ROBERT DUNBAR

Reidel, Marlene (1923–), German painter, graphic artist, children's book illustrator, author, and set designer. The oldest of seven children, Reidel grew up on a remote farm in Lower Bavaria. After completing her studies at the Munich Art Academy she wrote and illustrated *Kasimir's Weltreise* (1957; English trans., *Kasimir's Journey*, 1958), a picture book that takes readers on a lively, playful, childlike fantasy trip. This debut book was a breakthrough for Reidel, both in Germany and internationally. The linoleum block print method she used underscores the simple graphic design, while brilliant colors bring out special effects. Reidel developed her own naive, traditional, and at the same time bucolic style using woodcuts, stamps, and other unconventional printing methods. Her picture books make use of counting rhymes, lullabies, and street ballads as a basis for the text, and are geared toward the youngest readers (for example, *Der Jakob und die Räuber*, 1965; English trans., *Jacob and the Robbers*, 1967). Aside from doing illustrations for the Grimms' fairy tales and many of her own picture books, Reidel also works in other artistic fields such as stage set design, graphic arts, and film.

[*See also* Book Design; Germany; *and* Illustrations.]

CAROLINE ROEDER

Reinick, Robert (1805–1852), German painter, poet, and author whose children's poems and fairy tales were popular in the second half of the 19th century. Born into a merchant family in Danzig, Reinick became a painter in Berlin, studied at the art academy in Düsseldorf, and in 1844 settled in Dresden. Here he concentrated on writing children's literature, attaching himself to the artistic circle surrounding Ludwig Richter (1803–1884). Reinick's development is evident in his contribution to one of the most important contemporary German youth magazines, the *Deutsche Jugendkalender* (German Youth Calendar). In 1847 he started working regularly for the magazine and in 1849 became coeditor, and from that time until 1853 he wrote all the texts in the magazine. His work strongly inclined toward the literary conventions of the Biedermeier, and his writings for children were often cautionary. The intensity of his pedagogical intentions varies from book to book. His humorous lyrics, strongly influenced by Clemens Brentano and Achim von Arnim's collection *Des Knaben Wunderhorn* (The Boy's Wonder Horn) are less instructive than his prose. Works like *Die freche Gesellschaft* (The Jolly Company) or *Was geh'n den Spitz die Gänse an* (What's the Dog Got to Do with the Geese) appeared in anthologies and schoolbooks well into the 20th century. Music was composed for many of Reinick's poems because of their explicit musicality. His most famous fairy tale, *Die Wurzelprinzessin* (1848; English trans., *The King of Root Valley and His Curious Daughter*, 1856), is influenced by E. T. A. Hoffmann's *The Nutcracker and the Mouse King*, and with its cute attitude toward nature it is a predecessor of similar works of children's literature in the early 20th century. Reinick's stories have been collected in several anthologies such as the *Märchen-, Lieder-, und Geschichtenbuch* (Book of Fairy Tales, Songs, and Stories, 1873), first published twenty years after his death.

[*See also* Children's Magazines; Fairy Tales and Folk Tales; Germany; Poetry; *and biographies of figures mentioned in this article.*]

BERND DOLLE-WEINKAUFF

Reiniger, Lotte (1899–1981), German artist best known as a creator of animated films, producer of children's television programs, and founder of the production group Fantasia Productions Ltd. Reiniger began her career cutting title vignettes for Paul Wegener's film *The Pied Piper of Hamlin* (1918). She is famous for her remarkable silhouette animated films, such as the full-length feature *The Adventures of Prince Achmed* (1923–1926), based on stories from the *Arabian Nights* and produced by her husband Carl Kock, and *Aucassin and Nicolette* (1974), for which she won the Jury Prize in 1976 at the International Animated Film Festival in Ottawa. Her other animated films include adaptations of Hugh Lofting's *Doctor Doolittle* series and parodies of operas, such as Bizet's *Carmen* and Mozart's *The Magic Flute*. She also lectured on shadow animation. For young people she wrote *Shadow Theaters and Shadow Film* (1970), and illustrated

Roger L. Green's *King Arthur and His Knights of the Round Table* (1980).

[*See also* Animated Films; *Arabian Nights, The*; *and* Pied Piper of Hamelin, The.]

HELENE EHRIANDER

Reiss, Johanna (1932–), Dutch American author raised in the Netherlands who, at the age of eight during World War II, had to hide with her elder sister because they were Jewish. After the end of the war Reiss went to school again and became a teacher. She emigrated to the United States in 1955, where she has worked as a journalist in New York City since 1978. In 1972 she published her first juvenile book, the autobiographical *The Upstairs Room*. Annie de Leeuw, a ten-year-old Dutch girl, and her elder sister Sini have to separate from part of their family because of Nazi persecution of the Jews, and they hide in the upstairs room of a farmer's house for more than two years. The story describes the development of racial prejudices in neighbors and friends, but also focuses on the few people who support the two sisters during their time of hiding. Reiss tells the story from the child's point of view, portraying the details of daily life in confinement—showing the suffering, but also a spirit of optimism. The sequel *The Journey Back* (1976) follows Annie after 1945, as she leaves the family who hid her and her sister, faces the difficulties of returning to her father and a new stepmother, and experiences the long healing process. Both books have been translated into several languages. *The Upstairs Room* earned numerous honors, including a Newbery Honor, the Jewish Book Council Children's Book Award, and, in 1976, the Buxtehuder Bulle Prize, a German award for children's books promoting peace.

[*See also* Historical Fiction; Holocaust Literature for Children; Netherlands; *and* Young Adult Literature.]

EVA GRESSNICH

Religious Instruction and Education. Religious instruction implies an induction into a faith; religious education suggests learning about various faiths, though it is sometimes used as a false synonym of "Christian instruction." Both use story to give children knowledge and understanding, placing profound philosophical ideas into a form that people can wrestle with. Religious instruction in one's heritage faith or an adopted faith also offers a sense of belonging and ownership. Typically, stories relate to founders or key people, key events, and religious teaching such as parables, mythology, and explanations of festivals.

For groups of children from various faiths, instruction has to be fair to all and allow faith members and others to develop their understanding, ideally giving rise to honest and unthreatening dialogue from which all benefit without judging or ranking religions or life stances. This can teach children how to think seriously and analytically about life, relationships, and values, as well as about religions. Instruction in one's heritage or chosen religion will assume particular truth claims. Discussions can include themes such as goodness, evil, love, generosity, greed, ambition, ethics, caring, friendship, loss, conscience, and responsibility. These are the essence of children's stories; when they are explored in life and not explicitly in religious writings, they are sometimes called "implicit religious education," although others see this as personal, social, or moral education. These stories may focus on the death of a loved one, or the need to share, or the value of behaving kindly. Stories can run the risk of becoming moral homilies; the best stories show children wrestling with complexity and working out personal issues and solutions for themselves.

Explicit learning about religion uses stories from sacred writings and stories about how the religion is lived, with titles such as *I Am a Sikh*. These can be prosaic, historical, or creative, information-giving or thought-provoking. Basic stories about such people as Abraham, Moses, David and Goliath, Buddha, Jesus, Paul, Muhammad, and Guru Nanak abound. They mix biography and hagiography (reverential legendary stories about esteemed founders). Stories link myth, legend, and history together in ways now difficult to disentangle: it is important for children to appreciate and enjoy the deeper meaning. Festivals are explained through stories of their origins, bringing out theological meanings about natures both of God and of humanity. Other stories may focus on ritual—a child being baptized, confirmed, or having a bar mitzvah—as examples of life's milestones or "rites of passage." Religious instruction assumes religious truth that others find contestable. Truth and belief are contested within and between faiths, so open discussion is needed in mixed classes. Stories can help children understand religious issues if they are open-ended and require an emotional and intellectual response. Children can then make up their own minds about what is true, and begin a philosophical debate.

[*See also* Legends; Multiculturalism and Children's Books; Myths; *and* Religious Writing.]

BIBLIOGRAPHY

Broadbent, Lynne, and Alan Brown. *Issues in Religious Education*. London: Routledge, 2002.

Jackson, R. *Religious Education: An Interpretative Approach*. London: Hodder, 1997.

STEPHEN BIGGER

Religious Tract Society, publisher and distributor of children's literature in England. Founded in 1799, the interdenominational Religious Tract Society (RTS) was established to promote the dissemination of religious tracts among the poor. Following the example of Hannah More's Cheap Repository Tracts (1795–1798), the evangelical RTS sought to counteract the effect of radical, antireligious, and sensational writing of the time by providing cheap "improving" literature designed for a semiliterate audience. Tracts were published in large numbers and widely distributed for free by charitable volunteers, street hawkers, and peddlers in rural areas. Although the tracts were intended for modestly educated adults, juveniles also consumed them, partly because so little other reading matter for children was available before the later nineteenth century. The RTS soon became aware of this important sector of the reading market and appealed directly to younger readers by publishing pious narratives, such as the Reverend Legh Richmond's *The Dairyman's Daughter* (1810), which were reprinted often and consumed by generations of children throughout the nineteenth century. Such books were provided by the RTS at reduced cost to Sunday schools for working-class and poor children, who received them as rewards. In 1824 the RTS started its first periodical for children, *The Child's Companion; or, Sunday Scholar's Reward*, which was renamed *The Child's Companion and Juvenile Instructor* in 1846 and continued to be published until 1932.

In its early years, the RTS's publications for juveniles were explicitly religious and morally instructive. Two common story types were the conversion narrative, in which a wicked individual sees the error of his or her ways and experiences joyful salvation through God's grace; and the child-deathbed story, in which a pious child is happily released through death to a well-deserved home with God in heaven. As the century progressed, more secular material was introduced into RTS publications, and two different lines of children's books were developed for two different juvenile markets: adventure stories and narratives about family life for middle-class families and the boarding schools to which their children were sent, and tales of "street arabs" like those by Hesba Stretton (1832–1911) for charitable schools for children of the poor. By the latter part of the century, the RTS was publishing juvenile periodicals free of overtly religious content and with wide appeal for young readers of all classes. Like other publishers of the day, the RTS recognized the importance of marketing by gender, as the popularity of *Boy's Own Paper* (1879–1967) and *Girl's Own Paper* (1880–1956) testify. The RTS, along with similar religious organizations and missionary societies, greatly facilitated the rise of children's literacy and the growth of the juvenile sector of the book trade in the nineteenth century by developing a system of mass distribution that served as a model for those used in the commercial publishing industry today. In the 1930s, the RTS became the Lutterworth Press.

BIBLIOGRAPHY

Altick, Richard D. *The English Common Reader: A Social History of the Mass Reading Public, 1800–1900*. 2d ed. Columbus: Ohio University Press, 1998.

Darton, F. J. *Children's Books in England: Five Centuries of Social Life*. 3d ed. Cambridge: Cambridge University Press, 1982.

CAROL A. BOCK

Religious Writing. There is a vast range of books for children and schools exploring religious writings and stories, in addition to factual books on religions from devotional and school publishers. Religions are wide and varied, with some well known (Judaism, Christianity, Islam, Hinduism, Buddhism, Sikhism) and others less so (for instance, Bahais, Zoroastrians, Rastafarians, Jains). Some are disparagingly called "sects," and others "primitive" or "tribal." The term "pagan" has developed new status in New Age religion. Jews, Christians, and Muslims form a family, since Jewish figures (such as Abraham, Moses, and David) were adopted by the other two faiths. Jesus and John the Baptist are also Muslim prophets. Children's stories about these common characters abound in all three faiths. The Bahai faith is a more recent member of this family, a modernizing mainstream world faith from Iran. Indian faiths also form a family, with Hinduism being the ancestral faith from which new ideas developed. What we now know as "Hinduism" is an amalgam of many local traditions, harmonized by the Brahmans (the priests) and later by Western scholarship. Yoga is one form of spiritual discipline that has adapted to the West. Buddhism is a philosophy that repudiates ideas of self and desire. Originally with little mythology, Mahayana Buddhism developed symbolism and myth in local adaptations, for example, in Tibet, China, and Japan around deities such as Quan Yin, goddess of mercy. Jains are best known for the doctrine of nonviolence (ahimsa).

Judaism and Christianity

Religions claim to express truth, but various versions of the truth can be either inclusive or exclusive. Where exclusive truth is claimed (that is, the only truth), issues of genre can be controversial, since myths, legends, and fiction will all be viewed as objective fact. The biblical creation story is treated by some as historical fact and even dated to 4004 BC. Scholars separate Genesis 1, creation in six days, from the older Garden of Eden story that follows. A body of traditional stories has been edited into a theological framework. Most biblical stories cannot technically be treated as historical fact since they do not tie well into historical records or archaeology. Historicity has to be surmised or treated as an act of faith. To call a story a legend assumes that the hero existed but that details are exaggerated or fabricated. Myths explore eternal truths such as origins, the nature of humankind, good and evil, and may be populated with divine beings. Theological meaning is at the fore, not historical veracity. The biblical creation and flood stories are often classified as myths, which greatly annoys conservative Christians and Jews. The God of such "myths," worried that "man has become like one of us, knowing good and evil" (Genesis 3:2) and became sorry to have created humans (Genesis 6:5–7); the sons of God intermarried with human women (Genesis 6:2), and when concerned about human inventiveness at the tower of Babel, God said, "Come; let us go down and there confuse their language" (Genesis 11:7).

Myths are timeless stories, traditionally told and collected rather than made up. Fictions, on the other hand, are deliberately created stories. Bible stories such as those of Ruth, Esther, Jonah, and Daniel are likely to be popular fictions, telling the stories of an alien made good: Ruth the Moabite became an ancestress of King David; a pious Jew defeats genocide (Esther from the royal harem overcomes anti-Semitic and genocidal Haman in the story of the Jewish Purim festival); a xenophobic prophet sees good in foreigners (the reluctant prophet Jonah prophesies the destruction of Nineveh, only to find that they repent and are forgiven); and a persecuted Jew receives divine assistance (Daniel, who was faithful even when this was perilous and was rescued by divine intervention). Christian stories are the same mix of history, legend, and fiction; the Word becoming flesh and dwelling among humanity (John 3) is a fine example of myth, as are the divine titles such as "son of God" and "son of man." The theme of preplanned messianic history, with Jesus as the fulfillment of prophecy, assumes the divine intervention so common in myth. The doctrine of the virgin birth, confined largely to Matthew's gospel, stems from the misinterpretation of Isaiah: a "young woman shall conceive" is read as "a virgin shall conceive," following Greek versions. The devil in the wilderness temptation story (Luke 4) turns temptation into a personal battle of divine wills, good and evil. The miracle stories are examples of legend, with some, like the raising of Lazarus from the dead (John 11), beyond the possibility of medical misdiagnosis. The ultimate miracle, the Resurrection, forms the basis of Christian theology and creed and places Jesus mythically at the right hand of God (Acts 7:55). Rastafarians use biblical symbolism (exodus, exile, promised land) to shed light on black experience and aspirations. Babylon, the evil power, symbolizes white Western dominance. Jill Paton Walsh's *Babylon* (1982) turns this into story.

In children's books, Bible characters are generally presented in simplistic stories, assumed to be factual. Most of these books are intended for church or synagogue instruction. Just as the title the "Old Testament" for the Hebrew Bible suggests that the New Testament has superseded it, so Alan T. Dale's *Winding Quest* (1972), a children's version of the Hebrew Bible, assumes a quest that is completed in *New World* (1966), his version of the New Testament. Books for children do not tend to depict Jesus as Jewish, nor, outside Muslim devotional publications, do they show Abraham, Moses, David, Jesus, and others as Muslim prophets. Christian books on Jesus tend to present negative stereotypes of Jews, and in particular of the Pharisees as opponents of Jesus and as "Hypocrites"; they were actually in the process of founding Talmudic Judaism. Children's stories of Jesus tend to be simplistic and not controversial; there are, however, some more complex books on Jesus. Malcolm Saville's *Strange Story* (1966) tells the story of the crucifixion through the eyes of a Roman soldier as told to his grandchildren; Saville's *King of Kings* (1958) was also popular in its day. Stuart Jackman's *The Davidson File* (1982) puts together a dossier of His Grace the Lord Caiaphus on the case of "Jesus Davidson": letters, reports, memos, newspaper cuttings, and telephone transcripts are included. *The Lion Graphic Bible* (1998) presents Bible stories through picture sequences, as in classic comic strips. Geraldine McCaughrean's *The Jesse Tree* (2003) uses a vivid and contemporary story format seeing events through the eyes of witnesses.

Islam

In Islam, a children's Qur'an is not an acceptable concept to Muslims, since this would suggest a watering down of the sacred text. Muslims believe that the whole original text should be studied and that Muslim children should learn it by heart in Arabic. However, many devotional Muslim books take aspects such as the prophets, fasting, and prayer to help children understand religious teachings. Many books that depict the traditions (hadith) vary in authenticity. Elsa Marston's *Muhammad of Mecca: Prophet of Islam* (2001) for school pupils is an accessible Western text. The story of Muhammad is that of reestablishing strict monotheism in Mecca at the ancient house of Abraham (the Kaaba, the focus of prayer and pilgrimage). After persecution, the idolators are thrown out by force and a new political order is established in which Jews and Christians are respected as "people of the book," that is, as people of divine revelation. The Qur'an is recognized as the final revealed Word of God.

Hinduism

Children's versions of Hindu stories in India are often cheap graphic texts that offer vivid portrayals, and there are in addition a number of good written texts. The Ramayana, the scripture behind the Divali festival story, tells the adventure of Prince Rama and his wife Sita, kidnapped by King Ravana and taken to and rescued from Sri Lanka. The story appears in drama and puppetry, especially in Java, where shadow and solid puppets (wayang) are used. An ancient Thai royal family modeled itself on the story. Rama was considered to be an incarnation of the deity Vishnu, incarnated to rid the world of the evil ("demon") King Ravana, who combined spiritual power and dictatorship. This is a magical world where spiritual power can move mountains and kill or curse the unwary. Rama was the perfect model of a son. About to be crowned regent, he was exiled through court machinations. In the adventures that followed, his wife, Sita, was kidnapped by Ravana, who disguised himself as a monk. Rama and allies located her, besieged the palace in Lanka, and in a mighty battle, Ravana was killed and world order restored. Rama then returned to his kingdom in triumph. Abridged children's versions are by R. K. Narayan (1972), G. Krishnamurti (1974), Sally Hubble-Jackson (2000), and Anita Ganeri (2003); A. K. Banker's novelized *Prince of Ayodhya* (2003) and sequels are also noteworthy. The Mahabharata (Great Struggle) is a traditional Indian tale of a dysfunctional ruling family with two warring factors; the Pandavas and the Kauravas wipe each other out after the Kauravas cheated the Pandavas out of their kingdom through a game of dice. A body of spiritual and philosophical commentary discusses the nature of responsibility, power, jealousy, and duty. One minor character, Krishna, is revealed as a divine incarnation, and one purple passage, the Bhagavad Gita, has become particularly devotional. It ends with visions of hell and paradise, revealing both to be delusions, and the whole concept of future reward and punishment is questioned. Versions for children are available by S. R. Rao (1986) and R. K. Narayan (1978); Kerena Marchant's *Krishna and Hinduism* (2002) is aimed at schools, as is Cyaring and Lipner's *Stories of Krishna* (2000). Versions of Hindu stories for children concerning deities and heroes are also available. Hinduism is rich in symbolism, in which the idea of one God lies comfortably alongside stories and symbolic personifications of divine qualities: Sarasvati represents wisdom, Lakshmi success, Ganesh inner strength, Shiva the life energy (and through this creation, change and destruction), and so on. Theological symbolism is not always clearly visible through such stories as why Ganesh has an elephant's head. A good treatment of spiritual insight for young children focusing on Ganesh and other religious stories is given in Grimmitt's *Gift to the Child* (1995).

Buddhism

Buddhist stories generally depict the life of Siddhartha Gautama, the current Buddha. His story tells of how as a prince he was protected from illness, old age, death, and monastic abstinence; when he accidentally discovered these he began a path to religious enlightenment called "the middle way" as it avoided extremes. The four noble truths and the eightfold path teach people to cast aside delusion and self-conceit, the causes of suffering, and follow a path of right living and contemplation. Landlaw's *Prince Siddhartha* (1994) and Anne Rockwell's *The Prince Who Ran Away: The Story of Gautama Buddha* (2001) provide illustrated stories. On the scriptures is Anita Ganeri's *The Tipitaka* (2003). Although Buddhism does not teach personal reincarnation, there are folk stories ("jatakas") about Buddha's previous incarnations showing exceptional personal achievements. The story about his time as a monkey king sacrificing his life to help his people cross a gorge is the best known. The definitive collection, written some decades ago and still available, is *Twenty Jataka Tales* by Noor Inayat Khan.

Sikhism

Sikh scriptures contain some simple poetry and songs that are collected into anthologies for children, often combined with the life story of gurus such as Guru Nanak. Nanak brought together Hindu and Muslim insights to make a new spiritual and moral harmony that rejected tribalism and enmity. His disciples (Sikhs) give their name to the faith. Of the ten gurus, the last, Gobind Singh, also features in the story. The Sikh Missionary Society produces simple books for Sikh children. Panesar's *Guru Nanak and Sikhism* (2002) gives a good version; Anita Ganeri's *The Guru Granth Sahib and Sikhism* (2004) focuses on the scriptures.

[*See also* Bible in Children's Literature, The; Evangelical Writing; Legends; Myths; Religious Instruction and Education; Qur'an in Children's Literature, The; *and biographies of figures mentioned in this article.*]

BIBLIOGRAPHY

Bigger, S. F., ed. *Creating the Old Testament*. Oxford: Blackwell, 1989.

Drane, J. *Nelson's Illustrated Encyclopedia of the Bible*. London: Nelson, 1998.

Rogers, K. *Encyclopedia of World Religions*. Tulsa, Okla.: Education Development Corporation/Usborne, 2002.

STEPHEN BIGGER

Reuter, Bjarne (1950–), Danish author. His novels for children and young adults often combine realism with imagination, humor, and suspense. *Busters verden* (1979; English trans., *Buster's World*, 1988), the story of a highly vital loser, is a picaresque, farcelike tale. Reuter's universe is not idyllic, but shaped by basic existential themes, with underlying desperation spurring grotesque realism. From his debut in 1975 his novels focus on boy protagonists, set in a children's collective, and with reference to a wider social and historic context. The novel series starting with *Zappa* (1977) describes a boy's life and development in the Denmark of the 1960s and 1970s. Longing for self-fulfillment is here mixed with social and existential criticism.

HELENE HØYRUP

Reward Books. There is a long tradition of giving young people books as rewards or prizes to mark an achievement or reinforce a lesson. Isaac Watts suggested that children who learned verses from his *Divine Songs* be given a copy of the book for themselves, and even today books are regularly given during annual prize-giving events at schools. Originally the giving of reward books was done on an informal, individual basis: a parent, tutor, or other adult might choose to reward a child for any number of reasons at any time of the year, perhaps inscribing on the flyleaf the date and reason for the reward. With the rise of commercial publishing and the increased availability of handsome and affordable books, institutions recognized the commercial and social advantages of giving books as rewards; by the end of the 18th century, many private schools and Sunday schools in Britain and in many of its dominions and former colonies, including the United States and Canada, had initiated formal occasions when books were presented to children to celebrate achievements, including good attendance, collecting for a society, good conduct, "knowledge of the golden text," Scripture, drawing, and composition, position in class, and even popularity.

It soon became customary to insert ornamental bookplates in reward books; the bookplates not only recorded the date and nature of the prize, but also included details about the awarding institution. Any collection of reward fiction will contain a wide range of prizes awarded by a wide range of denominational groups, such as the Wesleyan Methodist Juvenile Foreign Missionary Society, the Salvation Army, and the Band of Hope, alongside those awarded by school boards, groups such as the National Temperance League, and a variety of youth organizations. Reward bookplates helped to develop a sense of belonging and allegiance to such institutions, and also advertised them. In addition, the giving of reward books to students was a good public relations exercise with fee-paying parents who were likely to be gratified by the reward, which suggested that their investment had been worthwhile.

Whatever the reason for the reward or the class of the recipient, books given as rewards were intended to be improving, wholesome, and safe in terms of the mores of the time. As the practice of giving books as rewards and prizes became widespread and institutionalized, the need for a substantial body of appropriate books became apparent. Publishers began to identify, commission, and advertise books suited for this purpose. In 1864 the Christmas number of the British trade journal *The Bookseller* included "A Complete List of Illustrated and Other Books suitable for Presents, School Prizes or Rewards." By the final decades of the 19th century, in both Britain and the United States, producing reward fiction was a major area of publishing activity. In both countries, religious publishing houses such as the Religious Tract Society in Britain and the American Tract Society dominated the reward book market. Though the kind of books produced in the two countries was similar, with many shared titles, over time specifically American settings and characters, including Native Americans and a range of wild animals, appeared. Often more attention was paid to appearance than to content and selection—reward books tended to be judged by their covers while their contents often disappointed or angered recipients, who found them boring and patronizing. There were, however, some notable exceptions. Works such as *The Wide, Wide World* (1850) and novels by Evelyn Everett-Green were best sellers whose sales reflected in part the frequency with which they were given as rewards, and encouraged the publishing houses to be more flexible in what they regarded to be suitable—and profitable—to publish.

Although appearance was an important aspect of reward and prize books, reward books should not be confused with "gift books," a term used in the antiquarian book trade to describe a particular kind of heavily illustrated, handsomely bound limited edition of a "classic" text issued by a trade publisher, as opposed to a fine art press, often for the Christmas market. Gift books are associated with the early 20th century, and in particular with the artists Edmund Dulac, Kay Nielsen, and Arthur Rackham.

[*See also* American Tract Society; Publishers and Publishing; Religious Tract Society; *and biographies of figures mentioned in this article.*]

BIBLIOGRAPHY

Alderson, B. "Tracts, Rewards, and Fairies: The Victorian Contribution to Children's Literature." In *A History of Publishing in Celebration of the 250th Anniversary of the House of Longman, 1724–1974*, edited by Asa Briggs. London: Longman, 1974.

Avery, Gillian. *Behold the Child: American Children and Their Books, 1621–1922*. London: Bodley Head, 1994.

Avery, Gillian. *Nineteenth-Century Children: Heroes and Heroines in English Children's Stories, 1780–1900*. London: Hodder and Stoughton, 1965.

Bratton, J. S. *The Impact of Victorian Children's Fiction*. London: Croom Helm, 1981.

Cutt, M. N. *Ministering Angels: A Study of Nineteenth-Century Evangelical Writing for Children*. Wormley, U.K.: Five Owls, 1979.

Entwistle, D. "Counteracting Street Culture: Book Prizes in English Sunday Schools at the Turn of the Century." *History of Education Society Bulletin* 55 (1995): 26–34.

KIMBERLEY REYNOLDS

Rewards and Fairies. *See* Kipling, Rudyard.

Rey, H. A. (1898–1977), and **Margret Rey** (1906–1996), authors and illustrators born in Hamburg, Germany, who emigrated to the United States in 1940. H. A. Rey, born Hans Augusto Reyersbach, had no formal art training; Margret, born Margarete Waldstein, studied art at the Bauhaus. With Hitler in power, Margret emigrated to Brazil, where she married H. A., after which they moved to Paris. Children born after 1950 will easily recognize the name of Curious George. This mischievous monkey is the product of two closely intertwined talents. Always interested in animals, H. A. had been a frequent visitor at Hamburg's Hagenbeck Zoo. In Paris, after drawing a giraffe for a periodical, a book editor contacted him about doing a book for the young. The Reys accepted the offer and wrote their first children's book,

The Reys. Front cover of *Curious George Learns the Alphabet* by H. A. Rey (Boston, Houghton Mifflin, 1963). REPRODUCED COURTESY OF THE COTSEN CHILDREN'S LIBRARY, PRINCETON UNIVERSITY LIBRARY

Rafi et les 9 Singes (English trans., *Raffy and the Nine Monkeys*, 1939). In 1940, hours before the Nazis arrived in Paris, H. A. and Margret fled south on bicycles with nothing but their coats and their book manuscripts, "Curious George" among them. After a brief stay in Brazil, they came to New York, and soon had a contract with Houghton Mifflin. They did flap books such as *How Do You Get There?* (1942) and books in verse such as *See the Circus* (1956). H. A. illustrated books of other authors, including Margaret Wise Brown's *The Polite Penguin* (1941) and Charlotte Zolotow's *The Park Book* (1944). But it is as the creators of Curious George that the Reys will be remembered.

In their distinctive yellow covers, the *Curious George* books have enchanted children since the first book in the series, H. A.'s *Curious George*, appeared in 1941. Thereafter, Margret and H. A. collaborated on the series, and Margret also wrote picture book texts of her own (for instance, *Pretzel*, 1944, and *Spotty*, 1945, illustrated by H. A.). Rey's illustrations are simple watercolors, done in saturated bright colors and rounded shapes outlined in black or gray pencil. They have a gay dynamism and goofiness that appeal to the very young. Since the early *George* books do not have a controlled vocabulary, they are intended as books to be read to youngsters. *Curious George Flies a Kite* (1958) was the one controlled-vocabulary book designed for beginning readers.

George is definitely the center of these stories, with other characters usually identified by their occupations (for instance, zookeeper or farmer) and not by name. The stories are episodic, with three or four situations typically arising in each one. George's caregiver, introduced in the first book when he catches George, is "the man in the yellow hat." Yellow appears on almost every page and may be seen as a symbol of control. George may be allowed to let his curiosity lead him into silly scrapes, but when things threaten to get out of control, "the man in the yellow hat" shows up like a guardian spirit to take care of things. This sends a strong message: it is okay to be curious, but you must keep things in control. Though some of the situations are ones children would find familiar, as in *Curious George Goes to the Hospital* (1966), most of them are far-fetched (for instance, as when George goes into outer space in *Curious George Gets a Medal*, 1957). Children may well equate their own shenanigans with those of Curious George and understand that it is all right to indulge their curiosity, but only so far.

The Reys also produced "The Zozo Page for Children" for *Good Housekeeping Magazine* in 1951. This cartoon page contained a number of ideas that later found their way into the *Curious George* books. After H. A.'s death in 1977, Margret joined the faculty of Brandeis University as professor of creative writing (1979) and continued to control the content of the *Curious George* series (although she apparently did not write any more of the stories). A series of short films was created between 1984 and 1990, edited by Alan Shalleck, with new *Curious George* titles being prepared from the artwork from these films. In 1998, Anita Silvey discovered a previously unpublished manuscript in the Reys' papers at the University of Southern Mississippi, and under her guidance, Margret Rey's text for *Whiteblack the Penguin Sees the World* was published in 2000.

[*See also* Picture Books *and biographies of figures mentioned in this article.*]

JACQUE ROETHLER

Reynard the Fox. Reynard the fox is the bawdy and crafty hero of the medieval French *Roman de Renart* and a ubiquitous trickster figure of European folklore. He first appears in the Latin poem *Ysengrimus*, c. 1150, describing the adventures of Isengrin the wolf and his nephew Reinardus the fox. The first version in French dates to the mid-1170s. Piecemeal additions by various authors resulted in the twenty-six tales or branches now known, fifteen of them composed about 1205 and the rest by mid-century. The core story of Reynard's summons by King Noble the Lion to answer complaints about him by Isengrin and other animals forms the starting point for the loosely connected tales, most of them satirizing the upper classes and the clergy. Testament to his popularity, Reinardus became Reynard and eventually *renard*, the common French word for fox, displacing the earlier *goupil*. Reynard appears in manuscript illuminations, in church decorations, and in ballads, and his character was adopted by various medieval French poets to lampoon individuals of their time. Among somewhat later versions, the Flemish poem *Reinaert de Vos* focused on Reynard's dispute with Isengrin and was translated into Latin and, in prose versions, into several other tongues. Reynard had already appeared in England in the 13th-century poem *Of the Fox and the Wolf* and then in Chaucer's *Nun's Priest's Tale*, where he is known as Daun Russell. Caxton's 1481 translation of a prose version of the Flemish poem made Reynard widely known in modern English literature. Among his modern incarnations, he appears in the hunting poem "Reynard the Fox" by John Masefield and in the traditional English ballad that bears his name. Recent retellings for children include one adapted and illustrated by Alain Vaës, one adapted by Selina Hastings and illustrated by Graham Percy, and one adapted by Roy Brown (based on the version by folklorist Joseph Jacobs) and illustrated by John Vernon Lord.

[*See also* Trickster Tales *and biographies of figures mentioned in this article.*]

BIBLIOGRAPHY

Owen, D. D. R. *The Romance of Reynard the Fox*. New York: Oxford University Press, 1994.

AMANDA COCKRELL

Rhoden, Emmy von (1829–1885), real name Emmy Friedrich-Friedrich, German writer, whose father was a wealthy banker. In 1854 she married the writer Hermann Friedrich (who later changed his name to Friedrich-Friedrich) and lived in Berlin starting in 1867. Five years later she moved with her family to Eisenach, in 1876 to Leipzig, and in 1885 to Dresden. Inspired by her daughter's experiences at a boarding school, she wrote her famous girls' story *Der Trotzkopf* (1885; English trans., *Taming a Tomboy*,

1898). In contrast to "Backfischbuch" (books for teenage girls) and the model morality story for children, this novel of education describes the psychological development of a young girl standing at the threshold of adulthood. Since von Rhoden died before the publication of her novel, she did not witness its enormous success. Her daughter Else Wildhagen wrote three sequels: *Trotzkopfs Brautzeit* (Tomboy's Bridal Time, 1892), *Aus Trotzkopfs Ehe* (Tomboy's Marriage, 1895), and *Trotzkopfs Nachkommen* (Tomboy's Descendants, 1930). Further sequels were written by Suse la Chapelle-Roobol, Marie von Felseneck, and Doris Mix. With *Der Trotzkopf*, von Rhoden contributed to the innovation of the genre in Germany and influenced many authors of girls' stories, such as Magda Trott and Else Ury.

Bettina Kümmerling-Meibauer

Ribeiro, Aquilino (1885–1963), writer born in the north of Portugal who died in Lisbon. His book *O Romance da Raposa* (The Romance of the Fox, 1924) is considered one of the greatest classics of Portuguese children's literature, initiating an extremely rich period in literary publishing for young people. In this book the hero is a cunning little fox called Salta-Pocinhas, who steals and kills for food. However, these actions are not morally condemned because they are driven by the laws of survival. As in a fable, the animals are anthropomorphized, yet the moral classifications that distinguish good from evil are not present. The text is full of humor and suspense, with an original use of language, very erudite and musical, where the pleasure of language per se often precedes the decoding of meaning. The book was dedicated to the author's son, and the illustrations are by Benjamin Rabier.

In 1936 Aquilino published a collection of stories for schools under the title of *Arca de Noé III Classe* (Noah's Ark, Third Year). The quality of these texts, which are full of humor and some of which descend directly from themes existent in traditional folklore, contrasts with the poverty of the texts found in primary school books at the time. In 1967, *O Livro da Marianinha* (The Book of Marianinha) was published. The book includes small stories in verse, some of which criticize the use of corporal punishment in school. Aquilino is also the author of one of the many children's adaptations of classic texts published in the 1930s.

[*See also* Fairy Tales and Folk Tales *and* Portugal.]

Claudia Sousa Pereira

Rice, Eve (1951–), American illustrator and writer. Rice grew up in Bedford, New York, and studied history at Yale University. After her graduation in 1972, she worked full-time as a picture book creator, providing both the text and illustrations for family tales such as *Ebbie* (1975) and *Benny Bakes a Cake* (1981). Her drawings were typically simple and cartoonlike, sometimes featuring anthropomorphized animals as in *Papa's Lemonade, and Other Stories* (1976), but Rice was also capable of subtle, textured work such as the detailed, charcoal-hued cityscapes of *Goodnight, Goodnight* (1980). Rice also penned a droll mystery novel for intermediate readers entitled *The Remarkable Return of Winston Potter Crisply* (1978) and eventually shifted her focus solely to writing, collaborating with artists such as Peter Sís and Nancy Winslow Parker. She graduated from the Mount Sinai School of Medicine in 1989 and became a professor of psychiatry at Cornell University.

[*See also* Parker, Nancy Winslow *and* Sís, Peter.]

Peggy Lin Duthie

Richard, Adrienne (1921–), American author of well-researched young adult novels set in diverse locations and time periods. The first was *Pistol* (1969), the story of Billy's experiences as a horse wrangler on a Montana ranch at the dawn of the Depression. The book is alive with detailed descriptions of western landscapes and the hard work of ranching. The author's gift for evoking far-off places and times is evident in all of her subsequent novels, including *The Accomplice* (1973), which concerns a boy's visit to modern Israel. A National Book Award finalist, *Wings* (1974) introduces young Pip and the colorfully offbeat people she encounters growing up in the1920s in Southern California. *Into the Road* (1976) is set in the contemporary world of motorcycle riding, as Nat and his older brother tour New England on their bikes. Although she is not a prolific author, each of Richard's novels is a distinct and memorable reading experience.

Peter D. Sieruta

Richards, Anna Matlack (1835–1900), American poet, playwright, and children's author. Her husband, William Trost Richards, and her daughter, Anna Richards Brewster, were well-known American artists. Brought up as a Quaker in Pennsylvania, Richards had already established a reputation as a poet before her marriage in 1856. Her children's fantasy, *A New Alice in the Old Wonderland* (1895), both imitates and satirizes Lewis Carroll's *Alice* books, as do the Tenniel-like illustrations by Richards's daughter, Anna. Richards's independent and assertive "New Alice" embodies characteristics of the fin de siècle "new woman," challenging and transforming the "old Wonderland's" repressive characters and situations.

[*See also* Alice Imitations; Carroll, Lewis; Fantasy; *and* Tenniel, John.]

Carolyn Sigler

Richards, Frank. *See* Hamilton, Charles.

Richards, Laura E. (1850–1943), American writer. A lifelong resident of New England, Richards was the daughter of Samuel Gridley Howe, a renowned physician and educator, and Julia Ward Howe, a poet and activist. Cowritten with two of her sisters, Richards's 1916 book about her mother won the inaugural Pulitzer Prize for biography. During her lifetime, Richards was recognized as a versatile and engaging writer, producing more than ninety books and contributing to magazines such as *St. Nicholas*, *Youth's Companion*, and *Ladies Home Journal* (the last with illustrations by Kate Greenaway). Richards's output included sentimental novels such as *Captain January* (1891), memoirs such as *When I Was Your Age* (1893), volumes of fables such as *The Golden Windows* (1903), and biographies of luminaries such as fellow Unitarians Florence Nightingale (1909)—godmother to one of Richards's sisters—and Abigail Adams (1917). Richards's Hildegarde series for girls (1891–1897) generated a substantial following and eventually overlapped with her Margaret series (1897–1904). *Tirra Lirra: Rhymes Old and New* (1932) cemented her reputation as a leading nonsense poet. Although most of Richards's work is no longer in print, individual poems such as "Eletelephony" have retained their appeal and are still anthologized and circulated.

[*See also* Biography; Girls' Books and Fiction; Greenaway, Kate; Nonsense; St. Nicholas Magazine; *and* Youth's Companion.]

Peggy Lin Duthie

Richardson, Samuel (1689–1761), British novelist, printer, and publisher, born in Derbyshire. As a child Richardson gained a reputation as an expert letter writer for local lovesick young women, a skill that he later employed in his epistolary novels. At age seventeen, although intended for the church, he was forced by reduced family finances to enter a printing apprenticeship. He was so successful that by age thirty he had established his own prestigious business in London, where in 1740 he published an illustrated edition of Roger L'Estrange's translation of *Aesop's Fables*, intended for children. Immensely popular, Richardson's edition was a meticulously revised text eminently well suited to its young audience. Commissioned by two publishers to produce a manual of model letters, he began instead to write *Pamela* (1740), which, because of its psychological realism and working-class setting, is considered to be the first modern novel. Richardson intended *Pamela*, and his later epistolary novels *Clarissa Harlowe* (7 vols.; 1747–1748) and *Sir Charles Grandison* (6 vols.; 1753–1754), as moral instruction for "the Youth of Both Sexes," and all three novels remained staples of adolescent reading for over a century. *Sir Charles Grandison* was Jane Austen's favorite novel, and Macaulay read it to his family. For children, an abridged version of all three lengthy novels, *The Paths of Virtue Delineated* (1756), published by John Newbery, is traditionally attributed to Oliver Goldsmith.

[*See also* Moral Tales; Publishers and Publishing; *and biographies of figures mentioned in this article*.]

Bridget Carrington

Richler, Mordecai (1931–2001), Canadian author. A native of Montreal and the grandson of a rabbi, Richler grew up on St. Urbain Street, part of a working-class Jewish neighborhood he later immortalized in *The Apprenticeship of Duddy Kravitz* (1959). Both comic and caustic in its portrait of an ambitious Jewish teenager and his land-acquisition schemes, the novel upset some readers because of its use of unflattering stereotypes; some critics accused Richler of encouraging anti-Semitism, but others were impressed by the novel's brutal truth. Frequently assigned to Canadian students, the story was adapted into a movie in 1974, for which Richler received a Screenwriters Guild Award, and into a musical in 1987 (Richler cowrote the libretto).

A freelance journalist and screenwriter, Richler lived in Europe from 1959 to 1972 and wrote primarily for adults. He was named a Companion to the Order of Canada for his achievements in literature, twice won the Governor-General's Award, and received the 1997 Giller Prize. Irascible and outspoken, Richler considered everyone fair game for criticism and often drew fire for his political and social verdicts. Richler reportedly began his Jacob Two-Two series to amuse his children, whom he judged to be too young to enjoy his other work; the children in the books share the same names as Daniel, Noah, Emma, Marfa, and Jacob Richler. The first book, *Jacob Two-Two Meets the Hooded Fang* (1975), was named the Canadian Library Association's Book of the Year for Children. It was also the winner of the first Ruth Schwartz Children's Book Award. Noting how it had outsold all of his other books, Richler followed it with *Jacob Two-Two and the Dinosaur* (1987) and *Jacob Two-Two's First Spy Case* (1995). Irreverent and fanciful, the books display Richler's characteristic blend of humor, outrageousness, and realism as he describes Jacob's attempts to cope with patronizing siblings and corrupt adults.

[*See also* Canada; Humor; Realism; *and* Young Adult Literature.]

BIBLIOGRAPHY

"Mordecai Richler." *Children's Literature Review* 17 (1989): 63–81.

PEGGY LIN DUTHIE

Richter, Hans Peter (1926–), German author of *Friedrich* (1961; English trans., 1970), a story loosely based on Richter's own childhood during the Third Reich. Richter details the gradually tightening restrictions on the central friendship between the narrator and Friedrich, his Jewish neighbor and classmate, in a style that is deliberately sober and stark. He conveys information without narrative commentary, so that the reader is left to make moral or political judgments and to imagine the emotional responses of the protagonists. *Friedrich*, published in Germany in 1961, was one of the first children's texts to address the subject of a Nazi childhood for a child audience. Richter portrays the indecisiveness and inactivity of the German population in the face of the treatment of Jewish citizens with an honesty that was rare at the time. A year after *Friedrich*, Richter published a more direct account of his own youth, *I Was There* (1962; English trans., 1972), that offers further insights into political polarization in 1930s Germany. A final volume, *Time of the Young Soldiers* (1976; English trans., 1978), follows the three friends at the center of *I Was There* in their first years of service in the German army.

The reception given Richter's work reflects Germany's tortuous reckoning with the Nazi era. *Friedrich* became a best seller in Germany and has been required reading on the school syllabus in a number of German regions. Outside Germany, the book has introduced many young readers to the dilemmas faced by young people in the Germany of the 1930s, but has also attracted criticism. Israeli academic Zohar Shavit (2003) accused Richter of adopting a philosemitic perspective in order to sidestep the issue of national responsibility. Richter's fictional recreation of the Third Reich should be judged as an early and commendable, if flawed, attempt to address Germany's past.

BIBLIOGRAPHY

Shavit, Zohar. "On the Use of Books for Children in Creating the German National Myth." In *The Presence of the Past in Children's Literature*, edited by Ann Lawson Lucas, 123–133. Westport, Conn.: Praeger, 2003.

GILLIAN LATHEY

Richter, Jutta (1955–), German author who writes novels, stories, radio plays, stage plays, and songs for adults, teenagers, and children. Richter studied theology, German philology, and communication studies in Münster. Her works are distinguished by their characteristic language, and often deal with children's environments and the conflicts of adolescence. Her children's book *Der Hund mit dem gelben Herzen* (The Dog with the Yellow Heart, 1998) became very popular and was performed on stage. *Der Tag, als ich lernte die Spinnen zu zähmen* (The Day I Learned to Tame the Spiders, 2000) treats topics such as exclusion and isolation, as well as courage; it was honored with the German Youth Literature Prize in 2001. The young adult book *Hechtsommer* (Pike Summer, 2005) broaches the subject of death within a family and how the relatives respond to it. In 2004 Richter received the Hermann Hesse fellowship for her complete works.

[*See also* Germany *and* Young Adult Literature.]

EVA GRESSNICH

Richter, Ludwig (1803–1884), popular German artist known for his woodcut illustrations of German fairy tales and folk life. The son of a copperplate engraver, Adrian Ludwig Richter was always expected to become an artist. At the age of twelve, he began learning his craft while working at his father's business and attending the Dresden Academy. At seventeen, he was chosen to travel through France with the entourage of the Russian prince Narischkin as one of a coterie of artists who were to document the journey. Much of Richter's early work consists of landscapes, such as *Aus Avignon* (1820), a stark, simple rendering of the famous bridge. From 1823 to 1827, Richter perfected his technique

Ludwig Richter. Illustration by Richter from *Deutsches Märchenbuch* by Ludwig Bechstein (1857). COLLECTION OF JACK ZIPES

in Rome, where he became friendly with a Swede, Ludwig von Maydell, who later persuaded him to work in the unfashionable medium of woodcut, a form the German eventually made his own. While in Rome, Richter also experienced a religious rebirth, which inspired him to use the woodcut as an economical method of reproduction, a decision that allowed the distribution of his religious and family-themed works to a wider audience. He produced illustrations of stories from the Bible, as well as modern scenes such as a family beside the Christmas tree or angels watching over pious children, a particular favorite revisited by the artist throughout his career.

Upon his return to Germany, Richter married and took a low-paying job as an art teacher. This period in his life was an unhappy one, as he suffered from poor health and nostalgia for his carefree days in Italy. His fortunes took a turn for the better following a journey to the upper Elbe valley that led to his falling in love with his own country for the first time and his appointment to a professorship at the Dresden Academy in 1836. Richter subsequently found inspiration in the depiction of German folk life—its farmers, lovers, drunkards in taverns, poignant deathbed and graveside scenes, religious holidays, parties in the forest, and other secular celebrations. His scenes of ordinary life have a romantic air, thanks to their borders of entwined flowers and vines. Richter's peasant mothers cradling their infants often recall the grace of the Madonna and Christ child. In some pictures, such as *Die Weisen aus dem Morgenland* (The Wise Men from the Orient, 1850), the peasant mother's loving eyes shine with greater beauty than those of the Virgin Mary. Like many German artists of his time, Richter was also attracted to his country's popular folk tales as subjects. His set of pictures for Johann Karl August Musäus's *Volksmärchen der Deutschen* (Folk Tales of the Germans, 1842) won him fame and other commissions for fairy tale illustrations. His style, which blended realism and romanticism, was perfectly suited to the representation of a world where children lost in the woods might encounter supernatural trials. For his masterpiece, *Bechsteins Märchenbuch* (Bechstein's Fairy Tale Book, 1853), Richter produced 174 woodcuts, bringing to life scenes such as Hansel and Gretel wandering in the forest, Little Red Riding Hood finding the wolf in her grandmother's bed, the dwarfs discovering Snow White strangled, and the prince awakening Briar Rose from her sleep. These illustrations are still reproduced in modern editions, and continue to appeal to today's readers as they did to Richter's contemporaries.

[*See also* Fairy Tales and Folk Tales; Germany; *and* Illustrations.]

BIBLIOGRAPHY

Fraser, Catherine. *Problems in a New Medium: Autobiographies by Three Artists*. New York: Lang, 1984.

MONICA FRIEDMAN

Riddell, Chris (1962–), British cartoonist, illustrator, and author of picture books. Riddell was born in South Africa before moving to the United Kingdom in 1963. He studied under Raymond Briggs at Brighton Polytechnic and has worked prolifically and diversely ever since as a freelance illustrator. Ridley's deft line drawing is in the tradition of Heath Robinson and Mervyn Peake, his exaggerated style demonstrating an affinity for the grotesque and fantastic. He has worked as a political cartoonist for various British journals and newspapers, such as *The Economist*, *The Independent*, and *The Observer*. He has illustrated several volumes of Ted Hughes's poetry; his absurd menagerie in Hughes's *The Iron Wolf* (1995) is typical of his work. As an illustrator of children's fiction, Riddell has collaborated with Philip Ridley, Susan Price, Terry Pratchett, and Brian Patten, and he cocreated *The Edge Chronicles* books with Paul Stewart. Venturing into historical "faction," Riddell "illuminated" Richard Platt's *Castle Diary* (1999) and won the Kate Greenaway Medal for Platt's *Pirate Diary* (2001). Riddell has also illustrated picture books with Paul Stewart, Alan Durant, and Katherine Cave, a partnership that claimed the UNESCO prize for *Something Else* (1994), and he has written his own picture books, including *Mr. Underbed* (1986), *The Trouble with Elephants* (1988), and *Platypus* (2001).

[*See also* Illustrations *and biographies of figures mentioned in this article.*]

LISA SAINSBURY

Riddle, Tohby (1965–), Australian picture-book author-illustrator, novelist, and newspaper cartoonist. Riddle is best known for *The Great Escape from City Zoo* (1997), which, in deceptively simple line drawings, encapsulates his characteristic mix of quirky humor, subtle (often ironical) wit, wide-ranging cultural reference, and willingness to engage with quite abstract social themes. Shaped by surreal storylines (an old man discarded at a rubbish dump; an unlikely quartet of animals staging a zoo-break; a bird nesting on a man's head), and incorporating numerous images from modern culture, from Mondrian to the Beatles, Riddle's picture books affirm cultural depth against a postmodern drift toward culture as surface.

[*See also* Australia *and* Picture Books.]

JOHN STEPHENS

Riddles. Riddles are enigmatic questions that are frequently used in narratives as contests and puzzles. While constrained literary writing like poetry has received much attention, riddles, perhaps by virtue of their puzzling form, are less often mentioned. Like poetry, riddles rely on the unusual use of everyday language for description. Using language in confusing or unusual ways, riddles ask questions or make statements in such a way as to make guessing the answer or meaning more difficult. While riddles were originally seen as advanced language play for adults, riddles were quickly incorporated into children's books—for example, Lewis Carroll's multiple riddles in the *Alice* books, because of their playful format, and J. R. R. Tolkien's riddling contest in *The Hobbit*.

In addition to the general form of the riddle, which has answers to its questions, particularly difficult or confusing questions are held within the larger category of enigmas, which includes questions that do not have answers. Other enigma forms include proverbs and fables, in which the meaning must be drawn from the stories. Riddles, because they create a contest between the one asking the riddle (the riddler) and the one answering the riddle (the riddlee), are inherently performative. The riddle differs from proverbs and fables because the riddle makes an explicit connection to its meaning through metaphor, while at the same time avoiding that connection through creative language usage to confuse the riddlee. Metaphor, which is the process by which two unlike objects are compared, is used in common riddles to connect things like people and fog or people and chess game pieces to allow for more creative description. In using metaphor to connect the two objects, riddles become questions to find both the manner in which the words are intended and the object to which the riddle refers.

Riddles are most often oral, as with riddling contests and games, or written, with books of riddles available as brain teasers and riddling games. There are multiple variations of the riddle in oral and written form. One of the oral variations includes conundrums, which rely on the multiple meanings of a single word instead of on metaphor. One popular conundrum is, "What's black and white and read all over?" The answer is a newspaper because the conundrum puns on the sound of the words "read" and "red." Other riddle forms include rebuses, which are riddles that combine images and text to confuse the reader and which visually appear in much the same form as concrete poetry. Still other forms include charades, in which the riddle is drawn or performed as a parlor game while others try to guess the answer.

One of the earlier examples of an oral riddle is the riddling contest tale between Oedipus and the Sphinx. In the tale, the land of Thebes was plagued by a monster called the Sphinx, who blocked the main road and made travelers who wished to pass answer a riddle. If the person failed, the Sphinx killed them. Until Oedipus, all of the travelers had been slain. The Sphinx asked Oedipus, "What animal in the morning goes on four feet, at noon on two, and in the evening on three?" To this, Oedipus replied, "Man." The answer to this riddle is man because a man crawls on hands and knees in childhood, stands on two feet in adulthood, and walks with a cane in old age. This riddle uses the metaphor of a day for a lifespan to make the answer more difficult. Other riddling contests have been more difficult because they are more enigmatic than true riddles, as with the riddling contest between Bilbo Baggins and Gollum in *The Hobbit*. In it, Bilbo asks Gollum to name the contents of Bilbo's pocket. This is not a true riddle, because it does not use metaphor and has no clear answer, but Gollum accepts it as a riddle. Because Gollum accepts it, the rules of riddling contests make it an allowable riddle.

Other riddling contests act as simple contests of wits, while others are used to decide marriages. Many stories and fables of princes and princesses who do not wish to marry or who wish to find the best marriage ask their suitors riddles, in order to refrain from marriage or to find the best marriage partner. Still other riddling contests are used to prove the intelligence of women in stories where men are dominant, showing that riddles are often subversive. In addition to the more elaborate and structure form of the riddling contest, other oral riddles are simply puzzles. One example of this sort of riddle is the nursery rhyme of Humpty Dumpty, which uses metaphor to describe an egg as a man. While the rhyme has lost its puzzle in more recent years, thanks largely to illustrated books of nursery rhymes, the rhyme was once a riddle.

Pictorial riddles are another, less recognized, form. Pictorial riddles often take the form of statements made with images, with clear answers. Other pictorial riddles include rebuses, which use images as language to convey the riddle. For these riddles, the riddlee must be able to understand the images in order to answer the riddle. Rebuses, like many pictorial riddles, draw heavily on hieroglyphics for their form. While pictorial riddles are less common than their oral and written counterparts, even less common are musical riddles. Tchaikovsky and Edward Elgar both created musical riddles where the music was meant to have an answer. Riddles in children's music are far less common, but they are becoming more common as children's digital media works emphasize sound and musical riddles. Children's riddles today are found in fiction works that ask riddles within the narrative; in word game puzzles like the altered meaning of the questions for crossword puzzles; in comic books with villains like the Riddler and Mr. Mxyzptlk; in board games that package charades into a game system with points; and in digital media that ask written riddles or that present visual riddles that players must solve.

[*See also* Humpty Dumpty; Nonsense; Poetry; *and biographies of figures mentioned in this article*.]

BIBLIOGRAPHY

Bryant, Mark. *Dictionary of Riddles*. New York: Routledge, 1990.

Dundas, Marjorie. *Riddling Tales from around the World*. Jackson: University Press of Mississippi, 2003.

McDowell, John Holmes. *Children's Riddling*. Bloomington: Indiana University Press, 1979.

LAURIE N. TAYLOR

Ridley, Philip (1964–), British writer. Ridley, born in London, had his own theater group at age six, wrote his first novel at age seven, and mounted a solo art exhibition at fourteen. While studying painting at London's St Martin's School of Art, he had his first book published at nineteen; he has since written plays and novels for both children and adults while also directing films and writing screenplays. Ridley's novels for children take on contemporary issues such as family breakdown and homelessness, but these are often seen through the prism of magical realism. The best example of this idiosyncratic approach is *Krindlekrax* (winner of the 1991 Smarties Prize), his third children's book, which tells the story of young Ruskin Splinter, up against not just the school bully but also a crocodile-dragon emerging from the sewers of London, whose name is the title of the book.

NICHOLAS TUCKER

Riley, James Whitcomb (1849–1916), American journalist and poet, a lifelong resident of Indiana. Riley began his career as a newspaper writer, humorist, and poet in the 1870s. In 1877 he started work at the *Indianapolis Journal* as resident poet and humorist. His first book of poetry, *The Old Swimmin' Hole and 'Leven More Poems*, was published in 1883, and from this time until 1903, rarely a year passed in which he did not publish a book. The poems were not always new, as later in his career he mostly reworked poems for collections. Several of these collections, such as *Rhymes of Childhood* (1890), *The Child-World* (1896), and *The Book of Joyous Children* (1902), were ostensibly aimed at children, though it has been argued that most of Riley's "children's poems" are poems about children but are meant to be read and appreciated by adults.

Nonetheless, many children in the early 20th century grew up thrilling to the words "The Gobble-uns'll git you ef you don't watch out!"—the refrain of Riley's most famous poem, "Little Orphant Annie" (1885), which was to gain tremendous popularity and, later, to give its adapted name to the famous comic strip. *The Old Swimmin' Hole* includes other well-known poems: "When the Frost Is on the Punkin" became a figure of speech as well as a widely recognized verse, while "Raggedy Man" (along with "Little Orphant Annie") inspired fellow Midwesterner Johnny Gruelle to name his doll creation Raggedy Ann.

Riley was one of the foremost practitioners of the regionalized dialect writing of the late 19th century, and the "Hoosier Poet" popularized his material further through his skill on the lecture circuit; as a result, Riley became probably the best-known poet of his, or any other, time in America. The dialect poem, with its attendant difficulties for child readers, has since fallen out of favor, and Riley is little read today. He nonetheless deserves to be remembered for his historical significance and for his creation of durable, if not eternal, standards of American children's verse.

[*See also* Poetry *and* United States.]

BIBLIOGRAPHY

Van Allen, Elizabeth J. *James Whitcomb Riley: A Life*. Bloomington: Indiana University Press, 1999.

JACQUE ROETHLER

Rinaldi, Ann (1934–), young adult and middle-grade historical fiction novelist. Rinaldi developed a passion for history by participating in American Revolution reenactments with her family in the 1970s. After publishing three contemporary realistic young adult novels in the early 1980s, Rinaldi incorporated her knowledge of the American Revolution into *Time Enough for Drums* (1986). Since then Rinaldi has written historical novels almost exclusively. Virtually all of her historical novels are set within the United States, most often during the Civil War or the American Revolution, and feature female protagonists whose stories are narrated in the first person. While most of Rinaldi's protagonists are of European American descent, she has written from an African American character's point of view in eight novels. Rinaldi's historical novels have received numerous awards, but her depiction of Nannie Rose, a Lakota Sioux attending boarding school in *My Heart Is on the Ground* (1999), has met with criticism on the grounds of cultural authenticity.

[*See also* Historical Fiction; Multiculturalism and Children's Books; *and* Native American Children's Literature.]

MARY ANN CAPPIELLO

Ring-a-ring-a-rosy. Also known as "Ring around the Rosie," one of the best-known nursery rhymes, as well an example of the tendency for children's material to attract theories of hidden, especially dark, meaning. The popular and widely repeated belief that this rhyme refers to the Black Death (or, in some versions, the 17th-century plague) continues to thrive, despite the absence of any historical support; the interpretation, doubted by folklore scholars, seems to have sprung up only in the 1960s. Antiquarians and folklorists, including Peter and Iona Opie, report Kate Greenaway's *Mother Goose* (1881) as its first print appearance and note several mentions of the verse (and suggestions of American origin) in folklore studies shortly thereafter. The rhyme's style and structure suggest a children's dancing game, and folklorists have theorized that it, like other "ring" rhymes, was in fact a game for the adolescent play-party, which was essentially a musicless square dance that allowed young people to evade bans on dancing.

[*See also* Fairy Tales and Folk Tales; Greenaway, Kate; Nursery Rhymes; *and* Opie, Iona, and Peter Opie.]

DEBORAH STEVENSON

Ringelnatz, Joachim (1883–1934), German cabaret artist, painter, and author, whose father Georg Bötticher also was a well-known children's author. Ringelnatz, whose real name was Hans Bötticher, served in the German Navy off and on from 1902 to 1918, but weak eyesight disqualified him from a full commission. He worked primarily as a librarian and archivist after World War I, while writing and reading his poetry in cabarets. Ringelnatz is best known for his humorous nonsense verse, such as the poems collected in *Kuttel Daddeldu oder das schlüpfrige Leid* (The Sailor Kuttel Daddeldu, or Underhanded Sorrow, 1920). His most famous children's books, *Geheimes Kinder-Spiel-Buch* (Secret Children's Game Book, 1924) and *Kinder-Verwirr-Buch* (Children's Confusion Book, 1931), are at times a grotesque affront to traditional order and respectability, while admirers see his playful verse as delightfully subversive—which is the reason they were republished during the antiauthoritarian period of the 1960s and 1970s.

[*See also* Germany; Nonsense; *and* Poetry.]

LUKE SPRINGMAN

Ringgold, Faith (1930–), African American artist raised in Harlem and internationally known for her paintings, fabric sculptures, and story quilts (a combination of painting, sewing, and storytelling). Ringgold's works typically combine

African American social history and African design elements. She was not initially convinced that story quilt scenes could be transferred to the picture book medium, but her first effort, *Tar Beach* (1991), became a Coretta Scott King Award winner and a Caldecott Honor book. The protagonist believes she can see much more by flying and thus improve life for her family—a conviction that grows as she soars over the bridge her father helped build. African American history is integral to the plot: for instance, the father is both Native American and African American; he is denied labor union membership; and his airborne daughter represents the flight-to-freedom motif that is ongoing in black culture. *Aunt Harriet's Underground Railroad in the Sky* (1992) features children who come to know the conductor on the "Railroad." Harriet Tubman is treated as both a presence and a voice, guiding the youngsters along the slave's dangerous path to Canada.

Ringgold's typical narrative strategy is to bring contemporary children into the realm of magic, a place in which historical events are dramatized. In *Dinner at Aunt Connie's House* (1993), she introduces achievements by African American women (for example, Sojourner Truth and Rosa Parks). *Bonjour Lonnie* (1996) highlights extended families and portrays black soldiers in World Wars I and II. Lonnie is the orphaned offspring of a father killed in battle and a Jewish mother killed by Nazis. Ringgold's art is highly stylized in its treatment of space, color, texture, and perspective. Her creations are thematically strong (for instance, sharply censuring ethnic and gender discrimination). Ringgold comments: "Art can envision our history and illustrate proud events in people's lives. And what's more, it can be magical!"

[*See also* African American Literature.]

Bibliography

Farrington, Lisa E. *Faith Ringgold*. San Francisco, Calif.: Pomegranate, 2004.

Ringgold, Faith. *Dinner at Aunt Connie's House*. New York: Hyperion Books for Children, 1993.

Donnarae MacCann

Rin Tin Tin. Rin Tin Tin was a German shepherd puppy discovered in the rubble of a German kennel in France at the end of World War I (1918). His rescuer, Corporal Lee Duncan, brought the dog home to Los Angeles and trained him. In 1922 the movie producer Darryl Zanuck saw the dog perform and made him a silent-film superstar. Since his death in 1932, his descendants have starred in movies, in an American Western television series (1954–1959), and in scores of books and comics. James English's 1949 biography outlines the affection between Duncan and Rin Tin Tin and his descendants. Some of the descendants were also trained to assist handicapped children through ARFKids.

[*See also* Animal Stories; Films: Original Feature Films; *and* Television and Children.]

Bibliography

English, James. *The Rin Tin Tin Story*. New York: Dodd Mead, 1949.

Arf Kids—Special Service Dogs for Special Kids. http://www.arfkids.com.

Rin Tin Tin. http://www.rintintin.com/story.htm.

Janice M. Bogstad

Rip Van Winkle. *See* Irving, Washington.

Riquet with the Tuft. "Riquet with the Tuft" is a French literary fairy tale in which a hideous suitor grants intelligence to a beautiful but witless woman in exchange for her hand in marriage. Versions of this story appear in Charles Perrault's *Histoires ou contes du temps passé* (Stories or Tales of Past Times, 1697) and Catherine Bernard's *Inès de Cordoue* (1697). In contrast to Perrault's optimistic rendering, which hints at the transformative power of love, Bernard's treatment of the theme reads as biting criticism of the folly of contractual marriages. No one has yet definitively proved which writer originated the tale, but both probably drew on motifs from beast bridegroom folk tales of the oral tradition.

[*See also* Fairy Tales and Folk Tales; France; *and* Perrault, Charles.]

Meera Lee Sethi

Ritchie, Anne Thackeray (1837–1919), English writer; daughter of William Makepeace Thackeray, who ensured that she had a good education in spite of her mother's bouts of mental illness, and gave her the opportunity to meet many of the major writers and public figures of the time. In later life, through her stepniece Virginia Woolf—whose work Ritchie influenced—she met the next generation of writers, including Henry James, Thomas Hardy, and Robert Louis Stevenson. Ritchie wrote a number of novels and tragedies in her early teens, "but then my father forbade me to waste my time any more scribbling, and desired me to read *other* people's books." For some time after that she wrote fairy tales exclusively, and this is the area in which she may be said to have contributed to children's literature. Ritchie's two volumes of contemporary tales, *Five Old Friends and a Young Prince* (1868; U.S. title, *Fairy Tales for Grown Folks*) and *Bluebeard's Keys* (1874), are largely based on classic tales. She also wrote an introduction to *The Fairy Tales of Madame d'Aulnoy* (1895). However, her implied audience was not one of children; Nina Auerbach and Uli Knoepflmacher include two of her tales in *Forbidden Journeys*, acknowledging Ritchie's early feminist leanings. The heroine of her "Sleeping Beauty" is an heiress who is stifled by the dullness of her "castle," and who has herself become dull, providing a critique of society's treatment of girls and women. The equivalent of the prince does come, but he finds her not particularly welcoming; they marry anyway.

Ritchie's reworking of "Cinderella" has a heroine who always thinks the best of people, and who receives help from a fairy godmother who "in her kind imperious way" overrides the petty unfairness of Cinderella's stepmother and stepsisters. The stature of this godmother is satirically undermined by revelations such as the fact that she "fattens up" workhouse boys and employs them as outriders to enhance her own dignity.

[*See also* Fairy Tales and Folk Tales *and* Thackerary, William Makepeace.]

FRANCES ARMSTRONG

Ritson, Joseph (1752–1803), English antiquary and book collector whose passion for preserving ballads and other traditional English songs included those of the nursery. The formidably learned Ritson was an atheist, vegetarian, and political radical with a gift for making enemies, thanks to his instigation of bitter controversies with other editors of historic literary texts, whom he abused for sloppiness, ignorance, and fraud. Ritson was regarded as a crackpot pedant consumed by trifles, a reputation exacerbated by his increasingly peculiar behavior during his descent into clinical dementia. By the end of his life, he had fallen out with most of his friends, including William Godwin, who nevertheless wrote a sympathetic obituary. By profession a lawyer but by avocation a scholar, Ritson edited several anthologies of traditional English and Scottish poetry between 1783 and 1795; his editions contain accurate transcriptions of the texts instead of versions rewritten to conform with contemporary taste, as was the practice during this period. Two volumes were issued at his own expense, handsomely produced with illustrations by John Bewick: *Pieces of Ancient Popular Poetry* (1791), which included a version of "Tom Thumb," and the monumental *Robin Hood: A Collection of All the Ancient Poems, Songs, and Ballads* (1795). The research for *Robin Hood* has proven so thorough that only a handful of ballads unknown to Ritson have been discovered subsequently. Using his collection of provincial chapbooks, Ritson compiled an anthology of nursery rhymes, *Gammer Gurton's Garland* (1783), one of the most important early sources for the genre. Possibly inspired by *Mother Goose's Melody*, a work Ritson presented to his little nephew, *Gammer Gurton* was first published as a twopenny chapbook for children. In 1810 Ritson's biographer Haslewood arranged for the publication of a new, much enlarged edition for adults. For his interest in collecting and publishing popular print culture and folklore for both learned and general audiences, Ritson should be seen as the first great scholar-collector of children's books and traditional lore, in whose footsteps James Halliwell-Phillipps and Iona and Peter Opie followed.

[*See also* Ballads; Collecting and Collectors; Nursery Rhymes; Robin Hood; *and biographies of figures mentioned in this article.*]

BIBLIOGRAPHY

Bronson, Bertrand. *Joseph Ritson: Scholar-at-Arms*. Berkeley: University of California Press, 1938.

ANDREA IMMEL

Rivero Oramas, Rafael (1904–1997), educator, journalist, painter, writer, and promoter of Venezuelan culture for children. He founded the first children's newspaper in Venezuela in 1938, *Onza, Tigre y León* (Otter-cat, Tiger, and Lion). In 1950 he founded and directed another magazine, *Tricolor*, which has published most of the major writers for children in Venezuela. It includes stories, biographies, poems, and articles on Venezuelan culture. His own stories, *Cuentos del tío Nicolás* (The Stories of Uncle Nicholas; some of them collected in *El mundo de Tio Conejo*, The World of Uncle Rabbit, 1985), were published in a national newspaper beginning in 1935. The stories were inspired by local legends and are set in the tropical landscape of his country—stories such as "El hombre, el tigre y la luna" (The Man, the Tiger, and the Moon), about the Camaracoto Indians, in which a man outwits a fierce tiger by pretending to catch and eat the moon. Others are humorous tales about stock animal characters and their tricks, such as "Tío Conejo y el Venado Sabio" (Uncle Rabbit and the Wise Deer).

[*See also* Children's Magazines; Journals and Periodicals; *and* South America, Spanish-Speaking.]

EVELYN ARIZPE

Riverside Magazine for Young People. Published between 1867 and 1870, *The Riverside Magazine for Young People: An Illustrated Monthly* was an innovative magazine for children with the highest literary and artistic standards. It was edited by Horace Scudder for Hurd and Houghton of New York and Boston, and was handsomely designed and illustrated by artists like John La Farge, Winslow Homer, and Thomas Nast. Scudder, a demanding editor, wrote a thoughtful column on children's reading, and selected contributors with care, among them Mary Mapes Dodge, Frank Stockton, and Sarah Orne Jewett. Scudder even taught himself Danish in order to cultivate a professional relationship with Hans Christian Andersen, managing to secure seventeen of his stories, ten of which were first published in *The Riverside*. Deemed a financial burden by its publishers, *The Riverside* disappeared in 1870 when sold to Scribner and Company; but it served as an excellent model for that publisher's *St. Nicholas Magazine*, edited by Scudder's friend Mary Mapes Dodge.

BIBLIOGRAPHY

Greene, David L. "*The Riverside Magazine for Young People*." In *Children's Periodicals of the United States*, edited by R. Gordon Kelly, 367–370. Westport, Conn., and London: Greenwood Press, 1984.

SUSAN R. GANNON

Roberts, Charles (1860–1943), Canadian poet, author, journalist, and editor who is often referred to as the father of Canadian literature. Roberts achieved popularity in the early 1900s as an innovator in the genre of the animal story. His writing depicts outdoor life in maritime Canada and portrays animals as intelligent and rational. He believed that animals do not act on instinct alone, contradicting prevalent notions of Darwinian determinism. President Theodore Roosevelt accused Roberts of being a "nature-fakir." Roberts, however, maintained that his stories were based on close observation. In any case, he is a precursor to modern environmental awareness and a significant contributor to the naturalist tradition in Canada. A popular example of his work is the novel *Red Fox* (1905), in which the title character, a fox, survives in the wilderness through superior cunning and wisdom. Red Fox learns from experience and overcomes obstacles, both man-made and natural, from traps set by men to confrontations with other predators to drought and fire. Human characters are secondary or not present at all. One human character, known only as Boy, is sympathetic to Red Fox and serves as a link to the target audience—the young adult reader. Roberts avoids symbolism in his writing and instead uses a straightforward, realistic, and descriptive voice. His upbringing near marshlands in rural New Brunswick served as a source of inspiration. Roberts's other works include *Earth's Enigmas* (1895), *Kindred of the Wild* (1902), *The Watchers of the Trails* (1904), *Haunters of the Silences* (1907), and *The Feet of the Furtive* (1912). A prominent member of the "Confederation Poets," Roberts wrote an elegy to Percy Bysshe Shelley and other poetry that varied from lyrical to free verse, with themes from pastoral to patriotic. He was knighted in 1935.

[*See also* Animal Stories; Canada; *and* Ecology and Environment.]

BRIAN J. HAMISTER

Roberts, Elizabeth (1881–1941), American novelist and poet. Elizabeth Madox Roberts's novels for adults were extremely popular during the 1920s and 1930s. Her reputation in children's literature rests on one book, a small volume of poetry published early in her career, *Under the Tree* (1922), available in the mid-2000s in its entirety online from the University of North Carolina. A revised edition with seven new poems was published in 1930, with lovely illustrations by F. D. Bedford, reprinted by the University Press of Kentucky in 1985. As the second of eight children, the young Elizabeth escaped the drudgery of household work by inventing a wealthy fantasy family, foreshadowing the vivid imagination that is evident in her poems. Roberts spent most of her life in Springfield, Kentucky, although she completed a degree in English at the University of Chicago at the age of forty. The poet David McCord waxed eloquent about the quality of her poetry in an essay in *Twentieth Century Children's Writers* (1983), describing her as "absolutely unique in the field of verse for children" and "the only poet . . . writing in the English language who possessed and consistently used the undisguised, uninterrupted voice of childhood." Roberts's poems continue to be anthologized in children's poetry collections.

[*See also* McCord, David *and* Poetry.]

LINNEA HENDRICKSON

Robertson, Keith (1914–1991), American writer of adventures, detective stories, historical sea tales, animal stories, and (under the pseudonym Carlton Keith) six adult mysteries. After graduating from the United States Naval

Academy and serving during World War II as the captain of a destroyer, Robertson published his first book, *Ticktock and Jim* (1948); the following year he published a sequel, *Ticktock and Jim, Deputy Sheriffs*. During the next three decades he published more than thirty books, including the animal stories *The Dog Next Door* (1950) and *In Search of a Sandhill Crane* (1973), mysteries such as *The Missing Brother* (1950) and *Three Stuffed Owls* (1954), and tales of suspense and adventure such as *Ice to India* (1955) and *The Crow and the Castle* (1957). He also published a single work of children's nonfiction, *The Wreck of the Saginaw* (1954). Robertson won the New Jersey Author's Award for *The Money Machine* (1969), a suspense thriller in his Carson Street Detectives series. He was best known for his award-winning Henry Reed series, comprising *Henry Reed, Inc.* (1958), *Henry Reed's Journey* (1963), *Henry Reed's Baby-Sitting Service* (1966), *Henry Reed's Big Show* (1970), and *Henry Reed's Think Tank* (1986). The series was widely praised for its comedy, most obvious in the dry wit of Henry's first-person narratives but also apparent in the unusual events that occur whenever Henry is around. Robertson focused on the adventures of believable characters in realistic situations and often rural surroundings. Moreover, he adhered to a strict code of ethics in his writing: he believed in using good grammar, making meaning clear, presenting accurate facts, avoiding foul language, and creating protagonists who achieved something independently of the adults around them.

[*See also* Adventure Books; Animal Stories; *and* Mystery and Detective Stories.]

ANNE HIEBERT ALTON

Robin Hood. Robin Hood stories in the modern age follow the wider trajectory of children's literature from adventure story and historical novel to introspective narratives engaging with issues of gender, ethnicity, ethics, and other issues that shape subjectivity. Because Robin Hood is known from a diverse bundle of sources, with no single, integrated narrative coming down from antiquity, the legend sustains diverse representations and genres, although a tendency to contain its growth within the bounds of the already told is evidenced in retellings as far apart as Rosemary Sutcliff's *The Chronicles of Robin Hood* (1950) and Robert Leeson's *The Story of Robin Hood* (1994).

Early references to Robin Hood, from the 14th century, can be found in "rymes" or songs, and most of the sources are described as ballads. The earliest extended narrative is *A Gest of Robyn Hode*, originating in the late 15th century. At this stage, Robin is a bandit yet to evolve into the modern romantic and chivalric figure. Although some of his named companions are familiar, such as Little John, Much the Miller's son, and Will Scathelock, others, particularly Friar Tuck and Maid Marian, have not yet appeared.

Numerous retellings for young readers were published in the 19th century, but by far the most distinguished of these is Howard Pyle's 1883 *The Merry Adventures of Robin Hood of Great Renown in Nottinghamshire*, which attempts to link episodes through character motivation and cause-and-effect processes. Pyle still influences modern retellings, especially in the United States. The outstanding retellings in the first half of the 20th century are by Henry Gilbert (1912), Geoffrey Trease (1934), and Roger Lancelyn Green (1956). Green, in his usual syncretic fashion, draws material from many sources, including the ballads, Walter Scott's *Ivanhoe* (1819)—in which, crucially, Robin is first represented as an Anglo-Saxon resisting the tyranny of the conquering Normans—and Thomas Love Peacock's *Maid Marian* (1822).

Retellings may be classified into two types. The first, which comprises most existing texts, is characterized by identification of Robin as "one of the first in a long line of men and women who believed that freedom is more precious than life itself" (Miles). These retellings take three forms: novelistic renditions with a developed sense of coherence and an inclination toward inventiveness; replications, which are characteristically episodic in structure and re-present a traditional selection of ballads; and illustrated and comic books, which usually focus on only a small selection of incidents.

The second type of retelling, "alternative" reversions, is represented by a very small group, consisting of Trease's *Bows against the Barons* (1934) and the novelized spin-offs from Richard Carpenter's television series *Robin of Sherwood* (1984–1986). These works are very different and widely separated in time but share a politicized, radical narrative stance that refuses the Royalist ideology on which the majority of retellings rest. Rather, they seek to exploit the differences between their versions and the traditional motifs and outcomes in order to suggest that new social formations will interrogate old narratives, reshaping them not merely into new shapes and plots but also into new significances.

More generally, however, the multiplicity of sources means that retellers choose between alternative possibilities with a potential for vastly different story outcomes. Interpretations pivot especially on the following: the class origins of Robin; the circumstances of Robin's outlawry; the class origins of Marian, and her relationship with the outlaws and

Robin Hood Engraving by Thomas Bewick from *Robin Hood* by Joseph Ritson (London, 1795). Collection of Jack Zipes

Sherwood; the presentation of setting, especially the idea of "merry England"; the functions of the Royalist ideology commonly attributed to Robin since the time of the *Gest* (whereby Robin punishes the wicked among the social elite but remains loyal to the true monarch); and the existence of multiple possible endings in which, for example, Robin may be murdered by the Prioress of Kirklees, join King Richard at the Crusades, resume or be awarded his aristocratic station as Robin of Loxley, or live out his days in Sherwood. If to this list are added such generic choices as that between novelistic or illustrated narrative, or that of any mix of historiography, legend, fantasy, and adventure story, there would seem to be an infinite number of ways of retelling the story. But although each retelling is distinct, there are two consistent elements: first, the majority of retellings center on representations of chivalric behavior and of the defense of the weak and ruled against tyrannical rulers, and second, the significant ideologically alternative texts construct their oppositional stances not by reworking traditional stories but by inventing new ones.

Trease's *Bows against the Barons* is notable for two main reasons: its depiction of class warfare, which introduces overt polemic into the narrative, and its harnessing of a device common in children's historical fiction in which the story is narrated from the point of view of a character, often a child, who is on the periphery of events but develops and matures as a consequence of exposure to them. This innovation reflects how subsequent retellings reproduce contemporary narrative strategies in children's literature, especially in the way fictive point of view is that of a single protagonist and theme hinges on the psychology and maturation of that protagonist. In contrast, the ballad origins had established a particular mode for narrating Robin Hood stories: characters are seen from outside, and reactions and responses are stated within narration rather than explored through inner mental processes or dialogue.

A second major trend is the assigning of central roles to female characters. Indebted to the feminist notion of the "green witch" evolved during the 1970s, such narratives depict women as healers and nurturers who bring range and depth to the episodic adventures of male characters: principal examples are Theresa Tomlinson's *The Forestwife* (1993) and *Child of the May* (1998), Nancy Springer's *Rowan Hood: Outlaw Girl of Sherwood Forest* (2001), and Robin McKinley's *The Outlaws of Sherwood* (1988). The standout version here is McKinley's, because of its capacity to elude event-focused narration and depict the characters focalizing incidents and events. A particularly impressive character-focalized retelling is Michael Cadnum's first Robin Hood novel, *In a Dark Wood* (2002), in which the Sheriff of Nottingham is protagonist. Here the sheriff is a solitary, introspective pragmatist who is humanized by his oblique and direct encounters with Robin.

Few stories have been retold as often as Robin Hood, but very few retellings have been able to find new possibilities in the story. Effective rereadings are achieved, as Trease, Carpenter, McKinley, and Cadnum demonstrate, by embedding the old stories within new frames.

BIBLIOGRAPHY

Barnhouse, Rebecca. "Robin Hood Comes of Age." *ALAN Review* 30, no. 2 (Winter 2003): 25–29.

Holt, James Clarke. *Robin Hood*. London: Thames and Hudson, 1982.

Knight, Stephen. *Robin Hood: A Mythic Biography*. Ithaca, N.Y.: Cornell University Press, 2003.

Miles, Bernard. *Robin Hood: His Life and Legend*. Chicago: Childrens Press Choice, 1984.

Singman, Jeffrey L. *Robin Hood: The Shaping of the Legend*. Westport, Conn.: Greenwood, 1998.

JOHN STEPHENS

Robinson, Charles (1870–1937), English illustrator. The second son of the wood engraver and illustrator Thomas Robinson, Charles Robinson was born in Islington, London. Unlike his artist brothers Tom and William, he was never able to study art full-time. On leaving school he was apprenticed to the lithographic printers Waterlow and Sons, completing his studies at evening classes. His first published drawings were for three children's primers, and their favorable review in *The Studio* magazine in 1895 led to an introduction to John Lane, who commissioned him to illustrate Robert Louis Stevenson's *A Child's Garden of Verses* (1895). Drawing on a variety of sources for inspiration, including Dürer's engravings, early Venetian printing, and the more contemporary ideas of William Morris and Walter Crane, Robinson produced a series of decorative and original illustrations that, together with his overall design for the book, won him wide acclaim. Over the next ten years he was inundated with commissions for book and magazine work, initially in black and white, but increasingly in color as well. At his best he showed a sureness and facility of line and an unfailing appreciation of the decorative possibilities of illustration rarely equaled by his contemporaries. Some of his finest work includes *The Secret Garden* (1911), *The Sensitive Plant* (1911), *The Big Book of Fables* (1912), and *The Happy Prince* (1913). After World War I, work from magazines enabled him to earn a modest living. Later he concentrated on watercolor for magazine and commercial work. He was elected to the Royal Institute of Painters in Watercolours in 1932.

[*See also* Book Design; Illustrations; *and biographies of figures mentioned in this article.*]

GEOFFREY BEARE

Robinson, W. Heath (1872–1944), English illustrator. In the 1930s, William Heath Robinson was best known for his drawings of mad inventions, and is still most widely remembered for his wonderful humorous work. But illustrating was only his third choice of career, one that he turned to almost by accident. On leaving the Royal Academy Schools in 1895 his ambition was to become a landscape painter. Realizing that it would not pay the bills, he followed his two older brothers (Thomas and Charles) into book illustration. With his fine control of line, original vision, and ability to adapt his style to the text, he quickly established himself. In 1903, following the publication of *The Adventures of Uncle Lubin* (1902), which he both wrote and illustrated, he felt sufficiently secure to marry. However, a publisher who had commissioned a large quantity of drawings was declared bankrupt. Heath Robinson, now the father of a baby girl, had quickly to find a new source of income. He turned to magazines, such as *The Sketch* and *The Tatler*, that paid well for humorous drawings, and within a year was being acclaimed as a unique talent in the field of humorous art. For many years, he combined illustration and humor with equal and growing success. He was ranked with Rackham and Dulac as an illustrator of gift books; outstanding examples include *Bill the Minder* (1912), which he also wrote; *Andersen's Fairy Tales* (1913); and *The Water Babies* (1915). But by the end of World War I the market for lavishly illustrated gift books had all but disappeared. Nevertheless his talents as a hu-

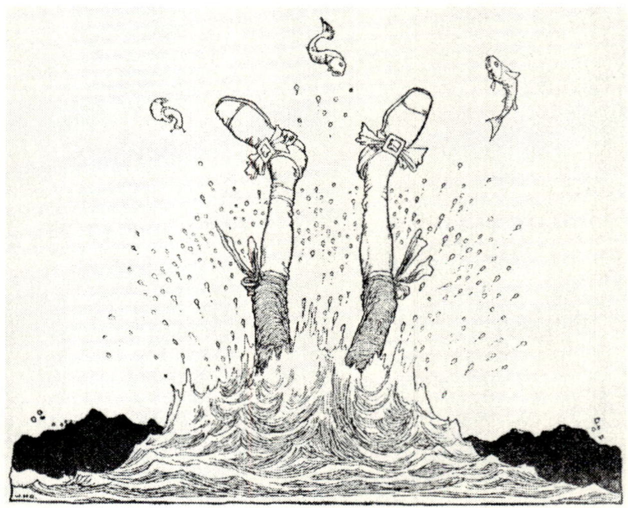

W. Heath Robinson. Illustration from *Bill the Minder* (London: Hodder & Stoughton, 1933), p. 10. REPRODUCED COURTESY OF THE COTSEN CHILDREN'S LIBRARY, PRINCETON UNIVERSITY LIBRARY

morist were in ever-increasing demand, especially for advertising. At his death in 1944 only a few remembered his work as a serious illustrator, but like Hogarth and Rowlandson before him, the appeal of his humorous art was largely the result of his considerable talents as a serious artist.

[*See also* Humor; Illustrations; *and biographies of figures mentioned in this article.*]

Geoffrey Beare

Robinson Crusoe. *See* Defoe, Daniel

Robinsonnades. Daniel Defoe's *Robinson Crusoe* (1719) was so popular that it began almost immediately to inspire a host of imitations throughout Europe. It became the prototype of a new literary genre known as the Robinsonnade that spread rapidly across Europe and beyond. Although the first Robinsonnades were for adults, the new genre, like the novel that had spawned it, soon became extremely popular with children. Several European countries produced great Robinsonnades that, in turn, would inspire others. Joachim Heinrich Campe published *Robinson der Jüngere* (1779; English trans., *Robinson the Younger*, 1781), which was one of Germany's most successful children's books. A Swiss pastor, Johann David Wyss, wrote the most famous Robinsonnade, *Der Schweizerische Robinson* (1812–1813; English trans., *The Swiss Family Robinson*, 1814), which engendered many adaptations and continuations, including Jules Verne's sequel, *Seconde patrie* (Second Fatherland, 1900).

Defoe's novel established the formal conventions of a realistic genre that combines the adventure story and the psychological novel, although the former generally prevails in juvenile Robinsonnades. Authors adhere with varying degrees of fidelity to its codes, but the narrative of the traditional Robinsonnade generally begins with a shipwreck and the arrival on a desert island, and ends with a return to civilization, usually accompanied by a spiritual regeneration. In addition to the ordeals involved in the struggle to survive, the protagonist must deal with such problems as solitude, fear, and depression. The archetypal motif of the desert island serves as a metaphor of solitude. This solitude may be an opportunity for new self-awareness, but it can also be the occasion for a regression into animality and insanity. The Robinsonnade has an amazing capacity to adapt to different cultural contexts and to lend itself to the social and literary preoccupations of the time. Just as Jean-Jacques Rousseau considered *Robinson Crusoe* to be an educational treatise, declaring it would be Émile's only book, the Robinsonnade has often had a didactic intent. Madame de Genlis's *L'île aux enfants* (The Children's Island) was a pedagogical treatise for young children. In Wyss's family Robinsonnade, the father imparts his knowledge to his four sons as well as young readers. Victorian boys' book writers often wrote didactic Robinsonnades that served to glorify God and country, for example Frederick Marryat's *Masterman Ready* (1841) and R. M. Ballantyne's *The Coral Island* (1857). Many 19th-century Robinsonnades extolled the values of colonialism and imperialism. Robinsonnades may accept, question, or renounce the original text. Contemporary Robinsonnades tend to interrogate and subvert the Crusoe myth, often with the use of irony, as does Michel Tournier's *Vendredi ou la vie sauvage* (1971; English trans., *Friday and Robinson*, 1972). Critics sometimes refer to certain inversions as anti-Robinsonnades. William Golding's *Lord of the Flies* has been called the first modern Robinsonnade. Golding deliberately exploits the genre to subvert the Crusoe myth, creating a tragic, dystopian Robinsonnade of the type that is common in adult novels. Contemporary authors work within the tradition of the Robinsonnade to examine modern social problems such as technology, environmental concerns, gender issues, and racism.

In Robinsonnades for children, the protagonist is generally a child. It can be a boy, a girl, a brother and sister (*Robinson et Robinsonne* by Pierre Maël, 1895), or even two sisters (*Baby Island* by Carol Ryrie Brinks, 1937). Sometimes it is a family, as in *The Swiss Family Robinson* or *Die Familie Waldmann* (1842), or a child in the company of adults, as in Jules Verne's *L'île mystérieuse* (1874; English trans., *The Mysterious Island*, 1875). It can also be a group composed only of children, generally boys, as in Verne's *Deux ans de vacances* (1888) and Vincent Serventy's *Crusoe Boys* (1995). The casting of a female in the role of the protagonist is not a new phenomenon. Madame Woillez's *Le Robinson des demoiselles* (The Young Ladies' Robinson) was published in France in 1835. Sometimes authors create a female Robinson, as in Marie Majerová's *Robinsonka* (Little Miss Robinson, 1984) and Elfie Stejskal's *Malediven: Das Mädchen Robinson* (Maldives: The Girl Robinson, 1986); sometimes the protagonist is another character, as in Jane Gardam's *Crusoe's Daughter* (1985). In Klaus Kordon's *Robinson, Mittwoch und Julchen* (Robinson, Wednesday, and Juliette, 1991), a feminine character is added to the two traditional male figures. Numerous Robinsonnades, in particular those for younger children, present an animal protagonist. The hero of William Steig's *Abel's Island* (1976) is a

FRONTISPIECE.

Family Robinson Crusoe.

THE
FAMILY
Robinson Crusoe:
OR,
JOURNAL
OF A FATHER SHIPWRECKED, WITH HIS
WIFE AND CHILDREN, ON AN
UNINHABITED ISLAND.

TRANSLATED FROM THE GERMAN OF
M. WISS.

IN TWO VOLUMES.
VOL. I.

London:
PRINTED FOR M. J. GODWIN AND Co.,
At the JUVENILE LIBRARY, 41, Skinner-Street.
1814.

Robinsonnades. Frontispiece and title page from *The Family Robinson Crusoe* by J. Wiss (London: M. J. Godwin, 1814). REPRODUCED COURTESY OF THE COTSEN CHILDREN'S LIBRARY, PRINCETON UNIVERSITY LIBRARY

mouse, whereas Janosch tells the story of a Robinson rabbit in *Robinson Hase* (Robinson Rabbit, 1988). In Anne Parrish's *Floating Island* (1930), the characters are dolls.

Although the island archetype is synonymous with the Crusoe myth, Robinsonnades take place in a wide range of settings. Other wilderness settings include the forest, the desert, and the polar regions. Catherine Parr Traill's *Canadian Crusoes* (1852) is set in the Ontario forest, and Mayne Reid's *The Desert Home* (1852) is set in the American desert. Urban Robinsonnades include *Slake's Limbo*, set in the New York City area; Doeschka Meijsing's *Robinson* (1976), set in Haarlem; and Uri Orlev's *The Island on Bird Street*, set in the Jewish ghetto of Warsaw. Settings range from the depths of the ocean (Gianni Padoan's *Robinson degli oceani*, 1973) to outer space, where the protagonist can be stranded on the moon (Padoan's *Robinson dello spazio*, 1971) or another planet (Robert Heinlein's *Tunnel in the Sky*, 1955). Science fiction Robinsonnades have flourished since the time of Verne. Fantasy Robinsonnades include a number of time travelers, such as the protagonists of Maurice Bitter's 1980s series *Les Robinsons du temps*. The Robinsonnade has been appropriated by most genres of children's literature. Many picture books, such as *Ich, Kater Robinson* (I, Robinson Cat) by Peter Schössow and Harry Rowohlt, and *Robinson couteau suisse* (Swiss Knife Robinson, 2002) by Bruno Heitz, are what some critics refer to as pseudo-Robinsonnades, because they retain little more than the intertextual reference in the title. The largest number of Robinsonnades, however, are realistic novels for adolescents, such as Scott O'Dell's *Island of the Blue Dolphins* (1960), Monique Peyrouton de Ladebat's *Le village aux yeux fermés* (1961; English trans., *The Village That Slept*, 1963), Ivan Southall's *To the Wild Sky* (1967), Richard Armstrong's *The Mutineers* (1968), Theodore Taylor's *The Cay* (1969), Nicholas Fisk's *High Way Home* (1973), and Arthur Roth's *The Iceberg Hermit* (1974).

[*See also* Adventure Books; Colonial Fiction; Sea Stories; *and biographies of figures mentioned in this article.*]

BIBLIOGRAPHY

Green, Martin. *The Robinson Crusoe Story*. University Park: Pennsylvania State University Press, 1990.

Hanlon, Tina. "The Descendents of Robinson Crusoe in North American Children's Literature." In *The Presence of the Past in Children's Literature*, edited by Ann Lawson Lucas, 61–69. Westport, Conn.: Greenwood, 2003.

Loxley, Diana. *Problematic Shores: The Literature of the Islands*. London: Macmillan, 1992.

SANDRA L. BECKETT

Robles, Antonio (1895–1983), also known as "Antoniorrobles," real name Antonio J. Robles Soler, Spanish author and journalist. Influenced by the avant-garde, he worked with several magazines specializing in the humor of the absurd. In the mid-1930s he became involved in children's literature, publishing two collections of stories that made him famous in Spain: *Hermanos Monigotes* (Puppet Brothers, 1935) and *Rompetacones y Azulita* (Break-Heels and Little Blue, 1936). In his stories, Antoniorrobles reveals his liking for minor, everyday matters as well as the great scientific and technical advances of his times. At the end of the Spanish civil war (1939), Robles went into exile in Mexico, where he continued working on a number of related projects.

BIBLIOGRAPHY

García Padrino, Jaime, ed. *Nuestro Antoniorrobles*. Madrid: Asociación de Amigos del Libro Infantil y Juvenil, 1996.

MARISA FERNÁNDEZ-LÓPEZ

Robson, Jenny (1952–), award-winning South African–born writer. Born Jennifer Marion Murray, Robson grew up amid apartheid, witnessing firsthand the results of prejudice. As an adult, she studied teaching and became a music educator in Botswana. Her books for children stress themes of identity, individuality, and acceptance. Among the many awards garnered by her work are four consecutive Sanlam Youth Novel Competitions, for *Don't Panic, Mechanic* (1994), *One Magic Moment* (1996), *The Denials of Kow-Ten* (1998), and *Because Pula Means Rain* (2000), which also earned a UNESCO Children's Book Prize in 2003. Additionally, Robson writes short stories and has published a novel for adults.

[*See also* Africa: Southern Africa.]

MONICA FRIEDMAN

Rockwell, Anne (1934–), prolific author-illustrator born in Tennessee and educated at the Pratt Graphic Arts Center in New York. Rockwell adapts, writes, and illustrates picture books of every sort: folk tales (*The Monkey's Whiskers*, 1971), books about things (*Fire Engines*, 1986), and books about places (*I Like the Library*, 1977), not to mention song books, game books, and nursery rhyme collections. Until his death in 1988, her husband, Harlow Rockwell, was sometimes a collaborator, as in *My Barber* (1981). In supporting the child's first haircut, the Rockwells develop an aura of equanimity in this book, using understatement in their forms and shading.

Albert B. Cub and Zebra: An Alphabet Storybook (1977) also demonstrates Anne Rockwell's skillful coordination of picture and text. Since this work is a learning game, a narrative, and an alphabet book, she must design illustrations that carry a storyline and at the same time accommodate exercises in word building. Moreover, since locating numerous objects is part of the game, she must make room for them with a minimum of clutter. Rockwell arranges all this with considerable spontaneity. Her style is decorative, simple, orderly, and appealing in its use of watercolor and fresh white spaces. For variations in tone, she lets her paint make occasional puddles of color. In illustrating Clyde Bulla's *The Stubborn Old Woman* (1980), a tale highlighting the encounter of child wisdom with adult foolishness, Rockwell combines many small objects into naive, unpretentious patterns. But the woman's form is a very strong shape—one that serves as a bold accent against an unobtrusive, geometric landscape. In her stream of books about springtime, playtime, daytime, nighttime, vacation time, and so on, Rockwell is serving the needs of teachers. But in using her skill as an artist, she is raising such formula-confining projects to a higher level—to an artistic standard where the child's aesthetic sensibilities can be easily engaged.

[*See also* ABC Books or Alphabet Books; Bulla, Clyde Robert; Illustrations; Information Books; *and* Picture Books.]

DONNARAE MACCANN

Rockwell, Harlow (1910–1988), American author and illustrator of books for very young children. After many years in commercial art, Harlow began creating picture books in 1961 with his *ABC Book*. He followed with just six other books, all written by others, in the rest of the decade. Then through the 1970s and 1980s, working sometimes alone and more often collaborating with his wife, Anne, he created more than thirty books presenting common experiences of preschool children. *The Toolbox* (1971), one of several titles selected for the American Institute of Graphic Arts Children's Book Show, became a kind of prototype with minimal, clear text and simple, clean drawings, flat in perspective and richly colored against white pages. Often, as in *My Back Yard* (1984), a young child is the narrator. Whatever the subject, from visiting the dentist to watching pollywogs, each book beautifully encapsulates the viewpoint of the young child.

[*See also* Anne Rockwell.]

MARGARET BUSH

Rockwell, Thomas (1933–), American writer. Rockwell is best known for his novel *How to Eat Fried Worms* (1973). He is the second son of the renowned painter Norman Rockwell, who regularly published in the *Saturday Evening Post*. Although surrounded by art while growing up in Vermont, Thomas Rockwell developed a greater interest in writing than in visual art. He earned a BA at Bard College (1956), but only when he became a father did he pursue his interest in writing, publishing his first children's text in 1969: *Rackety-Bang and Other Verses*. Rockwell's imaginative work is characterized by unconventional, child-centered humor that children enjoy but some adults find distasteful. In *How to Eat Fried Worms*, protagonist Billy Forrester accepts a fifty-dollar bet with his friends to eat fifteen worms in fifteen days. Rockwell continued Billy's story in two sequels, *How to Fight a Girl* (1987) and *How to Get Fabulously Rich* (1990).

MICHELLE H. MARTIN

Rodari, Gianni (1920–1980), Italian author. Rodari was the foremost writer for children in 20th-century Italy; his idealism, critical independence, experiments, and innovations changed the direction of Italian children's literature and gained Rodari an international reputation. Born to a poor northern Italian family, Rodari briefly became a teacher. After that he devoted his life to journalism, educational reform, and writing, inspired, like many other intellectuals in postwar Italy, by a utopian Marxism. His fundamental preoccupation was always with education in the broadest sense. As a writer for the young in both prose and verse, he was intensely original, imaginative, and creative.

Rodari became a staff journalist in 1947, working in Milan and Rome for the respected Communist daily *L'unità*;

Gianni Rodari. COLLECTION OF JACK ZIPES

in 1950 he became editor of *Il pioniere*, a children's weekly paper linked to the Communist Party. In 1958 he was appointed special correspondent and lead writer for *Paese sera*, a role he maintained until the end of his life. Rodari's abundant publications include travel writings resulting from journeys in Russia and China. In the 1950s, as the cold war began, Rodari was condemned by the Catholic Church for his promotion of communism; at the time the Church and the Italian Communist Party were the two great power blocs of Italian politics. In the 1960s Rodari traveled around schools, working closely with teachers and parents to regenerate education under the auspices of the Movimento di Cooperazione Educativa (Movement for Educational Cooperation). From 1968 to 1971 he was editor of *Il giornale dei genitori*, a periodical for parents. From the outset he was a deeply convinced campaigner for the application of egalitarian and humanitarian ideals to the education system and to teaching methods.

During the reconstruction of war-torn and impoverished Italy in the 1950s, Rodari began to introduce into reading matter for children new themes that demonstrated and encouraged social commitment—pacifism, class, and the exploitation and solidarity of workers. At this time, in *Il romanzo di Cipollino* (The Story of Little Onion, 1951), with its traditional peasant inspiration, Rodari reworked features of popular folklore. His early writings include his collection of new nursery rhymes, *Filastrocche in cielo e in terra* (Nursery Rhymes of Heaven and Earth, 1960), and the very short stories narrated by a traveling salesman to his child over the telephone each evening, *Favole al telefono* (1962; English trans., *Telephone Tales*, 1965). These texts have now become classics in Italy. His taste for parody was apparent: the title of the book of verse echoes a pompous title invented by the grandiloquent prewar poet Gabriele D'Annunzio. Rodari also relished wordplay and games with rhyme. A sense of joyous play is constantly present in his writings, and the stories frequently emphasize the contrast between the natural freedom of children's life and the regulated habits of the adult world. While there are many allusions to popular legend through variations on the themes of Cockayne and the World Upside Down, he also featured the technological advances of the modern world (telephones, television, machines). With *La torta in cielo* (1966; English trans., *A Pie in the Sky*, 1971), Rodari devised a comic science fiction novel developed from the idea of the flying saucer. More in line with the Romantic and fairy-tale tradition is *Gli affari del Signor Gatto* (1972; English trans., *Mr Cat in Business*, 1975), though Rodari's emblematic cat was derived from a personal childhood experience. His narrative masterpiece is the comic novel *C'era due volte il barone Lamberto* (Twice upon a Time There Was the Baron Lambert, 1978), in which, against the idyllic setting of his native Lake Orta, the author ridicules convention and the capitalist and commercial world, while elaborating the hilariously optimistic fantasy of a very old man who grows ever younger: the story urges heroic independence and laughs in the face of death.

In 1973 Rodari had published an extraordinary book for parents and teachers, *La grammatica della fantasia* (English trans., *The Grammar of Fantasy*, 1996), in which he explained his intentions and methods as an inventive storyteller and exhorted others to join him in his educational crusade to encourage creativity. The posthumous *Esercizi di fantasia* (Exercises in Imagination, 1981) further revealed his techniques and provided more coaching. These books offer remarkable insight into Rodari's thinking. His creative works combine a concern for the mundane world with flights of improbable fancy; however, he makes clear in his *Grammatica* that fantasy is not, for him, an escape but rather a key to understanding reality.

Rodari had embarked on his career at a time of radical political and social change; his work marks the definitive break of contemporary Italian children's literature with the social, literary, and linguistic assumptions of the first half of its history. Postwar Italy would establish education for all, while radio and television would unify a still deeply regional and multidialectal country. In order to gather all children in his audience, including the rural and urban poor, Rodari developed a new language and style not constrained by social class or region, a language that was not abstruse or sentimental but vivid and direct. For him language and imagination were interdependent. At the heart of his creative genius, therefore, is his bold and sparkling use of words.

BIBLIOGRAPHY

Argilli, Marcello, Lucio Del Cornò, and Carmine De Luca, eds. *Le provocazioni della fantasia: Gianni Rodari scrittore e educatore*. Rome: Riuniti, 1993.

Boero, Pino. *Una storia tante storie: Guida all'opera di Gianni Rodari*. Turin: Einaudi, 1992.

Cambi, Franco. *Collodi, De Amicis, Rodari: Tre immagini d'infanzia*. Bari: Dedalo, 1985.

De Luca, Carmine. *Gianni Rodari: La gaia scienza della fantasia*. Catanzaro: Abramo, 1991.

Rodari, Gianni. *The Grammar of Fantasy*. Translated and with an introduction by Jack Zipes. New York: Teachers and Writers Collaborative, 1996.

Zagni, Patrizia. *Gianni Rodari*. Florence: La Nuova Italia, 1975.

ANN LAWSON LUCAS

Rodda, Emily (1948–), real name Jennifer Rowe; Australian author also known for her work as an editor and as a writer of adult mysteries. Many of Rodda's children's stories employ fantasy elements within the real world or link this world to another (fantastic) realm. Beginning with *Something Special* in 1984, Rodda wrote several children's fantasies based on these structures, including *Pigs Might Fly* (1986), *The Best-Kept Secret* (1988), and *Crumbs!* (1990). After writing *The Timekeeper* (1992), a sequel to her fantasy *Finders Keepers* (1990), about a young boy's involvement in the events of another world that runs on a different time scheme than our own, Rodda began to write series fiction, several of which have become the high points of her oeuvre. The Rowan series, beginning with *Rowan of Rin* (1993), is a substantial contribution to Australian children's fantasy. Set in a fantasy otherworld, the five books of the series explore the way in which Rowan, though small and different, nevertheless has something to offer his community and his world. While the Rowan series is significant, Rodda's subsequent two Deltora Quest series have won her even more popularity among young readers. The Deltora Quest series, beginning with *The Forests of Silence* (2000), are structured around quests to recover magical objects that will assist characters to save the fantasy kingdom of Deltora from a great evil. Originally published under the name Mary-Anne Dickinson as the Storytelling Charms series in 1994, another fantasy series, the Fairy Realm books (2000), returns to her earlier dual world structure. Less well known is Rodda's nonfantasy series Teen Power Inc. (1994–1999), a collection of thirty books about a group of teenagers solving mysteries. Rodda has also written other stand-alone works and a variety of picture books, including *Bob the Builder and the Elves* (1998).

[*See also* Australia *and* Fantasy.]

SHELLEY CHAPPELL

Rodgers, Mary (1931–), American novelist, screenwriter, composer, and lyricist; daughter of composer Richard Rodgers and author Dorothy Rodgers. As a child Rodgers studied music privately, and during her teens she composed a series of songs for two pianos. During her twenties and thirties she wrote a number of musical scripts, including *Three to Make Music* (1959) and *Young Mark Twain* (1964). Her most famous composition was the popular *Once upon a Mattress* (1959), a musical adaptation of Hans Christian Andersen's "The Princess and the Pea," still performed regularly by amateur theatrical groups throughout America. From 1957 to 1971, while assistant to the producer of the New York Philharmonic's Young People's Concerts, she worked as an editor for Leonard Bernstein. In addition to acting as contributing editor to the best-selling book and recording *Free to Be . . . You and Me* (1974), Rodgers published the picture book *The Rotten Book* (1969), illustrated by Steven Kellogg, and a novel cowritten with her mother entitled *A Word to the Wives* (1970). She is best known for *Freaky Friday* (1972), which presents a humorous exploration of Annabel Andrews's adventures when she and her mother switch bodies for a day. The novel became tremendously popular, won numerous awards, and has been filmed three times, with Rodgers writing the screenplay for the earliest version (1977). Rodgers also wrote two sequels, *A Billion for Boris* (1974) and *Summer Switch* (1982), the latter of which applies *Freaky Friday*'s premise to Annabel's younger brother, Ben "Ape Face" Andrews, and his "second banana" advertising executive father. Rodgers's novels consistently focus on the interactions between siblings, parent-child relationships, and growing up into an adult-dominated world while managing to retain a both a sense of humor and balance.

[*See also* Andersen, Hans Christian; Kellogg, Steven; *and* Young Adult Literature.]

ANNE HIEBERT ALTON

Rodrian, Fred (1926–1985), chief editor and later director of the German publishing house Kinderbuchverlag, in East Berlin, from 1952 to 1985. Rodrian became a well-known children's book writer with *Das Wolkenschaf* (The Cloud Sheep, 1958), *Minni und die Kuh Mariken* (Minni and the Cow, Mariken, 1965), and *Pantommel malt das Meer* (Pantommel Paints the Sea, 1980). He studied writing at the J. R. Becher Institut in Leipzig from 1957 to 1958 and held many public positions. His varied writings are characterized by a focus on life in the socialist community, a close relationship to nature, a playful use of language, and touches of irony and satire. These elements can be seen in his picture books *Der Märchenschimmel* (The Fairy Tale Mold, 1962), *Paul und Janni finden einen Teddy* (Paul and Janni Find a Teddy Bear, 1978), and *Wir gehen mal zu Fridolin* (We're Going to Fridolin, 1971). They are also evident in his humorous short stories and anecdotes, as in *Die Räuber gehen baden* (The Robbers Go Swimming, 1977) and *Die hellgrüne Tür* (The Bright Green Door, 1986), as well as his poetry, as in *Ein Pferd schwebt durch den Himmel* (A Horse Sways through the Sky, 1989).

Sylvia Warnecke

Rogasky, Barbara (1933–), American editor and writer known for her retellings of fairy tales illustrated by Trina Schart Hyman, her poetry anthologies, and her award-winning history of the Holocaust, *Smoke and Ashes* (1988, 2002). Rogasky worked as an editor and freelance editorial consultant before she was urged by Trina Schart Hyman to create her first children's book, a retelling of *Rapunzel* (1982), an ALA Notable book that Hyman illustrated. The well-received *The Water of Life: A Tale from the Brothers Grimm* (1986), also illustrated by Hyman, followed. Other retellings of folk tales include a lengthy version of *The Golem* (1996) and *Dybbuk* (2005), illustrated by Leonard Everett Fisher. Rogasky has also been the selector and editor for several books of poetry, including *Winter Poems* (1994), illustrated by Hyman, and *Leaf by Leaf: Autumn Poems* (2001), with photographs by Marc Tauss. She also illustrated Myra Cohn Livingston's *Light and Shadow* (1992) with photographs.

[*See also* Collections; Fairy Tales and Folk Tales; Holocaust Literature for Children; Publishers and Publishing; *and biographies of figures mentioned in this article.*]

Linnea Hendrickson

Rogers, Fred (1928–2003), American television host, minister, educational consultant, and author; best known for his children's television program *Mister Rogers' Neighborhood.* Born in Latrobe, Pennsylvania, he attended first Dartmouth College, then Rollins College, earning a bachelor's degree in music in 1951. He continued his education at the Pittsburgh Theological Seminary, where he was ordained as a Presbyterian minister in 1963, and studied child development at the graduate level at the University of Pittsburgh from 1964 to 1967.

Rogers managed to combine all these areas of expertise in his television programming for children. He began work in the field as an assistant producer for NBC in New York City, which led to his serving from 1954 to 1961 as writer, producer, composer, and puppeteer of *Children's Corner*, a precursor of the landmark *Mister Rogers' Neighborhood.* The show first appeared on Pittsburgh's public television station in 1966. Boston added it the same year, and it was broadcast nationwide in 1968.

On the program, Rogers played himself, worked the puppets, and wrote and sang the songs. Each episode began with him entering his living room and putting on his cardigan and tennis shoes—Rogers believed that preschool children wanted and needed predictability. Through field trips to common places, like the barbershop or the post office, and in a blend of fantasy and reality, through puppet segments in the Neighborhood of Make Believe, the program showed children how to deal with common fears and problems while teaching them something new. Throughout it all, the overarching message of being accepted for who one is was emphasized. Although Rogers retired from the show in 2001, it continued to run daily on more than 260 public television stations. As of 2003, the slow-paced, quiet show was the longest-running PBS program.

Rogers's simple messages and straightforward talk on his television program carried over to other areas. He wrote more than two hundred songs, many for his program. His twenty-eight books include titles for both children and adults. His series of books, *Let's Talk about It* and *First Experiences*, help children to learn about and cope with scary topics, such as divorce and death, while his parenting books teach adults how to reassure their children and talk to them about major events in their lives. Along those same lines, he made public service announcements for children and their parents.

Rogers's efforts and accomplishments did no go unnoticed or unappreciated. He won four Emmy Awards and two Peabody Awards for *Mister Rogers' Neighborhood*, and both the National Academy of Television Arts and Sciences and the TV Critics Association granted him lifetime achievement awards. More than forty universities awarded him honorary degrees, and in 2002, Rogers was presented with the highest civilian honor, the Presidential Medal of Freedom. In his later years, he continued to foster children's emotional health and well-being through work on his Web site and his nonprofit organization, Family Communications, Inc. Rogers died of stomach cancer at the age of seventy-four.

Bibliography

Collins, Mark, and Margaret Mary Kimmel, eds. *Mister Rogers' Neighborhood: Children, Television, and Fred Rogers.* Pittsburgh: University of Pittsburgh Press, 1996.

Rebecca Hogue Wojahn

Rogers, Gregory (1957–), Australian illustrator, author, and musician. Rogers was awarded the Greenaway Medal for

Way Home (1993) by Libby Hathorn. His picture books include *Tracks* (1992) by Gary Crew, *Running Away from Home* (1996) by Nigel Gray, and *Princess Max* (2001) by Laurie Stiller. Rogers's first solo picture book, *The Boy, the Bear, the Baron, the Bard* (2004), uses a comic strip format. Rogers's realist style is most effective for portraiture. His use of dry media such as pencil, pastel, and charcoal is well suited to his expressive, lifelike approach, and also is well suited for capturing fine detail and the subtleties of light and shading.

[*See also* Australia; Illustrations; Picture Books; *and biographies of figures mentioned in this article.*]

KERRY MALLAN

Rohmer, Harriet (1938–), American author, editor, and founder of Children's Book Press, a pioneer in publishing multicultural books since 1975. After working with Third World cultural programs for UNESCO in Paris, Rohmer moved to New York and founded a small press devoted to poetry. Later, living in the Mission district of San Francisco, as the mother of a Head Start child, she became aware of a gap in children's publishing. There were few books in which Spanish-speaking children (as well as children from other cultural groups in the Head Start Program) could see themselves represented. With three different grants, Rohmer launched Children's Book Press, which has published numerous exciting, award-winning books by writers and illustrators from Asian, African American, Native American, and Latino/Latina cultures. Authors whose works have been published by Rohmer's company include Carmen Lomas Garza, Francisco X. Alarcón, and Juan Felipe Herrera.

[*See also* Multiculturalism and Children's Books *and* Publishers and Publishing.]

BIBLIOGRAPHY

Carger, Chris Liska. "Harriet Rohmer on New Voices and Visions in Multicultural Literature: Interview." *New Advocate* 14 (Spring 2001): 119–126.

LINNEA HENDRICKSON

Roi et l'oiseau, Le. *See* Prévert, Jacques.

Rojankovsky, Feodor (1891–1970), Russian illustrator. Rojankovsky studied the fine arts in Moscow. He rallied the White Army in 1919, ended up in Poland, settled in France in 1925, and earned his living with advertising drawings. His first publisher in France was Esther Averill. In 1931 he illustrated for Averill the large and splendid book on Daniel Boone, published at the same time in French and English. He collaborated for the major portion of his French career with the publisher Paul Faucher. He illustrated for Faucher twenty-seven of the Père Castor picture books, among them the eight wild animal books that came out between 1934 and 1939. Those eight picture books were quickly translated in England by Rose Fyleman and in the United States by Georges Duplaix under slightly different titles: *Froux le lièvre* (1934) became *Frou the Hare* in England and *Fluff, the Little Wild Rabbit* in the United States. By that time Rojankovsky had shortened his name to Rojan. The best-selling picture book of his French period remains *Michka* (1941; English trans., *Christmas Bear*, 1966), with seven hundred thousand copies sold in 2001. Though Rojankovsky was best known as an animal illustrator, he set about depicting human characters for some classical tales, such as Charles Perrault's *Cendrillon* (Cinderella, 1942) or the Grimms' *Les musiciens de la ville de Brême* (The Town Musicians from Bremen, 1942). With the onset of World War II, Rojankovsky left France in 1941 for the United States, where he resettled. His American career was as rich as the French one. He illustrated many Golden Books—the most famous being *The Three Bears* (1948)—and he received the Caldecott Medal in 1956 for *Frog Went A-Courtin'*. Rojankovsky was famous for his keen, unaffected, and realistic drawings, the gaiety of his colors, and the skillfulness of his layouts.

BIBLIOGRAPHY

La Maison des Trois Ours: Hommage à Rojankovsky. Paris: Edition Les Trois Ourses, 1998.

Rojankovsky, Nina. *Rojankovsky's Wonderful Picture Book: An Anthology*. New York: Golden Press, 1972.

Saint-Rat, A. L. "Children's Books by Russian Émigré Artists: 1921–1940." *The Journal of Decorative and Propaganda Arts* (Winter 1989).

ISABELLE NIÈRES-CHEVREL

Rollins, Charlemae (1897–1979), African American children's librarian at the George C. Hall Branch of the Chicago Public Library from 1932 to 1963. Rollins was educated at Columbia University and the University of Chicago, and published the groundbreaking bibliography *We Build Together: A Reader's Guide to Negro Life and Literature for Elementary and High School Use* (1941; reissued periodically). Always fighting stereotypes and stressing pride in an African heritage, she included criteria in the bibliography for realistic portrayals of blacks. Rollins was president of the children's services division of the American Library Association (1957–1958), and in 1963 she published *Christmas Gif': An Anthology of Christmas Poems, Songs and Stories, Written by and about Negroes* (the latter word in the title was amended to *African-Americans* in the 1993 edition). Additional books for children by Rollins include *Famous Negro Entertainers of Stage, Screen, and TV* (1967) and *Black Troubadour: Langston Hughes* (1971; a Coretta Scott King Award winner). Rollins received the Grolier Award for outstanding achievement in 1955 and an honorary doctorate from Columbia University in 1974.

Michelle H. Martin

Rollo. *See* Abbott, Jacob.

Ronskley, William (fl. c. 1680–1712), 17th-century English author of the speller, *The Child's Weeks-work* (1712), and sometime school master. Dissatisfied with the prevailing method of teaching reading, Ronskley developed a more child-friendly way of building the foundation for future learning that did not require children to memorize the rules of orthography or to decipher texts too serious and difficult for beginners. Pupils were addressed in a firm but affectionate tone. The text was written in verse to facilitate retention, using the stanza familiar to children from memorizing the Psalms. To avoid overwhelming them, the material was presented in stages, broken up in two two-hour lessons per day, and the vocabulary restricted mostly to monosyllables. The largely secular contents consisted of fables, riddles, proverbs, and precepts about behavior and health to keep up pupils' interest. Although Ronskley departed significantly from the educational practice of his times, it is difficult to determine what impact his speller may have had.

Bibliography

Michael, Ian. *The Teaching of English from the Sixteenth Century to 1870*. Cambridge, U.K.: Cambridge University Press, 1987.

Andrea Immel

Roop, Peter (1951–), and **Connie Roop** (1951–), American writers and educators who collaborate in their creation of nonfiction and fiction books for young readers. Peter was born in Winchester, Massachusetts, and Connie in Elkhorn, Wisconsin. They crossed paths while earning bachelor's degrees—Connie's in science education and Peter's in elementary education—at Lawrence University in Appleton, Wisconsin. They married in 1973. After teaching for several years, including a year as Fulbright exchange teachers in England in 1976, both returned to school in Boston to earn master's degrees in 1980—Peter's in children's literature from Simmons College and Connie's in education from Boston College. It was during this period that Peter began writing for children, first magazine articles, then nonfiction books that drew on his interest in history. They began writing together in 1984 and together have written a hundred books for elementary- and middle-school-aged children.

Many of the Roops' books showcase Connie's science background by treating science topics in books such as *One Earth, a Multitude of Creatures* (1992) and their Great Mysteries series (1988–1989). Their nonfiction and historical fiction books often feature history from a young person's point of view and involve primary source material or first-hand research, as in *Keep the Lights Burning, Abbie* (1985), which was a *Reading Rainbow* feature, and *Off the Map: The Journals of Lewis and Clark* (1993). Their books have received recognition from the National Association of Science Teachers, the National Council of Teachers of English, the Children's Book Council, and the American Library Association. Peter retired from teaching in 1999 to write and speak full-time and is an educational consultant for *Booklinks* magazine. Connie continues to teach environmental education in the Appleton, Wisconsin, school district as well as write.

Rebecca Hogue Wojahn

Root, Kimberly Bulcken (1957–), American illustrator of picture books and story collections. A graduate of the Parsons School of Design in New York, Root works in pen, ink, and watercolor. Her earth-toned palettes reflect subtleties of era, setting, and emotion, a stylistic choice that works well with folk tales and regional stories. Dusty colors recreate a rural Russian village in *The Peddler's Gift* by Maxine Rose Schur (1999). Her illustrations for Margaret Hodges's *The True Tale of Johnny Appleseed* (1997) are lighthearted in tone and detail. Attention to detail reveals the multifaceted personalities of each Appalachian character in *When the Whippoorwill Calls* by Candice F. Ransom (1995), *Junk Pile!* by Lady Borton (1997), and *Granny Will Your Dog Bite* by Gerald Milnes (1990). Full-page scenes and smaller vignettes provide period detail for Robert San Souci's colonial story, *The Birds of Killingworth* (2002). Root consistently delivers a captivating blend of realism and fantasy, capturing the spirit of the story.

[*See also* Hodges, Margaret *and* San Souci, Robert.]

JUDY A. TEAFORD

Rootabaga Stories. *See* Sandburg, Carl.

Roscoe, William (1791–1871), Liverpool lawyer, banker, book collector, writer, scholar, and botanist, whose abolitionist activities lost him his seat in Parliament. Largely self-educated, he wrote many books, including a life of Lorenzo de' Medici, but he is remembered for his poem *The Butterfly's Ball and the Grasshopper's Feast*, written for one of his sons (he had ten children). In rhyming couplets it lists the animals and insects who make their way to a feast and revels. The poem appeared in the November 1806 issue of the *Gentleman's Magazine* and also in the *Ladies' Monthly Museum.* On January 1, 1807, it was published in book form by John Harris, with copperplate engravers by William Mulready (1786–1863). In 1808, Harris published an expanded version with new engravings; this was repeatedly reissued: Harris described the 1841 edition as the twenty-first. There were many imitations, one of the best-known being Catherine Ann Dorset's *The Peacock "At Home"* (1807).

[*See also* Harris, John; Peacock "At Home," The *and* Poetry.]

GILLIAN AVERY

Rose, Gerald (1935–), British author and illustrator, winner of the 1960 Kate Greenaway Medal for *Old Winkle and the Seagulls.* The text is by Elizabeth Rose, with whom he collaborated on several picture books. His bold, urgent lines and bright colors impart a sense of vibrancy and movement to his subjects, but the gentler, more painterly style of *The Fisherman and the Cormorants* (1987) shows his versatility. His most distinguished work includes artwork for James Joyce's *The Cat and the Devil* (1965), in which the devil resembles Joyce. Most recent titles include *Horrible Hair* (2001) and *Millie's BIG Surprise* (2003), for which he created both text and artwork.

[*See also* Illustrations *and* Picture Books.]

VALERIE COGHLAN

Rose and the Ring, The. *See* Thackeray, William Makepeace.

Rosegger, Peter (1843–1918), Austrian poet and author of literature set in the province of Styria. In 1870, while studying at the Academy of Trade and Industry in Graz, Rosegger published his first volume of verse, which provided him with the financial support to begin his career as a writer. In 1876 he edited a three-volume selection of stories and sketches of village life in Styria for children, *Als ich noch der Waldbauernbub war* (Back When I Was Still a Forest Country Boy), which became one of the best-selling works of its time and has since become a classic in the German juvenile literary canon. In the same year he founded the journal *Heimgarten* (Home Garden) as a vehicle for his own ethnographic portraits and stories. Educators in Germany embraced Rosegger as an exemplary author for young people, and he was honored in his own time as a great man of letters.

LUKE SPRINGMAN

Rosen, Billi (1942–), writer born in Greece, educated in Sweden, and finally settled in England. Her best-known work, a realist trilogy for young adults—*Andi's War* (1988), *The Other Side of the Mountain* (1990), and *A Swallow in Winter* (1994)—is written with strong characters and contemporary themes, including the search for national identity and self-identity, racism, tolerance, and forgiveness. Awards for this trilogy include first prize for *Andi's War* in the Faber/Guardian/Jackanory Children's Competition (1987) and the Prix Enfance du Monde Natha Caputo (UNICEF; 1993). Further books by Rosen include *Sophie's Cat* (1993) and *Catch Me a Godzilla* (1994).

[*See also* Realism *and* Young Adult Literature.]

DOMINIQUE SANDIS

Rosen, Michael (1946–), British poet and writer. Rosen was born in Harrow, England, and educated at Oxford University. Although he originally intended to be a doctor, his decision to become a poet and writer is not surprising because both of his parents were involved in language education, Harold Rosen as a professor at the Institute of Education at London University and Connie Rosen as a lecturer at a college of education.

Rosen is one of a number of poets (e.g., Allan Ahlberg, Roger McGough, Spike Milligan, Gareth Owen, Brian Patten and Kit Wright) who from the 1960s on have changed the nature of poetry for children. They have written not so much for children as about them, and in many cases, about their own childhood. Although they have sometimes been accused of sacrificing reflection by pandering to humor, much of their work is both sensitive and perceptive. In addition, changing social mores have meant that their often abrasive questioning of the respectable has been accepted more readily than it might have been forty years earlier.

Since 1973 Rosen has published more than forty books of fiction and poetry. A criticism sometimes leveled at his work is that it can be difficult to establish where the poetry ends and the prose begins. Thus, storybooks such as *We're Going on a Bear Hunt* (1989) and *Cinderella* (1989) can look like long poems, and some of his poetry seems to be more dialogue than verse. Rosen responds calmly to such criticism, claiming that the supposed contradictions are of little import. A close examination of his poetry shows that its repetition and near-rhyme often convey a rhythm more likely to be identified with poetry than with prose.

Rosen's earliest poetry books were enhanced by the illustrations of Quentin Blake. The drawings, particularly on the covers, reflect the chaos and fun of childhood beyond the classroom. Some of the titles—*Mind Your Own Business* (1974), *Wouldn't You Like to Know* (1977), *Quick, Let's Get Out of Here* (1983), *You Can't Catch Me* (1981) and *That'd Be Telling* (1988)—are redolent of the language of the playground. Many of his poems are about his own childhood and, in particular, about his life with his parents and elder brother

It is a measure of Rosen's ability that he is not only a respected poet but also an effective broadcaster. For much of the 1990s he presented a program about children's literature for BBC Radio 4. He is also interested in teaching about writing, especially children's work. He participates in classroom teaching, is a sought-after speaker, and conducts in-service courses on language and children's literature. Rosen won the Signal Award for Poetry for his collection *You Can't Catch Me* in 1981, the Smarties Prize in 1989 for the picture book *We're Going on a Bear Hunt* (1989), and the Eleanor Farjeon Award for services to children's literature in 1997.

Geoffrey Fenwick

Rosenbach, A. S. W. (1876–1952), American bookseller and collector. A lifelong resident of Philadelphia, Abraham Simon Wolf Rosenbach attended the University of Pennsylvania and received his doctorate in 1901, specializing in Elizabethan and Stuart drama. A nephew of the antiquarian dealer Moses Polock, Rosenbach took charge of his uncle's inventory in 1903. He became notorious as "The Napoleon of Books" for his combination of showmanship and scholarship. His coups included the original manuscript of *Alice's Adventures in Wonderland*, which he purchased in 1928. In partnership with other major collectors, he returned it to England in 1946 as a gift from the Library of Congress.

Although a confirmed bachelor, Rosenbach maintained a keen interest in juvenilia; the catalog of his extensive personal collection, *Early American Children's Books* (1933), remains a reference classic. The collection was donated to the Free Library of Philadelphia in 1947. Rosenbach's house, now a museum and library, has become the chief repository for Maurice Sendak's archives.

[*See also* Collecting and Collectors.]

BIBLIOGRAPHY

Wolf, Edwin, II, and John F. Fleming. *Rosenbach: A Biography*. Cleveland: The World, 1960. Chatty and comprehensive; co-written by two former Rosenbach employees.

Peggy Lin Duthie

Ross, Diana (1910–2000), British writer and illustrator. Ross was born in Malta but spent most of her life in England. She was educated at Girton College, Cambridge, and the Central School of Art in London. A talented teller of tales from an early age, she made a substantial part of her contribution to children's literature in the stories she wrote for two of BBC Radio's most popular programs—*Children's Hour* and *Listen with Mother*. She also wrote scripts for the successful television program *Camberwick Green*.

Ross is best remembered for her Little Red Engine series of picture books. *The Little Red Engine Gets a Name* (1942) was followed by eight more titles written in 1945 and 1946. They coincided with the publication of the first of the W. V. Awdry's *Thomas the Tank Engine* stories. Together, these writers stimulated an enduring juvenile fascination with anthropomorphic steam engines.

Geoffrey Fenwick

Ross, Gayle (1951–), Cherokee storyteller, one of the most popular Native American speakers at schools, festivals, and national celebrations since the late 1970s. The Texas native tells about her mixed-blood family, including John

Ross, principal chief during the Trail of Tears, the forced removal of the Cherokee Nation from southern Appalachia to Oklahoma in 1838. Ross's performances deftly weave Native American history and culture with humor and legends passed down by her people. With Joseph Bruchac, Ross collected Native American tales about women and girls in *The Girl Who Married the Moon* (1994). Her audio recordings and picture books, such as *How Turtle's Back Was Cracked* (1995), also contain Cherokee and other Native American stories, stressing reverence for oral traditions and humanity's relations with the natural world. *How Rabbit Tricked Otter, and Other Cherokee Trickster Stories* (1994) smoothly links fifteen lively trickster and *pourquoi* tales about the perpetually mischievous cultural hero Rabbit.

[*See also* Animal Stories *and* Native American Children's Literature.]

TINA L. HANLON

Ross, Ramon Royal (1930–), American author and teacher, born in Walla Walla, Washington and recipient of an EdD from the University of Oregon (1961). His first novel, *Prune* (1984), received the award for notable fiction from the Southern California Council of Literature for Children and Young People. *Harper and Moon* (1993), set in Walla Walla during World War II, is a mystery story about boys whose friendship is solidly built on integrity and trust. The novel was recognized as a Notable Book by the American Library Association. In *The Dancing Tree* (1995) Ross turned his attention to parental desertion and its toll on the young. Yet the story's young protagonist finds some comfort in her grandmother's girlhood story of a Romany ("Gypsy") princess and a mysterious "Dancing Tree." Ross has been a professor of education at San Diego State University and a visiting lecturer on other campuses, including the State University of New York at Buffalo.

[*See also* Historical Fiction.]

SANDRA BOLTON

Ross, Tony (1938–), British writer and illustrator. Ross trained at the Liverpool School of Art and has worked as a cartoonist, graphic designer, art director of an advertising agency, and lecturer. He is well known for his series of traditional fairy tales retold and updated. The first was *Goldilocks and the Three Bears* (1976), with Goldilocks stumping around in oversized track shoes. *The Greedy Little Cobbler* (1979) outlines the perils of ambition and discontent and the worth of good friends, while in *Puss in Boots* (1981) the spirit of the text, which evinces daring, energy, and ingenuity, is matched by the spirit of the interpretation and the design of the layout. *Jack the Giant Killer* (1983) is an art lover's object in itself, with macabre images in densely colored, richly textured little pictures. Ross gives the old tale *Lazy Jack* (1985) a robust modern text, adding a dash of Thomas Rowlandson and a hint of Edward Lear to his own style to evoke a comic rural world. Ross also produced a successful series for young children, including *I Want My Potty* (1986), which won the Dutch Silver Pencil Award, *I Want to Be* (1993), *I Want My Dinner* (1995), *I Want a Sister* (1999), and *I Don't Want To Go to Hospital* (2000). The hero of Ross's Towser series, a scruffy, lovable dog, has appeared in award-winning books, a comic strip, and twenty-six short animated films.

Ross has illustrated juvenile fiction titles for several publishers in the United Kingdom, France, and the United States. His collaborations include the Mr. Browser series by Philip Curtis for young readers, and Hazel Townson's stories for beginner readers in the Andersen Press Tiger series. He and the writer Jeanne Willis have also collaborated. The first book in their Dr. Xargle series, *Dr. Xargle's Book of Earthlets*, was published in 1988. Each book purports to be a lesson in which Dr. Xargle, a teacher from outer space, sheds light on human behavior, customs, weather, and pets on planet Earth, for the benefit of his class of aliens; the books also introduce satire to young Earthling readers. Ross and Willis's other collaborations include *The Wind in the Wallows* (1998), a scatological visit to the Riverbank; *The Boy Who Lost His Bellybutton* (1999); and *Tadpole's Promise* (2002), in which black humor and high irony are appropriately shaped for children who know all about the life cycle of frogs and butterflies; clever layout exploits the material construction of the book, which has to be turned through 90 degrees for reading.

Ross's style is an apparently effortless partnership of unerring line and color, with the former given variety and vitality, and the latter employed for decorative, structural, and symbolic purposes, whether as a skimming wash or a rich mix of pastel, crayon, gouache, and paint. He limns a company of mostly genial grotesques and eccentric figures, while his literary tale-telling favors deadpan humor.

BIBLIOGRAPHY

Magic Pencil: Children's Book Illustration Today. Catalog to the British Council exhibition, selected by Quentin Blake. London: British Council/British Library, 2002.

JANE DOONAN

Rosselson, Leon (1934–), English songwriter, performance artist, and author. *Rosa's Singing Grandfather*, Rosselson's first book, was followed by *Rosa's Grandfather Sings Again* (both 1991; combined as *Rosa and Her Singing Grandfather*, 1991). These stories deal with teaching a child how the power of singing can overcome her fear of the dark and aid her in finding her own unique voice. Grandfather's devotion to Rosa is rewarded with a whispered "I love you, Grandad" when he is hospitalized. This close bond contrasts with the contentious yet affectionate relationship Grandfather has with Rosa's mother. Rosselson's works (seventeen titles by 2005) often center on family and identity (as in *Where's My Mum?*, 1994, and *Home Is a Place Called Nowhere*, 2002). He has done concert tours for children in Europe and North America, and many of his stories have been anthologized in volumes such as *Bedtime Stories for the Very Young* (1991).

Sandra Bolton

Rossetti, Christina (1830–1894), poet born in London, the daughter of an Italian exile. Rossetti grew up in an artistic and literary household that was also deeply infused with religious passion. She and her sister and mother were pious Anglicans, but Rossetti's faith was also influenced by the high church Oxford Movement and its theories of reserve and salvation. Almost all of her writing owes something to her vigorous social and religious conscience. Her writing is also influenced by the English Romantic poets and by a strong appreciation for beauty, especially in its more sensuous forms. Much of her poetry explores the effects of rhyme and rhythm, often using unconventional structures and styles.

Most of Rossetti's writing is for adults; even *Goblin Market* (1862) was not originally for children, but rather was the title poem for her first collection, written for adults. In 1872 she published *Sing-Song* specifically for children; here she experimented with form. In 1874 her remarkable fiction for children, *Speaking Likenesses*, appeared. Originally titled "Nowhere," the text tells the stories of three little girls, Flora, Edith, and Maggie, all of whom undergo trials. The book features a narrator, the Aunt, who is stern with her girls and proclaims, "no work no story"; Rossetti's work ethic is plain in this character, who is loving but not demonstrative. The story is sometimes described as an imitation of *Alice's Adventures in Wonderland*, and indeed Carroll knew Rossetti and he thought he saw similarities. But *Speaking Likenesses* is highly original; it contains little of Carroll's whimsy and instead builds on his darker undertones. Flora, a Sleeping Beauty type, is woken by her mother on her eighth birthday and proceeds to be fractious and disagreeable during her party; she falls asleep in a side path in the garden and dreams of a horrible Birthday Queen and several horrific children whose bodies reflect their morals (Quills, Slimy, Hooks, and so on). After being thoroughly terrorized, Flora awakes and learns the lesson of self-control. Edith, whose story reflects Cinderella's, wants nothing more than to light a kettle for a garden party, but is completely unable to do so even with the help of a variety of talking animals. Maggie, the most interesting protagonist, is a working-class girl whose one Christmas wish is to see the doctor's Christmas tree. She undertakes a perilous journey through the woods, like Little Red Riding Hood, and after a nasty fall on the ice encounters the embodiments of her deep desires to play, eat, and sleep. She is denied all three, as well as a glimpse of the tree, but on the way home is rewarded with a spectacular viewing of the northern lights and, finally, the continuing love of her grandmother. *Speaking Likenesses* explores issues of class, desire, consumerism, and need.

Similarly, *Goblin Market* combines a sensuous enjoyment of rhyme, rhythm, and imagery with a Christian message about redemption and salvation. Although readers today are often struck by the sexualized relationship between the sisters Laura and Lizzie, Rossetti bases her poetic work not on sex but on religion, forging a narrative that understands the relationship with Christ as one that is itself intensely physical and sensuous. When Laura eats the fruit of the goblin men and begins to pine away, Lizzie must sacrifice herself so that her sister may live again. The poem conflates the sisterly with the divine, concluding that "there is no friend like a sister."

[*See also* Alice Imitations; Poetry; *and* Religious Writing.]

BIBLIOGRAPHY

Knoepflmacher, U. C. "Avenging Alice: Christina Rossetti and Lewis Carroll." *Nineteenth-Century Literature* 41 (1986): 299–328.

McGillis, Roderick. "Simple Surfaces: Christina Rossetti's Work for Children." In *The Achievement of Christina Rossetti*, edited by David A. Kent, 208–230. Ithaca, N.Y.: Cornell University Press, 1989.

Jacqueline M. Labbe

Rostkowski, Margaret (b. 1945–), American author of three coming-of-age novels for young adults, *After the Dancing Days* (1986), *The Best of Friends* (1989), and *Moon*

Dancer (1995). Rostkowski first became interested in writing during her high school days in Seattle, thanks to the inspiration of a talented writing teacher. After obtaining her MA, Rostkowski turned to teaching and did not publish her first novel until she was thirty-seven. Much of the material for her books is drawn from her experiences with students and events from her own life. In all her books Rostkowski explores how history entwines with and shapes the lives of young people and their families. Her first two novels investigate the impact of World War I and the Vietnam War, while *Moon Dancer* delves into the more subtle connections between past individuals and societies by exploring a modern young woman's ties to the Hisatsinom Native Americans.

KATHERINE M. ADAMS

Rothmann, M. E. (1875–1975), South African author, teacher, and headmaster in Swellendam, editor of the journal the *Boervrou*, and second chairwoman of the National Party of Kaapland in 1933. She was member of the South African Academy of Arts and Sciences and was given three honorary doctorates by the universities of Capetown (1950), Stellenbosch (1950), and Pretoria (1973). Her historical novel *Kinders van de Voortrek* (Children of the Foretrail, 1921), which appeared in a revised version with the new title *De tweeling trek saam* (The Twins Move Away) in 1960, is now regarded as a children's classic.

[*See also* Africa: Southern Africa *and* Historical Fiction.]

BETTINA KÜMMERLING-MEIBAUER

Roubaud, Jacques (1932–), mathematician and one of the most distinguished contemporary French writers. He has been a member of the literary group OULIPO ("workshop for potential literature," founded by Raymond Queneau) since 1966. His literary invention is ruled by mathematical structures and formal constraints. He wrote children's books in many different genres. Among his rewritings of medieval literature, one finds *Le roi Arthur: au temps des chevaliers et des enchanteurs* (King Arthur; in the Time of Chivalry and Wizardry, 1983); in his "oulipian" fictions, *La princesse Hoppy; ou, Le conte du Labrador* (Princess Hoppy or the Tale of the Labrador, 1990); in his poetry, *Les animaux de tout le monde* (Animals for Everybody, 1983), *Les animaux de personne* (Animals for Nobody, 1991), *M. Goodman rêve de chats* (Mr. Goodman Dreams of Cats, 1994), and *Menu, menu* (A So Small Menu, 2000). Yet only Roubaud's books of verse are still in print.

ISABELLE NIÈRES-CHEVREL

Roughsey, Dick (1920–1985), Aboriginal author and artist of Lardil descent, born on Mornington Island in Queensland, Australia. After his education at a mission school, Dick (Goobalathaldin) Roughsey became a stockman and seaman, emerging as an artist in the 1960s. His first picture books, *The Giant Devil Dingo* (1973) and *The Rainbow Serpent* (1975), were landmark works, introducing Aboriginal art and cultures to Australian children. From the early 1960s Roughsey worked with the artist and author Percy Trezise, and they collaborated on six picture books from *The Quinkins* (1978) to *The Flying Fox Warriors* (1985). Roughsey's illustrations are characterized by their brilliance of color and fluidity of composition. Taking from a combination of Aboriginal and Western artistic traditions, his illustrations powerfully evoke relations between humans, spirits, and the natural world. In addition to his children's books, Roughsey exhibited his work on bark and paper in major galleries in Australia.

[*See also* Australia; Illustrations; Picture Books; *and* Trezise, Percy.]

CLARE BRADFORD

Rounds, Glen (1906–2002), prolific American author and illustrator. Rounds was born in a sod house in the South Dakota badlands and grew up on a ranch in Montana. He worked variously as a cowboy, cook, sign painter, and carnival barker. His first book, *Ol' Paul, the Mighty Logger* (1936), established his style of humorous exaggeration, vernacular dialogue, and scraggly black-and-white line drawings. Over six decades he published adventure-filled stories of the western frontier and authentic nonfiction about the people and wildlife of the Great Plains. Because of his economy of style, his books are often used for high-interest, low-vocabulary readers. Among his best-known works are *The Blind Colt* (1941), *Buffalo Harvest* (1952), *The Treeless Plains* (1967), *Wild Horses of the Red Desert* (1969), and his two series, Whitey the Cowboy (1942–1963) and Mr. Yowder, "the World's Bestest and Fastest Sign Painter" (1976–1983). Rounds's career almost ended in 1989 because of arthritis, but he taught himself to draw left-handed and published *Cowboys* (1991) and *Beavers* (1999).

[*See also* Illustrations *and* Westerns.]

SUSAN GARNESS

Rousseau, Jean-Jacques (1712–1778), Swiss author in French, autodidact, and educational philosopher. Rousseau's conception of childhood and his criticism of children's books played an important role in children's literature of the eighteenth and nineteenth centuries. His societal analysis (*Discours sur l'origine et les fondements de l'inégalité parmi les hommes*, 1754; English trans., *On Inequality among Mankind*) and his political ideas (*Du contrat social; ou, Principes du droit politique*, 1762; English trans., *A Treatise on the Social Contract; or, The Principles of Political Law*, 1764) contributed to revolutionary thought during the French Revolution of 1789. His sentimentalist novel *Julie; ou, La nouvelle Héloïse* (1758; English trans., *Eloisa: or, A Series of Original Letters Collected and Published by J.-J. Rousseau*, translated by William Kenrick, 1761) sold on a large scale and moved its readers. His posthumously published *Les confessions* (1782; English trans., *The Confessions*, 1783) became a literary reference for all succeeding French autobiographies. His varied genus also showed through *Émile; ou, De l'éducation* (1762; English trans., *Emilius; or, An Essay on Education*, translated by Nugent, 1763), which revolutionized pedagogic thought and founded active methods aimed toward autonomous liberal education.

Jean-Jacques Rousseau. Portrait by Maurice-Quentin de La Tour, 1753.

Émile, both fiction and treatise, had an important impact on children's literature. Dismissing the classical vision of a child as an incomplete person, Rousseau underlines the positivism and necessary function of childhood as a foundation to the construction of the singular human being. He saw the child through the reality of cognitive and emotional being, and that opened new perspectives for writing children's books. Observing children and their particular psychology to reproduce the specificity of their behavior in literary characters is a consequence of Rousseau's approach to childhood. Thus, Madame de Genlis, though opposed to the philosophes who claimed Rousseau as a leading light, referred to the knowledge of children evident in *Émile*. In his text, Rousseau directly faced the problem of children's literature. He began by stating, "I hate books, they teach you to speak only of what we ignore" (*Émile*). Émile was to be educated first by the world and the objects around him; books should only arrive when he reached puberty.

Only one book—*Robinson Crusoe* by Daniel Defoe—earned Rousseau's approval for younger readers, although he urged that this perfect pedagogical myth be "lightened of its lumber" to become more suitable. (His emulators rushed to pen new "Robinson" stories.) Rousseau also criticized La Fontaine's *Fables* as laden with cultural references, immoral, disguising the truth in animal fictions, using obsolete language, and thus out of reach for young minds. In effect, Rousseau condemned children's literature that anticipates the child's own personal experiences, a viewpoint still defended today by those who believe that children's literature can constitute an individual initiation.

BIBLIOGRAPHY

Bloch, Jean. *Rousseauism and Education in XVIIIth Century France*. Oxford: Voltaire Foundation, 1995.

Vargas, Yves. *Introduction à l'Émile de Jean-Jacques Rousseau*. Paris: Presses Universitaires de France, 1995.

MICHEL MANSON

Routledge, George (1812–1888), British publisher, born in Brampton, Cumberland. Routledge set up business as a retail bookseller in Leicester Square, London, in 1836 and as a publisher in 1843 at Soho Square with an assistant, later partner, William Henry Warne, his wife's brother. He founded George Routledge and Co. in 1851, taking his son-in-law Frederick Warne into partnership. The firm became

Routledge, Warne and Routledge when his son Robert became a partner in 1858. In 1865, when Frederick Warne left to establish his own company and Routledge's son Edward joined the firm, it became known as George Routledge and Sons. He was very active in issuing popular literature both for adults and children. His notable contribution to children's literature was the publication of cheap picture books known as toy books, which included works produced in collaboration with the engraver-printer Edmund Evans and artists such as Walter Crane and Randolph Caldecott.

TOMOKO MASAKI

Rowe, Richard (1828–1879), Victorian writer of adventure stories for boys and girls. Born in Dorchester, England, to the Wesleyan minister Thomas Rowe, Richard followed in his father's footsteps and became a minister. He was poor but well educated in the classics. In his youth, he spent several years in Australia, often in the company of a group of writers described in Ann Mari Jorden's *The Stenhouse Circle* (1979). Rowe became a regular contributor to Australian journals, and eventually published *Peter 'Possum's Portfolio* (1858), a collection of prose, poetry, and translations. Dedicated to Stenhouse, it is considered one of the first such Australian collections of serious literature, and was very well received. In the year of its publication, Rowe returned to England, married, and eventually settled in London's East End to become a Methodist minister for the working classes. His first novel, *The Boy in the Bush* (1869), originally serialized in *Good Words* under the pseudonym Edward Howe, was published anonymously in 1869 and again, posthumously, in 1885. Chronicling the exploits of two young colonials in Australia's cattle country, one of whom is captured by Aborigines, *The Boy* belongs to a genre of British empire adventure stories espousing imperialism and the excitement of the colonies. After *The Boy*'s publication, Rowe spent five years publishing accounts from his journals, which detailed the lives and the characters of the poor to whom he ministered. He returned to children's literature in the last five years of his life, writing volumes for children's compendiums of stories, appealing to the burgeoning children's literature market with more stories of adventure in the colonies. *Roughing It in Van Diemen's Land* (1880), published a year after Rowe's death and under the pseudonym Edward Howe, shows that his connection to Australia never faded. Posthumous publication of Rowe's work continued until 1925.

[*See also* Adventure Books; Australia; *and* Colonial Fiction.]

SIMON FARRELL

Rowling, J. K. (1965–), the British children's author responsible for the "Harry Potter Phenomenon," born in Gloucestershire, England. Joanne K. Rowling's Harry Potter books gained worldwide recognition when the fourth book in the series, *The Goblet of Fire* (2000), broke all children's book publishing records and was even instrumental in creating a Children's Literature category in the *New York Times* Best Seller listings. The seven-book series, six of which have been published, follows the education and adventures of Harry Potter at Hogwarts School of Witchcraft and Wizardry. Readers of all ages have been drawn to Rowling's books. Although she has taken all her story components from "the great cauldron of story," she has combined them in such a way that many adults as well as children enjoy her books. Rowling's narrative style helps her achieve this broad readership. Gone is the cushioning narrative voice of J. R. R. Tolkien. Gone is C. S. Lewis's intervening omniscient narrator who, like Uncle Digory in *The Lion, the Witch, and the Wardrobe*, seems to shake his head and ask, "Whatever are they teaching them in school nowadays?" Rowling's child protagonists' are never patronized by an authoritative narrator's voice. Albus Dumbledore comes closest to being the gentle avuncular adult who makes Harry, at least, feel safe, protected, and relatively sure of his abilities to succeed in his battle with Voldemort and his minions, but Harry comes to realize that Dumbledore, like other wizards, has human limitations, and in books five and six new tensions develop in their relationship.

Rowlingiana. Front covers of *Quidditch through the Ages* by Kennilworthy Whisp (New York: Arthur A. Levine, 2001); *Harry Potter and the Philosopher's Stone* (illustration by Thomas Taylor) (London: Bloomsbury, 1997); and *Fantastic Beasts & Where to Find Them* by Newt Salamander (New York: Arthur A. Levine, 2001). REPRODUCED COURTESY OF THE COTSEN CHILDREN'S LIBRARY, PRINCETON UNIVERSITY LIBRARY

Rowling's books have spawned renewed interest in children's fantasy literature. Her innovative combination of plot devices and techniques familiar to fantasy writers also contributes to their success. Like many fantasies, the *Potter* series may be classed as adventure, coming of age, or quest for identity stories, the latter being also closely identified with the Bildungsroman tradition. Rowling's books also share an affinity with the detective novel, with her characters often searching for a felon while trying to come to terms with a maze of bizarre situations, confusing clues, and circumstantial evidence. The most pressing question in the *Potter* books is, "Who can be trusted?" Learning to distinguish between appearance and reality, a lesson common to fairy tale literature, presents a major hurdle for Harry, Ron, and Hermione, the young protagonists in these stories. The fairy tale premise that both children and adults act true to type in given situations is shattered in Rowling's books; red herrings keep readers in suspense and pondering whether, for example, the potions teacher Severus Snape is on the side of Harry and the headmaster Dumbledore, or is true to his earlier allegiance to Voldemort. Hermione Granger, who has been termed the "stereotypical female," is more complex than most critics commenting on Rowling's treatment of females suggest; despite her initial adherence to Hogwarts' rules, Hermione later begins to challenge authority figures.

Rowling does not soft-pedal the darker aspects of her novels. She addresses crucial questions about right and wrong to provide her readers with coping strategies for what are essentially moral issues. Although children remain the focus of her novels, adult characters figure prominently and are more fully developed as individuals than is usual in children's literature. The grotesque, bizarre, and terrifying are not just part of the curriculum to be studied at Hogwarts—as Voldemort's fragile existence in book one and the staging of his physical resurrection in book four of the series attest. Rowling announced that the books would become darker as the series advanced, and book five, *Harry Potter and the Order of the Phoenix* (2003), did strike a more somber note. In contrast, humor serves an important function in the pacing of Rowling's narratives. She intersperses humor to alleviate the darker side of the action. The humor, at times almost slapstick and "stupid" in an adolescent way, is prevalent in a lighter vein in the marginal comments made by the various owners of the Hogwarts textbooks that Rowling published to accompany the series, *Fantastic Beasts and Where to Find Them*, by Newt Scamander, and *Quidditch Through the Ages*, by Kennilworthy Whisp.

The best fantasies are not escapist literature transporting us to another world, but rather they show us our own world in a new guise. Juxtaposing the Muggle and Wizarding worlds, as Rowling does in the *Harry Potter* books, brings the similarities between them into clearer focus. "The Harry Potter Phenomenon" continues to raise the profile of children's books: adults and children are sharing books, and the Potter books and films have stimulated J. K. Rowling–sanctioned Web site discussions as well as television programs and other media coverage. Reader/viewer response to the sixth book in the series, *Harry Potter and the Half-Blood Prince* (2005), and to the fourth Potter film (November 2005) confirm Rowling's continuing success with readers of all ages.

[*See also* Fantasy; Lewis, C. S.; Tolkien, J. R. R.; Witches; *and* Wizards.]

BIBLIOGRAPHY

Billone, Amy. "The Boy Who Lived: from Carroll's Alice and Barrie's Peter Pan to Rowling's Harry Potter." Children's Literature 32 (2004): 178–202.

Fraser, Lindsey. *Conversations with J. K. Rowling*. New York: Scholastic, 2000.

Gupta, Suman. *Re-Reading Harry Potter*. Basingstoke, U.K.: Palgrave, 2003.

Nel, Philip. *J. K. Rowling's Harry Potter Novels: A Reader's Guide*. New York: Continuum, 2001.

Zipes, Jack. *Sticks and Stones: The Troublesome Success of Children's Literature from Slovenly Peter to Harry Potter*. New York: Routledge, 2001.

Barbara Carman Garner

Roy, Atanu (1950–), Indian illustrator, artist, cartoonist, and designer whose work reflects his willingness to experiment and seek new styles. Thus in *What's Right What's Wrong* (2001) by Deepa Agarwal, Roy's illustrations match the realism of the text. Roy shows a tendency to exaggerate the world around him and, not surprisingly, his illustrations are fiercely individual and captivating in their originality. In *Who's Smarter* (1995) by Gita Iyengar, Roy focuses on the prominent physical features of both humans and animals. In *Alamelu's Appetite* (1998) by Jaya Paramasivan, this tendency is fine-tuned to a point where its grotesqueness is sure to appeal to children. The greedy Alamelu always has her mouth wide open. In *Wingless* (2003) by Paro Anand, Roy's illustrations are brilliant. The black-and-white illustrations march along the margins of the book and Roy constructs a parallel dialogue. These comments and jokes, which are sometimes beyond the understanding of children, display a close reading of the text and establish the illustrator as part of the book. Roy's presence permeates the book he is illustrating, resulting in a multilayered, many-voiced narrative.

[*See also* Illustrations; India; *and* Picture Books.]

NANDINI NAYAR

Roy, Claude (1915–1997), French writer. Claude Roy, whose real name was Claude Orland, experimented in a variety of genres: novels, poems, criticism, memoirs, chronicles, and travel stories. His first contribution to children's literature, published by the innovating publisher Robert Delpire, was the social satire *C'est le bouquet* (Bouquet Story, 1964), the appeal of which is well supported by the illustrations of Alain Le Foll. Other stories, fables, and novels followed, among them *La maison qui s'envole* (The House That Takes Off, 1977) and *Le chat qui parlait malgré lui* (The Cat Who Speaks in Spite of Himself, 1982). Roy is widely known for his poetry for children, such as *Enfantasques* (Children's Fantasies, 1974), a collection of poems accompanied by collages. These poems, with their humor, absurd logic, and animals characters, align themselves with the works of prominent children's authors, among them Lewis Carroll, Edward Lear, and Jacques Prévert.

[*See also* France; Poetry; Nonsense; *and biographies of figures mentioned in this article.*]

SOPHIE VAN DER LINDEN

Rubel, Nicole (1953–), American illustrator and author. Rubel began drawing early in her childhood, and pursued art education with a joint BA degree from Tufts and the Boston Museum School of Fine Arts (1975). She wrote and illustrated works such as *Sam and Violet Are Twins* (1981), which resulted in a series about a topic she understands well, being a twin herself. Rubel is best known, however, for her collaboration with Jack Gantos on *Rotten Ralph* (1976) and its sequels. Rotten Ralph, a cat with major behavior problems, resonates with young children. Despite his sometimes reprehensible actions, his owner patiently criticizes his behavior while continuing to love him. In *Worse than Rotten Ralph* (1979), Ralph leads a group of alley cats in a pie-throwing fight at a bakery and causes amusing chaos in a poodle-grooming salon. Rubel's bright, flat, folk art paintings help to keep the stories on a cartoonlike level. Her approach makes it clear that Ralph's misdeeds are overblown for the sake of humor. Rubel collaborates on other projects as well. She illustrates the Katy Hall and Lisa Eisenberg Riddle series (for instance, *Grizzly Riddles*, 1989), and a nonfiction teaching series for young children, Learning through Play. The American Institute of Graphic Arts honored *Rotten Ralph* with an award in 1979.

[*See also* Gantos, Jack *and* Picture Books.]

CHARLOTTE CUBBAGE

Rubino, Antonio (1880–1964), Italian poet, writer, painter, illustrator, and, from 1909, a major contributor to the children's weekly *Corriere dei piccoli*. Rubino had a leading role in the development of Italian children's literature in the first half of the 20th century. His first book, *Versi e disegni* (Verses and Drawings, 1911), established an exaggerated style, a macabre form of Art Nouveau. His love for the grotesque and the florid promoted an anarchic disruption of standard values—the foundation of his cartoons, both strip and animated.

Starting with *Pierino* (1909), *Pino and Pina* (1910), *Pippotto* (1910), and *Lalla and Lola* (1912), Rubino was to create more than fifty cartoon characters in drawings that combined the absurd and the surreal with graphic control and in stories that balanced moral expectations with the urge to transgress: Pierino hates a toy but cannot rid himself of it; Pino and Pina try not to be late for school but always fail. In the next decade, Rubino often directed his mordant satire at aspects of the education system. Comically iconoclastic, he invariably undermined current conventions, fashions, and assumptions: he undermined the exotic and colonialist in the adventures of an African boy, *Tidna Danna* (1920), the histrionics of the theater in *Lionello* (1925), and devotion to literature and poetic posturing in *Pico and Rocco* (1919) and *Girondello* (1940). After World War I, Rubino published two illustrated short novels (still in print) that represent the climax of his art: *Viperetta* (Little Viper, 1919) and *Tic e Tac; overossia, l'orologio di Pampalona* (Tick and Tock; or, The Clock of Pampalona, 1922). The first, about a nasty little girl, is a kind of paradoxical bildungsroman that develops the symbolism of the moon and lunacy. The contradictions of the world upside-down also pervade *Tic e Tac*, in which the toys revolt against their maltreatment by children. In the 1930s, Rubino's stories paid lip service to fascism, but his fundamental ridiculing of conventional rhetoric always resisted the worst sentimentality, moralism, and patriotism.

[*See also* Comic Books; Illustrations; Italy; *and* Parody.]

BIBLIOGRAPHY

Bertieri, C. *Le rotte dell'immaginario*. Genoa, Italy: Edizioni Esagraph, 1985.

Faeti, Antonio. *Guardare le figure*. Turin, Italy: Einaudi, 1972.
Pallottino, Paola. *La matita di zucchero*. Bologna, Italy: Cappelli, 1978.

ANN LAWSON LUCAS

Rubinstein, Gillian (1942–), also known as Lian Hearn and G. M. Hanson; Australian writer of children's and young adult books in a variety of genres, as well as playwright and freelance journalist. A most challenging writer who has published over thirty-five titles, Rubinstein was born in Potten End, Hertfordshire. She had a disruptive adolescence caused by her parents' divorce (and her father's premature death). She divided her time among boarding school, another family, and holidays with her mother and stepfather in Nigeria. She admits that the anger and insecurity caused by this dislocation affected her deeply and still allows her to tap into the psyche of young people.

Rubinstein received a degree in modern languages from Oxford, married, traveled in Europe, divorced, and then worked in England as a film critic, editor, arts journalist, and script assessor. In 1970 she traveled and worked in Australia before returning to study for a diploma in education at Stockwell College (London University). In 1973 she married Philip Rubinstein and they emigrated to Australia. She has said that she has learned about her adopted country and its literature through her three children.

Rubinstein constructs multilayered narratives, exploiting metaphor and allegory to examine power and gender relationships in families and in society, yet her style is always accessible. She is also particularly interested in animal-human interaction. Whether creating alternate worlds, blending fantasy with reality, or focusing in depth on contemporary life, she always expresses a strong ethical sense, with young people providing the moral consciousness in an imperfect world. Rubinstein has periodically worked in youth theater as well, creating original scripts and adapting her own and others' material. *Wake Baby* was a critical success in Australia and the United States.

Since the publication of her first novel, *Space Demons* (1986), a computer fantasy that focuses on the emotional upheavals of adolescence amid familial instability, Rubinstein has won myriad prizes, including Children's Book Council of Australia Awards as well as prizes in the United States and the United Kingdom. Her commercial and critical success, however, for both speculative and realistic fictions, has also generated controversy. She has not been afraid to tackle challenging subjects or use explicit language. The award-winning *Beyond the Labyrinth* (1988) provoked criticism because of a few episodes, as well as for its strategy of alternative endings. The novel concerns a sensitive fourteen-year-old boy, Brenton, who is addicted to choose-your-own-adventure games. He meets an alien anthropologist, Cal, who reinforces his perception that his society is doomed. Rubinstein maintains that young people have a right to read realistic portrayals of the complex world in which they live. The truth can be empowering. This belief has led her to incorporate social and environmental themes into many of her adventures. In *Answers to Brut* (1988), a short novel about dog fighting, Rubinstein investigates the pathology of intimidation and fear, revealing how adults can be as vulnerable as children. In *Foxspell* (1994), Rubinstein brilliantly weaves European myth into a domestic landscape to deal not only with adolescent alienation but also with the repercussions of migration.

Rubinstein's noteworthy series include Space Demons, Skymaze (1989), and Shinkei (1996). *Galax-Arena* (1992), one of her most disturbing speculative novels, which focuses on the powerlessness of children (especially from developing nations) and the misuse of science and technology, was followed by *Terra-Farma* (2001), which expands the narrative viewpoint and themes of its predecessor. In *Galax-Arena*, Rubinstein exploits her linguistic background by creating a pidgin language for the peb, child gymnasts supposedly kidnapped from earth to perform for the Vexa, an alien race.

Rubinstein has also published innovative picture books, including the visually clever *Dog In, Cat Out* (1991) and *Mr Plunkett's Pool* (1992), which won the 1993 Australian Multicultural Children's Book Award. In the rhyming *Sharon, Keep Your Hair On* (1996), *Hooray for the Kafe Karaoke* (1998), and *Prue Theroux, the Cool Librarian* (2000), Rubinstein revels in wordplay. *The Giant's Tooth* (1993), *The Fairy's Wings* (1998), and *The Pirate's Ship* (1998) provide dual narratives: a conventional one for the human children, speech bubbles for the giants. The *Jake and Pete* chapter books for younger readers create a witty vocabulary for the kittens, or "kitkids," and include *Jake and Pete* (1995), *Jake and Pete and the Stray Dogs* (1996), *Jake and Pete and the Catcrowbats* (1999), and *Jake and Pete and the Magpies' Wedding* (2000).

Since 2002, Rubinstein has also been publishing as Lian Hearn: "Lian" for a childhood nickname, "Hearn" for Lafcadio Hearn, an Irish-American writer who lived in Japan. *Across the Nightingale Floor* (2002), *Grass for His Pillow* (2003), and *Brilliance of the Moon* (2004) make up the historical fantasy trilogy *Tales of the Otori*, best-selling crossover books marketed under adult, children's, and young adult imprints. In an imaginary feudal world based on medieval Japan, Takeo, an orphaned teenager, is torn between loyalty to his patron, Lord Otori, to the Tribe, assassins with mystical powers that he has inherited, and to his lover, Lady Kaede, a beautiful, intelligent innocent who must learn how to cope in a ruthless patriarchal society. Rubinstein reinvigorates this quest and coming-of-age story with supernatural and feminist elements.

[*See also* Australia; Fantasy; Science Fiction; *and* Young Adult Literature.]

BIBLIOGRAPHY

Kroll, Jeri. "Gillian Rubinstein's *Beyond the Labyrinth*: A Court Case and its Aftermath." *Para*doxa: Studies in World Literary Genres* 3.3–4 (1996): 332–345.

Nieuwenhuizen, Agnes, ed. "Gillian Rubinstein." In *No Kidding: Top Writers for Young People Talk About Their Work*, 225–255. Chippendale: Pan Macmillan Australia, 1991.

Scutter, Heather. *Displaced Fictions: Contemporary Australian Fiction for Teenagers and Young Adults*. Melbourne, Australia: Melbourne University Press, 1999.

JERI KROLL

Ruck-Pauquèt, Gina (1931–), one of the most productive contemporary German authors. Since 1958 she has published over eighty books. Her work is primarily composed of picture books (*Der kleine Igel*, 1959; English trans., *Little Hegdehog*), anthologies (*Sandmännchen erzählt von seinen kleinen Freunden*, 1966; English trans., *Little Sandman Tells of His Little Friends*), and plays, poems, and songs for children. *Gespenster essen kein Sauerkraut* (1963, 25th ed., 1995; English trans., *Ghosts Don't Eat Sausages*, 1964) has been her most successful book. It stands in the tradition of oral storytelling, also used by other better-known German authors of that time (e.g., Otfried Preussler and James Krüss). Typical in her early works (*Vierzehn höllenschwarze Kisten*, 1962; English trans., *Fourteen Cases of Dynamite*, 1968, and *Die bezauberndsten Kinder der Welt*, 1969; English trans., *The Loveliest Children of the World*) are her casual reflections about childhood and children's impressions of grown-ups.

ANDREA WEINMANN

Ruffins, Reynold (1930–), African American illustrator and writer. Born in New York City and educated at Cooper Union, Ruffins established himself as a successful graphic designer before becoming a children's book illustrator. His first picture book illustrations were for Harry Hartwick's *The Amazing Maze* (1969; coillustrated by Simms Taback). Through the 1970s and early 1980s, Ruffins frequently collaborated with the writer Jane Sarnoff, and Ruffins's stylistic versatility, vibrant colors, and penchant for fanciful creatures is apparent in *The Chess Book* (1973) and *The Monster Riddle Book* (1975; filmstrip adaptation in 1981). Ruffins's author-illustrated titles include *My Brother Never Feeds the Cat* (1979), and he has illustrated retellings of traditional tales and rhymes such as Judy Sierra's *The Gift of the Crocodile: A Cinderella Story* (2000). Ruffins's many awards include a Coretta Scott King Illustrator Honor Award for *Running the Road to ABC* (1996) by Denizé Lauture.

[*See also* African American Literature; Illustrations; *and biographies of figures mentioned in this article.*]

ADRIENNE E. GAVIN

Rumpelstiltskin. One of the classical tales in the Grimms' *Kinder- und Hausmärchen* (1812–1857; English, *Children's and Household Tales*), "Rumpelstiltskin" has variants in several countries; different names for the character Rumpelstiltskin are Zorobubù (Italy); Titeliture (Sweden); Ricdin-Ricdon (France); Tom Tit Tot (England); and Batzibitzili, Panzimanzi, and Whuppity Stoorie (Scotland).

The Grimms' 1812 version of "Rumpelstiltskin" was based on variants heard from the Hassenplug family and from Dortchen Wild, who later married Wilhelm Grimm. The story is as follows: a miller boasts falsely that his daughter can spin straw into gold. When the king hears this, the girl is invited to the castle to prove her skill. For three nights, she is locked up with a spinning wheel and a heap of straw. Each night, a dwarf appears who spins the straw into gold in exchange for her ring, her necklace, and on the final night, the promise of her firstborn child. The miller's daughter marries the king, and when their first baby is born, the dwarf claims it, unless she can guess his name. A servant overhears the dwarf singing: "Tomorrow I brew, today I bake, and then the child away I'll take. For little deems my royal dame that Rumpelstiltskin is my name!" The servant tells the queen, who tells the dwarf his name, and the child is saved.

In their second edition (1819), the Grimms added a more spectacular ending to the tale after hearing a new variant from Lisette Wild: Rumpelstiltskin gets so angry that he tears himself in two. The Grimms also changed the girl's problem. In the Ölenberg manuscript version (1810), she can only spin gold, not thread. Ruth Bottigheimer has noted that the miller's daughter gradually loses agency in the later editions, and that her lonely suffering increases. Contemporary retellings can be found in, among others, Olga Broumas's

Rumpelstiltskin Approaches the Miller's Daughter. Illustration by Charles Folkard from *Grimm's Fairy Tales* (London: Adam and Charles Black, 1911). COLLECTION OF JACK ZIPES

Beginning with O (1977), Anne Sexton's *Transformations* (1979), Emma Donoghue's *Kissing the Witch* (1997), and Donna Jo Napoli's *Spinners* (1999).

[*See also* Fairy Tales and Folk Tales *and* Grimm, Jacob, and Wilhelm.]

BIBLIOGRAPHY

Zipes, Jack. "Spinning with Fate: Rumpelstiltskin and the Decline of Female Productivity." In his *Fairy Tale as Myth/Myth as Fairy Tale*. Lexington: University of Kentucky Press, 1994.

VANESSA JOOSEN

Rupert Bear. A comic strip character, originating in the *Daily Express* (London) in 1920, with a distinctive check trousers, jersey, and scarf, Rupert Bear was the creation of Mary Tourtel (1874–1948). She drew the strip and wrote the versified stories, establishing the basic framework of Nutwood village and Rupert's friends, Bill Badger, Algy Pug, Podgy Pig, and Edward Trunk. Though her verses are pedestrian, Tourtel's drawings are evocative and atmospheric. The stories, combining fantasy with the everyday, were a great success and started to appear in book format in 1921.

Declining eyesight forced Tourtel to retire in 1935, when Alfred Bestall (1892–1986) took over. Already an established illustrator, notably of A. A. Milne's work, Bestall brought new vitality to Rupert, making him more human and gradually refashioning the idyllic Nutwood. Bestall also established the well-known format of the Rupert stories, albeit unintentionally, when he submitted a present-tense prose summary of what was happening in each illustration. To his surprise, his prose appeared in print alongside the verses (written by others). This format became prominent in the Rupert annuals, first appearing in 1936 with *The New Adventures of Rupert*. In 1950, when the first of the celebrated endpapers was included, the format was complete: four stories, often depicting seasonal variation, told at different levels, with a few child-centered activities, including instructions on making a piece of origami related to one of the stories.

The different levels of story start with a headline—a bald declarative sentence at the top of each page—below which are four uniform pictures, each (with the addition of a verse couplet) forming a square. At the bottom of the page, like erudite footnotes, are the prose paragraphs. The pictures are more regular than those of *Tintin* or *Asterix* and, more significantly, have no speech bubbles. The multilayering gives the reader a notion of the stories having different perspectives and depths (each starts with an abstract and a pictorial collage, too). The shifting perspective is present in the illustrations as well, where Bestall, much influenced by early cinema, used closeup, medium, long, and shot-reverse-shot techniques. More generally, he delighted in depicting scenes from different angles, injecting a sense of dynamism into what might otherwise seem a static, unchanging world. Bestall also made Rupert's world more technologically sophisticated, even having the weather controlled by gadgetry. Wonderfully retro machines are common, taking the reader through the earth and, more frequently, up into the clouds. Bestall's world is, finally, less threatening than Tourtel's. Plots are rarely motivated by either lack or villainy. It is curiosity about the unfamiliar that moves Rupert into adventure, and the reader with him.

Until 1973 Bestall produced all the material for the annuals. Since then there have been a number of different artists and storytellers involved, with varying degrees of success. But they have managed to keep Rupert fresh and inventive for a modern child audience, assisted by an animated TV series and Paul McCartney's successful video animation and song, the 1984 hit "We All Stand Together" (known as "the Frog Song," inspired by the 1958 Bestall endpaper). They have thus kept Rupert in touch with contemporary culture, while also managing to cater for a more conservative adult readership, complete with its own Followers of Rupert society.

BIBLIOGRAPHY

Bott, Caroline G. *The Life and Works of Alfred Bestall: Illustrator of Rupert Bear*. London: Bloomsbury, 2003.

Crago, Hugh. "Rupert in Space and Time." *Signal* 73 (1994): 3–6.

Perry, George. *A Bear's Life: Rupert*. London: Pavilion, 1985.

Stewart, Brian. *Rupert: The Rupert Bear Dossier*. London: Hawk, 1997.

DAVID RUDD

Rushdie, Salman (1947–), Indian novelist living in England. Ahmed Salman Rushdie, born in Bombay and educated at Cambridge University, is famed for his complex and controversial novels for adults but has also written one children's book: *Haroun and the Sea of Stories* (1990), initially composed for his young son. Though witty and enjoyable on the surface level—the son, Haroun, saves not only his storytelling father (the "Shah of Blah"), but also stories in general—*Haroun* is a multilayered text. It points up the intertextuality of all tales, weaving together sources as diverse as the *Arabian Nights*, Dickens, Carroll, and the Beatles. Structurally, it draws especially on the Sanskrit *Kathasaritsagara*, the "Ocean of the Sea of Story," and *The Wizard of Oz*, about which Rushdie has written affectionately, acknowledging similarities with the quest of Dorothy and her companions. But Rushdie's postmodern medley of creativity also has a darker side, allegorically depicting a writer's plight as Khattam-Shud seeks to silence free expression—just as Rushdie found himself oppressed when Iran's Ayatollah Khomeini declared the novelist a blasphemer and issued a religious decree calling for Rushdie's assassination.

BIBLIOGRAPHY

Ellerby, Janet Mason. "Fiction under Siege: Rushdie's Quest for Narrative Emancipation in *Haroun and the Sea of Stories*." *The Lion and the Unicorn* 22 (1998): 211–220.

Hassumani, Sabrina. *Salman Rushdie: A Postmodern Reading of His Major Works*. Madison, N.J.: Fairleigh Dickinson University Press, 2002.

DAVID RUDD

Rusher, John Golby (1784–1877), printer in Banbury, Oxfordshire, who was a major publisher of children's chapbooks. He inherited the printing business from his father William and built it up into one of the most successful firms of its kind. Like the chapbooks of his contemporary James Kendrew in York, Rusher's pamphlets are small, decently printed, and generously illustrated with relief cuts that rarely rise above competence. Rusher's backlist is characteristic of the 19th-century provincial printer, dominated by material circulating in the public domain. Popular titles included alphabets; items of popular interest such as the cries of Banbury, versions of Jack Sprat, the Children in the Wood, Mother Hubbard, Cock Robin, Dick Whittington, Jack the Giant-Killer, and Cinderella; and abridgments of classics such as Isaac Watts's *Divine Songs* and Daniel Defoe's *Robinson Crusoe*. Rusher occasionally published excerpts from books by London publishers, such as *The Trial of an Ox for Killing a Man*, which originally appeared in John Newbery's *The Fables of the Wise Aesop*. Judging by their widespread availability on the antiquarian market throughout the 20th century, Rusher issued great quantities of halfpenny and penny chapbooks, but it is difficult to determine when individual titles were issued and how long they circulated because so few have dated title pages.

[*See also* Chapbooks *and articles on tales and biographies of figures mentioned in this article.*]

ANDREA IMMEL

Ruskin, John (1819–1900), author, artist, and social reformer. His *The King of the Golden River, or The Black Brothers, a Legend of Stiria* (1851) was one of the earliest English fantasy stories for children. The book, illustrated by Richard Doyle, appeared anonymously. The introduction explains that the story was written in 1841 "at the request of a very young lady." This was Euphemia Gray, then age twelve. Seven years later she married Ruskin, but the marriage was annulled in 1854. He said of the tale that it was "a fairly good imitation of Grimm and Dickens, mixed with some true Alpine feeling of my own." The story tells of three brothers living in a fertile Alpine valley. The two elder, cruel and grasping, bully the youngest, Gluck, and their inhospitality to an uninvited guest—the South West Wind—brings about the destruction of the valley. The valley is eventually restored through the agency of the golden dwarf who comes from Gluck's prized mug when his brothers smelt it for its gold.

[*See also* Doyle, Richard *and* Fantasy.]

GILLIAN AVERY

Russia. Although the first Russian ABC book was published in 1574, and although magazines for the enlightenment of youth existed in the eighteenth century, the emergence of children's literature reflects a late establishment of Russian national literature. Folk tales were not adapted for children until 1870, but literary fairy tales by mainstream Romantic authors appeared considerably earlier. *The Black Hen: or, the Underground People* (1829), by Antony Pogorelsky, bears a close resemblance to *The Nutcracker*. Overt didacticism marks *The Town in the Snuff-Box* (1834) by Vladimir Odoyevsky. The Russian national poet Alexander Pushkin's versified fairy tales, Ivan Krylov's fables, and Pyotr Yershov's chapbook pastiche *The Little Humpbacked Horse* (1834) were not intended for children, but they became integrated into children's reading by virtue of their "child-friendly" genres.

During the nineteenth century, two trends can be traced in Russian children's literature. First, there were occasional children's books by major writers: Nikolai Nekrasov's poetry featuring peasant children, Sergei Aksakov's "Beauty and the Beast" version *The Scarlet Flower* (1859), Vsevolod Garshin's *Frog the Traveler* (1887), and stories of miserable childhood by several mainstream writers of the 1880s and 1890s. These works established high standards in writing for and about children. Leo Tolstoy published school primers for peasant children, including fairy tales and stories, and Anton Chekhov wrote a number of short stories portraying children and animals. During the Silver Age of Russian literature, the turn of the 20th century to 1917, symbolist poets wrote fairy tales addressed to adults and modernist poetry that looked like children's verse. This tradition of major authors writing for children continued throughout the 20th century.

The other trend encompassed sentimental and didactic stories by predominantly female writers such as Alexandra Ishimova. It culminated by the beginning of the 20th century in the works of the prolific and famous Lidia Charskaya, who wrote boarding school novels and adventure stories with exotic settings. It was against this kind of pulp fiction that a new generation of writers, led by Kornei Chukovsky, protested when creating children's literature for young Soviet citizens.

The literary climate of the 1920s was favorable for all kinds of experiments, and in children's literature this period was marked by a flood of modernistic picture books employing a radically new visual language. Vladimir Lebedev was the most prominent artist within this tradition, collaborating with Samuil Marshak, who wrote the texts. Chukovsky's versified stories for children were illustrated by the leading artists of the time, while a number of outstanding futurist poets, including Vladimir Mayakovsky and Daniil Kharms, wrote innovative and playful poetry for children. Published in popular children's magazines, these stories and poems created the foundation for a new children's literature. However, these initiatives were eventually suppressed as incompatible with Soviet cultural policy. In 1934 the first congress of the Writers' Union proclaimed "socialist realism" as the only appropriate way to depict reality. Whatever the official explanation, this artificial pseudo-method basically means describing life not as it is but as it should be according to the ruling ideology, which significantly limited the choice of themes and styles available for children's writers. Quite a few of them were among the horrible toll of 2,500 writers arrested, deported, and murdered during the Great Terror of the 1930s.

In order to assess the development of children's literature from the 1930s on, it is necessary to understand which styles and genres were approved by official Soviet doctrine, and why. Overtly patriotic works glorifying the achievements of the first socialist state were given highest priority. Among these we find hagiographies of communist leaders starting with Lenin, heroes of the Revolution, the civil war and the Great Patriotic War (the official Soviet name of World War II), and outstandingly loyal Soviet citizens. Few such novels display any literary quality. A closely related genre is historical fiction, featuring figures in Russian and world history acceptable from the point of view of the regime: rebels, revolutionaries, and certain political leaders. Adventure was tolerated as long as it contained appropriate patriotic messages—for instance, capitalist spies are exposed by courageous Soviet schoolchildren in Anatoly Rybakov's *The Dagger* (1948) and *The Bronze Bird* (1956). Adventure could be a frame for revolutionary activity, as in Arkady Gaidar's *Military Secret* (1935) and *A Drum-boy's Fate* (1939), and Valentin Katayev's *A Lonely Sail Gleams White* (1936); it could also follow the glorious career of a young Soviet citizen in Veniamin Kaverin's *Two Captains* (1938–1940) or be incorporated into a description of the Soviet variant of the scouting movement in Gaidar's *Timur and His Gang* (1941).

Russia. Illustration by Aleksandr Deineka for *Pervoe maia* by Agniia Barto (Moscow: Gosudarstvennoe izdatel'stvo, 1928). REPRODUCED COURTESY OF THE COTSEN CHILDREN'S LIBRARY, PRINCETON UNIVERSITY LIBRARY

The young protagonists were supposed to serve as models for readers.

Science fiction was employed to propagate Communist ideas by depicting Soviet citizens helping oppressed people on Mars or other planets to start a revolution, as in Alexei Tolstoy's *Aelita* (1922–1923). Soviet science, technology, and space exploration invariably proved superior to the West in Alexander Belyayev's novels. Nature and animal stories were considered harmless and ideologically neutral and could therefore flourish—for instance, in the works of Vitaly Bianki and Yevgeny Charushin. Nonfiction was seen as beneficial for the education of young Soviet citizens. One of the first fictionalized encyclopedias for children, *What I Saw* (1939) by Boris Zhitkov, became an immediate success. After the playful poetic experiments of the 1920s, poetry for children was mostly narrative and satirical. Sergei Mikhalkov and Agniya Barto, two leading representatives, propagated the official ideology and condemned greed, laziness, and individualism.

School and family stories were acceptable, provided that they were not critical of any authority, including teachers and parents. Conflicts in school stories involve a lazy student who gradually reforms and becomes the pride of family, school, and motherland, as in Nikolai Nosov's *Vitya Maleyev at School and at Home* (1951). Individual desires are generally condemned and collective achievements given highest praise, as in Valentina Oseyeva's *Vasyok Trubachov and His Comrades* (1947–1952). Among domestic stories, childhood memoirs are prominent; Oseyeva's *Dinka* (1959) does not fail to mention the young protagonist's father being a revolutionary. Occasionally, in a novel addressed to adolescent readers, such as *Wild Dog Dingo; or, The Story of the First Love* (1939) by Ruvim Fraierman, some daring themes could be explored. More typical are Max Bremener's teenage novels and stories from the 1950s, from which any expression of personal emotion is conspicuously absent.

"Multinational" Soviet children's literature was a hypocritical label covering Russian imperialist policy toward the national republics, where writers, including children's writers, were forcibly russified. Most children's writers in the republics and ethnic areas wrote in Russian or translated their works from their native tongues into Russian, as in the case of the Moldavian Spiridon Vangeli. The topics were either neutral or emphasized the benefits of the socialist regime for minority cultures and the harmonious relationship between children of different ethnic groups.

Fairy tales and fantasy occupied an ambivalent position. On the one hand, they were repeatedly pronounced dangerous, escapist, and undesirable, not least by Lenin's influential widow, Nadezhda Krupskaya. Lev Kassil's *The Grade Book* (1929) shows, apparently against the author's intention, how a child's creative play involving an imaginary country is suppressed by Communist ideology. On the other hand, fairy tales for children were the only genre in which authors, including major adult authors, were relatively free from the prescriptions of socialist realism. Yury Olesha's fairy-tale novel *The Three Fat Men* (1928) is an allegory of oppression. During the worst years of Communist terror, fairy tales were a legitimate genre for many writers: Veniamin Kaverin and Yevgeni Schwartz depicted the abstract struggle between good and evil, easily translated into contemporary Soviet conditions. Thus, fairy tales and fantasy for children became a main channel for subversive literature by mainstream writers. It may be argued whether the use of political satire was conscious, yet it is transparent when the falsehood of the tyrant is accentuated in *The Land of Crooked Mirrors* (1951) by Vitaly Gubarev. The official understanding was that the depicted country embodied hateful capitalism, and that the protagonist, wearing a Soviet school uniform, represented the victorious ideas of Communism. However, reading between the lines became a habit for the Soviet adult audience, resuscitating the old phenomenon called "Aesopian language" in Russian.

The majority of fantasy stories exploited the motif of limitlessly fulfilled wishes, for instance Katayev's *The Rainbow Flower* (1940). The tendency to use an everyday setting rather than sending the protagonist to an alternative world is typical of Soviet writers, presumably as a compromise to the demands of socialist realism. Thus, in *The New Adven-*

Russia. Front cover illustration by Mstislav Dobushinskii for *Tri tol'staia* by Yuri Olesha (Moscow: Zemlia I Fabrika, 1928). Reproduced courtesy of the Cotsen Children's Library, Princeton University Library

tures of Puss in Boots (1937), Schwartz places the famous character in a Young Communist summer camp. Another familiar figure, an Oriental genie, appears in *Old Man Khottabson* (1938) by Lazar Lagin, a free adaptation of *The Brass Bottle* by F. Anstey, in which the released genie's ways and morals come into conflict with his young Communist rescuer. Adapting foreign sources to the declared needs of the Soviet audience was a common practice, possibly because of the cultural isolation of the Soviet Union. Thus, the most popular Russian fantasy novel ever written, *The Wizard of the Emerald City* (1939) by Alexander Volkov, is a retelling of *The Wizard of Oz*. For the most part, adaptations focused on social improvement and group achievement rather than on individual development manifest in the models. In the Russian version of *Pinocchio*, Alexei Tolstoy's *The Golden Key; or, The Adventures of Buratino* (1935), the object of the wooden boy's quest is not becoming human but finding a key to a secret door concealing a puppet theater, where the hero and his friends achieve happiness through socially beneficial labor. Another popular strategy for a successful fantasy was educational, attained by sending the protagonist to a country inhabited by numbers, colors, or musical instruments, so that readers acquired useful knowledge alongside the hero.

At best, fantasy created a childhood utopia comparable with the utopian promises of Communist doctrine, as in the trilogy by Nikolai Nosov, *Dunno and His Friends* (1954), portraying an idyllic society of miniature people. Most of the later fantasy novels, marked by obtrusive didacticism, continue exploiting the motif of a wish-granting magical object used to teach the protagonist a moral lesson. In works by Yuri Tomin, Sofia Prokofyeva, or Valery Medvedev, the struggle between ostensibly right and wrong values, explicitly or implicitly connected to Soviet versus Western ideology, is the central theme. In contrast, Eduard Uspensky's nonsensical fantasy tales were written with great respect for the child, especially in *Uncle Fedya, the Dog, and the Cat* (1974). Two other prominent exceptions are Radi Pogodin and Vladislav Krapivin, authors of philosophical, existential fantasy, completely free from ideology or didacticism.

The late 1960s and 1970s are generally referred to as "years of stagnation" when literature, art, theater, and film were under heavy censorial pressure. In children's literature, however, this was a period of innovation and flowering. A new generation of nonsense poets appeared, including Boris Zakhoder, Valentin Berestov, and Irina Tokmakova. Realistic, psychological children's novels became more candid and engaging than most adult fiction, as in the work of Yuri Korinets and Yuri Koval. Since children's literature was not considered dangerous or potentially subversive, writers started exploring subjects usually regarded as suspicious in literature for adults. It was still inconceivable to criticize the regime, but the interrogation of teachers' or parents' authority was daring enough. A child's point of view, rather than the authoritative omniscient perspective, became the trademark of Viktor Dragunsky. A more liberal attitude to personal relationships, including sexuality, began to appear in children's and young adult fiction. A poignant novel by Vladimir Zheleznikov, *The Scarecrow* (1981), portraying peer bullying, received much attention after it was made into a major film.

After the fall of the Soviet Union in 1991, children's literature was no longer a matter of consequence for the state, but it became a source of profit for private publishers. Since many writers, liberated from censorship, happily abandoned their young audience for more prestigious and better-paid general fiction, children's literature was for a while dominated by translations of formerly outlawed Western mass-market literature and reprints of pre-1917 sentimental stories. Religious literature for children, banned during the Soviet regime, became a flourishing genre, often of very low quality. Some young writers, such as Maria Semyonova, ventured into fantasy based on Slavic mythology. Nonsense poetry and prose for children saw a revival, especially in the works of Grigory Oster. Yet the best Russian illustrators, such as Gennady Spirin, Alexander Koshkin, and Boris Diodorov, either emigrated or began to work for foreign publishers. Consequently, by the mid-2000s a new picture-book tradition had not emerged. The gap was filled by translated supermarket books and comics. The most recent major event in Russian children's literature is a series of *Harry Potter* imitations by Dmitri Yemets, starting with *Tanya Grotter and the Magic Bass Guitar* (2002), which resulted in a lawsuit for plagiarism. At the outset of the 21st century, the serendipitous isolation of Russian children's literature had come to an end.

[*See also* Nutcracker, The *and biographies of figures mentioned in this article.*]

BIBLIOGRAPHY

Hellman, Ben. *Barn- och ungdomsboken i Sovjet-Ryssland: Från oktoberrevolutionen 1917 till perestrojkan 1986*. Stockholm: Rabén and Sjögren, 1991.

Mäeots, Olga. "Topsy-Turvy World: New Trends in Modern Russian Children's Literature." In *Reflections of Change: Children's Literature since 1945*, edited by Sandra L. Beckett, 171–176. Westport, Conn.: Greenwood, 1997.

Mitrokhina, Xenia. "The Land of Oz in the Land of the Soviets." *Children's Literature Association Quarterly* 21 (1996): 183–188.

Nikolajeva, Maria. "Fairy Tales in Society's Service." *Marvels and Tales* 16 (2002): 171–187.
Nikolajeva, Maria. "Russian Children's Literature before and after Perestroika." *Children's Literature Association Quarterly* 20 (1995): 105–111.
Nikolajeva, Maria. "The 'Serendipity' of Censorship." *Para*doxa* (1996): 379–386.
Nikolajeva, Maria. "Social Utopias." In her *From Mythic to Linear. Time in Children's Literature*, 61–85. Lanham, Md.: Scarecrow, 2000.
O'Dell, Felicity Ann. *Socialization through Literature: The Soviet Example*. Cambridge, U.K.: Cambridge University Press, 1978.
Prosalkova, Julia. "Bits and Pieces about Twentieth-Century Russian Science Fiction." *Bookbird* 35 (1997): 22–25.
Salminen, Jenniliisa. "Politics: Gubarev's Kingdoms of Crooked Mirrors." In *Children's Literature as Communication*, edited by Roger D. Sell, 201–212. Amsterdam: John Benjamins, 2002.
Sokol, Elena. *Russian Poetry for Children*. Knoxville: University of Tennessee Press, 1994.
Steiner, Eugeny. *Stories for Little Comrades: Revolutionary Artists and the Making of Early Soviet Children's Books*. Seattle: University of Washington Press, 1999.
Tumanov Klein, Larisa. "Writing for a Dual Audience in the Former Soviet Union: The Aesopian Children's Literature of Kornei Chukovsky, Mikhail Zhoshchenko, and Daniil Kharms." In *Transcending Boundaries: Writing for a Dual Audience of Children and Adults*, edited by Sandra L. Beckett, 129–148. New York: Garland, 1999.

Maria Nikolajeva

Russo, Marisabina (1950–), American author/illustrator of more than twenty picture books, many of which are family stories featuring children's experiences with parents, grandparents, and siblings. Russo's interest in art and writing developed through childhood, and after graduating from Mount Holyoke College she did freelance illustrating, including magazine covers, adult books, and a few children's books by other writers. Her writing and full-page gouache paintings in *The Line Up Book* (1986) established a style followed in one or two books per year—simple, amusing plots and pictures with strong colors and flat perspectives. Some later books move beyond daily dilemmas to include a novel about a seventh grader, *The House of Sports* (2002), and a longer, more complex picture book recounting the Holocaust as experienced by members of Russo's family, *Always Remember Me: How One Family Survived World War II* (2005). Many of her books have been on annual book lists and have won children's choice awards.

[*See also* Holocaust Literature for Children; Illustrations; *and* Picture Books.]

Margaret Bush

Rutgers van der Loeff-Basenau, An (1910–1990), Dutch author of a large oeuvre, consisting chiefly of realistic novels for older children. In her opinion, the main value of literature is that children can experience the world through the eyes of others. Although her work contains educational elements, the "message" is always hidden and everything is seen through the eyes of the characters.

Her first book for children became a classic: *De kinderkaravaan* (1949; English trans., *Children on the Oregon Trail*, 1961). This story, based on historical facts, relates the difficult experiences of seven pioneer children in the 19th century who continue on their way to Oregon, "the promised land," after the death of their parents.

She also had great success with a book about a Swiss children's village for victims of World War II, *Lawines razen* (1954; English trans., *Avalanche*, 1958).

Anne de Vries

Ruy-Vidal, François (1931–), French publisher. Ruy-Vidal was a schoolmaster from 1951 to 1963. In 1964 he met a young American publisher who was just starting to publish picture books. In 1966 they founded a French publishing house, intending that some of their books could be published on both sides of the Atlantic. They issued thirty-three picture books between 1967 and 1972 under the label "Un livre d'Harlin Quist." Ruy-Vidal wanted to break away from the rather dull French production styles of the time and stressed graphic inventiveness and new subjects. His picture books were not meant to guide or comfort children. They embodied an uncanny representation of childhood and questioned the power of adults over children. The publishers' American connection played a part in breaking with traditional themes. However, the books' spirit of nonsense has been badly misunderstood and read as transgressive. Children's librarians were rather puzzled and reluctant; some of them found the books unsuitable for young readers.

Ruy-Vidal published picture books nearly exclusively, and a new generation of French illustrators rose up around him, including Nicole Claveloux, Frédéric Clément, Alain Gauthier, Michel Gay, and Claude Lapointe. He also published some great French authors, such as Marguerite Duras (*Ah! Ernesto*, 1971) Eugène Ionesco (*Conte no. 1, 2, 3, 4* [Story Number 1, 2, 3, 4], 1969, 1970, and 1976). After a rather short existence, however, the French publishing house encountered financial difficulties, and the two publishers parted in 1972. Ruy-Vidal went on in publishing as an editor for Grasset (1973–1976), Jean-Pierre Delarge (1976–1978), and Éditions de l'amitié (1978–1981), striving to remain faithful to his aesthetic, moral, and literary choices. He published about eighty books during those years, among them *L'histoire du prince Pipo* by Pierre Gripari (The Story of Prince Pipo, 1976) and a retelling of *Le petit poucet* (Tom Thumb, 1974). His edition of *Alice's Adventures in Wonderland* received an award at the Bratislava Biennial in 1974. Ruy-Vidal was a leading figure of the revival of the French picture book in the 1970s.

BIBLIOGRAPHY

Nières-Chevrel, Isabelle. "François Ruy-Vidal et la révolution de l'album pour enfants dans les années 1970." In *La Licorn, L' image pour enfants: Pratiques, normes, discours (France et pays francophones, XVI*e*–XX*e *siècles)*, 251–263. Poitiers : UFR Langues Littératures, 2003.

ISABELLE NIÈRES-CHEVREL

Rwakasisi, Rose (1945–), Ugandan writer, curriculum developer, educator, and deputy head teacher of Kyamate Secondary School in Ntungamo. Born in Buhweju, Rwakasisi gained fame through Fountain Publishers' Our Heritage series, through which she published works such as *How Friends Became Enemies* (1993) and *The Old Woman and the Shell* (1994). Recent works such as *Sunshine after Rain* (2002) and *Why Mother Left Home* (2003) engage with issues like HIV-AIDS and drug addiction among youth. A mother and veteran educator who has taught in many schools and written some fifty children's books, Rwakasisi sees her mission as an instructor for the young generation.

[*See also* Africa: Sub-Saharan Africa *and* Nonfiction.]

AARON MUSHENGYEZI

Rydberg, Viktor (1828–1895), Swedish poet, member of the Swedish (Nobel Prize) Academy, and professor. Born poor, he worked early on as journalist, from 1855 to 1876 at the newspaper *Göteborgs Handels- och Sjöfartstidning*. Rydberg was a late-Romantic writer of sometimes idealistic poems and novels (*Singoalla*, 1857). He translated Goethe's *Faust* into Swedish, preferred Old Norse mythology to strict Christianity, and was against foreign words in Swedish. His famous poem "Tomten" (The Tomten), recited in many Swedish Schools in December, has been adapted into prose by Astrid Lindgren and illustrator Harald Wiberg as a picture book (1960); as shown by Lena Törnqvist, some translations replace Rydberg's name with Lindgren's, apparently for marketing reasons. The novella *Lille Viggs äfventyr på julafton* (1875; Eng. trans., *The Christmas Tomten*, 1981), illustrated by Jenny Nyström, is regarded as one of the earliest Swedish tales of fantasy.

[*See also* Lindgren, Astrid; Nordic Countries; *and* Poetry.]

ASTRID SURMATZ

Ryder, Joanne (1946–), American editor and prolific author of children's books, most of which focus on the natural world. Ryder's informative, image-rich picture books have received critical praise for combining poetic text with scientifically accurate information about nature and animals within fantastic plots that encourage young readers to consider their own roles in the web of life. Author of the Just for a Day, First Grade Is the Best, and Night and Morning series, Ryder has won awards for many of her titles, including *The Snail's Spell* (1982) and *Night Gliders* (1996). In 1968 Ryder received her BA in journalism from Marquette University, where she met the author Laurence Yep, whom she later married. After a year of studying library science at the University of Chicago, she moved to New York City, where she began her career as a children's book editor with Harper & Row. In the mid 2000s she was a full-time author of children's books.

[*See also* Animal Stories; Ecology and Environment; Picture Books; *and* Laurence Yep.]

MICHELLE H. MARTIN

Rylant, Cynthia (1954–), American author of over one hundred books, including picture books, poetry, short stories, and novels. Rylant was educated at Morris Harvey College and Marshall University in West Virginia, and at Kent State University (MLS, 1981). She has been a children's librarian and a university lecturer. Her first picture book, *When I Was Young in the Mountains* (1982), was chosen as a Caldecott Honor Book, as was *The Relatives Came* (1985), and both are set in the rural West Virginia of her childhood. Her young adult novels *A Fine White Dust* (1986) and *Missing May* (1992) focus on deep feelings about religion and death as each young protagonist struggles to reconcile personal needs with the outside world and with the people closest to them. *A Fine White Dust* was a Newbery Honor Book, and *Missing May* was a winner. In a lighter vein she wrote the twenty-eight-volume Henry and Mudge series (1987–1999), stories that unite the small, lonely Henry with Mudge, who quickly develops from a puppy to an ungainly hound. In 2000 she created a fanciful, animal-mystery series, the

High Rise Private Eyes, in which Bunny Brown, a rabbit, and Jack Jones, a raccoon, solve animal-related mysteries. Many of her stories depict caring, but also wary, relationships between people in unusual, self-formed families, and she does not hesitate in adding supernatural forces into the lives of her characters. For example, *The Van Gogh Café* (1995) is a special place to ten-year-old Clara and her father, and magical stories are lyrically told from Clara's perspective as she interprets them through the agency of visiting possums, gulls, and even lightning. *The Islander* (1998) incorporates a mermaid into a young boy's efforts to save birds. Additional stories and poems use simple language in exploring bonds within and between families, animals, nature, and the supernatural as a continuum in human experience.

BIBLIOGRAPHY

McGinty, Alice B. *Cynthia Rylant*. New York: Rosen, 2004.

JANICE M. BOGSTAD

S

S., Svend Otto (1916–), Danish illustrator. Svend Otto Sørenson, who signs his work "Svend Otto S.," is an Andersen Medal winner (1978), best known for his illustrations of folk and fairy tales, notably those of the Grimm brothers and Hans Christian Andersen. His picture books based on Andersen's fairy tales include *The Fir Tree* (1968; English trans., 1971), *The Tinder Box* (1972; English trans., 1971), and *The Ugly Duckling* (1975). Among his many versions of the Grimms' stories are *Little Red Riding Hood* (1970), *Hansel and Gretel* (1971; English trans., 1983), *Puss in Boots* (1972), *Briar Rose, the Sleeping Beauty* (1973; English trans., 1975), *Musicians from Bremen* (1974; English trans., 1974), *Snow White and the Seven Dwarfs* (1975; English trans., 1975), *Tom Thumb* (1976; English trans., 1979), *The Wolf and the Seven Little Kids* (1977; English trans., 1977), *Cinderella* (1978; English trans., 1978), and *Brave Little Tailor* (1979; English trans., 1979). More illustrated stories are collected in *Andersen's Fairytales* (1972; English trans., 1990) and *The Best of Grimm's Fairy Tales* (1970; English trans., 1979). Picture books with the artist's own text include *Taxi Dog* (1977; English trans., 1978), *The Giant Fish* (1981; English trans., 1982) and the folk-inspired but highly original *Tim and Trisha* (1976; English trans., 1977), featuring a friendship between a lonely child and a lonely troll. He has also illustrated Aesop's fables and Danish, Norwegian, and Russian folk tales; collaborated with the Swedish writer Lennart Hellsing on the picture book *The Wonderful Pumpkin* (1975; English trans., 1976); illustrated books by Danish and Swedish children's authors including Cecil Bødker, Astrid Lindgren, and Gunnel Linde; and provided covers for many adult novels. His illustrations are characterized by rich detail, elaborate technique, and warm humor. They also show a clear tendency to counterbalance the Disney style. This difference has gained S. a worldwide reputation as his illustrations have appeared in fairy tale volumes in several countries. Unlike many contemporary illustrators of classical fairy tales, S. addresses primarily an audience of children, avoiding adult connotations or allusions.

Maria Nikolajeva

Svend Otto S. Illustration from *Die schönsten Märchen der Brüder Grimm* (Oldenburg, Germany: Lappan, 1986). Reproduced courtesy of the Cotsen Children's Library, Princeton University Library

Sabuda, Robert (1965–), American illustrator and author. The innovative Sabuda is best known for his work with pop-up books. Fascinated from childhood by both the study of art and the craft of book making, Sabuda graduated from Pratt Institute in New York City and embarked on a career in illustration. His books are marked by complexity of design and expert execution, whether he works with mosaics, linoleum block prints, faux stained glass, batik, or cut paper. He is a self-taught paper engineer, and his creativity with three-dimensional design has led to a very sophisticated array of pop-up books. Many of his works feature animals or Christmas themes (e.g., *The Christmas Alphabet*, 1994) but recent publications, like his editions of *The Wizard of Oz* (2000) and *Alice's Adventures in Wonderland* (2003), include longer texts and complex visual dramas, which Sabuda brings elegantly to life. Sabuda's work as an illustrator of pop-up books has raised the profile of this artistic technique and has expanded the age range for which such books are designed.

MEGAN LYNN ISAAC

Sachar, Louis (1954–), American author of short stories and novels for early and middle-grade readers. He graduated from the University of California, Berkeley, and received a law degree from the University of California, San Francisco. Years of vacillating between a career as a writer and one as a lawyer ended once his books began to receive warm praise and a wide readership. Of Sachar's many fine qualities as a writer, humor is perhaps the most notable. His first publication, *Sideways Stories from Wayside School* (1978), describes a thirty-floor school peopled by teachers who know how to turn children into apples and instruct students in upside-down reading. The characters also include Louis the Yard Teacher, who oversees recess and bears more than a passing resemblance to the author himself. The popularity of the Wayside School stories led Sachar to write three sequels.

The episodic quality of the Wayside School stories provides much of their charm, but it is also one of their weaknesses. Sachar began to develop his skills in plotting and characterization with a handful of novels aimed at middle school readers. *Johnny's in the Basement* (1981) chronicles the humorous trials and tribulations of Johnny Laxatayl, who finds the responsibilities of being eleven years old entirely too much to bear. *Someday Angeline* (1983) features an eight-year-old genius who finds a friend in "Goon" Boone, who also does not fit the conventional mold. In his very popular *There's a Boy in the Girl's Bathroom* (1987), Sachar takes the point of view of Bradley Chalkers, the class bully and homework reprobate, and poignantly yet humorously demonstrates his transformation through the help of the school counselor and a friend. *Sixth Grade Secrets* (1987) and *Dogs Don't Tell Jokes* (1991) also demonstrate Sachar's ability to capture both the humor and the pain typical of preadolescent life.

Sachar's next set of literary ventures, the *Marvin Redpost* books, are aimed at younger readers and appeal equally to anyone who enjoys a good read-aloud. Hapless nine-year-old Marvin stumbles from one problem to the next. In the first volume, *Marvin Redpost: Kidnapped at Birth?* (1992), he fears only foul play can explain why he is the lone redhead in his family. In succeeding volumes he is unjustly accused of nose picking, fails at dog sitting, and finds himself enchanted by a magic crystal, or maybe just the girl who owns it.

Sachar's most memorable book is, however, *Holes* (1998), which was awarded the Newbery Medal as well as being made into a very successful film. Sent to the juvenile detention facility Camp Green Lake, Stanley Yelnats is sentenced to dig holes in a miserable desert populated by dangerous yellow spotted lizards and a variety of other nasty critters that walk and stalk on two or more legs. Along with his new buddy, Zero, Stanley manages both to escape the camp and to evade his legendary family curse. Although Sachar's wacky humor, penchant for strange circumstances, and deft rendering of friendship is as evident as ever in this tale, Sachar's writing rises to new heights.

[*See also* Easy Readers; Humor; *and* School Stories.]

MEGAN LYNN ISAAC

Sachs, Marilyn (1927–), American librarian and children's author of more than forty novels. Sachs was among the first authors to embrace a realist approach to children's fiction, not just in the characters but also in the social problems they face. Neither children nor adults are perfect in Sachs's books, nor do they inhabit a perfect world. The Great Depression colors the world of the Stern sisters in their three books, beginning with *Amy Moves In* (1964), and Sachs also addresses immigrant problems (*Call Me Ruth*, 1982) and the Holocaust (*A Pocket Full of Seeds*, 1973). Even the happy endings Sachs often provides have bittersweet aspects. The characters learn valuable lessons in tolerance, self-reliance, and understanding without the books ever crossing the line into preaching. Earlier books may look outdated to a modern reader: few people would suggest today that the title character of *Veronica Ganz* (1968) should trade physical bullying for stereotypically feminine wiles, batting her lashes. However, Sachs has changed with the times, and her characters remain vivid and contemporary to their own times.

[*See also* Historical Fiction; Holocaust Literature for Children; Librarians in the United States; *and* Realism.]

MARISSA K. LINGEN

Sadji, Aboulaye (1910–1961), Senegalese writer. Born in Rufisque, Senegal, Sadji taught school in Rufisque and Dakar, wrote articles for *Présence africaine* and *Bingo*, and created the first radio stations in Senegal for the nation's diverse languages. In 1959 he became an elementary school inspector, a post he held until he died. His talent as a storyteller is proven in the legend of *Tounka* (1965) and in heroic stories collected in *Ce que dit la musique africaine* (What African Music Says, 1985). Sadji is especially admired as the author of *La belle histoire de Leuk le lièvre* (The Beautiful Story of Leuk the Hare, 1953), a folk tale for children written in collaboration with Léopold Sédar Senghor. This book, designed to serve as a reader for African schoolchildren when there were few school books available, is still one of the most enchanting works of children's literature in Africa.

[*See also* Africa: Sub-Saharan Africa; Fairy Tales and Folk Tales; Primers; *and* Senghor, Léopold Sédar.]

Mahoumbah Klobah

Saint-Dizier, Marie (1944–), French novelist, known as Marie-Raymond Farré when she, together with her husband Raymond, translated the work of Roald Dahl in 1977. She is known for her humor and portrayal of family life through whimsical parody. Thus, sisterly conflicts rise to a grotesque climax in *Les aventures de Papagayo* (Papagayo's Adventures, 1983), while *L'incroyable secret de Bobbie Boulon* (The Incredible Secret of Bobbie Nuts, 1979) plays on a child's liking for automats. She and her husband wrote a set of successful picture books illustrated by Amato Soro, including *Papa est un ogre* (Dad Is an Ogre, 1983). On her own, Saint-Dizier began writing works with more complex plots set in Paris, such as *Ne jouez pas sur mon piano* (Don't Play on My Piano, 1996), and she also published many funny detective stories, such as *Qui a tué l'écrivain?* (Who Killed the Writer?, 1997). In 2003 she wrote an autobiographical novel, *Je reviens* (I Am Coming Back).

Jean Perrot

Saint-Exupéry, Antoine de (1900–1944), French writer. Saint-Exupéry was a commercial pilot during the 1930s and wrote three books based on his experiences. He returned to flying during World War II but was soon demobilized because of his age. The French defeat left him bewildered. In 1941 he went to the United States, where his fame as a writer was already established, to receive the National Book Award for *Wind, Sand, and Stars* (1939; French, *Terre des Hommes*, 1939). After three years in New York, he went to Algeria to serve with Free French forces and disappeared on a reconnaissance flight over the Mediterranean. He wrote two books during his stay in New York: *Pilote de guerre* (1942; English trans., *Flight to Arras*, 1942) and his only children's book, *Le petit prince* (1943; English trans., *The Little Prince*, 1943). Sketches of a little man appear in some of his letters as early as 1939, and it seems that by that time Saint-Exupéry was already considering writing a tale for children. Perhaps persuaded by his American publisher, Saint-Exupéry started to write *The Little Prince* in 1941 and to do the illustrations in watercolor and pencil. Reynal and Hitchcock brought out the book in April 1943; it is not certain that the layout of the illustrations was Saint-Exupéry's choice. One week later, Saint-Exupéry embarked for North Africa, never to return. The book was a success: thirty thousand copies of the English translation were sold by the summer of 1943. The first French edition, published by Gallimard, did not appear in Paris until November 1945. A project by Orson Welles to film the story in 1944 was never carried out (the script is in the Lilly Library at Indiana University).

The Little Prince is dedicated to Saint-Exupéry's close friend Léon Werth, a French Jewish journalist and writer who remained hidden in France throughout the war. The dedication is addressed to Werth both as an adult and as a child, suggesting that this is not merely a children's book but is also meant for adults. There are autobiographical allusions in the text: the narrator is a pilot; Saint-Exupéry experienced a serious plane crash in the desert in 1936; and the Little Prince's relationships with his rose may refer to Saint-Exupéry's complicated relations with his wife, Consuelo, and with women in general. Most critics agree, however, that the book is far more than that, and they emphasize its philosophical and symbolic meanings. The young hero—a *puer æternus* (eternal child)—judges the adults' ways of behaving and reveals to the narrator the secret of human wisdom, as the fox has taught him: "It is only with the heart that one can see rightly; what is essential is invisible to the eye." The drawings underline the opposition between appearance and meaning. "If you please—draw me a sheep," asks the Little Prince. If "words are the source of misunderstandings," drawings could be the way to restore the spirit of childhood. A mere sketch is enough for the Little Prince to see the sheep he wanted through the holes in a box. The lonely, depressed pilot of the beginning becomes by the end of the tale the comforted adult of a reclaimed childhood.

From a literary point of view, it is better not to consider *The Little Prince* as a modern fairy tale, but rather as an attempt to create a French fantasy genre, perhaps in the mode of André Maurois or Marcel Aymé. Saint-Exupéry must have been familiar with Kipling's *Just So Stories*, well known in France, and he may have borrowed one of its stylistic

Antoine de Saint-Exupéry. Illustration by Saint-Exupéry from *Le petit prince* (New York: Harcourt, Brace & World, 1943), p. 15. REPRODUCED COURTESY OF THE COTSEN CHILDREN'S LIBRARY, PRINCETON UNIVERSITY LIBRARY

devices: the expression "a thousand miles from any human habitation" is repeated four times in the second chapter. Linked with English children's fantasy, *The Little Prince* also belongs to a French narrative tradition, halfway between novel and poetry, for which Jean-Yves Tadié has coined the term *récit poétique* (poetic fiction); its elements include a character without social and historical background, a poetic link between the hero and the setting, a slow, retrospective narrative full of metaphors and symbols, and constant iteration of the weakness of language in grasping human experience. As early as the end of the war, *The Little Prince* had been translated into the major European languages, and by the mid-2000s it was known all over the world, translated into 102 languages.

Bibliography

Curtis, Cate. *Antoine de Saint-Exupéry: His Life and Times*. New York: Putnam, 1970.

de la Bruyère, Stacy. *Saint-Exupéry: A Star Crossed Life*. New York: Knopf, 1994.

Higgins, James E. *The Little Prince: A Reverie of Substance*. New York: Twayne, 1996.

Major, Jean-Louis. *Saint-Exupéry: L'écriture et la pensée*. Ottawa: Éditions de l'Université d'Ottawa, 1968.

Montandon, Alain. *Du récit merveilleux ou l'ailleurs de l'enfance : Le Petit Prince, Pinocchio, Le Magicien d'Oz, Peter Pan, E.T., L'histoire sans fin*. Paris: Imago, 2001.

von Franz, Marie Louise. *Puer Aeternus: A Psychological Study of the Adult Struggle with the Paradise of Childhood*. 2d ed. Santa Monica, Calif.: Sigo, 1981.

Isabelle Nières-Chevrel

Salassi, Otto (1939–1993), American writer and librarian. Salassi, whose real name was Otto Russell, was born in Vicksburg, Mississippi and earned a BS from Memphis State University and an MLS and MFA from the University of Arkansas. He worked primarily as a librarian at several colleges. Salassi's first young adult novel, *On the Ropes*, was published in 1981. His most enduring novel is *Jimmy D., Sidewinder, and Me* (1987). Its protagonist, hoping to get a more lenient sentence, writes a series of letters to the judge from jail, explaining why he acted as he did. The novel received a Notable Book citation from the American Library Association.

Nancy J. Keane

Sales, Francesc (1947–), Spanish author, translator, and publisher who has been writing novels for young people and adults and short stories for children in Catalan since 1980. His experiences as a teacher of Catalan language and literature in a secondary school have given him a sound knowledge of the world and speech patterns of teenagers. This has enabled him to achieve a good rapport with his readers. In 1992 he received the "Premio Gran Angular" (a prestigious Spanish prize) for his novel *El pes de la càrrega* (The weight of the load, 1993), in which an adolescent recounts episodes from his life to a psychiatrist (in the first person, so that the reader identifies with the character). Among other works are *Les cartes de la Mila* (Mila's Letters, 1985), *El meu amic Pau* (My friend Paul, 1992) and *Ibrahim, un noi del Marroc* (Ibrahim, a Boy from Morocco, 1984; English trans., *Ibrahim*, 1989).

Marisa Fernández-Lopez

Salgari, Emilio (1862–1911), first and foremost Italian writer of adventure novels. Salgari also played a significant role in early journalism for the young. Extraordinarily popular and frequently translated, especially into Spanish, Salgari began by writing exotic light fiction for adults, which was serialized in a Verona daily. At twenty-one he achieved local renown with *La Tigre della Malesia* (The Tiger of Malaysia, 1883–1884), which, reworked for children and adolescents, would become a classic adventure novel, *Le Tigri di Mompracem* (The Tigers of Mompracem, 1900); perhaps the most distinctive of his eighty-one novels, it has been in print ever since. The similarly imaginative *I misteri della Jungla Nera* (Mysteries of the Black Jungle, 1895), set in the Ganges delta, was also a conversion of an early serial.

After the publication of five adult tales describing tropical countries (foreign settings were an innovation in Italian novels), the editor of a children's weekly commissioned a serial, *La Scimitarra di Budda* (The Buddha's Scimitar, 1891); thereafter Salgari specialized in writing for the young. A period of sea stories followed, including *Un dramma nell'Oceano Pacifico* (A Drama on the Pacific Ocean, 1895), which included among its characters the first of many strong and active heroines. In the 1890s Salgari's novels were published by nine different houses and, after his move to Turin, his short stories and informative articles appeared in numerous periodicals for different age groups, both sexes, and families: girls loved his work as much as boys. From 1896 Salgari had exclusive contracts, first with Donath in Genoa (with whom he managed to escape the limits of his contract for financial reasons, by means of four main pseudonyms) and then with Bemporad, the distinguished Florentine publisher. In 1897 the king honored Salgari as "Cavaliere." Strongly identified with his Orientalist tales of modern Borneo pirates, Salgari in 1898 introduced his second great piracy series with *Il Corsaro Nero* (The Black Corsair), concerning 17th-century Caribbean freebooters. The exquisite Italian "Black Corsair" joined Sandokan, dispossessed Borneo sultan, as Salgari's most famous heroes and ultimately as figures in Italian cultural mythology. In 1904 Donath launched a new periodical as a vehicle for Salgari's writing and editorship: *Per Terra e per Mare* (By Land and Sea) was defined as a travel and adventure weekly for all the family. Some of Salgari's new novels appeared first as serials in its pages, and for it he wrote innumerable short stories, anecdotes, and articles on topics from around the world. In 1906 Bemporad recruited Salgari for the new children's newspaper, *Il Giornalino della Domenica*, which was to offer a galaxy of the finest writers and illustrators. Henceforth, until his suicide in 1911, Salgari's novels were published by Bemporad.

Still read today, Salgari introduced adventure novels to Italy, his colorful, operatic, encyclopedic oeuvre encompassing almost all types within the genre: pirates, freedom fighters, love across boundaries, quests, lost treasure, sea stories, futurist speculation, natural hazards, the slave trade, castaways, rescues, polar and transcontinental exploration, gold diggers, frontiersmen, Red Indians, Siberian salt miners, pearl divers, wars ancient and modern. Notable for their lyrical descriptions of nature and their feminism, some are historical novels, some are tragedies; all—despite fascist propaganda—are anticolonialist.

[*See also* Adventure Books; Colonial Fiction; Italy; *and* Sea Stories.]

BIBLIOGRAPHY

Di Biase, Carmine, ed. *Il "caso Salgari."* Naples: CUEN, 1997.
Lawson Lucas, Ann. "Decadence for Kids: Salgari's *Corsaro Nero* in Context." In *Children's Literature and the Fin de Siècle*, edited by Roderick McGillis, 81–90. Westport, Conn.: Praeger, 2003.
Lawson Lucas, Ann. "Fascism and Literature: 'Il caso Salgari.'" *Italian Studies* 45, (1990): 32–47.
Lawson Lucas, Ann. *La ricerca dell'ignoto: I romanzi d'avventura di Emilio Salgari*. Florence: Olschki, 2000.
Pozzo, Felice. *Emilio Salgari e Dintorni*. Naples: Liguori Editore, 2000.
Traversetti, Bruno. *Introduzione a Salgari*. Bari: Laterza, 1989.

ANN LAWSON LUCAS

Salinger, J. D. (1919–), American writer. Jerome David Salinger, the chronicler of the quintessential adolescent experience in his first novel, *The Catcher in the Rye* (1951), was born in New York City and served in the U.S. Army in Europe during World War II. Before *The Catcher in the Rye*, he published short stories in popular magazines (especially the *New Yorker*), but with the novel's publication he achieved instant fame, particularly with young readers who identified with the protagonist Holden Caulfield's struggle to reject all things "phony." Holden runs away from his prep school because he is miserable and about to flunk out, setting off on a journey to escape the "phoniness" of the adult world. Although this first-person tale became an immediate hit, critical approval did not follow until after the publication of Salinger's *Nine Stories* (1953). That collection was succeeded by the Glass family stories: *Franny and Zooey* (1961) and *Raise High the Roof Beam, Carpenters, and Seymour: An Introduction* (1963). "Hapworth 16, 1924," a Glass family novella in the form of a letter, appeared in the *New Yorker* in 1965. After that Salinger abandoned publication altogether, although he apparently continued to write, and interest in his work has faded somewhat. The appeal of *The Catcher in the Rye* has nonetheless given the novel the status of a classic and a classroom standard, despite frequent problems with censorship, a response to the profanity it contains.

Little is known about the reclusive Salinger's private life, but critics have concluded that much of his writing is autobiographical. Like the Glass children, he was a child of mixed parentage, with a Jewish father and Scottish-Irish mother. His difficulties in school as an adolescent prompted his father to send him to Valley Forge Military Academy in Pennsylvania, from which he graduated in 1936 and which was the model for Pencey Prep in *The Catcher in the Rye*. His examination of conflict between spiritual quests and materialism, and the search for real love despite the "phoniness" of most human relationships, place him in the ranks of postmodern writers. He joined many of his generation in responding to a sense of despair and paranoia in relation to events in the postwar world.

Salinger, living in almost total seclusion in rural New Hampshire, has continued to shun publicity and any contact with the publishing world, and to express his contempt for literary critics. He has also adamantly refused to allow republication of his earliest work. In 1974 *The Complete Uncollected Short Stories of J. D. Salinger*, a two-volume unauthorized edition, appeared, and Salinger was not able to suppress it until about twenty-five thousand copies had been distributed. In 1987 Salinger blocked publication of an unauthorized biography by Ian Hamilton, claiming copyright infringement of private letters from which Hamilton had quoted. Hamilton was forced to withdraw the book, and in 1988 a completely revised version appeared under the title *In Search of J. D. Salinger*.

BIBLIOGRAPHY

Bloom, Harold, ed. *J. D. Salinger: Modern Critical Views*. Broomall, Pa.: Chelsea House, 1987.
French, Warren. *J. D. Salinger, Revisited*. New York: Twayne, 1988.
Hamilton, Ian. *In Search of J. D. Salinger*. New York: Random House, 1988.
Salzman, Jack, ed. *New Essays on The Catcher in the Rye*. New York: Cambridge University Press, 1992

AMANDA COCKRELL

Salisbury, Graham (1944–), American fiction writer born in Philadelphia, Pennsylvania, and raised in Hawaii. Salisbury graduated magna cum laude from California State University at Northbridge and received an MFA from Vermont College of Norwich University in 1990. He has worked as a dockhand, graphic artist, and teacher, turning to writing in his thirties after the birth of his first child. Though not previously an avid reader, he found then that he began to enjoy reading, and subsequently became interested in writing. His first book, *Blue Skin of the Sea*, won many awards and was included on the American Library Association's list of Best Books for Young Adults (1992), and ensuing works have similarly garnered high praise. All of his novels take place at least partially in Hawaii, setting their stories of American history (*Under the Blood Red Sun*, 1994) and family relationships (*Lord of the Deep*, 2001) against the backdrop of the islands or out at sea.

[*See also* Historical Fiction *and* Young Adult Literature.]

NANCY J. KEANE

Salkey, Andrew (1928–1995), celebrated novelist, anthologist, broadcast journalist, poet, and dramatist who also taught writing at Hampshire College in Massachusetts. Born of Jamaican parents in Panama, Salkey was educated at St. George's College (Jamaica) and at the University of London. In addition to his adult novels and short stories, his work included a poetry collection and eight novels for the young, as well as over thirty plays for the British Broadcasting Corporation. *Hurricane* (1964) and *Earthquake* (1965) were for children, and *Jonah Simpson* (1969) was for young adults. In *Earthquake*, the quake of 1907 is graphically described, but the novel is essentially about the delicate balances characters achieve in their relationships. Grandparents, grandchildren, and a Rastafarian preacher show the way people often tease and compete, but not at the expense of gentleness and respect. The child's special talent for imaginative play stands out in this novel. In 1979 Salkey turned to poetry with *In the Hills Where Her Dreams Live: Poems for Chile, 1973–1980*.

[*See also* Caribbean Countries *and* Young Adult Literature.]

MAWUENA KOSSI LOGAN

Sally Series. A trilogy by Eilís Ní Dhuibhne (1954–) written under the name of Elizabeth O'Hara, the Sally series features Sally Gallagher in her struggle to make a living and a life in 19th-century Ireland. In the first book, *The Hiring Fair* (1993), thirteen-year-old Sally and her sister Katie are "bought" as domestic laborers to serve in well-to-do families in the County of Tyrone. In the second book, *Blaeberry Sunday* (1994), Sally is back in County of Donegal where she comes from. The last of the series, *Penny-Farthing Sally* (1996), pictures Sally as a young woman working as a governess in Dublin. Given Ní Dhuibhne's background as social historian and folklorist, it is not surprising that the *Sally* books contain a wealth of vividly reported details about the living conditions of 19th-century Ireland. In this series she manages to combine social history with compelling narrative and thorough characterization.

[*See also* Historical Fiction *and* Ireland.]

BJÖRN SUNDMARK

Salmon, Michael (1949–), prolific writer and illustrator of children's picture books, born in Wellington, New Zealand. Salmon came to Australia in 1966. He has published more than a hundred and fifty books in Australia and overseas, and many of his works have been translated into other languages. Salmon has won Children's Choice awards such as the Young Australians Best Book Award (YABBA) and Kids' Own Australian Literature Awards (KOALA) for works such as *The Monster Who Ate Australia*. He has worked as a cartoonist, held exhibitions of his artworks, designed sets and costumes for various theater productions, worked as a puppeteer with the Tintookies puppet theater (1968), and created the Alexander Bunyip series (1978–1988) for ABC children's television, as well as the spin-off series of Alexander Bunyip picture books. He has created many picture book series including Dinosaur Swamp, Animal Antics, and Junior Detective. His comic-style illustrations and jaunty text create humor that appeals to young readers. Many of his stories embrace gothic elements such as monsters, often with a comic flair, as in *The Little Monster Book: Rhymes for all Monsters* (1989). One of his best-known stories, originally published in 1972, *The Monster Who Ate Canberra*, was republished in a special thirty-second anniversary edition.

[*See also* Australia *and* Picture Books.]

WENDY FAYE MICHAELS

Salten, Felix (1869–1945), Austrian writer. Salten, whose real name was Siegmund Salzmann, wrote *Bambi*

(1923; English trans., 1929), which was transformed into a classic Disney film in 1942. He grew up in Vienna and became a journalist, theater critic, essayist, and novelist, and served as president of the Austrian PEN club from 1925 to 1934. He also worked in Berlin for a number of years from 1906 on and traveled extensively in Europe, Israel, and America. Once anti-Semitism took hold in Austria, Salten left his native country in 1939 for a life of exile in Switzerland.

Salten wrote essays, plays, and both contemporary and historical novels, but it is his realistic stories about animals that have been translated into many languages. Although Salten's creatures may share language and consciousness with human beings, their animal instincts remain intact to ensure survival in a harsh and unpredictable world. *Bambi* is not the romanticized tale of forest life that Disney's film leads one to expect. Bambi's mother suddenly and inexplicably departs, leaving Bambi to become self-reliant and independent and to learn that "He," the huntsman, is a constant threat. Indeed, one of Bambi's companions loses his essential animal fear and alertness after living with humans. Salten's sequel to *Bambi*, *Bambi's Children: The Story of a Forest Family* (1939; German, 1940) follows the terror of hunters and wariness of human contact into the next generation. Since *Bambi*'s publication coincided with the rise of the Third Reich, some critics have read an antifascist message into this negative portrayal of humanity and the social collective, with a note of optimism when a poacher is killed and the animals realize that man is not invincible. Yet Salten also wrote stories in which animals and human beings form a close bond. *Perri, the Youth of a Squirrel* (1938; English trans., 1938) tells of the friendship between two squirrels and a three-year-old child; *Renni, the Rescuer: A Dog of the Battlefield* (1940; German, 1941) depicts the perfect understanding between man and dog in wartime, and in *A Forest World* (1942; German, 1944) a disfigured orphan finds consolation in the companionship of animals.

Felix Salten.

Salten's representation of animal life and his particular brand of anthropomorphism developed the existing tradition of animal stories in children's literature toward a more naturalistic depiction of the animal world. Others were writing in a similar vein at the time; the work of Salten's predecessors and contemporaries Jack London, Rudyard Kipling, and Henry Williamson appears in the collection *Felix Salten's Favorite Animal Stories* (1948), edited by Salten's daughter. But it is as the inspiration for the Disney film rather than as a pioneer of realism in the animal story that Salten is best remembered. Although Disney's Bambi is cute in a way that Salten never intended, the film is one of the greatest animations ever made and has ensured the survival of Salten's original text.

BIBLIOGRAPHY

Fuss Phillips, Zlata. "Felix Salten." In *German Children's and Youth Literature in Exile, 1933–50: Biographies and Bibliographies*, 182–191. Munich: K. G. Saur, 2001.

GILLIAN LATHEY

Salwi, Dilip (1952–2004), Indian writer who pioneered science fiction writing for children. Salwi has authored stories, plays, novel, biographies, and several books based on science. His attempt was to make science interesting and fun for children. *Strange Place, This School!* (1996) is a play that takes an ironic look at a typical school where the emphasis is on rote learning, and where fun in the classroom is rare. Salwi himself took great pains to write well-researched books, focusing on little-known facts about science and scientists. His writing, however, is seldom simply informative: Salwi's talent makes science interesting. He ensures that each story differs from the other, and cleverly avoids the trap of formulaic science fiction. Salwi has experimented with a variety of genres and styles in his attempt to produce interesting books. He offers comments on the environment, education, lifestyles, and attitudes; what makes these comments especially interesting is that they are always voiced by aliens. In his stories Salwi speculates on life in the future, creating worlds with several problems, mostly of man's making. However, it is not a wholly hopeless scenario, and Salwi shows how, with some care, our earth can be saved.

[*See also* India *and* Science Fiction.]

NANDINI NAYAR

Samplers. Beginning in the Renaissance and extending into the mid-19th century and beyond, many educated European and American girls learned how to stitch a sampler, a work of embroidery frequently consisting of the alphabet, a verse, numbers, and decorative flowers or other images. Adults, often highly regarded schoolmistresses, designed patterns and chose text for the girls to stitch on cloth. While perfecting their stitches, the girls also reflected on whatever text or images they were so carefully executing. In this way adults indirectly conveyed religious and cultural values that were considered appropriate for girls and young women at the time. Bible verses, reminders to avoid idleness, and moral lessons were popular choices for texts. Like hornbooks, samplers reinforced knowledge of the alphabet and familiarity with religious and moral verses. Work related to samplers was originally viewed as a means to discipline the mind, learn practical stitches, and improve a child's character; today these samplers are considered works of art.

[*See also* ABC Books or Alphabet Books; Counting Books; *and* Religious Instruction and Education.]

NATALIE ZIARNIK

Sampson, Fay (1935–), English author of more than twenty-five novels, many of them juvenile fiction in the tradition of C. S. Lewis's Narnia books. Sampson's interest in Celtic history is demonstrated in the series of six Pangur Ban books, which are set in the Dark Ages of Celtic Britain. In the first book, *Pangur Ban: The White Cat* (1983), she combined Christian and indigenous British belief systems. The book presents a kingdom of talking animals and well-meaning but fallible humans—all living in a moral world in which self-sacrifice and redemption are imperative. In the Daughter of Tintagel series (1992), which is also based on early English history, she recounts the childhood, convent education, and adulthood of Morgan le Fay, King Arthur's half-sister. Other works include *Josh's Panther* (1988) and *A Free Man On Sunday* (1989). Besides her writing career, Sampson has taught mathematics, and from 1962 to 1964 she served as a librarian in Zambia.

SANDRA BOLTON

Sánchez-Silva, José María (1911–2002), Spanish journalist and writer. His childhood was worthy of a Dickens novel and is reflected in the character that made him famous: Marcelino. During the Spanish Civil War (1936–1939) he secretly helped the Phalange (Spanish Fascist Party). At the end of the war Sánchez-Silva was closely linked to the dictatorship's propaganda apparatus, but in 1952 he resigned from newspaper work and wrote the book that would bring him fame: *Marcelino pan y vino* (English trans., Miracle of Marcelino, 1963), followed by two sequels. The story tells of an orphan, sheltered by friars, who establishes a friendship with Jesus. The narrative is well put together, dealing with love and fraternity without declining into the sentimentalism typical in those days of Spanish children's stories connected with religion. In the 1960s Sánchez-Silva wrote *Adios Josefina!: Cuento de verano* (1962; English trans., The Boy and the Whale, 1963) and a series about the character Ladis. He received the Andersen Prize in 1968 for his work as a whole.

BIBLIOGRAPHY

Pascual, Emilio. "Sánchez-Silva y Marcelino." *Lazarillo* 1 (2000): 8–28.

MARISA FERNÁNDEZ-LOPEZ

Sand, George (1804–1876), one of the great French Romantic feminists, who helped shape the image of the independent girl and woman. Her *Contes d'une grand-mère* appeared in two volumes in 1873 and 1876 (English trans., *Wings of Courage, and Other Stories*, 1878) and exerted a strong influence on the work of feminist writers (*éditions des femmes*) for children in 1970s France. This can be seen from *Brise et rose* (The Zephyr and the Rose, 1977), drawn from her *Ce que disent les fleurs* (What the Flowers Say, 1873). Sand, whose name was Amandine-Aurore-Lucille Dupin, Baroness Dudevant, was the daughter of Maurice Dupin de Francueil, heir of Marshall De Saxe, who was related to the Polish dynasty, and Sophie Victoire Delaborde, whose father had sold birds near the Seine in Paris. Sand's mixed social origin helps explain her support of an elite education for the common people and her participation in the French government of the Second Republic in 1848, as well as her entrée into the high society of the Second Empire. One need only remember Sand's love affair, after the 1832 publication of her first feminist novel, *Indiana*, with the aristocratic poet Alfred de Musset in Venice during 1833–1834. Yet Sand was above all a politically engaged *femme de lettres*, as shown in her novel *Horace*, published in 1841 in *La revue indépendante* (The Independent Review), which she founded with Pierre Leroux. *Consuelo* (1842–1843), which is still read by adolescents, depicts the splendid development of a young artist. It should also be noted that Sand's grandmother often invited Jean-Jacques Rousseau as a guest, and his ideas on the education of children as expounded in *Émile; ou, De l'éducation* (1762; *Emile; or, An Essay on Education*, 1763) led to the original theories articulated by the main character of Sand's *Lucrezia Floriani* (1847). Lucrezia bears five children by four fathers and raises them as genuinely happy creatures living in harmony with nature. Rousseau's approach to both learning and humor is also obvious in one of her tales from *Contes d'une grand-mère*: *Le chêne parlant* (The Talking Oak), in which children are taught the fundamentals of the natural sciences and geology.

When the publisher Jules Hetzel first requested that she write a book for children, Sand responded with *Histoire du véritable Gribouille* (1850; English trans., *The Mysterious Tale of Gentle Jack and Lord Bumblebee*, 1988), a mixture of the supernatural and a historical Bildungsroman, which recounts the dramatic life of a boy who sacrifices himself to stop a war between rival nations. The idea of self-sacrifice inspires what has been called Sand's *romans champêtres* (rural stories): *La mare au diable* (1846; English trans., *The Devil's Pool*, 1861), *La petite Fadette* (1849; English trans., *Fadette, a Domestic Story*, 1851), and *François le champi* (1850; English trans., *François the Waif*, 1889), longtime favorite books in French schools. Another lighter novel commissioned by Hetzel was *Laura, voyage dans le crystal* (1864; English trans., *Laura, Journey within the Crystal*, 1892), which has the same spirit of adventure that marks Jules Verne's *A Journey to the Center of the Earth*, published the same year.

JEAN PERROT

Sandberg, Inger (1930–), and **Lasse Sandberg** (1924–), Swedish author and illustrator team. The Sandbergs developed a specific picture book style with sparse details and no backgrounds. Their focus on the everyday experience of very young children is reflected in titles such as *Little Anna's Mama Has a Birthday* (1966; English trans., 1966), *Nicholas' Favorite Pet* (1967; English trans., 1969), *Daniel and the Coconut Cakes* (1968; English trans., 1973), and *Dusty Wants To Help* (1987; English trans., 1987). They created a large gallery of characters, of whom perhaps the most popular is Little Spook, a young ghost who behaves just like an ordinary child. The texts are very simple, and the naive, unpretentious illustrations imitate children's drawings. The Sandbergs have also produced ABC and counting books involving their favorite characters, as well as books about colors and other primary themes. The straightforward pedagogical approach is a deliberate feature of their individual aesthetics, affecting the verbal as well as the visual level of the stories. Despite their superficial simplicity, many of the books carry deep social and existential messages, promoting peace, friendship, ethnic and gender equity, and mutual respect between children and adults. Inger Sandberg has also written children's novels, and Lasse Sandberg has produced picture books with his own text.

MARIA NIKOLAJEVA

Sandburg, Carl (1878–1967), Pulitzer Prize–winning American poet, writer, and folk musician, born in Galesburg, Illinois, to Swedish immigrant parents. After irregular schooling, Sandburg joined the thousands of itinerant workers who stowed away in railroad boxcars in search of jobs. He served briefly with the Illinois Volunteers in the Spanish-American War, then studied at Lombard College in his hometown. He left in 1902 without graduating and roamed the country as a salesman, giving occasional lectures, campaigning for social democracy, and writing free-verse poetry. Sandburg's career as a poet gathered momentum when six of his poems were published in the Chicago journal *Poetry*, and his *Chicago Poems* (1916) established him as the poet of the American people. He worked as a journalist and also as an entertainer, singing American folk songs. These were published in *The American Songbag* (1927).

The strength of Sandburg's feeling for the Midwest shines through the nonsense stories he told to his three children—*Rootabaga Stories* (1922), *Rootabaga Pigeons* (1923), *Rootabaga Country* (1929), and *Potato Face* (1930). Often incantatory with an air of improvisation, they work best read aloud. Sandburg evokes the landscape he saw when he was riding the rails in his youth; he re-creates the speech patterns of his fellow travelers, and repeats strings of place names. The romance of those journeyings stayed with him. In "The Two Skyscrapers Who Decided to Have a Child" in the first *Rootabaga* book, the skyscrapers standing on a street corner wistfully looking out on the distant lakes and prairies decide to have a *free* child. When it comes, it is a long-distance railroad train "running as far as the farthest mountains and sea coasts touched by the North-west Wind." Sandburg also wrote two books of poems for children, *Early Moon* (1930) and *Wind Song* (1960). His *Abe Lincoln Grows Up* (1928) was adapted from earlier chapters in his massive biography of Lincoln, which ultimately reached six volumes.

[*See also* Nonsense; Poetry; *and* United States.]

BIBLIOGRAPHY

Avery, Gillian. *Behold the Child: American Children and Their Books, 1621–1922*, page 213. Baltimore, Md.: Johns Hopkins University Press, 1994.

Crowder, Richard. *Carl Sandburg*. New York: Twayne, 1964.

GILLIAN AVERY

Sanders, Dori (1934–), African American writer whose first novel, *Clover* (1990), was a work marketed for adults but adopted by young readers. Set in rural South Carolina, the story is told by a ten-year-old black girl, whose father is killed hours after marrying a white woman from the North. In addition to coping with their grief, the two must overcome their own racial and cultural differences as well as the well-meaning opposition of the extended family. Sanders uses widely held stereotypes about customs and values to demonstrate racial divisions on both sides, while telling a story of growth and resolution. In 1997 the book was made into a television movie. Her second adult novel was *Her Own Place* (1993).

BIBLIOGRAPHY

Zaidman, Laura. "A Sense of Place in Dori Sanders' Clover." *ALAN Review* 22, no. 3 (Spring 1995): 16–18.

GRETA D. LITTLE

Sanderson, Ruth (1951–), American illustrator. Born in Ware, Massachusetts, Sanderson studied at the Paier School of Art, and began her career as an illustrator of others' work, including new editions of the Nancy Drew, Bobbsey Twins, and Black Stallion books. Her first picture book was Ilka List's *Grandma's Beach Surprise* (1975). Since then she has illustrated reissued classics including Johanna Spyri's *Heidi* (1984) and Frances Hodgson Burnett's *The Secret Garden* (1988) and the texts of numerous authors including Jane Yolen, working in many media: watercolor, oils, acrylic, air brush, colored pencil, and alkyd. In 1990 Sanderson began to illustrate her own work, beginning with her retelling of the fairy tale *The Twelve Dancing Princesses*. Her later work is noted for its sumptuous color and photographic attention to detail. For her fairy tale illustrations she paints from photographs of her young models, in elaborate medieval costumes which she sews herself, posing them to suit the intended picture, and taking up to a roll of film per scene. Especially remarkable in the resulting paintings are her uses of light and texture. Sanderson's work has a glow reminiscent of Maxfield Parrish and N. C. Wyeth, both of whom she claims as influences, accompanied by a startling realism.

AMANDA COCKRELL

Sandford and Merton. *See* Day, Thomas.

Sandham, Elizabeth, one of the publisher John Harris's popular writers. Until recently Sandham, whose name always appeared on her books' title pages, was believed to be the same person as Elizabeth Semple, whose works John Harris issued under the initials "E.S." Like many of her contemporaries, Sandham wrote across the spectrum of children's genres: animal stories such as *The Adventures of Poor Puss* (1809), moral tales such as her best-known work *The Twin Sisters* (1805), and works of classical history, popular science, geography, and Bible history in fictional form, such as *The History of Britannicus and His Sister Octavia* (1815), *Conversations on Natural History* (c. 1818), *Maria's First Visit to London* (c. 1818), and *The Travels of St. Paul in Letters Supposed to Be Written from a Mother to Her Daughter* (1812). Reviewers generally praised Sandham's children's books for promoting excellent ethical and religious values, but noted that her style was far from lively.

[*See also* Animal Stories; John Harris; Moral Tales; *and* Nonfiction.]

BIBLIOGRAPHY

Marks, Sylvia Kasey. *Writing for the Rising Generation: British Fiction for Young People, 1672–1839*. Victoria, British Columbia: University of Victoria Press, 2003.

Moon, Marjorie. *John Harris's Books for Youth, 1801–1843*. Revised and enlarged edition. Folkestone, U.K.: Dawson, 1992.

ANDREA IMMEL

Sandin, Joan (1942–), American author, illustrator, and translator of books from Swedish, including Christina Björk's *Linnea in Monet's Garden* (1987) and *The Other Alice: The Story of Alice Liddell and Alice in Wonderland* (1993). Sandin received her BFA from the University of Arizona, and has illustrated dozens of books by other authors, including Thomas P. Lewis's *Hill of Fire* (1971), about the origin of a volcano in Mexico, and Elizabeth Winthrop's *As the Crow Flies* (1998), which captures the desert in vivid watercolors. She has also authored and illustrated several works, including two Notable Books selected by the American Library Association, *The Long Way to a New Land* (1981) and *The Long Way Westward* (1989), both beginning readers about a Swedish immigrant family. The innovative *Coyote School News* (2003), based on an actual school, is told through "facsimiles" of a newspaper created by children in a one-room school in southern Arizona during the 1930s.

[*See also* Easy Readers; Historical Fiction; *and* Translation.]

LINNEA HENDRICKSON

Sandman Lilius, Irmelin (1936–), Finno-Swedish writer, best known for her novels, short stories, and picture books for children. Most of her books, such as *The Maharajah Adventure* (1964; English trans., 1966) or the trilogy *Gold Crown Lane* (1969; English trans., 1980), *The Goldmaker's House* (1970; English trans., 1980), and *Horses of the Night* (1971; English trans., 1980), take place in a half-imaginary magical universe that nonetheless bears close resemblance to Finland. Sandman Lilius combines myth, history, folk tradition, and family legends in a manner reminiscent of British fantasy. Her poetic language and imagery are highly original, as is her sharp social protest. The books are not very accessible to young readers because of their slow and disparate plots, large gallery of characters, and long descriptive and reflexive passages, yet their status as children's literature has not been questioned in Finland.

In her most recent children's stories, Sandman Lilius, who also illustrates most of her books, presents fairy–tale–flavored memories of her wartime childhood.

MARIA NIKOLAJEVA

Sansom, Clive (1910–1981), English poet, playwright, and teacher. Sansom was educated at London Polytechnic, the Speech Institute, and the University of London. His interest in spoken and written language is represented in plays, poems, and writings on speech education and poetic theory. In *Speech and Communication in the Primary School* (1966, 1979), he noted how such education was often neglected but deserved a central role in the curriculum. His dramas for children include *The Green Dragon and Other Plays* (1941). In *The Golden Unicorn* (1965) we see his keen observations of ladybugs, among other creatures: "Tiniest of turtles! / Your shining back / Is a shell of orange / With spots of black. . . . Your small wire legs, / So frail, so thin, / Their touch is swansdown / Upon my skin." This collection recalls *The Child's Garden of Verses* (1885) by Robert Louis Stevenson and A. A. Milne's *When We Were Very Young* (1924). As a writer for adults, Sansom won the Arts Council Festival of Britain Prize.

SANDRA BOLTON

San Souci, Daniel (1948–), American author and illustrator who grew up in Berkeley, California, and studied at the College of Arts and Crafts in Oakland. He has taught classes in book illustration both at his alma mater and at the University of California, Berkeley, and he is currently a faculty member at the Academy of Art University in San Francisco. His most successful self-illustrated book, *Country Roads* (1995), follows a father and son walking through the country together. The story is not dynamic, but the accompanying double-page spreads in watercolors beautifully show the details of the ordinary countryside, with particular attention given to the animals. San Souci has also collaborated as illustrator with several authors, most notably his brother, Robert. Together, the two have produced various picture books, including *Sootface: An Ojibwa Cinderella Story* (1994), *The Legend of Sleepy Hollow* (1986), and *The Legend of Scarface: A Blackfeet Indian Tale* (1978).

[*See also* Illustrations; Picture Books; *and* San Souci, Robert.]

KIRA B. HOMO

San Souci, Robert (1946–), American author and adapter of folk tales. Born and educated in California, San Souci has authored or retold more than eighty stories, selecting his materials from such locales as Africa, Japan, the Caribbean, and Europe. San Souci's greatest strength is in reviving interest in oral traditions, using such basic devices of orality as rhythm, rhyme, and repetition. His ghost story collections, beginning with *Short and Shivery: Thirty Chilling Tales* (1987), reflect this interest. His picture books—including *The Legend of Scarface: A Blackfeet Indian Tale* (1978), *A Weave of Words: An Armenian Tale Retold* (1998), and *Brave Margaret: An Irish Adventure* (1999)—reveal a similar commitment to traditional narrative styles. His retellings have led to impressive picture book collaborations, most notably with the African American father–son illustrators Jerry and Brian Pinkney. The drawings in *The Talking Eggs: A Folktale from the American South* (1989) are the work of Jerry Pinkney, and Brian Pinkney illustrated San Souci's *The Faithful Friend* (1995). Both titles were Coretta Scott King and Caldecott Honor selections. *Fa Mulan: The Story of a Woman Warrior* (1998) was the basis for the animated Disney film about a legendary Chinese woman who fights her country's invaders; San Souci wrote the movie's screenplay. The common theme throughout his varied body of work is cultural identity, and although he has often been praised for his cultural and historical research his record on ethnic authenticity is uneven. He has been severely criticized for distorting the Inuit myth retold in his *Song of Sedna* (1981). Nonetheless, it is fair to say that San Souci has been a prolific and sometimes eloquent contributor to the literature beyond national boundaries.

ELISSA GERSHOWITZ

Santa Claus. *See* Father Christmas.

Santucci, Luigi (1918–1999), Italian essayist and novelist who took active part in the Resistance. His religious commitment was in the manner of Bruce Marshall and his ironical style was compared to that of G. K. Chesterton. His first publication was *Limiti e ragioni della letteratura infantile* (Limits and Reasons of Children's Literature, 1942). He published a biography of Pinocchio's creator, *Collodi* (1961), and *Racconti e fiabe* (Tales and Fairy Tales, 1967), published in the United States. *Il bambino della strega* (The Witch's Child, 1981) and particularly *Le storie del regno* (Tales of the Kingdom, 1988) collect stories and folk tales drawn from the Gospels as well as medieval and regional Italian sources. *Le frittate di Clorinda* (Clorinda's Omelettes, 1996) features the turtle Clorinda, her colossal omelettes, and the goblins Pinch, Bagpipe, and Inkpot engaged in perpetual strife against ogre Pigtrotter and the bog's Witch. Other publications include *Tra pirati e delfini* (Between Pirates and Dolphins, 1996) and *Leggende di Natale* (Christmas Legends, 2002).

KATIA PIZZI

Sapkowski, Andrzej (1948–), one of the most popular Polish fantasy writers. He created three collections of stories about Geralt, a mutant witcher trained to kill monsters, and a thematically related cycle of fantasy novels, *Saga o wiedźminie* (The Saga about the Witcher, 1990–1999). He also published two parts the Narrenturm trilogy, a humorous tale about the Middle Ages. Although Sapkowski has been influenced by R. E. Howard, J. R. R. Tolkien, and Ursula Le Guin, he often refers to fairy tales and Slavic mythology. He also published *Rękopis znaleziony w Smoczej Jaskini* (A Manuscript Found in a Dragon's Cave, 2001), a guidebook to fantasy.

JUSTYNA DESZCZ-TRYHUBCZAK

Sapper, Agnes (1852–1929), German author of juvenile literature and books on child rearing. Born Agnes Brater Sapper began writing in 1882; her first published children's story, "In Wasserfluten" (In Floodwaters), appeared in the magazine *Immergrün* (English trans., *Evergreen*) in 1892. In the same year she published her first collection of stories for girls. In 1899, after the death of her husband, Sapper moved to Würzburg and then began her full-time career as an author. Sapper attained immense popularity with her novel *Die Familie Pfäffling* (1906; English trans., *The Pfäffling Family*), which depicts a year in the life of a large family in a Bavarian village. The familial idyll of the Pfäfflings departed from customary overwrought sentimentality in its more realistic characterizations—inept father, misbehaving children, social inequities. Nevertheless, in the end it reaffirmed patriarchal authority, propriety, and respectability, a formula consistent in her writings.

[*See also* Germany *and* Girls' Books and Fiction.]

LUKE SPRINGMAN

Sarg, Tony (1880–1942), American puppeteer, illustrator, and creator of humorous books. Sarg was born in Guatemala, where his German father owned sugar and coffee plantations. At age seven he was sent to Germany to be educated, and by the time he graduated he had a commission in the German army. But he disliked military service, and at twenty-five, he left Germany to settle in London, becoming a British citizen before World War I. However, because of anti-German sentiment, he immigrated to the United States, where he became a citizen in 1921.

Sarg had a life-long interest in marionettes that began at the age of six when he created a complicated system of pulleys and strings to avoid getting out of bed to feed the family's large flock of chickens. The interest was pursued in London and continued in the United States. By the late 1930s his marionettes were well known, and he had six touring companies and workshops in New York and Nantucket.

Sarg's humorous drawings appeared in the *Saturday Evening Post* and other magazines before he began focusing on children's books. One of his best-known works, *Tony Sarg's Book for Children from Six to Sixty* (1924), included seven hundred drawings with hand-lettered text. He wrote and illustrated more than a dozen other books, including *Tony Sarg's Book of Animals* (1925), *Tony Sarg's Wonder Zoo* (1925), and *Tony Sarg's New York* (1926). In the 1940s he produced three novelty books: *Tony Sarg's Surprise Book* (1941), *Tony Sarg's Treasure Book* (1942), and *Tony Sarg's Magic Movie Book* (1943), each with movable pictures.

Although best remembered now for his puppetry, Sarg was an energetic and prolific creator. He was a mural painter, designer of large mechanical window displays, toys, textiles, and puppets. He also created the large gas-filled balloons used in the annual Macy's Thanksgiving Day Parade.

ANN R. MONTANARO

Saro-Wiwa, Ken (1941–1995), Nigerian playwright, novelist, television producer, and children's author who devoted his relatively short life to the defense of the rights of his people, the Ogoni. Amid an international outcry, Saro-Wiwa was hanged by the military dictatorship of Sani Abacha after criticizing the government's oil policy with regard to the corporation Dutch/Shell (a policy that impaired people's health, land, and livelihood). Saro-Wiwa's children's novel *Mr. B* (1987) led to many sequels and to a TV series featuring comical ne'er-do-wells taken from the novels. The animals in his collection, *The Singing Anthill: Ogoni Folk Tales* (1991), resemble Mr. B and his rascally cohorts: all tricksters, all object lessons about human behavior.

[*See also* Africa: Sub-Saharan Africa; Collections; *and* Fairy Tales and Folk Tales.]

MAWUENA KOSSI LOGAN

Sasek, Miroslav (1916–1980), Czech author and illustrator who moved to France after the Communists invaded his country in the 1940s. He studied at the École des Beaux-Arts in Paris and settled in the United States. During a vacation in Paris he was inspired to write travel books for children, beginning with *This Is Paris* (1959) and followed by more than twenty books that featured European, American, and Asian cities (*This Is Munich*, 1961; *This Is San Francisco*, 1962; *This Is Hongkong*, 1967), countries (*This Is Israel*, 1962; *This Is Australia*, 1970), and institutions (*This Is the United Nations*, 1968). These large-format picture books captivate with their cartoonlike watercolor paintings whose impact is stressed by the humorous text. *This Is London* (1959) and *This Is New York* (1960) were each selected as the New York Times Best Illustrated Children's Book of the Year; *This Is New York* was also produced as a filmstrip.

[*See also* Geography and Travel Books *and* Picture Books.]

BETTINA KÜMMERLING-MEIBAUER

Sattler, Helen Roney (1921–1992), American author of highly respected nonfiction, known especially for her outstanding reference works on dinosaurs. Before becoming a writer, Sattler was a teacher, librarian, mother, and scout leader. The subjects of her first books and magazine articles were puzzles (including several books of Bible puzzles) and crafts. Sattler believed that puzzles stimulated children's minds, and that most children could learn to work with their hands and be creative if given a few designs to get them started. Her many successful craft books included *Kitchen Carton Crafts* (1970), a collection of projects to be made out of various kinds of packaging material, and the well-received *Recipes for Art and Craft Materials* (1973, 1987). *Train Whistles: A Language in Code* (1977, 1985), which was republished in a revised edition with colorful illustrations by Giulio Maestro, was originally written for her grandson, who wanted a book about trains. The story incorporated many kinds of train whistles and explained what they meant. A list of the signals and their meanings was appended. Another request for a dinosaur book "that didn't have any mistakes in it" inspired the first of several outstanding books on dinosaurs. Sattler's books were widely praised for their thoroughness and accuracy, and for the exceptional level of detail they provided in a readable fashion, making them useful for readers from elementary through high school. The extraordinary *Dinosaurs of North America* (1981), with its introduction by noted paleontologist John H. Ostrom and beautiful sepia illustrations by Anthony Rao, was followed by the outstanding *Illustrated Dinosaur Dictionary* (1983, 1990), which contained the name of practically every identified dinosaur and prehistoric creature, together with a pronunciation guide, name source, description, and classification. These carefully researched, well-written books were followed by a number of well-received books on pterosaurs, sharks, whales, hominids, and giraffes.

[*See also* Information Books; Maestro, Giulio; Nonfiction; *and* Science Books.]

Linnea Hendrickson

Saunders, Marshall (1861–1947), a Baptist clergyman's daughter born in Milton, Nova Scotia. Saunders, whose given name was Margaret, attended finishing school in Edinburgh, Scotland, and lived in Toronto for the last three decades of her life. She was a prolific writer best known for animal fiction. Her most famous work, *Beautiful Joe: The Autobiography of a Dog* (1894), won a competition held by the American Humane Education Society for a companion book to Anna Sewell's *Black Beauty* (1877). Like *Black Beauty*, *Beautiful Joe* is an animal autobiography that transmits a message of kindness to animals through depiction of cruel and kind treatment, but Saunders's novel is more sentimental than Sewell's. It became a best-selling novel in Canada and remains part of the canon of Canadian children's literature. Saunders's sequel, *Beautiful Joe's Paradise: or, The Island of Brotherly Love* (1902), which deals with animal immortality, and other animal and nonanimal books, including *The King of the Park* (1897), which tells of an orphan who comes to realize that wealth and rank are less significant than love, were not as successful as *Beautiful Joe*. Sometimes regarded as overly sentimental, Saunders's fiction has been accused of simplistic anthropomorphizing of animals and inelegant moralizing.

[*See also* Animal Stories; Canada; *and* Sewell, Anna.]

Adrienne E. Gavin

Saville, Malcolm (1901–1982), English author who published eighty-seven books for children. The Lone Pine series (1943–1978) started with *Mystery at Witchend*, in which children form a secret club. All stories are set in real, often countryside places, which Saville encouraged readers to visit—Shropshire and Sussex particularly. The Jillies series (1948–1953) started in Norfolk with two families meeting on holiday. In the Buckinghams series (1950–1974), children befriend the son of an exiled Polish violinist. For older teenagers, the Marston Baines (1963–1978) thrillers echo James Bond; they feature a master spy whose college student friends get into serious difficulties with terrorists, anti-Semites, drug dealers, black magic, and so forth. For younger children, Mary and Michael (1945–1957) were Londoners who were sent to the country: the first book, *Trouble at Townsend* (1945), was made into a film. Susan and Bill (1954–1961) were children who moved to a new town: stories describe their settling-in experiences and later their holidays. The Nettleford series details experiences of village life. Saville also wrote nonfiction, generally on country themes, with two religious books, *King of Kings* (1958; a life of Jesus) and *Strange Story* (1967; the crucifixion through Roman eyes). Saville's books are optimistic: good triumphs and loyalty and friendship prevail. Relationships reflect the complexity of adolescent feelings.

[*See also* Series Books.]

BIBLIOGRAPHY

O'Hanlon, Mark. *Beyond the Lone Pine: A Biography of Malcolm Saville*. Worcester, U.K.: Mark O'Hanlon, 2001.

O'Hanlon, Mark. *The Complete Lone Pine*. Worcester, U.K.: Mark O'Hanlon, 1996.

Stephen Bigger

Savino, Irene (1953–), Venezuelan artist who studied graphic design at the Instituto de Diseño Neumann, and later studied illustration at the Parsons School of Design in New York. She has worked as Art Director for the Ekaré publishing house, and as an illustration teacher at the Instituto ProDiseño in Caracas. She has illustrated *Once cuentos maravillosos* (1990; English trans., *Eleven Wonderful Stories*), *Cuentos y leyendas de amor para niños* (1992; English trans., *Love Stories and Legends for Children*), *María Tolete* (1993; a Venezuelan folk tale), and *El dueño de la luz* (1994; English trans., *The Owner of Light*), a Warao myth. In order to illustrate this myth, Savino traveled to Waranoko, in the Orinoco Delta, where the Warao people live. The work received the Fundalibro Award for the best children's book of the year in 1996, was selected for the Honor List of the Best Books for Children, Banco del Libro, 1996, and earned a Noma Award in 1996.

[*See also* Fairy Tales and Folk Tales; Illustrations; Myths; *and* South America, Spanish-Speaking.]

Olga García-Larralde

Sawyer, Ruth (1880–1970), American storyteller who collected folk tales in Ireland and Spain, as well as writing extensively for both children and adults. From the Garland Kindergarten Training School, Sawyer went to Cuba in 1900 to teach storytelling to teachers organizing kindergartens for orphans. She received a BS from Columbia University in 1904 with a major in folklore and storytelling, after which she told stories to immigrant children via the New York Lecture Bureau and public school system. After her 1910 debut as a storyteller with the New York Public Library (at the invitation of Anne Carroll Moore), she extended her work nationally in various venues, including rural communities and reformatories. Sawyer's tempestuous childhood—heavily influenced by an Irish storytelling nanny named Johanna—provided lively background for her 1937 Newbery Medal Book, *Roller Skates* (1936), about a young girl's exploration of New York City, with characters reflecting many facets of social class and ethnicity. Her grounding in folklore enriched the 1945 and 1954 Caldecott Honor books that she authored, *The Christmas Anna Angel* (1944) and *Journey Cake, Ho!* (1953). Sawyer's oral presentations were mesmerizing, and her writing style was personable. *The Way of the Storyteller* (1942) still enriches storytelling courses, combining historical, theoretical, and practical knowledge with some of her favorite tales. Sawyer's written texts are stylistically cadenced and folklorically structured in accordance with her belief that oral literature served as a bridge of literacy between children and reading. Most fundamental, however, was the idea that stories were first and foremost entertaining and thus extended children's sense of humanity. Sawyer won the Regina Medal and the Laura Ingalls Wilder Medal for her versatile lifetime achievements. Married to Dr. Albert Durand, with two children (her daughter was a children's librarian married to the author-illustrator Robert McCloskey), Sawyer maintained her work at the crossroads of folklore and literature into old age, returning to the Austrian Tyrol in 1961 to do extensive research on the Alpine trickster-goblin King Laurin for one of her last books.

[*See also* McCloskey, Robert *and* Moore, Anne Carroll.]

BIBLIOGRAPHY

Haviland, Virginia. *Ruth Sawyer*. London: Bodley Head, 1965.

BETSY HEARNE

Saxby, Maurice (1924–), one of Australia's foremost authorities on Australian children's literature. The first national president of the Children's Book Council of Australia, he has been granted life membership in recognition of his achievements, also receiving a Children's Book Council National Council Citation in 1990. Among his many other awards are the Nan Chauncy Award (2002), the Lady Cutler Award (1989), the Dromkeen Medal (1983), and, in 1995, Member in the Order of Australia (AM).

Saxby is a prolific reviewer of Australian children's books, with reviews published in *Magpies*, *Reading Time*, *Viewpoint*, and *Orana*, as well as in national newspapers. He has edited anthologies of poetry, short stories, myths, and legends. His children's literature criticism appears in various journals and in a number of significant works that document the history and significance of Australian children's literature, including *Give Them Wings: The Experience of Children's Literature* (1987), *The Proof of the Puddin': Australian Children's Literature 1970–1990* (1993), *Books in the Life of the Child: Bridges to Literature and Learning* (1997), *Offered to Children: A History of Australian Children's Literature 1841–1941* (1998), and *Images of Australia: A History of Australian Children's Literature 1941–1970* (2002).

[*See also* Australia *and* Critical Approaches to Children's Literature.]

WENDY FAYE MICHAELS

Say, Allen (1937–), Asian American children's author and illustrator born in Yokohama, Japan, to a Korean father and an American Japanese mother. Say's parents divorced when he was twelve, at which time he moved to Tokyo. There he became apprenticed to Noro Shinpei, a renowned Japanese cartoonist. Say credits Shinpei for his training in classical art and regards him as both a spiritual and an artistic mentor. This period of his life and the relationship with Shinpei is reflected in *The Ink-keeper's Apprentice* (1979), a novel for young adults about growing up in postwar Japan. Say remained in Tokyo until he was sixteen, then immigrated to California with his father's new family. In the early stages of his writing and illustrating career, Say primarily freelanced while working as a commercial photographer. His first picture book was *Dr. Smith's Safari* (1972).

In 1988 Say was commissioned to illustrate *The Boy of the Three-Year Nap*, a retelling by Dianne Snyder of a traditional Japanese folk tale. It was awarded both the Caldecott Honor Award and the Boston Globe–Horn Book Award. Soon afterward Say turned to a full-time career as a writer and illustrator. His critically acclaimed work often has autobiographical elements, particularly in relation to its explo-

Allen Say. Illustration by Say from *How My Parents Learned to Eat* by Ina R. Friedman (Boston: Houghton Mifflin, 1984), p. 27. Reproduced courtesy of the Cotsen Children's Library, Princeton University Library

ration of cross-cultural (that is, Asian American) experiences and identity. *The Bicycle Man* (1982), set in Japan during World War II, about two American soldiers who interact with and entertain a group of Japanese schoolchildren, is a simple story of cross-cultural interaction in which Say's illustrations perfectly capture the intricacies of nonverbal communication. *El Chino* (1990), *Tree of Cranes* (1991), and *Tea with Milk* (1999), a personal story about the life of Say's mother, also revolve around questions of immigrant identity and the search for a place of belonging. *Grandfather's Journey* (1994), Say's most celebrated examination of these themes, was awarded the Caldecott Medal. It charts the journey of Say's grandfather from Japan to America, subtly capturing the effects of cultural dislocation on him and subsequent generations of his family, including Say in his position as narrator. The book's minimalist prose is complemented by watercolor illustrations in contrasting styles—a boating scene in impressionist style, the Grand Canyon as abstract art, perspective found in traditional Japanese painting, and about half the pictures reminiscent of a family photograph album. Say's most confronting work on intercultural experience has been *Home of the Brave* (2002), which examines the trauma of incarceration for Japanese Americans in internment camps during World War II. Other publications, such as *Emma's Rug* (1996) and *The Sign Painter* (2000), have focused on the theme of artistic inspiration and expression. In *Emma's Rug*, which centers on a blanket that provides the stimulus for a child's artwork, Say deals with the issue of artistic imagination in vibrant watercolors that evoke great painters of Western art from Bosch to Monet. Say's picture books provide emotionally compelling visual and narrative accounts of immigrant identity and experience, using a variety of story strategies to investigate the intersection of Asian and American cultures.

[*See also* Asian American Literature; Multiculturalism and Children's Books; *and* Picture Books.]

John Stephens

Sayers, Dorothy L. (1893–1957), British novelist, religious writer, playwright, and translator, best known for her detective stories. Dorothy Leigh Sayers was born in Oxford, and educated there. Her essay "The Lost Tools of Learning," first presented at Oxford in 1947, argues that children are not being taught *how* to learn and makes a case for revival of classical education. Her stories for children were published as *Even the Parrot: Exemplary Conversations for Enlightened Children* (1944) and her radio play, *The Man Born To Be King*, written for the BBC children's hour and first aired in 1941, caused a storm of protest, as she allowed Jesus to speak in modern English.

Amanda Cockrell

Sayers, Frances Clarke (1897–1989), American librarian, educator, and writer. Raised in Texas, Sayers attended the University of Texas and the Carnegie Library School. As Anne Carroll Moore's protégé, she worked for the New York Public Library (1918–1923) and became superintendent of work with children (1941–1952). Sayers taught librarianship at the University of California, Berkeley, from 1934 to 1941, and later joined the English and Library Science faculties at the University of California at Los Angeles (1954–1965). She was a fierce proponent of literary standards, creating a firestorm when she denounced Walt Disney's adaptations as revisionist and reductionist travesties. Her own writing ranged from *Bluebonnets for Lucinda* (1934), a children's story, to *Anne Carroll Moore: A Biography* (1972), and her extraordinary wit and wisdom are preserved in the anthology compiled by Marjeanne Blinn, *Summoned by Books: Essays and Speeches by Frances Clarke*

Sayers (1965). The Catholic Library Association awarded Sayers the Regina Medal for lifetime achievement in 1973.

[*See also* Disney, Walt; Librarians in the United States; *and* Libraries.]

PEGGY LIN DUTHIE

Scannell, Vernon (1926–), writer born in Spilsby, Lincolnshire, and educated at Queen's Park School, Aylesbury. He served in the Gordon Highlanders, an army regiment, during World War II and subsequently studied at Leeds University. He has been at one time or another a fairground worker, a professional boxer, and, from 1955 to 1962, a teacher in a secondary school. Thereafter Scannell has been a novelist, poet, playwright, and editor. He has gained a number of awards for his poetry and has been a visiting poet at Shrewsbury School (1978–1979) and King's School, Canterbury (1979).

Most of Scannell's writing has been for an adult audience. Since 1947 he has written eight novels, three plays for radio, and twenty collections of verse. In 1962 he edited *New Poems* with Pat Beer and Ted Hughes. His work for children is slighter and consists of two novels and five collections of poetry. It is his poetry that is generally regarded as his outstanding contribution to children's literature. *Mastering the Craft* (1970), *The Apple Raid and Other Poems* (1974), *Catching the Light* (with Gregory Harmson; 1982), and *The Clever Potato* (illustrated by Tony Ross; 1988) were followed by *Collected Verse* (1995).

A considerable number of Scannell's poems are still anthologized and are studied with some frequency in both primary and secondary schools in Great Britain. Always more than reflective, many of his poems contain clear evidence of the poet's own experiences, notably his experience as a teacher in "School on a Wet Afternoon," and in "The Apple Raid" where he combines boyhood memories with his knowledge of military action. Scannell has never written down to his young readers. Even when the subjects are mundane, as in "Hide and Seek" and "Gunpowder Plot," his poetry is vigorous, original, and challenging.

[*See also* Hughes, Ted; Poetry; *and* Ross, Tony.]

GEOFFREY FENWICK

Scarry, Richard (1919–1994), American author and illustrator born in Boston, Massachusetts, and educated at Boston's Museum of Fine Arts School. A highly prolific author and illustrator, producing more than three hundred books, Scarry began illustrating for Little Golden Books in 1949 with Margaret Wise Brown and Edith Thacher Hurd's *Two Little Miners*. Other titles produced that year show Scarry's penchant for using anthropomorphic animals as main characters. For example, in Kathryn and Byron Jackson's *Mouse's House* (1949) and *Duck and His Friends* (1949), where a rabbit and mouse teach their friend the duck how to overcome his fear of water, Scarry's colorful and vibrant images present animals that seem to live between the human and the natural world—animals that wear clothes and are able to perform human tasks but that also face the frictions real animals contend with. This vulnerability continues into later works to some extent, but is largely dealt with through humor. In *Richard Scarry's Best Mother Goose Ever* (1964) and *Richard Scarry's Nursery Tales* (1975), Scarry is able to portray characters that possess an optimistic wit that is highly reminiscent of the innocent fun children enjoy.

Richard Scarry. Front cover of *The Great Big Car and Truck Book* (New York: Golden Press, 1951). REPRODUCED COURTESY OF THE COTSEN CHILDREN'S LIBRARY, PRINCETON UNIVERSITY LIBRARY

Scarry is perhaps best known for his later works, such as *Richard Scarry's Best World Book Ever* (1963), *Richard Scarry's Busy, Busy World* (1965), and *Richard Scarry's Storybook Dictionary* (1967), where his style and approach to writing and illustrating changed considerably. Creatively he developed a new technique for constructing his illustrations, whereby he made line drawings on an overlay and then painted colors separately onto blueboards ready for printing. Conceptually he began to create books that combined narrative with factual detail, using vignette images to explain the world to his readers. For example, in *Richard Scarry's Great Big Air Book* (1971) and *Richard Scarry's Best First Book Ever!* (1980) he combined the text and layout found in encyclopedias with a simple sequential fictional narrative revolving around favorite characters such as Huckle Cat, Lowly Worm, Miss Honey, and Rudolf Strudel to deal with themes such as jobs, colors, weather, transport, food, and so on. This unusual combination of positing the book between fact and fiction has proved to be extremely successful in helping young readers to understand how the world and its people work. This was a continuing theme for Scarry, as later titles such as *Richard Scarry's Just Right Word Book!* (1990) and *Richard Scarry's Things to Know* (1976) focus on the basic daily activities of the child in order to explain new objects, counting, fruits, and playthings. In all these books Scarry has demonstrated an uncanny knack for writing about things that interest the child. As an author and illustrator he was fascinated with transport, people's busy lives, basic science, and human relationships and communities, and he recognized that because animals are culturally ambiguous and many children feel an affinity for them, using animals instead of people would make his work appealing. His work has been translated into many languages and has been adapted into animated series.

[*See also* ABC Books or Alphabet Books; Anthropomorphism; Book Design; Counting Books; Easy Readers; *and* Information Books.]

BIBLIOGRAPHY

Retan, Walter, and Ole Risom. *The Busy, Busy World of Richard Scarry*. New York: Harry N. Abrams, 1997.

LINDA KNIGHT

Schami, Rafik (1946–), German-language children's author of Syrian origin. Born Suheil Fadéla, into the minority Christian community in Damascus, Schami emigrated to Germany at the age of twenty-five, after the authorities had suppressed the subversive newspaper he edited and threatened his freedom as a writer. For some time after his arrival in Germany, Schami wrote in Arabic and translated his own work; he began to write directly in German in 1977.

Schami is above all a passionate storyteller whose craft owes a great deal to his engagement with Arabic oral and literary traditions. As a child he learned classical poetry by heart, and for almost three years listened eagerly to nightly Radio Cairo broadcasts of all of Scheherazade's thousand and one stories. In Germany, Schami found a ready audience of all ages for tales inspired by Arabic narratives; one of the most popular of his longer works, *Damascus Nights* (1989; English trans., 1993) clearly owes its structure to *The Arabian Nights*. An exception to this love of the fantastical is the semiautobiographical *A Handful of Stars* (1987; English trans., 1990), a diary that records an adolescent boy's loves and trials against a background of political unrest and repression.

Schami has also collaborated with some of Germany's most prominent illustrators on picture books and illustrated stories. *Das ist Kein Papagei* (That's Not a Parrot, 1994) is the amusing domestic tale of a parrot who refuses to talk, enhanced by Wolf Erlbruch's quirky drawings. Together with Peter Knorr, Schami created in *Der Wunderkasten* (The Box of Delights, 1990) an ingenious representation of the negative influence of Western culture on the narrative of an itinerant storyteller in Damascus. Picture books with a text by Schami published in English include *Fatima and the Dream Thief* (1996; English trans., 1996) and *The Crow Who Stood on His Beak* (1995; English trans., 1996), both illustrated by Oliver Streich.

[*See also* Arabian Nights, The; Germany; Picture Books; *and biographies of figures mentioned in this article.*]

GILLIAN LATHEY

Schanz, Frida (1859–1944), author and publisher of books for children and young people during the German Empire (1871–1918). Her mother, Pauline Schanz (neé Leich), was also a children's author. In 1887 Frida Schanz, later known as Frida Schanz-Soyaux or Frida Soyaux, published her first book, *Mit Ränzel und Stab* (With Satchel and Walking Stick). In the ensuing period she wrote poems for small children, short stories for older ones, and a series of tales and novels that established her popularity as a writer of girls' books, among others *Komteßchen* (Little Countess, 1892) and *O du selige Backfischzeit* (Little Women, 1892). In general her work can be characterized as sentimental and patriotic. In addition, she collaborated with Julius Lohmeyer (1835–

1903), the editor of the magazine *Deutsche Jugend* (German Youth), and she herself published the annuals *Kinderlust* (Children's Enjoyment) from 1887 until 1905 and *Junge Mädchen* (Young Girls) from 1895 until 1904. Although the main period of Schanz's creativity lay before World War I, her works were reprinted in collections and were influential and popular into the 1920s.

[*See also* Children's Magazines; Girls' Books and Fiction; *and* Poetry.]

BERND DOLLE-WEINKAUFF

Scheffler, Axel (1957–), born in Hamburg, came to Britain in 1982 to study at the Bath Academy of Art. A successful illustrator ever since, his work has been published in over twenty different languages. He is best known for his collaboration with Julia Donaldson on their famous best-selling picture book *The Gruffalo* (1999). Fascinated by animals since he was a child, Scheffler portrays a strange but ultimately loveable monster living in a vast and mysterious forest. The book won the Smarties Gold Medal Award for Picture Books in 1999, and has since been adapted for the stage. Its success was followed up when the same team produced *The Gruffalo's Child* (2004). Scheffler has also provided illustrations for Ian Whybrow's *The Bedtime Bear* (1996). Packed with flaps to lift and tabs to pull, this affectionate bedtime story has proved particularly popular with young readers.

[*See also* Illustrations; Movable Books and Pop-Up Books; *and* Picture Books.]

NICHOLAS TUCKER

Scherf, Walter (1920–), German author of critical studies on literature for children and young people and on fairy tales. In the 1950s he also wrote children's books inspired by the German youth movement. From 1957 until 1982 he was director of the International Youth Library in Munich, and in 1986 he earned a doctorate at the University of Munich with a thesis about the form and function of violence in the fairy tale. It was this work, along with other research on motifs and narrative, that formed the basis of his important books such as *Lexikon der Zaubermärchen* (Encyclopedia of Fairy Tales, 1982) and *Die Herausforderung des Dämons* (The Challenge of the Demon, 1987). Scherf analyzed the fairy tale with psychological approaches and stressed that cruelty and violence in the fairy tale have to be seen in a positive light with regard to the development of the young reader. Other of his books contain critical evaluations of contemporary children's literature and narratological studies, for example in *Strukturanalyse der Kinder- und Jugendliteratur* (Structural Analyses of Literature for Children and Young People, 1978).

[*See also* Critical Approaches to Children's Literature *and* Fairy Tales and Folk Tales.]

BERND DOLLE-WEINKAUFF

Schertle, Alice (1941–), American poet and picture book author of over forty books hailed for their vivid and rhythmic language, their sensitivity, and their insight into the imaginative lives of young children. Her second book, *The April Fool* (1981), illustrated by Emily Arnold McCully, is a fanciful tale of a king looking for comfortable shoes. Other well-regarded books, some for preschoolers, and some for slightly older children, followed in rapid succession. *When the Moon Is High* (2003), illustrated by Julia Noonan, portrays a pajama-clad father walking with his sleepless baby in the country moonlight. Schertle is also noted for her poetry and her poetry collections, including *Keepers* (1996), *How Now, Brown Cow?* (1994), *I Am the Cat* (1999), *A Lucky Thing* (1999), and *Teddy Bear, Teddy Bear* (2004). Her skillful adaptation into English of *¡Pio Peep!: Traditional Spanish Nursery Rhymes* (2003), by Alma Flor Ada and F. Isabel Campoy, received high praise.

LINNEA HENDRICKSON

Schick, Eleanor (1942–), American author and illustrator of more than thirty picture books, mainly centering on everyday events. Drawing on her own background as a New Yorker, her first books were groundbreaking in their portrayal of city children. And as a professional dancer, Schick also wrote about children's encounters with dance, music, and art in books such as *The Dancing School* (1966), *A Piano for Julie* (1984), and *Art Lessons* (1987). After moving to New Mexico, Schick turned to Southwestern themes, working with the Navajo poet Lucy Tapahonso on *Navajo ABC: A Diné Alphabet Book* (1995), and writing and illustrating two other books set on the Navajo reservation. These were also her first books illustrated in color. In *Mama* (2000) she tells the story of a young girl's coming to terms with her mother's death. Most of Schick's books stem from her life experiences, and have been praised for their respect and authenticity in capturing the inner lives of children.

[*See also* ABC Books or Alphabet Books *and* Native American Children's Literature.]

LINNEA HENDRICKSON

Schindel, Morton (1918–), American children's film producer and educator, best known for his work with Weston Woods, a film studio he founded in 1953 in order to produce films based on high-quality children's books. A 1947 graduate of Columbia Teachers College, he studied audiovisual communication for his MA degree and began working for the short-lived Teaching Films, Inc., in 1948. Schindel produced his first Weston Woods picture book film in 1954. In 1964, he produced his first animated feature, *The Snowy Day*, based on the picture book by Ezra Jack Keats, and continued working on film versions of dozens of classics, such as the live-action film *The Doughnuts* (1963), based on Robert McCloskey's *Homer Price*, and an animated film based on Maurice Sendak's *Where the Wild Things Are* (film version, 1973), directed by Gene Deitch, whom Schindel met in Czechoslovakia, and who directed many Weston Woods films. Together they pioneered the "iconographic technique" of children's filmmaking and have described how they work the camera to move over still pictures, or they move the pictures in front of a stationary camera. Then, sound elements are methodically juxtaposed to impart an illusion of motion. Some of the most acclaimed of the Weston Woods films include *Doctor de Soto* (1984), based on the picture book of the same name by William Steig, which received an Academy Award nomination for best animated short, and *Chrysanthemum* (1999; narrated by Meryl Streep) based on the picture book by Kevin Henkes, which won a Cine Golden Eagle Award, among others. For fifteen years, the children's program *Captain Kangaroo* on CBS featured Weston Woods films. They have also been widely distributed in schools and libraries. Schindel's respect for the artistic ability of children's book authors and illustrators and his commitment to producing high-quality children's films based on distinguished children's books have resulted in a lasting contribution to children's media. He has produced a number of films that feature interviews with children's book creators, such as Sendak, McCloskey, and Tomi Ungerer.

[*See also* Animated Films; Films: Film Adaptations of Children's and Young Adult Literature; Television and Children; *and biographies of figures mentioned in this article.*]

J. D. STAHL

Schindler, S. D. (1952–), American illustrator born in Kenosha, Wisconsin, and a graduate in biology from the University of Pennsylvania. Artistically active since childhood, although not formally trained in art, Schindler is the prolific illustrator of a wide variety of children's books including fiction, nonfiction, poetry, and folk tales. Characterized by stylistic versatility, precise interpretation, and accurate detailing, his illustrations include those for works such as Phyllis Krasilovsky's *The First Tulips in Holland* (1982), Cynthia Rylant's *Every Living Thing* (1985), Ursula K. Le Guin's *Catwings* (1988) and sequels, Stephen Krensky's *How Santa Got His Job* (1998) and *How Santa Lost His Job* (2001), and Alan Armstrong's *Whittington* (2005). Schindler's series illustrations include those for Seymour Simon's Einstein Anderson, Science Detective series, about a boy sleuth who solves scientific mysteries, and Judy Delton's Lottery Luck series, about a family who wins the lottery.

[*See also* Illustrations *and biographies of figures mentioned in this article.*]

ADRIENNE E. GAVIN

Schmid, Christoph von (1768–1854), German Catholic theologian and writer of children's literature. Schmid was the most popular writer of the 19th century in Germany. His more than one hundred narratives for children, published in numerous editions and translated into more than twenty languages, initiated a renascence of religious children's literature. Schmid, who studied theology and worked as a priest and schoolteacher, considered his narratives a suitable medium to instill religious ideas and Christian moral principles. From 1801 to 1807 he published *Biblische Geschichte für Kinder* (Biblical History for Children) in six volumes. In 1810 his adaptation of the legend *Genovefa* brought him his first literary success. In 1816 his best-known narrative, *Die Ostereyer* (1816; English trans., *Easter Eggs*, 1829), appeared, which was then translated into many European languages. Schmid tells the story of the noble, virtuous Rosalinde, who flees from war and persecution to a remote village, where she lives modestly and according to God's commandments. She cares for the welfare of the community and the religious instruction of the children until her husband finally finds her again. The plot, which weaves adventures with sufferings to form a happy ending, serves as a model for Schmid's allegorical stories. His allegorical stories illustrate the act of Providence rewarding the good with wealth and happiness. Schmid turns the idealized images of a traditional, well-ordered patriarchal society, and of rural and family idylls, into religious critiques. His visions are criticisms of a restless present, marked by war and crises, alongside the social changes of the 19th century. Schmid's image of childhood, which gives romantic traditions a specific religious shape, is part of his restorationist worldview, in which the children embody the Christian virtues of innocence, trustfulness, and humility, and guarantee the maintenance of an authoritarian family structure.

[*See also* Germany *and* Religious Writing.]

UTE DETTMAR

Schmid, Eleonore (1939–), Swiss author and illustrator educated at Lucerne's School of Arts and Crafts. Schmid's picture books range from animal stories (*Der Weihnachtshase*; Hare's Christmas Gift, 2000) to science books (*Eine Wasserreise*; The Water's Journey, 1989). As a writer, she uses a spare, realistic style to accompany her lush illustrations. *Hare's Christmas Gift* presents the Nativity story as immensely meaningful, yet only as an observant hare could know it. Illustrations in Regine Schindler's *Der Esel Napoleon* (Napoleon the Donkey, 1988) reveal Schmid's characteristic use of colored pencils in stroking forms into existence and leaving soft edges throughout the composition. In addition, her muted, shaded colors are a harmonizing, unifying feature, while in her simple science books she adds the pleasure of panoramic space. She has been a prizewinner at the Bologna Book Fair and the Biennale of Illustrations in Bratislava.

[*See also* Illustrations; Picture Books; *and* Science Books.]

DONNARAE MACCANN

Schmidt, Annie M. G. (1911–1995), Dutch author of children's books, song texts, poetry for adults, columns, radio and television plays, stage plays, and musicals. She was generally recognized as the most versatile and talented children's book author in the Netherlands. Her work is the most striking example of a new tone in Dutch children's literature after World War II. From the very beginning, her children's books showed a happily anarchistic world, which was completely new at that time. She showed not even a vestige of moralism, and there was often a rebellion against decorum. She began with poetry (from 1947 in the newspaper *Het Parool*, and from 1950 in books). The form of her poems has much in common with nursery rhymes: for instance, repetitions, alliteration, and a great richness of sound. In content there are analogies as well, especially in the many nonsense poems with mysterious formulas and illogical associations. We meet eccentric characters, such as the mayor who paints ducks on the walls of the town hall, but overcomes this habit in the end: "now he paints tigers on the walls." There are also subdued poems about major events in a child's life ("The Loose Tooth") or a lullaby for a little porcupine. An anthology of her poetry, *Pink Lemonade*, was published in English in the United States in 1981. She also wrote stories for young children, which three generations of Dutch children have now grown up with: *Jip en Janneke* (8 vols., 1953–1960; English trans., *Mick and Mandy*, 3 vols., 1961, and *Bob and Jilly*, 3 vols., 1976–1980). Among the highlights of her work are fantasy stories: *Minoes* (1970; English trans., *Minnie*, 1992), about a cat that becomes a young woman after eating something from the garbage can of the Institute for Bio-Chemical Research; *Pluk van de Petteflet* (1971), about a little boy living alone in a small house on top of an apartment building; and *Otje* (1980). The main theme of all three novels is the struggle of the protagonists, children and childlike adults, against establishment and officialdom. The stories have a realistic, modern setting, but the world is "enchanted" and includes fairy tale elements, for example talking animals who assist the protagonists in their fight against injustice, as an "animal secret service." The structure shows the author's mastery; although the story appears to be told in a casual way, all threads come together in the end and every detail has a meaning. In 1988 Schmidt received the Hans Christian Andersen Award. In her acceptance speech she said, "It is a bit curious and frustrating to make a speech in English, when my best books are not available in that language. The international jury had to read my work in German or Japanese or Danish." She became incredibly popular: she was even called "the real queen of the Netherlands." Many of the next generation of Dutch children's book authors stated that they were greatly indebted to her.

[*See also* Fantasy; Netherlands; *and* Poetry.]

ANNE DE VRIES

Schoenherr, John (1935–), American author, illustrator, and wildlife artist, born in New York City to immigrant parents. Schoenherr started drawing as a means of communication and eventually attended the Art Students' League and then the Pratt Institute, from which he received his BFA in 1956. After he started in the book trade as a science fiction illustrator, a move to a New Jersey farm precipitated his gradual switch to wildlife illustration. He illustrated Sterling North's Newbery Honor book *Rascal* (1963) with detailed black-and-white drawings of the eponymous raccoon and other animals. Schoenherr contributed images in the same style to many other works of fiction, including *Incident at Hawk's Hill* (1971) by Allan W. Eckert and *Julie of the Wolves* (1971) by Jean Craighead George. His pictures, always lively and realistic, add an extra dimension to the words of the novel without intruding into the narrative. In addition to his illustrations for novels and nonfiction, he has also successfully illustrated picture books and is well known and respected in this field. His watercolor paintings for Jane Yolen's *Owl Moon* (1987), for which he won the Caldecott Award, were crucial in communicating the wonder and stillness of the woods at night. Schoenherr has also received acclaim for *Rebel* (1995), his self-illustrated story about a family of five goslings and their mother. His clean, fluid illustrations show the wanderings of one independent gosling, telling a slightly different version of what is, in the text, a cozy, safe family tale. Schoenherr's gift in illustration lies in his ability to depict animals unsentimentally while still communicating his great love for nature.

[*See also* Animal Stories; Ecology and Environment; Illustrations; Picture Books; *and biographies of figures mentioned in this article.*]

Kira B. Homo

Schönlank, Bruno (1891–1965), German author who wrote for the proletarian youth movement during the Weimar Republic (1918–1933). His father was chief editor for the social-democratic newspaper *Leipzig Volkszeitung* (Leipzig People's Newspaper). Schönlank attended preparatory school, but abandoned his studies and wandered through a number of lower-skilled jobs. After brief involvement with the communist Spartacus movement, he worked for various social-democratic newspapers and became politically active in the German Socialist Party. Schönlank's agitprop dramatic recitation works (*Sprechchorwerke*) propagated visionary ideals of a future socialist utopia, while condemning the abuses of capitalism, war, and oppression. Schönlank also published two collections of political fairy tales, *Großstadt-Märchen* (Urban Fairy Tales, 1923) and *Die Kraftbonbon und andere Großstadtmärchen* (The Power Bonbon and Other Urban Fairy Tales, 1928). In 1933, Schönlank emigrated from Nazi Germany to Switzerland, where he remained. He continued writing political fairy tales and *Sprechchorwerke*, although his popularity dwindled.

[*See also* Fairy Tales and Folk Tales; Germany; *and* Propaganda.]

Luke Springman

School Friend. A British weekly magazine for girls, *School Friend* appeared from 1919 to 1940 and from 1950 to 1965. Amalgamated Press launched the magazine as a girls' version of *The Magnet*, and tried introducing Bessie Bunter as a sister of *The Magnet*'s Billy Bunter. Although the same writer wrote both stories (Charles Hamilton, writing as Hilda Richards and Frank Richards), Bessie was not popular, and two more writers were needed to make her acceptable to the new readers. Although few readers had experienced boarding school life firsthand, stories in such settings were popular, especially those featuring secret societies whose members, in hooded cloaks, faced exciting challenges. When publication of *School Friend* resumed in 1950, the new editor, Stewart Pride, included *The Silent Three*, which he had written (as Dorothy Page) with Horace ("Enid") Boyton. These later issues included more stories in comic strip form than earlier ones. Most illustrators and writers were men.

[*See also* Girls' Magazines; Hamilton, Charles; The Magnet; *and* School Stories.]

Frances Armstrong

School Stories. Children's stories are often set in schools, but "school story" is a term of art referring to a genre, British in origin, in which school is not just a backdrop but rather is the raison d'être of the novel. The school stands for particular ideals yet also offers a place where pupils grow through the exercise of independent self-will rather than being crushed into conformity. The school story had its origins in the domestic tales of the mid-18th to mid-19th centuries whose object was to show moral development through personal hardship. *The Governess; or, Little Female Academy* by Sarah Fielding (the sister of Henry Fielding of

School Stories. "Tom's Departure from Rugby"; illustration by Arthur Hughes from *Tom Brown's School Days* by Thomas Hughes (London: Macmillan, 1869). COLLECTION OF JACK ZIPES

Tom Jones fame) is thought to be the first such story set in a school. Following its publication in 1749, novels for boys set in boys' schools as well as novels for girls set in girls' schools were produced, often by the same writers. The settings (small private or village establishments) and the messages (the sad consequences of disobedience and folly, the need for repentance and forgiveness) were similar, and the plots often involved a deathbed or near deathbed scene. That the majority of the authors of these tales were female (among them, Maria Edgeworth, Harriet Martineau, and Matilda Betham-Edwards) demonstrates not simply the association of women with the "maternal" function of education of the young but also the lack of barriers to women's getting work of this kind published when other avenues were closed to them. Not surprisingly, school stories soon became vehicles for evangelical influence, leading to a branch of the genre that survived right up to the mid-20th century (in, for example, the work of Dorothy Dennison and Helen S. Humphries).

The school story proper was a product of the educational developments of Victorian Britain. Thomas Hughes's *Tom Brown's School-Days* (1857), generally considered to be the first boys' school story, celebrated Rugby School, a former grammar school that under the headmastership of Dr. Arnold (1828–1842) was transformed into a modern public (i.e., large private) school for boys of the rising middle class. This reformed model was copied by other schools such as Repton and Uppingham and by new foundations like Cheltenham College (1841) and Marlborough (1843).

Girls' education, however, remained largely at the "manners and accomplishments" stage, constrained by an ideology that saw women's role as essentially private and domestic and therefore not requiring any academic training. Victorian feminists recognized the need for girls to be better educated to equip themselves for a career that was a genuine alternative to marriage, in an era when all aimed for marriage but many were not chosen. Frances Mary Buss set up the North London Collegiate School for Ladies in 1850, and Dorothea Beale became headmistress of Cheltenham Ladies' College in 1858. Emily Davies persuaded the Taunton Commission to investigate girls' as well as boys' schools, and their report, published in 1868, recognized the poor provision for girls and led to state support under the Endowed Schools Act of 1869. The same year Davies founded the first women's college at a British university, Girton (Cambridge). The 1870 and 1880 Education Acts, which made elementary education available and compulsory to all children, included girls on equal terms with boys.

In consequence of the new attitudes, the private sector saw the launch in 1872 of the Girls' Public Day School Company, which set up high schools throughout the country, and the foundation of girls' public schools such as St. Leonard's (1877), Roedean (1885), and Wycombe Abbey (1896), which adopted a modified academic curriculum and many other features such as games and prefects from the boys' schools. Just as many writers of boys' school stories were old public school boys, so several of the women who subsequently wrote girls' school stories were educated or taught, or both, at the new girls' high schools or public schools—for example, Winifred Darch and Evelyn Smith.

In spite of these developments, however, secondary education remained the province of a privileged few in British society—and, of those few, a much higher proportion were boys, since boys were expected to have a career and support a family, while girls would look forward to marriage and withdrawal from the workplace, if indeed they ever entered it. Not until 1944 was free secondary education made available to all children in England and Wales. The result was that education was valued, especially by girls, and school was viewed by the aspiring but less affluent as a privilege that opened doors to greater opportunity and choice. This goes a long way toward explaining the popularity of the school story in the first half of the 20th century and its subsequent decline when education was freely available and taken for granted, if not actively disliked. It also explains the development of two separate genres, boys' and girls' school stories, mirroring the separate educational provision for middle-class children in Britain and the Commonwealth until well after World War II, when coeducation became more common.

Boys' School Stories

Tom Brown's School-Days focused the boys' school story squarely on the public school, with its arcane norms and traditions. Its huge popularity established the genre firmly in the affections of its juvenile market. The publication of a second, very different, school story the following year, F. W. Farrar's *Eric; or, Little by Little*, demonstrated the flexibility of the genre; while Hughes portrayed a muscular Christian ideal, *Eric* perpetuated the more sentimental approach, and for this reason has worn less well. From this point on, Robert Kirkpatrick explains, the boys' school story took three paths: the "penny dreadful" melodrama (stories and serials in story papers and magazines, some later published in book form); the evangelical school story put out by religious publishers, with its delicate hero and fervent friendships; and, finally, the form that was to establish itself as the paradigmatic school story, which treated in a predominantly entertaining way the various facets of the schoolboy code of honor in the context of sport, fagging, fights, dormitory feasts, and breaking rules, with or without the addition of adventure or mystery elements. This was the formula that, at its best—as in the work of Talbot Baines Reed, Harold Avery, R. Warren Bell, Richard Bird, Hylton Cleaver, and R. A. H. Goodyear—caught the imagination of generations of boys from the 1880s to the 1940s, many of the stories appearing first as serials in the *Boy's Own Paper* and other story papers.

Perhaps the greatest exponent of the boys' school story was Gunby Hadath, whose forty-four novels (from 1913) were typical examples of the moral message in the school context, told with style and humor. With the advent of World War II, Hadath focused on the continuing relevance, or not, of the traditional values and ethos of the boys' public school, thus demonstrating an ability to move the genre forward with the times. In another sense, however (not a literary one), the boys' school story reached its apotheosis in the work of Frank Richards (Charles Hamilton), whose 72 million words (the equivalent of one thousand novels) adorned the pages of the boys' story papers (*Magnet*, *Gem*, *Boys' Friend*) for more than half a century. Greyfriars and Billy Bunter became household names, and boys learned their moral lessons (as well as a quantity of classical allusions) from their reading. It was the work of Hamilton that George Orwell had in mind when he wrote his famous critique of "Boys' Weeklies" in *Horizon* in 1940, targeting in particular their avoidance of real-life issues such as class friction, depression, unemployment, fascism, and civil war. Yet this was, of course, a major part of their appeal, especially for working-class readers. It is true that the values of the school story were assimilationist rather than radical. As Robert Roberts observed in *The Classic Slum* (1971), "In the final estimate it may well be found that Frank Richards during the first quarter of the twentieth century had more influence on the mind and outlook of young working-class England than any other person, not excepting Baden-Powell" (quoted in Tucker, ed., p. 29).

With the school story in decline, it is perhaps not surprising that the two outstanding writers of boys' school stories after World War II wrote about younger boys. *A Swarm in May* (1955) was the first of four delightfully whimsical novels about Canterbury Cathedral Choir School by William Mayne, one of the 20th century's most prolific and highly regarded writers for children, who had himself attended the school. The twenty-five-strong series of books about Jennings (1950–1994) by Anthony Buckeridge are funny, sympathetic tales about an eleven-year-old at preparatory school. They represent the last gasp of the traditional boys' school story. From the 1950s onward its place has gradually been taken by books set in state schools, first single-sex (as in the Barry novels by A. Stephen Tring [Laurence Meynell] and in E. W. Hildick's Jim Starling series) and then coeducational, best exemplified by the Grange Hill stories by Phil Redmond, Robert Leeson, and others, spin-offs from the successful television series. These pride themselves on tackling every kind of contemporary issue from drugs to teenage pregnancy and from bullying to obesity. In attempting to address the real educational needs of young people today, such novels have moved far beyond the "timeless" values and nostalgic settings of the conventional school story, but at the cost of the escapism that was the hallmark of the genre's appeal.

Girls' School Stories

The history of girls' school stories is independent from that of boys'. It starts around 1880 when L. T. Meade, always on the lookout for a current issue to write about, lit on the recent progress in women's education as a fruitful theme to pursue. Starting with *A World of Girls* (1886), she wrote about forty girls' school stories among a much larger output, mostly set in small, family-style establishments, though a few were based on large boarding schools like Cheltenham Ladies' College and St. Leonard's. She also wrote about higher education for women in novels like *A Sweet Girl Graduate* (1891). May Baldwin was the first prolific writer for girls to produce, from 1901, a majority of school stories; she, too, took account of educational developments, and her stories were mostly set in high schools and public schools. Raymond Jacberns (Georgiana Selby Ash) wrote the first school story series (from 1902). But it is Angela Brazil who made the school story her own. All but a handful of her fifty-seven books were girls' school stories, and they were immensely popular, establishing the genre as a commercial success that managed to appeal to the school and Sunday school "reward" market as well as to the girls who received those prizes, though not to teachers and critics, who generally deplored Brazil's entertaining purpose and her breezy, over-the-top style.

Brazil was one of a number of writers who set some of her novels abroad (Baldwin was another), offering readers the vicarious thrill of experiencing foreign climes (albeit not *very* foreign and from a very British perspective). Elsie J. Oxenham, best known for her Abbey series, which is only occasionally linked to school, wrote a four-book series about a girls' school and neighboring boys' school in the Bernese Oberland; Elinor M. Brent-Dyer picked up the Alpine location (and later the associated sanatorium) in *The School at the Chalet* (1925), the first in a series that lasted through fifty-nine novels over forty-five years, making her the best-known girls' school story writer of all time and first in the affections of many fans. But there are other, less celebrated authors of her generation whose work lays claim to greater originality or quality, among them Dorita Fairlie Bruce, Winifred Darch, Josephine Elder, and Evelyn Smith, whose books celebrated the modern girls' school with its emerging traditions (an academic curriculum, games, prefects, and schoolgirl honor), all the while focusing on personal development and the working out of relationships with peers and the wider community. As those traditions became more established, a later generation of writers—Joanna Lloyd, Jessie McAlpine, Nancy Breary—were able to adopt a deliberately amusing tone in novels that critiqued but never ridiculed the customs and values of girls' schools and girls' school stories.

The interwar period was the heyday of the girls' school story in terms of quantity as well as quality. The most lucrative of all the juvenile literary markets, it attracted the attention of many writers less suited to its particular constraints. Bessie Marchant, for example, wrote five school stories in the 1920s (out of about 150 novels for children), but her efforts had more in common with the genres in which she was most at ease—adventure stories, mysteries, and spy thrillers. This was also true of a small number of male authors of girls' school stories such as Ernest Protheroe, who had at least ten female pseudonyms, and Charles Hamilton, who, as "Hilda Richards," wrote about Bessie Bunter of Cliff House School.

Despite (or perhaps because of) the entry of Enid Blyton into the field in 1940 (her Naughtiest Girl sequence is unusually set in a progressive, coeducational school, and her Malory Towers books are considered to be her best work), World War II marked the start of a decline in the genre's appeal. School stories gave way to career novels, family adventures, "problem" stories, and teen romances. A few names kept the genre alive. In the hands of Mary K. Harris, the school story evolved in novels published between 1941 and 1967 from a boarding-school setting through grammar to secondary modern schools, with increasing emphasis on home life. Antonia Forest's four school stories, part of her longer series about the Marlow family, transcend their traditional setting thanks to writing of high literary quality. Anne Digby's Trebizon series (1978–1994) was popular, but the trend since the 1980s has been to use school simply as a setting, not a rationale, for stories that explore a whole range of issues. School is no longer viewed (in reality or in books) as special, wonderful, inspiring lasting loyalty and affection, but rather as normal, mundane, often tedious, and sometimes an ordeal to be got through as quickly and as best one can.

Adult School Stories

Mention must be made of a small number of school stories intended for the adult market, but apparently enjoyed by young readers as well, that deliberately debunked the ethos and values of the public school. Rudyard Kipling's *Stalky and Co.* (1899), the early novels of P. G. Wodehouse, and Alec Waugh's *The Loom of Youth* (1917) had no female equivalents, although Charlotte Brontë's *Jane Eyre* (1847), Henry Handel Richardson's (Australian) *The Getting of Wisdom* (1910), and Antonia White's *Frost in May* (1933) were certainly critical of the schools they described. The genre of boys' school stories also encompasses some novels that celebrated school as a place where close, quasi-homosexual friendships could be nurtured: H. O. Sturgis's *Tim* (1891), H. A. Vachell's *The Hill* (1905), and E. F. Benson's *David Blaize* (1916) are examples. Again, readers of girls' school stories have not embraced any female versions of this type of novel, although some were written: Clemence Dane's (Winifred Ashton)'s *Regiment of Women* (1917), Rosalind Wade's *Children, Be Happy* (1931), Dorothy Bussy's *Olivia* (1949), and Angela Lambert's *No Talking After Lights* (1990).

School Stories outside Britain

The lack of a comparable boarding-school tradition in the United States accounts for the relative absence of American school stories, although *Tom Brown's School-Days* was a significant influence on what came to be called boy books or bad boy books, starting with Thomas Bailey Aldrich's *The Story of a Bad Boy* (1869), while the high-spirited heroines of girls' school stories in Britain clearly owed a great deal to Susan Coolidge's *What Katy Did at School* (1873). At the turn of the century, college stories enjoyed a brief vogue, together with separate boys' and girls' series in which the school and college experiences of the hero or heroine occupied a few early volumes. Many 20th-century American children's novels have been set in schools, but other elements (such as mystery solving or relationships with the opposite sex) predominate, and the schools themselves are rarely reified in the manner of the British school story.

Before the Harry Potter books, British school stories were not usually marketed in the United States. This was not the case with the English-speaking Commonwealth countries such as Australia, New Zealand, Canada, and the former African colonies, where school stories were freely distributed and sometimes reprinted in local editions, and where, in the days before television, many children gleaned their knowledge of British culture (and assimilated its values) from the pages of school stories. In Australia and New Zealand there were some indigenous examples of the genre, although the trend was not a strong one. The New Zealand author Clare Mallory is one of the most accomplished writers of girls' school stories, but her work was better received in the United Kingdom than at home. Phillis Garrard wrote successful school stories set in New Zealand and Canada. In Australia, Ethel Turner wrote one undistinguished school story, *Judy and Punch* (1928, a retrospective account of the boarding-school experiences of the heroine she had killed off in *Seven Little Australians*, 1894), while Louise Mack's *Teens* (1897) is the sole school story of a trilogy. Other Australian school stories were written by Eustace Boylan, Constance Mackness, Margaret Parker, Lillian Pyke, and Dora Joan Potter.

The Tradition Revived?

In the second half of the 20th century critics lost no opportunity to draw attention to the school story's irrelevance, false values, and lack of realism. The bugbear of librarians and teachers, school stories began to be removed from school and library shelves, causing publishers to curtail their lists even though there was still a reading market for them. By the 1970s the genre appeared to be in terminal decline. Then, just as one could confidently claim that the school story was dead, along came Harry Potter. J. K. Rowling's novels combine several genres, but a convincing case could be (and has been) made that they are first and foremost school stories. Not only can one point to the hallmarks of the conventional school story—the prefect system, emphasis on games, uniforms, interhouse rivalries—but the plots themselves focus on the forging of character and relationships and the lessons learned (of which the academic are never the most important) in a closed community, where different people must learn to get along and the young are prepared for adult life.

The success of the Harry Potter novels in Britain has been ascribed to the British public's familiarity with their setting, but that familiarity is not with the reality of boarding-school life—very few British children have ever attended private schools, and an even smaller number go to boarding school—but with the fictional version of the school story. This is so deeply embedded in the British cultural heritage that it is recognized even by those who never read school stories in their youth. Girls' school stories in particular have been the butt of popular satire, the exotic and (in a patriarchal society) suspect nature of their single-sex canvas attracting innuendo both heterosexual (Ronald Searle's St. Trinian's stories of 1946–1953, for example) and lesbian (as in Denise Deegan's playful West End parody, *Daisy Pulls It Off*, 1985). Such lampooning can make sense only if the object of ridicule is instantly recognizable. Boys' school stories have not been subject to such raillery, perhaps (as Sheila Ray suggests) because of their association with adult school stories written by authors respected in the literary canon.

Scholarly interest in boys' school stories as social phenomena predated that in girls' school stories, but, largely as a result of the feminist rehabilitation of women's culture toward the end of the 20th century, girls' school stories have been reclaimed as offering readers an admittedly circumscribed space to put themselves first as well as a range of positive role models of female agency. At the same time the recent growth of fan associations, journals, and Web sites has ensured a lively market in secondhand school stories and reprints. It remains to be seen whether J. K. Rowling's coeducational and fantastic but in many respects conventional school stories will revive the genre in Britain and increase its appeal abroad.

[*See also* Boy's Own Paper, The; Children's Magazines; Penny Dreadful; Religious Writing; United Kingdom; *and biographies of figures mentioned in this article.*]

BIBLIOGRAPHY

Auchmuty, Rosemary. *A World of Girls: The Appeal of the Girls' School Story*. London: Women's Press, 1992.

Auchmuty, Rosemary. *A World of Women: Growing Up in the Girls' School Story*. London: Women's Press, 1999.

Cadogan, Mary, and Patricia Craig. *You're a Brick, Angela!: A New Look at Girls' Fiction, 1939–1975*. London: Gollancz, 1976.

Clark, Beverly Lyon. *Regendering the School Story: Sassy Sissies and Tattling Tomboys*. New York: Garland, 1996.

Foster, Shirley, and Judy Simons. *What Katy Read: Feminist Re-readings of "Classic" Stories for Girls*. Basingstoke, U.K.: Macmillan, 1995; Iowa City: University of Iowa, 1995.

Kirkpatrick, Robert J., ed. *The Encyclopaedia of Boys' School Stories*. Aldershot, U.K.: Ashgate, 2000.

Quigly, Isabel. *The Heirs of Tom Brown: The English School Story*. London: Chatto & Windus, 1982.

Richards, Jeffrey. *Happiest Days: The Public Schools in English Fiction*. Manchester, U.K.: Manchester University Press, 1988.

Sims, Sue, and Hilary Clare. *The Encyclopaedia of Girls' School Stories*. Aldershot, U.K.: Ashgate, 2000.

Tucker, Nicholas, ed. *School Stories from Bunter to Buckeridge*. London: National Centre for Research in Children's Literature, 1999.

ROSEMARY AUCHMUTY

Schroeder, Binette (1939–), German fine artist and picture book maker. Schroeder was born in Hamburg and trained at the School of Design, Basel. Important influences on her work were an introduction to early Netherlands art through the volumes in her grandfather's library, the English classics read to her as a child, and a love of the works of surrealists such as Max Ernst. The art of her picture books has moved through three distinguishable phases. The first is concerned with the creation of colorful toy worlds, as in *Lupinchen* (1969), which has become a modern classic in France, *Archibald und sein kleines Rot* (Archibald and His Little Red, 1970), and *Florian und Traktor Max* (Florian and Tractor Max, 1971). The second group has historical stylistic visual links: the "belle epoque" in *Krokodil Krokodil* (Crocodile Crocodile, 1975), by Peter Nickl; rococo art in *Die wunderbaren Reisen und Abenteuer des Freiherrn von Munchhausen* (The Marvelous Travels and Adventures of Baron Munchhausen, 1977), retold by Peter Nickl; and Renaissance elements in *Die Schöne und das Tier* (Beauty and the Beast, 1986), retold by Ann Carter. In the third group the picture books show strong affinities to theater, with the page-frame functioning as a stage on which the action is performed in a series of dramatically lit dynamic scenes, as in the Grimm brothers' *Der Froschkönig oder der Eiserne Heinrich* (The Frog Prince or Iron Henry, 1989) and *Laura*, translated by Rosemary Lanning (1999). *The Frog Prince* is highly innovative in its visual concept. Schroeder subordinates the narrator's speech by designing it as part of the spatial composition. Long vertical strip-frame sequences carry episodes of greatest emotional charge, and the differences in a landscape setting common to both front and back endpapers symbolize the transformations in appearance and values that the main characters undergo. Schroeder has exhibited her art worldwide, and her books have won awards in Germany, Switzerland, Japan, the United States, the Netherlands, and Slovakia.

[*See also* Illustrations; Picture Books; *and biographies of figures mentioned in this article.*]

BIBLIOGRAPHY

Doornkaat, Ten Hans. *The Art of Binette Schroeder*. Bilingual catalogue (English and German). Zurich, Switzerland: Lieferbare Publikationen, 1995.

JANE DOONAN

Schubiger, Jürg (1936–), Swiss writer for children and adults, with experiences in diverse professional activities and an academic background. His early story collections *Die vorgezeigten Dinge* (1972; All Things Presented) and *Dieser Hund heisst Himmel: Tag- und Nachtgeschichten* (1978; This Dog Is Called Sky: Day and Night Stories) depict everyday life, including subtle humor and asking philosophical questions that interest children and adults. *Als die Welt noch jung war* (1995; When the World Was New) made him famous as an author of children's literature. The family story *Vater Mutter ich und sie* (1997; Father, Mother, Me, and Her) depicts characters of different generations with a delicate psychological approach. His books *Die Geschichte von Wilhelm Tell* (2003; The Story of William Tell) and *Seltsame Abenteuer des Don Quijote* (2003; Strange Adventures of Don Quixote) provide children with the opportunity to get close to myths and classics.

ELISABETH STUCK

Schulz, Charles M. (1922–2000), American cartoonist known for the comic strip *Peanuts*. Launched on October 2, 1950, *Peanuts* flouted the conventions of comic strips in post–World War II popular culture. An immediate success, it is renowned for its cast of philosophical, humorous children who, in addition to living the lives of children, gave an unruffled commentary on literature, politics, and society at large.

Charles Monroe Schulz was able to translate lifelong feelings of inadequacy, insecurity, and isolation into his work,

Charles M. Schulz.

and many felt that his singular character Charlie Brown was a reflection of Schulz's own personality. The two even shared a similar parentage, both being sons of barbers. A pimple-faced, big-eared boy with a slight physique, who continuously had drawings rejected by his high school yearbook editors, Schulz was shadowed throughout his life by hardship. In 1943, while he was a twenty-year-old army private serving in World War II, his mother died from colon cancer, the same disease that would claim Schulz's own life in 2000.

Schulz developed a unique visual style early on. A crow-quill pen and ink was his signature medium for *Peanuts*. While marketing it to companies, Schulz received a letter from United Feature Syndicate (UFS) in 1950. The editor of UFS wished to expand *L'il Folks*, as it was then called, from a one-panel to a four-panel feature. Schulz was more than happy to accommodate. However, because of legal issues surrounding the title, Schulz was forced to rename the strip. UFS dubbed it *Peanuts*, to the dismay of Schulz. He felt the title made the strip seem insignificant and would imply a triviality about the characters, but the name stayed. When the strip debuted, the featured characters were Charlie Brown, Snoopy, Shermy, and Patty. The original cast of child characters had not yet made the transformation into the popular formula that we have all grown accustomed to with their quick-witted quirks, intense relationships, reassuring security blankets, and mythical air battles. Initially, critics noted that the characters were interchangeable.

When the *Peanuts* audience was introduced to the infant Schroeder, who grew to be a piano prodigy who played Beethoven, the interchangeable nature of the characters ceased, and the strip changed from a generic comedy to a unique window on the psychological, emotional, and physical needs of the generations after World War II. The characters assumed idiosyncrasies and neuroses, and participated in emotional dramas, while still remaining childlike. When Schulz brought the Van Pelt family into the neighborhood in 1952, Lucy and Linus Van Pelt demonstrated the sometimes damaging cruelty between brother and sister. Charlie Brown became an older brother in 1959 with the birth of Sally. The dog Snoopy became engaged in his battle with the Red Baron, a World War I fighter pilot. The characters developed strong personalities that thoroughly set them apart from those in other comic strips of the day. Lucy's humor was crabbier and more psychological, Linus was the faithful philosopher, and Charlie Brown looked inward. Each of these characters reflected the growth of Schulz's work, his internal struggles, and changes in society.

In the 1960s the Peanuts gang moved into the mainstream of mass-market merchandising, starting with a desk calendar in 1961. They appeared on the cover of *Time* magazine, and gained the recognition of NASA when the Lunar Excursion Module from the 1969 moon landing was named Snoopy. American soldiers in Vietnam adopted Snoopy as their mascot, sketching him on their helmets. As *Peanuts* went on to have television specials, such as *It's the Great Pumpkin, Charlie Brown* (1966) and the Emmy Award–winning *A Charlie Brown Christmas* (1969), as well as Broadway productions, Schulz felt constant anxiety. Despite living his dream of being a cartoonist, becoming in fact the highest-paid cartoonist in history, Schulz felt a prisoner of his success and became increasingly reclusive.

[*See also* Comic Books.]

BIBLIOGRAPHY

Inge, M. Thomas, ed. *Charles M. Schulz: Conversations*. Jackson: University Press of Mississippi, 2000.

Johnson, Rheta Grimsley. *Good Grief: The Story of Charles M. Schulz*. New York: Pharos, 1989.

Schulz, Charles M. *Peanuts: A Golden Celebration: The Art and the Story of the World's Best-Loved Comic Strip*. New York: HarperCollins, 1999.

Whiting, Jim. *Charles Schulz*. Bear, Del.: Mitchell Lane, 2003.

ANTHONY S. BURDGE

Schwab, Gustav (1792–1850), German theologian, preacher, and teacher of classical languages and literatures. Schwab is best known for collecting and editing collections of German folk literature, first published in *Buch der schönsten Geschichten und Sagen: Für Alt und Jung wiedererzählt* (Book of the Finest Tales and Sagas: Retold for Old and Young, 1836–1837). Schwab worked as an editor for German literary journals, and cultivated relations with prominent German Romantic authors such as Ludwig Uhland (1787–1862). Later Schwab reedited his collection as *Die deutschen Volksbücher* (German Folk Books, 1843), emphasizing Germanness during a time before the 1848 revolutions when nationalist sentiments excited the German middle class. A separate collection, *Die schönsten Sagen des klassischen Altertums* (The Finest Legends of Classical Antiquity, 1838–1840), helped the educated to adopt ideals of the neo-humanistic classical age. Together these entertaining, albeit bowdlerized, tales popularized ancient mythology and stimulated patriotic consciousness in young German readers for generations, and the collection remains one of the best-selling works of German literature of all time.

[*See also* Collections; Fairy Tales and Folk Tales; Germany; *and* Propaganda.]

LUKE SPRINGMAN

Schwartz, Alvin (1927–1992), best-selling author, known for his collections of humorous and scary folk tales. Born in Brooklyn, he briefly attended City College in New York, served in the U.S. Navy, then earned a BA from Colby College in 1949 and an MA in journalism from Northwestern University in 1951. Upon graduating, he found work in journalism, but turned to freelance writing in 1963. His early children's writing explored social issues; his first book for children was *The Night Workers* (1966) and featured people who worked at night. When the book market began to change in the 1970s because of decreased funding from the Elementary and Secondary Education Act, Schwartz started to explore something he had enjoyed since childhood: folklore. He collected folk tales from people young and old, then tapped into his journalism background and extensively researched the stories and their different versions through his scholarly contacts. His titles ranged from collections of tongue twisters, like *A Twister of Twists, a Tangler of Tongues* (1972), to tall tales, like *Whoppers* (1975), to poetry, like *And the Green Grass Grew All Around: Folk Poetry from Everyone* (1992), to humorous, like *Witcracks: Jokes and Jests from American Folklore* (1973). He is perhaps best known for his *Scary Stories* books: *Scary Stories to Tell in the Dark* (1981), *More Scary Stories to Tell in the Dark* (1984), and *Scary Stories, No. 3: More Tales to Chill Your Bones* (1991). Despite being immensely popular with children, the books topped the American Library Association's "100 Most Frequently Challenged Books of 1990–2000" list because of their scary, violent, and supernatural content. Nevertheless, his collections were often best sellers and were recognized by the National Council of Teachers of English, the American Library Association, the National Council of Social Studies, and the International Reading Association for their outstanding quality.

[*See also* Fairy Tales and Folk Tales; Ghost Stories; Horror Stories; *and* United States.]

REBECCA HOGUE WOJAHN

Schwartz, Amy (1954–), American illustrator and writer. Born in San Diego, California, and educated at Antioch College, Ohio, and the California College of Arts and Crafts before moving to New York City, Schwartz is an award-winning illustrator and author-illustrator of children's books. Frequently produced in watercolor and pen and ink, and typically featuring round-shaped figures, her illustrations, like her stories, depict childhood experience from the child's perspective. Characterized by humor, Schwartz's stories often focus on everyday activities. Her illustrations of other writers' works include Donna Guthrie's *The Witch Who Lives down the Hall* (1985), the Christopher Award–winning *The Purple Coat* (1986) by Amy Hest, and several titles authored by her father, Henry Schwartz. Award-winning author-illustrated titles include her first book *Bea and Mr. Jones* (1982), *Mrs. Moskowitz and the Sabbath Candlesticks* (1983), *A Teeny, Tiny Baby* (1994), and *What James Likes Best* (2003), winner of the 2004 Charlotte Zolotow Award.

[*See also* Illustrations; Picture Books; *and biographies of figures mentioned in this article.*]

ADRIENNE E. GAVIN

Schwartz, Yevgeni (1896–1958), Russian playwright and writer. In the 1920s he contributed regularly to the first Soviet children's magazines. His fairy tales have a clear didactic tone, most notably in an original sequel to *Puss in Boots* (1937), in which he places the famous character in a contemporary Soviet setting. *Two Brothers* (1943; English trans., 1973) is based on the common motif of enchantment and rescue, introducing a parody of the Father Frost figure, the cruel and cynical wizard Great-Grandfather Frost. *A Tale of Stolen Time* (1948; English trans., 1966) portrays a lazy schoolboy transformed into an old man by wicked wizards. In a number of realistic stories, such as *The First Grader* (1949), Schwartz depicts the everyday life of ordinary Soviet children.

Schwartz is best known for his fairy tale plays such as *Little Red Riding Hood* (1937), one of the earliest contemporary versions in which the girl outsmarts the wolf, or *Cinderella* (1947), originally a film script, abounding in funny, everyday details and introducing colorful secondary characters. Plays based on Andersen's fairy tales are primarily addressed to an adult audience. *The Naked King* (1934; published 1960) follows the plot of "The Emperor's New Clothes," incorporating elements from "The Swineherd" and "The Princess and the Pea," as well as a good deal of social satire. *The Snow Queen* (1939) and *The Shadow* (1940) are closer to the originals, while they have a clear satirical focus, the latter portraying a country ruled by a dictator. *The*

Dragon (1944; English trans., 1963) makes use of the dragon-slayer motif to show how slavery corrupts people and how easily the oppressed become oppressors. *The Two Maple-Trees* (1953) features a conceited witch, the traditional Baba Yaga of Russian folklore, and the lyrical comedy *The Ordinary Miracle* (1956) is an inversion of "Beauty and the Beast." Many of Schwartz's plays were banned when the Communist censors detected possible satire of the regime in their motifs of power and falseness.

[*See also* Fairy Tales and Folk Tales; Puss in Boots; *and* Russia.]

BIBLIOGRAPHY

Corten, Irina A. "Evgeni Shvarts as an Adapter of Hans Christian Andersen and Charles Perrault." *Russian Review* 37 (1978): 51–67.

MARIA NIKOLAJEVA

Schwind, Moritz von (1804–1871), German painter and illustrator. Born in Vienna, Schwind spent most of his life in Munich, where he became a professor at the Academy of Arts in 1847. His fame rests mainly on his paintings of historical subjects, in particular his series of cartoons for the Wartburg castle, which epitomize his penchant for idealized medieval settings and his skill in dramatic composition and picturesque landscapes, as well as his keen eye for details. Equally important are his paintings of idyllic scenes of contemporary rural life, and of motifs from legends and fairy tales. His fairy tale cycles—*Cinderella* (1854), *The Seven Ravens* (1857/8), and *Of Beautiful Melusine* (1869)—highlight his talent for narrative art; they were widely distributed in the form of etchings and photographs. Schwind also produced illustrations of children's books and woodcuts of fairy tale motifs (for instance, *Puss-in-Boots*) for a publication called *Münchner Bilderbogen*, a series of illustrated broadsheets that reached a large public of all ages.

[*See also* Fairy Tales and Folk Tales; Germany; *and* Illustrations.]

DIETER PETZOLD

Schwitters, Kurt (1887–1948), German artist associated with the Dada movement. Schwitters experimented with poetic collages using bits of paper, wood, and everyday objects since he did not believe in restricting himself to one single material. Always striving to expand the frontiers of art, Schwitters took the same approach in three children's booklets: *Die Märchen vom Paradies* (The Fairy Tales about Paradise, 1924; coauthored with Käte Steinitz), *Familie Hahnpeter* (The Family Hahnpeter, 1924; coauthored with Käte Steinitz), and *Die Scheuche, Märchen* (1925; Eng. trans., *Scarecrow Fairy Tales*; with the collaborating typographers Käte Steinitz and Theo van Doesburg). He did not particularly think of children as his readers, and adults sometimes found the associations and use of creative typography incomprehensible. But characteristically Schwitters made use of common stereotypes for the purpose of giving them new meaning. In 1937 he was compelled to flee Germany, first to Norway and finally to Great Britain (where he died). Throughout his life he was intensely involved with the international avant-garde, and his Dada-inspired poems, for example, "An Anna Blume" and "Ursonate," bear witness to his joy in experimentation. His pen name "Merz" became both a pseudonym and a term for his works and found its programmatic form in *Merz* (1923–1932), a periodical and series of booklets that Schwitters edited and published.

[*See also* Book Design; Fairy Tales and Folk Tales; Germany; *and* Illustrations.]

HELENE EHRIANDER

Science Books. The majority of science books for children in the United States date from the 1960s, after the Russians placed the Sputnik satellite in orbit around the earth in 1957. U.S. politicians and the educational community began to realize that American science teaching lagged behind that of the Soviet Union and indeed behind that of much of Europe. In fact, when the United States began to concentrate on building up the space program, children were encouraged to subscribe for free to a little monthly magazine called *NASA Facts*, which provided pictures and stories about the program. The space program caused a paradigm shift in U.S. views of science for children.

There were, of course, earlier attempts to interest some children in science and mathematics, including late 19th-century magazines for young adults, such as the ones that published Jules Verne's fiction. These were created with a pedagogical intent and with the idea, as stated by Verne's editor and publisher, Hetzel, in his *Journal of Scientific Education*, that one had to transform science from dry facts into something more colorful and adventurous. He could almost have been speaking for educational reformers in the 1960s and again in the late 1980s, as they tried a range of techniques and curricula to interest children in pursing scientific careers. Organizations like the American Association of Uni-

Science Book. Front cover illustration by Bruce Degen for *The Magic School Bus on the Ocean Floor* by Joanna Cole (New York: Scholastic, c. 1992). REPRODUCED COURTESY OF THE COTSEN CHILDREN'S LIBRARY, PRINCETON UNIVERSITY LIBRARY

versity Women also provided research and statistics on gender and racial biases in science teaching, as did the National Association of Science Teachers.

Series Books

Publishing of science books for children, other than the textbooks to be used in schools, is motivated by parents' and teachers' conception of what is both entertaining and useful, often as supplements to the curriculum. Thus, over time, the major publishers such as Raintree (RSVP), UXL/Gale, Franklin Watts/Grolier, Scholastic Books, and the American Library Association, as well science museums in various cities, have linked their science books to curricula units and competitive science fairs. The books are published usually in slightly oversized trade form, with sturdy covers on heavy paper, suitable for use in a school or public library and usually too expensive for a family with an average income. A few series are also issued in trade paperback editions, but this is not a large part of the market sector for children's science books.

In science publishing for children, the book series predominates. Books are published in series, with similar format and vocabulary level, so that they can fit into or supplement units on astronomy, health sciences, natural sciences, mathematics, and so on, as needed. Some of the earliest science series were written by Isaac Asimov, a prolific writer who trained in chemistry and taught at Columbia University's medical school. Asimov first published science fiction and was also well known for books addressed to the lay reader on almost every aspect of science. He also published children's science picture books on a wide range of topics, including the planets and space as well as everything from ecology to health. Some of his series have been reedited and republished. The science fiction writer Arthur C. Clarke also published series on space for children as well as for adults. Clarke was especially associated with selling the space program to the American public and was acknowledged for this by NASA. The earlier versions of series books were not as closely tied to curricular needs as at present, but in the series titles for younger children, the characteristic combination of colorful photographs and drawings, and of small amounts of text, sometimes with one connected narrative and with little aside texts that introduce a famous physicist or a famous discovery, has often been repeated in the more modern series titles.

While even the earlier science books for younger children focus more on illustration than text, the newer texts are yet more visually oriented, and it is more common for the illustrations to be photographs rather than drawings. Thus children will find a series on pond animals, one per book, with photographs of the animals in their natural habitat and in stages of the life cycle, or of planets and galaxies, some of them doubtless available through observatory photographs or the Hubble space telescope. In fact, some current children's books on planets, stars, galaxies, and other astronomical phenomena, including the space program and artificial satellites, acknowledge NASA as one of their sources. And while early series were written by scientists, more recent ones seem to be by professional writers like Kit and Ray Spanenburg, who have done almost all the books in a series devoted to artificial satellites and acknowledge both NASA and the Hayden Planetarium in their credits. Series books for middle-grade readers focus on biographies of famous scientists and experiments to try at home. One of the more popular series is *How Things Work* (2d ed., 2001), which uses both illustration and text to explicate the science of technologies in our everyday life.

The Audience

While many science books for children may have more appeal to parents and teachers than to children themselves, there are other strategies, with children's books, that are used to interest children in science—for example, curricular packages that use books like *Make Way for Ducklings* to teach about wildlife habitat. It is also well known by librarians and teachers that at least some children will read anything about dinosaurs, so there are a multiplicity of dinosaur series and fictional works. In this case, the creatures sell the books.

Additionally, one of the more famous science series is not strictly factual. This is the immensely successful *Magic School Bus* series, with the teacher Mrs. Frizzle, who actually takes her class off to live in a pond, or become clouds and raindrops, or become animals in a rain forest, and so on. This series by Joanna Cole, an established writer of other kinds of literature, was illustrated by Bruce Dergen and first published in the 1980s. Like some of the more sober series books that provide actual science activities, Cole's stories are created around the idea that children learn experientially, even if it is only by reading about the experiences of other children. And the books have become so popular that some of the stories have become animated television productions.

Because the books are so visually stimulating, it is difficult to distinguish good writing from mediocre. One can depend on only a few awards as guidance. Science books usually compete for awards with all other nonfiction (for example, Horn Book for Outstanding Nonfiction, Newbery, and Caldecott); there are a few awards specifically for science books, like the NSTA/CBS Outstanding Science Trade Books for Children, which was won by Joanna Cole. Also, one can depend on some reviews of science books in *Kirkus* and in the *School Library Journal*. But the interest in science books, and more recently, videos, DVDs, and computer-interactive materials, has so much increased in the last two decades that a magazine recommending the best purchases, *Science Books and Films*, has developed from a small newspaper format to a glossy monthly magazine recommending everything from reference books to Web sites. And science museums, planetariums, and aquariums are mentioned as resources somewhere in the text or bibliographies of both books written for children and curricular guides for teachers.

The experiential theory is expressed very clearly on the verso of the title page in the *Eyewitness* series, an oversize group of books that combine colorful pictures and charts and drawings in pages that are a mishmash of images and texts. On one two-page spread in the chemistry volume, you can expect to find a microscope, a picture of an early chemist like Mendeleev, and microscopic organisms and text interspersed in boxes and balloons of different colors. But the focus of the series, which covers electricity, light, force and motion, matter and energy, and evolution, is expressed thus: "It will help families to answer their questions about why and how things work—from daily occurrences in the home to the mysteries of space. In school, these books are valuable resources. Teachers will find them useful for work in many subjects, and the experiments and demonstrations in the book can serve as an inspiration for classroom activities." It is clear that the books speak to adults who will recommend them to children. Whether or not the children will pick the books up on their own is another question.

[*See also* Information Books; Nonfiction; Photography in Nonfiction for Children; Science Fiction; *and biographies of figures mentioned in this article*.]

Bibliography

Kelsey, Kathryn, and Ashley Steel. *The Truth About Science*. Arlington, Va.: NSTA Press, 2001.

Latridis, Mary D. *Teaching Science to Children: A Resourcebook*. New York: Garland, 1986.

Lynch, Sharon J. *Equity and Science Education Reform*. Mahwah, N.J.: Lawrence Erlbaum Associates, 2003.

Newmark, Dr. Ann. *Chemistry: Eyewitness Science*. New York: Dorling Kindersley, 1993.

Phelan, Carolyn. *Science Books for Young People*. Chicago: American Library Association, 1996.

Janice M. Bogstad

Science Fiction. The origins of science fiction have been widely debated, and a generally accepted definition of the term—first invented by William Wilson in 1851 to describe science-based poetry—has eluded literary theorists. Indeed, various writers and critics in the field have periodically suggested a variety of alternative labels for the genre, including "science fantasy," "speculative fiction," and "structural fabulation." Brian Aldiss, in his influential critical study *Trillion Year Spree* (1986), defined science fiction as "post-gothic" and named Mary Shelley's *Frankenstein* (1818) as the first true work of science fiction. Other scholars have privileged the older tradition of the imaginary voyage and have emphasized everything from Lucian's *True History* (c. A.D. 180) to Thomas More's *Utopia* (1551) to Jonathan Swift's *Gulliver's Travels* (1726) as key precursors of the genre. More frequently mentioned as founders, of course, are Edgar Allan Poe, Jules Verne, and H. G. Wells. Other scholars, however, have argued for Hugo Gernsback, whose *Amazing Stories* (1926) was arguably the first true science fiction magazine.

Essentially, as used here, the term "science fiction" refers to that subset of fantasy stories whose fantastic elements can be seen as resulting from unusual scientific phenomena, whether real or imagined. Stories that include such phenomena may also be seen as "science fictional" despite also containing elements of the supernatural, as in, for example, Madeleine L'Engle's *A Wrinkle in Time* (1962). Also related to science fiction is dystopian fiction, which may be defined as stories set in worlds distinctly worse than our own, usually with the intent of suggesting that our world is moving in the direction depicted. Not all dystopias are science fictional in nature—some take place in what are clearly fantasy worlds, while others may be set in the more or less realistically depicted present or past—but to the extent that dystopia attempts to depict the future it becomes science fiction, and, similarly, to the extent that science fiction attempts to warn its readers concerning the future, it becomes dystopian fiction. Much young adult science fiction—for example, Lois Lowry's *The Giver* (1993)—is thus clearly dystopian in nature.

Interestingly enough, with the possible exceptions of Lucian and More, all of the authors mentioned above as possible founders of the genre science fiction have also been popular with children, as have other purveyors of the fantastic from Homer to J. R. R. Tolkien. In a very real sense, then, fantasy and science fiction have always been children's literature. When David Hartwell wrote in *Age of Wonders* (1984) that "the golden age of science fiction is twelve," he was making a joke, but was also pointing to something very real. Twelve is the approximate age when children who will become lifelong readers of science fiction frequently begin to do so, and historically they have tended to read omnivorously without regard to age categories. It is thus, once again, entirely accurate to define the work of Verne, Wells, Edgar Rice Burroughs, Robert Heinlein, Arthur C. Clarke, Arkady and Boris Strugatski, Herbert Franke, and most of the other 19th- and 20th-century giants in the field as, at least in part, children's literature. A question then emerges: does children's or young adult science fiction differ in any appreciable way from adult science fiction? Heinlein, arguably the most significant writer in the field, insisted that his children's books were essentially identical to his other work, except that he left out the romance. Most young adult science fiction does tend to be didactic, of course, preaching the gospel of progress, and it does tend toward the Bildungsroman, but the same can also be said of much adult science fiction. Beginning in the 1970s, however, as writers like H. M. Hoover and Monica Hughes, who specialized in young adult science fiction, began to dominate the field, similarities could be noted between their work and the emerging genre of contemporary realistic fiction. To this day a significant number of works of young adult science fiction clearly qualify as problem novels.

Early Science Fiction for Children

In looking for work that was explicitly written for children, however, we might well begin with the dime novels of the late 19th and early 20th centuries, which appeared in such American and European publications as *The Boys of New York* (1875–1894), *The Boy's Own Paper* (1879–1967), and *Aus dem Reiche der Phantasie* (From the Realms of Imagination, 1901). Among the early science fiction stories published in various dime-novel formats were *The Steam Man of the Prairie* (1868); the entire host of Frank Reade and

Science Fiction. Front cover illustration by Darrell K. Sweet for *Have Space Suit—Will Travel* by Robert A. Heinlein (New York: Ballantine, 1977). COLLECTION OF JACK ZIPES

Frank Reade, Jr. stories, beginning in 1876; and the Tom Edison, Jr. stories, which first appeared in 1891, all of which heavily emphasized marvelous inventions and were clearly influenced by Verne. Aware of the success of these dime novels, the Stratemeyer Syndicate, a book packager run by Edward Stratemeyer and specializing in popular series, soon began to commission science fiction for boys in their Great Marvel series, beginning with *Through the Air to the North Pole* (1906) by "Roy Rockwood." Serials, often written for younger readers and also modeled on the work of Jules Verne, were equally popular in Italy and Germany, among them Enrico Novelli's *Atlantide* (1901) and Robert Kraft's *Der Herr der Lüfte* (Lord of the Air, 1909).

Not long after appeared Stratemeyer's *Tom Swift and His Motor Cycle* (1910) by "Victor Appleton." The Tom Swift books eventually totaled thirty-eight titles published over several decades, and were later followed by three Tom Swift, Jr. series, beginning with *Tom Swift and His Flying Lab* (1954), making the books a true publishing phenomenon. Numerous imitators also flourished throughout the 20th century, including Carl Claudy's Adventures in the Unknown series, most notably *The Mystery Men of Mars* (1933), and, somewhat later, the Rick Brant and the Tom Corbett series. Also worth mentioning are Buck Rogers and Flash Gordon. The former made his first appearance in Philip Nowlan's short story "Armageddon 2419 A.D." in *Amazing Stories* (1928) and then, in 1929, became the protagonist of the first science fiction comic strip, written by Nowlan and drawn by Dick Calkins. Alex Raymond's comic strip *Flash Gordon* followed in 1934. The first European science fiction comic strip may well have been René Pelos's *Futuropolis* (1937–1938).

The Victorian era and into the early 20th century was arguably the first great age of children's literature, of course, and this included a strong tradition of more literary fantastic fiction as well. Works such as Lewis Carroll's *Alice's Adventures in Wonderland* (1865) and L. Frank Baum's *The Wonderful Wizard of Oz* (1900) were clearly fantasy, but others, including Baum's *The Master Key* (1901) and Hugh Lofting's *Doctor Dolittle in the Moon* (1929), included elements of science fiction such as robots, antigravity, and space travel.

After World War II

In the United States in particular, however, children who had outgrown the dime novel and Tom Swift naturally moved on to the pulps, sensational and somewhat dubious magazines like *Amazing* and *Air Wonder Stories*, ostensibly written for adults, wherein they encountered the joys of reading Burroughs, A. Merritt, E. E. Smith, and other pulp science fiction authors. Indeed, no less a writer than Isaac Asimov has commented on the powerful effect that such publications had on him as a teenager. Although well-done science fiction novels intended for children did appear occasionally in the 1930s and early to mid-1940s—the best of these being John Keir Cross's *The Angry Planet* (1945) and William Pène du Bois's Newbery Award–winning utopian novel *The Twenty-One Balloons* (1947)—it was not until a few years after World War II that young adult science fiction really took off as a clearly defined publishing category. In 1947 Scribners brought out the first of a line of true young adult (or "juvenile" as they were called) science fiction novels by Robert Heinlein. *Rocket Ship Galileo* told the exciting tale of three teens who built and flew an atomic-powered spaceship to the moon, where they encountered Nazis and the remains of an ancient alien civilization. Other Heinlein juveniles that appeared from Scribners included such classics as *The Rolling Stones* (1952) and *Citizen of the Galaxy* (1957), books that remain popular to this day. Other major science fiction writers soon joined Heinlein in producing young adult fiction. Isaac Asimov (as Paul French) began his Lucky Starr series with *David Starr: Space Ranger* in 1952. The Winston Company published a popular series of juvenile science fiction novels, featuring such classics as Paul Anderson's *Vault of the Ages* (1952) and Arthur C. Clarke's *Islands in the Sky* (1952). Andre Norton had made her fiction debut in the 1930s but began to devote her career to young adult science fiction with *Star Man's Son: 2250 A.D.* (1952) and *Star Rangers* (1953). Indeed, as the above list makes clear, 1952 was a watershed year for the genre.

Most of the juvenile novels Heinlein and company were producing differed very little from the adult science fiction of the era, except in their exclusive focus on teen protagonists. They tended to feature all of the standard science fiction tropes of the day, from spaceships and robots to aliens and time travel. Most were "hard" science fiction, in that they emphasized technology. Authors like Heinlein, Clarke, and Norton were particularly fond of portraying lived-in futures, featuring young people making it in space as, for example, farmers on Mars or crewmen on interstellar cargo ships. A few books—Anderson's *Vault of the Ages* and Norton's *Star Man's Son*, for example—responding to Cold War worries, featured post-Holocaust scenarios, often centered on the recovery of civilization through the rediscovery of lost technology. Norton was also unusual in her willingness to mix science fiction and fantasy motifs in *Witch World* (1963) and its successors.

Most of the best young adult science fiction published in the 1950s was produced by authors who had cut their teeth writing adult science fiction. Francis J. Molson and Susan G. Miles, in *Anatomy of Wonder*, go so far as to speculate that only income from the growing young adult science fiction market made it possible for many science fiction writers to make a living at their craft. Other writers of adult science fiction who entered the young adult field in the 1960s and 1970s included Alan Nourse, whose *Star Surgeon* (1960) centered on the future of medicine; Robert Silverberg, whose *Time of the Great Freeze* (1964), featured the science of archaeology; John Christopher, who produced such dystopian masterpieces as *The White Mountains* (1967) and *The Guardians* (1970); and Anne McCaffrey, whose *Dragonsong* (1976) shared with some of Norton's work the tendency to mix science fiction with fantasy.

Young Adult Science Fiction by Young Adult Writers

In the 1950s, however, new authors emerged who wrote high-quality science fiction for children without having done adult work in the genre. The first of these writers mostly produced lightweight, often humorous work more appropriate for younger readers than those attracted to the Scribners and Winston novels, and thus served as a bridge between the comics and Tom Swift, Jr. books on the one hand and Heinlein and Norton on the other. Particularly notable were Ellen MacGregor's *Miss Pickerel Goes to Mars* (1951), Eleanor Cameron's *The Wonderful Flight to the Mushroom Planet* (1954), and Jay Williams and Raymond Abrashkin's *Danny Dunn and the Anti-Gravity Paint* (1956), each of which had several sequels. In the 1960s and 1970s, two young adult authors who produced particularly significant science fiction for older readers were Madeleine L'Engle, whose Newbery Award–winning *A Wrinkle in Time* (1962) and its sequels dealt seriously with the nature of good and evil, and Virginia Hamilton, whose trilogy, beginning with *Justice and Her Brothers* (1978), centered on the responsible use of psychic powers. Other noteworthy books from this period were Ludek Pesek's Deutscher Jugendliteraturpreis–winning *Die Erde Ist Nah* (1970; English trans., *The Earth Is Near*, 1974), Sylvia Engdahl's Newbery Honor book *Enchantress from the Stars* (1970), Louise Lawrence's *Andra* (1971), and Laurence Yep's *Sweetwater* (1973). Reflecting the tensions of the Cold War era, many young adult novels delved into the possibility of surviving a nuclear holocaust or environmental disaster. The best of these was probably Robert C. O'Brien's *Z for Zachariah* (1975). Still other novels, perhaps responding to a perceived increase in teenage skepticism about the adult world, were set in repressive, dystopian societies. William Sleator's *House of Stairs* (1974) particularly stood out in this regard. Also worthy of mention here are the enormously popular, if rather pulpish, Perry Rhodan series, first published in Germany in 1961, and the work of the Russian Kir Bulychev, author of, among many other books, such short-story collections as *Chudesa v Gusliare* (1972; English trans., *Gusliar Wonders*, 1983).

By the late 1970s and 1980s, Heinlein, Clarke, and the other big guns had long ceased writing for children, and the field came to be dominated by books written by authors who specialized in young adult fiction. Sleator and Lawrence were two of the most important writers of this period. Sleator produced a number of well-done novels, among them *Interstellar Pig* (1985), the engagingly gross tale of a boy who saved Earth from invasion by playing an interactive board game. Lawrence published the dark post-Holocaust tale *Children of the Dust* (1985), among other novels. Two other fine writers were the Canadian Monica Hughes, best remembered for her Phoenix Award–winning *The Keeper of the Isis Light* (1980) and its sequels, which told the tale of a young woman who had been surgically altered to survive in an alien world, and H. M. Hoover, whose *The Rains of Eridan* (1977) is also a superior planetary adventure. Also producing excellent work were the German Gudrun Pausewang, author of the devastating post-Holocaust novel *Die Letzen Kinder von Schewenborn* (1983; English trans., *Last Children*, 1988), and the British Robert Westall, whose *Futuretrack Five* (1983) was set in a nightmarish future England.

Science fiction for young adults is often didactic in nature. Its tendency toward Bildungsroman, stories about young people finding a place for themselves in adult society, has already been mentioned. Since this is by definition an activity that requires thinking about the future, the science fiction novel can serve quite nicely as a metaphor for the scary choices facing young readers. Further, children, teens particularly, often find the adult world enormously restrictive, and dystopian science fiction, including a number of the books discussed above, can easily symbolize those concerns. Therefore key issues in the lives of children and teens, both those particular to the young and those of general concern to society, have always been reflected in young adult science fiction, and this has been especially true since the 1980s. Thus a novel such as Gillian Rubinstein's *Space De-*

Science Fiction. Illustration by David Wiesner from *June 29, 1999* (New York: Clarion Books, 1992), p. 32. Reproduced courtesy of the Cotsen Children's Library, Princeton University Library

mons (1986) explores both the joys and the dangers of computer games. Peter Dickinson's *Eva* (1988) concerns the possibilities of primate intelligence and the problem of teen sexuality. In Monica Hughes's *Invitation to the Game* (1990), teens ponder survival in a future where unemployment is the rule. In Lois Lowry's Newbery Award–winning *The Giver* (1993), a boy discovers how much his society has given up in order to achieve the appearance of contentment. Nancy Farmer's *The Ear, the Eye, and the Arm* (1994) explores the future of sub-Saharan Africa. Margaret Peterson Haddix's *Among the Hidden* (2000) centers on overpopulation. Cloning is central to Farmer's National Book Award–winning *House of the Scorpion* (2002). Philip Reeve's *Mortal Engines* (2001) and M. T. Anderson's *Feed* (2002) center on compulsive consumption, while Jennifer Armstrong and Nancy Butcher's *The Kiln* (2002) explores the dangers of both biological warfare and millennialism, and Alison Goodman's *Singing the Dogstar Blues* (2002) deals with racism. Any number of young adult science fiction novels, including those by Reeve and Armstrong above, have dealt with gender issues.

Science Fiction for Younger Children

So far little mention has been made of contemporary science fiction for younger readers, largely because there is relatively little of it and much of what exists is not very good. New works for preteens comparable to the *Miss Pickerel* and *Danny Dunn* books do continue to appear, for example K. A. Applegate's popular *Animorphs* series, but most are fantasies with the smallest tinge of science content and few are of significant literary quality. As Farah Mendlesohn pointed out in her essay in the April 2004 issue of *The Lion and the Unicorn*, most supposed science fiction picture books (and, she argues, many young adult science fiction novels for that matter) may not even qualify as true science fiction because they merely use the trappings of the genre for purposes incongruent with what Mendlesohn, building on the work of

John Clute, calls "full science fiction." Nonetheless, a small number of picture books do seem worthy of particular mention, most notably Arthur Yorinks and David Small's *Company's Coming* (1988), in which an elderly human couple deal with what must be the least frightening alien invasion in the history of the genre; David Wiesner's *June 29, 1999* (1995), which concerns a little girl's science experiment gone humorously awry; and Jeanne Willis and Tony Ross's *Dr. Xarggle's Book of Earthlets* (2002), which centers delightfully on an alien scientist's misunderstanding of how Earth babies operate.

Trends

In the 1950s and 1960s the great names in children's and young adult science fiction were Heinlein and Norton. In the 1970s and 1980s they were replaced in part by Hoover, Hughes, Sleator, and others who specialized exclusively in books for young adults. European writers like Bulychev and Pausewang also gained an audience in their native lands. Since then, new names have achieved success, from Lois Lowry to Nancy Farmer to M. T. Anderson. While most fantastic fiction for children and young adults qualifies as fantasy rather than science fiction, as can easily be ascertained by a quick survey of the reviews in magazines like *VOYA* or *Horn Book*, the regular publication of significant works such as *The Giver*, *House of the Scorpion*, and *Feed* bodes well for the continuing health of science fiction for young readers.

[*See also* Bildungsroman or Novel of Education; Fantasy; Series Books; Utopia and Dystopia; Young Adult Literature; *and biographies of figures mentioned in this article.*]

BIBLIOGRAPHY

Antczak, Janice. *Science Fiction: The Mythos of a New Romance*. New York: Neal-Schuman, 1985. Somewhat dated study centering on young adult science fiction and mythology.

Beetz, Kirk H., and Suzanne Niemeyer, eds. *Beacham's Guide to Literature for Young Adults*. Vol. 4, *Science Fiction, Mystery, Adventure, and Mythology*. Washington, D.C.: Beacham, 1993.

Clute, John, and Peter Nicholls. *The Encyclopedia of Science Fiction*. New York: St. Martin's, 1993. Standard reference work in the field.

Foundation: The International Review of Science Fiction 70 (Summer 1997): 1–82. Special "Young SF" issue.

Hintz, Carrie, and Elaine Ostry, eds. *Utopian and Dystopian Writing for Children and Young Adults*. New York: Routledge, 2002. Fine collection of scholarly essays.

Lenz, Millicent. *Nuclear Age Literature for Youth: The Quest for a Life-Affirming Ethic*. Chicago: ALA, 1990. Well-done study of nuclear war fiction.

The Lion and the Unicorn 28.2 (2004): 171–313. Special children's and young adult science fiction issue.

Molson, Francis J., and Susan G. Miles. "Young Adult Science Fiction." In *Anatomy of Wonder: A Critical Guide to Science Fiction*, 4th ed., edited by Neil Barron. New Providence, N.J.: Bowker, 1995. Fine short history of the field, with excellent annotated bibliography; the 5th edition dropped its separate chapter on young adult science fiction.

Sullivan, C. W., III. *Science Fiction for Young Readers*. Westport, Conn.: Greenwood, 1993. Scholarly essay collection.

Sullivan, C. W., III. *Young Adult Science Fiction*. Westport, Conn.: Greenwood, 1999. Scholarly essay collection; includes an extensive bibliography of secondary materials.

MICHAEL LEVY

Scieszka, Jon (1954–), American author of picture books and middle-grade fiction. Scieszka is the author most associated with the postmodern pastiche that became popular in children's literature toward the end of the 20th century. Born in Flint, Michigan, Scieszka (pronounced SHEH-ska) grew up second oldest of six boys, and he was early taken with the comedy of books such as Dr. Seuss's *Green Eggs and Ham* (1960), which he characterizes as "goofy." Though nearly diverted into a career in medicine, Scieszka followed his youthful dreams and received an MFA in writing from Columbia University. Ten years of teaching elementary school in New York gave him a close acquaintanceship with the reading tastes of young people, but it was his 1986 meeting with illustrator Lane Smith that really precipitated his entry into children's literature.

Their first book together was *The True Story of the Three Little Pigs by A. Wolf* (1989), a satirical comedy that allows the protesting wolf to plead his case from prison with his version of the famous tale. An immediate critics' and audience favorite for its sly humor and slick, contemporary illustrations and design (by Smith's wife, Molly Leach), the book also fortuitously coincided with a burgeoning interest in folk tale revision and expansion, a direction in turn galvanized by the success of Scieszka and Smith's works. Their next project, *The Stinky Cheese Man and Other Fairly Stupid Tales* (1992), won a Caldecott Honor, and it remains arguably the team's touchstone work. Linked by the commentary of Jack the Narrator, revisited stories range from Andersen's "The Ugly Duckling" ("The Really Ugly Duckling" "grew up to be just a really ugly duck") to the Grimms' Little Red Riding Hood ("Little Red Running Shorts" bails out of her story in a fit of pique) to the internationally told "The Gingerbread Man" ("The Stinky Cheese Man" has such a stench that nobody wants to catch him). The work spoofs not only folklore but also books themselves: the title page is emblazoned with the words "Title Page," the table of contents falls on Chicken Licken, Jack moves the closing endpaper into the body of the book to dupe the giant into thinking the book is over, and the Little Red Hen clucks disparagingly about the ISBN bar code on the back cover.

In the pair's next picture book, *Math Curse* (1995), a girl finds herself viewing her daily life in terms of math problems, so slicing up a pizza becomes a question about fractions, a trip on the school bus becomes a logic problem, and jokey multiple-choice quizzes combine rueful comedy with practical responses. *Squids Will Be Squids: Fresh Morals, Beastly Fables* (1998) is a neo-Aesop collection with quirkily comic fables such as "Piece of Toast and Froot Loops" (the moral is, "Breakfast is the most important meal of the day"). Departing from the duo's tendency toward interrogation of established genres or curricular subjects is *Baloney (Henry P.)* (2001), though wordplay is rife in this shaggy-dog story of an alien kid's spinning a wild space-travel story to explain his tardiness to his extraterrestrial teacher. *Science Verse* (2004) treats or lampoons scientific subjects to the tune of recognizable poems and songs (the poetic treatise on "Evolution" can be sung to the tune of "The Battle Hymn of the Republic"). Scieszka also plays with familiar folklore in the picture books *The Frog Prince, Continued* (1991), illustrated by Steve Johnson, and *The Book That Jack Wrote* (1994), illustrated by Daniel Adel, but these titles are overshadowed by his partnerships with Smith.

Outside of the picture book genre, Scieszka is the author of the *Time Warp Trio* series of easy readers (many illustrated by Lane Smith), wherein a magical book transports three friends through time in comic, playfully titled adventures such as *Knights of the Kitchen Table* (1991), *Tut, Tut* (1996), and *See You Later, Gladiator* (2000). Concerned with statistics showing boys lagging behind on reading ability, Scieszka developed a literacy program for boys in the Web site www.guysread.com (supported by his short-story anthology *Guys Write for Guys Read*, 2005), where men are encouraged to be literacy role models and boys can seek and offer book recommendations. Scieszka's own titles are firm audience favorites with boys and with girls, fulfilling Scieszka's faith in a young audience that is both "silly *and* smart." The books' affection for corny humor and freewheeling irreverence is inviting, their high-styled visual emphasis makes them both unintimidating and sophisticated enough for older readers, and their quirky yet ebullient embrace of narrative sends a clear message: come on in, it's fun in here.

[*See also* Easy Readers; Fairy Tales and Folk Tales; Literacy; Parody; Picture Books; *and biographies of figures mentioned in this article.*]

BIBLIOGRAPHY

Apseloff, Marilyn. "The Big Bad Wolf: New Approaches to an Old Folk Tale." *Children's Literature Association Quarterly* 15, no. 3 (1990): 135–137.

McGillis, Roderick. " 'Ages All': Readers, Texts, and Intertexts in *The Stinky Cheese Man and Other Fairly Stupid Tales.*" In *Transcending Boundaries: Writing for a Dual Audience of Children and Adults*, edited by Sandra Beckett, 111–126. New York: Garland, 1999.

Stevenson, Deborah. " 'If You Read This Last Sentence, It Won't Tell You Anything': Postmodernism, Self-Referentiality, and *The Stinky Cheese Man.*" *Children's Literature Association Quarterly* 19, no. 1 (1994): 32–34.

DEBORAH STEVENSON

Scott, Ann Herbert (1926–), American author of children's picture books that embrace themes concerning the American West, ethnicity, and family. Scott earned a BA from the University of Pennsylvania in 1948 and an MA in 1958 from Yale. While working in housing projects in New Haven in the 1950s, she was appalled at the paucity of books depicting urban neighborhoods and children of color. Among other books, she wrote *Sam* to address this void. In *Sam* (1967), named an ALA Notable Book, the young African American protagonist attempts repeatedly to get the attention of his busy parents and siblings. When the family realizes that they have all chastised Sam one after the other, together they affirm his role in the family and give him a useful task. Scott's works such as *Not Just One* (1968), *On Mother's Lap* (1972), *A Brand Is Forever* (1993), and *Brave as a Mountain Lion* (1996) have been praised for their simplicity and for the author's ability to convey universal themes in particularized settings such as the inner city or a ranch in Nevada.

[*See also* African American Literature *and* Multiculturalism and Children's Books.]

MICHELLE H. MARTIN

Scott, Hugh, Scottish novelist. Promoted by Walker Books as the "Master of Menace," Scott has mostly produced supernatural thrillers since his debut, *The Shaman's Stone* (1988), though he has also written two after-the-bomb novels, *The Plant That Ate the World* (1989) and *Why Weeps the Brogan?* (1989), and humorous stories for younger readers: *Freddie and the Enormouse* (1989), *The Summertime Santa* (1990), and *Change the King!* (1991). Scott published ten books between 1989 and 1991. *Why Weeps the Brogan?* (which won the Whitbread Award) explores the child's confused feelings about codependency with the mother, and about venturing into the wider world. The confined, postcatastrophe setting and, most noticeably, the ending pay homage to Arthur Golding's *Lord of the Flies*. Like the Palace of Green Porcelain in H. G. Wells's *The Time Machine*, Scott's damaged museum demonstrates that history and memory are fragmented. *Why Weeps the Brogan?* epitomizes Scott's cliffhanger-packed taut plotting, as well as his conspicuous style: striking metaphors, defamiliarization, minor sentences, and split paragraphs. Bullied Spindletrim Tom in *The Camera Obscura* (1990) becomes more assertive and broadminded under his grandfather's tutelage. In an eerie scene, Spindletrim encounters a false grandfather in an ersatz antique shop and a church minister who eats boys—unpleasant clerics often appear in Scott's work. In *A Box of Tricks* (1991), an accumulation of odd happenings cascades to a dramatic climax after John and Maggie's magician great-grandfather conjure up Simon Welkin, an 18th-century stonemason whose fondness for a bet is his undoing in the past and the present. The title of *The Place Between* (1994) refers not only to the parallel world impinging though Bosky Wood, but also to the narrator Stella's transition into adolescent sexual awareness. Harry Rothwell's perception, in *Giants* (1999), that the cathedral is "like a vast machine" turns out to be more than a stylistic quirk.

[*See also* Fantasy; Science Fiction; *and* Young Adult Literature.]

PETER BRAMWELL

Scott, Michael (1959–), award-winning Irish author of more than ninety books for children and teenagers. Called "the king of Irish fantasy," Scott has his adventure stories invoke Irish legends and the supernatural, as in his fantasy trilogy *The De Danann Tales* (1991–1993), *The Last of the Fianna* (1987), the *Arcana* series written with Morgan Llywelyn, and his horror novels set in contemporary Ireland, *October Moon* (1992) and *Wolf Moon* (1995). An international expert on Celtic mythology, he has written several definitive collections of Irish folklore for young readers: *Irish Myths and Legends* (1983), *Irish Animal Tales* (1989), and *Irish Hero Tales* (1989).

[*See also* Fantasy; Ireland; Irish Mythology; Llywelyn, Morgan; *and* Myths.]

PATRICIA KENNON

Scott, Walter (1771–1832), pioneer historical novelist of the 19th century. Scottish-born Sir Walter Scott influenced many novelists, including James Fenimore Cooper and Edgar Allen Poe (American), Jules Verne (French), and Charles Dickens (British). Scott struggled most of his life to achieve financial stability as a lawyer (he was admitted to the Edinburgh Bar in 1792) and then as deputy sheriff of Silkirkshire (1799). However, he continued to pursue his passion for literature, as evidenced by his vast body of literary work and by antiquarian artifacts that he kept on display in his somewhat fantastic Abbotsford residence. His frequent visits to ruined abbeys in the north of England, such as Riveleaux and Fountains, are also reflected in his fiction.

Scott purchased an interest in Ballantyne publishing in 1805 and worked tirelessly as an editor until 1826, when the business failed. A methodical, prolific writer, he romanticized medieval Europe for an emerging middle-class audience, and appealed to the English nostalgia for an imagined past as an escape from the social and economic turbulent changes of the Industrial Revolution. He began his publishing career with a long poetic work, *The Lay of the Last Minstrel* (1805). Another more popular work, *The Lady of the Lake* (1810), was one of many he completed in the genres of poetry, nonfiction, and drama. His plays were staged in London and Edinburgh during his lifetime. He is remembered today, however, for his historical novels. His first, *Waverly* (1814), published anonymously, began a series of twenty-five fictional works later known as the *Waverly* novels. Some were attributed to "the author of *Waverly*," others were under the pseudonyms Jebediah Cleisbotham, Mr. Laurence Templeton, and Chrystal Crogangry, and most were published by A. Constable out of Edinburgh. The series has been perennially reprinted under Scott's own name. His novels were so popular with the English Regent that Scott was granted a baronetcy in 1819.

Most of the Waverly novels are no longer read, but a few, such as *Ivanhoe* (1820; made into several 20th-century movies and TV productions), nevertheless have become the source for popular images of knights, kings, queens, princesses, and the all-important jousting contests of the late Middle Ages. The novels appeal to young readers looking for tales of long-ago adventure and heroism, although Scott's grasp of history has been seriously criticized. His novel *Rob Roy* (1817) is still popular and is typical of a group of novels, including *Heart of Midlothian* (1818) and *The Bride of Lammermoor* (1819), through which he presented the history of Scotland to a larger world. Considered by critics like Pope-Hennessy as one of his weaker works, *Rob Roy* chronicles the heroic attempts of a highland chief fallen on hard times to take care of his people. Rob Roy overcomes the machinations of his English overlords through strength, skill, and guile, but principally because he is an honorable man, a quality shared by most of Scott's heroes. Readers are attracted to the heroism, vivid historical settings, and even the anachronistic language. But Scott is also credited with stabilizing the popularity of the gothic and the historical novel, and so his formal legacy is at least as important as his historical subjects. His critics, not all of them flattering, have attempted to explain away his popular, as well as his literary, successes, attributing them to his appeal to a wide range of readers. That popularity persists to the present day in media recreations of his works and references to them in the fiction of others.

[*See also* Historical Fiction.]

BIBLIOGRAPHY

Lauber, John. *Sir Walter Scott*. Rev. ed. Boston: Twayne, 1989.
Sutherland, John. *The Life of Walter Scott: A Critical Biography*. Oxford: Blackwell, 1995.

Janice M. Bogstad

Scudder, Horace E. (1838–1902), American editor and author of children's books, a descendant of New England Puritans. According to Horace Elisha Scudder, his parents (who were orthodox Congregationalists) zealously preserved Puritan traditions and principles. He later joined the Episcopal Church, but he recognized the virtues of Puritanism—praising its emphasis on family life—as well as its drawbacks. Nonetheless, his own childhood was very happy. "The tendency of the system was to ignore childhood," he said; and to the Puritan way of thought, works of the imagination, being untrue, were abhorrent. As a writer and an editor he devoted himself to promoting both. The *Dictionary of American Biography* states that he "rendered notable service as a pioneer in the provision of the best reading for the young."

Scudder received a classical education at Williams College, where at age seventeen he edited the *Williams Quarterly*. After graduating he taught privately in New York and published his first collection of fantasy stories, *Seven Little People and Their Friends* (1862). Two more collections followed, all written before he was thirty-two. Many of the stories derive from Hans Christian Andersen or George MacDonald (or, as in the case of "A Christmas Stocking with a Hole in It," from Charles Dickens's *A Christmas Carol*), but have American settings. In his second collection, the evocation of Cape Cod in "Carl's Voyaging" is memorable, and in "The Pot of Gold" he uses that landscape again for a story of a quest that owes much to MacDonald. These were his last original fairy stories.

In 1864 Scudder went back to Boston as reader and editorial assistant to the publishers Hurd & Houghton (later Houghton Mifflin), for whom he worked until his death. His eight Bodley Family travelogues, written between 1875 and 1885, were undertaken at their suggestion. Scudder made the series a distinguished one in a genre often regarded as hackwork. The Bodley family has an endearing life and warmth, and poems and traditional tales are woven into the accounts of their doings and travels. For him it was far more important that a book should stimulate the imagination than preach. He acted on this principle in his editorship of the *Riverside Magazine for Young People*, whose first issue appeared in January 1867 and whose name is synonymous with high literary quality. Distinguished writers, including Hans Christian Andersen, contributed to it, together with the finest illustrators of the day.

When *Riverside* ceased publication at the end of 1870 (having been financially unsuccessful), Scudder went on to edit the *Atlantic Monthly* for Houghton. In 1894 he published *Childhood in Literature and Art*, a collection of four lectures he had given at the Lowell Institute, among them an evaluation of the work of Hans Christian Andersen.

BIBLIOGRAPHY

Greene, David L. "The Riverside Magazine for Young People." In *Children's Periodicals of the United States*, edited by R. Gordon Kelly, 367–370. Westport, Conn.: Greenwood Press, 1984.
Haviland, Virginia. "The Travelogue Storybook of the Nineteenth Century." In *The Hewins Lectures, 1947–1962*, edited by Siri Andrews, 25–63. Boston: Horn Book, 1963.

Gillian Avery

Sealsfield, Charles (1793–1864), Austrian writer of novels about America that were widely read as adventure stories. Born in the Austrian province of Moravia (now part of the Czech Republic), Sealsfield, whose real name was Karl Anton Postl, became a student, and later secretary, at a Jesuit convent in Prague, from which he absconded in 1823 for unknown reasons. He resurfaced in America under the name Charles Sealsfield and returned to Europe in 1826, where he published both German and English versions of his first book on America, using yet another pseudonym, Charles Sidons. After more travels between Europe and America he lived mainly in Switzerland. The bulk of his writings appeared between 1833 and 1843, which also marks the apex of his popularity. His real identity became known only after his death in 1864.

Today Sealsfield is studied mainly as a historical and political writer who described the development of America, on the whole admiringly though not altogether uncritically, from the point of view of an impassioned opponent to the reactionary tendencies in post-Napoleonic Europe. Locating America's strength and utopian potential primarily at its frontier, he set his novels mostly in the South and Southwest. It is mainly because of their vivid descriptions of pristine nature, harsh living conditions, and incessant fights that the books survived, in suitably curtailed adaptations, as adventure stories for the young. Among Sealsfield's most frequently reprinted and adapted stories are his novels *Der Legitime und die Republikaner* (The Legitimate Man and the Republicans, 1833), a revised edition of his *Tokeah, or The White Rose*, first published in English in 1829, and *Nathan der Squatter-Regulator, oder Der erste Amerikaner in Texas* (Nathan the Squatter-Regulator, or The First American in Texas, 1837), and especially the novella "Die Prärie am Jacinto," from his *Das Cajütenbuch oder Nationale Charakteristiken* (The Prairie on the Jacinto, in The Cabin Book, or National Character Portraits, 1841). Sealsfield is the first in a series of German writers of the American frontier (his followers being, among others, Friedrich Gerstäcker and Karl May) who shaped the image, popular well into the 20th century, of America as a land of wilderness, adventure, and rugged individualism.

[*See also* Adventure Books; United States; *and* Westerns.]

BIBLIOGRAPHY

Sammons, Jeffrey L. *Ideology, Mimesis, Fantasy: Charles Sealsfield, Friedrich Gerstäcker, Karl May, and Other German Novelists of America*. Chapel Hill: University of North Carolina Press, 1998.

DIETER PETZOLD

Searle, Ronald (1920–), graphic artist of international stature born in Cambridge, England. Searle's harrowing sketches of life as a Japanese prisoner of war brought him to public notice in the late 1940s, but he is best remembered for his cartoons of unruly pupils at a fictitious girls school called St. Trinian's. The girls, whose rakish hats, abbreviated gym-slips, black stockings, and suspenders hinted at a sexual precocity in keeping with the rebellious anarchy that made them more than a match for teachers, appealed to the public in general and boys in particular. In the usually staid world of schoolgirl fiction they remain unique.

Down with Skool (1953), a collaboration with the journalist Geoffrey Willans, was also a success. It chronicled, in the first person, the exploits of "nigel molesworth," a pupil at "st. custard's," an imaginary boys' preparatory school. Spelling and punctuation might not have been Molesworth's strong points, but his subtlety, craft, wit, and philosophical bent placed him firmly in charge of his school environment. Three more successful *Molesworth* books followed before Willans's early death in 1958.

[*See also* Boys' Books and Fiction; Comic Books; Girls' Books and Fiction; Graphic Novels; *and* School Stories.]

GEOFFREY FENWICK

Sea Stories. Sea stories have charmed children for as long as coastal fishers could tell tales by the fire at night. Stories of Sinbad the sailor and Odysseus have been told and retold in dozens of languages over the course of millennia. The changeable nature of the sea itself and the number of cultures bordering on its bounty or its harshness combine to make it a remarkably versatile element of metaphor, sometimes symbolizing opposite aspects of human life from story to story or even within the same story.

Isolation and Camaraderie

The ocean can isolate island cultures and individuals. The classic shipwreck stories, Daniel Defoe's *Robinson Crusoe* (1719) and Johann David Wyss's *Swiss Family Robinson* (1812; English trans., 1814), allow the author to create microcosms of human experience and studies in loneliness in an adventurous setting young people can connect with. In 1954, William Golding's *Lord of the Flies* presented a more modern take on the same theme: in isolation a group of young boys devolves into all the dysfunctions of human adult cultures in a remarkably short time. John Steinbeck's *The Pearl*, from 1947, takes on the isolation of an island culture from a more colonialist perspective: the natural sea environment provides bounty, but human corruption sometimes loses sight of its wonders. Scott O'Dell's *Island of the Blue Dolphins* (1960), winner of the Newbery Medal and many other honors, shows how the isolation of island life can deepen self-reliance and appreciation of nature. Its lush depictions of ocean flora and fauna could make almost any child into a budding marine biologist.

On the other hand, sea stories are sometimes tales of camaraderie, largely when the work of surviving ocean voyages requires people to draw together in ways that otherwise would be impossible for them. Two novels written over a century apart, both aimed at young people, embody different aspects of sea-story camaraderie: Rudyard Kipling's *Cap-*

Sea Story. Endpaper design for *Swallows and Amazons* by Arthur Ransome (London: Junior Literary Guild, 1931). Reproduced courtesy of the Cotsen Children's Library, Princeton University Library

tains Courageous (1897), like Avi's *The True Confessions of Charlotte Doyle* (1990), tells the story of a somewhat sheltered young person who learns leadership, hard work, and teamwork in a turbulent ocean voyage. However, *Charlotte Doyle* is in some ways *Captains Courageous* turned on its ear: from the vantage of the late 20th century, Avi can see that his young heroine's new role would have been as unexpected and contrary to social norms as Kipling's hero's transformation would have been welcomed by those around him. In each case, the physical distance of the sea from the expectations of proper society allows young people to shed constraints, internal or external. For some societies, the sea provided such freedom for entire groups of people, and children's books like Clyde Robert Bulla's *Viking Adventure* (1963) have been written to depict that type of culture in microcosm, with their own constraints and social systems. Other books, such as Katherine Paterson's *Jacob Have I Loved* from 1980, depict more socially closed, constrained fishing villages, no matter what the century.

Arthur Ransome's twelve-book Swallows and Amazons series, starting with the volume of the same title, describes a different kind of camaraderie entirely. The bands of 1930s British children in these books (published between 1930 and 1947) have been steeped in the sea stories of the past, as well as in other tales of exploration and empire. As the series progresses, the lines blur between the stories the children tell and their actual adventures: *Peter Duck* takes them into the mid-Atlantic, and *Missee Lee* depicts them sailing in the China Seas, but the old sailor Peter Duck himself is referred to as imaginary in other books, and it becomes hard not to see Missee Lee in the same light. For these children, too, sailing provides both camaraderie and freedom from expectations, including gender role expectations for the girls.

Changing Genre

The archetypal book the Swallows and the Amazons devoured, as many real-life children have through the years, was Robert Louis Stevenson's *Treasure Island*. From its publication in 1881–1882, *Treasure Island* became a classic of the sea story genre, and the characters, especially Long John Silver, have become watchwords for the handling of pirates in fiction. With this work and *Kidnapped*, Stevenson set the tone for an entire subgenre. Later books like Sid Fleischman's *The Ghost in the Noonday Sun* (1965) take on the traditional tropes of pirates and a desert island, with a more modern consciousness. In 1924 the Newbery Medal–winning *The Dark Frigate* by Charles Boardman Hawes had a much more traditional take on pirates, and the change in writing style between the two is indicative of the time in which each was written. In the 1990s, Sam Llewelyn's *Deadeye* (1991) replaced the old pirates with the new: environmental criminals dumping toxins in the ocean. As society changes, so do the social constraints from which the sea provides freedom, and not all of the ways of flaunting convention are equally good.

And not all sea stories are tales of unadulterated freedom. Starting, probably not coincidentally, in the aftermath of the 1960s civil rights movement, authors began to be interested in the slave ships that crisscrossed the Atlantic until the 19th century. Outstanding examples of this subgenre include *Dark Venture* (1968) by Audrey White Beyer and *The Slave Dancer* (1973) by Paula Fox. While there is ultimate escape in most slave-trade books, there is no illusion that anyone touched by it escaped unscathed, no matter how young they were. Compared with a lighthearted, straightforward sailing story, the slave-transport stories bring a somber note to the sea story genre.

Like and yet unlike the rest of the sea story genres are the stories that use the sea in fantastical settings. High adventures in deep-sea submarines have been popular ever since Jules Verne's *Twenty Thousand Leagues under the Sea* appeared in 1870. Some young people are also content to stay closer to the shore, exploring the science fictional possibilities of dolphin intelligence in books like Madeleine L'Engle's *A Ring of Endless Light* (1980). On the other hand, popular fantasy series like Ursula K. LeGuin's Earthsea books and the multiauthored Voyage of the *Bassett* series use sea voyages through fantastical realms as quest structures for the personal growth of characters—just as Homer's *Odyssey* did.

[*See also* Adventure Books; Colonial Fiction; Fantasy; *and biographies of figures mentioned in this article.*]

BIBLIOGRAPHY

Furnas, J. C. *Voyage to Windward: The Life of Robert Louis Stevenson*. New York: Sloane, 1951.

Hunt, Peter. *Arthur Ransome*. Boston: Twayne, 1991.

Stanford, William Bedell. *The Ulysses Theme: A Study in the Adaptability of a Traditional Hero*. Oxford: Blackwell, 1954.

MARISSA K. LINGEN

Sebestyen, Ouida (1924–), American novelist born in Vernon, Texas, and a graduate of the University of Colorado. Sebestyen began writing in high school, submitting her first manuscript to publishers (who rejected it) at the age of twenty. She first found success in writing short stories for magazines. Finally, in 1979, she published *Words by Heart*, the emotional story of an African American girl's struggle against the violent bigotry of her community and times. The novel received much recognition, including the 1980 International Reading Association Children's Book Award and a Best Book of the Year citation from the *New York Times*. In addition to a sequel (*On Fire*, 1985), Sebestyen has authored several other novels, mostly set in her beloved American West, and often dealing similarly with attempts to find worth and beauty in the face of bitter hardship. She has also authored short stories under the name Igen Sebestyen.

[*See also* African American Literature *and* Multiculturalism and Children's Books.]

NANCY J. KEANE

Secret Garden, The. *See* Burnett, Frances Hodgson.

Secret Seven Series. *See* Blyton, Enid.

Sedgwick, Catharine Maria (1789–1867), American author who used didacticism in her writing for both children and adults. Educated mainly at home, Sedgwick refused several marriage proposals, preferring to remain single and live with her brothers' families throughout her life. Wanting to extol the strict Calvinism of her youth and champion honesty, kindness, and self-improvement, she began writing a novel, *A New-England Tale* (1822), followed by *Redwood* (1824) and *Hope Leslie* (1827), which established her as one of the founders of American literature along with Washington Irving and James Fenimore Cooper. Her two children's books, *The Travellers: A Tale Designed for Young People* (1825) and *The Deformed Boy* (1826), both stressed humility and sympathy for others. Especially concerned about education, Sedgwick also published collections of tales for children, *A Love Token for Children* (1838) and *Stories for Young Persons* (1841), and for young adults, *Tales and Sketches* (1835 and 1844). Additional stories appeared in magazines such as *Juvenile Miscellany* and *Godey's Lady's Book*, anthologies, annual gift books, and pamphlets. Intended mainly for Sunday school reading, they presented the virtues of hard work, the significance of choosing right over wrong, the value of charity for the poor, the worth of kindness to animals, and the importance of forgiveness. Other books for children included a biography of the Romantic poet Lucretia Maria Davidson and *Letters from Abroad to Kindred at Home* (1841), about her fifteen-month tour of Europe in 1839 and 1840. Sedgwick thought that inadequate home life and poor manners were the major problems in America, her topic in *Morals or Manners, or Hints for Our Young People* (1846). Sedgwick also founded the Society for the Aid and Relief of Poor Women and organized the first free school in New York. She simultaneously worked many years with the Women's Prison Association of New York, serving as its president from 1848 to 1863.

[*See also* Cooper, James Fenimore; Irving, Washington; *and* Moral Tales.]

LYNDA G. ADAMSON

Seed, Jenny (1930–), a South African writer of the last quarter of the 20th century, best known for her closely researched historical novels. She also wrote stories for young children, mostly with a modern setting, featuring both white and black children. She has been criticized for her stereotyping and clichéd style, and for setting black savagery as a foil to white civilization. Her admirers reject the charge of racism, praising her sympathetic portrayal of black characters (*The New Fire*, 1983; *The Hungry People*, 1992), her even-handed portrayal of historical events, and her explicit rejection of prejudice (*Place among the Stones*, 1987).

ELWYN JENKINS

Sefton, Catherine. *See* Waddell, Martin.

Segal, Lore (1928–), Austrian-born Jewish American children's book translator and writer. Born Lore Groszmann in Vienna, Segal lived "the first ten comfortable years" of her life as an only child and her grandparents' only grandchild. After Hitler annexed Austria, her family was persecuted. She was sent to England with the *Kindertransport* (she is interviewed in the documentary film *Into the Arms of Strangers: Stories of the Kindertransport*, 2000, in which she is one of the most articulate witnesses). A "tear-jerking letter full of sunsets" she wrote at age ten to a refugee committee enabled her parents to go to England. She has written a number of children's books, including the award-winning *Tell Me a Mitzi* (1970), but perhaps her most enduring contribution to children's literature is her fine translation (with Randall Jarrell) of the Grimm brothers' fairy tales in *The Juniper Tree and Other Tales from Grimm* (1973), illustrated by Maurice Sendak.

[*See also* Fairy Tales and Folk Tales; *and biographies of figures mentioned in this article.*]

J. D. STAHL

Segawa Yasuo (1932–), Japanese artist and picture book artist born in Okazaki, Aichi, Japan. After working as an illustrator in Tokyo, he met Tadashi Matsui of Fukuinkan Shoten Publishers and started publishing picture books. His first picture book was *Kitsune no Yomeiri* (1960; English trans., *The Fox's Wedding*, 1963), a Japanese folk tale with text by Miyoko Matsutani. He has experimented with lines and forms following old Japanese styles. His art has richness, humor, and dramatic process. *Fushigina Takenoko* (1963; English trans., *Taro and the Bamboo Shoot*, 1974), written by Masako Matsuno, was awarded the Grand Prix of the first BIB in 1967.

[*See also* Illustrations; Japan; Picture Books; *and biographies of figures mentioned in this article.*]

TOMOKO MASAKI

Segun, Mabel (1930–), Nigerian poet and author of children's books. Segun is also a teacher, editor, copywriter, broadcaster, head of an English and social studies department, executive secretary of the Nigerian book development council, inspector of education, research fellow, director of the Children's Literature Documentation and Research Center, president of the Children's Literature Association, consultant of African children's literature programs, and trustee of the Association of Nigerian Authors and the Nigerian Book Foundation. Segun was born in a family with a strong literary tradition. Her brothers, sister, daughter, and father (her role model for hard work, creativity, and service to humanity) are all accomplished authors. *My Father's Daughter* (1965), her first publication for children, and *My Mother's Daughter* (1985) are autobiographical readers that discuss a happy childhood relationship with her parents. Her desire to make poetry accessible, lively, and enjoyable, while promoting cultural identity for African children through creative methods, led her to coedit the publication of a two-volume poetry anthology, *Under the Mango Tree* (1980). In *The Twins and the Tree Spirits* (1991) and *Respect for Life* (1997), Segun passes on to children her concerns about humanity's struggle for equilibrium in human rights, the environment, and peaceful coexistence.

[*See also* Africa: Northern Africa; Poetry; *and* Teaching Children's Literature.]

MAHOUMBAH KLOBAH

Comtesse de Ségur. Illustration by Françoise Franc-Nohain from *Les malheurs de Sophie* (Tours, France: Alfred Mame, 1930). REPRODUCED COURTESY OF THE COTSEN CHILDREN'S LIBRARY, PRINCETON UNIVERSITY LIBRARY

Ségur, Sophie, Comtesse de (1799–1874), French novelist of Russian origin, born Sophie Rostopchine. At the age of fifty-seven she published *Nouveaux contes de fées* (English trans., *Fairy Tales for Little Folks*, 1869) with the great publisher Hachette, but gave up the fairy tales to write some twenty novels, which made the fortune of the *Bibliothèque rose illustrée*. In the Fleurville trilogy, Ségur introduces the château de Fleurville, where aristocratic happiness exists alongside bourgeois virtues. This women's world rests on gentleness and on refusal of adventure. However, violence is still looming: for instance, in *Les malheurs de Sophie* (1859; English trans., *The Misfortunes of Sophy*, 1937) Mme de Réan, despite her distinction, is not a good mother who corrects her daughter's failings; rather, she actually provokes them. The meaning of this book has often been misinterpreted: for instance, it was translated in 1929 in New York as *Sophie, the Story of a Bad Little Girl*. By giving her own first name to Sophie, the author emphasizes an autobiographic link. This darkly humorous novel, marked by a dramatic and repetitive concentration, has had a huge success that calls for study. The events happen before *Les petites filles modèles* (Small Model Girls, 1858), where Sophie has forgotten this emotional tragedy. She will actually remember it in the last book of the Fleurville trilogy, *Les vacances* (The Holidays, 1859), an astonishingly beautiful novel, full of different characters appearing successively in the foreground.

In the novels following the trilogy, all set in the province of Normandy, where Fleurville was located, Ségur worked through different social situations. For example, in *Les mémoires d'un âne* (1860; English trans., *Adventures of a Donkey*, 1881) and *Pauvre Blaise* (Poor Blaise, 1861), the point of view is different, and the rich are criticized. *La soeur de Gribouille* (Gribouille's Sister, 1862) marks another turning point: the aristocratic world is left behind for a confrontation between the ordinary people and the bourgeoisie.

At this point, Ségur seemed to face a dilemma: leave Fleurville and open up to other questions, or to go back to Fleurville and explore social concerns; she did both. In *Francois le bossu* (1864; English trans., *The Little Hunchback*, 1883) and *Diloy le chemineau* (Diloy the Tramp, 1868), the author offers some melancholy lines marked by religious austerity. Then everything goes wrong at the estate of Plaisance in *Après la pluie le beau temps* (After Rain, Good Weather, 1871), the last novel before Ségur's death.

In contrast, *L'auberge de l'ange gardien* (1863; English trans., *The Inn of the Guardian Angel*, 1897) was not a repetition. This novel was about two ordinary little boys, as sweet as perfect little girls: "are they kind, good boys, well mannered? I do believe it! They are real darlings! As polite as ladies are, as calm as priests are!" In the sequel, *Le général Dourakine* (General Dourakine, 1863), Ségur returns to her remote childhood in Russia through a journey both regressive and liberating. While rejecting the Russian feudal system, she finds inspiration in her own family estate, Voronovo, and turns the inn of the guardian angel into a new castle with extensive grounds. Although the hosts are fair and benevolent, they still are unreasonably wealthy, and the nearly magic intervention of the very rich General Dourakine reveals the difficulty Ségur faced in maintaining a sense of realism.

Ségur produced a serious body of work, moving between autobiography and reflection on society. Some critics even think that *La fortune de Gaspard* (Gaspard's Fortune, 1866), which deals with ambition and industrial development, is a book for adults. Ségur can sometimes also be satirical, as in *Les deux nigauds* (The Two Ninnies, 1862), *Un bon petit diable* (A Good Little Devil, 1865), and *Jean qui grogne et Jean qui rit* (Jean Who Grumbles and Jean Who Laughs, 1865), where we can find the influences of vaudeville and operetta. And she likes ridiculous characters, who inspire illustrators' vigor. The endings of some novels can be very sudden: "Holidays and the cousins arrived at last" (the last sentence in *Les petites filles modèles*), or "End of M Dormère, of Georges and of the book" (*Après la pluie le beau temps*). Together with cruel irony and casualness—the characters just disappear once they are not useful anymore—it is certainly in this style that her greatest originality can be found.

[*See also* Fairy Tales and Folk Tales; France; *and* Girls' Books and Fiction.]

BIBLIOGRAPHY

Diesbach, Ghislain de. *La Comtesse de Ségur, née Rostopchine*. Paris: Perrin, 1999.

Kreyder, Laura. *L'enfance des saints et des autres: Essai sur la comtesse de Ségur*. Fasano di Puglia, Italy: Schena-Nizet, 1987.

Marcoin, Francis. *La Comtesse de Ségur; ou, Le bonheur immobile*. Arras, France: Artois Presses Université, 1999.

FRANCIS MARCOIN

Seidel, Heinrich (1842–1906), German writer of idyllic, post-Romantic children's literature at the dawn of industrialization. After 1866, Seidel became an engineer, until 1880 when he began to concentrate full-time on writing. An author of fantastic novels, novellas, collections of poems, stories, essays, and fairy tales for both adults and children, Seidel mostly portrayed the idyllic aspects of bourgeois life in the country. He was strongly influenced by Theodor Fontane (1819–1898), Theodor Storm (1817–1888), and Hans Christian Andersen, and like Andersen, Seidel often employed a witness external to the story for credibility. Seidel's tales contain a moral and compassionate tone as if to counter the social pressures of industrialization. His novellas about *Leberecht Hühnchen* (1882, 1888, 1890) are mostly known among adults, while his collections *Ernst und Scherz: Kindergedichte* (Earnestness and Jest: Children's Poems, 1884) and *Wintermärchen* (Winter Tales, 1885) are mainly addressed to children. In 1902, Seidel received an honorary doctorate from the University of Rostock.

[*See also* Fairy Tales and Folk Tales; Fantasy; Germany; Poetry; *and biographies of figures mentioned in this article*.]

IRIS SCHUBERT

Seidel, Ina (1885–1974), German author of poetry, prose, and essays, who during the1920s and 1930s was recognized as among the best known and most widely read writers in Germany. Her most popular work, the novel *Das Wunschkind* (The Planned Child, 1930), is a historical narrative about a woman and her family in Germany before and during the Napoleonic wars of liberation (1792–1813). Seidel's themes and topics include a broad range of historical subjects, biographical writings, sentimental poetry, and essays on German literature. Seidel's Christian nationalist ideology led to a short-lived embrace of National Socialism, and she devoted a great deal of writing after 1945 to coming to terms with her actions. Her dedication to subjects related to women, including women's roles in history and literature, mark Seidel as prominent figure in German women's history. Seidel's only book written intentionally for children was *Das wunderbare Geißleinbuch: Neue Geschichten für Kinder, die die alten Märchen gut kennen* (The Miraculous Baby Goat Book, 1925).

[*See also* Germany.]

LUKE SPRINGMAN

Seidmann-Freud, Tom (1892–1930), German picture book author and illustrator. The niece of renowned psychoanalyst Sigmund Freud, Seidmann-Freud was a precocious and reportedly high-strung child. As an adult, she was noted for her eccentricities as well as her artistic talent—in particular, her decisions to adopt a man's first name and to wear men's clothing. A long history of emotional instability preceded a major breakdown after the failure of her husband's publishing venture and his suicide in 1929; she took her own life the following year. Seidmann-Freud has been characterized as a member of the *Jugendstil* (German Art Nouveau) movement. Her artwork often featured people and objects simply but precisely rendered in ink, their outlines carefully filled in with watercolors using the *pochoir* (stencil and layering) technique. The seemingly unsophisticated, artless look of her illustrations was counterbalanced by the thought clearly invested in their composition, especially in her ingenious movable books, *Das Wunderhaus* (The House of Wonders, 1927) and *Das Zauberboot* (The Magic Boat, 1929). *Das Zauberboot* consisted of six story-games featuring mechanical illustrations with tabs, wheels, and grids; its translations include a 1981 American edition. The stylized quality of Seidmann-Freud's work complemented her interest in fairy tales and fantasies, which she illustrated throughout her career, including *Kleine Märchen* (Little Fairy Tales, 1921), *Die Fischreise* (The Fish's Journey, 1923), *Buch der Hasengeschichten* (Book of Stories about Hares, 1924), and *Buch der erfüllten Wünsche* (Book of Wishes Come True, 1929). She also produced the charming counting book *Hurra, wir rechnen!* (Hurrah, We Are Counting! 1931) and illustrated the work of other authors, including the American Ralph Bergengren's *David the Dreamer* (1922). She provided a second set of illustrations for Chaim Bialik's Hebrew translation of her *Kleine Märchen* (*Esser Sichot Liyladim*, 1923). Because Seidmann-Freud was Jewish, many copies of her books vanished during Hitler's regime and have become comparatively difficult to find on the antiquarian market.

[*See also* Bialik, Chaim; Fairy Tales and Folk Tales; Germany; *and* Movable Books and Pop-Up Books.]

PEGGY LIN DUTHIE

Selden, George (1929–1989), American author, biographer, and playwright, born in Hartford, Connecticut, as George Selden Thompson. After graduating from Yale University, he spent a year in Italy on a Fulbright scholarship. In 1952 Selden began his career as a freelance writer in New York and wrote several plays before he began writing children's books.

His third children's book, *The Cricket in Times Square* (1960), brought Selden both success and critical acclaim: a Newbery Honor book citation in 1961 and the Lewis Carroll Shelf Award in 1963. Following the tradition of using anthropomorphized animals, Selden explores the friendship between a country cricket who accidentally comes to Times Square and a cat and mouse who live in a subway station. He brings life to these distinctive characters through lively and witty dialogue. With its theme of friendship, this book that has been called a minor modern classic strongly reminds us of *Charlotte's Web*, but Selden's uniqueness lies in the setting and the originality of the plot: the animals intend to save the financially troubled newsstand in the subway station by the cricket's musical performances.

Selden produced six more stories featuring these animals, all illustrated by Garth Williams, but these did not equal the first. In the second book, *Tucker's Countryside* (1969), the animals deal with the conservation of a Connecticut meadow by deceiving the humans with an ingenious and morally dubious trick. Though Selden shows his ability to produce mild satire, the lack of villains or death in his tales produces a sentimental and nostalgic tone that has little appeal to modern audiences.

He also wrote two biographies and several other fantasy stories. *Sparrow Socks* (1965), illustrated by Peter Lippman, is his most engaging book for younger readers. Set in Scotland, the book depicts the friendship between a boy and sparrows. Its usage of red for selected passages of the text and for the illustrations of socks, in otherwise monochrome drawings, is both striking and effective.

JUNKO NISHIMURA

Seligson, Susan, American writer. Seligson attended the State University of New York at Binghamton and contributed essays to the *New York Times*, *Atlantic Monthly*, and other major periodicals. Her best-known creation in children's books is Amos, an exuberant Irish setter who learns that his couch can miraculously travel about town in *The Story of an Old Dog and His Couch* (1987). In a 1989 sequel, *The Amazing Amos and the Greatest Couch on Earth*, the agile old dog practices his performing skills and becomes a circus star. Illustrator Howie Schneider adds to the fun with comical characterizations of Amos and impressive aerial views of street traffic and circus performers. Among the many genial hounds in children's stories, Amos stands out for the way his delightful sociability is combined with the presence of an ingenious magical helper. On land and sea (e.g., *Amos Camps Out*, 1992, and *Amos Ahoy*, 1990), Amos finds adventure on his bouncy, self-propelled sofa.

SANDRA BOLTON

Selsam, Millicent E. (1912–1996), American writer of nonfiction for children and young adults. Born in Brooklyn, New York, and having completed a bachelor's degree in biology at Brooklyn College and a master's degree in botany at Columbia University, Selsam was a high school science teacher for a decade, and in 1936 married the writer Howard B. Selsam (d. 1970), before becoming the prolific author of more than one hundred nonfiction books for children and young adults. Known for works on science and nature, she focuses especially on species and aspects of plants and animals. Characterized by enthusiasm for her subject and an ability to communicate with young readers, Selsam emphasizes the excitements of science, of discovering the hows and whys of nature's operation, and of thinking scientifically. Her first book, *Egg to Chick* (1946), was followed by titles including *Play with Leaves and Flowers* (1952), *All Kinds of Babies and How They Grow* (1953), *Benny's Animals and How He Put Them in Order* (1966), *Tyrannosaurus Rex* (1978), and *Eat the Fruit, Plant the Seed* (1980). She also produced books on historical travelers, such as *Around the World with Darwin* (1960), *Stars, Mosquitoes, and Crocodiles: The American Travels of Alexander Von Humboldt* (editor; 1962), and *The Quest of Captain Cook* (1962). Following her 1972 appointment as juvenile science editor at Walker and Company Publishers, New York, Selsam edited the *How Did We Find Out* series by Isaac Asimov and coedited the *First Look* science series for young readers. Selsam won several awards for her work, including in 1964 the first Eva L. Gordon Award of the American Nature Study Society and in 1977 the Washington Children's Book Guild Nonfiction Award for her overall contribution to children's literature. In 1980 she was a nominee for the Laura Ingalls Wilder Award.

[*See also* Ecology and Environment; Nonfiction; *and* Science Books.]

ADRIENNE E. GAVIN

Sempé (1932–), famous French illustrator for adults. Jean-Jacques Sempé created a child character, Nicolas, for a children's magazine in 1954. In 1960, he illustrated *Les Aventures du Petit Nicolas* (Little Nicolas's Adventures), written by René Goscinny, in the magazine *Pilote*. Afterward five successful volumes of short stories (1960–1964) with this character were published and are still reprinted. Sempé's thick strokes in black and white distinguish the different characters in Nicolas's primary school class. With tender irony Nicolas recounts their adventures, opposing the children's universe—that of the children and their friends—to that of the adults, parents, teachers, and neighbors. Sempé also wrote and illustrated *Marcellin Caillou* (1969) about a child named Marcellin, who keeps blushing, and René Rateau, who is always sneezing; the two become close friends because the other children make fun of them. When René moves away, the two friends are separated, but, fortunately, they meet again thirty years later and rekindle their childish spirit. Tenderness, melancholy, and optimism characterize this work.

[*See also* France *and* Illustrations.]

JACQUES TRAMSON

Sendak, Jack (1923–1995), writer born in Brooklyn, New York. Sendak began his writing career at an early age and collaborated with his brother Maurice. Together they illustrated, wrote, and bound their own books, and then presented them to their family and friends. Sendak wrote six children's books, starting with *The Happy Rain* (1956) and *Circus Girl* (1957), which were both illustrated by Maurice. The books that followed were *The Second Witch* (1965), *The King of the Hermits and Other Stories* (1966), and *Martze* (1968). In 1972, Sendak's last book, *The Magic Tears*, received the Children's Book Showcase Award, and secured his significance as a children's author. Sendak's ingenuity is apparent throughout his works; he creates magical, humorous, and mysterious tales that can be enjoyed by both child and adult.

[*See also* Book Design; Picture Books; *and* Sendak, Maurice.]

TIM SKRZYDLEWSKI

Sendak, Maurice (1928–), American illustrator and writer, one of the most esteemed and influential international contributors to the field of children's literature. He has illustrated more than eighty books for children, eleven of which also carry his stories, and has adapted several of these for the stage. Since the 1980s he has designed sets and costumes for numerous operas, including Wolfgang Amadeus Mozart's *The Magic Flute*, Sergey Prokofiev's *The Love of Three Oranges*, and Leos Janácek's *The Cunning Little Vixen*. He is also founder of Night Kitchen, a national children's theater. Maurice Sendak was born in Brooklyn in 1928, the youngest of three children of Polish immigrants who had come to New York before World War I. His father had a narrative gift, improvising stories for the children's entertainment; the implied values of the tales he told them, together with comics and the family visits to the cinema, were to have a direct influence on Sendak's work. His gift for art was recognized at Lafayette High School and in his senior year his earliest published illustrations for which he was

Maurice Sendak. PHOTOGRAPH BY FRANK WOJCIECHOWSKI, 2000

paid appeared in a physics textbook, *Atomics for the Millions* (1947).

Early Career

After leaving school, Sendak worked with a Manhattan window display company while attending evening classes at the Art Students League in New York. An introduction to Ursula Nordstrom, the children's book editor at Harper and Brothers, resulted in Sendak receiving illustration commissions. He illustrated more than fifty books between 1951 and 1961, developed his visual narrative techniques, and consciously expanded his command of graphic styles through study of great illustrators past and present. Sendak determined that for him, the role of the illustrator is to interpret the text, just as a musical conductor interprets a score. Sendak's major collaborations during this decade were with Ruth Krauss, Else Holmelund Minarik, and Meindert DeJong.

Illustrator

Sendak made his name with Krauss's *A Hole Is to Dig: A First Book of First Definitions* (1952), improvising on her text, responding to its rhythms by varying his designs for layout, and finding pictorial equivalence for the irrepressible energy of children. Their next book, *A Very Special House* (1953), features an exuberant child on tiny twinkling feet, who is both a character in and coillustrator of his own story. Sendak's collaboration with Minarik produced six books in a decade, with *No Fighting, No Biting* (1958) followed by five readers that make up the *Little Bear* series (1957–1968). For the overall design of the series, Sendak draws inspiration from the 19th-century English Arts and Crafts movement and dresses comely Mother Bear in a crinoline. Sendak's collaboration with DeJong, who writes junior novels, resulted in a Newbery Medal for their third book, *The Wheel on the School* (1954).

A constant characteristic of Sendak's work is his adoption of a particular style for each story. One of the most popular and reflective of Sendak's early collaborations is Charlotte Zolotow's *Mr. Rabbit and the Lovely Present* (1962), for which the dominant influence is the American painter Winslow Homer. Light dapples the woodland and river scenes as a sedate little girl searches for a present for her mother with the help of an elegant human-size talking rabbit. In stylistic contrast, for *Swine Lake* (1999) by James Marshall, the tale of a wolf who goes to the Boarshoi Ballet intent on finding his next meal but is so transported by the performance that art conquers appetite, Sendak cartoons a drama from a drama with visual puns and outrageous jokes leaping off the pages.

Author and Illustrator

The earlier of Sendak's books for which he is wholly responsible record how children are able to escape reality through fantasy or the power of imaginative play. He sets his marker on this territory in *Kenny's Window* (1956), about a young daydreamer, swiftly followed by *Very Far Away* (1957), the title of which refers to the location of a boy's fantasy kingdom. *The Sign on Rosie's Door* (1960) is a collection of stories about a girl who entertains her friends through acting out her fantasies, though not without taking risks. An animated film, *Really Rosie, Starring the Nutshell Kids* (1975) and a Broadway musical, *Broadway Rosie*, in the early 1980s bear witness to the character's enduring appeal. Continuing to explore the theme of make-believe, in 1962 he published the four miniature books in rhyme that make up *The Nutshell Library*: an alphabet book, a counting book, a seasons book, and a moral tale. The wit and originality of this work engages both children and adults.

One year later Sendak published *Where the Wild Things Are* (1963), the first of his self-styled trilogy that gives form to the more profound idea that through fantasy children achieve catharsis for their otherwise ungovernable feelings. Each of his initially troubled protagonists undertakes a journey, encounters extreme danger that has to be surmounted unaided, and in the resolution of each tale achieves an integrated self. *Where the Wild Things Are*, which received the

Caldecott Medal, changed perceptions of what a children's picture book might be, both in theme and in the general understanding of how the material form of the book, as a three dimensional sequential art object, may be exploited by design to serve the narrative act. The young hero, Max, misbehaves in more ways than one, and is sent to his room without any supper. The fantasy begins as the room changes into a jungle with a shore line, and Max sails away on a boat to the place where the wild things are. He celebrates with them, then tames them. Impossible lunar shifts accompany events; at their conclusion the full moon benevolently exemplifies the state of wholeness that Max achieves.

In the Night Kitchen (1970), the second in the trilogy, is more complex and open to interpretation on many levels: as an entertaining comic-book adventure, an allegory of childhood sensuality and sexuality, a mythic journey into the underworld where the hero overcomes dark forces, and no doubt many more. The tale takes the form of a dream fantasy set in New York, which Sendak transforms into a surreal kitchen-furnished skyline, together with props designed in authentic 1930s period detail. With a debt to the American cartoonist Winsor McCay, Sendak adopts the style of comics art, and the skillful layout seamlessly transports Mickey, the unsettled young hero, from his bed to the night kitchen, presided over by a trio of Oliver Hardy look-alikes, where he narrowly escapes being baked in the oven, then over the top of the Milky Way, and back to bed, carefree. Muted unmodulated color is held in a thick contour line.

The third and most complex book of the trilogy, *Outside Over There* (1981), is set in the last decade of the 18th century, written when Sendak was working on his first opera design, for Mozart's *The Magic Flute*. To complement the historical period, Sendak adopted the visionary style and iconography of the early northern Romantic artists, principally Philipp Otto Runge, Caspar David Friedrich, and William Blake. The story records the adventures of Ida, a young girl who has to rescue her baby sister kidnapped by goblins; the destructive feelings that Ida overcomes include sibling antagonism, jealousy, resentment, and complex feelings for her father.

Stylistically, Sendak returns to the northern Romantic mythic realm visited in *Outside Over There* to picture *Dear Mili* (1988) with a text by Wilhelm Grimm. A woman sends her daughter into the forest to save her from approaching war. Here the child meets her guardian angel and Saint Joseph, and believes three days have gone by, although she has died. Mili is miraculously reunited with her mother thirty years later, and leads her to heaven. Sendak meets the mystery at the heart of the tale by picturing the whole on a metaphysical level. The figures are lofty symbols exemplifying the suffering of the innocent in time of war, and the endurance of the human spirit. Philipp Otto Runge is the presiding genius of the visual narrative, which is replete with transhistorical cultural allusions.

Nursery Rhymes and Folk Tales

Nursery rhymes from Mother Goose have been a continuous source of inspiration for Sendak. *Hector Protector and As I Went Over the Water* (1965) is both his homage to the 19th-century artist Randolph Caldecott and a demonstration of his own ability to invest simple verses with additional meaning and drama. *Higglety Pigglety Pop!; or, There Must Be More to Life* (1967), a picture storybook, arguably Sendak's masterpiece in immortalizing his Sealyham terrier Jennie (who makes guest appearances in many of his works), also has roots in a nursery rhyme. The enigmatic story, with its surreal humor, irony, and capacity for bearing multiple meanings, is all Sendak's own; he pictures the impossible in precise pen-and-ink drawings, the close hatching settling the image on the page. Jennie is dissatisfied with all the material comforts she enjoys and leaves home. After enigmatic adventures she finds herself in a heavenly place, fulfilled through performing in The World Mother Goose Theatre. Life mirrored art in 1985, when the Glyndebourne Opera staged a production of *Higglety Pigglety Pop!* with a libretto by Sendak.

The source for the text of *We Are All in the Dumps with Jack and Guy* (1993) is two nonsense nursery rhymes also from Mother Goose; but this time Sendak unites them through his visual narrative, drawing inspiration from the real lives of dispossessed children who live on the streets. To amplify the rhymes Sendak writes his own text, which he sites on newspapers and boxes used as clothing and shelters or puts in speech balloons. The result is a story set in a cardboard city, under somewhere like the Brooklyn Bridge, occupied by a group of homeless children and their pet kittens, that confronts the social, political, and economic realities of such an existence. On a symbolic level, the story functions like a parable revealing a universal truth about the redemptive power of love. Images include Sendak's reworking of Christian iconography and Andrea Mantegna's beautiful yet terrifying painting, *Descent into Limbo* (c. 1470). The design for the layout and the compositions give the sequential art the immediacy of dramatic performance.

Traditional verses and rhymes also have been animated by Sendak's art. In 1965 he illustrated *Lullabies and Night*

Songs edited by William Engvick, music by Alec Wilder, a handsome large-format song book. Many of the pictures reflect Sendak's admiration for William Blake, George Cruikshank, Samuel Palmer, Thomas Rowlandson, and Randolph Caldecott. *I Saw Esau* (1992) is an equally handsome but small pocket book of children's rhymes, first compiled by Iona and Peter Opie in the late 1940s. Sendak's blithe, subversive little images are as uninhibited as the playground chants they partner.

Sendak's interpretations of the folk tales of the Brothers Grimm are further evidence of the range of his vision and graphic style. The setting for *King Grisly-Beard* (1973) is a playhouse, and the action is intended to raise smiles with a very young audience. In the same year, but in a very different vein, *The Juniper Tree* was published, comprising two volumes of twenty-seven stories by the Brothers Grimm, translated by Lore Segal, and illustrated by Sendak with great distinction. In the preparatory stage Sendak had traveled to Europe, visiting the places from which the tales had originated, and steeping himself in German art. The influence, in form and effect, of Albrecht Dürer's set of etchings, *The Little Passion*, is evident in Sendak's tightly framed black-and-white drawings, one for each tale. They not only resemble etched plates, but are almost the same size as Dürer's; furthermore, the perspective and the scale of the figures in relation to the frame causes the images to bulge against the picture plane, increasing their emotional intensity by seeming to invade the viewer's space.

Sendak's experimental approach to the picture book medium and his commitment to operatic art continue in a collaboration with playwright Tony Kushner. *Brundibar* (2003), a dual-narrative picture book with a Holocaust theme, is based on the opera of the same name by Hans Krása and Adolf Hoffmeister. In the 1940s, the children of Terezin, a concentration camp in Czechoslovakia, gave fifty-five performances of the opera, in which determination, courage, and collective action overcome evil. In tribute to this act of immense moral courage (most of the children in the opera's casts were to die in Auschwitz, as did Hans Krása), *Brundibar* is designed as an imaginary recreation of the opera, with the page for a stage and the words of songs forming a substantial proportion of the text. Sendak includes visual references to many of his other works, which add additional layers of meaning, particularly relating to the tenacity and bravery of children. Sendak and Kushner also have designed and translated a new version of the opera.

Awards

In addition to numerous awards for individual works, in 1970 Maurice Sendak won the Hans Christian Andersen Medal—he was the first American illustrator to be so honored; in 2003, as joint winner with the Austrian author Christine Nöstlinger, he received the inaugural Astrid Lindgren Award for Literature. Sendak received the Laura Ingalls Wilder Award from the American Library Association in recognition of his entire body of work in 1983, and in 1996 he received a National Medal of Arts in recognition of his contribution to the arts in America.

[*See also* Fairy Tales and Folk Tales; Illustrations; Nursery Rhymes; Picture Books; *and biographies of figures mentioned in this article.*]

BIBLIOGRAPHY

Cech, John, *Angels and Wild Things: The Archetypal Poetics of Maurice Sendak*. University Park: Pennsylvania State University Press, 1996.

Lanes, Selma. *The Art of Maurice Sendak*. New York: Abrams, 1980.

Sonheim, Amy. *Maurice Sendak*. New York: Twayne, 1991.

JANE DOONAN

Senghor, Léopold Sédar (1906–2001), poet and the first president of Senegal (1960–1980). He helped coin the word *negritude*, defined as "this *spirit* of Negro-African civilization . . . which is offered to the world . . . to unify it, to *understand* and to show it." He believed in the coming together of two different ways of life—European and African—and his works embody his fight for cultural and political independence. For children he collaborated with Abdoulaye Sadji on a collection of folk tales, *La belle histoire de Leuk-le-lièvre* (1953; English trans., *The Beautiful Story of Leuk the Hare*, 1965), and he provided a preface for the folk tale collection, *Les nouveaux contes d'Amadou Koumba* (1958) by the Senegalese writer Birago Diop.

[*See also* Africa: Northern Africa; Fairy Tales and Folk Tales; *and* Sadji, Aboulaye.]

BIBLIOGRAPHY

Senghor, Léopold, Sédar. "Negritude and the Concept of Universal Civilization." *Présence Africaine* 18.46 (March 1963): 8–13.

Zell, Hans M., Carol Bundy, and Virginia Coulon. "Léopold Sédar Senghor." In *A New Reader's Guide to African Literature*, 2d ed., 476–479. London: Heinemann, 1983.

JEAN FOUCAULT

Sengupta, Subhadra (1952–), Indian author of travelogues, stories, comic strips, biographies, and novels. Extremely prolific, she is also an experimentalist with form. *Kartik's War* and its sequel, *Kartik and the Lost Gold*, are set in King Ashoka's time, while *A Clown for Tenali Rama* is set in Sri Krishnadevaraya's reign. Fascinatingly, and tellingly, commoners and children are astute critics of politics, and are even instrumental in decisive actions or events in the court or the political arena. Hence the action is more often situated in kitchens, in the narrow lanes of the city or marketplaces, than in palaces. Historical figures are humanized in stories such as "A Rose for the Princess," and in sensitive retellings of the lives of *Jodh Bai* and *Jahanara*.

Strong, determined, and quick-witted child protagonists help adults ("Dal Delight") and ghosts ("A Dancer in the Rain," "Office Ghost"), or solve mysteries ("Hasan and the Lost Pigeons," "A Sword for Deva Raya"). These children are frequently from less affluent classes: Bishnu in *Bishnu the Dhobi Singer* (Bishnu the Washerman Singer) is a washerman's son chosen to train under the great Tansen, while Basava and Sivakka in *A Clown for Tenali Rama* are a poor farmer's children. Their talents, courage, and willingness to use available opportunities help them rise above their station in life.

The past is sharply delineated, and contrasted with the fast-paced 20th century in *A Clown for Tenali Rama*. In *Kartik's War* the paradoxes of history—such as Emperor Ashoka's peace policy—are portrayed. Food and music are central to most stories: in "Salim Husain Quwwal" selling biryani is the only means for Salim to earn money, while in "Salim's Song," Salim escapes the drudgery of kitchen work because of his voice. Sengupta has also tried her hand at a typical adventure tale in *The Mussoorie Mystery*.

[*See also* Historical Fiction *and* India.]

NANDINI NAYAR

Seredy, Kate (1899–1975), Hungarian American author and illustrator. Seredy had already established a career as an illustrator in Hungary before she came to the United States in 1922. She worked in a factory and made a second start painting lamp shades; magazine-cover and fashion-plate designers then started giving her work. Seredy illustrated textbooks and trade books before May Massee, an editor at Viking Press, suggested that she could write her own stories. *The White Stag* (1937), a novel of early Hungary, won the Newbery Medal. Seredy also received Newbery Honors for *The Good Master* (1935) and *The Singing Tree* (1939), both based on her own childhood. She received Caldecott Honors for illustrating *The Christmas Anna Angel* (1944), whose text was written by Ruth Sawyer; it tells the tale of a Hungarian child during World War II. Seredy's front-line nursing work during World War I influenced her lifelong opposition to war, expressed through stirring passages about peace, understanding, and the brotherhood of humanity in her children's books.

[*See also* Historical Fiction; Illustrations; *and* Massee, May.]

BIBLIOGRAPHY

Helbig, Althea K. "Kate Seredy." In *Writers for Children: Critical Studies of the Major Authors since the Seventeenth Century*, edited by Jane M. Bingham. New York: Scribners, 1988.

MARISSA K. LINGEN

Series Books. A series is a sequence of separate narratives, mostly about the same characters and usually written by one author. Series fictions have traditionally been grouped generically as ballet stories, school stories, holiday adventure stories, and so on. These groupings have given rise to the impression that series fiction is intrinsically formulaic. However, it has become increasingly acknowledged that series fiction plays an important part in children's reading development, and recent critical commentary has shown that some writers have used an extended sequence of narratives to pursue sustained and complex artistic purposes. Series fictions can be divided into two types, the progressive and the successive. A progressive series is one in which a developing story is told in installments, each book telling a different part of a sequential narrative. The novels in a progressive series have their own place and should ideally be read in the correct order. Since a series provides extended opportunities for representing the development of character, maturation is often a predominant theme. The North American family sagas popular between 1860 and 1920 are progressive series, since the main interest is the growth of the protagonists from childhood to parenthood. Ballet series—and career series in general—are usually progressive, following the careers of their characters from childhood to professional achievement.

A successive series is one in which the characters show few signs of growing older or changing in any significant way, though they may nevertheless be subtly represented. The works in most successive series may be read in any order, since none is structurally dependent on its place in the sequence. Richmal Crompton's William Brown stories (from 1922) are a successive series, and so are most of the post–World War II series by Enid Blyton. Series for very young readers are usually successive. However, some that began as early readers for very young children have matured along with their protagonists: the eponymous heroine of the Katie Morag picture books (from 1984), by Mairi Hedderwick, grows older as the series progresses, as does the famous heroine of Maud Hart Lovelace's Betsy-Tacy series (from 1940). Fantasy series whose narratives are tied in with a quest structure are invariably progressive, their extended length enabling the author to accumulate incrementally the complexity of secondary worlds. The Chronicles of Prydain by Lloyd Alexander (from 1964) is an example. However, other prolonged fantasy series are successive—L. Frank Baum's Oz series (from 1900), for example.

Trends

Series fiction began with James Fenimore Cooper's *Leather-Stocking Tales* (from 1823). Since then, different genres have dominated children's fiction at different periods. First there were the great North American family sagas, which began with Louisa May Alcott's *Little Women* (1868), followed by series by Susan Coolidge, Kate Douglas Wiggin, Eleanor H. Porter, and L. M. Montgomery. In the United Kingdom after World War I there was a great outpouring of school series. The most successful were by Elsie J. Oxenham, Dorita Fairlie Bruce, Angela Brazil, and Elinor Brent-Dyer. Enid Blyton—queen of series-writers—wrote the first of her St. Clare's School stories in 1941, and Malory Towers followed in 1946. The first of Anthony Buckeridge's Jennings books appeared in 1950.

Between 1930 and 1960, camping-and-tramping series fiction dominated children's reading in Britain. The greatest and most influential was the Swallows and Amazons (from 1930) series by Arthur Ransome, but there were others by M. E. Atkinson, Katharine Hull and Pamela Whitlock, Aubrey de Selincourt, Elinor Lyon, David Severn, and Marjorie Lloyd. The pony story—a close relative of the camping-and-tramping story—made its first significant appearance in series form with Monica Edwards's Punchbowl Farm and Romney Marsh series (both from 1947) and Ruby Ferguson's *Jill* series (from 1949). However, throughout the 20th century new series appeared by authors whose work was completely individualistic: Hugh Lofting's twelve Doctor Dolittle books (from 1920); Richmal Crompton's Just William stories; and Captain W. E. Johns's Biggles series (from 1932). In 1932 Laura Ingalls Wilder's *Little House in the Big Woods* was published, Norman Hunter's Professor Branestawm stories began in 1933, and P. L. Travers's *Mary Poppins* was published in 1934. Although the 1940s and 1950s were dominated in Britain by Enid Blyton and Malcolm Saville, new authors challenged the perceived blandness of their prolific output. In 1948 the first of Antonia Forest's Marlow series appeared; in 1949 Geoffrey Trease published the first of the Bannermere stories; and Tove Jansson's Moomintroll books (from 1945) were first translated into English in 1950. It was a time of great innovativeness, exemplified by C. S. Lewis's Chronicles of Narnia (1950), Mary Norton's The Borrowers (from 1952), and Lucy Boston's The Children of Green Knowe (from 1954). Among the many series for younger readers were Dorothy Edwards's My Naughty Little Sister (from 1951) and the Clever Polly series by Catherine Storr (from 1955).

Fantasy and Science Fiction

In the 1960s several notable fantasy, science fiction, and comic history series began to appear—the Miss Bianca series by Margery Sharp (from 1959), and Madeleine L'Engle's great unclassifiable series, which began with *A Wrinkle in Time* (1962). Joan Aiken's James III series started in 1962, and Lloyd Alexander's The Chronicles of Prydain first appeared in 1964. Susan Cooper's The Dark Is Rising series began in 1965 with the publication of *Over Sea, Under Stone*. In the age of J. K. Rowling's Harry Potter (from 1997) and Philip Pullman's His Dark Materials (from 1995), fantasy is currently in the ascendancy. Trilogies are plentiful. However, even before these two remarkable publishing successes, fantasy series were becoming more inventive and creatively mischievous, ignoring the usual generic boundaries. None better illustrates this than Diana Wynne Jones's Chrestomanci series (from 1977), which triumphantly challenges the usual expectations of series readers.

Toward the end of the 20th century, publishers' format series became immensely popular. They consist of works, often written by a syndicate of authors, bound together by theme, characters or genre, and marketed as a recognizable commodity. Format series may aspire to the conditions of either the progressive or the successive series. They are not, however, a recent phenomenon: in the United States, the Bobbsey Twins were created by Edward Stratemeyer in 1904, and his syndicate released the first of the Hardy Boys series by "F. W. Dixon" in 1927. Nancy Drew made her first appearance in 1930 in *The Secret of the Old Clock*. The appeal of series fiction lies in the combination of endings with continuity. A series is not simply an extremely long serial: it is a sequence of narratives each with its own closure, providing points of completeness while allowing for the renewal of acquaintance with familiar characters and situations.

[*See also* Baby-Sitters Club Series; Hardy Boys Series; Sally Series; School Stories; Stratemeyer Syndicate; Sweet Valley High Series; *and biographies of figures mentioned in this article*.]

BIBLIOGRAPHY

Cadogan, Mary, and Patricia Craig. *You're a Brick, Angela! A New Look at Girls' Fiction from 1939–1975*. London: Gollancz, 1976.

Campbell, Alasdair, and Deborah Gibbons. *Outstanding Sequence Stories*. Swansea, U.K.: Librarians of Institutions and Schools of Education, 1998.

Watson, Victor. *Reading Series Fiction: From Arthur Ransome to Gene Kemp*. London: RoutledgeFalmer, 2000.

VICTOR WATSON

Serraillier, Ian (1912–1994), British writer and publisher. Ian Lucien Serraillier was born in London and earned an MA at Oxford University in 1935. He was a teacher for many years, notably at Midhurst School in Surrey between 1946 and 1961. In 1950 he and his wife, Anne, founded the New Windmill Series, a branch of Heinemann Educational Books specializing in children's literature and the teaching of reading. From 1941 on, Serraillier wrote twenty-one books of verse for children, some of them retellings of ancient ballads. He also wrote eight novels for children, all except one of which are unremarkable. In addition, he contributed twenty retellings to the New Windmill series as well as creating three plays in verse.

The most significant of Serraillier's novels is *The Silver Sword* (American edition, *Escape from Warsaw*, 1956), the story of a Polish family during World War II and its aftermath. Admirably illustrated by C. Walter Hodges, it is written in a straightforward manner and has a plot that is quick-moving and full of suspense. Ruth, a teenager, her slightly younger brother Edek, and their infant sister Bronia seek shelter in a cellar in war-torn Warsaw after their mother and father have been taken away and their house blown up. They are joined by Jan, a streetwise but emotionally damaged orphan. As the war ends, the four children cross Poland and Germany to Switzerland, where they hope their parents have found sanctuary. Helped by Poles, Russians, Germans, Swiss, and Americans, the family is reunited thanks to a silver paper knife that establishes their identity. *The Silver Sword*, a masterpiece of children's literature, has twice been serialized for television and remains in print.

GEOFFREY FENWICK

Service, Robert W. (1874–1958), Scottish poet and author. After working in Canada and vagabonding in western America in the early 20th century, Service was a bank clerk in Whitehorse and Dawson, Yukon Territory. Here stories of the Klondike gold rush were fresh, and Service began writing poetry based on this history. His first book of verse, *Songs of a Sourdough* (1907; *Spell of the Yukon* in the U.S.), contained his two most popular poems, "The Shooting of Dan McGrew" and "The Cremation of Sam McGee." Other poetry and novels followed. His poetry is one step above doggerel, with its relentless rhymes and regular rhythm, its unapologetic bathos, its awful addiction to alliteration—and Service was aware of this. He claimed to be a versifier rather than a poet, and always said he was a poet of the common man. This is true—his poetry was, and still is, immensely popular with plain folk and children.

[*See also* Canada *and* Poetry.]

BIBLIOGRAPHY

MacKay, James. *Vagabond of Verse: Robert Service, a Biography*. Edinburgh: Mainstream, 1995. Containing a bibliography of Service's works and a good source bibliography, this biography does a good job of disentangling some of the incomplete information provided by Service in his two autobiographical works, *Harper of Heaven* and *Ploughman of the Moon*.

JACQUE ROETHLER

***Sesame Street*.** An educational television program for young children, *Sesame Street* first appeared in 1969 on National Educational Television (NET), precursor to the Public Broadcasting System (PBS), and is known for its cast of Muppets, the colorful "marionette puppets" created by Jim Henson. Combining Muppet characters like Bert and Ernie, Grover, Oscar the Grouch, Cookie Monster, The Count, Big Bird, Kermit the Frog, and later Elmo with live action, animation, and film shorts, *Sesame Street* teaches preschoolers basic information such as numbers, the days of the week, and the letters of the alphabet; essential life skills like brushing your teeth, washing your hands, and calling 911 for emergencies; and important social skills like asking permission and saying "please" and "thank you." The first children's television program to use empirical research for both its curriculum and its programming decisions, *Sesame Street* is designed to address the interests, concerns, and fears of children at all developmental stages.

What distinguished *Sesame Street* from the beginning was not simply its educational focus or use of colorful characters, but its urban sensibility and multicultural emphasis. The

Sesame Street. Frontispiece to *Sesame Street Songbook* (New York: Macmillan, c. 1992). REPRODUCED COURTESY OF THE COTSEN CHILDREN'S LIBRARY, PRINCETON UNIVERSITY LIBRARY

Sesame Street stage itself mirrors a city street, with brownstone apartment facades, front porch steps, neighborhood grocery and five-and-dime stores, and an assorted cast of neighborhood characters. From the start, *Sesame Street* featured children, senior citizens, and teenagers; single-parent families and characters of different religions; African American, Afro-Caribbean, and Hispanic actors; and disabled or differently abled characters. The show is known for dealing courageously and empathetically with difficult issues, as in the 1982 episode in which Big Bird came to grips with the death of the longtime *Sesame Street* veteran Mr. Hooper (played by Will Lee). *Sesame Street* also broke new ground in 2002 when its South African version introduced an HIV-positive character, Kami. The show has not been without its critics, however, particularly from the American right wing, which questions the efficacy of public funding for such potentially controversial, supposedly liberal, causes.

Sesame Street has also demonstrated a sly humor—in witty dialogue, pop-culture references, and parodies—that appeal to adults as well as children. Another testimony to *Sesame Street*'s quality and popularity is the plethora of A-list personalities who have appeared on the show: comedians (Carol Burnett, Bill Cosby, Steve Martin), actors (James Earl Jones, Robert De Niro, Mel Gibson), athletes (Arthur Ashe, Julius "Dr. J" Erving, Venus Williams), and even politicians (U.N. Secretary-General Kofi Annan, Ralph Nader). Singers and bands also have been favorites (Harry Belafonte, Johnny Cash, Destiny's Child), especially when they parody their own hits (R.E.M singing "Funny Happy Monsters" instead of "Shiny Happy People") or sing a spiced-up version of the ABCs (Ray Charles).

Sesame Street has produced more than 4,000 programs, won more than fifty Emmies, has two dozen international affiliates, and appears in more than 120 countries. It has been spun off into myriad children's products, and the Muppet characters have taken on lives of their own with network TV specials, soundtracks ("Fraggle Rock"), cartoon series (*Muppet Babies*), stage shows ("Sesame Street Live"), and feature films (six so far). Most successful of these ventures is *The Muppet Show*, a syndicated program that caters to the more adult-oriented sensibility glimpsed in *Sesame Street* through characters like the hecklers Stadler and Waldorf, the Swedish Chef, Gonzo the Great, Fozzie Bear, and the inimitable Miss Piggy. Fueled by the imaginative creativity of founder Jim Henson, who died unexpectedly of bacterial pneumonia in 1990, *Sesame Street* and the Muppets have become not just educators but cultural icons.

[*See also* Henson, Jim; Multiculturalism; *and* Television and Children.]

BIBLIOGRAPHY

Finch, Christopher, Charles S. Finch, and Jim Henson. *Jim Henson: The Works—The Art, the Magic, the Imagination*. New York: David McKay, 1993.

Fisch, Shalom M. *Children's Learning from Educational Television: Sesame Street and Beyond*. Mahwah, N.J.: L. Erlbaum, 2004.

Fisch, Shalom M., and Rosemarie T. Truglio, eds. *"G" is for Growing: Thirty Years of Research on Children and Sesame Street*. Lea's Communication Series. Mahwah, N.J.: L. Erlbaum, 2000.

Polsky, Richard M. *Getting to Sesame Street: Origins of the Children's Television Workshop*. New York: Praeger, 1974.

DANIEL T. KLINE

Seton, Ernest Thompson (1860–1946), author, wildlife artist, and naturalist. Born Ernest Thompson in South Shields, County Durham, England, he emigrated to Ontario, Canada, at the age of six and was educated in Toronto before studying art at the Royal Academy in London. After returning to Canada, he spent time in Manitoba, Toronto, and New York, becoming a naturalist, writer, and wildlife illustrator before undertaking further art training in Paris. He then became official naturalist to the government of Manitoba. He moved to Connecticut in 1908, eventually settling in Santa Fe, New Mexico. In 1902 Seton founded the Woodcraft Indians (later Woodcraft League), the first outdoor organization for boys, and in 1910 cofounded the Boy Scouts of America, becoming chief scout. He was a strong advocate of First Nations cultures, and the Sioux gave him the name "Black Wolf," which he widely used. Twice married, he had two children, one of whom was the historical novelist Anya Seton.

Seton's contribution to children's literature lies in the many realist "animal biographies" he wrote and abundantly illustrated. These novels follow the manner of Anna Sewell's *Black Beauty* in being written from the animal's perspective, but they focus on animals in the wild. His bestselling classic, *Wild Animals I Have Known* (1898), began as stories such as "Wully, the Story of a Yaller Dog," "Raggylug, the Story of a Cottontail Rabbit," and "Silverspot, the Story of a Crow," which influenced Rudyard Kipling's *Jungle Books*. His other animal novels include *The Biography of a Grizzly* (1900), *Biography of a Silver Fox* (1909), and *Bannertail: The Story of a Gray Squirrel* (1922). He also wrote books related to the Woodcraft and Scouting movements, including *The Book of Woodcraft and Indian Lore* (1912) and *The Woodcraft Manual for Boys* and *The Woodcraft Manual for Girls* (1918).

BIBLIOGRAPHY

Samson, John G., ed. *The Worlds of Ernest Thompson Seton*. New York: Knopf, 1976.

Seton, Julia M. *By a Thousand Fires*. New York: Doubleday, 1967.

ADRIENNE E. GAVIN

Seuss, Dr. (1904–1991), pseudonym of Theodor Seuss Geisel, American author and illustrator of more than forty children's books, all notable for their imaginative stories, quirky characters, distinctive illustrations, and memorable rhymes or rhythms. Born in Springfield, Massachusetts, Geisel attended Springfield's Central High School during the period of anti-German sentiment aroused by World War I. He graduated from Dartmouth College and did graduate work in literature at Lincoln College, Oxford, before working as an illustrator, cartoonist, and humorist for *Judge*,

Dr. Seuss. Front cover of *If I Ran the Circus* (New York: Random House, 1956). REPRODUCED COURTESY OF THE COTSEN CHILDREN'S LIBRARY, PRINCETON UNIVERSITY LIBRARY

Life, and *Vanity Fair* magazines. At Oxford he met Helen Marion Palmer, whom he married in 1927, and in 1928 the couple moved to La Jolla, California. After Helen Palmer Geisel died in 1967, Geisel married Audrey Stone Diamond in 1968. He headed Random House's Beginner Books division from its establishment in 1957 until his death. Interestingly, Dr. Seuss never won a Newbery or Caldecott Medal, but he was awarded an honorary doctorate from Dartmouth in 1956 and a Pulitzer Prize in 1984 for his "special contribution over nearly half a century to the education and enjoyment of America's children and their parents."

In the 1920s, Geisel wrote advertising copy and created slogans for such products as Flit bug spray—"Quick, Henry, the Flit!" became a national catchphrase. He also worked for General Electric, NBC, and other companies, and his ads for Esso Motor Oil featured such monsters as Karbo-nockus and Moto-raspu. During World War II Geisel became an editorial cartoonist for *PM*, a New York newspaper, and created more than four hundred cartoons. In 1943 he joined the army, where he was assigned to Frank Capra's Signal Corps unit and wrote films and pamphlets, some featuring Pvt. Snafu (an acronym for "situation normal, all fouled up"). Two of his documentary films, *Hitler Lives* (1946) and *Design for Death* (1947), won Academy Awards. He won a third Oscar in 1951 for the animated *Gerald McBoing Boing*.

Although Geisel illustrated two books in 1931 (*Boners* and *More Boners*, collections of children's sayings), his first children's book was *And to Think That I Saw It on Mulberry Street* (1937), whose rhythms were inspired by the throbbing engine of a passenger liner. Following his World War II work, Geisel turned out a series of enduringly popular books, including *Horton Hatches the Egg* (1940), *McElligot's Pool* (1947), *Horton Hears a Who* (1954), *On Beyond Zebra* (1955), *Yertle the Turtle and Other Stories* (1958), *The Lorax* (1971), and culminating with *Oh, the Places You'll Go!* (1990). The famous animator Chuck Jones turned *How the Grinch Stole Christmas* (1957) into a well-loved Christmas television special in 1966.

Reacting to John Hershey's famous *Life* magazine article entitled "Why Johnny Can't Read" (1954)—an indictment of dull primers used to teach children to read—Geisel's publisher challenged him to write an entertaining book for beginning readers. The result, *The Cat in the Hat* (1957), used only 220 different words and forever changed the face of literature and language instruction. Geisel's publisher, Bennett Cerf, upped the stakes and asked the author if he could write a book using only fifty words. The rebuttal to that question, *Green Eggs and Ham* (1960), echoes in the minds of generations of readers who have absorbed its irresistible rhymes. Sam-I-am, a persistent host, tries to persuade his friend to try a peculiar breakfast dish:

> I do not like them, Sam-I-am.
> I do not like green eggs and ham.

Dr. Seuss continued writing such Beginner Books throughout much of his career, including the well-known titles *One Fish Two Fish Red Fish Blue Fish* (1960), *Hop on Pop* (1963), and *Fox in Socks* (1965). The Beginner Books also featured other well-known authors and illustrators, for instance, Stan and Jan Berenstain, creators of the Berenstain Bears series.

Dr. Seuss's books are often described as "whimsical," a term he apparently disliked. His humor was, in fact, constructed with more than obvious incongruities and rowdiness: he combined the recognizable with the novel in creating characters, settings, and story lines. *Green Eggs and Ham* illustrates these Seussian characteristics. In the first illustration "Sam-I-am" is a smiling, furry, four-fingered mouse-child with tufted ears. He carries a placard with his name while perched atop a floppy-eared "dogimal." Sam-I-am and his mount whirl around the corner of a blue wall and past the unnamed antagonist, a "manimal" reading a newspaper. Immediately the contrast between Sam-I-am and the manlike character sets the dramatic wheels turning: Sam and his companion smile and stride lazily past the older character, who turns to see them pass. The tension increases in the third panel, when Sam-I-am returns atop an even larger, catlike animal and startles the older figure, who harrumphs and shakes his fist: "I do not like/ that Sam-I-am." On the next page, Sam-I-am pops the famous question "Do you like/ green eggs and ham?" and extends the platter of food on a fishing pole that is equal parts organic vine and mechanical contraption.

Green Eggs and Ham moves from this opening of tension and divisiveness—older versus younger, smaller versus larger, stationary versus kinetic—toward unity and concord. From its initial illustration of discomfort to its images of acceptance and friendship, *Green Eggs and Ham* is alive with movement and gesture. There are no straight lines in a Dr. Seuss book. The older figure walks purposefully away from Sam-I-am, who then scoops him up into a swooshing blue car that eventually lands on a yellow boat. As the boat and its furry denizens blithely sink into the sea, the older figure finally takes a bite of the breakfast concoction:

Say!
I like green eggs and ham!
I do! I like them, Sam-I-am!
And I would eat them in a boat.
And I would eat them with a goat.

Poetically, the regular rhythm of the line pushes against the variety in the rhyming couplets. Again we see the merging of consistency with variety, structure with innovation.

Although Geisel came under some criticism for the political undercurrents in his books, it is clear that he continually addressed social, cultural, and political concerns, from his *PM* cartoons to his books for the young. In fact, many of his works can be read allegorically: *Yertle the Turtle* critiques fascism, *The Butter Battle Book* (1984) parodies the Cold War's arms race, and *The Lorax* concerns environmental conservation. Several books also have appeared posthumously, including *Daisy-Head Mayzie* (1995) and *My Many Colored Days* (1996). In 1993 Audrey Geisel founded Dr. Seuss Enterprises to license the commercial use of Geisel's famous characters, something he resisted throughout his career. Accordingly, his work can now be found in a theme park, a board game, videos, DVDs, CD-ROMs, Hollywood movies, clothing, collectibles, and tie-ins with Hallmark Cards and Esprit. His works have been translated into fifteen languages and have sold more than 20 million copies.

[*See also* Berenstain, Stanley, and Janice Berenstain; Easy Readers; Humor; Poetry; Primers; *and* Reading Schemes.]

BIBLIOGRAPHY

Cohen, Charles. *The Seuss, the Whole Seuss, and Nothing But the Seuss: A Visual Biography of Theodor Seuss Geisel*. New York: Random House, 2004.

Minnear, Richard, ed. *Dr. Seuss Goes to War: The World War II Editorial Cartoons of Theodor Seuss Geisel*. New York: New Press, 2001.

Morgan, Judith, and Neil Morgan. *Dr. Seuss and Mr. Geisel: A Biography*. New York: Random House, 1996.

Nel, Philip. *Dr. Seuss: American Icon*. New York and London: Continuum, 2004.

DANIEL T. KLINE

Seven Champions of Christendom, The. A prolix romance by Richard Johnson (1573–1659?), a London writer of popular literature, *The Seven Champions of Christendom* was first published in two parts in 1596 and 1597. Very considerably shortened, the stories in it long remained favorite chapbook material; the précis of the contents given by the publisher of a 1746 version, R. Ware, shows its attractions: "The Illustrious and Renown'd History of the Seven Champions of Christendom. Containing their Honourable Births, Victories, and Noble Achievements by Sea and Land in divers strange Countries; their Combats with Giants, Monsters; Wonderful Adventures, Fortunes and Misfortunes in Desarts, Wildernesses, inchanted Castles, their Conquests of Empires, Kingdoms, relived distressed Ladies, with their Faithful Love to them; Honour they won in Tilts and Tournaments, and Success against the Enemies of Christendom." The champions were Saint George (England), Saint James (Spain), Saint Anthony (Italy), Saint Andrew (Scotland), Saint Patrick (Ireland), Saint Denis (France), and Saint David (Wales). However, as F. J. Harvey Darton pointed out in a retelling in 1913, "The champions have nothing whatever to do with the saints whose names they bear . . . Strictly 'Saint' should be read as 'Sir' [as for a knight], and Christendom would be better spelt 'chivalry.'" *The Seven Champions* was favorite reading with John Bunyan as a boy; elements from it can be found in *The Pilgrim's Progress*. Sir Richard Steele reported in *The Tatler* in 1709 that his eight-year-old godson "Loved Saint George for being the champion of England." By the 19th century, adult readers had grown out of such stories, but there were adaptations for children until the early 20th century, including a highly moral version of 1861 by the boys' writer W. H. G. Kingston.

[*See also* Bible in Children's Literature, The; Chapbooks; *and biographies of figures mentioned in this article*.]

GILLIAN AVERY

Severn, David (1918–), British writer and author of twenty-one children's books, mainly school holiday adventures. His real name is David Storr Unwin, and he is the son of Stanley Unwin. His first series, beginning with *Rick Afire!* (1942), featured "Crusoe" Robinson befriended by youngsters in holiday adventures, many featuring a Romany group. The Warner Family series (1947–1952) featured ponies and country life. *Foxy Boy* (1959) portrays a young boy brought up by foxes, behaving like a fox, hunted like a fox, but saved by a girl. A number of books experimented with the paranormal. *Dream Gold* (1948) shows the hypnotic power of one boy over another, with dreams retelling the conflicts of their ancestors. In *Drumbeats!* (1953) a native drum produces visions of the fate of a lost expedition to Africa. In *The Future Took Us* (1957) two boys are vortexed a millennium into a future feudal dictatorship. *The Girl in the Grove* (1974) is a powerful ghost story. Severn also produced illustrated books for younger children.

[*See also* Fantasy; Ghost Stories; *and* Series Books.]

BIBLIOGRAPHY

Bigger, Steven F. *David Severn: David Unwin's Stories for Children*. Worcester, U.K.: University College Worcester, 2003.

Unwin, David. *Fifty Years with Father*. London: Allen and Unwin, 1982.

STEPHEN BIGGER

Sewall, Marcia (1935–), American author-illustrator born in Providence, Rhode Island, and educated at the Rhode Island School of Design and the Boston Museum School. She worked as a staff artist at the Boston Children's Museum. Sewall is known for illustrating stories that have a distinctive, primitive American or New England flavor. She has written and illustrated ten books of her own, most notably *The Pilgrims of Plimoth* (1986), winner of the Boston Globe–Horn Book Award for nonfiction, which tells the story of the Pilgrims with first-person dignity. *People of the Breaking Day* (1990), the companion volume to *The Pilgrims of Plimoth*, gives a similar treatment to the Wampanoag nation, and ends shortly before the Pilgrims arrive. Several of Sewall's books are adaptations of folk tales and ballads. Best known may be the illustrations she created for Richard Kennedy's award-winning books, including her affectionate and poignant black-and-white illustrations for *The Porcelain Man* (1976) and *Come Again in the Spring* (1976). The latter was selected for an exhibition by the American Institute of Graphic Arts in 1955, as were her illustrations for Kennedy's *The Leprechaun's Story* (1979). *The Song of the Horse* (1981) was chosen for the 1983 Bratislava International Biennale exhibition. Sewall is versatile in medium, using gouache, crayon, scratchboard, oils, and varied formats as appropriate. She also shows stylistic versatility with illustrations ranging from the gentleness she uses for Kennedy's work, to the intense lines and energy of John Reynolds Gardiner's acclaimed *Stone Fox* (1980), or the flowing watercolor-and-sepia-ink illustrations of *James Towne: Struggle for Survival* (2001). In Barbara Joosse's *Nobody's Cat* (1992), she presents color and pattern in a natural, straightforward way, giving emphasis to the relationship between forms. Always her sense of design is exceptional and her illustrations show respect and affection for their subjects.

DEBORAH KAPLAN

Sewell, Anna (1820–1878), British author, born in Norfolk into a Quaker family. First educated at home by her mother, at twelve Sewell began attending a day school in Stoke Newington, London. At fourteen, an accident when running home from that school resulted in the lameness that subsequently dictated Sewell's reliance on horse transport and precipitated further chronic illnesses. Sewell and her mother, Mary, herself the author of several works of practical advice for children and workers, worked tirelessly for the cause of temperance and the benefit of the poor. A fervent Christian, the Quaker insistence on plain speaking, obedience, self-denial, and independence remained Sewell's guiding principles throughout life.

During her years of travel, Sewell had witnessed much cruelty to the horses upon which society—and she herself—depended. This prompted the writing of her only book, *Black Beauty: His Grooms and Companions; The Autobiography of a Horse* (1877), which she asserted she had "translated from the equine" to "induce kindness, sympathy and an understanding treatment of horses." Originally intended for those working with horses, and written therefore in simple, direct vocabulary and syntax, with each chapter propounding a clear moral, it swiftly became popular with children, and is now regarded as a classic of children's literature. Drawing on an earlier literary tradition of animal autobiography, and much imitated ever since, *Black Beauty* tells the life story of a horse, from his idyllic early life through times of mistreatment and consequent decline, eventually resolved by Beauty's return to green pastures. Although Sewell died before its immense popularity and influence became evident, *Black Beauty* quickly became an enduring best seller, widely translated and abridged, frequently adapted for other media, and a landmark of anthropomorphic fiction.

BRIDGET CARRINGTON

Sewell, Elizabeth Missing (1815–1906), English author who was born into a religiously strict family and lived on the Isle of Wight. She attended boarding school in Bath, later helping teach her younger sisters and founding her own school. Sewell wrote in part to pay off family debts. A polemical writer, like her friend Charlotte Yonge she was a High Church Anglican novelist inspired by the Oxford movement, and she wrote for educated girls and women. She produced a range of nonfiction and devotional works as well as didactic novels that promote religious duty and domestic life for women. These novels include the very successful *Amy Herbert* (1844) and *Laneton Parsonage: A Tale for Children, on the Practical Use of a Portion of the Church Catechism* (1846), which are both about moral behavior and issues of doctrine. Her most popular book was *The Experience of Life* (1853), based on her own youth.

ADRIENNE E. GAVIN

Sewell, Helen (1896–1957), American author and illustrator. Born on Mare Island, California, she spent her early years in Guam with her father, a naval commander, her mother having died when she was young. When she was seven her father also died, and she and her sister went to live with an aunt in Brooklyn, New York, where she studied art at the Pratt Institute, at twelve the youngest student ever admitted. Initially a greeting-card designer, she developed a career as a book illustrator, starting by illustrating Susanne Langer's *The Cruise of the Little Dipper, and Other Fairy Tales* (1924) and going on to illustrate almost sixty children's books. Her most famous works are her illustrations for Laura Ingalls Wilder's *Little House* series beginning in 1932, the first three of which she illustrated herself, collaborating with Mildred Boyle on later volumes. She received a Caldecott Honor for her illustrations to Alice Dalgliesh's *The Thanksgiving Story* (1954). Sewell also wrote and illustrated her own books, beginning with *ABC for Everyday* (1930), and including *Peggy and the Pony* (1936) and, with Elena Eleska, the comic strip–style book *Three Tall Tales* (1947). In addition, she illustrated a string of adult books and classics and contributed drawings to the *New Yorker*.

[*See also* Dalgliesh, Alice *and* Wilder, Laura Ingalls.]

ADRIENNE E. GAVIN

Sexton Blake. Popular British fictional detective who from 1893 to the 1970s featured in stories, novels, annuals, comics, and films written by more than 150 authors and pictured by a string of illustrators. Later known as "The World's Greatest Detective" and the "prince of the penny dreadfuls," Sexton Blake first appeared in 1893 in a story published in *The Halfpenny Marvel* by Hal Meredith (thought to be the pseudonym of Harry Blyth), who wrote the first few stories. Blake mysteries soon appeared in other magazines, including regular publication in *Union Jack* until 1933, in *Detective Weekly* from 1933 to 1940, in *Sexton Blake Library* from 1940 to 1963, and in paperbacks published by Howard Baker.

Created six years after Arthur Conan Doyle's Sherlock Holmes, Blake echoes Holmes by having an intent expression, a housekeeper, and a home in Baker Street, London. Blake's cases, however, focus heavily on action and adventure, and his strong and resilient physical abilities play a more prominent role in the cases' solutions than Holmesian intellectual deduction. In locales both English and exotic he outwits and fights villains such as Mr. Mist (the Invisible Man) and Miss Death, and escapes from perils as various as poisonous cobras and being tied to a moon rocket. Having a bloodhound named Pedro, a Rolls-Royce called the Grey Panther, a pilot's license, and medical training, Blake solves crimes with a series of sidekicks. Most notable of these assistants is the streetwise, irrepressible, Blake-worshipping Tinker, who entered the stories in 1904 but is overshadowed in stories of the 1950s and 1960s by Blake's new secretary, Paula Dane. Dubbed "the office-boy's Sherlock Holmes," Blake enjoyed particular popularity with young male readers.

[*See also* Doyle, Arthur Conan; Mystery and Detective Stories; *and* Penny Dreadful.]

BIBLIOGRAPHY

Turner, E. S. *Boys Will Be Boys: The Story of Sweeney Todd, Deadwood Dick, Sexton Blake, Billy Bunter, Dick Barton, et al.* Harmondsworth, U.K.: Penguin, 1976.

ADRIENNE E. GAVIN

Shakespeare Adaptations. Shakespeare's plays have long been revised for purposes ranging from accessibility to parody. Among familiar prose versions for young readers are Charles and Mary Lamb's *Tales from Shakespeare* (1807), E. Nesbit's *Beautiful Stories from Shakespeare for Children* (1907), and Leon Garfield's *Shakespeare's Stories I* (1985) and *II* (1994), widely regarded as the definitive contemporary collection. Complete adaptations either abridge the originals, as in Cass Foster's 60-Minute Shakespeare series; retell the plays in prose, as in Lamb, Nesbit, and Garfield; rewrite the plays in greatly simplified poetry, as in Lois Burdett's Shakespeare Can Be Fun! series; or combine techniques—for example, by retaining famous quotations but summarizing action in prose, as in Hilary Burningham's Graphic Shakespeare series.

Recently adaptations for children have proliferated. The introductions to several passionately state the adaptors' desire to include younger and younger readers in the pleasure of reading or performing the plays. Bruce Coville, in his prose picture book *Romeo and Juliet* (1999), writes, "our hope is to sharpen readers' appetite for Shakespeare and give them a hint of the treasures waiting to be found." However, Coville's is one of the best retellings. Others are not so good—and therein lies the rub. Versions, often for performance, are being written for children as young as seven or eight years old, though it is questionable whether cognitively immature children are really experiencing Shakespeare or are merely enjoying dressing up for teachers and parents.

Burdett claims that "Reading aloud to my own children has convinced me that the sooner you spark their interest, the better. From Gertrude and Hamlet to Green Eggs and Ham, they soak it all in like water in sand." Critics have asked, however, whether Gertrude is really equivalent to Green Eggs or Hamlet to Ham, no matter how indiscriminately one defines "it all." Nor is water renowned for its staying power in sand.

Prose versions retold by professional writers like Garfield, Coville, and Andrew Matthews are all lavishly illustrated, and the overall quality of production as well as of text is superior to retellings for younger readers. Author-illustrator Marcia Williams's *Tales from Shakespeare* (1998) and *Bravo, Mr. Shakespeare!* (2001) stand out for their imaginative layout and opportunities for multitasking by readers, with their running border cartoonishly depicting the playgoers of Shakespeare's time watching the action center page. Additionally, Julius Lester's *Othello: A Novel* (1995), Gary Blackwood's historical fictions *The Shakespeare Stealer* (1998) and *Shakespeare's Scribe* (2000), Avi's *Romeo and Juliet: Together (and Alive!) at Last* (1987), Wishbone Classics' *Romeo and Juliet* (1996), and Sweet Valley Twins' *Romeo and 2 Juliets* indicate the range of Shakespeare-based literature available.

[*See also* Abridgment; Adaptation; *and biographies of figures mentioned in this article.*]

BIBLIOGRAPHY

Burt, Richard, and Lynda Boose, eds. *Shakespeare, the Movie II: Popularizing the Plays on Film, TV, Video, and DVD*. New York: Routledge, 2003.

Foster, Cass. *Shakespeare—To Teach or Not to Teach: Teaching Shakespeare from Elementary to High School*. Scottsdale, Ariz.: Five Star, 2002.

Miller, Naomi, ed. *Reimagining Shakespeare for Children and Young Adults*. New York: Routledge, 2002.

Alida Allison

Shankar. *See* Pillai, Keshaw Shankar.

Shannon, David (1959–), American author and illustrator of picture books. Educated at the Art Center College of Design in Pasadena, California, Shannon has worked with a number of the most famous writers in American children's literature including Audrey Wood, Jane Yolen, and Julius Lester. His artistic style ranges widely and deftly captures the mood of each story whether he is illustrating Columbus's first mysterious contact with the people of the Americas in Yolen's *Encounter* (1992) or bringing jolly buccaneers to life with Melinda Long in *How I Became a Pirate* (2003). His own books have, however, been his most successful creations. Shannon won a 1999 Caldecott Honor for *No, David!* (1998) a book inspired by a series of drawings he created at age five. The book employs a childlike style of drawing to show David moving from one sort of mischief to another. His adventures continue in *David Goes to School* (1999), *David Gets in Trouble* (2002), and *Oh, David!* (2005).

Megan Lynn Isaac

Shannon, George (1952–), American picture book author, born in Caldwell, Kansas. He was educated at Western Kentucky University (BS, 1974) and the University of Kentucky (MSLS, 1976) and worked as a librarian in public schools and public libraries in Kentucky. Shannon is known for his oral storytelling, as well as for rhyming- and song-stories for young children, such as *Lizard's Song* (1981), still a favorite, now with two sequels; *The Piney Woods Peddler* (1981), adapted from a Grimm brothers' fairy tale; *Climbing Kansas Mountains* (1993), about a young boy and his father; and the more recent *Tippy-Toe Chick, Go!* (2003), a Charlotte Zolotow honor book. His young adult novel, *Unlived Affections* (1989), concerning issues of sexuality and families, won the Friends of American Writers Award in 1990. His books have lavish and colorful illustrations by talented artists such as Jose Aruego and Ariane Dewey, who illustrated his Lizard series. He has also written a popular series of story collections that allow middle-grade readers to solve problems for characters in the fiction, called simply *Stories to Solve* (1985), *More Stories to Solve* (1990), and *Still More Stories to Solve* (1994). They are based on riddles from around the world. His books often feature family relationships or animals and are very busy, upbeat, and joyful.

Janice M. Bogstad

Shannon, Monica (1905?–1965), Canadian-born author whose writing career spanned only a few years, yet produced a Newbery Award–winning novel. Moving to the United States as an infant, Shannon grew up in the American West, and her first book, *California Fairy Tales* (1926), blends the Golden State's natural history with magical storylines. This work was followed by *Goose Grass Rhymes* (1930) and by the pirate story *Tawnymore* (1931). Though these books have been long forgotten, she is still remembered for *Dobry* (1934), the story of a Bulgarian peasant boy with a talent for art. In writing this novel, Shannon drew on the reminiscences of Bulgarian ranch hands she knew as a child, as well as the memories of Atanas Katchamakoff, who illustrated the book. Evocative, quietly affecting prose brings historical Bulgaria to life and captures the growth of one artistic spirit. Though not a particularly popular Newbery winner among modern readers, it still holds up as one of the award's best selections.

PETER D. SIERUTA

Sharkey, Niamh (1972–), Irish artist and illustrator who studied at the Dublin College of Marketing and Design. Her books are known for her attention to design. Texture and depth are built by oil paint on layers of gesso; her images are highly stylized, displaying meticulous attention to detail. The layout of the page is significant, and perspective is often distorted, giving weight and meaning to particular characters and scenes. In 1999 Sharkey won the British Mother Goose award for *Tales of Wisdom and Wonder* (1998, text Hugh Lupton) and *The Gigantic Turnip* (1998, text Aleksei Tolstoy). The former also won the 1998/1999 Children's Books Ireland Bisto Book of the Year Award. Interpretations of traditional stories, including *Tales from Old Ireland* (2000, text Malachy Doyle), established her reputation. Publication of *The Ravenous Beast* (2003) and *Santasaurus* (2004), for which she wrote the text and designed the font, showed a lighter palette; these books for younger readers also demonstrate Sharkey's quirky humor.

BIBLIOGRAPHY

Short, John. "The Quirky World of Niamh Sharkey." *Inis: the Children's Books Ireland Magazine* 9 (Summer 2004).

VALERIE COGHLAN

Sharmat, Marjorie Weinman (1928–), prolific American author of children's and young adult books. Sharmat is best known for her beginning reader books featuring Nate the Great, boy detective. In *Nate the Great* (1972), the first in the series, Nate starts out with a breakfast of pancakes and then helps solve the minor mysterious occurrences on his block and among his friends. Marc Simont's simple yet action-filled illustrations complement Sharmat's basic yet lively text in a partnership that lasted for more than twenty "Nate the Great" titles. Sharmat and her husband, Mitchell Sharmat, are coauthors of the "Olivia Sharp, Agent for Secrets" series, which includes *The Pizza Monster* (1989), *The Princess of the Fillmore Street* (1989), and *The Sly Spy* (1990). Sharmat is also the author of the young adult series "Sorority Sisters" (1986–1987) as well as several young adult novels written under the pen name Wendy Andrews.

DEBRA MITTS-SMITH

Sharp, Edith Lambert (1917–), Canadian writer, born in Manitoba and raised in British Columbia. Sharp studied at the Vancouver School of Fine Arts and later at the Smithsonian Institute in Washington, D.C. Despite a notable stint with the Canadian Broadcasting Corporation, Sharp is best known for her only children's book, *Nkwala* (1958). She received several prestigious awards for *Nkwala*, including the Governor General's Award in Canada (1959) and the Hans Christian Andersen Award from Luxembourg (1960). *Nkwala* is widely considered one of Canada's best children's novels about early First Nations society, and is still considered a popular book in elementary schools today.

DIANA KINDRON

Sharp, Evelyn (1869–1955), British journalist, novelist, feminist, and author of fantasy and realistic fiction for children. As the ninth of eleven children in a Victorian middle-class family, Sharp could hardly expect to be sent to Cambridge, as her brothers were. She was lucky to go to school at all. Later she moved in avant-garde circles (contributing to *The Yellow Book*) and became a leading suffragist (for several years editing *Votes for Women*); later still she worked with a Quaker relief agency in Germany and Russia. As for her writing, she was primarily a journalist but also wrote fantasy, novels, an account of dance, studies of children, a biography, an autobiography, and a comic libretto. In her works for children Sharp followed her own advice in "The Books Children Like" (1922), writing fiction that makes children "feel on a level with the author." Her eponymous Micky (1905) feels "it won't never be tea time again" while his mother is away, and he proceeds to act out his favorite fairy tales, for good or ill. Sharp also explored new gender roles. The boy of "The Boy Who Looked Like a Girl" (*Wymps*, 1897) wants to leave his family of girls—until he experiences a land of boys. Firefly, the active heroine of "The Spell of the Magician's Daughter" (*Round the World to Wympland*, 1902), redefines witchcraft as positive and empowering. In *The Youngest Girl in the School* (1901) Sharp infuses the standard girls' school story with questions about the roles available to women. In *The Making of a Schoolgirl* (1897) she brilliantly undermines the patriarchal pronouncements of Becky's older brother without undermining the affection between the two siblings. Sharp excelled when she balanced on the precarious borderline between fact and fiction, probing for irony; when she wrote a kind of fictionalized nonfiction in stories of suffragists (*Rebel Women*, 1910); or when, as in *The Making of a Schoolgirl*, she wrote fiction that drew directly on her experiences as a girl.

[*See also* School Stories.]

BEVERLY LYON CLARK

Sharp, Margery (1905–1991), British author who lived principally in London and published adult and juvenile fiction as well as articles and plays. Sharp enjoyed a modest success with her adult novels and plays. The best known of these is *The Nutmeg Tree* (1937), produced in New York under the title *Lady in Waiting* (1940) and later as a feature film entitled *Julia Misbehaves* (MGM, 1948), featuring Greer Garson, Peter Lawford, Walter Pidgeon, and Elizabeth Taylor. Sharp achieved her widest fame for her juvenile titles in the "Miss Bianca" series published between 1959 and 1979. *The Rescuers* (1959), first of these, is an enchanting story of the Prisoners' Aid Society, a mouse organization dedicated to serving prisoners everywhere. It became an ALA Notable Book in 1959 and introduces the two mice who dominate the series. The first of these is the glamorous Miss Bianca, a white mouse who is the pet of the ambassador's son and lives in a lovely miniature palace. Bernard, hero of the last two stories, *Bernard the Brave* (1977) and *Bernard into Battle* (1979), is her faithful sidekick and devoted admirer in the earlier books. Together, they extend the work of the society from cheering up prisoners to rescuing those unfairly imprisoned. In most cases, these are human children who have been kidnapped or hidden away. Miss Bianca is self-confident, beautiful, and clever. Bernard is a prosaic, brown, simple working-class mouse who is also strong, able, creative, practical, and always modest. While simple, the books are very well written, with sophisticated language, subtle characterization, and imaginative plots that allude to a broader mistreatment of children by adults. The first and second (*Miss Bianca*, 1962) became a feature-length animated film (*The Rescuers*, Walt Disney, 1977), which was both successful and the focus of related merchandise sales such as dolls, picture books, and coloring books. Sharp's books still attract a wide readership of both children and adults.

JANICE M. BOGSTAD

Sharratt, Nick (1962–), British author and illustrator who began his career in children's books illustrating poetry anthologies. A prolific illustrator, popular for his bold, colorful, and simplified style, Sharratt regularly subverts the traditional format of picture books. *Ketchup on Your Cornflakes?* (1994) is ring-bound and contains pages that are divided horizontally into sections so that the reader can create various combinations around the theme of food. *Shark in the Park* (2002) features a boy who believes that there is a shark in the park whenever he sees a black fin shape through a hole in the recto page. In each case the "fin" is revealed to be a benign object. Sharratt's work displays a carnivalesque humor and a sense of the absurd, as seen in *Mixed Up Fairy Tales* (with Hilary Robinson, 2004) and *Pants* (with Giles Andreae, 2002). He also produces conventional interactive books with flaps and holes that give a surprise element to his stories. Sharratt has worked with many authors, including Kes Gray, Sue Heap, and Julia Donaldson. In 1991 he began his most famous collaboration by illustrating *The Story of Tracy Beaker* by Jacqueline Wilson. Since then he has illustrated all of her books.

[*See also* Wilson, Jacqueline.]

PHYLLIS RAMAGE

Shaw, Flora Louisa (1852–1929), British writer who wrote her first novel, *Castle Blair* (1877), reflecting her experiences of the Irish Republican movement during childhood visits to her Anglo-Irish grandfather, at the recommendation of her friend and mentor John Ruskin and of Charlotte M. Yonge. Her heroes Winnie and Murtagh anticipate the independent child characters of Kenneth Grahame, S. R. Crockett, and Edith Nesbit. The book's popularity swiftly spread to North America and Europe, as did that of *Hector* (1881) and *Phyllis Browne* (1882). Her last novels, *A Sea Change* (1885) and *Colonel Cheswick's Campaign* (1886), were increasingly oriented toward young adults.

BRIDGET CARRINGTON

Shedlock, Marie (1854–1935), actress and teacher who became a professional storyteller in the 1890s. Born in France but spending most of her life in England, she lectured on storytelling and demonstrated her skills in England, France, and the United States.

Shedlock's style brought a freshness to storytelling, which had in Victorian times become too dependent on elocution.

Her more natural, less stilted delivery was particularly suited to folk and fairy tales. In particular she made good use of Hans Christian Andersen's stories, "The Swineherd," "The Princess and the Pea," "The Steadfast Tin Soldier," and, most of all, "The Nightingale." In the last mentioned she contrasted the living bird with its clockwork rival to remarkable effect.

In *The Art of the Storyteller* (1915), which is regarded as a classic of its kind, she recorded a number of skills that she considered to be essential to her art. The selection of the right story was paramount, as was timing; the build-up of suspense was vital, and, most important of all, the teller needed to create the impression of being part of the story.

Shedlock's most important work was probably done during her several visits to the United States. Storytelling in the public library service there can be traced back to 1886 in The Free Library of Brooklyn, but it was her first visit in 1900 that galvanized interest in public library service across the nation. During her seven-year stay, she visited Boston, Pittsburgh, Cleveland, Chicago, and the West Coast, and consolidated her work in an extended trip between 1915 and 1920. Her inspiration to storytellers in public libraries is beyond doubt.

GEOFFREY FENWICK

Shelley, Noreen (1920–1985), Australian novelist who worked also as a scriptwriter for children's radio and as editor of the *School Magazine* (1960–1970). Her settings in Sydney and the surrounding region depict an Australia of the 1970s and show the tensions emerging in a period of change. Five books about a small pig, Piggy Grunter (e.g., *Piggy Grunter's Red Umbrella*, 1944) recount the escapades of a naughty, childlike animal. For older readers she wrote *Family at the Lookout* (1972; illustrated by Robert Micklewright), which won the Book of the Year Award from the Children's Book Council of Australia (1973). Within a mystery set in the Blue Mountains out of Sydney, this work exposes prejudice in a small community. *Faces in a Looking-Glass* (1974; illustrated by Astra Lacis) has the protagonist, Kylie, misunderstanding a mother/child relationship. Shelley adapted folk tales for *Legends of the Gods* (1976), also illustrated by Astra Lacis.

STELLA LEES and PAM MACINTYRE

Shepard, E. H. (1879–1976), British illustrator whose drawing ability was recognized and fostered when he was still at school. Ernest Howard Shepard trained at Heatherley's, and then won a scholarship to the Royal Academy Schools. Shepard is regarded as the last of the great English "black and white artists." As a young man he was called a "giddy kipper," a slang term implying that he had a happy-go-lucky nature, which was shortened to Kipper or Kip and became his lifelong nickname. His early career, which included placing two drawings with the periodical *Punch* in 1906, was interrupted by World War I, during which he saw combat at the Somme, Arras, and Ypres, and in Italy, and was awarded the Military Cross. Shepard sent drawings to *Punch* during the war, after which he was offered a regular staff position. Through this he met E. V. Lucas, chairman of Methuen, who suggested that Shepard might illustrate some of the verses written by A. A. Milne. Shepard made eleven

E. H. Shepard. The boy meets the Reluctant Dragon; illustration by Shepard from *Dream Days* (London: John Lane, 1930.) COLLECTION OF JACK ZIPES

drawings, and the subsequent book, *When We Were Very Young* (1924), was a huge success. Shepard's drawings were dropped in and around the text in an informal layout that was very unusual for the period. *Winnie-the-Pooh* (1926), *Now We Are Six* (1927), and *The House at Pooh Corner* (1928) followed swiftly.

Although the universe of the story for the *Pooh* books is the imaginary one of an only child and his observing father, the participants and setting existed in reality. Pooh, Eeyore, Piglet, Kanga, and Roo are all based on real soft toys; the Hundred Acre Wood where Owl lived was actually the Ashdown forest where A. A. Milne took his son, Christopher. Milne expected his illustrator to make sketches of scenes described in the text, and to use photographic sources as references for the drawings of Christopher and his toys. Shepard's line drawings, with their sure light touch, delicate strokes, and tonal hatching, catch the playfulness of the language and the sense of intimacy between participants. Robust little figures generally are caught in action, often defying gravity with their hops and jumps; sensitive portrayals of Christopher Robin record the vulnerable nape of the neck, the back of the knees, the curve of a turned-away cheek; air seems to tremble, and light seems to stream through forest foliage.

In 1931 Shepard was invited to illustrate Kenneth Grahame's *Wind in the Willows* and went to Berkshire to meet yet another author with a highly developed sense of place; Grahame sent him off to make sketches of the riverbank, the meadows, and the wood. The anthropomorphic animals that later come to life on the page coexist convincingly in their natural world and in the human one through Shepard's skillfully adapting their scale to suit the particular situation. Shepard also illustrated Kenneth Grahame's *Bertie's Escapade* (1949). After he left *Punch* in 1953, he wrote two autobiographies, *Drawn from Memory* (1957) and *Drawn from Life* (1961), and two children's books. Shepard was preparing colored editions of the Pooh books when he died in his early nineties.

[*See also* Anthropomorphism; Illustrations; Picture Books; *and biographies of figures mentioned in this article.*]

BIBLIOGRAPHY

Chandler, Arthur. *The Story of E. H. Shepard: The Man Who Drew Pooh*. Winkinswoof Farm, U.K.: Jaydem Books, 2000.

Meyer, Susan E. "Ernest H. Shepard." In *A Treasury of the Great Children's Book Illustrators*, 143–156. New York: Harry N. Abrams, 1987.

JANE DOONAN

Sherlock, Erica.

See Chapman, Jean.

Sherlock Holmes.

See Doyle, Arthur Conan.

Sherwood, Mary Martha

Sherwood, Mary Martha (1775–1851), English writer. Often considered one of the most severely moralistic English writers, Sherwood's religious beliefs dominated her writing for children. Mary Martha Butt Sherwood was raised in a Worcestershire village by strict but kind parents; her father was an Anglican clergyman who allowed his only daughter a more expansive education than that usually given to girls, teaching her Latin and encouraging her to write stories. After her father's death when she was twenty, she began to examine her religious beliefs seriously. She started teaching Sunday school and began to write stories featuring the rewards of piety, such as *Susan Gray* (1802), whose servant protagonist protects her virtue against an amorous employer and eventually dies a happy Christian death. After marrying her cousin, Captain Henry Sherwood, in 1803, Sherwood traveled with him to India, leaving behind her first child, and in India had two more, Lucy and Henry. She became friends with the missionary Henry Martyn and soon converted to his evangelical brand of religion; when Lucy died of dysentery in 1808, Sherwood felt it as a direct rebuke from God for loving her too much. This sense of God's personal interventions and the necessity to subordinate all earthly loves to religious faith informs her subsequent writing for children.

Sherwood wrote more than 350 books, tracts, and essays, but she is best known for two: "Little Henry and His Bearer" (1814) and the three-volume *History of the Fairchild Family* (1818; 1842; 1847). "Little Henry" contributes to the evangelical fervor to convert Indians to Christianity; its protagonist, an orphan left to the care of his Hindu bearer Boosy, learns at the age of five that all humanity is sinful, and that the punishment of sin is damnation. Through his great piety and love for Boosy, Henry begins to convert his bearer in order to save him from eternal death, but dies before the job is completed. Sherwood closes her text by extolling her child readers, especially those in India, to follow his evangelical example: "*go and do likewise*." This story was immensely popular and long-lived, going through thirty editions by 1840 and numerous translations.

Sherwood was equally celebrated for *The Fairchild Family*, which sought "to shew the Importance and Effects of a

Religious Education"; it remained in print until well after World War I, albeit in abridged form. The original text describes all children as inherently sinful, and in need of constant correction and an education in their own unworthiness. It contains some shocking incidents: one child, the spoiled and irreligious Augusta Noble, is burned to death unshriven (that is, not having received the sacrament of reconciliation), illustrating "the fatal effects of disobedience to parents," while the Fairchild children are subjected to the sight of a decomposed body on a gibbet to show the uncompromising "effects of filial wrath." However, the text also contains affection for and understanding of children and their foibles. Volumes two and three tone down the religious elements, reflecting Sherwood's own eventual turn to a belief in unconditional salvation and a merciful Redeemer.

[*See also* Evangelical Writing; Moral Tales; *and* Religious Writing.]

BIBLIOGRAPHY

Demers, Patricia. "Mrs. Sherwood and Hesba Stretton: The Letter and the Spirit of Evangelical Writing of and for Children." In *Romanticism and Children's Literature in Nineteenth-Century England*, edited by James Holt McGavran, 129–149. Athens: University of Georgia Press, 1991.

Vallone, Lynne. " 'A Humble Spirit Under Correction': Tracts, Hymns, and the Ideology of Evangelical Fiction for Children, 1780–1820." *The Lion and the Unicorn* 15 (1991): 72–95.

Cutt, M. Nancy. *Mrs. Sherwood and Her Books for Children*. Oxford: Oxford University Press, 1974.

JACQUELINE M. LABBE

Shimin, Symeon (1902–1984), prolific illustrator of more than fifty children's books, including two that he wrote. Shimin was born in Astrakhan, Russia, and immigrated to the United States with his parents when he was ten years old. In addition to illustrating children's books, he worked as a freelance commercial artist, and was commissioned to create a mural in the Department of Justice Building in Washington, D.C., in 1938. The first book he illustrated was a revised edition of Herman and Nina Schneider's *How Big Is Big?* (1950), published by William R. Scott. He illustrated several other books published by Scott, including those by Miriam Schlein and Margaret Wise Brown, and illustrated three books for Byrd Baylor, including one of his favorites, *One Small Blue Bead* (1965). He also provided the illustrations for Joseph Krumgold's Newbery Award winner, *Onion John* (1959) and Virginia Hamilton's *Zeely* (1967). He drew from live models, and his pencil, ink, and watercolor illustrations are fluid and lifelike.

[*See also biographies of figures mentioned in this article.*]

LINNEA HENDRICKSON

Sholem Aleichem (1859–1916), Russian-Jewish author and the most beloved of Yiddish writers. Sholem Aleichem, whose real name was Sholem Rabinowitz, adopted his pseudonym from the Hebrew phrase meaning "peace be with you." He grew up in a *shtetl* and was influenced by a Hasidic upbringing as well as modern Haskalah (enlightenment) ideals. In over forty volumes of stories he documents *shtetl* life and the modern world's encroachment on Jewish tradition. He eventually immigrated to America to escape anti-Semitism.

Tevye's Daughters (1895–1918; novel in short stories published in various permutations), the basis for the Broadway musical *Fiddler on the Roof*, examines the rejection of arranged marriage for romantic attachment. "Song of Songs" (1909–1911; published in two parts) portrays a passionate, innocent childhood love destroyed by the narrator's rejection of traditional Jewish values. Many of his children's stories, such as "What Will Become of Me?," are commentaries on secular temptation in a spiritual community.

BIBLIOGRAPHY

Samuel, Maurice. *The World of Sholem Aleichem*. New York: Atheneum, 1986. See especially chapters entitled "The Children's World" and "The Cheder" for keys to understanding the place of the child in the *shtetl* and Aleichem's stories.

MONICA FRIEDMAN

Short Story. The short story eludes definition, and this is part of its charm and success. The magical ambiguity of the form enables it to inspire many writers, serve many purposes, and entertain a wide variety of readers. Typically short stories are limited in length, written in prose, include a narrator, focus on the development of only one or two characters, have a single-stranded plot, and come to a resolution with a tidy conclusion. However, finding stories that violate one or more of these conventions is not difficult. Even the most basic question—what are the length limits of the short story—has no distinct answer. Simply put, in addition to being entertaining, the best short stories are sticky. They adhere to the imagination; they nudge the reader off balance; they sharpen the reader's awareness; they transform the mundane into the thought provoking; they grab hold of the reader. Some critics have attempted to define the short story less by what it looks like than what it does, and here the most common conclusion is that the short story intensifies the narrative process. Like a photograph, it draws the reader's attention to a moment, but also challenges the reader both to notice the frame that holds the picture and to look beyond it.

The brevity of the short story also makes it ideal not only for telling conventional tales but also for exploring experimental ones. Writers use short stories to reshape readers' expectations about place, time, voice, point of view, and structure. This very variety makes it impossible to define the genre and sustains its viability. The best definitions, then, are dialogic, taking into account what the short story is and what it is becoming.

Many traditional works for children, like fairy tales, folk tales, legends, myths, and fables, share features with the short story, but their constant reshaping through oral transmission and the creative innovation of modern authors distinguishes them as something different from the true short story. In general, however, the study of the short story as a genre has been severely neglected. Anthologies and textbooks focusing on the academic study of children's literature virtually never include a discussion of the short story. Choosing a starting point for the history of the short story would merely be an invitation to argument, but it is well recognized that the form received much of its definition from the early 19th-century American writers Washington Irving (1783–1859), Edgar Allan Poe (1809–1849), and Nathaniel Hawthorne (1804–1864). Although none of these men, with the exception of Hawthorne, wrote for children in particular, their work has been adopted by young readers.

The earliest short stories specifically for children were often lightly veiled moral and instructional texts, one of the most influential writers of which was Maria Edgeworth (1767–1849). In this period, the value of fiction for children, especially fairy tales, was a matter of speculation and concern. Stories were usually restricted to domestic and school settings. They featured either exemplary protagonists, naughty youngsters who learned a lesson and repented of earlier folly, or bad children who came too late to wisdom and suffered accordingly. Yet, the construction of such stories could not have been much more fun for the authors than reading them was for their audiences, and rather sooner than later authors began to indulge themselves and their audiences with wit and spunk, as in the work of Rudyard Kipling and Louisa May Alcott, and humor and suspense later in the tales of Joan Aiken and Philippa Pearce. The chronologically organized *Oxford Book of Children's Stories* (edited by Jan Mark, 1993) showcases this shift from a self-assuredly didactic intent to a more varied set of purposes.

For many decades the short story reached most young readers through periodicals. *St. Nicholas*, *The Youth's Companion*, *Boy's Own Paper*, and *Girl's Own Paper* were popular venues for short stories about school life, adventure, history, and friendship. Many, many smaller periodicals also flourished. Today periodicals are substantially less influential, but important magazines like *Highlights for Children* continue to publish short stories for very young readers. Today short stories tend to reach their audiences through anthologies; often these are organized by genre. Phillipa Pearce traces a history of ghost stories for children in *Dread and Delight* (1995). *Trip Trap* (Farrukh Dhondy, 1982), *Shades of Dark* (edited by Aidan Chambers, 1984), and *Ghosts, Ghouls, and Other Nightmares: Spooky Stories* (edited by Gene Kemp, 1995) are other standouts in this genre. Other fields rich in short stories include fantasy, which is well represented by Robin McKinley in *A Knot in the Grain* (1994) and *Water: Tales of Elemental Spirits* (with Peter Dickinson, 2002); science fiction, as seen in *Tomorrowland* (edited by Michael Cart, 1999); and humor, in Michael Rosen's anthology *Funny Stories* (1988) and Paul Jenning's many quirky volumes including *Unmentionable!* (1991). Common, too, are collections of loosely linked short stories like Donald Sobol's small mysteries in *Encyclopedia Brown* (1963) or the silly school stories of Louis Sachar in *Sideways Stories from the Wayside School* (1978).

Anthologies for young adult readers are more frequently built around themes. Marilyn Singer has produced several of these collections including *I Believe in Water: Twelve Brushes with Religion* (2000). *Am I Blue?* (edited by Marion Dane Bauer, 1994) explores questions of gay and lesbian experiences, and *Fractures: Family Stories* (Budge Wilson, 2002) confronts the difficulty, disappointment, and struggle that family life too often entails. Jennifer Armstrong has edited collections exploring war in *Shattered: Stories of Children and War* (2002) and using music as an organizing principle in *What a Song Can Do: Twelve Riffs on the Power of Music* (2004). Finally, Don Gallo has edited many anthologies that range from sport stories to a collection of immigrant experiences.

Short stories have also provided an avenue into children's and young adult literature for many writers of color in recent years. Single-authored collections and edited anthologies designed to this purpose include: *145th Street* (Walter Dean

Myers, 2001), *American Dragons: Twenty-Five Asian American Voices* (edited by Laurence Yep, 1993), *Local News* (Gary Soto, 1994), and *Moccasin Thunder: American Indian Stories for Today* (edited by Lori Marie Carlson, 2005).

[*See also* Children's Magazines; Journals and Periodicals; *and articles on journals and biographies of figures mentioned in this article.*]

BIBLIOGRAPHY

Commager, Henry Steele, ed. *The St. Nicholas Anthology*. New York: Random House, 1948.

Mark, Jan. *The Oxford Book of Children's Stories*. Oxford: Oxford University Press, 1993.

May, Charles E. *The New Short Story Theories*. Athens: Ohio University Press, 1994.

Shaw, Valerie. *The Short Story: A Critical Introduction*. New York: Longman, 1983.

MEGAN LYNN ISAAC

Shulevitz, Uri (1936–), Polish author and illustrator known for his "writing with pictures." In 1939, Shulevitz and his family escaped Nazi persecution in Poland and ultimately settled in Israel, where he attended the Art Institute in Tel Aviv (1953–1955) and Teacher's College (1956) before emigrating to New York City (1959). He studied at the Brooklyn Museum Art School and began illustrating for a Hebrew children's publisher. As an author and illustrator, his first work was *The Moon in My Room* (1963), followed by *One Monday Morning* (1967). His illustrations for Arthur Ransome's *The Fool of the World and the Flying Ship* (1968) earned him the Caldecott Medal, and both *The Treasure* (1979) and *Snow* (1998) were Caldecott Honor books. Shulevitz's approach to picture books includes his effort to suggest, imply, and stir imagination rather than delineate images in literal terms. He shares this philosophy, as well as ideas about graphic design, in *Writing with Pictures: How to Write and Illustrate Children's Books* (1985). All told, his career has many dimensions: museums and galleries exhibit his works, art students are instructed in his classes (for instance, at the New School for Social Research), and children are enriched by his exceptional artistic virtuosity.

[*See also* Illustrations; Picture Books; *and* Ransome, Arthur.]

BIBLIOGRAPHY

Shulevitz, Uri. "Writing With Pictures." *Horn Book* 58 (1982): 17–22.

REBECCA HOGUE WOJAHN

Sidjakov, Nicolas (1924–), picture book illustrator, born in Latvia of Russian parents and educated at the École des Beaux-Arts. Sidjakov worked for the French film industry (1950–1955); then, after marrying an American, he settled in San Francisco. He became a freelance designer and illustrated his first book, Laura N. Baker's *The Friendly Beasts* (1957). His next assignment—Ruth Robbins's adaptation of *Baboushka and the Three Kings* (1960)—was a Caldecott winner. Both books are characterized by bold, contemporary designs in conjunction with medieval (mostly Byzantine) traditions. In *Baboushka* he flattens his forms in order to emphasize geometric spaces and embellishes them with colors, textures, and minute ornamental details. He achieves great richness with this style. *The Friendly Beasts* was chosen for the American Institute of Graphic Arts Children's Book Show for 1955–1957; in 1962 another important work, *The Emperor and the Drummer Boy*, was cited by the *New York Times* as one of the year's best illustrated children's books.

DONNARAE MACCANN

Sidney, Margaret (1844–1924), author of domestic stories for children. Born Harriet Mulford Stone in New Haven, Connecticut, her writing career began in 1878 when she became a contributor to *Wide Awake*. Two years later her best-known book, *Five Little Peppers and How They Grew*, was serialized there and was published in book form in 1881. In that year she married her publisher, Daniel Lothrop. She was to share many of his interests in cultural and civic affairs. *Five Little Peppers* is a euphoric account of how poverty becomes prosperity through the benevolence of a wealthy man whose cold heart is thawed by contact with the indomitable Pepper family. The widowed Mrs. Pepper "had met life too bravely to be beaten down . . . so with a stout heart and a cheery face she had worked away day after day . . . and she had seen with pride that couldn't be concealed, her noisy happy brood growing up around her, and filling her heart with comfort, and making the little brown house fairly ring with jollity and fun." There is difficulty in paying the rent and in feeding the five children, but into their lives comes Jasper, charismatic schoolboy son of a rich and invalid businessman. Captivated by the household, he begs that Polly, the eldest Pepper, come and live with them. Then Phronsie, the youngest, joins her, and becomes the cherished pet of Jasper's father. Finally the whole family is absorbed, and it is discovered that Mrs. Pepper is the long-lost cousin of Jasper's brother-in-law. Readers found the story so entrancing that two million copies had been sold by the time of Mrs. Lothrop's death. She wrote many sequels about the doings of Polly, Ben, Joel, Davie, and Phronsie at school, grown up, and abroad, but none approached the popularity of the first book.

[*See also* Wide Awake.]

GILLIAN AVERY

Siebert, Diane (1948–), American poet born in Chicago. Siebert trained as a nurse before spending many years motorcycling with her husband throughout the United States and Mexico. These travels and her passion for running encouraged the close connection with the rhythms of the American landscape she expresses in her poetry in *Heartland* (1989):

I am the Heartland.
Smell the fields,
The rich, dark earth, and all it yields;
The air before a coming storm,
The newborn calf, so damp and warm; . . .

Produced as picture books illustrated by painters such as Wendell Minor (*Mojave*, 1988), Siebert's poetry combines lyricism, vivid imagery, and ecological accuracy. Her regional works, such as *Mississippi* (2001), celebrate the landscape from the perspective of the land itself, while another series reflects the rhythms of mechanical travel, as in *Motorcycle Song* (2002) and *Plane Song* (1993):

quick planes
slick planes
doing-fancy-trick planes . . .

ADRIENNE E. GAVIN

Siegal, Aranka (1929–), Hungarian-born novelist. Aranka Davidowitz Siegal was thirteen when Germany invaded her native Hungary in 1942. She and her family were incarcerated in the Beregszasz Jewish ghetto before their deportation to Auschwitz in May 1944. She and her elder sister were later sent to Bergen-Belsen, another concentration camp. No one else in their family survived. The Red Cross took the sisters to Sweden, where they lived for three years before emigrating to America. Siegal's two autobiographical novels, *Upon the Head of the Goat: A Childhood in Hungary, 1939–1944* (1982) and *Grace in the Wilderness: After the Liberation, 1945–1948* (1985), are narrated by Piri, which was Aranka's nickname. Both titles have won a number of prestigious prizes. The former received the Janusz Korczak Literary Award and the 1982 Boston Globe–Horn Book Award for Nonfiction as well as being a Newbery Honor Book. The latter was selected as a Notable Trade Book in the Field of Social Studies by the National Council for Social Studies Children's Book Council Joint Committee.

LYDIA KOKKOLA

Sienkiewicz, Henryk (1846–1916), Polish novelist of distinction, awarded the Nobel Prize for literature in 1905. He traveled widely in Europe and America. A stylist, realist, and critic of social and political evils, his 17th-century war trilogy captures the authentic voices of the past. Translations into English include *Quo Vadis?* (1896), about Christians in Ancient Rome, from 1912 popularized in numerous films. The children's adventure story, *In Desert and Wilderness* (1912), was the result of a hunting expedition in East Africa. A blend of Walter Scott, French romances, and epic, his work contributed to international enthusiasm for historical and adventure novels.

[*See also* Eastern European Countries *and* Historical Fiction.]

BIBLIOGRAPHY

Gardner, Monica M. *The Patriot Novelist of Poland, Henryk Sienkiewicz*. London: Dent, 1926.

ANN LAWSON LUCAS

Sierra i Fabra, Jordi (1947–), multifaceted and prolific Spanish writer. He has published over two hundred novels with all sorts of themes. His knowledge as a music critic and his liking for rock have been of use to him in writing works for young adults that have been successful in Spain, such as *El joven Lennon* (Young Lennon, 1988). Many of his works explicitly handle topics like urban violence or drugs, for example *Campos de fresas* (Strawberry Fields, 1997). However, he also treats themes like terrorism in *El tiempo del olvido* (A Time to Forget, 1995) or illegal immigration in *Noche de luna en el estrecho* (A Moonlit Night At the Straits of Gibraltar, 1996).

[*See also* Spain *and* Young Adult Literature.]

MARISA FERNÁNDEZ-LOPEZ

Signal: Approaches to Children's Literature. *Signal* was an independent children's literature journal that ran for one hundred issues and published over five hundred articles between 1970 and 2003. It was founded by Nancy and Aidan Chambers, under the aegis of their small publishing house, The Thimble Press, in rural Gloucestershire, U.K., and established very high standards of editing and production. *Signal* became one of the outstanding journals in its field, with a reputation for integrity, accessibility, and innovation. It catered to a wide audience, and its interests centered on the theoretical and practical interaction between child and book, and on the relationship between literary values, literacy, and publishing. Although it was based on a firm liberal-humanist stance on relative values, its policy was eclectic; as editor, Nancy Chambers continually encouraged her contributors to pursue original lines of cross-disciplinary research and to question academic conventions. A characteristic piece was Aidan Chambers's "The Reader in the Book" (1977) which effectively introduced reader-response theory to children's literature studies, and which won the first Children's Literature Association Award for criticism.

The international list of contributors included academics such as Lissa Paul, Hugh Crago, Sanjay Sircar, Jane Doonan, and John Goldthwaite, and authors such as Philip Pullman, Ursula Le Guin, Astrid Lindgren, and Joke Linders. Between 1983 and 1990 *Signal* also produced annual reviewing journals that pioneered collaborative reviewing, and notable books such as Lance Salway's *A Peculiar Gift: 19th Century Writings on Books for Children* (1976) originated in its pages. The annual Signal Poetry Award was highly respected, and was supported by a distinguished series of analytical essays. The Thimble Press continues with its award-winning list of short texts on children's literature, such as Margaret Meek's *How Texts Teach What Readers Learn* (1988) and Peter Hollindale's *Signs of Childness in Children's Books* (1997).

[*See also* Critical Approaches to Children's Literature; Journals and Periodicals; *and biographies of figures mentioned in this article.*]

BIBLIOGRAPHY

Moss, Elaine, and Nancy Chambers. *The "Signal" Companion: A Classified Guide to 25 Years of Signal Approaches to Children's Books, 1970–1994.* South Woodchester, U.K.: The Thimble Press, 1996.

PETER HUNT

Sigsgaard, Jens (1910–1991), Danish educator and children's writer, director of the Froebel Institute in Copenhagen, 1941–1974. His most famous picture book, illustrated by Arne Ungermann, *Paul Alone in the World* (1942; English trans., 1964), was inspired by a psychological study of a thousand children interviewed about their most secret desires. It is a didactic story about a boy who wakes up one day to discover that he is alone in the world and can do whatever he wants; he learns that it is not fun to be without anybody to play with, and in the end the experience turns out to be a dream. The book was translated into thirty languages. Sigsgaard wrote several other picture books in collaboration with Ungermann, mostly about everyday life. A good example is *Kathy and the Doll Buggy* (1958; English trans., 1961). He also collected and edited Danish nursery rhymes.

[*See also* Nordic Countries *and* Picture Books.]

MARIA NIKOLAJEVA

Sikuade, Yemi (1948–), a sociologist by training, who has written two works for children: *Ehanna and Friends* (1978) for young children and *Sisi* (1981) for adolescents. They both have a sociological stamp in their attention to sociocultural details. *Ehanna and Friends* describes African youngsters' pranks and adventures. Ehanna, the leader of a gang of three who plays numerous pranks in his village, is kidnapped along with the rest of the gang and two other children, and they are all taken across the country's border for sale. But they are eventually rescued through Ehanna's setting ablaze the thatch house they were hidden in. In *Sisi*, while staying in the home of his father's friend as a student in Lagos, a Hausa youth, Ibrahim, falls in love with Sisi, and they finally marry after a misunderstanding is cleared. This love and marriage between Ibrahim and Sisi indicates that ethnic and religious differences are no impediment where genuine love exists. Also, it strengthens their parents' old friendship and, by extrapolation, brings Nigeria's diverse ethnic groups together.

[*See also* Africa: Sub-Saharan Africa.]

OSAYIMWENSE OSA

Silverstein, Alvin (1933–), and **Virginia Silverstein** (1937–), husband and wife writing team who are known for their outstanding informational science books. Alvin was born in New York City and Virginia in Philadelphia. Both grew up avid readers with a leaning toward science. They met in a chemistry lab at the University of Pennsylvania and married in 1958. Alvin went on to earn a PhD from New York University in biology and is a professor at the College of Staten Island of the City University of New York. Virginia earned a degree in chemistry and works as a Russian to English translator of scientific publications. The first book they wrote was *Life in the Universe*, in 1967, and they have since gone on to collaborate on more than two hundred informational science books for children. Their books have garnered notice on many fronts, such as a New Jersey Institute of Technology award for *Guinea Pigs: All About Them* (1972), *Aging* (1979), *The Robots Are Here* (1983), *The Story of Your Mouth* (1984), and *Glasses and Contact Lenses* (1989); the Outstanding Science Books for Children for the National Science Teachers Association and Children's Book Council lists for *The Long Voyage* (1972), *The Muscular System* (1972), *The Skeletal System* (1972), *Cancer* (1977), *Life in a Bucket of Soil* (1972; published under the pseudonym Richard Rhine), *Rabbits: All About Them* (1973), *Animal Invaders* (1974), *Hamsters: All About Them* (1974), *Potatoes: All About Them* (1976), *Gerbils: All About Them* (1976), *Heartbeats* (1983), *The Story of Your Foot* (1987), *Wonders of Speech* (1988), *Nature's Living Lights* (1988), and *Overcoming Acne* (1990). This list of titles illustrates the breadth of their writing interests. It is because of this broad range, as well as their accessible writing style and their science expertise, that they are often considered the premier science writers for older children in the United States. Most recently, they have expanded their collaboration to include two of their children, Robert Silverstein and Laura Silverstein Nunn.

[*See also* Information Books *and* Science Books.]

REBECCA HOGUE WOJAHN

Silverstein, Shel (1932–1999), composer, folksinger, artist, playwright, poet, and prose writer; perhaps the most popular and best-known contemporary poet among American children. Because Shelby Silverstein was such an intensely private man, little is known about his life; even the year of his birth is contested. When Silverstein was a teenager, he wanted to be athletic and popular, but because he was not, he began to write. In the 1950s, when Silverstein served in the military in Korea and Japan, he worked as a cartoonist for a military publication, *Stars and Stripes*. When he returned home, he worked for *Playboy*, where he began publishing his humorous artwork. He also began writing country music, and during his career, he recorded a country music album, *The Great Conch Train Robbery* (1993) and wrote songs (most famously "A Boy Named Sue") that have been recorded by artists such as Johnny Cash, Dr. Hook, and the Irish Rovers.

Silverstein is best known for *The Giving Tree* (1964), *Where the Sidewalk Ends* (1974), and *A Light in the Attic* (1981), all of which he illustrated himself. *The Giving Tree*, as controversial as much of Silverstein's other work, tells the story of the relationship between a female tree and a little boy who grows into adulthood and old age, using up everything that the tree has to give, which she always gives willingly. At the end of the story, only a stump remains because the boy has used her fruit, her leaves, her branches, and finally her trunk for his own needs and desires. Yet "The tree was happy." While many readers interpret this story as a tribute to the selflessness and self-sacrifice of the maternal figure, still others read this story as representing a master/slave relationship or a gender imbalanced relationship in which the male wields all power and destroys the helpless, giving female. The simplicity of this text and several others that Silverstein composed and illustrated allow for wildly disparate interpretations, but despite the longstanding debate over the meaning of this text, *The Giving Tree* continues to win the favor of both child and adult readers.

Where the Sidewalk Ends and *A Light in the Attic*, both anthologies of primarily humorous poetry, include poems such as "Sarah Cynthia Sylvia Stout Would Not Take the Garbage Out," and "They've Put a Brassiere on the Camel." The former, a poem rich in imagery, lists, in lively detail, all of the items in the garbage that pile up when Sarah Cynthia refuses to take the garbage out. Characteristic of Silverstein's characters who make unwise decisions, this protagonist meets an "awful fate" that the narrator hints at but does not reveal. In the latter poem, the speaker wonders what they'll do to the cow, given what they've done to the camel to make its humps decent. Like Edward Lear, his predecessor within the nonsense tradition, Silverstein excelled at pointing out the foolishness of human behavior. In the poetic world that Silverstein creates, a child can get swallowed by a boa constrictor while he waxes poetic about his destruction, and a girl can say she will die if her parents do not buy her a pony . . . and she does. Not surprisingly, the elements of Silverstein's poetry that have made it memorable and popular with children have also made it a frequent target of censorship.

BIBLIOGRAPHY

Kean, John M. "Finding Humor and Value in *Where the Sidewalk Ends* and *A Light in the Attic*." In *Censored Books: Critical View-*

points, edited by Nicholas J. Karolides, Lee Burress, and John M. Kean, 485–489. Metuchen, N.J.: Scarecrow, 1993.
MacDonald, Ruth K. "The Weirdness of Shel Silverstein." *Studies in American Humor* 5, no. 4 (1986–1987): 267–279.

MICHELLE H. MARTIN

Simmonds, Posy (1945–), British author and illustrator who trained as a graphic designer and began her career drawing for *The Guardian* newspaper, where she created several long-running comic strip series. *Gemma Bovery* (1999), which tilts at the pretensions of the British class system, was subsequently published as a book. The same cartoon style is used in her children's books, in which the illustrations carry the weight of the narrative. Her drawings are lightly but brightly colored with watercolor or pencil and are a slyly humorous reflection on contemporary life. *Fred* (1987) is the story of a cat who sleeps all day, but after his death his human family discovers just what a lively character Fred was when all the neighborhood felines gather to hold a wake for him. The two Lulu books merge reality and fantasy when cherubs in an art gallery and the figures from a wedding cake come to life. *Lavender* (2003) is stylistically softer but still brings an edge to the story of a little rabbit who has a very timid disposition, encapsulating Simmonds's wry stance and warm regard for her subjects.

VALERIE COGHLAN

Simms, George Otto (1910–1991), born in County Donegal, Ireland, Simms, sometime Anglican archbishop of Armagh, wrote and lectured extensively on early Irish Christian manuscripts. His expertise on the *Book of Kells* is widely regarded. Simms's scholarship is accessible to younger readers in three children's books. *The Book of Kells* (1988) is an account of the creation of one of Ireland's great treasures; *Brendan the Navigator* (1989) tells the story of a monk who crossed the Atlantic in a coracle, and *St. Patrick* (1991) is the story of the man credited with bringing Christianity to Ireland.

VALERIE COGHLAN

Simon, Seymour (1931–), American writer. Born in New York City and educated at City College, New York, including graduate work in animal behavior, Simon served in the U.S. Army from 1953 to 1955 and then taught science in New York public schools until 1979, when he became a full-time writer. He is the award-winning and prolific author of over two hundred science books for children. Focusing on outer space, oceanography, computers, species of animals and plants, and scientific experiments and activities, his books are designed to inspire in children a passion for science, and they often encourage readers to discover their own answers to scientific questions. His first book, *Animals in Field and Laboratory: Science Projects in Animal Behavior* (1968), was followed by titles that include the widely admired *The Paper Airplane Book* (1971), *How to Be a Space Scientist in Your Own Home* (1982), *Bits and Bytes: A Computer Dictionary for Beginners* (1985), and many animal titles, such as *Cats* (2004). Simon's several series include the "Discovering" titles, such as *Discovering What Garter Snakes Do* (1975); the "Space Photos" series, illustrated with satellite photographs, including *Mars* (1987) and *Venus* (1992); and the "Let's Try it Out" series, including *Let's Try it Out with Towers and Bridges* (2003). Simon has also produced fiction with a science bent in his "Einstein Anderson, Science Detective" series, about a comical boy sleuth who solves mysteries through science. Over one hundred of Simon's works have been judged Outstanding Trade Science Books for Children by the National Science Teachers Association. He was awarded the 1984 Eva L. Gordon Award by the American Nature Study Society and the 1993 *Washington Post* Children's Book Guild Nonfiction Award, both for his overall contribution to children's literature. In 2002 he received the Jeremiah Ludington Memorial Award for contributions to educational paperbacks.

ADRIENNE E. GAVIN

Simont, Marc (1915–), born in France, spending much of his childhood in France, Spain, and the United States, Simont is a prolific illustrator, and an occasional author. He became a citizen of the United States in 1936. Although Simont never graduated from high school, he speaks several languages fluently and attended art schools in both Paris (Academies Ranson and Julian) and New York City (National Academy of Design). His father, sister, and two uncles were also professional artists. He worked as an illustrator for an advertising firm before moving on to children's books in 1939. Frequently working in watercolor and line drawings, Simont employs a deceptively simple, at times cartoon-like style. He excels in adding humorous details from everyday life. Simont gained fame with a 1950 Caldecott Honor Medal for Ruth Krauss's *Happy Day* (1949), and consolidated his reputation with the Caldecott Medal for illustrating Janice Udry's *A Tree Is Nice* (1956). In the 1970s he began a partnership with Marjorie Sharmat on the Nate the Great detective series that continued through 2001. These humorous beginning reader books are so popular with elementary school children that a thirtieth anniversary edition of the original *Nate the Great* (1972) was published in 2002. In the 1980s he created two whimsical, yet realistic, books with Karla Kuskin, *The Philharmonic Gets Dressed* (1982) and *The Dallas Titans Get Ready for Bed* (1986). Both books present everyday aspects from the lives of the anonymous members of two well-known organizations. Other authors he collaborated with include Margaret Wise Brown, Betsy Byars, Betty Bao Lord, Faith McNulty, James Thurber, and Charlotte Zolotow. Simont's popularity with children shows no sign of flagging, and he earned another Caldecott Honor Book Award in 2002 for *The Stray Dog* (2001).

[*See also biographies of figures mentioned in this article.*]

CHARLOTTE CUBBAGE

Simple Simon. Simple Simon is a nursery rhyme character who is a silly. It is unclear whether the name is proverbial or comes from the character's "adventures" revealing that he has no concept of money and thinks whales swim in buckets. This Simon does not resemble the abused husband of the same name in 18th-century ballads and chapbooks, *Simple Simon's Misfortunes*. As the rhyme first appeared in chapbooks for children during the 1820s, it may be an original poem whose source has yet to be discovered, similar to Sarah Catherine Martin's expanded version of *Mother Hubbard* (1805), which put an old character in a new dress.

ANDREA IMMEL

Simpsons, The. An animated television series on the Fox network, *The Simpsons* features Homer (dad), Marge (mom), Bart (age ten), Lisa (age eight), and Maggie (an infant), who live at 742 Evergreen Terrace in Springfield, an "Everytown" peopled with eccentric townspeople like Moe the Bartender, Reverend Lovejoy, Principal Skinner, and Apu the storekeeper. Many episodes center on Bart's irascible behavior or Homer's well-meaning but ineffectual attempts to better himself or the family. Homer's epithet, "D'oh!"—a catch-phrase for general consternation and befuddlement—now warrants an entry in the *Oxford English Dictionary*. Known for its witty and satirical take on contemporary culture, *The Simpsons* is a subversive parody of conservative stodginess, Middle-American values, and liberal pretension ("I'm a fifth degree vegan," said one character, "I don't eat anything that casts a shadow"). Created by Matt Groening, *The Simpsons* first aired as a cartoon short on *The Tracey Ullman Show* on April 19, 1987, and has appeared on Fox as a series since 1989. *The Simpsons* is the longest-running situation comedy in American history.

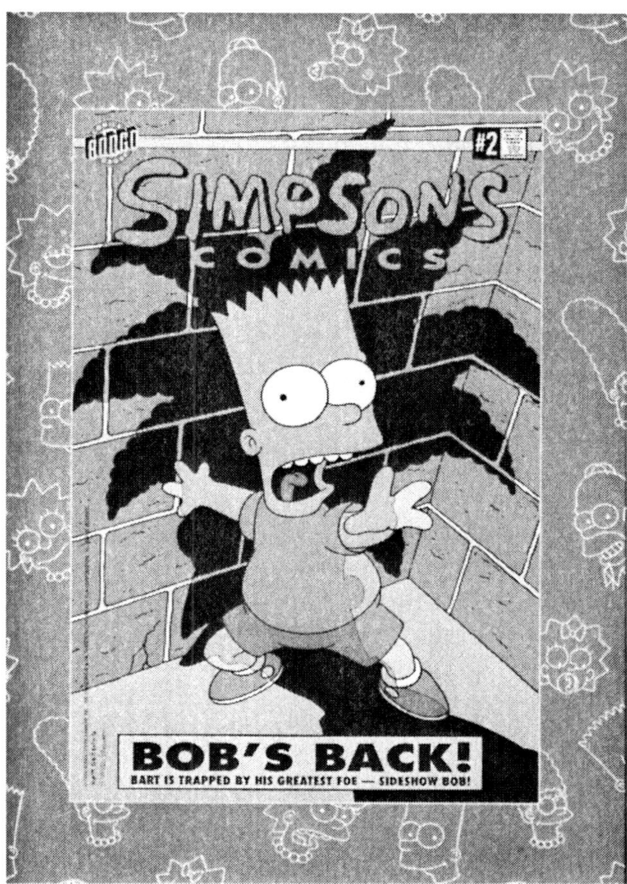

The Simpsons. Front cover of *Simpsons Comics* (Los Angeles: Bongo Comics Group, 1994). COLLECTION OF ANDREA IMMEL

BIBLIOGRAPHY

Groenig, Matt. *Bart Simpson's Guide to Life: A Wee Handbook for the Perplexed.* New York: HarperCollins, 1993.

Groenig, Matt. *The Simpsons Beyond Forever!: A Complete Guide to Our Favorite Family . . . Still Continued.* New York: HarperCollins, 2002.

Holtz, Mark, and Dave Hall. *The Simpsons Archive.* http://www.snpp.com.

Irwin, William, Mark T. Conard, and Aeon J. Skoble, eds. *The Simpsons and Philosophy: The D'oh! of Homer.* Chicago: Open Court Press, 2001.

DANIEL T. KLINE

Simrock, Karl (1802–1876), German author, literary scholar, and professor of German literature and language at the University of Bonn. As a substantial collector and editor, Simrock made contributions to numerous important editions of literature for children and young people. Among these are translations of Middle High German texts, as in the six-volume *Heldenbuch* (1843–1849; English trans., *The Book of Heroes*), and a nearly complete edition of the thirteen-volume *Deutsche Volksbücher* (1845–1867; English trans., *German Books of Folk Tales*). Most popular was his *Das deutsche Kinderbuch* (English trans., *The German Children's Book*), first published in 1856 and containing a collection of traditional rhymes, games, pleasantries, riddles, and songs for children.

BERND DOLLE-WEINKAUFF

Sinclair, Catherine (1780–1864), Scottish novelist born in Edinburgh, where her philanthropic work is commemorated by an impressive gothic memorial. From the age of fourteen she served as secretary to her father, the reformer Sir John Sinclair of Ulbster. As was often the case with women writers of this period, her father's death (in 1835) signaled the start of her own creative life. Although she had previously produced one children's novel, *Charlie Seymour; or, The Good Aunt and the Bad Aunt* (1832), she wrote and published steadily from 1836 to 1864. Although she wrote novels and travel guides for adults as well as children's books, Catherine Sinclair is now best remembered for one children's book: *Holiday House* (1839).

Published a quarter of a century before *Alice in Wonderland*, *Holiday House* is notable for its vindication of children's right to be childlike, its recognition and appreciation of children's inner worlds, and its reassuring attitude to naughtiness. Sinclair claimed that she wrote *Holiday House* because she was perturbed by the way children were being raised and educated so that "the minds of young people are now manufactured like webs of linen, all alike, and nothing left to nature." She feared the consequence would be no poets or other creative thinkers in future generations.

Sinclair wanted children to enjoy the freedoms of childhood, but she also understood that children lack understanding of themselves, have very little power or respect in society, and are often ruled over tyrannically. In *Holiday House* her two mischievous protagonists eventually grow up to be as pious and decorous as their better behaved peers.

In the 1860s Sinclair began to produce letters for children written in hieroglyphics, including *Letters for Children* (1862) and *The Bible Picture Letter* (1863). Best sellers in their day, they are now remembered only by collectors and bibliographers.

BIBLIOGRAPHY

Rudd, David. "The Froebellious Child in Catherine Sinclair's *Holiday House*." *The Lion and the Unicorn* 28 (2004): 53–69.

KIMBERLEY REYNOLDS

Sindbad the Sailor. "Sindbad the Sailor" is one of two popular stories from a cornerstone of children's literature, *The Arabian Nights*, a series of anonymous tales that first appeared in Arabic around A.D. 850. The tales stem from the storytelling traditions of India, Persia, and the Arabic cultures. The stories of Sindbad comprise seven adventures, which form an exciting heroic cycle, each beginning where the previous one ends. The hero, Sindbad, relates his daring journeys to a gathering of noblemen. Sindbad is a merchant who uses intelligence, bravery, strength, and ingenuity to overcome obstacles in strange lands and encounters with dangerous creatures, and return safely to his home in Baghdad. Sindbad does not possess superhuman abilities; therefore, he does not fit the classical hero in a mythical perspective. Indeed, Sindbad is a common man and a hero of common proportions, but he has the ability to overcome the odds through his will to live.

[*See also* Arabian Nights, The *and* Children's Literature in the Arab World.]

ANTHONY S. BURDGE

Singer, Isaac Bashevis (1904–1991), master storyteller for children and adults. By the time Polish-born Singer won the Nobel Prize for Literature in 1978, he had published fourteen children's books, beginning in 1966 with *Zlateh the Goat*, a collection of seven stories that won a Newbery Honor award. So did the single-story picture book *The Fearsome Inn* (1967) and the collection *When Shlemiel Went to Warsaw* (1968). In 1969 his autobiographical *A Day of Pleasure: Stories of a Boy Growing Up in Warsaw* garnered the National Book Award for Children's Literature. *The Golem* (1982) and *Stories for Children* (1984) were ALA Notable Books for Children. Clearly, Singer's depictions of the story-rich and history-burdened world of eastern European Jewish culture were as successful in his children's books as in those for adults. In 1984, Singer himself selected the thirty-seven stories in his crowning achievement, *Stories for Children*.

Singer was already a famous author and in his early sixties when his old friend, editor, and Yiddish translator Elizabeth Shub finally persuaded him to write for youngsters. His first story, "Zlateh the Goat," regarded as among his finest, is the realistic tale of a young boy and the family goat who survive a blizzard in Russia. In the eponymous collection, in addition to this original tale, is another kind of story characteristic of Singer, the folk tale transformed into fiction. Singer's personal fund of folklore was unusually well stocked. His father was a Hasidic rabbi, his mother the daughter of an Orthodox rabbi, and his older brother, I. J. Singer (also an author), an atheist; all were storytellers. A traditional religious education schooled Singer in Jewish scripture. And in the family's front room, his father's rabbinical "court," Singer heard the neighborhood's dramas and tales of faraway places. Born in a *shtetl* (Jewish village), at age three Singer moved with his family to Warsaw. Pressures leading to World War I forced the family's return to the countryside when Singer was in his early teens. Thus, while young, he experienced both rural and city life. He developed folk-tale characters like *shlemiels* (an inept type prominent in Jewish humor) and the Fools of Chelm into cycles of hilarious stories vividly set in, to quote the title of one of his brother's books, "a world that is no more."

In addition to original fictions and fictionalized folktales, Singer wrote autobiography, depicting himself as a philosophical child in *A Day of Pleasure* and also in *When Shlemiel Went to Warsaw*; *Naftali the Storyteller and His Horse, Sus* (1976); and *The Power of Light* (1980), eight stories centered on Hanukkah.

Among his best-known works are "Menaseh's Dream," about an orphan who imagines himself in heaven with his family, "Naftali the Storyteller and His Horse, Sus," about a poor boy whose single-minded vision of lifelong storytelling comes true, and *The Golem*, based on a famous Jewish legend. Singer's respect for the child both as character and as reader is also evident in his essays such as "Are Children the Ultimate Literary Critics?"

Singer spoke no English when he arrived in New York in 1935 at age thirty-one; though he acquired fluency, he continued to write in Yiddish. He became a citizen, lived in Manhattan, and died in Miami Beach, where a street is named after him.

BIBLIOGRAPHY

Allison, Alida. *Isaac Bashevis Singer: Children's Stories and Childhood Memoirs*. New York: Twayne, 1996.

Hadda, Janet. *Isaac Bachevis Singer: A Life*. Madison: University of Wisconsin Press, 2003.

Morse, Naomi. "Values for Children in the Stories of Isaac Bashevis Singer." In *Children's Literature: Selected Essays and Bibliographies*, edited by Anne MacLeod, vol. 9, 16–31. Baltimore: College of Library Information Services, University of Maryland, 1977.

ALIDA ALLISON

Singer, Marilyn (1948–), versatile and prolific American author of more than seventy titles. Her audiences range from children through young adults, and her genres include picture books, novels, mysteries, fairy tales, nonfiction, short stories, and poems. Singer loves animals, and they are featured in some of her most successful works including the picture book *The Dog Who Insisted He Wasn't* (1976), several of her books of poetry including *Turtle in July* (1989) and *Fireflies at Midnight* (2003), and most of her nonfiction titles including the humorous *Bottoms Up!* (1998) and *A Pair of Wings* (2001). Singer has taken on plenty of other topics, however. Her settings stretch from New York to China, and her books wrestle with matters as challenging as juvenile heart surgery in *It Can't Hurt Forever* (1978) and the meaning of faith in *I Believe in Water: Twelve Brushes with Religion* (2000), a collection of stories she edited.

MEGAN LYNN ISAAC

Sinha, Nilima (1939–), Indian author of stories, picture books, retellings of Indian history, and novels for children. Sinha's fiction is characterized by action-driven, well-conceived plots. In *Swan Song* and other books that focus on ecological issues, the morals about "progress" are woven into the story. A distinct ecological slant is visible in all her books, with children often preventing harmful development projects. Landlords, an army of faithful servants, and a comfortable life: This is the world Sinha portrays in her fiction. Strong girl characters—Sarika in *Vanishing Trick at Chandipur*, Nina in *Adventure on the Golden Lake*, and Richa in *Mystery of the Falling Mountains*—play a key role in the adventures, often providing the sane voice of caution. In the tradition of adventure fiction, parents and family do not play a role in the action. Instead, grandparents provide the affection and support system. In *Rishabh in the Land of the Flying Magicians* the grandmother whisks Rishabh and his sister away to a land of magic. In *The Chandipur Jewels*, Praveen, Sarika, and Sunil bring their estranged mother and grandfather together again.

[*See also* Adventure Books; Ecology and Environment; *and* India.]

NANDINI NAYAR

Sís, Peter (1949–), Czech American illustrator, author, and filmmaker. A native of Brno, Sís is admired for the virtuosic draftsmanship on display in his intricate, richly imagined drawings both for his own texts and for more than three dozen works by other authors, including multiple collaborations with George Shannon, Jack Prelutsky, and Sid Fleischman. Sís was the illustrator for Fleischman's *The Whipping Boy*, which won the 1987 Newbery Medal, and he has been a runner-up for the Caldecott Medal twice, for *Starry Messenger: Galileo Galilei* (1996) and *Tibet: Through the Red Box* (1998). His other prizes include a MacArthur Fellowship (popularly known as a "genius grant") in 2003 and over half a dozen appearances on the *New York Times* "Best Illustrated Children's Books of the Year" lists.

Raised in Prague, Sís attended its Academy of Applied Arts and continued his studies at London's Royal College of Art. Frustrated and uneasy with the restrictions his native government imposed on his work and travels, Sís defected to the United States in 1982 while in Los Angeles working on a film; he became an American citizen in 1989. Sís's art has often been characterized as multilayered and sophisticated, and his command of multiple techniques can be seen in *Madlenka* (2000) and *Madlenka's Dog* (2002), which feature playful cutouts, flaps, and inset maps; unconventionally typeset text; and strikingly strong contrasts between brightly colored figures and extensively crosshatched black-and-white backgrounds. A self-described perfectionist, Sís often uses pointillism and washes, and other manipulations of texture infuse his work with a delicate yet precise quality that well complements both the fairy tales and fantasy-tinged stories he favors and also his biographical accounts of explorers and scientists such as Christopher Columbus (*Follow the Dream*, 1991), Jan Welzl (*A Small Tall Tale from the Far Far North*, 1993), and Charles Darwin (*The Tree of Life*, 2003).

Peter Sís. Front cover of *Madlenka* (New York: Farrar, Straus Giroux, 2000). Reproduced courtesy of the Cotsen Children's Library, Princeton University Library

[*See also* Biography; Illustrations; Movable Books and Pop-Up Books; *and biographies of figures mentioned in this article.*]

Peggy Lin Duthie

Sixtus, Albert (1892–1960), German author of books for children and young people, who achieved popularity into the 21st century for his verses in the picture book *Die Häschenschule* (Rabbits at School, 1924). After his education at a teachers' seminar in Pirna, Saxony, and a brief period working in school, he was drafted into military service and severely wounded. His career as an author of books for children began with the publication of the fairy tales *Mein Guckkästchen* (My Little Peep Show) in 1922. More fairy tales followed, as well as a series of detective novels addressing older children: *Die wilden Jungen von der Feuerburg* (The Wild Boys of Feuerburg, 1925). One of his greatest successes was *Die Häschenschule*, illustrated by the famous caricaturist Fritz Koch-Gotha, 100,000 copies of which were sold in just one year after its publication. The story in verse is an endearing parody of contemporary school life and its rituals with animals in place of humans. In the following years Sixtus wrote verses for numerous other picture books, including some by Else Wenz-Viëtor. He also contributed articles for children's magazines, and from 1937 to 1943 was editor of the well-known traditional periodical *Auerbachs Deutscher Kinderkalendar* (Auerbach's Children's Calendar).

[*See also* Fairy Tales and Folk Tales; Germany; Picture Books; *and* Poetry.]

Bernd Dolle-Weinkauff

Skurzynski, Gloria (1930–), American fiction writer born in Duquesne, Pennsylvania. Skurzynski began writing with the encouragement of the poet Phyllis McGinley. After writing a fan letter to McGinley, the two began a lifelong correspondence. The first of her more than thirty children's books was published in 1971. *The Magic Pumpkin* (1971) is a fairy tale about a woman who rides through the jungle in her magic pumpkin trying to outwit the animals that are trying to eat her for dinner. Skurzynski turned to her love of historical fiction in *The Tempering* (1983). Based partly on her father's life, the story tells of three young men who lose their jobs in the steel mills of Pennsylvania in 1911. Skurzynski has written many more historical fiction books, but she has also drawn on her love of science to create many high-tech novels. *Virtual War* (1997) is the first in the series about a future world where three young people come together to wage a war in virtual reality. Skurzynski has collaborated with her daughter, Alane Ferguson, on a series of mystery novels set in America's national parks and published by National Geographic. In addition to her works of fiction, Skurzynski has written several nonfiction science and technology books for elementary-age students.

[*See also* Historical Fiction; Nonfiction; *and* Science Fiction.]

NANCY J. KEANE

Sleator, William (1945–), American children's author and musician. Sleator's dark-edged whimsy and speculation are as thoughtful as they are entertaining. While his telling of *The Angry Moon* (1970) received Caldecott Honor mention for Blair Lent's illustrations, most of Sleator's work has been aimed at older children and teenagers. His most popular book, *Interstellar Pig* (1984), and its sequel, *Parasite Pig* (2002), place Earth in the middle of a rapacious game in which the main character, Barney, has to save himself, his home, and his species. While the board game starts out amusing and a trifle silly with its focus on a Piggy, the stakes become much higher as the game is shown to be real. In novels such as *Others See Us* (1993), Sleator takes wild ideas to their logical conclusions: teens suddenly given mind-reading powers find out that their grandmother and cousin are deeply unpleasant and manipulative, and the happy ending they win for themselves is tinged with the possibility of more trouble later. *The Boy Who Couldn't Die* (2004) deals with the darker possibilities of immortality. Even lighter fare like *The Boy Who Reversed Himself* (1986) deals with very logical extrapolations from greater than three-dimensional spatial systems. Sleator's broad research in the sciences serves him well in all of his novels; in multiple interviews he has credited his family for this interest.

Sleator's love of Thailand, where he spends half of each year, shines through in his stylistically atypical *The Spirit House* (1991), which introduces traditional Thai beliefs, and its sequel, *Dangerous Wishes* (1995), set in Thailand. Even more clearly influenced by Sleator's personal life is *Oddballs* (1993), a slightly fictionalized set of stories about his childhood. Sleator has also written short stories for popular anthologies. He is the composer of scores for ballets, films, and plays, both professional and amateur.

[*See also* Lent, Blair.]

BIBLIOGRAPHY

Davis, James E., and Hazel K. Davis. *Presenting William Sleator*. New York: Twayne, 1992.

MARISSA K. LINGEN

Sleeping Beauty. "Sleeping Beauty" is a fairy tale also known as "Briar Rose." Variants of this tale appear in Giambattista Basile's *Pentamerone*, Charles Perrault's *Histoires; ou, Contes du temps passé* (1697; English trans., *Stories; or, Tales of Times Past*), and the Grimm brothers' *Kinder- und Hausmärchen* (1812; English trans., *Children's and Household Tales*). When a little princess is born, the king and queen invite only twelve of the thirteen wise women in the country to celebrate. The thirteenth fairy appears at the party and curses the baby. When the princess is fifteen, she pricks her finger on a spinning wheel and falls asleep for a hundred years. During this period, a briar of roses grows around the castle. Sleeping Beauty awakes only when a prince comes to the rescue and (in the Grimms' version) kisses her. In the 14th-century romance *Perceforest* and in Basile's "Sun, Moon, and Talia," the sleeping princess does not awake, and the prince rapes her. Perrault and Basile's stories continue after she wakes up: the princess gets twins, which are threatened to be cooked by the prince's evil wife (Basile) or mother (Perrault). Once again, the prince comes to the rescue in the end.

Bruno Bettelheim has interpreted the tale of "Sleeping Beauty" psychologically, stating that the hundred years of sleep are symbolic of a period of passivity that most adolescents go through before they awake to sexual maturity. Feminist writers and critics have often attacked Sleeping Beauty because she incarnates the patriarchal ideal of passive and helpless beautiful women. In some popular versions, the princess's passivity is enhanced even more. In the Disney film version (1959), for instance, the prince gets a much

Sleeping Beauty. Illustration by Ludwig Grimm from *Kinder- und Hausmärchen* (Berlin: G. Reimer, 1825). REPRODUCED COURTESY OF THE COTSEN CHILDREN'S LIBRARY, PRINCETON UNIVERSITY LIBRARY

more active part to play. This image is often corrected in many contemporary literary adaptations, which feature in the work of Jane Yolen, Sandra Henderson Hay, Angela Carter, Anne Sexton, Adèle Geras, Emma Donoghue, Francesca Lia Block, Olga Broumas, and Robert Coover.

[*See also* Fairy Tales and Folk Tales *and biographies of figures mentioned in this article.*]

BIBLIOGRAPHY

Zipes, Jack. "Fairy Tale As Myth/Myth As Fairy Tale: The Immortality of Sleeping Beauty and Storytelling." In *The Brothers Grimm: From Enchanted Forests to the Modern World*, 207–229. New York: Palgrave Macmillan, 2002. In this chapter, Zipes discusses variants of "Sleeping Beauty" in history, popular culture, and contemporary literature.

VANESSA JOOSEN

Sleigh, Barbara (1906–1982), British author of fantasy. Her trilogy *Carbonel* (1955), *The Kingdom of Carbonel* (1960), and *Carbonel and Calidor* (1978) features a talking cat who is the king of his magical realm, invisible to humans, but he also lives as an ordinary cat in the real world. The protagonist Rosemary has to assist Carbonel in a number of tasks to fight his evil enemies. Flying on a broom is one of Rosemary's accomplishments in this series. *Jessamy* (1967) is a time-slip fantasy in which the protagonist enters the past through a wardrobe and turns into her namesake two generations back. She visits the past twice, learning to adapt to her new identity, but is denied further chances when the magical agent is destroyed. The novel lacks the subtlety and psychological poignancy of Philippa Pearce's *Tom's Midnight Garden* (1958), yet it belongs to the same postwar trend in British time fantasy toward exploration of character through time displacement.

[*See also* Fantasy.]

BIBLIOGRAPHY

Moss, Elaine. "Barbara Sleigh: The Voice of Magic." *Signal* 8 (1972): 43–48.

MARIA NIKOLAJEVA

Slepian, Jan (1921–), author of young adult novels and coauthor of reading series for children. While working in speech therapy, Slepian collaborated with the physician Ann Seidler and the illustrator Richard E. Martin to produce the *Listen/Hear* series. Though written with a pragmatic purpose in mind, the stories were quite entertaining, especially *Bendemolena* (1967) and *The Hungry Thing* (1967). Both stories feature a character either hearing or saying something slightly inaccurate, allowing the reader to reinterpret the statement correctly. Later, Slepian drew from several aspects of her own life, especially her experience with a mentally retarded brother and her training in clinical psychology, to write *The Alfred Summer* (1980), which features several children with some form of handicap or challenging experience and describes the special ways they learn to cope with their obstacles. Later novels *The Night of the Bozos* (1983) and *The Broccoli Tapes* (1989) explore similar themes.

THOMAS R. PITCHFORD

Slingsby, Peter (1946–), South African environmental educator and cartographer, who pours his love of the Western Cape into his children's fiction and guide books. His stories feature strongly drawn boys on the brink of adolescence. He has made the settings and their inhabitants—past (*Tomas*, 1988), present (*Flood Sunday*, 1992), and mythical (*Leopard Boy*, 1989)—his unique preserve, compassionately recalling the idyllic lives that the early inhabitants led until they encountered new arrivals (*Jedro's Bane*, 2002). Most dramatically, in *The Joining* (1996), a group of children travel into the past, where they join a band of Xam hunter-gatherers and opt never to return.

ELWYN JENKINS

Slobodkin, Louis (1903–1975), American sculptor, illustrator, and author. Slobodkin's first and better-known career was in sculpture. He decided to try his hand at illustration when the author Eleanor Estes suggested it. He later illustrated her Newbery Honor books, *The Hundred Dresses* (1944), *Rufus M.* (1943), and *The Middle Moffat* (1942). He also illustrated the Caldecott Medal–winning book *Many Moons* (1943), written by James Thurber. After doing illustrations for a few books, Slobodkin decided to write some of his own texts as well. Among the books that he wrote as well as illustrated is *The Space-Ship under the Apple Tree* (1952), the tale of a little boy alien who visits a boy on a farm and participates in typical country pursuits like a three-legged race and feeding the chickens. In the midst of the whimsy of the spaceship premise, Slobodkin emphasized fair play and other "Earthling" values. Others of his books were more purely didactic in nature. Books like *Thank You, You're Welcome* (1957) taught children the importance of manners. After winning the Caldecott, Slobodkin was asked to illustrate new editions of Mark Twain, Charles Dickens, and Washington Irving; he also illustrated his wife Florence's book, *Sarah Somebody* (1970), as well as collaborating with her on four shared works.

[*See also biographies of figures mentioned in this article.*]

MARISSA K. LINGEN

Slobodkina, Esphyr (1908–2002), Russian American children's book artist and author. Perhaps best known for her illustrations for W. R. Scott's *Caps for Sale* (1940)—the story of a cap seller who falls asleep under a tree and has his caps stolen by a flock of monkeys—Slobodkina was also a painter, sculptor, and interior decorator, strongly influenced by avant garde art of the early to mid-twentieth century, beginning with Soviet Constructivist art. Born in Cheliabinsk, Siberia, she emigrated to the United States in 1928. She studied at the National Academy of Design and was an active member of the artists' group American Abstract Artists. In 1938 she became friends with Margaret Wise Brown and illustrated her children's books *The Little Fireman* (1938), *The Little Farmer* (1948), and *The Little Cowboy* (1949), as well as others by Brown. Her career as a children's book illustrator spanned the decades into the 1980s, with works such as *The Wonderful Feast* (1955) and *Pezzo the Peddler and the Circus Elephant* (1968).

J. D. STAHL

Slote, Alfred (1926–), American writer best known for his sports-themed and science fiction novels. Slote was born in New York City and served with the U.S. Navy during World War II. After the war, he earned a B.A. and an M.A. from the University of Michigan. He spent two years in France and then taught at Williams College before taking a position to write for educational television in Michigan. During this time, he published several works for adults and one picture book, but he did not shift his career toward children's writing until his agent asked him to take the place of an author who wrote baseball books. Since 1970, Slote has been known for books that integrate sports with other themes, such as racism in *Finding Buck McHenry* (1991) and divorce in *The Trading Game* (1990). Additionally, Slote has had success in writing science fiction; he was nominated for an Edgar Award for *Clone Catcher* (1982).

[*See also* Science Fiction *and* Sports Books.]

REBECCA HOGUE WOJAHN